U^{the}nofficial Guide® to

Walt Disney World 2005

the Unofficial Guide® to Walt Disney World* 2005

Bob Sehlinger

WILEY

*Walt Disney World® is officially known as Walt Disney World® Resort

Please note that prices fluctuate in the course of time, and travel information changes under the impact of many factors that influence the travel industry. We therefore suggest that you write or call ahead for confirmation when making your travel plans. Every effort has been made to ensure the accuracy of information throughout this book, and the contents of this publication are believed correct at the time of printing. Nevertheless, the publishers cannot accept responsibility for errors or omissions or for changes in details given in this guide or for the consequences of any reliance on the information provided by the same. Assessments of attractions and so forth are based upon the author's own experience, and therefore, descriptions given in this guide necessarily contain an element of subjective opinion, which may not reflect the publisher's opinion or dictate a reader's own experience on another occasion. Readers are invited to write the publisher with ideas, comments, and suggestions for future editions.

Published by:

John Wiley & Sons, Inc.

111 River Street

Hoboken, NJ 07030

Produced by Menasha Ridge Press
Cover design by Michael J. Freeland
Interior design by Michele Laseau

For information on our other products and services or to obtain technical support please contact our Customer Care Department within the U.S. at (800) 762-2974, outside the U.S. at (317) 572-3993 or fax (317) 572-4002.

John Wiley & Sons, Inc. also publishes its books in a variety of electronic formats. Some content that appears in print may not be available in electronic formats.

ISBN 0-7645-5972-9

Manufactured in the United States of America

5 4 3 2 1

Contents

Part Four   The Disney Cruise Line   225

List of Maps

Acknowledgments

Special thanks to our field-research team, who rendered a Herculean effort in what must have seemed like a fantasy version of Sartre's No Exit to the tune of "It's a Small World." We hope you all recover to tour another day.

Lynne Bachleda	Georgia Goff	Christina Koshzow
Molly Merkle	Chris Mohney	Fred Hazleton
Holly Cross	Nathan Lott	Grace Walton
Leslie Cummins	Luke Skurman	Barbara Williams
Shannon Dobbs	Kai Brueckerhoff	

Peals of laughter and much appreciation to nationally renowned cartoonist Tami Knight for her brilliant and insightful work.

Many thanks to Pam Brandon, who braved mountains of Disney merchandise and scoured countless central Florida shopping venues to provide us with our new comprehensive shopping chapter.

Psychologists Dr. Karen Turnbow, Dr. Gayle Janzen, and Dr. Joan Burns provided much insight concerning the experiences of young children at Walt Disney World. "Hotel Women" and Nathan Lott inspected many dozens of hotels. *Unofficial Guide to Cruises* author Kay Showker assisted with our coverage of the Disney Cruise Line.

Many thanks also to Molly Merkle, Chris Mohney, Gabbie Oates, and Marie Hillin for production and editorial work on this book. Steve Jones and Annie Long earned our appreciation for their fine work and for keeping tight deadlines in providing the typography. Cartography was provided by Steve Jones, Tim Krasnansky, Brian Taylor, and Gary Antonetti, and the index was prepared by Ann Cassar. Finally, thanks to Shane Kennedy, who tallied survey results and handled reader-mail.

Introduction

Why "Unofficial"?

Declaration of Independence

The author and researchers of this guide specifically and categorically declare that they are and always have been totally independent of the Walt Disney Company, Inc.; of Disneyland, Inc.; of Walt Disney World, Inc.; and of any and all other members of the Disney corporate family not listed.

The material in this guide originated with the author and researchers and has not been reviewed, edited, or approved by the Walt Disney Company, Inc.; Disneyland, Inc.; or Walt Disney World, Inc.

This guidebook represents the first comprehensive *critical* appraisal of Walt Disney World. Its purpose is to provide the reader with the information necessary to tour Walt Disney World with the greatest efficiency and economy and with the least hassle.

In this guide, we represent and serve you. If a restaurant serves bad food, or a gift item is overpriced, or a ride isn't worth the wait, we say so, and in the process we hope to make your visit more fun, efficient, and economical.

Dance to the Music

A dance has a beginning and an end. But when you're dancing, you're not concerned about getting to the end or where on the dance floor you might wind up. In other words, you're totally in the moment. That's the way you should be on your Walt Disney World vacation.

You may feel a bit of pressure concerning your vacation. Vacations, after all, are very special events, and expensive ones to boot. So you work hard to make your vacation the best that it can be. Planning and organizing are essential to a successful Walt Disney World vacation, but if they become your focus, you won't be able to hear the music and enjoy the dance.

So think of us as your dancing coach. We'll teach you the steps to the dance in advance so that when you're on vacation and the music plays, you will dance with effortless grace and ease.

The Importance of Being Goofy

Disney's park operations manager summoned his assistant. "Bill, there's something I don't understand about these quarterly numbers."

"What's that, boss?" asked the assistant.

The manager flipped through a huge stack of expense reports. "The character meals. We're still packing in the same number of guests, but our food budget is skyrocketing. What's the story?"

"Well," said the assistant, "it's the characters. They're eating more. A lot more, and they're eating pricier food."

Dumbfounded, the manager rechecked his figures. "That's crazy! How could they be eating enough to cost us this much? Didn't I fire the chubby ones after that 'incident' in the narrow seats on Splash Mountain? And I know I told Pooh and his freeloader friends to stay away from the dessert carts."

The assistant shook his head. "That's all true, sir, but we're looking at a variety of problems here. Take Uncle Scrooge ... ever since we forced him to cut out the cigars, he's been bingeing on truffles flown in from France. He's always had expensive tastes."

The manager groaned. "Expensive for everyone but him. What else?"

Flipping open a notepad, the assistant continued. "All of the characters are generally overweight, just like a rising percentage of the population at large. You may have noticed that Genie and Ballou use big cowboy belts to hold in their guts, and that Grumpy, Doc, and the Beast are wearing Hawaiian shirts outside their pants. "

"I can't believe it. They seem so fit."

"Well that's not all. The Little Mermaid has gone up two cup ... er, shell sizes. Another couple of pounds and she'll be sporting giant clams. Captain Hook and the Fairy Godmother are wearing lycra stretch pants, and Cinderella looks like she's got a little Prince Charming in the oven. Worst of all, the FAA has grounded Aladdin for exceeding the weight limit of his flying carpet."

"Why are they gaining so much weight?" asked the manager.

"Something about being cooped up in a roomful of rambunctious kids with an everlasting buffet seems to make them want to gorge." He looked up. "Must be the stress."

"I'll give them stress," the manager snapped. "Can't we get them on an exercise routine?"

"We tried that, sir," sighed the assistant. "Sam the Eagle led calisthenics out at Wide World of Sports. But he got a little too ... enthusiastic. They were burning so many calories that they became ravenous and ate even more than before."

"This is ridiculous," said the manager. "We get that buffet food in information is unique. In addition to *The Unofficial Guide to Walt Disney World,* these titles are available:

Mini-Mickey: The Pocket-Sized Unofficial Guide to Walt Disney World, by Bob Sehlinger

Inside Disney: The Incredible Story of Walt Disney World and the Man Behind the Mouse, by Eve Zibart

The Unofficial Guide to Walt Disney World for Grown-Ups, by Eve Zibart

The Unofficial Guide to Walt Disney World with Kids, by Bob Sehlinger

Beyond Disney: The Unofficial Guide to Universal, SeaWorld, and the Best of Central Florida, by Bob Sehlinger and Chris Mohney

Mini-Mickey is a portable, *Cliffs Notes* version of *The Unofficial Guide to Walt Disney World.* It distills information from this comprehensive guide to help short-stay or last-minute visitors decide quickly how to plan their limited hours at Disney World. *Inside Disney* is a behind-the-scenes, unauthorized history of Walt Disney World loaded with all the amazing facts and great stories we can't squeeze into this guide. *The Unofficial Guide to Walt Disney World for Grown-Ups* helps adults traveling without children make the most of their Disney vacation, while *The Unofficial Guide to Walt Disney World with Kids* presents planning and touring tips for a family vacation. Finally, *Beyond Disney* is a guide to non-Disney attractions, restaurants, outdoor recreation, and nightlife in Orlando and central Florida. All of the guides are available from Wiley Publishing and at most bookstores.

The Death of Spontaneity

One of our all-time favorite letters came from a man in Chapel Hill, North Carolina:

Your book reads like the operations plan for an amphibious landing ... Go here, do this, proceed to Step 15. ... You must think that everyone [who visits Walt Disney World] is a hyperactive, type-A, theme-park commando. What happened to the satisfaction of self-discovery or the joy of spontaneity? Next you will be telling us when to empty our bladders.

As it happens, *Unofficial Guide* researchers are a pretty existential crew. We are big on self-discovery if the activity is walking in the woods or watching birds. Some of us are able to improvise jazz, and others can whip up a mean pot of chili without a recipe. When it comes to Disney World, however, we all agree that you need either a good plan or a frontal lobotomy. The operational definition of self-discovery and spontaneity at Walt Disney World is the "pleasure" of heat prostration and the "joy" of standing in line.

Face it: Walt Disney World is not a very existential place. In many ways it's the quintessential system, the ultimate in mass-produced entertainment, the most planned and programmed environment anywhere.

We aren't saying that you can't have a great time at Walt Disney World. It is, after all, one of the world's most happy, delightful, and amazing destinations. What we *are* saying is that you need a plan. You don't have to be compulsive or inflexible; just think about what you want to do before you go. Don't delude yourself by rationalizing that the information in this guide is only for the pathological and the superorganized. Ask not for whom the tome tells, Bubba—it tells for thee.

A Word to Our Readers about Annual Revisions

Some who purchase each new edition of the *Unofficial Guide* chastise us for retaining examples, comments, and descriptions from previous editions. This letter from a Grand Rapids, Michigan, reader is typical:

You guidebook still has the same little example stories. When I got my [new] book I expected a true update and new stuff, not the same-old, same-old!

First, the *Unofficial Guide* is a reference work. Though we're flattered that some users read the guide from cover to cover and that some find it entertaining, our objective is to provide information that will enable you to have the best possible Walt Disney World vacation.

Each year during our revision research, we check every theme park, water park, attraction, hotel, restaurant, nightspot, shop, and entertainment offering. While there are many changes (most attributable to Disney World's growth), much remains the same from year to year. When we profile and critique an attraction, we try to provide the reader with the most insightful, relevant, and useful information, written in the clearest possible language. If an attraction doesn't change, it makes little sense to risk clarity for the sake of freshening the prose. Disney World guests who try the Mad Tea Party, the Haunted Mansion, or the *Country Bear Jamboree* today, for example, experience exactly the same presentation as guests who visited Disney World in 2004, 1990, or 1986. Moreover, according to our patron surveys (several thousand each year), today's guests respond to these attractions in the same way as prior-year patrons.

The bottom line: We believe our readers are better served if we devote our time to what's changing and new as opposed to what remains the same. The success or failure of the *Unofficial Guide* is determined not by the writing style but by the accuracy of the information and, ultimately, whether you have a positive experience at Walt Disney World. Every change we make (or don't make) is evaluated in this context.

Corrections, Updates, and Breaking News

Corrections and updates can be found online at the *Unofficial Guide* Web site **www.touringplans.com.** Also available on the site are custom touring plans, trip planning and organizing tools, research reports, and breaking Walt Disney World news.

We Got Attitude

Some readers disagree about our attitude toward Disney. A woman from Golden, Colorado, lambasted us:

*I read your book cover to cover and felt you were way too hard on Disney. It's
disappointing when you're all enthused about going [to Walt Disney World]
to be slammed with all these criticisms and possible pitfalls.*

A reader from Little Rock, Arkansas, took us to task for the opposite
prejudice:

*Your book was quite complimentary of Disney, perhaps too complimentary.
Maybe the free trips you travel writers get at Disney World are chipping
away at your objectivity.*

And from a Williamsport, Pennsylvania, mother of three:

*Reading your book irritated me before we went [to Walt Disney World]
because of all the warnings and cautions. I guess I'm used to having guidebooks pump me up about where I'm going. But once I arrived I found I
was fully prepared and we had a great time. In retrospect, I have to admit
you were right on the money. What I regarded as you being negative was
just a good dose of reality.*

Finally, a reader from Phoenixville, Pennsylvania, prefers no opinions
at all, writing:

*While each person has the right to his or her own opinion, I did not purchase
the book for an opinion.*

For the record, we've always paid our own way at Walt Disney World:
hotels, admissions, meals, the works. We don't dislike Disney, and we
don't have an ax to grind. We're positive by nature and much prefer to
praise than to criticize. Personally, we have enjoyed the Disney parks
immensely over the years, both experiencing them and writing about
them. Disney, however, as with all corporations (and all people), is better
at some things than others. Because our readers shell out big bucks to go
to Walt Disney World, we believe they have the right to know in advance
what's good and what's not. For those who think we're overly positive,
please understand that the *Unofficial Guide* is a guidebook, not an
exposé. Our objective is for you to enjoy your visit. To that end we report
fairly and objectively. When readers disagree with our opinions, we, in
the interest of fairness, publish their viewpoint alongside ours. To the
best of our knowledge, the *Unofficial Guides* are the only travel guides in
print that do this.

The Sum of All Fears

Every writer who expresses an opinion is accustomed to readers who
strongly agree or disagree: It comes with the territory. Extremely troubling, however, is the possibility that our efforts to be objective have
frightened some readers away from Walt Disney World or made others
apprehensive. For the record, if you enjoy theme parks, Disney World is

as good as it gets, absolute nirvana. It's upbeat, safe, fun, eye-popping, happy, and exciting. If you arrive without knowing a thing about the place and make every possible mistake, chances are about 90% that you'll have a wonderful vacation anyway. In the end, guidebooks don't make or break great destinations. They are simply tools to help you enhance your experience and get the most for your money.

As wonderful as Walt Disney World is, however, it's a complex destination. Even so, it isn't nearly as challenging or difficult as New York, San Francisco, Paris, Acapulco, or any other large city or destination. And, happily, there are numerous ways to save money, minimize hassle, and make the most of your time. That's what this guide is about: giving you a heads-up regarding potential problems or opportunities. Unfortunately, some *Unofficial Guide* readers add up the warnings and critical advice and conclude that Walt Disney World is too intimidating, too expensive, or too much work. They lose track of the wonder of Disney World and focus instead on what might go wrong.

Our philosophy is that knowledge is power (and time and money, too). You're free to follow our advice or not at your discretion. But you can't exercise that discretion if we fail to present the issues.

With or without a guidebook, you'll have a great time at Walt Disney World. If you let us, we'll help you smooth the potential bumps. We're certain we can help you turn a great vacation into an absolutely superb one. Either way, once there, you'll get the feel of the place and quickly reach a comfort level that will allay your apprehensions and allow you to have a great experience.

Too Many Cooks in the Kitchen?

We received this query from a Manchester, Vermont, reader, and feel it deserves a serious response:

I read a review on the Internet criticizing the Unofficial Guide because it was "written by a team of researchers." The reviewer doesn't say why he thinks the team approach is inferior, but the inference is along the lines of "too many cooks spoil the soup." Why do you use the team approach?

There are several reasons. Foremost is that the team approach gives us the capability to undertake much more sophisticated and extensive research. Collecting waiting-time data for our touring-plan software (see pages 66–71), for example, required more than a dozen researchers to visit the Disney parks for several days at four or more different times of year. Another project, monitoring the Disney transportation system, requires riding and timing every bus, boat, and monorail route, a task that takes four researchers almost a week to complete. In covering lodging, the *Unofficial Guide* reviews, rates, and ranks about 250 Disney World–area hotels—over four times as many as other guidebooks. On any research trip, we have one or two teams of hotel inspectors checking hotels all day long.

No other guides do this, nor can they, because the scope of the research and processing of data require time, experience, and resources beyond the capabilities of a single author or even several co-authors. An entire organization collects and compiles information for the *Unofficial Guide,* an organization guided by individuals with extensive training and experience in research design as well as data collection and analysis. Known and respected in both the travel industry and academe, *Unofficial Guide* researchers have served as consultants or project planners for the Busch Entertainment Corporation, H.B.J. Theme Park Division, the Utah Ski Association, the Eastern Professional River Outfitters Association, and the Boy Scouts of America, among others.

Not all *Unofficial Guide* research relates to the parks and resorts. We also conduct extensive research on you, the reader. From the concept up, you see, *Unofficial Guides* are different from other guidebooks. Other guides (regardless of how information is formatted) are researched and developed by individual authors or co-authors, usually travel writers. Thus, everything is filtered through the lens of those authors' tastes, preferences, and opinions. Publishers of these guides hope the information the author presents is compatible with the needs of the reader, but if it is, the compatibility is largely accidental. In *Unofficial Guides,* by contrast, it's your tastes, preferences, and opinions that dictate the content of the guides. In other words, we start with the needs of our readers, identified through exhaustive research, and build a book that meets those needs.

Another reason for using a team approach is to minimize author bias. As discussed earlier, a single author incorporates his (or her) own tastes and opinions in his work. Our researchers, by contrast, include individuals ranging in age from 16 to 60 and sometimes, for special assignments, children as young as 8. Thus, the opinions and advice in the *Unofficial Guide* are informed by the perspectives of a diverse group of researchers, a process that, we believe, achieves the highest level of objectivity.

A final reason for the team approach is the need for expertise in specific areas. No individual author can possibly be qualified to write about every topic in the vast range of important subjects that make up a good guide to Walt Disney World. Thus, our chapter "Walt Disney World with Kids" was developed in consultation with three nationally respected child psychologists and an advisory group of parents. Similarly, we have professional culinary experts dedicated to the task of rating restaurants. Our golf coverage, likewise, is handled by professional golf writer Larry Olmsted, and our database and touring plan program are developed and managed by programmer and software developer Len Testa. When you cover shopping, you want a local who lives to shop and knows where to find every back-counter deal within 50 miles. Guess what? We've got her!

The bottom line is that there are more of us so that we can do more for you. I (Bob) put the fruits of our research into words, but behind me is an organization unequaled in travel publishing.

The Unofficial Team

So who are all these folks? Allow me to introduce them all, except for our dining critic who shall remain anonymous:

Bob Sehlinger	Author and executive publisher
Len Testa	Touring plans software developer, data collection director, touringplans.com webmaster
Fred Hazelton	Statistician
Dr. Karen Turnbow	Child psychologist
Jim Hill	Disney historian
Pam Brandon	Shopping guru
Steve Jones	Cartographer
Tami Knight	Cartoonist
Marie Hillin	Fact checker
Shane Kennedy	*Unofficial Guide* mail manager and survey collator

Data Collectors	**Hotel Inspectors**	**Production and Editorial**
Rob Sutton, supervisor	Luke Skurman	Chris Mohney, editor
Kai Brueckerhoff	Christina Koshzow	Gabriela Oates
Kenny Contrell	Grace Walton	Molly Merkle
Linda Sutton	Holly Cross	Mopsy Gascon
Christine Testa		Annie Long
Mike Testa		Jackie Doyle
Mais Testa		Ann Cassar
Guy Garguilo		

While we're acknowledging people, allow me to express sincere thanks to reader Tom Dorans, who personifies the concept of constructive criticism. A careful and thoughtful reader, Tom found errors we had missed in our 2004 edition. Instead of just chucking the guide or making a big deal of our mistakes, Tom very kindly brought them to our attention. We all make mistakes. At the *Unofficial Guide,* we admit them, take responsibility, and try to do better next time. We're grateful to Tom for making the effort to contact us and for giving us the opportunity to straighten things out.

The How and the Why of It

A Dayton, Ohio, reader offered this comment:

> I used several guides preparing for our [Disney World] trip. One of them dumped on the Unofficial Guide for referring to Dumbo as a "cycle ride." Though my kids are totally infatuated with Dumbo, I found your section about how the various types of rides work to be both interesting and useful. Dumbo's charm and appeal doesn't change the fact that it's a cycle ride. Get a life!

Most guidebooks do a reasonably good job with what and where. *Unofficial Guides* add the how and why. Describing attractions like

Dumbo, or hotels or restaurants (the what) at a given destination (the where) is the foundation of other travel guidebooks. We know from our research, however, that our readers like to know how things work. Take hotels, for example. In the *Unofficial Guide,* we not only provide hotel choices (rated and ranked, of course) but also explain the economic and operational logic of the lodging industry (the why) and offer instructions (the how) that enable the reader to take advantage of opportunities for hotel discounts, room upgrades, and the like. In this and all of our *Unofficial Guides,* whether we're discussing cruise ships, theme parks, ski resorts, casinos, or golf courses, we reveal the travel industry's inner workings and demonstrate how to use such insight in selecting and purchasing travel and for planning itineraries. For the reader, knowledge is power, which translates into informed decisions and confidence.

Most guides give the reader a plate of fish to choose from. An *Unofficial Guide* additionally says which fish are best. More important, however, an *Unofficial Guide* teaches the reader how to fish. Anyone who has read the hotel chapter in any *Unofficial Guide* can use the information to book a great room at a bargain price anywhere in the world.

The *Unofficial Guide* Publishing Year

We receive many queries asking when the next edition of the *Unofficial Guide* will be available. Usually our new editions are in stores by late August or early September. Thus, the 2006 edition will be on the shelves in August or September 2005.

Letters and Comments from Readers

Many who use *The Unofficial Guide to Walt Disney World* write us to comment or share their own strategies for visiting Disney World. We appreciate all such input, both positive and critical, and encourage our readers to continue writing. Their comments and observations are frequently incorporated into revised editions of the *Unofficial Guide* and have contributed immeasurably to its improvement. If you write us or return our reader-survey form, rest assured that we won't release your name and address to any mailing-list companies, direct-mail advertisers, or other third party. Unless you instruct us otherwise, we'll assume that you don't object to being quoted in the *Unofficial Guide.*

Reader Questionnaire and Restaurant Survey

At the back of this guide is a questionnaire you can use to express opinions about your Walt Disney World visit. The questionnaire allows every member of your party, regardless of age, to tell us what he or she thinks. Use the separate restaurant survey to describe your Disney World dining experiences. Clip the questionnaire and restaurant survey and mail them to:

Reader Survey, The *Unofficial Guide* Series, P.O. Box 43673, Birmingham, AL 35243.

How to Contact the Author

Bob Sehlinger
The Unofficial Guide to Walt Disney World
P.O. Box 43673
Birmingham, AL 35243
unofficialguides@menasharidge.com

When you write, put your address on both your letter and envelope; the two sometimes get separated. It's also a good idea to include your phone number. If you e-mail us, please tell us where you're from. Remember, as travel writers, we're often out of the office for long periods of time, so forgive us if our response is slow. *Unofficial Guide* e-mail isn't forwarded to us when we're traveling, but we'll respond as soon as possible after we return.

Walt Disney World: An Overview

If you're choosing a United States tourist destination, the question is not whether to visit Walt Disney World, but how to see its best offerings with some economy of time, effort, and finances.

What Walt Disney World Encompasses

Walt Disney World encompasses 43 square miles, an area twice as large as Manhattan Island or roughly the size of Boston. Situated strategically in this vast expanse are the Magic Kingdom, Epcot, Disney-MGM Studios, and the Animal Kingdom theme parks; two swimming theme parks; two nighttime-entertainment areas; a sports complex; several golf courses, hotels, and campgrounds; more than 100 restaurants; four interconnected lakes; a shopping complex; three convention venues; a nature preserve; and a transportation system consisting of four-lane highways, elevated monorails, and a network of canals.

The Major Theme Parks

The Magic Kingdom

When people think of Walt Disney World, most think of the Magic Kingdom. It consists of the adventures, rides, and shows symbolizing the Disney cartoon characters, and Cinderella Castle. Although the Magic Kingdom is only one element of Disney World, it remains the heart.

The Magic Kingdom is subdivided into seven "lands," six of which are arranged around a central hub. First encountered is Main Street, U.S.A., which connects the Magic Kingdom entrance with the hub. Clockwise around the hub are Adventureland, Frontierland, Liberty Square, Fantasyland, and Tomorrowland. Mickey's Toontown Fair (originally Mickey's Birthdayland), the first new land added since the Magic Kingdom opened, is along the Walt Disney Railroad on three acres between Fantasyland and Tomorrowland. Access is through Fantasyland or Tomorrowland or via the railroad. Main Street and the other six lands will be detailed later. Three hotels (the Contemporary, Polynesian, and Grand Floridian Beach Resorts) are near the Magic Kingdom and directly connected to it by monorail and boat. Two additional hotels, Shades of Green and Disney's Wilderness Lodge Resort and Villas, are nearby but aren't served by the monorail.

Epcot

Opened in October 1982, Epcot is twice as big as the Magic Kingdom and comparable in scope. It has two major areas: Future World consists of pavilions concerning human creativity and technological advancement; World Showcase, arranged around a 41-acre lagoon, presents the architectural, social, and cultural heritages of almost a dozen nations, each country represented by replicas of famous landmarks and settings familiar to world travelers. Epcot is more educational than the Magic Kingdom and has been characterized as a permanent World's Fair.

The Epcot resort hotels—Disney's Beach Club Resort and Villas, Disney's Yacht Club, Disney's BoardWalk Inn and Villas Resort, the Walt Disney World Swan, and the Walt Disney World Dolphin—are within a 5- to 15-minute walk of the International Gateway entrance to the theme park. The hotels are also linked to the park by canal. Epcot is connected to the Magic Kingdom and its hotels by monorail.

Disney-MGM Studios

Opened in 1989 and about the size of the Magic Kingdom, Disney-MGM Studios has two areas. The first is a theme park focused on the past, present, and future of the motion-picture and television industries. This section contains movie-theme rides and shows and covers about half of the complex. Park highlights include a re-creation of Hollywood and Sunset Boulevards from Hollywood's Golden Age, stunt demonstrations, a children's play area, shows on sound effects, and four high-tech rides.

The second area is a working motion-picture and television production facility encompassing three sound stages, a backlot of streets and sets, and support services. Public access is limited to tours that take visitors behind the scenes for crash courses on Disney animation and moviemaking, including (on occasion) the opportunity to witness the shooting of a film, television show, or commercial.

Disney-MGM Studios is connected to other Walt Disney World areas by highway and canal but not by monorail. Guests can park in the Studios' pay parking lot or commute by bus. Guests at Epcot resort hotels can reach the Studios by boat or on foot.

Disney's Animal Kingdom

More than five times the size of the Magic Kingdom, the Animal Kingdom combines zoological exhibits with rides, shows, and live entertainment. The park is arranged somewhat like the Magic Kingdom, in a hub-and-spoke configuration. A lush tropical rain forest serves as Main

Street, funneling visitors to Discovery Island, the park's hub. Dominated by the park's central icon, the 14-story-tall, hand-carved Tree of Life, Discovery Island offers services, shopping, and dining. From there, guests can access the theme areas: Africa, Asia, DinoLand U.S.A., and Camp Minnie-Mickey. Discovery Island, Africa, Camp Minnie-Mickey, and DinoLand U.S.A. opened in 1998, followed by Asia in 1999. Africa, the largest theme area, at 100 acres, features free-roaming herds in a re-creation of the Serengeti Plain. Guests tour in open-air safari vehicles.

Animal Kingdom has its own pay parking lot and is connected to other Disney World destinations by the Disney bus system. Although there are no hotels at the Animal Kingdom, the All-Star, Animal Kingdom Lodge, and Coronado Springs Resorts are nearby.

The Water Parks

Disney World has two major water parks: Typhoon Lagoon and Blizzard Beach. Typhoon Lagoon is distinguished by a wave pool capable of making six-foot waves. Blizzard Beach is newer and features more slides. Both parks are beautifully landscaped, and great attention is paid to atmosphere and aesthetics. Typhoon Lagoon and Blizzard Beach have their own adjacent parking lots and can be reached via Disney bus.

Other Walt Disney World Venues

Downtown Disney (Downtown Disney Marketplace, Pleasure Island, and Disney's West Side)

Downtown Disney is a large shopping, dining, and entertainment complex encompassing the Downtown Disney Marketplace on the east, the gated (admission-required) Pleasure Island nighttime entertainment venue in the middle, and Disney's West Side on the west. Downtown Disney Marketplace contains the world's largest Disney character merchandise store, upscale resort-wear and specialty shops, and several restaurants, including the tacky but popular Rainforest Café. Pleasure Island offers the nightclubs described below plus several upscale restaurants and shops. Disney's West Side opened in 1997 and combines nightlife, shopping, dining, and entertainment. The House of Blues serves Cajun-Creole dishes in its restaurant and electric blues in its music hall. Bongos, a nightclub and café created by Gloria and Emilio Estefan, offers Cuban rhythms and flavors. Wolfgang Puck Café, sandwiched among pricey boutiques (including a three-level Virgin Records mega-store), is the West Side's prestige eatery. For entertainment, you'll find a 24-screen cinema; a permanent showplace for the extraordinary, 70-person cast of Cirque du Soleil's *La Nouba;* and Disney-Quest, an interactive virtual reality and electronic games venue. Access Downtown Disney via Disney buses from most Disney World locations.

Pleasure Island

Part of the Downtown Disney complex, Pleasure Island is a six-acre nighttime-entertainment center where one cover charge gets a visitor into eight nightclubs. The clubs have different themes and feature a variety of shows and activities. Music ranges from pop rock to hip-hop to jazz. For the sedentary (or exhausted), there's an adjacent 24-screen movie complex, and for the hungry, restaurants include a much-hyped Planet Hollywood.

Disney's BoardWalk

Located near Epcot, Disney's BoardWalk is an idealized replication of an East Coast turn-of-the-nineteenth-century waterfront resort. Open all day, BoardWalk features upscale restaurants, shops and galleries, a brew pub, and an ESPN sports bar. In the evening, a nightclub with dueling pianos and a DJ dance club join the lineup. There's no admission fee for BoardWalk, but individual clubs levy cover charges at night. In addition to public facilities are a 378-room deluxe hotel and a 532-unit time-share development. BoardWalk is within walking distance of the Epcot resorts and Epcot's International Gateway. Boat transportation is available from Disney-MGM Studios; buses serve other Disney World locations.

Disney's Wide World of Sports

Disney's 200-acre Wide World of Sports is a state-of-the-art competition and training facility consisting of a 7,500-seat ballpark, a field house, and venues for baseball, softball, tennis, track and field, beach volleyball, and 27 other sports. The spring-training home of the Atlanta Braves, the complex also hosts a mind-boggling calendar of professional and amateur competitions. Disney World guests are welcome as paid spectators but can't use the facilities unless they're participants in a scheduled competition.

Disney Cruise Line

In 1998, Disney launched (literally) its own cruise line with the 2,400-passenger *Disney Magic*. Its twin ship, the *Disney Wonder*, first sailed in 1999. Cruises depart from Port Canaveral (about a 90-minute drive from Walt Disney World) on 3-, 4-, 7-, and 14-day itineraries, and in the summer of 2005, from Los Angeles. Caribbean cruises include a day at Castaway Cay, Disney's private island. Cruises can be packaged with a stay at Disney World, and in 2005 with a stay at Disneyland. Although the cruises are family-oriented, extensive children's programs and elaborate child-care facilities allow parents plenty of opportunity for time away from the kids.

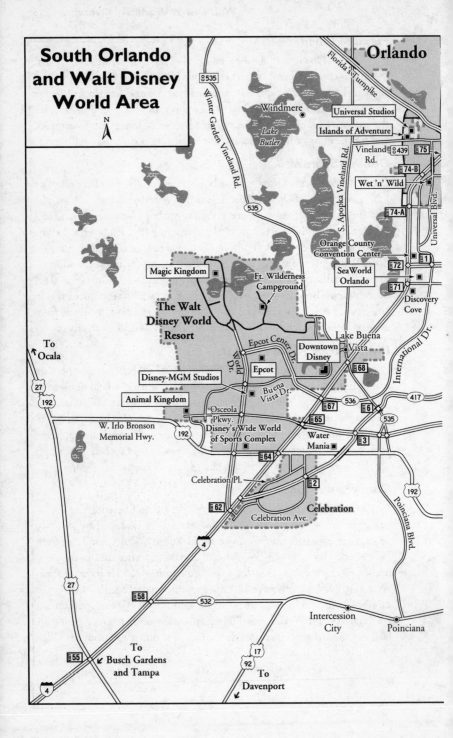

South Orlando and Walt Disney World Area

Orlando

Florida's Turnpike

Winter Garden Vineland Rd.

535

Windmere

Lake Butler

Universal Studios

Islands of Adventure

Vineland Rd.

439

75

74-B

Wet 'n' Wild

74-A

S. Apopka Vineland Rd.

Orange County Convention Center

SeaWorld Orlando

72

1

71

Discovery Cove

Magic Kingdom

Ft. Wilderness Campground

The Walt Disney World Resort

Epcot Center Dr.

Lake Buena Vista

Downtown Disney

68

World Dr.

Epcot

Disney-MGM Studios

Buena Vista Dr.

International Dr.

Animal Kingdom

Osceola Pkwy.

Disney's Wide World of Sports Complex

67

536

6

65

417

535

Water Mania

3

64

To Ocala

27

192

W. Irlo Bronson Memorial Hwy.

192

Celebration Pl.

2

62

Celebration

Celebration Ave.

Poinciana Blvd.

4

27

58

532

192

Intercession City

Poinciana

55

To Busch Gardens and Tampa

17

92

To Davenport

4

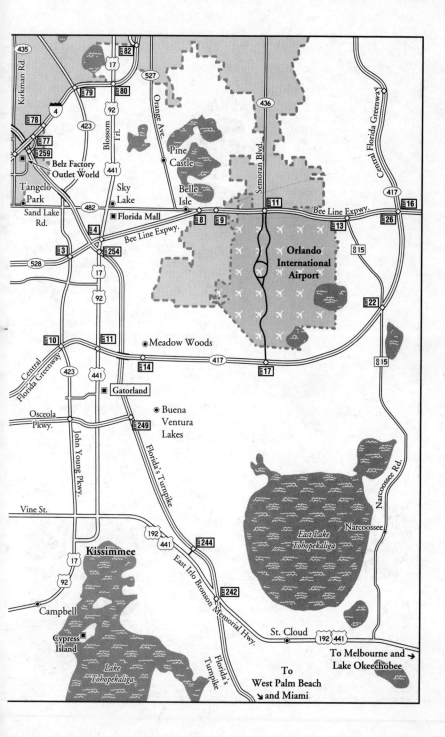

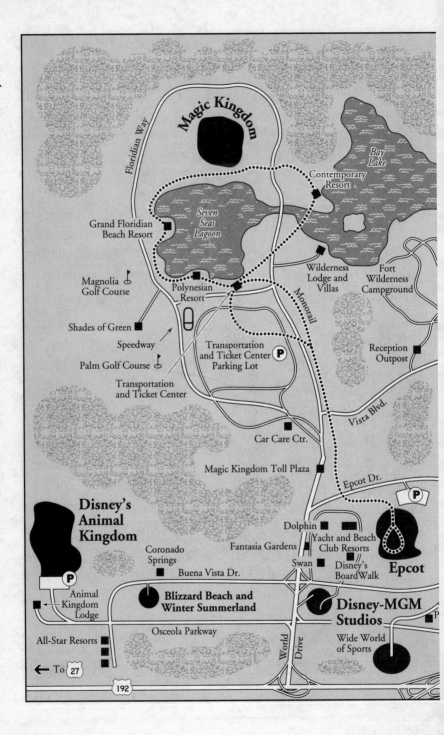

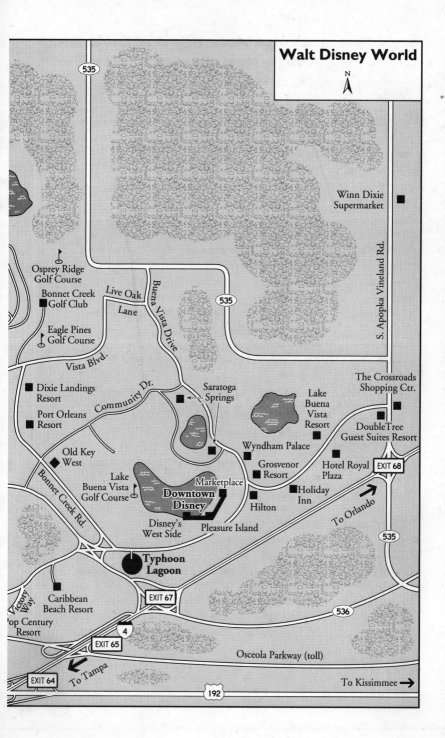

Walt Disney World

N

Winn Dixie
Supermarket

Osprey Ridge
Golf Course

Bonnet Creek
Golf Club

Live Oak Lane

Buena Vista Drive

Eagle Pines
Golf Course

Vista Blvd.

S. Apopka Vineland Rd.

535

The Crossroads
Shopping Ctr.

Dixie Landings
Resort

Community Dr.

Saratoga
Springs

Lake
Buena
Vista
Resort

DoubleTree
Guest Suites Resort

Port Orleans
Resort

Wyndham Palace

Grosvenor
Resort

Hotel Royal
Plaza

EXIT 68

Old Key
West

Lake
Buena Vista
Golf Course

Marketplace

Downtown
Disney

Hilton

Holiday
Inn

To Orlando

535

Bonnet Creek Rd.

Disney's
West Side

Pleasure Island

Typhoon
Lagoon

EXIT 67

536

Victory Way

Caribbean
Beach Resort

Pop Century
Resort

4

EXIT 65

To Tampa

Osceola Parkway (toll)

EXIT 64

192

To Kissimmee

DISNEYSPEAK POCKET TRANSLATOR

Disney has its own somewhat peculiar language. Here are terms you're likely to encounter:

DisneySpeak	English Definition
Adventure	Ride
Attraction	Ride or theater show
Attraction Host	Ride operator
Audience	Crowd
Backstage	Behind the scenes, out of view of customers
Bull Pen	Queuing area
Cast Member	Employee
Character	Disney cartoon character impersonated by an employee
Costume	Work attire or uniform
Dark Ride	Indoor ride
Day Guest	Any customer not staying at a Disney resort
Face Character	A character that does not wear a head-covering costume (Snow White, Cinderella, Jasmine)
General Public	Same as day-guest
Greeter	Employee positioned at the entrance of an attraction
Guest	Customer
Hidden Mickeys	Frontal silhouette of Mickey's head worked subtly into the design of buildings, railings, vehicles, golf greens, attractions, and just about anything else
In Rehearsal or In Preview	Operating though not officially open
Lead	Foreman or manager, the person in charge of an attraction
On Stage	In full view of customers
Preshow	Entertainment at an attraction prior to the feature presentation
Resort Guest	A customer staying at a Disney resort
Role	An employee's job
Security Host	Security guard
Soft Opening	A park or attraction becoming operational before its stated opening date
Transitional Experience	An element of the queuing area and/or preshow that provides a story line or information essential to understanding the attraction

Part One

Planning before You Leave Home

Visiting Walt Disney World is a bit like childbirth—you never really believe what people tell you, but once you have been through it yourself, you know exactly what they were saying!

> —Hilary Wolfe, a mother and Unofficial Guide reader
> from Swansea, United Kingdom

Your guide was a little overwhelming (like a research project to plan our vacation), but then so were all the choices at Disney.

> —Mother of two from Greenfield, Indiana

Gathering Information

In addition to this guide, we recommend that you obtain:

1. The Walt Disney Travel Company Florida Vacations Brochure and Video/DVD   This video/DVD and brochure describe Walt Disney World in its entirety, list rates for all Disney resort hotels and campgrounds, and describe Disney World package vacations. They're available from most travel agents or by calling the Walt Disney Travel Company at (407) 828-8101 or (407) 934-7639. Be prepared to hold. When you get a representative, tell them you want the video or DVD vacation planner that lists the benefits and costs of the various packages.

2. The Disney Cruise Line Brochure and DVD   The brochure provides details on vacation packages that combine a cruise on the Disney Cruise Line with a stay at Disney World. Disney Cruise Line also offers a free DVD that tells all you need to know about Disney cruises and then some. To obtain a copy, call (888) DCL-2500 or order at **www.disneycruise.com.**

3. Orlando MagiCard   If you're considering lodging outside Disney World or if you think you might patronize attractions and restaurants outside the park, obtain an Orlando MagiCard, a Vacation Planner, and the *Orlando Official Accommodations Guide* (all free) from the Orlando Visitors Center. The MagiCard makes you eligible for discounts at hotels, restaurants, and attractions outside Disney World. To order the accommodations guide, call (800) 943-9492. For additional information and materials, call (407) 363-5872 weekdays during business hours. Allow four weeks for delivery. On the Internet, see **www.orlandoinfo.com.** The MagiCard and accompanying brochure can be printed from a personal computer.

4. *Florida Traveler Discount Guide* Another good source of discounts on lodging, restaurants, and attractions statewide is the *Florida Traveler Discount Guide,* published by Exit Information Guide. The guide is free, but you pay $3 for handling ($5 shipped to Canada). Call (352) 371-3948, Monday–Friday, 8 a.m.–5 p.m. EST, or go to **www. travelerdiscountguide.com** and order online. Order by mail at 4205 NW 6th Street, Gainesville, FL 32609. Similar guides to other states are available at the same number. Also, print hotel coupons free from their **www.roomsaver.com** Web site.

5. *Kissimmee–St. Cloud Tour and Travel Sales Guide* This full-color directory of hotels and attractions is one of the most complete available and is of particular interest to those who intend to lodge outside Disney World. It also lists rental houses, time-shares, and condominiums. For a copy, call the Kissimmee–St. Cloud Convention and Visitors Bureau at (800) 327-9159, (407) 939-6244, or (407) 827-5141 (TTY); or access **www.floridakiss.com.**

6. *Guidebook for Guests with Disabilities* Each park's *Guidebook for Guests with Disabilities* is available online at **www.disneyworld.com.**

Request Information Early

Request information as far in advance as possible and allow four weeks for delivery. Make a checklist of information you requested, and follow up if you haven't received your materials within six weeks.

Disney Magazine

If you're really a Disneyholic, this quarterly magazine will supply full-color hype of all developments in the Walt Disney Company, including theme parks, movies, Disney art, collectibles, and merchandise. Though there isn't much useful information, the magazine is usually a fun read. A two-year subscription is $19.95. Write *Disney Magazine,* P.O. Box 37265, Boone, IA 50037-0265, call (800) 333-8734, or log on to **www.disney.com/disneymagazine.**

The Organizer

The *PassPorter Walt Disney World Resort Planner and Organizer* is a perfect companion to the *Unofficial Guide.* In addition to being a fine guidebook, it offers all the bells and whistles of a desk organizer, including pockets for tickets, coupons, and receipts, and blank daily itinerary forms. The spiral-bound organizer sells for $22 and is available from PassPorter Travel Press at (877) 929-3273 or **www.passporter.com.**

Walt Disney World on the Web

Searching the Internet for Disney information is like navigating an immense maze for a very small piece of cheese. There's a lot of information available, but you may have to wade through list after list until you find the Internet addresses you want and need.

Disney's official Web site offers much of the same information as the Walt Disney Travel Company's vacation guidebook, but the guidebook has better pictures. Supposedly, the Web site is updated daily, but we frequently find errors. You can buy theme-park admissions and make resort and dining reservations online. The Web site also offers online shopping, weather forecasts, and information on renovations and special events. Disney's Web site is **www.disney.com.** (Universal Orlando's home page is **www.universalorlando.com.**)

Many individuals maintain elaborate Disney-related Web sites. Individuals also maintain Disney chat groups, which can provide both correct and incorrect information, depending on who's chatting. Disneyphile techies worldwide help maintain lists. There are lists of hidden Mickeys, lists of attractions ranked and rated, lists of characters, and more lists of lists. You could explore the Web for weeks on end.

Recommended Web Sites

Len Testa, Internet guru and *Unofficial Guide* data collection director, has combed the Web, looking for the best Disney sites. Here are Len's picks:

Best Official Theme-park Site   The official Walt Disney World Web site (**www.disneyworld.com**) gets the nod over the official Universal Studios site (**www.universalorlando.com**) and the official SeaWorld site (**www.seaworld.com**). Each contains information on ticket options, park hours, and attractions. Disney's site is more comprehensive, providing downloadable color maps of each park and lists of attractions closed for maintenance.

Best General Unofficial Site   The Walt Disney World Information Guide (**www.allearsnet.com**) is the first Web site we recommend to friends interested in going to Disney World. It contains information on virtually every hotel, restaurant, and activity in the World. Want to know what the rooms look like at Disney resorts before you book one? This site has photos—sometimes for each floor of a resort. The Web site is updated several times per week and includes menus from Disney restaurants, ticketing information, maps, driving directions, and more.

A good site that has gotten even better over the past year is **www.mouseplanet.com.** Besides timely information, MousePlanet has shown a commitment to delivering detailed, multipart stories on a wide range of Disney theme-park subjects. We've even had the opportunity to visit Disney World with MousePlanet's park-touring expert, Mike Scopa, whose enthusiasm for Disney World shows in his weekly column.

Best Money-saving Site   Mary Waring's **www.mousesavers.com** is the kind of Web site for which the Internet was invented. It keeps an updated list of discounts and reservation codes for use at Disney resorts. The codes are separated into categories such as "For anyone" and "For residents of certain states." Anyone calling the Disney central reservations office (phone (407) W-DISNEY) can use a current code and get the discounted rate. Savings can be considerable. On a recent trip, we used a discount code and paid about $89 per night for a room in the Casitas at Coronado Springs. The family two doors down paid the full rate of $180 per night for essentially the same room, but they probably didn't sleep as well as we did. Two often-overlooked features are the discount codes for rental cars and non-Disney hotels in the area.

Best Disney Discussion Boards   The best online discussions of all things Disney can be found at **www.disboards.com.** Containing more than 60,000 members and 5 million postings, the discussion boards here are the most active and popular on the Web. Posting a question on any aspect of an upcoming trip is likely to get helpful responses from lots of folks who've been in the same situation. We love the interactive nature of these boards and often answer questions, post experimental touring plans, and solicit opinions on upcoming *Unofficial Guide* subjects.

Best Site for Breaking News and Rumors   We try to check **www.wdw magic.com** every few days for the latest news and rumors on Disney World. The site is popular with Disney fans and park cast members, who often provide insider information on upcoming attractions and developments. WDWMagic also has pages dedicated to major rides, parades, and shows in each park, including audio and video. User forums allow you to read and post messages to other Disney fans. A close second: **www.scream scape.com.** Lance and crew continue to do an excellent job of uncovering the very latest on Disney projects still in development. Years after its debut, Screamscape is one of the sites we check a couple times per week.

Best "Theme-park Insider" Site   If *E! True Hollywood Stories* did an episode on theme-park development, it would end up with something like **www.jimhillmedia.com.** Well-researched and supplied with seemingly limitless inside information, Jim's columns guide you through the internal squabbles, shareholder revolts, budget compromises, and outside competition that made (and makes) Walt Disney World what it is.

Best Orlando Weather Information   Printable 15-day forecasts for the Orlando area are available from **www.accuweather.com.** The site is especially useful in winter and spring, when temperatures can vary dramatically. During summer the ultraviolet index forecasts will help you choose between a tube and a keg of sunscreen.

Best Safety Site   All children younger than age 6 must be properly restrained when traveling by car. Check **www.buckleupflorida.com** to learn about Florida child-restraint requirements.

Best Website for Orlando Traffic, Road Work, and Construction Information   Visit **www.expresswayauthority.com** for the latest information on road work in the Orlando and Orange County areas. The site also contains detailed maps, directions, and toll-rate information for the most popular tourist destinations.

Best Driving Directions   The printable directions at **www.mapquest.com** are accurate and efficient. We especially like the feature that allows you to get driving directions for the drive home. Perhaps future maps will be able to flag every Stuckey's along your route, too.

Finally, we've added quite a few useful features to our own Web site, **www.touringplans.com.** Probably the one we're most excited about is our free online trip organizer. The organizer allows you to keep track of all your trip details, including packing checklists, flight information, ground transportation, lodging, budgets, and daily activities in each of the parks. Best of all, you can optionally share trip details with family, friends, and others. So, for example, your travel agent can update your organizer, and you'll be able to see the new information immediately.

When it's time for your trip, you can print the organizer's pages in any of three different sizes: The "pocket" size is handy for on-the-go types interested in traveling as light as possible; a "standard" size fits many off-the-shelf binders; and the "large" format is for folks who prefer more room. Free refills and blank templates for all formats are also available.

There are hundreds of other Disney sites, as well as sites that rate and contrast thrill rides in theme parks in the United States and all over the world. Start with sites listed above and follow the links.

Information about Disney World is also available at public libraries, travel agencies, AAA, or by contacting any of the following:

IMPORTANT WALT DISNEY WORLD ADDRESSES

Walt Disney World Info/Guest Letters/ Letters to Mickey Mouse P.O. Box 10040 Lake Buena Vista, FL 32830-0040	Lake Buena Vista, FL 32830-1000 Merchandise Mail Order (Guest Service Mail Order) P.O. Box 10070 Lake Buena Vista, FL 32830-0070
Walt Disney World Central Reservations P.O. Box 10100 Lake Buena Vista, FL 32830-0100	Walt Disney World Ticket Mail Order P.O. Box 10100 Lake Buena Vista, FL 32830-0140
Convention and Banquet Information Walt Disney World Resort South P.O. Box 10000 Lake Buena Vista, FL 32830-1000	Compliments, Complaints, and Suggestions Walt Disney World Guest Communications P.O. Box 10040 Lake Buena Vista, FL 32830-1000
Walt Disney World Educational Programs P.O. Box 10000	

Important Walt Disney World Telephone Numbers

When you call the main information number, you'll be offered a menu of options for recorded information on operating hours, recreation areas, shopping, entertainment, tickets, reservations, and driving directions. If you're using a rotary telephone, your call will be forwarded to a representative. If you're using a touch-tone phone and have a question not covered by recorded information, press 8 at any time to speak to a representative.

General Information	(407) 824-4321
Accommodations/Reservations	(407) W-DISNEY or (407) 824-8000
All-Star Café	(407) 827-8326
All-Star Movie Resort	(407) 939-7000
All-Star Music Resort	(407) 939-6000
All-Star Sports Resort	(407) 939-5000
AMC Theaters Pleasure Island	(407) 298-4488
Animal Kingdom Lodge	(407) 938-4760
Beach Club Resort	(407) 934-8000
Blizzard Beach	(407) 560-3400
BoardWalk Resort	(407) 939-5100
Caribbean Beach Resort	(407) 934-3400
Celebration Realty Office	(407) 566-4663
Centracare	(407) 238-3000
The Crossroads	(407) 239-7777
Disney Main Gate	(407) 397-7032
Kissimmee	(407) 390-1888
Lake Buena Vista	(407) 934-2273
Cirque du Soleil	(407) 939-7600
Contemporary Resort	(407) 824-1000
Convention Information	(407) 828-3200
Coronado Springs Resort	(407) 939-1000
Dining Priority Seating	(407) WDW-DINE
Disabled Guests Special Requests	(407) 939-7807
DisneyQuest	(407) 828-4600
Disney's Wide World of Sports	(407) 363-6600
Disney Professional Seminars	(407) 824-7997
Downtown Disney Guest Services	(407) 934-6374
Downtown Disney Marketplace	(407) 828-3800
Fantasia Gardens Miniature Golf	(407) 560-8760
Fort Wilderness Campground	(407) 824-2900
Golf Reservations and Information	(407) WDW-GOLF
Grand Floridian Beach Resort and Spa	(407) 824-3000

Group Camping	(407) 939-7807
Guided Tour Information	(407) 939-TOUR
Guided VIP Solo Tours	(407) 560-6233
House of Blues Tickets and Information	(407) 934-2583
Lost and Found for articles lost:	
Yesterday or before (All Disney parks)	(407) 824-4245
Today at Magic Kingdom	(407) 824-4245
Today at Epcot	(407) 560-7500
Today at Disney-MGM	(407) 560-3764
Today at Animal Kingdom	(407) 938-2265
Today at Universal Orlando	(407) 224-4244
Main Street Physicians	(407) 239-1195
Merchandise Guest Services Department	(407) 363-6200
Ocala Chamber of Commerce	(352) 629-8051
Ocala Disney Information Center	(352) 854-0770
Old Key West Resort	(407) 827-7700
Outdoor Recreation Reservations and Information	(407) WDW-PLAY
Pleasure Island Information	(407) 939-2648
Polynesian Resort	(407) 824-2000
Pop Century Resort	(407) 938-4000
Port Orleans Resort	(407) 934-5000
Resort Dining and Recreational Information	(407) WDW-DINE
Saratoga Springs Resort	(407) 827-1100
Shades of Green U.S. Armed Forces Hotel	(407) 824-3400
Telecommunication for the Deaf Reservations	(407) 939-7670
WDW Information	(407) 939-8255
Tennis Reservations/Lessons	(407) 939-7529
Typhoon Lagoon Information	(407) 560-4141
Walt Disney Travel Company	(407) 828-3232
Walt Disney World Dolphin	(407) 934-4000
Walt Disney World Speedway	(407) 939-0130
Walt Disney World Swan	(407) 934-3000
Weather Information	(407) 827-4545
Wilderness Lodge and Villas Resort	(407) 824-3200
Winter Summerland Miniature Golf	(407) 560-3000
Wrecker Service	(407) 824-0976
Yacht Club Resort	(407) 934-7000

This Year's Buzz: Magical Gatherings

If you watch TV, read magazines, or are one of millions of earthlings with a Disney receptor surreptitiously embedded in your brain, you've probably heard of Magical Gatherings. Defined simply, a Magical Gathering is a large group of friends or extended family vacationing together at Walt Disney World. It's also an ingenious Disney marketing campaign aimed at getting guests to haul a couple of platoons of closest friends or relatives along with them on vacation. All things considered, Magical Gatherings work pretty well: guests enjoy a nice reunion with family or buddies, and Disney bumps up its numbers and sells a lot of private functions and catered events.

More Buzz: Disneyland's 50th Anniversary

Disneyland's 50th Anniversary will be celebrated at Disney theme parks worldwide with new shows, parades, live entertainment, and at some parks, new attractions. We don't think the celebration will measurably affect park attendance except at Disneyland Park and Disney's California Adventures in Anaheim.

When to Go to Walt Disney World

Why do they call it tourist season if we can't shoot them?

—Palatka, Florida, outdoorsman

Selecting the Time of Year for Your Visit

Walt Disney World is busiest Christmas Day through New Year's Day. Also extremely busy are Thanksgiving weekend, the week of Washington's birthday, the Martin Luther King holiday weekend, spring break for colleges, and the two weeks around Easter. On a single day in these peak times, as many as 92,000 people have toured the Magic Kingdom alone! While this level of attendance isn't typical, only those who absolutely cannot go at any other time should challenge the parks at their peak.

The least busy time is after the Thanksgiving weekend until the week before Christmas. Next slowest are November through the weekend preceding Thanksgiving, September (after Labor Day) and October, January 4 through the first week of February, and the week after Easter through early June. Late February, March, and early April are dicey. Crowds ebb and flow according to spring-break schedules and the timing of Presidents' Day weekend. Though crowds have grown markedly in September and October as a result of promotions aimed at locals and the international market, these months continue to be good for weekday touring at the Magic Kingdom, Disney-MGM Studios, and Animal Kingdom, and for weekend visits to Epcot.

Many readers share their thoughts about the best time to visit Walt Disney World. These letters are representative.

From a Centerville, Ohio, family:

Catching on to the "off-season," we took the kids out of school and went to WDW in mid-May. So did a lot of other people. In fact, there were enough people there for me to think crowds must be increasing in the off-season as more people wise up about avoiding the masses. If I'm wrong, and this really was half the summer crowd, "high season" these days must be total and complete gridlock.

A mom from West Plains, Missouri, writes:

We visited WDW three times in the past eight years, each time in the second week of June. Each time the crowds were worse, and this time they were so big that we won't go at this time of year anymore.

The Downside of Off-season Touring

Though we strongly recommend going in the fall, winter, or spring, there are trade-offs. The parks often open late and close early during off-season. When they open as late as 9 a.m., everyone arrives about the same time. A late opening coupled with an early closing drastically reduces available touring hours. Even when crowds are small, it's difficult to see big parks like the Magic Kingdom between 9 a.m. and 6 p.m. Early closing (before 8 p.m.) also usually means that evening parades or fireworks are eliminated. And, because these are slow times at Disney World, some rides and attractions may be closed. Finally, central Florida temperatures fluctuate wildly during late fall, winter, and early spring; daytime highs in the 40s and 50s aren't uncommon.

Given the choice, however, smaller crowds, bargain prices, and stress-free touring are worth risking cold weather or closed attractions. Touring in fall and other "off" periods is so much easier that our research team, at the risk of being blasphemous, would advise taking children out of school for a Disney World visit.

Most readers who have tried Disney World at various times agree. A gentleman from Ottawa, Ontario, who toured in early December writes:

It was the most enjoyable trip [to Walt Disney World] I have ever had, and I can't imagine going [back] to Disney World when it is crowded. Even without the crowds, we were still very tired by afternoon. … We will never go again at any other time.

A father of two from Reynoldsburg, Ohio, offers this opinion:

Taking your kids out of school. Is it worth it? Yes! … It used to be true that missing a week of school would place your child so far behind it could take months for him/her to regain that lost week. Not so today. With advance preparations and informing the teachers months before our departure, this was no problem. With less than an hour of homework after dinner, our kids went back to school with assignments completed and no makeup work. But it was all those other hours with no lines and no heat that were the real payoff.

There is another side to this story, and we have received some well-considered letters from parents and teachers who don't think taking kids out of school is such a hot idea. From a Fairfax, Virginia, dad:

My wife and I are disappointed in that you seem to be encouraging families to take their children out of school to avoid the crowds at WDW during the summer months. My wife is an eighth-grade science teacher of chemistry and physics. She has parents pull their children, some honor-roll students, out of school for vacations, only to discover when they return that the students are unable to comprehend the material. … Parental suspicions [about] the quality of their children's education should be raised when children go to school for six hours a day yet supposedly can complete this same instruction with "less than an hour of homework" each night.

Likewise, a teacher from Louisville, Kentucky, didn't mince words:

Teachers absolutely hate it when a kid misses school for a week, because: (a) parents expect a neat little educational packet to take with them as if every minute can be planned—not practicable; (b) when the kid returns he is going to be behind, and it is difficult to make up classroom instruction.

If a parent bothers to ask my opinion, I tell them bluntly it's their choice. If the student's grades go down, they have to accept that as part of their family decision. I have a student out this entire week, skiing in Colorado. There's no way she can make up some of the class activities (and that's exactly what I told her mom).

TOP TEN AMERICAN THEME PARKS

Compared with 2002 figures, 2003 theme-park attendance was flat at the Magic Kingdom and the Animal Kingdom, up 4% at Epcot, and down 2% at the Disney MGM Studios. Both Universal Orlando parks were also flat, while SeaWorld Orlando was up 4%. The big winner in 2003 was Disney's California Adventure, up 13%. Down 12%, the big loser was Universal Studios Hollywood.

Theme Park	Annual Attendance	Average Daily Attendance
Magic Kingdom	14 million	38,356
Disneyland	12.7 million	34,795
Epcot	8.6 million	23,561
Disney-MGM Studios	7.8 million	21,369
Animal Kingdom	7.3 million	20,000
Universal Studios Orlando	6.8 million	18,630
Islands of Adventure	6.0 million	16,038
Disney's California Adventure	5.3 million	14,520
SeaWorld	5.2 million	14,245
Universal Studios Hollywood	4.5 million	12,328

2003 attendance figures. Source: Amusement Business magazine.

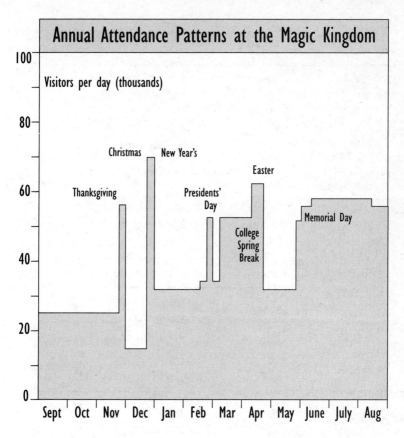

Annual Attendance Patterns at the Magic Kingdom

Visitors per day (thousands)

Labels on chart: Thanksgiving, Christmas, New Year's, Presidents' Day, College Spring Break, Easter, Memorial Day

Y-axis: 0, 20, 40, 60, 80, 100

X-axis: Sept, Oct, Nov, Dec, Jan, Feb, Mar, Apr, May, June, July, Aug

High Low, High Low, It's Off to Disney We Go   Though we recommend off-season touring, we realize many families can't do that. We want to make it clear, therefore, that you can have a wonderful experience regardless of when you go. Our advice, irrespective of season, is to arrive early at the parks and avoid the crowds by using one of our touring plans. If attendance is light, kick back and forget the touring plans.

We Got Weather!   Long before Walt Disney World, tourists visited Florida year round to enjoy the temperate tropical and subtropical climates. The best weather months generally are October, November, February, March, and April. Fall is usually dry, spring wetter. December and January are mild, with average highs of 66–74° intermixed with highs in the 50–65° range. May is hot but tolerable. June, July, August, and September are the warmest months. Rain is possible anytime, usually in the form of scattered thunderstorms. An entire day of rain is unusual.

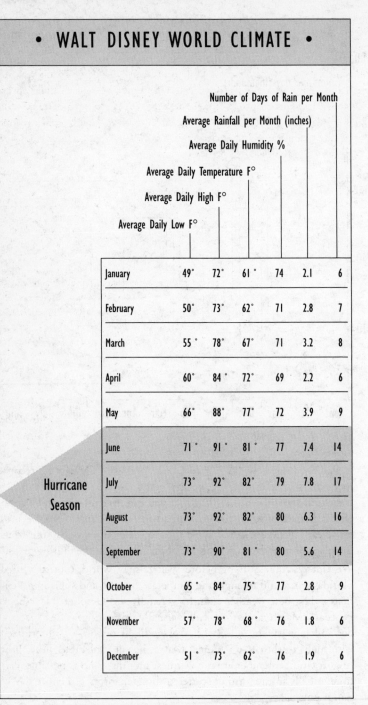

• WALT DISNEY WORLD CLIMATE •

	Average Daily Low F°	Average Daily High F°	Average Daily Temperature F°	Average Daily Humidity %	Average Rainfall per Month (inches)	Number of Days of Rain per Month
January	49°	72°	61°	74	2.1	6
February	50°	73°	62°	71	2.8	7
March	55°	78°	67°	71	3.2	8
April	60°	84°	72°	69	2.2	6
May	66°	88°	77°	72	3.9	9
June	71°	91°	81°	77	7.4	14
July	73°	92°	82°	79	7.8	17
August	73°	92°	82°	80	6.3	16
September	73°	90°	81°	80	5.6	14
October	65°	84°	75°	77	2.8	9
November	57°	78°	68°	76	1.8	6
December	51°	73°	62°	76	1.9	6

Hurricane Season

Unofficial Guide Crowd-Level Calendar

Each year, we receive over a thousand e-mails and letters inquiring about crowd conditions on specific dates throughout the year. Readers also want to know which park is best to visit on each day of their stay. To make things easier for you (and us!), we provide below a calendar covering the last four months of 2004 and all of 2005. For each date, we offer a crowd-level index based on a scale of 1 to 10, with 1 being least crowded conditions and 10 being most crowded. Our calendar takes into account all holidays and special events.

CROWD-LEVEL INDEX

1. Lightest crowd conditions of the year.
2. Very light crowd conditions.
3. Light crowd conditions.
4. Moderately busy. Crowds primarily affect headliner attractions.
5. Busy. Crowds affect headliner attractions and major attractions.
6. Moderately crowded. Expect all attractions to be affected.
7. Crowded. Expect waits of 65 minutes or more at headliner attractions and 40 minutes or more at major attractions.
8. Very crowded. Expect waits of 80 minutes or more at headliner attractions and 45 minutes or more at major attractions.
9. Exceedingly crowded. Expect waits of 100 minutes or more at headliner attractions and 60 minutes at major attractions.
10. Jam packed. Most crowded conditions of the year.

In addition to the 1–10 crowd-level index, we also list the best park and the worst park for visitation on each day of the year. If you visit a park on a day with a crowd-level index of 1–3, you probably won't need our touring plans except as an organizational aid. For crowd levels of 4–8, our touring plans will keep you one step ahead of the crowd and keep your wait times quite tolerable. Days with crowd levels of 9 or 10 are relatively few (usually major holidays). On these days, seeing the attractions is difficult, but there's a wealth of spectacular live entertainment and events to enjoy. Space limitations preclude publishing special touring plans for 9–10 crowd-level days in this guide, but such plans are available at our Web site **www.touringplans.com.**

Least Crowded Days

Use our Crowd-level Calendar to check out the best and worst parks (in terms of crowd conditions) on a given day. As for the parks not mentioned, use the information following the chart (page 40) to get a grip on crowd conditions for those parks.

Magic Kingdom   Wednesday and Saturday are least crowded in summer, and Friday and Wednesday are least crowded the rest of the year.

2004

SEPTEMBER	1	2	3	4	5	6	7
crowd level	2	3	3	5	7	7	2
best park(s)	MK	DS, AK	MK, DS	EP, AK	EP	DS	AK
park(s) to avoid	EP	MK	AK	DS	MK	AK	DS

	8	9	10	11	12	13	14
crowd level	2	2	2	2	2	2	2
best park(s)	MK	DS, AK	MK, DS	EP, AK	EP	DS	AK
park(s) to avoid	EP	MK	AK	DS	MK	AK	DS

	15	16	17	18	19	20	21
crowd level	2	2	2	2	2	2	2
best park(s)	MK	DS, AK	MK, DS	EP, AK	EP	DS	AK
park(s) to avoid	EP	MK	AK	DS	MK	AK	DS

	22	23	24	25	26	27	28
crowd level	2	2	2	2	2	2	2
best park(s)	MK	DS, AK	MK, DS	EP, AK	EP	DS	AK
park(s) to avoid	EP	MK	AK	DS	MK	AK	DS

	29	30	OCTOBER	1	2	3
crowd level	2	2		2	2	2
best park(s)	MK	DS, AK		MK, DS	EP, AK	EP
park(s) to avoid	EP	MK		AK	DS	MK

OCTOBER (cont)	4	5	6	7	8	9	10
crowd level	2	2	2	2	2	2	3
best park(s)	DS	AK	MK	DS, AK	MK, DS	EP, AK	EP
park(s) to avoid	AK	DS	EP	MK	AK	DS	MK

	11	12	13	14	15	16	17
crowd level	4	3	2	2	2	2	2
best park(s)	DS	AK	MK	DS, AK	MK, DS	EP, AK	EP
park(s) to avoid	AK	DS	EP	MK	AK	DS	MK

	18	19	20	21	22	23	24
crowd level	2	2	2	2	2	2	2
best park(s)	DS	AK	MK	DS, AK	MK, DS	EP, AK	EP
park(s) to avoid	AK	DS	EP	MK	AK	DS	MK

	25	26	27	28	29	30	31
crowd level	2	2	2	3	3	3	3
best park(s)	DS	AK	MK	DS, AK	MK, DS	EP, AK	EP
park(s) to avoid	AK	DS	EP	MK	AK	DS	MK

NOVEMBER	1	2	3	4	5	6	7
crowd level	2	2	2	2	2	2	2
best park(s)	EP	AK	MK	EP, DS, AK	MK, DS	AK	EP, AK
park(s) to avoid	AK	DS	EP	MK	AK	DS	MK

	8	9	10	11	12	13	14
crowd level	2	2	2	2	2	2	2
best park(s)	EP	AK	MK	EP, DS, AK	MK, DS	AK	EP, AK
park(s) to avoid	AK	DS	EP	MK	AK	DS	MK

NOVEMBER (cont)	15	16	17	18	19	20	21
crowd level	2	2	2	2	2	2	2
best park(s)	AP	AK	MK	EP, DS, AK	MK, DS	AK	EP, AK
park(s) to avoid	AK	DS	EP	MK	AK	DS	MK
	22	23	24	25	26	27	28
crowd level	3	3	5	8	8	8	8
best park(s)	EP	AK	MK	EP, DS, AK	EP, DS	MK, EP, AK	EP
park(s) to avoid	AK	DS	EP	MK	AK	DS	MK
	29	30	DECEMBER	1	2	3	
crowd level	2	1		1	1	1	
best park(s)	EP	AK		MK	EP, DS, AK	MK,DS	
park(s) to avoid	AK	DS		EP	MK	AK	

DECEMBER (cont)	4	5	6	7	8	9	10
crowd level	1	1	1	1	1	1	1
best park(s)	AK	EP, AK	EP	AK	MK	EP, DS, AK	MK, DS
park(s) to avoid	DS	MK	AK	DS	EP	MK	AK
	11	12	13	14	15	16	17
crowd level	1	1	1	1	1	1	2
best park(s)	AK	EP, AK	EP	AK	MK	EP, DS, AK	MK, DS
park(s) to avoid	DS	MK	AK	DS	EP	MK	AK
	18	19	20	21	22	23	24
crowd level	2	3	3	4	5	7	10
best park(s)	AK	EP, AK	EP	AK	MK	EP, DS, AK	EP, DS
park(s) to avoid	AK	DS	MK	AK	DS	EP	MK
	25	26	27	28	29	30	31
crowd level	10	8	9	9	9	10	10
best park(s)	MK, EP, AK	EP	EP	EP, AK	MK	EP, DS, AK	EP, DS
park(s) to avoid	DS	MK	AK	DS	EP	MK	AK

2005

JANUARY	1	2	3	4	5	6	7
crowd level	10	8	3	3	3	3	3
best park(s)	MK, EP, AK	EP	EP	AK	MK	EP, DS, AK	MK, DS
park(s) to avoid	DS	MK	AK	DS	EP	MK	AK
	8	9	10	11	12	13	14
crowd level	3	3	3	3	3	3	3
best park(s)	AK	EP, AK	EP	AK	MK	EP, DS, AK	MK, DS
park(s) to avoid	DS	MK	AK	DS	EP	MK	AK
	15	16	17	18	19	20	21
crowd level	3	5	5	3	3	3	3
best park(s)	AK	EP, AK	EP	AK	MK	EP, DS, AK	MK, DS
park(s) to avoid	DS	MK	AK	DS	EP	MK	AK
	22	23	24	25	26	27	28
crowd level	3	3	3	3	3	3	3
best park(s)	AK	EP, AK	EP	AK	MK	EP, DS, AK	MK, DS
park(s) to avoid	DS	MK	AK	DS	EP	MK	AK

MK = Magic Kingdom, EP = Epcot, DS = Disney-MGM Studios, AK = Animal Kingdom

JANUARY (cont)	29	30	31	FEBRUARY	1	2	3
crowd level	3	3	3		3	3	3
best park(s)	AK	EP, AK	EP		AK	MK	EP, DS, AK
park(s) to avoid	DS	MK	AK		DS	EP	MK

FEBRUARY (cont)	4	5	6	7	8	9	10
crowd level	3	3	3	3	3	3	3
best park(s)	MK, DS	AK	EP, AK	EP	AK	MK	EP, DS, AK
park(s) to avoid	AK	DS	MK	AK	DS	EP	MK

	11	12	13	14	15	16	17
crowd level	3	4	4	4	3	4	4
best park(s)	MK, DS	AK	EP, AK	EP	AK	MK	EP, DS, AK
park(s) to avoid	AK	DS	MK	AK	DS	EP	MK

	18	19	20	21	22	23	24
crowd level	5	7	7	7	4	3	3
best park(s)	MK, DS	MK, AK	EP, AK	EP	AK	MK	EP, DS, AK
park(s) to avoid	AK	DS	MK	AK	DS	EP	MK

	25	26	27	28			
crowd level	4	4	4	4			
best park(s)	MK, DS	AK	EP, AK	EP			
park(s) to avoid	AK	DS	MK	AK			

MARCH	1	2	3	4	5	6	7
crowd level	4	4	4	4	5	6	6
best park(s)	AK	MK	EP, DS, AK	MK, DS	AK	EP, AK	EP
park(s) to avoid	DS	EP	MK	AK	DS	MK	AK

	8	9	10	11	12	13	14
crowd level	6	6	6	7	7	7	7
best park(s)	AK	MK	EP, DS, AK	DS	MK, AK	EP, AK	EP
park(s) to avoid	AK	DS	MK	AK	DS	EP	MK

	15	16	17	18	19	20	21
crowd level	7	7	7	7	7	7	6
best park(s)	AK	MK	EP, DS, AK	DS	MK, AK	EP, AK	EP
park(s) to avoid	DS	EP	MK	AK	DS	MK	AK

	22	23	24	25	26	27	28
crowd level	5	6	6	8	9	10	8
best park(s)	AK	MK	EP, DS, AK	EP, DS	MK, EP, AK	EP	EP
park(s) to avoid	DS	EP	MK	AK	DS	MK	AK

	29	30	31	APRIL	1	2	3
crowd level	6	3	3		4	4	4
best park(s)	AK	MK	EP, DS, AK		MK, DS	AK	EP, AK
park(s) to avoid	DS	EP	MK		AK	DS	MK

APRIL (cont)	4	5	6	7	8	9	10
crowd level	4	4	4	4	4	4	4
best park(s)	EP	AK	MK	EP, DS, AK	MK, DS	AK	EP, AK
park(s) to avoid	AK	DS	MK	AK	DS	EP	MK

APRIL (cont)	11	12	13	14	15	16	17
crowd level	4	4	4	4	4	4	4
best park(s)	EP	AK	MK	EP, DS, AK	MK, DS	AK	EP, AK
park(s) to avoid	AK	DS	EP	MK	AK	DS	MK
	18	19	20	21	22	23	24
crowd level	4	4	4	4	5	5	5
best park(s)	EP	AK	MK	EP, DS, AK	MK, DS	AK	EP, AK
park(s) to avoid	AK	DS	EP	MK	AK	DS	MK
	25	26	27	28	29	30	
crowd level	3	3	3	3	3	3	
best park(s)	EP	AK	MK	EP, DS, AK	MK, DS	AK	
park(s) to avoid	AK	DS	EP	MK	AK	DS	
MAY	1	2	3	4	5	6	7
crowd level	3	3	3	3	4	3	3
best park(s)	EP, AK	EP	AK	MK	EP, DS, AK	MK, DS	AK
park(s) to avoid	MK	AK	DS	EP	MK	AK	DS
	8	9	10	11	12	13	14
crowd level	4	3	3	3	3	3	3
best park(s)	EP, AK	EP	AK	MK	EP, DS, AK	MK, DS	AK
park(s) to avoid	MK	AK	DS	EP	MK	AK	DS
	15	16	17	18	19	20	21
crowd level	3	3	3	3	3	3	3
best park(s)	EP, AK	EP	AK	MK	EP, DS, AK	MK, DS	AK
park(s) to avoid	MK	AK	DS	EP	MK	AK	DS
	22	23	24	25	26	27	28
crowd level	3	3	3	3	4	6	8
best park(s)	EP, AK	EP	AK	MK	EP, DS, AK	MK, DS	MK, EP, AK
park(s) to avoid	MK	AK	DS	EP	MK	AK	DS
	29	30	31	JUNE	1	2	3
crowd level	8	8	8		6	5	6
best park(s)	EP	EP, DS	EP, AK		MK	AK	DS
park(s) to avoid	MK	AK	DS		EP	MK	MK, AK
JUNE (cont)	4	5	6	7	8	9	10
crowd level	8	6	6	6	6	7	7
best park(s)	EP, AK	EP	MK, DS	AK	MK	AK	DS
park(s) to avoid	MK, AK	MK	AK	DS	EP	MK	AK
	11	12	13	14	15	16	17
crowd level	8	8	8	8	8	8	8
best park(s)	MK, EP, AK	EP	MK, EP, DS	EP, AK	MK	EP, AK	EP, DS
park(s) to avoid	DS	MK	AK	DS	EP	MK	AK
	18	19	20	21	22	23	24
crowd level	8	8	8	8	8	8	8
best park(s)	MK, EP, AK	EP	MK, AP, DS	EP, AK	MK	EP, AK	EP, DS
park(s) to avoid	DS	MK	AK	DS	EP	MK	AK

MK = Magic Kingdom, EP = Epcot, DS = Disney-MGM Studios, AK = Animal Kingdom

JUNE (cont)	24	25	26	27	28	29	30
crowd level	8	8	8	8	8	8	8
best park(s)	EP, DS	MK, EP, AK	EP	MK, EP, DS	EP, AK	MK	EP, AK
park(s) to avoid	AK	DS	MK	AK	DS	EP	MK

JULY	1	2	3	4	5	6	7
crowd level	8	9	9	9	8	8	8
best park(s)	EP, DS	MK, EP, AK	EP	MK, EP, DS	EP, AK	MK	EP, AK
park(s) to avoid	AK	DS	MK	AK	DS	EP	MK

	8	9	10	11	12	13	14
crowd level	8	8	8	8	8	8	8
best park(s)	EP, DS	MK, EP, AK	EP	MK, EP, DS	EP, AK	MK	EP, AK
park(s) to avoid	AK	DS	MK	AK	DS	EP	MK

	15	16	17	18	19	20	21
crowd level	8	8	8	8	8	8	8
best park(s)	EP, DS	MK, EP, AK	EP	MK, EP, AK	EP, AK	MK	EP, AK
park(s) to avoid	AK	DS	MK	AK	DS	EP	MK

	22	23	24	25	26	27	28
crowd level	8	8	8	8	8	8	8
best park(s)	EP, DS	MK, EP, AK	EP	MK, EP, DS	EP, AK	MK	EP
park(s) to avoid	AK	DS	MK	AK	DS	EP	MK

	29	30	31	AUGUST	1	2	3
crowd level	8	8	8		8	8	8
best park(s)	EP, DS	MK, EP, AK	EP		MK, EP, AK	EP, AK	MK
park(s) to avoid	AK	DS	MK		AK	DS	EP

AUGUST (cont)	4	5	6	7	8	9	10
crowd level	8	8	8	8	7	7	7
best park(s)	EP, AK	EP, DS	MK, EP, AK	EP	MK, DS	AK	MK
park(s) to avoid	MK	AK	DS	MK	AK	DS	EP

	11	12	13	14	15	16	17
crowd level	7	7	7	6	6	6	6
best park(s)	AK	DS	MK, EP, AK	EP	MK, DS	AK	MK
park(s) to avoid	MK	AK	DS	MK	AK	DS	EP

	18	19	20	21	22	23	24
crowd level	6	6	6	5	5	5	5
best park(s)	AK	MK, DS	MK, EP, AK	EP	MK, DS	AK	MK
park(s) to avoid	MK	AK	DS	MK	AK	DS	EP

	25	26	27	28	29	30	31
crowd level	5	5	5	4	4	4	4
best park(s)	AK	MK, DS	MK, EP, AK	EP	MK, DS	AK	MK
park(s) to avoid	MK	AK	DS	MK	AK	DS	EP

SEPTEMBER	1	2	3	4	5	6	7
crowd level	3	5	7	7	2	2	2
best park(s)	DS, AK	MK, DS	MK, EP, AK	EP	DS	AK	MK
park(s) to avoid	MK	AK	DS	MK	AK	DS	EP

SEPTEMBER (cont)	8	9	10	11	12	13	14
crowd level	2	2	2	2	2	2	2
best park(s)	DS, AK	MK, DS	EP, AK	EP	DS	AK	MK
park(s) to avoid	MK	AK	DS	MK	AK	DS	EP
	15	16	17	18	19	20	21
crowd level	2	2	2	2	2	2	2
best park(s)	DS, AK	MK, DS	EP, AK	EP	DS	AK	MK
park(s) to avoid	MK	AK	DS	MK	AK	DS	EP
	22	23	24	25	26	27	28
crowd level	2	2	2	2	2	2	2
best park(s)	DS, AK	MK, DS	EP, AK	EP	DS	AK	MK
park(s) to avoid	MK	AK	DS	MK	AK	DS	EP
	29	30	OCTOBER 1	2	3	4	
crowd level	2	2	2	2	2	2	
best park(s)	DS, AK	MK, DS	EP, AK	EP	DS	AK	
park(s) to avoid	MK	AK	DS	MK	AK	DS	

OCTOBER (cont)	5	6	7	8	9	10	11
crowd level	2	2	2	2	3	4	3
best park(s)	MK	DS, AK	MK, DS	EP, AK	EP	DS	AK
park(s) to avoid	EP	MK	AK	DS	MK	AK	DS
	12	13	14	15	16	17	18
crowd level	2	2	2	2	2	2	2
best park(s)	MK	DS, AK	MK, DS	EP, AK	EP	DS	AK
park(s) to avoid	EP	MK	AK	DS	MK	AK	DS
	19	20	21	22	23	24	25
crowd level	2	2	2	2	2	2	2
best park(s)	MK	DS, AK	MK, DS	EP, AK	EP	DS	AK
park(s) to avoid	EP	MK	AK	DS	MK	AK	DS
	26	27	28	29	30	31	
crowd level	2	2	3	3	3	3	
best park(s)	MK	DS, AK	MK, DS	EP, AK	EP	DS	
park(s) to avoid	EP	MK	AK	DS	MK	AK	

NOVEMBER	1	2	3	4	5	6	7
crowd level	2	2	2	2	2	2	2
best park(s)	AK	MK	EP, DS, AK	MK, DS	MK, DS	EP, AK	EP
park(s) to avoid	DS	EP	MK	AK	DS	MK	AK
	8	9	10	11	12	13	14
crowd level	2	2	2	2	2	2	2
best park(s)	AK	MK	EP, DS, AK	MK, DS	AK	EP, AK	EP
park(s) to avoid	DS	EP	MK	AK	DS	MK	AK
	15	16	17	18	19	20	21
crowd level	2	2	2	2	2	2	2
best park(s)	AK	MK	EP, DS, AK	MK, DS	AK	EP, AK	EP
park(s) to avoid	DS	EP	MK	AK	DS	MK	AK

MK = Magic Kingdom, EP = Epcot, DS = Disney-MGM Studios, AK = Animal Kingdom

NOVEMBER (cont)	22	23	24	25	26	27	28
crowd level	3	3	8	8	8	8	2
best park(s)	AK	MK	EP, DS, AK	EP, DS	MK, EP, AK	EP	EP
park(s) to avoid	DS	EP	MK	AK	DS	MK	AK

	29	30	DECEMBER	1	2	3	4
crowd level	1	1		1	1	1	1
best park(s)	AK	MK		EP, DS, AK	MK, DS	AK	EP, AK
park(s) to avoid	DS	EP		MK	AK	DS	MK

DECEMBER (cont)	5	6	7	8	9	10	11
crowd level	1	1	1	1	1	1	1
best park(s)	EP	AK	MK	EP, DS, AK	MK, DS	AK	EP, AK
park(s) to avoid	AK	DS	EP	MK	AK	DS	MK

	12	13	14	15	16	17	18
crowd level	1	1	1	1	1	2	2
best park(s)	EP	AK	MK	EP, DS, AK	MK, DS	AK	EP, AK
park(s) to avoid	AK	DS	EP	MK	AK	DS	MK

	19	20	21	22	23	24	25
crowd level	2	3	4	5	7	10	10
best park(s)	EP	AK	MK	EP, DS, AK	DS	MK, EP, AK	EP
park(s) to avoid	AK	DS	EP	MK	AK	DS	MK

	26	27	28	29	30	31	
crowd level	8	9	9	9	10	10	
best park(s)	EP	EP, AK	MK	EP, DS, AK	EP, DS	MK, EP, AK	
park(s) to avoid	AK	DS	EP	MK	AK	DS	

MK = Magic Kingdom, EP = Epcot, DS = Disney-MGM Studios, AK = Animal Kingdom

Disney-MGM Studios   Monday and Friday are best during summer. Off-season, try Thursday and Friday.

Epcot   Monday and Thursday are least crowded from January through May, as well as in November and December. During summer, crowds are smaller Saturday and Sunday. In September and October, when school groups inundate Epcot, visit on Saturday and Sunday.

Animal Kingdom   Visit on Tuesday, Thursday, or Saturday.

Early Entry (a.k.a. Extra Magic Hour)

The early-entry program applies to the Magic Kingdom, Epcot, Animal Kingdom, and Disney-MGM Studios. Each day of the week, lodging guests are invited to enter a designated theme park one hour before the general public. During the early-entry hour, guests can enjoy attractions opened early just for them. At the Magic Kingdom, for example, most attractions in Fantasyland and Tomorrowland are open to early arrivals. At Epcot, Spaceship Earth, Mission: Space, the Universe of Energy, and Test Track open early; and at Disney-MGM Studios, early entrants can enjoy the *Twilight Zone* Tower of Terror, Star Tours, Rock 'n' Roller

Coaster, and *MuppetVision 3-D,* among others. Kilimanjaro Safaris, *It's Tough to Be a Bug,* the Tree of Life, and the Discovery Island Trails are open early at Animal Kingdom. Be advised that attractions open for early entry change periodically.

EARLY-ENTRY (EXTRA MAGIC HOUR) DAYS	
Magic Kingdom	Thursday and Sunday
Epcot	Wednesday
Disney-MGM Studios	Tuesday and Saturday
Animal Kingdom	Monday and Friday

Though the early-entry program is a perk for Disney hotel guests, no guest identification was required to enter the parks early during much of 2004. Thus, if you're staying at a non-Disney hotel and want to take a chance, you very well might gain admittance.

How Early Entry Affects Attendance at the Theme Parks

Early entry strongly affects attendance at the theme parks, especially during busier times of year. Each day, vast numbers of Disney resort guests tour whichever theme park is designated for early entry. If the Magic Kingdom is tapped for early entry on Thursday, for example, it will be more crowded that day, and Epcot, Animal Kingdom, and Disney-MGM Studios will be less crowded. Epcot, the Animal Kingdom, and Disney-MGM Studios will be more crowded when those parks are slated for early entry.

During holiday periods and summer, when Disney hotels are full, early entry makes a tremendous difference in crowds at the designated park. The program funnels so many people into the early-entry park that it fills by about 10 a.m. and is practically gridlocked by noon. Whatever edge resort guests gain by taking advantage of early entry is offset by horrendous crowds later in the day. During busier times of year, regardless of your hotel, avoid any park on the day it's scheduled for early entry.

If you elect to use your early-entry privileges, be among the first early entrants. A mother of three from Lee Summit, Missouri, writes:

Our first full day at WDW, we went to the Magic Kingdom. This was on a Monday, an early-entry day for resort guests. We were there at 7:30 a.m. and were able to walk onto all the rides in Fantasyland with no wait. At 8:45 a.m. we positioned ourselves at the Adventureland rope and ran toward Splash Mountain when the rope dropped. We were able to ride Splash Mountain with no wait (switching off), and then Big Thunder with about a 15-minute wait (switching off). We then went straight to the Jungle Cruise and the wait was already 30 minutes, so we skipped it. The park became incredibly crowded as the day progressed, and we were all exhausted from getting up so early to get there for early entry. We left the park around noon. After that day, I resolved to avoid early-entry days and instead be at a non-early-entry park about a half hour before official opening time. This worked much better for us.

This note from a North Bend, Washington, dad emphasizes the importance of arriving at the beginning of the early-entry period.

We only used early entry once—to [Disney-]MGM. We got there 20 minutes after early entry opened and the wait for Tower of Terror was already one-and-a-half hours long [without FASTPASS]. We skipped it.

A lady from Ann Arbor, Michigan, who is clearly working overtime trying to figure all this stuff out, says:

We are starting to think that reverse-reverse psychology might work: Disney opens one park earlier for all their guests, so all the guests go to that park, but then, everyone buys your book in which you tell them not to go to that park because all Disney guests are there, so no one goes to that park, therefore we can go to that park because people think it is going to be packed and they avoid it. What do you think?

Because Disney has changed the early-entry program numerous times, we suggest you call Walt Disney Information at (407) 824-4321 before you leave home to verify the early-entry schedule during your stay.

Early Entry and Park-hopping

An alternative strategy for Disney resort guests is to take advantage of early entry, but only until the designated park gets crowded. At that time, move to another park. This plan works particularly well at the Magic Kingdom for families with young children who love the attractions in Fantasyland. However, it will take you about an hour to commute to the second park of the day. If, for example, you depart the Magic Kingdom for the Disney-MGM Studios at 10 a.m., you'll find the Studios pretty crowded when you arrive at about 11 a.m. Keeping these and other considerations in mind, here are some guidelines:

1. Use the Early Entry–Park Hopping strategy during the less busy times of year when the parks close early. You'll get a jump on the general public and add an hour to what, in the off-season, is an already short touring day.

A reader from Providence found early admission to be an advantage:

During the off-season, the early admission was great. Only on Saturday did the crowd get so large that there were lines and bottlenecks. The mother behind me at Dumbo told me that they had waited three hours to ride Dumbo during their last visit to WDW. She took advantage of early admission to let her kid ride three times in a row with no waiting.

2. Use the Early Entry–Park Hopping strategy to complete touring a second park that you've already visited on a previous day, or specifically to see live entertainment in the second park.

It rarely makes sense to hop to the Animal Kingdom. The Animal Kingdom is almost always the first park to close each evening, so arriving later than 2 p.m. for the handful of remaining hours is not generally a good use of time.

On any day except Wednesday, hopping to Epcot is usually good. Epcot is able to handle large crowds better than any other Disney park, minimizing the effects of a midday arrival. Also, World Showcase has a large selection of interesting dining options, making it a good choice for evening touring.

Don't hop to the park with early entry (Extra Magic Hour). The idea is to avoid crowds, not join them.

Limit your hopping to two parks per day. Park hopping to a third park in one day would result in more time spent in transportation than saved by avoiding crowds.

Finally, except as stated in 1 and 2 above, never hop to the Magic Kingdom. It will be too crowded by the time you arrive.

E-Ride Night is the lazy man's alternative to early entry. Operated now at various times of year, E-Ride Night is a program where resort guests with multiday passes can (for around $13 extra per adult) remain in the Magic Kingdom after official closing and ride all the biggies with little or no waiting. Needless to say, E-Ride Night (detailed on page 479) is the best thing since catsup on fries for folks who want to sleep in. Like most programs, it's subject to termination.

Nighttime Version of Extra Magic Hour

In May of 2004, Disney began testing an Extra Magic Hour(s) program that allows guests from "select" Disney resorts to enjoy a different theme park each night for three hours after it closes to the general public. Unlike E-Ride Night, guests pay no additional charge to participate. Two hours before the park closes, eligible guests obtain an after-hours wristband by showing their Key to the World card or Resort I.D. Inquire at park Guest Relations for the locations of the four or five wristband distribution centers. To determine which Disney resorts are participating and which theme park is offering the program on a given night, inquire at your Disney hotel.

More attractions operate during the extended evening period than during the early-entry hour in the morning. Certain fast-food and full-service restaurants remain open as well. The program is experimental and may or may not be adopted. It is presumably in response to perks extended to Universal Orlando hotel guests that allow them to go to the front of the line at any attraction. Disney has thus far maintained a level playing field, rejecting programs that allow resort guests line-breaking privileges.

Summer and Holidays

A reader from Columbus, Ohio, once observed, "The main thing I learned from your book is not to go during the summer or at holiday times. Once you know that, you don't need a guidebook."

While we might argue with the reader's conclusion, we agree that avoiding summer and holidays is a wise strategy. That said, we also understand that many folks have no choice concerning the time of year they visit Disney World. Much of this book, in fact, is dedicated to making sure those readers who visit during busier times enjoy their experience. Sure, off-season touring is preferable, but, armed with knowledge and some strategy, you can have a great time whenever you visit.

To put it in perspective, early summer (up to about June 15) and late summer (after August 15) aren't nearly as crowded as the intervening period. And even midsummer crowds pale in comparison to the hordes during holiday periods. If you visit in midsummer or during a holiday, the first thing you need to know is that the theme parks' guest capacity is not infinite. In fact, once a park reaches capacity, only Disney resort guests arriving via the Disney transportation system are allowed to enter. If you aren't a Disney resort guest, you may find yourself in a situation similar to this Boise, Idaho, dad's:

> This is the worst of it. The Magic Kingdom and the [Disney-]MGM Studios were so full they closed the parks. For three days we could not enter those parks, so we were forced to go to Epcot and use up two days of our four-day pass. We decided to pay for another night at our hotel to see if the crowds would let up, but no luck. All we could do was just drive around Orlando and sight-see.

The reader didn't tell us what time he arrived at the Magic Kingdom or the Studios, but we can assume he wasn't on hand for opening. If you roll out of bed early and get to a park 30 minutes or so before official opening, you're almost certain to be admitted.

The thought of teeming throngs jockeying for position in endless lines under the baking Fourth of July sun is enough to wilt the will and ears of the most ardent Mouseketeer. Disney, however, feeling bad about those long lines and challenging touring conditions on packed holidays, compensates patrons with a no-less-than-incredible array of first-rate live entertainment and events.

Shows, parades, concerts, and pageantry continue throughout the day. In the evening, so much is going on that you have to make tough choices. Concerts, parades, light shows, laser shows, fireworks, and dance productions occur almost continually. No question about it: You can go to Walt Disney World on the Fourth of July (or any extended-hours, crowded day), never get on a ride, and still have a good time. Admittedly, the situation isn't ideal for a first-timer who wants to experience the attractions, but for anyone else it's a great party.

Disney provides colorful decorations for most holidays, plus special parades and live entertainment for Christmas, New Year's, Easter, and Fourth of July, among others. Regarding Christmas, we advise visiting in early December when you can enjoy the decorations and festivities without the crowds. If you must tour during the holidays and New Year, skip the Magic Kingdom; consider visiting Epcot or Disney-MGM instead.

To project attendance, Disney monitors occupancy of area hotels. On days when huge crowds are expected, Disney will sometimes open the parks ahead of the official opening time. This applies to all the parks and is done to prevent the overwhelming of parking-toll booths, ticket windows, transportation systems, and entrance plazas. When the early-opening plan is in operation, the parks don't discriminate between Disney resort guests and day guests (those not staying at Disney hotels). In short, when really big crowds are expected, Disney will often open all parks early and admit any guest.

Unfortunately, Disney doesn't announce in advance that it will open the parks early, nor will operators at Disney's main information number clue you in. You must guess based on the time of year whether early opening is likely. During 2003 and early 2004, with the recession, the war on terrorism, and the war with Iraq, attendance at the parks was below normal. Consequently, this special early opening was rare.

If you visit on a nonholiday midsummer day, arrive at the turnstile 30 minutes before the stated opening on a non-early-entry day. If you visit during a major holiday period, arrive 40 minutes before. Hit your favorite rides early using one of our touring plans, then return to your hotel for lunch, a swim, and perhaps a nap. (Don't forget to have your hand stamped for re-entry when you exit.) If you're interested in the special parades and shows, return to the park in late afternoon or early evening. Assume that unless you use FASTPASS, early morning will be the only time you can experience the attractions without long waits. Finally, don't wait until the last minute in the evening to leave the park. The exodus at closing is truly mind-boggling.

Epcot is usually the least-crowded park during holiday periods. Expect the other parks to be mobbed. To save time in the morning, buy your admission in advance. Also, consider bringing your own stroller or wheelchair instead of renting one of Disney's. If you're touring Epcot or the Magic Kingdom and plan to spend the day, try exiting the park for lunch at a nearby resort hotel. Above all, bring your sense of humor and pay attention to your group's morale. Bail out when touring is more work than fun.

The Disney Calendar

Walt Disney World Marathon   Usually the first weekend after New Year's, the marathon pulls in about 20,000 runners and their families, enough people to affect crowd conditions in the parks. Additionally, the race disrupts both vehicular and pedestrian traffic throughout Disney World.

Mardi Gras   A Mardi Gras party is held at Pleasure Island from the Friday before Mardi Gras through Fat Tuesday. Paying Pleasure Island admission is required. The area is mobbed, but the rest of the World is largely unaffected.

Black History Month   Black History Month is celebrated throughout Walt Disney World in February with displays, artisans, storytellers, and entertainers. There is no extra charge for the activities, and the celebration's effect on crowd levels is negligible.

Atlanta Braves Spring Training   The Atlanta Braves hold spring training at Disney's Wide World of Sports from mid-February through March. Admission is required to watch the training. Attendance levels at the theme parks aren't affected by the activities.

Epcot International Flower and Garden Festival   A celebration of flowers, gardening, and landscaping, the festival is held annually; in 2005 it's from April 15 through July 5. Expert horticulturalists showcase exotic floral displays, share gardening tips, and demonstrate techniques for planting, cultivating, and pest control. Even if you don't have a green thumb, the 20 million blooms from some 1,200 species will make your eyes pop. And the best thing about the event is that it doesn't noticeably impact crowd levels at Epcot.

Gay Day   Since 1991, gay men and lesbians from around the world have converged in and around Disney World for a long weekend of events centered around the theme parks. Gay Day attendance has grown considerably, attracting more than 100,000 gays, bisexuals, and family and friends. Universal Studios, SeaWorld, and Busch Gardens also participate. The event, actually a week long, will run in 2005 from June 1 to June 7, with most major events over the weekend of June 3–5. For additional information, access **www.gayday.com.**

Minor League Baseball   The Orlando Rays, the AA farm club of the Tampa Bay Devil Rays, play about 70 Southern League home games at Disney's Wide World of Sports between the first week of April and the first week of September. There's an admission charge. Rays games don't affect attendance at the theme parks.

Epcot International Food and Wine Festival   From September 30th through November 14, about 30 nations trot out their most famous cuisine, wine, and entertainment. Held in the World Showcase, the celebration includes demonstrations, wine seminars, tastings, and opportunities to see some of the world's (i.e., the real world's) top chefs. Although many activities are included in Epcot admission, the best workshops and tastings are by reservation only and cost extra. Call (407) WDW-DINE well in advance for details. Crowd conditions are impacted only slightly.

Mickey's Not-So-Scary Halloween Party   Held each year on two-dozen-or-so nights before Halloween, plus Halloween night, the party runs from 7 p.m. to midnight at the Magic Kingdom. The event includes trick-or-treating in costume, parades, live music, storytelling, and a fireworks show. Aimed primarily at younger children, the party is happy and upbeat rather than spooky and scary. It's by reservation only. Admission is about $32 for adults and $27 for ages 3–9 if purchased in advance. Tickets at the gate (assuming they're available) run $36 for adults and $30 for children. For reservations and details, call (407) W-DISNEY. Teens and young adults looking for a Halloween happening should check out parties at Pleasure Island, Universal CityWalk, and at the Universal theme parks.

A woman from Nokomis, Florida, reports that crowds were the only scary thing at the Not-So-Scary Halloween Party:

> I've been to Mickey's Not-So-Scary Halloween Party twice, and both times it has been an overcrowded nightmare! Don't even bother to try and ride anything.

A mother from Kissimmee who attends with her school-age children every year, likes the party, writing:

> For me the festive nature of the [Not-So-Scary Halloween] Party makes up for the crowds. I love seeing all the kids and characters (!) in their costumes.

What makes Disney Halloween and Christmas events special are the partying and entertainment. These celebrations aren't a good choice if your primary agenda is to experience the attractions.

Christmas and New Year's at the Theme Parks   Don't expect to see all of the attractions in a single day of touring at any park. Skip the Magic Kingdom, if possible, if you tour the week between Christmas and New Year's. We love the Magic Kingdom. Really. But that love is tempered by the fact that women will wait up to 20 minutes to use the restrooms during this week. Thirty-minute waits are typical at counter-service restaurants. Ask a teenager what happens in a "mosh pit," and you'll have some idea what Fantasyland looks like by midafternoon, only with more strollers and peppier music.

Epcot, on the other hand, is at its best during the holidays. Touring in the evening will reward you with stunning displays of holiday decorations and slightly smaller crowds than in daytime. Exceptional live entertainment abounds, too. The American Pavilion, for example, has two choral groups—easily over 150 singers total—performing holiday favorites during this week.

Disney-MGM Studios is also a good choice for evening touring. Crowds will be larger than normal, but the decorations make up for it. One "must see" is the Osborne Family Spectacle of Lights, which returns to the Studios after a brief absence. The aptly named Spectacle contains a staggering five million Christmas lights, including 3-D images that can be seen using special glasses. The Studios simulates winter during the festivities by mounting bubble-making machines atop buildings in the New York Street area. At night, millions of small bubbles cascade onto park guests. The effect is striking—it took us a moment to realize it wasn't really snowing. An outstanding effect, we hope it becomes a permanent part of the holiday display.

Mickey's Very Merry Christmas Party   The party is staged from 8 p.m. to 1 a.m. (after regular park hours) on several evenings in December. Advance tickets cost $36 for adults and $26 for ages 3–9, while tickets at the gate run about $42 and $32, respectively. For dates and prices, call (407) W-DISNEY. Included are use of all attractions during party hours, holiday-theme stage shows featuring Disney characters, cookies and hot chocolate, performances of Mickey's Very Merry Christmas Parade, a party memento (usually a family photo), carolers, "a magical snowfall on Main Street," and fireworks.

A reader from Pineville, Louisiana, tried the Very Merry Christmas Party and found the guest list too large for her liking:

Another thing I will not do again is buy tickets and go to the Very Merry Christmas Party. We went in December to avoid crowds and were taken by surprise to find wall-to-wall people at the Very Merry Christmas Party. They offered some great shows, but we could not get to them. The parade at 9 p.m. and the fireworks at 10 p.m., then fighting our way back to the parking lot was all we could muster. . . . We did not ride anything, and there were some things that we had wanted to go back and ride. Mickey's Very Merry Christmas Party is not the time for rides!

Until last year, most reader mail described huge crowds and long lines. More recently, however, either because of the dip in Disney World attendance or because Disney limited the number of tickets sold each night (supposedly to about 20,000), readers reported very tolerable crowds and short lines at the Very Merry Christmas Party. (The Magic Kingdom can absorb 20,000 guests quite handily; that's a couple thousand fewer than average attendance on an off-season day.) Our advice is to nail Disney down on the max-attendance number before you plunk down your cash.

Remember: During major holiday periods such as Christmas, many of the festive extras can be enjoyed in the weeks before the actual week in which the holiday occurs.

Part Two

Making the Most of Your Time and Money

Allocating Money

Did Walt really intend for it to be so expensive that the average family couldn't afford it?

—*Unofficial Guide* reader and mother of one from Amarillo, Texas

How much you spend depends on how long you stay at Walt Disney World. But even if you stop for only an afternoon, be prepared to drop a bundle. In Part Three, we'll show you how to save money on lodging, and in Part Nine, you'll find tips for economizing on meals. This section will give some sense of what admission will cost, as well as which admission option will best meet your needs.

Walt Disney World Admission Options

In an effort to accommodate vacations of various durations and activities, Disney currently offers more than 180 different admission options to its theme parks. These options range from the basic "One Day, One Park" ticket, good for a single entry into any one of Disney's theme parks, to the top of the line Premium Annual Pass, good for 365 days of admission into every theme and water park Disney operates, plus DisneyQuest and Pleasure Island.

The sheer number of ticket options available makes it difficult and, yes, daunting, for a family to sort out which option represents the least expensive way to see and do everything they want. Of course, not all of the 180 ticket options are relevant to every guest. Moreover, to purchase a goodly number of the admissions, you must meet some specific qualification, for example, being a Florida resident. An average family staying for a week at an off-World hotel and planning a couple of activities outside the theme parks generally has about a dozen different ticket options to consider. To complicate matters, comparing options requires detailed knowledge of the myriad perks included with specific admissions, such as the "Plus" features on certain Park Hopper tickets. Finding the optimum admission, or combination of admissions, however, could save our average family a nice little bundle.

Many families, we suspect, become overwhelmed trying to sort out the different options, and simply purchase a more expensive ticket with features they will probably never use. Adding to the frustration, Disney's reservation agents are generally trained to avoid answering subjective questions such as which ticket option is "best." We don't think Disney is intentionally confusing anyone, but we do note that if you're a company running a theme park, having guests pay for features they'll never use is a nice way to pad your bottom line.

To simplify things, *Unofficial Guide* researchers tried to define four or five guidelines to help you choose the best ticket options for your vacation. Eight hours into this project, we sounded like a theme-park version of Forrest Gump. You know that scene where Forrest rattles off seven thousand different ways to prepare shrimp? That was us, babbling about Park Hopper tickets. Even saying some of the ticket names ("Adult Advance Purchase Internet-Only Seven-Day Park Hopper Plus Four") made us sound like our local Starbucks barista, just not as perky. We did, however, feel like we needed a drink.

After a day or so, we realized that a handful of general guidelines was an impossible task, so we wrote a computer program to figure it out (for anyone interested, it's an optimization model for the classic bin-packing problem in operations research). You can use the program to determine the best ticket options for you by visiting our Web site at **www.touringplans.com.** The program is free and considers almost all of the 180 different ticket options. It also takes into account discounts for Florida residents, members of the military, and families able to take advantage of advance-purchase tickets. All you have to do is answer a few simple questions relating to the theme parks you intend to visit, whether you intend to stay at a Disney or non-Disney hotel, etc. (nothing personal). The program will then identify the four least-expensive ticket options for your vacation.

The program will also make recommendations concerning considerations other than price. For example, annual passes, though they might cost more, may make sense in certain circumstances because Disney often offers substantial resort discounts and other deals to annual passholders. Those resort discounts, especially during off-season times, can more than offset a small incremental charge for the annual pass.

Basic Admission Options

Happily, we need only discuss about 10 or so of those 180 admission options. Though the program on our Web site considers practically all of the ticket alternatives, these are the ones (many with silly names) that the majority of Walt Disney World guests purchase. Note that the prices below include sales tax; prices quoted in Disney literature or on the Disney information phone line don't.

Speaking of prices, Disney World ticket prices change almost as often as the prime rate. In fact, since the first edition of the *Unofficial Guide* in 1985, prices have escalated 160%! Prices quoted below are current at press time. Increases historically have been in the 3–5% per year range.

Type of Pass	Front Gate Adult Price w/ Tax	Front Gate Child Price w/ Tax
1-Day/One-Park Only Pass*	$58	$47
1-Day/One-Park Bounce-Back Pass*	$52	$40
4-Day Park-Hopper Pass	$233	$187
5-Day Park-Hopper Pass	$265	$213
5-Day Park-Hopper Plus Pass	$300	$240
6-Day Park-Hopper Plus Pass	$332	$266
7-Day Park-Hopper Plus Pass	$364	$292
Ultimate Park-Hopper Pass	*Varies according to length of stay*	
Annual Passports**	$404	$343
Florida Resident/Seasonal	$212	$180

* *Sold only at the theme parks.*

** *More expensive Annual Passports include water parks, Pleasure Island, and Disney's Wide World of Sports.*

The **1-Day/One-Park Only Pass** is good for admission and unlimited use of attractions at the Magic Kingdom, Epcot, Animal Kingdom, or Disney-MGM Studios but provides same-day admission to only one of the four.

The **1-Day/One-Park Bounce-Back Pass** works as follows: If you buy a 1-Day/One-Park Only Pass at the regular price, you're eligible to buy a 1-Day/One-Park Bounce-Back Pass at a discounted rate, *as long as you buy it the same day you bought the original pass.* Wait, there's more: If you buy a 1-Day/One-Park Only Pass and a second, discounted 1-Day/One-Park Bounce-Back Pass, you're eligible to buy a third and fourth 1-Day/One-Park Bounce-Back Pass at an even greater discount. All must be bought the same day.

The 1-Day/One-Park Bounce-Back Pass is a good example of why Disney World doesn't have a toll-free number. When introduced, it took an information operator over 12 minutes to explain how it works, and she had to consult her supervisor twice. When we phoned to check on the Bounce-Back, we made upward of five calls just to get an operator to admit it exists. Frustrated by our persistence, an operator finally said the Bounce-Back is available but that "Disney doesn't want anyone to know about it." Because the Bounce-Back was trumpeted only a few years ago, we asked, "Why have it if you don't want anyone to know about it?" The answer, according to Disney, is that ticket sellers at the parks are instructed to try to talk guests into buying multiday Park Hopper passes instead of 1-Day/One-Park Only tickets. If a guest balks at buying the more-expensive multiday pass, the seller is authorized to offer the Bounce-Back in order to prolong the guest's visit. The bottom line, evidently, is that Bounce-Backs were cannibalizing sales of multiday Park Hoppers, so they were withdrawn, except as an incentive to keep one-day guests on property.

If you buy four 1-Day/One-Park Only admissions under the Bounce-Back arrangement, you pay $58 for the first pass, and $53 for the second, third, and fourth or $217 total ($170 for a child's passes). This is about $16 per adult ($17 per child) less than you would pay for 4-Day Park Hopper Passes (see below). For the savings, you forfeit two features of the Park Hopper: You give up the right to visit more than one park in a day, and Bounce-Back passes expire, whereas Park Hoppers are good forever. If you buy a 1-Day/One-Park Only Pass and then buy a 1-Day/One-Park Bounce-Back Pass, the Bounce-Back expires four days from the purchase date. If you buy three Bounce-Backs, the first expires in four days, the second in six, and the third in eight.

It's a pretty good deal for anyone who wants to visit the theme parks over three or four days and doesn't care about hopping from park to park on the same day.

The **4-Day** and **5-Day Park Hopper Passes** provide same-day admission to the Magic Kingdom, Animal Kingdom, Epcot, and Disney-MGM Studios. You can tour the Studios in the morning, have lunch at Animal Kingdom and dinner at Epcot, then stop by the Magic Kingdom for the evening parades. Unused days don't expire.

The **5-Day, 6-Day,** and **7-Day Park Hopper Plus Passes** provide unlimited use of the major theme parks plus limited visits to Pleasure Island, Blizzard Beach, Typhoon Lagoon, and Wide World of Sports for the number of days stated on the pass. They don't expire and don't have to be used during one stay or on consecutive days.

Regarding the water parks, Pleasure Island, and Wide World of Sports, the 5-Day Park Hopper Plus allows two visits to the venues of your choice. The 6- and 7-Day Plus Passes allow three and four visits, respectively. Unused admissions are good forever, including admissions to minor parks (water parks, Pleasure Island, and the sports complex). You can't hop from water park to water park as you can among the major theme parks. If you buy a 5-Day Park Hopper Plus Pass and visit Typhoon Lagoon in the morning and Blizzard Beach in the afternoon, you'll use up both of your admissions to the water parks and minor entertainment venues.

The **Ultimate Park Hopper Pass,** for Disney lodging and campground guests, provides the same benefits as the Park Hopper Plus Pass but can be purchased for any stay two days or longer. It offers comprehensive admission (all major and minor parks) for stays of any length. These passes are incredibly convenient: Guests receive a card that functions as a combination park pass and credit card. The card can be used at restaurants, shops, and other facilities throughout Disney World, and purchases are charged to the guest's room. The negative: Ultimate Park Hopper Passes are good only for the guest's stay.

Also, because the Ultimate Park Hopper Pass is available only to Disney resort guests, prices aren't published. This makes prices subject to manipulation and increases the difficulty of comparing admission options. We can say, however, that the Ultimate Park Hopper Pass is more expensive than regular Park Hopper passes because it includes the water parks and entertainment venues. If you don't intend to spend much time at the water parks, Pleasure Island, or Wide World of Sports, or plan to spend a day or two outside the World, you're much better off buying a Park Hopper pass. However, the Ultimate Park Hopper Pass allows you to hop from water park to water park to Pleasure Island, etc., on the same day.

The **Annual Passport** provides unlimited use of the major theme parks for one year. An add-on is available to provide unlimited use of the minor theme parks. Annual Passport holders also get perks, including free parking and seasonal offers such as room-rate discounts at Disney resorts. This pass isn't valid for special events.

For Additional Information on Passes

If you have a question or concern regarding admissions that can be addressed only through a person-to-person conversation, call Disney Ticket Services at (407) 827-4166. If you need prices or routine information, call (407) 824-4321 for recorded info.

Which Admission Should You Buy?

If you have only one day at Walt Disney World, select the park that most interests you and buy the 1-Day/One-Park Only ticket. If you have two days and don't plan to return for a couple of years, buy two 1-Day tickets, a Bounce-Back Pass, or an Ultimate Park Hopper Pass if you're a Disney lodging guest. If you think you might revisit the area in the next year or two, spring for a 4-, 5-, 6-, or 7-day pass. Use two days of admission to see as much as you can, and save the remaining days for another trip.

If you plan to spend three or more days, buy a 4- or 5-day pass. If you live in Florida or plan to spend seven or more days in the major theme parks, the Annual Passport is a good buy. If you live in Florida and don't mind being restricted to visiting Disney World at designated off-peak times, consider the Florida Resident's Seasonal Pass.

If you visit Disney World every year, here's how to save big bucks. Let's say you usually vacation during summer. This year, go in July and buy an

Annual Passport. Next year, go in June. Because Annual Passports start on the purchase date, those you buy this year will still be good for next year's vacation if you go a month earlier! If you spend four days each year at Disney World (eight days in the two consecutive years), you'll cut your daily admission to about $50 per adult, including tax. The longer your Disney vacation, of course, the more you save with the Annual Passport. If you visit two parks seven days each year (14 days total), your admission will be less than $29 per day.

Another Tip for Saving Money on Admissions

You can also save by planning ahead and watching the calendar, as this mom from Broomfield, Colorado, explains:

If you are planning a trip well in advance, purchase your Park Hopper Passes before the end of the year. Our travel agent recommended this because Disney usually increases their prices in the new year. So we purchased our tickets for June back in December, and sure enough, I found out that the price for a Park Hopper Pass had increased $20 per person. That's an $80 [savings] for our family!

Discounts on Admissions

Admission Discounts Available to Anyone

Surprisingly, deals available to anyone are about the same as those offered to special groups (with the exception of military and civil service personnel). Whoever you deal with, check to see if their price includes tax. If you order over the phone or on the Internet, buy from sellers who will ship your tickets to you in advance.

Advance Purchase on the Walt Disney World Web Site   You can save 3–8% off front-gate prices by purchasing your passes at **www.disney world.com.** This applies to all admissions except Annual Passports, which are cheaper and far less hassle to buy at each theme park's Guest Services window. Shipping and handling costs $3.

Advance Purchase from the Disney Store   If you have a Disney Store nearby, you get roughly the same discount there that's available online. Disney stores outside Florida sell Park Hopper and Park Hopper Plus passes only.

Advance Purchase by Calling (407) W-DISNEY   If you don't have Web access or a Disney Store handy, you can buy Park Hopper and Park Hopper Plus tickets by phone. There is a $3 per order mailing charge.

TicketMania   offers discounts on tickets for almost all central Florida attractions, including Disney, Universal, SeaWorld, and Cirque du Soleil. Shop online at **www.ticketmania.com.** Discounts for the major theme parks are about 4%. Discounts of up to 7% are available for some Universal and SeaWorld combo passes. Tickets for other attractions are more deeply discounted. Ticketmania offers free shipping with 5- to 10-day delivery. Rush shipping costs extra. Ticketmania confirms orders via e-mail and specifies when the tickets will be shipped and when they should arrive. Ticketmania is primarily set up to do business on the Internet, but customers can reach it by phone at (877) 822-7299, 9:30 a.m. to 4 p.m. EST, seven days a week.

Floridaorlandotickets.net frequently beats TicketMania's prices but charges for shipping and handling.

Orlando Convention and Visitors Bureau Official Visitors Center If you're staying at a Universal Orlando hotel or in the International Drive area, you can save about 2–3% off regular prices at the Visitor Center. It's at 8723 International Drive, about a half-mile south of the intersection with Sand Lake Road. From I-4, take Exit 29A. Open 8 a.m. to 6 p.m. daily. Phone (407) 363-5872. The bureau also sells tickets online at **www.orlandoticketsales.com.**

Admission Discounts Available to Certain Groups and Individuals

Canadians Canadians purchasing their admission at a Disney Store in Canada will save about 6% by avoiding taxes.

AAA Members Members of AAA can buy Park Hopper and Park Hopper Plus passes for a discount of 3–5%. AAA offers the best discount available at the time of this writing for regular Park Hopper passes (that is, no "Plus" features).

Disney Vacation Club Members receive a 4–5% discount on admissions.

Disney Corporate Sponsors If you work for a Disney World corporate sponsor, you might be eligible for discounted admissions or preferential treatment at the parks. Ask your personnel or employee-benefits office.

Military, Department of Defense, Civil Service Active-duty and retired military, Department of Defense civilian employees, some civil service employees, and dependents of these groups can buy Disney multiday admissions at a 9–10% discount. At most military and DOD installations, the passes are available from the Morale, Welfare, and Recreation office. Civil service employees should contact their personnel office to see if they're eligible and for instructions on how and where to purchase tickets. Military personnel can buy a discounted admission for nonmilitary guests as long as the military member accompanies the nonmilitary member. If a group, 50% must be eligible for the military discount.

Special Passes

Walt Disney World offers a number of special and situational passes that are not known to the general public and are not sold at any Disney World ticket booth. The list includes convention passes and even 3-Day Park

Hopper Plus passes. The best information we've found on these passes is available on the internet at **www.mousesavers.com.**

Buying Your Admission on Arrival

Admission passes are available at Walt Disney World resorts and theme parks. Passes are also available at hotels, some grocery stores, and through various independent ticket brokers. Because Disney admissions are not discounted in the greater Walt Disney World–Orlando area, the only reason to purchase from an independent broker is convenience.

Partially Used Passes

Many readers ask if they can use remaining admissions on 4- through 7-day passes brought home by relatives. Whoever bought the pass agreed that "the pass must be used by the same person for all days." Because most passes sold in recent years don't bear the buyer's photograph or signature—or even name—guests have generally had no difficulty gaining admission with a partially used pass acquired from a friend or relative. This makes the pass perfectly, though illegally, transferable.

A corollary question concerns what to do with unused admissions on 4-, 5-, 6-, or 7-day passes purchased legally during your vacation. We advise hanging onto the passes. First, resale of unused multiday passes is a misdemeanor. Second, because Disney raises admission prices almost every year, using an old pass during your next visit will save you money.

Recently, black-market ticket sellers have become bolder. Although it's true that most theme-park tickets offered at a deep discount involve suffering through a time-share pitch, there's now an active market in unused admissions on multiday passes. Most of this activity is on US 192 in stores with signs reading "We Buy Unused Days on Park Passes" or similar language. Savings on "pre-owned" passes may be more than 50%, and salespersons claim that buying and reselling passes is legal. Disney has yet to challenge these operations. We advise buying only new passes from a legitimate source. The modern plastic pass must be computer-scanned to ascertain the number of days left on it. When you purchase a partially used card from a stranger, you can't verify how many, if any, unused days remain.

How Much Does It Cost per Day at Walt Disney World?

A typical day would cost $459.10, excluding lodging and transportation, for a family of four—Mom, Dad, 12-year-old Tim, and 8-year-old Sandy—driving their own car and staying outside "the World." They plan to be in the area for a week, so they buy 5-Day Park Hopper Passes. Here's a breakdown:

HOW MUCH DOES A DAY COST?

Breakfast for four at Denny's with tax and tip	$26.00
Epcot parking fee	8.00
One day's admission on a 5-Day Park Hopper Pass	
Dad: Adult 5-Day with tax = $265 divided by five (days)	53.00
Mom: Adult 5-Day with tax = $265 divided by five (days)	53.00
Tim: Adult 5-Day with tax = $265 divided by five (days)	53.00
Sandy: Child 5-Day with tax = $213 divided by five (days)	42.60
Morning break (soda or coffee)	13.50
Fast-food lunch (sandwich or burger, fries, soda), no tip	35.00
Afternoon break (soda and popcorn)	18.00
Dinner at Italy (no alcoholic beverages) with tax & tip	118.00
Souvenirs (Mickey T-shirts for Tim and Sandy) with tax*	39.00

One-Day Total (without lodging or transportation)   **$459.10**

* Cheer up; you won't have to buy souvenirs every day.

Allocating Time

During Disney World's first decade, a family with a week's vacation could enjoy the Magic Kingdom and the now-closed River Country and still have several days for the beach or other area attractions. Since Epcot opened in 1982, however, Disney World has steadily been enlarging to monopolize the family's entire week. Today, with the addition of Blizzard Beach, Typhoon Lagoon, Disney-MGM Studios, the Animal Kingdom, and Downtown Disney, you should allocate six days for a whirlwind tour (seven to ten if you insist on a little relaxation during your vacation). If you don't have six or more days or think you might want to venture outside the World, be prepared to make some hard choices.

The theme parks and water parks are huge and require a lot of walking and, sometimes, a lot of waiting in lines. Approach Disney World the same way you would an eight-course Italian dinner: with plenty of time between courses. Don't cram too much into too little time.

Which Park to See First?

This question is less academic than it appears, especially if your party includes children or teenagers. Children who see the Magic Kingdom first expect the same type of entertainment at the other parks. At Epcot, they're often disappointed by the educational orientation and serious tone (many adults react the same way). Disney-MGM offers some wild action, but the general presentation is educational and more adult. Though most children enjoy zoos, animals can't be programmed to entertain. Thus, children may not find the Animal Kingdom as exciting as the Magic Kingdom or Disney-MGM.

First-time visitors should see Epcot first; you'll be able to enjoy it without having been preconditioned to think of Disney entertainment as solely fantasy or adventure.

See the Animal Kingdom second. Like Epcot, it's educational, but its live animals provide a change of pace.

Next, see Disney-MGM Studios, which helps all ages transition from the educational Epcot and Animal Kingdom to the fanciful Magic Kingdom. Also, because Disney-MGM Studios is smaller, you won't walk as much or stay as long.

Save the Magic Kingdom for last.

Operating Hours

Disney runs a dozen or more schedules each year. Call (407) 824-4321 for the exact hours before you arrive. Off-season, parks may be open as few as eight hours (9 a.m. to 5 p.m.). At busy times (particularly holidays), they may operate from 8 a.m. until 2 a.m.

Official Opening versus Real Opening

When you call, you're given "official hours." Sometimes, parks open earlier. If official hours are 9 a.m.–9 p.m., for example, Main Street in the Magic Kingdom might open at 8:30 a.m., the remainder of the park at 9 a.m.

Disney publishes hours well in advance but reacts to gate conditions. Disney surveys local hotel reservations, estimates how many visitors to expect on a given day, and opens the theme parks early to avoid bottlenecks at parking facilities and ticket windows and to absorb crowds as they arrive.

Rides and attractions shut down at approximately the official closing time. Main Street in the Magic Kingdom remains open 30 minutes to an hour after the rest of the park has closed.

The Vacation that Fights Back

Visiting Disney World requires levels of industry and stamina more often associated with running marathons. A mother from Middletown, New York, spells it out:

A vacation at WDW is not a vacation in the usual sense—sleeping late, total relaxation, leisurely meals, etc. It is a vacation that's frankly exhausting, but definitely worth doing. WDW is a magical place, where the visitor feels welcomed from the minute they arrive at their accommodations to the last second before boarding the shuttle bus back to the airport.

A British gentleman, thinking we exaggerated about the walking required, measured his outings using a pedometer. His discovery:

I decided to wear a pedometer for our recent visit to WDW. Our visits to the theme parks were spread over five days, during which my wife and I (ages 51 and 55) walked a total of 68 miles for an average of 13 miles per day!

The point is: At Walt Disney World, less is more. Take the World in small doses, with plenty of swimming, napping, reading, and relaxing in between. If you don't see everything, guess what? You can come back!

Also, you can prepare. An Ohio reader discovered this secret too late:

> The only thing missing from your book is more strongly worded advice about being able to walk unlimited miles and stand for an infinite amount of time. I fly a desk for a living and don't get near enough walking or standing exercise to prepare myself for the rigors of the World. My wife and I have determined that before we go to Disney World again, we will be able to walk at least five miles without a rest or feeling any pain the next day. After pounding the pavement for hours on end, we were so exhausted that we had no choice but to spend two of our vacation days just recovering from the previous day's walking.

Hitting the Wall

As you plan your time at Disney World, consider your physical limitations. It's exhausting to rise at dawn and run around a theme park for 8–12 hours day after day. Sooner or later (usually sooner), you hit the wall. Every Disney World vacation itinerary should include days when you don't go to a theme park and days when you sleep in and take the morning off. Plan these to follow unusually long and arduous days, particularly those when you stay in the parks to see the evening parades or fireworks. Keep telling yourself that you'll enjoy your vacation more if you're rested.

A Suwanee, Georgia, reader makes this suggestion:

> The one area that I think you can expand on in your book is preparing people for the overall pace that this type of vacation warrants. My initial plan for the family entailed a day at MK, one day each at Epcot, AK, Disney-MGM, Universal Studios, and Islands of Adventure, one down day, and a leftover day for a second visit to something we hadn't finished. By day two, I became acutely aware that there was no way we would be able to keep up that pace.

A mom from La Grange, Illinois, tried to sidestep our advice to stay rested:

> As I was planning, I was very sure we would not be taking a swim/nap break in the middle of the day. No way! On the very first day of touring (at the Magic Kingdom), my seven-year-old said (at 9:30 a.m.—after only two hours at the park), "I'm hot—when can we go back to the hotel and swim?" Needless to say, we took that little break every day.

If you don't pace yourself, you'll be writing us letters like this one from a father of three from Unionville, Connecticut:

> It's difficult to follow your [touring plans] for more than one day in a row. The kids are too exhausted to last through the fireworks.

A Tolland, Connecticut, family altered their touring for an "easy day":

There is so much to do and see at WDW, we inevitably push the kids, and then pay the price. One day, when they were tired, we went to MGM and only did shows. We got there in time for Indiana Jones, then moved to the Hunchback of Notre Dame [now closed], then to lunch. Since most of the day was seated, the kids got time to rest and weren't too cranky.

A Narberth, Pennsylvania, mom changed their dinner time:

We found that getting up as early as we did, it was important to make early dinner reservations—6:30 p.m. at the latest. The one time we tried to eat at 8 p.m., our younger son fell asleep at the table and could not be awakened.

The Practicality of Returning to Your Hotel for Rest

Many readers write about the practicality of departing the theme park for a nap and swim at the hotel. A dad from Sequim, Washington, made this request:

I would like to see nearness to the parks emphasized in your accommodation guide, taking traffic and hotel access into account. We tried going back to the hotel for midday breaks, but it was too time consuming. By the time you got to the car, negotiated traffic, rested, and reversed the process to get back to the park, it took two–three hours for a short rest and was not worth it!

First, in response to the reader's request, we now publish a chart in Part Three, Selecting Your Hotel, that provides the commuting times to each of the Disney theme parks from virtually every hotel within 20 miles of Walt Disney World. But to address the larger issue, we think the reader was overly anxious about the time away from the parks. Two to three hours really won't cut it. If he had resigned himself to a four- to five-hour break, his family would have stayed rested and relaxed.

Here's the scoop: At the Animal Kingdom, Disney-MGM Studios, and Epcot, you can get to your car in the parking lot in about 15–20 minutes. From the Magic Kingdom, it will take you 30–35 minutes. Obviously, if you're at the farthest point from the park entrance when you decide to return to the hotel, or you barely miss a parking-lot tram, it will take longer, but from most places in the parks, the above times are correct. Once in your car, you'll be able to commute to most US 192 hotels, all Disney World hotels, all Lake Buena Vista hotels, and most I-4 corridor and southbound International Drive (I-Drive) hotels in 20 minutes or less. It will take about the same time to reach hotels on I-Drive north of Sand Lake Road and in the Universal-Orlando area.

So, for most people, the one-way commute will average 30 minutes. But here's what you get for your time: a less-expensive lunch at a restaurant of your choosing; a swim; and a one-and-a-half to two-hour nap. If you add up the times, you'll be away from the parks about four to four-

and-a-half hours, counting the commute. If you want, eat dinner outside the World before returning. Clearly, this won't work during times of year when the parks close early, but these aren't times when most families go to Disney World. If you visit when the parks close early, you'll see more attractions in less time, owing to reduced attendance, and will be able to leave the parks earlier and take your break in the late afternoon or early evening. Not ideal, but neither are the crowds and heat of summer.

A corollary to this discussion is what you do the next day. If you're getting a three- to five-hour break each day and not keeping late hours, you'll be fine. If you forgo the break, you'll need to alternate full days with very easy, sleep-late days in order to recharge your batteries. If you do neither, you'll say hello to the wall by your third day.

Arrival-Day Blues:
What to Do When You Have Only a Half Day

On arrival and departure days, you probably will have only part of a day for touring or other recreational pursuits. It's a common problem: You roll into the World about 1 p.m., excited and ready to go … but where?

The first question: Do you feel comfortable blowing an expensive day's admission to the parks when you have less than a full day to tour? Certainly, your arrival time and the parks' closing times are considerations, but so is the touring disadvantage you suffer by not being there when a park opens. FASTPASS, a type of reservation system for popular attractions (see pages 79–85), provides some relief from long afternoon lines, but FASTPASS isn't available for every attraction, nor is there an unlimited supply of passes.

Opting for a Partial Day at the Theme Parks

If you decide to splurge and burn a pass on a half day or less, refer to our *Unofficial Guide* Crowd-level Calendar (pages 33–40).

One option, if you can reach the park by 1 p.m. and stay until closing (5–8 p.m., depending on season), is the Animal Kingdom, which requires the least time to tour. Because guests who arrive at opening frequently complete their tour by about 2 p.m., crowds thin in late afternoon. As a bonus, FASTPASS is offered for the three most popular attractions. If you arrive much after 1 p.m., however, the daily allocation of FASTPASSes, especially for Kilimanjaro Safaris, might be exhausted. And Animal Kingdom closes earlier than the other parks.

Whenever you arrive at a theme park (including Universal parks) after 10 a.m., go to higher-capacity attractions where waiting time is relatively brief even during the most crowded part of the day. In Disney parks, you can also cut your time in line by using FASTPASS. Another time-saver at Mission: Space and Test Track in Epcot, and at several Universal Studios and Islands of Adventure attractions is the "singles line." Found only at rides, it's a separate line for individuals who are alone or don't mind riding alone. The objective is to fill odd spaces left by groups that don't quite fill the entire ride vehicle. Because there aren't many singles and most groups are unwilling to split up, singles lines are usually much shorter than regular lines.

Disney parks are better for partial-day touring than Universal parks because Disney parks generally operate more high-capacity attractions than Universal does. However, the Universal Express program has more perks than Disney's equivalent FASTPASS (especially if you're staying at a Universal resort). This means that those who use Universal Express may tour more efficiently than a similar guest at Disney. Even so, nothing is guaranteed. We like the Universal parks and admire their cutting-edge technology, but the best way to see them is to be there at opening and follow our touring plans.

Our Touring Plan Companions (back of this book) list attractions in each Disney park that require the least waiting during the most crowded part of the day. Although the queues for these attractions may seem humongous, they move quickly. Also check out parades, stage shows, and other live entertainment. Popular attractions generally stay packed until an hour or so before closing; however, they often require little waiting during evening parades, fireworks, or, in the case of Disney-MGM Studios, *Fantasmic!*

Alternatives to the Theme Parks on Arrival Day

Before you head out for fun on arrival day, you must check in, unpack, and buy admissions, and you probably will detour to the grocery or convenience store to buy snacks, drinks, and breakfast food. At all Disney resorts and many non-Disney hotels, you cannot occupy your room until after 3 p.m.; however, many properties will check you in, sell you tickets, and store your luggage before that hour.

The least expensive way to spend your arrival day is to check in, unpack, do your chores, and relax at your hotel swimming pool. (Be careful not to get sunburned; it's the last thing you want at the beginning of your vacation.)

Other daytime options include a trip to a local water park. Because the Disney water parks are so crowded (during summer you need to be on hand for opening, just like at the major Disney parks), we recommend **Water Mania** on US 192, about 10–15 minutes from most hotels in and around Disney World. Water Mania has great slides but hardly a shadow of the long lines at Blizzard Beach or Typhoon Lagoon. Plus, it's much less expensive. **Wet 'n' Wild** on International Drive is also excellent. Generally it's less crowded than Disney water parks but more packed than Water Mania, and more expensive. What's great about Wet 'n' Wild is that it stays open late in summer. Any water park that stays open past 5 p.m. is worth a look because crowds at all parks clear out substantially after 4 p.m. If the park is open late and you get hungry, you'll find ample fast food. No matter which water park you choose, lather up with waterproof sunscreen. For details on water parks, see Part Fourteen, The Water Parks.

If you want something drier, we heartily recommend **Gatorland,** a quirky attraction on US 441 near Kissimmee (about 20 minutes from Walt Disney World). Gatorland, a slice of pre-Disney Florida, is exceptionally interesting and well-managed. It's perfect for a half-day outing, providing you like alligators, snakes, and lizards. For information, call Gatorland at (800) 393-JAWS or check its Web site at **www.gatorland.com.**

If none of the above fires your boiler, consider miniature golf (expensive in the World; more reasonable outside it) or **DisneyQuest,** Disney's venue featuring interactive games and simulator technology. Alas, like the Disney parks, DisneyQuest is expensive and doesn't handle crowds particularly well. It's at Disney's West Side. Late mornings and early afternoons are the best times to go.

In the Evening

Dinner provides a great opportunity to plan the next day's activities. If you're hungry for entertainment, too, try a dinner show or take in a show after dinner. If you go the show route, we recommend Cirque du Soleil's *La Nouba* at Disney's West Side. Cirque is expensive, but we think it's the single best thing in all of Walt Disney World. Disney also offers some dinner shows, of which the *Hoop-Dee-Doo Revue* is our pick of the litter. Both Cirque and *Hoop-Dee-Doo* are extremely popular; make reservations far in advance. A dozen or so non-Disney dinner shows are advertised in visitor magazines (often with discount coupons) available free at any non-Disney hotel.

If you don't try Cirque or a dinner show, consider Pleasure Island, Disney's nightclub complex, or Universal's club scene, CityWalk. Both are best appreciated by adults—energetic adults, at that. Whatever you do, don't wear yourself out the first day.

Departure Days

Departure days don't seem to cause as much consternation as arrival days. If you want to visit a theme park on your departure day, get up early and be there when it opens. If you have a lot of time, check out and store your luggage with the bell desk or in your car. Or, if you can arrange a late check-out, you might want to return to your hotel for a shower and change of clothes before departing. Some hotels are quite liberal regarding late check-outs; others assess a charge.

Optimum Touring Situation

We don't believe there's one ideal itinerary. Tastes, energy levels, and perspectives on what constitutes entertainment and relaxation vary. This said, here are some considerations for developing your ideal itinerary.

Optimum touring at Disney World requires a good itinerary, at least six days on site (excluding travel time), and a fair amount of money. It also requires a prodigious appetite for Disney entertainment. The essence of optimum touring is to see the attractions in a series of shorter, less-exhausting visits during cooler, less-crowded times of day, with plenty of rest and relaxation between excursions.

Since optimum touring calls for leaving and returning to the theme parks on most days, it makes sense to stay in a Disney resort hotel or a non-Disney hotel no more than 12 minutes away. Disney resort guests have freer use of the bus, boat, and monorail systems and have more choices for baby-sitting and children's programs. Sound good? It is, but be prepared to pay.

If you visit during busy times (see pages 28–31), you need to get up early to beat the crowds. Short lines and stress-free touring are incompatible with sleeping in. If you want to sleep late and enjoy your touring, visit Disney World when attendance is lighter.

The Cardinal Rules for Successful Touring

Many visitors don't have six days to devote to Disney. Some are en route to other destinations or may wish to sample additional central Florida attractions. For these visitors, efficient touring is a must.

Even the most time-effective touring plan won't allow you to comprehensively cover two or more major theme parks in one day. Plan to allocate an entire day to each park (an exception to this is when the parks close at different times, allowing you to tour one park until closing then proceed to another). If your schedule permits only one day of touring, concentrate on one theme park and save the others for another visit.

One-Day Touring

A comprehensive, one-day tour of the Magic Kingdom, Animal Kingdom, Epcot, or Disney-MGM Studios is possible, but requires knowledge of the park, good planning, good navigation, and plenty of energy and endurance. One-day touring leaves little time for sit-down meals, prolonged browsing in shops, or lengthy breaks. One-day touring can be fun and rewarding, but allocating two days per park, especially for the Magic Kingdom and Epcot, is preferable.

Successful touring of the Magic Kingdom, Animal Kingdom, Epcot, or Disney-MGM Studios hinges on three rules:

1. Determine in Advance What You Really Want to See

Which rides and attractions appeal most to you? Which ones would you like to experience if you have time left? What are you willing to forgo?

To help you set your touring priorities, we describe the theme parks and every attraction in detail in this book. In each description, we include the author's evaluation of the attraction and the opinions of Disney World guests expressed as star ratings. Five stars is the highest rating.

Finally, because attractions range from midway-type rides and horse-drawn trolleys to high-tech extravaganzas, we have developed a hierarchy of categories to pinpoint an attraction's magnitude:

Super Headliners   The best attractions the theme park has to offer. Mind-boggling in size, scope, and imagination. Represents the cutting edge of attraction technology and design.

Headliners   Multimillion-dollar, full-scale, themed adventures and theater presentations. Modern in technology and design and employing a full range of special effects.

Major Attractions   More modest themed adventures, but incorporating state-of-the-art technologies. Or, larger-scale attractions of older design.

Minor Attractions   Midway-type rides, small "dark" rides (cars on a track, zig-zagging through the dark), small theater presentations, transportation rides, and elaborate walk-through attractions.

Diversions   Exhibits, both passive and interactive. Includes playgrounds, video arcades, and street theater.

Though not every attraction fits neatly into these descriptions, the categories provide a comparison of attraction size and scope. Remember that bigger and more elaborate doesn't always mean better. Peter Pan's Flight, a minor attraction in the Magic Kingdom, continues to be one of the park's most beloved rides. Likewise, for many young children, no attraction, regardless of size, surpasses Dumbo.

2. Arrive Early! Arrive Early! Arrive Early!

This is the single most important key to efficient touring and avoiding long lines. First thing in the morning, there are no lines and fewer people. The same four rides you experience in one hour in early morning can take as long as three hours after 10:30 a.m. Eat breakfast before you arrive; don't waste prime touring time sitting in a restaurant.

The earlier a park opens, the greater your advantage. This is because most vacationers won't rise early and get to a park before it opens. Fewer people are willing to be on hand for an 8 a.m. opening than for a 9 a.m. opening. On those rare occasions when a park opens at 10 a.m., almost everyone arrives at the same time, so it's almost impossible to beat the crowd. If you visit during midsummer, arrive at the turnstile 30–40 minutes before opening. During holiday periods, arrive 45–60 minutes early.

3. Avoid Bottlenecks

Helping you avoid bottlenecks is what this guide is about. Bottlenecks are caused by crowd concentrations and/or faulty crowd management. Avoiding bottlenecks involves being able to predict where, when, and why they occur. Concentrations of hungry people create bottlenecks at restaurants during lunch and dinner; concentrations of people moving toward the exit near closing time create bottlenecks in gift shops en route; concentrations of visitors at new and popular rides, and at rides slow to load and unload, create bottlenecks and long lines.

We provide touring plans for the Magic Kingdom, Animal Kingdom, Epcot, Disney-MGM Studios, and Pleasure Island to help you avoid bottlenecks. We also provide detailed information on all rides and performances, enabling you to estimate how long you may have to wait in line and allowing you to compare rides for their crowd capacity. Touring plans for the Magic Kingdom begin on page 470; Epcot, page 531; Animal Kingdom, page 571; Disney-MGM Studios, page 608; and Pleasure Island, page 716. We also include one-day touring plans for Universal Studios Florida on page 631 and Universal's Islands of Adventure on page 647.

In response to reader requests, we have clip-out versions of the plans at the end of this book.

What's a Queue?

Although it's not commonly used in the United States, "queue" is the universal English word for a line (such as you wait in to cash a check at the bank or to board a ride in a theme park). There's a mathematical area of specialization within the field of operations research that studies and models how lines work (queuing theory). Because the *Unofficial Guide* draws heavily on this discipline, we use some of its terminology. In addition to the noun, the verb "to queue" means to get in line, and a "queuing area" is a waiting area that accommodates a line. When guests decline to join a queue because they perceive the wait to be too long, they are said to "balk."

Touring Plans: What They Are and How They Work

We followed your plans to the letter—which at times was troublesome to the dad in our party . . . somewhat akin to testing the strength of your marriage by wallpapering together!

—Unofficial Guide reader and mother of two

See More, Do More, Wait Less

From the first edition of the *Unofficial Guide,* minimizing our readers' wait in lines has been a top priority. We know from our research and that of others that theme-park patrons measure overall satisfaction based on the number of attractions they're able to experience during a visit: the more attractions, the better. Thus, we developed and offered our readers field-tested touring plans that allow them to experience as many attractions as possible with the least amount of waiting in line.

Our touring plans have always been based on theme-park traffic flow, attraction capacity, the maximum time a guest is willing to wait (called a "balking constraint"), walking distance between attractions, and waiting-time data collected at specific intervals throughout the day and at various times of year. The touring plans derived from a combinatorial model (for anyone who cares) that married the well-known assignment problem of linear programming with queuing (waiting-line) theory. The model approximated the most time-efficient sequence in which to visit the attractions of a specific park. After we derived a preliminary touring plan from the model, we field-tested it in the park, using a test group who followed our plan and a control group (who didn't have our plan) who toured according to their own best judgment.

The two groups were compared, and the results were amazing. On days of heavy attendance, the groups touring without our plans spent an average of three-and-a-half hours more in line and experienced 37% fewer attractions than did those who used our touring plans.

Over the years, this research has been recognized by both the travel industry and academe, having been cited by such diverse sources as *USA Today, Travel Weekly, Bottom Line, Money, Operations Research Forum,* CBS News, Fox News, the BBC, the Travel Channel, and the *Dallas Morning News,* among others.

John Henry and the Nail-Driving Machine

As sophisticated as our model may sound, we recognized that it was cumbersome, slow, and didn't approximate the "perfect" touring plan as closely as we desired. Moreover, advances in computer technology and science, specifically in the field of genetic algorithms, demonstrated that it wouldn't be long before a model, or program, was created that would leave ours in the dust.

Do you remember the story of John Henry, the fastest nail driver on the railroad? One day a man appeared with a machine he claimed could drive spikes faster than any man. John Henry challenged the machine to a race, which he won, but which killed him in the process. We felt a bit like John Henry. We were still very good at what we did, but knew with absolute certainty that sooner or later we'd have to confront the touring-plan version of a nail-driving machine.

Our response was to build our own nail-driving machine. We teamed up during the mid-1990s with Len Testa, a cutting-edge scientist and programmer who was working in the field of evolutionary algorithms and who, coincidentally, was a theme-park junkie. Marrying our many years of collecting Walt Disney World observations and data to Len's vision and programming expertise, we developed a state-of-the-art program for creating nearly perfect touring plans.

Several university professors, many of them leaders in their fields, have contributed research or ideas to the new software program. Results from early versions of the software have been published in peer-reviewed academic journals. The most recent versions of the program are protected through pending patent applications. Special thanks go to Dr. Albert C. Esterline of North Carolina A&T State University and Dr. Gerry V. Dozier of Auburn University. Credit is also due to Dr. Nikolas Sahinidis as well as his graduate students at the University of Illinois at Urbana-Champaign, who have contributed a number of exceptionally helpful studies. Chryssi Malandraki, Ph.D., from United Parcel Service, and Robert Dial, Ph.D., from the Volpe National Transportation System Center, likewise provided assistance and encouragement over the years.

It has been a process of evolution and refinement, but in each year of its development, the new program came closer to beating the results of our long-lived model. In 2002, at field trials during the busy spring-break period, the new program beat the best touring plan generated by the traditional *Unofficial* model by 90 minutes at the Magic Kingdom. This was in addition to the three hours saved by the earlier model. Getting there, however, wasn't easy.

The Challenge

Creating effective, dependable touring plans has always been difficult and remains so. The main problem is that there are many ways to see the same attractions. For example, if we want to visit Space Mountain, Pirates of the Caribbean, and Splash Mountain as soon as the Magic Kingdom opens, there are six ways to do so:

1. First ride Space Mountain, then Pirates of the Caribbean, then Splash Mountain.
2. First ride Space Mountain, then Splash Mountain, then Pirates of the Caribbean.
3. First ride Splash Mountain, then Space Mountain, then Pirates of the Caribbean.
4. First ride Splash Mountain, then Pirates of the Caribbean, then Space Mountain.
5. First ride Pirates of the Caribbean, then Splash Mountain, then Space Mountain.
6. First ride Pirates of the Caribbean, then Space Mountain, then Splash Mountain.

Some of these combinations make better touring plans than others. Since the queue for Space Mountain increases rapidly, it's best to see Space Mountain first thing in the morning. For similar reasons, it would be better to see Splash Mountain before Pirates. In this example, touring plan number 2 would probably save us the most time standing in line. Touring plan 5 would probably result in the most waiting in line.

As we add attractions to our list, the number of possible touring plans grows rapidly. Adding a fourth attraction would result in 24 possible touring plans, since there are four possible variations for each of the six plans listed above. In general, the number of possible touring plans for n attractions is $n \times (n-1) \times (n-2) \times \ldots \times 1$ (Don't let the mathematical notation throw you. If we plug real numbers in, it's quite simple.) For five attractions, as an example, there are $5 \times 4 \times 3 \times 2 \times 1$ possible touring plans. If you don't have a calculator handy, that adds up to 120 potential plans. For six attractions, there are $6 \times 5 \times 4 \times 3 \times 2 \times 1$, or 720 possible plans. A list of ten attractions has over three million possible plans. The 21 attractions in the Magic Kingdom One-Day Touring Plan for Adults have a staggering 51,090,942,171,709,440,000 possible touring plans. That's over 51 million billion combinations, or roughly six times more than the estimated number of grains of sand on Earth. Adding in complexities such as FAST-PASS, parades, meals, and breaks further increases the combinations.

Scientists have been working on similar problems for years. Companies that deliver packages, for example, plan each driver's route to minimize the distance driven, saving time and fuel. In fact, finding ways to visit many places with minimum effort is such a common problem that it has its own nickname: the traveling-salesman problem.

For more than a small number of attractions, the number of possible touring plans is so large it would take a very long time for even a powerful computer to find the single best plan. A number of proposed techniques give very good, but not necessarily exact, solutions to the traveling-salesman problem in a reasonable amount of time.

The *Unofficial Guide* Touring Plan program contains two algorithms that allow it to quickly analyze tens of millions of possible plans in a very short time. (An algorithm is to a computer like a recipe is to a chef. Just as a chef takes specific steps to make a cake, a computer takes specific steps to process information. Those steps, when grouped, form an algorithm.) The program can analyze FASTPASS distribution patterns at all attractions, for example, and suggest the best times and attractions to use FASTPASS. The software can also schedule rest breaks throughout the day. If you're going to eat lunch in the park, the software can suggest restaurants near where you'll be at lunchtime that will minimize the time you spend looking for food. Numerous other features are available, many of which we'll discuss later, in the section "Custom Touring Plans."

The new program, however, is only part of what's needed to create a good touring plan. Good data are also important. For more than six years, we've been collecting data in the theme parks at every conceivable time of year. At each park, researchers recorded the estimated wait at every attraction, show, FASTPASS booth, and restaurant, every thirty minutes, from park opening to closing. On a typical day at the Magic Kingdom, for example, each researcher walked about 18 miles and collected around 500 pieces of data. One of several research routes would start researchers at the Swiss Family Treehouse in Adventureland. After collecting data on all of Adventureland, they would continue to the attractions and restaurants in Frontierland. After that came Liberty Square, then finally through half of Fantasyland, before returning to Swiss Family Treehouse for an eight-minute break before starting the next round of data collection. A platoon of additional volunteers collected data in the other half of the park.

So how good are the new touring plans in the *Unofficial Guide?* Our computer program typically gets within about 2% of the optimal touring plan. To put this in perspective, if the hypothetical "perfect" Adult One-Day touring plan took about 10 hours to complete, the *Unofficial* touring plan would take about 10 hours and 12 minutes. Since it would take about 30 years for a really powerful computer to find that "perfect" plan, the extra 12 minutes is a reasonable trade-off.

In the 2003 edition of this guidebook, we noted the possibility of using our touring-plan software to see all of the more than 40 attractions in the Magic Kingdom in one day. We dubbed this the Ultimate Magic Kingdom Touring Plan and offered it free to anyone up for the challenge. Several people have completed this plan since that time, and many have come close. The current record holder is Rich Vosburgh of Hutto, Texas. On June 10, 2003, Rich experienced the 41 open Magic Kingdom attractions in 10 hours, 40 minutes. The current record for most unique attractions seen in one day is 42 by Scott Hughes, Lynn Gurnee, and Rob Sutton, in 9 hours, 59 minutes, on December 4, 2003. Drop us a line if you're interested in challenging either of these records. Note that this touring plan isn't intended for families, first-time visitors, or anyone simply wanting a nice day in the Magic Kingdom. Attempting this plan is like running a marathon.

Custom Touring Plans

The *Unofficial Guide* Touring Plan program allows us to offer readers customized touring plans to all Disney parks. *The best touring plans our program can produce are the ones published in this guide.* Most of the plans, however, require that you be on hand when the park opens. If you are able to meet this requirement you will not need a custom touring plan. If you want to sleep in, arrive at the park at 11 a.m. instead of at park opening, or if you want to commence touring at 3 p.m., a customized plan will guarantee the least time waiting in line.

One customized plan costs $16. You can download a Custom Touring Plan Questionnaire from **www.touringplans.com** or e-mail a request to **orders@touringplans.com.** On the questionnaire, specify the dates of your vacation; the park you intend to visit; what time you want to arrive; attractions you want to experience; whether you want to watch a parade, fireworks, or other live performances; when and where you'd like to eat (the plan makes suggestions based on where in the park you'll be at your desired mealtime); and when you want to depart. Because park hours can change without notice, the best time to request your custom plan is two to four weeks before leaving home. Your customized plan will be e-mailed to you within three business days of receipt of your questionnaire.

Allow us to underscore that the most efficient possible touring plans are those included in this guide. They allow you to see more attractions with less waiting because they require you to be on hand when the parks open. If you can't get the kids up and out early, or if you want to take a morning off, or if you prefer attractions different from those we include in our touring plans, a custom plan is a good option for you.

Overview of the Touring Plans

Our touring plans are step-by-step guides for seeing as much as possible with a minimum of standing in line. They're designed to help you avoid crowds and bottlenecks on days of moderate-to-heavy attendance. On days of lighter attendance (see "Selecting the Time of Year for Your Visit," pages 28–31), the plans will still save time but won't be as critical to successful touring.

What You Can Realistically Expect from the Touring Plans

Though we present one-day touring plans for each theme park, be aware that the Magic Kingdom and Epcot have more attractions than you can reasonably expect to see in one day. Because the *two-day plans* for the Magic Kingdom and Epcot are the most comprehensive, efficient, and relaxing, we strongly recommend them over the one-day plans. However, if you must cram your visit into a single day, the one-day plans will allow you to see as much as is humanly possible. You may not complete the plan, and you definitely won't be able to see everything. Although Disney-MGM Studios has grown considerably since its 1989 debut, seeing everything in one day is no problem. Likewise, the Animal Kingdom is a one-day outing.

Variables that Will Affect the Success of the Touring Plans

The plans' success will be affected by how quickly you move from ride to ride; when and how many refreshment and rest-room breaks you take; when, where, and how you eat meals; and your ability (or lack thereof) to find your way around. Smaller groups almost always move faster than larger groups, and parties of adults generally cover more ground than families with young children. Switching off (pages 266–268), among other things, inhibits families with little ones from moving expeditiously among attractions. Plus, some children simply cannot conform to the plans' "early-to-rise" conditions.

A mom from Nutley, New Jersey, writes:

[Although] the touring plans all advise getting to parks at opening, we just couldn't burn the candle at both ends. Our kids (10, 7, and 4) would not go to sleep early and couldn't be up at dawn and still stay sane. It worked well for us to let them sleep a little later, go out, and bring breakfast back to the room while they slept, and still get a relatively early start by not spending time on eating breakfast out. We managed to avoid long lines with an occasional early morning, and hitting popular attractions during parades, mealtimes, and late evenings.

And a family from Centerville, Ohio, says:

The toughest thing about your touring plans was getting the rest of the family to stay with them, at least to some degree. Getting them to pass by attractions in order to hit something across the park was no easy task (sometimes impossible).

If you have young children in your party, be prepared for character encounters. The appearance of a Disney character usually stops a touring plan in its tracks. While some characters stroll the parks, it's equally common that they assemble in a specific venue (such as the Hall of Fame at Mickey's Toontown Fair) where families queue up for photos and autographs. Meeting characters, posing for photos, and collecting autographs can burn hours of touring time. If your kids collect character autographs, you need to anticipate these interruptions and negotiate some understanding with your children about when you will follow the plan and when you will collect autographs. Our advice is to go with the flow or set aside a specific morning or afternoon for photos and autographs. Note that queues for autographs, especially in Toontown at the Magic Kingdom and Camp Minnie-Mickey at the Animal Kingdom, are sometimes as long as the queues for major attractions. The only time-efficient way to collect autographs is to line up at the character-greeting areas first thing in the morning. Because this is also the best time to experience the popular attractions, you may have tough choices to make.

While we realize that following the plans isn't always easy, we nevertheless recommend continuous, expeditious touring until around noon. After noon, breaks and diversions won't affect the plans significantly.

Some variables that can profoundly affect the plans are beyond your control. Chief among these are the manner and timing of bringing a particular ride to capacity. For example, Big Thunder Mountain Railroad, a roller coaster in the Magic Kingdom, has five trains. On a given morning, it may begin operation with two of the five, then add the other three when needed. If the waiting line builds rapidly before operators go to full capacity, you could have a long wait, even in early morning.

Another variable relates to the time you arrive for a theater performance. Usually, you'll wait from the time you arrive to the end of the presentation then in progress. Thus, if Country Bear Jamboree is 15 minutes long and you arrive one minute after a show has begun, your wait for the next show will be 14 minutes. Conversely, if you arrive as the show is wrapping up, your wait will be only a minute or two.

What to Do if You Lose the Thread

Anything from a blister to a broken attraction can throw off a touring plan. If unforeseen events interrupt a plan:

1. Skip one step on the plan for every 20 minutes delay. If, for example, you lose your billfold and spend an hour finding it, skip three steps and pick up from there.

2. Forget the plan and organize the remainder of your day using the Recommended Attraction Visitation Times clip-out lists at the back of this guide. These timetables summarize the best times to visit each attraction.

What to Expect When You Arrive at the Parks

Because most touring plans are based on being present when the theme park opens, you need to know about opening procedures. Disney transportation to the parks, as well as their parking lots, begins an hour and a half to two hours before official opening.

Each park has an entrance plaza outside the turnstiles. Usually, you're held there until 30 minutes before the official opening time, when you'll be admitted through the turnstiles. What happens next depends on the season and the day's anticipated crowds.

1. Low Season At slower times, you will usually be confined outside the turnstiles or in a small section of the park until the official opening time. At the Magic Kingdom you might be admitted to Main Street, U.S.A.; at Animal Kingdom, to the Oasis and sometimes to Discovery Island; at Epcot, to the fountain area around Spaceship Earth; and at Disney-MGM Studios, to Hollywood Boulevard. Rope barriers supervised by Disney cast members keep you there until the "rope drop," when the barrier is removed and the park and its attractions are opened at the official start time.

2. High-Attendance Days When large crowds are expected, you will be admitted through the turnstiles 30 minutes before official opening and the entire park will be operating. However, with the recession and the depressed travel market, this didn't happen often in 2003 or 2004.

3. Variations Sometimes, Disney will run a variation of those two procedures. In this, you'll be permitted through the turnstiles and find that one or several specific attractions are open early. At Epcot, Spaceship Earth and sometimes Test Track will be operating. At Animal Kingdom, you may find Kilimanjaro Safaris and *It's Tough to Be a Bug!* running early. At Disney-MGM Studios, look for Tower of Terror and/or Rock 'n' Roller Coaster. The Magic Kingdom almost never runs a variation. Instead, you'll usually encounter number 1, or occasionally 2.

4. A Word about the Rope Drop Until recently, at all four parks, Disney cast members would dive for cover when the rope was dropped as thousands of adrenaline-crazed guests stampeded to the parks' most popular attractions. This practice occasioned the legendary Space Mountain Morning Mini-Marathon and the Splash Mountain Rapid Rampage at the Magic Kingdom, the Tower of Terror Trot at Disney-MGM Studios, and the Safari Sprint at Animal Kingdom, among others. Each morning, a throng would crowd the rope barriers, waiting to sprint to their favorite ride. It was each person for himself—parents against offspring, brother against sister, coeds against truck drivers, nuns against beauticians. There was nothing to do but tie up your Reeboks and get ready to run.

Well, this ritual insanity no longer exists—at least not in the tumultuous versions of years past. Disney has increased the number of cast members supervising the rope drop in order to suppress the melee. In some cases, the rope isn't even "dropped." Instead, it's walked back: Cast members lead you with the rope at a fast walk toward the attraction you're straining to reach, forcing you (and everyone else) to maintain their pace. Not until they near the attraction do cast members step aside. A New Jersey mom described it thus:

You are no longer allowed to sprint to these [attractions] because of people being trampled. Now there is a phalanx of cast members lined up at the rope who instruct you in friendly but no uncertain terms that when the rope drops they will lead you to the rides at a fast walk. However, you are not allowed to pass them. (No one ever said what would happen if you did pass). To my surprise, everyone followed the rules and we were splish-splashing within five minutes after 9 a.m.

You never know with Disney. The current rope-drop procedure may be abandoned and the traditional insanity allowed to resume. But we don't think so. And while we'll miss the passion of the early-morning races, we admit that the new practice is safer.

So, here's the straight poop. If Disney persists in walking the rope back, the only way you can gain an advantage is to arrive early enough to be up front near the rope. Be alert, though; cast members sometimes step out of the way after about fifty yards. If this happens, fire up the afterburners and speed the remaining distance to your destination.

Touring Plan Clip-Out Pocket Outlines

For your convenience, we have prepared outlines of all touring plans in this guide. These pocket versions present the same itineraries as the detailed plans, but with maps and abbreviated directions. Select the plan appropriate for your party and familiarize yourself with the detailed version. Then clip the pocket version from the back of this guide and carry it with you as a quick reference at the theme park.

Will the Plans Continue to Work Once the Secret Is Out?

Yes! First, all of the plans require that a patron be there when a park opens. Many Disney World patrons simply won't get up early while on vacation. Second, less than 1% of any day's attendance has been exposed to the plans—too few to affect results. Last, most groups tailor the plans, skipping rides or shows according to taste.

How Frequently Are the Touring Plans Revised?

Because Disney is always adding new attractions and changing operations, we revise the plans every year. Most complaints we receive about them come from readers using out-of-date editions of the *Unofficial*

Guide. Be prepared, however, for surprises. Opening procedures and show times may change, for example, and you can't predict when an attraction might break down.

Tour Groups from Hell

We have discovered that tour groups of up to 200 people sometimes use our plans. A lady from Memphis writes:

> When we arrived at The Land [pavilion at Epcot], a tour guide was holding your book and shouting into a bullhorn, "Step 7. Proceed to Journey into Imagination." With this, about 65 Japanese tourists in red T-shirts ran out the door.

Unless your party is as large as the Japanese group, this development shouldn't alarm you. Because tour groups are big, they move slowly and have to stop to collect stragglers. The tour guide also has to accommodate the unpredictability of five dozen or so bladders. In short, you should have no problem passing a group after the initial encounter.

"Bouncing Around"

Many readers object to crisscrossing a theme park as our touring plans sometimes require. A lady from Decatur, Georgia, said she "got dizzy from all the bouncing around." We empathize, but here's the rub, park by park.

In the Magic Kingdom, the most popular attractions are positioned across the park from one another. This is no accident. It's a method of more equally distributing guests throughout the park. If you want to experience the most popular attractions in one day without long waits, you can arrive before the park fills and see those attractions first (requires crisscrossing the park), or you can enjoy the main attractions on one side of the park first, then try the most popular attractions on the other side during the hour or so before closing, when crowds presumably have thinned. Using FASTPASS lessens the time you wait in line but tends to increase the bouncing around because you must visit the same attraction twice: once to obtain your FASTPASS and again to use it.

The best way to minimize "bouncing around" at the Magic Kingdom is to use the Magic Kingdom Two-Day Touring Plan, which spreads the more popular attractions over two mornings and works beautifully even when the park closes at 8 p.m. or earlier.

We have revised the Epcot plans to eliminate most of the "bouncing around" and have added instructions to further minimize walking.

Disney-MGM Studios is configured in a way that precludes an orderly approach to touring, or to a clockwise or counterclockwise rotation. Orderly touring is further confounded by live entertainment that prompts guests to interrupt their touring to head for whichever theater is about to crank up. At the Studios, therefore, you're stuck with "bouncing around" whether you use our plan or not. In our opinion, when it comes to Disney parks, it's best to have a plan.

The Animal Kingdom is arranged in a spoke-and-hub configuration like the Magic Kingdom, simplifying crisscrossing the park. Even so, the only way to catch various shows is to stop what you're doing and troop across the park to the next performance.

Touring Plans and the Obsessive-Compulsive Reader

We suggest you follow the touring plans religiously, especially in the mornings, if you're visiting during busy times. The consequence of touring spontaneity in peak season is hours of standing in line. During quieter times, there's no need to be compulsive about following the plans.

A mom in Atlanta, Georgia, suggests:

Emphasize perhaps not following [the touring plans] in off-season. There is no reason to crisscross the park when there are no lines.

A mother in Minneapolis advises:

Please let your readers know to stop along the way to various attractions to appreciate what else may be going on around them. We encountered many families using the Unofficial Guide [who] became too serious about getting from one place to the next, missing the fun in between.

We realize the touring plans can contribute to some stress and fatigue. A mother from Stillwater, Maine, writes:

We were thankful for the touring plan and were able to get through the most popular rides early before the lines got long. One drawback was all the bouncing around we did, backtracking through different parts of the Magic Kingdom in order to follow the touring plan. It was tiring.

What can we say? It's a lesser-of-two-evils situation. If you visit Walt Disney World at a busy time, you can either rise early and hustle around, or you can sleep in and see less.

When using the plans, however, relax and always be prepared for surprises and setbacks. When your Type-A brain does cartwheels, reflect on the advice of a woman from Trappe, Pennsylvania:

You cannot emphasize enough the dangers of using your touring plans that were printed in the back of the book, especially if the person using them has a compulsive personality. I have a compulsive personality. I planned for this trip for two years, researched it by use of guidebooks, computer programs, video tapes, and information received from WDW. I had a two-page itinerary for our one-week trip in addition to your touring plans of the theme parks. On night three of our trip, I ended up taking a non-scheduled trip to the emergency room of Sand Lake Hospital in Lake Buena Vista. When the doctor asked what seemed to be the problem, I responded with "I don't know, but I can't stop shaking, and I can't stay here very long because I have to get up in a couple hours to go to MGM according to my itinerary." Diagnosis: an anxiety attack caused by my excessive itinerary. He gave me a shot of something, and I slept through the first four attractions the next morning. This was our third trip to WDW (not including one trip to

Disneyland); on all previous trips I used only the Steve Birnbaum book, and I suffered no ill effects. I am not saying your book was not good. It was excellent! However, it should come with a warning label for people with compulsive personalities.

Touring-Plan Rejection

Some folks don't respond well to the regimentation of a touring plan. If you encounter this problem with someone in your party, roll with the punches as this Maryland couple did:

The rest of the group was not receptive to the use of the touring plans. I think they all thought I was being a little too regimented about planning this vacation. Rather than argue, I left the touring plans behind as we ventured off for the parks. You can guess the outcome. We took our camcorder with us and watched the movies when we returned home. About every five minutes or so there is a shot of us all gathered around a park map trying to decide what to do next.

Finally, as a Connecticut woman alleges, the plans are incompatible with some readers' bladders and personalities:

I want to know if next year when you write those "day" schedules you could schedule bathroom breaks in there, too. You expect us to be at a certain ride at a certain time and with no stops in between. In one of the letters in your book, a guy writes, "You expect everyone to be theme-park commandos." When I read that, I thought there is a man who really knows what a problem the schedules are if you are a laid-back, slow-moving, careful detail noticer. What were you thinking when you made these schedules?

Touring Plans for Low-Attendance Days

We receive a number of letters each year similar to this one from Lebanon, New Jersey:

The guide always assumed there would be large crowds. We had no lines. An alternate tour for low traffic days would be helpful.

If attendance is low, you don't need a touring plan. Just go where your taste and instinct direct and glory in the hassle-free touring. Having said that, however, there are attractions in each park that bottleneck even if attendance is low. These are Space Mountain, Splash Mountain, Dumbo, The Many Adventures of Winnie the Pooh, and Peter Pan's Flight in the Magic Kingdom; Test Track and Mission: Space at Epcot, Kilimanjaro Safari at Animal Kingdom; and Tower of Terror and Rock 'n' Roller Coaster at the Disney-MGM Studios. All are FASTPASS attractions. Experience them immediately after park opening or use FASTPASS. Remember that crowd size is relative and that large crowds can gather at certain attractions even during less-busy times. We recommend following a touring plan through the first five or six steps. If you're pretty much walking onto every attraction, feel free to scrap the remainder of the plan.

A Clamor for Additional Touring Plans

We're inundated by letters urging us to create additional plans. These include a plan for ninth- and tenth-graders, a plan for rainy days, a seniors' plan, a plan for folks who sleep late, a plan omitting rides that "bump, jerk, and clonk," a plan for gardening enthusiasts, a plan for kids who are afraid of skeletons, and a plan for single women.

The plans in this book are flexible. Adapt them to your preferences. If you don't like rides that bump and jerk, skip those when they come up in a plan. If you want to sleep in and go to the park at noon, use the afternoon part of a plan. If you're a ninth-grader and want to ride Space Mountain three times in a row, do it. Will it decrease the plans' effectiveness? Sure, but they were created only to help you have fun. It's your day. If you feel it's impossible to adapt our plans to your situation, consider ordering a custom plan (see pages 70–71).

Early Entry and the Touring Plans

If you're a Disney resort guest and use your early-entry privileges, complete your early-entry touring before the general public is admitted and position yourself to follow the touring plan. When the public is admitted, the park will suddenly swarm. A Wilmington, Delaware, mother advises:

The early-entry times went like clockwork. We were finishing up the Great Movie Ride when Disney-MGM opened [to the public], and [we] had to wait in line quite a while for Voyage of the Little Mermaid, which sort of screwed up everything thereafter. Early-opening attractions should be finished up well before regular opening time so you can be at the plan's first stop as early as possible.

In the Magic Kingdom, the early-entry attractions are in Fantasyland and Tomorrowland. At Epcot, they're in the Future World section. At Disney-MGM Studios, they're dispersed. Practically speaking, see any attractions on the touring plan that are open for early entry, crossing them off as you do. If you finish all early-entry attractions on the touring plan and have time left before the general public is admitted, sample early-entry attractions not included in the plan. Stop touring about ten minutes before the public is admitted and position yourself for the first attraction on the plan that wasn't open for early entry. During early entry in the Magic Kingdom, for example, you can usually experience Peter Pan's Flight and It's a Small World in Fantasyland, plus Space Mountain and Stitch's Great Escape in Tomorrowland. As official opening nears, go to the boundary between Fantasyland and Liberty Square and be ready to blitz to Splash Mountain and Big Thunder Mountain according to the touring plan when the rest of the park opens.

FASTPASS

In 1999, Disney launched a system for moderating the wait at popular attractions. Called FASTPASS, it was originally tried at Animal Kingdom then expanded to attractions at the other parks.

Here's how it works. Your handout park map and signage at attractions will tell you which attractions are included. Attractions operating FAST-PASS will have a regular line and a FASTPASS line. A sign at the entrance will say how long the wait is in the regular line. If the wait is acceptable to you, hop in line. If it seems too long, insert your park admission pass into a FASTPASS machine and receive an appointment time (for later in the day) to return and ride. When you return at the designated time, you enter the FASTPASS line and proceed directly to the attraction's preshow or boarding area. Interestingly, this procedure was pioneered by Universal Studios Hollywood years ago and had been virtually ignored by theme parks since (Universal now has a reworked variation called Universal Express). The system works well, however, and can save a lot of waiting time. There's no extra charge to use FASTPASS.

FASTPASS is evolving, and attractions continue to be added and deleted from the lineup. Changes aside, here's an example of how to use FASTPASS: Say you have only one day to tour the Magic Kingdom. You arrive early and ride Space Mountain and Buzz Lightyear with minimal waits. Then you cross the park to Splash Mountain and find a substantial line. Because Splash Mountain is a FASTPASS attraction, you can insert your admission pass into the machine and receive an appointment to come back and ride, thus avoiding a long wait.

FASTPASS works remarkably well, primarily because FASTPASS holders get amazingly preferential treatment. In fact, the effort to accommodate FASTPASS holders makes anyone in the regular line feel second class. And a telling indication of their status is that they're called "standby guests." Indeed, we watched people in regular lines despondently stand by and stand by, while dozens and sometimes hundreds of FASTPASS holders were ushered into the boarding area ahead of them. Disney is sending a message here: FASTPASS is heaven; anything else is limbo at best and probably purgatory. In any event, you'll think you've been in hell if you're stuck in the regular line during the hot, crowded part of the day.

Readers regularly send standby-line horror stories. Here's one from a Pequea, Pennsylvania, family:

We, a group of four 12-year-olds and five adults, decided to ride Test Track when we arrived at Epcot at 11:00 a.m. FASTPASSes were being issued for [late that night] and the singles line was not open yet, so we decided to brave the 120-minute wait (at MK and MGM many waits ended up being less than the posted time). What a disaster! Once inside the building, the FASTPASS and singles line (which opened when we were very near the building) sped ahead while the standby line barely moved. ... After 3 hours and 20 minutes, we finally made it to the car! One man who was in the FASTPASS line said that he counted 12:1 ratio between FASTPASSers and standby people being let into the [boarding] area. ... Disney needs to seriously reconsider their boarding policy!

FASTPASS doesn't eliminate the need to arrive early at a theme park. Because each park offers a limited number of FASTPASS attractions, you still need an early start if you want to see as much as possible in one day. Plus, there's a limited supply of FASTPASSes available for each attraction on any day. If you don't arrive until midafternoon, you might find that no more FASTPASSes are available. FASTPASS does make it possible to see more with less waiting, and it's a great benefit to those who like to sleep late or who choose an afternoon or evening at the parks on their arrival day. It also allows you to postpone wet rides such as Kali River Rapids at Animal Kingdom or Splash Mountain at the Magic Kingdom, until a warmer time of day.

Do guests like FASTPASS? This note from a Surrey, British Columbia, family is typical:

Please, please do not emphasize how great FASTPASS is! It is (so far) the best-kept secret at WDW. For the popular rides, it's the only way to go during peak times. It saved us hours of waiting in lines. We couldn't believe everyone wasn't using it—but we were glad they weren't!

Understanding the FASTPASS System

The purpose of FASTPASS is to reduce the wait for designated attractions by distributing guests at those attractions throughout the day. This is accomplished by providing an incentive (a shorter wait) for guests willing to postpone experiencing the attraction until later in the day. The system also, in effect, imposes a penalty (standby status) on those who don't use it. However, spreading out guest arrivals sometimes also decreases the wait for standby guests.

When you insert your admission pass into a FASTPASS time clock, the machine spits out a slip of paper about two-thirds the size of a credit card—small enough to fit in your wallet but also small enough to lose easily. Printed on it is the attraction's name and a one-hour window, for example 1:15–2:15 p.m., during which you can return to ride.

When you report back during your one-hour window, you'll enter a line marked "FASTPASS Return" that routes you more or less directly to the boarding or preshow area. Each person in your party must have his own FASTPASS and be ready to show it at the entrance of the FAST-PASS Return line. Before you enter the boarding area or theater, another cast member will collect your FASTPASS.

You may show up any time during the specified window, and from our observation, no time within it is better or worse. This holds true because cast members are instructed to minimize waits for FASTPASS holders. Thus, if the FASTPASS Return line is suddenly inundated (something that occurs by chance), cast members intervene to reduce the FASTPASS line. As many as 25 FASTPASS holders will be admitted for each standby guest until the FASTPASS line is reduced to an acceptable length. Although FASTPASS usually eliminates 80% or more of the wait you'd experience in the regular line, you can still expect a short wait, usually less than 20 minutes.

You can ordinarily obtain a FASTPASS anytime after a park opens (some attractions are a little tardy getting their FASTPASS system up), but the FASTPASS Return lines don't usually begin operating until 60–120 minutes after opening.

Whenever you obtain a FASTPASS, you can be assured of a period of time between when you receive your FASTPASS and when you report back. The interval can be as short as 30 minutes or as long as three to seven hours, depending on park attendance and the attraction's popularity and hourly capacity. Generally, the earlier in the day you obtain a FAST-PASS, the shorter the interval before your return window. If the park opens at 9 a.m. and you obtain a FASTPASS for Splash Mountain at 9:25 a.m., your appointment for returning to ride would be 10–11 a.m. or 10:10–11:10 a.m. The exact time will be determined by how many other guests have obtained FASTPASSes before you.

To more effectively distribute guests over the day, FASTPASS machines bump the one-hour return period back five minutes for a set number of passes issued (usually about 6% of the attraction's hourly capacity). For example, when Splash Mountain opens at 9 a.m., the first 125 people to obtain a FASTPASS will get a 9:40–10:40 a.m. return window. The next 125 guests are issued FASTPASSes with a 9:45–10:45 a.m. window. And so it goes, with the time window dropping back five minutes for every 125 guests. The fewer guests who obtain FASTPASSes for an attraction, the shorter the interval between receipt of your pass and the return window. Conversely, the more guests issued FASTPASSes, the longer the interval. If an attraction is exceptionally popular and/or its hourly capacity is relatively small, the return window might be pushed back to park closing time. When this happens the FASTPASS machines shut down and a sign is posted saying all FASTPASSes are gone for the day. It's not unusual, for example, for Test Track at Epcot or Winnie the Pooh at the Magic Kingdom to distribute all available FASTPASSes by 1 p.m.

Rides routinely exhaust their daily FASTPASS supply, but shows almost never do. FASTPASS machines at theaters try to balance attendance at each show so that the audience of any given performance is divided about evenly between standby and FASTPASS guests. Consequently, standby guests for shows aren't discriminated against to the degree experienced by standby guests for rides. In practice, FASTPASS diminishes the wait for standby guests. With few exceptions, the standby line at theater attractions requires less waiting than using FASTPASS.

A more interesting exception concerns the Haunted Mansion and the Jungle Cruise at the Magic Kingdom. When you obtain a FASTPASS at either of these, the FASTPASS states that you can acquire another FAST-PASS at any other FASTPASS attraction in just five minutes. We aren't sure whether this is an experiment or a glitch in the system, or if it will last, but it's potentially a big timesaver for those in the know.

When to Use FASTPASS   Except as discussed below, there's no reason to use FASTPASS during the first 30–40 minutes a park is open. Lines for most attractions are manageable during this period, and this is the only time of day when FASTPASS attractions exclusively serve those in the regular line. Regardless of the hour, however, if the wait in the regular line at a FASTPASS attraction is 25–30 minutes or less, join the regular line.

Using FASTPASS requires two trips to the same attraction: one to obtain the pass and another to use it. You must invest time to obtain the pass (sometimes FASTPASS machines have lines!), then interrupt your touring later and backtrack to use your FASTPASS. The additional time, effort, and touring modification are justified only if you can save more than 30 minutes. Don't forget: Even the FASTPASS line requires waiting.

Six attractions in the Disney parks build lines so quickly in the morning that failing to queue up within the first six or so minutes of operation will mean a long wait—Test Track and Mission: Space at Epcot, Kilimanjaro Safaris at the Animal Kingdom, Space Mountain at the Magic Kingdom, and Tower of Terror and Rock 'n' Roller Coaster at Disney-MGM Studios. With these attractions, you can be present when the park opens and race directly to the attractions or obtain a FASTPASS.

Another four FASTPASS attractions—Splash Mountain, Winnie the Pooh, Peter Pan's Flight, and Jungle Cruise in the Magic Kingdom—develop long lines within 30–50 minutes of park opening. If you can get to one or more of these before the wait becomes intolerable, great. Otherwise, your options are FASTPASS or a long wait.

If you're wondering how FASTPASS waits compare with waits in the standby line, here's what we observed at Space Mountain during spring break on a day when the park opened at 9 a.m. From 9 to 10 a.m. both sides of Space Mountain served standby guests (there are two identical roller coasters in the Space Mountain building). Before 10 a.m. the entire right side was cleared and at 10 a.m. became dedicated to FASTPASS. At 10:45 a.m., the posted standby wait time was 45 minutes; for FAST-PASS, only 10 minutes. At 1:45 p.m., the posted standby wait time was 60 minutes, with 10 minutes for FASTPASS. These observations document the benefit of FASTPASS, and interestingly, also reveal shorter waits in the regular line than those observed at the same time of day before the advent of FASTPASS.

FASTPASS Rules   Disney received hundreds of letters similar to one we received from a Newport News, Virginia, reader:

> *About 1 [p.m.] there was a long line at Winnie the Pooh, so we walked up and got a FASTPASS without bothering to notice what the return time was. When I looked at my [FASTPASS] ticket, it said to come back between 6:45 and 7:45 [p.m.]! I tried to get the Disney person at the FASTPASS machine to take it back, but she said there was nothing she could do. According to the rules, I was stuck and could not get another FASTPASS for the rest of the afternoon. As it worked out, we left the park before it was time to use the FASTPASS. That was our last day and I never did get to ride Winnie the Pooh.*

Because situations (and complaints) like this one were legion, Disney amended the rules to allow you to obtain a second FASTPASS at the time printed on the bottom of your most recent FASTPASS, usually two hours or less from the time the first was issued. The lesson here is to check the posted return time before obtaining a FASTPASS, as a father of two from Cranston, Rhode Island, advises:

> *Always check on the sign above the FASTPASS machines to see the [return] time that you will receive. We made the mistake of not looking at the time before we got our FASTPASSes for Space Mountain. The time we received was not for two hours and was at a time when we could not ride because of lunch reservations. So we couldn't take advantage of FASTPASS at Space Mountain and couldn't get any other FASTPASSes until after lunch.*

If the return time is hours away, forgo FASTPASS. Especially in the Magic Kingdom, there will be other FASTPASS attractions where the return time is only an hour or so away.

At a number of attractions, the time gap between issuance and return can be three to seven hours. If you think you might want to use FAST-PASS on the following attractions, obtain it before 11 a.m.:

Magic Kingdom	Disney-MGM Studios	Epcot
Winnie the Pooh	Rock 'n' Roller Coaster	Test Track
Peter Pan's Flight		Mission: Space
Space Mountain		Soarin' (opens 2005)
Splash Mountain		
Buzz Lightyear		

FASTPASS Oddities and Exceptions   Generally, you can obtain a second FASTPASS when you enter your return window, at the time printed at the bottom of the FASTPASS, or two hours after time of issue, whichever is first. An exception is the Tower of Terror at the Disney-MGM Studios, where you're eligible to obtain a second FASTPASS after one hour.

In 2004, Disney experimented with something called "Surprise FAST-PASS." At Test Track in Epcot, the FASTPASS machines sometimes spit out a second, unrequested FASTPASS for *Honey, I Shrunk the Audience* at the Imagination pavilion. Receiving a Surprise FASTPASS isn't automatic: Sometimes you get one, sometimes you don't. On days when the Surprise FASTPASSes are issued, the wait in the standby line for *Honey, I Shrunk the Audience* often exceeds an hour.

Tricks of the Trade   It's possible to acquire a second FASTPASS before using the first one (and sooner than two hours after getting it). Say you obtain a FASTPASS to Kilimanjaro Safaris at Animal Kingdom with a return time of 10:15–11:15 a.m. Any time after your FASTPASS window begins, you can obtain another FASTPASS, say for Kali River Rapids. This is possible because the FASTPASS computer monitors only the distribution of passes, ignoring whether or when a FASTPASS is used.

Disney finally chose to demystify the rules for acquiring a second FASTPASS. Now when a FASTPASS is issued, the time when you can obtain another is printed on the bottom of the front of the first. This time is consistent with the beginning of your return time slot. Thus if your window to return to ride is 11 a.m. to noon, your FASTPASS will say you can acquire a second FASTPASS anytime after 11 a.m.

When obtaining FASTPASSes, it's quicker and more considerate if one person obtains passes for your entire party. This means entrusting one individual with your valuable park-admission passes and your FAST-PASSes, so choose wisely.

Obtain FASTPASSes for all members of your party, including those who are too short, too young, or simply not interested in riding, as this family of four recommends:

Utilize the FASTPASSes of people in your group who don't want to ride. Our six-year-old didn't want to ride anything rough. All four of us got FAST-PASSes for each ride. [When] the six-year-old didn't want to ride, my husband and I took turns riding with the twelve-year-old. It was our version of the FASTPASS child swap and the twelve-year-old got double rides.

If you're going to baby swap at a FASTPASS attraction, your nonriding children (over age 3) do not require FASTPASSes to enter the FASTPASS line. Moreover, you can use those children's admission passes to obtain FASTPASSes for yourself. For example, enter Frontierland at the Magic Kingdom and use your admission pass and that of your spouse to obtain FASTPASSes at Splash Mountain. Then go next door to Big Thunder Mountain and obtain FASTPASSes for you and your spouse by using the passes of your children who are too short or too young to ride.

Don't pack too much into the time between obtaining your FAST-PASSes and the end of your return window. We interviewed families who missed their FASTPASS time slot by trying to cram an extra attraction or two into their touring before returning to use their FASTPASSes.

FASTPASS GUIDELINES

- Don't mess with FASTPASS unless it can save you 30 minutes or more.

- If you arrive after a park opens, obtain a FASTPASS for your preferred FASTPASS attraction first thing.

- Do not obtain a FASTPASS for a theater attraction until you have experienced all the FASTPASS rides on your itinerary. (Using FASTPASS at theater attractions usually requires more time than using the standby line.)

- Always check the FASTPASS return period before obtaining your FASTPASS.

- Obtain FASTPASSes for Rock 'n' Roller Coaster at MGM-Studios, Mission: Space and Test Track at Epcot, and Winnie the Pooh, Peter Pan's Flight, Space Mountain, and Splash Mountain at the Magic Kingdom as early in the day as practicable.

- Try to obtain FASTPASSes for rides not mentioned on page 83 by 1 p.m.

- Don't depend on FASTPASSes being available after 2 p.m. during busier times.

- Make sure everyone in your party has their own FASTPASS.

- You can obtain a second FASTPASS as soon as you enter the return period for your first FASTPASS or two hours after issuance, whichever is first.

- Note your FASTPASS return slot and plan activities accordingly.

Understanding Walt Disney World Attractions

Disney World's primary appeal is in its rides and shows. Understanding how these are engineered to accommodate guests is interesting and invaluable to developing an efficient itinerary.

All attractions, regardless of location, are affected by two elements: capacity and popularity. Capacity is how many guests the attraction can serve at one time—in an hour or in a day. Popularity shows how well visitors like an attraction. Capacity can be adjusted at some attractions. It's possible, for example, to add trams at the Disney-MGM Studios Backlot Tour or put extra boats on the Magic Kingdom's Jungle Cruise. Generally, however, capacity remains relatively fixed.

Designers try to match capacity and popularity as closely as possible. A high-capacity ride that isn't popular is a failure. Lots of money, space, and equipment have been poured into the attraction, yet there are empty seats. El Río del Tiempo, a ride in Epcot, fits this profile.

It's extremely unusual for a new attraction not to measure up, but it's fairly common for an older ride to lose appeal. The Magic Kingdom's *Enchanted Tiki Birds,* for example, played to half-capacity audiences until its 1998 renovation.

Generally, attractions are immensely popular when they're new. Some, like Space Mountain (Magic Kingdom), have sustained great appeal years beyond their debut, while others, such as Epcot's The Living Seas and the Journey Into Your Imagination ride declined in popularity after a few years. Most attractions, however, work through the honeymoon, then settle down to handle the level of demand for which they were designed. When this happens, there are enough interested guests during peak hours to fill almost every seat, but not so many that long lines develop.

Sometimes Disney correctly estimates an attraction's popularity but fouls the equation by mixing in a third variable such as location. Spaceship Earth, the ride inside the geosphere at Epcot, is a good example. Placing the ride squarely in the path of every person entering the park assures that it will be inundated during morning when the park is filling. On the flip side, *The American Adventure,* at the opposite end of Epcot, has huge capacity but plays to a partially filled theater until midafternoon, when guests finally reach that part of the park.

If demand is high and capacity is low, large lines materialize. Dumbo the Flying Elephant in the Magic Kingdom has the smallest capacity of almost any Disney World attraction, yet it probably is the most popular ride among young children. The result of this mismatch is that children and parents often suffer long, long waits for a one-and-a-half-minute ride. Dumbo is a simple yet visually appealing midway ride. Its capacity is limited by the very characteristics that make it popular.

Capacity design is predicated on averages: the average number of people in the park, the normal distribution of traffic to specific areas, and the average number of staff needed to operate the ride. On a holiday weekend, when all the averages are exceeded, all but a few attractions operate at maximum capacity, and even then they are overwhelmed by the huge crowds. On low-attendance autumn days, capacity is often not even approximated, and guests can ride without waiting.

The Magic Kingdom offers the greatest variety in capacity and popularity, with vastly differing rides and shows. Only the Magic Kingdom and Animal Kingdom offer low-capacity midway rides and spook-house "dark" rides. They range from state-of-the-art to antiquated. This diversity makes efficient touring of the Magic Kingdom much more challenging. If guests don't understand the capacity–popularity relationship and plan accordingly, they might spend most of the day in line.

While Epcot, Animal Kingdom, and Disney-MGM Studios have fewer rides and shows than the Magic Kingdom, almost all of their attractions are major features on par with the Magic Kingdom's Pirates of the Caribbean and the Haunted Mansion in scope, detail, imagination, and spectacle. All but one or two Epcot, Animal Kingdom, and Disney-MGM Studios rides are fast-loading, and most have large capacities. Because Epcot, Animal Kingdom, and Disney-MGM Studios attractions are generally well engineered and efficient, lines may appear longer than those in the Magic Kingdom but usually move more quickly. There are no midway rides at Epcot or Disney-MGM Studios, and fewer attractions are intended for children.

In the Magic Kingdom, crowds are more a function of the popularity and engineering of individual attractions. At Epcot and the Animal Kingdom, traffic flow and crowding are more affected by park layout. For touring efficiency, it's important to understand how Magic Kingdom rides and shows operate. At Epcot and Animal Kingdom, this knowledge is less important.

Crowds at Disney-MGM Studios have been larger than anticipated since the park opened. Disney has added attractions, making a touring plan essential. Likewise, the Animal Kingdom is operating with only five of its six originally planned theme areas open. Lack of capacity plus the allure of a newer park translates into lengthy queues.

To develop an efficient touring plan, it's necessary to understand how rides and shows are designed and function. We'll examine both.

Cutting Your Time in Line by Understanding the Rides

There are many types of rides at Walt Disney World. Some, like the Great Movie Ride at Disney-MGM Studios, can carry more than 3,000 people every hour. At the other extreme, Dumbo the Flying Elephant can accommodate only around 400 people an hour. Most rides fall somewhere in between. Many factors figure into how long you'll wait to experience a ride: its popularity; how it loads and unloads; how many persons can ride at once; how many units (cars, rockets, boats, flying elephants, etc.) are in service at a time; and how many staff are available to operate the ride. Let's take the factors one by one.

1. How Popular Is the Ride?

Newer rides like the Rock 'n' Roller Coaster at Disney-MGM Studios, and Mission: Space and Test Track at Epcot attract a lot of people, as do such longtime favorites as the Magic Kingdom's Jungle Cruise. If a ride is popular, you need to know how it operates in order to determine the best time to ride. But a ride need not be especially popular to generate long lines; the lines can result from weak traffic engineering (i.e., it takes so long to load and unload that a line builds regardless). This is the case at the Mad Tea Party and Cinderella's Golden Carrousel (among others) in Fantasyland. Since mostly children and teens ride the Mad Tea Party, it serves only a small percentage of any day's attendance at the Magic Kingdom. Yet, because it takes so long to load and unload, long lines form.

2. How Does the Ride Load and Unload?

Some rides never stop. They are like conveyor belts that go around and around. These are "continuous loaders." The Magic Kingdom's Haunted Mansion and Epcot's Spaceship Earth are continuous loaders. The number of people that can be moved through in an hour depends on how many cars—"doom buggies" or whatever—are on the conveyor. The

Haunted Mansion and Spaceship Earth have lots of cars on the conveyor, and each consequently can move more than 2,000 people an hour.

Other rides are "interval loaders." Cars are unloaded, loaded, and dispatched at set intervals (sometimes controlled manually, sometimes by computer). Space Mountain in Tomorrowland is an interval loader. It has two tracks (the ride has been duplicated in the same facility). Each track can run as many as 14 space capsules, released at 36-, 26-, or 21-second intervals. (The bigger the crowd, the shorter the interval.)

In one kind of interval loader (Space Mountain), empty cars (space capsules) return to where they reload. In a second type, one group of riders enters the vehicle while the previous group departs. These are "in-and-out" interval loaders. Splash Mountain is an in-and-out loader. As a boat docks, those who have just completed their ride exit to the left. At almost the same time, those waiting to ride enter the boat from the right. The reloaded boat is released to the dispatch point a few yards down the line, where it is launched according to the interval being used.

Interval loaders of both types can be very efficient people movers if (1) the dispatch (launch) interval is relatively short and (2) the ride can accommodate many vehicles at one time. Since many boats can float through Pirates of the Caribbean at one time, and since the dispatch interval is short, almost 3,000 people can see this attraction each hour.

The least efficient rides, in terms of traffic engineering, are "cycle rides," also called "stop-and-go" rides. On cycle rides, those waiting to ride exchange places with those who have just ridden. Unlike in-and-out interval rides, cycle rides shut down during loading and unloading. While one boat is loading and unloading in It's a Small World (an interval loader), many other boats are advancing through the ride. But when Dumbo the Flying Elephant touches down, the whole ride is at a standstill until the next flight launches (ditto Cinderella's Golden Carrousel).

In cycle rides, the time in motion is "ride time." The time the ride idles while loading and unloading is "load time." Load time plus ride time equals "cycle time," or the time from the start of one run of the ride until the start of the next. The only cycle rides in Disney World are in the Magic Kingdom and the Animal Kingdom.

3. How Many Persons Can Ride at One Time?

This figure expresses "per-ride capacity" or "system capacity." It's the number of people who can ride at one time. The greater the carrying capacity of a ride (all other things being equal), the more visitors it can accommodate per hour. Some rides can add extra units (cars, boats, etc.) as crowds build, to increase capacity, while others, like the Astro Orbiter in Tomorrowland, have a fixed capacity (it's impossible to add rockets).

4. How Many "Units" Are in Service at a Given Time?

"Unit" is our term for the vehicle in which you ride. At the Mad Tea Party the unit is a teacup; at Peter Pan's Flight, a pirate ship. On some rides (mostly cycle rides), the number of units operating at one time is fixed. There are always 16 flying elephants at Dumbo and 90 horses on Cinderella's carrousel. There is no way to increase the capacity of such rides by adding units. On a busy day, the only way to carry more people each hour on a fixed-unit cycle ride is to shorten the loading time or decrease the ride time. The bottom line: On a busy day for a cycle ride, you'll wait longer and possibly be rewarded with a shorter ride. This is why we steer you away from cycle rides unless you're willing to ride them early in the morning or late at night. These are cycle rides:

Magic Kingdom   Dumbo the Flying Elephant, Cinderella's Golden Carrousel, Mad Tea Party, Magic Carpets of Aladdin, Astro Orbiter, Goofy's Barnstormer

Animal Kingdom   TriceraTop Spin

Many other rides throughout Disney World can increase their capacity by adding units as crowds build. For example, if attendance is light, Big Thunder Mountain Railroad in Frontierland can start the day by running only one of its five mine trains from one of two available loading platforms. If lines build, the other platform is opened and more mine trains are placed into operation. At capacity, the five trains can carry about 2,400 persons an hour. Likewise, Star Tours at Disney-MGM Studios can increase its capacity by using all of its simulators, and the Maelstrom boat ride at Epcot can add more Viking ships. Sometimes a long queue will disappear almost instantly when new units are brought. When an interval loader places more units into operation, it usually shortens the dispatch intervals, allowing more units to be dispatched more often.

5. How Many Staff Are Available to Operate the Ride?

Adding staff to a ride can allow more units to operate or additional loading or holding areas to open. In the Magic Kingdom, Pirates of the Caribbean and It's a Small World can run two waiting lines and loading zones. The Haunted Mansion has a one-and-a-half-minute preshow staged in a "stretch room." On busy days, a second stretch room can be activated, permitting a more continuous flow of visitors to the actual loading area.

Additional staff makes a world of difference to some cycle rides. Often, the Mad Tea Party has only one attendant. This person alone must clear visitors from the ride just completed, admit and seat visitors for the upcoming ride, check that each teacup is secured, return to the control panel, issue instructions to the riders, and finally activate the ride (whew!). A second attendant divides these responsibilities and cuts loading time by 25–50%.

Cutting Your Time in Line by Understanding the Shows

Many featured attractions at Disney World are theater presentations. While they aren't as complex as rides, from a traffic-engineering standpoint, understanding their operation may save touring time.

Most theater attractions operate in three phases:

1. Guests are in the theater viewing the presentation.
2. Guests who have passed through the turnstile wait in a holding area or lobby. They will be admitted to the theater as soon as the show in progress concludes. Several attractions offer a preshow in their lobby to entertain guests until they're admitted to the main show. Examples include *Enchanted Tiki Birds* and *Stitch's Great Escape* in the Magic Kingdom; *The Living Seas* and *Honey, I Shrunk the Audience* at Epcot; and *Sounds Dangerous* and *MuppetVision 3-D* at Disney-MGM.
3. A line waits outside. Guests in line enter the lobby when there is room, and will ultimately move into the theater.

Theater capacity, the presentation's popularity, and park attendance determine how long lines will be at a theater attraction. Except for holidays and other days of heavy attendance, the longest wait for a show usually doesn't exceed the length of one performance.

Since almost all theater attractions run continuously, stopping only long enough for the previous audience to leave and the waiting audience to enter, a performance will be in progress when you arrive. *Impressions de France* in the French pavilion at Epcot is 18 minutes in duration; your longest wait under normal circumstances is about 18 minutes if you arrive just after the show has begun.

All theaters (except a few amphitheater productions) are very strict about access. You can't enter during a performance. This means you will always have at least a short wait. Most theaters hold a lot of people. When a new audience is admitted, any outside line will usually disappear. Exceptions are *Honey, I Shrunk the Audience* in the Imagination pavilion at Epcot; *Voyage of the Little Mermaid* and *MuppetVision 3-D* at Disney-MGM Studios; and *It's Tough to Be a Bug!* at the Animal Kingdom. Because these shows are so popular, you may have to wait through more than one show before you're admitted (unless you go early in the morning or after 4:30 p.m.).

A Word about Disney Thrill Rides

Readers of all ages should attempt to be open-minded about Disney "thrill rides." In comparison with rides at other theme parks, the Disney attractions are quite tame, with more emphasis on sights, atmosphere, and special effects than on the motion, speed, or feel of the ride. While we suggest you take Disney's preride warnings seriously, we can tell you that guests of all ages report enjoying rides such as Tower of Terror, Big Thunder Mountain, and Splash Mountain. The baddest thrill rides in Florida are the Montu coaster at Busch Gardens, the Incredible Hulk and Fire and Ice coasters at Universal Islands of Adventure, and SeaWorld's Kraken coaster.

A Washington reader sums up the situation well:

Our boys and I are used to imagining typical amusement park rides when it comes to roller coasters. So, when we thought of Big Thunder Mountain and Space Mountain, what came to mind was gigantic hills, upside-down loops, huge vertical drops, etc. I actually hate roller coasters, especially the unpleasant sensation of a long drop, and I have never taken a ride that loops you upside down.

In fact, the Disney [thrill rides] are all tame in comparison. There are never any long and steep hills (except Splash Mountain, and it is there for anyone to see, so you have informed consent going on the ride). I was able to build up courage to go on all of them, and the more I rode them, the more I enjoyed them—the less you tense up expecting a big, long drop, the more you enjoy the special effects and even swinging around curves. Swinging around curves is really the primary motion challenge of Disney roller coasters.

Seniors who experience Disney thrills generally enjoy the smoother rides like Splash Mountain, Big Thunder Mountain, and Tower of Terror and tend to dislike more jerky attractions. This letter from a Gig Harbor, Washington, woman is typical:

I am a senior woman of small stature and good health. I am writing my comments on Space Mountain, Splash Mountain, Big Thunder Mountain, and Star Tours. My experience [is that] all of the rides, with the exception of Star Tours, were wonderful rides. Star Tours is too jerky and fast, the music is too loud, and I found it to be unacceptable.

Notwithstanding this letter, most comments we receive from seniors about Star Tours are positive. The Rock 'n' Roller Coaster, however, is a different story. Rock 'n' Roller Coaster is a serious coaster that shares more in common with Hulk and Montu than with Space Mountain or Big Thunder Mountain.

Mission: Space, a new, high-tech simulation ride at Epcot, is a toss-up (pun intended). It absolutely has the potential to make you sick. Disney, however, tinkered with it throughout its first year of operation to minimize the likelihood of motion sickness without compromising the thrill. The ride vehicles are constructed with an "easy-clean" design that allows cast members to quickly hose down any mess that occurs. But don't worry. Disney is as interested in avoiding this unpleasant exercise as you are in keeping your cookies right where they belong.

"Unheralded Treasures" Touring

Unheralded treasures are special features found in all of the Disney theme parks and add texture, context, beauty, depth, and subtlety to your visit. Generally speaking, Unheralded treasures are nice surprises that should be accorded a little time. They are the proverbial Disney roses that you should stop and smell. Mike Scopa, *Unofficial Guide* friend and writer for **www.mouseplanet.com,** knows them all. His list follows.

The Magic Kingdom

Treasure   Roy Disney Statue

Location   Magic Kingdom Town Square

In the center of the town square near the flagpole is a statue of Roy Disney sitting on a bench. Few guests are aware of this tribute to Walt Disney's brother, whose contribution to the success of the Disney Company rivaled Walt's. Roy was somewhat unheralded, and his statue is also. Take an opportunity to sit next to Roy and have your picture taken with the lesser-known Disney.

Treasure   Animated Mural

Location   Disneyana Building

When you enter the Magic Kingdom from underneath the train station, to your right is the building where Tony's Town Square Restaurant resides. The far right side of that building used to be home to an attraction known as the Walt Disney Story, which featured a film on Walt Disney's life and showed how Walt and Mickey first got started, as well as Walt's work in television and eventual leap into the world of theme-park entertainment.

Although the attraction has been moved, something essential has remained. Prior to the showing of the movie, the guests were treated to a brief introduction by the attraction's cast-member host. The cast member delivered this introduction in front of a wall upon which was drawn all the major animated characters from Walt Disney animation. New characters were added to the mural as they emerged. That mural is still there. To see the mural, walk down the hallway lined with vintage WDW photos. At the end of the hallway, turn to your left to view this masterpiece.

Treasure   Mickey's Firehouse

Location   Magic Kingdom Town Square

On the left as you emerge from under the train station, you will see the Magic Kingdom City Hall. To the right of the city hall is the Magic Kingdom Firehouse. Within the firehouse, you will find several glass displays that contain fire-department patches given to WDW from guests who have visited the resort. The shop is usually sparsely attended, and it offers a chance to inspect the glass cases. There are more patches than space to display them all.

Treasure   Magic Kingdom Barbershop

Location   Magic Kingdom Town Square

To the right of the firehouse, hidden in a corner to the left of the emporium, is the Magic Kingdom Barbershop. A few years back, it was moved from Main Street, U.S.A., to its present location. Visit the shop, and you may be lucky to receive a magical trim while being serenaded by the Dapper Dans. At last check, a Magic Kingdom haircut was $15.

Treasure   Dapper Dans

Location   Main Street, U.S.A.

Dapper Dans are synonymous with Main Street, U.S.A. Guests can find them most anywhere on the street and sometimes in the shops. These stripe-clad cast members offer guests a chance to begin their day with a smile and a song. If you happen to see the Dapper Dans, let them know if it's your birthday. You might just stir up a song or two.

Epcot

Treasure   Leapfrog Fountains

Location   Future World

To the left of *Honey, I Shrunk the Audience* are Future World's Leapfrog Fountains. This group of fountains offers guests a unique look at how water can be appear to "leap" from fountain to fountain. On a warm day, you can sit and enjoy the amused guests, especially children, reveling at the unusual fountains and catching a welcome shower. We don't hear much about these fountains, but they are a joy to watch.

Treasure   Fiber-optic Sidewalks

Location   Innoventions Plaza

A delightful part of the Innoventions Plaza is the collection of fiber-optic lights buried in the ground just outside the entrance to Innoventions. These are best seen at night, and if you happen to be in the area toward the park's closing hour, you will sense the calming effect of these designs and lights … a great way to end an evening at Epcot.

Treasure   Stave Church

Location   World Showcase, Norway

The stave church exhibit in Norway shows how this architectural design evolved with informative photographs and accounts of its design and development. However, the real beauty of this stave church is the singing that you hear while inside. A few moments in the stave church offer a nice respite from the crowds.

Treasure   Miniature Train

Location   World Showcase, Germany

Many guests may not realize that between Germany and Italy is an area that contains a miniature train display (often called the railway garden), complete with trains, buildings, and miniature people. The detail of this display, including the landscaping, is a wonder to behold. Look for the full-scale train light that draws guests' attention to the display at night.

Treasure   Japanese Pavilion Garden

Location   World Showcase, Japan

There are many gardens to explore in Epcot's World Showcase. However, the garden found at the Japan pavilion is very special because almost all its plants and flowers are native to Japan. Great care was taken to accurately represent Japanese horticulture. Of all the World Showcase gardens, this one is by far the best-kept secret.

Disney-MGM Studios

Treasure   Indiana Jones Set

Location   Next to the Indiana Jones Outpost

As you walk past the Prime Time Café and the Indiana Jones Outpost, you will see, tucked away in a corner, a display of props used in the movie *Indiana Jones and the Last Crusade*. You will recognize the vehicles (especially that famous tank). Unless you happen to attend the *Indiana Jones Stunt Spectacular* and exit to the left, you might never know this exhibit is there.

Treasure   Cement Footprint

Location   The Great Movie Ride Plaza

The plaza in front of the Great Movie Ride contains cement blocks that have hand- and shoe-prints from famous celebrities. Not every block "made" by celebrities is displayed; they are often rotated, with special consideration given to celebrities currently getting a lot of press. Prints made by celebrities who have passed away also get special attention.

Treasure   Ewok Village

Location   Star Tours

During the day there is a lot of activity in this area near the Star Tours attraction. However, if you are in this portion of Disney-MGM after dark, you may want to hang around and listen to the sounds of the Ewok village that you were not able to hear during the day.

Treasure   Academy of Television Arts and Sciences Hall of Fame Busts

Location   Between ABC Theater and *Sounds Dangerous*

This relatively small alcove contains marble busts of some of the most influential people in television history. This attraction is not listed on the official guidemap, making it easy to miss. It offers guests a place to sit and reflect on some of the great television entertainers of all time.

Treasure   Streetmosphere

Location   Hollywood Boulevard Area

First-time visitors to this park may be surprised by a face-to-face with a movie starlet, janitor, taxi driver, or movie director. These Streetmosphere cast members interact with each other and park guests, and over the years they have developed some very entertaining skits.

Disney's Animal Kingdom

Treasure   Discovery Island Trails

Location   Base of Tree of Life

If you walk around the base of the Tree of Life, you will find many extraordinary animal figures carved into this structure. Look for the owl, the scorpion, the gorilla, and especially the six-foot rabbit.

Treasure   Goofy and Friends Fishing

Location   Camp Minnie-Mickey

As you walk toward Camp Minnie-Mickey, you may not notice the old watering hole where fisherman Goofy and some of his closest friends enjoy a lazy fishing trip. Look for this watering hole just after crossing the large bridge that brings you to Camp Minnie-Mickey.

Treasure   DeVine

Location   Asia

If you are lucky when walking through Asia, you may see DeVine, a cast member who you would swear is a walking vine. DeVine is often found up against a building and moves ever so slightly, if at all. The talent of this cast member brings smiles to guests, especially children. How do you know it's DeVine and not a regular plant? Look for her eyes.

Treasure   *Pocahontas and Her Forest Friends*

Location   Camp Minnie-Mickey

This treasure offers entertainment and education to children. Tucked away in Camp Minnie-Mickey, this show is a great attraction for young children who love nature and animals. The songs, mixed with very informative dialogue, make this one of the most worthwhile attractions guests can show their children.

Treasure   Talking Palm Tree

Location   Turnstile Area

Just before you approach the Animal Kingdom turnstile area, you may notice a very mobile palm tree conversing with guests, especially children. This treasure introduces young guests to the environment they are about to enter. The fascination on the faces of the children as this tree converses with them is priceless. The adults can have fun trying to figure out how the tree works.

Part Three

Selecting Your Hotel

The Basic Considerations

Locating a suitable hotel or condo is critical to planning any Walt Disney World vacation. The basic question is whether to stay inside the World. Luxury lodging can be found both in and out of Disney World. Budget lodging is another story. In the World, room rates range from about $80 a night to more than $500. Outside, rooms are as low as $35 a night at some independent motels.

Beyond affordability is convenience. We've lodged both in and out of Disney World, and there's special magic and peace of mind associated with staying inside the World. "I feel more a part of everything and less like a visitor," one guest writes.

There's no real hardship in staying outside Disney World and driving or taking a hotel shuttle to the theme parks. Meals can be less expensive, and rooming outside the World makes you more receptive toward other Orlando-area attractions and eating spots. Universal Studios, Universal's Islands of Adventure, Kennedy Space Center Visitor Complex, Sea-World, and Gatorland, among others, are well worth your attention.

Because Disney World is so large, some off-property hotels are closer in time and distance to many of the theme parks than are some Disney resorts. Check our chart on pages 210–223 that lists commuting time from both Disney and non-Disney hotels.

Lodging prices are subject to change, but our researchers lodged in an excellent (though not plush) motel surrounded by beautiful orange groves for half the cost of staying in the least expensive Disney hotel. Our one-way commute to the Magic Kingdom or Epcot parking lots was 17 minutes.

If you have young children, read Part Five, Walt Disney World with Kids (page 235), before choosing lodging. Similarly, seniors, couples on a honeymoon or romantic holiday, and disabled guests should read the applicable sections of Part Six, Special Tips for Special People (page 291), before booking.

About Hotel Renovations

We inspected several hundred hotels in the Disney World area to compile the *Unofficial Guide's* list of lodging choices. Each year we phone each hotel to verify contact information and inquire about renovations or refurbishments. If a hotel has been renovated or has refurbished its guest rooms, we reinspect that hotel, along with any new hotels, for the next edition of the *Guide.* Hotels reporting no improvements are rechecked every two years.

Most hotels over five years old, both in and out of the World, refurbish 10–20% of their guest rooms each year. This incremental approach minimizes disruption but makes your room assignment a crap shoot. You might luck into a newly renovated room or be assigned a threadbare room. Disney resorts won't guarantee specific rooms but will note your request for a recently refurbished room and will try to accommodate you. Non-Disney hotels will often guarantee an updated room when you book.

Benefits of Staying in the World

Disney resort hotel and campground guests have privileges and amenities unavailable to those staying outside the World. Though some of these perks are advertising gimmicks, others are real and potentially valuable.

Here are the benefits and what they mean:

1. Convenience   If you don't have a car, commuting to the parks is easy via the Disney Transportation System. This is especially advantageous if you stay in a hotel connected by monorail or boat service. If you have a car, however, there are dozens of hotels outside Disney World that are within 5 to 10 minutes of theme-park parking lots.

2. Early Entry at the Theme Parks   Disney World lodging guests (excluding guests at the independent hotels of Downtown Disney Resort Area, except for the Hilton) are invited to enter a designated park one hour earlier than the general public each day. Disney guests are also offered specials on admission, including a passport good for the exact number of days of their visit and discount tickets to the water parks. These benefits are subject to change without notice.

Early entry can be quite valuable if you know how to use it. It can also land you in gridlock. See our detailed discussion of early entry on pages 40–43. Disney has additionally been running a program called E-Ride Night (about $13 extra) that allows resort guests with certain multiday passes to remain in the park two to three hours after official closing. For details, see 481.

3. Baby-sitting and Childcare Options   Disney hotel and campground guests have several options for baby-sitting, childcare, and children's programs. Each resort hotel connected by the monorail, as well as several other Disney hotels, offers "clubs" (themed childcare centers), where potty-trained children ages 3–12 can stay while the adults go out.

Though somewhat expensive, the clubs are highly regarded by children and parents. On the negative side, they're open only in the evening, and not all Disney hotels have them. If you're staying at a Disney hotel without a club, you're better off using a private in-room baby-sitting service (page 287). In-room baby-sitting is also available at hotels outside Disney World.

4. Guaranteed Theme-park Admissions   On days of unusually heavy attendance, Disney resort guests are guaranteed admission to the parks. In practice, no guest is turned away until a park's parking lot is full. When this happens, that park will be packed to gridlock. Under such conditions, you would exhibit the common sense of an amoeba to exercise your guaranteed-admission privilege. The privilege, by the way, does not extend to the water parks (Blizzard Beach and Typhoon Lagoon).

5. Children Sharing a Room with Their Parents   There's no extra charge per night for children younger than 18 sharing a room with their parents. Many hotels outside Disney World also offer this.

6. Free Parking   Disney resort guests with cars pay nothing to park in theme-park lots. This saves about $8 per day.

7. Recreational Privileges   Disney guests get preferential treatment for tee times at the golf courses.

Staying in or out of the World: Weighing the Pros and Cons

1. Cost   If cost is a primary consideration, you'll lodge much less expensively outside Disney World. Our ratings of hotel quality, cost, and commuting times to the theme parks (pages 210–223) compare hotels both in and out of the World.

2. Ease of Access   Even if you stay in Disney World, you're dependent on some mode of transportation. It may be less stressful to use the Disney transportation system, but with the single exception of commuting to the Magic Kingdom, the fastest, most efficient, and most flexible way to get around is usually a car. If you're at Epcot, for example, and want to take the kids back to Disney's Contemporary Resort for a nap, forget the monorail. You'll get back much faster by car.

A reader from Raynham, Massachusetts, who stayed at the Caribbean Beach Resort, writes:

> Even though the resort is on the Disney bus line, I recommend renting a car if it fits one's budget. The buses do not go directly to many destinations, and often you have to switch [buses]. Getting a [bus] seat in the morning is no problem [because] they allow standing. Getting a bus back to the hotel after a hard day can mean a long wait in line.

The Disney transportation system, particularly the bus system, is about as efficient as humanly possible. No matter where you're going, you rarely wait more than 15–20 minutes for a bus, monorail, or boat. Although it's only for the use and benefit of Disney guests, it is nonetheless public transportation, and users must expect inconveniences: conveyances that arrive and depart on their schedule, not yours; the occasional need to transfer; multiple stops; time lost loading and unloading passengers; and, generally, the challenge of understanding and using a large, complex transportation network.

If you plan to have a car, consider this: Disney World is so large that some destinations within the World can be reached more quickly from off-property hotels than from Disney hotels. For example, guests at lodgings on US 192 (near the so-called Walt Disney World main entrance) are closer to Disney-MGM Studios, the Animal Kingdom, and Blizzard Beach water park than guests at many hotels inside Disney World.

A Kentucky dad overruled his family about staying at a Disney resort and was glad he did:

> My wife read in another guidebook that it can take two hours to commute to the parks if you stay outside Walt Disney World. What nonsense! I guess it could take two hours if you stayed in Tampa, but from our hotel on [US] 192 we could commute to any of the parks except the Magic Kingdom, and have at least one ride under our belt in about an hour. We found out later that the writer of the other guidebook is a writer for Disney Magazine.

For commuting times from specific non-Disney hotels, see our hotel chart on pages 210–233.

3. Young Children   Although the hassle of commuting to most non-World hotels is only slightly (if at all) greater than that of commuting to Disney hotels, a definite peace of mind results from staying in the World. Regardless of where you stay, make sure you get your young children back to the hotel for a nap each day.

4. Splitting Up   If you're in a party that will probably split up to tour (as frequently happens in families with teens or children of widely varying ages), staying in the World offers more transportation options and, thus, more independence. Mom and Dad can take the car and return to the hotel for a relaxed dinner and early bedtime while the teens remain in the park for evening parades and fireworks.

5. Feeding the Army of the Potomac   If you have a large crew that chows down like cattle on a finishing lot, you may do better staying outside the World, where food is far less expensive.

6. Visiting Other Orlando-area Attractions   If you will visit SeaWorld, Kennedy Space Center Visitor Complex, Universal Orlando, or other area attractions, it may be more convenient to stay outside the World.

The Disney Resorts

Disney Resorts 101

Before making decisions, understand these basics regarding Disney resorts.

1. Resort Classifications   Disney loves to categorize, so it's not surprising that they have developed a hierarchy of resort classifications. Deluxe resorts are Disney's top-of-the-line hotels. Home Away from Home resorts offer suites, some with full kitchens. Many of these resorts equal or surpass deluxe resorts in quality; others are actually attached to a deluxe resort. Moderate resorts are a step down in guest-room quality, amenities, and cost. Anchoring the bottom of the list are value resorts, with smaller rooms, limited amenities, and the lowest rates of any Disney-owned hotels. Finally, there's the Fort Wilderness Campground, which offers both campsites and fully equipped Home Away from Home cabins.

DISNEY RESORT CATEGORIES: Prices and Amenities			
Value	Moderate	Home Away from Home	Deluxe
$77–$126	$133–$209	$254–$1,460	$199–$840
Food courts	Food courts	Food courts	Food courts
Snack bars	Snack bars	Snack bars	Snack bars
Lounges/bars	Lounges/bars	Lounges/bars	Lounges/bars
Pools	Pools	Pools	Pools
Playgrounds	Playgrounds	Playgrounds	Playgrounds
	Bell services	Bell services	Bell services
	Whirlpools	Whirlpools	Whirlpools
	Table-service dining	Table-service dining	Table-service dining
	Water sports	Water sports	Water sports
		Beach	Beach
		Fine dining	Fine dining
		Room service	Room service
		Character breakfasts	Character breakfasts
		Powerboat rental	Powerboat rental
		Fishing	Fishing
		Valet parking	Valet parking
		Kids' programs	Kids' programs
		Tennis courts	Tennis courts
		Walking/jogging paths	Walking/jogging paths
		Fitness center/spa	Fitness center/spa *
		Kitchens/kitchenettes	Concierge service

* Except Polynesian Resort

		Home Away	
Value	Moderate	from Home	Deluxe

DISNEY RESORT CATEGORIES: Prices and Amenities (continued)

			Monorail access
			Closest to parks
			Larger rooms
			Suites

2. Making Reservations   Whether you book through Disney, your travel agent, online, with a tour operator, or through an organization like AAA, you will save by booking the room exclusive of any vacation package. This is called a "room-only" reservation. Though later in this chapter we'll scrutinize the advantages and disadvantages of buying a package, we'll say now that Disney World packages rarely save you money (though sometimes they're worthwhile for the convenience and peace of mind).

In dealing with Disney for room-only, call the Disney Reservations Center (DRC) at (407) W-DISNEY. Because of some administrative and operational consolidation in 2004, reservationists at the DRC are now trained only to sell Walt Disney Travel Company packages. Even if you insist that you just want a room, they'll try to bundle your room with some small extra like miniature golf passes so your purchase can be counted as a "basic" package. This seems innocuous enough, and you might even appreciate the mini-golf passes, but classifying your reservation as a package allows Disney to apply numerous restrictions and cancellation policies that you won't be saddled with if you buy room-only. When you call, politely but persistently specify that you want a room-only reservation. If the first agent you speak to isn't accommodating, hang up and call back. There are a couple hundred agents, and some are more helpful than others.

Understand that the DRC and Walt Disney Travel Company representatives don't possess detailed personal knowledge of the resorts. If you need specific information, call the resort directly, ask for the front desk, and pose your question before phoning the DRC. If your desired dates aren't available, keep calling back. Something might open up.

3. A Most Confusing View   Rates at Disney hotels vary from season to season (see the next section) and from room to room according to view. Further, each Disney resort has its own seasonal calendar. Seasons such as "regular, value, peak, and holiday" come and go at the whim of the resort with little or no coordination with other resorts or that tired old January-to-December calendar the rest of us use. But confusing as Disney seasons are, they're logic personified compared to the panoply of guest-room views the resorts offer. Depending on the resort, you can choose standard views, water views, parking-lot views, pool views, lagoon views, garden views, or savanna views, among others.

Standard view, the most ambiguous category, crops up at about three-fourths of Disney resorts. It's usually interpreted as a view that doesn't fit any other view classification the hotel offers. At the Animal Kingdom Lodge, for example, you have savanna views, water views, and standard views. Savanna views overlook the replicated African savanna, water views overlook the swimming pool, and standard views offer stunning vistas of other stuff, whatever it might be.

With a standard view, however, you at least can pinpoint what you won't be seeing. Every resort defines water views differently. According to a manager at the Grand Floridian, for example, a water fiew is a direct, unobstructed, frontal view of Seven Seas Lagoon. Views of swimming pools or sideways views of the lagoon don't count. If the Grand Floridian sells you a water-view room, by George, you're going to see some water.

Zip over to the Yacht Club Resort, another deluxe property, and the definition of water view is completely different. Like the Grand Floridian, the Yacht Club is on a lake, but booking a water-view room doesn't guarantee you'll see the lake. At the Yacht Club, anything wet counts, whether it's in front of you or so far to the side you have to crane your neck. If somehow you can glimpse the lake, a creek, or a swimming pool, you have a water view.

Our favorite is the Contemporary Resort. Extending out toward Bay Lake from the giant A-frame are two "Garden Buildings." Some of the best lake views in Walt Disney World can be had from rooms in these three-story buildings. Many of these rooms are so near the water you could spit a prune seed into the lake from your room. And their category? Garden views.

We could go on and on, but pinning Disney down on precisely what will be outside your window is the point. In our discussion of individual resorts later in this chapter, we'll tell you which rooms have the good views.

4. How to Get the Room You Want   Disney won't guarantee a specific room when you book but will post your request on your reservation record. Our experience indicates that if you give them your first, second, and third choices, you'll probably get one of the three. If they balk at listing specific rooms (as in "Room 1231," for example), you can either call back and talk to another reservationist, or tell the agent exactly what you want in descriptive terms, the more specific the better. For example: "I'd like a nonsmoking room with a full balcony on the fifth floor with an unobstructed view of the Seven Seas Lagoon and the Magic Kingdom."

Be direct and politely assertive when speaking to the Disney agent. Port Orleans Resort, for example, offers either standard or water-view rooms. Water view could mean a view of the river or a swimming pool. If you want to overlook the river, say so; likewise, if you want a pool view, say so. Similarly, state clearly such preferences as a particular floor, a corner room, a room near restaurants, a room away from elevators and ice machines, a nonsmoking room, or a room with a certain type of balcony. If you have a laundry list of preferences, type it in order of importance, and e-mail, fax, or mail it to the Disney Reservations Center. Include your contact information and reservation confirmation number. Call in a couple of days to make sure your preferences were posted to your record.

We'll provide info needed for each resort to frame your requests, including a resort layout map and our recommendations for specific rooms or buildings. We'll use "to" to indicate a range of rooms. Thus, "rooms 2230 to 2260" refers to the 31 rooms within that range. Sometimes we'll specify even or odd number rooms within a range, for example, "odd-numbered rooms 631 to 639." In this case we're referring to rooms 631, 633, 635, 637, and 639, eliminating intervening even-numbered rooms. For brevity, we may refer to "rooms 15-11, 22, 31, and 40." In this instance, "15-" is a numerical prefix that applies to all of the rooms listed. The actual room numbers are 1511, 1522, 1531, and 1540.

How to Get Discounts on Lodging

There are so many guest rooms in and around Disney World that competition is brisk, and everyone, including Disney, wheels and deals to fill them. This has led to a more flexible discount policy for Disney hotels. Here are tips for getting price breaks:

1. Seasonal Savings   Save from $15 to $50 per night on a Disney hotel room by scheduling your visit during slower times of year. However, Disney uses so many adjectives (regular, holiday, peak, value, etc.) to describe its seasonal calendar, that it's hard to keep up. Plus, dates for each "season" vary among resorts. If you're set on staying at a Disney resort, obtain a copy of Disney's Walt Disney World Florida Vacations video/DVD brochure described on page 21.

Forget trying to find seasonal dates on the Disney World Web site. Easier by far is checking them on **www.mousesavers.com,** an independent site described below.

Understand that Disney seasonal dates aren't sequential like spring, summer, fall, and winter. That would be way too simple. For any specific resort, there often are four or more seasonal changes in a month. This is important, because your rate per night will be determined by the season prevailing when you check in. Let's say you check into the Animal Kingdom Lodge on April 19 for a five-night stay. April 19 is in the more expensive peak season that ends April 20, followed by the less pricey regular season beginning April 21. Because you arrived during peak season, the peak rate will apply to your entire stay even though more than half of it was in regular season. Your strategy, therefore, is to shift your dates (if possible) to arrive during a less expensive season. If your dates are non-negotiable, book back-to-back reservations. In our example above, you'd first book a one-night stay on April 19 at peak-season rates and then a separate four-night reservation at regular-season rates from April 20–23.

2. Ask about Specials   When you talk to Disney reservationists, ask specifically about specials. For example, "What special rates or discounts are available at Disney hotels during the time of our visit?" Being specific and assertive paid off for an Illinois reader:

> I called Disney's reservations number and asked for availability and rates . . . [Because] of the Unofficial Guide warning about Disney reservationists answering only the questions posed, I specifically asked, "Are there any special rates or discounts for that room during the month of October?" She replied, "Yes, we have that room available at a special price. . . ." [For] the price of one phone call, I saved $440.

Similarly, a Warren, New Jersey, dad reports:

> Your tip about asking Disney employees about discounts was invaluable. They will not volunteer this information, but by asking we saved almost $500 on our hotel room using a AAA discount.

3. "Trade-up" or "Upsell" Rates   If you request a room at a Disney value resort and none is available, you may be offered a discounted room in the next category up (moderate resorts, in this example). Similarly, if you ask for a room in a moderate resort and none is available, Disney will usually offer a deal for Home-Away-from-Home rooms or a deluxe resort. You can angle for a trade-up rate by asking for a resort category that's more likely to be sold out. For part of 2004, because some hotels were closed, there was limited availability of rooms at moderate resorts. Several readers reported scoring a bargain room at a deluxe resort by requesting accommodations at the French Quarter section of Port Orleans, which closed in 2003 and didn't reopen until April 2004.

4. Know the Secret Code   The folks at **www.mousesavers.com** keep an updated list of discounts and reservation codes for Disney resorts. The codes are separated into categories such as "For anyone," "For residents of certain states," and "For annual passport holders." For example, the site listed code "CVZ," published in an ad in some Spanish-language newspapers and magazines, offering a rate of $65 per night for Disney's All-Star Resorts from April 22 through August 8 and $49 per night from August 9 through October 3. Dozens of discounts are usually listed on the site, covering most Disney hotels. Anyone calling the Disney Reservations Center at (407) W-DISNEY can use a current code and get the discounted rate.

The site also features a great links page with short descriptions and Web addresses of the best Disney-related Web sites, as well as a current seasonal rates calendar for each Disney resort. Two other sites, **www.allearsnet.com**

and **www.wdwinfo.com,** have discount codes we've used to get up to 50% off rack rates at the Swan and Dolphin.

5. Expedia   Online travel seller Expedia (**www.expedia.com**) discounts Disney hotels. Most breaks are in the 7–25% range, but they can go as deep as 40%.

6. Walt Disney World Web Site   Disney has become more aggressive about offering deals on its Web site. Go to **www.disneyworld.com** and look for the icon "Vacation Savings." Click on it to see what's available. The icon doesn't appear consistently. It comes up periodically or seasonally when Disney needs to boost occupancy. You must click on "Vacation Savings" to get the discounts. If you click on "Reservations and Tickets" in the upper right corner, you'll be charged full rack rate with no mention of available discounts. You must cancel reservations for rooms sold at discount 46 days before arrival if you want a full refund. Reservations booked through "Reservations and Tickets" may be canceled six days before arrival. In any event, before booking rooms on Disney's or any Web site, click on "Terms and Conditions" and read the fine print.

7. Annual Passholder Discounts   Annual Passholders are eligible for discounts on dining, shopping, and lodging. If you visit Disney World once a year or more, of if you plan to visit five or more days, you might save money overall by purchasing annual passes. During the past year, we saw resort discounts as deep as 45% for annual passholders. It doesn't take long to recoup the extra bucks for an annual pass when you're saving that kind of money. Discounts in the 10–25% range are more the norm.

8. Renting Disney Vacation Club Points   The Disney Vacation Club (DVC) is Disney's time-share condominium program. DVC resorts at Walt Disney World include Old Key West, Saratoga Springs, the Beach Club Villas, Villas at Wilderness Lodge, and the BoardWalk Villas. Each resort offers studios and one- and two-bedroom villas (some resorts also offer three-bedroom villas). All accommodations are roomy and luxurious. The studios are equipped with wet bars and fridges, and the villas come with full kitchens. Most accommodations have patios or balconies.

DVC members receive annually a number of "points" that they use to pay for their Disney accommodations. Sometimes members elect to "rent" (sell) their points instead of using them in a given year. Though Disney is not involved in the transaction, it allows DVC members to make these points available to the general public. The going rental rate is usually in the range of $10 per point. A studio for a week at the BoardWalk Villas would run you $2,303 plus tax for regular season if you booked through the Disney Reservation Center. The same studio costs the DVC member 123 points for a week. If you rented his points at $10 per point, the BoardWalk Villas Studio would cost you $1,230, that is, more than $1,000 less.

When you rent points, you deal with the selling DVC member and pay him or her directly. The DVC member makes a reservation in your name and pays Disney the requisite number of points. Arrangements vary widely, but some trust is required from both parties. Usually your reservation is documented by a confirmation sent from Disney to the owner, and then passed along to you. Though the deal you cut is strictly up to you and the owner, you should always insist on receiving the aforementioned confirmation before making more than a one-night deposit.

Owners post points for sale and prospective buyers solicit points on **www.wdwinfo.com.** The site, like Disney, is merely a facilitator and is not involved in, or in any way liable for, the success of the transaction.

9. Travel Agents   Travel agents are active players and particularly good sources of information on limited-time programs and discounts. We believe a good travel agent is the best friend a traveler can have. And though we at the *Unofficial Guide* know a thing or two about the travel industry, we always give our agent a chance to beat any deal we find. If she can't beat it, we let her book it anyway if it's commissionable. We nurture a relationship that gives her plenty of incentive to roll up her sleeves and work on our behalf.

10. Organizations and Auto Clubs   Disney has developed time-limited programs with some auto clubs and organizations. Recently, for example, AAA members were offered 10–20% savings on Disney hotels, preferred parking at the theme parks, and discounts on Disney package vacations. Such deals come and go, but the market suggests there will be more. If you're a member of AARP, AAA, or any travel or auto club, ask whether the group has a program before shopping elsewhere.

11. Room Upgrades   Sometimes a room upgrade is as good as a discount. If you're visiting Disney World during a slower time, book the least expensive room your discounts will allow. Checking in, ask very politely about being upgraded to a "water-" or "pool-view" room. A fair percentage of the time, you'll get one at no additional charge.

12. Extra-night Discounts   During slower times, book your Disney hotel for half the period you intend to stay. Often, the hotel will offer extra nights at a discounted rate to get you to stay longer.

13. Military Discounts   The Shades of Green Armed Forces Recreation Center, near the Grand Floridian Resort, offers luxury accommodations and attraction tickets to WDW at rates based on a service member's rank. Shades of Green completed an extensive renovation and expansion in 2004 that doubled the number of rooms and upgraded most public areas. For rates and other information, see **www.shadesof green.org** or call (888) 593-2242.

14. Ocala Disney Information Center   The Ocala Disney Information Center off I-75 in Ocala, Florida, once booked Disney hotel rooms at discounts of up to 43%. Now the Center is run by AAA and offers discounts of 10% or so—discounts than can be had in easier ways than scheduling a special stop at the Info Center.

WHAT IT COSTS TO STAY IN A DISNEY RESORT HOTEL	
Grand Floridian	$339–$2,450
Polynesian Resort	$299–$2,490
Swan (Westin)	$289–$2,700
Dolphin (Sheraton)	$289–$3,100
Beach Club Resort	$289–$2,110
Beach Club Villas	$289–$1,010
Yacht Club Resort	$289–$2,290
BoardWalk Inn	$289–$2,340
BoardWalk Villas	$289–$1,915
Wilderness Lodge	$199–$1,190
Wilderness Lodge Villas	$279–$985
Saratoga Springs	$254–$1,460
Old Key West Resort	$254–$1,460
Contemporary Resort	$239–$2,405
Fort Wilderness Resort	$229–$329
Coronado Springs Resort	$133–$1,105
Caribbean Beach Resort	$133–$209
Port Orleans Resort	$133–$209
All-Star Resorts	$77–$126
Pop Century Resorts	$77–$126

WHAT IT COSTS TO STAY IN THE DOWNTOWN DISNEY RESORT AREA	
DoubleTree Guest Suites Resort	$139–$250
Hilton	$129–$279
Wyndham Palace	$119–$248
Hotel Royal Plaza	$74–$210
Holiday Inn at Walt Disney World	$109–$180
Grosvenor Resort	$78–$220
Lake Buena Vista Resort	$83–$150

Walt Disney World Lodging Areas

The Grand Floridian, Polynesian, Contemporary, Wilderness Lodge and Villas, and Shades of Green Resorts are near the Magic Kingdom. The Swan and Dolphin hotels, the Yacht and Beach Club resorts, and Disney's BoardWalk Inn and Villas are near Epcot. The All-Star, Coronado

Springs, and Animal Kingdom Lodge resorts are on the far southwest side. Saratoga Springs Resort and the independent hotels of the Walt Disney World Hotel Plaza are on the far east side of Walt Disney World near Downtown Disney. Centrally located are the Caribbean Beach Resort and Disney's Pop Century Resort. Along Bonnet Creek, Old Key West and Port Orleans resorts also offer a central location.

Choosing a Walt Disney World Hotel

If you want to stay in the World but don't know which hotel to choose, consider:

1. Cost   Consider your budget. Hotel rooms start at about $77 a night at the All-Star and Pop Century Resorts during Value Season and top out near $840 at the Grand Floridian during Holiday Season. Suites, of course, are more expensive.

BoardWalk Villas, Wilderness Lodge Villas, Old Key West Resort, Saratoga Springs, and Beach Club Villas offer condo-type accommodations with one-, two-, and (at Saratoga Springs, BoardWalk Villas, and Old Key West) three-bedroom units with kitchens, living rooms, VCRs, and washers and dryers. Prices range from about $254 per night for a studio suite at Saratoga Springs to more than $1,915 per night for a three-bedroom villa at BoardWalk Villas. Fully equipped cabins at Fort Wilderness Resort and Campground cost $229–$329 per night. A limited number of suites are available at the more expensive Disney resorts, but they don't have kitchens.

Also at Disney World are the seven hotels of the Downtown Disney Resort Area (DDRA), formerly known as the Disney Village Hotel Plaza. Accommodations range from fairly luxurious to Holiday Inn quality. Though not typically good candidates for bargains, these hotels surprised us with some great deals during 2004. While the DDRA is technically part of Disney World, staying there is like visiting a colony rather than the motherland. Free parking at theme parks isn't offered—nor is early entry, with one exception, the Hilton—and hotels operate their own buses rather than use Disney transportation. For more information on the properties of the Downtown Disney Resort Area, see our evaluation and comparison on pages 167–170.

2. Location   Once you determine your budget, think about what you want to do at Disney World. Will you go to all four theme parks or concentrate on one or two?

If you will have a car, your Disney hotel's location isn't especially important unless you plan to spend most of your time at the Magic Kingdom. (Disney transportation is always more efficient than your car in this case because it bypasses the Transportation and Ticket Center, the World's transportation hub, and deposits you at the theme-park entrance.) If you haven't decided whether you want a car for your Disney vacation, see "How to Travel around the World" (page 313).

Most convenient to the Magic Kingdom are the three resorts linked by monorail: Grand Floridian, Contemporary, and Polynesian. Commuting to the Magic Kingdom via monorail is quick and simple, allowing visitors to return to their hotel for a nap, swim, or meal.

The Contemporary Resort, in addition to being on the monorail, is only a 10–15-minute walk to the Magic Kingdom. Contemporary Resort guests reach Epcot by monorail but must transfer at the Transportation and Ticket Center. Buses connect the Contemporary to Disney-MGM Studios and Animal Kingdom. No transfer is required, but the bus makes several stops before reaching either destination.

The Polynesian Resort is served by the Magic Kingdom monorail and is an easy walk from the transportation center. At the center, you can catch an express monorail to Epcot. This makes the Polynesian the only Disney resort with direct monorail access to both Epcot and the Magic Kingdom. To minimize your walk to the transportation center, book a room in the Rapa Nui, Tahiti, or Tokelau guest buildings.

The Wilderness Lodge Resort and Villas, along with Fort Wilderness Campground, are linked to the Magic Kingdom by boat, and to everywhere else in the World by somewhat convoluted bus service.

Most convenient to Epcot and Disney-MGM Studios are the Board-Walk Inn, BoardWalk Villas, Yacht and Beach Club Resorts, Beach Club Villas, and Swan and Dolphin. Though all are within easy walking distance of Epcot's International Gateway, boat service is also available. Vessels also connect Epcot hotels to Disney-MGM Studios. Epcot hotels are best for guests planning to spend most of their time at Epcot or Disney-MGM Studios.

If you plan to use Disney transportation to visit all four major parks and one or both of the water parks, book a centrally located resort with good transportation connections. The Epcot resorts and the Polynesian, Caribbean Beach, Pop Century, and Port Orleans resorts fill the bill. Old Key West Resort is centrally located but offers only limited bus service between noon and 6 p.m.

Though not centrally located, the All-Star, Coronado Springs, and Animal Kingdom resorts have very good bus service to all Disney World destinations and are closest to the Animal Kingdom. Wilderness Lodge and Villas and Fort Wilderness Campground have the most convoluted transportation service.

If you plan to golf, book Old Key West Resort or the new Saratoga Springs Resort. They're built around golf courses. Shades of Green, the military-only resort, is adjacent to two golf courses. Near but not on a golf course are the Grand Floridian, Polynesian, and Port Orleans resorts. For boating and water sports, try the Polynesian, Contemporary, or Grand

Floridian resorts, Fort Wilderness Campground, or the Wilderness Lodge and Villas. The lodge and the campground are also the best for hikers, bikers, and joggers.

3. Room Quality   Few Disney guests spend much time in their hotel rooms, though they're among the best designed and most well appointed anywhere. Plus, they're meticulously maintained. Top of the line are the spacious and luxurious rooms of the Grand Floridian. Bringing up the rear are the small, garish rooms of the All-Star Resorts. But even these are sparkling clean and livable.

Here's how Disney hotels (along with Swan and Dolphin, which are Westin and Sheraton hotels, respectively) stack up for quality:

Hotel	Room Quality Rating
1. Grand Floridian Beach Resort	93
2. Beach Club Resort	92
3. Yacht Club Resort	92
4. Old Key West Resort (studio)	92
5. BoardWalk Villas (studio)	91
6. Saratoga Springs (studio)	91
7. Animal Kingdom Lodge	90
8. BoardWalk Inn	90
9. Beach Club Villas	90
10. Swan	90
11. Wilderness Lodge Villas (studio)	90
12. Polynesian Resort	89
13. Contemporary Resort	87
14. Dolphin	86
15. Wilderness Lodge	86
16. Port Orleans Resort (French Quarter)	84
17. Coronado Springs Resort	83
18. Caribbean Beach Resort	80
19. Port Orleans Resort (Riverside)	79
20. Pop Century Resorts	74
21. All-Star Resorts	73

4. The Size of Your Group   Larger families and groups may be interested in how many persons a Disney resort room can accommodate, but only Lilliputians would be comfortable in a room filled to capacity. Groups requiring two or more guest rooms should consider condo/villa accommodations in or out of the World. The most cost-efficient Disney lodging for groups of five or six persons are the cabins at Fort Wilderness Campground. They sleep six adults plus a child or toddler in a crib. If there are more than six in your party, you will need either two hotel rooms, a suite, or a condo. The Disney room layout schematics on the following pages show the rooms' relative size and configuration and the maximum number of persons per room.

5. Theme   All Disney hotels are themed. Each is designed to make you feel you're in a special place or period of history. Here are the themes:

Hotel	Theme
All-Star Resorts	Sports, music, and movies
Animal Kingdom Lodge	African game preserve
Beach Club Resort and Villas	New England beach club of the 1870s
BoardWalk Inn	East Coast boardwalk hotel of the early 1900s
BoardWalk Villas	East Coast beach cottage of the early 1900s
Caribbean Beach Resort	Caribbean islands
Contemporary Resort	Future as perceived by past, present generations
Coronado Springs Resort	Northern Mexico and the American Southwest
Dolphin	Modern Florida resort
Grand Floridian Beach Resort	Turn-of-the-nineteenth-century luxury hotel
Old Key West Resort	Key West
Polynesian Resort	Hawaii/South Sea islands
Pop Century Resorts	Icons from various decades of the twentieth century
Port Orleans	Turn-of-the-nineteenth century New Orleans and Mardi Gras
Saratoga Springs	Upstate New York 1880s Victorian lakeside retreat
Swan	Modern Florida resort
Villas at the Disney Institute	Combo rustic villas and country club atmosphere
Wilderness Lodge and Villas	National park grand lodge of the early 1900s in the American Northwest
Yacht Club Resort	New England seashore hotel of the 1880s

Some resorts carry off their themes better than others, and some themes are more exciting. The Wilderness Lodge and Villas, for example, is extraordinary. The lobby opens eight stories to a timbered ceiling supported by giant columns of bundled logs. One look eases you into the Northwest-wilderness theme. Romantic and isolated, the lodge is a great choice for couples and seniors and is heaven for children.

The Animal Kingdom Lodge replicates grand safari lodges of Kenya and Tanzania and overlooks its own African game preserve. By far the most exotic Disney resort, it's made to order for couples on a romantic getaway, and families with children. The Polynesian, likewise dramatic, conveys the feeling of the Pacific Islands. It's great for romantics and families. Many waterfront rooms offer a perfect view of Cinderella Castle and the Magic Kingdom fireworks across Seven Seas Lagoon.

Grandeur, nostalgia, and privilege are central to the Grand Floridian and Yacht and Beach Club Resorts and the BoardWalk Inn and Villas.

Deluxe Resorts Room Diagrams

Contemporary Resort

Typical Room 394 Square Feet
*Rooms accommodate 5 guests,
plus 1 child under age 3 in a crib.*

Polynesian Resort

Typical Room 391 Square Feet
*Rooms accommodate 5 guests,
plus 1 child under age 3 in a crib.*

Grand Floridian Resort & Spa

Typical Room 440 Square Feet
*Rooms accommodate 5 guests,
plus 1 child under age 3 in a crib.*

BoardWalk Inn

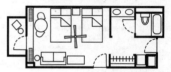

Typical Room 385 Square Feet
*Rooms accommodate 4 guests,
plus 1 child under age 3 in a crib.*

Beach Club Resort

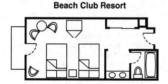

Typical Room 381 Square Feet
*Rooms accommodate 5 guests,
plus 1 child under age 3 in a crib.*

Yacht Club Resort

Typical Room 381 Square Feet
*Rooms accommodate 5 guests,
plus 1 child under age 3 in a crib.*

Wilderness Lodge

Typical Room 344 Square Feet
*Rooms accommodate 4 guests,
plus 1 child under age 3 in a crib.*

Animal Kingdom Lodge

Typical Room 344 Square Feet
*Rooms accommodate 2 to 5 guests,
plus 1 child under age 3 in a crib.*

Home-Away-from-Home Resorts Room Diagrams

Old Key West Resort

Queen Sleeper Sofa

Typical Villas, 4 to 12 guests,
plus 1 child under age 3 in a crib
One Bedroom – 942 square feet
Two Bedroom – 1,333 square feet
Grand Villa – 2,202 square feet
Studio (gray) – 376 square feet

Disney's
BoardWalk Villas

Typical Villas, 4 to 12 guests,
plus 1 child under age 3 in a crib
One Bedroom – 814 square feet
Two Bedroom – 1,236 square feet
Grand Villa – 2,491 square feet
Studio (gray) – 412 square feet

Villas at Disney's
Wilderness Lodge

Typical Villas, 4 to 8 guests,
plus 1 child under age 3 in a crib
One Bedroom – 727 square feet
Two Bedroom – 1,080 square feet
Grand Villa – 2,202 square feet
Studio (gray) – 356 square feet

Disney's
Beach Club Villas

Typical Villas, 4 to 8 guests,
plus 1 child under age 3 in a crib
One Bedroom – 726 square feet
Two Bedroom – 1,083 square feet
Studio (gray) – 356 square feet

Saratoga Springs
Resort & Spa

Typical Villas, 4 to 12 guests,
plus 1 child under age 3 in a crib
One Bedroom – 714 square feet
Two Bedroom – 1,075 square feet
Grand Villa – 2,113 square feet
Studio (gray) – 355 square feet

Moderate Resorts Room Diagrams

Caribbean Beach Resort

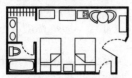

Typical Room, 314 square feet
*Rooms accommodate 4 guests,
plus 1 child under age 3 in a crib.*

Port Orleans French Quarter Resort

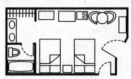

Typical Room, 314 square feet
*Rooms accommodate 4 guests,
plus 1 child under age 3 in a crib.*

Coronado Springs Resort

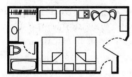

Typical Room, 314 square feet
*Rooms accommodate 4 guests,
plus 1 child under age 3 in a crib.*

Port Orleans Resort Riverside

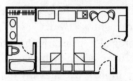

Typical Room, 314 square feet
*Rooms accommodate 4 guests,
plus 1 child under age 3 in a crib.
Alligator Bayou has trundle bed for
extra child (54" long), for extra cost.*

Value Resorts Room Diagrams

All-Star Resorts

Typical Room, 260 square feet
*Rooms accommodate 4 guests,
plus 1 child under age 3 in a crib.*

Pop Century Resort

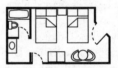

Typical Room, 260 square feet
*Rooms accommodate 4 guests,
plus 1 child under age 3 in a crib.*

Fort Wilderness Campground Log Cabin Diagram

Fort Wilderness Resort and Campground

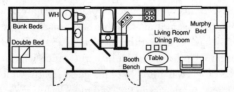

Cabins, 504 square feet
*Cabins accommodate 6 guests,
plus 1 child under age 3 in a crib.*

Although modeled after Eastern seaboard seaside hotels of different eras, the resorts are similar. Saratoga Springs, supposedly representative of an upstate New York country retreat, looks like what you'd get if you crossed the Beach Club with the Wilderness Lodge. For all of the resorts inspired by northeastern resorts, thematic distinctions are subtle and lost on many guests.

The Port Orleans French Quarter Resort lacks the mystery and sultriness of the New Orleans French Quarter, but captures enough of its architectural essence to carry off the theme. Port Orleans Riverside Resort likewise succeeds with its plantation and bayou setting. Old Key West Resort gets the architecture right, but cloning Key West on such a large scale totally glosses over Key West's idiosyncratic, patchwork personality. The Caribbean Beach Resort's theme is much more effective at night, thanks to creative lighting. By day, it looks like a Miami condo development.

Coronado Springs Resort offers several styles of Mexican and Southwestern American architecture. Though the lake setting is lovely and the resort is attractive and inviting, the theme (with the exception of the main swimming area) isn't especially stimulating. Coronado Springs feels more like a Scottsdale, Arizona, country club than a Disney resort.

The All-Star Resorts comprise 30 three-story, T-shaped hotels with almost 6,000 guest rooms. There are 15 themed areas: five celebrate sports (surfing, basketball, tennis, football, and baseball), five recall Hollywood movies, and five have musical motifs. The resort's design, with entrances shaped like giant Dalmatians, Coke cups, footballs, and the like, is pretty adolescent, sacrificing grace and beauty for energy and novelty. Guest rooms are small, with décor reminiscent of a teenage boy's bedroom. Despite the theme, there are no sports, music, or movies at All-Star Resorts. The Pop Century Resort is pretty much a clone of All-Star Resorts, only this time the giant icons symbolize decades of the twentieth century (Big Wheels, 45 rpm records, silhouettes of people doing period dances, etc.), and period memorabilia decorate the rooms.

Pretense aside, the Contemporary, Swan, and Dolphin are essentially themeless though architecturally interesting. The Contemporary is a 15-story, A-frame building with monorails running through the middle. Views from guest rooms in the Contemporary Tower are among the best at Disney World. Swan and Dolphin are massive yet whimsical. Designed by Michael Graves, they're excellent examples of "entertainment architecture." Unfortunately, a little too much whimsy and entertainment worked their way into Dolphin's guest rooms, which border on garish. Swan's guest rooms, originally even more avant-garde, were totally redesigned in 2004. Although still visually interesting, they're now more restful and easier on the eye.

6. Dining   The best resorts for dining quality and selection are the Epcot resorts: Swan, Dolphin, Yacht and Beach Club Resorts, Beach Club Villas, and BoardWalk Inn and Villas. Each has good restaurants and is within easy walking distance of the others (and of the ten ethnic restaurants in Epcot's World Showcase section). If you stay at an Epcot resort, you have 21 of Disney World's finest restaurants within a 5- to 12-minute walk.

The only other place in Disney World where restaurants and hotels are similarly concentrated is in the Downtown Disney Resort Area. In addition to restaurants in the hotels themselves, the Hilton, Holiday Inn at Walt Disney World, Grosvenor Resort, and Wyndham Palace, as well as Disney's Saratoga Springs Resort, are within walking distance of restaurants in Downtown Disney.

Guests at the Contemporary, Polynesian, and Grand Floridian can eat in their hotel, or they can commute to restaurants in the Magic Kingdom (not recommended) or in other monorail-linked hotels. Riding the monorail to another hotel or to the Magic Kingdom takes about ten minutes each way, plus waiting for the train.

All other Disney resorts are somewhat isolated. This means you're stuck dining at your hotel unless (1) you have a car and can go anywhere or (2) you eat at the theme parks or Downtown Disney.

Here's the deal. Disney transportation works fine for commuting from hotels to theme parks and Downtown Disney, but it's hopeless for getting from one hotel to another. If you're staying at Port Orleans and want to dine at the Swan, forget it. It can take you up to an hour and a half each way by bus. You could take a bus to the Magic Kingdom and catch a train to one of the monorail-served hotels for dinner. That would take "only" 45 minutes each way.

Of the more isolated resorts, Wilderness Lodge and Villas and Animal Kingdom Lodge serve the best, most varied food. Coronado Springs, Port Orleans, Old Key West, and Caribbean Beach resorts each have a full-service restaurant of acceptable quality, a food court, and in-room pizza delivery. None of the isolated resorts, however, offers enough variety for the average person to be happy eating in his/her hotel every day. Pop Century Resorts and All-Star Resorts (Disney's most isolated hotel) have nearly 6,000 guest rooms but no full-service restaurant. There are three food courts, but you have to get to them before 11 p.m.

7. Amenities and Recreation   Disney resorts offer a staggering variety of amenities and recreational opportunities (chart on pages 118–119). All provide elaborate swimming pools, themed shops, restaurants or food courts, bars or lounges, and access to five Disney golf courses. The more you pay for your lodging, the more amenities and opportunities are at your disposal. The Grand Floridian, Animal Kingdom Lodge,

DISNEY RESORT AMENITIES AND RECREATION

Resort	Suites	Concierge	Number of Rooms	Room Service
All-Star Resorts			5,760	
Animal Kingdom Lodge	✓	✓	1,293	✓
Beach and Yacht Club Resorts	✓	✓	1,197	✓
Beach Club Villas	✓		354	✓
BoardWalk Inn	✓	✓	372	✓
BoardWalk Villas	✓		532	✓
Caribbean Beach Resort			2,112	
Contemporary Resort	✓	✓	1,008	✓
Coronado Springs Resort	✓		1,967	
Dolphin	✓	✓	1,466	✓
Fort Wilderness Homes			408	
Grand Floridian Beach Resort	✓	✓	867	✓
Old Key West Resort	✓		761	
Polynesian Resort	✓	✓	847	✓
Pop Century Resort			2,880	
Port Orleans Resort			3,056	
Saratoga Springs	✓		840	
Shades of Green		✓	587	✓
Swan		✓	758	✓
Wilderness Lodge and Villas	✓		909	✓
Yacht and Beach Club Resorts	✓	✓	1,197	✓

Yacht and Beach Club Resorts, and Swan and Dolphin, for example, offer concierge floors.

For sunning and swimming, the Contemporary, Polynesian, Wilderness Lodge and Villas, and Grand Floridian offer both pools and white-sand beaches on Bay Lake or Seven Seas Lagoon. The Caribbean Beach Resort also provides both pools and beaches. Though lacking a lakefront beach, Saratoga Springs, Animal Kingdom Lodge, Yacht and Beach Club, Port Orleans, and Coronado Springs resorts and the BoardWalk Inn and Villas have exceptionally creative pools. Here's how we ranked and rated swimming facilities at each Disney resort:

Fitness Center	Water Sports	Marina	Beach	Tennis	Biking
✓					
✓	✓	✓	✓	✓	
✓	✓	✓	✓	✓	
✓		✓		✓	✓
✓		✓		✓	✓
	✓	✓	✓		✓
✓	✓	✓	✓	✓	
✓	✓	✓			✓
✓	✓	✓	✓	✓	
	✓	✓	✓	✓	✓
✓		✓	✓	✓	
✓	✓	✓		✓	✓
	✓	✓	✓		
	✓	✓			✓
✓	✓	✓		✓	✓
✓				✓	
✓		✓	✓	✓	
✓	✓	✓	✓		✓
✓	✓	✓	✓	✓	

Hotel	Pool Rating
1. Yacht and Beach Club Resorts (shared complex)	★★★★★
2. Port Orleans	★★★★½
3. Saratoga Springs	★★★★½
4. Wilderness Lodge and Villas	★★★★½
5. Animal Kingdom Lodge	★★★★
6. Coronado Springs Resort	★★★★
7. Polynesian Resort	★★★★
8. BoardWalk Inn and Villas	★★★½
9. Contemporary Resort	★★★½
10. Dolphin	★★★½

Hotel	Pool Rating (continued)
11. Grand Floridian Resort	★★★½
12. Swan	★★★½
13. All-Star Resorts	★★★
14. Caribbean Beach Resort	★★★
15. Fort Wilderness Resort and Campground	★★★
16. Old Key West Resort	★★★
17. Pop Century Resort	★★★
18. Shades of Green	★★½

Bay Lake and the Seven Seas Lagoon are the best venues for boating. Resorts fronting these lakes are the Contemporary, Polynesian, Wilderness Lodge and Villas, Grand Floridian, and Fort Wilderness Resort and Campground. Though on smaller bodies of water, Caribbean Beach, Old Key West, Port Orleans, Coronado Springs, Saratoga Springs, and Yacht and Beach Club resorts also rent watercraft.

Most convenient for golf are Shades of Green, Saratoga Springs, Old Key West, Contemporary, Polynesian, Grand Floridian, and Port Orleans. Tennis is available at all deluxe and home-away-from-home resorts, as well as at Swan and Dolphin. Disney resorts with fitness and weight-training facilities are rated and ranked as follows (resorts not listed don't have such facilities):

Hotel	Fitness Center Rating
1. Saratoga Springs	★★★★★
2. Grand Floridian Resort and Spa	★★★★½
3. Animal Kingdom Lodge	★★★★
4. BoardWalk Inn and Villas	★★★★
5. Yacht and Beach Club Resorts (shared facility)	★★★★
6. Contemporary Resort	★★★½
7. Coronado Springs Resort	★★★½
8. Wilderness Lodge and Villas	★★★½
9. Dolphin Resort	★★★
10. Swan Resort	★★★
11. Old Key West Resort	★½

While there are many places to bike or jog at Disney World (including golf-cart paths), the best biking and jogging are at Fort Wilderness Resort and Campground and the adjacent Wilderness Lodge and Villas. Caribbean Beach Resort offers a lovely hiking, biking, and jogging trail around the lake. Also good for biking and jogging is the area along Bonnet Creek extending through Port Orleans and Old Key West toward

Downtown Disney. Epcot resorts offer a lakefront promenade and bike path, as well as a roadside walkway suitable for jogging.

On-site childcare programs are offered at Grand Floridian, Animal Kingdom Lodge, Yacht and Beach Club, Polynesian, Wilderness Lodge and Villas, and BoardWalk Inn and Villas. All other resorts offer in-room baby-sitting (options detailed on page 287).

8. Nightlife   The boardwalk at BoardWalk Inn and Villas has an upscale dance club (that has never lived up to its potential), a club with dueling pianos and sing-alongs, a brew pub, and a sports bar. BoardWalk clubs are within easy walking distance of all Epcot resorts. Most non-Disney hotels in Downtown Disney Resort Area are within walking distance of Downtown Disney nightspots. Nightlife at other Disney resorts is limited to lounges that stay open late. The best are Mizner's Lounge at the Grand Floridian, Kimono's at Swan, and the California Grill Lounge on the 15th floor of the Contemporary Resort. At the California Grill Lounge, you can relax over dinner and watch the fireworks at the nearby Magic Kingdom.

9. Reader Reports   Many readers share with us their experiences and criticisms regarding Disney hotels. Some copy us on letters of complaint sent to Disney. If you wrote or copied us about a bad experience, you might be surprised that we did not quote your letter. Any business can have a bad day, even a Disney hotel, and a single incident might not be indicative of the hotel's general level of quality and service. In our experience, if a problem is endemic, the same complaint will usually surface in a number of letters. But even with our voluminous mail, reader comments often paint a mixed picture. For example, for every letter critical of Disney's Grand Floridian, it's not unusual to receive another letter telling us it's the best place the reader ever stayed.

We tend to hear more often from readers when things go badly than when everything is fine. Whether your experience was positive or negative, we encourage you to share it with us. The more comments we receive, the more accurate and complete a picture we can provide.

Readers' 2004 Disney Resort Report Card

Each year, several thousand readers mail or e-mail us their responses to the survey at the end of the guide. The "Report Card" below documents their opinion of the respective Disney resorts, as well as of Swan, Dolphin, and Shades of Green. Room Quality reflects their level of satisfaction with their room. Value indicates how the hotel stacks up in value for the dollar. Check-in Efficiency grade rates the speed and efficiency of check-in. Quietness of Room measures how well their room is insulated from external noise. The Shuttle Service grade rates Disney bus, boat, and/or monorail service at their hotel. Pool Facilities reflects reader satisfaction with the pool(s). The Overall Rating represents an average of all five grades. The new Pop Century and Saratoga Springs resorts had only been open a few months when we went to press, so their scores may reflect problems characteristic of any resort in its first year of operation. Or, expressed differently, cut them some slack.

Readers were pretty tough on the resorts, especially in grading room quality. In this category, readers generally rate the rooms lower than do the *Unofficial Guide* hotel inspectors. In assessing this difference, remember that readers are rating one guest room during a specific visit, while the *Unofficial Guide* inspectors provide a comparative rating of more than 200 Disney and non-Disney hotels in and around Walt Disney World. For *Unofficial Guide* hotel ratings, see "How the Hotels Compare" on pages 210–233.

READERS' DISNEY RESORT REPORT CARD

Resort	Room Quality	Value	Check-in Efficiency	Quietness of Room	Shuttle Service	Pool Facilities	Overall Rating
All-Star Movies	B	A	B	B	B	B	B
All-Star Music	C	C	C	C	C	B	C
All-Star Sports	B	A	B	B	B	B	B
Animal Kingdom Lodge	B	B	C	C	C	A	B–
Beach Club	B	B	A	A	A	A	A–
Beach Club Villas	B	B	A	C	A	C	B
BoardWalk Inn	B	D	B	B	C	B	B
BoardWalk Villas	B	C	B	B	B	B	B
Caribbean Beach Resort	B	B	C	B	C	A	B
Contemporary	C	D	C	B	C	C	C
Coronado Springs Resort	B	B	A	B	A	B	B+
Dolphin	B	C	B	B	A	A	B
Grand Floridian	A	C	B	A	B	A	B+
Old Key West	A	A	B	A	B	B	A
Polynesian	B	C	B	A	B	A	B
Pop Century	B	B	B	B	B	B	B
Port Orleans	B	B	B	B	B	A	B
Shades of Green	A	A	B	A	C	B	B+
Saratoga Springs	B	B	B	A	C	B	B
Swan	A	B	B	A	B	B	B+
Wilderness Lodge	A	B	B	A	B	A	B+
Yacht Club	A	C	A	A	B	A	B+

Walt Disney World Hotel Profiles

For those of you who plowed though the forgoing and remain undecided, here are our profiles of each Disney resort. For both exterior and interior photos of the Walt Disney World resorts, check out **www.allearsnet.com/acc/gallery.htm.**

The Magic Kingdom Resorts

Disney's Grand Floridian Resort andSpa

Disney World's flagship hotel is inspired by Florida's grand Victorian sea-side resorts at the turn of the last century. A complex of four- and five-story white frame buildings, the Grand Floridian integrates verandas, intricate latticework, dormers, and turrets beneath a red shingle roof to capture the most memorable elements of nineteenth-century ocean-resort architecture. A five-story domed lobby encircled by enameled balustrades and overhung by crystal chandeliers establishes the resort's understated opulence. Covering 40 acres along the Seven Seas Lagoon, the Grand Floridian offers lovely pools, white-sand beaches, and a multifaceted marina.

The 867 guest rooms, while luxurious with wood trim and beachy pastel soft goods, are warm and inviting without being stuffy or overly feminine. Armoires, marble-topped sinks, and ceiling fans amplify the Victorian theme. The typical room is 440 square feet (dormer rooms are smaller), large by any standard, and furnished with two queen beds, a daybed, a reading chair, and a table with two side chairs. Many rooms have a balcony.

With a high ratio of staff to guests, service is outstanding. The resort has several full-service restaurants, and others are a short monorail ride away. The hotel is connected directly to the Magic Kingdom by monorail and to other Disney World destinations by bus. Walking time to the monorail and bus loading areas from the most remote guest rooms is about seven to ten minutes.

GRAND FLORIDIAN BEACH RESORT

Strengths	Weaknesses
Beautiful guest rooms	Distant guest self-parking
Outstanding public areas	Inadequate capacity of self-park lot
On Magic Kingdom monorail	
Restaurant selection via monorail	
Excellent lounge	
Recreational options	
Fitness center and spa	
Childcare facility on site	

Good Rooms and Not-So-Good Rooms at the Grand Floridian The resort is spread over a peninsula jutting into Seven Seas Lagoon. In addition to the main building, there are five dispersed, rectangular buildings also hosting guests. Most rooms have a balcony, and most balconies are enclosed by a rail that affords good visibility. Rooms just beneath the roof in each building (dormer rooms) have smaller, inset, solidly enclosed balconies that limit visibility when you're seated. Most dormer rooms, however, have vaulted ceilings and a coziness that compensates for the less-desirable balconies.

If you want to be near the bus and monorail stations, most of the restaurants, and shopping, ask for a room in the main building. The best rooms are 4322 to 4329 and 4422 to 4429, which have full balconies and overlook the lagoon in the direction of the beach and the Polynesian Resort. Other excellent main-building rooms are 4401 to 4409, with full balconies overlooking the marina and an unobstructed view of Cinderella Castle across the lagoon.

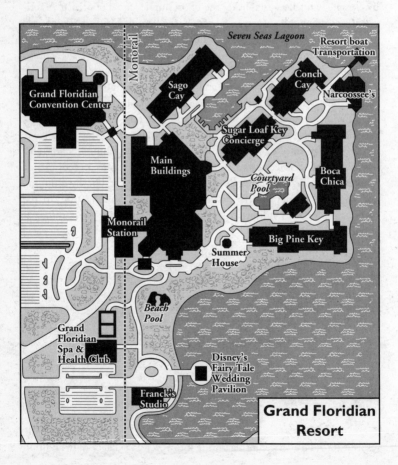

Grand Floridian Resort

Of the five lodges, three (Conch Key, Boca Chica, and Big Pine Key) have one long side facing the lagoon and the other facing inner courtyards and swimming pools. At Conch Key, full-balcony rooms 7228 to 7231, 7328 to 7331, and 7425 to 7431 offer vistas across the lagoon to the Magic Kingdom and castle. Less expensive rooms in the same building that offer good views are 72-, 73-, 74-11, 13, 15, 17, 19, 21, and 72-, 73-, 74-12 and 14. (Grand Floridian room numbers are coded. Take Room 7213: 7 is the building number, 2 is the floor, and 13 is the room number.) In Boca Chita and Big Pine Key, ask for a lagoon view room on the first, second, or third floor. Many garden-view rooms in Big Pine Key, and a few in Boca Chica, have views obstructed by a poolside building. These are the worst views from any Grand Floridian room.

The two remaining buildings, Sugar Loaf Key and Sago Cay, face each other across the marina. The opposite side of Sugar Loaf Key faces a courtyard, while the other side of Sago Cay faces a finger of the lagoon and a forested area. All of these views are pleasant but not in the same league as those from rooms listed above. Exceptions are end rooms in Sago Cay (rooms 5139, 5144, 5145, 5242 to 5245, 5342 to 5345) that have a view of the lagoon and Cinderella Castle.

Disney's Polynesian Resort

South Pacific tropics are recreated at this deluxe resort. The Polynesian consists of 11 two- and three-story Hawaiian "longhouses" situated around the four-story "Great Ceremonial House." Buildings at the Polynesian feature wood tones, with exposed-beam roofs and tribal-inspired geometric inlays in the cornices. The Great Ceremonial House contains restaurants, shops, and a rain-forest atrium lobby with a rocky waterfall and over 70 species of tropical plants. Spread across many acres along Seven Seas Lagoon, the resort has a white-sand beach with volleyball courts. Its pool complex was completely redesigned in 2001.

Many of the Polynesian's 847 guest rooms offer lagoon views, and many have balconies. Typical rooms measure 391 square feet. While rooms are smaller than most Disney deluxe rooms, they're quite comfortable. Each contains two queen-size beds, a daybed, an armoire, and a table and chairs. Batik-design bedspreads and curtains and bamboo furniture continue the island theme and are visually interesting. Bathrooms are somewhat small, although well designed.

A problem unique to the Polynesian is the proximity of the Walt Disney World Speedway. A number of guests have written complaining about the noise of roaring racecars while they were trying to nap. Rooms with parking-lot views are most likely to be affected.

Service at the Polynesian is excellent. There are two full-service restaurants, and others in the Magic Kingdom are accessed easily via monorail.

The Polynesian has a monorail station on site and is within easy walking distance of the Transportation and Ticket Center. Bus service is available to other Disney destinations. Walking time to the bus and monorail loading areas from the most remote rooms is 8–11 minutes.

POLYNESIAN RESORT

Strengths	Weaknesses
On Magic Kingdom monorail	Inadequate on-site dining
Adjacent to Epcot monorail	Confusing layout
Restaurant selection via monorail	Noise from nearby motor speedway
Recreational options	No fitness center
Childcare facility on site	
Exotic theme	
Swimming complex	
Easily accessible self-parking	

Good Rooms and Not-So-Good Rooms at the Polynesian Resort   The Polynesian's 11 guest-room buildings, called "longhouses," are spread over a long strip of land bordered by the monorail on one side and Seven Seas Lagoon on the other. Though periodically refurbished, all of the buildings, except the more recently added Tahiti, Rapa Nui, Tonga, and Tokelau, were part of the original hotel, which opened with the Magic Kingdom in 1971. All buildings offer first-floor patios and third-floor balconies. The older buildings have fake balconies on their second floors, and vegetation obstructs views from a goodly number of first-floor patios. Thus, if you stay in one of the seven older longhouses, ask for a third-floor room. The newer buildings offer full balconies on the second and third floors and patios on the first.

Most restaurants and shops, as well as the resort lobby, guest services, and bus and monorail stations, are in the Great Ceremonial House. Unfortunately, longhouses most convenient to the Great Ceremonial House (Fiji, Tonga, Rarotonga, Niue, and Samoa) offer views of the swimming complex, a small marina, or inner gardens. There are no lagoon views except for oblique views from the upper floors of Fiji and Samoa, and a tunnel view from Tonga. Samoa, however, by virtue of its proximity to the main swimming complex is a good choice for families who plan to spend time at the pool. If your children are under eight, request a first-floor room on the Nanea Volcano Pool side of Samoa. If your children are older, rooms 2915 to 2918 and 3015 to 3018 offer good, though slightly oblique, views of the lagoon from full balconies.

For an unobstructed lagoon view, request lagoon-side rooms on the second or third floor in Tahiti, the first or third floor in Hawaii, or the third floor in Tuvalu. Landscaping is superb, so garden-view rooms are generally a cut above garden- or standard-view rooms at other resorts.

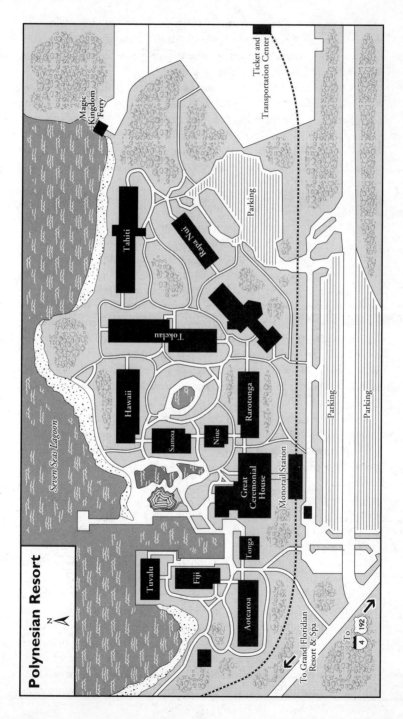

Polynesian Resort

N

Seven Seas Lagoon

Magic Kingdom Ferry

Ticket and Transportation Center

Parking

Tahiti

Rapa Nui

Tokelau

Hawaii

Rarotonga

Samoa

Niue

Great Ceremonial House

Monorail Station

Parking

Parking

Tuvalu

Fiji

Tonga

Aotearoa

To Grand Floridian Resort & Spa

To 4 192

Aside from second-floor rooms in the older buildings (with fake balconies), also avoid the monorail-side rooms in Rarotonga and Rapa Nui. Garden-view rooms in Aotearoa are especially nice, but the monorail, though quiet, runs within spitting distance.

If you plan to spend a lot of time at Epcot, Tahiti and Rapa Nui are within easy walking distance of the Ticket and Transportation Center (TTC) and the Epcot monorail. Even if you're going to the Magic Kingdom, it's a shorter walk to the TTC and Magic Kingdom monorail from Tahiti and Rapa Nui than to the monorail station at the Great Ceremonial House. Conversely, Tahiti and Rapa Nui are the most distant accommodations from the Polynesian's bus stop.

Disney's Wilderness Lodge and Villas

This deluxe resort is inspired by national-park lodges of the early twentieth century. The Wilderness Lodge and Villas ranks with Animal Kingdom Lodge as the most impressively themed and meticulously detailed Disney resorts. On Bay Lake, the lodge features an eight-story central building flanked by two seven-story guest-room wings and a new wing of studio and one- and two-bedroom condominiums. The hotel features exposed timber columns, log cabin–style façades, and dormer windows. The grounds are landscaped with evergreen pines and pampas grass. The lobby boasts an 87-foot-tall stone fireplace and two 55-foot Pacific Northwest totem poles. Timber pillars, giant tepee chandeliers, and stone, wood, and marble-inlaid floors reflect the resort's rustic luxury. Although the resort isn't on vast acreage, it does have a beach and a delightful pool modeled on a mountain stream complete with waterfall and geyser.

The lodge's 909 guest rooms have darkly stained mission-style furniture accented by primary colors in the décor. The Native American–patterned bedspreads, animal-motif armoires, and faux-calfskin fixtures create a sort of log cabin coziness. At 344 square feet each, average rooms at the lodge are the World's smallest deluxe rooms. Typical rooms have two queen-size beds, and some have one queen bed and bunk beds. All rooms have a table and chairs, and a vanity outside the bathroom. Most rooms have balconies.

Part of the Disney Vacation Club time-share program, Wilderness Villas are studio and one- and two-bedroom units in a freestanding building to the right of the lodge. Studios offer kitchenettes; one- and two- bedroom villas come with full kitchens. The lodge's rustic décor extends to the villas, which can be booked by non–Vacation Club members as space allows. The villas share restaurants, pools, and other amenities with Wilderness Lodge.

Service at Wilderness Lodge and Villas is excellent. There are two full-service restaurants, with several more a boat ride away. The resort is connected to the Magic Kingdom by boat and to other Disney parks by bus. Walking time to bus and boat loading areas from the most remote rooms is about five to eight minutes.

WILDERNESS LODGE AND VILLAS

Strengths	Weaknesses
Magnificently rendered theme	Boat service only to Magic Kingdom
Good on-site dining	No direct bus to many destinations
Great views from guest rooms	
Interesting architecture	
Extensive recreational options	
Romantic setting	
Swimming complex	
Health and fitness center	
Childcare facility on site	
Convenient self-parking	

Good Rooms and Not-So-Good Rooms at Wilderness Lodge   The lodge is shaped like a very blocky V. The main entrance and lobby are at the closed end of the V. Next are middle wings that connect the lobby to the parallel end sections, which extend to the open part of the V. The V's open end flanks pools and gardens and overlooks Bay Lake directly or obliquely. The better rooms are on floors four, five, and six toward the V's open end. On the very end of the V, odd- and even-numbered rooms 4000 to 4003, 4166 to 4169, 5000 to 5003, 5166 to 5169, 6000 to 6003, and 6166 to 6169 offer a direct frontal view of the lake. Toward the end of the V on the parallel wings, but facing inward, odd-numbered rooms 4005 to 4023, 4147 to 4165, 5005 to 5023, 5147 to 5165, 6005 to 6023, and 6147 to 6165 face the courtyard, but with excellent oblique lake views. Even-numbered rooms 5004 to 5030 and 6004 to 6030 front a woods northwest of the lodge, and beyond the woods, the Magic Kingdom. Rooms on the sixth floor (6604 to 6030) have a particularly good view of Magic Kingdom fireworks. Odd-numbered rooms 5035 to 5041, 5123 to 29, 6035 to 6041, and 6123 to 6129, on the lake end of the parallel middle wings, offer a direct but distant view of the lake, with pools and gardens in the foreground. Rooms looking southeast face the Wilderness Villas, a garden area, and woods. The map suggests that these rooms offer a lake view, but the woods block the line of sight.

There are only a handful of rooms at the lodge that overlook parking lots, service areas, and such. The rooms listed above afford the most desirable views, but if you can't score one of them, you're pretty much assured of a woods view or a room fronting the faux rocks and creek in the V's inner courtyard. Concierge rooms on the seventh floor aren't

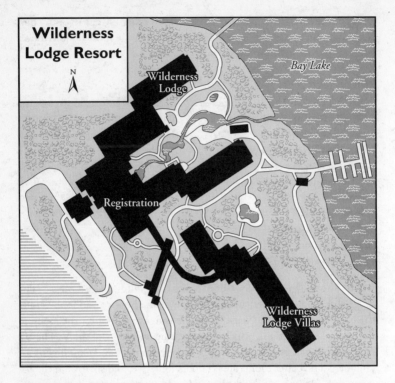

Wilderness Lodge Resort

N

Wilderness Lodge

Bay Lake

Registration

Wilderness Lodge Villas

recommended. Only those facing the Magic Kingdom have nice views, and even those have a service area in the foreground. Almost all rooms at the lodge have balconies.

Except for a few rooms overlooking the pool, rooms at Wilderness Villas offer woods views. The best are odd-numbered rooms 2531 to 2563 and 3531 to 3563, which open to the northeast, or lake side of the resort (though you can't see the lake). Rooms on the opposite side of the same wing offer similar views, but with some roads and parking lots visible, and with traffic noise.

Disney's Contemporary Resort

This deluxe resort on Bay Lake is the least themed of the Disney-owned properties. The Contemporary is unique in its A-frame design that permits the Magic Kingdom monorail to pass through the structure's cavernous atrium. The only real source of color in the atrium is a 90-foot mosaic depicting Native American children and nature. The off-white A-frame tower is flanked by two three-story "garden" buildings. Landscaping at the Contemporary is a little bizarre, with trees and shrubs trimmed like overgrown poodles. The Contemporary offers a marina and a white-sand beach, and its 6,500-square-foot swimming pool is the largest at any Disney World resort.

Rooms in the tower enjoy fantastic views of Bay Lake or the Magic Kingdom, and all have balconies. At 394 square feet each, they're only slightly smaller than those at the Grand Floridian. All rooms are tasteful, albeit somewhat dull, with simple lines and neutral colors. We think the Contemporary is a bit cold, and the angular lines of furnishings make the ambiance somewhat sterile. Most rooms have two queen-size beds, a daybed, and a table and chair.

The Contemporary's pool has slides and waterfalls. The resort has two full-service restaurants (including the well-known California Grill), a buffet, and a counter-service restaurant. There are six shops. The resort is within easy walking distance of the Magic Kingdom, and monorail transportation is available to both the Magic Kingdom and Epcot. Other destinations can be accessed by bus or boat. Walking time to transportation loading areas from the most remote rooms is six to nine minutes.

CONTEMPORARY RESORT

Strengths	Weaknesses
On Magic Kingdom monorail	Sterility of theme and décor
Ten-minute walk to Magic Kingdom	
Interesting architecture	
Great views from guest rooms	
Good on-site dining	
Best lounge at Walt Disney World	
Restaurant selection via monorail	
Recreational options	
Swimming complex	
Childcare facility on site	
Health and fitness center	

Good Rooms and Not-So-Good Rooms at the Contemporary Resort
There are three guest-room buildings at the Contemporary: the A-frame tower, and the North and South Garden buildings. Rooms in the A-frame overlook either Bay Lake and the marina and swimming complex on one side, or the parking lot with Seven Seas Lagoon and the Magic Kingdom in the background on the other. All guest rooms have a balcony furnished with two chairs and a table. If you stay on the Magic Kingdom side, ask for a room on the ninth floor or higher. The parking lot and connecting roads are less distracting (and noisy) there. On the Bay Lake side, the view is fine from all floors, though higher floors are preferable.

In the garden buildings, all ground-floor rooms have patios. Only end rooms on the second and third floors of the buildings nearest Bay Lake have full balconies. All other rooms have balconies only a foot deep—fine for standing at the rail, but not wide enough to sit outdoors. Both garden buildings are a fair walk from the restaurants, shops, front desk,

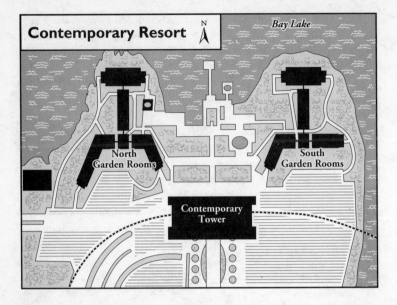

guest services, and monorail station in the A-frame. This isolation, how-ever, is a plus when it comes to the scenery and peaceful tranquillity offered by some guest rooms.

In general, the North Garden building is more serene and offers better views than the South Garden building does. In the North building, rooms 8108 to 8124, 8208 to 8224, and 8308 to 8324 are so close to the lake that you could cast a fishing line from your patio. The view is of the lake's quietest part, with just a slip of a sand beach graced by stately cypress trees between you and the water. The same view can be enjoyed from rooms 7129 to 7139, 7229 to 7251, and 7329 to 7351, though from a bit farther across a lawn. These rooms, particularly those on the first floor, provide the best views for the dollar at any Disney resort.

There's a lot of boat traffic in the lake and canal alongside the South Garden building. Nearest the lake and quietest are rooms 6116 to 6123, 6216 to 6223, and 6316 to 6323. At water's edge but noisier are rooms 6107 to 6115, 6207 to 6215, and 6307 to 6315. Flanking the canal con-necting Bay Lake and Seven Seas Lagoon are rooms 5128 to 5143, 5228 to 5251, and 5328 to 5351. All of these have nice canal and lake views, but they're subjected to a lot of noise from passing watercraft.

Both buildings have rooms facing the marina, pool, and playground; that works well for families with young children. The view isn't compara-ble to views from the rooms previously listed, but ground-floor rooms 7101 to 7126 in the North building, and 5110 to 5125 in the South pro-vide easy access to the pool.

In addition to offering some of the most scenic and tranquil guest rooms in Disney World, the North and South Garden buildings likewise contain some of the most undesirable rooms. In the North building, avoid any room with a number ending with 58 through 88. In the South, avoid room numbers ending with 52 through 70. Almost all of these rooms look directly onto a parking lot.

Shades of Green

This deluxe resort is owned and operated by the U.S. Armed Forces and is available only to U.S. military personnel (including the National Guard, reserves, retired military, Public Health Service, and Department of Defense). Shades of Green consists of one three-story building nestled among three golf courses. Tastefully nondescript, Shades of Green is at the same time pure peace and quiet. There's no beach or lake, but there are several pools, including one shaped like Mickey's head. The resort is open only to the military, but surrounding golf courses are open to all Disney guests.

At 455 square feet each, the 587 guest rooms at Shades of Green are larger than those at the Grand Floridian. They're luxuriously decorated in an English-countryside theme, with light-oak furniture, dust ruffles, and soft colors. Most rooms have two queen-size beds, a daybed, and a table and four chairs, as well as a television in an armoire. All rooms have a patio or balcony.

According to a serviceman from Fort Worth, Texas, Shades of Green is the way to go:

Shades of Green is the best-kept secret in Disney. It is actually a [military] resort in the Disney complex with all the benefits of being a Disney resort. It was a great deal, and military members usually look for the best deals. When my wife and I stayed there in May, we paid $58 a night [rates now start at $72]. That is not per person. That was the total price. . . . The rooms were huge. It had two double beds and a lot of room to spare. They also had VCRs in the rooms and a movie-vending machine on the second floor. Shades of Green is right across the street from the Polynesian Resort. It is about a 10–15 minute walk to the Ticket and Transportation Center. The hotel does have shuttle buses that take you to the TTC (about a two-minute ride). Our overall stay at Shades of Green was wonderful.

Even though the resort isn't operated by Disney, service is comparable to that at deluxe Disney properties. Transportation to all theme parks is by bus, with a transfer required to almost all destinations. Walking time to the bus loading area from the most remote rooms is about five minutes. The resort is immensely popular; make reservations seven months in advance.

SHADES OF GREEN

Strengths	Weaknesses
Large, beautiful guest rooms	Limited on-site dining
Informality	Limited bus service
Quiet setting	
Views of golf course from guest rooms	
Convenient self-parking	

Shades of Green completed a major expansion in 2004. The project added 299 guest rooms, 10 suites, a multilevel parking structure, an Italian restaurant, and a new family-style restaurant. You don't have to worry much about bad rooms at Shades of Green. Except for a small percentage that overlook the entrance road and parking lot, most offer views of the golf courses that surround the hotel, or the swimming area. When you book your reservation, make your preference known. Shades of Green has its own Web site at **www.shadesofgreen.org.**

The Epcot Resorts

The Epcot Resorts are arrayed around Crescent Lake between Epcot and the Disney-MGM Studios (but closer to Epcot). Both theme parks are accessible by boat and on foot. No Epcot resort offers transportation to Epcot's main entrance. As a Greenville, South Carolina, mom reports, this can be a problem:

I would like to point out one inconvenience of staying in the Epcot-area resorts. The only transportation to Epcot is by boat or foot. There is no bus available to take you to the front gates of Epcot. We had to walk through the International Gateway and all the way to the front of Epcot to ride Future World attractions. And if we finished Epcot at the end of the day near the front entrance, the only way back home was a long hike through Future World and the International Gateway.

Disney's Yacht and Beach Club Resorts and Villas

These adjoined five-story deluxe resorts are similarly themed. Both have clapboard facades with whitewashed-wood trim. The Yacht Club is painted a subdued gray, while the Beach Club is painted a brighter blue. The Yacht Club has a nautical theme with model ships and antique navigational instruments in public areas. The Beach Club is embellished with beach scenes in foam green and white. Both resorts have themed lobbies, with a giant globe in the Yacht Club's and sea-horse fixtures in the Beach Club's. The resorts face 25-acre Crescent Lake and share an elaborate swimming complex.

There are 621 guest rooms at the Yacht Club, 576 at the Beach Club, and 354 studio and one- and two-bedroom villas at the Beach Club

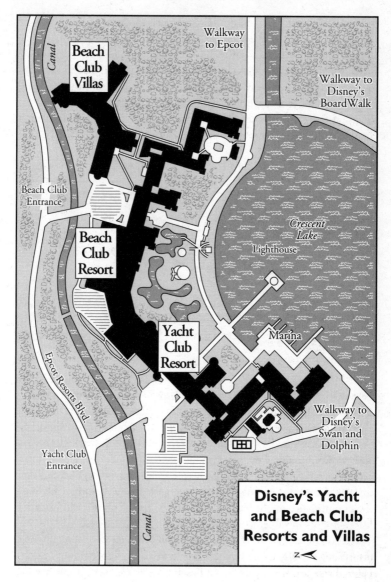

Beach
Club
Villas

Walkway
to Epcot

Canal

Walkway to
Disney's
BoardWalk

Beach Club
Entrance

Beach
Club
Resort

Crescent
Lake

Lighthouse

Yacht
Club
Resort

Marina

Epcot Resorts Blvd.

Walkway to
Disney's
Swan and
Dolphin

Yacht Club
Entrance

Canal

**Disney's Yacht
and Beach Club
Resorts and Villas**

z

Villas, part of the Disney Vacation Club time-share program. Most of the
hotel rooms are 381 square feet and have two queen-size beds, a daybed,
and a table and two chairs. Like the Grand Floridian's, rooms have a lot
of drawer space. Yacht Club rooms are decorated in navy blue and white;
Beach Club's offer soft green tones. Some rooms have balconies.

The Beach Club Villas evoke seaside Victorian cottages. Studio accommodations offer kitchenettes; one- and two-bedroom villas have a full

kitchen. Subject to availability, villas are open to the public as well as to Vacation Club (time-share) members. The villas share restaurants, pools, and other amenities with the Yacht and Beach Club resorts.

As deluxe Disney resorts, the Yacht and Beach Clubs provide excellent service. They offer nine restaurants and lounges and are within walking distance of Epcot and Disney's BoardWalk. Transportation to other destinations is by bus or boat. Walking time to the transportation loading areas from the most remote rooms is seven minutes.

YACHT AND BEACH CLUB RESORTS AND VILLAS

Strengths	Weaknesses
Attractive guest rooms	No transportation to Epcot main
Good on-site dining	entrance
Selection of nearby off-site dining	Distant guest self-parking
Ten-minute walk to Epcot	
Ten-minute walk to BoardWalk nightlife	
Swimming complex	
Health and fitness center	
View from waterside guest rooms	
Childcare facility on site	
Nautical/New England theme	

Although the Yacht and Beach Club resorts are arrayed along Crescent Lake opposite Disney's BoardWalk, a relatively small percentage of guest rooms actually overlook the lake. Many additional rooms have an oblique view of the lake but face a courtyard or garden. To complicate matters, the resorts don't differentiate between a room with a lake view and one overlooking a swimming pool, pond, or canal. All are considered water views. We receive letters each year from readers complaining that their "water view" was a distant, sidelong peek at a swimming pool. Such disappointments might explain why many readers grade the resorts a mediocre "C" in value.

The Beach Club consists of a long main building with several wings protruding toward Crescent Lake. Looking at the resort from Crescent Lake, the Beach Club adjoins the Yacht on the left and spreads toward Epcot on the right. The main building and the various wings range from three to five stories. Most rooms have balconies, or on the ground floor, patios. Balconies are either big enough for a couple of chairs, or about six inches deep (stand at the rail or sit in a chair inside the room). Top-floor rooms often have enclosed balconies inset into the roof. Unless you're standing, visibility is somewhat limited from these dormer balconies.

Good Rooms and Not-So-Good Rooms at the Beach Club Resorts   The Beach Club's better views are from rooms with full balconies, and from those that overlook the lake. Other good rooms include those facing woods, with Epcot in the background. The latter are the resort's quietest, most peaceful rooms, in terms of both noise and scenery. They're also nearest to Epcot's International Gateway entrance if you're walking, but farthest from the resort's main pool area, lobby, and restaurants. Of the remaining rooms, most face courtyards, with some of these providing oblique views of the lake, and others overlooking parking lots and the resort's front entrance.

Here are our recommendations for good Beach Club rooms. All room numbers are four digits, with the first digit specifying the floor and the remaining three digits the room number.

Water-view Rooms with Full Balconies Facing the Lake Odd-numbered rooms: 2641 to 2647, 3501 to 3511, 3683 to 3691, 3725 to 3795, 5607 to 5623, 5683 to 5691, 5725 to 5795. (The Beach Club will charge you for a water-view room if there's so much as a birdbath in sight. If you're going to pay the price, get a real water view.)

Standard-view Rooms with Full Balconies Facing the Woods and Epcot Even-numbered rooms 3512 to 3536, 4578 to 4598.

Good Rooms and Not-So-Good Rooms at the Yacht Club Resort Looking at the Yacht Club from Crescent Lake, the resort is connected to the Beach Club on the right and angles toward the Dolphin hotel on the left. All Yacht Club rooms offer full balconies or, on the ground floor, patios. Rooms with the best views are as follows (the higher the last three digits in the room number, the closer to lobby, main pool area, and restaurants):

Rooms with Full Balconies Directly Facing the Lake with Disney's BoardWalk in the Background Odd-numbered rooms 2003 to 2009, 3003 to 3009, 3057 to 3065, 3161 to 3163, 3201 to 3209, 4057 to 4065, 4161 to 4163, 4201 to 4209, 5161 to 5163, 5201 to 5209.

Rooms Directly Facing the Lake with Epcot in the Background Odd-numbered rooms 2011 to 2025, 2067 to 2081, 3011 to 3025, 3067 to 3081, 4067 to 4081, 5067 to 5081.

Some other rooms face the BoardWalk or Epcot across Crescent Lake, but they're inferior to the rooms listed above.

Avoid standard-view rooms at either resort except for rooms 3512 to 3536 and 4578 to 4598 at the Beach Club, which overlook a dense pine thicket. In addition to offering a nice vista for a standard-view rate, these are the closest rooms to Epcot available at any resort on Crescent Lake.

Disney's Beach Club Villas

The Beach Club Villas is a Disney Vacation Club (time-share) property supposedly inspired by the grand Atlantic seaside homes of the early twentieth century. We'll bet the villas don't resemble any seaside home you ever saw. Thematically, there's little we can discern to differentiate the Beach Club Villas from the Yacht and Beach Club resorts, or from the parts of the BoardWalk Inn and Villas that don't front the BoardWalk.

Configured roughly in the shape of a fat Y, or slingshot, the Beach Club Villas are away from the lake adjoining the front of the Beach Club Resort. Arrayed in connected four- and five-story taffy-blue buildings topped with cupolas, the villas are festooned with white woodwork and slat-railed balconies. It's clean, breezy, and evocative, though we're not certain of what. Accommodations include studios, with a kitchenette, one queen bed and a sofa sleeper, and one- and two-bedroom villas with full kitchens. The rooms are a bit small but attractively furnished in pastels with New England-style summer-home furniture. Patterned carpets and seashore-themed art complete the package.

We don't like the Beach Villas as well as the Wilderness Lodge Villas (more visually interesting) or the villas of Old Key West (roomier, more luxurious, more private). Beach Club Villas has its own modest pool, but otherwise shares the restaurants, facilities, and transportation options of the adjoining Yacht and Beach Club resorts. The Beach Club Villas' strengths and weaknesses are identical to those of the Yacht and Beach Club resorts except that the villas offer no lake view.

Good Rooms and Not-So-Good Rooms at the Beach Club Villas   Though the studios and villas are attractive and livable, the location of the Beach Club Villas, between parking lots, roads, and canals, leaves much to be desired. Rooms facing the pool offer a limited view of a small canal but are subject to traffic noise. Ditto the rooms on the northeast side, except without the pool. Only southeast-facing rooms provide both scenic landscape (woods) and relative relief from traffic noise. The nearby road is only two-lane, and traffic noise probably won't bother you if you're indoors with the balcony door closed, but for the bucks you shell out to stay at the villas, you can find nicer, quieter accommodations elsewhere on Disney property. If you elect to stay at the Beach Club Villas, go for odd-numbered rooms 229 to 251, 329 to 351, 429 to 451, and 529 to 551.

Disney's BoardWalk Inn and BoardWalk Villas

On Crescent Lake across from the Yacht and Beach Club resorts, the BoardWalk Inn is another of the Walt Disney World deluxe resorts. The complex is a detailed replica of an early-twentieth-century Atlantic coast boardwalk. Facades of hotels, diners, and shops create an inviting and exciting waterfront skyline. In reality, the BoardWalk Inn and Villas are a single integrated structure behind the facades. Restaurants and shops occupy the boardwalk level, while accommodations rise up to six stories above. Painted bright red and yellow along with weathered pastel greens and blues, the BoardWalk resorts are the only Disney hotels that use neon signage as architectural detail. The complex shares one pool having an old-fashioned amusement-park theme. The BoardWalk Inn's 372 deluxe rooms measure 385 square feet each, and most contain two queen-size brass beds, a child's cherry daybed, a cherry table and two chairs, and ceiling fans. Décor includes blue and yellow gingham wall-paper and print curtains with a blue postcard pattern. Closet space exceeds that in other deluxe Disney rooms. Most rooms have balconies.

The 532 BoardWalk Villas are decorated in warmer tones and primary colors, with bright tiles in the kitchens and bathrooms. Villas range from 412 to 2,491 square feet (studio through three-bedroom), and sleep 4–12 people. Many villas have full kitchens, laundry rooms, and whirlpool bathtubs. The villas tend to be more expensive than similar accommodations at other Disney resorts—you pay for the address.

The inn and villas are well staffed and offer excellent service. They also are home to some of Disney World's finest restaurants and shops. The complex is within walking distance of Epcot and is connected to other destinations by bus and boat. Walking time to transportation loading areas from the most remote rooms is five to six minutes.

BOARDWALK INN AND VILLAS

Strengths	Weaknesses
Attractive guest rooms	No transportation to Epcot main
Ten-minute walk to Epcot	entrance
Swimming complex	No restaurants in hotel
Health and fitness center	Distant guest self-parking
Three-minute walk to BoardWalk nightlife	
Selection of off-site dining within walking distance	
View from waterside guest rooms	
Childcare facility on site	
Nautical/New England theme	

Good Rooms and Not-So-Good Rooms at the BoardWalk Inn and Villas   The complex consists of several wings radiating from the lobby complex, roughly in the shape of a giant H. Crescent Lake and the Prom-enade (pedestrian boardwalk) are to the north, the entrance is to the south, and the canal that runs to Disney-MGM Studios is to the west. At the BoardWalk, the "water" part of "water view" can mean Crescent Lake, the canal, or a small pool. There are two concierge floors for those want-ing extra service.

Most rooms at the inn and villas have a balcony or patio, though bal-conies on the standard upper-floor rooms alternate between large and medium. The BoardWalk Inn and Villas each share about half the frontage on the Promenade, which overlooks Crescent Lake. The Prome-nade's clubs, stores, and attractions are spread about equally between the two sections, leading to similar levels of noise and commotion. However, the inn side is closer to Epcot and the nearby access road; this provides better views of Epcot fireworks and easier access to that park, but it also means more road noise.

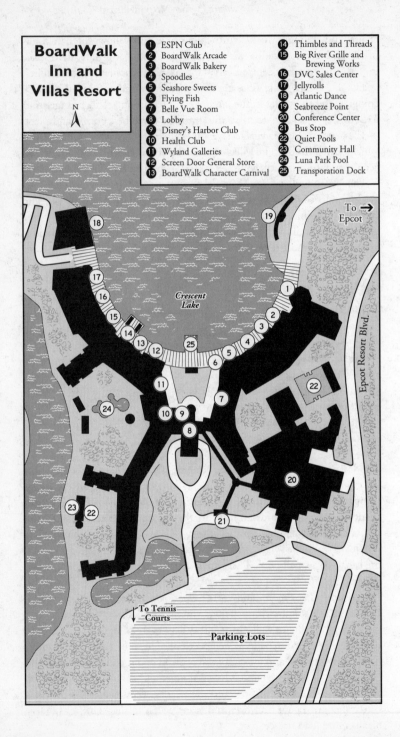

BoardWalk Inn and Villas Resort

N

1. ESPN Club
2. BoardWalk Arcade
3. BoardWalk Bakery
4. Spoodles
5. Seashore Sweets
6. Flying Fish
7. Belle Vue Room
8. Lobby
9. Disney's Harbor Club
10. Health Club
11. Wyland Galleries
12. Screen Door General Store
13. BoardWalk Character Carnival
14. Thimbles and Threads
15. Big River Grille and Brewing Works
16. DVC Sales Center
17. Jellyrolls
18. Atlantic Dance
19. Seabreeze Point
20. Conference Center
21. Bus Stop
22. Quiet Pools
23. Community Hall
24. Luna Park Pool
25. Transporation Dock

To Epcot

Crescent Lake

Epcot Resort Blvd.

To Tennis Courts

Parking Lots

Otherwise, the inn is actually less noisy than the more expensive villas; there's one tranquil, enclosed courtyard, and another half-enclosed area with a quiet pool (where BoardWalk's Garden Suites are located). There are many rooms to avoid at the inn, starting with rooms overlooking access roads and parking lots, and rooms looking down on the unattractive roof of the adjacent conference center. And although the aforementioned quiet rooms face courtyards, the views are pretty are ho-hum. When you get right down to it, the only rooms with decent views are those fronting the Promenade and lake, specifically odd-numbered rooms 3213 to 3255 and 4213 to 4255. As for the others, you're more likely to get a better view at the far less expensive Port Orleans, Caribbean Beach, or Coronado Springs resorts.

The villas are somewhat better. Most overlook a canal to the west with the Swan resort with its access road and parking lots on the far side. Worse are the rooms that front BoardWalk's entrance and car lots. As at the inn, the villas offer only a handful of rooms with good views. Odd-numbered rooms 3001 to 3033, 3001 to 4033, and 5001 to 5033 afford dynamic views of the Promenade and Crescent Lake, with Epcot in the background. They're a little noisy if you open your balcony door, but otherwise offer a glimpse of one of Disney World's more happening places. Unless you bag one of these rooms, however, you'll spend a bundle for a very average (or worse) view.

Promenade-facing villa rooms have noise issues identical to their inn counterparts. The midsection of the canal-facing villas look out on Luna Park Pool, a carnival-themed family-pool complex that gets extremely noisy during the day. Some of the quieter villas are away from the Promenade with views of the canal and a partially enclosed quiet pool. Noise is practically nonexistent; the only downside is that the rooms are relatively distant from the Promenade and Epcot. Rooms on the opposite side of this wing are almost as quiet, but they face BoardWalk's parking lot and thus are less desirable.

The Swan and Dolphin Resorts

Although these resorts are inside the World and Disney handles their reservations, they're owned by Sheraton (Dolphin) and Westin (Swan). The resorts face each other on either side of an inlet of Crescent Lake. Dolphin is a 27-story triangular turquoise building. On its roof are two 56-foot-tall fish balanced with their tails in the air. Swan has a 12-story main building flanked by two seven-story towers. Two 47-foot-tall swans adorn its roof, staring incredulously at the fish across the way. Swan and Dolphin have been described as "bizarre" and stylistically disjointed. At the very least, they're eclectic in their theming. Disney says you'll step into a "fantasy world." We think the experience is more akin to art deco

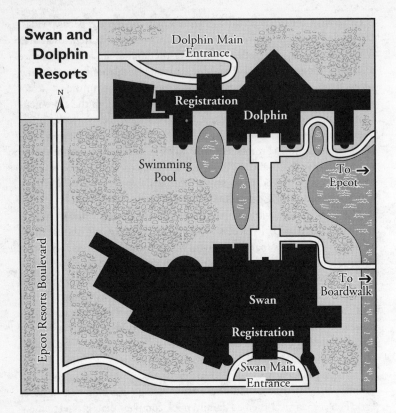

gone haywire. The giant swans look swanlike, but Dolphin's fish are more like catfish from outer space. The atmosphere at these properties could be described as adventurous or confusing, depending on how much you value the work of a good interior decorator.

Dolphin's restyled lobby is the more ornate, featuring a rotunda with spoke-like corridors branching off to shops, restaurants, and other public areas. At the other end of the spectrum, the Swan's lobby is so small that it seems an afterthought. Both resorts feature art of wildly different styles and eras (from Matisse to Roy Lichtenstein). Each resort has its own pool. Dolphin's "Grotto" is shaped like a seashell and has a waterfall, while Swan's pool is a conventional rectangle.

Dolphin's rooms underwent a complete redesign in 2004, deep-sixing most of the garish décor that characterized (some say branded) its rooms for years. The new design incorporates light-colored woods, floral earth-tone carpeting, and pastel-blue draperies. Plush "Heavenly" beds are buttressed by oversized wood headboards adorned with abstract murals. A sleek, contemporary combination dresser/desk and a reading chair complete the furnishings. Some rooms have balconies.

Swan's guest rooms were redecorated in 2003. The once eye-poppingly bold colors have given way to restful earth-tone pastels and handsome Scandinavian-modern blond bedsteads and dressers. The new rooms have great light for reading, in or out of bed. A huge, round mirror framed in blond wood hangs above the dresser. The bath is small for a Disney World hotel but elegantly appointed.

Since Swan and Dolphin aren't run by Disney, the service at these resorts is less sugar-coated than at other Disney resorts. Swan and Dolphin collectively house more than a dozen restaurants and lounges and are within easy walking distance of Epcot and the BoardWalk. The resorts are connected to other destinations by bus and boat. Walking time from the most remote rooms to the transportation loading areas is seven to nine minutes.

SWAN AND DOLPHIN RESORTS

Strengths	Weaknesses
Exotic architecture	No transportation to Epcot main
Good on-site and nearby dining	entrance
Health and fitness center	Distant guest self-parking
View from guest rooms	Confusing layout
Ten-minute walk to BoardWalk nightlife	

Good Rooms and Not-So-Good Rooms at Swan and Dolphin These sprawling hotels are configured very differently, and their irregular shapes mean it's easier to discuss groups of rooms in relation to exterior landmarks and compass directions rather than by room numbers. When speaking with a Disney reservationist, use our tips to ask for a particular view or area.

Swan Swan's prime views are from its east-facing rooms, particularly in the upper half of the eight-story wing above the Palio restaurant. From this vantage point, guests overlook a canal and the BoardWalk, with Epcot in the distance. *IllumiNations* fireworks enliven the view nightly. Balcony rooms are available on floors five, six, and seven. However, rooms in the wing nearest the hotel's main section have the southern portion of their view obscured by the building's easternmost portion, which juts east beyond the eight-story wing. There are some east-facing rooms on that portion of the main section, sans balconies. Lofty palm trees obscure the view from east-facing rooms below the fourth floor. The best rooms with an Epcot view are 626AQ and 726AQ.

North-facing rooms afford views of Dolphin and (generally) of the courtyard. Exceptions are the north-facing rooms on the easternmost portion of the main section, which look across Crescent Terrace to the BoardWalk. These afford angled views of Epcot and are buffered by palms on the lowest three floors. The few north-facing rooms at the end of the Swan's two eight-story wings directly overlook Crescent Lake.

However, the bulk of north-facing rooms are in the main section and overlook the courtyard, with greenery, fountains, and an indoor café in its center. Courtyard-facing rooms are subject to noise from below, though never much.

Above the eighth floor, north-facing rooms in the main section overlook roofs of the shorter wings. In these rooms, height enhances the vista from your window, but only near the center of the hotel is the view not seriously marred by rooftops below.

North-facing main-section rooms have a more direct view of Dolphin across the lake than the courtyard-facing rooms in either eight-story wing. However, most wing rooms can view the lake at an angle. Those on the northern edge of the western wing also view the BoardWalk at an angle.

Most courtyard-facing rooms have balconies; 224 rooms are so equipped, and these balconies offer panoramic 180-degree views. Of course, from most rooms at Swan, part of any 180-degree view will include another section of the hotel.

Swan's worst views are from west-facing rooms above the fourth floor, which overlook the unsightly roof of the hotel's western wing. The northernmost rooms in the wing directly above Kimonos restaurant are an exception to this, as their balconies overlook the pool and the beach on Crescent Lake's western shore. Good pool-view rooms are rooms 680–691.

Above Swan's main entrance, south-facing rooms overlook the parking lot, with forest and Disney-MGM Studios in the distance. However, the canal is also visible to the east. These rooms lack balconies.

Dolphin   Consisting of a central A-frame with large wings jutting off each side and four smaller arms extending from the rear of the building, Dolphin is attached to a large conference center, which means that the majority of guests are ostensibly there on business. Many vacation amenities found at true Disney properties are absent (such as extensive playgrounds) or available in limited supply (Dolphin has only one pool). All parks are accessible from a shuttle stop or a boat dock between Dolphin and Swan.

If you want a room with easy access to shopping, dining, and transport to and from the parks, almost any Dolphin room will do. The shuttle (outside the main entrance) and boat dock are equidistant from the main front and rear exits. Restaurants and shopping are primarily on the first and third floors. If you also would also like a view of something other than parking-lot asphalt, your choices narrow considerably. Rooms in Dolphin with pleasant views are in the four arms on the rear of the building. Rooms on all the arms sport balconies from the first through fourth floors, then offer balconies or windows alternatively on floors five through nine.

One of Dolphin's best views overlooks the Grotto pool on the far west side of the building. A man-made beach with a small waterfall is visible from rooms at the very end of the large west wing. None of these rooms has a balcony, but that might be a blessing, since the pool comes with canned tiki music and a bar. A better bet would be to ask for a room on the far west side of the first rear arm. These outer rooms have balconies and are more removed from the pool. Rooms on the inner, west part of that arm overlook a bladderwort-encrusted reflecting pool; these aren't recommended. Nor are the facing rooms on the next arm.

Between the second and third arms looms the monstrous Dolphin fountain, and the better choices here are on the top two floors. There, from arm two you can see the BoardWalk (including any nighttime fireworks), and from arm three the Grotto pool. Otherwise, you may find you have a view of massive, green-concrete fish scales. The noise from the water is loud, and the fountain geysers, continuously. Depending upon your personality, this is either soothing or maddening.

Arm three and arm four are situated around a reflecting pool. A concern for rooms in this area is that the ferry toots its horn every time it approaches and departs the dock. Its path runs right by these rooms, and the horn blows just as it passes. The first time that happens, it's quaint. By the 117th, your hair will be coming out in clumps.

The Crescent Lake side of arm four, and the small jut of the large Dolphin wing perpendicular to it, offer arguably the best views. You have an unobstructed view of the lake and Epcot fireworks, a fine BoardWalk view for people-watching, and, from higher floors, a view of the beach at Beach Club. There's ferry noise, but these rooms still have the most going for them. The best of the best in this arm are rooms 8015, 7015, 5015, 4015, and 3015. Balcony rooms at Dolphin generally run $30 a day more than rooms without balconies.

Disney's Caribbean Beach Resort

The Caribbean Beach Resort occupies 200 acres surrounding a 45-acre lake called Barefoot Bay. This mid-price resort, modeled after resorts in the Caribbean, consists of the registration area ("Custom House") and five two-story "villages" named after Caribbean islands. Each village has its own pool, laundry room, and beach. The Caribbean motif is maintained with red-tile roofs, widow's walks, and wooden railed porches. The atmosphere is cheerful, with buildings painted blue, lime green, and sherbet orange. In addition to the five village pools, the resort's main swimming pool is themed as an old Spanish fort, complete with slides and water cannons.

Most of the 2,112 guest rooms are 314 square feet and contain two double beds and a table and two chairs. Some are decorated with bright tropical colors, while others are decorated with neutral beach tones. All rooms are suited with the same light-oak furniture. Rooms don't have balconies, though the access passageways are external and have railings. Many guests bring a yard chair and use the external passageway as a balcony.

One of the most centrally located resorts, the Caribbean Beach offers transportation to all Disney World destinations by bus. Though it has one full-service restaurant and a food court, food service is woefully inadequate for a resort of this size. Because food service is limited and it's immensely time-consuming to commute to other resorts by Disney bus, guests at the Caribbean Beach should seriously consider having a car. Walking time to the bus loading area from the most remote rooms is seven to ten minutes.

CARIBBEAN BEACH RESORT

Strengths	Weaknesses
Attractive Caribbean theme	Guest rooms
Children's play areas	On-site dining
Convenient self-parking	No easily accessible off-site dining
Walking, jogging, biking around the lake	Extreme distance of many guest rooms from dining and services
	Large, confusing layout
	Poor bus service

Good Rooms and Not-So-Good Rooms at the Caribbean Beach Resort   The resort's grounds are quite pleasant. Landscaping—lots of ferns and palm trees—is verdant, especially in the courtyards. The six "islands" or groups of buildings clustered around Barefoot Bay are identical. The motel-style, two-story structures are arranged in various ways to face courtyards, pools, the bay, and so forth. The setup is similar to Disney's Coronado Springs Resort in nearly every way but theme.

In general, corner rooms at Caribbean Beach Resort are preferable since they have more windows. Standard-view rooms face either the parking lots or courtyards, and the usual broad interpretation of water views is in play here. Beyond that, your main choices will revolve around your preference for proximity to (or distance from) the Custom House, pools, parking lots, or beaches on Barefoot Bay. Each island has direct access to at least one beach, playground, bus stop, and parking lot.

The island of Barbados is nearest the Custom House, but its central location guarantees that it also experiences the most foot traffic and road noise. It also shares its only beach and playground with Martinique, which probably is the best area for families. (Martinique has access to two beaches, is adjacent to the main pool and playground at the Old Port Royale Town Centre, and yet is removed enough from the Custom House to offer a little serenity for parents.) The islands of Aruba and Jamaica are similar in character to Martinique, but each has only one beach, and guests must cross a footbridge to reach Old Port Royale center. Trinidad North comprises three buildings, and its thin

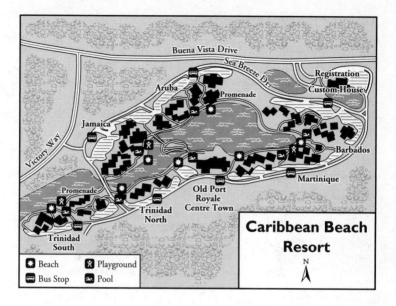

layout means that noise penetrates its courtyard from surrounding roads and from rambunctious kids at Old Port Royale next door. The quietest island is Trinidad South, which is most remote from resort facilities. It has its own playground and beach, and the beach has a bonus—the view across Barefoot Bay is of wild, undeveloped Florida forest, a rarity on a Disney property.

After you've sorted out your convenience and location priorities, think about the view. Avoid standard-view rooms; all look onto a parking lot, road, or tiny, claustrophobic garden. Water views at the Caribbean overlook swimming pools or Barefoot Bay. Pool views are less than enchanting, and there's lots of noise and activity around the pools. Bay views are the pick of the litter at the Caribbean. Such rooms in Barbados, Martinique, Trinidad North, and Trinidad South catch the afternoon sun. Bay-view rooms in Aruba and Jamaica catch the morning sun. Because we like the sun at our back in the evening, we always go for rooms 4245 to 4252 in Jamaica or rooms 5253 to 5264 and 5541 to 5548 in Aruba. If you don't mind the sun in your eyes during cocktail time, rooms 2245 to 2256 and 2413 to 2416 in Martinique, 1246 to 1248 in Barbados, and all lake-facing second-story rooms in buildings 35, 38, and 39 in Trinidad South are good bets. We're not crazy about any room in Trinidad North. Be aware that the aging air-conditioning units for individual buildings at the resort are pretty loud. One of our favorite bay-view rooms (2525 in Martinique) isn't recommended because of its proximity to a clunky air-conditioner.

The Bonnet Creek Resorts

Saratoga Springs Resort

Replacing the defunct Disney Institute, the theme at Saratoga Springs recalls an "1880s, Victorian, upstate New York lakeside retreat" amid "pastoral landscapes, formal gardens, bubbling springs, and natural surrounds." Ain't that a mouthful! How does Disney come up with this stuff? And what is a "natural surround"?

A Disney Vacation Club property, the resort offers 840 studio and one-, two-, and three-bedroom villas across the lake from Downtown Disney. Housed in 12 buildings, most accommodations are new constructions, though the existing fitness center, check-in building, and spa have been retained and rethemed. The fitness center is by far the best in Walt Disney World, and the spa was named one of the top five destination spas in North America and the Caribbean by readers of *Condé Nast Traveler* magazine. Saratoga Springs is surrounded on three sides by golf courses. It is the only Disney-owned resort that affords direct access to the links (the military-only Shades of Green also provides golf on property).

The main pool is the resort's focal point. Called High Rock Springs, it tumbles over boulders into a clear, free-form, heated pool. The area offers a water slide that winds among the rocks, two whirlpool spas, and an interactive children's wet play area. Two quiet pools serve villas far from the main pool. Other recreational features include tennis courts, playgrounds, and paths for jogging, walking, and biking. Disney buses provide transportation to the theme parks. Downtown Disney is accessible by boat, or from some accommodations by foot.

Furnishings and soft goods in the villas and studios are less whimsical, and a little more upscale and masculine, than in Disney resorts modeled on a beach theme. Chairs, sofas, and tables are quite substantial, perhaps a little too large for the rooms they inhabit. The overall effect, however, is restful and sophisticated.

SARATOGA SPRINGS

Strengths	Weaknesses
Extremely nice studio rooms and villas	No full-service restaurant on site
Lushly landscaped setting	Traffic congestion at resort's south- east entrance
Convenient self-parking	
Close to Downtown Disney	Distance of some accommodations from dining and services
Golf on property	
Best spa at Walt Disney World	Noise from Downtown Disney
Best fitness center at Walt Disney World	
Excellent themed swimming complex	
Hiking, jogging, and water recreation	

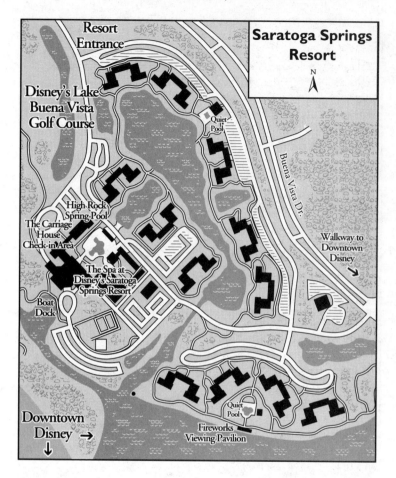

Good Rooms and Not-So-Good Rooms at Saratoga Springs   Villas near the Buena Vista Drive entrance and those situated along the north-easternmost shore of the lake are within easy walking distance of Down-town Disney shops, restaurants, and entertainment. These same villas, however, are also subject to the din of Pleasure Island, with its outdoor rock bands and late-night fireworks. If you book Saratoga Springs, ask for a water view or fairway view on the southwest side of the resort. If you want quiet as well as a nice view, ask for a water view away from Downtown Disney and closer to the spa.

Disney's Old Key West Resort

This was the first Disney Vacation Club property. Although the resort is a time-share property, units not being used by owners are rented on a nightly basis. Old Key West is a large aggregation of two- to three-story buildings

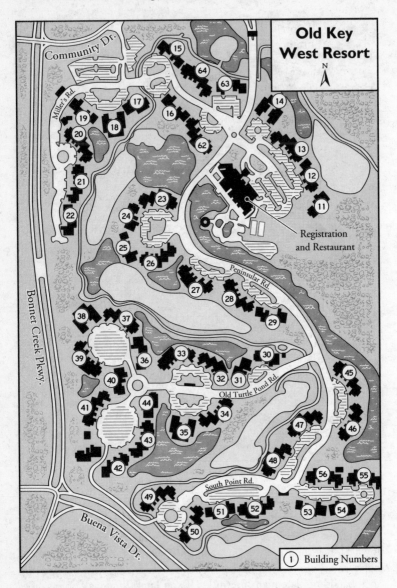

modeled after Caribbean residences and guesthouses of the Florida Keys. Arranged subdivision-style around a golf course and along Bonnet Creek, the buildings are in small neighborhood-like clusters. They feature pastel facades, white trim, and shuttered windows. The registration area is in Conch Flats Community Hall, along with a full-service restaurant, modest fitness center, marina, and sundries shop. Each cluster of accommodations has a quiet pool; a larger pool is at the community hall.

This resort offers some of the roomiest accommodations at Disney World. Studios are 376 square feet; one-bedroom villas, 942; and two-bedroom villas, 1,333. Studios contain two queen-size beds, a table and two chairs, and an extra vanity outside the bathroom. One-bedroom villas have a king-size bed in the master bedroom, a queen-size sleeper sofa in the living room, a laundry room, and a full kitchen. Two-bedroom villas include an additional bedroom with two queen-size beds. All villas have enough closet space to contain your entire wardrobe. Studios and villas are tastefully decorated with wicker and upholstered furniture, and peach and light-green color schemes. Each villa has a private balcony that opens onto a delightfully landscaped private courtyard.

As a Disney Vacation Club resort, Old Key West's service is very personal. Transportation to other Disney World destinations is by bus. Walking time to transportation loading areas from the most remote rooms is about six minutes.

OLD KEY WEST RESORT

Strengths	Weaknesses
Extremely nice studios and villas	Substandard bus service
Quiet, lushly landscaped setting	Limited on-site dining
Convenient self-parking	No easily accessible off-site dining
Old Key West theme	Large, confusing layout
	Extreme distance of many guest rooms from dining and services

Good Rooms and Not-So-Good Rooms at Old Key West Resort Old Key West is huge, with 56 three-story villa buildings. Each contains a mix of studio and multiroom villas. Views are nice from almost all villas. To enhance the view, all multiroom villas and some studios have a large balcony furnished with a table and chairs. Though nice vistas are easy to come by, quiet is more elusive. Because the resort is bordered by busy Bonnet Creek Parkway and even busier Buena Vista Drive, the best villas are those as far from the highway noise as possible. For quiet isolation and a lovely river view, ask for building 55, 46, or 45, in that order. For a lake and golf-course view away from road noise but closest to restaurants, recreation, the marina, the main swimming complex, and shopping, ask for building 13. Nearby buildings 12 and 11 are likewise quiet and convenient but offer primarily golf-course views. Next-best choices are buildings 32 and 34. Building 32 looks onto a lake with the golf course in the background, while 34 faces the golf course with tennis courts to the left and a lake to the right. None of the buildings recommended is more than a two- to five-minute walk to the nearest bus stop or pool. Avoid buildings 19–22, 38 and 39, 41 and 42, and 49–51.

Ground-floor villas make lugging in suitcases and groceries less taxing. Though the top floor requires a three-story climb, views from on high are superior. The top floor also ensures that you'll have no noisy neighbors clomping above you.

Disney's Port Orleans Resort

The Port Orleans and Dixie Landings Resorts were merged in 2001. The combined midprice resort, called Port Orleans, is divided into two sections. The smaller, southern part that previously was Port Orleans is now called the French Quarter. The larger section encompassing the former Dixie Landings is labeled Riverside.

PORT ORLEANS RESORT

Strengths	Weaknesses
Swimming areas	Insufficient on-site dining
Nice guest rooms, especially in	No easily accessible off-site dining
French Quarter	Large, confusing layout
Food courts	Extreme distance of many guest
Convenient self-parking	rooms from dining and services
Children's play areas	

Port Orleans French Quarter   The 1,008 room French Quarter section is a sanitized Disney version of the New Orleans French Quarter. Consisting of seven three-story guest-room buildings next to Bonnet Creek, the resort suggests what New Orleans would look like if its buildings were painted every year and garbage collectors never went on strike. There are prim pink-and-blue guest buildings with wrought-iron filigree, shuttered windows, and old-fashioned iron lampposts. In keeping with the Crescent City theme, the French Quarter is landscaped with magnolia trees and overgrown vines. The centrally located "Mint" contains the registration area and food court, and is a reproduction of a turn-of-the-nineteenth-century building where Mississippi Delta farmers sold their harvests. The registration desk features a vibrant Mardi Gras mural and old-fashioned bank-teller windows. The section's "Doubloon Lagoon" surrounds a colorful fiberglass creation depicting Neptune riding a sea serpent.

French Quarter rooms measure 314 square feet. Most contain two double beds, a table and two chairs, a dresser/credenza, and a vanity outside the bathroom. All guest rooms were refurbished from bow to stern in 2004, resulting in the most attractive and tasteful rooms of any of the Disney moderate resorts. With their dark cherry headboards, Mardi Gras pastel bedspreads, cherry with oak inlaid credenza, and dark blue, floral carpet, we think the rooms rival those of several deluxe resorts. None of the rooms has a balcony, but ornamental, iron-railed accessways on each floor provide a good (though less private) substitute.

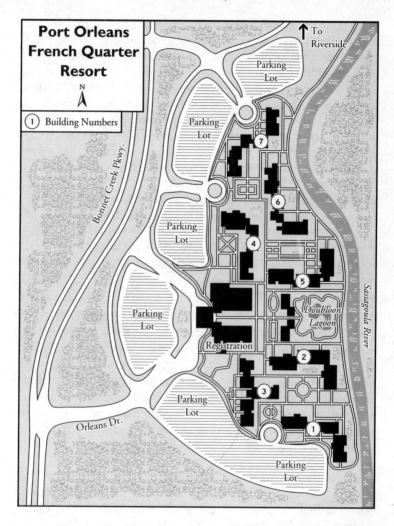

There's a food court, but no full-service restaurant. The closest full-service eatery is in the adjacent Riverside section of the resort, about a 15-plus-minute walk. The commute to restaurants in other hotels may be 40–60 minutes each way. The Disney bus system links the French Quarter to all Disney World destinations. Walking time to bus loading areas from the most remote French Quarter rooms is seven to ten minutes.

Good Rooms and Not-So-Good Rooms at the Port Orleans French Quarter Resort   Seven guest-room buildings flank the pool and guest-services building and bus stop. The best views are from rooms directly facing the river and natural pine forest on the opposite bank. Wings of buildings 1, 2, 5, 6, and 7 flank the river and provide the best river views in either the French Quarter or Riverside sections of Port Orleans. River-view rooms in buildings 1, 6, and 7 are a long walk from French Quarter public facilities, but they're the most tranquil. Families with children should request river-view rooms in buildings 2 and 5, nearest the swimming complex. Make sure the reservationist understands that you are requesting a "river-view," not a "water-view" room. All river-view rooms are also water-view rooms, but not vice versa.

Following are the best river-view rooms in each building:

Building 1 Rooms 1127 to 1132, 1227 to 1232, 1327 to 1332

Building 2 Rooms 2127 to 2132, 2227 to 2232, 2327 to 2332

Building 5 Rooms 5117 to 5122, 5217 to 5222, 5317 to 5322

Building 6 Rooms 6123 to 6126, 6223 to 6226, 6323 to 6326, 6133 to 6140, 6233 to 6240, 6333 to 6340, 6141 to 6148, 6241 to 6248, 6341 to 6348

Building 7 Rooms 7141 to 7148, 7241 to 7248, 7341 to 7348

Standard-view rooms look onto a courtyard or a parking lot. Although there are no private balconies, you can bring a lawn chair and sit on the exterior accessway. You'll have to make way for fellow guests coming and going to their rooms, but most of the time you'll be undisturbed.

Port Orleans Riverside   Riverside draws on the lifestyle and architecture of Mississippi River communities in antebellum Louisiana. Spread along Bonnet Creek, which encircles "Ol' Man Island" (the section's main swimming area), Riverside is subdivided into two more themed areas: the "mansion" area, which features plantation-style architecture, and the "bayou" area, with tin-roofed rustic (imitation) wooden buildings. Mansions are three stories tall, while bayou guesthouses are a story shorter. The river-life theme is augmented by groves of azalea and juniper. Riverside's food court houses a working cotton press powered by a 32-foot waterwheel.

Each of Riverside's 2,048 rooms measures 314 square feet. Most provide two double beds, a table and two chairs, and two pedestal sinks outside the bathroom. Some rooms also contain a child's trundle bed. Rooms in the Alligator Bayou section of Riverside feature brass bathroom fixtures, hickory-branch bedposts, and quilted bedspreads. Rooms in the plantation-themed Magnolia Bend section of Riverside are more conventional with light yellow walls, dark wood furnishings, and teal carpets with dark blue floral patterns. Room refurbishment is underway throughout Riverside, but the look will be substantially the same as before.

Riverside has one full-service restaurant and a food court. The restaurant is a 15-minute walk from many of the guest buildings. The Disney bus system links the resort to all Disney World destinations. The commute to restaurants in other hotels may be 40–60 minutes each way. Walking time from the most remote rooms to the transportation loading areas is ten minutes.

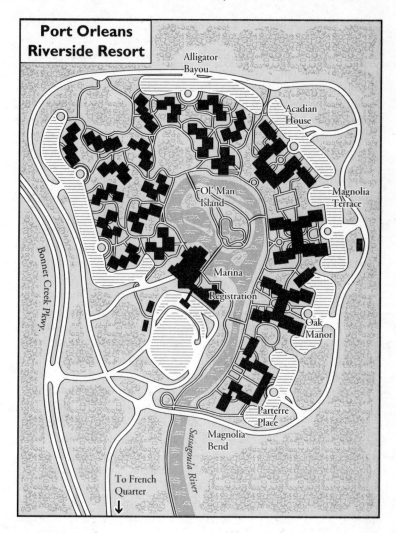

Port Orleans Riverside Resort

Alligator Bayou

Acadian House

Magnolia Terrace

Ol' Man Island

Bonnet Creek Pkwy.

Marina

Registration

Oak Manor

Parterre Place

Magnolia Bend

Sassagoula River

To French Quarter

Good Rooms and Not-So-Good Rooms at the Port Orleans Riverside Resort Riverside is so large that we use bicycles whenever we work there. All told, there are 20 guest-room buildings (not counting flanking wings on two buildings). Divided into two sections, Alligator Bayou and Magnolia Bend, the resort is arrayed around two pine groves and a watercourse that Disney calls the Sassagoula River. Magnolia Bend consists of four three-story, grand plantation–style complexes named Acadian House, Magnolia Terrace, Oak Manor, and Parterre Place. Though on the river, only about 15% of the guest rooms have an unobstructed view of the water. The vast majority of rooms overlook a courtyard or parking lot. Trees and other vegetation block the view of many rooms actually facing the river. The best views in Magnolia Bend are from the third-floor river side of Acadian House (building 80), which overlooks the river and Ol' Man Island.

To the south are Magnolia Terrace (building 85) and Oak Manor (building 90), each an H shape. In them, only second- and third-floor rooms on the very top of the H (facing the river) have an unobstructed water view. Ask for rooms 9416, 9417, 9039, 9042, and 9239 to 9242. Both H-shape buildings, however, are nearer the front desk, restaurant, lounge, and shopping complex than is Acadian House. Continuing south, Panterre Place (building 95) has a number of rooms overlooking the river, but they also overlook the parking lot on the far shore. Generally, with the few exceptions described above, if you really want a nice river view, opt for Port Orleans French Quarter downriver.

Alligator Bayou, the other part of Port Orleans Riverside, forms an arch around the resort's northern half. Sixteen smaller, two-story guest-room buildings, set among pine groves and abundant gardens, offer a cozy, tranquil alternative to the more-imposing structures of the Magnolia Bend section of Riverside and Port Orleans French Quarter. If you want a river view, ask for a second-story water-view room in buildings 27 or 38. Building 14 also offers some river-view rooms, and it's quite convenient to shops, front desk, and restaurant, but it's in a noisy, high-traffic area. A good compromise building for families is building 18. It's insulated from traffic and noise by landscaping, yet is next to a satellite swimming pool and within an easy walk of the guest-services building.

Disney's Port Orleans Riverside map shows two lakes north of the river bend, suggesting additional water views in Alligator Bayou. But these are dried-up lakes now forested with pine. This area, however, is richly land-scaped to complement the "pine islands," and though out of sight of water, it offers the most peaceful and serene accommodations in the Port Orleans resort. In this area, we recommend buildings 26, 25, and 39, in that order. Note that these buildings are somewhat distant from the resort's central facilities, and there's is no adjacent parking. In Alligator Bayou, avoid buildings 15, 16, 17, and 24, all of which are subject to traffic noise from nearby Bonnet Creek Parkway.

Remember: All Port Orleans guest buildings have exterior corridors. When you look out your window, a safety rail will be in the foreground, and other guests will periodically walk past.

The Animal Kingdom Resorts

Animal Kingdom Lodge

The Animal Kingdom Lodge, in the far southwest corner of the World and a short distance from Animal Kingdom theme park, opened in April 2001. Designed by Peter Dominick of Disney's Wilderness Lodge fame,

Animal Kingdom Lodge fuses African tribal architecture with the exotic, rugged style of grand East African national park lodges. Five-story, thatched-roof guest-room wings fan out from a vast central rotunda housing the lobby and featuring a huge mud fireplace. Public areas and about half of the guest rooms offer panoramic views of a private 33-acre plain punctuated with streams and elevated kopje (rock outcroppings) and populated with 200 free-roaming animals and 130 birds. Most of the 1,293 guest rooms are 344 square feet and boast hand-carved furnishings and richly colored soft goods. Almost all have full balconies.

Billed as a deluxe property, the lodge offers fine dining in a casual setting at Jiko. Twin wood-burning ovens are the focal point of the restaurant, which serves primarily light, simple meals. Boma, the family restaurant, is an African version of the Whispering Canyon eatery at Wilderness Lodge and Villas. Boma serves a buffet with food prepared in an exhibition kitchen featuring a wood-burning grill and rotisserie. Tables are under thatched roofs. Mara, a quick-service restaurant with extended hours, and Victoria Falls, a delightful mezzanine lounge overlooking Boma, round out the lodge's food and beverage service. Other amenities include an elaborate swimming area and a village marketplace.

The lodge is connected to the rest of Disney World by bus, but because of the lodge's remote location, you should seriously consider having a car if you stay there.

ANIMAL KINGDOM LODGE

Strengths	Weakness
Exotic theme	Remote location
Uniquely appointed guest rooms	
Views from guest rooms	
Swimming area	
On-site dining	
Health and fitness center	
Childcare center on site	
Recreational options	

Good Rooms and Not-So-Good Rooms at Animal Kingdom Lodge   A glance at the resort map will tell you where the best rooms are. Two wings branching from the rear of the main lodge, respectively called Kudu Trail and Zebra Trail, form a half-circle around the central wildlife savanna. On each wing are seven five-story buildings with guest rooms on floors two through five. Five buildings on each wing form the semicircle, while the remaining two jut away from the center. The best rooms are on floors three and four, facing into the circle. These rooms are high enough to survey the entire savanna, but low enough to let you appreciate the ground-level detail of this amazing wildlife exhibit. Second-floor rooms

really can't take in the panorama, and fifth-floor rooms are a little too high for intimate views of the animals. For the best wildlife viewing plus easy access to the main lodge, book a third- or fourth-floor, interior-facing room in the third building from the end of either trail.

Most rooms in the outward-jutting buildings, as well as rooms facing away from the interior, also survey a savanna, but one not as compelling as that of the inner circle. On the Zebra Trail, the first two buildings plus the first jutting building provide savanna views on one side and look onto the swimming complex on the other.

Less attractive still are two smaller wings, Ostrich Trail and Giraffe Trail, branching from either side of the lodge near the main entrance. Some rooms in Ostrich Trail, on the left, overlook a small savanna. Rooms on the opposite side of the same buildings overlook the front entrance. Least desirable is Giraffe Trail, extending from the right side of the lobby. Rooms in this wing overlook either the pool (water view) or the resort entrance (standard view).

Disney's Coronado Springs Resort

Coronado Springs Resort, near the Animal Kingdom, is Disney's only midprice convention property. Inspired by northern Mexico and the

American Southwest, the resort is divided into three separately themed areas. The two- and three-story Ranchos call to mind Southwestern cattle ranches, while the two- and three-story Cabanas are modeled after Mexican beach resorts. The multistoried Casitas embody elements of Spanish architecture found in Mexico's great cities. The lobby, part of Casitas, features a mosaic ceiling and tiled floor. The vast resort surrounds a 15-acre lake, and there are three small pools as well as one large swimming complex. The main pool features a reproduction of a Mayan steppe pyramid with a waterfall cascading down its side.

Most of the resort's 1,967 guest rooms measure 314 square feet and contain two double beds, a table and chairs, and a vanity outside the bathroom. Rooms are decorated with sunset colors and feature hand-painted Mexican wall hangings. All have coffeemakers. No room has its own balcony.

Coronado Springs offers one full-service restaurant as well as Disney World's most interesting food court. Unfortunately, there's not nearly enough food service for a resort this large and remote. If you book Coronado Springs, we suggest you have a car to expand your dining options. The resort is connected to other Disney destinations by bus only. Walking time from the most remote rooms to the bus stop is eight to ten minutes.

As a convention hotel, Coronado Springs is peculiar. Unlike most convention hotels, where everything is centrally located with guest rooms in close proximity, rooms at this resort are arrayed around a huge lake. If you're assigned a room on the opposite side of the lake from the meeting area (and restaurants!) plan on an 11- to 15-minute hike every time you leave your room. If your organization books Coronado Springs for a meeting, consider having your meals catered. The hotel's restaurants simply don't have the capacity during a large convention to accommodate the breakfast rush or to serve a quick lunch between sessions.

CORONADO SPRINGS RESORT

Strengths	Weaknesses
View from waterside guest rooms	Remote location
Themed swimming area	Insufficient on-site dining
Nice guest rooms	Extreme distance of many guest
Food court	rooms from dining and
Convenient self-parking	services

Good Rooms and Not-So-Good Rooms at Coronado Springs Resort
Coronado Springs encircles a large, man-made lake called Lago Dorado. In addition to the main building (El Centro), which contains shopping venues, restaurants, and a conference center, there are three communities of accommodations, each different in appearance and layout. Moving clockwise around the lake, the Casitas are near the lobby, restaurants,

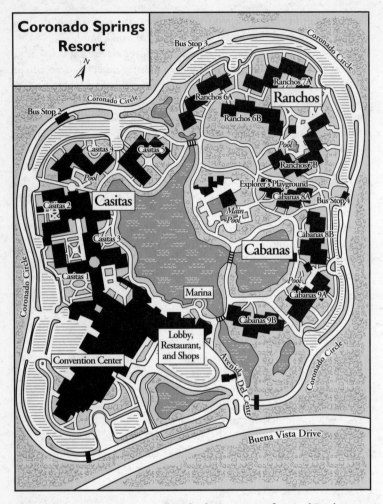

shops, and convention center. Standard-view rooms face parking lots or a courtyard. Water-view rooms cover pools, lake, birdbaths, and so on. For a good view of Lago Dorado, go for these rooms:

3220 to 3287 (except 3224, 3230, 3260, 3261, 3265 to 67, and 3274)

3320 to 3387 (except 3324, 3330, 3360, 3361, 3365 to 67, and 3374)

3420 to 3487 (except 3424, 3430, 3460, 3461, 3465 to 67, and 3474)

4230 to 4266

5200 to 5213, 5223 to 5263 (except 5250)

5300 to 5313, 5323 to 5363 (except 5350)

5400 to 5413, 5423 to 5463 (except 5450)

Next in our rotation are the Ranchos, set back from the lake. The desert theme translates to plenty of cactus and gravel, not much water or shade, and almost no good views. Though near the main swimming facility, Ranchos are a hike from everything else. Best room views are:

6103, 6203, 6303, 6225, 6226, 6325, 6326, 6245, 6246 (water views);

6600 to 6604, 6610 (water views); 6750 to 6760 (woods views)

Next are the Cabanas, which offer some very nice lake views. Cabana 9B is our favorite, near restaurants and the convention center, and only a moderate walk to the main pool. Best-view rooms are 9500 to 9507, 9600 to 9611, and 9650 to 9657 with lake views, and 4640 to 4647 and 9640 to 9647 with a view of a small lagoon. Rooms overlooking the lake are subject to some generally tolerable traffic noise.

Other lake-view rooms we recommend include:

8120, 8121, 8124 to 8126, 8128 to 8131, and 8140 to 8147

8500 to 8511, 8550 to 8553, 8571, and 8573

8600 to 8611, 8650 to 8653, 8671, and 8673

9108 to 9110, 9150 to 9153, 9170 to 9173, 9203 to 9210, 9250 to 9253, and 9270 to 9273

As at Port Orleans and the Caribbean Beach Resort, external railed walkways to guest rooms double as balconies. Because there's not a lot of traffic along them, you can pull a chair from your room onto the walkway and enjoy the view. We always bring lawn chairs expressly for "balcony" use when we stay at Coronado Springs.

Disney's All-Star Sports, All-Star Music, and All-Star Movie Resorts

Disney's version of a budget resort features three distinct themes executed in the same hyperbolic style. Spread over a vast expanse, the resorts comprise almost 35 three-story motel-style guest-room buildings. Although the three resorts are neighbors, each has its own lobby, food court, and registration area. All-Star Sports Resort features huge sports icons: bright football helmets, tennis rackets, and baseball bats, all taller than the buildings they adorn. Similarly, All-Star Music Resort features 40-foot guitars, maracas, and saxophones, while All-Star Movie Resort showcases giant popcorn boxes and icons from Disney films. Lobbies of all are loud (in both decibels and brightness) and cartoonish, with checkerboard walls and photographs of famous athletes, musicians, and film stars. There's even a photo of Mickey Mouse with Alice Cooper. The Music Resort's swimming pool is shaped like a guitar, and the Sports Resort's pool features plastic replicas of Disney characters shooting water pistols. The Movie Resort's pool is star-shaped.

At 260 square feet, guest rooms at the All-Star Resorts are very small. They're so small that a family of four attempting to stay in one room might redefine family values by week's end. Each room has two double beds, a separate vanity area, and a table and chairs. The bedspreads feature athletes, movie stars, and musicians, and the light fixtures are star-shaped. No rooms have balconies.

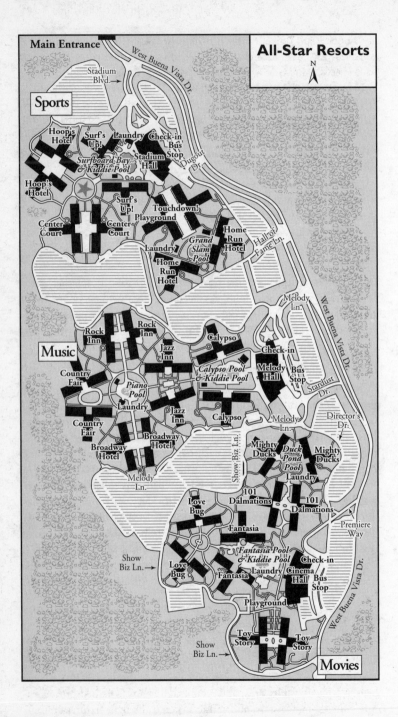

All-Star Resorts

Main Entrance

West Buena Vista Dr.

Stadium Blvd. →

Sports

Hoop's Hotel
Surf's Up!
Laundry
Check-in
Bus Stop

Surfboard Bay & Kiddie Pool

Stadium Hall

Dugout Dr.

Hoop's Hotel

Surf's Up!

Center Court

Center Court

Touchdown! Playground

Home Run Hotel

Laundry

Grand Slam Pool

Hall of Fame Ln.

Home Run Hotel

Rock Inn

Rock Inn

Melody Ln.

West Buena Vista Dr.

Music

Jazz Inn

Calypso

Check-in

Country Fair

Piano Pool

Calypso Pool & Kiddie Pool

Melody Hall

Bus Stop

Stardust Dr.

Laundry

Jazz Inn

Calypso

Melody Ln.

Director's Dr.

Country Fair

Broadway Hotel

Broadway Hotel

Mighty Ducks

Duck Pond Pool

Mighty Ducks

Melody Ln.

Show Biz Ln.

Laundry

101 Dalmations

101 Dalmations

Love Bug

Fantasia

Premiere Way

Show Biz Ln. →

Love Bug

Fantasia Pool & Kiddie Pool

Check-in

Fantasia

Laundry

Cinema Hall

Bus Stop

West Buena Vista Dr.

Playground

Show Biz Ln. →

Toy Story

Toy Story

Movies

If you're planning to save for a Disney vacation, save enough for a bigger room. Also, young children running wild makes the All-Stars the noisiest Disney resorts, though guest rooms are well soundproofed and quiet.

With a low staff-to-guests ratio, service is not the greatest. Also, there are no full-service restaurants, and the bus ride from the remote All-Stars to a full-service restaurant at another resort is about 45 minutes each way. There is, however, a McDonald's about a quarter-mile away. Bus service to the theme and water parks is pretty efficient. Walking time to the bus stop from the most remote guest rooms is about eight minutes.

We receive a lot of letters commenting on the All-Star Resorts. The following are representative:

From a family group of 13 from East Greenbush, New York:

The All-Star Resorts are perfectly family-oriented. Some nice touches that were not mentioned in your guide—a small amphitheater set up in the lobby to occupy the kids while you check in, soft sidewalk material surrounding the kiddie pool, which is only about ten inches deep. And the playground has two separate jungle gyms—one for older kids and one for younger kids.

Regardless of your personal preference, if you are going to stay at an All-Star Resort, stay at Sports. The sole reason is that the shuttle buses pick up and drop off at the All-Star Resorts in this order: Sports, Music, Movies. That little difference can mean a lot when traveling with kids or with a group.

An Orland Park, Illinois, family had a tough time with their All-Star neighbors, copying us on a letter to Disney:

I am not a person who usually complains, but I had to write and tell you how extremely disappointed I was with the accommodations we had at the All-Star Sports. I was expecting that a Disney resort would be geared toward families. Boy was I mistaken! What we mostly had staying with us were young teenagers who were extremely loud and foul mouthed. We could hardly get any rest. We had groups of people outside our room partying on the football field one night until midnight before someone finally closed them down. Then in the morning (one time as early as 6:30 a.m.) we had cheerleaders practicing right outside our door, shouting their cheers.

A Canadian family had a similar experience:

The guide did not prepare us for the large groups of students that take over the resorts. They are very noisy and very pushy when it comes to getting on buses. Our scariest experience was when we tried getting on a bus and got mobbed by about 100 students. We didn't know if our children would come out alive from the experience. We don't think we would go back to the All-Star Resort for this reason (they offer packages to student groups). Also, the motel does not want to hear your complaints at all.

But a Baltimore family had a very positive experience:

We decided early on that we'd rather spend more money on food than lodging. We love to eat, and figured that we wouldn't spend that much time in
the room, so we picked the All-Star Movies resort. We were pleasantly surprised. Yes, the rooms are small. But the overall magic there is amazing. The
lobby played Disney movies, which is perfect if you get up early and the
buses aren't running yet. There are great photo ops everywhere (Donald
and Daisy were awesome). It's heaven for fans of Fantasia 2000. Customer service was impeccable. Everyone seems to bust on the food court,
which—let's face it—is crap ... except for the refrigerator cases where you
can buy (albeit expensive) fresh-tasting fruit, water, healthy snacks, and
great chicken-salad sandwiches. Further, despite forewarnings of loud children, we were in the Love Bug building and found it very quiet. The express
checkout service was also a godsend.

From a Massachusetts family of four:

I would never recommend the All-Star for a family. It was like dormitory living.
Our room was about one mile from the bus stop, and the food court got
old very quickly. Buses were great, but the room was tiny. I'm in the hotel
business, and it was one of the smallest I've been in. You needed to step
into the bathroom, shut the door, then step around the toilet that blocked
half the tub.

And finally, a family from the United Kingdom reports:

We stayed at All-Star Sports. For younger kids the other themed hotels can be a
bit too adult—my kids don't know much about Dixie/N'Awlins (yet!), but they
loved the theme at All-Star Sports. Perhaps again it is a foreign thing, but we
all loved the over-the-top décor. Can you say something nice about it, please?

ALL-STAR RESORTS

Strengths	Weaknesses
Low (for Disney) rates	No full-service dining
Food courts	Small guest rooms
Convenient self-parking	Remote location
	Large, confusing layout

Good Rooms and Not-So-Good Rooms at the All-Star Resorts   Though
the layout of All-Star Resorts' movies, music, and sports sections are different, the buildings are identical three-story, three-winged structures. The
T-shaped buildings are further grouped into pairs, generally facing each
other, and share a common subtheme. For example, there's a *Toy Story* pair
in the movies section. In addition to being named by theme, such as *Fantasia,* buildings are numbered 1–10 in each section. Rooms are accessed via
a motel-style outdoor walkway, but each building has an elevator.

Parking is plentiful, all in sprawling lots buffering the three sections. A room near a parking lot means easier loading and unloading but also unsightly views of the lot during your stay. (The resort offers a luggage service, but it often takes up to an hour for your bags to arrive.)

The sure way to avoid a parking-lot vista is to request a room facing a courtyard or pool. The trade-off is noise. Cars starting in the parking lot are no match for shrieking children or hooting teenagers in the pool. But don't count on a good view of the pool, even if your room faces it directly. The buildings' themed façade decorations are placed on their widest face—the top of the T—which is also the side facing the pool or courtyard. In some cases, as with the surfboards in the sports section, these significantly obstruct the view from nearby rooms. Also, floodlights are trained on these facades. If you step out of your room at night to view the action below, looking down may result in temporary blindness.

The sort of traveler you are should dictate the room you request at All-Star Resorts. If you choose the resort because you'd rather spend time and money at the parks, opt to be near the bus stop your link to the rest of the World. Note that buses leave from the central public buildings of each section, which are near the larger, noisier pools. If you're planning to return to your room for an afternoon nap, request a room farther from the pools. Also consider an upper-story room to minimize foot traffic past your door. On the other hand, if you choose All-Star for its kid-friendly aspects, consider roosting near the action. A bottom-floor room provides easy pool access, and a room looking out on a courtyard or pool allows you to keep an eye on children playing outside.

For travelers without young children (infants excluded), the best bets for privacy and quiet are buildings that overlook the forest behind the resort, buildings 2–4 in All-Star Sports and 4–7 in All-Star Music. Interior-facing rooms in these buildings (and their partners) also fill the bill, since they overlook courtyards farthest from the large pools. The courtyards vary with theme but are generally only mildly amusing.

If you're traveling with children, opt for a section and building with a theme that appeals to your kids. Often, that will be a film—movies are the lifeblood of the Disney empire—but it might be a sport. If you're staying in Home Run Hotel, don't forget the ball and gloves to maximize the experience. (Just keep games of catch away from the pool.) Older elementary- and middle-school children probably will want to spend hotel time in or near the bigger pools or arcades in nearby halls. Periodically, cadres of teenagers—too cool for their younger siblings—effectively commandeer the smaller secondary pools. Playgrounds are tucked behind building 9 in All-Star Music and behind building 6 in All-Star Sports. Rooms facing these are ideal for families with children too young or timid for the often-chaotic larger pools. In All-Star Movies, the playground is nearer the food court than to any rooms.

Disney's Pop Century Resort

Located on Victory Way near Disney's Wide World of Sports, the Pop Century is the newest Disney value resort. It's to be completed in phases, but the first section, scheduled to open in December 2001, was actually opened in early 2004. The second phase, which would complete the planned 5,760 guest rooms, is still in limbo.

Pop Century is an economy resort; rooms run about $77–$126 per night. In terms of layout, architecture, and facilities, Pop Century is almost a clone of the All-Star Resorts (that is, three-story, motel-style buildings built around a central pool, food court, and registration area). Decorative touches make the difference. Where the All-Star Resorts display larger-than-life icons from sports, music, and movies, Pop Century draws its icons from decades of the twentieth century. Look for such oddities as building-size Big Wheels, Hula-Hoops, and the like, punctuated by silhouettes of people dancing the decade's fad dance.

Public areas at Pop Century are marginally more sophisticated than the All-Star Resorts, with twentieth-century period furniture and décor rolled up in a saccharine, those-were-the-days theme. Food courts, bars, playgrounds, pools, and so on emulate the All-Star Resorts model in size and location. A Pop Century departure from the All-Star precedent has merchandise retailers thrown in with the fast-food concessions in a combination dining and shopping area. This apparently is what happens when a giant corporation tries to combine selling pizza with hawking Goofy hats. You just know the word "synergy" was used like cheap cologne in those design meetings. As at the All-Star Resorts, there is no full-service restaurant. The resort is connected to the rest of Disney World by bus, but because of the limited dining options, we recommend having a car.

Guest rooms at Pop Century are small at 260 square feet. The décor is upbeat, with print bedspreads and wall art depicting pop memorabilia from decades past. Light-finish wood-inlaid furniture and dark, patterned carpet provide an upscale touch, but these are not rooms you'd want to spend a lot of time in. Bathrooms are tiny and counter space is a scarce commodity. A lake separating the resort's two halves offers water views not available at the All-Star Resorts.

POP CENTURY RESORT

Strengths	Weaknesses
Low (for Disney) rates	No full-service dining
Food courts	Small guest rooms
	Remote location
	Large, confusing layout
	Construction noise

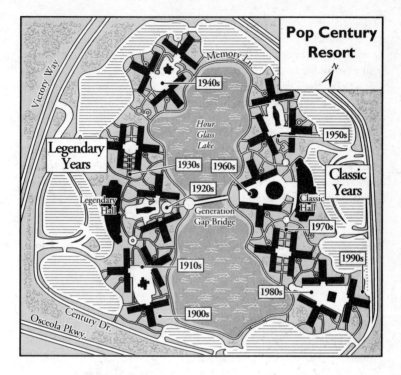

Good Rooms and Not-So-Good Rooms at the Pop Century Resort   Guest rooms don't have private patios or balconies. If you bring a lawn chair, however, you can sit on the railed walkway that serves as the guest-room access corridor on each floor. The best rooms in both view and convenience are the lake-view rooms in buildings 4 and 5, representing the 1960s. These rooms are subject to highway noise from Victory Way and Osceola Parkway across the lake. If work resumes on the other half of Pop Century, these rooms will also contend with the sights and noise of construction. A safer short-term bet, though with a less compelling view, would be east-facing rooms in the same building, that is, rooms facing the registration and food-court building. Next-best choices would be the east-facing rooms of building 3 in the 1950s, and of building 6 in the 1970s. Avoid south-facing rooms in 1980s building 7 and 1990s building 8. Both are echo chambers for noise from nearby Osceola Parkway.

Independent Hotels of the Downtown Disney Resort Area

The seven hotels of the Downtown Disney Resort Area (DDRA) were created in the days when Disney had far fewer of its own resorts. The hotels—the Holiday Inn at Walt Disney World, DoubleTree Guest Suites,

Grosvenor Resort, Hilton, Hotel Royal Plaza, Lake Buena Vista Resort, and Wyndham Palace—are chain-style hotels with minimal or nonexistent theming, though the Wyndham Palace, especially, is pretty upscale. All were hit hard by the tourism slump in recent years, and several of the larger properties shifted their focus to convention and business travelers. Now that Disney has trouble filling its own massive inventory of rooms, DDRA properties are struggling to refurbish or re-create themselves while clinging tenaciously to the Disney World connection.

The main advantage to staying in the DDRA is being in Disney World and proximal to Downtown Disney. Guests at the Hilton, Grosvenor Resort, Wyndham Palace, or Holiday Inn at Walt Disney World are an easy 5- to15-minute walk from Disney Marketplace on the east side of Downtown Disney. Guests at the Hotel Royal Plaza, Lake Buena Vista Resort, or DoubleTree Guest Suites are about ten minutes farther by foot. Disney transportation can be accessed at Downtown Disney, though the Disney buses take a notoriously long time to leave due to the number of stops throughout the shopping and entertainment complex. Although all DDRA hotels offer shuttle buses to the theme parks, the service is provided by private contractors and is somewhat inferior to Disney Transportation in frequency of service, number of buses, and hours of operation. Get firm details in advance about shuttle service from any DDRA hotel you're considering. All these hotels are easily accessible by car and are only marginally farther from the Disney parks than several of the Disney resorts (and DDRA hotels are quite close to Typhoon Lagoon water park).

All DDRA hotels try to appeal to families, even the business and meeting hotels. Some have pool complexes that rival those at any Disney resort, while others offer a food court or all-suite rooms. A few sponsor Disney character meals and organized children's activities; all have counters for buying Disney tickets, and most have Disney gift shops. In addition, we've seen some real room deals in the DDRA, especially off-season. To help you decide if the DDRA is right for you, here are descriptions. Plus, check the comparative chart (page 170).

Holiday Inn at Walt Disney World   1805 Hotel Plaza Boulevard; (407) 828-8888; **www.holidayinnwdw.com**   Fairly representative of the chain, the Holiday Inn consists of a hotel tower and one wing. The tower rooms are built around an atrium and face outward while the wing rooms overlook the pool. For quick meals and snacks, the 2GO snack bar features Pizza Hut pizza, sandwiches, and TCBY yogurt. A breakfast buffet, as well as dinner, is served in the Café and Grille. The Tipsy Parrot cocktail lounge rounds out the food and beverage offerings. Two pools (plus whirlpool and children's pool) are chain-typical, but they're large and clean. Organized children's programs aren't available, but there's a game room.

DoubleTree Guest Suites   2305 Hotel Plaza Boulevard; (407) 934-1000; **www.doubletree.com**   This giant white bunker of a hotel is the only all-suite establishment on Disney World property. The 229 suites have advantages similar to all-suite hotels everywhere, with separate bedroom and living room and minikitchen (fridge, microwave, coffeemaker). The usual recreation options prevail: medium-sized hotel pool with snack bar, kiddie pool, lighted tennis courts, and exercise room. Streamers restaurant serves American standards for breakfast, lunch, and dinner, and the attached lounge pours cocktails. Kids have their own check-in desk, plus a theater and arcade, but there are no organized children's programs.

Grosvenor Resort   1850 Hotel Plaza Boulevard; (407) 828-4444; **www.grosvenorresort.com**   The Grosvenor's 626 rooms are appointed with Holiday Inn–style décor and are comparably comfortable and clean. The hotel does offer a great roster of amenities, including character breakfasts in Baskvervilles restaurant (sandwiches, salads, beef, and so on). Moriarty's Pub serves a quiet drink on the mezzanine, and there's also a lobby lounge and snack bar. Outdoors are two pools, a whirlpool, kiddie pool, playground, and lighted courts for tennis, basketball, volleyball, and shuffleboard. "Kid's Night Out" is a dinner-inclusive evening program offering games and other activities.

Hilton Walt Disney World   1751 Hotel Plaza Boulevard; (407) 827-4000; **www.hilton-wdwv.com**   (See page 200 for full profile.) This upscale Hilton is the nicest hotel in the Downtown Disney Resort Area, challenged only by the Wyndham Palace. It's also the only DDRA hotel offering Disney's early-entry program to its guests. Rooms are a cut above others in the DDRA. Dining on site includes the Covington Mill Restaurant, offering American sandwiches and pasta; Finn's Grill, a seafood house; and Benihana, a Japanese steakhouse and sushi bar. Covington Mill hosts a Disney character breakfast on Sundays. A large selection of microbrews is available at John T's lounge. The two pools are matched with a children's "spray pool," a small spa, and a volleyball court. An exercise room and game room are available. There are no organized children's programs.

Hotel Royal Plaza   1905 Hotel Plaza Boulevard; (407) 828-2828; **www.royalplaza.com**   The Hotel Royal Plaza has 394 rooms decorated in pleasant but generic hotel style. Giraffe Café serves American breakfast, lunch, and dinner; the attached Giraffe Tavern is the main hotel bar, though Sips is open seasonally poolside. The pool itself is comfortable and pleasant though not flashy or particularly kid-oriented. Four lighted tennis courts and an exercise room are available. A "Kid's Night Out" program (dinner included) provides an evening of games, arts and crafts, movies, swimming, and the like.

Lake Buena Vista Resort   2000 Hotel Plaza Boulevard; (407) 828-2424; **www.orlandoresorthotel.com**   Formerly known by the name of its corporate parent (Best Western), Lake Buena Vista Resort completed a substantial renovation in 2003 of all guest rooms and public areas. The improvements help compensate for offering fewer of the extras common to most other DDRA properties. A breakfast buffet and dinner service of American fare are available in the Trader's Island Grill, while the Parakeet Café offers sandwiches, pizza, and snacks. The poolside Flamingo Cove Lounge provides its own menu of pub standards as well as alcoholic refreshment. The pool is small though pleasantly landscaped, and there's a kiddie pool. Also offered are a fitness room, game room, and playground, but there are no organized children's programs.

Wyndham Palace   1900 Buena Vista Drive; (407) 827-2727; **www. wyndham.com**   Though it has no Disneyesque theme, the sprawling Wyndham Palace Resort and Spa can compete with Disney's best resorts in number and variety of amenities. Its rooms aren't quite as nice as the nearby Hilton's, but it's larger and offers a bit more of everything. The resort's 1,014 rooms and suites are spread over 27 acres and four towers, and the spa and fitness center is one of the most comprehensive on Disney World property (60 spa services and treatments, including private outdoor whirlpools). Dining options abound, including continental cuisine at the 27th-floor Arthur's 27, which provides a decent view of Disney fireworks; the Outback Restaurant (not affiliated with the chain of the same name), specializing in steaks and seafood; Watercress Café (breakfast, lunch, and dinner buffets, plus healthful "spa cuisine"); and a poolside snack bar. The Watercress Café also hosts a Disney character breakfast each Sunday. For lounge action and live entertainment, visit the Laughing Kookabura Good Time Bar, Lobby Lounge, and Top of the Palace Lounge. The wet set will enjoy three tropical-themed pools, a whirlpool, and sauna. Three lighted tennis courts, jogging trails, a white-sand volleyball court, and an arcade and playground round out recreational offerings, and supervised children's programs are available at the hotel year-round.

AMENITIES AT DOWNTOWN DISNEY RESORT AREA HOTELS					
Name	Children's Programs	Dining	Kid-Friendly	Pool(s)	Recreation
DoubleTree Guest Suites	—	★★	★★★	★★½	★★½
Grosvenor Resort	★★½	★★½	★★★	★★★½	★★★
Hilton	—	★★★½	★★½	★★★	★★½
Holiday Inn	—	★★½	★★½	★★★	★★½
Hotel Royal Plaza	★★½	★★	★★½	★★½	★★★
Lake Buena Vista Resort	—	★★½	★★★	★★½	★★
Wyndham Palace	★★★★	★★★★	★★★½	★★★★	★★★★

Camping at Walt Disney World

Fort Wilderness Campground is a spacious resort campground for tent and RV camping. Fully equipped, air-conditioned prefab log cabins are also available for rent.

Sites with water and electric only are $36–$69 per night, depending on season. Sites with water, electric, and sewer run $41–$81. Add cable, and the price is $49–$86. All sites are arranged on loops accessible from one of three main roads. There are 28 loops, with loops 100–2000 for tent and RV campers, and loops 2100–2800 offering cabins. All sites are level and provide a picnic table, waste container, and grill. No fires are permitted except in the grills. RV sites are roomy by eastern U.S. standards, but tent campers will probably feel cramped. On any given day, 90% or more of campers will be RVers.

Fort Wilderness Campground arguably offers the most recreational facilities and activities of any Disney resort. Among them are two video arcades; nightly campfire programs; Disney movies; a dinner theater; two swimming pools; a beach; walking paths; bike, boat, canoe, golf cart, and water ski rentals; a petting zoo; horseback riding; hay rides; fishing; and tennis, basketball, and volleyball courts. There are two convenience stores, a restaurant, and a tavern. Comfort stations with toilets, showers, pay phones, ice machine, and laundry facilities are within easy walking distance of all campsites.

Access to the Magic Kingdom is by boat from Fort Wilderness Landing, and to Epcot by bus with a transfer at the Ticket and Transportation Center to the Epcot Monorail. Transportation to all other Disney destinations is by bus. Motor traffic within the campground is permitted only when entering or exiting. Get around within the campground by bus, golf cart, or bike, the latter two available for rent.

FORT WILDERNESS CAMPGROUND

Strengths	Weaknesses
Informality	Complicated bus service
Children's play areas	Lack of privacy
Recreational options	Very limited dining options
Special day and evening programs	Confusing campground layout
Campsite amenities	Small baths in cabins and trailers
Number of shower/toilet facilities	Distance to store and restaurant from many campsites

For tent and RV campers, there's a fairly stark trade-off between sites convenient to pools, restaurant, trading posts, and other amenities, and those that are most scenic, shady, and quiet. RVers who prefer to be near guest services, the marina, the beach, and the restaurant and tavern

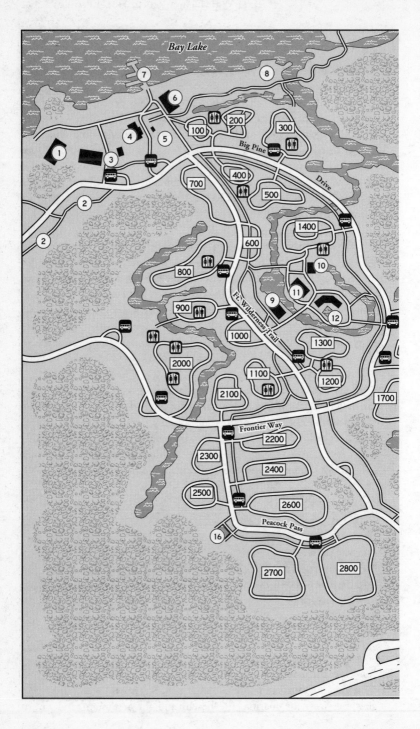

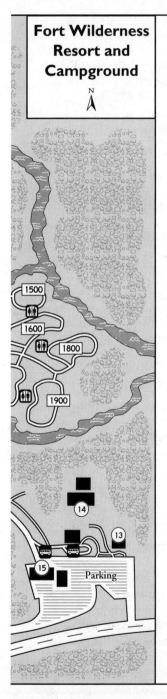

Fort Wilderness Resort and Campground

N
↑

1. Mickey's Backyard BBQ
2. Exercise Trail
3. Petting Farm/Ranch
4. Pioneer Hall
    Guest Services
    Trail's End Restaurant
    Crockett's Tavern
    Hoop-Dee-Doo Revue
5. Coachmen RV Display
6. Settlement Trading Post
7. Marina
8. Nature Trail
9. Meadow Trading Post
10. Campfire Program
11. Bike Barn
12. Meadow, Pool, and Tennis Courts
13. Kennel
14. Trail Ride
15. Reception Outpost
16. Peacock Pass Pool

Campsite Loops

100. Bay Tree Lake
200. Palmetto Path
300. Cypress Knee Circle
400. Whispering Pine Way
500. Buffalo Bend
600. Sunny Sage Way
700. Cinnamon Fern Way
800. Jack Rabbit Run
900. Quail Trail
1000. Raccoon Lane
1100. Possum Path
1200. Dogwood Drive
1300. Tumblewood Turn
1400. Little Bear Path and Big Bear Path
1500. Cottonwood Curl
1600. Timber Trail
1700. Hickory Hollow
1800. Conestoga Trail
1900. Wagon Wheel Way
2000. Spanish Moss Lane
2100. Bobcat Bend
2200. Arrowhead Way
2300. Shawnee Bend
2400. Settler's Bend
2500. Cedar Circle
2600. Moccasin Trail
2700. Heron Hollow
2800. Willow Way

🚌 Bus Stop
🚻 Comfort Station/Laundry Facility

should go for loops 100, 200, 700, and 400 (in that order). Loops near
the campground's secondary facility area with pool, trading post, bike
and golf-cart rentals, and campfire program, are 1400, 1300, 600, 1000,
and 1500 in order of preference. If you're looking for a tranquil, scenic
setting among mature trees, we recommend loops 1800, 1900, 1700,
and 1600, in that order, and the backside sites on the 700 loop. The best
loop of all, and the only one to offer both a lovely setting and close proximity to key amenities, is loop 300. The best loops for tents and pop-up
campers are loops 1500 and 2000, with 1500 being nearest a pool, convenience store, and the campfire program.

With the exception of loops 1800 and 1900, avoid sites within 40
yards of the loop entrance. These sites are almost always flanked by one
of the main traffic arteries within Fort Wilderness. Further, sites on the
outside of the loop are almost always preferable to those in the center of
the loop. RVers should be forewarned that all sites are back-ins, and that
although most sites will accommodate large rigs, the loop access roads are
pretty tight and narrow.

Rental cabins offer a double bed and two bunk beds in the only bedroom, augmented by a Murphy bed (pulls down from the wall) in the living room. There's one rather small bathroom with shower and tub.

All cabins offer air-conditioning, color television with VCR, a fully
equipped kitchen, and a dining table. Housekeeping is provided daily.
Most readers are crazy about the cabins. Here are representative comments:

From a Lancaster, New York, family of five:

Fort Wilderness Cabins are underrated. It's a great place for our family of five.
If you don't mind cooking breakfast and a few other meals during your
stay, you can actually save on food at restaurants. This makes up for the
extra money spent on accommodations. The cabins are more spacious and
much more comfortable than a basic hotel room. The bedroom is great for
the kids to have an afternoon rest or for getting them to bed early so parents can relax and unwind after a long day.

Another New York family, this one from Wappingers Falls, writes:

We stayed at Fort Wilderness Campgrounds in a cabin because:
- We wanted a separate bedroom area.
- We wanted a kitchen.
- Our kids are very lively and the cabins were apart from each other
  so we wouldn't disturb other guests.
- We thought the kids might meet other children to play with. ...

The cabins worked out just right for us. Although the kids did not meet
any other children to play with, they had a ball chasing the little lizards and
frogs, kicking around pinecones, sitting on the deck to eat ice pops, and
sleeping in bunk beds. We went to the campfire twice (we brought our own
marshmallows and sticks). Our cabin was a short walk to our bus stop and

two "blocks" away from the pool and laundry. I loved the dishwasher, the generous storage space, the extra towels, the air conditioning, and the daily cleaning service. There was no canned music or fake bird calls in the trees, just peace and quiet.

Bus service at Fort Wilderness leaves a lot to be desired, so much in fact, that we wouldn't stay there unless we had our own car. To go anywhere you first have to catch an internal bus, which makes many, many stops. If your destination is outside Fort Wilderness, you then have to transfer to a second bus. To complicate things, buses serving destinations outside the campground depart from two locations, the Reception Outpost and Pioneer Hall. This means that you have to keep track of which destinations each transfer center serves.

Finally, if you rent a cabin or camp in a tent or RV, particularly in fall or spring, keep abreast of local weather conditions. This is not the place to be in a tornado.

How to Evaluate a Walt Disney World Travel Package

Hundreds of Walt Disney World package vacations are offered each year. Some are created by the Walt Disney Travel Company, others by airline touring companies, independent travel agents, and wholesalers. Almost all include lodging at or near Disney World and theme-park admissions. Packages offered by airlines include air transportation.

Prices vary seasonally; mid-March through Easter, summer, and holiday periods are the most expensive. Off-season, forget packages: there are plenty of empty rooms, and you can negotiate great discounts, especially at non-Disney properties. Similarly, airfares and rental cars are cheaper off-peak.

Almost all package ads are headlined "5 Days at Walt Disney World from $645" (or such). The key word is "from." The rock-bottom price includes the least desirable hotels. If you want better or more convenient digs, you'll pay more, often much more.

Packages offer a wide selection of hotels. Some, like the Disney resorts, are very dependable. Others run the gamut of quality. If you consider a non-Disney hotel, check its quality as reported in an independent rating such as those from *Unofficial Guides*, *AAA Directories*, *Mobil Guides*, or *Frommer's Guides*. Checking two or three independent sources is best. Also, before you book, ask how old the hotel is and when the guest rooms were last refurbished. Locate the hotel on a map to verify its proximity to Disney World. If you won't have a car, make sure the hotel has an adequate shuttle service.

Packages with non-Disney lodging are much less expensive. But guests at Disney-owned properties get early-entry privileges, free parking, and access to the Disney transportation system. These privileges (except early entry for Hilton guests) don't apply to guests at the independent hotels of the Downtown Disney Resort Area (Wyndham Palace, Grosvenor Resort, DoubleTree Guest Suites Resort, Hilton, Holiday Inn at Walt Disney World, Hotel Royal Plaza, and Lake Buena Vista Resort).

Packages should be a win-win proposition for both buyer and seller. The buyer makes only one phone call and deals with one salesperson to set up the whole vacation (transportation, rental car, admissions, lodging, meals, and even golf and tennis). The seller, likewise, deals with the buyer only once. Some packagers also buy airfares in bulk on contract, like a broker playing the commodities market. By buying a large number of airfares in advance, the packager saves significantly over posted fares. The practice is also applied to hotel rooms. Because selling packages is efficient and because the packager often can buy package components in bulk at discount, the seller's savings in operating expenses are sometimes passed on to the buyer, making the package both convenient and an exceptional value.

In practice, however, the seller may realize all of the economies and pass on no savings. Packages sometimes are loaded with extras that cost the packager almost nothing but run the package's price sky-high. Savings passed on to customers are still somewhere in Fantasyland.

Choose a package that includes features you're sure to use. You'll pay for all of them whether you use them or not. If price is more important than convenience, call around to see what the package would cost if you booked its components on your own. If the package price is less than the à la carte cost, the package is a good deal. If costs are about equal, the package probably is worth it for the convenience. Much of the time, however, you'll find you save significantly by buying the components individually.

Walt Disney Travel Company Packages

After years of stratospheric prices, the Walt Disney Travel Company (WDTC), at least for the moment, has descended to Earth. In late 2003, WDTC began offering packages where the cost of the package was only 5–10% more than the price of the package components if purchased separately. Several special packages, including one that offered seven nights for the price of five (offered again in 2004), were actually very good deals. WDTC continues to maintain this more reasonable pricing model and occasionally even discounts a package or two.

The Walt Disney Travel Company's Dream Maker Package is Disney's current starter package. For an additional investment, you can upgrade the Dream Maker Package to Silver, Gold, or Platinum. It's like buying a car. You start with the basic car, then add leather seats, a stereo, automatic windows, and whatever other features you want and can afford. But before we dazzle you with a barge load of options, let's define the basic Dream Maker package. It includes:

1. Three or more nights of accommodation at your choice of any Disney resort. Rates vary with lodging choice; the Grand Floridian is the most expensive, and All-Star Resorts are the least expensive.
2. Unlimited use of the Disney transportation system.
3. Admission and unlimited use of all Disney theme parks during your stay.
4. Admission and unlimited use of Pleasure Island nighttime entertainment venue, Typhoon Lagoon and Blizzard Beach swimming parks, the DisneyQuest interactive virtual entertainment complex, and Disney's Wide World of Sports during your stay. (Admission becomes effective upon check-in and is valid until midnight of your check-out day.)
5. Free theme-park parking.
6. Two trading pins and two lanyards per room.

Disney's Dream Maker plan also includes a "Choice Feature," which consists of one of the following per person:

1. A round of miniature golf.
2. One Disney character poster.
3. Up to two images displayed on a "Leave a Legacy" tile at Epcot.
4. $25 coupon for dining at Planet Hollywood.

Obviously the heart of the package is the lodging and admissions. The rest can be categorized as either fluff, for example, minor purchase incentives of nominal value (lanyards, mini-golf, etc.), or things like free theme-park parking and use of the transportation system that are available to all Disney resort guests.

If the lodging in the package costs approximately what you'd pay if you booked room-only, it's a nonissue. So the purchase decision on the Dream Maker package pretty much revolves around the admissions component. If you intend to tour the four major theme parks, you're not going to have a lot of time left to visit all of the swimming, sports, and entertainment venues included (unless you plan to vacation for more than a week). Further, the pass is good from when you check in until midnight on the day you check out. That means effectively that you paying a whole day's admission for days when you'll probably be traveling. When you add it up, it's very hard to get full use of the Dream Maker unless you plan to stay for significantly more than a week and use a goodly part of your travel days for touring.

Another problem with the Dream Maker admission is that whatever you don't use, you lose. Admissions are good only for the days of the package, unlike the nonpackage passes. Unused days on most other passes are good forever.

Silver Plan   For about $70 for adults and $35 for children ages 3–9, you can upgrade the Dream Maker package to Silver. The Silver Plan is Disney's most complex and confusing package, one that keeps travel agents and WDTC reservationists on the phone until they're hoarse trying to explain it.

With the Silver Plan, you get everything in the Dream Maker package. In addition, each member of your party gets two "Magical Wishes" for each day that you stay in a Disney Resort. The Magical Wishes can be redeemed for full-service and counter-service meals, character breakfasts, Disney dinner shows, golf, watercraft rental, behind-the-scenes tours, childcare at Disney's children's activity "clubs," spa treatments, and Disney merchandise. Most of the forgoing cost one wish, but some cost two. You receive all of your wishes at once when you check in. So two adults and two school-age kids staying seven nights would rack up at total of 56 wishes (2 per night × 2 adults plus 2 kids × 7 nights). The wishes are credited to the family rather than to specific family members in a sort of pooled account to be drawn down as the wishes are redeemed. You can use your wishes whenever you want: all on your first day, apportioned over your entire stay, whatever. Any wishes you don't use expire at midnight on the day you check out.

Once the wishes are in your pooled account, they all have equal value. In other words, there's no such thing as a child wish or an adult wish (even though you paid twice as much for the adults as for the kids). Thus, you get more dish for your wish if you redeem your wishes for adult meals, admissions, etc., and pay cash for children's meals, admissions, and entertainment.

Gold and Platinum Plans   Though you can exact more value from your Silver Plan by savvy management of your Magical Wishes, with the Gold Plan and Platinum Plans you essentially pay Disney a kazillion dollars in advance then do whatever you want short of eloping with Minnie. You get lodging, Ultimate Park Hopper passes; breakfast, lunch, and dinner in full-service restaurants; unlimited golf, tennis, boating, and recreation; unlimited dinner shows and character breakfasts; Cirque du Soleil; unlimited use of childcare facilities … in other words, everything you can think of, except alcoholic beverages. The Platinum Plan offers everything in the Gold Plan plus personalized itinerary planning, dinner at Victoria & Albert's restaurant, spa treatments, a fireworks cruise, private in-room childcare, reserved seating for *Fantasmic!,* and (here's the kicker) nightly turndown service. The Gold Plan costs about $140 per adult per night and $95 per child (ages 3–9) per night over the cost of the Dream Maker package. The add-on for the Platinum Plan is $200 per adult per night and $120 per child.

Coming next year is the Disney Ice Maker Plan where all of the deceased members of your party get to sleep in the freezer with Walt. Disney, needless to say, has built a nice profit into every component of the Dream Maker plan and all upgraded plans. If you don't use all features of a given plan (and most people don't) Disney makes out even better.

Number Crunching

Comparing a Dream Maker package with purchasing the package components separately is a breeze.

1. Pick a Disney resort and decide how many nights you want to stay.

2. Next, work out a rough plan of what you want to do and see so you can determine the admission passes you'll require.

3. When you're ready, call the Disney Reservations Center (DRC) at (407) W-DISNEY and price a Dream Maker package with tax for your selected resort and dates. The package will include both admissions and lodging.

4. Now, to calculate the costs of buying your accommodations and admission passes separately, call the DRC a second time. This time price a room-only rate for the same resort and dates. Be sure to ask about the availability of any special deals. While you're still on the line, obtain the prices, with tax, for the admissions you require. If you're not sure which of the various admission options will best serve you, consult our free Admissions Option analizer at www.touringplans.com.

5. Add the room-only rates and the admission prices. Compare this sum to the DRC quote for the Dream Maker package.

6. Check for deals and discounts for packages, room-only rates, and admission.

When you upgrade to a Silver, Gold, or Platinum plan, you load the plan with so many features that it's extremely difficult to cost them individually. For a rough comparison, price the plan of your choice using the steps above. To complete the picture, work up a dining budget, excluding alcohol. Add your estimated dining costs to the room-only quote and admissions quote and compare to the price of the plan.

Throw Me a Line!

If you buy a package from Disney, don't expect reservationists to offer suggestions or help you sort out your options. Generally, they respond only to your specific questions, ducking queries that require an opinion. A reader from North Riverside, Illinois, complains:

> I have received various pieces of literature from WDW, and it is very confusing to figure out everything. My wife made two telephone calls, and the representatives from WDW were very courteous. However, they only answered the questions posed and were not eager to give advice on what might be most cost-effective. [The] WDW reps would not say if we would be better off doing one thing over the other. I feel a person could spend eight hours on the phone with WDW reps and not have any more input than you get from reading the literature.

If you can't get the information you need from Disney, contact a good travel agent. Chances are the agent can help you weigh your options.

Packages from a Different Perspective

We've always evaluated packages from a dollar-and-cents perspective, paying scant attention to other consideration such as time economy and convenience. A reader from Westchester County, New York, finally got our attention, writing:

I fully understand your position not to recommend the [Silver, Gold, and
   Platinum] plans in your guide as they are not a good buy by financial
   comparison. However, when one books six rooms, as I have, with guests
   ages 4 through 59 including a wife, grandchildren, children, sons- and
   daughters-in-law, and a nanny, the thought of trying to find out what way
   each family segment would like to go and then arranging for it on a daily
   basis is a scary scenario. With the Gold Plan, they can go where they want,
   eat where they want, and Gramps and his roommate don't have the hassle.

Purchasing Room-only Plus Passes versus a Package

Sue Pisaturo of Small World Vacations, a travel agency that specializes in
Disney, also thinks there is more involved in a package purchase decision
than money. Below she shares a planning questionnaire she uses with her
clients to determine if a package is right for them.

Should you purchase a Walt Disney World package, or buy all the
components of the package separately? There is no single answer to this
confusing question.

A Walt Disney World package can be compared to a store-bought
child's LunchAble meal, the kind with the little compartments filled with
meat, cheese, crackers, drink, and dessert. You just grab the package and
go. It's easy, and if it's on sale, why bother doing it yourself? If it's not on
sale, it still may be worth the extra money for convenience.

Purchasing the components of your vacation separately is like buying
each of the LunchAble ingredients, cutting them up into neat piles and
packaging the lunch yourself. Is it worth the extra time and effort to do it
this way? Will you save money if you do it this way?

You have two budgets to balance when you plan your Disney World
vacation: time and money. Satisfying both is your ultimate goal. To make
sure you are making the most of your time, create your itinerary before
making your final decision on whether to get a package. Mapping your
itinerary will help you assess whether you'll have enough time to use all of
the features a package might offer. Remember, with a package, you'll be
paying for all of the features regardless of whether you use them or not. It's
critical, therefore, to be realistic about what you'll have time to do.

The Ultimate Park Hopper passes that come with packages are only
valid for the length of your stay. Passes purchased separately are good forever. Many guests go home with unused days on their separately purchased passes. Great if you plan visit Walt Disney World again in the next
year or two; not so good if your Disney vacation is a one-time fling. Bear
in mind, time is money; always buy the passes that fit your plans.

Buying your room and admission separately might be best for you if
you answer yes to one or more of these questions:

1. Am I the type of person who is willing to price out each separate feature of my vacation to save money? If not, a package might be easier.

2. Will I be arriving late on the day I check in?

3. Will I be departing early on the day I check out?

4. Do I plan to take a day or more to hang around my resort, go to non-Disney attractions, schedule a day at the beach, or visit local friends? If so, I won't need passes for every day of my vacation.

5. Do I have leftover Park Hopper passes from another trip?

6. Do I have smaller children who will not be going to DisneyQuest, water parks, Pleasure Island, or Disney's Wide World of Sports (included in most Disney packages)?

7. Am I going during the cooler months of the year when visits to the swimming parks are unlikely?

8. Am I comfortable with the cancellation penalties on a room-only reservation? (You risk losing one night's room charge if you cancel within five days of arrival.)

9. Do I prefer to pay for my room balance on arrival as opposed to 45 days prior to arrival as required with a package?

10. Do I plan to tour the theme parks for more than eight days? If so, an annual pass might be my best value.

11. Do I plan to return to tour the theme parks more than once in a year? If so, an annual pass might be my best value.

12. Am I eligible for any exclusive room-only or theme-park pass discounts not offered on a package (AAA, military, annual passholder, Florida or other location resident, teacher, government worker, nurse, etc.)?

13. Am I aware that separately purchased Park Hoppers passes are nonrefundable (so if I cancel my vacation, I'll still have my passes)?

A Walt Disney World Vacation Package may be best for you if you answer yes to one or more of these questions:

1. Do I want to do this as easily as possible? Is convenience a priority? (Remember the LunchAble.)

2. Are there discounts on a Walt Disney Travel Company package? (Those that offer a percentage off the entire package are the best.)

3. Am I eligible for a special discount on a Walt Disney Travel Company package (Disney Visa cardholder, Kids Free, Canadian at Par discounts, etc.)?

4. Do I plan to go to the water parks, Pleasure Island, DisneyQuest, and/or the Wide World of Sports on several occasions?

5. Do I want to add airfare, car rental, travel insurance, transfers, meals, and so on to my package?

6. Do I like an all-inclusive plan so I know in advance how much everything will cost?

7. Am I the type of person who does not want to keep track of how many days I can go to the parks, water parks, Pleasure Island, etc?

8. Do I want to lock into my theme-park pass price now (If you book your room and wait to purchase your passes, Disney might raise the price of admission)?

9. Am I comfortable with the fact that any unused features in my package such as theme-park passes, Magical Wishes, and so on expire at midnight the day I check out?

10. Am I comfortable with all restrictions and cancellation policies that apply to my package?

SOME TIPS FROM MARY WARING

Mary Waring, webmaster at www.mousesavers.com (see page 24), knows more about Disney packages than anyone on the planet. Here's what she suggests:

Book "room-only." Disney likes to sell packages because they're easy and profitable. When you buy a package, you're typically paying a premium for convenience. You can often save money by assembling your own "package." It's not difficult. Just book "room-only" at a resort, and buy passes, meals, and extras separately.

Recently, Disney started pricing its standard packages at the same rates as if you had purchased individual components separately at full price. This is better than previous years, when packages were often way more expensive than buying the room, tickets, and meals separately at full price! However, what Disney doesn't tell you is that components can usually be purchased separately at a discount—and those discounts are never reflected in brochure prices of Disney's packages. (Sometimes you can get "special offer" packages that include discounts; see below.)

Keep in mind that Disney's packages are designed to include extras you're unlikely to use. Also, packages require full payment well in advance and have less desirable change and cancellation policies than "room-only" bookings—although Disney has begun imposing tighter policies on some "room-only" reservations, and I predict the trend will continue. Generally, booking "room-only" requires a deposit of one night's room rate with the remainder due at check-in. Your reservation can be changed or canceled for any reason until five days before check-in.

For best results when booking a Disney resort reservation, keep these points in mind:

- Know how to work with Disney's phone reservations agents. All reservations calls go to the Disney Reservations Center (DRC). Tell the agent pleasantly but firmly that you want a "room-only" reservation. If the first agent isn't helpful, politely end the call and try again. There are hundreds of agents, and you're unlikely to reach the same one twice. The DRC phone number is (407) W-DISNEY.

- Use discount codes to reduce your "room-only" rate by up to 45%. Discount codes are used by Disney to push unsold rooms at certain times of year. They're published in newspaper ads, on Disney's Web site, and in e-mails and postcards sent by Disney. Check a Web site like www.mousesavers.com to learn about any codes that may be available for your vacation dates. Many codes are available to anyone, though a few are specific to residents of certain states, annual passholders, and so on.

Discount codes aren't always available for every hotel or every date, and they typically don't appear until two to six months in advance. The good news is you can usually apply

Hotels outside Walt Disney World

Selecting and Booking a Hotel outside Walt Disney World

Lodging costs outside Disney World vary incredibly. If you shop around, you can find a clean motel with a pool within 5–20 minutes of the World for as low as $35 a night. You also can find luxurious, expensive hotels. Because of hot competition, discounts abound, particularly for AAA and AARP members.

a code to an existing "room-only" reservation. Simply call the DRC and ask whether any rooms are available at your preferred hotel for your preferred dates, using the code.

- Use discount codes to reduce your package rate by up to 25%. Disney also offers some discounted packages that include resort discounts similar to those offered with the "room-only" discount codes. Sometimes these special offers include 10% off the advance-purchase price of the Ultimate Park Hopper passes that Disney includes with its packages. Even more amazing, Disney last year offered seven-day packages for the price of four-day packages—a great deal. For those who like the convenience of packages, these offers are a real breakthrough. If the travel market remains flat, there undoubtedly will be more such deals.

You'll need a discount code to get the special package rates. The codes are published in newspaper ads, on Disney's Web site, and in e-mails and postcards sent by Disney. Check a Web site like www.mousesavers.com to learn about codes that may be available for your vacation dates. Many of the codes are available to anyone.

Package discount codes aren't always available for every hotel or every date, and they typically don't appear until two to six months in advance. You can usually apply a code to an existing package reservation. Simply call the DRC and ask whether any rooms are available at your preferred hotel for your preferred dates, using the package code.

Be flexible. Buying a room or package with a discount code is a little like shopping for clothes at a discount store. If you wear size XX-small or XXXX-large, or you like green when everyone else is wearing pink, you're a lot more likely to score a bargain. Likewise, resort discounts are going to happen only when Disney has excess rooms. You're more likely to get a discount during less-popular times (such as value season) and at larger or less-popular resorts. Animal Kingdom Lodge and Old Key West seem to have discounted rooms available more often than other resorts do.

Be persistent. This is the most important tip. Disney allots a certain number of rooms to each discount; reportedly this averages 100 rooms per night per code. Once the discounted rooms are gone, you won't get that rate unless someone cancels. Fortunately, people change and cancel reservations all the time. If you can't get your preferred dates or hotel with one discount code, try another code (if available) or keep calling back first thing in the morning to check for cancellations. The system resets overnight, and any reservations with unpaid deposits are automatically released for resale.

There are three primary out-of-the-World areas to consider:

1. **International Drive Area**   This area, about 15–25 minutes northeast of the World, parallels I-4 on its eastern side and offers a wide selection of hotels and restaurants. Prices range from $40 to $320 per night. The chief drawbacks of this area are its terribly congested roads, countless traffic signals, and inadequate access to westbound I-4. While International's biggest bottleneck is its intersection with Sand Lake Road, the mile between Kirkman and Sand Lake roads is almost always gridlocked.

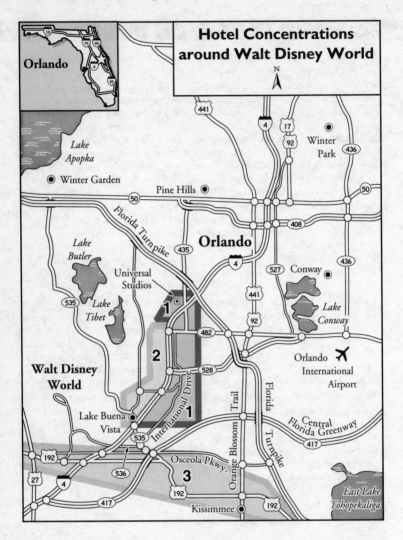

It's common to lose 25–35 minutes trying to navigate this stretch. We provide tips for avoiding this traffic in Part Seven, Arriving and Getting Around (see pages 317–318).

Regarding International Drive (known locally as I-Drive) traffic, these comments are representative. From a Seattle mom:

After spending half our trip sitting in traffic on International Drive, those Disney hotels didn't sound so expensive, after all.

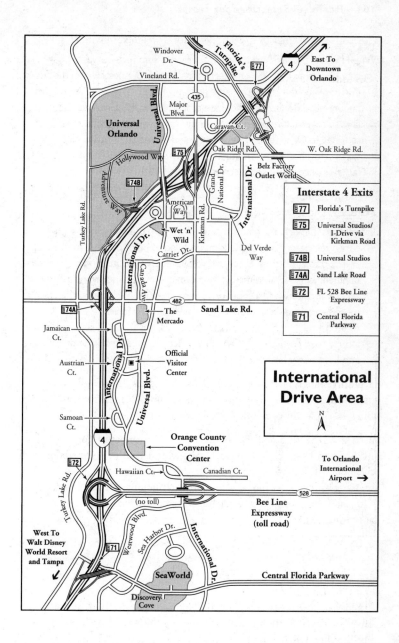

International Drive Area

N

Interstate 4 Exits

77	Florida's Turnpike
75	Universal Studios/ I-Drive via Kirkman Road
74B	Universal Studios
74A	Sand Lake Road
72	FL 528 Bee Line Expressway
71	Central Florida Parkway

Windover Dr.

Vineland Rd.

Florida's Turnpike

77

4

East To Downtown Orlando

435

Major Blvd.

Universal Orlando

Universal Blvd.

Caravan Ct.

Oak Ridge Rd.

W. Oak Ridge Rd.

75

Belz Factory Outlet World

Hollywood Way

74B

Adventure Way

Turkey Lake Rd.

American Way

Grand National Dr.

International Dr.

Kirkman Rd.

Wet 'n' Wild

Del Verde Way

Carrier Dr.

International Dr.

Canada Ave.

74A

482

Sand Lake Rd.

The Mercado

Jamaican Ct.

Austrian Ct.

Official Visitor Center

Universal Blvd.

Samoan Ct.

4

Orange County Convention Center

To Orlando International Airport →

72

Hawaiian Ct.

Canadian Ct.

Turkey Lake Rd.

(no toll)

528

Bee Line Expressway (toll road)

West To Walt Disney World Resort and Tampa

71

Westwood Blvd.

Sea Harbor Dr.

International Dr.

Central Florida Parkway

SeaWorld

Discovery Cove

A convention-goer from Islip, New York, weighed in with this:

When I visited Disney World with my family last summer, we wasted huge chunks of time in traffic on International Drive. Our hotel was in the section between the big McDonald's [at Sand Lake Drive] and Wet 'n' Wild [at Universal Boulevard]. There are practically no left-turn lanes in this section, so anyone turning left can hold up traffic for a long time. Recently, I returned to Orlando for a trade show and stayed at a hotel on International Drive near the convention center. This section was much saner and far less congested. It's also closer to Disney World.

Traffic aside, a man from Ottawa, Canada, sings the praises of his I-Drive experience:

International Drive is the place to stay when going to Disney. Your single-paragraph description of this location failed to point out that [there are] several discount stores, boutiques, restaurants, mini-putts, and other entertainment facilities, all within walking distance of remarkably inexpensive accommodations and a short drive away from WDW. Many of the chain motels and hotels are located in this area, and the local merchants have created a mini-resort to cater to the tourists. It is the ideal place to unwind after a hard day visiting WDW. I have recommended this location for years and have never heard anything but raves about the wisdom of this advice.

I-Drive hotels are listed in the *Orlando Official Accommodations Guide* published by the Orlando and Orange County Convention and Visitors Bureau. For a copy, call (800) 255-5786 or (407) 363-5872.

2. Lake Buena Vista and the I-4 Corridor   A number of hotels are along FL 535 and west of I-4 between Disney World and I-4's intersection with the Florida Turnpike. They're easily reached from the interstate and are near many restaurants, including those on International Drive. The Orlando Official Accommodations Guide lists most of them. For some traffic avoidance tips, see page 319 in Part Seven, Arriving and Getting Around.

3. US 192/Irlo Bronson Parkway   This is the highway to Kissimmee to the south of Disney World. In addition to large, full-service hotels, there are many small, privately owned motels that are often a good value. Several dozen properties on US 192 are nearer Disney parks than are more expensive hotels inside the World. The number and variety of restaurants on US 192 has increased markedly, easing the area's primary shortcoming. Locally, US 192 is called Irlo Bronson Parkway. The section to the west of I-4 and the Disney "Maingate" is designated Irlo Bronson Parkway West while the section from I-4 running southeast toward Kissimmee is Irlo Bronson Parkway East.

We're happy to report that construction on US 192 east and west of the entrance to Disney World has been completed. The highway has

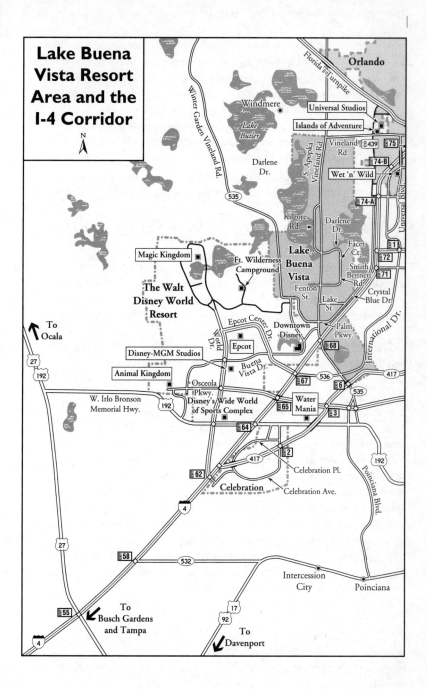

Lake Buena Vista Resort Area and the I-4 Corridor

N

Orlando

Windmere

Lake Butler

Winter Garden Vineland Rd.

Darlene Dr.

Universal Studios

Islands of Adventure

Vineland Rd.

439

75

74-B

Wet 'n' Wild

74-A

S. Apopka Vineland Rd.

535

Kilgore Rd.

Darlene Dr.

Facet Ct.

1

72

Lake Buena Vista

Smith Bennett Rd.

71

Magic Kingdom

Ft. Wilderness Campground

Fenton St.

Lake St.

Crystal Blue Dr.

The Walt Disney World Resort

Downtown Disney

Palm Pkwy.

68

To Ocala

Epcot Center Dr.

World Dr.

Epcot

Disney-MGM Studios

Buena Vista Dr.

International Dr.

27

192

Animal Kingdom

Osceola Pkwy.

67

536

417

Disney's Wide World of Sports Complex

W. Irlo Bronson Memorial Hwy.

192

65

Water Mania

6

535

64

3

2

417

62

Celebration Pl.

Celebration

Celebration Ave.

4

Poinciana Blvd.

192

58

532

Intercession City

Poinciana

27

55

To Busch Gardens and Tampa

4

17

92

To Davenport

been widened and medians added. Traffic flow has improved considerably. Still, a little insider knowledge will save you time in traffic. See our tips on pages 318–319 in Part Seven, Arriving and Getting Around.

A senior citizen from Brookfield, Connecticut, was pleased with lodging in the US 192/Kissimmee area:

> We were amazed to find that from our cheaper and superior accommodations in Kissimmee it took only five minutes longer to reach the park turnstiles than it did from the Disney accommodations.

Hotels on US 192 and in Kissimmee are listed in the *Kissimmee–St. Cloud Visitor's Guide.* Call (800) 327-9159 or see **www.floridakiss.com.**

Driving Time to the Theme Parks for Visitors Lodging outside Walt Disney World

Our "How the Hotels Compare" chart on pages 210–233 shows the commuting time to the Disney theme parks from each hotel listed. Those commuting times represent an average of several test runs. Your actual time may be shorter or longer depending on traffic, road construction (if any), and delays at traffic signals.

The commuting times in "How the Hotels Compare" show conclusively that distance from the theme parks is not necessarily the dominant factor in determining commuting times. Among those we list, the hotels on Major Boulevard opposite the Kirkman Road entrance to Universal Orlando, for example, are the most distant (in miles) from the Disney parks. But because they're only one traffic signal from easy access to I-4, commuting time to the parks is significantly less than for many closer hotels.

Note that times in the chart differ from those in "Door-to-Door Commuting Times" in Part Seven, Arriving and Getting Around. The door-to-door chart in Part Seven compares using the Disney Transportation System versus driving your own car *inside* Walt Disney World. These times include actual transportation time plus tram, monorail, or other connections required to get from the parking lots to the entrance turnstiles. The hotel chart's commuting times, by contrast, represent only the driving time to and from the parks, with no consideration of getting to and from the parking lot to the turnstiles.

Add to the commuting times in our "How the Hotels Compare" chart a few minutes for paying your parking fee and parking. Once parked at the Transportation and Ticket Center (Magic Kingdom parking lot), it takes 20–30 minutes more to reach the Magic Kingdom via monorail or ferry. To reach Epcot from its parking lot, add 7–10 minutes. At Disney-MGM Studios and Animal Kingdom, the lot-to-gate transit is 5–10 minutes. If you haven't purchased your theme-park admission in advance, tack on another 10–20 minutes.

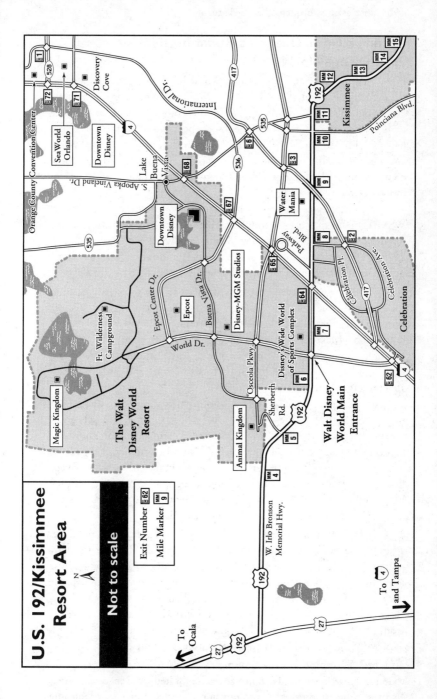

U.S. 192/Kissimmee Resort Area

N

Not to scale

Exit Number 62
Mile Marker 9

189

Getting a Good Deal on a Room outside Walt Disney World

Hotel development at Walt Disney World has sharpened competition among lodgings throughout the Disney World/Orlando/Kissimmee area. Hotels outside the World struggle to fill their rooms. Unable to compete with Disney resorts for convenience or perks, off-World hotels lure patrons with bargain rates. These deals vary with season, day of the week, and area events. In high-season, during holiday periods, and during large conventions at the Orange County Convention Center, even the most modest property is sold out.

Here are strategies for getting a good deal on a room outside Disney World. The list may refer to travel-market players unfamiliar to you, but many tips we provide for Disney World deals work equally well almost any place you need a hotel. Once you understand these strategies, you'll be able to routinely obtain rooms for the lowest possible rates.

1. Orlando MagiCard   Orlando MagiCard is a discount program sponsored by the Orlando/Orange County Convention and Visitors Bureau. Cardholders are eligible for discounts of 20–50% at about 50 hotels. The MagiCard is also good for discounts at area attractions, including SeaWorld, the Universal parks, several dinner theaters, and Disney's Pleasure Island. Valid for up to six persons, the card isn't available for larger groups or conventions.

To obtain a free MagiCard and a list of participating hotels and attractions, call (800) 255-5786 or (407) 363-5874. On the Internet, go to **www.orlandoinfo.com;** the MagiCard and accompanying brochure can be printed from a personal computer. Anyone 18 or older is eligible. If you miss getting one before you leave home, obtain one at the Convention and Visitors Bureau Information Center at 8723 International Drive. When you call for a MagiCard, also request the *Orlando Official Accommodations Guide* and the Orlando Vacation Planner.

2. Exit Information Guide   Exit Information Guide (EIG) publishes a book of coupons for discounts at hotels statewide. It's free in many restaurants and motels on main highways leading to Florida. Because most travelers make reservations before leaving home, picking up the book en route doesn't help much. If you call and use a credit card, EIG will send the guide first class for $3 ($5 U.S. for Canadian delivery). Contact Exit Information Guide at 4205 NW 6th Street, Gainesville, FL 32609; (352) 371-3948; **www.travelersdiscountguide.com.**

3. Hotel Shopping on the Internet   Hotels use the Internet to fill rooms during slow periods and to advertise limited-time specials. Hotels also use more traditional communication avenues such as promoting specials through travel agents. If you enjoy cyber-shopping, have at it, but hotel shopping on the Internet isn't as quick or convenient as hand-ing the task to your travel agent. When we bump into a great deal on the Web, we call our agent. Often she can beat the deal or improve on it (perhaps with an upgrade). Although a good agent working alone can achieve great things, the same agent working with a savvy, helpful client can work wonders.

Here are Web sites we've found most dependable for discounts on Disney-area hotels:

mousesavers.com	Best site for hotels in Disney World
dreamsunlimitedtravel.com	Excellent for both Disney and non-Disney hotels
2000orlando-florida.com	Comprehensive hotel site
valuetrips.com	Specializes in budget accommodations
travelocity.com	Multi-destination travel superstore
roomsaver.com	Provides discount coupons for hotels
floridakiss.com	Primarily US 192/Kissimmee area hotels
orlandoinfo.com	Good info; not user-friendly for booking
orlandovacation.com	Great rates for a small number of properties, including condos and home rentals
expedia.com	Largest of the multi-destination travel sites
hotels.com	Largest Internet hotel-booking service; many other sites link to hotels.com and their subsidiary, www.hoteldiscounts.com
accommodationsexpress.com	Discounts on 1,500 hotels in 190 U.S. cities

The secret to shopping on the Internet is: shopping. When we're really looking for a deal, we check all the above sites. Flexibility on dates and location are helpful, and we always give our travel agent the opportunity to beat any deal we find.

We recommend choosing a hotel based on location, room quality, price, commuting time to the parks (all summarized in the chart on pages 210–233) plus any features important to you. Next, check each of the applicable sites above. You'll be able to ferret out the best Internet deal in about 30 minutes. Then call the hotel to see if you can save more by booking directly. Start by asking the hotel for specials. If their response doesn't beat the Internet deal, tell them what you've found and ask if they can do better.

So Who Offers the Best Deals on the Net?   *Unofficial Guide* statistician Fred Hazelton analyzed over two million rate quotes from Internet sellers, individual and chain-hotel Web sites, and hotel reservations departments for 350 Disney and Orlando-area hotels. The idea was to determine which sellers had the best deals most (or a high percentage) of the time.

The ranking of the sellers in the chart below is based on how often a seller's rate was lower than all of its competitors. Thus, a success rate of 70% means that the seller beat all competitors who market the same hotels 70% of the time. The numbers can be tricky, though. A seller who offers hotels not sold by others is obviously going to have the best deals on those properties most (if not all) of the time, and consequently score high. Conversely, a seller that lists a large number of hotels also sold by many competitors will offer the best price a lower percentage of the time.

We collected rates from most of the Web sites that offer rates for hotels in and around the Orlando/Kissimmee area. Then we also obtained rates from the hotel front desk and from the hotel's Web site. When we compared all the rates from all sellers, we found that **www.octopustravel.com** and **www.floridakiss.com** had the best bang for your Internet buck. The rates offered by these Web sites beat out all others about 81% of the time. These sites, however, offer a much smaller selection of hotels than biggies like Expedia and Travelocity. The best of the large Web sites was **www.hotel kingdom.com,** with an impressive 75% success rate. Also note that the hotel front desk and the hotel Web site offered the lowest rate about two-thirds of the time (65% and 60%, respectively). **Mousesavers.com,** a site that specializes in discount codes for hotels, is not listed because the site doesn't actually sell rooms. To use the codes, you quote the relevant code to an actual seller—the Walt Disney Travel Company, for example.

One thing we noticed when getting rates from all the different sellers is that no one seller offered the best rate all the time. Rankings are ordered from top to bottom, best to worst.

Seller	Percentage of Winning Quotes	Number of Hotels Represented
1. floridakiss.com	81%	Small
2. octopustravel.com	81%	Small
3. hotelkingdom.com	75%	Large
4. hotel reservation department	65%	One hotel
5. dreamsunlimitedtravel.com	64%	Small
6. expedia.com	63%	Large
7. travelocity.com	62%	Large
8. hotel Web sites	60%	One hotel
9. inntopia.com	53%	Small
10. travelworm.com	51%	Large
11. 2000-orlando.com	50%	TK
12. orbitz.com	42%	Medium
13. aanhotels.com	37%	Medium
14. onetravel.com	36%	Medium
15. hotels.com	33%	Medium
16. placestostay.com	31%	Medium
17. lodging.com	23%	Medium

While Expedia is often able to offer better deals on some larger properties (for example, Hilton and Doubletree), some Disney-centric travel sites, such as **www.dreamsunlimitedtravel.com** and **www.mousesavers.com,** form special relationships with specific hotels that result in unusually juicy discounts. Because the megasites like Orbitz, Expedia, and **www.hotels. com** have neither the time nor inclination to nurture such relationships, they can't obtain these sweetheart deals. At the boutique Celebration Hotel, for example, Dreams Unlimited's rate was more than 35% lower than Expedia's.

The following chart summarizes how much you can expect to save on average from each of the Internet sellers listed above (only these for which we have a minimum of 1,000 observations are included).

Seller	Number of Observations	Average Savings (Method 1)	Average Savings (Method 2)
octopustravel.com	2,118	21%	34%
aanhotels.com	5,424	12%	20%
onetravel.com	3,600	11%	24%
placestostay.com	6,371	9%	17%
hotelkingdom.com	456,524	7%	8%
hotels.com	17,990	7%	13%
orbitz.com	15,822	7%	13%
lodging.com	9,883	5%	7%
travelocity.com	255,533	5%	6%
inntopia.com	1,188	4%	5%
travelworm.com	163,209	4%	5%
expedia.com	257,998	3%	4%

Method 1: Average percentage by which the seller beats its nearest competitor.
Method 2: Average percentage by which the seller beats the highest rate advertised.

Another tool in the hotel-hunting arsenal is **www.travelaxe.com.** Travelaxe offers free software you can download on your PC (won't run on Macs) that will scan an assortment of hotel-discount sites and find the cheapest rate for each of over 200 Disney-area hotels. The site offers filters such as price, quality rating, and proximity to a specific location (Walt Disney World, SeaWorld, the convention center, airport, and so on) to allow you to narrow your search. The same software also scans for the best rates in cities throughout the United States and the world.

4. If You Make Your Own Reservation   Always call the hotel in question, not the chain's national toll-free number. Often, reservationists at the toll-free number are unaware of local specials. Always ask about specials before you inquire about corporate rates. Don't hesitate to bargain, but do it before you check in. If you're buying a hotel's weekend package and want to extend your stay, for example, you can often obtain at least the corporate rate for the extra days.

5. Condominium and Vacation Home Deals   A large number of condo resorts, time-shares, and all-suite properties in the Kissimmee–

RENTING A VACATION HOME

April Arnatt, an Unofficial Guide reader from the United Kingdom, always rents a vacation home when she visits Walt Disney World. Here is her advice on researching and selecting a rental that's right for you.

There are hundreds of vacation-home rentals in the Walt Disney World area, ranging from condos to large, seven-bed, five-bath, single-family homes with heated pools and spas. Many are in neighborhoods with large pools, movie theaters, tennis courts, or golf courses that renters can use.

However, there are choices and consequences. You will have more space than in any hotel room and will almost certainly save money for any party size, especially for longer stays. You will not have all the services of a hotel, nor a corporate standard. You will not have a shuttle bus to the parks, but then, at the end of a long day, you will not have to wait for one, either. This does mean you will need a car.

What you will get is a property set up for vacation guests but with individual touches. Even similarly sized neighboring homes will have different outlooks and décor. Many homes are owned by individuals who rent their properties for short periods when they are not in residence, so the property will usually have all the amenities from home you miss when traveling. Homes often include items such as radios, extra TVs, grills, toy boxes, or Disney-themed rooms for kids.

A large percentage of vacationers become annual regulars once they experience the relaxed balance of life in a vacation home. Many convene get-togethers for extended families, allowing everyone to be "together" but not on top of each other.

Before you begin your search, know what's important to you and your family.

Privacy   Sharing even two hotel rooms will test your patience after a few days. In a vacation rental, you get a whole condo or house to yourselves, so you can escape from each other when togetherness becomes just too much. Rent a home with a pool, and you will have that to yourselves too; no pool hours, no competition for the loungers, and all the drinks and snacks you require. If privacy is important, ask the exact location of the home you're considering. Does it back onto other homes with a fence in between, or does it have an open view over a lake, golf course, or woodland?

Facilities   If you enjoy having (and paying for) hot- and cold-running room service at a top-class hotel, then a home rental is not likely to be for you. Homes should be clean for your arrival, but unless you arrange (and pay for) maid service, the home will probably not be cleaned again until after you leave. There will not be any room service, laundry service, or anyone to carry your bags. However, you are likely to have an equipped kitchen and laundry, as well as space to entertain and chill out.

Cost   Vacation homes near Highway 192 typically cost $110–$200 per night, depending on size and facilities; you may find discounts for booking for longer periods and quiet seasons. Always ask homeowners about discounts. If the nightly rate seems stiff, remember that you're getting the equivalent of at least two suites in a hotel. You get your own kitchen and laundry, so you can keep costs down by eating in. You can easily pack your own lunches for an early-morning arrival at a theme park.

How much pre-vacation research are you prepared to do? Some, or you would not be reading this book. But if you are going to enjoy your vacation, be sure you have the right property for you and your group. Because these are homes, they are individual in style, and no two are alike.

If you do not want to do much work to find your home, book one via a travel agent, a property-management company, or a travel company as part of a package. This is often more expensive, and you may not be able to guarantee which home will be assigned to you until you arrive; thus, you lose many of the benefits of renting a home. We recommend finding vacation homes through personal contact, classified ads in your local newspaper, specialist magazines, or Web sites.

For large Web sites offering hundreds of homes across Florida, check www. villas2000.com or www.vrbo.com; both have listings with photographs of individual homes and allow you to contact the owner directly. Once in contact and before booking, ask specific questions. Many other Web sites offer homes managed by one agent or company.

Travel Time to Attractions and Shops   Trekking back and forth to the attractions can rob you of precious vacation time. Not everywhere can really be "ten minutes from Disney." There are indeed plenty of rental homes within a five-mile or ten-minute radius, but some are farther away. If you plan to visit attractions every day, ask the number of miles (and minutes) your home is from your favorite attractions.

Convenience   If you have preschool kids in your party, do you want strollers, cribs, child seats, and a DVD player for cartoons? Are there patio door alarms to guard the pool area? You might want to have a little more space in the living areas to provide kids' and adults' zones; you might also want to split the kids into separate bedrooms without having to convert one of the sofas into a guest bed each evening.

If you enjoy making new friends around the hotel pool, consider a home with community facilities where you can meet others. Check that you will have membership or free access to them.

Amenities and Intangibles   Homes shown on Web sites and in brochures usually have several photos so you can see what you would be getting. Ask the owners if they have more photos they can e-mail, or a brochure or floorplan they can send. Many properties are second homes for their owners, so they will have personal touches and high standards of décor.

Consider whether you require a grill, a hot tub, pool heating, or additional maid service. How much patio furniture do you need? Do you want extra bedding, a microwave oven, or ceiling fans?

The best recommendations are from previous guests and personal contacts. Most vacation-home owners are happy to talk to you about the home and can offer advice about travel arrangements, local services, and attractions, as well as details of what the rental fee includes.

Pricing   Vacation homes are usually rented by the week, though some will rent for shorter periods (usually at a premium). Many offer discounts for longer stays (especially for more than 14 nights) and for quiet periods, or if owners are trying to fill gaps between bookings. Costs vary enormously depending on the size and location of rental home and season. Prices usually are higher during holiday periods and in July and early August.

Before you book, check if the rental fee quoted includes taxes. Ask about charges for additional equipment, such as cribs or grills.

Orlando area rent to vacationers for a week or less. Look for bargains, especially off-peak. Some numbers below are for reservations services that serve as rental agents for multiple, generally unrelated condo and resort owners. Other numbers are for time-shares that rent vacant condos when available. If you rent a time-share unit, you may be invited to a sales presentation, but accepting the invitation is entirely at your discretion. For reservations and information, contact:

AAA Dream Homes (multi-property reservation service) (888) 658-8535

Condolink (multi-property reservation service) (800) 733-4445

Disney Rents (multi-property reservation service) (877) 357-3685

East and West of Disney Condos (multi-property reservation service) (800) 633-7108

Embassy Sunterra Grand Beach (time-share) (800) 350-3382

Fairfield Orlando at Cypress Point (time-share) (800) 438-6493

Florida Supreme Villas Rentals (multi-property reservation service) (888) 353-9188

Hilton Grand Vacations Club (time-share) (800) 448-2736

Hilton Grand Vacations Club Sea World (time-share) (800) 448-2736

Holiday Inn Family Suites (all-suite hotel) (877) 387-5437

Holiday Villas (multi-property reservation service) (800) 344-3959

Kissimmee–St. Cloud Reservations (multi-property reservation service) (800) 333-5477

Liki Tiki Village (time-share) (800) 634-3119

Marriott Vacation Club (four time-share resorts) (800) 845-5279

Orange Lake Country Club (time-share) (888) 657-3529

Polynesian Isles Resort (time-share) (800) 424-1943

Ramada Inn All Suites (all-suite hotel) (800) 272-6232

Silver Lake Resort (time-share) (407) 397-9721 Ext. 5145

Star Island Resort (time-share) (800) 513-2820

Vacation Homes at Disney (multi-property reservation service) (800) 288-6608

Vistana Resort (time-share) (800) 877-8787

Westgate Resorts (six time-share resorts) (888) 808-7410

Wyndam Palms (time-share) (407) 390-1991

We frequently receive letters from readers extolling the virtues of renting a condo or vacation home. This endorsement by a family from Ellington, Connecticut, is typical:

Our choice to stay outside Disney was based on cost and sanity. We found over the last couple of years that our children can't share the same bed. We have also gotten tired of having to turn off the lights at 8 p.m. and lie quietly in the dark waiting for our children to fall asleep. With this in mind, we needed a kind of condo/suite layout. Anything in Disney offering this option (e.g. BoardWalk Villas, [Beach Club Villas, Old Key West, etc.]) was going to cost approximately $400–$500 a night. This was not built into our

Disney budget. We decided on the Sheraton Vistana Resort. We had a two-bedroom villa with full kitchen, living room, three TVs and washer/dryer. I packed for half the trip and did laundry almost every night. The facilities offered a daily children's program and several pools, kiddy pools, and "playscapes." Located on FL 535, we had a 5–10 minute drive to most attractions, including SeaWorld, Disney, and Universal.

A St. Joe, Indiana, family also had a good experience, writing:

We rented a home in Kissimmee this time and we'll never stay in a hotel at WDW again. It was by far the nicest, most relaxing time we've ever had down there. Our rental home was within 10–15 minutes of all the Disney parks, and 25 minutes from SeaWorld. We had three bedrooms, two baths, and an in-ground pool in a screened enclosure out back. We paid $90 per night for the whole shootin' match. We did spring for the pool heating, $25/night extra. (February) We used AAA Dream Homes Rental Company and they did a great job by us. They provided us with detailed info before we went down, so we would know what we needed to bring.

Many rental condos are listed with travel agents. Owners often pay an enhanced commission to agents who rent units at reduced consumer rates.

Best Hotels for Families outside Disney World

What makes a super family hotel? Roomy accommodations, in-room fridge, great pool, complimentary breakfast, childcare options, and programs for kids are a few of the things the *Unofficial Guide* hotel team researched in selecting the top hotels for families from among hundreds of properties in the Disney World area. Some of our picks are expensive, others are more reasonable, and some are a bargain. Regardless of price, be assured that these hotels understand a family's needs.

Though all hotels listed below offer some type of shuttle to the theme parks, some offer very limited service. Call the hotel before you book and ask what the shuttle schedule will be when you visit. Since families, like individuals, have different wants and needs, we haven't ranked the following properties here; they're listed by zone and alphabetically.

Zone 1: International Drive

DoubleTree Castle Hotel

8629 International Drive, Orlando; (407) 345-1511 or (800) 952-2785; www.doubletreecastle.com

Rate per Night $120 Pool ★★★ Fridge in Room Yes Shuttle to Parks Yes (Disney, Universal, and SeaWorld) Maximum Persons per Room 4

Special Comments Add $10 to room rate, and up to four people receive continental breakfast; two signature chocolate-chip cookies come with every room

You can't miss this one; it's the only castle on I-Drive. Inside you'll find royal colors (purple dominates), opulent fixtures, European art, Renaissance music, and a mystical Castle

Creature at the door. The 216 guest rooms also receive the royal treatment in décor, though some guests may find them gaudy. All, however, are fairly large and well equipped with TV with PlayStation, fridge, three phones, coffeemaker, iron and board, hair dryer, and safe. The Castle Café off the lobby serves full or continental breakfast. A court jester appears at breakfast four days a week to entertain with juggling and balloon sculptures. For lunch or dinner, you might walk next door to Vito's Chop House or Café Tu Tu Tango (an Unofficial favorite). The heated circular pool is five feet deep and features a fountain in the center, a poolside bar, and a whirlpool. There's no separate kiddie pool. Other amenities include a fitness center, arcade, gift shop, lounge, valet laundry service and facilities, and guest services desk with park passes for sale and baby-sitting recommendations. Security feature: Elevators require an electronic guest card key.

Hard Rock Hotel

5800 Universal Boulevard, Orlando; (407) 503-ROCK; www.universalorlando.com

Rate per Night $249 Pool ★★★★ Fridge in Room Available, $10 per day Shuttle to Parks Yes (Universal, SeaWorld, and Wet 'n' Wild) Maximum Persons per Room 4

Special Comments Microwaves available for $15 per day

Located on Universal property, the 650-room Hard Rock Hotel is nirvana for any kid older than eight, especially those interested in music. Architecture is California mission–style, and rock memorabilia is displayed throughout. If you plan to spend at least a few days at Universal parks, this is an excellent upscale option. Guests get theme-park privileges such as early admission on select days and all-day access to the Universal Express line-breaking program, plus delivery of packages to their room and priority seating at select Universal restaurants. The music-filled pool area has a white-sand beach, water slide, underwater audio system, and ultra-hip pool bar. You'll also find two restaurants, including the Palm chophouse, a chic lounge, fitness center, and Hard Rock merchandise store. Guest rooms are ultra-hip too, with cutting-edge contemporary décor, a CD sound system, TV with pay-per-view movies and video games, coffeemaker, iron and board, robes, hair dryer, and two phones. A supervised activity center serves kids ages 4–14.

Holiday Inn Family Suites Resort

14500 Continental Gateway, Orlando; (407) 387-5437 or (877) 387-5437; www.hifamilysuites.com/bro

Rate per Night $152 Pools ★★★★ Fridge in Room Yes Shuttle to Parks Yes (Disney only) Maximum Persons per Room 7

Special Comments Complimentary hot breakfast buffet

Set on 24 acres, this resort is as kid-friendly as they come. Little ones will love the locomotive theme; they're engaged the moment they arrive with a kids' check-in desk designed to look like a caboose. Watch the tykes, or they might hop the kiddie train for a ride around the property. Guests can choose among two- and three- bedroom Kid-Suites executed in a number of different themes, including Jungle, Magic of Disney, Manatee, and Camp Kellogg. There are also smaller suites. All are about 485 square feet and include microwave, fridge, coffeemaker, TV and VCR, iron and board, two hair dryers, and a safe. Kidsuites feature a semiprivate kids' bedroom with bunk beds, pull-out sleeper bed, 20-inch TV and VCR, Nintendo 64, CD/cassette player, and activity table. All suites offer contemporary and comfortable décor but are a bit chopped up and don't receive much natural light. You can stay in the family-oriented East Track Courtyard or the West Track Courtyard, which has a more adult atmosphere. Additional amenities include high-tech game room, casual-dining restaurant (12 and younger eat free with a paying adult), food court, convenience store, lounge, gift shop, fitness center, washer and dryer in each courtyard, and guest activities desk (buy Disney tickets and get recommendations on baby-sitting). Adults will enjoy the Olympic-size lap pool, while kids will like the huge zero-depth-entry pool with fountains, water toys, kiddie pool, and tubular playground with slide. Afternoon pool activities for kids are scheduled seasonally. The resort teems with families even in the off-season; it's huge but can get crowded.

Portofino Bay Hotel

5601 Universal Boulevard, Orlando; (407) 503-1000; www.universalorlando.com

Rate per Night $269 Pools ★★★★ Fridge in Room Minibar; fridge available for $10 per day Shuttle to Parks Yes (Universal, SeaWorld, and Wet 'n' Wild) Maximum Persons per Room 4

Special Comments Character dinner on Monday and Friday

Located in Universal, the 750-room Portofino Bay Hotel is themed like an Italian Riviera village. Guests receive theme-park privileges such as early admission on select days and all-day access to the Universal Express line-breaking program, plus delivery of packages to their room and priority seating at select Universal restaurants. Rooms are ultra luxurious, with Italian furnishings, opulent baths, and soothing neutral hues. Standard guestroom amenities include minibar, coffeemaker, iron and board, hair dryer, safe, umbrella, and TV with pay-per-view movies. Microwaves are available ($15 a day). Camp Portofino offers supervised activities (movies, video games, crafts, etc.) from 5 to 11:30 p.m. for children ages 4–14. Cost is $45 per child and $35 for each additional child in the same family; dinner is included. Trattoria del Porto, one of the Portofino's casual-dining restaurants, offers a character dinner 6–9 p.m. on Friday. Characters such as Scooby Doo and Woody Woodpecker attend. Cost is $19.50 for adults, $12.75 for 12 and younger. Portofino has four other Italian restaurants (each with children's menu), an Italian bakery (also serves gelato), and two bars. Three elaborate pools, gardens, jogging trails, and a spa and fitness center round out major amenities. If you have the bank account to pay for it and plan to spend time at Universal, you can't go wrong here.

Sheraton World Resort

10100 International Drive, Orlando; (407) 352-1100 or (800) 327-0363; www.sheratonworld.com

Rate per Night $289–$329 Pools ★★★½ Fridge in Room Yes Shuttle to Parks Yes (Disney only) Maximum Persons per Room 4

Special Comments A good option if you're visiting SeaWorld

Set on 28 acres, the Sheraton World Resort offers plenty of room for kids to roam. And with three heated pools, two kiddie pools, a small playground, an arcade, and a free minigolf course (very mini), this resort offers ample kid-friendly diversions. The main pool is especially pleasant, with fountains, lush landscaping, and poolside bar. Other amenities and services include fitness center, massage therapy, gift shop, guest services desk, and lounge. Book a room in the new tower if possible, even though it's away from the kiddie pools and playground. Tower rooms are a bit larger and more upscale than low-rise rooms, some of which could use renovation. All 1,102 rooms include fridge, coffeemaker, TV with Nintendo, iron and board, hair dryer, and safe. The Sheraton has one restaurant and a deli with a Pizza Hut. If your family loves SeaWorld, you're in luck: Shamu and friends are within walking distance.

Zone 2: Lake Buena Vista and I-4 Corridor

Hilton Walt Disney World

1751 Hotel Plaza Boulevard, Lake Buena Vista; (407) 827-4000 or (800) 782-4414; www.hilton-wdwv.com

Rate per Night $129 Pools ★★★½ Fridge in Room Minibar Shuttle to Parks Yes (Disney theme and water parks only) Maximum Persons per Room 4
Special Comments Sunday character breakfast and Disney early-entry program

The Hilton occupies 23 acres in the Downtown Disney Resort Area. Since it's an official Walt Disney World hotel, guests can take advantage of the Disney early-entry program, which allows entry to a selected Disney park one hour before official opening. The Hilton's 814 guest rooms and suites are spacious, luxurious, and tasteful. Decorated in earth tones, all standard rooms have marble baths, iron and board, hair dryer, two phones, desk, minibar, coffeemaker, and cable TV with pay-per-view movies and video games. One big plus family amenity is the character breakfast, offered 8:30–11 a.m. on Sunday. (Reservations aren't accepted.) Food is served buffet style, and four characters attend (only two are present at a time). Other important family amenities include the Hilton Vacation Station, where kids ages 4–12 can join supervised activities; baby-sitting services; an arcade and pool table; and two beautifully landscaped heated swimming pools, as well as a kiddie pool. Adults and older children can relax in the fitness center after a long day touring. Nine restaurants, including Benihana, add to the hotel's convenience.

Holiday Inn Sun Spree Resort

13351 State Road 535, Lake Buena Vista; (407) 239-4500 or (800) 366-6299; www.kidsuites.com

Rate per Night $118 Pool ★★★ Fridge in Room Yes Shuttle to Parks Yes (Disney only) Maximum Persons per Room 4–6
Special Comments The first hotel in the world to offer KidSuites

Put on your sunglasses. You'll know you're here when the hot pink, bright blue, green, and yellow exterior comes into view. Inside, kids have their own check-in counter, where they'll receive a free goody bag. Character mascots Max, Maxine, and the Kidsuite Gang come out to play at scheduled times. But the big lure is KidSuites, 405-square-foot rooms with a separate children's area. Themes include a tree house, circus tent, jail, space capsule, igloo, and fort. The kids' area sleeps three to four children in two sets of bunk beds or one bunk bed and a twin; it has a cable TV and VCR, Nintendo, radio/cassette or CD player, fun phone, and game table. The separate adult area has its own TV and VCR, safe, hair dryer, and mini-kitchenette with fridge, microwave, sink, and coffeemaker. Standard guest rooms offer these adult amenities. Other kid-friendly amenities include free bedtime tuck-in by a member of the KidSuite Gang (reservations required); the tiny Castle Movie Theater, which shows continuous movies daily and clown and magic shows nightly; a playground; an arcade with Sega games and air hockey, among many games; a basketball court; and Camp Holiday, a free supervised program for ages 3–12. Held every day in Max's Magic Castle, Camp Holiday might include movies and cartoons, bingo, face painting, and karaoke. Also offered are a large, free-form pool complete with kiddie pool and two whirlpools, and a fitness center ($6 hour per child, 10 a.m.–10 p.m.). Maxine's Food Emporium, open 7 a.m.–10 p.m., includes Little Caesars, A&W Restaurant, Otis Spunkmeyer Cookies and Muffins, TCBY, and more. There's also a mini-mart. Another perk: Kids 12 and younger eat free from a special menu when dining with one paying adult (maximum four kids per adult).

Hyatt Regency Grand Cypress

One Grand Cypress Boulevard, Lake Buena Vista; (407) 239-1234;
www. hyattgrandcypress.com

Rate per Night $199 Pool ★★★★★ Fridge in Room Minibar; fridge available on
request Shuttle to Parks Yes (Disney only) Maximum Persons per Room 4
Special Comments Wow, what a pool!

There are myriad reasons to stay at this 1,500-acre resort, but the pool ranks as number one. The 800,000-gallon tropical paradise has a 125-foot water slide, waterfalls, caves
and grottos, and a suspension bridge. Your kids may never want to leave the pool to visit
the theme parks. The Hyatt also is a golfer's paradise. With a 45-hole championship Jack
Nicklaus–designed course, an 18-hole course, a 9-hole pitch and putt course, and a golf
academy, there's something for golfers of all abilities. Other recreational perks include a
racquet facility with hard and clay courts, a private lake with beach, a fitness center, and
miles of trails for biking, walking, jogging, and horseback riding. The 750 standard guest
rooms are 360 square feet and have a Florida ambience, with green and reddish hues,
touches of rattan, and private balconies. Amenities include minibar, iron and board, safe,
hair dryer, ceiling fan, and cable TV with pay-per-view movies and video games. Suite and
villa accommodations offer even more amenities. Camp Hyatt provides supervised programs for kids, and in-room baby-sitting is available. Five restaurants offer dining options.
Four lounges provide nighttime entertainment. If outdoor recreation is high on your
family's list, Hyatt is an excellent high-end choice.

Marriott Village at Little Lake Bryan

8623 Vineland Avenue, Lake Buena Vista; (407) 938-9001 or (877) 682-8552;
www.marriottvillage.com

Rate per Night $79–$89 Pools ★★★ Fridge in Room Yes Shuttle to Parks Yes
(Disney, Universal, SeaWorld, and Wet 'n' Wild) Maximum Persons per Room 4
Special Comments Free continental breakfast at Fairfield Inn and Spring Hill Suites

This gated community includes a 388-room Fairfield Inn, a 400-suite Spring Hill Suites,
and 312-room Courtyard. Whatever your budget, you'll find a room here to fit it. For a
bit more space, book Spring Hill Suites; if you're looking for value, try the Fairfield Inn; if
you need limited business amenities, reserve at the Courtyard. Amenities at all three
properties include fridge, cable TV with PlayStation, iron and board, and hair dryer. Additionally, all Spring Hill suites have microwaves, and all Courtyard rooms feature Web TV.
Cribs and rollaway beds are available free at all locations. Pools at all three hotels are
attractive and medium-sized, with children's interactive splash zones and whirlpools.
Each property has a fitness center. The incredibly convenient Village Marketplace food
court includes Pizza Hut, TCBY, Oscar Mayer Hot Dog Construction Company, Oscar
Mayer 1883 Deli, Village Grill, Gourmet Bean Coffee and Pastry Shop, and a 24-hour
convenience store. The Bahama Breeze, Fish Bones, and Golden Corral full-service
restaurants are within walking distance. Each hotel has a Kids Club (no extra charge) for
ages 4–8. Kids Clubs are themed (backyard, tree house, and library) and feature a big-
screen TV, computer stations, and three educational centers (math and science, reading,
and creative activities). They operate about six hours daily; a staff member is on duty at
all times. Marriott Village also offers a supervised Kids Night Out program (ages 4–10)
from 6 to 10 p.m. on select nights. Cost is $35 per child, which includes activities and
dinner. Other services and amenities include a Disney planning station and ticket sales,
an arcade, and a Hertz car-rental desk. Shoppers will find the Orlando Premium Outlets
adjacent. You'll get a lot of bang for your buck at Marriott Village.

Sheraton Royal Safari

12205 Apopka-Vineland Road, Lake Buena Vista; (407) 239-0444 or (800) 423-3297; www.sheraton.com

Rate per Night $149 Pool ★★★ Fridge in Room Safari suites only Shuttle to Parks Yes (Disney free; other parks for fee) Maximum Persons per Room 4–6
Special Comments Cool python water slide

The safari theme is nicely executed throughout the property—from the lobby dotted with African artifacts and native décor to the 79-foot python water slide dominating the pool. The 393 guest rooms and 90 safari suites sport African-inspired art and tasteful animal-print soft goods in brown, beige, and jewel tones. Amenities include cable TV with PlayStation, coffeemaker, iron and board, hair dryer, and safe. Suites are a good option for families since they provide added space with a separate sitting room and a kitchenette with a fridge, microwave, and sink. The first thing your kids will probably want to do is take a turn on the python water slide. It's pretty impressive, but as one Unofficial Guide researcher pointed out, it's somewhat of a letdown: The python doesn't actually spit you out of its mouth. Instead you're deposited below its chin. Other on-site amenities include a restaurant (children's menu available), deli, lounge, arcade, and fitness center. Baby-sitting is available.

Sheraton Vistana Resort

8800 Vistana Center Drive, Lake Buena Vista; (866) 208-0003; www.starwoodvo.com

Rate per Night $289 Pools ★★★½ Fridge in Room Minibar Shuttle to Parks Yes (Disney) Maximum Persons per Room 6
Special Comments Though time-shares, the villas are rented nightly as well

Sheraton Vistana is deceptively large, stretching across both sides of Vistana Center Drive. Since Sheraton's emphasis is on selling the time-shares, the rental angle is little known. But families should consider it; the Vistana is one of Orlando's best off-Disney properties. If you want a serene retreat from your days in the theme parks, this is an excellent base. The spacious villas come in one-bedroom, two-bedroom, and two-bedroom-with-lock-off models. All are decorated in beachy pastels, but the emphasis is on the profusion of amenities. Each villa has a full kitchen (including fridge/freezer, microwave, oven/range, dishwasher, toaster, and coffeemaker, with an option to pre-stock with groceries), clothes washer and dryer, TVs in the living room and each bedroom (one with VCR), stereo with CD player, separate dining area, and private patio or balcony in most. Grounds offer seven swimming pools (four with bars), four playgrounds, three restaurants, game rooms, fitness centers, a minigolf course, sports equipment rental (including bikes), and courts for basketball, volleyball, tennis, and shuffleboard. A mind-boggling array of activities for kids (and adults) ranges from crafts to games and sports tournaments. Of special note: Vistana is highly secure, with locked gates bordering all guest areas, so children can have the run of the place without parents worrying about them wandering off.

Wyndham Palace

1900 Buena Vista Drive, Lake Buena Vista; (407) 827-2727 or (800) WYNDHAM; www.wyndham.com

Rate per Night $145 Pools ★★★½ Fridge in Room Minibar Shuttle to Parks Yes (Disney only) Maximum Persons per Room 4
Special Comments Sunday character breakfast available

In the Downtown Disney Resort Area, the Wyndham Palace is upscale and convenient. Surrounded by a man-made lake and plenty of palms, the spacious pool area contains three heated pools, the largest of which is partially covered (nice for when you need a little shade); a whirlpool; and a sand volleyball court. Plus, a pool concierge will fetch your favorite magazine or fruity drink. On Sunday, the Watercress Café hosts a character breakfast ($19 for adults and $11 for children). The 1,014 guest rooms are posh and spacious; each comes with a desk, coffeemaker, hair dryer, cable TV with pay-per-view movies, iron and board, and minibar. There are also 112 suites. Children ages 4–12 can participate in supervised programs of Wyndy Harbour Kids' Klub (where spelling is obviously not in the curriculum). In-room baby-sitting is available through the All about Kids service. Three lighted tennis courts, a European-style spa offering 60 services, a fitness center, an arcade, a playground, and a beauty salon round out amenities. Three restaurants and a mini-market are on site. And if you aren't wiped out after time in the parks, consider the Laughing Kookaburra Good Time Bar for live entertainment and dancing. Note: All these amenities and services come at a price; an $8 per night resort fee will be added to your bill.

Zone 3: US 192

Comfort Suites Maingate Resort

7888 West US 192, Kissimmee; (407) 390-9888

Rate per Night $90 Pool ★★★ Fridge in Room Yes Shuttle to Parks Yes (Disney, Universal, SeaWorld, and Wet 'n' Wild) Maximum Persons per Room 6
Special Comments Complimentary continental breakfast daily

This property has 150 spacious one-room suites with double sofa bed, microwave, fridge, coffeemaker, TV, hair dryer, and safe. The suites aren't lavish but are clean and contemporary, with muted deep-purple and beige tones. Extra bathroom counter space is especially convenient for larger families. The heated pool is large and has plenty of lounge chairs and moderate landscaping. A kiddie pool, whirlpool, and poolside bar complete the courtyard. Other amenities include an arcade and gift shop. But Maingate's big plus is its location: next door to a shopping center with about everything a family could need. There, you'll find seven dining options, including Outback Steakhouse, Dairy Queen, Subway, TGI Friday's, and Chinese, Japanese, and Italian eateries; a Goodings supermarket; one-hour film developing; hair salon; bank; dry cleaner; tourist information center with park passes for sale; and a Centra Care walk-in clinic, among other services. All this a short walk from your room.

Gaylord Palms Resort

6000 West Osceola Parkway, Kissimmee; (407) 586-0000; www.gaylordpalms.com

Rate per Night $169 Pool ★★★★ Fridge in Room Yes Shuttle to Parks Yes (Disney) Maximum Persons per Room 4
Special Comments Probably the closest off-World to Disney-level extravagance

This decidedly upscale resort has a colossal convention facility and strongly caters to business clientele but still is a nice (if pricey) family resort. Hotel wings are defined by the three themed, glass-roofed atriums they overlook. Key West's design is reminiscent of island life in the Florida Keys; Everglades is an overgrown spectacle of shabby swamp chic, complete with piped-in cricket noise and a robotic alligator; and the immense, central St. Augustine hearkens to Spanish Colonial Florida. Lagoons, streams, and waterfalls cut through and connect all three, and walkways and bridges abound. Rooms reflect the colors of their respective areas, though there's no particular connection in décor (St. Augustine atrium-view rooms are the most opulent, but they're not Spanish).

A fourth wing, Emerald Tower, overlooks the Emerald Bay shopping and dining area of the St. Augustine atrium. These rooms are the nicest and most expensive, and they're mostly used by convention-goers. Though rooms have fridges and stereos with CD (as well as other high-end perks, like high-speed Internet access), the rooms themselves really work better as retreats for adults rather than kids. However, children will enjoy wandering the themed areas, playing in the family pool (with water-squirting octopus), or participating in La Petite Academy Kids Station, which organizes games and activities.

Holiday Inn Nikki Bird Resort

7300 West US 192, Kissimmee; (407) 396-7300 or (800) 20-OASIS

Rate per Night $83 Pools ★★★½ Fridge in Room Yes Shuttle to Parks Yes (Disney only) Maximum Persons per Room 5 (2 adults; 3 small children)

Special Comments Kids 12 and younger eat free from special menus with a paying adult; room service includes Pizza Hut pizza

In the Orlando hotel world, you're nobody unless you have a mascot. Here it's Nikki Bird and Wacky the Wizard, who stroll the resort interacting with kids and posing for photos. This Holiday Inn offers standard rooms and Kidsuites. All feature microwave, fridge, TV with PlayStation, coffeemaker, iron and board, hair dryer, and safe. Kidsuites also offer a children's area with kid-size bunk beds and twin bed, TV/VCR, radio/CD player, and PlayStation. Kidsuites are most suitable for families with children nine and younger; older children will have a hard time fitting into the kids' beds. Parents beware: Kidsuites come with extremely bright décor; sunglasses are recommended. Standard rooms are fairly large, but the Kidsuites are a bit cramped by the children's area. This sprawling resort offers three pools with whirlpools and two kiddie pools with squirt fountains and small playgrounds. On-site volleyball and tennis provide more outdoor recreation. Fitness equipment is available, and a large arcade has air hockey, pool, and Sega games. Services include car rental and a tour desk selling park passes. The resort can arrange baby-sitting for $10 per hour (minimum four hours), plus a $10 transportation fee. The full-service Angel's Diner has 1950s décor and a good buffet with American cuisine and some theme nights. After dinner, find nightly family entertainment at "Nikki's Nest" with songs, puppet and magic shows, and games.

Howard Johnson EnchantedLand

4985 West Highway 192, Kissimmee; (407) 396-4343 or (888) 753-4343

Rate per Night $80 Pool ★★ Fridge in Room Yes Shuttle to Parks Yes (Disney, Universal, and SeaWorld) Maximum Persons per Room 4

Special Comments Complimentary ice cream party; free video library

Fairies, dragons, and superheroes have invaded the HoJo. Book a Family Value Room—a standard room transformed into a kids' suite. About 300 square feet, these rooms feature a themed kids' area (choose from tree house, fairies, or action heroes) with a twin daybed that converts to two twins or one king, TV and VCR, microwave, fridge, coffeemaker, and safe. The kids' area is separated from the double bed by a half-wall, so parents looking for privacy probably won't find it here. Kids check in at a tree house. Based in a small playroom, the Adventure Club ($5 per child) offers supervised activities, games, and movies Thursday–Saturday evenings. A small market is on site, and breakfast is 7 to 11 a.m. daily (kids 12 and younger eat free with a paying adult). Other amenities include a small arcade and a whirlpool. EnchantedLand may not offer the myriad amenities found in more-deluxe properties, but it is a good value.

Radisson Resort Parkway

2900 Parkway Boulevard, Kissimmee; (407) 396-7000 or (800) 634-4774

Rate per Night $145 Pool ★★★★½ Fridge in Room Minibar Shuttle to Parks Yes (Disney, Universal, and SeaWorld) Maximum Persons per Room 4
Special Comments Kids 10 and younger eat free with a paying adult at any hotel restaurant

The pool alone is worth a stay here, but the Radisson Resort gets high marks in all areas. The free-form pool is huge, with a waterfall and water slide surrounded by palms and flowering plants, plus a smaller heated pool, two whirlpools, and a kiddie pool. Other outdoor amenities include two lighted tennis courts, volleyball, a playground, and jogging areas. Kids can also blow off steam at the arcade, while adults might visit the fitness center. Rooms are elegant, featuring Italian furnishings and marble baths. They're above average size and include minibar, coffeemaker, color TV, iron and board, hair dryer, and safe. Dining options include The Court for breakfast and dinner buffets and a 1950s-style diner serving burgers, sandwiches, shakes, and Pizza Hut pizza, among other fare. A sports lounge with 11-by-6-foot TV offers nighttime entertainment. Guest services can help with tours, park passes, car rental, and baby-sitting. The only downside: no children's programs.

Hotels and Motels: Rated and Ranked

In this section, we compare hotels in three main areas outside Walt Disney World (pages 182–205) with those inside the World.

In addition to Disney properties, we rate hotels in the three lodging areas defined earlier in this chapter. There are additional hotels at the intersection of US 27 and I-4, on US 441 (Orange Blossom Trail), and in downtown Orlando. Most of these require more than 30 minutes of commuting to Disney World and thus are not rated. We also haven't rated lodging east of Siesta Lago Road on US 192.

What's in a Room?

Except for cleanliness, state of repair, and décor, travelers pay little attention to hotel rooms. There is, of course, a clear standard of quality and luxury that differentiates Motel 6 from Holiday Inn, Holiday Inn from Marriott, and so on. Many guests, however, fail to appreciate that some rooms are better engineered than others. Making the room usable to its occupants is an art that combines both form and function.

Décor and taste are important. No one wants to stay in a room that's dated, garish, or ugly. But beyond décor, how "livable" is the room? In Orlando, for example, we have seen some beautifully appointed rooms that aren't well designed for human habitation. The next time you stay in a hotel, note your room's details and design elements. Even more than décor, these are the things that will make you feel comfortable and at home.

Room Ratings

To evaluate properties for their quality, tastefulness, state of repair, cleanliness, and size of their standard rooms, we have grouped the hotels and motels into classifications denoted by stars—the overall star rating. Star ratings in this guide apply only to Orlando-area properties and don't necessarily correspond to ratings awarded by Frommer's, Mobil, AAA, or other travel critics. Because stars have little relevance when awarded in the absence of recognized standards of comparison, we have tied our ratings to expected levels of quality established by specific American hotel corporations.

OVERALL STAR RATINGS

★★★★★	Superior Rooms	Tasteful and luxurious by any standard
★★★★	Extremely Nice Rooms	What you would expect at a Hyatt Regency or Marriott
★★★	Nice Rooms	Holiday Inn or comparable quality
★★	Adequate Rooms	Clean, comfortable, and functional without frills—like a Motel 6
★	Super Budget	These exist but are not included in our coverage

Overall star ratings apply only to room quality and describe the property's standard accommodations. For most hotels, a standard accommodation is a room with one king bed or two queen beds. In an all-suite property, the standard accommodation is either a studio or one-bedroom suite. In addition to standard accommodations, many hotels offer luxury rooms and special suites, which aren't rated in this guide. Star ratings for rooms are assigned without regard to whether a property has restaurant(s), recreational facilities, entertainment, or other extras.

In addition to stars (which delineate broad categories), we use a numerical rating system—the room quality rating. Our scale is 0–100, with 100 the best possible rating and zero (0) the worst. Numerical ratings show the difference we perceive between one property and another. Rooms at both the Hawthorne Suites Universal and Grosvenor Resort are rated three-and-a-half stars (★★★½). In the supplemental numerical ratings, Hawthorne Suites Universal is an 82, and Grosvenor a 76. This means that within the three-and-a-half-star category, Hawthorne Suites Universal has slightly nicer rooms than Grosvenor.

The location column identifies the area around Walt Disney World where you'll find a particular property. The designation "WDW" means the property is inside Walt Disney World. A "1" means it's on or near International Drive. Properties on or near US 192 (a.k.a. Irlo Bronson Memorial Highway, Vine Street, and Space Coast Parkway) are indicated by a "3." All others are marked with "2" and for the most part are along the FL 535 and the I-4 Corridor, though some are in nearby locations that don't meet any other criteria.

Names of properties along US 192 also designate location; for example, Holiday Inn Maingate West. The consensus in Orlando seems to be that the main entrance to Disney World is the broad interstate-type road that runs off of US 192. This is called Maingate. Properties along US 192 call themselves Maingate East or West to differentiate their positions along the highway. So, driving southeast from Clermont or the Florida Turnpike, the properties before you reach the Maingate turnoff are called Maingate West, while the properties after you pass the Maingate turnoff are called Maingate East.

LODGING AREAS

WDW	Walt Disney World
1	International Drive
2	I-4 Corridor
3	US 192 (Irlo Bronson Memorial Highway)

Cost estimates are based on the hotel's published rack rates for standard rooms. Each "$" represents $50. Thus a cost symbol of "$$$" means that a room (or suite) at that hotel will be about $150 a night.

We've focused on room quality and excluded consideration of location, services, recreation, or amenities. In some instances, a one- or two-room suite is available for the same price or less than that of a single standard hotel room.

If you've used an earlier edition of this guide, you'll notice that new properties have been added and many ratings and rankings have changed, some because of room renovation or improved maintenance or housekeeping. Failure to maintain rooms or lax housekeeping can bring down ratings.

Before you shop for a hotel, consider this letter from a man in Hot Springs, Arkansas:

We canceled our room reservations to follow the advice in your book and reserved a hotel highly ranked by the Unofficial Guide. We wanted inexpensive, but clean and cheerful. We got inexpensive, but [also] dirty, grim, and depressing. I really felt disappointed in your advice and the room. It was the pits. That was the one real piece of information I needed from your book! The room spoiled the holiday for me aside from our touring.

This letter was as unsettling to us as the bad room was to our reader. Our integrity as travel journalists is based on the quality of the information we provide. When rechecking the hotel our reader disliked, we found our rating was representative, but he had been assigned one of a small number of threadbare rooms scheduled for renovation.

The key to avoiding disappointment is to snoop in advance. Ask the hotel to send a photo of its standard guest room before you book, or get a copy of the hotel's promotional brochure. Note that some chains use the same guest-room photo in promotional literature for all of its hotels and that the room in a specific property may not resemble the photo. When you or your travel agent call, ask how old the property is and when the guest room you're being assigned was last renovated. If you are assigned a room inferior to expectations, demand to be moved.

The Top 30 Best Deals

Let's look at the best combinations of quality and value in a room. Rankings are made without consideration of location or the availability of restaurant(s), recreational facilities, entertainment, and/or amenities.

A reader recently wrote to complain that he had booked one of our top-ranked rooms in terms of value and had been very disappointed in the room. We noticed that the room the reader occupied had a quality rating of ★★½. Remember that the list of top deals is intended to give you some sense of value received for dollars spent. A ★★½ room at $40 may have the same value as a ★★★★ room at $115, but that doesn't mean the rooms will be of comparable quality. Regardless of whether it's a good deal, a ★★½ room is still a ★★½ room.

THE TOP 30 BEST DEALS					
Hotel	Location	Phone (area code 407)	Quality Rating	Overall Rating	Cost ($ = $50)
1. DoubleTree Universal	1	351-1000	★★★★	88	$$–
2. Hilton Grand Vacations Club	1	(800) 448-2736	★★★★	88	$$–
3. Lake Buena Vista Resort	WDW	828-2424	★★★★	85	$$–
4. Grosvenor Resort	WDW	828-4444	★★★½	76	$+
5. Extended Stay Convention Center	1	352-1708	★★★	72	$
6. Extended Stay Universal	1	351-1788	★★★	72	$
7. Holiday Inn Nikki Bird Resort	3	396-7300	★★★½	80	$$–
8. Marriott Imperial Palm Villas	1	239-4200	★★★★	86	$$+
9. Country Inn and Suites Calypso Cay	3	997-1400	★★★½	82	$$–
10. Studio Plus Convention Center	1	(800) 804-3274	★★★	73	$+
11. Studio Plus Universal	1	(800) 804-3274	★★★	73	$+
12. Vacation Village Parkway	3	396-4086	★★★★½	91	$$$–

THE TOP 30 BEST DEALS (continued)

Hotel	Location	Phone (area code 407)	Quality Rating	Overall Rating	Cost ($ = $50)
13. Fairfield Orlando Cypress Point	3	(800) 438-6493	★★★★	86	$$+
14. Orange Lake Country Club	3	239-0000	★★★★	85	$$
15. Celebrity Resorts Resort World	3	396-8300	★★★★	84	$$
16. Embassy Sunterra Grand Beach	1	(800) 350-3382	★★★★½	93	$$$–
17. Days Inn Eastgate	3	396-7700	★★½	64	$–
18. Best Western Movieland	1	351-3900	★★★	68	$+
19. Red Horse Inn	1	351-4100	★★★	69	$+
20. Embassy Vacation Resort	2	238-2500	★★★★½	92	$$$–
21. Residence Inn SeaWorld	1	313-3600	★★★★	85	$$+
22. AmeriSuites Lake Buena Vista South	3	997-1300	★★★½	82	$$
23. Hampton Inn Maingate West	3	396-6300	★★★	69	$+
24. AmeriSuites Orlando Convention Ctr.	1	370-4720	★★★½	81	$$
25. Fairfield Inn and Suites Universal	1	581-5600	★★★	73	$$–
26. Marriott Cypress Harbour	1	238-1300	★★★★	86	$$$–
27. Pop Century Resort	WDW	934-7639	★★★	74	$$–
28. Travelodge Suites Eastgate	3	396-7666	★★★	67	$+
29. Hawthorne Suites Lake Buena Vista	2	597-5000	★★★★	87	$$$–
30. Star Island Resort	3	997-8000	★★★★	84	$$$–

HOW THE HOTELS COMPARE

Hotel	Zone	Phone (area code 407)	Overall Quality Rating	Room Quality Rating
All-Star Resort	WDW	934-7639	★★★	73
AmeriHost Resort	3	396-6000	★★½	64
AmeriSuites Lake Buena Vista South	3	997-1300	★★★½	82
AmeriSuites Orlando Convention Ctr.	1	370-4720	★★★½	81
AmeriSuites Universal	1	351-0627	★★★½	76
Animal Kingdom Lodge	WDW	934-7639	★★★★½	90
Baymont Inn Kissimmee	3	787-3555	★★½	62
Beach Club Resort	WDW	934-7639	★★★★½	92
Beach Club Villas	WDW	934-7639	★★★★½	90
Best Value Inn	3	396-2333	★★	51
Best Western Movieland	1	351-3900	★★★	68
Best Western Plaza I-Drive	1	345-8195	★★½	62
Best Western Universal Inn	1	226-9119	★★½	63
BoardWalk Inn	WDW	934-7639	★★★★½	90
BoardWalk Villas	WDW	934-7639	★★★★½	91
Buena Vista Motel	3	396-2100	★★	55
Buena Vista Suites	3	239-8588	★★★★	83
Caribbean Beach Resort	WDW	934-7639	★★★½	80
Caribe Royale Resort Suites	3	238-8000	★★★½	80
Celebration Hotel	WDW	566-6000	★★★★½	90
Celebrity Resorts Lake Buena Vista	2	238-1700	★★★	66
Celebrity Resorts Resort World	3	396-8300	★★★★	84
Clarion Maingate	3	396-4000	★★★	71
Clarion Universal	1	351-5009	★★★	67
Club Hotel by DoubleTree	2	239-4646	★★★½	81
Comfort Inn I-Drive	1	313-4000	★★½	60
Comfort Inn Lake Buena Vista	2	239-7300	★★½	64
Comfort Inn Maingate West	3	(863) 424-9670	★★½	64
Comfort Inn Sandlake	1	363-7886	★★★	66
Comfort Suites Maingate	3	390-9888	★★★	73
Comfort Suites Orlando	2	351-5050	★★★	69
Comfort Suites Universal	1	363-1967	★★★	66
Contemporary Resort	WDW	934-7639	★★★★	87
Coronado Springs Resort	WDW	934-7639	★★★★	83
Country Inn & Suites (Rooms)	2	239-1115	★★★	72
Country Inn & Suites (Suites)	2	239-1115	★★★½	78
Country Inn & Suites Calypso Cay	3	997-1400	★★★½	82
Country Inn & Suites I-Drive	1	313-4200	★★½	63
Courtyard by Marriott I-Drive	1	351-2244	★★★½	76

Cost ($=$50)	COMMUTING TIMES TO THE PARKS			
	Magic Kingdom	Epcot	Disney-MGM	Animal Kingdom
$$–	6:15	5:45	5:15	4:15
$+	8:15	7:30	7:15	5:00
$$	13:30	11:00	13:30	11:30
$$	21:00	17:30	20:00	20:30
$$	19:00	14:15	16:45	17:45
$$$$$–	8:15	6:15	6:00	2:15
$$–	14:30	14:00	13:00	12:30
$$$$$$$–	7:15	5:15	4:00	6:45
$$$$$$$–	7:15	5:15	4:00	6:45
$–	18:15	17:45	16:45	16:15
$+	20:30	15:45	18:15	18:45
$+	22:00	17:15	19:45	20:15
$$–	17:30	13:00	15:30	16:00
$$$$$$$–	7:15	5:30	3:00	7:00
$$$$$$$$	7:15	5:30	3:00	7:00
$–	14:30	14:00	13:30	12:30
$$$–	9:15	4:30	8:15	7:30
$$$–	8:00	6:00	4:15	7:15
$$$–	9:15	4:45	8:15	7:45
$$$$	13:30	13:00	12:30	13:00
$$$+	13:15	8:30	11:00	11:30
$$	16:30	16:15	15:30	14:30
$$–	8:30	8:00	7:30	5:30
$$	20:30	15:45	18:30	18:45
$$+	13:00	8:30	11:00	11:30
$$+	20:00	15:30	18:00	18:30
$+	13:15	8:30	11:00	11:30
$+	14:00	13:15	13:00	11:00
$$–	22:15	17:30	20:00	20:30
$$–	10:00	9:15	9:00	7:00
$$–	20:45	16:00	18:30	19:00
$$$–	17:45	13:15	15:15	16:15
$$$$$+	on monorail	11:00	14:15	17:15
$$$–	5:30	4:00	4:45	4:45
$$–	14:00	9:15	11:45	12:15
$$	14:00	9:15	11:45	12:15
$$–	13:30	13:00	12:30	11:30
$$–	21:00	16:15	18:45	19:15
$$	21:45	17:00	19:30	20:00

HOW THE HOTELS COMPARE *(continued)*

Hotel	Zone	Phone (area code 407)	Overall Quality Rating	Room Quality Rating
Courtyard by Marriott Lake Buena Vista	2	239-6900	★★★	67
Crowne Plaza Resort	1	239-1222	★★★★	87
Crowne Plaza Universal	1	355-0550	★★★★	86
Cypress Pointe Resort	2	238-2300	★★★★	83
Days Inn Eastgate	3	396-7700	★★½	64
Days Inn I-Drive	1	351-1200	★★½	58
Days Inn West Kissimmee	3	(800) 544-5713	★★½	62
Days Inn Lake Buena Vista	2	239-4441	★★★	65
Days Inn Suites Maingate East	3	396-7900	★★½	61
Days Inn Maingate West	3	977-1000	★★½	58
Days Inn Orlando Lakeside	1	351-1900	★★½	60
Days Inn SeaWorld/ Convention Center	1	352-8700	★★½	60
Days Inn Universal Studios	1	351-3800	★★½	60
Delta Orlando Resort	1	351-3340	★★★	67
Dolphin	WDW	934-7639	★★★★	86
DoubleTree Castle Hotel	1	345-1511	★★★½	82
DoubleTree Guest Suites	WDW	934-1000	★★★★	84
DoubleTree Orlando Suites & Villas	3	397-0555	★★★½	81
DoubleTree Universal	1	351-1000	★★★★	88
Eastgate Inn	3	396-0707	★★½	57
Econo Lodge Maingate Resort	3	396-2000	★★½	59
Econo Lodge Polynesian Resort	3	396-2121	★★½	62
Econo Lodge Universal	1	354-3996	★★	52
Embassy Suites Orlando I-Drive	1	352-1400	★★★★	84
Embassy Suites Plaza I-Drive	1	345-8250	★★★½	80
Embassy Suites Resort Lake Buena Vista	2	239-1144	★★★½	81
Embassy Sunterra Grand Beach	1	(800) 350-3382	★★★★½	93
Embassy Vacation Resort	2	238-2500	★★★★½	92
Enclave Suites	1	351-1155	★★★	67
Extended Stay Convention Center	1	352-1708	★★★	72
Extended Stay Universal	1	351-1788	★★★	72
Fairfield Inn & Suites Universal	1	581-5600	★★★	73
Fairfield Inn I-Drive	1	363-1944	★★½	59
Fairfield Orlando Cypress Point	3	(800) 438-6493	★★★★	86
Fort Wilderness Resort (Cabins)	WDW	934-7639	★★★½	76
Gaylord Palms Resort	3	586-0000	★★★★½	90
Golden Link Motel	3	396-0555	★★	54

Cost ($=$50)	COMMUTING TIMES TO THE PARKS			
	Magic Kingdom	Epcot	Disney-MGM	Animal Kingdom
$$	13:15	8:30	11:00	11:30
$$$–	14:45	10:00	12:30	13:00
$$$$$+	21:15	16:30	19:00	19:30
$$$+	14:15	9:30	12:00	12:30
$–	15:45	15:30	15:15	13:45
$	20:30	15:45	18:15	18:45
$	14:00	13:15	13:00	11:00
$+	11:45	7:00	9:30	10:00
$$–	11:15	11:00	10:30	9:15
$	10:30	9:45	9:45	7:30
$–	20:00	14:15	16:45	17:15
$	18:45	14:00	16:30	17:00
$+	18:45	14:00	16:30	17:00
$$$	18:00	13:30	16:00	16:30
$$$$$$$–	6:45	5:00	4:00	6:15
$$+	22:30	17:45	20:15	20:45
$$$–	13:00	8:30	10:00	12:30
$$+	18:15	17:45	17:30	16:15
$$–	19:00	14:15	16:45	17:15
$+	13:30	13:15	12:15	11:30
$	8:15	7:45	7:30	5:15
$+	13:45	13:15	12:45	11:45
$–	18:00	13:30	16:00	16:30
$$$–	22:00	17:15	19:45	20:15
$$$	20:15	15:30	18:00	18:30
$$$≠	12:45	8:00	10:30	11:00
$$$–	13:15	8:30	11:15	11:45
$$$–	12:00	7:15	9:45	10:15
$$$–	20:45	16:15	18:45	19:15
$	17:30	12:45	15:30	15:45
$	18:00	14:15	16:00	18:00
$$–	17:30	12:45	15:15	15:45
$+	20:15	15:30	18:00	18:30
$$+	15:15	15:00	14:45	14:45
$$$$$–	13:15	8:30	14:00	20:00
$$$+	9:00	8:45	8:15	7:00
$–	16:15	16:00	15:45	14:15

HOW THE HOTELS COMPARE *(continued)*

Hotel	Zone	Phone (area code 407)	Overall Quality Rating	Room Quality Rating
Grand Floridian Resort	WDW	934-7639	★★★★★	96
Grand Lake Resort	3	396-3000	★★★½	76
Grosvenor Resort	WDW	828-4444	★★★½	76
Hampton Inn Convention Center	1	354-4447	★★★	65
Hampton Inn Kirkman	1	345-1112	★★½	64
Hampton Inn Lake Buena Vista	2	465-8150	★★★	65
Hampton Inn Maingate	3	396-8484	★★★	66
Hampton Inn Maingate West	3	396-6300	★★★	69
Hampton Inn Universal	1	351-6716	★★★	67
Hard Rock Hotel	1	503-ROCK	★★★★★	96
Hawthorne Suites Lake Buena Vista	2	597-5000	★★★★	87
Hawthorne Suites Orlando	1	351-6600	★★★	74
Hawthorne Suites Universal	1	581-2151	★★★½	82
Hilton Garden Inn	1	354-1500	★★★½	77
Hilton Grand Vacations Club	1	(800) 448-2736	★★★★	88
Hilton Grand Vacations Club SeaWorld	1	239-0100	★★★★	89
Hilton Walt Disney World	WDW	827-4000	★★★★	85
Holiday Inn Express	1	351-4430	★★½	63
Holiday Inn Express Summerbay Resort	3	239-8315	★★½	62
Holiday Inn Family Suites Resort	1	387-5437	★★★½	82
Holiday Inn Hotel & Suites Convention Center	1	581-9001	★★★	74
Holiday Inn Hotel & Suites Maingate East (Rooms)	3	396-4488	★★★	71
Holiday Inn Hotel & Suites Maingate East (Suites)	3	396-4488	★★★	66
Holiday Inn International Resort	1	351-3500	★★★	73
Holiday Inn Maingate West	3	396-1100	★★★	68
Holiday Inn Nikki Bird Resort	3	396-7300	★★★½	80
Holiday Inn Sun Spree Resort	2	239-4500	★★★	69
Holiday Inn Universal Studios	1	351-3333	★★★	74
Holiday Inn WDW Resort	WDW	828-8888	★★★½	75
Homewood Suites I-Drive	1	248-2232	★★★½	79
Homewood Suites Lake Buena Vista	2	465-8200	★★★	69
Homewood Suites Maingate	3	396-2229	★★★	74
Hotel Royal Plaza (Garden)	WDW	828-2828	★★★★	68
Hotel Royal Plaza (Tower)	WDW	828-2828	★★★★	85
Howard Johnson Enchanted Land Resort Hotel	3	396-4343	★★★	66

Cost ($=$50)	COMMUTING TIMES TO THE PARKS			
	Magic Kingdom	Epcot	Disney-MGM	Animal Kingdom
$$$$$$$$–	on monorail	4:45	6:45	11:45
$$	9:15	8:30	8:30	6:15
$+	15:15	10:45	12:15	14:45
$$	21:30	17:00	19:30	20:00
$+	21:15	16:45	19:15	19:45
$+	12:45	8:00	10:30	11:00
$$–	8:30	8:00	10:30	6:30
$+	8:15	7:30	7:15	5:15
$+	19:00	14:15	16:45	17:15
$$$$$	21:45	17:00	19:30	20:00
$$$–	20:15	15:30	18:00	18:30
$$$–	17:30	12:45	15:30	15:45
$$$–	20:15	15:45	19:15	18:45
$$+	15:30	11:00	13:30	14:00
$$–	16:15	14:00	16:30	17:00
$$$	17:00	12:30	15:30	16:30
$$$–	15:15	10:30	12:15	14:30
$$+	20:45	16:00	18:30	19:00
$$–	14:00	9:15	13:15	11:30
$$$	9:45	5:00	7:30	8:00
$$+	23:00	18:15	20:45	21:15
$$–	12:15	12:00	11:30	10:15
$$–	12:30	12:15	11:45	10:30
$$	21:15	16:45	19:15	19:45
$$–	8:30	8:15	7:45	5:30
$$–	8:15	8:00	7:45	5:00
$$+	10:45	6:00	8:30	9:00
$$	19:00	14:15	16:45	17:15
$$	15:30	10:45	12:30	14:45
$$$–	21:45	17:00	19:30	20:00
$$	13:45	9:15	11:45	12:15
$$$–	8:30	8:15	7:45	6:30
$$+	15:45	11:00	12:45	15:00
$$$–	15:45	11:00	12:45	15:00
$$–	16:15	16:00	15:45	14:15

HOW THE HOTELS COMPARE (continued)

Hotel	Zone	Phone (area code 407)	Overall Quality Rating	Room Quality Rating
Howard Johnson Express Inn and Suites (Rooms)	3	396-4762	★★½	57
Howard Johnson Express Inn and Suites (Suites)	3	396-4762	★★½	62
Howard Johnson Inn Orlando	1	351-2900	★★½	59
Howard Johnson Inn South I-Drive	1	351-5100	★★½	63
Howard Johnson Plaza Resort	1	351-2000	★★½	61
Howard Johnson Inn Maingate East	3	396-1748	★★½	57
Howard Johnson Inn Maingate West	3	396-9300	★★½	64
Hyatt Regency Grand Cypress	2	239-1234	★★★★½	90
Inn at Summer Bay	3	(888) 742-1100	★★½	63
Key Motel	3	396-6200	★★	51
Knights Inn Kissimmee	3	396-4200	★★	55
Knights Inn Maingate East	3	396-8186	★★	52
La Quinta Inn I-Drive	1	351-1660	★★★	73
La Quinta Inn Lakeside	3	396-2222	★★★	67
Lake Buena Vista Resort	WDW	828-2424	★★★★	85
Liki Tiki Village	3	(800) 634-3119	★★★½	82
Magic Castle	3	396-2212	★★½	59
Mainstay Suites	3	396-2056	★★½	61
Marriott Cypress Harbour	1	238-1300	★★★★	86
Marriott Imperial Palm Villas	1	239-4200	★★★★	86
Marriott Orlando World Center	2	239-4200	★★★★½	92
Marriott Grande Vista	1	238-7676	★★★★½	92
Marriott Village Courtyard	2	938-9001	★★★	71
Marriott Village Fairfield Inn	2	938-9001	★★½	64
Marriott Village Spring Hill Suites	2	938-9001	★★★	74
Master's Inn I-Drive	1	345-1172	★★	50
Masters Inn Kissimmee	3	396-4020	★★	55
Masters Inn Maingate	3	396-7743	★★	55
Microtel Inn & Suites	1	226-9887	★★½	63
Monte Carlo	3	396-4700	★★	48
Motel 6 I-Drive	1	351-6500	★★½	61
Motel 6 Maingate East	3	396-6333	★★	52
Motel 6 Maingate West	3	396-6427	★★	52
Old Key West Resort	WDW	934-7639	★★★★½	92
Orange Lake Country Club	3	239-0000	★★★★	85
Orlando International Resort Florida Center	1	351-4600	★★½	64

Cost ($=$50)	COMMUTING TIMES TO THE PARKS			
	Magic Kingdom	Epcot	Disney-MGM	Animal Kingdom
$–	16:30	16:15	15:45	14:30
$	16:35	16:15	15:45	14:30
$$–	21:00	16:30	19:00	19:30
$$–	19:30	14:15	16:45	17:15
$+	22:00	16:30	19:00	19:30
$+	11:15	11:00	10:30	8:15
$+	13:45	13:45	13:00	10:4
$$$$	13:30	8:45	11:15	11:45
$+	14:15	13:45	13:30	11:15
$–	16:30	16:15	15:45	14:30
$–	8:15	7:45	7:30	5:45
$–	15:45	15:30	15:00	13:45
$$–	21:45	17:15	19:45	20:15
$$–	9:15	8:30	8:30	6:30
$$–	16:00	11:15	13:00	15:15
$$+	9:00	8:45	8:15	5:15
$–	14:15	13:45	13:30	12:15
$$	16:45	16:15	16:00	14:45
$$$–	17:45	13:15	16:15	17:45
$$+	9:45	5:00	7:30	8:00
$$$+	9:45	5:00	7:30	8:00
$$$+	15:00	12:45	15:15	15:45
$$–	12:00	7:15	9:45	10:15
$$–	12:00	7:15	9:45	10:15
$$–	12:00	7:15	9:45	10:15
$+	8:30	8:15	10:45	11:15
$	13:45	13:30	13:00	11:45
$$	8:30	8:30	7:45	6:45
$+	20:15	15:45	18:15	18:45
$	18:30	18:15	17:45	16:30
$	20:15	16:00	18:30	19:00
$–	12:30	12:00	11:45	10:30
$–	7:15	6:45	6:30	4:45
$$$$$	10:45	6:00	10:30	14:30
$$	8:45	8:30	8:00	5:30
$$$–	20:00	15:30	18:00	18:30

HOW THE HOTELS COMPARE *(continued)*

Hotel	Zone	Phone (area code 407)	Overall Quality Rating	Room Quality Rating
Orlando Worldgate Resort	3	396-1400	★★★½	77
Park Inn & Suites Maingate East	3	396-6100	★★½	58
Parkway International Resort	3	396-6600	★★★½	75
Peabody Orlando	1	352-4000	★★★★½	90
Polynesian Resort	WDW	934-7639	★★★★	89
Polynesian Isles Resort	3	396-1622	★★★★	83
Pop Century Resort	WDW	934-7639	★★★	74
Port Orleans Resort (French Qtr.)	WDW	934-7639	★★★½	79
Port Orleans Resort (Riverside)	WDW	934-7639	★★★½	82
Portofino Bay Hotel	1	503-1000	★★★★½	94
Quality Inn I-Drive	1	351-1600	★★★	65
Quality Inn Maingate West	3	396-1828	★★½	58
Quality Inn Plaza	1	345-8585	★★½	62
Quality Inn & Suites Eastgate	3	396-1376	★★★	66
Quality Inn & Suites Universal	1	370-5100	★★★	67
Quality Suites I-Drive	1	363-0332	★★★½	75
Quality Suites Maingate East	3	396-8040	★★★	73
Radisson Barcelo Inn I-Drive (Garden)	1	345-0505	★★★½	76
Radisson Barcelo Inn I-Drive (Tower)	1	345-0505	★★★★	85
Radisson Inn Lake Buena Vista	2	239-8400	★★★½	81
Radisson Resort Parkway	3	396-7000	★★★★	84
Ramada Eastgate Fountain Park	3	396-1111	★★★	66
Ramada Inn I-Drive	1	351-4410	★★½	61
Ramada Inn I-Drive Orlando	1	345-5340	★★★	72
Ramada Inn Westgate	3	(863) 424-2621	★★½	62
Ramada Plaza & Inn Gateway (Garden)	3	396-4400	★★½	64
Ramada Plaza & Inn Gateway (Tower)	3	396-4400	★★★	71
Ramada Resort Maingate	3	396-4466	★★½	61
Red Carpet Inn East	3	396-1133	★★	50
Red Horse Inn	1	351-4100	★★★	69
Red Roof Inn Convention Center	1	352-1507	★★½	58
Red Roof Inn Kissimmee	3	396-0065	★★½	62
Red Roof Inn Universal	1	313-3100	★★½	63
Renaissance Orlando Resort	1	351-5555	★★★½	80
Residence Inn Convention Center	1	226-0288	★★★½	77
Residence Inn Lake Buena Vista	2	465-0075	★★★½	76
Residence Inn Orlando	1	345-0117	★★★½	76
Residence Inn SeaWorld	1	313-3600	★★★★	85
Riande Continental Plaza	1	352-8211	★★½	56

COMMUTING TIMES TO THE PARKS

Cost ($=$50)	Magic Kingdom	Epcot	Disney-MGM	Animal Kingdom
$$	8:15	7:45	7:45	5:45
$$−	10:15	9:45	9:30	7:30
$$$$	8:30	8:15	7:45	6:15
$$$$$$$$	19:30	15:15	17:45	18:15
$$$$$$	on monorail	4:45	6:45	11:30
$$$−	14:30	14:15	14:00	12:30
$$−	8:30	6:30	5:00	6:15
$$$−	12:00	8:00	12:30	16:15
$$$−	12:00	8:00	12:30	16:15
$$$$$+	21:45	17:15	19:45	20:15
$+	19:45	15:00	17:30	18:00
$	9:15	8:45	8:30	6:30
$$−	22:15	17:30	20:00	20:30
$+	15:45	15:30	14:45	13:45
$+	19:00	14:15	16:45	17:15
$$$−	20:30	15:45	18:15	18:45
$$−	11:15	11:00	10:30	9:15
$$$	21:15	16:30	19:00	19:30
$$$$−	21:15	16:30	19:00	19:30
$$$+	14:15	9:45	12:15	12:45
$$$	8:30	8:00	7:45	6:30
$+	15:45	15:15	15:00	13:45
$$−	20:30	16:00	18:30	19:00
$$−	21:30	16:45	19:15	19:45
$+	13:45	13:15	13:00	10:45
$$+	8:15	8:00	7:45	6:00
$$+	8:15	8:00	7:45	6:00
$$	7:00	6:45	6:15	5:15
$−	18:30	18:00	17:45	16:30
$+	20:30	16:00	18:30	19:00
$$−	19:00	14:15	16:45	17:15
$	16:45	16:15	16:00	14:45
$$	18:00	13:15	16:00	16:15
$$$−	16:45	12:15	14:45	15:15
$$	22:00	17:30	20:00	20:30
$$+	15:40	11:00	13:30	14:00
$$$−	20:00	15:15	17:45	18:15
$$+	15:45	11:15	13:45	14:15
$	20:30	15:45	18:30	18:45

HOW THE HOTELS COMPARE (continued)

Hotel	Zone	Phone (area code 407)	Overall Quality Rating	Room Quality Rating
Ritz-Carlton Orlando Grand Lakes	1	206-2400	★★★★½	94
Rodeway Inn I-Drive	1	351-4444	★★½	56
Rodeway Inn Maingate	3	396-4300	★★½	59
Rosen Centre Hotel	1	354-9840	★★★½	80
Rosen Plaza Hotel	1	352-9700	★★★★	84
Royal Pacific Resort	1	224-6222	★★★★½	90
RUI Orlando	2	239-8500	★★★	74
Saratoga Springs	WDW	934-7639	★★★★½	91
Shades of Green	WDW	824-3400	★★★★½	91
Sheraton Royal Safari	2	(800) 423-3297	★★★½	82
Sheraton Studio City	1	351-2100	★★★½	82
Sheraton Vistana Resort	2	(866) 208-0003	★★★★	84
Sheraton World Resort (Garden)	1	352-1100	★★★	68
Sheraton World Resort (Tower)	1	352-1100	★★★½	79
Sierra Suites Convention Center	1	363-1333	★★½	58
Sierra Suites Lake Buena Vista	2	239-4300	★★★★	83
Sierra Suites Pointe Orlando	1	903-1500	★★★★	83
Silver Lake Resort	3	397-9721 x5145	★★½	64
Sleep Inn Convention Center	1	313-4100	★★	54
Sleep Inn Maingate	3	396-1600	★★½	63
Spring Hill Suites by Marriott	1	345-9073	★★★	72
Star Island Resort	3	997-8000	★★★★	84
Studio Plus Convention Center	1	(800) 804-3274	★★★	73
Studio Plus Universal	1	(800) 804-3274	★★★	73
Suburban Lodge Universal	1	313-2000	★★★	65
Summer Bay Resort	3	(800) 654-6102	★★★	65
Summerfield Suites	1	352-2400	★★★½	82
Summerfield Suites Lake Buena Vista	2	238-0777	★★★★	83
Sun Inn & Suites	3	396-2673	★★	53
Super 8 Lakeside	3	396-1144	★★½	58
Super 8 East	3	396-8883	★★½	57
Super 8 Kissimmee	3	847-6121	★★½	60
Super 8 Universal	1	352-8383	★★	52
Swan	WDW	934-7639	★★★★	90
Traveler's Inn	3	396-1668	★★	52
Travelodge Convention Center	1	(800) 346-1551	★★½	59
Travelodge I-Drive	1	(800) 327-0750	★★½	60
Travelodge Maingate	3	396-0100	★★½	59

COMMUTING TIMES TO THE PARKS

Cost ($=$50)	Magic Kingdom	Epcot	Disney-MGM	Animal Kingdom
$$$$	23:00	18:15	20:45	21:30
$+	21:00	16:15	18:45	19:15
$	11:15	11:00	10:30	9:15
$$$$$$$	19:45	15:15	17:45	18:15
$$$$$–	20:45	16:15	18:45	19:15
$$$$+	20:00	15:15	17:45	18:15
$$$$–	14:45	10:00	12:30	13:00
$$$$$	14:45	8:45	14:30	18:15
$+ (Military Only)	3:30	4:45	6:15	9:30
$$$	13:45	9:00	11:30	12:00
$$$$–	20:30	15:45	18:15	18:45
$$$$$$–	11:15	6:30	9:00	9:30
$$$$$$–	17:45	13:00	15:30	16:00
$$$$$$$–	17:45	13:00	15:35	16:00
$$$	17:45	13:00	15:30	17:00
$$$	13:45	9:00	11:30	12:00
$$$–	22:15	17:45	18:15	20:45
$$+	8:15	8:00	7:30	4:30
$+	17:45	13:00	15:30	16:00
$+	13:45	13:15	13:00	11:00
$$+	22:30	17:50	20:20	20:45
$$$–	15:45	15:15	13:30	14:15
$+	17:30	12:45	15:30	15:45
$+	18:00	14:15	16:00	18:00
$+	17:45	13:15	15:45	16:15
$+	14:00	13:30	13:15	12:00
$$$$$$–	21:15	16:30	19:00	19:30
$$$+	14:15	9:30	12:00	12:30
$–	16:00	15:45	15:15	14:00
$–	16:30	16:00	15:45	14:30
$–	11:45	11:15	11:00	9:45
$–	8:30	8:00	7:45	5:45
$–	21:15	16:30	19:00	19:30
$$$$$$$–	6:30	4:45	4:00	6:15
$	15:15	15:00	14:30	13:15
$	17:45	13:15	12:45	11:45
$	21:15	16:30	19:00	19:30
$+	13:30	13:00	12:45	11:30

HOW THE HOTELS COMPARE *(continued)*

Hotel	Zone	Phone (area code 407)	Overall Quality Rating	Room Quality Rating
Travelodge Maingate East	3	396-4222	★★★	65
Travelodge Suites Eastgate	3	396-7666	★★★	67
Travelodge Suites Maingate	3	396-1780	★★½	56
Universal Inn	1	351-4100	★★½	66
Vacation Village Parkway	3	396-4086	★★★★½	91
Wellesley Inn Kissimmee/Lake Cecile	3	396-4455	★★½	61
Westgate Lakes	2	(888) 808-7410	★★★★½	92
Westgate Palace	1	(888) 808-7410	★★★	68
Westgate Resorts (Tower)	3	(800) 925-9999	★★★½	78
Westgate Resorts (Town Center)	3	(800) 925-9999	★★★★½	93
Westgate Resorts (Villas)	3	(800) 925-9999	★★★★½	90
Westgate Towers	3	396-2500	★★★½	76
Wilderness Lodge	WDW	934-7639	★★★★	86
Wilderness Lodge Villas	WDW	934-7639	★★★★½	90
Wyndham Orlando	1	351-2420	★★★½	82
Wyndham Palace	WDW	827-2727	★★★★	86
Wyndham Palms	3	390-1991	★★★★½	87
Yacht Club Resort	WDW	934-7639	★★★★	92

COMMUTING TIMES TO THE PARKS

Cost ($=$50)	Magic Kingdom	Epcot	Disney-MGM	Animal Kingdom
$+	12:15	12:00	11:30	10:15
$+	13:30	13:15	12:45	11:45
$	18:30	18:00	17:45	16:30
$$$$–	21:15	16:45	19:15	19:45
$$$–	8:30	8:15	7:45	6:45
$+	15:45	15:30	15:00	13:45
$$$+	17:30	14:30	18:00	19:15
$$$$–	20:45	16:15	18:45	19:15
$$$+	8:45	8:30	8:00	5:45
$$$+	8:45	8:30	8:00	5:45
$$$+	8:45	8:30	8:00	5:45
$$$	8:30	8:15	7:45	5:30
$$$$$–	n/a	10:00	13:30	15:15
$$$$$$+	n/a	10:00	13:30	15:15
$$$$	19:45	15:00	17:30	18:15
$$$	16:00	11:15	13:00	15:15
$$$–	10:45	10:30	10:00	7:45
$$$$$–	7:15	5:15	4:00	6:45

Part Four

The Disney Cruise Line

The Mouse at Sea

In case you've been raising chinchillas on Venus, here's the news: The Walt Disney Company is in the cruise business with two almost-identical ships, *Disney Wonder* and *Disney Magic*. Cruises leave Port Canaveral (about an hour from the Orlando airport) and visit Nassau in the Bahamas, and Castaway Cay, Disney's private Bahamian island, on three-and four-day itineraries. Seven-day eastern-Caribbean itineraries include calls at St. Maarten and St. Thomas, plus Castaway Cay. Western itineraries are offered on alternate weeks. Ports include Key West, Grand Cayman Island, Cozumel, and Castaway Cay. The ten-day cruise stops at Key West, St. Maarten, St. Lucia, Antigua and St. Thomas, with excursions to St. John, before heading to Castaway Cay. All itineraries can be bundled with a stay at Walt Disney World.

Between May 28 and August 20, 2005, the *Disney Magic* will operate seven-day cruises to the Mexican Riviera out of Los Angeles with calls at Puerto Vallarto, Mazatlan, and Cabo San Lucas. Before and after the dates listed above, you can enjoy a repositioning cruise from and to the Caribbean that includes transiting the Panama Canal. Cruises out of Los Angeles can be bundled with a stay at Disneyland.

Cruises can be purchased separately or as part of weeklong packages that also include three or four days at Disney World, or two or three days at Disneyland. You get your Disney hotel, theme park admissions, the cruise, and transportation (called transfers) from the airport to Disney World or Disneyland, and to the ship.

At the outset, Disney assembled a team of respected cruise-industry veterans, dozens of the world's best-known ship designers, and Disney's own unrivaled creative talent. Together, they created the Disney ships, recognizing that every detail would be critical to the line's success. Their task was to design a product that makes every adult on board feel that the vacation is intended for them, while giving every child the same impression.

DISNEY CRUISE LINE STANDARD FEATURES

Officers   Multinational

Staffs   Cabin, dining/Multinational; cruise/American

Dining   Three themed family restaurants with "rotation" dining; alternative adults-only restaurant; indoor/outdoor cafe for breakfast, lunch, snacks, and buffet dinner for children; pool bar/grill for burgers, pizza, and sandwiches; ice-cream bar

Special Diets   On request; health-conscious cuisine program

Room Service   24 hours

Dress Code   Casual by day; casual and informal in the evenings

Cabin Amenities   Direct-dial telephone with voice mail; tub and shower; TV; safe; hair dryer; mini-bar stocked for fee

Electrical Outlets   110 AC

Wheelchair Access   Yes

Smoking   Smoking allowed only in designated areas

Disney Suggested Tipping   Dining-room server: $3.50–$4 per night. Assistant server: $2.50 per night. Dining room head server: 3- and 4-night cruise, $3 and $4;. 7-night cruise, $5; 10-night cruise, $8. Stateroom Host: $4 per night. Dining Manager and Room service, your discretion. A 15% service charge is added automatically to bar bills

Credit Cards   For cruise payment and on-board charges, all major credit cards

The first surprise is the ships' appearance. They're simultaneously classic and innovative. Exteriors are traditional, reminiscent of great ocean liners of the past, but even in that you'll find a Disney twist or two. Inside, they're up-to-the-minute technologically, and full of novel ideas for dining, entertainment, and cabin design. Disney's exclusive cruise terminal at Port Canaveral is integral to the overall strategy, which aims to make even embarkation and debarkation enjoyable. Likewise, Disney's private island, Castaway Cay, was chosen in order to avoid the hassle of tendering. As for dining, each evening you dine in a different restaurant with a different motif, but your waiters and dining companions move with you.

Disney's plan has been to create a "seamless vacation package" by combining a stay at Disney World with a cruise. Cruise passengers are met at the airport by Disney staff and transported to Port Canaveral in easily identifiable Disney Cruise Line buses. During the hour-long ride, passengers watch a video preview of the cruise. To smooth embarkation, check-in is streamlined. When your cruise is packaged with a Disney World stay, you check in once. The key that unlocks your hotel room opens the door to your cruise cabin.

The company targets first-time cruisers, counting on Disney's reputation for quality, service, and entertainment to dispel noncruisers' doubts about cruise vacations. At the same time, much time and effort has been spent to ensure that the ships appeal to adults—with or without children—as much as to children and families. Adults are catered to in myriad ways, and presented with an extensive menu of adult-oriented activities. For example, the ships have an adults-only alternative restaurant, swimming pool, and nightclub, and entertainment ranges from family musicals to adults-only dueling pianos (what a concept!). Meanwhile, from virtually sunrise to midnight, children are offered equally varied programs. Because all programs are offered à la carte, families can choose how much time to spend together, or pursuing separate interests.

The children's programs are excellent. In fact, they're rated the best in the cruise industry in *The Unofficial Guide to Cruises,* by Kay Showker and Bob Sehlinger. Thus, it's no surprise that many parents see their kids only at breakfast and dinner. But while adults easily can get a breather from children, it's tougher to escape Disney's syrupy, wholesome, cuter-than-a-billion-Beanie-Babies entertainment, which permeates every cruise. Expressed differently, to enjoy a Disney cruise you'd better love Disney.

The Ships

Disney Magic and *Disney Wonder* are modern cruise ships with sleek lines, twin smokestacks, and nautical styling recalling classic ocean liners, but with instantly recognizable Disney signatures. The colors—black, white, red, and yellow—and the famous face-and-ears silhouette on the stacks are clearly those of Mickey Mouse. Look closely, and you'll see that *Magic*'s figurehead is a 15-foot Goofy (Donald Duck on *Wonder*) swinging upside down from a boatswain's chair, "painting" the stern.

Interiors combine nautical themes with art-deco inspiration. Disney images are everywhere, from Mickey's profile in the wrought-iron balustrades to the bronze statue of Helmsman Mickey at the center of the three-deck Grand Atrium. Disney art is on every wall, stairwell, and corridor. A grand staircase sweeps from the atrium lobby to shops selling Disney Cruise Line–themed clothing, collectibles, jewelry, sundries, and more. (The shops are always full of eager buyers; some observers speculate that the cruise line will derive as much revenue here as other lines do from their casinos, which Disney ships don't have.)

The ships have two lower decks with cabins, three decks with dining rooms and show rooms, then three decks of cabins. Two sports and sun decks offer separate pools and facilities for families, and for adults without kids. Signs point toward lounges and facilities, and all elevators are clearly marked forward, aft, or amidships.

Our main complaint concerning the ships' design is that outdoor public areas focus inward toward the pools instead of seaward, as if Disney wants you to forget you're on a cruise liner. There's no public place where you can curl up in the shade and watch the ocean (at least not without a

Plexiglas wall between you and it). If this quintessential cruise pleasure ranks high on your hit parade, spring for a cabin with a private veranda.

Another predictable but nonetheless irritating design characteristic is the extensive childproofing. There's enough Plexiglas on *Magic* and *Wonder* to build a subdivision of transparent homes. On the pool decks (Deck 9), especially, it feels as if the ships are hermetically sealed.

Cabins

Cabins and suites are spacious, with wood paneling throughout. About three-fourths are outside, almost half with private verandas. The 12 cabin categories range from standard to deluxe, deluxe with veranda, family suite, one- and two-bedroom suites, and royal suite. Categories are similar to those at Disney hotels. Passengers who spend three or four days at a Disney resort are assigned a cabin in a comparable category.

Cabin design reveals Disney's finely tuned sense of the needs of families and children and offers a cruise-industry first: a split bathroom with a bathtub and shower combo and sink in one room, and toilet, sink, and vanity in another. This configuration, found in all but standard inside cabins, allows any family member to use the bathroom without monopolizing it. All bathrooms have both tub and shower.

Decor includes unusual features such as bureaus designed to look like steamer trunks. Cabins also have a direct-dial telephone with voicemail; TV; hair dryer, and mini-bar. In some, pull-down Murphy beds allow for additional daytime floor space. Storage is generous, with deep drawers and large closets.

Each ship has 252 inside cabins and 625 outside cabins; 276 suites with verandas, 82 family suites, 16 one-bedroom suites, 2 two-bedroom suites, 2 royal suites; and 14 wheelchair-accessible cabins. Most cabins accommodate three people; inside cabins up to four; deluxe with verandas up to four; family and one-bedroom suites up to five.

Services and Amenities

Passengers lavishly praise Disney cast members. They're among the most accommodating you'll ever encounter in travel, and they try hard to smooth your way from boarding to departure. *Unofficial Guide* cruise writer Kay Showker writes, "More than once when I stopped to get my bearings, a Disney cast member was there within seconds to help me."

You'll receive a *Disney Magic* Passport, a purse-size booklet covering about everything you need to know for your cruise. Daily in your cabin, you'll receive "Your Personal Navigator" listing entertainment and activities, with options for teens, children, adults, and families, as well as information on shore excursions.

Dining

Dining is Disney's most innovative area. Ships have three family restaurants, plus an adults-only alternative restaurant. Each night, passengers move to a different family restaurant, each with a different theme and menu. Their table companions and wait staff move with them. In each restaurant, tableware, linens, menu covers, and waiters' uniforms fit the theme.

On *Magic*, **Lumière's,** named for the candlestick character in *Beauty and the Beast*, is a handsome, art-deco venue serving continental cuisine. A mural depicts *Beauty and the Beast*. (The equivalent restaurant on *Wonder* is **Triton,** themed after *The Little Mermaid*.)

Parrot Cay dishes up Caribbean-accented food in a colorful, fun, tropical setting that reminds Disney veterans of the Enchanted Tiki Room. Parrot Cay is the most popular of the three restaurants for breakfast. Children particularly enjoy the decor and festivity, but the food, although adequate, is a notch below that of the other restaurants.

Animator's Palate reflects the creative genius of Disney animation and is the ships' dining *pièce de résistance*. Diners are given the impression they have entered a black-and-white sketchbook. As the meal progresses, sketches on the walls are transformed through fiber optics into a full-color extravaganza. Waiters change their costumes from black-and-white to color. A montage of appetizers is served on a palette-shaped plate, and dessert—a tasteless mousse shaped like Mickey—comes by way of a parade of waiters bearing trays of colorful syrups—mango, chocolate, and strawberry—to decorate it. The food is less than inspired, and hot dishes are likely to arrive cold. But no ones seems to care; they're too absorbed in watching Disney perform its magic. Conversation is often difficult, and the entertainment, though creative, is the ultimate in Disney cute (and totally inescapable). Children love it, but adults may find it overwhelming.

Palo, the casual Italian restaurant named for the pole gondoliers use to navigate Venetian canals, is the intimate, adults-only restaurant. It's the best on board and has its own kitchen. The sophisticated, semicircular room has soft lighting, Venetian glass, inlaid wood, and a back-lit bar. Northern Italian cuisine is featured. Food and presentation are excellent. More than two dozen wines are available by the glass for $5.50–$30. There's a $10-per-person cover charge, but no signs in the restaurant, on the menu, or in ship's literature alert you. Service is attentive but leisurely, though it may just seem that way in comparison to the staccato pace in the other restaurants. Reservations are required; make them when you board or risk being shut out (Disney underestimated demand for this venue). In addition to dinner, Palo offers a champagne brunch for a $10 surcharge and high tea for $5.

There are two seatings (6 and 8:30 p.m.) for dinner at (Triton), Animator's Palate, and Parrot Cay. If your children are 12 or younger and you plan to dine as a family, we recommend the early seating. If your kids are involved in programs where they dine with other children, go with your preference. All three restaurants offer special meals if your picky eaters can't find something they like on the menu.

On a three-day cruise, your normal rotation will have you dine one night each at Lumière's (Triton), Animator's Palate, and Parrot Cay. If you book Palo (adults only), you'll skip the restaurant designated for that night on your rotation. Thus, choose your Palo night carefully. We view Parrot Cay as the most expendable in the rotation, and if you miss it for dinner, you can try it at lunch or breakfast. On a four-day cruise, one restaurant will pop up twice on your rotation. If you want to eat at all restaurants, including Palo, reserve Palo for the night you're scheduled to repeat one of the basic three.

Shortly after boarding, you're given the opportunity to make Palo reservations (taken in the restaurant) and/or change your restaurant rotation. We believe one night each at Animator's Palate or Parrot Cay is enough. If your rotation calls for you to repeat a night in either, book Palo or substitute a second night at Lumière's (Triton).

Wondering what to do with your children while you dine at Palo? You have several options: Make a late reservation for Palo, then keep your children company (but don't eat) while they dine at the regularly assigned restaurant (this works only if you eat at the first seating); enroll your children in a program where they'll eat with other kids; take your children to Pluto's Dog House (poolside on Deck 9) for hot dogs and burgers; or order them a room-service dinner and hire a private sitter.

Buffet and Fast Food   Other dining options include **Topsiders** (**Beach Blanket Buffet** on *Wonder*), an indoor/outdoor café serving breakfast, lunch, snacks, and a buffet dinner for children; a pool bar and grill for hamburgers, hot dogs, and sandwiches; **Pinocchio's Pizzeria;** an ice cream and frozen yogurt bar; and 24-hour room service. Topsiders is the weakest; it's OK for breakfast, but long on bulk and short on flavor for lunch. Pizza, dogs, burgers, yogurt, and ice cream are good.

Facilities and Entertainment

Nightly entertainment is unlike any other cruise line's. The 977-seat **Walt Disney Theater** stages a different show nightly, with talented actors, singers, and dancers. These family productions are on par with Disney parks' entertainment rather than Broadway and will probably appeal more to children than adults. Longer cruises present a welcome variety show and an end-of-cruise farewell show in addition to the productions described below.

The Golden Mickeys is an Academy Awards-style tribute to the music and characters of Disney films over the decades.

Disney Dreams has about every Disney character and song ever heard and offers a thin plot wherein Peter Pan visits a girl who dreams of Disney's characters. It's pure schmaltz, but audiences give it a standing ovation. At the late show, many kids dozed off before the curtain fell.

Another night offers *Hercules, The Muse-ical,* a musical comedy that's the least saccharine of the lot. The low-budget third production is the *Disney Trivia Game Show.* Do you know Goofy's middle name? On seven-night cruises, a *Welcome Aboard Variety Show,* magic show and *Magical Farewell* are added.

First-run movies and classic Disney films are shown daily in the **Buena Vista Theater,** with full screen and Dolby sound.

Studio Sea, modeled after a television- or film-production set, is a family-oriented nightclub offering dance music, cabaret acts, passenger game shows, karaoke and multimedia entertainment. The art-deco **Promenade Lounge** offers a haven for reading and relaxing by day, and cocktails and piano music by night. Cove Café is a quiet, secluded venue for reading over a designer coffee. *Magic* features **Beat Street,** an adult-oriented evening entertainment district with shops and three themed nightclubs: **Rockin' Bar D,** with live bands playing rock-and-roll, Top 40, and country music; **Diversions,** offering group sing-alongs and karaoke in what Disney calls "a cross between a golf clubhouse and a local neighborhood bar" (running on empty in the theme department, eh?); and **Sessions,** a casual place to enjoy easy-listening music and jazz. On *Wonder,* Beat Street is replaced with the **Route 66** three-club complex: **Wavebands** features live bands playing pop and oldies; **Barrel of Laughs** offers dueling pianos and sing-alongs; and **Cadillac Lounge** is the place for quiet music.

Disney ships have no casinos or libraries.

Children's Programs

Playrooms and other kids' facilities occupy more than 15,000 square feet of each ship. Age-specific programs are among the most extensive in cruising. They include challenging interactive activities and play areas supervised by trained counselors. Age groups are 3–7, 8–12, and teens. Baby-sitting (ages 12 weeks–3 years) is provided in the Flounders Reef nursery 2–4 p.m. and 7 p.m.–midnight daily. Cost is $6 per child per hour; $5 per hour for each additional child.

The **Oceaneer's Adventure** program encompasses **Oceaneer's Club** (ages 3–7), themed to resemble Captain Hook's pirate ship, with plenty of activity space; and **Oceaneer's Lab** (ages 8–12), with video games, computers, and lab equipment, and an area for listening to CDs. Kids wear ID bracelets, and parents receive pagers for staying in touch with them. Both parents and children give youth programs high marks. Children in the drop-off program eat dinner at Topsiders.

Common Grounds The Stack (Deck 9), is a teen area with a coffee-bar theme featuring a game arcade, videos, and CD-listening lounge. Located in a non-functioning smokestack on the top deck, the venue allows teens to rock out in arguably the most isolated part of the ship (chaperoned, of course). There are also organized activities including nighttime volleyball. Activities are supervised in a way that makes participants feel unfettered. For example, other than counselors, no adults are allowed in The StackCommon Grounds.

Sports, Fitness, and Beauty

Of three top-deck pools, one has a Mickey Mouse motif and water slide, and is intended for families. Another is set aside for team sports; the third is adults-only. At night the pool area can be a stage for deck parties and dancing.

The 8,500-square-foot, ocean-view **Vista Spa and Salon** above the bridge offers Cybex exercise equipment, an aerobics room, exercise instruction, a thermal-bath area, saunas, and steam rooms. A qualified fitness director supervises. The spa, run by British-based Steiner, offers pricey beauty treatments plus a sales pitch for Steiner products. Nevertheless, it has proved to be very popular and is generally sold out within hours of embarkation. Passengers in concierge-level suites can have a private massage in their suite or veranda (50 minutes for $108; prices vary).

The Sports Deck has a paddle tennis court, table tennis, basketball court, and shuffleboard. The full promenade deck lures walkers and joggers but has no lounge chairs.

Castaway Cay

Each cruise includes a day at Castaway Cay, Disney's 1,000-acre private island. The island's environment and beauty have been preserved. Miles of white-sand beaches are surrounded by emerald water. A pier allows access without tendering. A four-car open tram (like those at Disney parks) links the ship to **Scuttle's Cove** family beach. It runs every five minutes. You could walk the quarter-mile to the beach, but it's inadvisable in the blistering heat. (Bring sunblocksun block and wear a hat.) Strollers are available, as are rental floats, bikes, kayaks, and snorkel gear. Lounge chairs under pastel umbrellas are plentiful, and hammocks swing under the palms, but there's very little shade otherwise.

Disney Imagineers have created shops, rest rooms, and pavilions that give the impression they've been there for years. A supervised children's area includes a "dig" at a half-buried whale skeleton. Water sports are offered in a protected lagoon. One snorkeling course is near shore; the other, farther out, requires more endurance. On the distant course, snorkelers see fish they identify from a waterproof card provided with rental equipment. Lifeguards watch all snorkelers. The cruise line has planted several "shipwrecks." On one in about ten feet of water, snorkelers see Mickey Mouse riding the ship's bow. Rental equipment costs $25 for adults and $10 for ages 3–9. Nature trails and bike paths are available. The main beach offers kids' activities, live Bahamian music, and shops. **Cookie's Bar-B-Cue** serves a buffet lunch of burgers, pork ribs, hot dogs, baked beans, slaw, corn on the cob, fruit, and potato chips.

A second tram connects to **Serenity Bay,** the adult beach on the island's opposite side. A bar serves drinks, and passengers can enjoy a massage in one of the private cabanas opening on the sea. Passengers must be back aboard by 3:15 p.m. Many say they would have liked more time on the island.

Rates

Although Disney bundles its cruises with a stay at Disney World, you can usually beat the package price by buying your vacation components à la carte. Disney cruise-only brochure rates range from $410 per person (double occupancy) for a standard inside cabin on a three-day cruise to about $2,049 for a veranda cabin on a four-day cruise. Suites cost up to $3,200 for a four-day cruise. Seven-day packages that include a Disney World stay range from $829 to about $4,999 per person. Fares for children sharing a cabin with their parents are $139–$1,400. Prices include port charges.

Shop non-Disney cruise discount agencies. Some sell only cruises, but others sell the entire cruise and land package. However, we haven't seen a package that we couldn't beat by buying the components individually ourselves.

CRUISE DISCOUNT AGENCIES

All Cruise Travel	(800) 227-8473	**www.allcruise.com**
Crown Travel	(800) 869-7447	**www.crowncruise.com**
Cruise Mates Bazaar		**www.cruisemates.com**
Cruise Match	(800) 925-8572	**www.cruisematch.com**
Cruises Only/Sea Saver	(800) 895-3771	**www.mytravelco.com**
Last Minute Travel	(866) 210-3290	**www.lastminutetravel.com**
Mann Travel & Cruises	(800) 438-3709	**www.travelcruises.com**
Moments Notice	(718) 621-4548	**www.moments-notice.com**

Once you've shopped and determined the lowest price available, give your travel agent the opportunity to match or beat it. For savings in addition to discounts offered by cruise sellers like those listed, book in advance to get "early bird" discounts. If you prefer to buy directly from Disney, here's how to get in touch:

Disney Cruise Line

210 Celebration Place, Suite 400

Celebration, FL 34747-4600

(800) 951-6499 or (800) 951-3532

fax: (407) 566-7739; www.disneycruise.com

Disney Cruise Line offers a free planning DVD that tells all you'd need to know about Disney cruises and then some. To obtain a copy call (888) DCL-2500 or order online at **www.disneycruise.com.**

A Few Tips

1. If you opt for a week that includes the cruise and a Disney World stay, go first to Disney World. Cruising at the end of your vacation will ensure you arrive home rested.

2. Board the ship as early as possible. Check your dining rotation, and change it if desired. Make Palo reservations as soon as the restaurant's reservations desk opens, usually 2 p.m.

3. After setting your dining arrangements, register your children at **Oceaneer Club** (ages 3–7) and/or **Oceaneer Lab** (ages 8–12). If you board before 1:30 p.m., register your kids first, then arrange dining.

4. If you want spa services, sign up between 2 and 4 p.m. at the spa.

5. Disney requests that gentlemen wear jackets (no ties required) in the evening at **Palo** and **Lumière's** *(Triton)*.

6. If you're staying at a Disney resort before your cruise, complete and return your cruise forms at the hotel. Your shoresideshore-side room key card will allow you to bypass lines at the cruise terminal and board the ship directly. Cruise-only passengers may encounter a wait at check-in.

7. Most cabins have a mini-fridge; bring your own snacks and beverages.

8. The **Sessions (Cadillac Lounge)** piano bar is one of the most relaxing and beautiful lounges we've seen on a cruise ship. Make a before- or after-dinner drink there part of your routine. It's on Deck 3, forward.

9. Don't miss the kids' programs.

10. WARNING: Since September 11, 2001, Disney has tightened security on both ships. Knives of any kind, scissors, corkscrews, and anything else that can be used as a weapon are prohibited. Both carry-on and checked luggage are inspected. Confiscated items are returned at disembarkation.

Part Five

Walt Disney World with Kids

The Ecstasy and the Agony

So overwhelming is the Disney media and advertising presence that any child who watches TV or shops with Mom is likely to get revved up about going to Walt Disney World. Parents, if anything, are even more susceptible. Almost every parent brightens at the prospect of guiding their children through this special place. But the reality of taking a young child (particularly in summer) can be closer to the agony than to the ecstasy.

A Dayton, Ohio, mother took her five-year-old to Disney World in July:

> I felt so happy and excited before we went. I guess it was all worth it, but when I look back I think I should have had my head examined. The first day we went to [the Magic Kingdom] it was packed. By 11 in the morning we had walked so far and stood in so many lines that we were all exhausted. Kristy cried about going on anything that looked or even sounded scary and was frightened by all of the Disney characters (they are so big!) except Minnie and Snow White.
>
> We got hungry about the same time as everyone else, but the lines for food were too long and my husband said we would have to wait. By one in the afternoon we were just plugging along, not seeing anything we were really interested in, but picking rides because the lines were short, or because whatever it was was air-conditioned. ... At around 2:30 we finally got something to eat, but by then we were so hot and tired that it felt like we had worked in the yard all day. Kristy insisted on being carried, and we had 50 fights about not going on rides where the lines were too long. At the end, we were so P.O.'d and uncomfortable that we weren't having any fun. Mostly by this time we were just trying to get our money's worth.

Before you stiffen in denial, let me assure you that this family's experience is not unusual. Most young children are as picky about rides as they are about what they eat, and more than half of preschoolers are intimidated by the Disney characters. Few humans (of any age) are mentally or physically equipped to march all day in a throng of 50,000 people in the hot Florida sun. And would you be surprised to learn that almost 60% of preschoolers said the thing they liked best about their Disney vacation was the hotel swimming pool?

Reality Testing: Whose Dream Is It?

Remember when you were little and you got that nifty electric train for Christmas, the one Dad wouldn't let you play with? Did you wonder who the train was really for? Ask yourself that question about your vacation to Disney World. Whose dream are you trying to make come true: yours or your child's?

Young children read their parents' emotions. When you ask, "Honey, how would you like to go to Disney World?" your child will respond more to your smile and enthusiasm than to any notion of what Disney World is all about. The younger the child, the more this is true. From many preschoolers, you could elicit the same excitement by asking, "Honey, how would you like to go to Cambodia on a dogsled?"

So, is your happy fantasy of introducing your child to Disney magic a pipe dream? Not necessarily, but you have to be practical and open to reality testing. For example, would you increase the probability of a successful visit by waiting a couple of years? Is your child adventuresome enough to sample the variety of Disney World? Will your child have sufficient endurance and patience to cope with long lines and large crowds?

Recommendations for Making the Dream Come True

When planning a Disney World vacation with young children, consider:

Age   Although Disney World's color and festivity excite all children, and specific attractions delight toddlers and preschoolers, Disney entertainment is generally oriented to older children and adults. Children should be a fairly mature seven years old to *appreciate* the Magic Kingdom and the Animal Kingdom, and a year or two older to get much out of Epcot or Disney-MGM Studios.

Our readers have an ongoing debate on how old a child should be or the ideal age to go to Disney World. A Waldwick, New Jersey, mother reports:

> My kids, not in the least shy or clingy, were frightened of many attractions. I thought my six-year-old was the "perfect age" but quickly realized this was not the case. Disney makes even the most simple, child-friendly story into a major theatrical production, to the point where my kids couldn't associate their beloved movies to the attraction in front of them.

A Rockaway, New Jersey, mom writes:

> You were absolutely right about young kids—I found myself re-reading your section "The Ecstasy and the Agony." Unfortunately, our experience was

pure agony, with the exception of our hotel pool. It was the one and only thing our kids wanted to do. I planned this trip and saved for over a year and cried all week at the disappointment that our kids just wanted to swim.

A Dallas, Texas, dad says:

I must echo the thoughts of readers about parents who bring infants and toddlers to WDW. Are these people nuts? They should find a better way to waste their hard-earned vacation dollars. These children (and therefore their parents) cannot ride any of the best rides and won't remember the ones they do ride five minutes after they get off. It is tough enough walking these huge parks without pushing around one or more children in a stroller. My advice to these parents is to go to a nice beach, rest, let the kids play in the sand, spend less money, and come back in a few years. Disney World will still be there.

A Lexington, Kentucky, couple agrees:

To the folks with kids in strollers ... Six years ago we carried an infant in a Snugli, pushed another child in a stroller, and carried the diaper bag from hell. This year, all were on their own foot power. What a difference. Those of you with preschoolers, please wait until they are older. The kids will have just as much fun and may even remember it when they are older. You will actually enjoy the trip instead of being a Grand Canyon pack mule.

But a Cleveland, Ohio, mother takes exception:

The best advice for parents with young kids is to remember for whom you are there and if possible accommodate the kids' need to do things again and again. I think you underestimate Disney's appeal to young children. Since we've gotten home my four-year-old has said "I don't want to live in Cleveland. I want to live at Disney World" at least five times a day.

Mental preparation is key, says a New York mother of two:

I disagree with what you say about toddlers being too young. My two-year-old had a great time! He loved the Animal Kingdom, the characters, and many of the rides. Even my seven-month-old enjoyed Disney World. He had a good time just looking at the colors and lights. As long as you understand that going with babies will take a little extra work, you can have a good time. ... If one of my children was cranky, we just left.

A Lawrenceville, Georgia, mother of two toddlers advises maintaining the children's normal schedule:

The first day, we tried your suggestion about an early start, so we woke the children (ages four and two) and hurried them to get going. BAD IDEA with toddlers. This put them off schedule for naps and meals the rest of the day. It is best to let young ones stay on their regular schedule and see Disney at their own pace.

Finally, an Alabama woman encourages parents to be more open-minded about taking toddlers to Disney World:

Parents of toddlers, don't be afraid to bring your little ones! Ours absolutely loved it, and we have priceless photos and videos of our little ones and their grandparents with Mickey and the gang. For all those people in your book who complained about our little sweethearts crying, sorry, but we found your character-hogging, cursing, ill-mannered, cutting-in-line, screaming-in-our-ears-on-the-roller-coasters teens and preteens much more obnoxious.

When to Visit   Avoid the hot, crowded summer months, especially if you have preschoolers. Go in October, November (except Thanksgiving), early December, January, February, or May. If you have children of varied ages and they're good students, take the older ones out of school and visit during the cooler, less congested off-season. Arrange special assignments relating to educational aspects of Disney World. If your children can't afford to miss school, take your vacation as soon as the school year ends. Alternatively, try late August before school starts.

Build Naps and Rest into Your Itinerary   The parks are huge; don't try to see everything in one day. Tour in early morning and return to your hotel around 11:30 a.m. for lunch, a swim, and a nap. Even during off-season when crowds are smaller and the temperature more pleasant, the major parks' size will exhaust most children younger than eight by lunchtime. Return to the park in late afternoon or early evening and continue touring. A family from Texas underlines the importance of naps and rest:

Despite not following any of your "tours," we did follow the theme of visiting a specific park in the morning, leaving midafternoon for either a nap back at the room or a trip to the [hotel] pool, and then returning to one of the parks in the evening. On the few occasions when we skipped your advice, I was muttering to myself by dinner. I can't tell you what I was muttering ...

Regarding naps, this mom doesn't mince words:

For parents of small kids: take the book's advice and get out of the park and take the nap, take the nap, TAKE THE NAP! Never in my life have I seen so many parents screaming at, ridiculing, or slapping their kids. (What a vacation!) WDW is overwhelming for kids and adults. Even though the rental strollers recline for sleeping, we noticed that most of the toddlers and preschoolers didn't give up and sleep until 5 p.m., several hours after the fun had worn off, and right about the time their parents wanted them to be awake and polite in a restaurant.

A Rochester, New York, mom was adamant:

[You] absolutely must rest during the day. Kids went from 8 a.m. to 9 p.m. in the Magic Kingdom. Kids did great that day, but we were all completely

worthless the next day. Definitely must pace yourself. Don't ever try to do
two full days of park sight-seeing in a row. Rest during the day. Go to a
water park or sleep in every other day.

If you plan to return to your hotel at midday and want your room
made up, let housekeeping know.

Where to Stay The time and hassle involved in commuting to and
from the theme parks will be less if your hotel is close by. This doesn't
necessarily mean you have to lodge inside Disney World. Because the
World is so geographically dispersed, many off-property hotels are closer
to the parks than some Disney resorts (see our chart on pages 210–233
showing commuting times from Disney and non-Disney hotels).
Regardless where you stay, it's imperative that you take young children
out of the parks each day for a few hours of rest. Neglecting to relax will
get the whole family in a snit and ruin the day (or the vacation).

If you have young children, book a hotel within 20 minutes of the
theme parks. It's true you can revive somewhat by retreating to a Disney
hotel for lunch or by finding a quiet restaurant in the parks, but there's
no substitute for returning to the comfort of your hotel. Regardless of
what you've heard, children too large to sleep in a stroller won't relax
unless you take them back to your hotel. If it takes renting a car to make
returning to your hotel practicable, rent the car.

Thousands of new rooms have been built in and near Disney World,
many of them affordable. With planning, you should have no difficulty
finding lodging to meet your requirements.

If you're traveling with children 12 and younger and want to stay in
the World, we recommend the Polynesian, Grand Floridian, or Wilderness Lodge and Villas Resorts (in that order) if they fit your budget. For
less expensive rooms, try the Port Orleans Resort. Bargain lodging is
available at the All-Star and Pop Century resorts. Log cabins at Fort
Wilderness Campground are also economical. Outside the World, check
our top hotels for families on pages 197–205.

Be in Touch with Your Feelings When you or your children get tired
and irritable, call time-out. Trust your instincts. What would feel best?
Another ride, an ice-cream break, or going back to the room for a nap?

The way to protect your considerable investment in your Disney vacation is to stay happy and have a good time. You don't have to meet a
quota for experiencing attractions. Do what you want.

Least Common Denominators Somebody is going to run out of steam
first, and when they do, the whole family will be affected. Sometimes a
snack break will revive the flagging member. Sometimes, however, it's
better to return to your hotel. Pushing the tired or discontented beyond
their capacity will spoil the day for them—and you. Energy levels vary.

Be prepared to respond to members of your group who poop out. *Hint:* "We've driven a thousand miles to take you to Walt Disney World and now you're ruining everything!" is not an appropriate response.

Building Endurance Though most children are active, their normal play usually doesn't condition them for the exertion required to tour a Disney park. Start family walks four to six weeks before your trip to get in shape. A mother from Wesconsville, Pennsylvania, reports:

> We had our six-year-old begin walking with us a bit every day one month before leaving—when we arrived [at Walt Disney World], her little legs could carry her, and she had a lot of stamina.

Setting Limits and Making Plans Avoid arguments and disappointment by establishing guidelines for each day, and get everybody committed. Include:

1. Wake-up time and breakfast plans.
2. When to depart for the park.
3. What to take with you.
4. A policy for splitting the group or for staying together.
5. What to do if the group gets separated or someone is lost.
6. How long you intend to tour in the morning and what you want to see, including plans in the event an attraction is closed or too crowded.
7. A policy on what you can afford for snacks.
8. A time for returning to the hotel to rest.
9. When you will return to the park and how late you will stay.
10. Dinner plans.
11. A policy for buying souvenirs, including who pays: Mom and Dad or the kids.
12. Bedtimes.

Be Flexible Any day at Disney World includes surprises; be prepared to adjust your plan. Listen to your intuition.

Maintaining Some Semblance of Order and Discipline OK, OK, wipe that smirk off you face. Order and discipline on the road may seem like an oxymoron to you, but you won't be hooting when your five-year-old launches a screaming mimi in the middle of Fantasyland. Your willingness to give this subject serious consideration before you leave home may well be the most important element of your pre-trip preparation.

Discipline and maintaining order are more difficult when traveling than at home because everyone is, as a Boston mom put it, "in and out" —in strange surroundings and out of the normal routine. For children, it's hard to contain excitement and anticipation that pop to the surface in the form of fidgety hyperactivity, nervous energy, and sometimes, acting out. Confinement in a car, plane, or hotel room only exacerbates the situation, and kids often tend to be louder than normal, more aggressive with siblings, and much more inclined to push the envelope of parental patience. Once in the theme parks, it doesn't get much better. There's more elbow room, but there's also overstimulation, crowds, heat, and miles of walking. All this, coupled with marginal or inadequate rest, can lead to a meltdown in the most harmonious of families.

Sound parenting and standards of discipline practiced at home, applied consistently, will suffice to handle most situations on vacation. Still, it's instructive to study the hand you are dealt when traveling. For starters, aside from being jazzed and ablaze with adrenaline, your kids may believe that rules followed at home are somehow suspended when traveling. Parents reinforce this misguided intuition by being inordinately lenient in the interest of maintaining peace in the family. While some of your home protocols (cleaning your plate, going to bed at a set time, etc.) might be relaxed to good effect on vacation, differing from your normal approach to discipline can precipitate major misunderstanding and possibly disaster.

Children, not unexpectedly, are likely to believe that a vacation (especially a vacation to Walt Disney World) is expressly for them. This reinforces their focus on their own needs and largely erases any consideration of yours. Such a mindset dramatically increases their sense of hurt and disappointment when you correct them or deny them something they want. An incident that would hardly elicit a pouty lip at home could well escalate to tears or defiance when traveling. It's important before you depart on your trip, therefore, to discuss your vacation needs with your children, and to explore their wants and expectations as well.

The stakes are high for everyone on a vacation—for you because of the cost in time and dollars, but also because your vacation represents a rare opportunity for rejuvenation and renewal. The stakes are high for your children too. Children tend to romanticize travel, building anticipation to an almost unbearable level. Discussing the trip in advance can ground expectations to a certain extent, but a child's imagination will, in the end, trump reality every time. The good news is that you can take advantage of your children's emotional state to establish preagreed rules and conditions for their conduct while on vacation. Because your children want what's being offered sooooo badly, they will be unusually accepting and conscientious regarding whatever rules are agreed upon.

According to *Unofficial Guide* child psychologist Dr. Karen Turnbow, successful response to (or avoidance of) behavioral problems on the road begins with a clear-cut disciplinary policy at home. Both at home and on vacation the approach should be the same, and should be based on the following key concepts:

1. Let Expectations Be Known   Discuss what you expect from your children, but don't try to cover every imaginable situation (that's what lawyers are for—just kidding). Cover expectations regarding compliance with parental directives, treatment of siblings, resolution of disputes, schedules (including morning wake-up and bedtimes), courtesy and manners, staying together, and who pays for what.

2. Explain the Consequences of Noncompliance   Detail very clearly and firmly the consequence of not meeting expectations. This should be very straightforward and unambiguous. If you do X (or don't do X), this is what will happen.

3. Warning   You're dealing with excited, expectant children, not machines, so it's important to issue a warning before meting out discipline. It's critical to understand that we're talking about one unequivocal warning rather than multiple warnings or nagging. These last undermine your credibility and make your expectations appear relative or less than serious. Multiple warnings or nagging also effectively pass control of the situation from you to your child (who sometimes may continue acting out as an attention-getting strategy).

4. Follow Through   If you say you're going to do something, do it. Period. Children must understand that you are absolutely serious and committed.

5. Consistency   Inconsistency makes discipline a random event in the eyes of your children. Random discipline encourages random behavior, which translates to a nearly total loss of parental control. Long term, both at home and on the road, your response to a given situation or transgression must be perfectly predictable. Structure and repetition, essential for a child to learn, cannot be achieved in the absence of consistency.

Although the above are the five biggies, there are several corollary concepts and techniques that are worthy of consideration.

First, understand that whining, tantrums, defiance, sibling friction, and even holding up the group are ways in which children communicate with parents. Frequently the object or precipitant of a situation has little or no relation to the unacceptable behavior. A fit may on the surface appear to be about the ice cream you refused to buy little Robby, but there's almost always something deeper, a subtext that is closer to the truth (this is the reason why ill behavior often persists after you give in to a child's demands). As often as not, the real cause is a need for attention. This need is so powerful in some children that they will subject themselves to certain punishment and parental displeasure to garner the attention they crave, even if it is negative.

To get at the root cause of the behavior in question requires both active listening and empowering your child with a "feeling vocabulary." Active listening is a concept that's been around a long time. It involves being alert not only to what a child says, but also to the context in which it is said, to the words used and possible subtext, to the child's emotional state and body language, and even to what's not said. Sounds complicated, but it's basically being attentive to the larger picture and, more to the point, being aware that there is a larger picture.

Helping your child to develop a feeling vocabulary consists of teaching your child to use words to describe what's going on. The idea is to teach the child to articulate what's really troubling him, to be able to identify and express emotions and mood states in language. Of course, learning to express feelings is a lifelong learning experience, but it's much less dependent on innate sensitivity than being provided the tools for expression and being encouraged to use them.

It all begins with convincing your child that you're willing to listen attentively and take what he's saying seriously. Listening to your child, you help him transcend the topical by reframing the conversation to address the underlying emotional state(s). That his brother hit him may have precipitated the mood state, but the act is topical and of secondary importance. What you want is for your child to be able to communicate how that makes him feel, and to get in touch with those emotions. When you reduce an incident (hitting) to the emotions triggered (anger, hurt, rejection, etc.) you have the foundation for helping him to develop constructive coping strategies. Being in touch with one's feelings and developing constructive coping strategies are essential to emotional well being, and they also have a positive effect on behavior. A child who can tell his mother why he is distressed is a child who has discovered a coping strategy far more effective (not to mention easier for all concerned) than a tantrum.

Children are almost never too young to begin learning a feeling vocabulary. And helping your child to be in touch with—and communicate—his or her emotions will stimulate you to focus on your feelings and mood states in a similar way. In the end, with persistence and effort, the whole family will achieve a vastly improved ability to communicate.

Until you get the active listening and feeling vocabulary going, be careful not to become part of the problem. There's a whole laundry list of adult responses to bad behavior that only make things worse. Hitting, swatting, yelling, name-calling, insulting, belittling, using sarcasm, pleading, nagging, and inducing guilt (as in, "we've spent thousands of dollars to bring you to Disney World and now you're spoiling the trip for everyone") figure prominently on the list.

Responding to a child appropriately in a disciplinary situation requires thought and preparation. Following are things to keep in mind, and techniques to try, when your world blows up while waiting in line for Dumbo.

1. **Be the Adult**   It's well understood that children can punch their parents' buttons faster and more lethally than just about anyone or anything else. They've got your number, know precisely how to elicit a response, and are not reluctant to go for the jugular. Fortunately (or unfortunately), you're the adult, and to deal with a situation effectively, you've got to act

like one. If your kids get you ranting and caterwauling, you effectively abdicate your adult status. Worse, you suggest by way of example that being out of control is an acceptable expression of hurt or anger. No matter what happens, repeat the mantra, "I am the adult in this relationship."

2. Freeze the Action   Being the adult and maintaining control almost always translates to freezing the action, to borrow a sports term. Instead of a knee-jerk response (at a maturity level closer to your child's than yours), freeze the action by disengaging. Wherever you are or whatever the family is doing, stop in place and concentrate on one thing, and one thing only: getting all involved calmed down. Practically speaking this usually means initiating a time-out. It's essential that you take this action immediately. Grabbing your child by the arm or collar and dragging him toward the car or hotel room only escalates the turmoil by prolonging the confrontation and by adding a coercive physical dimension to an already volatile emotional event. If for the sake of people around you (as when a toddler throws a tantrum in church) it's essential to retreat to a more private place, chose the first place available. Firmly sit the child down and refrain from talking to him until you've both cooled off. This might take a little time, but the investment is worthwhile. Truncating the process is like trying to get on your feet too soon after surgery.

3. Isolate the Child   You'll be able to deal with the situation more effectively and expeditiously if the child is isolated with one parent. Dispatch the uninvolved members of your party for a Coke break or have them go on with the activity or itinerary without you (if possible) and arrange to rendezvous later at an agreed time and place. In addition to letting the others get on with their day, isolating the offending child with one parent relieves him of the pressure of being the group's focus of attention and object of anger. Equally important, isolation frees you from the scrutiny and expectations of the others in regard to how to handle the situation.

4. Review the Situation with the Child   If, as discussed above, you've made your expectations clear, stated the consequences of failing those expectations, and have administered a warning, review the situation with the child and follow through with the discipline warranted. If, as often occurs, things are not so black and white, encourage the child to communicate his feelings. Try to uncover what occasioned the acting out. Lecturing and accusatory language don't work well here, nor do threats. Dr. Turnbow suggests a better approach (after the child is calm) is to ask, "What can we do to make this a better day for you?"

5. Frequent Tantrums or Acting Out   The preceding four points relate to dealing with an incident as opposed to a chronic condition. If a child frequently acts out or throws tantrums, you'll need to employ a somewhat different strategy.

Tantrums are cyclical events evolved from learned behavior. A child learns that he can get your undivided attention by acting out. When you respond, whether by scolding, admonishing, threatening, or negotiating, your response further draws you into the cycle and prolongs the behavior. When you accede to the child's demands, you reinforce the effectiveness of the tantrum and raise the cost of capitulation next time around. When a child thus succeeds in monopolizing your attention, he effectively becomes the person in charge.

To break this cycle, you must disengage from the child. The object is to demonstrate that the cause-and-effect relationship (i.e., tantrum elicits parental attention) is no longer operative. This can be accomplished by refusing to interact with the child as long as the untoward behavior continues. Tell the child that you're unwilling to discuss his problem until he calms down. You can ignore the behavior, remove yourself from the child's presence (or visa versa), or isolate the child with a time-out. It's important to disengage quickly and decisively with no discussion or negotiation.

Most children don't pick the family vacation as the time to start throwing tantrums. The behavior will be evident before you leave home and home is the best place to deal with it. Be forewarned, however, that bad habits die hard, and that a child accustomed to getting attention by throwing tantrums will not simply give up after a single instance of disengagement. More likely, the child will at first escalate the intensity and length of his tantrums. By your consistent refusal over several weeks (or even months) to respond to his behavior, however, he will finally adjust to the new paradigm.

Children are cunning as well as observant. Many understand that a tantrum in public is embarrassing to you and that you're more likely to cave in than you would at home. Once again, consistency is the key, along with a bit of anticipation. When traveling, it's not necessary to retreat to the privacy of a hotel room to isolate your child. You can carve out space for time-out almost anywhere: on a theme park bench, in a park, in your car, in a restroom, even on a sidewalk.

You can often spot the warning signs of an impending tantrum and head it off by talking to the child before he reaches an explosive emotional pitch. And don't forget that tantrums are about getting attention. Giving you child attention when things are on an even keel often preempts acting out.

6. Salvage Operations Who knows what evil lurks in the hearts of children? What's for sure is that they are full of surprises, and sometimes the surprises are not good. If your sweet child manages to pull a boner of mammoth proportions, what do you do? This happened to an Ohio couple, resulting in the offending kid pretty much being grounded for life. Fortunately there were no injuries or lives lost, but the parents had to determine what to do for the remainder of the vacation. For starters, they split the group. One parent escorted the offending child back to the hotel, where he was effectively confined to his guest room for the duration. That evening, the parents arranged for in-room sitters for the rest of the stay. Expensive? You bet, but better than watching your whole vacation go down the tubes.

A family at Walt Disney World's Magic Kingdom theme park had a similar experience, although the offense was of a more modest order of magnitude. Because it was their last day of vacation, they elected to place the misbehaver in time-out, in the theme park, for the rest of the day. One parent monitored the culprit while the other parent and the siblings enjoyed the attractions. At agreed times the parents would switch places. Once again, not ideal, but preferable to stopping the vacation.

About the Unofficial Guide Touring Plans   Parents who use our touring plans are often frustrated by interruptions and delays caused by their young children. Here's what to expect:

1. Character encounters can wreak havoc with the touring plans. Many children will stop in their tracks whenever they see a Disney character. Attempting to haul your child away before he has satisfied his curiosity is likely to cause anything from whining to full-scale revolt. Either go with the flow or specify a morning or afternoon for photos and autographs. Be aware that queues for autographs, especially in Toontown at the Magic Kingdom and Camp Minnie-Mickey at the Animal Kingdom, are as long as the queues for major attractions.

2.   Our touring plans call for visiting attractions in a sequence, often skipping attractions along the way.   Children don't like skipping anything! If something catches their eye, they want to see it that moment. Some can be persuaded to skip attractions if parents explain their plans in advance. Other kids flip out at skipping something, particularly in Fantasyland. A mom from Charleston, South Carolina, writes:

We did not have too much trouble following the touring plans at [Disney-]
MGM and at Epcot. The Magic Kingdom plan, on the other hand, turned
out to be a train wreck. The main problem with the plan is that it starts in
Fantasyland. When we were on Dumbo, my five-year-old saw eight dozen
other things in Fantasyland she wanted to see. The long and the short is
that after Dumbo, there was no getting her out of there.

A mother of two from Burlington, Vermont, adds:

I found out that my kids were very curious about the castle because we had
read Cinderella at home. Whenever I wanted to leave Fantasyland, I would
just say, "Let's go to the castle and see if Cinderella is there." Once we got
as far as the front door to the castle, it was no problem going out to the
[central] hub and then to another land.

3. Children have an instinct for finding rest rooms.   We have seen adults with maps search interminably for a rest room. Young children, however, including those who can't read, will head for the nearest rest room with the certainty of a homing pigeon. You can be sure your children will ferret out (and want to use) every rest room in the park.

4. If you're using a stroller, you won't be able to take it into attractions or onto rides. This includes rides such as the Walt Disney World Railroad that are included in the touring plans as in-park transportation.

5. You probably won't finish the touring plan. Varying hours of operation, crowds, your group's size, your children's ages, and your stamina will all affect how much of the plan you'll complete. Tailor your expectations to this reality, or you'll be frustrated as this mother of two from Nazareth, Pennsylvania, was:

We do not understand how anyone could fit everything you have on your plans into the time allotted while attending to small children. We found that long lines, potty stops, diaper changes, stroller searches, and autograph breaks ate huge chunks of time. And we were there during the off-season.

While our touring plans allow you to make the most of your time at the parks, it's impossible to define what "most" will be. It differs from family to family. If you have two young children, you probably won't see as much as two adults will. If you have four children, you probably won't see as much as a couple with only two children.

Overheating, Sunburn, and Dehydration These are the most common problems of younger children at Disney World. Carry and use sunscreen. Be sure to apply it on children in strollers, even if the stroller has a canopy. Some of the worst sunburns we've seen were on the exposed foreheads and feet of toddlers and infants in strollers. To avoid overheating, rest regularly in the shade or in an air-conditioned restaurant or show.

Don't count on hydrating young children with soft drinks and stops at water fountains. Carry plastic bottles of water. Plastic squeeze bottles with caps are sold in all major parks for about $3. Remember: Excited children may not tell you when they're thirsty or hot.

Blisters and Sore Feet All guests should wear comfortable, broken-in shoes and socks that wick off perspiration, like Smart Wool socks. If you or your children are susceptible to blisters, bring precut Moleskin bandages. They offer the best protection, stick great, and won't sweat off. When you feel a hot spot, stop, air out your foot, and place a Moleskin bandage over the area before a blister forms. Moleskin is available at all drug stores. Preschoolers may not say they're developing blister until it's too late; inspect their feet two or more times a day. For a more expanded discussion about keeping your feet happy, see pages 330–331.

First Aid Each major theme park has a first-aid center. In the Magic Kingdom, it's behind the refreshment corner to the left after you enter. At Epcot, it's on the World Showcase side of Odyssey Center. At Disney-MGM, it's in the Guest Relations Building inside the main entrance. At

Animal Kingdom, it's in Discovery Island. If you or your children have a medical problem, go to a first-aid center. They're friendlier than most doctor's offices and are accustomed to treating everything from paper cuts to allergic reactions.

Children on Medication   Some parents of hyperactive children on medication discontinue or decrease the child's dosage at the end of the school year. If you have such a child, be aware that Disney World might overstimulate him/her. Consult your physician before altering your child's medication regimen.

Walkie-Talkies and Cell Phones   An increasing number of readers stay in touch while on vacation by using walkie-talkies. From a Cabot, Arkansas, family:

Borrow or get walkie-talkies! ... Our youngest was too scared or too short for some rides, plus I was expecting, so we would sit outside or go to a snack area, but we were always in contact. My husband could tell me how long the wait was, when he was about to come down Splash Mountain (for me to take a photo!), or where to meet.

A dad from Roanoke is on the same wavelength:

The single best purchase we made was Motorola TalkAbout walkie-talkies. They have a two-mile range and are about the size of a deck of cards. ... At the parks, the kids would invariably have diverse interests. With walkie-talkies, however, we could easily split up and simply communicate with each other when we wanted to meet back up. At least a half-dozen times, exasperated parents asked where they could rent/buy the walkie-talkies.

If you buy walkie-talkies, get a set that operates on multiple channels, or opt for cellular phones as a Duluth, Georgia, family did:

I spoke with a woman who invested $100 in walkie-talkies. All day long all she could hear were other people's conversations as so many people are using them. My husband and I used our cellular phones, and they worked beautifully. Even though I pay roaming charges on mine, there's no way I could use $100 worth!

Sunglasses   If your younger children wear sunglasses, put a strap or string on the frames so the glasses will stay on during rides and can hang from the child's neck while indoors. Works for adults, too.

Things You Forgot or Things You Ran Out Of   Rain gear, diapers, diaper pins, formula, film, aspirin, topical sunburn treatments, and other sundries are sold at all major theme parks and at Typhoon Lagoon, Blizzard Beach, and Downtown Disney. Rain gear is a bargain, but most other items are high. Ask for goods you don't see displayed.

Infants and Toddlers at the Theme Parks   The major parks have centralized facilities for infant and toddler care. Everything necessary for changing diapers, preparing formulas, and warming bottles and food is available. Supplies are for sale (two diapers plus ointment are $3.50, for example), and there are rockers and special chairs for nursing mothers. At the Magic Kingdom, the Baby Center is next to the Crystal Palace at the end of Main Street. At Epcot, Baby Services is near the Odyssey Center, right of the Test Track in Future World. At Disney-MGM Studios, Baby Care is in the Guest Relations Building left of the entrance. At Animal Kingdom, Baby Changing/Nursing is in Discovery Island in the park's center. Dads are welcome at the centers and can use most services. In addition, many men's rooms in the major parks have changing tables.

A mom from New Berlin, Wisconsin, offered this tip for families with babies on formula:

A note to families with infants: We got hot water from the food vendors at WDW and mixed the formula as we went. It eliminated keeping bottles cold and then warming them up.

Infants and toddlers are allowed in any attraction that doesn't have minimum height or age restrictions. But as a Minneapolis mother reports, some attractions are better for babies than others:

Theater and boat rides are easier for babies (ours was almost one year old, not yet walking). Rides where there's a bar that comes down are doable, but harder. Peter Pan was our first encounter with this type, and we had barely gotten situated when I realized he might fall out of my grasp. The standing auditorium films are too intense; the noise level is deafening, and the images inescapable. You don't have a rating system for babies, and I don't expect to see one, but I thought you might want to know what a baby thought (based on his reactions). [At the Magic Kingdom:] Jungle Cruise—Didn't get into it. Pirates—Slept through it. Riverboat—While at Aunt Polly's, the horn made him cry. Aunt Polly's—Ate while watching the birds in relative quiet. Small World—Wide-eyed, took it all in. Peter Pan— Couldn't really sit on the seat. A bit dangerous. He didn't get into it. Carousel of Progress—Long talks; hard to keep him quiet; danced during song. WDW RR—Liked the motion and scenery. Tiki Birds—Loved it. Danced, clapped, sang along. At Epcot: Honey, I Shrunk the Audience— We skipped due to recommendation of Disney worker that it got too loud and adults screamed throughout. Journey into Imagination—Loved it. Tried to catch things with his hands. Bounced up and down, chortled. The Land— Watchful, quiet during presentation. El Río del Tiempo—Loved it.

The same mom also advises:

We used a baby sling on our trip and thought it was great when standing in lines—much better than a stroller, which you have to park before getting in line (and navigate through crowds). The food at WDW [includes] almost nothing a baby can eat. No fruits or vegetables. My baby was still nursing when we went to WDW. The only really great place I found to nurse in MK was a hidden bench in the shade in Adventureland in between the freezee stand (next to Tiki Birds) and the small shops. It is impractical to go to the baby station every time, so a nursing mom better be comfortable about nursing in very public situations.

If you think you might try nursing during a theater attraction, be advised that most shows run about 17–20 minutes. Exceptions are *The Hall of Presidents* at the Magic Kingdom and *The American Adventure* at Epcot that run 23 and 29 minutes respectively.

Strollers   The good news: Strollers are available for a modest rental fee at all four theme parks. Even better, Disney has replaced the ancient blue clunkers at Epcot and the Magic Kingdom with brand-new strollers. If you rent a stroller at the Magic Kingdom and decide to go to Epcot, Animal Kingdom, or Disney-MGM Studios, turn in your Magic Kingdom stroller and present your receipt at the next park. You'll be issued another stroller without additional charge.

Obtain strollers to the right of the Magic Kingdom entrance, to the left of Epcot's Entrance Plaza, and at Oscar's Super Service just inside the entrance of Disney-MGM Studios. At Animal Kingdom, they're to the right just inside the entrance. Rental at all parks is fast and efficient, and returning the stroller is a breeze. If you don't mind forfeiting your dollar deposit, you can ditch your rental stroller anywhere in the park when you're ready to leave.

Readers inform us that there is a lively "gray market" in strollers at the parks. Families who arrive late look for families who are heading for the exit and "buy" their stroller at a bargain price. A Chester, New Hampshire, mom, ever vigilant for a bargain, reported: "We 'bought' strollers for $3 when we saw people returning them. Also, we 'sold' our strollers when leaving for $3."

When you enter a show or board a ride, you must park your stroller, usually in an open area. If it rains before you return, you'll need a cloth, towel, or diaper to dry it.

Strollers are a must for infants and toddlers, but we have observed many sharp parents renting strollers for somewhat older children (up to five or so). The stroller prevents parents from having to carry children when they sag and provides a convenient place to carry water and snacks.

If you go to your hotel for a break and intend to return to the park, leave your rental stroller by an attraction near the park entrance, marking it with something personal like a bandanna. When you return, your stroller will be waiting.

Rental strollers are too large for all infants and many toddlers. If you plan to rent a stroller for your infant or toddler, bring pillows, cushions, or rolled towels to buttress him in.

Bringing your own stroller is permitted. However, only collapsible strollers are allowed on monorails, parking-lot trams, and buses. Your stroller is unlikely to be stolen, but mark it with your name.

Having her own stroller was indispensable to a Mechanicsville, Virginia, mother of two toddlers:

How I was going to manage to get the kids from the parking lot to the park was a big worry for me before I made the trip. I didn't read anywhere that it was possible to walk to the entrance of the parks instead of taking the tram, so I wasn't sure I could do it.

I found that for me personally, since I have two kids aged one and two, it was easier to walk to the entrance of the park from the parking lot with the kids in [my own] stroller than to take the kids out of the stroller, fold the stroller (while trying to control the two kids and associated gear), load the stroller and the kids onto the tram, etc. ... No matter where I was parked I could always just walk to the entrance ... it sometimes took awhile but it was easier for me.

A Secaucus, New Jersey, mom weighed all the considerations in exemplary Type-A fashion:

If your child is under age two, bring your own stroller. Three reasons to bring your own: First, you have all the way from your car to the TTC to the monorail (or ferry) to the stroller rental without a stroller, but with your child, diaper bag, and own self and stuff in tow. Not half as bad as doing it in reverse when leaving, when you're exhausted and have added to your luggage with purchases and the toddler who might have walked in wants to be carried out. Second, the WDW stroller is simply too large for most children under two to be comfortable without significant padding. The seat is so low that the child is forced to keep their legs straight out in front of them. Third, despite being sooo big, there is NO PLACE to store anything. The body of the stroller is so low, there is no underneath storage for the diaper bag. There is a small net bag on the back of the carriage, but it seems designed to hold, at most, a small purse. If you hang a diaper bag by its straps from the handle, the stroller will tip backwards very, very easily. And you can't balance it on the top or the canopy won't stay open. It amazed me that the Disney folks did not provide ample space for all the souvenirs they want you to buy!

Now, if your child is past needing a diaper bag, the WDW strollers seem like a pretty good deal. You won't need the storage space, and they do maneuver very well. They seem especially good for children who no longer need a stroller at home (ages 4–6) but who won't make it walking all day.

If your child is between ages 2 and 3, it's a toss-up. If you're a Type-A mom, like me, who carries extra clothes, snacks, toys, enough diapers for three days, along with a pocketbook and extra-jackets-for-everyone-just-in-case, you've probably found a stroller that suits your needs, and will be miserable with the WDW kind. If you're a Type B, "we can get everything else we need at the park, I'll just throw a diaper in my back pocket" mom, you'll probably be tickled with the WDW strollers. Also consider your toddler's personality. Will his familiar stroller add a level of comfort to a pretty intense experience? Or will he enjoy the novelty of the new wheels?

Stroller Wars   Sometimes strollers disappear while you're enjoying a ride or show. Disney staff will often rearrange strollers parked outside an attraction. This may be done to "tidy up" or to clear a walkway. Don't assume your stroller is stolen because it isn't where you left it. It may be "neatly arranged" a few feet away.

Sometimes, however, strollers are taken by mistake or ripped off by people not wanting to spend time replacing one that's missing. Don't be alarmed if yours disappears. You won't have to buy it, and you'll be issued a new one. In the Magic Kingdom, replacements are available at Tinker Bell's Treasures in Fantasyland and at the main rental facility near the park entrance. At Epcot, get replacements at the Entrance Plaza rental headquarters and at the International Gateway (in World Showcase between the United Kingdom and France). Strollers at Disney-MGM can be replaced at the Animation Courtyard Shops next to *The Voyage of the Little Mermaid*. In Animal Kingdom, they're available at Garden Gate Gifts and Mombasa Marketplace.

While replacing a stroller is no big deal, it's inconvenient. A Minnesota family complained that their stroller was taken six times in one day at Epcot and five times in a day at Disney-MGM Studios. Even with free replacements, larceny on this scale represents a lot of wasted time. Through our own experiments and readers' suggestions, we developed techniques for hanging on to a rented stroller: Affix something personal (but expendable) to the handle. Evidently, most strollers are pirated by mistake (they all look alike) or because it's easier to swipe someone else's than to replace one that has disappeared. Since most stroller "theft" results from confusion or laziness, the average pram pincher will hesitate to haul off a stroller containing another person's property. We tried several items and concluded that a bright, inexpensive scarf or bandanna tied to the handle works well as I.D. A sock partially stuffed with rags or paper works even better (the weirder and more personal the object, the greater the deterrent). Best might be an Ann Arbor, Michigan, mother's strategy:

We used a variation on your stroller identification theme. We tied a clear plastic bag with a diaper in it on the stroller. Jon even poured a little root beer on the diaper for effect. Needless to say, no one took our stroller, and it was easy to identify.

Strollers as Lethal Weapons   A father of one from Purcellville, Virginia, complains about some inconsiderate parents:

The biggest problem is surviving the migrating herds of strollers. The drivers of these contraptions appear to believe they have the right-of-way in all situations and use the strollers as battering rams. ... I know they will not be banned from the parks, but how about putting speed governors on these things?

You'd be surprised at how many people are injured by strollers pushed by parents who are driving aggressively, in a hurry, or in the ozone. Though you may desire to use your stroller to wedge through crowds like Moses parting the seas, think twice. It's very un-Disney to steamroll other guests.

Lost Children

Although it's amazingly easy to lose a child (or two) in the theme parks, it usually isn't a serious problem. All Disney employees are schooled in handling the situation. If you lose a child in the Magic Kingdom, report it to a Disney employee, then check at the Baby Center and at City Hall, where lost-children "logs" are kept. At Epcot, report the loss, then check at Baby Services near the Odyssey Center. At Disney-MGM Studios, report the loss at the Guest Relations Building at the entrance end of Hollywood Boulevard. At Animal Kingdom, go to the Baby Center in Discovery Island. Paging isn't used, but in an emergency an "all-points bulletin" can be issued throughout the park(s) via internal communications. If a Disney employee encounters a lost child, he or she will take the child immediately to the park's guest relations center or its baby-care center.

We suggest that children younger than eight be color-coded by dressing them in purple T-shirts or equally distinctive clothes. Sew a label into each child's shirt that states his name, your name, the name of your hotel, and if you have one, your cell phone number. Accomplish the same thing by writing the information on a strip of masking tape. Security professionals suggest the information be printed in small letters and the tape be affixed to the outside of the child's shirt, five inches below the armpit. Also, name tags can be obtained at the major theme parks.

A Kingston, Washington, reader recommends recording vital info for each child on a plastic key tag or luggage tag and affixing it to the child's shoe. This reader also snaps a photo of the kids each morning to document what they're wearing. A mother from Rockville, Maryland reported a strategy one step short of a brand or tattoo:

Traveling with a three-year-old, I was very anxious about losing him. I wrote my cell phone number on his leg with a "sharpie" permanent marker, and felt much more confident that he'd get back to me quickly if lost.

How Kids Get Lost

Children get separated from their parents every day at Disney parks under remarkably similar (and predictable) circumstances:

1. Preoccupied Solo Parent   The party's only adult is preoccupied with something like buying refreshments, loading the camera, or using the rest room. Junior is there one second and gone the next.

2. The Hidden Exit   Sometimes parents wait on the sidelines while two or more young children experience a ride together. Parents expect the kids to exit in one place and the youngsters pop out elsewhere. Exits from some attractions are distant from entrances. Know exactly where your children will emerge before letting them ride by themselves.

3. After the Show   At the end of many shows and rides, a Disney staffer announces, "Check for personal belongings and take small children by the hand." When dozens, if not hundreds, of people leave an attraction simultaneously, it's easy for parents to lose their children unless they have direct contact.

4. Rest-Room Problems   Mom tells six-year-old Tommy, "I'll be sitting on this bench when you come out of the rest room." Three possibilities: One, Tommy exits through a different door and becomes disoriented (Mom may not know there is another door). Two, Mom decides she also will use the rest room, and Tommy emerges to find her gone. Three, Mom pokes around in a shop while keeping an eye on the bench, but misses Tommy when he comes out.

If you can't be with your child in the rest room, make sure there's only one exit. The rest room on a passageway between Frontierland and Adventureland in the Magic Kingdom is the all-time worst for disorienting visitors. Children and adults alike have walked in from the Adventureland side and walked out on the Frontierland side (and vice versa). Adults realize quickly that something is wrong. Children, however, sometimes fail to recognize the problem. Designate a distinctive meeting spot and give clear instructions: "I'll meet you by this flagpole. If you get out first, stay right here." Have your child repeat the directions back to you. When children are too young to leave alone, sometimes you have to think outside the box as our Rockville mom (quoted above) did:

It was very scary for me at times, being alone with children that had just turned one and two. I'm reminded of the time on the trip when I couldn't fit the double stroller into the bathroom. I was at Epcot inside one of the buildings and I had to leave my kids with a WDW employee outside of the rest room because the stroller just wouldn't fit inside with me. Thinking about the incident now makes me laugh. The good news is that I found that most WDW bathrooms can accommodate a front-and-back, double stroller inside the handicapped stall [with you].

5. Parades   There are many parades and shows at which the audience stands. Children tend to jockey for a better view. By moving a little this way and that, the child quickly puts distance between you and him before either of you notices.

6. Mass Movements   Be on guard when huge crowds disperse after fireworks or a parade, or at park closing. With 20,000–40,000 people at once in an area, it's very easy to get separated from a child or others in your party. Use extra caution after the evening parade and fireworks in the Magic Kingdom, *Fantasmic!* at the Disney-MGM Studios, and *IllumiNations* at Epcot. Families should plan where to meet if they get separated.

7. Character Greetings   When the Disney characters appear, children can slip out of sight. See "Then Some Confusion Happened" (page 255).

8. Getting Lost at the Animal Kingdom   It's especially easy to lose a child in Animal Kingdom, particularly at the Oasis entryway, on the Maharaja Jungle Trek, and on the Pangani Forest Exploration Trail. Mom and Dad will stop to observe an animal. Junior stays close for a minute or so, and then, losing patience, wanders to the exhibit's other side or to a different exhibit.

Especially in the multipath Oasis, finding a lost child can be maddening, as a Safety Harbor, Florida, mother describes:

Manny wandered off in the paths that lead to the jungle village while we were looking at a bird. It reminded me of losing somebody in the supermarket when you run back and forth looking down each aisle but can't find the person you're looking for because they are running around, too. I was nutso before we even got to the first ride.

A mother from Flint, Michigan, came up with yet another way to lose a kid: abandonment.

From the minute we hit the park it was gripe, whine, pout, cry, beg, scream, pick, pester, and aggravate. When he went to the rest room for the ninth time before 11 a.m., I thought I'M OUTTA HERE ... let the little snothead walk back to Flint. Unfortunately, I was brought up Catholic with lots of guilt so I didn't follow through.

Disney, Kids, and Scary Stuff

Disney rides and shows are adventures, and they focus on themes of all adventures: good and evil, death, beauty and the grotesque, fellowship and enmity. As you sample the attractions at Walt Disney World, you transcend the spinning and bouncing of midway rides to thought-provoking and emotionally powerful entertainment. All of the endings are happy, but the adventures' impact, given Disney's gift for special effects, often intimidates and occasionally frightens young children.

There are rides with menacing witches, burning towns, and ghouls popping out of their graves, all done with humor, provided you're old enough to understand the joke. And bones. There are bones everywhere: human bones, cattle bones, dinosaur bones, even whole skeletons. There's a stack of skulls at the headhunters' camp on the Jungle Cruise, a platoon of skeletons sailing ghost ships in Pirates of the Caribbean, and an assemblage of skulls and skeletons in The Haunted Mansion. Skulls, skeletons, and bones punctuate Snow White's Adventures, Peter Pan's Flight, and Big Thunder Mountain Railroad. The Animal Kingdom has an entire playground comprised exclusively of giant bones and skeletons.

Monsters and special effects at Disney-MGM Studios are more real and sinister than those in the other parks. If your child has difficulty coping with the witch in Snow White's Adventures, think twice about exposing him at the Studios to machine-gun battles, earthquakes, and the creature from *Alien* in the Great Movie Ride.

One reader tells of taking his preschool children on Star Tours:

> We took a four-year-old and a five-year-old, and they had the shit scared out of them at Star Tours. We did this first thing, and it took hours of Tom Sawyer Island and Small World to get back to normal. Our kids were the youngest by far in Star Tours. I assume other adults had more sense.

Preschoolers should start with Dumbo and work up to the Jungle Cruise in late morning, after being revved up and before getting hungry, thirsty, or tired. Pirates of the Caribbean is out for preschoolers. You get the idea.

You can reliably predict that Disney World will, at one time or another, send a young child into system overload. Be sensitive, alert, and prepared for almost anything, even behavior that is out of character for your child. Most children take Disney's macabre trappings in stride, and others are easily comforted by an arm around the shoulder or a squeeze of the hand. Parents who know that their children tend to become upset should take it slow and easy, sampling benign adventures like the Jungle Cruise, gauging reactions, and discussing with the children how they felt about what they saw.

Sometimes young children will rise above their anxiety in an effort to please their parents or siblings. This doesn't necessarily indicate a mastery of fear, much less enjoyment. If children leave a ride in apparently good shape, ask if they would like to go on it again (not necessarily now, but sometime). The response usually will indicate how much they actually enjoyed the experience.

Evaluating a child's capacity to handle the visual and tactile effects of Disney World requires patience, understanding, and experimentation. Each of us has our own demons. If a child balks at or is frightened by a ride, respond constructively. Let your children know that lots of people, adults and children, are scared by what they see and feel. Help them understand that it's okay if they get frightened and that their fear doesn't lessen your love or respect. Take pains not to compound the discomfort by making a child feel inadequate; try not to undermine self-esteem, impugn courage, or ridicule. Most of all, don't induce guilt by suggesting the child's trepidation might be ruining the family's fun. It's also some-times necessary to restrain older siblings' taunting.

A reader from New York City expressed strong feelings about pressur-ing children:

As a psychologist who works with children, I felt ethically torn (and nearly filed a report!) watching parents force their children to go on rides they didn't want to ride (especially the Tower of Terror and Dinosaur). The Disney staff were more than willing to organize a parental swap to save these children from such abuse!

A visit to Disney World is more than an outing or an adventure for a young child. It's a testing experience, a sort of controlled rite of passage. If you help your little one work through the challenges, the time can be immeasurably rewarding and a bonding experience for you both.

The Fright Factor

While each youngster is different, there are seven attraction elements that alone or combined could punch a child's buttons:

1. Name of the Attraction Young children will naturally be apprehen-sive about something called "The Haunted Mansion" or "Tower of Terror."

2. Visual Impact of the Attraction from Outside Splash Mountain and Big Thunder Mountain Railroad look scary enough to give adults second thoughts, and they terrify many young children.

3. Visual Impact of the Indoor Queuing Area Pirates of the Caribbean's caves and dungeons and The Haunted Mansion's "stretch rooms" can frighten children.

4. Intensity of the Attraction Some attractions are overwhelming, inundating the senses with sights, sounds, movement, and even smell. Epcot's *Honey, I Shrunk the Audience,* for example, combines loud sounds, lasers, lights, and 3-D cinematography to create a total sensory experience. For some preschoolers, this is two or three senses too many.

5. Visual Impact of the Attraction Itself Sights in various attractions range from falling boulders to lurking buzzards, from grazing dinosaurs to attacking white blood cells. What one child calmly absorbs may scare the bejabbers out of another the same age.

6. Dark Many Disney World attractions operate indoors in the dark. For some children, this triggers fear. A child frightened on one dark ride (Snow White's Adventures, for example) may be unwilling to try other indoor rides.

7. The Tactile Experience of the Ride Itself Some rides are wild enough to cause motion sickness, wrench backs, and discombobulate patrons of any age.

SMALL-CHILD FRIGHT-POTENTIAL CHART

Our "Fright-Potential Chart" is a quick reference to identify attractions to be wary of, and why. The chart represents a generalization, and all kids are different. It relates specifically to kids ages three to seven. On average, children at the younger end of the range are more likely to be frightened than children in their sixth or seventh year.

MAGIC KINGDOM

Main Street, U.S.A.
Walt Disney World Railroad   Not frightening in any respect.

Main Street Vehicles   Not frightening in any respect.

Adventureland
Swiss Family Treehouse   Not frightening in any respect.

Jungle Cruise   Moderately intense, some macabre sights. A good test attraction for little ones.

Enchanted Tiki Birds   A thunderstorm, loud volume level, and simulated explosions frighten some preschoolers.

Pirates of the Caribbean   Slightly intimidating queuing area; intense boat ride with gruesome (though humorously presented) sights and a short, unexpected slide down a flume.

Magic Carpets of Aladdin   Much like Dumbo. A favorite of most younger children.

Frontierland
Splash Mountain   Visually intimidating from outside, with moderately intense visual effects. The ride, culminating in a 52-foot plunge down a steep chute, is somewhat hair-raising for all ages. Switching off option provided (pages 266–268).

Big Thunder Mountain Railroad   Visually intimidating from outside, with moderately intense visual effects. The roller coaster is wild enough to frighten many adults, particularly seniors. Switching off provided (pages 266–268).

Tom Sawyer Island   Some very young children are intimidated by dark, walk-through tunnels that can be easily avoided.

Country Bear Jamboree   Not frightening in any respect.

Frontierland Shootin' Arcade   Not frightening in any respect.

Liberty Square
The Hall of Presidents   Not frightening, but boring for young ones.

Liberty Belle Riverboat   Not frightening in any respect.

Mike Fink Keelboats   Not frightening in any respect.

The Haunted Mansion   Name raises anxiety, as do sounds and sights of waiting area. Intense attraction with humorously presented macabre sights. The ride itself is gentle.

Fantasyland
Mad Tea Party   Midway-type ride can induce motion sickness in all ages.

The Many Adventures of Winnie the Pooh   Frightens a small percentage of preschoolers.

Snow White's Adventures   Moderately intense spook-house-genre attraction with some grim characters. Absolutely terrifies many preschoolers.

Dumbo the Flying Elephant   A tame midway ride; a great favorite of most young children.

Cinderella's Golden Carrousel   Not frightening in any respect.

It's a Small World   Not frightening in any respect.

Peter Pan's Flight   Not frightening in any respect.

Mickey's Toontown Fair

All attractions except roller coaster   Not frightening in any respect.

The Barnstormer at Goofy's Wiseacres Farm (children's roller coaster)   May frighten some preschoolers.

Tomorrowland

Buzz Lightyear's Space Ranger Spin   Dark ride with cartoonlike aliens may frighten some preschoolers.

Tomorrowland Transit Authority   Not frightening in any respect.

Space Mountain   Very intense roller coaster in the dark; the Magic Kingdom's wildest ride and a scary roller coaster by any standard. Switching off provided (pages 266–268).

Stitch's Great Escape   Very intense. May frighten children age 9 and younger. Switching off provided (pages 266–268).

Astro Orbiter   Visually intimidating from the waiting area. The ride is relatively tame.

Walt Disney's Carousel of Progress (open seasonally)   Not frightening in any respect.

Tomorrowland Speedway   Noise of waiting area slightly intimidates preschoolers; otherwise, not frightening.

Timekeeper (open seasonally)   Both loud and intense, with frightening film scenes. Audience must stand.

EPCOT

Future World

Spaceship Earth   Dark and imposing presentation intimidates a few preschoolers.

Innoventions East and West   Not frightening in any respect.

Universe of Energy   Dinosaur segment frightens some preschoolers; visually intense, with some intimidating effects.

Wonders of Life—Body Wars (open seasonally)   Very intense, with frightening visual effects. Ride causes motion sickness in riders of all ages. Switching off provided (pages 266–268).

Wonders of Life—Cranium Command (open seasonally)   Not frightening in any respect.

Wonders of Life—The Making of Me (open seasonally)   Not frightening in any respect.

Mission: Space   Extremely intense space simulation ride frightens guests of all ages. Switching off provided (pages 266–268).

Test Track   Intense thrill ride may frighten any age. Switching off provided (pages 266–268).

Journey into Imagination—Honey, I Shrunk the Audience   Extremely intense visual effects and loudness frighten many young children.

Journey into Your Imagination Ride   Loud noises and unexpected flashing lights startle younger children.

The Land—Living with the Land   Not frightening in any respect.

The Land—Circle of Life Theater   Not frightening in any respect.

The Land—Soarin'   Mellow, but may frighten children age 9 and younger.

SMALL-CHILD FRIGHT-POTENTIAL CHART *(continued)*

EPCOT *(continued)*

World Showcase

Mexico—El Río del Tiempo   Not frightening in any respect.

Norway—Maelstrom   Visually intense in parts. Ride ends with a plunge down a 20-foot flume. A few preschoolers are frightened.

China—Reflections of China   Not frightening in any respect.

Germany   Not frightening in any respect.

Italy   Not frightening in any respect.

The American Adventure   Not frightening in any respect.

Japan   Not frightening in any respect.

Morocco   Not frightening in any respect.

France—Impressions de France   Not frightening in any respect.

United Kingdom   Not frightening in any respect.

Canada—O Canada!   Not frightening in any respect, but audience must stand.

DISNEY-MGM STUDIOS

The Twilight Zone Tower of Terror   Visually intimidating to young children; contains intense and realistic special effects. The plummeting elevator at the ride's end frightens many adults. Switching off provided (pages 266–268).

The Great Movie Ride   Intense in parts, with very realistic special effects and some visually intimidating sights. Frightens many preschoolers.

Who Wants to Be a Millionaire   Not frightening in any respect.

Sounds Dangerous   Noises in the dark frighten some preschoolers.

Indiana Jones Epic Stunt Spectacular!   An intense show with powerful special effects, including explosions. Presented in an educational context that young children generally handle well.

Rock 'n' Roller Coaster   The wildest coaster at Walt Disney World. May frighten guests of any age. Switching off provided (pages 266–268).

Star Tours   Extremely intense visually for all ages. Not as likely to cause motion sickness as Body Wars at Epcot. Switching off provided (pages 266–268).

Disney-MGM Studios Backlot Tour   Sedate and nonintimidating except for "Catastrophe Canyon," where an earthquake and a flash flood are simulated. Prepare younger children for this part of the tour.

Backstage Walking Tours   Not frightening in any respect.

A Bit of Preparation

We receive many tips from parents telling how they prepared their young children for the Disney experience. A common strategy is to acquaint children with the characters and stories behind the attractions by reading Disney books and watching Disney videos at home. A more direct approach is to rent Walt Disney World travel videos that show the attractions. Of the latter, a father from Arlington, Virginia, reports:

My kids both loved The Haunted Mansion, with appropriate preparation. We rented a tape before going so they could see it, and then I told them it was all "Mickey Mouse Magic" and that Mickey was just "joking you," to

Jim Henson's MuppetVision 3-D   Intense and loud, but not frightening.

Honey, I Shrunk the Kids Movie Set Adventure Playground   Everything is oversized, but nothing is scary.

Voyage of the Little Mermaid   Not frightening in any respect.

The Magic of Disney Animation   Not frightening in any respect.

Walt Disney: One Man's Dream   Not frightening in any respect.

Playhouse Disney: Live on Stage   Not frightening in any respect.

Fantasmic!   Terrifies some preschoolers.

Lights! Motors! Action!   Superstunt spectacular intense with loud noises and explosions but not threatening in any way.

ANIMAL KINGDOM

The Boneyard   Not frightening in any respect.

Rafiki's Planet Watch   Not frightening in any respect.

Dinosaur   High-tech thrill ride rattles riders of all ages. Switching off provided (pages 266–268).

TriceraTop Spin   A midway-type ride that will frighten only a small percentage of younger children.

Pimeval Whirl   A beginner roller coaster. Most children age seven and over will take it in stride.

Festival of the Lion King   A bit loud, but otherwise not frightening in any respect.

Flights of Wonder   Swooping birds alarm a few small children.

Pangani Forest Exploration Trail   Not frightening in any respect.

Pocahontas and Her Forest Friends   Not frightening in any respect.

It's Tough to Be a Bug!   Very intense and loud with special effects that startle viewers of all ages and potentially terrify young children.

Kilimanjaro Safaris   A "collapsing" bridge and the proximity of real animals make a few young children anxious.

Maharaja Jungle Trek   Some children may balk at the bat exhibit.

The Oasis   Not frightening in any respect.

Kali River Rapids   Potentially frightening and certainly wet for guests of all ages. Switching off provided (pages 266–268).

Theater in the Wild   Not frightening in any respect, but loud.

Wildlife Express Train   Not frightening in any respect.

put it in their terms, and that there weren't any real ghosts, and that Mickey wouldn't let anyone actually get hurt.

A Teaneck, New Jersey, mother adds:

I rented movies to make my five-year-old more comfortable with rides (Star Wars; Indiana Jones; Honey, I Shrunk the Kids). If kids are afraid of rides in the dark (like ours), buy a light-up toy and let them take it on the ride.

If your video store doesn't rent Disney travel videos, you can order the free Walt Disney World Holiday Planning Video/DVD by calling Disney reservations at (407) 824-8000. Ignore all prompts, and the phone system will assume you're on a rotary phone and patch you through to a live person (though you may be on hold a couple minutes). This video/DVD isn't as comprehensive as travelogues you might rent, but it's adequate for giving your kids a sense of what they'll see. You can also ask for information on lodging, restaurants, etc. Allow at least one month for delivery. Because Disney is in a cost-containment fit, it's possible that the free video/DVD may be discontinued.

A Gloucester, Massachusetts, mom solved the fright problem on the spot:

The three-and-a-half-year-old liked It's a Small World, [but] was afraid of The Haunted Mansion. We just pulled his hat over his face and quietly talked to him while we enjoyed [the ride].

Sometimes children balk at any attraction that isn't a ride, reports a reader from Lenexa, Kansas:

The one thing I would do differently is prepare my kids for the different kinds of entertainment each park offers. Some have more rides, some more shows, some street performers (very fun), and some interesting things about the world. My eight-year-old especially had trouble admitting he liked anything that wasn't a ride (even if he did).

Attractions that Eat Adults

You may spend so much energy worrying about Junior that you forget to take care of yourself. If the motion of a ride is potentially disturbing, persons of any age may be affected. These attractions are likely to cause motion sickness or other problems for older children and adults:

Magic Kingdom	Tomorrowland—Space Mountain
	Fantasyland—Mad Tea Party
	Frontierland—Big Thunder Mountain Railroad
	Frontierland—Splash Mountain
Epcot	Future World—Body Wars
	Future World—Test Track
	Future World—Mission: Space
Disney-MGM Studios	Star Tours
	The Twilight Zone Tower of Terror
	Rock 'n' Roller Coaster
Animal Kingdom	Dinosaur
	Kali River Rapids

A Word about Height Requirements

A number of attractions require children to meet minimum height and age requirements. If you have children too short or too young to ride, you have several options, including switching off (described in this chapter). Although the alternatives may resolve some practical and logistical issues, your smaller children may nonetheless be resentful of their older (or taller) siblings who qualify to ride. A mom from Virginia writes of such a situation:

You mention height requirements for rides but not the intense sibling jealousy this can generate. Frontierland was a real problem in that respect. Our very petite five-year-old, to her outrage, was stuck hanging around while our eight-year-old went on Splash Mountain and [Big] Thunder Mountain with grandma and granddad, and the nearby alternatives weren't helpful [too long a line for rafts to Tom Sawyer Island, etc.]. If we had thought ahead, we would have left the younger kid back in Mickey's Toontown with one of the grown-ups for another roller-coaster ride or two and then met up later. … The best areas had a playground or other quick attractions for short people near the rides with height requirements, like the Boneyard near the dinosaur ride at the Animal Kingdom.

The reader makes a point, though splitting the group and meeting later can be more complicated than she imagines. If you split up, ask the Disney attendant (called a "greeter") at the entrance to the attraction(s) with height requirements how long the wait is. If you tack five minutes for riding onto the anticipated wait and add five or so minutes to exit and reach the meeting point, you'll have a sense of how long the younger kids (and their supervising adult) will have to do other stuff. Our guess is that even with a long line for the rafts, the reader would have had sufficient time to take her daughter to Tom Sawyer Island while the sibs rode Splash Mountain and Big Thunder Mountain with the grandparents. For sure, she had time to tour the Swiss Family Treehouse in adjacent Adventureland.

ATTRACTION AND RIDE RESTRICTIONS

Magic Kingdom

Stitch's Great Escape	44 inches minimum height
Big Thunder Mountain Railroad	40 inches minimum height
Goofy's Barnstormer	35 inches minimum height
Mickey's Toontown playground attractions	40 inches **maximum** height
Space Mountain	44 inches minimum height
Splash Mountain	40 inches minimum height
Tomorrowland Indy Speedway	52 inches minimum height (to drive unassisted)

Epcot

Body Wars	40 inches minimum height
Mission: Space	44 inches minimum height
Test Track	40 inches minimum height
Soarin'	40 inches minimum height

ATTRACTION AND RIDE RESTRICTIONS *(continued)*

Disney-MGM Studios

Honey, I Shrunk the Kids playground	4 years minimum age
Rock n' Roller Coaster	48 inches minimum height
Star Tours	40 inches minimum height
Tower of Terror	40 inches minimum height

Animal Kingdom

Dinosaur	40 inches minimum height
Kali River Rapids	38 inches minimum height
Primeval Whirl	48 inches minimum height

Blizzard Beach Water Park

Chair Lift	32 inches minimum height
Downhill Double Dipper slide	48 inches minimum height
Slush Gusher slide	48 inches minimum height
Summit Plummet slide	48 inches minimum height
T-Bar (in Ski Patrol Training Camp)	48 inches **maximum** height
Tike's Peak children's area	48 inches **maximum** height

Typhoon Lagoon Water Park

Humunga Kowabunga slide	48 inches minimum height
Ketchakiddee Creek children's area	48 inches **maximum** height
Mayday Falls raft ride	48 inches minimum height
Shark Reef saltwater reef swim	10 years minimum age unless accompanied by an adult
Wave Pool	Adult supervision required

Disney Quest

Buzz Lightyear's AstroBlasters	51 inches minimum height
CyberSpace Mountain	51 inches minimum height
Mighty Ducks Pinball Slam	48 inches minimum height

Waiting-Line Strategies for Adults with Young Children

Children hold up better through the day if you minimize the time they spend in lines. Arriving early and using our touring plans immensely reduce waiting. Here are additional ways to reduce stress for children:

1. Line Games Anticipate children to get restless in line, and plan activities to reduce the stress and boredom. In the morning, have waiting children discuss what they want to see and do during the day. Later, watch for and count Disney characters or play simple games like "20 Questions."

Lines move continuously; games requiring pen and paper are impractical. Waiting in the holding area of a theater attraction is a different
story. Here, tic-tac-toe, hangman, drawing, and coloring make the
time fly.

A Springfield, Ohio, mom reports on an unexpected but welcome
assist from her brother:

> I have a bachelor brother who joined my five-, seven-, and nine-year-olds
> and me for vacation. Pat surprised all of us with a bunch of plastic
> animal noses he had in his hip pack. When the kids got restless or
> cranky in line, he'd turn away and pull out a pig nose or a parrot nose
> or something. When he turned back around with the nose on, the kids
> would majorly crack up. The other people in line thought he was nuts,
> but he restored my kids' good humor more times than I can count.

2. Last-Minute Entry If an attraction can accommodate many
people at once, standing in line is often unnecessary. The Magic Kingdom's *Liberty Belle* Riverboat is an example. The boat holds about 450
people, usually more than are waiting in line. Instead of standing in a
crowd, grab a snack and sit in the shade until the boat arrives and loading is under way. When the line is almost gone, join it.

At large-capacity theaters like that for Epcot's *The American
Adventure,* ask the greeter how long it will be until guests are admitted for the next show. If it's 15 minutes or more, take a toilet break
or get a snack, returning a few minutes before show time. Food and
drink aren't allowed in the attraction; be sure you have time to finish
your snack before entering.

Attractions You Can Usually Enter at the Last Minute

Magic Kingdom

Liberty Square	*The Hall of Presidents*
	Liberty Belle Riverboat

Epcot

Future World	*The Circle of Life* (except during mealtimes)
World Showcase	*Reflections of China*
	The American Adventure
	O Canada!

Disney-MGM Studios

Sounds Dangerous	Backlot Tour

Animal Kingdom | *Flights of Wonder*

3. The Hail Mary Pass Certain lines are configured to allow you
and your smaller children to pass under the rail to join your partner
just before entry or boarding. This technique allows children and one
adult to rest, snack, cool off, or potty while another adult or older

sibling stands in line. Other guests are understanding about this strategy when used for young children. Expect opposition, however, if you try to pass older children or more than one adult under the rail.

Attractions Where You Can Usually Complete a Hail Mary Pass

Magic Kingdom

Adventureland	Swiss Family Treehouse
Frontierland	*Country Bear Jamboree*

Attractions Where You Can Usually Complete a Hail Mary Pass *(cont'd)*

Fantasyland	Mad Tea Party
	Snow White's Adventures
	Dumbo the Flying Elephant
	Cinderella's Golden Carrousel
	Peter Pan's Flight

Epcot

Future World	Spaceship Earth
	Living with the Land

Disney-MGM Studios

Sounds Dangerous	*Indiana Jones Epic Stunt Spectacular!*

Animal Kingdom

Dinoland USA	TriceraTop Spin

4. Switching Off (a.k.a. The Baby Swap)   Several attractions have minimum height and/or age requirements. Some couples with children too small or too young forgo these attractions, while others take turns riding. Missing some of Disney's best rides is an unnecessary sacrifice, and waiting in line twice for the same ride is a tremendous waste of time.

Instead, take advantage of the "switching off" option, also called "The Baby Swap." To switch off, there must be at least two adults. Adults and children wait in line together. When you reach an attendant, say you want to switch off. The cast member will allow everyone, including young children, to enter the attraction. When you reach the loading area, one adult rides while the other stays with the kids. Then the riding adult disembarks and takes charge of the children while the other adult rides. A third adult in the party can ride twice, once with each switching-off adult, so that the switching-off adults don't have to ride alone.

Most rides with age and height minimums load and unload in the same area. An exception is Space Mountain, where the first adult at the conclusion of the ride must inform the unloading attendant that he or she is switching off. The attendant then admits the first adult to an internal stairway that returns to the loading area.

Attractions where switching off is practiced are oriented to more-mature guests. Sometimes it takes a lot of courage for a child just to move

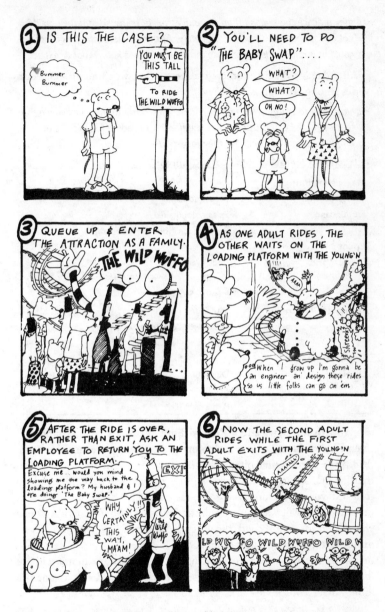

through the queue holding Dad's hand. In the boarding area, many children suddenly fear abandonment when one parent leaves to ride. Prepare your children for switching off, or you might have an emotional crisis on your hands. A mom from Edison, New Jersey, writes:

Once my son came to understand that the switch-off would not leave him abandoned, he did not seem to mind. I would recommend to your readers that they practice the switch-off on some dry runs at home, so that their child is not concerned that he will be left behind. At the very least, the procedure could be explained in advance so that the little ones know what to expect.

An Ada, Michigan, mother discovered the switching-off procedure varies among attractions. She says:

Parents need to tell the very first attendant they come to that they would like to switch off. Each attraction has a different procedure for this. Tell every other attendant too because they forget quickly.

Attractions Where Switching Off Is Common

Magic Kingdom

Tomorrowland	Space Mountain
Frontierland	Splash Mountain
	Big Thunder Mountain Railroad

Epcot

Future World	Body Wars
	Test Track
	Mission: Space
Disney-MGM Studios	Star Tours
	The Twilight Zone Tower of Terror
	Rock 'n' Roller Coaster

Animal Kingdom

DinoLand U.S.A.	Dinosaur
Asia	Kali River Rapids
	Primeval Whirl

5. How to Ride Twice in a Row without Waiting Many young children like to ride a favorite attraction two or more times in succession. Riding the second time often gives them a feeling of mastery and accomplishment. Unfortunately, even in early morning, repeat rides can eat time. If you ride Dumbo as soon as the Magic Kingdom opens, for instance, you will wait only a minute or two for your first ride. When you return for your second, the wait will be about 12–15 minutes. For a third, count on 20 minutes or longer.

The best way to get your child on the ride twice (or more) without blowing your morning is to use the "Chuck Bubba Relay" (named in honor of a Kentucky reader):

a. *Mom and little Bubba enter the waiting line.*

b. *Dad lets a specific number of people go in front of him (24 at Dumbo), then gets in line.*

c. *As soon as the ride stops, Mom exits with Bubba and passes him to Dad to ride the second time.*

d. *If everybody is really getting into this, Mom can hop in line again, at least 24 people behind Dad.*

The Chuck Bubba Relay won't work on every ride, because waiting areas are configured differently (i.e., it's impossible in some cases to exit the ride and make the pass). For those rides where the relay works, here are how many people to count off:

Magic Kingdom

Mad Tea Party 53	Snow White's Adventures 52
Dumbo the Flying Elephant 24	Cinderella's Golden Carrousel 75
Peter Pan's Flight 64	Magic Carpets of Aladdin 48

Animal Kingdom

TriceraTop Spin 56

If you're the relay's second adult, you'll reach a place in line where it's easiest to make the hand-off. This may be where those exiting the ride pass closest to those waiting to board. You'll know it when you see it. If you reach it and the first parent hasn't arrived with Bubba, let those behind you pass until Bubba shows up.

6. Last-Minute Cold Feet If your young child gets cold feet just before boarding a ride where there's no age or height requirement, you usually can arrange a switch-off with the loading attendant. This is a common occurrence after experiencing Pirates of the Caribbean's dungeon waiting area.

No law says you have to ride. If you reach the boarding area and someone is unhappy, tell an attendant you've changed your mind, and you'll be shown the way out.

7. Elevator Shoes for the Short and the Brave If you have a child begging to go on rides with height requirements but who is a little too short, slip heel lifts into his Nikes before he reaches the measuring point. Be sure to leave the lifts in, because he may be measured again before boarding.

A Huntsville, Alabama, mom has the heel-lift problem under control:

Knowing my wild three-year-old child as I do, I was interested in your comment regarding shoe lifts. I don't know about other places, but in the big city of Huntspatch where we live, one has to have a prescription for lifts. Normal shoe repair places don't make them. I couldn't think of a material with which to fashion a homemade lift that would be comfortable enough to stand on while waiting in line. I ended up purchasing some of those painfully ugly two-inch chunky-heeled sandals at my local mart where they carried these hideous shoes in unbelievably tiny sizes ($12). Since they didn't look too comfortable, we popped them on her right before we entered the ride lines. None of the height checkers ever asked her to remove them and she clip-clopped onto Splash Mountain, Big Thunder Railroad (Dat BIG Choo-Choo), Star Wars, and The Tower of Terror—twice! ... For adventuresome boys, I would suggest purchasing some of those equally hideous giant-heeled cowboy boots.

A Long Pond, Pennsylvania, mom has this to offer:

Tower of Terror, Star Tours, and Body Wars are 40" requirements. Being persistent with a 39" child, we tried these several times. She got on Tower of Terror two of three times, Body Wars one of one time, and Star Tours one of two tries. She wore elevator shoes and a bun hairstyle to increase height.

Note that boosting your child's height by a couple inches with a heel lift or the like will not compromise his safety on the ride.

8. Throw Yourself on the Grenade, Mildred! For conscientious parents determined to sacrifice themselves on behalf of their children, we provide a Magic Kingdom One-Day Touring Plan called the "Dumbo-or-Die-in-a-Day Touring Plan, for Parents with Small Children." This plan (pages 487–489) will ensure that you run yourself ragged. Designed to help you forfeit everything of personal interest for your children's pleasure, the plan guarantees you'll go home battered and exhausted, with extraordinary stories of devotion and perseverance. By the way, it really works. Anyone under eight will love it.

The Disney Characters

The large and friendly costumed versions of Mickey, Minnie, Donald, Goofy, and others—known as "Disney characters"—provide a link between Disney animated films and the theme parks. To people emotionally invested, the characters in Disney films are as real as next-door neighbors, never mind that they're drawings on plastic. In recent years, theme-park personifications of the characters also have become real to us. It's not a person in a mouse costume; it's Mickey himself. Similarly, meeting Goofy or Snow White is an encounter with a celebrity, a memory to be treasured.

While there are hundreds of Disney animated film characters, only about 250 have been brought to life in costume. Of these, fewer than a fifth are "greeters" (characters who mix with patrons). The others perform in shows or parades. Originally confined to the Magic Kingdom, characters are now found in all major theme parks and Disney hotels.

Character-Watching Watching characters has become a pastime. Families once were content to meet a character occasionally. They now pursue them relentlessly, armed with autograph books and cameras. Because some characters are only rarely seen, character-watching has become character-collecting. (To cash in on character-collecting, Disney sells autograph books throughout the World.) Mickey, Minnie, and Goofy are a snap to bag; they seem to be everywhere. But Daisy Duck seldom comes out. Other characters appear only in a location consistent with their starring role. Cinderella, predictably, reigns at Cinderella Castle in

Fantasyland, while Br'er Fox and Br'er Bear frolic in Frontierland near Splash Mountain.

A Brooklyn dad complains that character-collecting has gotten out of hand:

Whoever started the practice of collecting autographs from the characters should be subjected to Chinese water torture! We went to WDW eleven years ago, with an eight-year-old and an eleven-year-old. We would bump into characters, take pictures, and that was it. After a while, our children noticed that some of the other children were getting autographs. We managed to avoid joining in during our first day at the Magic Kingdom and our first day at Epcot, but by day three our children were collecting autographs. However, it did not get too out of hand, since it was limited to accidental character meeting.

This year when we took our youngest child (who is now eight), he had already seen his siblings' collection, and was determined to outdo them. However, rather than random meetings, the characters are now available practically all day long at different locations, according to a printed schedule, which our son was old enough to read. We spent more time standing in line for autographs than we did for the most popular rides!

A family from Birmingham, Alabama, found some benefit in their children's pursuit of characters:

We had no idea we would be caught up in this madness, but after my daughters grabbed your guidebook to get Pocahontas to sign it (we had no blank paper), we quickly bought a Disney autograph book and gave in. It was actually the highlight of their trip, and my son even got into the act by helping get places in line for his sisters. They LOVED looking for characters (I think it has all been planned by Kodak to sell film). The possibility of seeing a new character revived my seven-year-old's energy on many occasions. It was an amazing, totally unexpected part of our visit.

Preparing Your Children to Meet the Characters Almost all characters are quite large, and several, like Br'er Bear, are huge! Small children don't expect this, and preschoolers especially can be intimidated.

Discuss the characters with your children before you go. On first encounter, don't thrust your child at the character. Allow the little one to deal with this big thing from whatever distance feels safe. If two adults are present, one should stay near the youngster while the other approaches the character and demonstrates that it's safe and friendly. Some kids warm to the characters immediately; some never do. Most take a little time and several encounters.

There are two kinds of characters: those whose costume includes a face-covering headpiece (animal characters and such humanlike characters as

Captain Hook) and "face characters," those who resemble the characters so no mask or headpiece is necessary. These include Mary Poppins, Ariel, Jasmine, Aladdin, Cinderella, Belle, Snow White, Esmeralda, and Prince Charming.

Only face characters speak. Headpiece characters make no noises. Because cast members couldn't possibly imitate the character's distinctive cinema voice, Disney has determined it's more effective to keep them silent. Lack of speech notwithstanding, headpiece characters are warm and responsive and communicate effectively with gestures. Tell children in advance that headpiece characters don't talk.

Some character costumes are cumbersome and give cast members very poor visibility. (Eyeholes frequently are in the mouth of the costume or even on the neck or chest.) Children who approach the character from the back or side may not be noticed, even if the child touches the character. It's possible in this situation for the character to accidentally step on the child or knock him down. A child should approach a character from the front, but occasionally not even this works. Duck characters (Donald, Daisy, Uncle Scrooge), for example, have to peer around their bills. If a character appears to be ignoring your child, pick up your child and hold her in front of the character until the character responds.

It's okay for your child to touch, pat, or hug the character. Understanding the unpredictability of children, the character will keep his feet still, particularly refraining from moving backward or sideways. Most characters will pose for pictures or sign autographs. Costumes make it difficult for characters to wield a normal pen. If your child collects autographs, carry a pen the width of a magic marker.

The Big Hurt Many children expect to meet Mickey the minute they enter the park and are disappointed if they don't. If your children can't enjoy things until they see Mickey, ask a cast member where to find him. If the cast member doesn't know, he or she can phone to learn exactly where characters are.

"Then Some Confusion Happened" Children sometimes become lost at character encounters. Usually, there's a lot of activity around a character, with both adults and children touching it or posing for pictures. Most commonly, Mom and Dad stay in the crowd while Junior approaches the character. In the excitement and with the character moving around, Junior heads in the wrong direction to look for Mom and Dad. In the words of a Salt Lake City mom: "Milo was shaking hands with Dopey one minute, then some confusion happened and [Milo] was gone."

Families with several young children, and parents who are busy with cameras, can lose a youngster in a heartbeat. We recommend that parents with preschoolers stay with them when they meet characters, stepping back only to take a quick picture.

Character Hogs   While we're on the subject of cameras, give other families a chance. Especially if you're shooting video, consider the perspective of this Houston mom:

One of the worst parts to deal with are the people with movie cameras who take about three minutes filming their child with Mickey, asking everyone else to move. A 35mm camera takes about two seconds.

Meeting Characters for Free

You can *see* Disney characters in live shows at all the theme parks and in parades at the Magic Kingdom and Disney-MGM Studios. Your daily entertainment schedule lists times. If you want to *meet* the characters, get autographs, and take photos, consult the park map or the handout *Times Guide* sometimes provided with it. If there's a particular character you're itching to meet, ask any cast member to call the character hotline and ask if the character is out and about, and if so, where.

At the Magic Kingdom   Characters are encountered more frequently here than anywhere else in Walt Disney World. A character almost always will be next to City Hall on Main Street, and there will usually be one or more in Town Square or near the railroad station. If it's rainy, look for characters on the veranda of Tony's Town Square Restaurant or in the Town Square Exposition Hall next to Tony's. Characters appear in all the lands but are more plentiful in Fantasyland and Mickey's Toontown Fair. At Mickey's Toontown Fair, meet Mickey privately in his "Judge's Tent." Characters actually work shifts at the Toontown Hall of Fame next to Mickey's Country House. Here, you can line up to meet three different assortments of characters. Each assortment has its own greeting area and its own line. One group, variously labeled Mickey's Pals, Toon Pals, Famous Friends, or some such, will include Minnie, Pluto, Goofy, Donald, and sometimes Chip 'n' Dale, Daisy, and Uncle Scrooge. The other two assortments vary and are more ambiguously defined. The 100 Acre Wood Friends are mostly Winnie the Pooh characters, while Fairy Tale Friends include Snow White, assorted dwarfs, Sleeping Beauty, the Beast, Belle, Cinderella, Prince Charming, etc. Sometimes it's Villains (Captain Hook, Cruella DeVil, Jafar, et al.), and Princesses (Sleeping Beauty, Mary Poppins, yadda, yadda, yadda). In Fantasyland, Cinderella regularly greets diners at Cinderella's Royal Table in the castle, and Ariel holds court in her grotto. Nearby, check out the Fantasyland Character Festival by the lagoon opposite Dumbo. Also look for characters in the central hub and by Splash Mountain in Frontierland.

Characters are featured in afternoon and evening parades and also play a major role in Castle Forecourt shows (at the castle entrance on the central hub side) and at the Galaxy Palace Theater in Tomorrowland. Find performance times for shows and parades in the daily entertainment schedule or *Times Guide.* Characters sometimes stay to mingle after shows.

At Epcot Disney at first didn't think characters would fit the more serious, educational style of Epcot. Later, characters were imported to blunt criticism that Epcot lacked warmth and humor. To integrate them thematically, new and often bizarre costumes were created. Goofy was seen roaming Future World in a metallic silver cape reminiscent of Buck Rogers. Mickey greets guests at the American Adventure dressed like Ben Franklin.

Although chance encounters with characters are less frequent at Epcot than at other parks, Epcot compensates by periodically bringing in characters by the busload, literally. Eight to ten times a day, a platoon of characters piles into a British double-decker bus and visits one of the World Showcase countries. When the bus stops, characters hop off and mingle, posing for pictures and signing autographs. Mickey, Minnie, Goofy, Chip and Dale, and Pluto are almost always on the bus, and are frequently accompanied by Baloo, Tigger, Eeyore, the Genie from *Aladdin,* Jasmine, Mushu, Timon, and Snow White. The Epcot handout map or *Times Guide* lists the buses' times and stops. If you position yourself at a scheduled stop a few minutes before the bus arrives, you can score photos and autographs before other guests figure out what's happening. In fact, the bus offers the easiest access to the most characters in one place in all of Disney World. However, once people in the immediate area get the drift, the characters are mobbed. In addition to the bus, character shows are performed daily at the American Gardens Theater World Showcase and at Guest Relations. Check the daily entertainment schedule or *Times Guide* for times.

Characters may be rarer at Epcot, but they're often easier to meet. A father from Effingham, Illinois, writes:

Trying to get autographs and pictures with Disney characters in the Magic Kingdom was a nightmare. Every character we saw was mobbed by kids and adults. Our kids had no chance. But at Epcot and Disney-MGM, things were much better. We got autographs, pictures, and more involvement. Our kids danced with several characters and received a lot of personal attention.

At Disney-MGM Studios Characters are likely to turn up anywhere at the Studios but are most frequently found in front of the Animation Building, along Mickey Avenue (leading to the soundstages), and on New York Street. Mickey and his "friends" pose for keepsake photos (about $14 each) on Hollywood Boulevard and Sunset Boulevard. Characters are also prominent in shows, with *Voyage of the Little Mermaid* running almost continuously and an abbreviated version of *Beauty and the Beast* performed several times daily at the Theater of the Stars. Check the daily entertainment schedule or *Times Guide* for showtimes.

At the Animal Kingdom Camp Minnie-Mickey in the Animal Kingdom is designed specifically for meeting characters. Meet Mickey, Minnie, and various characters from *The Jungle Book* and *The Lion King* on designated character greeting "trails." Also at Camp Minnie-Mickey are two stage shows featuring characters from *The Lion King* and *Pocahontas.*

Disney has several initiatives intended to satisfy guests' inexhaustible desire to meet characters. Most important, Disney assigned Mickey and a number of other characters to all-day duty in Mickey's Toontown Fair in the Magic Kingdom and Camp Minnie-Mickey in Animal Kingdom. While making the characters more available has taken the guesswork out of finding them, it has robbed encounters of much of their spontaneity. To address this, especially at the Magic Kingdom, Disney has put a throng of characters back on the street. At park opening there are enough characters on hand to satisfy any child's desires. If you line up at one of the permanent character greeting venues, be aware that lines for face characters move m-u-c-h more slowly than do lines for nonspeaking characters. Because face characters are allowed to talk, they often engage children in lengthy conversations, much to the dismay of families still in the queue.

Character Dining

Fraternizing with characters has become so popular that Disney offers character breakfasts, brunches, and dinners where families can dine in the presence of Mickey, Minnie, Goofy, and other costumed versions of animated celebrities. Besides grabbing customers from Denny's and Hardee's, character meals provide a controlled setting in which young children can warm to characters. All meals are attended by several characters. Adult prices apply to persons 12 or older, children's prices to ages 3–11. Younger than three eat free. For more information on character dining, call (407) 939-3463 (WDW-DINE).

Because character dining is very popular, arrange priority seating as far in advance as possible by calling (407) 939-3463. Priority seating isn't a reservation, only a commitment to seat you ahead of walk-in patrons at the scheduled date and time. Even with priority seating, expect to wait 10–30 minutes to be seated. At very popular character meals like the breakfast at Cinderella's Royal Table, you are required to make a for-real reservation and to guarantee it with a for-real deposit.

Character Dining: What to Expect

Character meals are bustling affairs held in hotels' or theme parks' largest full-service restaurants. Character breakfasts offer a fixed menu served individually, family style, or on a buffet. The typical breakfast includes scrambled eggs; bacon, sausage, and ham; hash browns; waffles or French toast; biscuits, rolls, or pastries; and fruit. With family-style service, the meal is served in large skillets or platters at your table. Seconds (or thirds) are free. Buffets offer much the same fare, but you fetch it yourself.

CHARACTER MEAL HIT PARADE

Meals Rank/Restaurant	Location	Served	Characters
1. Cinderella's Royal Table	Magic Kingdom	Breakfast	Cinderella, Snow White, Belle, Jasmine, Aladdin
2. Akershus Princess Storybook Breakfast	Epcot	Breakfast	4–6 characters chosen from daily: Belle, Jasmine, Snow White, Sleeping Beauty, Esmeralda, Mary Poppins, Pocahontas, Mulan
3. Chef Mickey's	Contemporary	Breakfast	Minnie, Mickey, Chip, Pluto, Goofy
		Dinner	Mickey, Pluto, Chip, Dale, Goofy
4. Crystal Palace	Magic Kingdom	Breakfast	Pooh, Tigger, Eeyore, Piglet
		Lunch/Dinner	Pooh, Tigger, Eeyore
5. 1900 Park Fare	Grand Floridian	Breakfast	Mary Poppins and friends
		Dinner	Cinderella and friends
6. Garden Grill	Epcot	Lunch/Dinner	Chip, Dale, Mickey, Pluto
7. Liberty Tree Tavern	Magic Kingdom	Dinner	Minnie, Pluto, Donald Duck, Meeko, Chip and/or Dale
8. Donald's Breakfastosaurus	Animal Kingdom	Breakfast	Mickey, Donald, Pluto, Goofy
9. Cape May Cafe	Beach Club	Breakfast	Goofy, Chip, Dale, Pluto
10. Ohana	Polynesian Resort	Breakfast	Mickey, Goofy, Chip, Dale
11. Gulliver's Grill	Swan	Dinner	Goofy and Pluto or Rafiki and Timon

Character dinners range from a set menu served family-style to buffets or ordering off the menu. The character dinner at the Magic Kingdom's Liberty Tree Tavern, for example, is served family-style and consists of turkey, ham, marinated flank steak, salad, mashed potatoes, green vegetables, and, for kids, macaroni and cheese. Dessert is extra. Character dinner buffets, such as those at 1900 Park Fare at the Grand Floridian and Chef Mickey's at the Contemporary Resort, offer separate adults' and children's serving lines. Typically, the children's buffet includes hamburgers, hot dogs, pizza, fish sticks, fried chicken nuggets, macaroni and cheese, and peanut-butter-and-jelly sandwiches. Selections at the adult buffet usually include prime rib or other carved meat, baked or broiled

Served	Setting	Type of Service	Food Variety and Quality	Noise Level	Character to Guest Ratio
Daily	★★★★★	Buffet	★★★	Quiet	1 to 26
Daily	★★★★	Family Style	★★★½	Quiet	1 to 54
Daily	★★★	Buffet	★★★	Loud	1 to 56
Daily	★★★	Buffet	★★★½	Loud	1 to 56
Daily	★★★	Buffet	★★½	Very Loud	1 to 67
Daily	★★★	Buffet	★★★	Very Loud	1 to 89
Daily	★★★	Buffet	★★★	Moderate	1 to 54
Daily	★★★	Buffet	★★★½	Moderate	1 to 44
Daily	★★★★½	Family Style	★★½	Very Quiet	1 to 46
Daily	★★★½	Family Style	★★★	Moderate	1 to 47
Daily	★★★	Buffet	★★★	Very Loud	1 to 112
Daily	★★★	Buffet	★★½	Moderate	1 to 67
Daily	★★½	Family Style	★★½	Moderate	1 to 57
Daily	★★★	Buffet/Menu	★★★½	Moderate	1 to 198

Florida seafood, pasta, chicken, an ethnic dish or two, vegetables, potatoes, and salad.

At both breakfasts and dinners, characters circulate around the room while you eat. During your meal, each of the three to five characters present will visit your table, arriving one at a time to cuddle the kids (and sometimes the adults), pose for photos, and sign autographs. Keep autograph books (with pens) and loaded cameras handy. For the best photos, adults should sit across the table from their children. Seat the children where characters can easily reach them. If a table is against a wall, for example, adults should sit with their backs to the wall and children on the aisle.

At some larger restaurants, including 'Ohana at the Polynesian Resort and Chef Mickey's at the Contemporary, character meals involve impromptu parades of characters and children around the room, group singing, napkin waving, and other organized mayhem.

Servers don't rush you to leave after you have eaten. You can get seconds on coffee or juice and stay as long as you wish to enjoy the characters. Remember, however, that lots of eager children and adults are waiting not so patiently to be admitted.

When to Go

Attending a character breakfast usually prevents you from arriving at the theme parks in time for opening. Because early morning is best for touring and you don't want to burn daylight lingering over breakfast, we suggest:

1. Go to a character dinner or lunch instead of breakfast; it won't conflict with your touring schedule.

2. Substitute a late character breakfast for lunch. Have a light breakfast early from room service or your cooler to tide you over. Then tour the theme park for an hour or two before breaking off around 10:15 a.m. to go to the character breakfast. Make a big brunch of your character breakfast and skip lunch. You should be fueled until dinner.

3. Go on your arrival or departure day. The day you arrive and check in is usually good for a character dinner. Settle at your hotel, swim, then dine with the characters. This strategy has the added benefit of exposing your children to the characters before chance encounters at the parks. Some children, moreover, won't settle down to enjoy the parks until they have seen Mickey. Departure day also is good for a character meal. Schedule a character breakfast on your check-out day before you head for the airport or begin your drive home.

4. Go on a rest day. If you plan to stay five or more days, you'll probably take a day or half-day from touring to rest or do something else. These are perfect days for a character meal.

How to Choose a Character Meal

Many readers ask for advice about character meals. This question from a Waterloo, Iowa, mom is typical:

Are all character breakfasts pretty much the same or are some better than others? How should I go about choosing one?

In fact, some *are* better, sometimes much better. When we evaluate character meals, we look for:

1. The Characters   The meals offer a diverse assortment of characters. Select a meal that features your children's favorites. Check our Character Meal Hit Parade chart to see which characters are assigned to each meal. With the exception of 1900 Park Fare at the Grand Floridian, most restaurants stick with the same characters. Even so, check the lineup when you phone to make your priority seating. A mom from Austin, Texas, writes:

We went to two character meals at 1900 Park Fare. We ate dinner there the night we arrived unaware that the characters would all be villains.

My four-year-old was a little scared of the witch from Snow White but amaz-
ingly kept his cool! Cruella De Vil, Captain Hook, and Prince John (from Robin
Hood) were also there. My son asked the next morning if that witch was
going to be at the theme parks, too. Needless to say, we did not ride the
Snow White ride in MK! (The character breakfast was kinder and gentler.)

A Michigan family didn't fare as well:

Our character meal at 1900 Park Fare was a DISASTER!!! Please warn other
readers with younger children that if they make a priority seating and the
characters are villains, they may want to rethink their options. We went for
my daughter's fifth birthday, and she was scared to death. The Queen of
Hearts chased her sobbing and screaming down the hallway. Most young
children we saw at the dinner were very frightened. Captain Hook and
Prince John were laid-back, but Governor Ratcliff (from Pocahontas) and
the Queen were amazingly rude and intimidating.

The villains have abdicated 1900 Park Fare in favor of more benign
characters, but you never know where they might show up next. Moral?
Call before making priority seatings and ask which characters you'll be
dining with.

2. Attention from the Characters   At all character meals, characters
circulate among guests, hugging children, posing for pictures, and signing autographs. How much time a character spends with you and your
children depends primarily on the ratio of characters to guests. The more
characters and fewer guests, the better. Because many character meals
never fill to capacity, the Character-to-Guest Ratios found in our Character Meal Hit Parade chart have been adjusted to reflect an average
attendance. Even so, there's quite a range. The best ratio is at Cinderella's
Royal Table where there's approximately 1 character to every 26 guests.
The worst ratio is at Gulliver's Grill at the Swan Resort. Here, there's only
1 character for every 198 guests. In practical terms, this means your family will get eight times more attention from characters at Cinderella's
Royal Table than from those at Gulliver's Grill. Many children particularly enjoy meals with characters such as Snow White, Belle, Jasmine,
Cinderella, and Aladdin. These "face characters" speak and are able to
engage children in a way not possible for the mute animal characters.

3. The Setting   Some character meals are in exotic settings. For others,
moving the event to an elementary school cafeteria would be an improvement. Our chart rates each meal's setting with the familiar scale of 0–5
stars. Two restaurants, Cinderella's Royal Table in the Magic Kingdom and
the Garden Grill in the Land pavilion at Epcot, deserve special mention.
Cinderella's Royal Table is on the first and second floors of Cinderella Castle in Fantasyland, offering guests a look inside the castle. The Garden Grill
is a revolving restaurant overlooking several scenes from the Living with the

Land boat ride. Also at Epcot, the popular Princesses Character Breakfast is held in the castle-like Restaurant Akershus. Although Chef Mickey's at the Contemporary Resort is rather sterile in appearance, it affords a great view of the monorail running through the hotel. Themes and settings of the remaining character-meal venues, while apparent to adults, will be lost on most children.

4. The Food Although some food served at character meals is quite good, most is average (palatable but nothing to get excited about). In variety, consistency, and quality, restaurants generally do a better job with breakfast than with lunch or dinner (if served). Some restaurants offer a buffet, while others opt for "one-skillet," family-style service where all hot items are served from the same pot or skillet. To help you sort it out, we rate the food at each character meal in our chart using the five-star scale.

5. The Program Some larger restaurants stage modest performances where the characters dance, head a parade around the room, or lead songs and cheers. For some guests, these activities give the meal a celebratory air; for others, they turn what was already mayhem into absolute chaos. Either way, the antics consume time the characters could spend with families at their table.

6. Noise If you want to eat in peace, character meals are a bad choice. That said, some are much noisier than others. Our chart gives you an idea of what to expect.

7. Which Meal? Although breakfasts seem to be most popular, character lunches and dinners are usually more practical because they don't interfere with early-morning touring. During hot weather, a character lunch can be heavenly.

8. Cost Dinners cost more than lunches, and lunches are more than breakfasts. Prices for any meal vary only about $4 from the least expensive to the most expensive restaurant. Breakfasts run $14–$20 for adults and $6–$10 for ages 3–9. For character lunches, expect to pay $18–$20 for adults and $10 for kids. Dinners are $22–$24 for adults and $10–$11 for children. Little ones two and younger eat free.

9. Priority Seatings/Reservations The Disney dining reservations system makes priority seatings for character meals up to 90 days before you wish to dine. Priority seating for most character meals is easy to obtain even if you call only a couple of weeks before you leave home. Breakfasts at Cinderella's Royal Table are another story. To get breakfast table at Cinderella's, you'll need our strategy (pages 281–285), as well as help from Congress and the Pope.

10. Homeless Characters Because of decreased attendance at Disney World, several character meals have been eliminated. Reconfirm all character meal priority seatings three weeks or so before you leave home, by calling (407) WDW-DINE.

11. Friends For some venues, Disney has stopped specifying characters scheduled for a particular meal. Instead, they say it's a certain character "and friends." For example, "Pooh and friends," meaning Eeyore, Piglet, and Tigger, or some combination thereof, or "Mickey and friends" with some assortment chosen among Minnie, Goofy, Pluto, Donald, Daisy, Chip, and Dale. Most are self-evident, but others such as "Mary Poppins and friends" are unclear. Who knows whom Mary Poppins hangs out with? Don't expect Dick van Dyke.

12. Oddities Character meals are odd affairs, with the name "character meal" implying you eat the characters. We have seen characters gnawed, but we haven't seen one devoured. Semantics aside, we refer to oddities that may confuse or disappoint you. In the confusion department, the Garden Grove Café at the Swan Resort changes its name to Gulliver's Grill for dinner. If you ask, Garden Grove Café/Gulliver's Grill will tell you that two characters attend each meal. What you need to know, however, is that they work alternating 30-minute shifts, so there is usually only one character in the restaurant at a time.

Many people unable to obtain a priority seating for the character breakfast at Cinderella's Royal Table reserve a table there for lunch or dinner. Unfortunately, neither lunch nor dinner is a character meal. Although Cinderella and Snow White have been known to appear during lunch or dinner, there's no guarantee. Finally, 1900 Park Fare at the Grand Floridian Resort trots out five characters for dinner but only four for breakfast. Conversely, the Crystal Palace features four characters for breakfast but only three for lunch and dinner.

Getting a Priority Seating at Cinderella's Royal Table

The character breakfast at Cinderella's Royal Table is extremely popular as this frustrated reader from Golden, Colorado, complains:

I don't know what you have to do to get a priority seating for Cinderella's [Royal] Table in the castle. I called Disney Dining every morning at 7 [a.m.], which was 5 [a.m.] where I live! It was like calling into one of those radio shows where the first person to call wins a prize. Every time I finally got through, all the tables were gone. I am soooo frustrated and mad I could spit. What do you have to do to get a table for Cinderella's breakfast?

Admittedly, the toughest ticket at Disney World is a priority seating for the character breakfast at Cinderella's Royal Table in the castle at the Magic Kingdom. Why? Cinderella's Royal Table is Disney's tiniest character meal restaurant, accommodating only about 130 diners at a time. The only way to get a table is to obtain a priority seating through

939 3463

Disney reservations. You must call (407) WDW-DINE at 7 a.m. EST exactly 90 days before the day you want to eat at Cinderella's. Reservations can be made 90 days in advance.

Here's how it works. It's 6:50 a.m. EST and all the Disney dining reservationists are warming up their computers to begin filling available seats at 7 a.m. As the clock strikes seven, Disney dining is blasted with an avalanche of calls, all trying to make priority seatings for the character breakfast at Cinderella's Royal Table. There are over 100 reservationists on duty, and most priority seatings can be assigned in two minutes or less. Thus, the coveted seats go quickly, selling out as early as 7:02 a.m. on many days.

To be among the fortunate few who score a priority seating, try the following. First, call on the correct morning. Use a calendar and count backward exactly 90 days from (but not including) the day you wish to dine. (The computer doesn't understand months, so you can't, for example, call on February 1 to make a priority seating for May 1 because that's fewer than 90 days.) If you want to eat on May 1, for example, begin your 90-day backward count on April 30. If you count correctly, you'll find that the correct morning to call is January 31st. If you don't feel like counting days, call (407) WDW-DINE, and the Disney folks will calculate it for you. Call them during the afternoon when they're less busy about 100 days before your trip. Let them know when you'd like your priority seating, and they'll tell you the morning to call.

To get a table, you must dial at almost exactly 7 a.m. EST. Disney does not calibrate its clock with the correct time as determined by the U.S. Naval Observatory or the National Institute of Standards and Technology, but we conducted synchronizing tests and determined that Disney reservation system clocks are accurate to within 1–3 seconds. Several Internet sites will give you the exact time. Our favorite is **www.atomic time.net,** which offers the exact time in displays that show hours, minutes, and seconds. Once the Atomic Time home page is up, click on "html multizone continuous" and look for the Eastern Time Zone. Using this site or your local "Time of Day" number from the phone directory, synchronize your watch TO THE SECOND. About 18–20 seconds before 7 a.m., dial (407) WDW-DIN, waiting to dial the final "E" in "DINE" until 7 seconds before the hour.

Hang up and redial until your call is answered. When it is, you will hear one of two recorded messages:

1. "Thank you for calling the Disney Reservation Center. Our office is closed . . . " If you get this message hang up the instant you hear the words "Our office" and hit redial.

   OR

2. "Thank you for calling the Disney Reservation Center" followed by a pause. "If you are calling to make a Priority Seating for any location

except Victoria & Albert's at the Grand Floridian Resort and Spa, please press 1 or remain on the line. For Victoria & Albert's, please press 2.

Be ready. As soon as you hear the pause, press 1. Your call will be answered momentarily by a Disney Reservations Center (DRC) agent. Don't get nervous if you're on hold for a bit. The worst thing you can do now is hang up and try again.

As soon as a live DRC agent comes on the line, interrupt immediately and say, "I need Cindy's, for May 1st, for four people, any available time" (substituting your own dates, of course). Don't engage in "good mornings" or other pleasantries. Time is of the essence. You can apologize later to the DRC agent for your momentary rudeness if you feel the need, but she already knows what's going on. Don't try and pick a specific time. Even two seconds to ask for a specific time will seriously diminish your chances of getting a priority seating/reservation. If you ask for a specific time and it's full, you probably won't have time to make a second request before all times are filled.

If the atomic clock thing seems too complicated (not to mention anal), start dialing (407) WDW-DINE about 50 seconds before 7 a.m. If the reservation center isn't open yet, you'll get a recorded message saying so. When this happens, hang up and call back immediately. If you have a redial button on your phone, use it to speed the dialing process. Continue hanging up and redialing as fast as you can until you get the recording with the pause. This recording verifies that your call has been placed in the service queue in the order in which it was received. If you were among the first to get through, a reservationist will normally pick up in 3–20 seconds. What happens next depends on how many others got through ahead of you, but chances are good that you'll be able to get a priority seating. Bear in mind that while you're talking, other agents are confirming priority seatings for other guests, so you want the transaction to go down as fast as possible. Flexibility on your part counts. It's much harder to get a seating for a large group; give some thought to breaking your group into numbers that can be accommodated at tables for four or even tables for two.

All priority seatings/reservations for Cinderella's Royal Table character breakfast require a credit-card deposit (not guarantee) of $10 per adult and $5 per child at the time of the booking. The name on the booking can't be changed after the priority seating is made. Priority seatings may be canceled with the deposit refunded in full by calling (407) WDW-DINE at least 24 hours before the seating time.

While many readers have been successful using our strategies, some have not:

[Regarding] reservations for breakfast as Cinderella's castle. I did exactly what you suggested, five days in a row, and was unable to get through to an

actual person until after 7:15 each day (although I was connected and put on hold at exactly 7 a.m. each time). Of course, by then, all reservations were gone (this was for the first week in May, not a peak time).

On most days, a couple of hundred calls slam Disney's automated call queuing system within milliseconds of one another. With this call volume, 1/20 of a second or less can make the difference between getting and not getting a table. As it happens, there are variables beyond your control. When you hit the first digit of a long-distance number, your phone system leaps into action. As you continue entering digits, your phone system is already searching for the best path to the number you're calling. According to federal regulation, a phone system must connect the call to the target number within 20 seconds of your entering the last digit. In practice, most systems make the connection much faster, but your system could be pokey. How fast your call is connected, therefore, depends on your local phone system's connection speed, and even this varies according to traffic volume and available routing paths for individual calls. Distance counts too, although we're talking milliseconds. Thus, it takes just a bit longer for a call to reach Disney World from Chicago than from Atlanta, and longer yet if you're calling from San Francisco.

So, if you're having trouble getting a priority seating at Cinderella's Royal Table using the strategies outlined earlier, here are our suggestions. Make a test call to (407) WDW-DINE at 7 a.m. EST a couple of days before you call in earnest. Using a stopwatch or the stopwatch function on your watch, time the interval between entering the last digit of the number and when the phone starts to ring. This exercise will provide a rough approximation of the call connection speed at that time from your area, taking into account both speed of service and distance. For most of you, the connection interval will be very short. Some of you, however, might discover that your problem in getting through is because of slow service. Either way, factor in the connection interval in timing your call to Disney. Phone traffic is heavier on weekdays than weekends, so if you plan to call reservations on a weekday, conduct your test on a weekday. Finally, don't use a cell phone to make the call. The connection time will usually be slower and certainly less predictable.

Though this is one of the most widely used sections in this guidebook, we're amazed that anyone would go to this much trouble to eat with Cinderella . . . atomic clocks, split-second timing, test calls . . . yikes!

As a postscript, we've found it's often easier to get through to reservations if you call on Saturday or Sunday. Presumably, folks don't mind calling at the break of dawn if they're up getting ready for work but object to interrupting their beauty rest on weekends.

If You Can't Get a Priority Seating   If you insist on breakfast at Cinderella's but can't get a priority seating, go to the restaurant on the morning you wish to dine and try for a table as a walk-in. This is a long shot, though possible during the least busy times of year. There's also a fair shot at success on cold or rainy days when there's an above-average probability of no-shows. If you try to walk in, your chances are best during the last hour of serving.

If none of that works, consider this suggestion from a Providence, Rhode Island, mother of three:

> We were not able to get [priority seating] for Cinderella's breakfast at the castle, so we booked a character breakfast at our hotel and then lunch at [Cinderella's Royal Table] for later in the week. This way our kids were able to eat with Mickey one day and see the inside of the castle a few days later. Incidentally, getting the [priority seating] for lunch at the castle was easy.

Neither lunch nor dinner at Cinderella's is a character meal, but Cinderella or Snow White sometimes looks in (no guarantees). Even without characters, a meal in the castle costs a bundle, as this Snellville, Georgia, mom points out:

> We ate at Cinderella's Castle to fulfill my longtime dream. The menu was very limited and expensive. For three people, no appetizers or dessert, the bill was $100.

And no alcoholic beverages, either. Alcohol isn't served in the Magic Kingdom.

Other Character Events

A campfire and sing-along are held nightly (times vary with the season) near the Meadow Trading Post and Bike Barn at Fort Wilderness Campground. Chip 'n' Dale lead the songs, and two Disney films are shown. The program is free and open to resort guests (call (407) 824-2788).

Ice Cream Social   At 3 p.m., the Garden Grill in the Land pavilion at Epcot hosts an Ice Cream Social. The cost is $6.99 per person, plus tax and tip, for both children and adults. Mickey gets sticky with the kids (a lot of autograph books get chocolate-coated at this event). Usually uncrowded, it's a great break on a hot day and an easy way to see Mickey.

Wonderland Tea Party   Although the name of this enchanting soiree is enough to give most boys hives, it's nevertheless available at the Grand Floridian's 1900 Park Fare restaurant, Monday–Friday, at 1:30 p.m. for about $29 per child (ages 3–10). The program consists of making cupcakes, arranging flower bouquets, and having lunch and tea with characters from *Alice in Wonderland*. Reserve up to 90 days in advance by calling (407) WDW-DINE.

Baby-Sitting

Childcare Centers Childcare isn't available inside the theme parks, but each Magic Kingdom resort connected by monorail or boat, each Epcot resort (BoardWalk Inn and Villas, Yacht and Beach Club resorts), and Animal Kingdom Lodge have a childcare center for potty-trained children older than three. Services vary, but children generally can be left between 4:30 p.m. and midnight. Milk and cookies, and blankets and pillows are provided at all centers, and dinner is provided at most. Play is supervised but not organized, and toys, videos, and games are plentiful. Guests at any Disney resort or campground may use the services.

CHILDCARE CLUBS*			
Hotel	**Name of Program**	**Ages**	**Phone**
Animal Kingdom Lodge	Simba's Cubhouse	4–12	(407) 938-4785
Contemporary Resort	Mouseketeer Clubhouse	4–12	(407) 824-1000 ext. 3700
Dolphin	Dinner Camp	4–12	(407) 934-4241
Grand Floridian Beach Resort	Mouseketeer Club	4–12	(407) 824-1666
The Hilton	All About Kids	4–12	(407) 812-9300
Polynesian Resort	Neverland Club	4–12	(407) 824-2000
Swan	Dinner Camp	4–12	(407) 934-1621
Yacht and Beach Club Resorts	Sandcastle Club	4–12	(407) 934-7000
Wilderness Lodge & Villas	Cub's Den	4–12	(407) 824-1083
Wyndham Palace	All About Kids	All	(407) 812-9300

* Childcare clubs operate afternoons and evenings. Before 4 p.m., call the hotel rather than the number listed above. All programs require reservations.

The most elaborate of the childcare centers (variously called "clubs" or "camps") is Neverland Club at the Polynesian Resort. The rate for ages 4–12 is $10 per hour per child.

All clubs accept reservations (some six months in advance!) with a credit-card guarantee. Call the club directly or reserve through Disney central reservations at (407) WDW-DINE. Most clubs require a 24-hour cancellation notice and levy a hefty penalty of $15 per child for no-shows. A limited number of walk-ins are usually accepted on a first-come, first-served basis.

If you're staying in a Disney resort that doesn't offer a childcare club and you *don't* have a car, you're better off using in-room baby-sitting. Trying to take your child to a club in another hotel via Disney bus requires a 50- to 90-minute trip each way. By the time you have deposited your little one, it will almost be time to pick him up again.

Childcare clubs close at or before midnight. If you intend to stay out late, in-room baby-sitting is your best bet.

Kinder-Care Learning Centers also operate childcare facilities at Disney World. Developed for use by Disney employees, the centers now also take guests' children on a space-available basis. Kinder-Care provides services much like a hotel club's, except that the daytime "Learning While Playing Development Program" is more structured and educational. Employees are certified in CPR and first aid. Kinder-Care is open Monday–Friday, 6 a.m.–9 p.m., and Saturday and Sunday, 6 a.m.–6 p.m. Accepted are ages 1 (provided they're walking and can eat table food) through 12; $10 per hour, per child. For reservations, call (407) 827-5437 or (407) 824-3290.

In-Room Baby-Sitting Three companies provide in-room sitting in Walt Disney World and surrounding tourist areas, including the International Drive/Orange County Convention Center area, the Universal Orlando area, and the Lake Buena Vista area. They are **Kid's Nite Out** (a Kinder-Care company), **All About Kids,** and the **Fairy Godmothers** (no kidding). Kid's Nite Out also serves hotels in the greater Orlando area, including downtown. All three provide sitters older than age 18 who are insured, bonded, and trained in CPR. Some sitters have advanced medical/first-aid training and/or education credentials. All sitters are screened, reference-checked, and police-checked. In addition to caring for your children in your guest room, the sitters will, if you direct (and pay), take your children to the theme parks or other venues. Many sitters arrive loaded with reading books, coloring books, and games. All three services offer bilingual sitters.

Special Programs for Children

Several programs for children are available, and while all are fun, they're somewhat lacking in educational focus.

Let the Kids Play Pirate This program originates at the Grand Floridian and is open to all Disney resort guests ages 4–10. Children don bandannas and cruise to other resorts on Bay Lake and the Seven Seas Lagoon, following a treasure map and discovering clues along the way. At the final port, kids gobble a snack and locate the buried treasure (doubloons, beads, and rubber bugs!). The two-hour cruise operates Monday and Thursday and costs $29 per child. Reservations can be made up to 120 days in advance by calling (407) WDW-DINE.

Magic Kingdom Family Magic Tour This two-hour guided tour of the Magic Kingdom is for the entire family. Even children in strollers are welcome. The tour combines information about the Magic Kingdom with the gathering of clues that lead the group to a character greeting at tour's end. Definitely not for the self-conscious, the tour involves skipping, hopping, and walking sideways as you progress from land to land.

BABY-SITTING SERVICES

Service Name/Phone	Hotels Served	Sitters	Minimum Charges	Base Rates Per Hour
Kid's Nite Out (407) 827-5444 kidsniteout.com	All Orlando, WDW hotels, and WDW area hotels	Male and Female	4 hours	1 Child $14 2 Children $16 3 Children $19 4 Children $21
All About Kids (407) 812-9300 all-about-kids.com	All WDW hotels and some outside WDW	Male and Female	4 hours	1 Child $11 2 Children $12 3 Children $13 4 Children $ 14
Fairy Godmothers (407) 277-3724	All WDW hotels and all hotels in the general WDW area	Mothers and grandmothers	4 hours	1 Child $12 2 Children $12 3 Children $12 4 Children $14

There's usually a thin plot, such as saving Wendy from Captain Hook, in which case the character at tour's end is Wendy. The tour departs daily at 10 a.m. Cost is $25 per person, plus a valid Magic Kingdom admission. The maximum group size is 18 people. Make reservations up to one year in advance by calling (407) WDW-TOUR.

Disney's The Magic Behind Our Steam Trains   You must be 10 or older for this three-hour tour presented every Monday, Thursday, and Saturday. You join the crew of the Walt Disney World Railroad at 7:30 a.m. as they prepare their steam locomotives for the day. Cost is $40 per person, plus a valid Magic Kingdom admission. Call (407) WDW-TOUR for information and reservations.

Birthdays and Special Occasions

If someone in your family celebrates a birthday while you're at Disney World, don't keep it a secret. A Lombard, Illinois, mom put the word out and was glad she did:

Extra Charges	Cancellation Deadline	Form of Payment	Things Sitters Won't Do
Transportation Fee $8 Starting after 9 p.m. + $2 per hour	24 hours prior to service when reservation is made	VISA, MC, AmEx, Discover Gratuity in cash	Transport children in private vehicle. Take children swimming. Give baths.
Transportation Fee $8 Starting after 9 p.m. + $2 per hour	3 hours prior to service	Credit card to hold reservation	Transport children. Give baths.
Transportation Fee $12 Starting after 10 p.m. + $2 per hour	3 hours prior to service	Cash or Travelers checks for actual payment. Gratuity in cash.	Transport children. Give baths. Swimming is at sitter's discretion.

*My daughter was turning five while we were there and I asked about special
things that could be done. Our hotel asked me who her favorite character
was and did the rest. We came back to our room on her birthday and
there were helium balloons, a card, and a Cinderella 5x7 photo autographed in ink!! When we entered the Magic Kingdom, we received an "It's
My Birthday Today" pin (FREE!), and at the restaurant she got a huge cup-
cake with whipped cream, sprinkles, and a candle. IT PAYS TO ASK!!*

An Ohio mom celebrated her child's first haircut at the Magic Kingdom barber shop:

*The barber shop at the entrance of MK makes a big deal with baby's first hair-
cut—pixie dust, photos, a certificate, and "free" mouse ears hat! ($12 total).*

Part Six

Special Tips for Special People

Walt Disney World for Singles

Disney World is great for singles. It's safe, clean, and low-pressure. If you're looking for a place to relax without being hit on, Disney World is perfect. Bars, lounges, and nightclubs are the most laid-back and friendly you're likely to find. Parking lots are well lighted and constantly patrolled. For women alone, safety and comfort are unsurpassed.

There's also no need to spend evenings alone in your hotel. Between the BoardWalk and Downtown Disney, nightlife abounds. Virtually every type of entertainment performed fully clothed is available at a reasonable price at a Disney nightspot. If you over-imbibe and are a Disney resort guest, Disney buses will return you safely to your hotel.

Walt Disney World for Couples

So many couples marry or honeymoon in the World that a department was created to tend to their needs. Disney's Fairy Tale Weddings & Honeymoons offers a range of wedding venues and services, plus honeymoon packages.

Weddings

It takes big bucks to marry at Disney World. Disney's Intimate Wedding (maximum eight or fewer guests plus bride and groom) includes four nights' lodging for the wedding couple, admission to the parks, a wedding officiant, and one dinner at a Disney "fine-dining" establishment— for $3,000! This price also includes a musician, cake, bouquet, limousine ride, and wedding coordinator. If you invite more than eight guests, you must buy one of Disney's customized wedding packages, which start at $7,500 (Monday–Thursday) and $10,000 (Friday–Sunday).

If you're short on friends, you can rent Disney characters by the half hour to attend your wedding reception. Volume discounts are available;

TIPS FOR GOING SOLO

"Single" can mean traveling alone as well as unmarried, and being by yourself doesn't mean you can't have a great time in Disney World. Deb Wills, webmaster of **www.allearsnet.com,** offers this advice:

Some people say visiting Disney World by yourself can't possibly be fun. They couldn't be more wrong, as there are many reasons for going to WDW solo.

Whether you're in Orlando on business and visiting the parks to kill time, or you came to get away from it all, visiting the parks by yourself needn't be lonely. It affords you the opportunity to see and do what you want, when you want. For those of you who are hesitating—JUST DO IT! You'll be glad you did. Here are ways to maximize your experience when alone at WDW.

The tendency might be to plan your days full of activity. I suggest the opposite: Don't plan much at all. Keep your schedule as open as you can. One of the best parts about traveling solo is that you can be your own boss. Sleep in, have leisurely morning coffee on the balcony, relax by the pool ... or not. If you'd rather get up and go early, who's to stop you?

One of my favorite things to do when I'm traveling solo is to play photographer. If you encounter folks taking photos of each other, ask if they would like to be in one photo, then offer to snap the picture. This is a great way to make friends.

Get your favorite Disney snack, find a bench, and people-watch. You'll be amazed at what you see: the honeymooning couple wearing bride-and-groom mouse ears, toddlers giving Mickey and the characters their first hugs, grandparents smiling indulgently as the grandchildren smear ice cream all over their faces. If you're missing the

characters cost $675 for one, $1,020 for two, $1,365 for three, and so on. If character prices sound steep, be comforted that they don't eat or drink.

Indoor and outdoor wedding sites are available at theme parks, the Grand Floridian, Yacht Club, Beach Club, BoardWalk Inn and Villas, Contemporary, Wilderness Lodge and Villas, Polynesian, and Downtown Disney resorts. You can have a nautical wedding aboard the *Kingdom Queen* sternwheeler on Bay Lake or the riverboat adjacent to Pleasure Island at Downtown Disney. Pleasure Island nightclubs are available for nighttime weddings. If you want a short ceremony, you can tie the knot on a plummeting elevator at the Tower of Terror in Disney-MGM Studios. (I swear I'm not making this up.) The glass-enclosed Fairy Tale Wedding pavilion on a private island near the Grand Floridian is nondenominational and can accommodate up to 250 guests.

One of the more improbable services available is bachelor parties (phone (407) 828-3400 for information). What goes on at a Disney bachelor party? Stag cartoons?

To marry in the World, you need a marriage license. They're $89 at any Florida county courthouse (cash, traveler's checks, or money orders accepted). There's no waiting period; your license is issued when you apply. The ceremony must occur within 60 days. Blood tests aren't smiles of your own children, buy a couple of balloons and give them away. You'll help make the kids near you very, very happy.

Learn how some of the magic is created. Take a behind-the-scenes tour (see descriptions in each park's chapter) or one of the deluxe hotel tours.

Visit Animal Kingdom Lodge and relax at an animal-viewing area. Find an animal keeper; they'll gladly discuss care of the wild animals at the resort.

Don't hesitate to strike up conversations with cast members or guests in line with you. Foreign cast members in Epcot's World Showcase are happy to share stories about their homelands.

With no one pulling to go to Space Mountain, get a snack, or go to the bathroom, you can enjoy a leisurely shop around the World. Some stores (Arribas Brothers in Downtown Disney, and Mitsukoshi Department Store in the Japan section of World Showcase) have really neat displays and exhibits.

Go to that restaurant you've always wanted to try, but your picky eater has always declined. You don't have to order a full meal; try several appetizers, or, better yet, just dessert.

You don't want the folks at home to think you've forgotten them, so go to Innoventions in Epcot to e-mail a photo of yourself to your family.

Use common sense about your personal security. I feel very comfortable and safe traveling alone at Disney World (and have done so many times), but I still don't do things I wouldn't do at home (like announce to anyone listening that I'm traveling solo). If you aren't comfortable walking to your room alone, ask at the front desk for a security escort. Use extra caution in the parking lots at night (just like you would at home).

required, but you must present ID (driver's license, passport, or birth certificate). If you were divorced within the year, you must produce a copy of your decree. For more information, call the wedding consultant at (407) 939-4610 or (877) 566-0969, or visit **www.disneywedding.com.**

Honeymoons and Vow Renewals

Honeymoon packages are adaptations of regular Walt Disney Travel Company vacations. No special rooms are included unless you upgrade. Honeymoon features vary with the package purchased, and rates are $1,100–$5,700. Vow renewal packages are $1,800–$4,200. For more information, contact Disney's Fairy Tale Weddings and Honeymoons, P.O. Box 10000, Lake Buena Vista, FL 32830-0020; (800) 370-6009; **www.disneywedding.com.**

An Easton, Pennsylvania, couple enjoyed the reception they received and offer advice on how to make it even warmer:

We found that everyone, guests and cast members, bent over backwards for us when they learned it was our honeymoon. I highly recommend buying the bride-and-groom mouse ears, and wearing them everywhere. I know most men will be hesitant, as was my husband, but once you see what you get, you'll wear them gladly.

Romantic Getaways

Disney World is a favorite getaway for couples, but not all Disney hotels are equally romantic. Some are too family-oriented; others swarm with convention-goers. For romantic (though expensive) lodging, we recommend the Animal Kingdom Lodge, Polynesian Resort, Wilderness Lodge and Villas, Grand Floridian, BoardWalk Inn and Villas, and the Yacht and Beach Club Resorts.

The Alligator Bayou section at Port Orleans Riverside, a moderate Disney resort, also has secluded rooms. In Part Three, Selecting Your Hotel, we provide recommendations for the best rooms in each Disney resort, taking into consideration view, quiet, and convenience.

Quiet, Romantic Places to Eat

Quiet, romantic restaurants with good food are rare in the theme parks. Only the Coral Reef, the terrace at the Rose & Crown, and the San Angel Inn at Epcot satisfy both requirements. Waterfront dining is available at Fulton's Crab House at Pleasure Island, and Narcoossee's at the Grand Floridian.

The California Grill atop the Contemporary Resort has the best view at Walt Disney World. If window tables aren't available, ask to be served in the adjoining lounge. Victoria & Albert's at the Grand Floridian is the World's showcase gourmet restaurant; expect to pay big bucks. Other good choices for couples include Shula's Steakhouse at the Swan, Jiko at Animal Kingdom Lodge, and Spoodles and the Flying Fish Café at the BoardWalk.

Eating later in the evening and choosing a restaurant we've mentioned will improve your chances for intimate dining, but children—well-behaved or otherwise—are everywhere at Disney World, and you won't escape them. Honeymooners from Slidell, Louisiana, write:

> We made dinner reservations at some of the nicer Disney restaurants. When we made reservations, we made sure they were past the dinner hours and we tried to stress that we were on our honeymoon. [In] every restaurant we went to, we were seated next to large families. The kids were usually tired and cranky. After a whole day in the parks, the kids were not excited about sitting through a long meal. It's very difficult to enjoy a romantic dinner when there are small children crawling around under your table. We looked around the restaurant and always noticed lots of nonchildren couples. Our suggestion: Seat couples without children together and families with kids elsewhere. ... Some attempt should be made to keep romantic restaurants romantic.

A couple from Woodbridge, Virginia, adds:

> We found it very difficult to find a quiet restaurant for dinner anywhere. We tried a restaurant, which you recommended as quiet and pleasant. We

even waited until 8:30 p.m. to eat and we were still surrounded by out-of-control children. ... The food was very good, but after a long day in the park, our nerves were shot.

For complete information about Disney restaurants, plus recommendations for off-World dining, see Part Nine, Dining in and around Walt Disney World.

Walt Disney World for Expectant Mothers

It's said that a good shepherd will lay down his life for his sheep. Heaven knows we have tried to be good shepherds for you. While researching this guide, we have spun in teacups and been jostled in simulators until we turned green. We have baked in the sun, flapped in the wind, and been drenched in the rain. But we have failed expectant mothers. Try as he might, the author has never become pregnant. Consequently, the *Unofficial Guide* has never included first-hand information for mothers-to-be. Then, to the rescue came Debbie Grubbs, a reader from Colorado in her fifth month of pregnancy. Debbie fearlessly waddled all over Disney World, compiling observations and tips for expectant moms. Here are her conclusions:

Generally speaking, pregnant women can experience more attractions than not at Walt Disney World. Therefore, I will outline only those rides that are prohibited to pregnant women and the reasons why. There were several rides that I just knew I could ride even though they were restricted, so I sent my husband and friends to ride first and they reported why they thought I could or could not ride.

Magic Kingdom

Splash Mountain *is restricted obviously due to the drop, or so I thought. It turns out that the seat configuration in the "logs" has more to do with it than the drop. The seats are made so that your knees are higher than your rear, causing compression on the abdomen (when it is this large). This is potentially harmful to the baby. As always, better safe than sorry.*

Big Thunder Mountain Railroad *is restricted for obvious reasons as well. It's just not a good idea to ride roller coasters when you are pregnant.*

Mad Tea Party *may be okay if you don't spin the cups. We didn't ride this one because my doctor advised me not to ride things with centrifugal [or centripetal] force. Dumbo and the Astro Orbiter (Tomorrowland) are okay, but the Mad Tea Party is too fast if you spin the cups.*

Space Mountain *is one of my favorite rides, but a roller coaster nonetheless.*

Tomorrowland Speedway *is not recommended due to the amount of rear-ending that always occurs from overzealous younger drivers.*

Epcot

Body Wars, Mission: Space *and* **Test Track** *are restricted, as are all simulator rides. They are too rough and jerky, much like a roller coaster. [Nonmoving seats are available in some simulation attractions—ask a cast member.]*

Disney-MGM Studios

Tower of Terror *is restricted for the drop alone, and* **Star Tours** *is restricted because it is a simulator. Although not as rough as Mision: Space, Star Tours is still a no-no. The* **Rock 'n' Roller Coaster** *is clearly off limits.*

There might be some question about the **Backlot Tour** *due to Catastrophe Canyon, where there is a simulated earthquake. It is very tame compared to* **Earthquake!** *at Universal Studios. I rode with no problems.*

Animal Kingdom

Dinosaur *is very jerky and should be avoided. Same for* **Primeval Whirl.** **Kali River Rapids** *is a toss-up—it's somewhat bouncy and very wet.*

Water Parks

All of the slides are off-limits. Pregnant women can, however, do **Shark Reef** *at Typhoon Lagoon with an extra-large wetsuit vest. The wave pools and floating creeks are great for getting the weight off your feet.*

A mother of three from Bethesda, Maryland, adds:

First, anyone who is pregnant should go to their local golf shop and buy one of those canes that has a seat attached to it. They are lightweight and easy to carry. Without a seat, I would have been gone. Second, a pregnant woman must come with some type of support or "Belly Bra."

More Tips for Moms

In addition to Debbie's tips, here are a few of ours:

1. Go over your Disney vacation plans with your obstetrician before your trip.
2. Be prepared for a lot of walking. Get in shape by walking at home, gradually building endurance and distance.
3. Get as much rest as you need, even if you have to sacrifice some time at the theme parks. Try to nap each afternoon.
4. Eat properly. Drink plenty of water throughout the day, especially in warmer months.
5. Use in-park transportation whenever available to cut down on walking.
6. Stay in the World if possible. This will make it easier to return to your hotel for rest.

Walt Disney World for Seniors

Seniors' problems and concerns are common to Disney visitors of all ages. Seniors do, however, get into predicaments caused by touring with younger people. Pressured by grandchildren to endure a frantic pace, many seniors concentrate on surviving Disney World rather than enjoying it. Seniors must either set the pace or dispatch the young folks to tour on their own.

An older reader in Alabaster, Alabama, writes:

Being a senior is not for wussies. At Disney World particularly, it requires courage and pluck. Things that used to be easy take a lot of effort, and sometimes your brain has to wait for your body to catch up. Half the time, your grandchildren treat you like a crumbling ruin and then turn around and trick you into getting on a roller coaster in the dark. What you need to tell seniors is that they have to be alert and not trust anyone. Not their children or even the Disney people, and especially not their grandchildren. When your grandchildren want you to go on a ride, don't follow along blindly like a lamb to the slaughter. Make sure you know what the ride is all about. Stand your ground and do not waffle. He who hesitates is launched!

Most seniors we interview enjoy Disney World much more when they tour with folks their own age. If, however, you're considering visiting Disney World with your grandchildren, we recommend an orientation visit without them first. If you know first-hand what to expect, it's easier to establish limits, maintain control, and set a comfortable pace when you're with the youngsters.

If you're determined to take the grandkids, read carefully the sections of this book that discuss family touring. (*Hint:* The Dumbo-or-Die-in-a-Day Touring Plan has been known to bring grown-ups of any age to their knees.)

Because seniors are varied and willing, there aren't any attractions we'd suggest they avoid. Personal taste is more important than age. We hate to see mature visitors pass an exceptional attraction like Splash Mountain because it's called a "thrill ride." Splash Mountain is a full-blown adventure that gets its appeal more from music and visual effects than from the thrill of the ride. Because you must choose among attractions that might interest you, we provide facts to help you make informed decisions.

Getting Around

Many seniors like to walk, but a seven-hour visit to a theme park normally includes four to eight miles on foot. If you aren't up to that, let a member of your party push you in a rented wheelchair. The theme parks also offer fun-to-drive electric carts (electric convenience vehicles or ECVs). Don't let your pride keep you from having a good time. Sure you could march ten miles if you had to, *but you don't have to!*

Your wheelchair-rental deposit slip is good for a replacement wheelchair in any park during the same day. You can rent a chair at the Magic Kingdom in the morning, return it, go to Epcot, present your deposit slip, and get another chair at no additional charge.

Timing Your Visit

Retirees should make the most of their flexible schedules and go to Disney World in fall or spring (excluding holiday weeks), when the weather is nicest and crowds are thinnest. Crowds are also sparse from late January through early February, but weather is unpredictable. If you visit in winter, take coats and sweaters, plus warm-weather clothing. Be prepared for anything from near-freezing rain to afternoons in the 80s.

Lodging

If you can afford it, stay in Disney World. Rooms are among the Orlando/Kissimmee area's nicest, and transportation is always available to any Disney destination at no additional cost.

Disney hotels reserve rooms closer to restaurants and transportation for guests of any age who can't tolerate much walking. They also provide golf carts to pick up and deliver guests at their rooms. Service can vary dramatically depending on the time of day and the number of guests requesting carts. At check-in time (around 3 p.m.), for example, the wait for a ride can be as long as 40 minutes.

Here are five reasons to consider staying in Disney World:

1. The quality of the properties is consistently above average.
2. Buses run only hourly or so for "outside" hotels. Disney buses run continuously. Staying in the World guarantees transportation when you need it.
3. Boarding pets overnight at the kennels is available only to Disney resort guests.
4. You get free parking in major theme parks' lots.
5. You get preferential tee times on resort golf courses.

All Disney hotels are spread out. It's easy to avoid most stairs, but it's often a long hike to your room from parking lots, bus stops, or public areas. Seniors intending to spend more time at Epcot and Disney-MGM Studios than at the Magic Kingdom or Animal Kingdom should consider the Yacht and Beach Club Resorts, Swan and Dolphin, or Board-Walk Inn and Villas.

The Contemporary Resort is a good choice for seniors who want to be on the monorail system. So are the Grand Floridian and Polynesian resorts, though both sprawl over many acres, necessitating a lot of walking. For a restful, rustic feeling, choose the Wilderness Lodge and Villas. If you want a kitchen and comforts of home, book Old Key West Resort, the Beach Club Villas, or BoardWalk Villas. If you enjoy watching birds and animals, try Animal Kingdom Lodge. Try Saratoga Springs if you plan to golf.

RVers will find pleasant surroundings at Disney's Fort Wilderness Campground. There also are several KOA campgrounds within 20 minutes of Disney World. None offers the wilderness setting or amenities that Disney does, but they cost less.

Transportation

Roads in Disney World can be daunting. Armed with a moderate sense of direction and above-average sense of humor, however, even the most timid driver can get around.

If you drive, parking isn't a problem. Lots are served by trams linking the parking area and the theme park's entrance. Parking for the disabled is available adjacent to each park's entrance. Pay-booth attendants will provide a dashboard ticket and direct you to the reserved spaces. Disney requires that you be recognized officially as disabled to use this parking, but temporarily disabled or injured persons also are permitted access.

Senior Dining

Eat breakfast at your hotel restaurant or save money by having juice and rolls in your room. Carry snacks in a fannypack supplemented by fruit, fruit juice, and soft drinks purchased from vendors. Make your lunch priority seating for before noon to avoid the crowds. Follow with an early dinner and be out of the restaurants, ready for evening touring and fireworks, long before the main crowd even thinks about dinner.

We recommend seniors fit dining and rest into each day. Plan lunch as a break. Sit back, relax, and enjoy. Then return to your hotel for a nap or swim during the hot, crowded hours of the day.

Behind the Scenes Tours

Every senior should take at least one behind-the-scenes tour, most of which are at Epcot. They offer an in-depth look at Walt Disney World operations. Especially worthwhile are Hidden Treasures and Gardens of the World. If you don't have time for these lengthy tours, the shorter Greenhouse Tour at Epcot's The Land pavilion is a "must-see." Backstage Magic visits behind-the-scenes locations at several theme parks, while Keys to the Kingdom provides a glimpse of the Magic Kingdom's history and hidden operations. Ranging from one to seven hours long and $8 to $200 per person, all tours require a lot of walking and standing.

Walt Disney World for Disabled Guests

Disney World is so attuned to guests with disabilities that unscrupulous people have been known to fake a disability in order to take unfair advantage. If you have a disability, even a restricted diet, Disney World is prepared to meet your needs.

Valuable information for trip planning is available at **www.disney world.com.** Each major theme park offers a free booklet describing disabled services and facilities. Disney people are somewhat resistant to mailing you the booklets, but if you're polite and persistent they can be persuaded. The same information is on the Web site; type "disabled" in the search tool. Or, get a booklet at wheelchair-rental locations in parks.

For specific requests, including specialized accommodations at hotels or on the Disney Transportation System, call (407) 939-7807 (voice) or (407) 939-7670 (TTY). When the recorded menu comes up, press "1" on your touch-tone phone. Limit calls to this number to questions and requests regarding disabled services and accommodations. Address other questions to (407) 824-4321.

The following equipment, services, and facilities are available at Disney hotels, though not all hotels offer all items:

Wheelchairs	Refrigerators
Bed and bathroom rails	Knock and phone alerts
Wider bath doors	Closed-captioned televisions
Roll-in showers	TTYs
Shower benches	Strobe-light smoke detectors
Hand-held shower heads	Double peep holes in doors
Accessible vanities	Braille on signs and elevators
Rubber bed pads	Portable commodes
Lower beds	Lower kitchen appliances, cupboards

Much of the Disney transportation system is accessible. Monorails can be accessed by ramp or elevator, and all bus routes are served by vehicles with wheelchair lifts, though unusually wide or long wheelchairs (or motorized chairs) may not fit the lift. Watercraft accommodations for wheelchairs are iffier. If you plan to stay at Wilderness Lodge and Villas, Fort Wilderness Campground, or an Epcot resort, call the special-requests number (above) for the latest information on watercraft accessibility.

Food and merchandise locations at theme parks, Downtown Disney, and hotels are generally accessible, but some fast-food queues and shop aisles are too narrow for wheelchairs. At these locations, ask a cast member or member of your party for assistance.

Disabled guests and their families give high marks for accessibility and consideration for disabled patrons. An Arlington, Virginia, woman writes:

Before the trip, I thought of Disney as a sort of corporate monster that successfully accessed my pocketbook through my innocent and trusting children with its diabolical marketing expertise. I also considered a Disney vacation pretty ersatz. . . . However, I must say that Disney is dynamite in its treatment of handicapped vacationers, and this perspective has turned me into a fan. My mom has mobility problems that got a lot worse between the time my dad made reservations and the time we arrived, and she was worried about getting around. Disney supplied a free wheelchair, and every bus had kneeling steps for wheelchair users. The disabled brochures for each park were incredibly informative about access for each attraction, and the hosts sprang into action when they saw us coming.

Visitors with Special Needs

Wholly or Partially Nonambulatory   Guests may rent wheelchairs. Most rides, shows, attractions, rest rooms, and restaurants accommodate the nonambulatory disabled. If you're in a park and need assistance, go to Guest Relations.

A limited number of electric carts or ECVs (electric convenience vehicles) are available for rent. Easy to drive, they give nonambulatory guests tremendous freedom and mobility. For some reason, vehicles at the Magic Kingdom go much faster than those at other parks.

All Disney lots have close-in parking for disabled visitors. Request directions when you pay your parking fee. All monorails and most rides, shows, rest rooms, and restaurants accommodate wheelchairs.

Theme-park maps issued to each guest on admission are symbol-coded to show which attractions accommodate wheelchairs.

Wheelchairs rent for $8; ECVs are $40 per day, and each rental requires a refundable deposit. Rentals are available at Disney-MGM, Epcot, Animal Kingdom, and Downtown Disney, and they are welcome (though not available for rent) at both water parks.

Even if an attraction doesn't accommodate wheelchairs, nonambulatory guests may ride if they can transfer from their wheelchair to the ride's vehicle. Disney staff, however, aren't trained or permitted to assist in transfers. Guests must be able to board the ride unassisted or have a member of their party assist them. Either way, members of the nonambulatory guest's party will be permitted to ride with them.

Because waiting areas of most attractions won't accommodate wheelchairs, nonambulatory guests and their party should request boarding instructions as soon as they arrive at an attraction. Almost always, the entire group will be allowed to board without a lengthy wait. A New Orleans woman who traveled with a nonambulatory friend writes:

I went with a very dear friend of mine who is a paraplegic, confined to a wheelchair. It was his first trip to WDW, and I knew that it was a handicap-friendly place, but we were still a little apprehensive about how much we would be able to do. The official pamphlet distributed by the WDW staff is helpful, but it implies limitations, such as stating that one must be able to navigate (i.e., walk) the catwalks of Space Mountain in case of emergency. After reading this, Brian and I thought that we would end up walking around the MK looking at the rides, not riding them. The reality is, nonambulatory visitors are able to do much more—one only has to ask the cast members what is really allowed. Of course, I'm sure the WDW publication is written to cover liability purposes; also, Brian is a very active person who is able to transfer from his wheelchair without too much difficulty, so we were able to ride almost everything we wanted! We both had a terrific time. The only ride that it seems we should have been able to ride but

couldn't was Pirates of the Caribbean, and [this was] only because the rail-
ings at the loading site are just a few inches too close together for a wheel-
chair to pass through. Anyway, my point is that it may be encouraging to
disabled readers of the Unofficial Guide *to know that there are options*
available; of course, with the caveat that it depends on the individual's
mobility. I would recommend to anyone to not avoid a ride—ask first.

Dietary Restrictions   Visitors with dietary restrictions can be assisted at Guest Relations in the parks. For Disney World restaurants outside the parks, call a day ahead for assistance.

Sight- and/or Hearing-Impaired Guests   Guest Relations at the parks provides free tape cassettes and portable tape players to sight-impaired guests ($25 refundable deposit). At the same locations, TDDs are available for hearing-impaired guests. Many pay phones in the major parks are equipped with amplifying headsets. See your Disney map for locations.

Braille guidemaps are available from Guest Relations at all parks. Some rides provide closed captioning; many theater attractions provide reflective captioning. Disney will provide an interpreter for live shows; to reserve, call (407) 824-4321 (voice) or (407) 939-8255 (TTY).

Non-Apparent Disabilities   We receive many letters from readers whose traveling companion or child requires special assistance, but who, unlike a person in a wheelchair, is not visibly disabled. Autism, for example, makes it very difficult or impossible to wait in line for more than a few minutes, or in queues surrounded by a crowd.

A trip to Disney World can be positive and rewarding for guests with autism and similar conditions. And while any Disney vacation requires planning, a little extra effort to accommodate the affected person will pay large dividends.

One of the first things to do is obtain a letter from the disabled party's primary physician that explains the condition and any special needs it implies. The letter should clearly explain the condition to the Disney cast member reading the letter. The following template (on your doctor's letterhead) works well. This example is for a disabled child:

To Whom It May Concern:

[child's name] is a delightful child who has been diagnosed with [child's
condition]. This diagnosis impedes his ability to wait for extended periods of
time, and he struggles with sensory issues (e.g., touch) that may impact his
ability to wait in lines. Please offer whatever accommodation you can for
this young man and his family.

Sincerely,
[doctor's name]

Show your doctor's note at Guest Relations at any Disney theme park and request a Guest Assistance Card. The card is a pass allowing the disabled person and his companions to wait in a separate holding area, apart from the regular queues at most attractions. One card is good for all four parks. Also, obtain a copy of each park's *Guidebook for Guests with Disabilities* (also available online at **www.disneyworld.com**).

We have heard from several families with doctors' notes who were told by cast members that no "special assistance" card existed. To test awareness of the card, we sent research teams to ask for one at Guest Relations in each park. In three of four cases, the cast member knew exactly what we wanted and explained clearly how the card worked. At one park, however, we encountered a cast member who knew nothing about the card. Aware of the high standards Disney has in this area, we decided to give someone a call.

Disney's Park Operations group was shocked to hear our findings. Their explanation, which we can understand, is that Guest Relations is occasionally staffed by recently hired cast members who may not be familiar with every benefit Disney offers. If you encounter a cast member in training, Disney advises the following: Firmly but politely ask for the manager and explain the situation to the manager. Guest Relations managers are Disney veterans who are virtually certain to know about the Guest Assistance Card. In the unlikely event the manager doesn't know of the card, ask to speak to an "area manager." An area manager is responsible for the day-to-day operation of a significant section of the park, and we're assured that they will know about the card.

The card doesn't allow you to bypass normal waits at each attraction. It's designed to provide "more convenient entrance" into attractions. In some cases, this may be through the attraction's FASTPASS return line or the attraction's exit. The *Guidebook for Guests with Disabilities* lists the entrance to use at each attraction, as well as special effects (e.g., loud noises or flashing lights) inside.

More Tips for Visitors with Special Needs

Families have sent us their hotel, restaurant, and transportation tips. For example, a quiet hotel room can often help the affected individual unwind after a day in the parks. (See page 123 for the numbers of the best rooms in Disney resorts.) Other tips sent by readers include:

Schedule breaks. A midday nap or dip in the pool may relax weary, overstimulated members of your group.

Earplugs brought from home may help children in attractions with loud music or sound effects.

Consider using a town-car service from the Orlando airport to your hotel. Shuttle and bus services usually drop guests at several hotels, and it's common for the trip to take two or more hours. In contrast, most town-car services will drive you directly to your destination. Good town-car services are listed on pages 308–309.

If you'd like a meal with Disney characters, reviews starting on page 279 will help you choose a suitable experience. For example, Cinderella's Gala Feast at the Grand Floridian is a boisterous affair that may overwhelm any child.

Whenever possible, obtain priority seating (page 347) for meals, and consider asking for a table near an exit or window.

To save time, consider using a taxi to travel between Disney resorts.

Sensory-defensive children may enjoy the "deep pressure" sensation of the sandy beaches or whirlpools at some Disney resorts. The wave pool at Typhoon Lagoon also gets high marks from readers.

Pin trading (pages 684–685) with Disney cast members offers a safe, scripted opportunity for children to work on their social and communication skills.

We're grateful to the many families with autistic children who have shared their Disney experiences with us. Special thanks goes to the Cartwright family of Fon Du Lac, Wisconsin.

Friends of Bill   A Linthicum, Maryland, mom suggested this:

We went on this vacation with a recovering alcoholic. He was able to attend daily 3–4 p.m. meetings that were held just outside the park in one of the hotels. It would be helpful if you mentioned that there are meetings available for Alcoholics Anonymous. Disney does not sponsor them. This is a very sensitive issue for many that are too afraid to ask for fear of public ridicule. The person in our group took a cab from the resort the first time and never had to after that. There are regulars in the meetings that will pick up anyone from their resorts that needs a ride. Thanks for letting me include this. I wouldn't want someone to be afraid to come to Disney because they feared a setback in their recovery.

Guests Who Don't Speak English

Disney has developed a wireless device called Ears to the World that provides syncronized narration in French, German, Japanese, Portuguese, or Spanish for more than 25 attractions in the major theme parks. The wireless, lightweight headsets provide real-time translation allowing guests with limited fluency in English to understand the storylines of the designated attractions. The device is available free of charge at Guest Relations at all parks.

Part Seven

Arriving and
Getting Around

Getting There

Directions

Motorists can reach any Walt Disney World destination via World Drive off US 192, or via Epcot Drive off I-4 (map, pages 314–315).

Warning! I-4, connecting Daytona and Tampa, is an east/west highway but takes a north/south drop through the Orlando/Kissimmee area. This directional change complicates getting oriented in and around Disney World. Logic suggests that highways branching off I-4 should run north and south, but most run east and west here.

From I-10 Take I-10 east across Florida to I-75 southbound. Exit I-75 onto the Florida Turnpike. Exit onto I-4 westbound. Take Exit 67, marked Epcot/Downtown Disney, and follow the signs to your Disney destination.

From I-75 Southbound Follow I-75 south to the Florida Turnpike. Exit onto I-4 westbound. Take Exit 67, marked Epcot/Downtown Disney, and follow the signs.

From I-95 Southbound Follow I-95 south to I-4. Go west on I-4 through Orlando. Take Exit 67, marked Epcot/Downtown Disney, and follow the signs.

From Daytona or Orlando Go west on I-4 through Orlando. Take Exit 67, marked Epcot/Downtown Disney, and follow the signs.

From the Orlando International Airport Drive southwest on Central Florida Greenway (FL 417), a toll road. Take Exit 6 onto FL 535, then left onto FL 536. FL 536 will cross I-4 and become Epcot Drive. From here, follow signs to your Walt Disney World destination. If you are going to a hotel on US 192 (Irlo Bronson Highway), follow the same route until you reach I-4. Take I-4 west toward Tampa. Take the first US 192 exit if your hotel is on West Irlo Bronson, and the second exit if your

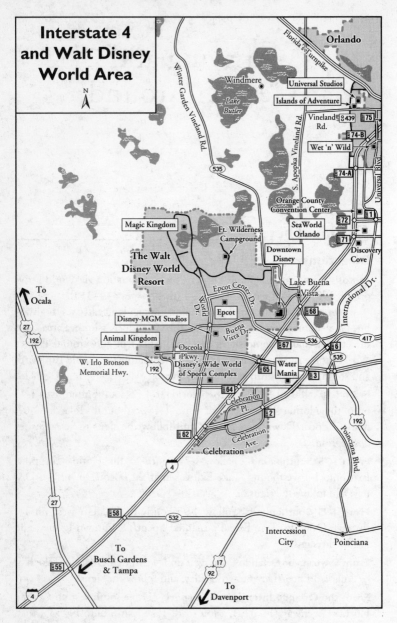

Interstate 4
and Walt Disney
World Area

N

Orlando

Windmere

Universal Studios

Islands of Adventure

Vineland Rd.

439

75

74-B

Wet 'n' Wild

74-A

Winter Garden Vineland Rd.

S. Apopka Vineland Rd.

Lake Butler

535

Orange County Convention Center

Magic Kingdom

Ft. Wilderness Campground

SeaWorld Orlando

The Walt Disney World Resort

Downtown Disney

Discovery Cove

To Ocala

Lake Buena Vista

Epcot Center Dr.

68

World Dr.

Epcot

Disney-MGM Studios

Buena Vista Dr.

67

536

6

417

Animal Kingdom

Osceola Pkwy.

535

W. Irlo Bronson Memorial Hwy.

192

Disney's Wide World of Sports Complex

65

Water Mania

3

27

192

64

Celebration Pl.

2

International Dr.

Poinciana Blvd.

62

Celebration Ave.

Celebration

192

4

27

58

532

Intercession City

Poinciana

To Busch Gardens & Tampa

55

17

92

To Davenport

4

hotel is on East Irlo Bronson. If your hotel is in Lake Buena Vista, exit
FL 417 onto FL 535 as described above, but continue straight on FL
535 instead of turning left onto FL 536.

Alternate route: Take FL 528 (Beeline Highway toll road) west for about 12 miles to the intersection with I-4. Go west on I-4 to Exit 67, marked Epcot/Downtown Disney, and follow the signs to your Walt Disney World destination. This is also the route to take if your hotel is on International Drive or Universal Boulevard, near Universal Studios, near SeaWorld, or near the Orange Country Convention Center. For these destinations, take I-4 east toward Orlando.

From Miami, Fort Lauderdale, and Southeastern Florida   Head north on the Florida Turnpike to I-4 westbound. Take Exit 67, marked Epcot/Downtown Disney, and follow the signs.

From Tampa and Southwestern Florida   Take I-75 northbound to I-4. Go east on I-4, take Exit 64 onto US 192 westbound, and follow the signs.

Walt Disney World Exits Off I-4

East to west (direction of Orlando to Tampa), four I-4 exits serve Disney World.

Exit 68 (marked FL 535/Lake Buena Vista) primarily serves the Downtown Disney Resort Area and Downtown Disney, including Disney Village Marketplace, Pleasure Island, and Disney's West Side. It also serves non-Disney hotels with a Lake Buena Vista address. This exit puts you on a road with lots of traffic signals. Avoid it unless you're headed to one of the above destinations.

Exit 67 (marked Epcot/Downtown Disney) delivers you to a four-lane expressway into the heart of Disney World. It's the fastest and most convenient way for westbound travelers to access almost all Disney destinations except Animal Kingdom and Wide World of Sports.

Exit 65 (marked Osceola Parkway) is the best exit for westbound travelers to access the Animal Kingdom, Animal Kingdom Lodge, Pop Century Resort, All Star Reorts, and Wide World of Sports.

Exit 64 (marked US 192/Magic Kingdom) is the best route for eastbound travelers to all Disney destinations.

Getting to Walt Disney World from the Airport

You have four options for getting from the Orlando airport to Disney World:

1. Taxi   Taxis carry four to eight passengers (depending on vehicle type). Rates vary according to distance. If your hotel is in the World, your fare will be about $36, plus tip. For the US 192 "Main Gate" area, it will be about $45. To International Drive or downtown Orlando, expect to pay about $36.

2. Shuttle Service   Mears Motor Transportation Service (phone (407) 423-5566) provides your transportation if your vacation package includes "airport transfers." But nonpackage travelers also can use the service. The shuttles collect passengers until they fill a van (or bus). They're then dispatched. Mears charges *per-person* rates (under age four ride free). One-way and round-trip services are available.

From the Airport to:	One-Way	Round-Trip
	Adult/Child	Adult/Child
International Drive	$15/$11	$25/$18
Downtown Orlando	$15/$11	$25/$18
Walt Disney World/Lake Buena Vista	$17/$13	$29/$21
US 192 "Main Gate" Area	$17/$13	$29/$21

You might have to wait at the airport until a vehicle fills. Once underway, the shuttle will probably stop several times to discharge passengers before it reaches your hotel. Nobody accuses the shuttles of being overly expeditious. Obviously, it takes less time to fill a van than a bus, and less time to deliver and unload those passengers.

Though Mears has a lot of capacity, it maxes out periodically, as this Philadelphia reader reports:

Mears should pay us to ride them! The confusion at the airport was atrocious! I'm kind of aggressive, so I got my husband and myself on the third bus that left, leaving 100 or more angry travelers behind. [Later] to get to Universal two times and SeaWorld once, we had to pay $12 a day. The bus was invariably late picking us up at either end and made us generally miserable.

From your hotel to the airport, you're likely to ride in a van (unless you're part of a tour group, for which Mears might send a bus). Because shuttles make several pick-ups, they ask you to leave much earlier than you would depart if you were taking a cab or returning a rental car.

3. Town-Car Service Similar to taxi service, town-car service will transport you directly from the airport to your hotel. The town-car driver usually will be waiting for you in your airline's baggage-claim area.

Each town-car service we surveyed offers large, well-appointed late-model sedans, such as the Lincoln Town Car ES series, or limousines. These hold four adults or two adults and three children comfortably. To reserve a child's car seat, call ahead. Trunks easily hold golf bags. We're sure it's just coincidence that every driver we interviewed quantified his car's trunk capacity using dead bodies as the unit of measure.

Tiffany Towncar Service (phone (888) 838-2161 or (407) 251-5431; **www.tiffanytowncar.com**) provides a prompt, clean ride. Tiffany also received the best reviews from Disney bellhops. Round-trip to a Disney resort costs $85–$90, while the round-trip fee to a non-Disney resort is $80–$90, plus tip. One way is about half as much. Only Tiffany offers a free stop at a Publix supermarket en route to your hotel. You can save time and money if you stock up on breakfast and snack items here rather than in the parks. Also, check Tiffany's Web site for a coupon worth $5 off a round-trip.

Quicksilver Tours & Transportation (phone (888) GO-TO-WDW or (407) 390-0113; **www.quicksilver-tours.com**) offers ten-person limos and vans in addition to Town Cars. Rates for a round-trip range from $90 to $100 depending on location. Like Tiffany, Quicksilver throws in a stop at the supermarket en route.

4. Rental Cars   Short- and long-term rentals are available. Most companies allow drop-off at certain hotels or subsidiary locations in the Disney area if you don't want the vehicle for your entire stay. Likewise, any time during your stay, you can pick up a car at those hotels and locations. Check **mousesavers.com** for rental-car discount codes. With a little effort, you may get a great deal.

Dollars and Sense   Which option is the best deal depends on how many people are in your party and how much you value your time. If you're traveling solo or have only two in your party, and you're pretty sure you won't need a rental car, the shuttle is your least expensive bet. A cab for two makes sense if you want to get to your hotel faster than the shuttle can arrange. The cab will cost about $36–$52, including tip. That's $18–$26 per person. The shuttle will cost $15 each, saving $4 per person. You must decide whether the cab's timeliness and convenience are worth the extra bucks. A one-day car rental costs $34–$70, plus you have to take time to complete the paperwork, get the vehicle, and fill the tank before you return it. The more people in your group, the more economical the cab becomes over the shuttle. Likewise with the rental car, though the cab will get you there faster. If saving time and hassle is worth the money, book a town car.

Renting a Car

Readers planning to stay in the World, frequently ask if they'll need a car. If your plans don't include restaurants, attractions, or destinations outside Disney World, the answer is a very qualified no. But consider the thoughts of this Snohomish, Washington, reader:

We rented a car and were glad we did. It gave us more options, though we used the [Disney] bus transportation quite extensively. With a car we could drive to the grocery store to restock our snack supply. It also came in handy for our night out. I shudder at how long it might have taken us to get from the Caribbean Beach to the Polynesian to leave our kids [at the childcare facility], then to Pleasure Island, then back to the Polynesian [to get the kids], and then back to the Caribbean Beach. At $10 an hour [for childcare] you don't want to waste time! It was also nice to drive to Typhoon Lagoon with a car full of clothes, lunches, and other paraphernalia. It was also easier to drive to the other hotels for special meals.

This reader will be open-minded about renting a car in the future:

I read what you said about using our own transportation between the parks but I did not believe you. Duh! That won't happen again. ... I had not been to "The World" since the early 1980s and did not remember having any problem getting around on the Disney Transportation System. I will never forget all of the waiting we did this trip. There is nothing more frustrating than to get in sight of your bus stop and see your bus driving off, because you know it is going to be near twenty minutes before the next one pulls up.

A dad from Avon Lake, Ohio, adds:

It was unbelievable how often we used our rental car. Although we stayed at the Grand Floridian, we found the monorail convenient only for the Magic Kingdom. Of the six nights we stayed, we used our car five days.

A family from Lynn Haven, Florida, reports:

The transportation system (buses specifically) was a mess. Nothing like the efficient system they had when we visited four years ago. What has happened? It took us an hour and 45 minutes to get from the BoardWalk to Fort Wilderness by bus. Bus transportation was very bad the whole time. Boat transportation was just fine.

A Portland, Maine, family had gripes with non-Disney transportation:

We stayed outside WDW and tried to commute on the bus furnished by our hotel. After two days, we gave up and rented a car.

Plan to Rent a Car

1. If your hotel is outside Walt Disney World.
2. If your hotel is in the World and you want to dine someplace other than the theme parks and your hotel.
3. If you plan to return to your hotel for naps or swimming during the day.
4. If you plan to visit other area theme parks or water parks (including Disney's).

Renting a Car at Orlando International Airport

The airport has two terminals: A and B. Airlines serving Orlando are assigned to one or the other. Each terminal has three levels and a parking garage. Ticket counters are on Level Three. Baggage claim is on Level Two. Level One is where car-rental counters are, or, if your rental company is off-site, where you'll catch a courtesy vehicle to its location.

Orlando is the world's largest rental-car market. At last count, 22 companies competed for your business. Five—**Avis, Budget, Dollar, L&M, and National**—have counters on Level One of both terminals. **Alamo, Enterprise, Hertz, Thrifty,** and 13 other companies have locations near the airport and provide courtesy shuttles outside Level One at both terminals. Most shuttles run continuously; you don't have to call for pick-up. We prefer using one of the five companies inside the airport because (1) you can complete your paperwork while you wait for your checked luggage to arrive at baggage claim and (2) it's a short walk to the garage to pick up your car (no shuttle needed).

If you rent from an on-site company, you'll return your car to the garage adjacent to the terminal where your airline is assigned. If you return your car to the wrong garage, you'll have to haul your luggage on foot from one side of the airport to the other in order to reach your check-in.

Prepay for a tank of gas (so you can return the car empty) or fill up near your hotel. There are no convenient gas stations near the airport, and most rental companies charge about $4 a gallon if they fill the tank.

How the Orlando Rental-Car Companies Stack Up

Unofficial Guide readers provide lots of information about the quality of the car and service they receive from Orlando car-rental companies. Most folks are looking for:

1. Quick, courteous, and efficient processing on pick-up.
2. A nice, well-maintained, late-model automobile.
3. A car that is clean and odor-free.
4. Quick, courteous, and efficient processing on return.
5. If applicable, an efficient shuttle between the rental agency and airport.

Most of our readers rent from Alamo, Avis, Budget, Dollar, Hertz, or National. On a scale of 0 (worst) to 100 (best), the following table shows how they rate the Orlando operations of each company, based on the points listed above. If you would like to participate in our rental-car survey, complete and return the form at the back of this book.

Company	Pick-Up Efficiency	Condition of the Car	Cleanliness of the Car	Return Efficiency	Shuttle Efficiency
Alamo	67	78	85	74	86
Avis	92	86	86	90	n/a
Budget	70	87	93	93	n/a
Dollar	81	90	87	90	n/a
Enterprise	88	88	92	90	91
Hertz	82	94	90	90	93
National	89	93	92	93	n/a
Payless	65	90	81	91	75

L&M, a lesser-known company, often offers to beat the rate you were quoted when you reserved with one of the majors. L&M's cars are new, in good condition, and at the airport. *Unofficial Guide* readers rank processing among the highest. Before picking up the car you reserved elsewhere, stop by the L&M counter to comparison-shop. If you want to check L&M's rates and specials before you go, see **www.lmcarrental.net.**

If you rent a car, a 6–7% sales tax, $2.35-per-day state surcharge, and $0.40-per-day vehicle license recovery fee will be heaped onto your final bill. If you rent from an agency with airport facilities or shuttles, a 10% airport tax will be added. Remember: You can rent a car at your hotel on the day you actually need it.

Getting Oriented

A Good Map

Readers frequently complain about signs and maps provided by Disney. While it's easy to find the major theme parks, locating other Disney destinations can be challenging. Many Disney-supplied maps are stylized and hard to read, while others provide incomplete information. The most easily obtained map is in the Walt Disney World "Once Upon A Visit" planning guide. Available at any resort or theme-park Guest Relations office, the guide has a reduced version of the Walt Disney World Property Map and Disney Transportation System information on its last two pages. The guide also covers dining, recreation, and shopping.

A very good map of the Orlando/Kissimmee/Disney World area is free at the AAA Car Care Center operated by Goodyear near the Magic Kingdom parking lot (see map, pages 314–315). Request the map at the counter.

Finding Your Way Around

Walt Disney World is like any big city. It's easy to get lost. Signs for the theme parks are excellent, but finding a restaurant or hotel is often confusing. The easiest way to orient yourself is to think in terms of five major areas, or clusters (see map on pages 314–315):

1. The first encompasses all hotels and theme parks around Seven Seas Lagoon. This includes the Magic Kingdom, hotels connected by the monorail, Shades of Green resort, and two golf courses.

2. The second includes developments on and around Bay Lake: Wilderness Lodge and Villas, Fort Wilderness Campground, and two golf courses.

3. Cluster three contains Epcot, Disney-MGM Studios, Disney's BoardWalk, Disney's Wide World of Sports, Epcot resort hotels, Pop Century Resorts, and Caribbean Beach Resort.

4. The fourth cluster encompasses Walt Disney World Village; Downtown Disney (including Disney Village Marketplace, Pleasure Island, and Disney's West Side); Typhoon Lagoon; a golf course; Downtown Disney Resort Area; and the Port Orleans, Saratoga Springs, and Old Key West resorts.

5. The fifth and newest cluster contains Animal Kingdom, Blizzard Beach, and the Disney All-Star, Coronado Springs, and Animal Kingdom Lodge resorts.

How to Travel around the World (or the *Real* Mr. Toad's Wild Ride)

Trying to commute around Walt Disney World can be frustrating. A Magic Kingdom street vendor, telling me how to get to Epcot, proposed, "You can take the ferry or the monorail to the Transportation and Ticket Center. Then you can get another monorail, or you can catch the bus, or you can take a tram out to your car and drive over there yourself." What he didn't say was that it would be easier to ride a mule than to take any conceivable combination from this transportation smorgasbord.

There's no simple way to travel around the World, but there are ways to make it easier. Just give yourself plenty of time.

Transportation Trade-Offs for Guests: Lodging outside Walt Disney World

Day-guests (those staying outside the World) can use the monorail, bus, and boat systems. Our most important advice for these guests is to park in the lot of the theme park (or other Disney destination) where you plan to finish your day. This is critical if you stay at a park until closing.

Moving Your Car from Lot to Lot on the Same Day

Once you've paid to park in any major theme-park lot, show your receipt and you'll be admitted into another park's lot on the same day without further charge. Disney lodging guests park free in any theme-park lot.

All You Need to Know about Driving to the Theme Parks

1. Positioning of the Parking Lots Animal Kingdom, Disney-MGM Studios, and Epcot parking lots are adjacent to each park's entrance. The Magic Kingdom lot is adjacent to the Transportation and Ticket Center. From the TTC, take a ferry or monorail to the park's entrance.

2. Paying to Park Disney resort guests and annual passholders park free. All others pay. If you pay to park and you move your car during that day, show your receipt and you won't have to pay at the new lot.

3. Finding Your Car when It's Time to Depart Parking lots are huge. Jot down the section and row where you park. If you're driving a rental car, note the license number (you wouldn't believe how many white rental cars there are).

4. Getting from Your Car to the Park Entrance Each lot provides trams to the park entrance or, at the Magic Kingdom, to the TTC. If you arrive early in the morning, it may be faster to walk to the entrance (or TTC) than to take the tram.

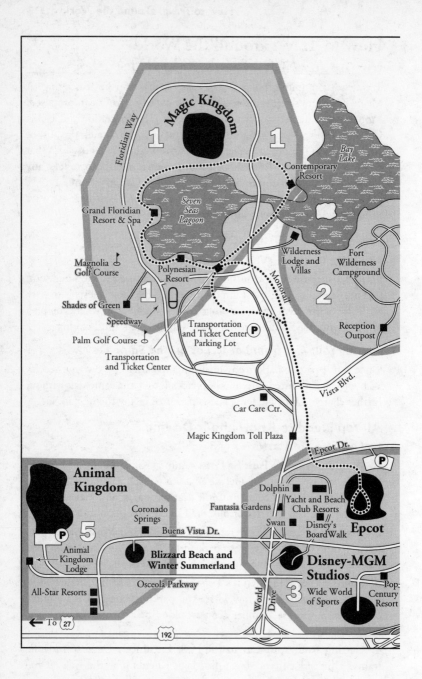

Magic Kingdom

1

1

Floridian Way

Bay Lake

Contemporary Resort

Grand Floridian Resort & Spa

Seven Seas Lagoon

Wilderness Lodge and Villas

Fort Wilderness Campground

Magnolia Golf Course

Polynesian Resort

2

Shades of Green

1

Monorail

Reception Outpost

Speedway

Palm Golf Course

Transportation and Ticket Center Parking Lot

P

Transportation and Ticket Center

Vista Blvd.

Car Care Ctr.

Magic Kingdom Toll Plaza

Epcot Dr.

P

Animal Kingdom

Dolphin

Yacht and Beach Club Resorts

Fantasia Gardens

Coronado Springs

Swan

Disney's BoardWalk

Epcot

5

Buena Vista Dr.

P

Animal Kingdom Lodge

Blizzard Beach and Winter Summerland

Disney-MGM Studios

Pop-Century Resort

All-Star Resorts

Osceola Parkway

3

Wide World of Sports

World Drive

← To 27

192

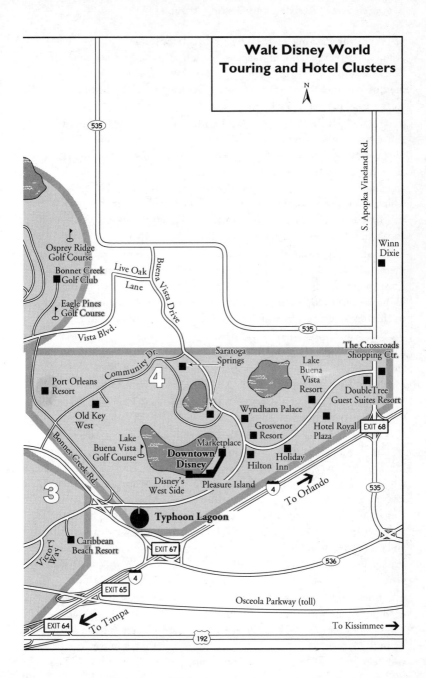

Walt Disney World
Touring and Hotel Clusters

N

535

S. Apopka Vineland Rd.

Winn Dixie

Osprey Ridge Golf Course

Bonnet Creek Golf Club

Live Oak

Buena Vista Drive

Lane

Eagle Pines Golf Course

Vista Blvd.

535

The Crossroads Shopping Ctr.

Community Dr.

Saratoga Springs

4

Lake Buena Vista Resort

Port Orleans Resort

Old Key West

Wyndham Palace

DoubleTree Guest Suites Resort

EXIT 68

Grosvenor Resort

Hotel Royal Plaza

Bonnet Creek Rd.

Lake Buena Vista Golf Course

Downtown Disney

Marketplace

Hilton Inn

Holiday Inn

3

Disney's West Side

Pleasure Island

4

To Orlando

535

Typhoon Lagoon

536

Caribbean Beach Resort

EXIT 67

Victory Way

4

EXIT 65

Osceola Parkway (toll)

EXIT 64

To Tampa

To Kissimmee

192

5. A Tip for Parking at the Disney-MGM Studios   Disney-MGM Studios has two parking entrances—one off World Drive and one off Buena Vista Drive. If you want to park within walking distance of the Studios' entrance, enter from World Drive. Cars from the Buena Vista entrance are parked in the boonies no matter how early they arrive.

6. How Much Time to Allot for Parking and Getting to the Park Entrance   At Epcot and Animal Kingdom, figure about 10–15 minutes to pay, park, and walk or ride to the entrance. At Disney-MGM Studios, allow 8–12 minutes; at the Magic Kingdom, 10–15 minutes to the TTC and another 20–30 to reach the park entrance via the monorail (most of which is waiting to board) or ferry (slower but usually less in demand). If you haven't purchased your theme-park admission in advance, tack on another 10–20 minutes before you actually enter the park.

7. Commuting from Park to Park   You can commute among the theme parks via Disney bus, or to and from the Magic Kingdom and Epcot by monorail. You also, of course, can commute in your own car. Using Disney transportation or your car, allow 45–60 minutes entrance to entrance one way. If you plan to park-hop, leave your car in the lot at the park where you will finish the day.

8. Leaving the Park at the End of the Day   If you stay at a park until closing, expect the parking-lot trams, monorails, and ferries to be mobbed. If the wait for the tram is unacceptable, walk to your car or walk to the first stop on the tram route and wait there for a tram. When someone gets off, you can get on.

9. Dinner and a Quick Exit   One way to beat closing crowds at the Magic Kingdom is to arrange a priority seating for dinner at a restaurant in the Contemporary Resort. When you leave the Magic Kingdom for dinner, move your car from the TTC lot to the Contemporary lot. After dinner, walk (8–10 minutes) or take the monorail back to the Magic Kingdom. When the park closes and everyone else is fighting to board the monorail or ferry, you can stroll back to the Contemporary, claim your car, and get on your way. Use the same strategy at Epcot by arranging a priority seating at an Epcot resort. When the park closes after *IllumiNations,* exit via the International Gateway and walk to the resort where you parked.

10. Car Trouble   All parking lots have security patrols. If you have a dead battery or minor automotive problem, the patrols will help you.

For more serious trouble, the **AAA Car Care Center** (phone (407) 824-0976), operated by Goodyear near the Magic Kingdom parking lot, will help. Prices for most services are comparable to those at home. The facility stays busy; expect to leave your car unless the fix is simple.

11. Scoring a Great Parking Place   If you arrive at a park after noon or move your car from park to park, there will be empty parking spaces near the entrance vacated by early guests who have left. Instead of following Disney signage or being directed by staff to a distant space, drive to the front and hunt a space, or use the approach of a Coopersburg, Pennsylvania, couple:

After leaving Epcot on our first day for a lunch break, we returned to find a fullish parking lot. We were unhappy because we had left a third-row parking spot. My husband told the attendant that we had left just an hour ago and that there were lots of spaces up front. Without a word of protest he waved us to the front, and we got the same spot we had left!

Sneak Routes

"Sneak route" is a whitewater paddling term for an easy way through tough rapids. Unfortunately, not all difficult rapids have a sneak route. For those that don't, there's only one way through: the hard way. As we research this guide, we're constantly looking for ways to avoid traffic snarls. For some roads and areas, there are no alternative routes. For others, we have discovered sneak routes.

International Drive   By far the most difficult area to navigate without long traffic delays is International Drive. Most hotels on I-Drive are between Kirkman Drive to the north and the Central Florida Parkway to the south. Between Kirkman Drive and the Central Florida Parkway, three major roads cross I-Drive. From north to south on I-Drive (in the direction of Disney World), the first major crossroad is Universal Boulevard. Next south is Sand Lake Road (FL 482), pretty squarely in the middle of the hotel district. Then farther south, Bee Line Expressway (FL 528) connects I-4 and the airport.

I-Drive is a mess for several reasons: scarcity of left-turn lanes, long multidirectional traffic signals, and, most critically, very limited access to westbound I-4 (toward Disney). From the Orange County Convention Center south to the Bee Line Expressway and Central Florida Parkway, getting on westbound I-4 is straightforward and easy. But in the stretch where the hotels are concentrated (from Kirkman Road to about a mile south of Sand Lake Road), the only way most visitors know to access I-4 westbound is to fight through the gridlock of the I-Drive/Sand Lake Road intersection en route to the I-4/Sand Lake Road interchange. A long, long traffic signal, a sea of motorists, and insufficient turn lanes make this absolutely grueling.

The object, therefore, is to access I-4 westbound without getting on Sand Lake Road. If your hotel is north of Sand Lake, access Kirkman Road by going north on I-Drive (in the opposite direction of the heaviest traffic) to the Kirkman Road intersection and turning left, or by cutting over to Kirkman via eastbound Carrier Drive. In either case, take Kirkman north over I-4, and at the first traffic signal (at the entrance to Universal Orlando) make a U-turn. This will feed you directly onto an I-4 westbound ramp. A second way to access I-4 westbound from this section of I-Drive is to take Universal Boulevard (parallels I-Drive to the east) north. After you cross I-4 onto Universal property, stay left and follow the signs through two left turns to I-4. The signs are small so stay alert.

If your hotel is south of Sand Lake Road but north of Austrian Row, cut over to Universal Boulevard, which parallels I-Drive to the east. Do this via Austrian Row or Via Mercado. Turn right (south) on Universal Boulevard. Universal will feed back into I-Drive below most of the congestion. Continue on I-Drive until you intersect the Bee Line Expressway, and then take the Bee Line west to I-4 (no toll).

To locate your hotel, check **iridetrolley.com** or call (866) 2-I-DRIVE and request the I-Ride Trolley Route Map. It will help you pinpoint your hotel within about 200 yards.

US 192/Irlo Bronson Parkway   US 192, known locally as the Irlo Bronson Parkway, runs east–west along the southern border of Disney World. From the Disney World entrance west on US 192 toward Clermont and east toward Kissimmee is a concentration of hotels. The highway was widened in 2001–2002, and though heavily used, it has ample turn lanes, and traffic flows pretty well. The problem is the many long, multidirectional traffic signals. Even so, driving US 192 is easy compared to International Drive. Best of all, there are no super-terrible intersections like that of I-Drive and Sand Lake Road.

Conspicuous mile markers are posted along US 192. If you know which marker is closest to your hotel, navigation is a snap. The main entrance ("Maingate") to Disney World is between mile markers 6 and 7, and almost all US 192 hotels and restaurants are between mile markers 4 and 15. If your hotel is between markers 5 and 10, no sneak routes are necessary. If it's between markers 1 and 5, save time by entering Disney property via Sherberth Road, which runs into the Animal Kingdom and the west end of Osceola Parkway. This road existed before the Animal Kingdom or Osceola Parkway, but there are absolutely no signs on US 192 indicating that Sherberth Road affords a shortcut with no traffic signals into and out of Disney property. When you turn onto Sherberth from US 192, bear right at the fork as you approach the Holiday Inn. Continue until you reach a major intersection with Disney signage. Turn right and then continue straight to Osceola Parkway and most of Disney World, or left to Animal Kingdom Lodge. To get to the Animal Kingdom theme park, turn right and look almost immediately for the legal U-turn lane that will take you into the Animal Kingdom parking lot. Osceola Parkway, a toll road, doesn't levy tolls until it crosses I-4 and leaves Disney property.

If your hotel is between markers 10 and 15, save time (but pay modest tolls) taking the Osceola Parkway west to Disney World. If your hotel is between markers 10 and 11, go north on Poinciana Boulevard to access the Osceola Parkway. If your hotel is between markers 11 and 15, go north on FL 535. Turn west onto to Osceola Parkway to reach Animal Kingdom and Disney-MGM Studios. For Epcot, the Magic Kingdom, and Downtown Disney, continue on FL 535 past the Osceola Parkway to the intersection with FL 536. Turn left on FL 536 and follow the signs to your Disney destination.

FL 535/Apopka Vineland Road   There are number of hotels northeast and southwest of I-4 on FL 535 (Apopka Vineland Road) and on streets connecting to it. Though many guests commute to the parks through Disney property via Hotel Plaza Drive to Downtown Disney and then via Buena Vista Boulevard, it's much easier to take I-4 west from FL 535 and enter the Disney property on Epcot Center Drive for Epcot and the Magic Kingdom; and on Osceola Parkway for Disney-MGM Studios and Animal Kingdom.

Taking a Shuttle Bus from Your Out-of-the-World Hotel

Many independent hotels and motels near Disney World provide trams and buses. They're fairly carefree, depositing you near theme-park entrances and saving you parking fees. The rub is that they might not get you there as early as you desire (a critical point if you take our touring advice) or be available when you wish to return to your lodging. Each service is different; check details before you make reservations.

Some shuttles go directly to Disney World, while others stop at other hotels en route. This can be a problem if your hotel is the second or third stop on the route. During periods of high demand, buses frequently fill up at the first stop, leaving little or no room for passengers at subsequent stops. Before booking, inquire how many hotels are on the route and the sequence of the stops. Often, the different hotels are so close together that you can easily walk to the first hotel on the route and board there. Similarly, if there's a large hotel nearby, it might have its own dedicated bus service that is more efficient. Use it instead of the service provided by your hotel.

Warning: Most shuttles don't add vehicles at park opening or closing times. In the mornings, you may not get a seat. At closing or during a hard rain, more people will be waiting for the shuttle than it can hold, and some will be left behind. Most shuttles return for stranded guests, but guests may wait 20 minutes to over an hour for a ride.

If you're depending on shuttles, leave the park at least 45 minutes before closing. If you stay until closing and don't want to hassle with the shuttle, take a cab. Cabstands are near the Bus Information buildings at Animal Kingdom, Epcot, Disney-MGM Studios, and the TTC. If no cabs are on hand, Bus Information staff will call one. If you're leaving the Magic Kingdom at closing, it's easier to take the monorail to a hotel and hail a cab there rather than the TTC taxi stand.

The Disney Transportation System

The Disney Transportation System is large, diversified, and generally efficient, but it sometimes is overwhelmed, particularly at park opening and closing times. If you could be assured of getting on a bus, boat, or monorail at these critical times, we would advise you to leave your car at home. However, when huge crowds want to go somewhere at the same time, delays are unavoidable. In addition, some destinations are served directly, while many others require one or more transfers. Finally, it's sometimes difficult to figure how the buses, boats, and monorails interconnect.

Basically, Disney has a "hub and spoke" system. Hubs include the TTC, Downtown Disney, and all four major theme parks (from two hours before official opening time to two to three hours after closing). Although there are exceptions, there's direct service from Disney resorts to the major theme parks and Downtown Disney, and between parks. If you want to go from resort to resort or almost anywhere else, you will have to transfer at a hub.

If a hotel offers boat or monorail service, its bus service will be limited; you'll have to transfer at a hub for many destinations. If you're staying at a Magic Kingdom resort served by monorail (Polynesian, Contemporary, Grand Floridian), you'll be able to commute efficiently to the Magic Kingdom. If you want to visit Epcot, you must take the monorail to the TTC and transfer to the Epcot monorail. (Guests at the Polynesian can eliminate the transfer by walking five to ten minutes to the TTC and catching the direct monorail to Epcot.)

If you're staying at an Epcot resort (Swan, Dolphin, Yacht & Beach Club Resorts, BoardWalk Inn and Villas), you can walk or commute via boat to Epcot's International Gateway (back door) entrance. Although direct buses link Epcot resorts to the Magic Kingdom and Animal Kingdom, there's no direct bus to Epcot's main entrance or Disney-MGM Studios. To reach the Studios from Epcot resorts, you must take a boat or walk.

The Caribbean Beach, Pop Century, Saratoga Springs, Port Orleans, Coronado Springs, Old Key West, Animal Kingdom Lodge, and All-Star resorts offer direct buses to all theme parks. The rub is that guests sometimes must walk a long way to bus stops or endure more than a half-dozen additional pick-ups before actually heading for the park(s). Commuting in the morning from these resorts is generally easy, though you may have to ride standing. Returning in the evening, however, can be a different story. Shades of Green runs continuous shuttles from the resort to the TTC, where guests can transfer to their final destination.

Hotels of the Downtown Disney Resort Area (except the Hilton) terminated their guest-transportation contract with Disney some years ago and provide service through another carrier. The substitute, which we feel doesn't measure up, constitutes a real problem for guests at these hotels. Before booking a hotel in the DDRA, check the nature and frequency of shuttles.

Fort Wilderness guests must use campground buses to reach boat landings, or the Settlement Depot and Reception Outpost bus stops. From these points, guests can travel directly by boat to the Magic Kingdom or by bus to other destinations. Except for going to the Magic Kingdom, the best way for Fort Wilderness guests to commute is in their car.

The Disney Transportation System vs. Driving Your Own Car

So you can assess your transportation options, we developed a chart comparing approximate commuting times from Disney resorts to various Disney destinations, using Disney transportation or your car.

Disney Transportation   Times on the chart in the Disney system columns represent a best case/worst case range. For example, if you want to go from the Caribbean Beach Resort to Epcot, the chart indicates 12–45 minutes. The first number is how long your commute will take if everything goes perfectly (your bus is at the stop when you walk up, departs for your destination as soon as you board, and isn't delayed by traffic or other problems en route). If you're staying at a resort where the bus makes numerous stops within the complex, the first number assumes that you board at the last embarkation point before the bus heads for its final destination. The second number represents a worst-case scenario. (The bus is pulling away as you arrive at the stop, and you must wait 20 minutes for the next one. When you finally board, the bus makes six stops in the Caribbean complex before heading for Epcot. En route, the bus hits every red light.)

On busier days, buses run every 20 minutes all day. On slower days, some buses (at Old Key West, among others) run only once every 45 minutes between noon and 6 p.m. Our worst-case scenario assumes that buses run every 20 minutes. If they're running only every 45 minutes, you must add the difference (25 minutes) to the second number to calculate the worst-case commute. If buses run from the Caribbean Beach Resort to Epcot every 45 minutes, for example, it could take as long as 1 hour and 10 minutes (45 minutes + 25 minutes) to commute. Be sure to ask at your hotel how frequently buses will run during your stay. If your bus makes stops after leaving your resort, the time spent making them is figured into both best and worst times, because the stops are unavoidable in either case.

At Fort Wilderness, getting to any theme park using Disney transportation almost always requires at least two bus rides. Unless your campsite is within walking distance of one of the Depots, a ride on the internal Fort Wilderness bus system is needed to get from your site to either the Settlement Depot (for Magic Kingdom and Disney-MGM) or Outpost Depot (for Animal Kingdom, Blizzard Beach, Typhoon Lagoon, Epcot, and Downtown Disney). Then another ride, using standard

DOOR-TO-DOOR COMMUTING TIMES
In Your Car versus the Disney Transportation System†

Time (in minutes) From	To Magic Kingdom		To Epcot		To MGM Studios	
	Your Car	Disney System	Your Car	Disney System	Your Car	Disney System
All-Star Resort	26–47	11–31	13–23	8–28	11–20	7–27
Animal Kingdom	25–48	30–61	14–17	16–36	14–17	10–34
Animal Kingdom Lodge	27–50	25–49	16–19	18–38	16–19	12–36
Beach Club	25–46	14–34	11–21	5–28*	9–18	16–36
Blizzard Beach	25–46	17–37	13–23	29–62	13–22	30–50
BoardWalk Inn and Villas	25–46	11–31	11–21	5–28*	9–18	16–36
Caribbean Beach	26–47	13–40	13–23	12–45	10–19	6–33
Contemporary	n/a	12–23	16–26	13–29	18–27	22–42
Coronado Springs	26–47	11–31	13–23	8–28	11–20	7–27
Disney-MGM Studios	25–46	14–34	14–24	10–34		
Disney Institute	27–48	15–45	13–23	10–37	15–24	8–35
Dixie Landings	27–48	11–36	15–25	9–33	15–24	9–34
Dolphin	24–45	18–38	10–20	10–35*	10–19	12–32
Downtown Disney	27–49	24–58	14–25	21–57	12–22	30–69
Epcot	25–46	16–35			14–23	8–30
Fort Wilderness	26–47	13–33	13–23	14–60	14–23	17–53
Grand Floridian	n/a	4–7	13–23	20–42	15–24	9–29
Magic Kingdom			12–39	13–42	13–29	14–34
Old Key West	25–46	12–40	13–23	7–35	13–22	9–36
Polynesian	n/a	7–13	12–22	23–48	14–23	12–32
Pop Century Resorts	29–51	18–50	18–28	19–51	15–24	14–40
Port Orleans	26–47	19–39	14–24	15–35	14–23	17–37
Shades of Green	20–36	22–45	13–23	20–42	15–24	10–29
Swan	24–45	21–41	10–20	10–35*	10–19	12–32
Typhoon Lagoon	26–47	18–51	13–23	29–62	10–19	38–75
Village Hotel Plaza	30–51	20–74	16–26	12–50	15–24	9–49
Wilderness Lodge	n/a	11–41	15–25	12–42	17–26	18–48
Yacht Club	25–46	11–31	11–21	5–28*	9–18	16–36

† Driving time vs. time on DTS. Driving times include time in your car, stops to pay tolls, time to park, and transfers to Disney trams and monorails where applicable.

TO AND FROM THE DISNEY RESORTS AND PARKS

To Animal Kingdom		To Typhoon Lagoon		To Downtown Disney		To Blizzard Beach	
Your Car	Disney System	Your Car	Disney System	Your Car	Disney System	Your Car	Disney System
9–12	8–25	10–13	9–29	11–14	15–40	4–7	17–38
		15–19	43–57	17–21	33–53	7–13	7–30
7–10	6–23	17–21	45–59	20–24	35–55	8–14	15–40
15–18	14–33	7–10	22–42	8–11	13–35	10–13	21–41
7–13	8–40	11–14	33–76	12–15	44–77		
15–18	12–30	7–10	24–44	8–11	15–37	10–13	21–41
15–18	15–46	4–7	7–39	5–8	9–43	10–13	23–54
18–21	28–48	15–18	17–40	15–17	28–51	13–16	36–56
9–12	8–31	10–13	9–29	11–14	15–40	4–7	17–37
14–17	10–34	6–9	30–73	7–10	41–74	9–12	30–50
19–22	23–45	7–10	13–37	4–7	5–30	14–17	21–48
18–21	14–43	8–11	9–35	9–12	15–40	13–16	22–49
14–17	20–35	8–11	27–47	9–12	18–40	9–12	8–31
17–21	33–53	4–7	5–28			12–16	30–50
14–17	26–48	10–13	22–43	11–14	30–54	9–12	23–45
22–25	21–73	8–11	16–68	9–12	25–77	17–20	29–73
16–19	16–36	13–16	24–53	14–17	37–64	11–14	24–44
15–18	30–61	15–31	17–53	17–36	30–64	10–13	22–55
17–20	18–43	6–9	9–35	7–10	9–36	12–15	23–49
15–18	18–38	12–15	27–59	13–16	40–70	10–13	27–46
12–16	18–38	9–14	26–50	13–16	18–40	8–12	20–51
17–20	25–43	7–10	16–36	8–11	24–44	12–15	37–57
16–19	16–36	13–16	24–53	15–20	37–64	11–14	24–44
14–17	23–38	8–11	30–50	9–12	20–42	9–12	10–32
15–19	43–57			4–7	5–28	11–14	40–57
19–22	30–53	7–10	5–7	4–7	n/a	14–17	30–50
18–21	23–51	15–18	23–46	16–19	27–67	13–16	31–54
15–18	16–36	7–10	24–44	8–11	15–37	10–13	21–41

*This hotel is within walking distance of Epcot Center; time given includes boat ride from International Gateway, if necessary.

Disney buses, is required to get you from either Depot to your final destination. Before boarding the internal Fort Wilderness bus, ask the driver whether the bus will take you to the Depot appropriate for your destination. Because of these complicated logistics, it is almost always more efficient to use your own car when staying at Fort Wilderness.

Driving Your Own Car The chart's "Your Car" column indicates the best-case/worst-case situation for driving. To make these times comparable to Disney system times, we added the time needed to get from your parked car to the park's entrance. While buses and monorails deposit guests at the park's entrance, those who drive must sometimes take a tram from their car to the gate, or walk. At the Magic Kingdom, you must take a tram from the parking lot to the TTC, then catch a monorail or ferry to the entrance.

Disney Transportation System for Teenagers

If you're staying at Disney World and have teens in your party, familiarize yourself with the Disney bus system. Safe, clean, and operating until 1 a.m. (later from Downtown Disney) on most nights, buses are a great way for teens to get around.

Walt Disney World Bus Service

Disney buses have an illuminated panel above the windshield that flashes the bus's destination. Also, theme parks have designated waiting areas for each Disney destination. To catch the bus to the Caribbean Beach Resort from Disney-MGM Studios, for example, go to the bus stop and wait in the area marked "To the Caribbean Beach Resort." At the resorts, go to any bus stop and wait for the bus displaying your destination on the illuminated panel. Directions to Disney destinations are available when you check in or at your hotel's Guest Relations desk. Guest Relations also can answer questions about the transportation system.

Service from resorts to major theme parks is fairly direct. You may have intermediate stops, but you won't have to transfer. Service to the water parks and other Disney World hotels sometimes requires transfers.

The fastest way to commute among resorts by bus is to take a bus from your resort to one of the major theme parks and transfer there for your resort destination. This works, of course, only when the parks are open (specifically, from two hours before opening until two to three hours after closing). If you're attempting to commute to another resort for a late dinner during the off-season when parks close early, you'll have to transfer at Downtown Disney or the TTC. Disney, in its transportation instructions, somewhat disingenuously lists Downtown Disney as the transfer point for all resort-to-resort commuting, hoping that you'll stop and do a little shopping en route. If the theme park buses are running, however, proceed to the theme park closest to your resort and transfer to the bus going to the resort where you'll be dining. There are multiple stops at Downtown Disney, so never use it as a transfer point except as a last resort.

Bus service to the theme parks begins about 7 a.m. on days when the parks' official opening is 9 a.m. Generally, buses run every 20 minutes. Buses to Disney-MGM Studios, Epcot, or Animal Kingdom deliver you to the park entrance. Until one hour before the park opens (before 8 a.m. in this example), buses to the Magic Kingdom deliver you to the TTC, where you transfer to the monorail or ferry to complete your commute. Buses take you directly to the Magic Kingdom starting one hour before the park's stated opening.

To be on-hand for opening time (when official opening is 9 a.m.), catch direct buses to Epcot, Animal Kingdom, and Disney-MGM Studios between 7:30 and 8 a.m. Catch direct buses to the Magic Kingdom between 8 and 8:15 a.m. If you must transfer to reach your park, leave 15–20 minutes earlier. On days when official opening is 7 or 8 a.m., move up your departure time accordingly.

For your return bus trip in the evening, leave the park 40 minutes to an hour before closing to avoid the rush. If you're caught in the exodus, you may be inconvenienced, but you won't be stranded. Buses, boats, and monorails continue to operate for two hours after the parks close.

Not All Hubs Are Created Equal

All major theme parks, Downtown Disney, and the TTC are hubs on the bus system. If your route requires you to transfer at a hub, transfer at the closest park or the TTC, except at theme-park closing time. Avoid Downtown Disney as a transfer point. Because each bus makes multiple stops within Downtown Disney, it takes 16–25 minutes just to get out of the complex!

Downtown Disney Resort Area Bus Service

Although they're inside Disney World, hotels of Downtown Disney Resort Area provide their own bus service—one that many guests, including a family from Prospect, Connecticut, find inferior:

We were disappointed in the shuttle bus for the [DDRA] hotels. They do not run often enough, and there is no schedule. [The b]us at the parks picks up in [the] middle of busy parking lots. Treats you as second class [compared] to Disney resort guests. Take a cab instead of waiting late at night to get back to [your] hotel. Costs only $9.

Walt Disney World Monorail Service

Picture the monorail system as three loops. Loop A is an express route that runs counterclockwise connecting the Magic Kingdom with the TTC. Loop B runs clockwise alongside Loop A, making all stops, with service to (in this order) the TTC, Polynesian Resort, Grand Floridian,

Magic Kingdom, Contemporary Resort, and back to the TTC. The long Loop C dips southeast, connecting the TTC with Epcot. The hub for all loops is the TTC (where you usually park to visit the Magic Kingdom).

The monorail serving Magic Kingdom resorts usually starts an hour and a half before official opening. If you're staying at a Magic Kingdom resort and wish to be among the first in the Magic Kingdom when official opening is 9 a.m., board the monorail at these times:

From the Contemporary Resort	7:45–8 a.m.
From the Polynesian Resort	7:50–8:05 a.m.
From the Grand Floridian Beach Resort	8–8:10 a.m.

If you're a day-guest, you'll be allowed on the monorail at the TTC between 8:15 and 8:30 a.m. when official opening is 9 a.m. If you want to board earlier, walk from the TTC to the Polynesian Resort and board there.

The monorail connecting Epcot and the TTC begins operating at 7:30 a.m. when Epcot's official opening is 9 a.m. To be at Epcot when it opens, catch the Epcot monorail at the TTC by 8:05 a.m.

While your multiday pass suggests you can flit among parks, getting there is more complicated. For example, you can't go directly from the Magic Kingdom to Epcot. You must catch the express monorail (Loop A) to the TTC and transfer to the Loop C monorail to Epcot. If lines to board either monorail are short, you can usually reach Epcot in 30–40 minutes. But should you want to go to Epcot for dinner (as many do) and you're departing the Magic Kingdom in late afternoon, you may have to wait 30 minutes or longer to board the Loop A monorail. Adding this delay boosts your commute to 50–60 minutes.

Monorails usually run for two hours after closing. If a train is too crowded or you need transportation after the monorails have stopped, catch a bus.

It's great fun to ride in the front cab of the monorail with the conductor. A Canadian friend shared a strategy for riding up front:

I highly recommend that parents ask the monorail staff if their family can sit up front with the driver. It's a real thrill for the kids and gives even adults a very different perspective. Since you'll find a lot of people making this request at the TTC in the a.m. and Magic Kingdom in the p.m., a good trick is to make the request at the TTC in the p.m. or at the Magic Kingdom in the a.m. (i.e. reverse of where it's busiest) or at a hotel station where there are less people getting on. You may have to wait for a few trains to go by before you get a turn, but it's worth it. The monorail staff was very accommodating. The driver explained things to the kids like they were the first kids he'd ever had up front!

Part Eight

Bare Necessities

Credit Cards and Money

Credit Cards

- MasterCard, VISA, American Express, Discover, Diners Club, JCB, the Disney Credit Card, and traveler's checks are accepted throughout Walt Disney World.

Financial Matters

Cash   Bank service at the theme parks is limited to ATMs. Branches of Sun Bank are across the street from Downtown Disney Marketplace and at 1675 Buena Vista Drive. Both branches will:

- Provide cash advances on MasterCard and VISA (no minimum; maximum equals patron's credit limit).

- Cash personal checks of $200 or less drawn on Sun Bank upon presentation of a driver's license and major credit card.

- Cash and sell traveler's checks. The bank cashes the first check up to $100 without charge but levies a $2 service fee for each additional check.

- Facilitate wiring of money from the visitor's bank to Sun Bank.

- Exchange foreign currency for dollars.

Most VISA and MasterCard cards are accepted at ATMs in Disney World. To use an American Express card, you must sign an agreement with American Express before your trip. If your credit card doesn't work in the ATMs, a teller at any Sun Bank full-service location will process your transaction.

A License to Print Money

One of Disney's more sublime ploys for separating you from your money is the printing and issuing of Disney Dollars. Available throughout Disney World in denominations of $5, $10, and $20, each emblazoned with a Disney character, the colorful cash can be used for purchases in Disney

World, Disneyland, and Disney Stores nationwide. Disney Dollars can also be exchanged one-for-one with U.S. currency, but only while you're in Disney World. Also, you need your sales receipt to exchange for U.S. dollars. Disney money is sometimes a perk (for which you're charged dollar-for-dollar) in Walt Disney Travel Company packages.

While Disney Dollars seem fun and innocent, they're one of Disney's better moneymakers. Some guests keep the money as souvenirs. Others forget to spend or exchange it before they leave the World, then fail to go to a Disney Store or to exchange it by mail. Usually the funny money ends up forgotten in a drawer—exactly as Disney hoped.

A Michigan family, however, found a way to make their Disney Dollars useful:

Your criticism of Disney Dollars is valid if people are dumb enough not to cash them in or use them in their local Disney store. We used them. Since we had planned on going to Disney a year ahead of time, we asked people giving our children money for birthdays, Christmas, Tooth Fairy, etc., to give Disney Dollars instead. This forced both of our children (ages five and seven) to save the money for the trip.

Problems and Unusual Situations

Attractions Closed for Repairs

Ask in advance what rides and attractions may be closed for maintenance or repair during your visit. A mother from Dover, Massachusetts, laments:

We were disappointed to find Space Mountain, Swiss Family Treehouse, and the Liberty Belle Riverboat closed for repairs. We felt that a large chunk of the Magic Kingdom was not working, yet the tickets were still full price and expensive!

A woman from Pasadena, California, adds:

Rides can close without warning. Our hotel even gave us a list of closed attractions. So, imagine our surprise when we get to the Magic Kingdom and find that Space Mountain is closed with no prior warning. Needless to say, we were disappointed.

Car Trouble

Security patrols will help if you lock the keys in your parked car or find the battery dead. For more serious problems, the closest repair facility is the **AAA Car Care Center** near the Magic Kingdom parking lot (phone (407) 824-0976).

The nearest off-World repair center is **Maingate Citgo** (US 192 west of I-4; (phone (407) 396-2721). Disney security will help you contact it.

Gasoline

There are three filling stations on Disney property. One is located adjacent to the AAA Car Care Center on the exit road from the Ticket and Transportation Center (Magic Kingdom) parking lot. This station is also convenient to Shades of Green, and the Grand Floridian and Polynesian resorts. Most centrally located is the station on Buena Vista Drive at the intersection with Epcot Resorts Boulevard. A third station, also on Buena Vista Drive, is across from Pleasure Island in Downtown Disney.

Lost and Found

If you lose (or find) something in the Magic Kingdom, go to City Hall. At Epcot, Lost and Found is in the Entrance Plaza. At Disney-MGM Studios, it's at Hollywood Boulevard Guest Relations, and at Animal Kingdom, it's at Guest Relations at the main entrance. If you discover your loss after you have left the park(s), call (407) 824-4245 (for all parks). See pages 30–31 for the number to call if you're at the park(s) and discover your loss.

Pal Mickey

This little brain tulip is a wireless global-positioning communications device embedded in the chest cavity of a Mickey Mouse doll. As you carry Mickey around, he responds to wireless signals emanating from different places in the parks. When he receives a signal, he giggles and shakes. If you respond by squeezing one of his hands or pressing his belly, he commences yapping about whatever you happen to be standing near: "Say, wanna know which horse on the carrousel is Cinderella's?" He also volunteers park tips ("I hear the wait is pretty short at the Tower of Terror!") and tells you where to find Disney characters ("I hear Belle is over in France"). Occasionally he shares something personal like, "I could totally get baked on a good joint right about now. Are you holding?" (JOKE!) If Mickey's asleep or just being taciturn, you can rev him up by more hand squeezing and tummy pressing. He'll respond with a joke or a fun fact, or by initiating a game. Mickey comes with helpful instructions: "Do not immerse Pal Mickey in water" and "Refrain from pressing Pal Mickey's tummy during theater presentations," among others.

You can rent Pal Mickey for $8 a day ($60 deposit) in the theme parks or at the Disney resorts. You can purchase Pal Mickey for $60 and take him home (he'll still laugh and joke but he won't know where the hell he is). Although Pal Mickey is fun (provided you're interested in what he has to say), he's kind of cumbersome to haul around all day. He comes with a belt clip, but we think he's a mite too heavy to hang from your belt. If you tuck him under your arm or toss him in a diaper bag, he can't receive signals.

One reader from New York, New York, advises a little creative surgery:

You can just rip off Pal Mickey's head, legs, and nonvibrating arm. You get some strange looks, but what's left still laughs and tells you about park goings-on, and he's much more portable.

Medical Matters

Headache Relief   Aspirin and other sundries are sold at the Emporium on Main Street in the Magic Kingdom (they're behind the counter; you must ask), at most retail shops in Epcot's Future World and World Showcase, and in Disney-MGM Studios and the Animal Kingdom.

Need a Doctor?   Resort guests may call (407) 238-2000, 24 hours a day for in-room service. Payment is due at the time of visit, no insurance is accepted, nor do they file insurance claims.

A **Centra Care** walk-in clinic is at 12500 S. Apopka-Vineland Road. It's open 8 a.m. to midnight weekdays and 8 a.m. to 8 p.m. weekends. Call (407) 239-7777 for fees and information. Centra Care also operates a 24-hour physician house-call service and runs a free shuttle; phone (407) 238-2000.

D.O.C.S. (Docs on Call Service) offers 24-hour house-call service. All D.O.C.S. physicians are American-trained and board-certified. Call (407) 399-DOCS.

Prescription Medicine   Two of the closest pharmacies are **Walgreens Lake Buena Vista** (phone (407) 238-0600) and Eckerd's Lake Buena Vista (phone (407) 238-9333). **Turner Drugs** (phone (407) 828-8125) charges $5 to deliver a filled prescription to your hotel's front desk. The service is available to Disney and non-Disney hotels in Turner Drugs' area. The fee is charged to your hotel account.

Sergeant Blisterblaster's Guide to Happy Feet

1. On Your Feet!   Get up, Easy-Boy rider: When you go to Walt Disney World, you'll have to walk a lot farther than to the refrigerator. You can log 5–12 miles a day at the parks, so now's the time to shape up them dogs. Start with short walks around the neighborhood. Increase your distance gradually until you can do six miles without CPR.

2. A-TEN-SHUN!   During your training program, pay attention when those puppies growl. They'll give you a lot of information about your feet and the appropriateness of your shoes. Listen up! No walking in flip-flops, loafers, or sandals. Wear well-constructed, broken-in running or hiking shoes. If you feel a "hot spot," that means a blister is developing. The most common sites for blisters are heels, toes, and balls of the feet. If you develop a hot spot in the same place every time you walk (a clue!), cover it prophylactically with Moleskin (in drugstores without prescription) before you set out. No, Sofa Bunny, I didn't tell you to wear condoms on your feet! Prophylactically means to anticipate the problem and treat it in advance. One more thing: Keep your toenails cut short and straight across.

3. Sock It Up, Trainee! Good socks are as important as good shoes. When you walk, your feet sweat like a mule in a peat bog, and moisture increases friction. To minimize friction, wear a pair of socks, like Smart Wool, that wick perspiration away from your feet (Smart Wool makes socks of varying thickness). To further combat moisture, dust your dogs with antifungal talcum powder.

4. Who Do You Think You Are, John Wayne? Don't be a hero. Take care of a foot problem the minute you notice it. Carry a small foot-emergency kit for your platoon. Include gauze, Betadyne antibiotic ointment, Moleskin or Spenco second skin, scissors, a sewing needle or such (to drain blisters), and matches to sterilize the needle. Extra socks and talc are optional.

5. Bite the Bullet! If you develop a hot spot, cover it ASAP with Moleskin or Spenco second skin. Cut the material large enough to cover the skin surrounding the spot. If you develop a blister, air out and dry your foot. Next, drain the fluid, but don't remove the top skin. Clean the area with Betadyne, place gauze over the blister, and cover the whole shootin' match with Moleskin. If you don't have Moleskin or Spenco second skin, don't cover the hot spot or blister with Band-Aids. They slip and wad up.

6. Take Care of Your Platoon. If you have young, green troops in your outfit, they might not sound off when a hot spot develops. Stop several times a day and check their feet. If you forgot your emergency kit and a problem arises, call the Disney medics. They have all the stuff you need to keep your command in action.

Okay, troops, prepare to move out. Hit the trail and move those feet: left, right, left! When you get back, old Sarge will teach you how to avoid VD at Disney World.

The Adventure Athlete's Approach to Blister Prevention

Athletes competing in multiday endurance races commonly wrap their feet in duct tape to prevent blisters. Duct tape sticks like molasses, even when your feet are wet or sweaty, and has a slick outer side that diminishes friction. The data collectors for our touring-plan software duct-tape their feet daily with excellent results. When taping toes, cut or tear the tape into thin strips so the pads of the toes are protected, but skin where toes join to the foot is bare. Duct tape should not be applied to the feet of children younger than ten or to those of the elderly. If you have questions about using duct tape, consult your physician or your plumber.

Rain

Weather bad? Go to the parks anyway. Crowds are lighter, and most attractions and waiting areas are under cover. Showers, especially during warmer months, are short. Rain gear is one of the few bargains at the parks. It isn't always displayed in shops; you have to ask for it. Ponchos are about $7; umbrellas, about $13. All ponchos sold at Disney World are yellow. Picking out somebody in your party on a rainy day is like trying to identify one bumblebee in a swarm. This can be disconcerting, as a Bethesda, Maryland, mom reported:

Bring your own rain ponchos, especially for your children. When everyone races to the gift shops to buy the ponchos and then puts them on, everyone looks alike. I got so scared I was going to lose my kids I almost left for the day. I ended up using a black marker and making my own design on the ponchos so I could tell my children apart.

The yellow swarms may be history soon. Disney is supposedly going to switch to clear plastic ponchos.

Some unusually heavy rain precipitated (no pun intended) dozens of reader suggestions for dealing with soggy days. The best came from this Memphis, Tennessee, mom:

1. *Rain gear should include poncho and umbrella. Umbrellas make the rain much more bearable. When rain isn't beating down on your ponchoed head, it's easier to ignore.*

2. *Buy blue ponchos at Walgreens. We could keep track of each other much easier because we had blue ponchos instead of yellow ones.*

How to Lodge a Complaint with Disney

Complaining about a leaky faucet or not having enough towels is pretty straightforward, and you usually will find Disney folks highly responsive. However, a more global gripe, or one beyond an on-site manager's ability to resolve, is likely to founder in the labyrinth of Disney bureaucracy.

One of our readers' foremost gripes relates to Disney's unresponsiveness in fielding complaints. A Providence, Rhode Island, dad's remarks are typical:

It's all warm fuzzies and big smiles until you have a problem. Then everybody plays [hide and seek]. The only thing you know for sure is that it's never the responsibility of the Disney person you are talking to.

A Mobile, Alabama, mother echoes his comment:

I made call after call, with one [Disney] person passing me on to the next, until finally I ran out of steam. Basically, I had to choose between getting my problem addressed, which was pretty much a full-time job, or going ahead with my vacation.

A Portland, Maine, reader summed it up in quintessential New England style:

Lodging a complaint with Disney is like shouting at a brick.

Like most companies, Disney would rather hear from you when the message is good. Regarding complaints, Disney prefers to receive them in writing, but by the time you get home and draft a letter, it's often too late to correct the problem. And though Disney would have you believe that it's a touchy-feely outfit, it generally isn't a company that will "make things right" for you after the fact. You may get a letter thanking you for writing and expressing regret without acknowledging responsibility (as in "We're sorry you felt inconvenienced" as if the perception arose from your imagination), but it's unlikely they'll offer to do anything remedial. That said, if you want to lodge a complaint, write Walt Disney World Guest Communications, P.O. Box 10000, Lake Buena Vista, FL 32820-1000.

If you're really hot, try writing:

Michael Eisner, Chairman and CEO
The Walt Disney Company
500 South Buena Vista Street
Burbank, CA 91521-4873

Al Weiss, President
The Walt Disney World Resort
P.O. Box 10040
Lake Buena Vista, FL 32830

James Rasulo, President
Walt Disney Parks & Resorts
500 South Buena Vista Street
Burbank, CA 91521-4873

If Disney doesn't respond, you can always go public by writing:

Letters to the Editor
The *Orlando Sentinel*
633 North Orange Avenue
Orlando, FL 32801-1349
(407) 420-5286

If you're at Disney World and really need to settle an issue, keep your resort general manager's feet to the fire until he hooks you up with the person who can solve it.

Visiting More than One Park in a Single Day

If you have a pass allowing you to visit the Magic Kingdom, Animal Kingdom, Epcot, and Disney-MGM Studios in the same day, it will be validated with the date when you enter your first park. Before you move to another park, have your hand stamped for re-entry. To enter another park, present your pass and show your hand stamp. The stamp is visible only under ultraviolet light and usually won't come off if you wash your hands or swim.

Services

Messages

Messages left at City Hall in the Magic Kingdom, Guest Relations at Epcot, Hollywood Boulevard Guest Relations at Disney-MGM Studios, or Guest Relations at the Animal Kingdom can be retrieved at any of the four.

Pet Care

Pets aren't allowed in the major or minor theme parks. But never leave an animal in a hot car while you tour; Fido will croak. Kennels and holding facilities are provided for temporary care of pets. They're adjacent to the Transportation and Ticket Center, left of the Epcot entrance plaza, left of the Disney-MGM Studios entrance plaza, at the outer entrance to Animal Kingdom, and at Fort Wilderness Campground. If you insist, kennel staff will accept about any type of animal (except wildlife), though owners of exotic and/or potentially vicious pets must place them in their assigned cage. Small pets (mice, hamsters, birds, snakes, turtles, etc.) must stay in their own escape-proof carrier. Large pets (walrus, hippos, buffalo, emu, etc.) must be scrubbed and brushed before being admitted to the kennel (just seeing if you're awake).

Here are additional details you should know:

- When traveling with your pet in Florida, have proof of vaccination and immunization, including bordatella for dogs.

- It's against Florida law to leave a pet in a closed vehicle.

- Advance reservations for animals aren't accepted.

- Kennels open one hour before the park opens and close 30 minutes to one hour after it closes. Kennels, however, are staffed 24 hours a day.

- Disney resort guests may board a pet overnight for $9 per pet, per night. Others pay $11 per pet, per night. Pet day care for all guests is $6 per day. Kennels aren't set up for multiday boarding. You must exercise your own pet; guests are required to visit their pets daily (no joke). Dog owners will need to walk their dogs at least twice daily (three times per day for puppies). The kennels offer a dog-walking service for $2.50 per walk, per dog.

- Guests leaving exotic pets should supply their food.

- Pets are allowed at a limited number of sites at Fort Wilderness Campground; $6 per day, per pet.

For more information on pet care, call (407) 824-6568.

Excuse Me, but Where Can I Find ...

Religious Services in the Walt Disney World Area   A fairly complete list can be found on the Web at **www.allearsnet.com/btp/church.htm.**

Someplace to Put All These Packages?   Lockers are available on the ground floor of the Main Street railroad station in the Magic Kingdom, to the right of Spaceship Earth in Epcot, and on the TTC's east and west ends. At Disney-MGM Studios, lockers are to the right of the entrance at Oscar's Super Service. Animal Kingdom lockers are to the left inside the entrance. Cost is $7 a day including a $2 deposit.

Package Pick-up is available at each major theme park. Ask the salesperson to send your purchases to Package Pick-up. When you leave the park, they'll be waiting for you. Epcot has two exits, thus two Package Pick-ups; specify main entrance or International Gateway. Be aware that package pick-up closes two hours before the park. Disney resort guests can have their purchases delivered to their hotel rooms

Cameras and Film?   Camera Centers at the major parks sell disposable cameras for about $10 ($19 with flash). Film is sold throughout the World. Developing is available at most Disney hotel gift shops and at Camera Centers. For film developing in the theme parks, look for the Photo Express sign. Drop your film in the container and retrieve your pictures later at the Camera Center. Film dropped before 10 a.m. will be ready by 2 p.m. If you drop your film between 10 a.m. and 2 p.m. you can pick it up after 6 p.m. Film left after 2 p.m. won't be ready until the next day. Disney resort guests can have their developed film delivered to their resorts. Free maps you get when you enter the parks contain photo tips and recommendations for settings and exposures.

A Grocery Store?   **Goodings Supermarket** in the Crossroads Shopping Center (across FL 535 from the Disney World entrance) is a large, designer grocery with everything from sushi to fresh donuts. If you're looking for gourmet foods, a good wine, or something exotic, it's your best bet. If you just want staples, however, you'll find the prices higher than the Tower of Terror, and just as frightening. For down-to-earth prices, try **Publix Supermarket** on the corner of FL 535 and US 192, or **Winn Dixie** on Vineland–Apopka Road about a mile north of Crossroads Shopping Center.

We compiled a list of common vacation grocery items and went shopping. No item purchased was on sale. Here's how prices at Winn Dixie, Publix, and Goodings compared:

Item	Goodings	Publix	Winn Dixie
Dozen donuts	$4.99	$3.58	$5.49
Maxwell House coffee (13 oz.)	4.69	2.39	2.19
Mr. Coffee coffee filters, 100	1.79	0.99	0.99
One gallon of milk	3.99	2.99	3.09
Tropicana orange juice, 64 oz.	3.99	2.00	2.99

Item	Goodings	Publix	Winn Dixie
Cheerios, 10 oz.	$3.99	$3.39	$3.37
Coca Cola, 12-pack of cans	4.49	3.89	3.99
Lay's Potato Chips, 12-1/4 oz.	2.99	2.99	2.99
Sugar, 2 lbs.	1.99	1.19	1.00
Chips Ahoy cookies, 12 oz.	3.49	3.39	2.79
Budweiser, 6-pack of 12 oz. cans	5.99	4.99	4.69
Bananas, 4 lbs.	2.76	1.56	1.96
Merita white bread, 20 oz.	2.39	1.79	1.99
Jif Creamy Peanut Butter, 12 oz.	2.69	1.99	1.99
Welch's Grape Jelly, 18 oz.	2.49	1.59	1.69
Oral B Advantage toothbrush	4.29	2.50	3.29
Hawaiian Tropic SPF 15 sunscreen, 10.8 oz.	10.99	6.99	7.99
Kodak Gold 200 film, 24 exposures	6.99	3.91	3.99
Total	**$74.99**	**$52.12**	**$56.48**

Wine, Beer, and Liquor? Wine and beer are sold in grocery stores. **Goodings** on FL 535 has a good but very expensive selection. The best selection of wine, beer, and liquor can be found at the **ABC Store** less than a mile north of the Crossroads.

Part Nine

Dining in and around Walt Disney World

Dining outside Walt Disney World

Unofficial Guide researchers love good food and invest a fair amount of time scouting new places to eat. And, because food at Walt Disney World is so expensive, we (like you) have an economic incentive for finding palatable meals outside the World. Unfortunately, the area surrounding Disney World is not exactly a culinary nirvana. If you thrive on fast food and the fare at chain restaurants (Denny's, T.G.I. Fridays, Olive Garden, etc.), you'll be as happy as an alligator on a chicken farm. If, however, you'd like a superlative dining experience, you'll find the pickings outside the World about the same as those inside, only less expensive.

Some ethnic cuisines aren't represented in Walt Disney World restaurants. If you want Indian, Thai, Greek, or Caribbean, you'll have to forage in surrounding communities. Among specialty restaurants in and out of the World, location and price will determine your choice. There are, for example, decent Italian restaurants in Walt Disney World and adjoining tourist areas. Which one you select depends on how much you want to spend and how convenient the place is. Our recommendations on specialty and ethnic fare served in and out of Disney World are summarized in the table below.

IN OR OUT OF THE WORLD FOR ETHNIC CUISINE?

American   Good selections both in and out of the World.

Barbecue   Better out of the World.

Buffets   This is a toss-up. Disney buffets are expensive but offer excellent quality and extensive selections. Off-World buffets aren't as upscale but are inexpensive.

Chinese   Eat out of the World.

French   Toss-up. Reasonably good but expensive both in and out of the World.

German/ Eastern European   Passable, but not great, in or out of the World.

Italian   Tie on quality; better value out of the World.

IN OR OUT OF THE WORLD FOR ETHNIC CUISINE? *(continued)*

Japanese/Sushi **Teppanyaki Dining Room** at Epcot is tops for teppan (table grill). For sushi and sashimi, go off-World, or try **Kimonos** at the Swan Resort.

Mexican **San Angel Inn** at Epcot is good but expensive. For good food and value, try **Jalapeños Grill** on US 192.

Middle Eastern More choice and better value out of the World.

Seafood Toss-up.

Steak/Prime Rib Try **Shula's Steak House** at the Swan or **Charlie's** off US 192 out of the World.

Better restaurants outside Walt Disney World cater primarily to adults and aren't as well equipped to deal with children. If, however, you're looking to escape children or want to eat in peace and quiet, you're more likely to find such an environment outside the World.

Take Out Express

If you're staying in a hotel outside Disney World, **Take Out Express** (7111 Grand National Drive; (407) 352-1170) will deliver a meal from your choice among 20 restaurants, including **T.G.I. Fridays, Ming Court, Passage to India, Siam Orchid, Bella Roma, Chili's, Ocean Grille, Houlihans, Italianni's,** and **Sizzler.** The delivery charge is $5–$10 per restaurant (depending on your distance from the restaurant), with a minimum $15 order. Tips aren't included. Cash, traveler's checks, MasterCard, VISA, and American Express are accepted. Hours are 4:30–11 p.m.

Dining at Universal's CityWalk

Universal rolled out its answer to Downtown Disney with a vengeance in 1999. Like Downtown Disney, CityWalk is a combination of entertainment and dining with a focus on adults. Restaurant tastes run the gamut, from the elegant (**Emeril's Orlando**) to the basic (**NASCAR Café**), or, if you prefer, from the sublime to the ridiculous. All the restaurants share one common trait: They are loud. But there is good food to be found inside some of them. Most of the restaurants are partners with Universal's culinary team.

Bob Marley—A Tribute to Freedom The Bob Marley place (a medium-sized and moderately loud tribute)

Emeril's Orlando Chief among these offerings, Emeril's Orlando is Emeril Lagasse's Florida version of his New Orleans restaurant. Lagasse is on hand from time to time, though he tends to stay in the kitchen. But even when he's not there, you're in for some good eating. The food is Louisiana style with a creative flair.

Hard Rock Café Food is so-so burgers, ribs, and other American fare. More remarkable is the extensive collection of music memorabilia, including a pink 1959 Cadillac revolving over the bar. It's the biggest such collection on display anywhere in the Hard Rock chain.

Jimmy Buffett's Margaritaville A large and noisy tribute to the head Parrothead. None of the food, including the cheeseburger, will make you think you're in paradise, but fans don't seem to care. The focal point is a volcano that erupts occasionally, spewing margarita mix instead of lava.

Latin Quarter Simple Latin cuisine is served here—beans and rice, plantains, flan. Most patrons come to dance and drink.

Motown Café This is the rhythm-and-blues version of Hard Rock Café. The food here is about as satisfying as trying to listen to an old 45-rpm record on a player without an adapter for the hole, but there is a good floor show with singers performing classic Motown hits.

NASCAR Café A large and noisy tribute to all things motorized. You may find yourself sitting under a full-sized race car that from time to time starts up and roars at a too-realistic sound level. The food? See all the logos for oil companies on the walls?

NBA City NBA City serves decent theme-restaurant eats. The dining area looks like a miniature basketball arena, and televisions throughout play videos of famous basketball players and key moments in roundball history.

Pastamoré This is the requisite Italian restaurant. The décor is modern and stylish, and the food—with portions big enough to share—is better than average.

Pat O'Brien's and **CityJazz** are mostly music venues that serve some food. Pat O'Brien's, behind a facade that looks remarkably like the New Orleans original, has the best bites (try the jambalaya).

One Man's Treasure

A man from Richland, Washington, urges:

I think that you should in future editions promote the Crossroads of Buena Vista [Shopping Center] a little stronger. There are plenty of non-WDW restaurants at non-WDW prices. The Crossroads is nothing less than a small city that can service all of your needs.

Crossroads Shopping Center is on FL 535 directly across from the entrance to Walt Disney World Village and Downtown Disney Resort Area. As the reader suggests, it offers about everything you need. Fast food is sold at **McDonald's** and **Taco Bell.** Up a notch are **T.G.I. Fridays, Jungle Jim's, Pizzeria Uno,** and **Red Lobster.** For a really nice meal, pick **Pebbles,** featuring fresh Florida seafood. When you finish eating, shop for sportswear, swimwear, and athletic shoes.

Buffets and Meal Deals outside Walt Disney World

Buffets, restaurant specials, and discount dining abound in the area surrounding Walt Disney World, especially on US 192 (locally known as the

WHERE TO EAT OUTSIDE WALT DISNEY WORLD

American

*La Boheme** 325 S. Orange Avenue, downtown Orlando; (407) 581-4700; expensive. Elegant, upscale setting, eclectic menu featuring seafood, steaks and game.

Café Tu Tu Tango 8625 International Drive, Orlando; (407) 248-2222; inexpensive to moderate. Mediterranean-style tapas in an artist's garret setting.

*Chatham's Place** 7575 Dr. Phillips Boulevard, Orlando; (407) 345-2992; moderate to expensive; New American cuisine: the dining room is small and unappealing, but the food and service are some of the best in Orlando.

*Hue 629** E. Central Boulevard, Orlando; (407) 849-1800; moderate. Chic hotspot in trendy Thornton Park. But the food is still star of the show—try the sea bass.

Pebbles 12551 FL 535, Crossroads Shopping Center, Lake Buena Vista; (407) 827-1111; moderate to expensive. A casual homegrown chain featuring a Florida version of California cuisine.

Seasons 52 7700 W. Sand Lake Road, Orlando; (407) 354-5212; moderate. Delicious, creative New American food (and low in fat and calories). Solid wine list.

Barbecue

Bubbalou's Bodacious B-B-Q 5818 Conroy Road, Orlando (near Universal Orlando); (407) 295-1212; inexpensive. Tender, smoky barbecue; tomato-based "killer" sauce.

Steak/Prime Rib

Charlie's Steak House 6107 S. Orange Blossom Trail, Orlando; (407) 851-7130; moderate. There are other locations for this small chain, including one just south of the I-4 interchange on US 192.

*Del Frisco's** 729 Lee Road, Orlando (quarter-mile west of I-4); (407) 645-4443; expensive. A little pricey, but if you're in the mood for a great steak, it's worth it.

Texas de Brazil 2559 International Drive, Orlando; (407) 355-0355; expensive. All-you-care-to-eat in an upscale, Brazilian-style churrascuria. Filet mignon, sausage, pork ribs, chicken, lamb, and more. Under age 6 free; ages 7 to 12 half price. Salad bar with more than 40 options.

Vito's Chop House 8633 International Drive, Orlando; (407) 354-2467; moderate. Surprisingly upscale meat house with a taste of Tuscany.

Caribbean

Bahama Breeze 8849 International Drive, Orlando; (407) 248-2499; moderate. A creative—and tasty—version of Caribbean cuisine from the owners of the Olive Garden and Red Lobster chains.

Chinese

Ming Court 9188 International Drive, Orlando; (407) 351-9988; expensive. Ask to see the dim sum menu.

Cuban

*Numero Uno** 2499 S. Orange Avenue, Orlando; (407) 841-3840; inexpensive. No trip to Florida is complete without a sampling of Cuban food.

*Rolando's Cuban Restaurant** 870 East Altamonte Drive, Altamonte Springs; (407) 767-9677; inexpensive. Some of the best Cuban food, served by some of the friendliest folks.

French

*Le Coq au Vin** 4800 S. Orange Avenue, Orlando; (407) 851-6980; moderate. A perennial local favorite featuring country French in a relaced atmosphere. Reservations required.

German/Eastern European

*Chef Henry's Café** 3716 Howell Branch Road, Winter Park; (407) 657-2230; moderate. A small, family-run café with authentic and delicious Eastern European dishes. Don't leave without having a slice (or five) of the apple streudel.

Gains German Restaurant* 5731 S. Orange Blossom Trail, Orlando; (407) 438-8997; moderate. Nothing special, but if you've just got to have some sauerbraten . . .

Indian

Memories of India 7625 Turkey Lake Road, Orlando; (407) 370-3277; moderate. A quiet atmosphere with some of the best Indian cuisine in the area. A bit more reasonable than some other I-Drive–area Indian restaurants.

Passage to India 5532 International Drive, Orlando; (407) 351-3456; moderate. A lot of locals brave International Drive just to dine here.

Shamiana 7040 International Drive, Orlando; (407) 354-1160; inexpensive. Also serves Pakistani cuisine.

Italian

Antonio's Bay Hill 7559 W. Sand Lake Road, Orlando; (407) 363-9191; moderate to expensive. Upscale Italian that's a popular choice among locals.

Capriccio Peabody Orlando, 9801 International Drive, Orlando; ; (407) 345-4450; moderate to expensive. This upscale Italian restaurant serves a good Sunday brunch.

Japanese/Sushi

Amura 7786 W. Sand Lake Road, Orlando; (407) 370-0007; moderate. A favorite sushi bar for locals. The tempura is popular, too.

Hanamizuki 8255 International Drive, Orlando; (407) 363-7200; moderate to expensive. Usually filled with Japanese visitors; expensive, but very authentic.

Ichiban* 19 S. Orange Avenue, Orlando; (407) 423-2688; moderate. Sit on the floor or at a table; good sushi and tempura.

Mexican

Don Pablo's 8717 International Drive, Orlando; (407) 354-1345; inexpensive. A pretty good chain that uses fresh ingredients. Can be a bit noisy.

Middle Eastern

Cedars 7732 W. Sand Lake Road, Orlando; (407) 351-6000; inexpensive. Traditional favorites from baba ghannouj to tabbouleh and lentil soup.

New World

Norman's 4000 Central Florida Parkway, in the Ritz-Carlton; (407) 206-2400; expensive. Norman Van Aken, patron of New World cuisine, offers a menu that changes daily—but you'll always find his sinfully delicious conch chowder. World-class wine menu.

Seafood

Bonefish 7830 Sand Lake Road, Orlando; (407) 355-7707; moderate. Casual setting along busy Restaurant Row on Sand Lake Road. Choose your fish, then choose a favorite sauce to accompany. Also steaks and chicken.

Crabby Bill's 5030 Irlo Bronson Highway (US 192), Kissimmee; ; (321) 677-0303; inexpensive to moderate. This new location of a Pinellas County landmark serves up some of the best seafood and shellfish in Florida. .

McCormick & Schmick's 200 Conroy Road, Mall at Millenia, Orlando; (407) 226-6515; expensive. Menu changes often based on freshness. Raw oysters are a big hit.

Thai

Siam Orchid 7575 Universal Boulevard, Orlando; (407) 351-0821; moderate to expensive. Fancier than most Thai places and a bit pricier, but the best Thai in the tourist areas.

Thai House* 2117 E. Colonial Drive, Orlando; (407) 898-0820; inexpensive. Locals love the "Thai hot" specials at this little diner near downtown.

*20 minutes or more from Walt Disney World.

Irlo Bronson Highway) and along International Drive. The local visitor magazines, distributed free at non-Disney hotels among other places, are packed with advertisements and discount coupons for seafood feasts, Chinese buffets, Indian buffets, breakfast buffets, and a host of combination specials for everything from lobster to barbecue. For a family trying to economize on meals, some of the come-ons are mighty appealing. But are these places any good? Is the food fresh, tasty, and appealing? Are the restaurants clean and inviting? Armed with little more than a roll of Tums, the *Unofficial* research team tried all the eateries that advertise heavily in the free tourist magazines. Here's what we discovered.

Chinese Super Buffets   Whoa! Talk about an oxymoron. If you've ever tried preparing Chinese food, especially a stir-fry, you know that split-second timing is required to avoid overcooking. So it should come as no big surprise that Chinese dishes languishing on a buffet lose their freshness, texture, and flavor in hurry. As a rule, Chinese dishes simply do not work on a buffet. The exception might be a busy local Chinese lunch spot where buffet items are replenished every five or so minutes. Even then, however, the food doesn't measure up to dishes that are cooked to order and served fresh out of the wok. At the so-called Chinese super buffets, the food often sits a long time. We tried all the buffets advertised in the visitor magazines (and a few that were not), and while a number of them had great eye appeal, the food was inevitably lackluster.

A notable exception is the **New York China Buffet** (phone (407) 238-9198) in the Buena Vista Shopping Center on Vineland Apopka Road about a mile north of the Disney Village entrance to Walt Disney World and the Crossroads Shopping Center. The buffet serves Chinese and American fare with a little Japanese and Korean thrown in for good measure. It also features a Mongolian barbecue, a cook-to-order stir-fry with meats, veggies, and seasoning of your choice. The buffet is replenished often, so in the main, the buffet items remain fresher than at other area Chinese buffets. Lunch and dinner are served daily.

Indian Buffets   Indian food works much better on a buffet than Chinese food. The mainstay of Indian buffets is curries. Curry, you may be surprised to know, is essentially the Indian word for stew. Curry powder, as sold in the United States, is nothing more than a blend of spices prepackaged to flavor a stew. In India, each curry is prepared with a different combination of spices, and no self-respecting cook would dream of using an off-the-shelf mix. The salient point about Indian buffets is that stews, unlike stir-frys, actually improve with a little aging. If you've ever heated a leftover stew at home and commented that it tasted better than when originally served, it's because the flavors and ingredients continued to marry during the storage period, making it richer and tastier.

In the Walt Disney World area, most Indian restaurants offer a buffet at lunch only—not too convenient if you plan on spending your day at the theme parks. If you're out shopping or taking a day off, here are some Indian buffets worth trying:

India Palace at Vista Shoppes	8530 Palm Parkway (off FL 535)	(407) 238-2322
Passage to India	5532 International Drive	(407) 351-3456
Punjab Indian Restaurant	7451 International Drive	(407) 352-7887
Shalimar Tandoor & Grill	7342 International Drive	(407) 226-9797

General Buffets   There are three buffets, the **Las Vegas Buffet** (5269 W. US 192; (407) 397-1288), **Stevie B's Southern Buffet** (4118 W. Vine (US 192); (407) 870-9983), and **Bill Wong's** (5668 International Drive; (407) 352-5373), that offer fair value. The Las Vegas Buffet, the better of the three, features a carving station with prime rib, ham, turkey, and sometimes lamb. Stevie B's specializes in Southern fare with fried chicken, catfish, roast beef, and vegetables flavored with ham or bacon. Bill Wong's represents itself as a Chinese buffet but shores up its Chinese selections with peel-and-eat shrimp, prime rib, and a nice selection of hot and cold vegetables. Discount coupons for all three buffets are usually available.

Seafood and Lobster Buffets   These affairs do not exactly fall under the category of inexpensive dining. Prices range from $18 to $24 for early birds (4–6 p.m.) and $23 to $29 after 6 p.m. The main draw (no pun intended) is all the lobster you can eat. The problem is lobsters, like Chinese food, don't wear well on a steam table. After a few minutes on the buffet line, they make better tennis balls than dinner. If, however, you have someone in the kitchen who knows how to steam a lobster, and if you grab your lobster immediately after a fresh batch has been brought out, it will probably be fine. There are two lobster buffets on US 192 and another two on International Drive. Although all four do a reasonable job, we prefer **Angel's** (7300 Irlo Bronson Highway; (407) 397-1960) and the **International Lobster Feast** (8735 International Drive; (407) 248-8606). In both cases, there's enough other good stuff on the buffet, including prime rib, to have a good meal even if the lobsters are sub-par. If you put our two favorites head-to-head, the International Lobster Feast offers greater variety, especially in terms of shellfish, but is also about $4 more expensive. Both places are cavernous, noisy joints. Finally, be aware that the other International Drive lobster buffet is called the International Lighthouse Lobster Feast. A lot of folks get the names and the restaurants confused. Discount coupons are available in local visitor magazines.

A buffet that's been running big ads in the local visitor mags is the **Coney Island Lobster and Seafood Feast** (5150 W. US 192; (407) 397-7077). Located between mile markers 10 and 11, Coney Island is a smaller buffet in a smaller venue, but it offers all of the usual headliner items: lobster, crab legs, oysters, clams, shrimp, prime rib, grilled, sirloin, salmon, etc. Prices are about $3–$5 less than competitors who offer more salad, side dish, and desert variety. Like the others, Coney Island offers discount coupons.

Breakfast Buffets and Entrée Buffets   Entrée buffets are offered by most of the area chain steakhouses such as **Ponderosa, Sizzler, Western Steer,** and **Golden Corral.** Between them, there are 18 locations in the Walt Disney World area. All serve breakfast, lunch, and dinner. At lunch and dinner, you get the buffet when you buy an entrée, usually a steak. Generally speaking, the buffets are less elaborate than a stand-alone buffet and considerably more varied than a salad bar. Breakfast service is a straightforward buffet (i.e., no obligation to buy an entrée). Concerning the food, it's chain-restaurant quality but pretty decent all the same. Prices are a bargain, and you can get in and out at lightning speed—important at breakfast when you're trying to get to the theme park early. Some locations offer lunch and dinner buffets at a set price without buying an entrée.

Though you can argue about which chain serves the best steak, Golden Corral wins the buffet contest hands downs with twice or more offerings than its three competitors. Where buffets at Golden Corral, Western Steer, and Ponderosa are pretty consistent from location to location, the buffets at the various Sizzlers vary a good deal. The pick of the Sizzlers is the 4006 W. US 192 location. In addition to the steakhouses, area **Shoney's** also offer breakfast, lunch, and dinner buffets. Local freebie visitor magazines are full of discount coupons for all of the above.

Meal Deals   Discount coupons are available for a wide range of restaurants, including some wonderful upscale ethnic places like **Siam Orchid** (Thai) and **Ming's** (Chinese). For those who crave both beef and a bargain, try **JT's Prime Time Restaurant & Bar** (16299 W. Irlo Bronson; (407) 239-6555). JT's serves all-you-can-eat prime rib for $15. They slice it a little thin but are very attentive in regard to bringing you additional helpings. Other prime rib specials can be found at **Cattleman's Steakhouse,** with locations at 8801 International Drive a quarter of a mile north of the convention center (phone (407) 354-9888) and on US 192 at FL 535 (2948 Vineland Road; (407) 397-1888). Our favorite prime rib option is **Wild Jack's Steaks & BBQ** (7364 International Drive; (407) 352-4407). The décor is strictly cowboy modern, but the beef is some of the best in town, and the price is right. The best steak deal in the Disney World area is the $12, 10-ounce New York strip at the **Black Angus Steak House.** The beef is served with salad, choice of vegetables or potato, and bread, and is available at both locations convenient to Disney: 7516 W. Irlo Bronson (US 192), (407) 390-4548; and 6231 International Drive, (407) 354-3333. Another meat-eater's delight is the Feast for Four at **Sonny's Real Pit Bar-B Q,** a Florida chain that turns out good barbecue. For $26–$30 per family of four, you get sliced pork or beef, plus chicken, ribs, beans, slaw, fries, garlic bread, and soft drinks or tea, all served family style. Locations include: 4220 Vine Street, Kissimmee, (407) 847-8888; 3189 S. John Young Parkway, (407) 847-8889; and on US 192 at 4475 13th Street, (407) 892-2285. No coupons are needed or available for JT's or Sonny's, but coupons are available for the other meateries.

Dining in Walt Disney World

This section aims to help you find good food without going broke or tripping over one of Disney World's many culinary landmines. More than 100 restaurants operate in Walt Disney World, including about 70 full-service restaurants, 23 of which are inside the theme parks. Collectively, Disney restaurants offer exceptional variety, serving everything from Moroccan to Texas barbecue. Most restaurants are expensive, and many serve less than distinguished fare, but the culinary scene at Disney World gets better every year. You can find good deals if you know where to look, and there are ethnic delights rarely found outside of America's largest cities.

Getting It Right

Although we work hard to be fair, objective, and accurate, many readers, like this one from Couderport, Pennsylvania, think we are too critical of Disney restaurants. He writes:

You are tough on all Disney dining ... Everyone has to eat while there, so it benefits no one to be this critical. Lighten up a little bit and make your dining recommendations in the same spirit as the rest of the book.

In a similar vein, a Charleston, West Virginia, woman came out swinging:

Get a life! It's crazy and unrealistic to be so snobbish about restaurants at a theme park. Considering the number of people Disney feeds each day, I think they do a darn good job. Also, you act so surprised that the food is expensive. Have you ever eaten at an airport? HELLO, IN THERE? ... Surprise, you're a captive! It's a theme park!

And a mom from Erie, Pennsylvania, struck a practical note, writing:

Most of the food [at Walt Disney World] is OK. Certainly in our experience, more of it is good than bad. If you pay attention to what other visitors say and what's in the guidebooks, you can avoid the yucky places. It's true that you pay more than you should, but it's more convenient [to eat in Walt Disney World] than to run around trying to find cheaper restaurants somewhere else. When it comes to Walt Disney World, who needs more running around.

As you might infer from the reader comments above, getting our dining coverage right is a bit of a challenge. While researching and reviewing restaurants may appear to be a straightforward endeavor, we can assure you that it is fraught with peril. We have read dining reviews by writers who turn up their noses at anything except four-star French restaurants (of which there are a whole lot fewer than people think). Likewise, we have seen reviewers who totally avoid Thai and Indian restaurants (among others) because they do not understand those cuisines. We have read reviews absolutely devoid of criticism, written by "experts" unwilling to risk offending the source of their free meals. Finally, we've seen reviews in dining guides that are wholly based on surveys submitted by diners whose credentials for evaluating fine dining are mysterious at best and questionable at least.

How, then, do you go about presenting the best possible dining coverage? What is the best way to get it right? At the *Unofficial Guide,* we have elected to begin with highly qualified culinary experts and then balance their opinions with those of our readers. It's necessary, we believe, to present both an expert and a popular opinion of each restaurant.

The expert opinion is essential because it's important to be able to differentiate what the restaurant really serves from what it purports to serve. Many years ago in Lexington, Kentucky, by way of example, there was only one Chinese restaurant. It was wildly successful in spite of the fact that it was Chinese in name only. Even so, its specialty dishes, essentially American vegetable casseroles smothered in cornstarch, were happily gobbled up by loyal patrons who had never been exposed to real Chinese cooking. The food was not bad, mind you, but it was not Chinese either. Visitors from out of town, inquiring about a good local Chinese restaurant, were often directed to this place. As you would expect, they were routinely horrified by the fare.

In this guide, we think you deserve to know whether or not you're getting the real thing. If we recommend the bastilla (a Moroccan pastry) at the Restaurant Marrakesh, it's pretty essential that our dining critics know what bastilla is, how it's properly prepared, how it should be served, and how it should taste. Likewise with the béarnaise sauce served at the Yachtsman Steakhouse, or the Jagerschnitzel at the Biergarten. In our opinion, it's almost impossible to publish a creditable restaurant review without the help of a knowledgeable, professional dining critic.

The ultimate test of success for a restaurant, however, is not the authenticity of its dishes, but the level of satisfaction of its patrons. If diners have a bad experience and don't come back, the restaurant will fail. Thus, in this guide, we regard our expert's opinion and our readers' opinions as two halves of a whole. Both are necessary to give you the information you need to make your dining decisions.

Our experts are knowledgeable, seasoned professionals who have studied culinary arts around the world and who have written cookbooks or columns. They are well versed in ethnic dishes and have studied many of the cuisines of the world in their native lands. As at home in a Tupelo, Mississippi, catfish shack as in an exclusive French restaurant on New York's Upper East Side, they have no prejudice about high or low cuisine. Equally important, our experts conduct their reviews anonymously, and always pay full menu prices for their meals.

To be as fair and thorough as possible, we display our readers' opinion of each restaurant right alongside that of our dining critics and encourage you to take both into consideration when selecting a restaurant. Likewise, we encourage you to send us the dining survey in the back of this guide so we can include your opinions in our tabulations. If you want to share your dining experience in great depth, write us at the address listed on page 12 or e-mail us at unofficialguides@menasharidge.com.

Disney Dining 101

Priority Seating

Disney ceaselessly tinkers with its restaurant reservations policy. Since 1997, reservations have been replaced with "Priority Seating." When you call, your name and essential information are taken as if you were making a reservation. The Disney representative then says you have priority seating for the restaurant on the date and time you requested and usually explains that priority seating means you will be seated ahead of walk-ins, i.e., those without priority seating.

Behind the Scenes at Priority Seating
Central Reservations

Disney restaurants operate on what they call a "template system." Instead of scheduling priority seatings for actual tables, reservationists fill time slots. The number of time slots available is based on the average observed length of time that guests occupy a table at a particular restaurant, adjusted for seasonality. Here's a rough example of how it works. Let's say the Coral Reef Restaurant at Epcot has 40 tables for four and 8 tables for six and that the average length of time for a family to be seated, order, eat, pay, and depart is 40 minutes. Add 5 minutes to bus the table and set it up for the next guests, and they are turning the table every 45 minutes. The restaurant provides Walt Disney World Dining (a.k.a. WDW-DINE) with a computer template of its capacity along with the average time the table is occupied. Thus, when WDW-DINE makes a priority seating for four people at 6:15 p.m., the system removes one table for four from overall capacity for 45 minutes. The template on the reservationist's computer indicates that the table will not be available for reassignment until 7 p.m. (45 minutes later). So it goes for all the tables in the restaurant, each being subtracted from overall capacity for 45 minutes, then listed as available again, and then assigned to other guests and subtracted again, and so on, throughout the meal period. WDW-DINE tries to fill every time slot for every seat in the restaurant or come as close to filling every slot as possible. No seats, repeat none, are reserved for walk-ins.

Templates are filled differently depending on the season of the year. During slower times of year when priority seatings are easier to get, WDW-DINE will overbook the restaurant for each time slot on the assumption that there will be a lot of no-shows. During busy times of year when priority seatings are harder to come by, there are very few no-shows, so the restaurant is booked according to its actual capacity. The no-show rate in January, a slow month, is about 33%, while in July it's less than 10%.

Even though, as discussed above, no seats are reserved for walk-ins, it's easy to get a walk-in seat during slower times of the year (with the exception of Cinderella's Royal Table). During high season, it's tougher to get seated as a walk-in, but by no means impossible. As we've seen, you can score a seat in the event of no-shows, but you can also sometimes get in if the tables turn over more rapidly than usual. Hosts in each restaurant are responsible for keeping every table full. If additional guests can be accommodated, you can bet the host will jump to fill those slots.

With priority seating, your wait almost always will be less than 20 minutes during peak hours, and often less than 10 minutes. If you just walk in, especially during busier seasons, expect to wait 40–75 minutes.

Getting Your Act Together

If you want to patronize any of the Walt Disney World Resort full-service restaurants, buffets, character meals, or dinner shows, you should make priority seatings in advance. Following is a listing of how far in advance you can make priority seating arrangements:

730 Days (two years) in advance
Hoop-Dee-Doo Revue

Spirit of Aloha

365 Days (one year) in advance
Mickey's All American Backyard BBQ (Fort Wilderness)

180 Days in advance
Victoria & Albert's

90 Days in advance
All Walt Disney World Resort hotel restaurants

All theme park full-service restaurants except Bistro de Paris

Downtown Disney's Fulton's Crab House, House of Blues
   and Portobello Yacht Club

All character meals

Afternoon Tea (Grand Floridian)

Ice Cream Social (Epcot)

60 Days in Advance
Wolfgang Puck Express (Downtown Disney)

30 Days in Advance
Bistro de Paris (Epcot)

Dine with a Disney Imagineer (Disney-MGM, Hollywood Brown Derby)

For most full-service restaurants, buffets, and character meals, you can make priority seatings 90 days in advance. Exceptions include Disney dinner shows such as the *Spirit of Aloha* and the *Hoop-Dee-Doo Revue* where priority seatings can be scheduled two years in advance.

If you fail to make priority seating before you leave home, or if you want to make your dining decisions spontaneously while at Walt Disney World, your chances of getting a table at the restaurant of your choice is pretty good, but not a slam dunk. The *Hoop-Dee-Doo Revue* and Cinderella's Royal Table breakfast will most certainly be sold out, as will several of the other more popular character meals. If, however, you visit Walt Disney World during a busier time of year, it's to your advantage to make priority seatings before you leave home. Except for Cinderella's Royal Table Character Breakfast, the *Hoop-Dee-Doo Review,* and Victoria & Albert's, don't worry about calling the maximum number of days in advance. It will suffice to call three or five weeks before you leave home, by which time you will have sorted out your dining preferences. If you change your mind once you arrive, you can try to change your priority seating by calling (407) WDW-DINE. If you poop out in the theme park and don't feel like using your priority seating that night, don't worry, there's no penalty for being a no-show—except at a couple of restaurants like Cinderella's Royal Table character breakfast, where a credit card deposit is required. In those cases, you'll be charged a cancellation fee if you don't show up. Incidentally, if you're ever asked for a credit card to secure a seating, it's a real reservation as opposed to a priority seating. If you're a no-show for a particular priority seating, it will not affect other priority seatings you've made.

It's a good idea if you've lined up a lot of priory seatings to phone (407) WDW-DINE a few days in advance of your vacation to make sure everything's in order. Similarly, if you stay in a Disney resort, guest services can print out a summary of all your priority seatings on request.

For each priority seating you make, you will be given a confirmation number. Bring this number with you to the restaurant. Snafus are relatively few, but it makes things a whole lot easier to straighten out if you have your confirmation number.

If you have a priority seating for a theme park restaurant at a time prior to opening, simply proceed to the turnstiles and inform a cast member. Be sure to have your confirmation number. The cast member will admit you to the park and direct you to the restaurant.

In the theme parks, you can make priority seatings in person at the door of the restaurant, at Guest Services, or at the kiosk at the intersection of Hollywood and Sunset Boulevards at the Disney-MGM Studios. With a few exceptions, you'll have no problem getting your priority seating at the park. If you fail to make priority seatings, most full-service theme park restaurants will take walk-ins between 2:30 and 4:30 p.m.

Dress

Dress is informal at all theme-park restaurants. While theme-park attire (shorts, T-shirts, sneakers, etc.) is tolerated at hotel restaurants, you probably would feel more comfortable if you dressed up a bit. The only restaurant requiring jackets for men and dressy clothes for women is Victoria & Albert's at the Grand Floridian.

Smoking

Walt Disney World restaurants adopted a nonsmoking policy several years ago, although smoking was allowed in the lounge areas of many restaurants. Florida voters recently passed an amendment to the state's constitution that also prohibits smoking in restaurant lounges. Freestanding bars—those that realize less than 10% of their revenues from food sales—are exempted. They're also hard to find on Disney property; Mizner's Lounge at Disney's Grand Floridian Resort is one possible exception. In most cases, however, diners may be required to go outside for a smoke—and in the theme parks, that might also mean going to one of the designated smoking areas.

A Few Caveats

Before you begin eating your way through the World, you need to know:

1. However creative and enticing the menu descriptions, avoid fancy food, especially at full-service restaurants in the Magic Kingdom and Disney-MGM Studios. Order dishes the kitchen is unlikely to botch. An exception to this caveat is the Brown Derby Restaurant at the Studios.

2. Don't order baked, broiled, poached, or grilled seafood unless the restaurant specializes in seafood or rates at least ★★★½ on our restaurant profile.

3. Theme-park restaurants rush their customers in order to make room for the next group of diners. Dining at high speed may appeal to a family with young, restless children, but for people wanting to relax, it's more like *Beat the Clock* than fine dining.

If you want to linger over your expensive meal, do not order your entire dinner at once. Order drinks. Study the menu while you sip, then order appetizers. Tell the waiter you need more time to decide among entrées. Order your main course only after appetizers have been served. Dawdle over coffee and dessert.

4. If you're dining in a theme park and cost is an issue, make lunch your main meal. Entrées are similar to those on the dinner menu, but prices are significantly lower.

Walt Disney World Restaurant Categories

In general, food and beverage offerings at Walt Disney World are defined by service, price, and convenience:

Full-Service Restaurants   Full-service restaurants are in all Disney resorts except the All-Star and Pop Century, and all major theme parks, Downtown Disney Marketplace, Pleasure Island, and Disney's West Side. Disney operates the restaurants in the theme parks and its hotels. Contractors or franchisees operate the restaurants in hotels of the Downtown Disney Resort Area, the Swan and Dolphin resorts, Pleasure Island, Disney's West Side, and some in the Marketplace. Priority seating (explained above), arranged in advance, is recommended for all full-service restaurants except those in the DDRA. The restaurants accept VISA, MasterCard, American Express, Discover, Diners Club, and the Disney Credit Card.

Buffets   There has been an explosion of buffets at Disney World during recent years. Many have Disney characters in attendance, and most have a separate children's menu featuring hot dogs, burgers, chicken nuggets, pizza, macaroni and cheese, and spaghetti and meatballs. In addition to the buffets, several restaurants serve a family-style, all-you-can-eat, fixed-price meal. Priority-seating arrangements are required for character buffets and recommended for all other buffets and family-style restaurants. Most major credit cards are accepted.

The table below lists buffets (where you can belly up for bulk loading) at Walt Disney World.

WALT DISNEY WORLD BUFFETS

Location	Restaurant	Cuisine	Meals Served	Disney Characters Present
Magic Kingdom	Crystal Palace	American	B, L, D	Yes
Magic Kingdom	Cinderella's Royal Table	American	B	Yes
Epcot	Biergarten	German	L, D	No
Epcot	Restaurant Akershus	Scandinavian	L, D	Yes (B)
Epcot	Garden Grill	American	B, L, D	Yes (L, D)
Disney-MGM Studios	Hollywood and Vine	American	L, D	No
Animal Kingdom	Restaurantosaurus	American	B	Yes
Contemporary Resort	Chef Mickey's	American	B, D	Yes
Beach Club Resort	Cape May Café	Clambake	B, D	Yes (B)
Grand Floridian	1900 Park Fare	American	B, D	Yes
Animal Kingdom Lodge	Boma	African	B, D	No
Wilderness Lodge	Whispering Canyon	American	B, L, D	No
Fort Wilderness	Trail's End	American	B, L, D	No
Swan	Garden Grove Café	American	B	Yes (Weekends)

If you want to eat a lot but don't feel like standing in yet another line, consider one of the all-you-can-eat, family-style restaurants. These feature platters of food brought to your table in courses by a server. You can sample everything on the menu and eat as much as you like. You can even go back to a favorite appetizer after you finish the main course. Food tends to be a little better than you'll find on a buffet line.

Family-style, all-you-can-eat service is available at the **Liberty Tree Tavern** in the Magic Kingdom and the **Garden Grill** in the Land pavilion in Epcot (both with character dining); or at **'Ohana** in the Polynesian Resort and **Whispering Canyon Café** in the Wilderness Lodge.

Cafeterias and Food Courts   Cafeterias in all the major theme parks offer a middle ground between full-service and counter-service dining. Food courts, featuring a collection of counter-service eateries under one roof, are found at the theme parks as well as at the moderate (Coronado Springs, Caribbean Beach, Port Orleans) and budget (All-Star and Pop Century) Disney resorts. No priority seating is required or available at cafeterias or food courts.

Counter Service   Counter-service fast food is available in all theme parks and at Downtown Disney Marketplace, Pleasure Island, Disney's BoardWalk, and Disney's West Side. The food compares in quality with McDonald's, Captain D's, or Taco Bell, but is more expensive, though often served in larger portions.

THE COST OF COUNTER-SERVICE FOOD

To help you develop your dining budget, here are prices of common counter-service items. Sales tax isn't included.

FOOD

Bagel/Muffin	$1.79–$2.29
Brownie	$1.79–$2.39
Cake or Pie	$2.29–$3.99
Cereal with Milk	$1.99–$3.50
Cheeseburger with Fries	$5.69–$7.19
Chicken Breast Sandwich (grilled)	$6.59–$7.59
Children's Meals	$4.99
Chips	$0.75–$2.59
Cookies	$0.80–$2.09
Sub/Deli Sandwich	$6.49–$7.50
Fish Basket (fried) with Fries	$6.39–$6.79
French Fries	$1.50–$3.29 (loaded)
Fried Chicken Strips with Fries	$3.49–$6.79
Fruit (whole piece)	$0.99–$3.29
Fruit Cup/Fruit Salad	$1.29–$3.29
Hot Dogs	$3.59–$3.69 (foot-long)
Ice Cream Bars	$2.50–$3.00
Nachos with Cheese	$3.25–$5.50

THE COST OF COUNTER-SERVICE FOOD (continued)

PBJ Sandwich	$2.99–$3.90
Pizza	$4.80–$6.29
Popcorn	$2.39–$3.49
Pretzel	$2.90–$3.90 (with cheese)
Salad (entrée)	$8.00
Salad (side)	$4.69
Smoked Turkey Leg	$4.50–$4.69
Soup/Chili	$1.79–$4.99
Tacos (2) with Beans and Salsa	$6.99
Taco Salad	$6.59
Veggie Burger	$6.09

DRINKS	Small	Large
Beer (not available in the Magic Kingdom)	$3.50	$5.00
Bottled Water	$1.25	$2.50
Cappuccino/Espresso	$1.79–$2.99	$2.49–$2.79
Coffee	$1.69	$1.89
Fruit Juice	$1.49	$2.39
Milk	$0.99–$1.29	$1.99
Milkshakes/Floats/Sundaes	$2.79–$3.99	n/a
Soft Drinks, Iced Tea, and Lemonade	$1.99	$2.29–$2.50
Refillable Souvenir Mug ($12 to buy)	n/a	$3.50–$4.99
Hot Tea and Cocoa	$1.39–$1.69	$1.89

Vendor Food   Vendors abound at the theme parks, Downtown Disney Marketplace, Pleasure Island, Disney's West Side, and Disney's Board-Walk. Offerings include popcorn, ice cream bars, churros (Mexican pastries), soft drinks, bottled water, and (in theme parks) fresh fruit. Prices include tax, and payment must be in cash.

Hard Choices

Dining choices will definitely impact your Walt Disney World experience. If you're short on time and you want to see the theme parks, avoid full-service restaurants. Ditto if you're short on funds. If you want to try a Disney full-service restaurant, arrange priority seating in advance. That won't reserve you a table, but it will minimize your wait.

Integrating Meals into the Unofficial Guide Touring Plans

Arrive before the park of your choice opens. Tour expeditiously, using your chosen plan (taking as few breaks as possible), until about 11–11:30 a.m. Once the park becomes crowded around midday, meals and other breaks won't affect the plan's efficiency. If you intend to stay in the park for evening parades, fireworks, or other events, eat dinner early enough to be finished in time for the festivities.

Character Dining

A number of restaurants, primarily those serving all-you-can-eat buffets and family-style meals, offer character dining. At character meals, you pay a fixed price and dine in the presence of one to five Disney characters that circulate throughout the restaurant, hugging children (and sometimes adults), posing for photos, and signing autographs. Character breakfasts, lunches, and dinners are served at restaurants in and out of the theme parks. For an extensive discussion of character dining, see Part Five, Walt Disney World with Kids (page 235).

Full-Service Dining for Families with Young Children

Disney restaurants offer an excellent (though expensive) opportunity to introduce young children to the variety and excitement of ethnic food. No matter how formal a restaurant appears, the staff is accustomed to wiggling, impatient, and often boisterous children. Chefs de France at Epcot, for example, may be the nation's only French restaurant where most patrons wear shorts and T-shirts and at least two dozen young diners are attired in basic black . . . mouse ears. Bottom line: young children are the rule, not the exception, at Disney restaurants.

Almost all Disney restaurants offer children's menus, and all have booster seats and highchairs. They understand how tough it may be for children to sit for an extended period, and waiters will supply little ones with crackers and rolls and serve your dinner much faster than in comparable restaurants elsewhere. Letters from readers suggest that being served too quickly is much more common than having a long wait.

Good Walt Disney World Theme-Park Restaurants for Children

In Epcot, preschoolers most enjoy the **Biergarten** in Germany, **San Angel Inn** in Mexico, and **Coral Reef** in The Living Seas pavilion in Future World. The Biergarten combines a rollicking and noisy atmosphere with good basic food, including roast chicken; a German oompah band entertains. Children often have the opportunity to participate in Bavarian dancing. San Angel Inn is in the Mexican village marketplace. From the table, children can watch boats on El Río del Tiempo drift beneath a smoking volcano. With a choice of chips, tacos, and other familiar items, picky children usually have no difficulty finding something to eat. The Coral Reef, with tables beside windows looking into The Living Seas aquarium, offers a satisfying mealtime diversion for all ages. If your kids don't eat fish, Coral Reef also serves chicken.

The Biergarten offers reasonable value, plus good food. The Coral Reef and San Angel Inn are overpriced, though the food is palatable.

Cinderella's Royal Table in Cinderella Castle is the big draw in the Magic Kingdom. Interestingly, other Magic Kingdom full-service restaurants hold little appeal for children. For the best combination of food and entertainment, book a character meal at the **Liberty Tree Tavern** or **Crystal Palace.**

At Disney-MGM Studios, all ages enjoy the atmosphere and entertainment at the **Sci-Fi Dine-In Theater Restaurant** and the **50's Prime Time Café.** Unfortunately, the Sci-Fi's food is close to dismal and the Prime Time's is uneven. Eat only dessert at these restaurants.

The only full-service restaurant at the Animal Kingdom is the **Rainforest Café,** which is a great favorite of children.

Fast Food in the Theme Parks

Because most meals during a Disney World vacation are consumed on the run while touring, we'll tackle counter-service and vendor foods first. Plentiful in all theme parks are hot dogs, hamburgers, chicken sandwiches, green salads, and pizza. They're augmented by special items that relate to the park's theme or the part of the park you're touring. In Epcot's Germany, for example, counter-service bratwurst and beer are sold. In Frontierland in the Magic Kingdom, vendors sell smoked turkey legs. Counter-service prices are fairly consistent from park to park. Expect to pay the same for your coffee or hot dog at the Animal Kingdom as at Disney-MGM Studios.

Getting your act together in regard to counter-service restaurants in the parks is more a matter of courtesy than necessity. Rude guests rank fifth among reader complaints. A mother from Fort Wayne, Indiana, points out that indecision can be as maddening as outright discourtesy, especially when you're hungry:

Every fast-food restaurant has menu signs the size of billboards, but do you think anybody reads them? People waiting in line spend enough time in front of these signs to memorize them, and still don't have a clue what they want when they finally get to the order taker. If by some miracle they've managed to choose between the hot dog and the hamburger, they then fiddle around another ten minutes deciding what size coke to order. Tell your readers PULEEEZ get their order together ahead of time!

Healthful Food in Walt Disney World

One of the most commendable developments in food service at Walt Disney World has been the introduction of more healthful foods and snacks. Diabetics, vegetarians, weight-watchers, those requiring kosher meals, and guests on restricted diets should have no trouble finding something to eat. Ditto for anyone seeking wholesome, nutritious food. Healthful food is available at most fast-food counters and even from vendors. All major theme parks, for example, have fruit stands.

A Nashville, Tennessee, mom was delighted to see the changes, writing:

I was very happy to see vegetarian items on almost every menu. What a difference from a couple of years ago.

g Your Dining Time at the Theme Parks

Even if you confine your meals to vendor and counter-service fast food, you lose a lot of time getting food in the theme parks. At Walt Disney World, everything begins with a line and ends with a cash register. When it comes to fast food, "fast" may apply to the time you spend eating it, not the time invested in obtaining it.

A New York reader agrees, writing:

In terms of lunch, we found the lines, staff, and general service incredibly slow, unappetizing, and annoying. How is it that ski resorts throughout the country feed hordes of people at precisely the same time and offer an extensive array of quality food with a broad selection, prompt service, and quick check out? Perhaps WDW should visit Vail or Steamboat and learn a thing or two.

Here are suggestions for minimizing the time you spend hunting and gathering food:

1. Eat breakfast before arriving. Don't waste touring time eating breakfast at the parks. Besides, restaurants outside the World offer some outstanding breakfast specials. Some hotels furnish small refrigerators in their guest rooms, or rent them. If you can get by on cold cereal, rolls, fruit, and juice, having a fridge in your room will save a ton of time. If you can't get a fridge, bring a cooler.

2. After a good breakfast, buy snacks from vendors in the parks as you tour, or stuff some snacks in a fanny pack. This is very important if you're on a tight schedule and can't spend a lot of time waiting in line for food.

3. All theme-park restaurants are busiest between 11:30 a.m. and 2:15 p.m. for lunch and 6 and 9 p.m. for dinner. For shorter lines and faster service, avoid eating during these hours.

4. Many counter-service restaurants sell cold sandwiches. Buy a cold lunch (except for drinks) before 11 a.m. and carry it until you're ready to eat. Ditto for dinner. Bring small plastic bags in which to pack the food. Purchase drinks at the appropriate time from any convenient vendor.

5. Most fast-food eateries have more than one service window. Regardless of time of day, check the lines at all windows before queuing. Sometimes a window that's manned but out of the way will have a much shorter line or none at all. Note, however, that some windows may offer only certain items. For example, some windows may serve only soup and salad, while others serve sandwiches.

6. If you're short on time and the park closes early, stay until closing and eat dinner outside Disney World before returning to your hotel. If the park stays open late, eat dinner about 4 or 4:30 p.m.

at the restaurant of your choice. You should miss the last wave of lunchers and sneak in just ahead of the dinner crowd.

Beyond Counter Service: Tips for Saving Money on Food

Though buying food from counter-service restaurants and vendors will save time and money (compared to full-service dining), additional strategies can bolster your budget and maintain your waistline. Here are some suggestions our readers have made over the years:

1. Go to Disney World during a period of fasting and abstinence. You can save a fortune and save your soul at the same time!

2. Wear clothes that are slightly too small and make you feel like dieting (no spandex allowed!).

3. Whenever you're feeling hungry, ride the Mad Tea Party, Body Wars, or other attractions that induce motion sickness.

4. Leave your cash and credit cards at your hotel. Buy food only with money your children fish out of fountains and wishing wells.

Cost-conscious readers also have volunteered ideas for stretching food dollars. A family from Lee's Summit, Missouri, tells us:

Last year we requested a small refrigerator for our room and were given one for no charge. This year we were charged $5 a day [now it's $10 a day!] for use of the fridge, but it was definitely worth it for us to be able to eat breakfast in the room to save time and money.

A Missouri mom writes:

I have shared our very successful meal plan with many families. We stayed six nights and arrived at WDW after some days on the beach south of Sarasota. We shopped there and arrived with our steel Coleman cooler well stocked with milk and sandwich fixings. I froze a block of ice in a milk bottle, and we replenished it daily with ice from the resort ice machine. I also froze small packages of deli-type meats for later in the week. We ate cereal, milk, and fruit each morning, with boxed juices. I also had a hot pot to boil water for instant coffee, oatmeal, and soup.

Each child had a belt bag of his own, which he filled from a special box of "goodies" each day. I made a great mystery of filling that box in the weeks before the trip. Some things were actual food, like packages of crackers and cheese, packets of peanuts and raisins. Some were worthless junk, like candy and gum. They grazed from their belt bags at will throughout the day, with no interference from Mom and Dad. Each also had a small, rectangular plastic water bottle that could hang on the belt. We filled these at water fountains before getting into lines and were the envy of many.

We left the park before noon, ate sandwiches, chips, and soda in the room, and napped. We purchased our evening meal in the park, at a counter-service eatery. We budgeted for both morning and evening snacks from a vendor but often did not need them. It made the occasional treat all the more special. Our cooler had been pretty much emptied by the end of the week, but the block of ice was still there.

We interviewed one woman who brought a huge picnic for her family of five packed in a large diaper/baby paraphernalia bag. She stowed the bag in a locker under the Main Street Station and retrieved it when the family was hungry. A Pennsylvania family adds:

Despite the warning against bringing food into the park, we packed a double picnic lunch in a backpack and a small shoulder bag. Even with a small discount, it cost $195 for the seven of us to tour the park for a day, and I felt that spending another $150 or so on two meals was not in the cards. We froze juice boxes to keep the meat sandwiches cool (it worked fine) and had an extra round of juice boxes and peanut butter sandwiches for a late-afternoon snack. We took raisins and a pack of fig bars for sweets, but didn't carry any other cookies or candy to avoid a "sugar-low" during the day. Fruit would have been nice, but it would have been squashed.

Note: Disney has a rule against bringing your own food and drink into the park. Although after 9/11, all packs, purses, diaper bags, etc., are being searched, security usually does not enforce this ban.

A mom from Whiteland, Indiana, who purchases drinks in the parks, offers this suggestion :

One "must take" item if you're traveling with younger kids is a supply of small paper or plastic cups to split drinks which are both huge and expensive.

Disney Dining Suggestions

Below are suggestions for dining at each of the major theme parks. If you are interested in trying a theme-park full-service restaurant, be aware that the restaurants continue to serve after the park's official closing time. For example, we showed up at the Hollywood Brown Derby just as Disney-MGM Studios closed at 8 p.m. We were seated almost immediately and enjoyed a leisurely dinner while the crowds cleared out. Incidentally, don't worry if you are depending on Disney transportation: buses, boats, and monorails run two to three hours after the parks close.

The Magic Kingdom

Food at the Magic Kingdom has improved noticeably over the past several years. The **Crystal Palace** at the end of Main Street offers a good (albeit pricey) buffet chaperoned by Disney characters, while the **Liberty Tree Tavern** in Liberty Square features hearty family-style dining, also with Disney characters in attendance. **Cinderella's Royal Table,** a full-service restaurant on the second floor of the castle, delivers palatable meals in one of the World's most unique settings.

THE MAGIC KINGDOM

Author's Favorite Counter-Service Restaurants

Cosmic Ray's (serves kosher food)—Tomorrowland

The Plaza Pavilion—Tomorrowland

Pecos Bill's Tall Tale Inn & Café—Frontierland

Fast food at the Magic Kingdom is, well, fast food. It's more expensive, of course, than what you would pay at McDonald's, but what do you expect? It's like dining at an airport—you're a captive audience. On the positive side, portions are large, sometimes large enough for children to share. Overall, the variety of fast food offerings provides a lot of choice, though the number of selections at any specific eatery remains quite limited. Check our mini-profiles of the park's counter-service restaurants before you queue up.

Here are dining recommendations for a day at the Magic Kingdom:

1. Take the monorail to one of the hotels for lunch. The trip over and back takes very little time, and because most guests have left the hotels for the parks, the resorts' restaurants are often uncrowded. The food is better than in the Magic Kingdom; the service is faster; the atmosphere is more relaxed; and beer, wine, and mixed drinks are available. Decent dinner buffets are served at **Chef Mickey's** at the Contemporary and at **1900 Park Fare** at the Grand Floridian. Both feature characters; don't expect quiet dining. Commuting to the buffets is a snap by monorail. A more adult option is the family-style skillet dinner served at **Whispering Canyon Café** in the Wilderness Lodge and Villas. Lunch is also available. To reach the Wilderness Lodge and Villas, take the boat from the Magic Kingdom docks.

2. Full-service restaurants that accept priority seating for lunch and/or dinner fill quickly in the summer and during holiday periods. To obtain priority seating in advance, call (407) 939-3463 or hotfoot to your chosen restaurant as soon as you enter the park. Priority seating is explained and all Magic Kingdom full-service restaurants are profiled later in this section.

3. Of the park's four full-service restaurants, **Liberty Tree Tavern** in Liberty Square is the best. **Tony's Town Square Restaurant** on Main Street and **Cinderella's Royal Table** in the castle also serve decent food. Because children love Cinderella and everyone's curious about the castle, you need to make a priority seating before you leave home if you want to eat breakfast at Cinderella's Royal Table (see pages 281–285). Priority seatings for lunch or dinner are easier to arrange.

4. A good rule at any full-service restaurant in the park is to keep it simple. Order sandwiches or basic dishes (roast turkey and mashed potatoes, for example).

Following are some comments from readers about Magic Kingdom full-service and counter-service restaurants. First, Cinderella's Royal Table character breakfast:

We were able to get into breakfast with Cinderella at the castle thanks to strategies described in your book. However, we were somewhat disappointed. The menu was extremely limited, space very tight, and the characters available for very brief amounts of time.

Is worth every bit of trouble; not only do the kids love it, the food is good, and you can have all you want.

The food was okay—a lot of characters: Snow White, Cinderella, Belle, Sleeping Beauty, Fairy Godmother, Mary Poppins. The place was not that big. but the characters spent a lot of time at each table—so much time that we only got to meet Snow White and Belle. The boys were bored. Was not worth the trouble of getting the seating.

Walked in for lunch with no reservations at 11:15. Waited 45 minutes, but it was inside the castle with air conditioning, and Cinderella and her Fairy Godmother sat on their thrones the first 15 minutes. $12 chicken Caesar salad and $5 kids' meals. My husband's sandwich was not good, and [when] he made a face, our waitress saw him. She came over and asked if he'd like something else and replaced it quick!

Fun, good food, and an unimaginable din was this reader's summation of the Crystal Palace character dinner:

Great food, great service, good price. Got to meet characters at dinner. We went at 4:30, and the din from small children was loud. (We did not care!!)

Pecos Bill's Café and Cosmic Ray's are two Magic Kingdom counter-service favorites among our readers:

If you are looking for heart-healthy meals, Pecos Bill's Café has a great chicken wrap. Pecos Bill's also has a pretty tasty hamburger with an outstanding fixin's bar (grilled onions and mushrooms, hot cheese and chili) for those not looking for a heart-healthy menu.

[At Cosmic Ray's], we had the "Family Meal" of a whole chicken and a generous serving of mashed potatoes for $15.99; with drinks the total was $21.00!! It was great, plus entertaining for the kids.

As a footnote, in 2003, Cosmic Ray's became the first counter-service restaurant in any of the Disney theme parks to offer a kosher menu.

Epcot

From the beginning, dining has been an integral component of Epcot's entertainment product. The importance of dining is reflected in the number of restaurants and in their ability to serve consistently interesting and well-prepared meals. This is in stark contrast to the Magic Kingdom, where, until recently, food service was seemingly an afterthought, with quality and selection a distant runner-up to logistical efficiency.

For the most part, Epcot's restaurants have always served decent food, though the World Showcase restaurants have occasionally been timid about delivering an honest representation of the host nation's cuisine. While these eateries have struggled with authenticity and have sometimes shied away from challenging the meat-and-potatoes palate of the average tourist, they are bolder now, encouraged by America's exponentially expanding appreciation of ethnic dining. True, the less adventuresome can still find sanitized and homogenized meals, but the same kitchens will serve up the real thing for anyone with a spark of curiosity and daring.

FULL-SERVICE RESTAURANTS IN EPCOT

Future World

Coral Reef	The Living Seas
The Garden Grill Restaurant	The Land

World Showcase

Biergarten	Germany
Bistro de Paris	France
Chefs de France	France
Le Cellier Steakhouse	Canada
L'Originale Alfredo di Roma Ristorante	Italy
Nine Dragons Restaurant	China
Restaurant Akershus	Norway
Restaurant Marrakesh	Morocco
Rose & Crown Dining Room	United Kingdom
San Angel Inn Restaurante	Mexico
Tempura Kiku	Japan
Teppanyaki Dining Room	Japan

EPCOT

Author's Favorite Counter-Service Restaurants

Kringla Bakeri og Kafé	Rose & Crown Pub
Sommerfest	Yakitori House

Many Epcot restaurants are overpriced, most conspicuously **Nine Dragons Restaurant** (China) and the **Coral Reef** (The Living Seas). Representing relatively good value through the combination of ambience and well-prepared food are **Chefs de France** (France), **Restaurant Akershus** (Norway), **Biergarten** (Germany), and **Restaurant Marrakesh** (Morocco). The Biergarten and the Marrakesh also have entertainment.

If cost is an issue, make lunch your main meal. Entrées are similar to those on the dinner menu, but prices are significantly lower.

Epcot has 13 full-service restaurants: 2 in Future World and 11 in World Showcase. With a couple of exceptions, these are among the best restaurants at Disney World, in or out of the theme parks. Profiles of Epcot full-service restaurants are presented at the end of this section.

While eating at Epcot can be a consummate hassle, an afternoon without priority seating for dinner in World Showcase is like not having a date on the day of the prom. Each pavilion has a beautifully seductive ethnic restaurant, offering the gastronomic delights of the world. To tour these exotic settings and not partake is almost beyond the limits of willpower. And although the fare in some World Showcase restaurants isn't always compelling, the overall experience is exhilarating. If you fail to dine in World Showcase, you'll miss one of Epcot's more delightful features.

If you want to sample the ethnic foods of World Showcase without eating in restaurants requiring priority seating, we recommend these counter-service specialties:

France	Boulangerie Pâtisserie, for French pastries
Germany	Sommerfest, for bratwurst and Beck's beer
Japan	Yakitori House, for yakitori (meat or vegetables on skewers)
Norway	Kringla Bakeri og Kafé, for pastries, open-face sandwiches, and Ringnes beer (our favorite)
United Kingdom	Rose & Crown Pub, for Guinness, Harp, and Bass beers and ales

(Epcot counter-service restaurants are profiled at the end of this section.)

Unofficial Guide readers have many diverse opinions of Epcot's full-service restaurants. Concerning the much-hyped Chefs de France:

Cafeteria food served on linen placemats. An expensive rip-off; [food] on par with Denny's.

What a joke!!! Pre-made food that anyone can get [where they live], served by snotty little princesses.

It was very noisy; the waiter broke glass on the floor three times during our meal.

And finally, from a United Kingdom reader, a detailed account of his experience:

We took dinner at the Chefs de France, expecting from previous experience a really classy meal, albeit expensive. The ambience was great—we could have been in Paris. The menu contained all the right items. But the entrées seriously disappointed. We tried sending one back because it arrived cold. The waiter took it away, stuck it under a hot lamp and brought it back minutes later. The top was now hot, sure enough, but the underside was still lukewarm, and the gravy was gaining a skin. This is not how it is done in France—we should have received a fresh entrée. Others in the party later admitted that their meals were not correctly heated. We also ordered a carafe of wine expecting European measures, but received only enough for three glasses. We had to order up another, so making the wine doubly expensive. Chefs de France needs to address its problems.

Though Chefs de France fares better with our *Unofficial Guide* restaurant critics and on our reader restaurant (thumbs up/thumbs down) survey, comments in our reader mail and e-mail have been pretty scathing. Maybe this year we'll hear more from readers who have a favorable opinion of Chefs de France. Negative feelings toward Chefs de France do not, incidentally, extend to **Bistro de Paris,** the other French restaurant. Bistro de Paris is generally highly regarded by all.

The Coral Reef Restaurant in the Living Seas pavilion fared a bit better:

Food was good; however service was poor and portions were small and overpriced. Music has added a lot of atmosphere.

Best desserts for children, but entrées are overpriced.

You were dead on; we went this year, and it was fairly disastrous. I think my dinner was prepared underwater.

Restaurant Marrakesh likewise garnered mixed reviews:

Restaurant Marrakesh is overrated. It may be a walk on the wild side for someone from say, Wichita, but I can find better and more exotic food at a dozen places in my neighborhood.

(For all you folks who are wondering where this reader is from: Arlington, Virginia.) More comments:

It's worth eating here just to see the interior. Going to Epcot and passing this gem up is like going to Paris and skipping Notre Dame.

The Rose & Crown Dining Room exceeded the expectations of many readers. This comment is fairly typical:

We were pleasantly surprised by the Rose & Crown [Dining Room], so much so that we have since been back several times. We love their sampler platter and the puff pastry with mushrooms. Simple but well prepared foods.

And finally, about the San Angel Inn:

Expensive, but where else can you drink Corona beer and dine under a moonlit sky at the base of a vaulted pyramid while serene boats drift by?

We love the view!!! The food was good, we enjoyed lunch there, since the portions are generous, and the prices are a little lower. [Priority seatings] are definitely recommended.

Disney-MGM Studios

Dining at Disney-MGM Studios is more interesting than in the Magic Kingdom and less ethnic than at Epcot. Disney-MGM has five restaurants where priority seating is recommended: The **Hollywood Brown Derby, 50's Prime Time Café, Sci-Fi Dine-In Theater Restaurant, Mama Melrose's Ristorante Italiano,** and the **Hollywood and Vine Cafeteria.** The upscale Brown Derby is by far the best restaurant at the Studios. For simple Italian food, including pizza, Mama Melrose's is fine. Just don't expect anything fancy. At the Sci-Fi Dine-In, you eat in little cars at a simulated drive-in movie of the 1950s. Though you won't find a more entertaining restaurant in Walt Disney World, the food is quite disappointing. Somewhat better is the 50's Prime Time Café, where you sit in Mom's kitchen of the 1950s and scarf down meat loaf while watching clips of vintage TV sitcoms. The 50's Prime Time Café is fun, and the food is a step up. The best way to experience either restaurant is to stop in for dessert or a drink between 2:30 and 4:30 p.m.

DISNEY-MGM STUDIOS	
Author's Favorite Counter-Service Restaurants	
Toy Story Pizza Planet	Backlot Express
ABC Commissary	Toluca Legs Turkey Co.

We receive considerable mail from readers recounting their Disney-MGM dining experiences. A man from Sumter, South Carolina, writes:

We had lunch at the Sci-Fi Dine-In. In the guide you gave it a terrible review, but I have always felt you guys are too hard on the Disney restaurants, so we went ahead and ate there. Well, on this one you were right on target! While the atmosphere was fun, and the clips were a hoot, the food was lousy ... and expensive!

A Mechanicsville, Virginia, family agreed:

You tried to warn us about the Sci-Fi Dine-In, but my four-year old was dying to eat there. The food was even worse than you said—and the cost! $9.50 for a hot dog and fries.

Readers respectively from Yakima, Washington and Glendale Heights, Illinois, chimed in, writing:

I admit I didn't follow your advice and we ate at the Sci-Fi. You were right, the food was expensive. It was actually our most expensive lunch on the trip.

Eating in miniature cars was original. But the food was mediocre and way overpriced. The proverbial hot dog and fries were $9.50.

The 50's Prime Time Café is always a hot topic. First from a Maryland reader:

50's Prime Time Café was a fun experience, but again, the food quality was, at best, mediocre. If my mom really did cook that way, I would have many times run away from home. Our poor reaction to the food quality pushed us quickly into the car and out of WDW. I never thought I would get down on my knees and kiss the sidewalk outside of a Perkins Pancake House.

But a West Newton, Massachusetts, family loved the Prime Time:

50's Prime Time Café: We know you guys didn't rate it very well, but we decided to go against your recommendation and give it a shot. We're so glad we did! For the five of us (ages 16–20), this dining experience was a blast. Our waiter (and big brother for the meal), "Leroy," came and sat at our table and helped us set our places so we wouldn't get in trouble with "Mom." When one member of our party cursed, "Mom" arrived to punish him, making him clear the table onto her tray, which he did shamefully. Overall, the experience was a total kick, which we talked about for the rest of the trip.

Other Prime Time advocates had this to say:

Best meal in park, but you must get into character [i.e., go along with the role-playing] to have fun.

The 50's Prime Time Café had very good food. It's hardly a gourmet dish, but I have had lots of chicken Caesar salads, many of them bad. The Prime Time Café's salad was really excellent! The chicken was amazingly moist, and the salad was very fresh tasting. Even the croutons were above par.

The Brown Derby was a favorite of a San Diego reader:

Delicious food, great selections, and an excellent end to an evening at the Studios.

While yet another reader made a culinary find at Mama Melrose's Ristorante:

Great flatbread pizza!! Our waiter was as slow as a snail, but the food was good.

If you arrive at Disney-MGM Studios without previously arranging priority seating for meals, do so at the the priority seating kiosk at the corner of Hollywood and Sunset boulevards or at the restaurants.

If you have no priority seating and become hungry during meal times, try Toy Story Pizza Planet (sometimes overlooked by the teeming hordes).

Disney-MGM Studios full-service and counter-service restaurants are profiled at the end of this chapter.

Animal Kingdom

Because touring the Animal Kingdom takes less than a day, crowds are heaviest from 9:30 a.m. until about 3:30 p.m. Expect a mob at lunch and thinner crowds at dinner. We recommend you tour early after a good breakfast, then eat a very late lunch or graze on vendor food. If you tour later in the day, eat lunch before you arrive, then enjoy dinner in or out of the theme park.

The Animal Kingdom mostly offers counter-service fast food. Although grilled meats are available, don't expect a broad choice of exotic dishes. Most Animal Kingdom eateries serve up traditional Disney theme-park fare: hot dogs, hamburgers, deli sandwiches, and the like. Even so, we found Animal Kingdom fast food to be a cut above the average Disney fare. **Flame Tree Barbeque** in Safari Village is our pick of the litter, both in terms of food quality and atmosphere. For a quiet refuge away from the crowds, you can't beat Flame Tree Barbeque's waterfront dining pavilions.

THE ANIMAL KINGDOM
Author's Favorite Counter-Service Restaurant
Flame Tree Barbecue

The only full-service restaurant is the **Rainforest Café,** with entrances both inside and outside the theme park (you don't have to purchase theme-park admission, in other words, to eat at the restaurant). Unlike the Rainforest Café at the Downtown Disney Marketplace, the Animal Kingdom branch accepts priority seatings.

More Readers' Comments about Walt Disney World Dining

Eating is a popular topic among *Unofficial Guide* readers. In addition to participating in our annual restaurant survey, many readers share their thoughts. The following comments are representative.

A reader from Carbondale, Illinois, exhorts other readers to be adventuresome in their choice of restaurants:

Please advise your readers to try "different" restaurants at Epcot! We had a blast dining at Akershus and Marrakesh! The service was great, food was different, but not weird. My husband is a picky eater, but even he was able to say that he tried Norwegian and Moroccan food at the end of our vacation! I feel like Marrakesh is not popular because people think the food is too ethnic. Well, it was ethnic enough, but not too hot or spicy, and the atmosphere was great. To me, it was the most themed restaurant—the inside SCREAMED Mediterranean, and the belly dancer was GREAT! I think it would be a fun restaurant for anyone with kids as well.

Another Illinois reader, this one from Glendale, had a positive experience with Disney food, writing:

On the food: In general, we were pleasantly surprised. I expected it to be over-priced, generally bad, and certainly unhealthy. There were a lot of options—and almost all restaurants (including counter service) had generally good food, and some healthy options. It is not the place to expect fine cuisine—and is certainly overpriced—but if you understand the parameter, you can eat quite well. One thing I appreciated was having a children's menu that did not consist only of hot dogs and fries. My children ate well, and we were able to get them a good variety of food—with plenty of fruits and vegetables.

Another big thumbs up from Terre Haute, Indiana, for the California Grill:

I had what might be the most memorable meal of my life at the California Grill. We left the kids with a sitter, (Vivian from Fairy Godmother's: "You'll like her—she's been with me 20 years."), and went out for a romantic evening. You mentioned being seated at the counter overlooking the show kitchen, which I'm sure would be great, but for a romantic dinner, you can't beat the smaller dining room. We didn't know it existed, but we were led through the end of the main dining room through large glass doors to a table in the corner of a smaller dining room with only seven other tables. Away from the cacophony of the main dining room, this was a quiet haven with a spectacular view. We watched as a thunderstorm with all its light-ning glory rolled toward, then over us. Afterward, we were awed by a stun-ning full rainbow. It was a nice treat for our 10th anniversary. The food was out of this world, and the service (by Judy) was impeccable.

A family of five loved Whispering Canyon at the Wilderness Lodge:

Our best experience for dining was at the Whispering Canyon. My girls (6, 10, and 11) thought the servers were great. They joked with each other, shouted and laughed with the kids. They had wooden pony races around the restaurant for the kids. Our waiter even sat down with our kids and helped my oldest "finish" her salad and showed my youngest how to eat whipped cream off her nose. Out of all the places we ate, this was my kids' (and Mom and Dad's) favorite. Oh, and the food was pretty good too.

We've received consistent raves for Boma:

Boma (the African Buffet at the Animal Kingdom Lodge) is terrific!!

A Lombard, Illinois, mom underscores the need to make priority seat-ings in advance:

Please stress that if you want a "normal" dining hour at a specific restaurant, call them 60 or 45 days in advance—IT IS WORTH IT! One reservation I wanted to change about two weeks before our arrival date, and I had a choice of dinner times of either 7:45 or 9 p.m. (not feasible with little ones).

A Baltimore, Maryland, reader thinks we failed to give Wolfgang Puck his due:

Bob, you greatly underestimated the Wolfgang Puck Express in Marketplace. It's not five-star, but it is a great fast-food alternative. We got yummy gourmet pizzas and rotisserie chicken ... but the best part were the beer barrels. We ended up eating there on two occasions.

I was apprehensive about the food, [but] our experiences were very good overall at both the full-service and counter-service restaurants. Face it, you don't go to Disney for the dinner bargains.

A Greenwood, Indiana, family agrees:

The food was certainly expensive, but contrary to many of the views expressed in the Unofficial Guide, *we all thought the quality was excellent. Everything we had, from chicken strips and hot dogs in the parks to dinner at the Coral Reef, tasted great and seemed very fresh.*

A family from Youngsville, Louisiana, got a leg up on other guests:

The best thing we ate were the smoked turkey legs.

A mom from Aberdeen, South Dakota, writes:

When we want great food, we'll be on a different vacation. Who wants to waste fun time with the kids at a sit-down restaurant when you know the food will be mediocre anyway?

A woman from Verona, Wisconsin, offers this:

We think the character meals are underrated in all guidebooks. These meals are in pleasant settings and provide an easy, efficient way for little kids to interact with characters while providing adults with an opportunity to relax. For value and good food, we especially like the breakfasts. Yes, they're a little pricey, but you get more than food. Probably our favorite is at the Garden Grill at The Land at Epcot. This year, they even gave us souvenir hats.

A mother of three from Jamaica, New York, waited two hours and 40 minutes for a table at the Rainforest Café and still had a good time:

The Rainforest Café was an absolute delight. Our six-year-old sat right next to a gorilla that ranted every few minutes; our ten-month-old loved the huge fish tanks; and they loved the food. Our wait for a table was two hours, so we went back to the hotel and returned two hours later. We still had to wait 40 minutes, but it was worth it. The gorilla room had more of a jungle feel than the elephant room.

But a Richardson, Texas, family had this to say:

A terrible dinning experience. It was wild, wet, loud, and the service was the worst in WDW.

A Lehi, Utah, woman also had a rough time:

Rainforest Café was awful!!!! It was so loud we couldn't even hear our wait-

ress or each other. The service was unorganized and food wasn't worth the price we paid.

It goes on. A Charleroi, Pennylvania, reader offered this report:

I walked in to find no host in sight so I stood and stood. When the host came, she said the servers were on break and I would be seated in fifteen minutes. I pointed out the three customers in a room of empty tables and questioned why I was not allowed to sit to examine the menu. The host huffed and walked away. When she came back, she said she would seat me after she seated the customers behind me. I told her they were not even in the building while I was looking for her. I got a table right away—after an argument.

We should note that most negative reader comments concerning the Rainforest Café pertain to the Downtown Disney location and not to the Animal Kingdom location.

On the topic of saving money, a Seattle woman offered the following:

For those wanting to save a few bucks (or in some cases several bucks) we definitely suggest eating outside WDW for as many meals as possible. To keep down our costs, we ate a large breakfast before leaving the hotel, had a fast-food lunch in the park, a snack later to hold us over, and then ate a good dinner outside the park. Several good restaurants in the area have excellent food at reasonable prices, notably Café Tu Tu Tango and Ming [Court], both on International Drive. We also obtained the "Entertainment Book" for Orlando, which offers 50% off meals all over town.

Counter-Service Restaurant Mini-Profiles

To help you find palatable fast-service food that suits your taste, we have developed mini-profiles of Walt Disney World theme-park counter-service restaurants. The restaurants are listed alphabetically by theme park.

For convenience, we've repeated our lists of favorite counter-service restaurants here. The restaurants profiled below are rated for quality and portion size (self-explanatory), as well as for value. The value rating ranges from A to F as follows:

A = Exceptional value, a real bargain
B = Good value
C = Fair value, you get exactly what you pay for
D = Somewhat overpriced
F = Extremely overpriced

THE MAGIC KINGDOM

Author's Favorite Counter-Service Restaurants

Cosmic Ray's (serves kosher food)—Tomorrowland

The Plaza Pavilion—Tomorrowland

Pecos Bill's Tall Tale Inn & Café—Frontierland

Aunt Polly's Dockside Inn (Seasonal)

QUALITY Good | VALUE B | PORTION Medium | LOCATION Frontierland/Tom Sawyer Island

Selection Desserts; ice-cream cones, floats, chocolate brownies, and apple pie.
Comments Scenic and off the beaten path. Closes at dusk.

Casey's Corner

QUALITY Good | VALUE B | PORTION Medium | LOCATION Main Street U.S.A

Selection Quarter-pound hot dogs; fries; and brownies.
Comments A little pricey on the dogs and very crowded—keep walking.

Columbia Harbour House

QUALITY Fair | VALUE C+ | PORTION Medium | LOCATION Liberty Square

Selection Fried fish and chicken strips; hummus, ham-and-cheese, veggie, and tuna-salad sandwiches; Starboard Deck sandwich; child's plate with bologna-and-cheese sandwich or macaroni and cheese, cookie, and child's beverage; New England clam chowder (in bread bowl) and vegetable chili; coleslaw; chips; fries; garden salad with chicken; and apple pie and cookies.
Comments Fried items aren't appetizing, but the soups and sandwiches and their unusual sides (hummus, carrots, broccoli slaw) are a nice change from the usual pizza/burger fare. Tables usually available upstairs. Quickest service within spitting distance of Fantasyland.

Cosmic Ray's Starlight Café

QUALITY Good | VALUE B | PORTION Large | LOCATION Tomorrowland

Selection Rotisserie chicken meal; deli sandwiches; stacked sandwiches; cheesesteak subs; burgers (including vegetarian); chicken strips; hot dogs; child's plate with corn dog–nuggets and fries; vegetable and cream-of-chicken soups; chicken Caesar salads; fries, mashed potatoes; and ice-cream bars.
Comments Big place. Tables inside usually available. Out-of-this-world entertainment on stage. This is the place if everybody in your party is picky—you'll have plenty of options. Nice burger-fixin' bar. Kosher items available.

El Pirata y el Perico (Seasonal)

QUALITY Fair | VALUE B | PORTION Medium to large | LOCATION Adventureland

Selection Nachos; taco salad; tacos; beef empanada with black beans and rice; chili with cheese; churros; and candy bars.
Comments Large, shaded eating area. Open seasonally and often overlooked.

The Lunching Pad

QUALITY Good | VALUE B– | PORTION Medium | LOCATION Tomorrowland

Selection Smoked turkey legs; Disney-character cookies; and frozen sodas.

Comments Smack in the middle of Tomorrowland, The Lunching Pad is good for a quick snack or for waiting for people on nearby rides.

Mrs. Potts' Cupboard

QUALITY Good | VALUE B | PORTION Medium | LOCATION Fantasyland

Selection Sundaes, including regular, fudge brownies and strawberry shortcakes; floats, shakes; cookies; drinks.

Comments An ice cream stop. Good options, decent value.

Pecos Bill's Tall Tale Inn & Café

QUALITY Good | VALUE B | PORTION Medium to large | LOCATION Frontierland

Selection Cheeseburgers; hot dogs; chicken wraps; chicken salad; chili; hot dogs, chili dogs; child's plate with hot dog and child's beverage; fries and chili cheese fries; chocolate cream pie.

Comments Use the great fixin's station to garnish your burger or dog. Combos come with fries or carrots.

The Pinocchio Village Haus

QUALITY Fair to good | VALUE B | PORTION Medium | LOCATION Fantasyland

Selection Quarter-pound cheeseburger; half-pound double cheeseburger; quarter-pound hot dog; turkey sandwich; combos come with carrots or fries; fries with the works; garden salad (with or without chicken); child's plate with peanut-butter-and-jelly sandwich or hot dog, chips, and a child's beverage; fries; fresh fruit; brownies and shakes.

Comments Almost always crowded. Try Columbia Harbour House on the border with Liberty Square. And for the same burger/dog fare, Pecos Bill's gets higher marks.

The Plaza Pavilion

QUALITY Good | VALUE B | PORTION Medium to large | LOCATION Tomorrowland

Selection Six-inch pizzas; pizza combo meal with small salad; bread sticks; regular tossed salads; chicken salads; chicken strips; Italian stacked sandwiches; child's plate with peanut-butter-and-jelly sandwiches, chips, and a child's beverage; fries; sugar-free brownies, and ice-cream bars.

Comments Usually not too crowded. Along with Cosmic Ray's, our pick for best menu selection in the Magic Kingdom.

Scuttle's Landing

QUALITY Fair to good | VALUE B | PORTION Medium | LOCATION Fantasyland

Selection Caramel corn; frozen cokes; pretzels (soft); chips; breakfast menu with muffins and bagels.

Comments Essentially a snack bar, but not a bad place to grab breakfast food.

EPCOT

Author's Favorite Counter-Service Restaurants

Kringla Bakeri og Kafé	Sommerfest
Rose & Crown Pub	Yakitori House

Boulangerie Pâtisserie

QUALITY Good | VALUE B | PORTION Small to medium | LOCATION World Showcase, France

Selection Coffee; croissants, pastries, chocolate mousse; sandwiches; baguettes; cheese plate; ham-and-cheese croissant; quiche Lorraine; and French wine and beer.

Comments Okay for a light meal, better for a snack. A few outside tables. Tucked away in the corner, a little hard to find.

Cantina de San Angel

QUALITY Fair to good | VALUE C+ | PORTION Medium | LOCATION World Showcase, Mexico

Selection Hard and soft chicken tacos; enchiladas; burritos; ensalada Mexicana; child's plate with burrito, chips, and child's beverage; nachos; churros; Dos Equis and frozen margaritas.

Comments Most meals are served with refried beans and salsa. Tables are outdoors.

Crêpes des Chefs de France

QUALITY Good | VALUE B+ | PORTION Medium | LOCATION World Showcase, France

Selection Crêpes with chocolate, orange, or strawberry ice cream (vanilla or chocolate). Specialty beer (Fischer la Belle). Espresso.

Comments Dessert bar and café attached to neighboring Chefs de France.

Electric Umbrella Restaurant

QUALITY Fair to good | VALUE B– | PORTION Medium | LOCATION Future World, Innoventions, Plaza East

Selection Cheese omelet meal, French toast and French toast sticks, cereal, bagel breakfast sandwich, sausage, bacon; burgers, veggie burgers, and chicken strips with fries; chicken sandwiches; child's plates with macaroni and cheese; chicken nuggets; chicken Caesar salad; fruit cups; cookies, including chocolate-chip; pies, including chocolate cream pie and cheesecake; Budweiser and Bud Light.

Comments All items are served with fries. Shaded outdoor seating; topping bar.

Fountain View Espresso & Bakery

QUALITY Good to Excellent | VALUE C+ | PORTION Small to medium | LOCATION InnoventionsWest

Selection Gourmet pastries, cookies, tarts, croissants, muffins, cakes; breakfast pockets; fruit cups; specialty smoothies, espresso products, sodas, and juices.

Comments Sugar-free options, indoor and outdoor seating. Overpriced but beautiful desserts.

Kringla Bakeri og Kafé

QUALITY Good to excellent | VALUE B | PORTION Small to medium | LOCATION World Showcase, Norway

Selection Pastries; sugar-free chocolate mousse; lefse (traditional potato bread); cakes and cookies; rice cream; yogurt; open-faced sandwiches (smoked ham, smoked turkey, smoked salmon); green salad, fruit cup; sweet pretzels with raisins and almonds; cinnamon rolls; waffles; wine and imported beers (Ringnes beer on tap, 20 oz. for $6.75).

Comments Good but pricey. Shaded outdoor seating.

Liberty Inn

QUALITY Fair | VALUE C | PORTION Medium | LOCATION World Showcase, *The American Adventure*

Selection Burgers and fries; hot dogs; chicken strips; turkey club and grilled-chicken sandwiches; vegetarian burger; tuna salad subs; chili cheese fries; fruit cups; chicken Caesar salad; child's hot dog and child's chicken-nugget plate; apple pie, chocolate-chip cookies, and root-beer floats; ice cream (regular or sugar-free/fat-free); Samuel Adams, Budweiser, and Bud Light.

Comments The only place in World Showcase for American fast food. Ample seating. Spacious atmosphere.

Lotus Blossom Café

QUALITY Fair | VALUE C | PORTION Medium | LOCATION World Showcase, China

Selection Beef and chicken rice bowls; sweet-and-sour chicken; vegetable lo mein; egg rolls; beef fried rice; crystal noodle salad; ginger ice cream, red-bean ice cream, strawberry and mango smoothies, bubble tea (tea with tapioca balls), fruit cup with lychee, almond cookies, fortune cookies; child's plate with egg roll and beef fried rice or sweet, crispy wonton ribbons in bag (includes beverage); and Chinese beer and wine.

Comments Marginal Chinese at fancy prices. Nothing terrible; nothing amazing.

Refreshment Outpost

QUALITY Good | VALUE B– | PORTION Small | LOCATION World Showcase, between Germany and China

Selection Gourmet ice cream (waffle cones or dish), snacks; frozen bananas; frozen slushes (frozen soda); coffee, hot cocoa or tea; bottled beer or on tap, Michelob and Redhook (20 oz. $5.50, 32 oz. $8.99).

Comments Mainly prepackaged food for a quick drink or snack.

Refreshment Port

Between the World Showcase and Future World

QUALITY Good | VALUE B | PORTION Medium | LOCATION Between World Showcase and Future World

Selection Chicken nuggets; fries; McFlurry dessert.

Comments Though now a thinly disguised McDonald's, it's still a convenient place for a snack.

Rose & Crown Pub

QUALITY Good | VALUE C | PORTION Medium | LOCATION World Showcase, U.K.

Selection Seasonal salad; smoked salmon; lamb barley; soup; shortbread; fruit and cheese plate; ham and cheese pastry; and Guinness, Harp, and Bass beers and ales, as well as other spirits.

Comments The attraction here is the pub atmosphere and the draft beer. Note that the restaurant requires priority seating while the pub does not. Order food at the bar to get anything to go or as a quick sit-down alternative. Outside the pub is Harry Ramsden Fish & Chips serving food to go. See also the full-service restaurant profile for the Rose & Crown Dining Room, later in this chapter.

Sommerfest

QUALITY Good | VALUE B– | PORTION Medium | LOCATION World Showcase, Germany

Selection Bratwurst and frankfurter sandwiches with kraut; smoked ham sandwiches; chicken schnitzel; soft pretzels; soup; apple strudel and Black Forest cake; and German wine and beer (Beck's).

Comments Tucked in the entrance to the Biergarten restaurant, Sommerfest is hard to find from the street. Very limited seating. Not for kids who are picky eaters.

Sunshine Season Food Fair

QUALITY Fair to good | VALUE C | PORTION Medium | LOCATION Future World, The Land

Selection Potatoes with cheese and bacon, and chicken and vegetables; soups and salads; barbecued chicken and ribs; smoked sandwiches with corn on the cob and fries; deli sandwiches; chicken Parmesan; pastas; veggie wrap; fruit-and-yogurt cups; brownies, cookies, ice cream and freshly baked goods; and beer.

Comments This is a food court with six different counters. Most of the counters offer adult and child combo meals, and several feature heart-healthy options. Most counters serve beverages, so you don't have to queue up twice. Very crowded at mealtimes, making empty tables difficult to find.

Tangierine Café

QUALITY Good | VALUE B | PORTION Medium | LOCATION World Showcase, Morocco

Selection Chicken and lamb shawarma; hummus; tabbouleh; lentil salad; chicken with couscous; chicken, or tabbouleh wraps; olives; child's meal of pizza or hamburger with fries and small beverage; Casablanca beer; baklava.

Comments You won't get the belly dancers that entertain inside the pavilion at Restaurant Marrakesh, but the food here is good with an authentic flavor. The best seating is at the outdoor tables. Sufficient shade under umbrellas and trees.

Yakitori House

QUALITY Excellent | VALUE B | PORTION Small to medium | LOCATION World Showcase, Japan

Selection Shogun combo meal with beef and chicken teriyaki and rice (adult and child versions); shrimp, chicken, and beef skewers with rice; beef curry; shrimp tempura and beef udon; side salad, fruit cup; sushi; seafood salad; pickled radishes; edamame; miso soup; child's fried chicken with vegetables and rice; ginger green tea, red-bean ice cream; Kirin beer, sake, and plum wine.

Comments A great place for a light meal. Nice cultural detailing. Limited seating.

Yorkshire County Fish Shop

QUALITY Good | VALUE B+ | PORTION Medium | LOCATION World Showcase, U.K.

Selection Fish 'n' chips, child's hot dog, crisps (English potato chips), shortbread. Bass Ale, Guinness, Woodpecker Sweet Cider (other specialty beers).

Comments A convenient fast-food window attached to the Rose & Crown Pub.

DISNEY-MGM STUDIOS

Author's Favorite Counter-Service Restaurants

Toy Story Pizza Planet	Backlot Express
ABC Commissary	Toluca Legs Turkey Co.

ABC Commissary

QUALITY Good | VALUE B+ | PORTION Medium to large | LOCATION Backlot

Selection Tabbouleh wrap; chicken; Cuban sandwiches, feijoada (Brazilian black beans), cheeseburgers; fries, white rice; vegetable noodle stir-fry; fish 'n' chips; marinated tomatoes; steamed white rice; child's chicken-nugget or fish 'n' chips plate; ice-cream bars; and pie; beer.

Comments Indoors, centrally located, air-conditioned, and usually not too crowded. Also offers a great traditional breakfast. Hard to find.

Backlot Express

QUALITY Good | VALUE B | PORTION Medium to large | LOCATION Backlot

Selection Burgers and fries or fruit; chicken salad; grilled turkey and cheese; children's lunch box (chicken nuggets); croissants; chicken strips; quarter-pound hot dogs; grilled vegetable sandwich; salad; desserts. Frozen soft drinks; beer.

Comments Often overlooked. Great burger-fixin' bar. Indoor and outdoor seating.

Catalina Eddie's

QUALITY Fair | VALUE B | PORTION Medium to large | LOCATION Sunset Boulevard

Selection Cheese, pepperoni, barbecue chicken pizzas; salads; apple pie, chocolate cake.

Comments Seldom crowded.

Dipsite

QUALITY Very good | VALUE A– | PORTION Large | LOCATION Backlot

Selection Steak sub sandwich, funnel cake with fruit toppings, snow cones; chips; beer and soda.

Comments A great place for a serious sandwich prepared right in front of you.

Min and Bill's Dockside Diner

QUALITY Fair | VALUE C | PORTION Small to medium | LOCATION Echo Lake

Selection Shakes and beverages, beer; chips; cookies and brownies; variety of pretzels, including spicy cheese stuffed, and apple cinnamon or cream cheese dessert pretzels.

Comments Limited outdoor seating.

Rosie's All American Café

QUALITY Good | VALUE B | PORTION Medium | LOCATION Sunset Boulevard

Selection Cheeseburgers, bacon cheeseburgers, double cheeesburgers, veggie burgers; chicken strips; soup; side salads; fries, chips; apple pie, chocolate cake.

Comments Sandwiches are premade. Backlot Express is a better option for the same fare.

Starring Rolls Café

QUALITY Fair to good | VALUE C | PORTION Small to medium | LOCATION Sunset Boulevard

Selection Deli sandwiches, salads, pastries, desserts, chocolates, coffee. Gourmet.

Comments Open for breakfast on some mornings. Slowest service of any counter-service eatery. Pastries look better than they taste. Expensive; prices not on display.

Studio Catering Co. (Seasonal)

QUALITY Good | VALUE B | PORTION Small to medium | LOCATION Backlot

Selection Pretzels; popcorn; chips; fruit cups.

Comments Ice cream has separate service lines. Good place for a break while your kids enjoy the Honey, I Shrunk the Kids playground. Shady outside seating.

Toluca Legs Turkey Co.

QUALITY Good | VALUE B | PORTION Medium to large | LOCATION Sunset Boulevard

Selection Smoked turkey legs, hot dogs; baked potatoes; cookies, chips, muffins, pastries, bagels, croissants, cereal; coffee, tea, hot chocolate, and bottled soda.

Comments This vendor stall serves up some of the tastiest fast food in the park. Often overlooked. Covered outside seating.

Toy Story Pizza Planet

QUALITY Good | VALUE B+ | PORTION Medium | LOCATION Backlot

Selection Cheese, pepperoni, or veggie pizzas; salads; cookies, and crisped rice treats.

Comments The place for pizza at the Studios. Fresh ingredients. Gets good marks from readers. Combo meals are not a good deal (same price as buying separately).

THE ANIMAL KINGDOM

Author's Favorite Counter-Service Restaurant
Flame Tree Barbecue

Chakranadi Chicken Shop

QUALITY Good | VALUE C | PORTION Small | LOCATION Asia

Selection Pot stickers; stir-fried chicken with rice; Thai beef salad; Chai tea.

Comments Tasty food, tiny portions.

Flame Tree Barbecue

QUALITY Good | VALUE B– | PORTION Large | LOCATION Safari Village

Selection Half-slab St. Louis ribs; smoked half chicken; beef, pork, and chicken sandwiches; barbecue chicken salad; combination barbecue platters; crisp green salad with chicken; child's plate of peanut-butter-and-jelly sandwich or mini–hot dogs and chips with cookie; steak fries (with or without cheese), baked beans, corn-on-the-cob, coleslaw, onion rings; chocolate cake; Safari Amber, Budweiser.

Comments Queues very long at lunch time, but seating is ample and well shaded. One of our favorites for lunch.

Pizzafari

QUALITY Good | VALUE B | PORTION Medium | LOCATION Safari Village

Selection Cheese and pepperoni personal pizzas; Caesar salad; bread sticks; Italian deli sandwiches; child's cheese pretzel; peanut butter and jelly; cinnamon apples on pizza shell; frozen strawberry lemonade; Budweiser and draft beer.

Comments A favorite with children. Hectic at peak mealtimes. The pizza is pretty unimpressive—toppings resemble those on a cheap frozen pizza.

Restaurantosaurus

QUALITY Good | VALUE B+ | PORTION Medium to large | LOCATION Dinoland U.S.A

Selection Hamburgers, cheeseburgers, hot dogs; McDonald's Chicken McNuggets and Happy Meals; mesquite-grilled chicken salad; fries, brownies, strawberry shortcake, and cookies; espresso products, coffee, tea, cocoa; apple and orange juice; and beer.

Comments Picky children might enjoy Restaurantosaurus. Topping bar available. Character breakfast every day.

Tamu Tamu

QUALITY Good | VALUE C | PORTION Large | LOCATION Africa

Selection Various flavors of yogurt or ice cream, available in cones or as sundaes; ice-cream floats; smoothies. Sugar-free options.

Comments Seating is behind building and could easily be overlooked.

Tusker House Restaurant

QUALITY Very good | VALUE B– | PORTION Medium to large | LOCATION Africa

Selection Half rotisserie chicken; grilled salmon; corn chowder; fried chicken sandwich; turkey wraps; smoked turkey or veggie focaccia; chicken salad; grilled-chicken sandwich; roasted vegetable sandwich with tabbouleh; peanut butter and jelly; child's plate with macaroni and cheese; cheesecake, chocolate or carrot cake.

Comments Excellent selections for health-conscious diners. Salads are refreshing. Separate line for bakery items. Also serves a nice sit-down breakfast.

Walt Disney World Restaurants: Rated and Ranked

To help you in your dining choices, we have developed profiles of full-service restaurants at Disney World. Each profile allows you to quickly check the restaurant's cuisine, location, star rating, cost range, quality rating, and value rating. Profiles are listed alphabetically by restaurant.

Star Rating The star rating represents the entire dining experience: style, service, and ambience, in addition to taste, presentation, and quality of food. Five stars is the highest rating and indicates that the restaurant offers the best of everything. Four-star restaurants are above average, and three-star restaurants offer good, though not necessarily memorable meals. Two-star restaurants serve mediocre fare, and one-star restaurants are below average. Our star ratings don't correspond to ratings awarded by AAA, Mobil, Zagat's, or other restaurant reviewers.

Cost Range The next rating tells how much a complete meal will cost. We include a main dish with vegetable or side dish, and a choice of soup or salad. Appetizers, desserts, drinks, and tips aren't included. We've rated the cost as inexpensive, moderate, or expensive.

Inexpensive	$12 or less per person
Moderate	$13–$23 per person
Expensive	More than $23 per person

Quality Rating The food quality is rated on a scale of one to five stars, five being the best rating attainable. The quality rating is based on the taste, freshness of ingredients, preparation, presentation, and creativity of food served. There is no consideration of price. If you are a person who wants the best food available and cost is not an issue, you need look no further than the quality ratings.

Value Rating   If, on the other hand, you are looking for both quality and value, then you should check the value rating, expressed as stars.

★★★★★	Exceptional value, a real bargain
★★★★	Good value
★★★	Fair value, you get exactly what you pay for
★★	Somewhat overpriced
★	Significantly overpriced

Payment   All Disney restaurants now accept American Express, MasterCard, VISA, Diners Club, Discover, Disney credit card, and JCB (Japanese Credit Bureau).

Readers' Restaurant Survey Responses

For each Disney World restaurant profiled, we include the results of last year's readers' survey responses. Results are expressed as a percentage of responding readers who liked the restaurant well enough to eat there again (Thumbs Up), as opposed to the percentage of responding readers who had a bad experience and wouldn't go back (Thumbs Down). (Readers tend to be less critical than our *Unofficial Guide* restaurant reviewers.) If you would like to participate in the survey, complete and return the restaurant form on the last page of this book.

WALT DISNEY WORLD RESTAURANTS BY CUISINE					
Cuisine	Location	Overall Rating	Cost	Quality Rating	Value Rating
African					
Jiko	Animal Kingdom Lodge	★★★½	Expensive	★★★★	★★★½
Boma	Animal Kingdom Lodge	★★★½	Moderate	★★★½	★★★★
American					
California Grill	Contemporary	★★★★½	Expensive	★★★★½	★★★
Artist Point	Wilderness Lodge	★★★½	Moderate	★★★★	★★★
Planet Hollywood	Pleasure Island	★★★	Moderate	★★★★	★★★
Olivia's Café	Old Key West	★★★	Moderate	★★★½	★★★
The Hollywood Brown Derby	Disney-MGM	★★★½	Expensive	★★★★	★★★
House of Blues	West Side	★★★	Moderate	★★★½	★★★
Yacht Club Galley	Yacht Club	★★★	Moderate	★★★½	★★★
Wolfgang Puck Café	West Side	★★★	Expensive	★★★½	★★★
All-Star Café	Wide World of Sports	★★½	Moderate	★★★	★★★

WALT DISNEY WORLD RESTAURANTS BY CUISINE (continued)

Cuisine	Location	Overall Rating	Cost	Quality Rating	Value Rating
American (continued)					
Whispering Canyon Café	Wilderness Lodge	★★★	Moderate	★★★½	★★★★
All Star Café	Disney-MGM	★★½	Moderate	★★★	★★★
Hollywood & Vine	Disney-MGM	★★½	Inexpensive	★★★	★★★
Liberty Tree Tavern	Magic Kingdom	★★½	Moderate	★★★	★★★
Boatwright's Dining Hall	Port Orleans	★★½	Moderate	★★★	★★
Rainforest Café	Downtown Disney and Animal Kingdom	★★½	Moderate	★★★	★★
Cinderella's Royal Table	Magic Kingdom	★★½	Moderate	★★	★★
ESPN Club	BoardWalk	★★½	Moderate	★★★	★★★
The Garden Grill Restaurant	Epcot	★★	Moderate	★★★	★★★
50's Prime Time Café	Disney-MGM	★★½	Moderate	★★★	★★
Grand Floridian Café	Grand Floridian	★★	Moderate	★★★	★★
Gulliver's Grill	Swan	★★	Expensive	★★★	★★
Sci-Fi Dine-In Theater Restaurant	Disney-MGM	★★	Moderate	★★½	★★
Baskervilles	Grosvenor Resort	★★	Moderate	★★	★★★
Big River Grille & Brewing Works	BoardWalk	★★	Moderate	★★	★★
The Plaza	Magic Kingdom	★★	Moderate	★★	★★
Buffet					
Boma	Animal Kingdom Lodge	★★★½	Moderate	★★★★	★★★★★
Cape May Café	Beach Club	★★★½	Moderate	★★★½	★★★★
Restaurant Akershus	Epcot	★★★½	Moderate	★★★★	★★★★
The Crystal Palace	Magic Kingdom	★★★	Moderate	★★★½	★★★
1900 Park Fare	Grand Floridian	★★½	Moderate	★★★	★★★
Biergarten	Epcot	★★½	Moderate	★★★	★★★★
Hollywood & Vine	Disney-MGM	★★½	Inexpensive	★★★	★★★
Chef Mickey's	Contemporary	★★½	Moderate	★★★	★★★
Chinese					
Nine Dragons Restaurant	Epcot	★★½	Expensive	★★★	★

WALT DISNEY WORLD RESTAURANTS BY CUISINE (continued)

Cuisine	Location	Overall Rating	Cost	Quality Rating	Value Rating
Cuban					
Bongos Cuban Café	West Side	★★	Moderate	★★	★★
English					
Rose & Crown Dining Room	Epcot	★★★	Moderate	★★★½	★★
French					
Chefs de France	Epcot	★★★★	Moderate	★★★★	★★★
Bistro de Paris	Epcot	★★★	Expensive	★★★½	★★
German					
Biergarten	Epcot	★★★	Moderate	★★★½	★★★★
Gourmet					
Victoria & Albert's	Grand Floridian	★★★★½	Expensive	★★★★★	★★★★
Arthur's 27	Wyndham Palace	★★★★	Expensive	★★★★	★★★
Italian					
Palio	Swan	★★★½	Expensive	★★★½	★★★
Portobello Yacht Club	Pleasure Island	★★★	Expensive	★★★	★★
Tony's Town Square Restaurant	Magic Kingdom	★★½	Moderate	★★★	★★
L'Originale Alfredo di Roma Ristorante	Epcot	★★½	Expensive	★★★	★★½
Mama Melrose's Ristorante Italiano	Disney-MGM	★★½	Moderate	★★★	★★
Japanese					
Kimonos	Swan	★★★★	Moderate	★★★★½	★★★
Mitsukoshi Teppanyaki Dining Room	Epcot	★★★½	Expensive	★★★★	★★★
Tempura Kiku	Epcot	★★★	Moderate	★★★★	★★★
Benihana— Steakhouse & Sushi	Hilton	★★★	Moderate	★★★½	★★★
Mediterranean					
Cítricos	Grand Floridian	★★★★	Expensive	★★★★½	★★★
Spoodles	BoardWalk	★★★½	Moderate	★★★★	★★★
Fresh	WDW Dolphin	★★½	Moderate	★★½	★★

WALT DISNEY WORLD RESTAURANTS BY CUISINE (continued)

Cuisine	Location	Overall Rating	Cost	Quality Rating	Value Rating
Mexican					
San Angel Inn Restaurante	Epcot	★★★	Expensive	★★★½	★★
Maya Grill	Coronado Springs	★★	Expensive	★★	★★
Moroccan					
Restaurant Marrakesh	Epcot	★★★	Moderate	★★★½	★★★
Norwegian					
Restaurant Akershus	Epcot	★★★½	Moderate	★★★★	★★★★
Polynesian/ Pan Asian					
'Ohana	Polynesian	★★★	Moderate	★★★½	★★★
Kona Café	Polynesian	★★★	Moderate	★★★	★★★★
Seafood					
Flying Fish Café	BoardWalk	★★★★	Expensive	★★★★	★★★
Artist Point	Wilderness Lodge	★★★½	Moderate	★★★★	★★★
Narcoossee's	Grand Floridian	★★★½	Expensive	★★★½	★★
bluezoo	WDW Dolphin	★★★	Expensive	★★★	★★
Cap'n Jack's Restaurant	Downtown Disney	★★½	Moderate	★★	★★
Coral Reef	Epcot	★★½	Expensive	★★★	★★
Fulton's Crab House	Pleasure Island	★★½	Expensive	★★★½	★★
Shutters at Old Port Royale	Caribbean Beach	★★	Moderate	★★½	★★
Finn's Grill	Hilton	★	Moderate	★★	★★
Steak					
Shula's Steak House	Dolphin	★★★★	Expensive	★★★★	★★★
Yachtsman Steakhouse	Yacht Club	★★★	Expensive	★★★½	★★
Le Cellier Steakhouse	Epcot	★★★	Moderate	★★★	★★★
Concourse Steakhouse	Contemporary	★★★	Moderate	★★★	★★
The Outback	Wyndham Palace	★★	Expensive	★★★	★★
Shutters at Old Port Royale	Caribbean Beach	★★	Moderate	★★½	★★

Full-Service Restaurant Profiles

ALL STAR CAFÉ ★★½

AMERICAN | MODERATE | QUALITY ★★★ | VALUE ★★★

READER'S SURVEY RESPONSES 82% 👍 18% 👎

Disney's Wide World of Sports; (407) 827-8326

Customers People attending sporting events **Reservations** Not necessary **When to go** Anytime **Entrée range** $9–$19 (child $6) **Service** ★★ **Friendliness** ★½ **Parking** Wide World of Sports' lot **Bar** Full service **Wine selection** Minimal **Dress** Jerseys if you've got 'em **Disabled access**: Yes

Lunch and dinner Daily, 11:30 a.m.–9 p.m. (fall/winter, Thursday–Sunday)

Setting and atmosphere Think Hard Rock Café but with sports memorabilia instead of musical instruments. More than 20 big-screen TVs play whatever game is on.

House specialties Burgers, sandwiches, fried chicken, ribs.

Entertainment and amenities Televised sporting events.

Summary and comments This originally was the Official All Star Café, part of the Planet Hollywood company backed by such sports stars as Shaquille O'Neal and Wayne Gretzky. Though it's changed hands, the food is still unpretentious American cuisine—giant cheeseburgers, nachos, piles of chicken wings and onion rings, chili, and ice cream sundaes. You wouldn't go out of your way to dine here, but this menu works for hungry fans at Disney's Wide World of Sports.

ARTHUR'S 27 ★★★★

GOURMET | EXPENSIVE | QUALITY ★★★★ | VALUE ★★★

READER'S SURVEY RESPONSES 78% 👍 22% 👎

Wyndham Palace, Downtown Disney Resort Area; (407) 827-3450

Customers Hotel guests and locals **Reservations** Necessary **When to go** Sunset or during fireworks at any of the three parks **Entrée range** $22–$40 **Service** ★★ **Friendliness** ★★ **Parking** Complementary valet **Bar** Full service **Wine selection** Award-winning **Dress** Jackets preferred, tie optional **Disabled access** Yes

Dinner Daily, 6–10 p.m.

Setting and atmosphere From its perch on the 27th floor of the Wyndham Palace, Arthur's gives a breathtaking view of the glittering lights of Downtown Disney and fireworks from the Disney parks—but only if you ask for a table with a view. Diners sit at large booths, all set apart from each other with their own windows.

House specialties À la carte menu; Florida red snapper; loin of North American buffalo; Colorado rack of lamb.

Other recommendations Citrus-crusted sea bass; pepper-seared shrimp and scallops; cherry balsamic glazed breast of duck; salmon in strudel leaves; chilled breast of chicken.

Entertainment and amenities Live entertainment in lounge.

Summary and comments The best values at this overpriced restaurant are the four-and five-course table d'hôte offerings for $66 and $72. If you're not looking for a lot of food, you'll pay too much for what you get. Call at least a week in advance for reservations. The Wyndham is a convention hotel, and the dining room is often packed with conventioneers.

Honors and awards DiRoNa winner.

ARTIST POINT   ★★★½

SEAFOOD | MODERATE | QUALITY ★★★★ | VALUE ★★★

READER'S SURVEY RESPONSES 74% 👍 26% 👎

Disney's Wilderness Lodge and Villas; (407) 824-3200

Customers Hotel guests, locals **Priority seatings** Recommended for dinner **When to go** Anytime **Entrée range** $19–$30 (child $6–$9) **Service** ★★★★ **Friendliness** ★★★★★ **Parking** Hotel lot **Bar** Full service **Wine selection** All wines from Pacific Northwest **Dress** Casual **Disabled access** Yes

Dinner Daily, 5:30–10 p.m.

Setting and atmosphere The dining room is inspired by the grand national park lodges from the early twentieth century—two-story-high paintings depict the landscape of the Pacific Northwest, and out the tall windows you'll see wildflowers, the lake, a waterfall off high rocks and even an erupting geyser. Cast-iron chandeliers hold 12 lanterns with milk-glass panes, tables are heavy wood, uncovered, and engraved with animals native to the Northwest.

House specialties Roasted cedar plank salmon; roasted free-range chicken; pan-seared scallops; berry cobbler.

Other recommendations Grilled buffalo top sirloin.

Summary and comments The kitchen has a chef who knows what he is doing. Big seller is the cedar plank salmon, but the buffalo runs a close second in today's fat- and carb-conscious world. The restaurant recently went to an all-Pacific Northwest wine list, with some boutique wines you won't find anywhere else east of the Mississippi. You'll get a great meal without the stuffiness of a "gourmet" dining room, in a setting that makes dining a pleasure.

BASKERVILLES   ★★

AMERICAN | MODERATE | QUALITY ★★ | VALUE ★★★

READER'S SURVEY RESPONSES 76% 👍 24% 👎

Grosvenor Resort, Downtown Disney Resort Area; (407) 828-4444

Customers Hotel guests **Reservations** Accepted **When to go** Anytime **Entrée range** $12–$23 **Service** ★★★ **Friendliness** ★★ **Parking** Hotel lot **Bar** Full service **Wine selection** Good **Dress** Casual **Disabled access** Yes

Breakfast Daily, 7–11:30 a.m.

Lunch Monday–Friday, 11:30 a.m.–1 p.m.
Dinner Daily, 5–10 p.m.

Setting and atmosphere This is a half-hearted attempt to create an English drawing-room atmosphere. Unfortunately, it looks way too much like a cafeteria in a college dormitory.

House specialties Prime rib; specialty buffets.

Other recommendations Steak; Cajun snapper; coconut shrimp; Sherlock's breakfast combo.

Entertainment and amenities Murderwatch-mystery theatre Saturdays where guests solve the crime (priority seatings required, adults $40, children $11). Disney character breakfast three days a week. Live jazz on Fridays.

Summary and comments There's nothing special about the cuisine, but the best reason to dine here is the Disney character breakfast three days a week, with an all-you-can-eat buffet and a kid-sized buffet just for little ones. Along with the regular menu there's always a themed buffet (barbecue on Mondays, Italian on Wednesdays), and the Saturday murder-mystery dinners are popular with locals. Friday nights the restaurant features live jazz and a substantial seafood buffet.

BENIHANA—STEAKHOUSE & SUSHI ★★★

JAPANESE | MODERATE | QUALITY ★★★½ | VALUE ★★★

READER'S SURVEY RESPONSES 60% 👍 40% 👎

The Hilton, Downtown Disney Resort Area; (407) 827-4865

Customers Hotel guests and some locals **Reservations** Recommended **When to go** Anytime **Entrée range** $16–$43 **Service** ★★★★ **Friendliness** ★★★★ **Parking** Hotel lot **Bar** Full service **Wine selection** Good **Dress** Casual **Disabled access** Yes

Dinner Monday–Thursday, 5–10 p.m.; Friday–Sunday, 5:30–10 p.m.

Setting and atmosphere Large tables with built-in grills are crammed into small rooms decorated with rice-paper panels and Japanese lanterns. Lighting is low and focused on the stage—the chef's grill.

House specialties Teppanyaki service at large tables (where the chef cooks dinner in front of you). Specialties include New York steak; lobster tail; hibachi vegetables.

Other recommendations Japanese onion soup.

Entertainment and amenities Dinner is the show at this teppanyaki-service restaurant, where the chef does a lot of noisy chopping and grilling.

Summary and comments If you're looking for a nice, quiet dinner, be aware that diners sit at tables of eight and private conversation is almost impossible.

BIERGARTEN ★★★

GERMAN | MODERATE | QUALITY ★★★½ | VALUE ★★★★

READER'S SURVEY RESPONSES 86% 👍 14% 👎

Germany, World Showcase, Epcot; (407) 939-3463

Customers Theme-park guests **Priority seatings** Recommended **When to go** After 6 p.m. **Entrée range** $15 lunch (child $6), $20 dinner (child $8) **Service** ★★★ **Friendliness** ★★★ **Parking** Epcot lot **Bar** Full service **Wine selection** German **Dress** Casual **Disabled access** Yes

Lunch Daily, noon–3:45 p.m.
Dinner Daily, 4 p.m.–park close

Setting and atmosphere Hungry? This is the place to make a priority seating if you want to graze at a hefty German buffet that includes schnitzel, various wursts, spaetzle, rotkraut and sauerkraut, roast chicken, and sauerbraten (dinner only). Salads, breads, and desserts round out the offerings. The light level is low, and décor is inspired by a German village town square, with seating at long tables in a tiered dining room that surrounds a stage and dance floor. It's Oktoberfest every day, with a lederhosen-clad oompah band (including a singing saw) playing on the stage and encouraging diners to sing-along and dance. After a 32-ounce Beck's beer, you may even find yourself swept up for the chicken dance or a polka.

House specialties German potato salad; lentil salad; various sausages and wieners; spaetzle with gravy; and sauerbraten in sauerkraut. There is also rotisserie chicken, which looks and tastes like the rotisserie chicken you would get at any other country in World Showcase—or in the world, for that matter. The buffet is set up on wooden barrels, and the food is served from vats.

Other recommendations Bratwurst; stuffed cabbage; roast pork; beer.

Entertainment and amenities Oompah band and German dancers perform after 12:30 p.m.

Summary and comments Unless you have a very big party, you will be seated with other guests. But the lively, 25-minute dinner show (one every hour) and noisy dining room are part of the fun, especially for families. This is a bargain if you're a big eater.

BIG RIVER GRILLE & BREWING WORKS   ★★

AMERICAN | MODERATE | QUALITY ★★ | VALUE ★★

READER'S SURVEY RESPONSES 85% 👍 15% 👎

Disney's BoardWalk; (407) 560-0253

Customers Tourists **Priority seatings** Not accepted **When to go** Anytime **Entrée range** $10–$25 (child $5) **Service** ★★ **Friendliness** ★★★ **Parking** BoardWalk lot; valet parking is free before 5 p.m., $6 after (for nonresort guests only) **Bar** Full service **Wine selection** Minimal **Dress** Casual **Disabled access** Good

Lunch and dinner Daily, 11:30 a.m.–midnight

Setting and atmosphere Industrial cubist murals of factories, machinist-metal and wood chairs and tables, and a midnight-blue neon river that flows along the ceiling of the restaurant set a working-class atmosphere. The place is small—it seems like the huge copper brewing tanks take up more room than that allotted to the diners.

House specialties Hazelnut-crusted chicken, sautéed and served in sundried cherry sauce; flame-grilled meat loaf, topped with rich brown gravy.

Summary and comments Big River is outsourced to a Tennessee company and is the first brewpub at Walt Disney World. The Brewing Works brews six beers, including a light lager, a robust ale, and two seasonal choices. If you're a beer drinker and like try-ing something new, you should like this. If you're a beer drinker and have a craving for your favorite brew, you're out of luck—the hand-crafted beers are the only beers sold here. The food is okay, though nothing special. It's another good late-night choice. There is outside seating and service, weather permitting.

BISTRO DE PARIS   ★★★

FRENCH | EXPENSIVE | QUALITY ★★★½ | VALUE ★★

READER'S SURVEY RESPONSES 76% 👍 24% 👎

France, World Showcase, Epcot; (407) 939-3463

Customers Theme-park guests **Priority seatings** Recommended **When to go** Late dinner **Entrée range** $29–$35 **Service** ★★★ **Friendliness** ★★★★ **Parking** Epcot lot or BoardWalk lot and enter through back gate **Bar** Full service **Wine selec-tion** Good but pricey; several by the glass **Dress** Casual **Disabled access** Elevator to second level

Dinner Daily, 6–8:45 p.m.

Setting and atmosphere This is the more upscale of the two restaurants at the Epcot France pavilion, up a flight of stairs with its own kitchen. Open only for dinner, request a table at the windows to view World Showcase Lagoon. The quiet dining room, painted yellow with dark red banquettes, seats just 120, so service is attentive and personal.

House specialties Grilled Bahamian lobster tail; roasted veal loin with thyme and potato blinis; seared medallion of lamb with thyme flower.

Summary and comments Most diners enjoy the hustle and bustle of the noisy bistro downstairs, but for a quiet dinner and conversation, this is the spot. Chef Bruno Vrignon, who trained with famed Chef Paul Bocuse in France, has been with the restau-rant since it opened, and continues to turn out authentic, indulgent fare. Start with a duo of foie gras, end with the Grand Marnier soufflé, you'll think you've been trans-ported to Paris or Lyon.

BLUEZOO   ★★★

SEAFOOD | EXPENSIVE | QUALITY ★★★ | VALUE ★★

Walt Disney World Dolphin; France; (407) 934-1111

Customers Hotel guests, locals **Reservations** Mandatory **Priority seatings** Required **When to go** Anytime **Entrée range** $22–$54 **Service** ★★★ **Friendli-ness** ★★ **Parking** Valet or self park **Bar** Full service **Wine selection** Excellent **Dress** Casual **Disabled access** Good

Open Daily, 3:30–11 p.m.

Setting and atmosphere A dreamy setting designed by noted architect Jeffrey Beers, the dining room is swathed in blues with iridescent bubbles suspended from the lights. The name is from Chef Todd English's 7-year-old son, who saw an under-the-sea movie and said it looked like a "blue zoo." Open kitchen, raw bar, "dancing fish" on a circular rotisserie.

House specialties Clam chowder, whole roasted fish, grilled fish, Cantonese lobster.

Other recommendations Lobster chive dumplings, oven-roasted filet of beef, shake-and-bake fries

Summary and comments Celebrity chef Todd English opened this stylish Florida outpost, frequented by conventioneers who don't mind the high prices ($2 for a single oyster) and expensive wine list. Food is sophisticated, from the hand-cut pasta with mussels to whole fried crispy sea bass, but you can make a meal from the simple bowl of clam chowder with salt-cured bacon and the roasted beet salad with greens, goat cheese, and candied walnuts. The dining room gets noisy, and you'll rarely find Chef English in the kitchen, but bluezoo adds panache to Central Florida's growing restaurant scene.

BOATWRIGHT'S DINING HALL ★★½

AMERICAN/CAJUN | MODERATE | QUALITY ★★★ | VALUE ★★

READER'S SURVEY RESPONSES 50% 👍 50% 👎

Disney's Port Orleans Resort; (407) 934-5000

Customers Hotel guests **Priority seatings** Recommended for dinner **When to go** Early evening **Entrée range** Breakfast $7–$11 (child $5), dinner $15–$20 (child $6) **Service** ★★ **Friendliness** ★★★★ **Parking** Hotel lot **Bar** Full service **Wine selection** Fair; the beer selection is better. **Dress** Casual **Disabled access** Good

Breakfast Daily, 7–11:30 a.m.
Dinner Daily, 5–10 p.m.

Setting and atmosphere Diners sit in a large, noisy room under the skeleton of a riverboat under construction that looks sort of like the carcass of a mastodon. Tables are set with a boatwright's tool kit that contains condiments instead of tools. The real tools—two-handed saws, hatchets, chisels, and a few that are too obscure to identify—hang along the walls.

House specialties Jambalaya with chicken and andouille sausage.

Other recommendations Barbecue glazed pork ribs; pot roast; crab-stuffed salmon.

Summary and comments With 200 seats, Boatwright's is there to serve the masses (basic fare with a Cajun flair), but cuisine is pretty homogenized to meet the tastes of middle America. It's the only table-service restaurant in Port Orleans Resort, so it gets busy and there can be waits. Order a regional beer—Dixie or Blackened Voodoo—and relax.

BOMA ★★★½

AFRICAN | MODERATE | QUALITY ★★★½ | VALUE ★★★★

READER'S SURVEY RESPONSES 83% 👍 17% 👎

Animal Kingdom Lodge; (407) 938-3000

Customers Hotel guests **Reservations** Mandatory **Priority seatings** Required **When to go** Anytime **Entrée range** Breakfast $15 (child $8), dinner $24 (child $10) **Service** ★★★ **Friendliness** ★★★ **Parking** Complementary valet or self park in hotel's lot **Bar** Full service **Wine selection** All South African **Dress** Casual **Disabled access** Good

Breakfast Daily, 7:30–11 a.m.
Dinner Daily, 5:30–10 p.m.

Setting and atmosphere An open area with a number of food stations that encourage diners to roam about and graze, just like the animals that wander about the lodge.

House specialties Watermelon rind salad; couscous salad; Moroccan seafood salad; chicken salad with cilantro.

Other recommendations Prime rib; zebra dome; crusted salmon; soups.

Summary and comments The quality of the food, the surroundings, and the selection of dishes make this a terrific deal. Disney doesn't use the word buffet, and indeed this is very different from the typical buffet (there are no steam tables for starters), but for those who like a major bang for their buck, this is the place to go.

BONGOS CUBAN CAFÉ ★★

CUBAN | MODERATE | QUALITY ★★ | VALUE ★★

READER'S SURVEY RESPONSES 79% 👍 21% 👎

Downtown Disney West Side; (407) 828-0999

Customers Gloria Estefan fans; Disney guests **Reservations** Accepted **When to go** Anytime **Entrée range** $8–$28 (child $6–$7) **Service** ★★★ **Friendliness** ★★★ **Parking** Downtown Disney lot **Bar** Full service **Wine selection** Moderate **Dress** Casual **Disabled access** Elevator to second level

Lunch and dinner Daily, 11 a.m.–11 p.m.

Setting and atmosphere This multilevel restaurant features an airy environment with a tropical theme built around a three-story pineapple. Other touches include a banana-leaf roof, banana-leaf ceiling fans, and palm tree–shaped columns. You'll expect Carmen Miranda to dance through the door any minute. Hand-painted murals and mosaics lend an artistic air. An open wrap-around porch provides pleasant outdoor dining.

House specialties Arroz con pollo (chicken with rice); camerones al ajillo (shrimp in garlic sauce); ropa vieja (shredded beef in tomato sauce); churrasco (grilled skirt steak).

Entertainment and amenities Latin music.

Summary and comments Miami resident and Latin singer Gloria Estefan and her husband-producer, Emilio, created this large restaurant that marries salsa music with Cuban cuisine. There are any number of mom-and-pop Cuban restaurants in the area (not that the Estefans aren't mom-and-pop) that do a better and more consistent job with this wonderful cuisine. If you've never had Cuban food, try it somewhere else. Come here to have a drink with an umbrella in it and listen to music. It's upbeat but noisy.

CALIFORNIA GRILL ★★★★½

AMERICAN | EXPENSIVE | QUALITY ★★★★½ | VALUE ★★★

READER'S SURVEY RESPONSES 81% 👍 19% 👎

Disney's Contemporary Resort; (407) 939-3463

Customers Locals and hotel guests **Priority seatings** Recommended **When to go** During evening fireworks **Entrée range** $18–$33 **Service** ★★★★ **Friendliness**

★★★★ **Parking** Valet on request **Bar** Full service **Wine selection** California wines
Dress Casual; no tank tops **Disabled access** Yes

Dinner Daily, 5:30–10 p.m.
Lounge Daily, 5:30 p.m.–midnight

Setting and atmosphere High atop the Contemporary Resort, award-winning California Grill set new standards for Disney dining when it opened in the mid-1990s, and continues to raise the bar. The view from the 15th floor is stellar, one of the best spots for watching the Magic Kingdom fireworks—so popular that the Grill no longer allows just anyone on the elevator for a ride to the top—you must have a dinner reservation (the restaurant now has a reservation podium on the hotel's fourth floor). A show kitchen is the centerpiece of the airy dining room.

House specialties The menu changes often to take advantage of seasonal produce, fish, and meats. Pristine sushi and oven-fired flatbreads are always on the menu, along with the grilled pork tenderloin with creamy polenta and zinfandel glaze, a favorite since Day One.

Other recommendations Sonoma goat cheese ravioli, oak-fired beef filet, whatever fresh fish is on the menu.

Entertainment and amenities The lights are dimmed during the Magic Kingdom fireworks, and the accompanying music is piped in. You can also step outside onto the 15th-floor deck for a closer look. Other entertainment includes watching the chefs; instead of begging for a window seat, sit at the counter. The chefs love to slip samples to the people sitting there.

Summary and comments Just ask the locals—if you're going to choose just one upscale dining experience at Disney, head for the California Grill. The setting is fabulous, and Chef John State knows how to cook. Even kids are right at home, with a menu that includes a kid-sized sirloin and rice cereal sushi. And now that the fireworks crowd in flip-flops and fanny packs has been banned (without a reservation for dinner), the sophisticated dining room is even more enjoyable.

CAPE MAY CAFÉ ★★★½

BUFFET | MODERATE | QUALITY ★★★½ | VALUE ★★★★

READER'S SURVEY RESPONSES 75% 👍 25% 👎

Disney's Beach Club Resort; (407) 934-3358

Customers Theme park and hotel guests **Priority seatings** Accepted and recommended **When to go** Anytime **Entrée range** Breakfast $17 (child $9), dinner $24 (child $10) **Service** ★★★★ **Friendliness** ★★★★ **Parking** Hotel lot **Bar** Full service **Wine selection** Limited **Dress** Casual **Disabled access** Yes

Breakfast Daily, 7:30–11 a.m.

Dinner Daily, 5:30–9:30 p.m.

Setting and atmosphere The natural-finish wood furniture and padded booths are in a clean, nautical New England style—bright, airy, and informal.

House specialties The buffet features peel-and-eat shrimp, tasty (albeit chewy) clams; mussels; baked fish; barbecued ribs; corn on the cob; Caesar salad; and a good dessert bar. Kids' bar includes chicken fingers, fried shrimp, and mac and cheese.

Other recommendations Lobster can be ordered as a supplement to the buffet, as can crab legs.

Entertainment and amenities Character breakfast.

Summary and comments This buffet consistently serves some of the best food available at Walt Disney World. While the restaurant is large and tables turn over rapidly, priority seatings are recommended. Because the Cape May is within easy walking distance of the World Showcase entrance to Epcot, it is a perfect and affordable place to dine before *IllumiNations*.

CAP'N JACK'S RESTAURANT ★★½

SEAFOOD | MODERATE | QUALITY ★★ | VALUE ★★

READER'S SURVEY RESPONSES 71% 👍 29% 👎

Downtown Disney Marketplace; (407) 828-3971

Customers Tourists **Priority seatings** Not accepted **When to go** Anytime **Entrée range** $20–$30 (child $6) **Service** ★★★★ **Friendliness** ★★★★ **Parking** Marketplace lot **Bar** Full service **Wine selection** Not a specialty **Dress** Casual **Disabled access** Yes

Lunch and dinner Daily, 11:30 a.m.–10:30 p.m.

Setting and atmosphere A pierhouse on the edge of the Buena Vista Lagoon.

House specialties Cap'n Jack's has a limited menu. Choices include New England clam chowder; spicy conch chowder with tomatoes, carrots, and onions; crab cakes made with lump crabmeat and onions; and peel-and-eat shrimp. You can also get a fresh-fish dinner—usually mahi mahi, tuna, or grouper—at a fair price.

Entertainment and amenities The lagoonside setting offers views of amateur boaters, and sunsets are pretty here.

Summary and comments Back in the 1970s, this was the place for sipping drinks and noshing on seafood. Today it's convenient for shoppers at Downtown Disney Marketplace—but not a dining destination. But it's a fine spot to sip a cold beer or a margarita (smoothies for the kids) and relax.

LE CELLIER STEAKHOUSE ★★★

STEAK | MODERATE | QUALITY ★★★ | VALUE ★★★

READER'S SURVEY RESPONSES 88% 👍 12% 👎

Canada, World Showcase, Epcot; (407) 939-3463

Customers Theme-park guests **Priority seatings** Recommended **When to go** Before 6 p.m. **Entrée range** $16–$27 **Service** ★★★ **Friendliness** ★★★★ **Parking** Epcot lot **Bar** Beer and wine only **Wine selection** Canadian wines are featured **Dress** Casual **Disabled access** Yes

Lunch Daily, 11:30 a.m.–3 p.m.

Dinner Daily, 4:30 p.m.–park close

Setting and atmosphere Designed to look like a wine cellar, Le Cellier is a pleasant respite from World Showcase once you adjust to the dim dining room. Décor is ordinary, but visible wine racks and wall sconces with fat candle lamps add to the ambience. Most of the servers are from provinces in Canada and enjoy sharing stories.

House specialties Canadian cheddar cheese soup, steaks, maple-glazed salmon.

Other recommendations Seared rainbow trout, salad with duck and green apples, free-range chicken, sautéed seafood pasta.

Summary and comments Plenty of Disney executives head here for lunch. Even at lunchtime, guests are chowing down on hearty steaks, but you can make a meal on the rich Canadian cheddar cheese soup and a salad, or one of the substantial sandwiches. Le Cellier is the only restaurant outside of Canada to feature Moosehead Pale Ale—pair it with the restaurant's mushroom filet mignon for a Canadian-style treat.

CHEF MICKEY'S ★★½

AMERICAN/BUFFET | MODERATE | QUALITY ★★★ | VALUE ★★★

READER'S SURVEY RESPONSES 80% 👍 20% 👎

Disney's Contemporary Resort; (407) 939-3463

Customers Theme-park guests **Priority seatings** Recommended **When to go** Early evening **Entrée range** Breakfast $17 (child $9), dinner $6 (child $11) **Service** ★★★ **Friendliness** ★★★★ **Parking** Resort valet or lot **Bar** None **Wine selection** Good **Dress** Casual **Disabled access** Yes

Breakfast Daily, 7–11:30 a.m.
Dinner Daily, 5–9:30 p.m.

Setting and atmosphere Colorful, open dining room with the monorail running overhead, this is one of the most popular Disney character restaurants—mostly because you're guaranteed an audience with the Big Cheese, Mickey Mouse, who dons a chef hat and visits every single table for photos. (Goofy and Minnie are there, too.) You get a solid meal and save time waiting in line in the theme park for a character moment. The buffet circles the center of the room. It's noisy, busy, and fun for families.

House specialties Breakfast: French toast; biscuits and gravy. Dinner: oven-roasted prime rib, slow-baked bone-in ham.

Other recommendations Fresh greens and mixed salads; pasta selections; Parmesan mashed potatoes and gravy.

Entertainment and amenities Character visits.

Summary and comments The all-you-can-eat breakfast buffet is a terrific value for families; there's plenty for picky eaters, and you can start the day with a full tummy and photos of the "A list" Disney characters already checked off your to-do list. Though no one is really here for the food, selections at both breakfast and dinner are freshly prepared and served in casseroles and platters on special heated countertops—a small step up from chafing dishes.

LES CHEFS DE FRANCE ★★★

FRENCH | MODERATE | QUALITY ★★★ | VALUE ★★★

READER'S SURVEY RESPONSES 81% 👍 19% 👎

France, World Showcase, Epcot; (407) 939-3463

Customers Theme-park guests **Priority seatings** Recommended **When to go** Anytime **Entrée range** Lunch $10–$18, dinner $16–$28 (child menu available) **Service** ★★★★ **Friendliness** ★★★★ **Parking** Epcot lot **Bar** None **Wine selection** Very good **Dress** Casual **Disabled access** Yes

Lunch Daily, noon–3 p.m.

Dinner Daily, 5–9 p.m.

Setting and atmosphere The smell of buttery croissants is as much a part of the décor here as the carefully placed copies of *Le Monde* and the huge mottled mirrors. White tablecloths and padded banquettes accentuate the classic bistro décor of the main dining room. Another room sits off to the side, this one a more casual sunroom with a better view of what's going on outside, but you're there for the illusion—insist on a seat in the main room.

House specialties Chefs de France features some of the dishes served at the real restaurants of the three chefs for whom this restaurant is named: Paul Bocuse, Roger Verge, and Gaston LeNotre. You may sample classic leg of lamb braised in tomatoes and wine, hangar steak with French fries, or a silky crème brûlée.

Other recommendations Onion soup topped with Gruyère, chicken crêpes (lunch only); baked goat cheese on walnut-raisin bread with arugula.

Summary and comments Here is your chance to eat in a restaurant supervised by three of France's best chefs. Paul Bocuse and Roger Verge take turns visiting from France and supervising the staff in the preparation of their creations (Gaston LeNotre doesn't make the trip too often anymore), so you just might get a chance to meet a culinary legend. But don't expect them to actually prepare your meal. And don't think what you're served here is even close to what you'd get at one of their hometown restaurants. Still, Executive Chef Bruno Vrignon, who trained in Lyon with Paul Bocuse, does a pretty good job in the kitchen, and the French servers make it an immersion experience. If you're on a budget, go for lunch: many of the dinner entrées are available midday for a reduced price (and smaller portion). The best deal is the three-course lunch ($15) that starts with French onion soup with Gruyère, then the classic croque monsieur (French toasted ham and cheese sandwich with a green salad), and a final course of crème brûlée.

CINDERELLA'S ROYAL TABLE ★★½

AMERICAN | MODERATE | QUALITY ★★ | VALUE ★★

READER'S SURVEY RESPONSES 74% 👍 26% 👎

Cinderella Castle, Fantasyland, Magic Kingdom; (407) 939-3463

Customers Theme-park guests **Priority seatings** Required **When to go** Early **Entrée range** Lunch $9–$26 (child 5$), dinner $21–$26 (child $5) **Service** ★★★ **Friendliness** ★★★ **Parking** Magic Kingdom lot **Bar** None **Wine selection** None **Dress** Casual **Disabled access** Limited

Breakfast Daily 8–11:30 a.m.
Lunch Daily, 11:30 a.m.–2:45 p.m.
Dinner Daily, 4 p.m.–park close

Setting and atmosphere A medieval banquet hall, appointed with the requisite banners and Round Table–like regalia, located on the second floor of Cinderella Castle. Stained-glass windows overlook Fantasyland, but the view is limited.

House specialties Prime rib; seafood.

Other recommendations Caesar salad; grilled salmon club (lunch); braised lamp shank (dinner).

Entertainment and amenities Cinderella makes occasional appearances. Character breakfast.

Summary and comments The Once Upon a Time breakfast here is perhaps the most coveted table at Disney World—for reasons unknown to many. Just the cache of dining in Cinderella Castle in the Magic Kingdom with a bevy of characters makes it hot, hot, hot. Lunch and dinner offerings are mediocre, but it is the fanciest full-service restaurant in the Magic Kingdom and there's always a crowd. And Cinderella isn't too dependable, she may or may not be there for your seating time at lunch and dinner.

CÍTRICOS ★★★★

MEDITERRANEAN | EXPENSIVE | QUALITY ★★★★½ | VALUE ★★★

READER'S SURVEY RESPONSES 85% 👍 15% 🗨

Disney's Grand Floridian Resort; (407) 824-2496

Customers Hotel guests and locals **Priority seatings** Required **When to go** Anytime **Entrée range** $26–$75 (child $6–$12) **Service** ★★★★ **Friendliness** ★★★★ **Parking** Valet; self-parking is deceptively far away. **Bar** Full service **Wine selection** Very good **Dress** Casually dressy **Disabled access** Good

Dinner Wednesday–Sunday, 5:30–9:30 p.m.

Setting and atmosphere The golds and yellows of the Mediterranean color this stylish dining room by noted designer Martin Dorf (who also designed California Grill and Flying Fish Café). Amiable Chef Gray Byrum is often in the restaurant's show kitchen, in full view of diners, where the ambience is upscale but not stuffy. White tablecloths and napkins embroidered with the restaurant's name add an elegant touch.

House specialties Sautéed shrimp with lemon, feta cheese and white wine; warm onion tart with walnut vinaigrette; basil-crusted rack of lamb; braised veal shank.

Other recommendations Foie gras ravioli; roasted duck breast; seared tuna with saffron, pappardelle, tomatoes, olives, and capers.

Summary and comments This is one of the "best-kept" dining secrets at Disney World—it's generally easy to get a priority seating in the spacious dining room, where you'll enjoy a superb meal. For an extra-special night, reserve the Chef's Domain, a private room for up to 12 where Chef Byrum can create a special menu. Any of the desserts are standouts, the creations of Grand Floridian Pastry Chef Erich Herbitschek.

CONCOURSE STEAKHOUSE ★★★

STEAK | MODERATE | QUALITY ★★★ | VALUE ★★

READER'S SURVEY RESPONSES 89% 👍 11% 🗨

Disney's Contemporary Resort; (407) 939-3463

Customers Hotel guests **Priority seatings** Recommended **When to go** Anytime **Entrée range** Breakfast and lunch $8–$12, dinner $25 (child, all meals, $5–$13) **Ser-**

vice ★★★ **Friendliness** ★★★ **Parking** Hotel lot **Bar** Full service **Wine selection** Limited **Dress** Casual **Disabled access** Yes

Breakfast Daily, 7:30–11 a.m.

Lunch Daily, noon–2:30 p.m.

Dinner Daily, 5:30–10 p.m.

Setting and atmosphere The décor is a cross between art deco and *2001: A Space Odyssey*. Large booths sit in the "open air" of the Contemporary's Concourse, with the monorails gliding by overhead on either side.

House specialties Although the name says steaks, sandwiches, burgers, pizzas, and pasta dishes are also available. The burgers are among the best at Walt Disney World.

Other recommendations Besides red meat: herb-crusted Atlantic salmon; barbe-cued chicken with smashed boniato sweet potatoes and Napa cabbage slaw.

Summary and comments You usually can slip in this casual little restaurant next door to Chef Mickey's without much of a wait for a well-prepared T-bone or filet mignon. Add a side of creamed spinach or beer-battered onion rings for satisfying hotel fare. Hotel guests who want to skip Chef Mickey's can find a substantial breakfast here, too, with eggs Benedict, French toast, steak and eggs, or go for a low-fat smoothie.

CORAL REEF   ★★½

SEAFOOD | EXPENSIVE | QUALITY ★★★ | VALUE ★★

READER'S SURVEY RESPONSES 48% 👍 52% 👎

The Living Seas, Future World, Epcot; (407) 939-3463

Customers Theme-park guests **Priority seatings** Recommended **When to go** Lunch **Entrée range** Lunch $14–$22, dinner $16–$27 (child $4–$9) **Service** ★★★ **Friendliness** ★★★ **Parking** Epcot lot **Bar** None **Wine selection** Good **Dress** Casual **Disabled access** Good

Lunch Daily, 11:30 a.m.–3 p.m.
Dinner Daily, 4:30 p.m.–park close

Setting and atmosphere Coral Reef offers one of the best views anywhere—below the water level of the humongous saltwater tank in The Living Seas pavilion. Sharks, rays, and even humans swim by, and every table has a great view. Seating still features tiers that afford perfect views, but now special lighting fixtures throw ripple patterns on the ceiling that make diners feel as though they're underwater.

House specialties Grilled swordfish with lobster and smoked Gouda mashed pota-toes; pan-seared tilapia with coconut rice.

Other recommendations Grilled New York strip loin.

Summary and comments Often overlooked at Epcot for dining rooms in World Showcase, Coral Reef is the only table-service restaurant in Future World where you can sip a nice glass of wine and enjoy good food in a quiet, informal setting. The creamy lobster soup, on the menu since the restaurant opened, is a decadent starter. Wines by the glass are paired with each dinner menu entrée, making it easy to order. It's a fun spot for marriage proposals—divers in the tank are willing to hold up a "Will you marry me?" sign for romantic diners.

THE CRYSTAL PALACE ★★★

AMERICAN/BUFFET | MODERATE | QUALITY ★★★½ | VALUE ★★★

READER'S SURVEY RESPONSES 80% 👍 20% 👎

Main Street, U.S.A., Magic Kingdom; (407) 939-3463

Customers Magic Kingdom guests **Priority seatings** Recommended **When to go** Anytime **Entrée range** Breakfast $17 (child $9), lunch $18 (child $10), dinner $22 (child $10) **Service** ★★ **Friendliness** ★★★ **Parking** Magic Kingdom lot **Bar** None **Wine selection** None **Dress** Casual **Disabled access** Yes

Breakfast Daily, 8–10:30 a.m.
Lunch Daily, 11:30 a.m.–2:45 p.m.
Dinner Daily, 4 p.m.–park close

Setting and atmosphere A turn-of-the-nineteenth-century glass pavilion awash with sunlight and decorated with plenty of summer greenery. Seating is comfortable (a pleasant respite), and buffet lines are open and accessible. There is a low buffet area for kids to help themselves.

House specialties Waffles and pancakes layered with fresh fruit; muesli; grilled vegetable platter; penne pasta tossed with romaine lettuce, grilled chicken, and Parmesan cheese; ham carving station; grilled peel-and-eat shrimp; prime rib carving station. Menu items change often.

Entertainment and amenities Winnie the Pooh characters dance about and pose with the kids.

Summary and comments Best value in the Magic Kingdom—go hungry and fill up. Winnie the Pooh and friends are an added bonus for fans, stopping by each table for photos. The food here continues to get better and better on the state-of-the-art buffet with no steam tables but casserole dishes and pans that sit on special heated countertops. From appetizers to dessert, you can get your money's worth, and there's plenty for picky eaters. Kids get their own buffet with mac and cheese, pizza, and chicken nuggets.

ESPN CLUB ★★½

AMERICAN/SANDWICHES | MODERATE | QUALITY ★★★ | VALUE ★★★

READER'S SURVEY RESPONSES 80% 👍 20% 👎

Disney's BoardWalk; (407) 939-5100

Customers Tourists **Priority seatings** Not accepted **When to go** Anytime **Entrée range** $8–$16 (child $6) **Service** ★★ **Friendliness** ★★★ **Parking** BoardWalk lot; valet parking is free before 5 p.m., $6 after **Bar** Full service **Wine selection** Minimal **Dress** Casual—helmets not required **Disabled access** Good

Open Sunday–Thursday, 11:30 a.m.–1 a.m.; Friday and Saturday, 11:30 a.m.–2 a.m.

Setting and atmosphere This is a sports bar to the nth degree, with basketball court flooring, sports memorabilia, and more television monitors than a network affiliate. The bar area has satellite sports-trivia video games. A large octagonal room with a wall of TV monitors serves as the main dining room.

House specialties Red wings (Buffalo-style wings); half-pound burger with cheddar or Swiss cheese; fresh fin tuna-salad sandwich; fresh fish grilled with garlic butter; marinated grilled chicken breast on a roll.

Entertainment and amenities Live sports-trivia contests and televised sports.

Summary and comments Service is a little more brusque than at other property restaurants. Portions are large, and the quality is in line with the price. This is a good choice for late-night dining or when you have to choose between going out for a bite and staying in the room to catch "the big game."

50'S PRIME TIME CAFÉ   ★★½

AMERICAN | MODERATE | QUALITY ★★★ | VALUE ★★

READER'S SURVEY RESPONSES 74% 👍 26% 👎

Disney-MGM Studios; (407) 939-3463

Customers Theme-park guests **Priority seatings** Suggested **When to go** Anytime **Entrée range** Lunch $10–$16, dinner $13–$20 **Service** ★★★★ **Friendliness** ★★★★ **Parking** Disney-MGM lot **Bar** Full service **Wine selection** Limited **Dress** Casual **Disabled access** Yes

Lunch Daily, 11 a.m.–3:55 p.m.; opens at 10:30 a.m. on Sunday and Wednesday

Dinner Daily, 4 p.m.–park close

Setting and atmosphere A meal at the 50's Prime Time Café is like eating a meal in your own kitchen, 1950s style. Pastel laminate, gooseneck lamps, and black-and-white televisions that run vintage sitcoms are the rule.

House specialties Meat loaf, pot roast, chicken, and other homey fare are featured. We get a lot of mail from readers who like the 50's Prime Time Café. Most say the food is good, the portions large, and that it is easy to find something the kids like. The peanut-butter-and-jelly milkshake is worth every calorie.

Entertainment and amenities 1950s sitcom clips on television.

Summary and comments Diners really get a kick out of the 1950s sitcoms playing on black-and-white TVs, and servers who insist you "take your elbows off the table" or "finish every last bite." This isn't haute cuisine—skip the appetizers and stick with filling fare like the pot roast or golden fried chicken, then save room for a plate of s'mores to share. This experience isn't for gourmands, but it's right for hungry vacationers who want a little fun with their food.

FINN'S GRILL   ★

SEAFOOD | MODERATE | QUALITY ★★ | VALUE ★★

READER'S SURVEY RESPONSES 41% 👍 59% 👎

The Hilton, Downtown Disney Resort Area; (407) 827-4000

Customers Unsuspecting hotel guests **Reservations** Not necessary **When to go** Anytime **Entrée range** $18–$27 **Service** ★ **Friendliness** ★★ **Parking** Valet or hotel lot **Bar** Full service **Wine selection** Fair **Dress** Casual **Disabled access** Yes

Dinner Daily, 5:30–10:30 p.m.

Setting and atmosphere Walls are painted with the bright colors of the sea and are decorated with stylized fish fins, sort of abstract abalone. The oyster bar is decorated with crab and lobster traps. Staff members wear silly fish hats that seem to denote some staffing hierarchy. The menu is fraught with puns on the word Finn, such as finnomenal, finn-icky, and finn-tastic.

House specialties Fresh fish, including snapper, salmon, and swordfish depending on availability, prepared blackened or grilled. Other items include shrimp scampi served with herb butter over yellow rice; Finn's gumbo, with shrimp, crabmeat, chicken, and sausage; and a number of pasta dishes.

Other recommendations Steamed Maine lobster; fresh oysters; stone crab claws (in season); shrimp.

Summary and comments It might not be bad for a bucket of steamers and a few cold beers, and if you're really, really tired and just don't want to walk over to Downtown Disney. You can probably find something to satisfy you here, but there isn't enough emphasis put on the food quality, and service has always been a disappointment.

FLYING FISH CAFÉ ★★★★

SEAFOOD | EXPENSIVE | QUALITY ★★★★ | VALUE ★★★

READER'S SURVEY RESPONSES 70% 👍 30% 👎

Disney's BoardWalk; (407) 939-3463

Customers Tourists and locals **Priority seatings** Recommended **When to go** Anytime **Entrée range** $18–$34 **Service** ★★★★ **Friendliness** ★★★★ **Parking** BoardWalk lot; valet parking is free before 5 p.m., $6 after **Bar** Full service **Wine selection** Excellent but pricey **Dress** Casual dressy **Disabled access** Good

Dinner Sunday–Thursday, 5:30–10 p.m.; Friday and Saturday, 5:30–10:30 p.m.

Setting and atmosphere A whimsical remembrance of a circa-1920 Coney Island roller coaster served as the inspiration for the décor and the name. Actually the coaster was called The Flying Turns, and one of the cars on the ride was dubbed The Flying Fish. Booth backs resemble the climbs and swoops of a coaster. On the far wall is a Ferris wheel, and overhead, fish fly on a parachute ride. Diners may choose to sit at the fish-scale-covered counter that overlooks the open kitchen. Children are given a list of "flaws" in the décor to spot, such as the one fish flying backward on the parachute ride. If the décor is reminiscent of California Grill, it's because they were both designed by Martin Dorf.

House specialties At press time, a new chef was coming on board, so expect his own creations on the menu. But you'll always find the potato-wrapped snapper, the restaurant's signature dish, with creamy leek fondue and a red wine reduction; charcrusted New York strip steak; and the Peeky Toe crab cakes. For desserts, the Valrhona chocolate soufflé is divine.

Summary and comments Locals love the Flying Fish, and for good reason. The seafood is fresh, the kitchen is bustling, and you can always find favorites on the menu. Though this is food for grown-ups, you'll often see children in the dining room because of the BoardWalk location (and their menu includes buttermilk-fried fish and chips and a grilled steak). If you can't get a table, check on seating availability at the counter. The food is just as good and the show in the kitchen is entertaining.

FRESH   ★★½

MEDITERRANEAN/AMERICAN | MODERATE | QUALITY ★★½ | VALUE ★★

Walt Disney World Dolphin; (407) 934-1609

Customers Hotel guests **Priority seatings** Available, not necessary **When to go**
Anytime **Entrée range** Breakfast, $4–$13; lunch, $10–$14; lunch buffet, $18, $11 children ages 3–11. **Service ★★★ Friendliness ★★★ Parking** Hotel lot **Bar** Beer,
wine, limited cocktails **Wine selection** Limited **Dress** Casual **Disabled access** Yes

Breakfast Daily, 6:30–11 a.m.

Lunch Daily, 11:30 a.m.–2 p.m.

Setting and atmosphere Brightly colored tiles, light woods, and big windows create
a pleasant spot for breakfast or lunch. Ask for a veranda table if you want to have a quiet
conversation away from the action in the open kitchen. A buffet encourages you to mix
and match meats, veggies, soups, and sandwiches, or you can order from the menu.

House specialties For breakfast, tableside yogurt cart with granola, fruit, berries, and
nuts; for lunch and dinner, panini with asparagus fries; seared tuna Nicoise; roasted
chicken; pork tenderloin; sangria.

Other recommendations For breakfast, crabmeat omelette with sun-dried tomatoes, spinach and Brie; fresh pressed juices.

Summary and comments Fresh is the next generation for buffets, with healthy,
customized options for diners. You can pick and choose from a delightful array—
imported meats and cheeses, olives, peppers, olives, and fresh greens—to create your
own sandwich or salad. If you don't want an interactive meal, order from the menu.
(There's even wireless Internet service, so you can work right through you meal in
this convention hotel.)

FULTON'S CRAB HOUSE   ★★½

SEAFOOD | EXPENSIVE | QUALITY ★★★½ | VALUE ★★

READER'S SURVEY RESPONSES 84% 👍 16% 👎

Empress Lilly, Pleasure Island; (407) 934-2627

Customers Locals, Disney guests **Priority seatings** Accepted **When to go** Early
evening **Entrée range** $26–$60 **Service ★★★ Friendliness ★★★ Parking** Pleasure Island lot **Bar** Full service **Wine selection** Good; mostly American **Dress** Casual
Disabled access Yes

Lunch Daily, 11:30 a.m.–4 p.m.
Dinner Daily, 5–11 p.m.

Setting and atmosphere In the early 1990s, Fulton's took over the entire three
decks of the *Empress Lilly,* which underwent extensive remodeling that removed the rear
paddle wheel and the smokestacks (they didn't really work anyway). The third deck is
used mainly for banquets. There is a large lounge on the first deck, where you will spend
a good deal of time waiting for your table. Separate dining areas include the Market
Room, which is a tribute to New York's Fulton Fish Market (for which the restaurant is

named); the Constellation Room, a semicircular room with a starlit night sky; and the Industry Room, which is a tribute to the commercial fishing industry.

House specialties Stone crab; fresh fish flown in daily (the airbills are on display inside the front door); fresh-oyster selection; Fulton's seafood chowder; cioppino with crab, shrimp, scallops, and fish in a tomato broth; Alaskan king crab; Alaskan Dungeness crab.

Other recommendations Charcoal-grilled Scottish salmon; Prince Edward Island mussels and clams; crab and lobster for two; rib eye and grilled shrimp.

Summary and comments Fulton's once had some of the best seafood in central Florida, but it has changed its focus from the cutting edge of seafood cuisine to a get-'em-in/get-'em-out volume feeding philosophy. Now selections are mundane, but prices are still high. Waits can be long—over an hour even on weeknights. Have an appetizer in the lounge or on the outside deck while you wait for a table.

THE GARDEN GRILL RESTAURANT ★★★

AMERICAN | MODERATE | QUALITY ★★★ | VALUE ★★★

READER'S SURVEY RESPONSES 84% 👍 16% 👎

The Land, Future World, Epcot; (407) 939-3463

Customers Theme-park guests **Priority seatings** Recommended **When to go** Anytime **Entrée range** $20 (child $10) **Service** ★★★ **Friendliness** ★★★★ **Parking** Epcot lot **Bar** Beer and wine **Wine selection** Fair **Dress** Casual **Disabled access** Yes **Lunch and dinner** Daily, 11:30 a.m. until park closing

Setting and atmosphere Diners step on a slowly revolving floor to make their way to tables that revolve above scenes from Living With the Land, the pavilion's ride-through attraction. About the time you finish a meal you've revolved around once, past scenes of a desert, a rain forest, and a farm (and a few mural-painted walls in between). But the big draw here, besides the all-you-can-eat fare, is the Disney characters: Mickey Mouse and his pals make stops at each table for photos.

House specialties All-you-can-eat family-style skillets for lunch and dinner include grilled flank steak, fried catfish, mashed potatoes and gravy, cornbread stuffing, and apple cobbler with vanilla ice cream. You can request a vegetarian meal with roasted veggies in marinara sauce with polenta and portobello mushrooms.

Entertainment and amenities The view. Character dining.

Summary and comments Salad greens are hydroponically grown right in The Land gardens downstairs. For families this is a good option: food, though ordinary, is filling, characters stop tableside, and there's beer or wine for grown-ups (at an extra charge).

GRAND FLORIDIAN CAFÉ ★★

AMERICAN | MODERATE | QUALITY ★★★ | VALUE ★★

READER'S SURVEY RESPONSES 76% 👍 24% 👎

Disney's Grand Floridian Resort; (407) 824-2496

Customers Hotel guests **Priority seatings** Required **When to go** Anytime **Entrée range** $9–$16 **Service** ★★ **Friendliness** ★★★ **Parking** Valet; self-parking is far away **Bar** Full service **Wine selection** Very good **Dress** Casual **Disabled access** Yes

Breakfast Daily, 7–11:30 a.m.

Lunch Daily, 11:30 a.m.–2 p.m.

Dinner Daily, 5–9 p.m.

Setting and atmosphere The large dining room, with high ceilings and decorative windows, looks out on the hotel's pool and center courtyard.

House specialties Breakfast includes eggs prepared just about every way known to mankind; waffles; French toast; and a traditional Japanese breakfast. Lunch and dinner include a decent burger, grilled mahi mahi, and prime rib (dinner only).

Other recommendations At lunch, the Asian grilled chicken salad is a standout; for dinner, shrimp pasta with prosciutto is good.

Summary and comments The impersonal service detracts from the overall quality. Try it for breakfast.

GULLIVER'S GRILL ★★

AMERICAN | EXPENSIVE | QUALITY ★★★ | VALUE ★★

READER'S SURVEY RESPONSES 71% 👍 29% 💬

Walt Disney World Swan; (407) 934-3000

Customers Hotel guests **Reservations** Required for dinner **When to go** Dinner **Entrée range** $26–$75 **Service** ★★ **Friendliness** ★★ **Parking** Hotel lot **Bar** Full service **Wine selection** Good **Dress** Casual **Disabled access** Yes

Dinner Daily, 5:30–10 p.m.

Setting and atmosphere A large greenhouse-like rotunda with tall palm trees and parrot figures attached to street lamps. Faux-stone tabletops are set with placemats and napkins.

House specialties Breakfast: eggs any style, including a lo-carb, all-protein omelette; French toast; Manhattan breakfast with bagel and smoked salmon; Japanese breakfast with miso soup. Dinner: crab-stuffed baked shrimp; filet mignon; meat loaf. Buffet is also available for breakfast, lunch, and dinner.

Entertainment and amenities Disney character breakfast on Saturday and Sunday; Disney character dinner nightly.

Summary and comments This restaurant is called Garden Grove during the day for breakfast and lunch, then changes its name to Gulliver's Grill for dinner. It's the catch-all restaurant for a busy hotel, so food is for sustenance, not winning awards. But the Disney characters nightly are a real plus for families. And the buffet is a good way to fill up—or you can eat light, with specially designated low-carb choices on all three menus. The menu also tells the story of Gulliver, a "direct descendant" of Jonathan Swift's fictitious character.

HOLLYWOOD & VINE ★★½

AMERICAN | INEXPENSIVE | QUALITY ★★★ | VALUE ★★★

READER'S SURVEY RESPONSES 88% 👍 12% 💬

Disney-MGM Studios; (407) 939-3463

Customers Theme-park guests **Priority seatings** Recommended **When to go** Dinner **Buffet** $22 (child $10) **Service** ★★★ **Friendliness** ★★★★ **Parking** Disney-MGM lot **Bar** Full service **Wine selection** Limited **Dress** Casual **Disabled access** Yes

Dinner Daily, 5:30 p.m–park close

Setting and atmosphere Large Art Deco–style cafeteria with tile floors and lots of chrome. Walls are decorated with huge murals that resemble old postcards with vintage scenes of old Hollywood and other California landmarks.

House specialties Rotisserie turkey; prime rib; mashed potatoes; vegetable lo mein.

Summary and comments If you feel the need to stuff yourself, try this all-you-can-eat buffet. Be prepared for lots of noise—with all the glass, tile, and chrome, the noise echoes for days.

THE HOLLYWOOD BROWN DERBY ★★★½

AMERICAN | EXPENSIVE | QUALITY ★★★★ | VALUE ★★★

READER'S SURVEY RESPONSES 84% 👍 16% 👎

Disney-MGM Studios; (407) 939-3463

Customers Theme-park guests **Priority seatings** Recommended **When to go** Early evening **Entrée range** Lunch $13–$18, dinner $19–$27 (child $2–$6) **Service** ★★★★ **Friendliness** ★★★★ **Parking** Disney-MGM lot **Bar** Full service **Wine selection** Very good **Dress** Casual **Disabled access** Yes

Lunch Daily, 11:30 a.m.–2:45 p.m.
Dinner Daily, 4:30 p.m.–park close

Setting and atmosphere A replica of the original Brown Derby restaurant (not the one shaped like a derby) in California, including duplicates of the celebrity caricatures that cover the paneled walls. The elegant sunken dining room has curved booths, tables draped with yards of white linen, and romantic shaded candles. Tall palm trees in huge pots stand in the center of the room and reach for the high ceiling. Waiters wear white jackets and are better dressed than most of the park guests.

House specialties Cobb salad (a Brown Derby creation named for Bob Cobb, not Lee J.); spiced pan-roasted pork tenderloin; pan-fried grouper; grapefruit cake.

Other recommendations Oyster Brie soup; Thai noodle bowl with coconut-crusted tofu; grilled salmon on sweet corn risotto.

Summary and comments The décor is so perfect you'll feel as though you're in 1930s Hollywood. It is so elegant that it is a shame it is located in a theme park full of T-shirted guests. Everyone should really dress in white ties and long chiffon gowns and do their best Fred Astaire and Ginger Rogers impersonations. Don't expect to see any real stars dining in the next booth, however. There is outdoor dining available, but it is much better to sit inside.

HOUSE OF BLUES ★★★

REGIONAL AMERICAN | MODERATE | QUALITY ★★★½ | VALUE ★★★

READER'S SURVEY RESPONSES 90% 👍 10% 👎

Downtown Disney West Side; (407) 934-2623

Customers Blues lovers **Priority seatings** Accepted **When to go** Early evening; Sunday gospel brunch **Entrée range** $10–$25; brunch $30 (child $15) **Service** ★★★ **Friendliness** ★★ **Parking** Downtown Disney lot; valet $6 **Bar** Full service **Wine selection** Modest **Dress** Casual **Disabled access** Good

Brunch 2 seatings on Sunday, 10:30 a.m. and 1 p.m.
Lunch and dinner Sunday–Wednesday, 11 a.m.–midnight; Thursday–Saturday, 11 a.m. –2 a.m.

Setting and atmosphere You'd think it was a ramshackle hut in the bayous of Louisiana if the place weren't bigger than all of Louisiana. Nearly every available inch of wall space displays some type of folk art, which has a voodoo sort of feel to it. The restaurant area is separate from the performance hall, where blues and rock groups perform. There is often a live band in the restaurant as well. Outdoor dining is available overlooking the lagoon. When recorded music is featured, monitors throughout the restaurant give a detailed description of the artist and the selection.

House specialties New Orleans–inspired cuisine, like étouffée, jambalaya, and po'boy sandwiches with shrimp or catfish.

Other recommendations Tennessee-style baby-back ribs; pecan-crusted catfish; white chocolate–banana bread pudding.

Summary and comments What Hard Rock Café is to rock music, House of Blues is to rhythm and blues. For a themed restaurant, House of Blues does an impressively good job with the food. If you're planning on taking in one of the acts at the performance space next door, you're better off going there first so you can assure yourself of a good seat and then eating afterwards.

JIKO—THE COOKING PLACE ★★★½

AFRICAN/EUROPEAN | EXPENSIVE | QUALITY ★★★★ | VALUE ★★★½

READER'S SURVEY RESPONSES 81% 👍 19% 👎

Disney's Animal Kingdom Lodge; (407) 938-3000

Customers Hotel guests, locals **Reservations** Mandatory **When to go** Anytime **Entrée range** $18–$27 (child $2–$9) **Service** ★★★ **Friendliness** ★★★ **Parking** Complementary valet or self park in hotel's lot **Bar** Full bar **Wine selection** All South African **Dress** Dressy casual **Disabled access** Good

Dinner Daily, 5–10 p.m.

Setting and atmosphere Young students from Africa, part of a yearlong cultural exchange program, greet guests as they enter Jiko's spacious dining room, created by noted designer Jeffrey Beers and inspired by the opening scenes of *The Lion King*. A large wood-burning oven dominates the center of the room, where diners can sit at a bar and watch the action in the open kitchen. The dining room is relatively quiet, with low lighting. Servers are professional, most of them sommeliers who guide diners through the South African wine list.

House specialties Kalamata olive flat bread; cucumber, tomato, and red onion salad; pan-roasted monkfish.

Other recommendations Marinated ahi tuna appetizer; braised lamb shank; seared jumbo scallops; oak-grilled filet mignon.

Summary and comments Jiko has been on a roll, winning awards and accolades for its interesting fare and stellar wine list—the largest collection of South African wines in any North American restaurant, with more than 1,800 bottles. And more than 20 of the servers are sommeliers, helping take the guesswork out of choosing a wine. Chef Anette Grecchi Gray continues to refine her cooking style, and the crowds keep coming, including a loyal following of locals. If you're an adventurous diner, give it a try—food is beautifully spiced, full of flavor, and made with TLC. Start with the three African dips and breads, and don't miss the Jiko Dream-sicle made with blood-orange sorbet and frozen buttermilk yogurt.

KIMONOS ★★★★

JAPANESE | MODERATE | QUALITY ★★★★½ | VALUE ★★★

READER'S SURVEY RESPONSES 88% 👍 12% 👎

Walt Disney World Swan; (407) 934-3000

Customers Hotel guests, locals **Reservations** Accepted for parties over 10 **When to go** Anytime **Entrée range** Sushi and rolls à la carte, $5–$23 **Service** ★★★★ **Friendliness** ★★★★ **Parking** Hotel lot; valet, $10 **Bar** Full service **Wine selection** Very good **Dress** Casual **Disabled access** Yes

Dinner Daily, 5:30 p.m.–1 a.m.; bar opens at 5 p.m.

Setting and atmosphere The décor consists of black lacquered tabletops and counters, tall pillars rising to bamboo rafters with rice-paper lanterns, and elegant kimonos that hang outstretched on the walls and between the dining sections. The chefs will greet you with a friendly welcome, and you'll be offered a hot towel to clean your hands. Even if you're not in the mood for sushi, this is a delightful place to just sit and sip sake.

House specialties Although sushi and sashimi are the focus, Kimonos also serves a number of hot appetizers, including tempura-battered shrimp, fish, and vegetables; skewered chicken yakitori; beef teriyaki and gyoza; and steamed dumplings stuffed with a pork mixture. The crispy soft-shell crab is wonderful.

Summary and comments The skill of the sushi artists is as much a joy to watch as is eating the wonderfully fresh creations. There are no full entrées here, just good sushi and appetizers. The Swan resort is host to many Japanese tourists, and you'll find many of them here on any given night. Enough said.

KONA CAFÉ ★★★

NEW AMERICAN/PAN-ASIAN | MODERATE | QUALITY ★★★ | VALUE ★★★★

READER'S SURVEY RESPONSES 84% 👍 16% 👎

Polynesian Resort; (407) 939-3463

Customers Mostly hotel guests; some locals **Priority seatings** Accepted **When to go** Anytime **Entrée range** $8–$25 (child $2–$6) **Service** ★★★ **Friendliness** ★★★★ **Parking** Polynesian lot; valet available **Bar** Full service **Wine selection** Moderate **Dress** Casual **Disabled access** Good

Breakfast Daily, 7–11:45 a.m.

Lunch Monday–Saturday, noon–2:45 p.m.; Sunday, 12:30–2:45 p.m.
Dinner Monday–Saturday, 5–9:45 p.m.

Setting and atmosphere Kona Café has a modest, postmodern décor with arched railings and grillwork on the ceiling, a step up from the previous coffee shop ambience. A dessert kitchen is right in the dining room so you can watch the pastry chef putting on the finishing touches on dessert. Still, it's nothing fancy, serving three meals a day, a good spot to remember if you want to escape the Magic Kingdom for a quiet lunch— hop on the monorail or take the resort launch to the Polynesian.

House specialties Breakfast: Tonga toast, a decadent French toast layered with bananas. Lunch: Asian noodle bowl; wok-seared mushroom pasta; barbecued pork sandwich; pot stickers; sticky wings. Dinner: macadamia mahi mahi; seared scallops and tempura shrimp; pork tenderloin.

Other recommendations Crab cakes; Kilauea torte (chocolate cake with a warm chocolate center); Kona coffee served in a press pot.

Summary and comments This isn't a fancy dining room, but the food is on a higher plane than your average java joint.

LIBERTY TREE TAVERN ★★½

AMERICAN | MODERATE | QUALITY ★★★ | VALUE ★★★

READER'S SURVEY RESPONSES 78% 👍 22% 👎

Liberty Square, Magic Kingdom; (407) 939-3463

Customers Theme-park guests **Priority seatings** Suggested **When to go** Anytime
Entrée range Lunch $11–$15 (child $5), dinner $22 (child $10) **Service** ★★★★
Friendliness ★★★★ **Parking** Magic Kingdom lot **Bar** None **Wine selection** None
Dress Casual **Disabled access** Yes

Lunch Daily, 11:30 a.m.–3 p.m.
Dinner Daily, 4 p.m.–park close

Setting and atmosphere Low, exposed-beam ceilings in rooms framed by pastel gray chair rails. Colonial-period wall art, much with a nautical theme, accents simple dark wood tables and chairs with woven seats.

House specialties New England pot roast; roast turkey; salmon on griddled pumpkin bread. Family-style character dining at dinner.

Other recommendations Sandwiches and salads are good here.

Summary and comments Though the Liberty Tree is the best of the Magic Kingdom's full-service restaurants, it is often overlooked at lunch. A good plan is to make a priority seating here for about an hour or so before parade time. After you eat, you can walk right out and watch the parade. Dinner is served family style, with Disney characters in attendance. The menu is all-you-can-eat turkey, beef, mashed potatoes, vegetables, stuffing, and macaroni and cheese.

MAMA MELROSE'S RISTORANTE ITALIANO ★★½

ITALIAN | MODERATE | QUALITY ★★★ | VALUE ★★

READER'S SURVEY RESPONSES 81% 👍 19% 👎

Disney-MGM Studios; (407) 939-3463

Customers Theme-park guests **Priority seatings** Suggested **When to go** Anytime **Entrée range** $12–$22 (child $5) **Service** ★★★★ **Friendliness** ★★★★ **Parking** Disney-MGM lot **Bar** Full service **Wine selection** Limited **Dress** Casual **Disabled access** Yes

Lunch Daily, 11:30 a.m.–3:30 p.m.
Dinner Daily, 3:30 p.m.–park close

Setting and atmosphere Mama Melrose's looks like a big-city neighborhood restaurant of the 1930s, with bare wooden floors, red-and-white checkered table-cloths, red vinyl booths, and grapevines hanging from the rafters. By far the most relaxing restaurant at Disney-MGM Studios, Mama Melrose's sports a worn, ethnic look that is as comfortable as an old sweatshirt.

House specialties Bruschetta; crispy calimari; panzanella (toasted bread tossed with cucumbers, tomatoes, arugula, onions, and red wine vinegar); eggplant parmesan; spicy Italian sausage.

Other recommendations Designer pizzas.

Summary and comments Because of its out-of-the-way location, you can some-times just walk into Mama Melrose's, especially in the evening.

MAYA GRILL ★★

MEXICAN | EXPENSIVE | QUALITY ★★ | VALUE ★★

READER'S SURVEY RESPONSES 77% 👍 23% 👎

Coronado Springs Resort; (407) 939-3463

Customers Hotel guests **Priority seatings** Recommended **When to go** Anytime **Entrée range** Dinner $15–$27 (child $9), breakfast buffet $12 (child $7) **Service** ★★ **Friendliness** ★★ **Parking** Hotel lot; no valet **Bar** Full service **Wine selection** Fair **Dress** Casual **Disabled access** Good

Breakfast Daily, 7–11 a.m.
Dinner Daily, 5–10 p.m.

Setting and atmosphere The dining room is meant to evoke the ancient world of the Maya, achieving (according to the menu) "a harmony of fire, sun, and water." The fire takes the form of "flames" made of fan-blown fabric at the top of two large columns. The kitchen is open to view, but so is the barren and starkly lit walkway outside, which detracts a bit from the atmosphere.

House specialties The kitchen has backed off a bit from their original Nuevo Latino concept and adopted a more mainstream menu of steak, ribs, and seafood. There are still a few hints of Latin America, such as a chimichurri dipping oil for the bread instead of butter, but most of the creativity has been muted. Steak seems to be the safest thing to order here.

Summary and comments Diners are meant to be swept away to another land, but we don't think this is what the Disney folks had in mind. This land is one where the usual good Disney service and friendliness are missing. As for the food, it ranges from mundane to poor (good steak, but really awful ribs). Overall, the quality doesn't come close to matching the prices, so you're better off eating somewhere else. The décor, too, isn't as upscale as when the restaurant first opened, and the corporate dining room atmosphere is a bit off-putting.

MITSUKOSHI TEPPANYAKI DINING ROOM ★★★½

JAPANESE | EXPENSIVE | QUALITY ★★★★ | VALUE ★★★

READER'S SURVEY RESPONSES 89% 👍 11% 👎

Japan, World Showcase, Epcot; (407) 939-3463

Customers Theme-park guests **Priority seatings** Required **When to go** Anytime **Entrée range** Lunch $9–$25 (child $8), dinner $13–$30 (child $5–$9) **Service** ★★★★ **Friendliness** ★★★★ **Parking** Epcot lot **Bar** Full service **Wine selection** Limited **Dress** Casual **Disabled access** Yes, via elevator

Lunch Daily, noon–3:45 p.m.

Dinner Daily, 4:30 p.m.–park close

Setting and atmosphere The décor is upscale Japanese, only roomier, with light wood-beam ceilings, grass-cloth walls, and lacquered oak chairs. Overall, very clean and spare.

House specialties Chicken, shrimp, beef, scallops, and Oriental vegetables stir-fried on a teppan grill by a knife-juggling chef. The Teppanyaki Dining Room is a fancy version of the Benihana restaurant chain.

Entertainment and amenities Watching the teppan chefs.

Summary and comments While this restaurant offers some of the best teppan dining you will find in the United States, it has missed a wonderful opportunity to introduce the diversity and beauty of authentic Japanese cuisine to the American public. Be aware that diners at the teppan tables (large tables with a grill in the middle) are seated with other parties. Finally, if you would like to try more traditional Japanese fare, consider Tempura Kiku, a small restaurant in the same building, or just opt for sushi in the bar.

NARCOOSSEE'S ★★★½

SEAFOOD | EXPENSIVE | QUALITY ★★★½ | VALUE ★★

READER'S SURVEY RESPONSES 74% 👍 26% 👎

Disney's Grand Floridian Beach Resort; (407) 939-3463

Customers Hotel guests, locals **Priority seatings** Recommended **When to go** Early evening **Entrée range** $26–$50 **Service** ★★★★ **Friendliness** ★★★★ **Parking** Valet; self-parking is deceptively far away. **Bar** Full service **Wine selection** Good **Dress** Casual **Disabled access** Yes

Dinner Daily, 5–10 p.m.; lounge open, 3–11 p.m.

Setting and atmosphere Part of the Grand Floridian Beach Resort complex, Narcoossee's is a free-standing octagonal building at the edge of Seven Seas Lagoon. It offers a great view of the Magic Kingdom and the boats that dock nearby to pick up guests and drop them off after a day at the park. The lack of carpet and tablecloths, and the high noise level, belie the fine-dining aspect.

House specialties Steamed seafood appetizer (shrimp, mussels, and clams); steamed Maine lobster tail; lobster and fish chowder.

Other recommendations Lobster and crab cakes; pan-seared flounder with garlic-herb risotto and lobster sauce.

Summary and comments Prices are steep for such a casual atmosphere, but it's one of the few places at Disney you can get fresh steamed lobster, and plenty of diners have it on their plates. Seafood is fresh, the wine list is decent, but it's noisy and small.

NINE DRAGONS RESTAURANT ★★½

CHINESE | EXPENSIVE | QUALITY ★★★ | VALUE ★

READER'S SURVEY RESPONSES 61% 👍 39% 👎

China, World Showcase, Epcot; (407) 939-3463

Customers Theme-park guests **Priority seatings** Suggested **When to go** Anytime **Entrée range** Lunch $10–$16, dinner $13–$40 **Service** ★★★ **Friendliness** ★★★★ **Parking** Epcot lot **Bar** Full service **Wine selection** Limited **Dress** Casual **Disabled access** Yes

Lunch Daily, noon–4:30 p.m.

Dinner Daily, 4:45 p.m.–park close

Setting and atmosphere One of the prettiest dining rooms in World Showcase, the spacious Nine Dragons is formal and elegant, with décor that reflects Asian artistry and sophistication—bright lacquered colors and natural wood hues. There are inlaid ceilings, large and elaborate wood sculptures, and a red, floral-patterned carpet. Friendly servers greet you at the door, and the thoughtful service continues throughout the meal.

House specialties New dim sum cart has more than a dozen choices, including savory and sweet choices, some warm, others cold. As the traditional trolley cart moves throughout the dining room, diners select the appetizer-sized dishes, and a small card is stamped each time they choose a basket or plate of dim sum. Dishes from the carts are priced from $4. Other specialties include three-course Peking whole duck dinner; crisp whole deboned fish glazed with sweet and sour sauce; honey sesame chicken.

Summary and comments Dim sum is a fun way to enjoy a variety of tastes in this traditional Chinese restaurant. Shrimp dumplings, barbecued pork buns, and spring rolls are the most popular. Sure, you can stick to the ordinary moo goo gai pan or wonton soup, but this is a good place to try something different. It's not as cheap as your favorite neighborhood Chinese, but prices are in line with other World Showcase table-service restaurants.

1900 PARK FARE ★★½

BUFFET | MODERATE | QUALITY ★★★ | VALUE ★★★

READER'S SURVEY RESPONSES 90% 👍 10% 👎

Disney's Grand Floridian Resort; (407) 824-3000

Customers Hotel and resort guests **Priority seating** Necessary **When to go** Breakfast or dinner **Buffet cost** Breakfast $17 (child $10), dinner $26 (child $11) **Service** ★★★ **Friendliness** ★★★ **Parking** Complementary valet **Bar** Full service **Wine selection** Limited **Dress** Theme-park casual **Disabled access** Yes

Breakfast Daily, 8–11 a.m.

Dinner Daily, 5:15–9 p.m.

Setting and atmosphere The cavernous, high-ceilinged, bright room is warmly appointed in pastels. Tables are set with linen. There are no windows. A calliope erupts periodically to provide musical accompaniment to dining (or add to the din, depending on your opinion of calliopes).

House specialties Buffet includes prime rib and nice pasta dishes.

Other recommendations Separate buffet for kids includes burgers, hot dogs, chicken nuggets, and macaroni and cheese.

Entertainment and amenities All meals feature character dining and the calliope.

Summary and comments A good choice for character dining, but too bright and loud for adults without children. The dinner buffet is on par with Chef Mickey's (Contemporary Resort) but not as good as the Cape May at the Beach Club. The prime rib is 1900 Park Fare's major draw at dinner, but go someplace else if you prefer your beef on the rare side of medium.

'OHANA ★★★

POLYNESIAN | MODERATE | QUALITY ★★★½ | VALUE ★★★

READER'S SURVEY RESPONSES 76% 👍 24% 👎

Disney's Polynesian Resort; (407) 939-3463

Customers Resort guests **Priority seatings** Recommended **When to go** Anytime **Entrée range** Breakfast $17 (child $9), dinner $24 (child $10) **Service** ★★★ **Friendliness** ★★★★ **Parking** Hotel lot **Bar** Full service **Wine selection** Limited **Dress** Casual **Disabled access** Yes

Breakfast Daily, 7:30–11 a.m.

Dinner Daily, 5–10 p.m.

Setting and atmosphere A large open pit is the centerpiece of the room. Here the grilled foods are prepared with a flare—literally. From time to time the chef will pour some liquid on the fire, causing huge flames to shoot up. This is usually in response to something one of the strolling entertainers has said, evoking a sign from the fire gods. At any given moment, there may be a hula-hoop contest or a coconut race, where the children are invited to push coconuts around the dining room with broomsticks.

House specialties Skewer service is the specialty here. There is no menu. As soon as you are seated, your server will begin to deliver food. First come stir-fried vegetables, salad, shrimp wontons, and honey-covered chicken wings. These are followed by smoked turkey, beef, pork, and shrimp. These are accompanied by assorted salads, placed on a lazy Susan in the center of the table, along with stir-fried rice.

Entertainment and amenities Strolling singers; games. Character meal.

Summary and comments 'Ohana, which means family, is a fun place. The food is good but not superior. The method of service and the fact that it just keeps coming make it all taste a little better. Insist on being seated in the main dining room, where the fire pit is located. There are tables around the back, but you can't see what's going on from back there.

OLIVIA'S CAFÉ   ★★★

AMERICAN | MODERATE | QUALITY ★★★½ | VALUE ★★★

READER'S SURVEY RESPONSES 73% 👍 27% 👎

Old Key West Resort; (407) 939-3463

Customers Resort guests **Priority seatings** Recommended **When to go** Lunch
Entrée range Breakfast $8–$11, lunch $9–$12, dinner $18–$32 (child, all meals,
$5–$7) **Service** ★★★★ **Friendliness** ★★★★ **Parking** Hotel lot **Bar** Full service
Wine selection Limited **Dress** Casual **Disabled access** Yes

Breakfast Daily, 7:30–10:15 a.m.

Lunch Daily, 11:30 a.m.–5 p.m.

Dinner Daily, 5–10 p.m.

Setting and atmosphere This is Disney's idea of Key West, with lots of pastels and
rough wood siding on the walls, mosaic tile floors, potted palms, and tropical trees in
the center of the room, and plenty of nautical gewgaws, including vintage photos of Key
West and its inhabitants of long ago. (Key West is nothing like this today.) There is some
outside seating, which looks out over the waterway. Tile, wood siding, and no tablecloths add up to a very noisy dining room.

House specialties Appetizers include conch chowder and lump blue crab cakes.
Entrées feature prime rib; coconut shrimp; fresh grilled fish.

Other recommendations Pan-seared Florida snapper; grilled Jamaican jerk chicken.

Summary and comments You may spot a few Disney cast members lunching in
this out-of-the-way spot. Olivia's is not a dining destination, but for guests at the resort,
it's a nice place for a quiet meal.

L'ORIGINALE ALFREDO DI ROMA RISTORANTE   ★★½

ITALIAN | EXPENSIVE | QUALITY ★★★ | VALUE ★★

READER'S SURVEY RESPONSES 84% 👍 16% 👎

Italy, World Showcase, Epcot; (407) 939-3463

Customers Theme-park guests **Priority seatings** Recommended **When to go**
Midafternoon **Entrée range** Lunch, $11–$22; dinner, $17–$34 **Service** ★★★★
Friendliness ★★★★ **Parking** Epcot lot **Bar** Beer and wine only **Wine selection**
All Italian **Dress** Casual **Disabled access** Yes

Lunch Daily, noon–4:15 p.m.

Dinner Daily, 4:30 p.m.–park close

Setting and atmosphere The elegant—some would say garish—Roman décor features huge murals of an Italian piazza along the wall behind the upholstered banquettes.
Dark woods and latticework on the high ceilings add to a sumptuous atmosphere. It is,
however, a noisy dining room, one that is nearly always filled. This is yet another location for the so-called famous restaurant of the inventor of fettucine Alfredo.

House specialties Fettucine Alfredo (what else?).

Other recommendations Slow-roasted pork shank; pan-seared veal medallions in
sauce of tomato, capers, and garlic.

Entertainment and amenities Strolling opera singers at dinner.

Summary and comments In spite of carb-counting Americans, this is the most popular World Showcase restaurant, and the fettuccine Alfredo is worth every calorie. Besides that, the menu is pretty ho-hum Italian, but crowd pleasing. Dishes are heavy, but just ask for a simple pasta with, for instance, basil and tomatoes, and they'll make it for you.

THE OUTBACK ★★

STEAK | EXPENSIVE | QUALITY ★★★ | VALUE ★★

READER'S SURVEY RESPONSES 83% 17% 🗨

Wyndham Palace, Downtown Disney Resort Area; (407) 827-2727

Customers Tourists, locals **Reservations** Recommended **When to go** Very early dinner **Entrée range** $14–$40 **Service** ★★ **Friendliness** ★★ **Parking** Complementary valet parking at the rear of the hotel **Bar** Full service **Wine selection** Excellent **Dress** Casual **Disabled access** Yes

Dinner Daily, 5:30–11 p.m.

Setting and atmosphere A large, open room with a two-story ceiling and a cascading waterfall. Servers are in khaki to look like bush outfits, but the menu is pretty straightforward American cuisine.

House specialties Try an appetizer of marinated kangaroo. The 4- to 6-pound lobsters or any of the steaks are a good bet (but the 5-to-6 lb. lobster is $100!).

Other recommendations Fried gator bites (just so you can say you tried them); grilled pork chops; barbecue baby back ribs.

Summary and comments Not a dining destination, but if you're in the mood for pricey Maine lobster or a decent steak and staying in the Downtown Disney Resort Area, give it a try.

PALIO ★★★½

ITALIAN | EXPENSIVE | QUALITY ★★★½ | VALUE ★★★

READER'S SURVEY RESPONSES 89% 11% 🗨

Walt Disney World Swan; (407) 934-3000

Customers Hotel guests **Reservations** Recommended **When to go** Anytime **Entrée range** $17–$36 **Service** ★★★ **Friendliness** ★★★ **Parking** Hotel lot **Bar** Full service **Wine selection** Very good **Dress** Casual **Disabled access** Yes

Dinner Daily, 6–11 p.m.

Setting and atmosphere The name means banner, and they're hanging all over this upscale Italian trattoria—even draped over the tables. It is a pretty place and bustles with excitement and the sounds of happy diners. Like just about everything else in the hotel, designer Michael Graves had a hand in the décor and design of the restaurant, and it shows. It is a beautiful place.

House specialties Wood-fired brick oven pizzas; linguini with clams, pancetta, and chili oil in a red sauce; cioppino; veal scallopine with Marsala wine sauce; pork tenderloin with prosciutto, mushrooms, and linguine.

Other recommendations   Gnocchi with Parma ham; tortellini sautéed with lobster, garlic, basil, and cream; marinated swordfish in garlic and rosemary.

Summary and comments   The food isn't bad, and the experience is satisfying overall, but there are more exciting dining options available. The roasted-garlic spread served with the hot bread is nice. Fill up on that and then order one of the reasonably priced pizzas.

PLANET HOLLYWOOD   ★★★

AMERICAN | MODERATE | QUALITY ★★★ | VALUE ★★★

READER'S SURVEY RESPONSES 62% 👍 38% 👎

Pleasure Island; (407) 827-7827

Customers Tourists, locals **Priority seatings** Accepted lunch and late-night only **When to go** Late lunch **Entrée range** $9–$22 **Service** ★★ **Friendliness** ★★ **Parking** Pleasure Island lot **Bar** Full service **Wine selection** Limited **Dress** Casual **Disabled access** Yes

Lunch and dinner Daily, 11 a.m.–1 a.m.

Setting and atmosphere   A large planet-shaped structure "floating" in the lagoon next to Pleasure Island. Planet Hollywood's décor is something of a movie museum, with memorabilia from famous movies. Orlando is world headquarters for the chain, and the hometown restaurant is really a special structure. Check out artifacts like the bus from the movie *Speed,* Marilyn Monroe's gloves, and life-sized likeness of Robin Williams.

House specialties   The menu is standard around the world, with pasta dishes, fajitas, burgers, dinner salads, and pizzas. Burgers are huge (the classic cheeseburger is a half pound). Desserts are incredible, especially the white-chocolate bread pudding.

Other recommendations   Chicken fajitas; linguini and sausage; grilled swordfish.

Summary and comments   Plenty of parties still happen here with film and music stars making appearances (check the Web site for upcoming events). Servings are gargantuan and good enough, so the place is usually crowded.

THE PLAZA   ★★

AMERICAN | MODERATE | QUALITY ★★ | VALUE ★★

Main Street, U.S.A., Magic Kingdom; (407) 939-3463

Customers Theme-park guests **Priority Seating** Suggested **When to go** Anytime **Entrée range** $9–$11 **Service** ★★★ **Friendliness** ★★★ **Parking** Magic Kingdom lot **Bar** None **Wine selection** None **Dress** Casual **Disabled access** Yes

Hours 11 a.m.–15 minutes before park closing

Setting and atmosphere   Tucked away on a side street at the end of Main Street, U.S.A., as you head to Fantasyland, the Plaza's old-fashioned décor is a spiffed-up version of small-town diners in hometowns across America. You pay top dollar for a tuna sandwich or a burger, but on a hot Florida day, it's a casual, air-conditioned respite.

House specialties   Reuben sandwich, club sandwich, chicken and pear salad, ice cream dessert, like the Plaza Special (two scoops of butter pecan ice cream with hot fudge and caramel sauce, topped with whipped cream, nuts, and a cherry).

Other recommendations   Burger, veggie sandwich, hot fudge sundae, banana split.

Summary and comments   You don't head here for a gourmet meal, though the pricey sandwiches are just fine. Or just skip the protein and go straight for a sweet ending with a giant sundae or triple-scoop banana split—that's what most everyone orders. If you're counting calories, order the Unicycle, just one scoop of ice cream with hot fudge. Or Café Mocha with coffee and chocolate.

PORTOBELLO YACHT CLUB ★★★

ITALIAN | EXPENSIVE | QUALITY ★★★ | VALUE ★★

READER'S SURVEY RESPONSES 82% 👍 18% 👎

Pleasure Island; (407) 934-8888

Customers Tourists, locals **Priority seatings** Recommended **When to go** Anytime **Entrée range** $16–$44 (child $5–$12) **Service** ★★★★ **Friendliness** ★★★★ **Parking** Pleasure Island lot **Bar** Full service **Wine selection** Very good; heavy on Italian selections **Dress** Casual **Disabled access** Yes

Lunch   Daily, 11:30 a.m.–3 p.m.
Dinner   Daily, 5–11 p.m.

Setting and atmosphere   This restaurant sports an upscale nautical theme with lots of polished brass, dark woods, and canvas window coverings. There is a patio overlooking the lagoon for those days with low humidity.

House specialties   Thin-crust pizzas; Spaghettini Portobello with scallops, shrimp, clams; Alaska king crab with tomatoes, garlic, olive oil, and wine; braised bison shank; Scottish salmon wrapped in pancetta; white chocolate custard with a crisp candy glaze and fresh berries.

Other recommendations   Fried calamari; wild mushroom ravioli; New Zealand rack of lamb; ribeye steak with garlic mashed potatoes.

Summary and comments   Levy Restaurants operates three Downtown Disney restaurants: Portobello, Fulton's Crab House, and Wolfgang Puck. Portobello is a longtime favorite, and the food is worth a visit if you're planning an evening at Downtown Disney—better than average, though prices are a bit steep.

RAINFOREST CAFÉ ★★½

AMERICAN | MODERATE | QUALITY ★★★ | VALUE ★★

READER'S SURVEY RESPONSES 67% 👍 33% 👎

Downtown Disney Marketplace; (407) 933-2800; Animal Kingdom; (407) 938-9100

Customers Tourists and locals **Priority seatings** Accepted at Animal Kingdom location only, until 1 hour after park closes **When to go** After lunch crunch, in late afternoon, and before dinner hour **Entrée range** $10–$40 (child $6–$8) **Service** ★★ **Friendliness** ★★★ **Parking** Marketplace lot **Bar** Full bar **Wine selection** Limited **Dress** Dressy casual **Disabled access** Good

Open *Downtown Disney Marketplace:* Sunday–Thursday, 11:30 a.m.–11 p.m.; Friday and Saturday, 11:30 a.m.–midnight; *Animal Kingdom:* Daily, 8:30 a.m.–park close

Setting and atmosphere   The Downtown Disney version of the national chain sits beneath a giant volcano that can be seen (and heard) erupting all over the Marketplace. The smoke coming from the volcano is nonpolluting, in accordance with the restaurant's conservation theme. Inside is a huge dining room designed to look like a jungle (imagine all the silk plants in the world tacked to the ceiling), complete with audio-animatronic elephants, bats, and monkeys (not the most realistic animatronics you've seen). There is occasional thunder and even some rainfall. Large aquariums connected with glass "swimways" serve as one of several waiting areas. Next to the dining room is a 5,000-square-foot retail shop. The Animal Kingdom version, featuring a huge waterfall, is easier on the eye externally. Once inside, however, you'll find the same food, décor, and retail space as at the Marketplace.

House specialties   Lettuce wraps with lime-grille chicken; Rasta Pasta with grilled chicken and walnut pesto; turkey wrap; crab cake sandwich; coconut shrimp; slow-roasted pork ribs.

Entertainment and amenities   After the wait you endure, a chair and some sustenance is all the entertainment you'll need. If you're willing to pay to avoid the long wait, stop by the day before and purchase a Safari Club membership for $15. By presenting your card on the day you want to dine, you will be seated immediately. Safari Club members can also call ahead for priority seating.

Summary and comments   Let us say upfront that while we are not impressed by the Rainforest Cafés, a lot of our readers rave about them. The slogan for Rainforest Café is "a wild place to shop and eat." The shopping experience must be the attraction because it certainly isn't the food. Preparations are spotty; spicing is uneven; and the quality is not as high as at other area theme restaurants such as Planet Hollywood and Hard Rock Café. Waits can be horrendous. Of course, you are expected to shop in the retail space during your wait time. By all means, visit the gift shop, but dine somewhere else.

RESTAURANT AKERSHUS ★★★½

NORWEGIAN/BUFFET | MODERATE | QUALITY ★★★★ | VALUE ★★★★

READER'S SURVEY RESPONSES 86% 👍 14% 👎

Norway, World Showcase, Epcot; (407) 939-3463

Customers Theme-park guests **Priority seatings** Required **When to go** Anytime **Entrée range** Lunch $14 (child $7), dinner $19 (child $5–$8) **Service** ★★★ **Friendliness** ★★★ **Parking** Epcot lot **Bar** Full service **Wine selection** Good **Dress** Casual **Disabled access** Yes

Lunch Daily, noon–4 p.m.
Dinner Daily, 4:30–9 p.m.

Setting and atmosphere   Modeled on a 14th-century fortress, Akershus entertains its guests in a great banquet hall under high A-framed ceilings and massive iron chandeliers. Stone arches divide the dining rooms. A red carpet alternates with patterned hardwood floors.

House specialties   A variety of fish and meats on the koltbord; braised lamb and cabbage; pan-fried trout; seared Atlantic salmon. Be sure to try the mashed rutabaga.

Other recommendations Cold Ringnes beer on tap.

Summary and comments A recent renovation of Restaurant Akershus changed the menu: It's still all you can eat, but diners start at the koltbord (or cold buffet), where there's a wonderful array of cheeses, meats, and salads, then order hot entrées from the kitchen. You may order more than one hot entrée, but only one at a time. Service can sometimes be slow, but the experience is mostly enjoyable as you chat with servers from Scandinavia and are introduced to Scandinavian cuisine of above-average quality.

RESTAURANT MARRAKESH ★★★

MOROCCAN | MODERATE | QUALITY ★★★½ | VALUE ★★★

READER'S SURVEY RESPONSES 79% 👍 21% 👎

Morocco, World Showcase, Epcot; (407) 939-3463

Customers Theme-park guests **Priority seatings** Required **When to go** Anytime **Entrée range** Lunch $12–$19, dinner $17–$30 (child $5–$6) **Service** ★★★ **Friendliness** ★★★★ **Parking** Epcot lot **Bar** Full service **Wine selection** Limited **Dress** Casual **Disabled access** Yes

Lunch Daily, 11:30 a.m.–3:30 p.m.

Dinner Daily, 4 p.m.–park close

Setting and atmosphere One of the more exotic World Showcase restaurants, Marrakesh re-creates a Moroccan palace with gleaming tile mosaics, high inlaid-wood ceilings with open beams and brass chandeliers, and red Bukhara carpets.

House specialties Start with bastila (a minced chicken pie sprinkled with cinnamon confectionary sugar), followed by roast lamb. Split an order of couscous. Beef and chicken kebabs are also available.

Other recommendations If you are hungry, curious, or both, go for one of the combination platters for two people.

Entertainment and amenities Moroccan band and belly dancing.

Summary and comments Interesting fare that is almost impossible to find except in the largest U.S. cities. Unlike diners at most Moroccan restaurants, those at Marrakesh sit at tables (instead of on the floor) and eat with utensils rather than with their hands. Because Moroccan food is unfamiliar to most visitors, Marrakesh sometimes has tables available for walk-ins.

ROSE & CROWN DINING ROOM ★★★

ENGLISH | MODERATE | QUALITY ★★★½ | VALUE ★★

READER'S SURVEY RESPONSES 80% 👍 20% 👎

United Kingdom, World Showcase, Epcot; (407) 939-3463

Customers Theme-park guests **Priority seatings** Recommended **When to go** Anytime **Entrée range** Lunch $11–$16, dinner $14–$22 (child $5–$7) **Service** ★★★★ **Friendliness** ★★★★ **Parking** Epcot lot **Wine selection** Limited **Bar** Full bar with Bass ale and Guinness and Harp beers on tap **Dress** Casual **Disabled access** Yes

Lunch Daily, 11:30 a.m.–4 p.m.
Dinner Daily, 4:30 p.m.–park close

Setting and atmosphere The Rose & Crown is both a pub and dining establishment. The traditional English pub has a large, cozy bar with rich wood appointments and trim, beamed ceilings, and a hardwood floor. The adjoining English country dining room is rustic and simple. Meals are served outdoors overlooking the World Showcase Lagoon when the weather is nice.

House specialties Fish and chips; bangers and mash (sausage and mashed potatoes); steak and batter-fried prawns—washed down with Bass ale.

Other recommendations Lamb barley soup; roast chicken with sage-onion stuffing; chilled lemon cream with fresh berries.

Summary and comments Rose & Crown has never been a stellar dining room—most of the patrons are there for the pub. But the restaurant is a prime spot for viewing *IllumiNations,* so book a table on the patio for late evening, order fish and chips, then sit back in your front-row seat for the fireworks-and-laser show.

SAN ANGEL INN RESTAURANTE ★★★

MEXICAN | EXPENSIVE | QUALITY ★★★½ | VALUE ★★

READER'S SURVEY RESPONSES 60% 👍 40% 👎

Mexico, World Showcase, Epcot; (407) 939-3463

Customers Theme-park guests **Priority seatings** Recommended **When to go** Anytime **Entrée range** Lunch $10–$18, dinner $18–$24 (child $5) **Service** ★★★
Friendliness ★★★ **Parking** Epcot lot **Bar** Full service **Wine selection** Limited **Dress** Casual **Disabled access** Yes

Lunch Daily, 11:30 a.m.–4 p.m.
Dinner Daily, 4:30 p.m.–park close

Setting and atmosphere The San Angel Inn is inside the great Aztec pyramid of the Mexican pavilion. A romantically crafted open-air cantina, the restaurant overlooks both El Río del Tiempo (The River of Time) and the bustling plaza of a small Mexican village.

House specialties In addition to enchiladas, tacos, and other routine Mexican fare, San Angel features (at dinner only) mole poblano (chicken with an exotic sauce made from several kinds of peppers and unsweetened Mexican chocolate) and some interesting regional fish preparations.

Other recommendations Grilled mahi mahi or grilled sea bass.

Entertainment and amenities Mariachi or marimba bands in the adjacent courtyard.

Summary and comments The San Angel Inn serves good (sometimes excellent) Mexican food at prices much higher than you would find at most Mexican restaurants. The shrimp grilled with pepper sauce, for example, is five medium-sized shrimp for the outrageous sum of $20 ($4 per shrimp!). The menu goes beyond normal Mexican selections, offering special and regional dishes that are difficult to find in the United States. If you go, we recommend you skip the tacos and try one of the unique dishes.

SCI-FI DINE-IN THEATER RESTAURANT ★★

AMERICAN | MODERATE | QUALITY ★★½ | VALUE ★★

READER'S SURVEY RESPONSES 39% 👍 61% 👎

Disney-MGM Studios; (407) 939-3463

Customers Theme-park guests **Priority seatings** Required **When to go** Anytime **Entrée range** Lunch $11–$18, dinner $13–$21 (child $5) **Service** ★★★★★ **Friendliness** ★★★★★ **Parking** Disney-MGM lot **Bar** Full service **Wine selection** Limited **Dress** Casual **Disabled access** Yes

Lunch Sunday and Wednesday, 10:30 a.m.–4 p.m.; Monday and Tuesday and Thursday–Saturday, 11 a.m.–4 p.m.

Dinner Daily, 4 p.m.–park close

Setting and atmosphere Everyone, especially diners over the age of 30, gets a kick out of this unusual dining room—a faux drive-in from the 1950s, with faux classic cars instead of tables. You hop in, order, and watch kitschy black-and-white clips. Servers, some on roller skates, take your order from the driver's seat.

House specialties The lunch fare consists of sandwiches, burgers, salads, and shakes. Dinner offerings include pasta, ribs, steaks, and fish. While we think the food quality is way out of line with the cost, you can have an adequate meal at the Sci-Fi if you stick with simple fare.

Entertainment and amenities Cartoons and clips of vintage horror and sci-fi movies are shown, such as *The Attack of the Fifty-foot Woman, Robot Monster*, and *Son of the Blob*. Also shown are lurid previews, proclaiming, "See a sultry beauty in the clutches of a half-crazed monster!"

Summary and comments We recommend making a late-afternoon or late-evening priority seating and ordering only dessert. In other words, think of the Sci-Fi as an attraction (which it is) as opposed to a good dining opportunity (which it is not). If you want to try the Sci-Fi Dine-In and do not have priority seatings, try walking in at 11 a.m. or around 3 p.m.

SHULA'S STEAK HOUSE ★★★★

STEAK | EXPENSIVE | QUALITY ★★★★ | VALUE ★★★

READER'S SURVEY RESPONSES 86% 👍 14% 👎

Walt Disney World Dolphin; (407) 934-1362

Customers Hotel guests and locals **Priority seatings** Recommended **When to go** Anytime **Entrée range** $22–$70 **Service** ★★★ **Friendliness** ★★★ **Parking** Hotel lot; complementary valet **Bar** Full service **Wine selection** Very good; expensive **Dress** Dressy casual **Disabled access** Yes

Dinner Daily, 5–11 p.m.

Setting and atmosphere Clubby and masculine with dark woods and darker lighting. Large black-and-white photographs of football players in action framed in gold gilt offer the only decorations. White tablecloths adorn tables.

House specialties Meat—really expensive but very high-quality meat. Only certified Angus beef is served, with filet mignon, porterhouse (including a 42-ounce version), lamb chops, and prime rib.

Other recommendations The steak tartare appetizer is special; split lobster cocktail appetizer.

Summary and comments This is the growing chain owned by former Miami Dolphins football coach Don Shula. It's classier than it is kitschy, though printing the menu on the side of a football and placing it on a kickoff tee in the center of the table is a bit over the top. They could also do without the rehearsed spiel from the waiters who present raw examples of the beef selections (not to mention a live lobster) at each table. Once you get past that, however, you're in for some wonderful steaks. And service here has improved so much that the staff is winning kudos from locals, many of whom are driving from downtown Orlando just for the great meat and terrific service.

SHUTTERS AT OLD PORT ROYALE ★★

STEAK AND SEAFOOD | MODERATE | QUALITY ★★½ | VALUE ★★

Disney's Caribbean Beach Resort; (407) 939-3463

Customers Hotel guests **Priority seatings** Recommended **When to go** Anytime **Entrée range** $15–$20 (child $6–$9) **Service** ★★★ **Friendliness** ★★★★ **Parking** Hotel lot **Bar** Full service **Wine selection** Moderate **Dress** Casual **Disabled access** Yes

Dinner Daily, 5–10 p.m.

Setting and atmosphere The small dining areas are claustrophobia-inducing, and the servers have to cross the food court's walkway to get to the kitchen. There isn't a thing about the décor that will make you wish you'd brought a camera.

House specialties Smoked prime rib; grilled mahi mahi; spicy chicken wings; citrus ginger pork chop.

Other recommendations French toast bread pudding with coconut ice cream.

Summary and comments Disney's Caribbean Beach Resort is huge—more than 2,000 rooms—and for years did not have a table-service restaurant. Shutters is there for that reason; you wouldn't drive to the resort for dinner, but if you need to sit down and have someone wait on you, this probably will meet your needs. Stick with simple dishes—the food leaves a lot to be desired.

SPOODLES ★★★½

MEDITERRANEAN | MODERATE | QUALITY ★★★★ | VALUE ★★★

READER'S SURVEY RESPONSES 90% 👍 10% 👎

Disney's BoardWalk; (407) 939-3463

Customers Tourists and locals **Priority seatings** Recommended **When to go** Anytime **Entrée range** Breakfast $7–$13 (child $5), dinner $16–$25 (child $6–$7), pizza window $3–$12 **Service** ★★★★ **Friendliness** ★★★★ **Parking** BoardWalk lot; valet parking is free before 5 p.m., $6 after **Bar** Full service **Wine selection** Good selection of Mediterranean countries **Dress** Casual **Disabled access** Good

Breakfast Daily, 7:30–11 a.m.

Dinner Daily, 5–9:30 p.m.

Pizza Window Daily, 5 p.m.–midnight

Setting and atmosphere The dining room is designed like a farmhouse you might find in the Mediterranean countryside—a really big farmhouse. Light fixtures of various sizes and styles (no two are alike), Fietsaware plates and cups stacked on wooden tables, and posters of Mediterranean countries reinforce the family-style atmosphere. The open kitchen adds to the noise, which is already extensive because of the size of the room and the sound of people enjoying themselves and passing around plates.

House specialties Frittatas at breakfast; for dinner, tapas ($5–$8) like Mediterranean dips, sautéed chili garlic shrimp, mussels, and grilled lamb skewers; seafood paella; Moroccan spiced tuna with braised greens.

Summary and comments The kitchen has seen several chefs come and go, but things seem to be settling down with Nick Pastis, a young chef of Greek heritage who is passionate about Mediterranean cuisine (paella is his big seller). You might skip the entrées and just make a meal on his tapas and a pitcher of sangria. The big, noisy dining room appeals to families, so ask for a booth at the back of the room if you want to have a conversation.

TEMPURA KIKU   ★★★

JAPANESE | MODERATE | QUALITY ★★★★ | VALUE ★★★

READER'S SURVEY RESPONSES 88% 👍 12% 👎

Japan, World Showcase, Epcot; (407) 939-3463

Customers Theme-park guests **Priority seatings** Not accepted **When to go** Lunch **Entrée range** Lunch $9–$15 (child $7), dinner $13–$25 (child $9) **Service** ★★★★ **Friendliness** ★★★ **Parking** Epcot lot **Bar** Full service **Wine selection** Limited **Dress** Casual **Disabled access** Yes

Lunch Daily, noon–3:45 p.m.

Dinner Daily, 4:30 p.m.–park close

Setting and atmosphere Tempura Kiku is a small (25-person) tempura bar. The setting is intimate, almost cramped, and very communal.

House specialties Tempura-battered deep-fried foods featuring chicken, shrimp, and vegetables. The menu tells the story of tempura, which apparently came about when some Portuguese sailors were shipwrecked on a Japanese shore. The Catholic Portuguese did not eat meat on the holy days, which came four times a year and were called quattuor tempora. On these days, the sailors ate fried shrimp. The Japanese adapted the word tempura to mean fried shrimp, and the rest of the world adapted it to mean all kinds of fried food.

Other recommendations Kabuki beef; sushi; sashimi.

Summary and comments Not the most appealing restaurant at Epcot, but the tempura is arguably the best in the Japan pavilion. The sushi and sashimi are not heavily marketed, but you can bet the sanitation—important in any restaurant but crucial where sushi is served—is impeccable.

TONY'S TOWN SQUARE RESTAURANT ★★½

ITALIAN | MODERATE | QUALITY ★★★ | VALUE ★★

READER'S SURVEY RESPONSES 59% 👍 41% 👎

Main Street, U.S.A., Magic Kingdom; (407) 939-3463

Customers Theme-park guests **Priority seatings** Recommended **When to go** Late lunch or early dinner **Entrée range** Lunch $12–$15, dinner $19–$30 (child $5) **Service** ★★★ **Friendliness** ★★★★ **Parking** Magic Kingdom lot **Bar** None **Wine selection** None **Dress** Casual **Disabled access** Yes
Lunch Daily, noon–2:45 p.m.
Dinner Daily, 4 p.m.–park close

Setting and atmosphere Right along Main Street, U.S.A. after you enter the Magic Kingdom, Tony's is a bit worn on the edges with tile floors, tablecloths, dark woods, and pictures and memorabilia from the Disney classic, *Lady and the Tramp,* on the walls. The nicest seats are on the glass-windowed porch.

House specialties For lunch, paninis and pizzas; for dinner, eggplant roulade, New York strip.

Summary and comments No one comes to the Magic Kingdom expecting haute cuisine, but Tony's does a decent job with pizzas and pasta. And the chef keeps gluten-free pasta on hand for diners on special diets. It's a nice respite from the crowds—we recommend lunch when the prices are not so steep. Go ahead, share a plate of over-priced spaghetti with someone you love.

VICTORIA & ALBERT'S ★★★★½

GOURMET | EXPENSIVE | QUALITY ★★★★★ | VALUE ★★★★

READER'S SURVEY RESPONSES 86% 👍 14% 👎

Disney's Grand Floridian Beach Resort; (407) 939-7707

Customers Hotel guests, locals **Priority seatings** Mandatory; must confirm by noon the day of your seating; call at least 120 days in advance to ensure a table **When to go** Anytime **Entrée range** Fixed price: $105 per person or up to $165 with wine pairings **Service** ★★★★ **Friendliness** ★★★ **Parking** Valet, $6; self-parking is deceptively far away **Wine selection** Excellent **Dress** Jacket required for men; proper evening attire for women **Disabled access** Yes

Dinner Two seatings nightly at 5:45–6:30 p.m. and 9–9:45 p.m.

Setting and atmosphere Frette linens, Riedel crystal, Christofle silver from France—with only 15 tables in the main dining room and the private Fireplace Room with five tables, this is the top dining experience at Disney World. A AAA Five-Diamond winner (the only one in Central Florida), Victoria & Albert's is civilized, lavish, and expensive. Instead of servers, each table is attended by a maid and butler named Victoria and Albert.

House specialties The seven-course menu changes daily, but chef Scott Hunnel's favorites include Jamison farm lamb; seared foie gras over brioche with imported Fuji apples; and African pheasant with summer truffles. The Stilton "cheesecake" with Bosc pears is divine.

Entertainment and amenities A harpist or violinist entertains from the foyer. But the best show is in the kitchen when you book the Chef's Table, where Chef Hunnel starts the evening with a champagne toast and crafts a personal menu, often up to 12 courses. All guests receive personalized souvenir menus, and women get a long-stemmed red rose.

Summary and comments Haute cuisine isn't for everyone, but Hunnel and his team prepare modern American cuisine with the best-of-the-best from around the world. We recommend the Chef's Table; while the main dining room is whisper quiet, the convivial Chef's Table is a whole other experience. For foodies, it's a bargain. The restaurant's wine cellar has more than 700 selections on the menu and 4,200 in the cellar.

Honors and awards AAA 4-Diamond Award.

WHISPERING CANYON CAFÉ ★★★

AMERICAN | MODERATE | QUALITY ★★★½ | VALUE ★★★★

READER'S SURVEY RESPONSES 72% 👍 28% 👎

Disney's Wilderness Lodge and Villas; (407) 939-3463

Customers Hotel guests **Priority seatings** Accepted **When to go** Anytime **Entrée range** Breakfast $7–$13, breakfast buffet $10 (child $6), lunch $14 (child $7), dinner $17–$23 (child $9) **Service** ★★★ **Friendliness** ★★★ **Parking** Hotel lot **Bar** Full service **Wine selection** Limited **Dress** Casual **Disabled access** Yes

Breakfast Daily, 8–11 a.m.

Lunch Daily, noon–3 p.m.

Dinner Daily, 5–10 p.m.

Setting and atmosphere Located just off the hotel's atrium lobby, the restaurant looks out on the lobby on one side and a mountain prairie, created by the Disney land-scapers, on the other. Tables have a barrel-top lazy Susan where the food is placed. The servers sometimes have amusing responses when asked for straws or ketchup, especially if asked by children.

House specialties All-you-can-eat skillets with cornbread, pork ribs, pulled pork, roast chicken, pork sausage, potatoes, baked beans, cole slaw, and corn on the cob.

Other recommendations Order off the menu: New York strip steak or pan-seared snapper.

Summary and comments The real value here is in the "family-style" service, with all-you-can eat servings brought to you on platters and in crocks to pass around (just your family—you don't have to share with others). There is also an à la carte option for those who don't care to share even with family members, but expect to pay more for your stinginess.

WOLFGANG PUCK CAFÉ ★★★

CREATIVE CALIFORNIAN | EXPENSIVE | QUALITY ★★★½ | VALUE ★★★

READER'S SURVEY RESPONSES 57% 👍 33% 👎

Downtown Disney West Side; (407) 938-9653

Customers Tourists and locals **Priority seatings** Upstairs only **When to go** Early evening **Entrée range** Café $11–$30 (child $7–$8), upstairs $65–$115 **Service** ★★ **Friendliness** ★★ **Parking** Downtown Disney lot; valet evenings, $6 **Bar** Full service **Wine selection** Very good **Dress** Casual in the café; collared shirt for men and no jeans upstairs **Disabled access** Good

Open *Café:* Daily, 11:30 a.m.–11 p.m. *Upstairs:* 6 p.m.–until last reservation; bar open until midnight

Setting and atmosphere These are actually two restaurants in one—four if you count the attached Wolfgang Puck Express (and there's no reason to count it for anything, except it serves breakfast, lunch, and dinner) and the sushi bar that does a freeform flow into the restaurant's lounge area. The downstairs is the actual café, with several open kitchen areas, colorful tile (one designer has called it a tile factory outlet store), and plenty of pictures of Wolfgang Puck hanging around the place. The upstairs is a more formal dining room, but in name only. Both spaces are inordinately loud, and conversation is difficult. Throughout the restaurant are TV monitors trained on various culinary stations. One supposes this is so diners can watch their food being prepared (they certainly can't talk to one another), but unless you have excellent vision—and we're talking something along the lines of Superman—you probably won't be able to see anything. The images are like the surveillance cameras in convenience stores.

House specialties Puck's gourmet pizzas made him famous in California in the 1980s, and you can try them here, including his famous smoked salmon with dill cream and chives. The Chinois chicken salad is the best seller, a gargantuan serving with a hot-mustard-based dressing with a kick. Sushi is also a hit. Upstairs the pricey menu features fresh pastas, fish, chicken, and beef.

Summary and comments Wolfgang hasn't been minding the store, and the quality at this Florida outpost is suffering. Levy Restaurants recently took over the operation, and we've seen the famous chef in the kitchen more often than usual, perhaps setting the place back on course. In spite of less-then-stellar food, there's usually a crowd, and we can always recommend grabbing a seat at the sushi bar. Or you can always skip the entrée and go straight for a sweet ending—desserts are worth the calories.

YACHT CLUB GALLEY ★★★

AMERICAN | MODERATE | QUALITY ★★★½ | VALUE ★★★

READER'S SURVEY RESPONSES 75% 👍 25% 👎

Disney's Yacht Club Resort; (407) 939-3463

Customers Hotel guests **Priority seatings** Not necessary **When to go** Breakfast or lunch **Entrée range** Breakfast buffet $14 (child $7), lunch $10–$16 (child $6) **Service** ★★★★ **Friendliness** ★★★★ **Parking** Hotel lot **Bar** Full service **Wine selection** Good **Dress** Casual **Disabled access** Yes

Breakfast Daily, 7–11 a.m.
Lunch Daily, 11:30 a.m.–2:30 p.m.
Dinner Daily, 5–9 p.m.

Setting and atmosphere This large and somewhat noisy dining room features a bright nautical theme with colorful pastels, blue-striped wallpaper, and tablecloths.

House specialties Breakfast features a buffet or an à la carte menu, with such selections as eggs with grilled sirloin steak. Lunch is coffee-shop fare, like grilled chicken, club, or reuben sandwiches. You can get a cold beer or glass of wine to accompany.

Summary and comments This is the catch-all restaurant for the resort, not a dining destination, but you'll see Disney cast members lunching here because it's quiet and service is quick.

YACHTSMAN STEAKHOUSE ★★★

STEAK | EXPENSIVE | QUALITY ★★★½ | VALUE ★★

READER'S SURVEY RESPONSES 76% 👍 24% 👎

Disney's Yacht Club Resort; (407) 939-3463

Customers Hotel guests, locals **Priority seatings** Required **When to go** Anytime **Entrée range** $20–$50 (child $6–$10) **Service** ★★★ **Friendliness** ★★★★ **Parking** Hotel lot **Bar** Full service **Wine selection** Very good **Dress** Casual **Disabled access** Yes

Dinner Daily, 5:30–10 p.m.

Setting and atmosphere Wood beams, white linens, and a view of the sandy lagoon at the resort make this steakhouse appealing. Unlike traditional steakhouses, the menu is expansive, with fish, pork, lamb, fowl, and even vegetarian creations. The adjacent Crew's Cup Lounge, with 40 types of beers and fine wines by the glass, is a fun place to start the evening. A refrigerated display case with big slabs of beef in various stages of aging allows you to see your steak before you're seated, then watch chefs in action in the show kitchen.

House specialties Start with chipotle barbecued shrimp or oysters Rockefeller. All steaks are cut and trimmed on the premises. The Australian barrel-cut tenderloin, Kansas City strip, and prime rib are just some of the cuts. And there's always a fresh fish creation on the menu.

Other recommendations Filet mignon with lobster tail; rack of lamb; Jack Daniels mousse cake. Side dishes, including creamed spinach and sautéed mushrooms, are enough to share.

Entertainment and amenities Strolling musicians (the same ones who stroll through the Yacht Club Galley).

Summary and comments Yachtsman has a loyal following of locals—die-hard meat lovers who don't mind paying for a good steak. International wines from every major wine-producing region of the world complement the menu.

Part Ten

The Magic Kingdom

Arriving

If you drive, the Magic Kingdom/Ticket and Transportation Center (TTC) parking lot opens about two hours before the park's official opening. After paying a fee, you are directed to a parking space, then transported by tram to the TTC, where you catch either a monorail or ferry to the park's entrance.

If you're staying at the Contemporary, Polynesian, or Grand Floridian Resorts, you can commute directly to the Magic Kingdom by monorail (guests at the Contemporary can walk there more quickly). If you stay at Wilderness Lodge and Villas or Fort Wilderness Campground, you can take a boat. Guests at other Disney resorts can reach the park by bus. All Disney lodging guests, whether they arrive by bus, monorail, or boat, are deposited at the park's entrance, bypassing the TTC.

Getting Oriented

At the Magic Kingdom, stroller and wheelchair rentals are to the right of the train station, and lockers are on the station's ground floor. On your left as you enter Main Street is City Hall, the center for information, lost and found, guided tours, and entertainment schedules.

If you don't already have a handout guidemap of the park, get one at City Hall. The guidemap lists all attractions, shops, and eating places; provides helpful information about first aid, baby care, and assistance for the disabled; and gives tips for good photos. It lists times for the day's special events, live entertainment, Disney character parades, and concerts, and it also tells when and where to find Disney characters. Often the guidemap is supplemented by a daily entertainment schedule known as a *Times Guide*. In addition to listing performance times, the *Times Guide* also provides info on Disney character appearances and what Disney calls "Special Hours." Special Hours usually refers to

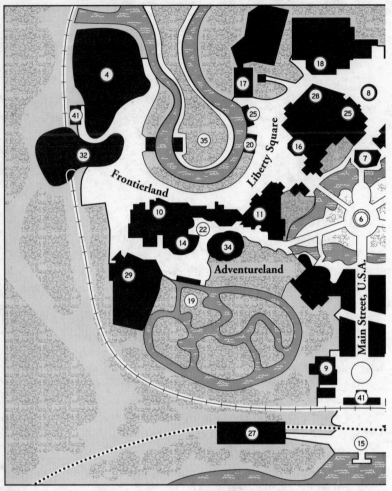

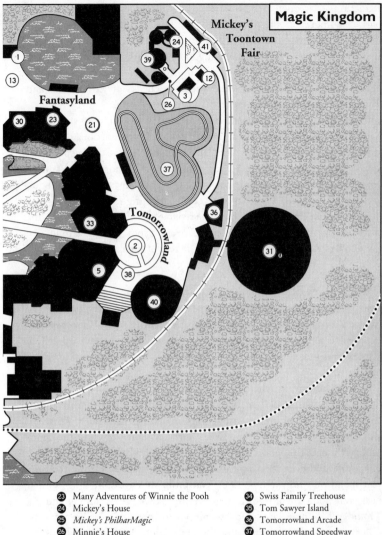

Magic Kingdom

Mickey's Toontown Fair

Fantasyland

Tomorrowland

㉓	Many Adventures of Winnie the Pooh	㉞	Swiss Family Treehouse
㉔	Mickey's House	㉟	Tom Sawyer Island
㉕	*Mickey's PhilharMagic*	㊱	Tomorrowland Arcade
㉖	Minnie's House	㊲	Tomorrowland Speedway
㉗	Monorail Station	㊳	Tomorrowland Transit Authority
㉘	Peter Pan's Flight	㊴	Toontown Hall of Fame
㉙	Pirates of the Caribbean	㊵	*Walt Disney's Carousel of Progress*
㉚	Snow White's Adventures	㊶	WDW Railroad Station
㉛	Space Mountain		
㉜	Splash Mountain		
㉝	*Stitch's Great Escape*		

attractions that open late or close early and to the operating hours of park restaurants.

Main Street ends at a central hub from which branch the entrances to five other sections of the Magic Kingdom: Adventureland, Frontierland, Liberty Square, Fantasyland, and Tomorrowland. Mickey's Toontown Fair is squeezed like a pimple between the cheeks of Fantasyland and Tomorrowland and doesn't connect to the central hub.

Cinderella Castle is the entrance to Fantasyland and is the Magic Kingdom's architectural icon and visual center. If you start in Adventureland and go clockwise around the Magic Kingdom, the castle spires will always be roughly on your right; if you start in Tomorrowland and go counterclockwise through the park, the spires will always be roughly on your left. Cinderella Castle is an excellent meeting place if your group decides to split up during the day or is separated accidentally. Because the castle is large, designate a very specific meeting spot, like the entrance to Cinderella's Royal Table restaurant at the rear of the castle.

Starting the Tour

Everyone soon finds their favorite and not-so-favorite attractions in the Magic Kingdom. Be open-minded and adventuresome. Our personal experience and research indicate that each visitor differs on which attraction is most enjoyable. Don't dismiss a ride or show until *after* you have tried it.

Take advantage of what Disney does best: the fantasy adventures of Splash Mountain and The Haunted Mansion and the various audio-animatronic (talking robots) attractions, including *The Hall of Presidents* and Pirates of the Caribbean. Don't burn daylight browsing the shops unless you plan to spend a minimum of two-and-a-half days at the Magic Kingdom, and even then wait until midday or later. Minimize the time you spend on midway-type rides; you probably have something similar near your hometown. (Don't, however, mistake Space Mountain and Big Thunder Mountain Railroad as amusement-park rides. They may be roller coasters, but they're pure Disney genius.) Eat a good breakfast early, and avoid lines at eateries by snacking during the day on food from vendors, or better yet, from you fannypack. Fare at most Magic Kingdom eateries is on a par with Subway or McDonald's.

FASTPASS at the Magic Kingdom

The Magic Kingdom offers ten FASTPASS attractions, the most in any Disney park. Strategies for using FASTPASS at the Magic Kingdom have been integrated into our touring plans.

MAGIC KINGDOM FASTPASS ATTRACTIONS

Adventureland	Jungle Cruise
Fantasyland	The Many Adventures of Winnie the Pooh
	Mickey's PhilharMagic
	Peter Pan's Flight
Frontierland	Splash Mountain
	Big Thunder Mountain Railroad
Liberty Square	The Haunted Mansion
Tomorrowland	Space Mountain
	Buzz Lightyear's Space Ranger Spin
	Stitch's Great Escape

NOT TO BE MISSED AT THE MAGIC KINGDOM

Adventureland	Pirates of the Caribbean
Fantasyland	The Many Adventures of Winnie the Pooh
	Mickey's PhilharMagic
	Peter Pan's Flight
Frontierland	Big Thunder Mountain Railroad
	Splash Mountain
Liberty Square	The Haunted Mansion
Special Events	Evening Parade
Tomorrowland	Space Mountain
	The Timekeeper (open seasonally)

Main Street, U.S.A.

You begin and end your Magic Kingdom visit on Main Street, which may open a half hour before, and closes a half hour to an hour after, the rest of the park. The Walt Disney World Railroad stops at the Main Street Station; board here for a grand tour of the park or a ride to Frontierland or Mickey's Toontown Fair.

Main Street is a sanitized Disney re-creation of a turn-of-the-nineteenth-century, small-town American street. Its buildings are real, not elaborate props. Attention to detail is exceptional: all interiors, furnishings, and fixtures are true to the period. Along the street are shops and eating places, City Hall, and a fire station. Occasionally, horse-drawn trolleys, fire engines, and horseless carriages transport visitors along Main Street to the central hub.

MAIN STREET SERVICES

Most park services are centered on Main Street, including:

Wheelchair and Stroller Rental	Right of the main entrance before passing under the railroad station
Banking Services	Automated tellers (ATMs) are underneath the Main Street railroad station

MAIN STREET SERVICES *(continued)*

Storage Lockers	Ground floor of the railroad station at the end of Main Street; all lockers are cleaned out each night
Lost and Found	City Hall at the railroad station end of Main Street
Live Entertainment and Parade Info	City Hall at the railroad station end of Main Street
Lost Persons	City Hall
Walt Disney World and Local Attraction Information	City Hall
First Aid	Next to The Crystal Palace, left around the central hub (toward Adventureland)
Baby Center/ Baby-Care Needs	Next to The Crystal Palace, left around the central hub (toward Adventureland)

Walt Disney World Railroad

What It Is Scenic railroad ride around perimeter of the Magic Kingdom, and transportation to Frontierland and Mickey's Toontown Fair

Scope and Scale Minor attraction

When to Go Anytime

Special Comments Main Street is usually the least congested station.

Author's Rating Plenty to see; ★★½

Appeal by Age Group

Preschool ★★★★	Teens ★★★	Over 30 ★★
Grade school ★★½	Young Adults ★★★	Seniors ★★★

Duration of Ride About 19 minutes for a complete circuit

Average Wait in Line per 100 People ahead of You 8 minutes

Assumes 2 or more trains operating

Loading Speed Moderate

Description and Comments A transportation ride blending an unusual variety of sights and experiences with an energy-saving way to get around the park. The train provides a glimpse of all lands except Adventureland.

A Princeton, New Jersey, dad disputes our comment that there's "plenty to see" on the Walt Disney World Railroad:

I'm not sure why you say there is "plenty to see." We got a great view of lots of trees, a brief glimpse of the queue for Splash Mountain and a scene inside it, an even briefer glimpse of Fantasyland, and a view of Toontown Fair, and that's about it. Yeah, it's kind of fun to ride an old steam engine, and our two-year-old sure likes trains, but I found the sights kind of boring.

Touring Tips Save the train ride until after you have seen the featured attractions, or use it when you need transportation. On busy days, lines form at the Frontierland Station, but rarely at the Main Street Station. Strollers aren't allowed on the train. Wheelchair access is available only at the Frontierland and Mickey's Toontown Fair stations.

You cannot take your rental stroller on the train, but you can obtain a replacement stroller at your destination. Just take your personal belongings, your stroller name card, and your rental receipt with you on the train.

Finally, be advised that the railroad shuts down immediately preceding and during parades. Check your park guidemap or *Times Guide* for parade times. Needless to say, this is not the time to queue up for the train.

A PEEK BEHIND THE SCENES WITH JIM HILL

That's a Mighty Lively Gator As you're riding the train, keep an eye out for the trio of robotic alligators serenading a bullfrog on a stump. Every so often, a real alligator swims up the canal directly below the plastic gators and pulls itself out of the water to challenge them. Over the years, the Imagineers have had to repaint these animatronic gators dozens of times to repair wounds the real gators have inflicted.

Transportation Rides

Description and Comments Trolleys, buses, etc., which add color to Main Street

Touring Tips Will save you a walk to the central hub. Not worth a wait.

Adventureland

Adventureland is the first land to the left of Main Street. It combines an African safari theme with a Caribbean atmosphere.

Swiss Family Treehouse

What It Is Outdoor walk-through treehouse

Scope and Scale Minor attraction

When to Go Before 11:30 a.m. or after 5 p.m.

Special Comments Requires climbing a lot of stairs

Author's Rating A visual delight; ★★★

Appeal by Age Group

Preschool ★★★	Teens ★★★	Over 30 ★★★
Grade school ★★★½	Young Adults ★★★	Seniors ★★★

Duration of Tour 10–15 minutes

Average Wait in Line per 100 People ahead of You 7 minutes

Loading Speed Doesn't apply

Description and Comments An immense replica of the shipwrecked family's treehouse home will turn your children into arboreal architects. It's the king of all treehouses, with its multiple stories, clever jerry-rigging, and mechanical wizardry.

Touring Tips A self-guided walk-through tour involves a lot of stairs up and down, but no ropes, ladders, or anything fancy. People who stop for extra-long looks or to rest sometimes create bottlenecks that slow the crowd flow. Visit in late afternoon or early evening if you're on a one-day tour, or in the morning of your second day.

A PEEK BEHIND THE SCENES WITH JIM HILL

For Sale: 3BR 0BA SPLIT-LEVEL / ONE OWNER
Given that Disneyland's Swiss Family Treehouse was re-themed back in 1999, Mouse House insiders suggest it will only be a matter of time 'til the Magic Kingdom's version also goes under the knife. The attraction can then be tied directly in with a more modern, more viable Disney franchise.

Jungle Cruise (FASTPASS)

What It Is Outdoor safari-themed boat ride adventure

Scope and Scale Major attraction

When to Go Before 10 a.m. or 2 hours before closing

Author's Rating A long-enduring Disney masterpiece; ★★★

Appeal by Age Group

Preschool ★★★½	Teens ★★½	Over 30 ★★★
Grade school ★★★½	Young Adults ★★★	Seniors ★★★

Duration of Ride 8–9 minutes

Average Wait in Line per 100 People ahead of You 3½ minutes

Assumes 10 boats operating

Loading Speed Moderate

Description and Comments An outdoor cruise through jungle waterways. Passengers encounter animatronic elephants, lions, hostile natives, and a menacing hippo. Boatman's spiel adds to the fun. Once one of the most grand and elaborate attractions at the Magic Kingdom, the Jungle Cruise's technology now seems dated and worn. Since the advent of the Animal Kingdom, the attraction's appeal has diminished, but in its defense, you can always depend on the Jungle Cruise's robotic critters being present as you motor past.

An Albany, New York, woman agrees that the Jungle Cruise is past its prime:

Jungle Cruise needs updating! My husband gave it a five on the "cheese factor" scale.

Touring Tips Among the park's oldest attractions and one that occupies a good third of Adventureland. A convoluted queuing area makes it very difficult to estimate the length of the wait for the Jungle Cruise. A mother from the Bronx, New York, complains:

A PEEK BEHIND THE SCENES WITH JIM HILL

George of the Jungle Cruise? When Disney's Animal Kingdom opened, the Imagineers pondered the fate of the Jungle Cruise. One of the ideas suggested was re-theming this entire attraction to celebrate the Disney 1997 hit film, "George of the Jungle." Imagine going through the "Sacred Elephant Bathing Pool" where the elephants really do have their trunks on . . . plus snorkels and swim fins. Fittingly, the Imagineer responsible for this brain fart was relegated to designing tutus for dancing hippos in *Fantasia* (just kidding).

The line for this ride is extremely deceiving. We got in line toward early evening; it was long but we really wanted to take this ride. Every time the winding line brought us near the loading dock and we thought we were going to get on, we'd discover a whole new section of winding lanes to go through. It was extremely frustrating. We must have waited 20–30 minutes before we finally gave up and got out.

Fortunately, the Jungle Cruise is a FASTPASS attraction. Before you obtain a FAST-PASS, however, ask a cast member what the estimated wait in the standby line is.

Magic Carpets of Aladdin

What It Is Elaborate midway ride

Scope and Scale Minor attraction

When to Go Before 10 a.m. or in the hour before park closing

Author's Rating An eye-appealing children's ride; ★★★

Appeal by Age Group

Preschool ★★★★½	Teens ★½	Over 30 ★½
Grade school ★★★★	Young Adults ½★	Seniors ★½

Duration of Ride 1½ minutes

Average Wait in Line per 100 People ahead of You 16 minutes

Loading Speed Slow

Description and Comments   Magic Carpets of Aladdin is a midway ride like Dumbo, except with magic carpets instead of elephants. Copying the water innovation of the One Fish, Two Fish attraction at Universal's Islands of Adventure, Disney's Aladdin ride has a spitting camel positioned to spray jets of water on carpet riders. Riders can maneuver their carpets up and down and side to side to avoid getting wet.

Touring Tips Like Dumbo, this ride has great eye appeal but extremely limited capacity (that is, it's slow-loading). If your younger children see it, they'll probably want to ride. Try to get them on during the first 30 minutes the park is open or try just before park closing.

A PEEK BEHIND THE SCENES WITH JIM HILL

Recycling Disney Style
The spitting camels that spritz riders on the Magic Carpets of Aladdin actually started life as parts of parade floats at the Disney-MGM Studios. There, the dromedaries unashamedly heaped spit on guests watching Aladdin's Royal Caravan, a parade that ran daily from December 1992 through August of 1995.

Pirates of the Caribbean

What It Is Indoor pirate-themed adventure boat ride

Scope and Scale Headliner

When to Go Before noon or after 5 p.m.

Special Comments Frightens some young children

Author's Rating Disney audio-animatronics at its best; not to be missed; ★★★★★

Appeal by Age Group

Preschool ★★★	Teens ★★★★	Over 30 ★★★★½
Grade school ★★★★★	Young Adults ★★★★	Seniors ★★★★½

Duration of Ride About 7½ minutes

Average Wait in Line per 100 People ahead of You 1½ minutes

Assumes Both waiting lines operating

Loading Speed Fast

Description and Comments An indoor cruise through a series of sets depicting a pirate raid on an island settlement, from bombardment of the fortress to debauchery after the victory. Regarding debauchery, Pirates of the Caribbean is one of several Disney attractions that has been administered a strong dose of political correctness. Even so, a Rockville, Maryland, mom was not prepared for what she saw:

I had not understood that it would be as visually violent and historically accurate as it was. I really didn't look forward to explaining to my son why those women had ropes around their necks, etc. I wish I'd been better warned that this isn't the "Captain Hook" view of piracy, but a much more realistic one.

Touring Tips Undoubtedly one of the park's most elaborate and timeless attractions. Engineered to move large crowds in a hurry, Pirates is a good attraction to see during later afternoon. It has two covered waiting lines.

A PEEK BEHIND THE SCENES WITH JIM HILL

Hey, That Pirate Looks Sorta Familiar
Following the success of Disney's *Pirates of the Caribbean* feature film, theme park guests have been asking where in the attraction to find Captain Jack Sparrow. Well, you can't… yet. But—if everything goes according to plan—you should be able to see an animatronic figure of Johnny Depp lurching through this ride at about the time that the first of two *Pirates of the Caribbean* sequels sail into theaters.

Enchanted Tiki Birds

What It Is Audio-animatronic Pacific island musical theater show

Scope and Scale Minor attraction

When to Go Before 11 a.m. or after 3:30 p.m.

Special Comments Frightens some preschoolers

Author's Rating Very, very unusual; ★★★½

Appeal by Age Group

Preschool ★★★★	Teens ★★★	Over 30 ★★★
Grade school ★★★½	Young Adults ★★★	Seniors ★★★

Duration of Presentation 15½ minutes

Preshow Entertainment Talking birds

Probable Waiting Time 15 minutes

Description and Comments   Upgraded in 1998, this theater presentation features two of Disney's most beloved bird characters: Iago from *Aladdin* and Zazu from *The Lion King*. A new song, "Friend Like Me," and a revamped plotline add some much-needed zip, but the production remains (pardon the pun) a featherweight in the Disney galaxy of attractions. Even so, the Tiki Birds are a great favorite of the eight-and-under set and guests on drugs. Although readers like the *Enchanted Tiki Birds* show, they caution that the new version is more frightening to younger children than was the old. Concerning the scary parts, a mother of three from Coleman, Michigan, was outspoken:

> *The Tiki Bird show was very scary, with a thunder and lightning storm and a loud volcano goddess with glowing red eyes. Can't Disney do anything without scaring young children? It's a bird show!*

  A New Jersey dad concurred, commenting:

> *Enchanted Tiki Birds are now REALLY intense—far more intense than I remember fondly from previous visits. Tiki Gods storming and smoking, the whole room plunged into utter darkness, and thunder and lightning that quite literally shakes the benches you're sitting on—our child (two and a half) was terrified. Definitely not recommended for very young children; it seems the attraction is aimed at older children now.*

Touring Tips   One of the more bizarre Magic Kingdom entertainments. Usually not too crowded. We go in the late afternoon when we especially appreciate sitting briefly in an air-conditioned theater with our brains in park.

A PEEK BEHIND THE SCENES WITH JIM HILL

Presidents Are More Boring than Birds
You'll have to wait in the *Enchanted Tiki Room* theater to the very end of the show. But—if you do so—you get to hear one Magic Kingdom show take a jab at another when Iago says: "Well, I'm exhausted. I think I'll go over to *The Hall of Presidents* and take a nap."

Frontierland

Frontierland adjoins Adventureland as you move clockwise around the Magic Kingdom. The focus is on the Old West, with stockade-type structures and pioneer trappings.

Splash Mountain (FASTPASS)

What It Is   Indoor/outdoor water-flume adventure ride

Scope and Scale   Super headliner

When to Go   As soon as the park opens, during afternoon or evening parades, just before closing, or use FASTPASS

Special Comments   Must be 40" tall to ride; children younger than 7 must ride with an adult. Switching off option provided (pages 266–268).

Author's Rating A wet winner; not to be missed; ★★★★★
Appeal by Age Group

Preschool †		Teens ★★★★★		Over 30 ★★★★★
Grade school ★★★★★	Young Adults ★★★★★		Seniors ★★★★★	

† *Many preschoolers are too short to meet the height requirement, and others are visually intimidated when they see the ride from the waiting line. Among preschoolers who actually ride, most give the attraction high marks (3–5 stars).*

Duration of Ride About 10 minutes

Average Wait in Line per 100 People ahead of You 3½ minutes

Assumes Operating at full capacity

Loading Speed Moderate

Description and Comments Amusement park flume ride, Disney-style. Bigger than life and more imaginative than anyone thought possible, Splash Mountain combines steep chutes with excellent special effects. The ride covers over half a mile, splashing through swamps, caves, and backwood bayous before climaxing in a five-story plunge and Br'er Rabbit's triumphant return home. More than 100 audio-animatronic characters, including Br'er Rabbit (a.k.a. Br'er Hare), Br'er Bear, and Br'er Fox, regale riders with songs, including "Zip-a-Dee-Doo-Dah."

WARNING!
For Bouffants, Rug Wearers, and Elvis Impersonators
This Ride Will Muss Your 'Do

Touring Tips This happy, exciting, adventuresome ride vies with Space Mountain in Tomorrowland as the park's most popular attraction. Crowds build fast in the morning, and waits of more than two hours can be expected once the park fills. Get in line first thing, certainly no later than 45 minutes after the park opens. Long lines will persist all day.

If you have only one day to see the Magic Kingdom, ride Space Mountain first, then Buzz Lightyear (also in Tomorrowland), then hot-foot it over to Splash Mountain. If the line isn't too long, go ahead and ride. Otherwise, obtain a FASTPASS and return later to enjoy Splash Mountain. FASTPASS strategies have been incorporated into the Magic Kingdom One-Day Touring Plans (see pages 481–482). If you have two mornings to devote to the Magic Kingdom, experience Space Mountain one morning and Buzz Lightyear, Splash Mountain, and Big Thunder Mountain the next. Spreading your visit over two mornings will eliminate much crisscrossing of the park as well as the backtracking that is inevitable when you use FASTPASS.

As occurs with Space Mountain, when the park opens, hundreds are poised to dash to Splash Mountain. The best strategy is to go to the end of Main Street and turn left to The Crystal Palace restaurant. In front of the restaurant is a bridge that provides a shortcut to Adventureland. Stake out a position at the barrier rope. When the park opens and the rope drops, move as fast as you comfortably can and cross the bridge to Adventureland.

Here's another shortcut: Just past the first group of buildings on your right, roughly across from the Swiss Family Treehouse, is a small passageway containing rest rooms and phones. Easy to overlook, it connects Adventureland to Frontierland. Go through the passageway into Frontierland and take a hard left. As you emerge along the waterfront, Splash Mountain is straight ahead. If you miss the passageway, don't fool around looking for it. Continue straight through Adventureland to Splash Mountain.

Less exhausting in the morning is to commute to Splash Mountain via the Walt Disney World Railroad. Board at Main Street Station and wait for the park to open. The train will pull out of the station a few minutes after the rope drops at the central hub end of Main Street. Ride to Frontierland Station (the first stop) and disembark. As you come down the stairs at the station, the entrance to Splash Mountain will be on your left. Because of the time required to unload at the station, train passengers will arrive at Splash Mountain about the same time as the lead element from the central hub.

A Suffolk, Virginia, mom contends that there are more important considerations than beating the crowds:

> The only recommendation I do have for the Magic Kingdom plan is to definitely wait to do Splash Mountain at the end of the day. We were seated in the front of the ride and needless to say we were soaked to the bone. If we had ridden the ride [first thing in the morning] according to your plan, I personally would have been miserable for the rest of the day. Parents, beware! It says you will get wet, not drowned.

At Splash Mountain, if you ride in the front seat, you almost certainly will get wet. Riders elsewhere get splashed, but usually not doused. Since you don't know which seat you'll be assigned, go prepared. On a cool day, carry a plastic garbage bag. Tear holes in the bottom and sides to make a water-resistant (not waterproof) sack dress. Be sure to tuck the bag under your bottom. Leave your camera with a nonriding member of your group or wrap it in plastic. An alternative to the garbage bag get-up is to store a change of clothes, including footwear, in one of the park's rental lockers. For any attraction where there's a distinct possibility of getting soaked, we recommend you wear Tevas or some other type of waterproof sandal. Change back to regular shoes after the ride.

The scariest part of this adventure ride is the steep chute you see when standing in line, but the drop looks worse than it is. Despite reassurances, however, many children wig out after watching it. A mom from Grand Rapids, Michigan, recalls her kids' rather unique reaction:

> We discovered after the fact that our children thought they would go underwater after the five-story drop and tried to hold their breath throughout the ride in preparation. They were really too preoccupied to enjoy the clever Br'er Rabbit story.

A PEEK BEHIND THE SCENES WITH JIM HILL

No Rhyme or Remus: Fans of "Song of the South" (The 1946 Disney film on which Splash Mountain was based) may notice one very important character from that movie missing from this attraction: Uncle Remus himself. Supposedly out of concern that this character might offend African Americans, the Imagineers just cut Uncle Remus out of the show, replacing him with a new narrator for the ride, Br'er Frog.

Big Thunder Mountain Railroad (FASTPASS)

What It Is Tame, Western-mining-themed roller coaster

Scope and Scale Headliner

When to Go Before 10 a.m., in the hour before closing, or use FASTPASS

Special Comments Must be 40" tall to ride; children younger than age 7 must ride with an adult. Switching off option provided (pages 266–268).

Author's Rating Great effects; relatively tame ride; not to be missed; ★★★★

Appeal by Age Group

Preschool ★★★	Teens ★★★★	Over 30 ★★★★
Grade school ★★★★	Young Adults ★★★★	Seniors ★★★

Duration of Ride Almost 3½ minutes

Average Wait in Line per 100 People ahead of You 2½ minutes

Assumes 5 trains operating

Loading Speed Moderate to fast

Description and Comments Roller coaster through and around a Disney "mountain." The idea is that you're on a runaway mine train during the Gold Rush. This roller coaster is about 5 on a "scary scale" of 10. First-rate examples of Disney creativity are showcased: realistic mining town, falling rocks, and an earthquake, all humorously animated.

Touring Tips A superb Disney experience, but not too wild a roller coaster. Emphasis is much more on the sights than on the thrill of the ride.

Nearby Splash Mountain affects the traffic flow to Big Thunder Mountain Railroad. Adventuresome guests ride Splash Mountain first, then go next door to ride Big Thunder. This means large crowds in Frontierland all day and long waits for Big Thunder Mountain. The best way to experience the Magic Kingdom's "mountains" is to ride Space Mountain one morning as soon as the park opens, and Splash Mountain and Big Thunder the next morning. If you only have one day, the order should be (1) Space Mountain (2) optional–Buzz Lightyear (3) Splash Mountain (4) Big Thunder Mountain. If the wait exceeds 30 minutes when you arrive, use FASTPASS.

Guests experience Disney attractions differently. Consider this letter from a lady in Brookline, Massachusetts:

Being in the senior citizens' category and having limited time, my friend and I confined our activities to those attractions rated as four or five stars for seniors. Because of your recommendation and because you listed it as "not to be missed," we waited for one hour to board the Big Thunder Mountain Railroad, [which you] rated a "5" on a scary scale of "10." After living through three-and-a-half minutes of pure terror, I will rate that attraction a "15" on a scary scale of "10." We were so busy holding on and screaming and even

praying for our safety that we did not see any falling rocks, a mining town, or an earth-quake. In our opinion, the Big Thunder Mountain Railroad should not be recommended for seniors or preschool children.

Another woman from New England writes:

My husband, who is 41, found Big Thunder Mountain too intense for his enjoyment, and feels that anyone who does not like roller coasters would not enjoy this ride.

A woman from Vermont discovered that there's more to consider about Big Thunder than being scared:

Big Thunder Mountain Railroad was rated a "5" on the scary scale. I won't say it warranted a higher scare rating, but it was much higher on the lose-your-lunch meter. One more sharp turn and the kids in front of me would have needed a dip in Splash Mountain!

However, a reader from West Newton, Massachusetts, dubbed Big Thunder Mountain "a roller coaster for people who don't like roller coasters."

A PEEK BEHIND THE SCENES WITH JIM HILL

Big Thunder. Laaaaarge Lightning.
Notice those pointy pieces of metal sticking out of the tops of all the spires on Big Thunder Mountain? Those are light-ning rods, designed to take the hit (instead of you) when one of those colossal Central Florida thunderstorms comes rolling through. In fact, if you'll pay close attention to the rooftops of Walt Disney World, you'll find lightning rods on top of virtually every structure around. Just another of the less-obvious ways the Mouse goes out of its way to ensure guest safety.

Country Bear Jamboree

What It Is Audio-animatronic country hoedown theater show

Scope and Scale Major attraction

When to Go Before 11:30 a.m., before a parade, or during the 2 hours before closing

Special Comments Shows change at Christmas

Author's Rating A Disney classic; ★★★

Appeal by Age Group

Preschool ★★★	Teens ★★½	Over 30 ★★★
Grade school ★★★	Young Adults ★★★	Seniors ★★★

Duration of Presentation 15 minutes

Preshow Entertainment None

Probable Waiting Time This attraction is moderately popular but has a compara-tively small capacity. Waiting time between noon and 5:30 p.m. on a busy day will aver-age 15–30 minutes.

Description and Comments A charming cast of audio-animatronic bears sing and stomp in a Western-style hoedown. Although one of the Magic Kingdom's most humor-ous and upbeat shows, *Country Bear Jamboree* hasn't been revised for so long that the bears are past retirement age.

Readers continue to debate the merits of *Country Bear Jamboree*. The following comments are representative.

First, from a woman who thinks the *Jamboree* is way past its prime:

Country Bear Jamboree—"A Disney classic 3.0"—You cannot be serious!! Although I must admit my ten-year-old daughter enjoyed it and got very angry about all the jokes we made about it for the remainder of the holiday!

A Sandy Hook, Connecticut, mom agrees, commenting:

I know they consider it a classic, and kids always seem to love it, but could they PLEASE update it after half a century?

A young woman from Carmel, Indiana, put her experience in perspective, writing:

Here is another half hour of my life that I cannot get back.

And from a New York woman:

Country Bear Jamboree should be retired. We walked in from the hot sun with a crowd and were sitting in the cool air-conditioning, which was nice. But then some cutesy voice said "The bears want you to stand up." The crowd shouted in unison, "NO WAY!" I was shocked to laughter by that reaction and was further amused by the complete disdain the audience held for the show.

A New Jersey family with a terrified child didn't have time to be bored:

We must disagree with your statement that Country Bear Jamboree has no fear factor whatsoever. When he was two years old, our son was so terrified by the talking heads on the wall that we had to remove him from the show.

But, a dad from Cape Coral defends the show:

Don't sell the Country Bear Jamboree short. It may be boring to repeat visitors, but the look on our three-year-old son's face as he saw the show was priceless. In addition, he was astounded when he left the theater and found the mounted heads on the wall of the restaurant still singing away. It was the best thing we saw for him that day.

Touring Tips The *Jamboree* remains popular and draws large crowds, from mid-morning on.

A PEEK BEHIND THE SCENES WITH JIM HILL

Country Bear Bed-and-Breakfast

Back in 1971, before they opened the Magic Kingdom to the public, Disney officials were worried about horrendous traffic on I-4. So worried in fact that they didn't want the theme park's opening crew to go home the night before the official grand opening, out of fear that these workers would get caught in some awful traffic jam and not be able to get to work the next morning. In the end, management persuaded a number of key cast members to stay overnight in the park, sleeping in the Country Bear Playhouse.

Tom Sawyer Island and Fort Langhorn

What It Is Outdoor walk-through exhibit/rustic playground

Scope and Scale Minor attraction

When to Go Midmorning through late afternoon

Special Comments Closes at dusk

Author's Rating The place for rambunctious kids; ★★★

Appeal by Age Group

Preschool ★★★★★	Teens ★★	Over 30 ★★
Grade school ★★★★★	Young Adults ★★	Seniors ★★

Description and Comments Tom Sawyer Island is a getaway within the park. It has hills to climb, a cave and windmill to explore, a tipsy barrel bridge to cross, and paths to follow. You can fire a toy rifle from the blockhouse of Fort Langhorn. It's a delight for adults and a godsend for children who have been in tow and closely supervised all day. They love the freedom to explore Fort Langhorn. There is even a "secret" escape tunnel.

Touring Tips Tom Sawyer Island isn't one of the Magic Kingdom's more celebrated attractions, but it's one of the park's better conceived ones. Attention to detail is excellent, and kids revel in its frontier atmosphere. It's a must for families with children ages 5–15. If your group is made up of adults, visit on your second day or on your first day after you've seen the attractions you most wanted to see.

Although children could spend a whole day on the island, plan on at least 20 minutes. Access is by raft from Frontierland; two operate simultaneously and the trip is pretty efficient, though you may have to stand in line to board both ways.

For a mother from Duncan, South Carolina, Tom Sawyer Island is as much a refuge as an attraction:

> I do have one tip for parents. In the afternoon when the crowds were at their peak, the weather [at] its hottest, and the kids started lagging behind, our organization began to suffer. We then retreated over to Tom Sawyer Island, which proved to be a true haven. My husband and I found a secluded bench and regrouped while sipping iced tea and eating delicious soft ice cream. Meanwhile, the kids were able to run freely in the shade. Afterward, we were ready to tackle the park again, refreshed and with direction once more.

According to a dad from Hampton, Connecticut, Tom Sawyer Island was a hit with three generations of his family:

> Tom Sawyer Island was Grandfather's favorite [attraction]—he fell asleep in the rocking chair on Aunt Polly's Landing while the kids explored the islands and Mom and Dad rested with cool drinks.

A PEEK BEHIND THE SCENES WITH JIM HILL

Enjoy It While You Can
Given that Disneyland has already shuttered Fort Wilderness on its own version of Tom Sawyer's Island (supposedly due to costs associated with disabled-access issues as well as safety concerns), it's only a matter of time 'til Disney's lawyers finally get around to closing down Fort Langhorn. So run up and down those extremely narrow and poorly lit stairs and fire off a politically incorrect rifle while you still can. The Imagineers expect to be playing "Taps" for this Frontierland icon in the very near future.

The Diamond Horseshoe Saloon

What It Is   Line-dance lessons hosted by Disney characters

Scope and Scale   Minor attraction

When to Go   Check the daily entertainment schedule

Special Comments   No food available

Author's Rating   Unorganized but fun; ★★★

Appeal by Age Group

Preschool ★★★★½	Teens ★★★	Over 30 ★★★½
Grade school ★★★★	Young Adults ★★★½	Seniors ★★★½

Duration of Presentation   About 20 minutes

Average Wait in Line per 100 People ahead of You   No wait

Description and Comments   Approximately 6–7 times each day, the Diamond Horseshoe Saloon hosts *Goofy's Country Dancin' Jamboree*. Much of the production takes place on the main floor of the saloon (as opposed to on the stage), and consists of audience-participation country line dancing lessons taught by a human performer, Sara Jo, with assistance from Goofy, Chip and Dale, and Woody, Jessie, and Bullseye from *Toy Story 2*.

Usually, four dances are presented at each show, about three and a half too many for preschoolers to learn in 15 minutes. The upshot is a lot of busy fumbling, bumping into other guests, and precious little dancing. The kids (and most adults) stay thoroughly confused for the duration. When it's over you're exhausted and left with the feeling that Disney might have been better off teaching the kids to make Baked Alaska. Ironically, the reality that the concept doesn't work particularly well makes it all the more fun and endearing. Needless to say, the little ones enjoy it immensely and the parents shoot some great photos.

Touring Tips   The jamboree takes place on the regular floor of the Diamond Horseshoe (which has been cleared of tables and chairs since the saloon no longer serves food or drinks). Parents and those opting not to dance can watch and photograph the melee from the wraparound balcony on the second floor. Participation, as well as seating in the balcony, are on a first-come, first-served basis. Most days you should queue up in front of the Saloon about 20 minutes before showtime.

Frontierland Shootin' Arcade

What It Is   Electronic shooting gallery

Scope and Scale   Diversion

When to Go   Whenever convenient

Special Comments   Costs 50 cents per play

Author's Rating   Very nifty shooting gallery; ★½

Appeal by Age Group

Preschool ★★★	Teens ★★★	Over 30 ★★
Grade school ★★★★	Young Adults ★★	Seniors ★★

Description and Comments   Very elaborate. One of few attractions not included in Magic Kingdom admission.

Touring Tips   Not a place to blow your time if you're on a tight schedule. If time allows, go on your second day. The fun is entirely in the target practice—no prizes can be won.

Walt Disney World Railroad

Description and Comments   Stops in Frontierland on its circle tour of the park. See the description under Main Street (page 429) for additional details.

Touring Tips   Pleasant, feet-saving link to Main Street and Mickey's Toontown Fair, but the Frontierland Station is usually more congested than those stations. You cannot take your rental stroller on the train. If you don't want to make a round-trip to pick up your stroller, take your personal belongings, your stroller name card, and your rental receipt with you on the train. You'll be issued a replacement stroller at your Walt Disney World Railroad destination.

A PEEK BEHIND THE SCENES WITH JIM HILL

Taming the Wild Frontier   Ah, it used to be that Disney World visitors were treated to the sight of a man with an arrow sticking out of his back as the riverboat floated past "The Burning Cabin" on the Rivers of America. But there were concerns that Native Americans might take offense to the suggestion that Indians had turned a settler into a pincushion. Consequently, the settler and the arrow were removed to the Disney warehouse of politically incorrect artifacts. In 1974 there were concerns that the immoderate amount of gas needed to keep "The Burning Cabin" burning looked bad during the energy crisis. Oil lobbyists apparently prevailed in the cabin controversy (when do they not?), and the cabin burns on as an icon of conspicuous consumption.

Liberty Square

Liberty Square re-creates Colonial America at the time of the American Revolution. The architecture is Federal or Colonial. A real, 130-year-old live oak (dubbed the "Liberty Tree") lends dignity and grace to the setting.

The Hall of Presidents

What It Is   Audio-animatronic historical theater presentation

Scope and Scale   Major attraction

When to Go   Anytime

Author's Rating   Impressive and moving; ★★★

Appeal by Age Group

Preschool ★	Teens ★★★	Over 30 ★★★★
Grade school ★★½	Young Adults ★★★½	Seniors ★★★★

Duration of Presentation   Almost 23 minutes

Preshow Entertainment   None

Probable Waiting Time   Lines for this attraction look awesome but are usually swallowed up as the theater exchanges audiences. Your wait will probably be the remaining time of the show that's in progress when you arrive. Even during the busiest times, waits rarely exceed 40 minutes.

Description and Comments   President George W. Bush was added in 2001, but the content of the presentation remains largely the same. A 23-minute, strongly inspirational and patriotic program highlights milestones in American history. The performance climaxes with a roll call of presidents from Washington through the present, with a few words of encouragement from President Lincoln. A very moving show, coupled with one of Disney's best and most ambitious audio-animatronic efforts.

Our high opinion notwithstanding, we receive a lot of mail from readers who get more than entertainment from *The Hall of Presidents*. A lady in St. Louis writes:

We always go to The Hall of Presidents *when my husband gets cranky so he can take a nice nap.*

A young mother in Marion, Ohio, adds:

The Hall of Presidents is a great place to breast-feed.

But for a Texas family, *The Hall of Presidents* was an unexpected hit:

We were sure our young children would not like The Hall of Presidents, *and so we avoided it for several years. This trip we tried it. What a pleasant surprise, both our eight- and ten-year-olds recognized George W. and the roll call was very moving without being the least sappy. We all loved it.*

Touring Tips   Detail and costumes are masterful. If your children fidget during the show, notice the Presidents do too. This attraction is one of the park's most popular among older visitors. Don't be put off by long lines. The theater holds more than 700 people, thus swallowing large lines at a single gulp when visitors are admitted.

A PEEK BEHIND THE SCENES WITH JIM HILL

Adding Their Own Finishing Touches   The Imagineers went to great pains to make sure that all of the robotic commanders-in-chief looked exactly right in WDW's *Hall of Presidents*. But the cast members who work at this attraction sometimes make their own little additions to these august figures. Condoms have been found in President Clinton's pockets and—during the Watergate hearings back in 1974—the Nixon figure was often found with his hands tied behind his back, as if about to be carted off to jail.

Liberty Belle Riverboat

What It Is   Outdoor scenic boat ride

Scope and Scale   Major attraction

When to Go   Anytime

Author's Rating   Slow, relaxing, and scenic; ★★½

Appeal by Age Group

Preschool ★★★½	Teens ★★½	Over 30 ★★★
Grade school ★★★	Young Adults ★★★	Seniors ★★★

Duration of Ride   About 16 minutes

Average Wait to Board   10–14 minutes

Description and Comments   Large-capacity paddle-wheel riverboat navigates the waters around Tom Sawyer Island and Fort Langhorn. A beautiful craft, the riverboat provides a lofty perspective of Frontierland and Liberty Square.

Touring Tips   The riverboat is a good attraction for the busy middle of the day. If you encounter huge crowds, chances are that the attraction has been inundated by a wave of guests coming from a just-concluded performance of *The Hall of Presidents.*

The Haunted Mansion (FASTPASS)

What It Is   Haunted-house dark ride

Scope and Scale   Major attraction

When to Go   Before 11:30 a.m., or use FASTPASS after 8 p.m.

Special Comments   Frightens some very young children

Author's Rating   Some of Walt Disney World's best special effects; not to be missed; ★★★★

Appeal by Age Group

Preschool [varies]	Teens ★★★★	Over 30 ★★★★
Grade school ★★★★★	Young Adults ★★★★	Seniors ★★★★

Duration of Ride   7-minute ride plus a 1½-minute preshow

Average Wait in Line per 100 People ahead of You   2½ minutes

Assumes   Both "stretch rooms" operating

Loading Speed   Fast

Description and Comments   More fun than scary, with some of the Magic Kingdom's best special effects, The Haunted Mansion is a masterpiece of detail. "Doom Buggies" on a conveyor belt transport you throughout the house from parlor to attic, and then through a graveyard. The story line is so thin and unemphasized you won't notice.

Although the story is not obvious to the casual observer, an Australian reader suggests that knowing it in advance really enhances the attraction:

During our behind-the-scenes tour, we were told the story line for [The Haunted Mansion]. It actually made it much more enjoyable. From my recollection, a lady was about to be married when her groom discovered her with the tailor's arms around her (probably just getting a dress fitting, but we'll never know!). The groom killed the tailor in a rage, and she jumped out the window in distress. This is very cleverly shown throughout the attraction: The carriages rise to the attic to see her in her wedding dress, and while descending, the broken window can be seen. At this point, the "guests" assume the role of her ghost, and the gravedigger and faithful dog shiver as the "ghost" passes. The story line really added another dimension to the attraction.

Some children become overly anxious about what they think they'll see. Almost nobody is scared by the actual sights.

The Haunted Mansion is one of veteran *Unofficial Guide* writer Eve Zibart's favorite attractions. She warns:

Don't let the childishness of the old-fashioned Haunted Mansion put you off: This is one of the best attractions in the Magic Kingdom. It's jam-packed with visual puns, special effects, hidden Mickeys, and really lovely Victorian-spooky sets. It's not scary, except in the sweetest of ways, but it will remind you of the days before ghost stories gave way to slasher flicks.

Touring Tips This attraction would be more at home in Fantasyland, but no matter. It's Disney at its best. Lines here ebb and flow more than those at most other Magic Kingdom hot spots because the Mansion is near *The Hall of Presidents* and the Liberty Belle Riverboat. These two attractions disgorge 700 and 450 people respectively when each show or ride ends, and many of these folks head straight for the Mansion. If you can't go before 11:30 a.m. or after 8 p.m., try to slip in between crowds. Note that The Haunted Mansion is such a fast-loading attraction that FASTPASS really isn't warranted. In the end, FASTPASS will cost you more time than it will save.

A PEEK BEHIND THE SCENES WITH JIM HILL

Getting Ready for a Scary Christmas Recently, Disney World's Haunted Mansion has gone through a number of rehabs and repairs. How come? Because—in the fall of 2005—the Magic Kingdom's Mansion is rumored to be getting a brand new tenant: Jack Skellington, the star of Touchstone Pictures' 1994 release, Tim Burton's *The Nightmare before Christmas*. As Jack and his friends remake the Mansion each holiday season in their own goofy, ghoulish image, look for this Haunted Mansion Holiday attraction to quickly become a holiday hit in Central Florida (as it has at Disneyland).

Fantasyland

Fantasyland is the heart of the Magic Kingdom, a truly enchanting place spread gracefully like a miniature Alpine village beneath the steepled towers of Cinderella Castle.

It's a Small World (Will remain closed for part of 2005)

What It Is World brotherhood–themed indoor boat ride

Scope and Scale Major attraction

When to Go Anytime

Author's Rating Exponentially "cute"; ★★★

Appeal by Age Group

Preschool ★★★½	Teens ★★½	Over 30 ★★½
Grade school ★★★	Young Adults ★★½	Seniors ★★★

Duration of Ride Approximately 11 minutes

Average Wait in Line per 100 People ahead of You 11 minutes

Assumes Busy conditions with 30 or more boats operating

Loading Speed Fast

Description and Comments Happy, upbeat indoor attraction with a catchy tune that will take over your mind for weeks. Small boats carry visitors on a tour around the world, with singing and dancing dolls showcasing the dress and culture of each nation. One of Disney's oldest entertainment offerings, It's a Small World first unleashed its brainwashing song and adorable ethnic dolls on the real world at the 1964 New York World's Fair. Though it bludgeons you with sappy redundancy, almost everyone enjoys It's a Small

World (at least the first time). It stands, however, along with *Enchanted Tiki Birds*, in the What-Kind-of-Drugs-Were-They-On-When-They-Thought-This-Up? category.

A woman from Holbrook, New York, apparently underwhelmed, suggests that "Small World" would be much better "if each person got three to four softballs on the way in!" (We continue to hear from the Softball Lady. She's still pitching.)

And a mother from Castleton, Vermont, added this:

> It's a Small World at Fantasyland was like a pit stop in the Twilight Zone. They were very slow in unloading the boats, and we were stuck in a line of about six boats waiting to get out while the endless chanting of that song grated on my nerves. I told my husband I was going to swim for it just to escape one more chorus.

Touring Tips Cool off here during the heat of the day. With two waiting lines, It's a Small World loads fast and usually is a good bet between 11 a.m. and 5 p.m. If you wear a hearing aid, turn it off.

A PEEK BEHIND THE SCENES WITH JIM HILL

Big Plans for Small World
This Fantasyland relic will be closed through part of 2005. When it re-opens it will feature a brand new, state-of-the-art lighting and sound system. The upgrade is absolutely necessary if Disney World is to present its first-ever holiday edition of this much beloved attraction starting in 2006.

Peter Pan's Flight (FASTPASS)

What It Is Indoor track ride

Scope and Scale Minor attraction

When to Go Before 10 a.m., or use FASTPASS after 6 p.m.

Author's Rating Happy, mellow, and well done; ★★★★

Appeal by Age Group

Preschool ★★★½	Teens ★★★½	Over 30 ★★★½
Grade school ★★★½	Young Adults ★★★½	Seniors ★★★½

Duration of Ride A little over 3 minutes

Average Wait in Line per 100 People ahead of You 5½ minutes

Loading Speed Moderate to slow

Description and Comments Though not considered a major attraction, Peter Pan's Flight is superbly designed and absolutely delightful, with a happy theme uniting some favorite Disney characters, beautiful effects, and charming music. An indoor attraction, Peter Pan's Flight offers a relaxing ride in a "flying pirate ship" over old London and thence to Never-Never Land. Unlike Snow White's Adventures, there's nothing here that will jump out at you or frighten young children.

Touring Tips Because Peter Pan's Flight is very popular, count on long lines all day. Ride before 10 a.m., during a parade, just before the park closes, or use FASTPASS. If you use FASTPASS, pick up your pass as early in the day as possible. Sometimes Peter Pan exhausts its whole day's supply of FASTPASSes by 2 p.m.

A PEEK BEHIND THE SCENES WITH JIM HILL

How Do They Do That? What's the secret behind those tiny cars you see rolling through the streets of London as you fly off to Neverland? Those aren't really autos at all, just dots of glow-in-the-dark paint on bicycle chains. As these chains are pulled through the miniature version of the city, they give the impression that cars—with their headlights on—are rolling through London.

Mickey's PhilharMagic (*FASTPASS*)

What It Is 3-D movie

Scope and Scale Major attraction

Special Comments Not to be missed

When to Go Before 11 a.m., during parades, or use FASTPASS

Author's Rating ★★★★ A masterpiece

Appeal by Age Group

Preschool ★★★½	Teens ★★★★	Over 30 ★★★★
Grade school ★★★★½	Young Adults ★★★★	Seniors ★★★★

Duration of Presentation About 20 minutes

Probable Waiting Time 12–30 minutes

Description and Comments With *Mickey's PhilharMagic* up and running, there is a 3-D movie attraction at each of the four Disney theme parks. The *PhilharMagic* features an odd collection of Disney characters, mixing Mickey and Donald with Simba, Ariel (from the *Little Mermaid*), as well as Jasmine and Aladdin. Presented in a theater large enough to accommodate a 150-foot-wide screen—huge by 3-D movie standards, the 3-D movie is augmented by an arsenal of special effects built into the theater. The plot involves Mickey, as the conductor of the PhilharMagic, leaving the theater to solve a mystery. In his absence Donald appears and attempts to take charge, with disastrous results.

The attraction is one of Disney's best 3-D efforts. Brilliantly conceived, furiously paced, and laugh-out-loud funny, *PhilharMagic* incorporates a hit parade of Disney's most beloved characters in a production that will leave you grinning. All of our reader comments concerning the *PhilharMagic* have been enthusiastic. This review from a Huntsville, Alabama, reader is typical:

The new PhilharMagic *was the best 3-D show that Disney offers!*

Touring Tips Though the other 3-D movies are intense, loud, in-your-face productions, *Mickey's PhilharMagic* is much softer and cuddlier. Things still pop out of the screen in keeping with the time-tested 3-D model, but they're not scary things. Children for once are enthusiastic and astonished instead of quaking in their Nikes. You should still proceed cautiously if you have kids under age 5 in your group, but it's the rare child who is frightened. Because it's new, the show is very popular, but on the other hand the theater is very large. Except on the busiest of days you shouldn't wait more than 35 minutes (usually less) in the standby line.

A Coming Attraction? The flying sequences where Donald is flying high over London with Peter Pan and Tinker Bell as well as zooming through the streets of Agrabah on a flying carpet are supposedly tests for a "Fantasy Flight" attraction that the Imagineers are considering. The proposed attraction would use the same ride system found in Epcot's Future World attraction, Soarin'.

Cinderella's Golden Carrousel

What It Is Merry-go-round

Scope and Scale Minor attraction

When to Go Before 11 a.m. or after 8 p.m.

Special Comments Adults enjoy the beauty and nostalgia of this ride

Author's Rating A beautiful children's ride; ★★★

Appeal by Age Group

Preschool ★★★★	Teens —	Over 30 —
Grade school ★★½	Young Adults —	Seniors —

Duration of Ride About 2 minutes

Average Wait in Line per 100 People ahead of You 5 minutes

Loading Speed Slow

Description and Comments One of the most elaborate and beautiful merry-go-rounds you'll ever see, especially when its lights are on.

A shy and retiring nine-year-old girl from Rockaway, New Jersey, thinks our rating of the carousel for grade schoolers should be higher:

> I am nine years old and I want to complain. I went on Cinderella's Golden Carrousel four times and I loved it! Raise those stars right now!! Also kids who don't like things jumping out at them should not go to Honey, I Shrunk the Audience [at Epcot].

Touring Tips Unless young children in your party insist on riding, appreciate this attraction from the sidelines. While lovely to look at, the carousel loads and unloads very slowly. (And yes, there's an extra old-style "r" in Cinderella's Carrousel, but not in the modern-themed *Walt Disney's Carousel of Progress*.)

The Many Adventures of Winnie the Pooh (FASTPASS)

What It Is Indoor track ride

Scope and Scale Minor attraction

When to Go Before 10 a.m., in the 2 hours before closing, or use FASTPASS

Author's Rating Cute as the Pooh-bear himself; ★★★½

Appeal by Age Group

Preschool ★★★★½	Teens ★★★	Over 30 ★★★
Grade school ★★★★	Young Adults ★★★	Seniors ★★★

Duration of Ride About 4 minutes

Average Wait in Line per 100 People ahead of You 4 minutes

Loading Speed Moderate

Description and Comments Opened in the summer of 1998, this addition to Fantasyland replaced the alternately praised and maligned Mr. Toad's Wild Ride (Toadsters are still pissed). Pooh is sunny, upbeat, and fun—more in the image of Peter Pan's Flight or Splash Mountain. You ride a "Hunny Pot" through the pages of a huge picture book into the Hundred Acre Wood, where you encounter Pooh, Piglet, Eeyore, Owl, Rabbit, Tigger, Kanga, and Roo as they contend with a blustery day. There's even a dream sequence with Heffalumps and Woozles, a favorite of this 30-something couple from Lexington, Massachusetts, who thinks Pooh has plenty to offer adults:

The attention to detail and special effects on this ride make it worth seeing even if you don't have children in your party. The Pooh dream sequence was great!

Touring Tips Because of its relatively small capacity, the daily allocation of FAST-PASSes for Winnie the Pooh is often distributed by noon or 1 p.m. For this same reason, your scheduled return time to enjoy the ride might be hours away. It's not unusual to pick up a FASTPASS for Winnie the Pooh at 12:30 p.m. with a scheduled return time of 5 p.m. or later.

A PEEK BEHIND THE SCENES WITH JIM HILL

Toad You So
The Many Adventures of Winnie the Pooh replaced the cult favorite Mr. Toad's Wild Ride in 1998. In an effort to make amends with disappointed Wild Ride fans, the Imagineers slipped a Toad tribute into Pooh. Keep a sharp eye out— you may see some very familiar faces in paintings on the floor near Owl's house.

Snow White's Adventures

What It Is Indoor track ride

Scope and Scale Minor attraction

When to Go Before 11 a.m. or after 6 p.m.

Special Comments Terrifying to many young children

Author's Rating Worth seeing if the wait isn't long; ★★½

Appeal by Age Group

Preschool ★	Teens ★★	Over 30 ★★½
Grade school ★★½	Young Adults ★★½	Seniors ★★½

Duration of Ride Almost 2½ minutes

Average Wait in Line per 100 People ahead of You 6¼ minutes

Loading Speed Moderate to slow

Description and Comments Mine cars travel through a spook house showing Snow White as she narrowly escapes harm at the hands of the wicked witch. Action and effects are not as good as Peter Pan's Flight or Winnie the Pooh.

Touring Tips We get more mail about this ride than any other Disney attraction. It terrifies many children age 6 and younger. Though a 1994 upgrade gave Snow White a larger role, the witch (who is relentless and ubiquitous) continues to be the focal character. Many readers tell us their children have refused to ride any attraction that operates in the dark after having experienced Snow White's Adventures.

A mother from Knoxville, Tennessee, writes:

The outside looks cute and fluffy, but inside, the evil witch just keeps coming at you. My five-year-old, who rode Space Mountain three times and took The Great Movie Ride's monster from Alien right in stride, was near panic when our car stopped unexpectedly twice during Snow White. [After Snow White] my six-year-old niece spent a lot of time asking "if a witch will jump out at you" before other rides. So I suggest that you explain a little more what this ride is about. It's tough on preschoolers who are expecting forest animals and dwarfs.

A mom from Long Island, New York, adds:

My daughter screamed the whole time and was shot for the day. Grampa kept asking, "Where in the hell is Snow White?"

Ride Snow White if lines aren't too long or on a second day at the park.

A PEEK BEHIND THE SCENES WITH JIM HILL

Who Am I Supposed to Be?
According to this attraction's original design, the guests riding were supposed to think that they were Snow White experiencing everything that happened to the animated heroine in the 1937 animated feature. Unfortunately, so few guests got the drift that Disney eventually had to admit defeat. So when this Fantasyland attraction was revamped in December 1994, the Imagineers actually put a figure of Snow White in the very first scene of the ride. As if to say: "Look! There she is! Now are you happy?"

Ariel's Grotto

What It Is Interactive fountain and character-greeting area

Scope and Scale Minor attraction

When to Go Before 10 a.m. or after 9 p.m.

Author's Rating One of the most elaborate of the character-greeting venues; ★★★

Appeal by Age Group

Preschool ★★★★★	Teens ★★	Over 30 ★
Grade school ★★★★	Young Adults ★	Seniors ★

Average Wait in Line per 100 People ahead of You 30 minutes

Description and Comments   On the lagoon side of Dumbo, Ariel's Grotto consists of a small children's play area with an interactive fountain and a rock grotto where Ariel, the Little Mermaid, poses for photos and signs autographs. If "interactive fountain" is new to you, it means an opportunity for your children to get ten times wetter than a trout. Can you say "hy-po-ther-mi-a"?

Touring Tips   The Grotto is small, and the wait to meet Ariel is usually long. Because kids in line are fresh from the fountain, it's very difficult for adults to remain dry.

A mother from Hagerstown, Maryland, said the experience was "like being packed in a pen with wet cocker spaniels."

If your children spot the Grotto before you do, there's no turning back. Count on a long queue and a 20–40-minute wait to see Ariel except the first 15 minutes she's open for business (usually 10 a.m.). Then there's the fountain. Allow your children to disrobe to the legal limit. (Don't bother with umbrellas or ponchos, because water squirts up from below.) When you're finished meeting Ariel, you will have to navigate an armada of variously aged males plowing upstream through the exit to admire the Little Mermaid's cleavage.

Dumbo the Flying Elephant

What It Is Disneyfied midway ride

Scope and Scale Minor attraction

When to Go Before 10 a.m. or after 9 p.m.

Author's Rating An attractive children's ride; ★★★

Appeal by Age Group

Preschool ★★★★★	Teens ★½	Over 30 ★½
Grade school ★★★★	Young Adults ★½	Seniors ★½

Duration of Ride 1½ minutes

Average Wait in Line per 100 People ahead of You 20 minutes

Loading Speed Slow

Description and Comments A tame, happy children's ride based on the lovable flying elephant, Dumbo. Despite being little different from rides at state fairs and amusement parks, Dumbo is the favorite Magic Kingdom attraction of many younger children.

A lot of readers take us to task for lumping Dumbo with carnival rides. A reader from Armdale, Nova Scotia, writes:

> I think you have acquired a jaded attitude. I know [Dumbo] is not for everybody, but when we took our oldest child (then just four), the sign at the end of the line said there would be a 90-minute wait. He knew and he didn't care, and he and I stood in the hot afternoon sun for 90 blissful minutes waiting for his 90-second flight. Anything that a four-year-old would wait for that long and that patiently must be pretty special.

Touring Tips If Dumbo is essential to your child's happiness, make it your first stop, preferably within 15 minutes of park opening. Also, consider this advice from an Arlington, Virginia, mom:

> Grown-ups, beware! Dumbo is really a tight fit with one adult and two kids. My kids threw me out of their Dumbo and I had to sit in a Dumbo all by myself! Pretty embarrassing, and my husband got lots of pictures.

Mad Tea Party

What It Is Midway-type spinning ride

Scope and Scale Minor attraction

When to Go Before 11 a.m. or after 5 p.m.

Special Comments You can make the teacups spin faster by turning the wheel in the center of the cup

Author's Rating Fun, but not worth the wait; ★★

Motion Sickness

WARNING!

Appeal by Age Group

Preschool ★★★★	Teens ★★★★	Over 30 ★★
Grade school ★★★★	Young Adults ★★★★	Seniors ★★

Duration of Ride 1½ minutes

Average Wait in Line per 100 People ahead of You 7½ minutes

Loading Speed Slow

Description and Comments   Riders whirl feverishly in big teacups. Alice in Wonderland's Mad Hatter provides the theme. A version of this ride, without Disney characters, can be found at every local carnival. Teenagers like to lure adults onto the tea cups, then turn the wheel in the middle (making the cup spin faster), until the adults are plastered against the sides and on the verge of throwing up. Unless your life's ambition is to be the test subject in a human centrifuge, don't even consider getting on this ride with anyone younger than 21.

Touring Tips   This ride, well done but not unique, is notoriously slow loading. Skip it on a busy schedule—if the kids will let you. Ride the morning of your second day if your schedule is more relaxed.

A PEEK BEHIND THE SCENES WITH JIM HILL

Hurling for Dollars
In an effort to raise money for Orlando-area charities, Disney cast members sometimes take part in ride-endurance contests. Among the more infamous fundraising events was the "Fantasyland 500," where WDW employees had to ride in these spinning teacups for over an hour.

Mickey's Toontown Fair

Mickey's Toontown Fair is the only new "land" to be added to the Magic Kingdom since its opening and the only land that doesn't connect to the central hub. Attractions include an opportunity to meet Mickey Mouse, tour Mickey's and Minnie's houses, and ride a child-sized roller coaster.

Mickey's Toontown Fair is sandwiched between Fantasyland and Tomorrowland, like an afterthought, on about three acres formerly part of the Tomorrowland Speedway. It's the smallest of the lands and more like an attraction than a separate section of the park. Though you can wander in on a somewhat obscure path from Fantasyland or on a totally obscure path from Tomorrowland, Mickey's Toontown Fair generally receives guests arriving by the Walt Disney World Railroad.

Opened in 1988 and reworked in 1996 with a county fair theme, Mickey's Toontown Fair now serves as the Magic Kingdom's character-greeting headquarters. The Fair provides a place where Disney characters are available to guests on a continuing and reliable schedule. Mickey, in the role of the Fair's chief judge, meets guests for photos and autographs in the Judge's Tent. Other characters appear in the Toontown Hall of Fame. Characters are available throughout the day except during parades.

In general, Mickey's Toontown Fair doesn't handle crowds very well. If your children are into collecting character autographs and want to enjoy the various Toontown attractions without extraordinary waits, we recommend touring first as soon as Toontown opens. If you have only one day to visit the Magic Kingdom, and the children-oriented attractions are a priority, head first to Fantasyland and ride Dumbo, Pooh, and Peter Pan, then split for Toontown. In Toontown, ride Goofy's Barnstormer first and then tour Mickey's and Minnie's houses. Go next to the Toontown Hall of Fame for character pics and autographs. Be advised that Mickey's Toontown Fair usually opens an hour later than the rest of the park. Consult your *Times Guide* (available at City Hall) for opening times on the day of your visit.

A South Euclid, Ohio, family took our advice and reported these results:

> We followed your advice and hit Fantasyland first (9 a.m.–10 a.m.). I would strongly urge parents with young children to head next to Mickey's Toontown! It opened at 10 a.m. and we went directly to meet Mickey in his house. Then we went to Toontown Hall of Fame. Due to the lack of lines our daughter got to meet all nine characters—in a row—with no line! Another MK guest told us the line had been an hour just the day before. Do Toontown when it opens!

If you plan to remain in the park until closing, follow the example of this family of four from Lewiston, Maine:

> A great time to visit [Toontown] is the final hour the Magic Kingdom is open. We rode the small roller coaster several times in a row without ever leaving our seats (a great thrill for a toddler who spent much of his day in lines). Also, no queues for a visit with Mickey. A great, fun, relaxing end to a busy day.

For adults without children, Toontown is visually interesting but otherwise expendable.

A PEEK BEHIND THE SCENES WITH JIM HILL

Now That's What I Call Fast

Back in February of 1988, Disney execs decided that the Magic Kingdom should do something special to celebrate Mickey's 60th birthday. Which is why—in just three months time—they designed and built an entire new "land": Mickey's Birthdayland. Though the name of this land has changed several times over the years (Mickey's Birthdayland to Mickey's Starland to Mickey's Toontown Fair), the Imagineers have yet to top that concept-to-ribbon-cutting speed record.

Mickey's Country House and Judge's Tent

What It Is Walk-through tour of Mickey's house and meeting with Mickey

Scope and Scale Minor attraction

When to Go Before 11:30 a.m. or after 4:30 p.m.

Author's Rating Well done; ★★★

Appeal by Age Group

Preschool ★★★½	Teens ★★½	Over 30 ★★½
Grade school ★★★	Young Adults ★★½	Seniors ★★½

Duration of Tour 15–30 minutes (depending on the crowd)

Average Wait in Line per 100 People ahead of You 20 minutes

Touring Speed Slow

Description and Comments Mickey's Country House is the starting point of a self-guided tour through the famous Mouse's house, into his backyard, and past Pluto's doghouse. If you want to tour Mickey's house, but skip meeting Mickey, you'll find an exit just before entering his tent.

Touring Tips Discerning observers will see immediately that Mickey's Country House is a cleverly devised queuing area for delivering guests to Mickey's Judge's Tent for the Mouse Encounter. It also heightens anticipation by revealing the corporate symbol on a more personal level. Mickey's Country House is well conceived and contains a lot of Disney memorabilia. Children touch *everything* as they proceed through the house, hoping to find some artifact not welded into the set. (An especially tenacious child actually ripped a couple of books from a bookcase.)

Meeting Mickey and touring his house are best done during the first hour Mickey's Toontown Fair is open, or in the evening. If meeting the great Mouse is your child's priority, you can be certain of finding Mickey here. Some children are so obsessed with seeing Mickey that they can't enjoy anything else until they have him in the rearview mirror.

Minnie's Country House

What It Is Walk-through exhibit

Scope and Scale Minor attraction

When to Go Before 11:30 a.m. or after 4:30 p.m.

Author's Rating Great detail; ★★

Appeal by Age Group

Preschool ★★★	Teens ★★½	Over 30 ★★½
Grade school ★★★★	Young Adults ★★½	Seniors ★★½

Duration of Tour About 10 minutes

Average Wait in Line per 100 People ahead of You 12 minutes

Touring Speed Slow

Description and Comments Minnie's Country House offers a self-guided tour through the rooms and backyard of Mickey's main squeeze. Similar to Mickey's Country House, only predictably more feminine, Minnie's also showcases fun Disney memorabilia. Among highlights of the short tour are the fanciful appliances in Minnie's kitchen.

Touring Tips The main difference between Mickey's and Minnie's houses is that Mickey is home to receive guests. Minnie was never home during our visits. We did, however, bump into her on the street and in the Toontown Hall of Fame. Minnie's

Country House is one of the more accessible attractions in the Fair, but we nonetheless recommend touring early or late in the day.

Toontown Hall of Fame

What It Is Character-greeting venue

Scope and Scale Minor attraction

When to Go Before 10:30 a.m. or after 5:30 p.m.

Author's Rating You want characters? We got 'em! ★★

Appeal by Age Group

Preschool ★★★★	Teens ★★	Over 30 ★★
Grade school ★★★★★	Young Adults ★★	Seniors ★★

Duration of Greeting About 7–10 minutes

Average Wait in Line per 100 People ahead of You 35 minutes

Touring Speed Slow

Description and Comments The Toontown Hall of Fame is at the end of a small plaza between Mickey's and Minnie's houses. It offers one of the largest and most dependably available collection of characters in Walt Disney World. Just inside to the right are entrances to three queuing areas. Signs over each suggest, somewhat ambiguously, which characters you will meet. Character assortments in each greeting area change, as do the names of the assortments themselves. Thus, on a given day you will find two or three groupings available: Famous Friends (also called Toon Pals and sometimes Minnie's Famous Pals) include Minnie, Goofy, Donald, Pluto, and sometimes Uncle Scrooge, Chip 'n' Dale, Roger Rabbit, and Daisy. The 100-Acre-Wood Pals are mostly Winnie the Pooh characters but may include any character that fits the forest theme. Storybook Friends are Snow White, various dwarfs, Belle, the Beast, Sleeping Beauty, Prince Charming, etc. Other categories include Mickey's Pals, Disney Princesses, Disney Villains, Characters on Weight Watchers, Corporate Symbols, and so on.

Each category of characters occupies a greeting room where 15–20 guests are admitted at a time. They're allowed to stay 7–10 minutes, long enough for a photo, autograph, and hug with each character.

Touring Tips If your children want to visit each category, you'll have to queue up three times. Each line is long and slow-moving, and during busier hours you can lose a lot of time here. While Famous Friends (a.k.a. Toon Pals and Minnie's Famous Pals) are slightly more popular than other categories, the longest wait is for groupings that include "face characters." Face characters are actors who strongly resemble the character they portray and don't wear any head-covering costume. They are allowed to speak and thus engage children in conversation, prolonging the visit. All characters work in 25-minute shifts, with breaks on the hour and half hour. Because characters in each category change frequently during the day, it's possible to see quite an assortment if you keep recirculating.

If the cast member can't tell you, walk over to the exit and ask departing guests which characters are on duty. Remember that there is some switching of characters on the hour and half hour.

A mother from Winchester, Virginia, reported her solution to seeing characters without waiting in lines:

Some of the things that surprised us, both good and bad, were the crowding and lines to see the characters. We stopped to visit a few, especially when we got lucky with a shorter line, but mostly we couldn't justify stopping at many because we would have missed so many attractions. The best thing we did with regard to the characters was to have the

Winnie the Pooh character dinner at The Crystal Palace. Tigger and Pooh are my kids' favorites, and the characters were VERY attentive; my just-turned three-year-old was in heaven and did not have to fight crowds.

A 30-something mother of two comments:

For parents with smaller children at the Magic Kingdom, take the train to Toontown as soon as [it] opens—my six-year-old and eight-year-old rode Goofy's Barnstormer roller coaster seven times without getting off. After others wanted on, they moved on to the Toontown Hall of Fame for autographs—no lines!!

On many days, during the first hour the park is open, a multitude of characters roam the Magic Kingdom Streets. It's just like the old days: spontaneous contact and no lines.

The Barnstormer at Goofy's Wiseacres Farm

What It Is Small roller coaster

Scope and Scale Minor attraction

When to Go Before 10:30 a.m., during parades, or in the evening just before the park closes

Special Comments Must be 35" or taller to ride

Author's Rating Great for little ones, but not worth the wait for adults; ★★

Appeal by Age Group

Preschool ★★★★	Teens ★★½	Over 30 ★★½
Grade school ★★★	Young Adults ★★½	Seniors ★★

Duration of Ride About 53 seconds

Average Wait in Line per 100 People ahead of You 7 minutes

Loading Speed Slow

Description and Comments The Barnstormer is a very small roller coaster. The ride is zippy but super short. In fact, of the 53 seconds the ride is in motion, 32 seconds are consumed in leaving the loading area, being racheted up the first hill, and braking into the off-loading area. The actual time you spend careering around the track is 21 seconds.

A 42-year-old woman from Westport, Connecticut, warns adults that the Barnstormer may not be as tame as it looks:

Goofy's Barnstormer was a nightmare that should have gone in your "Eats Adults" section. It looked so innocent—nothing hidden in the dark, over quickly ... It took hours to stop feeling nauseated, and my eight-year-old son and I were terrified.

Though the reader's point is well taken, the Barnstormer is a fairly benign introduction to the roller-coaster genre and a predictably positive way to help your children step up to more adventuresome rides. Simply put, a few circuits on the Barnstormer

will increase your little one's confidence and improve his chances for enjoying Disney's more-adult attractions. As always, be sensitive and encouraging, but respect your child's decision whether or not to ride.

Touring Tips The cars of this dinky coaster are too small for most adults and tend to whiplash taller people. This, plus the limited capacity, equals an engineering marvel along the lines of Dumbo. Parties without children should skip the Barnstormer. If you're touring with children, you have a problem. Like Dumbo, the ride is visually appealing. All kids want to ride, subjecting the whole family to slow-moving lines. If the Barnstormer is high on your children's hit parade, try to ride as soon as Mickey's Toontown Fair opens.

Donald's Boat

What It Is Playground and (when the water is running) interactive fountain

Scope and Scale Diversion

When to Go Anytime

Author's Rating A favorite of the 5-and-under set. ★★½

Appeal by Age Group

Preschool ★★★★	Teens ★	Over 30 ★½
Grade school ★★½	Young Adults ★½	Seniors ★½

Descriptions and Comments Donald's Boat is an interactive playground themed as a fat, cartoon-style tugboat.

Touring Tips A great opportunity for easing regimentation and allowing small children to expend pent-up energy.

Tomorrowland

Tomorrowland is a mix of rides and experiences relating to the technological development of man and what life will be like in the future. If this sounds like Epcot's theme, it's because Tomorrowland was a breeding ground for ideas that spawned Epcot. Yet, Tomorrowland and Epcot are very different in more than scale. Epcot is more educational. Tomorrowland is more for fun, depicting the future as envisioned in science fiction.

Exhaustive renovation of Tomorrowland was completed in 1995. Before refurbishing, Tomorrowland's 24-year-old buildings resembled 1970s motels more than anyone's vision of the future. The new design is ageless, revealing the future as imagined by dreamers and scientists in the 1920s and 1930s. Today's Tomorrowland conjures visions of Buck Rogers, fanciful mechanical rockets, and metallic cities spread beneath towering obelisks. Disney calls the renovated Tomorrowland the "Future That Never Was," while *Newsweek* dubbed it "retro-future."

Space Mountain (FASTPASS)

What It Is Roller coaster in the dark

Scope and Scale Super headliner

When to Go When the park opens, between 6 and 7 p.m., during the hour before closing, or use FASTPASS

Special Comments   Great fun and action; much wilder than Big Thunder Mountain Railroad. Must be 44" tall to ride; children younger than age 7 must be accompanied by an adult. Switching off option provided (pages 266–268).

Author's Rating   An unusual roller coaster with excellent special effects; not to be missed; ★★★★

Appeal by Age Group

Preschool †		Teens ★★★★★		Over 30 ★★★★
Grade school ★★★★★		Young Adults ★★★★½		Seniors †

† *Some preschoolers loved Space Mountain; others were frightened. The sample size of senior citizens who experienced this ride was too small to develop an accurate rating.*

Duration of Ride   Almost 3 minutes

Average Wait in Line per 100 People ahead of You   3 minutes

Assumes   Two tracks, one dedicated to FASTPASS riders, dispatching at 21-second intervals

Loading Speed   Moderate to fast

Motion Sickness

WARNING!

Description and Comments   Totally enclosed in a mammoth futuristic structure, Space Mountain has always been the Magic Kingdom's most popular attraction. The theme is a space flight through dark recesses of the galaxy. Effects are superb, and the ride is the fastest and wildest in the Magic Kingdom. As a roller coaster, Space Mountain is much zippier than Big Thunder Mountain Railroad, but much tamer than the Rock 'n' Roller Coaster at the Studios.

Roller-coaster aficionados will tell you (correctly) that Space Mountain is a designer version of The Wild Mouse, a midway ride that's been around for at least 50 years. There are no long drops or swooping hills like on a traditional roller coaster, only quick, unexpected turns and small drops. Disney's contribution essentially was to add a space theme to The Wild Mouse and put it in the dark. And indeed, this does make the Mouse seem wilder.

A teen from Colchester, Connecticut, wrote us about her bad-hair day:

WARN Space Mountain riders to take off hair scrunchies. I lost my best one on it and couldn't get it back. This ride was fast, curvy, and very hairdo-messing.

Touring Tips   People who can handle a fairly wild roller-coaster ride will take Space Mountain in stride. What sets Space Mountain apart is that cars plummet through darkness, with only occasional lighting. Half the fun of Space Mountain is not knowing where the car will go next.

Space Mountain is the favorite attraction of many Magic Kingdom visitors ages 7–60. Each morning before opening, particularly during summer and holiday periods, several hundred S.M. "junkies" crowd the rope barriers at the central hub, awaiting the signal to head to the ride's entrance. To get ahead of the competition, be one of the first in the park. Proceed to the end of Main Street and wait at the entrance to Tomorrowland.

Couples touring with children too small to ride Space Mountain can both ride without waiting in line twice by taking advantage of "switching off." Here's how it works: When you enter the Space Mountain line, tell the first Disney attendant (Greeter One) that you want to switch off. The attendant will allow you, your spouse, and your small child (or children) to continue together, phoning ahead to tell Greeter Two to expect you. When you reach Greeter Two (at the turnstile near the boarding area), you'll be given specific directions. One of you will proceed to ride, while the other stays with the kids. Whoever rides will be admitted by the unloading attendant to stairs leading back up to the boarding area.

Here you switch off. The second parent rides, and the first parent takes the kids down the stairs to the unloading area where everybody is reunited and exits together. Switching off is also available at Big Thunder Mountain Railroad and Splash Mountain.

Seats are one behind another, as opposed to side-by-side. Parents whose children meet the height and age requirements for Space Mountain can't sit next to their kids.

If you don't catch Space Mountain early in the morning, use FASTPASS or try again during the hour before closing. Often, would-be riders are held in line outside the entrance until all those previously in line have ridden, thus emptying the attraction. The appearance from the outside is that the line is enormous when, in fact, the only people waiting are those visible. This crowd-control technique, known as "stacking," discourages visitors from getting in line. Stacking is used in several Disney rides and attractions during the hour before closing to ensure that the ride will be able to close on schedule. It is also used to keep the number of people waiting inside from overwhelming the air-conditioning. Despite the apparently long line, the wait is usually no longer than if you had been allowed to queue inside.

Splash Mountain siphons off some guests who would have made Space Mountain their first stop. Even so, a mob rushes to Space Mountain as soon as the park opens. If you especially like the thrill attractions and have only one day, see Space Mountain first in the morning, followed by Splash Mountain and Big Thunder Mountain.

A PEEK BEHIND THE SCENES WITH JIM HILL

Strange but True, Folks

According to press materials predating Space Mountain's official opening in January 1975, guests were to "…board rocket cars on a space-station launching platform orbiting the Earth. As your journey begins, you'll race through a vast man-made solar field—energizing your rocket car for its dazzling plunge into super-space. Hold on tight! You're on your way as you blast off into the void of the universe."

See? And you thought that you were just riding an indoor roller coaster.

Tomorrowland Indy Speedway

What It Is   Drive-'em-yourself miniature cars

Scope and Scale   Major attraction

When to Go   Before 11 a.m. or after 5 p.m.

Special Comments   Must be 52" tall to drive unassisted

Author's Rating   Boring for adults (★); great for preschoolers

Appeal by Age Group

Preschool ★★★★	Teens ★	Over 30 ½
Grade school ★★★	Young Adults ½	Seniors ½

Duration of Ride   About 4¼ minutes

Average Wait in Line per 100 People ahead of You   4½ minutes

Assumes   285-car turnover every 20 minutes

Loading Speed   Slow

Description and Comments   An elaborate miniature raceway with gasoline-powered cars that travel up to seven mph. The raceway, with sleek cars and racing noises, is quite alluring. Unfortunately, the cars poke along on a guide rail, leaving the driver little to do. Pretty ho-hum for most adults and teenagers. The height requirement excludes small children who would enjoy the ride.

Touring Tips   This ride is visually appealing but definitely one adults can skip. Preschoolers, however, love it. If your child is too short to drive, ride along and allow the child to steer the car while you work the foot pedal.

A mom from North Billerica, Massachusetts, writes:

I was truly amazed by the number of adults in line. Please emphasize to your readers that these cars travel on a guided path and are not a whole lot of fun. The only reason I could think of for adults to be in the line would be an insane desire to go on absolutely every ride at Disney World. The other feature about the cars is that they tend to pile up at the end, so it takes almost as long to get off as it did to get on. Parents riding with their preschoolers should keep the car going as slow as [possible] without stalling. This prolongs the preschooler's joy and decreases the time you will have to wait at the end.

The line for the Tomorrowland Indy Speedway snakes across a pedestrian bridge to the loading areas. For a shorter wait, turn right off the bridge to the first loading area (rather than continuing to the second).

A PEEK BEHIND THE SCENES WITH JIM HILL

Speedway to Get a Tune-Up?
Among the ideas that the Imagineers are reportedly considering for improving Tomorrowland is re-theming the speedway to include the talking autos featured in Pixar Animation Studio's theatrical release *Cars*.

Astro Orbiter

Motion Sickness

WARNING!

What It Is   Buck Rogers–style rockets revolving around a central axis

Scope and Scale   Minor attraction

When to Go   Before 11 a.m. or after 5 p.m.

Special Comments   This attraction, formerly StarJets, is not as innocuous as it appears.

Author's Rating   Not worth the wait; ★★

Appeal by Age Group

Preschool ★★★★	Teens ★★½	Over 30 ★★
Grade school ★★★	Young Adults ★★½	Seniors ★

Duration of Ride   1½ minutes

Average Wait in Line per 100 People ahead of You   13½ minutes

Loading Speed   Slow

Description and Comments   Though visually appealing, the Astro Orbiter is still a slow-loading carnival ride. The fat little rocket ships simply fly in circles. The best thing about the Astro Orbiter is the nice view when you're aloft.

Touring Tips Expendable on any schedule. If you ride with preschoolers, seat them first, then board. The Astro Orbiter flies higher and faster than Dumbo and frightens some young children. It also apparently messes with some adults. A mother from Lev Hashomnon, Israel, attests:

I think your assessment of [Astro Orbiter] as "very mild" is way off. I was able to sit through all the "Mountains," the "Tours," and the "Wars" without my stomach reacting even a little, but after [Astro Orbiter] I thought I would be finished for the rest of the day. Very quickly I realized that my only chance for survival was to pick a point on the toe of my shoe and stare at it (and certainly not lift my eyes out of the "jet") until the ride was over. My four-year-old was my co-pilot, and she loved the ride (go figure), and she had us up high the whole time. It was a nightmare—people should be forewarned.

Tomorrowland Transit Authority

What It Is Scenic tour of Tomorrowland

Scope and Scale Minor attraction

When to Go During hot, crowded times of day (11:30 a.m.–4:30 p.m.)

Special Comments A good way to check out the FASTPASS line at Space Mountain

Author's Rating Scenic, relaxing, informative; ★★★

Appeal by Age Group

Preschool ★★★½	Teens ★★½	Over 30 ★★½
Grade school ★★★	Young Adults ★★½	Seniors ★★★

Duration of Ride 10 minutes

Average Wait in Line per 100 People ahead of You 1½ minutes

Assumes 39 trains operating

Loading Speed Fast

Description and Comments A once-unique prototype of a linear induction–powered mass-transit system, the Authority's tramlike cars carry riders on a leisurely tour of Tomorrowland, including a peek inside Space Mountain. The attraction was formerly called the WEDway PeopleMover.

Touring Tips A relaxing ride, where lines move quickly, and you seldom have to wait. It's a good choice during busier times of day, and it can double as a nursery.
A Texas mom writes:

The [Transit Authority] is an excellent ride for getting a tired infant to fall asleep. You can stay on for several times around. It is also a moderately private and comfortable place for nursing an infant.

A woman from upstate New York also found it relaxing:

Tomorrowland Transit Authority was a surprising treat; we rode it three times to see everything and to take a break from walking; it's especially nice when it goes through Space Mountain.

An Indiana reader really liked the Tomorrowland Transit Authority but isn't sure why:

I don't know why, but we really enjoyed this attraction. It was a neat way to see inside various rides, and it's a good way to take a load off to relax and still feel like you're doing something. I highly recommend this in the middle of the day.

A Peek at Futures Past   Ever wonder what Epcot Center would have actually looked like if Walt Disney had lived long enough to supervise the construction of his futuristic city? Then keep a sharp eye out during your trip on the Tomorrowland Transit Authority. You'll be able to catch a quick glimpse of a small section of the Epcot model that used to be on display in the post-show section of Disneyland's Carousel of Progress attraction.

Walt Disney's Carousel of Progress *(open seasonally)*

What It Is Audio-animatronic theater production

Scope and Scale Major attraction

When to Go Anytime

Author's Rating Nostalgic, warm, and happy; ★★★

Appeal by Age Group

Preschool ★★	Teens ★★½	Over 30 ★★★
Grade school ★★½	Young Adults ★★★	Seniors ★★★½

Duration of Presentation 18 minutes

Preshow Entertainment   Documentary on the attraction's long history

Probable Waiting Time Less than 10 minutes

Description and Comments   Updated and improved during the Tomorrowland renovation, *Walt Disney's Carousel of Progress* offers a delightful look at how technology and electricity have changed the lives of an audio-animatronic family over several generations. The family is easy to identify with, and a cheerful, sentimental tune bridges the generations.

Touring Tips   This attraction is a great favorite among repeat visitors and is included on all of our one-day touring plans. *The Carousel* handles big crowds effectively and is a good choice during busier times of day.

The Timekeeper *(open seasonally)*

What It Is Time-travel movie adventure

Scope and Scale Major attraction

When to Go Anytime

Special Comments Audience must stand throughout entire presentation

Author's Rating Outstanding; not to be missed; ★★★★

Appeal by Age Group

Preschool ★★	Teens ★★★★	Over 30 ★★★★
Grade school ★★★½	Young Adults ★★★★	Seniors ★★★★

Duration of Presentation About 20 minutes

Preshow Entertainment   Robots, lasers, and movies

Probable Waiting Time 8–15 minutes

Description and Comments   Developed as Le Visionarium for Disneyland Paris, *The Timekeeper* adds audio-animatronic characters and a story line to the long-successful Circle-Vision 360 technology. The preshow introduces *Timekeeper* (a humanoid) and 9-Eye (a time-traveling robot so-named because she has nine cameras that serve as eyes). Afterward, the audience enters the main theater, where *Timekeeper* places 9-Eye into a time machine and dispatches her on a crazed journey into the past and future. What 9-Eye sees on her odyssey is projected onto huge screens that surround the audience with action. The robot travels to prehistoric Europe and then forward to meet French author Jules Verne, who hitches a ride into the future. Audio-animatronics, Circle-Vision 360 technology, and high-tech special effects combine to make *The Timekeeper* one of Tomorrowland's premier attractions.

The Timekeeper may be the most underrated attraction in the Magic Kingdom, but as this Westport, Connecticut, family attests, it's a "must-see."

We thought The Timekeeper *was the best [audio-animatronics] in the whole of Disney World. Robin Williams was brilliant. We saw it twice—5 stars!*

A New England family of eight agrees, writing:

The Timekeeper *is an example of how far audio-animatronics has come and when done right, how convincing it can be. A must-see show.*

Touring Tips   Operating seasonally on days of expected high attendance, and occasionally when other Tomorrowland attractions are closed for maintenance, *The Timekeeper* draws crowds from mid-morning on. Because the theater accommodates more than 1,000 guests per show, there is never much of a wait. Go during early afternoon when the park is hot and crowded.

Buzz Lightyear's Space Ranger Spin (FASTPASS)

What It Is   Whimsical space travel–themed indoor ride

Scope and Scale   Minor attraction

When to Go   Before 10:30 a.m., after 6 p.m., or use FASTPASS

Author's Rating   A real winner! ★★★★

Appeal by Age Group

Preschool ★★★★	Teens ★★★★½	Over 30 ★★★★
Grade school ★★★★★	Young Adults ★★★★	Seniors ★★★★

Duration of Ride   About 4½ minutes

Average Wait in Line per 100 People ahead of You   3 minutes

Loading Speed   Fast

Description and Comments   This attraction is based on the space-commando character of Buzz Lightyear from the film *Toy Story*. The marginal story line has you and Buzz Lightyear trying to save the universe from the evil Emperor Zurg. The indoor ride is interactive to the extent that you can spin your car and shoot simulated "laser cannons" at Zurg and his minions.

Touring Tips   Each car is equipped with two laser cannons and a scorekeeping display. Each scorekeeping display is independent, so you can compete with your riding partner. A joystick allows you to spin the car to line up the various targets. Each time you pull the trigger you'll release a red laser beam that you can see hitting or missing the target. Most folks' first ride is occupied with learning how to use the equipment (fire off individual shots as opposed to keeping the trigger depressed) and figuring out how the targets work. The next ride (like certain potato chips, one is not enough), you'll surprise yourself by how much better you do. *Unofficial* readers are unanimous in their praise of Buzz Lightyear. Some, in fact, spend several hours on it, riding again and again. The following comments are representative:

From a Yorktown, Virginia, mom:

I am a 44-year-old woman who has never been fond of shoot-'em-up arcade games, but I decided I'd better check out Buzz Lightyear's Space Ranger Spin after the monorail driver told us that it, along with Space Mountain, were her favorite rides at the Magic Kingdom. What a blast! My husband and I enjoyed it every bit as much as our ten-year-old daughter. After riding it the first time, we couldn't wait to ride it again (and again) in an effort to improve our scores. Alas, I was never able to advance beyond Ranger 1st Class although my husband made it all the way to Space Ace. Warning—Buzz Lightyear is addictive!

From a father of three from Cleveland, Ohio:

Without question, the favorite ride of my 11-year-old son was the Buzz Lightyear Ride. Come to think about it, it was my favorite too!

From a Snow Hill, Maryland, dad:

Buzz Lightyear was so much fun it can't be legal! We hit it first on early-entry day and rode it ten times without stopping. The kids had fun, but it was Dad who spun himself silly trying to shoot the Zs. This is the most unique, creative ride ever devised.

And finally, from a Massachusetts couple:

Buzz Lightyear was the surprise hit of our trip! My husband and I enjoyed competing for the best score so much that we went on this ride several times during our stay. Definitely a must, especially when there's no wait!

See Buzz Lightyear after riding Space Mountain first thing in the morning or use FASTPASS.

A PEEK BEHIND THE SCENES WITH JIM HILL

Good Ideas Take Time Imagineers came up with the idea for a ride-through shooting gallery in the early 1970s. Back then, this proposed attraction was known as the UFO Show, and was supposed to allow Tomorrowland visitors to target swarms of little green men invading Earth. It took over 20 years, and the arrival of *Toy Story's* Buzz Lightyear in November 1995, before this particular ride concept finally made it off the drawing board.

Stitch's Great Escape

What It Is Theater-in-the-round sci-fi adventure show

Scope and Scale Headliner

When to Go Before 10 a.m. or after 4 p.m.; try during parades

Special Comments Frightens children 10 years or younger

Author's Rating *Not open at press time*

Appeal by Age Group *Not open at press time*

Duration of Presentation About 12 minutes

Preshow Entertainment About 6 minutes

Probable Waiting Time 12–35 minutes

Description and Comments   *Stitch's Great Escape* is a benign, humorous replacement for the oft-maligned *Alien Encounter* attraction. Same theater, same tele-transportation theme, but this time starring the cuddly, albeit havoc-wreaking, little alien from the feature film *Lilo & Stitch*. In *Great Escape*, Stitch is a prisoner of the galactic authorities and is being transferred to a processing facility en route to his final place of incarceration. He manages to escape by employing an efficient, though gross, trick, knocking out power to the facility in the process. At this juncture Stitch lumbers around in the dark in much the same way as the theater's previous resident *Alien*, but less menacing.

Touring Tips   Like in the *Alien Encounter* attraction, you're held in your seat by over-head restraints, and you're subjected to something weird clambering around you (and whispering to you) in a theater darker than a stack of black cats. The Stitch version is sweeter by far, but more than capable when it comes to frightening children ten years and younger. Our advice: sound out a couple of families exiting the attraction before you get in line.

Live Entertainment in the Magic Kingdom

Bands, Disney character appearances, parades, ceremonies, and singing and dancing further enliven the Magic Kingdom. For specific events the day you visit, check the live entertainment schedule in your Disney guidemap (free as you enter the park or at City Hall); or alternatively in the *Times Guide* available along with the guidemap.

Be aware: If you're short on time, it's impossible to see Magic Kingdom feature attractions *and* the live performances. Our one-day touring plans exclude live performances in favor of seeing as much of the park as time permits. This tactical decision is based on the fact that some parades and performances siphon crowds away from the more popular rides, thus shortening lines.

Nonetheless, the color and pageantry of live events are integral to the Magic Kingdom and a persuasive argument for a second day of touring. Here's a list and description of some performances and events presented with regularity that don't require reservations.

Fantasyland Pavilion   Site of various concerts in Fantasyland.

Frontierland Hoedown   Characters join square dancers and guests for a hoedown in front of the *Country Bear Jamboree;* check the daily enter-tainment schedule *(Times Guide).*

Castle Forecourt Stage   The forecourt show called *Cinderella's Surprise Celebration* features a plot, elaborate props (including the castle itself), and a veritable roll call of Disney characters. Like *Fantasmic!,* it's another good-versus-evil spectacular, though, in distinct contrast to *Fantasmic!,* not at all frightening to preschoolers. Because characters pop out of turrets and parapets high up on the castle as well as along the balustrades and on the stage, it's pretty hard to find a viewing perspective where you can see everything. Fortunately, the plot is so simplistic that missing a few things won't compromise your understanding or your enjoyment. The show is performed five to seven times each day according to the season with show-times listed the daily entertainment schedule *(Times Guide)*. During our last visit, we stood on the concrete benches in front of the statue of Mickey and Walt in the central hub. In 2005, a new show, called Cin-derellabration, will either join or replace Cinderella's Surprise Celebration. Imported from Tokyo Disneyland, the new show features Cinderella beginning her happily-ever-after life with her royal coronation.

Storytime with Belle at the Fairytale Garden   Belle and several helpers select children from the small amphitheater audience and dress them up as characters from *Beauty and the Beast*. As Belle tells the story, the chil-dren act out the roles. There is a 3–5-minute meet-and-greet with photo and autograph opportunities afterward. Storytime is staged six to eight times each day according to the daily entertainment schedule *(Times Guide)*. To find the Fairytale Garden, follow the path on the Fantasyland side of the castle moat toward Tomorrowland. A reader from Tyler, Texas, enjoyed the short production:

This was actually kind of cute, as the chosen children were hams and very famil-iar with the story already. The location is sort of set back and down into the ground, thus allowing for a lot of shade and a cooler breeze. It's definitely worth dropping in to sit down and rest in the middle of the afternoon.

Flag Retreat   At 5 p.m. daily at Town Square (railroad station end of Main Street). Sometimes performed with great fanfare and college marching bands, sometimes with a smaller Disney band.

Sword in the Stone Ceremony   Staged about six times each day behind Cinderella Castle; check the daily entertainment schedule *(Times Guide)*.

A ceremony based on the Disney animated feature of the same name. Merlin the Magician selects youngsters from the audience to test their courage and strength by removing the sword, Excalibur, from the stone.

Bay Lake and Seven Seas Lagoon Floating Electrical Pageant   Per-formed at nightfall (about 9 p.m. most of the year) on Seven Seas Lagoon and Bay Lake, this is one of our favorites among the Disney extras, but it's necessary to leave the Magic Kingdom to view it. The pageant is a stunning electric-light show afloat on small barges and set to nifty electronic music. Leave the Magic Kingdom and take the monorail to the Polynesian Resort. Get yourself a drink and walk to the end of the pier to watch the show.

Wishes   Memorable vignettes and music from beloved Disney Films com-bine with a stellar fireworks display while Jiminy Cricket narrates a lump-in-your-throat story about making wishes come true. For an uncluttered view and lighter crowds, watch from the terrace of The Plaza Pavilion restaurant in Tomorrowland. Another good fireworks viewing area is between Dumbo and the carousel.

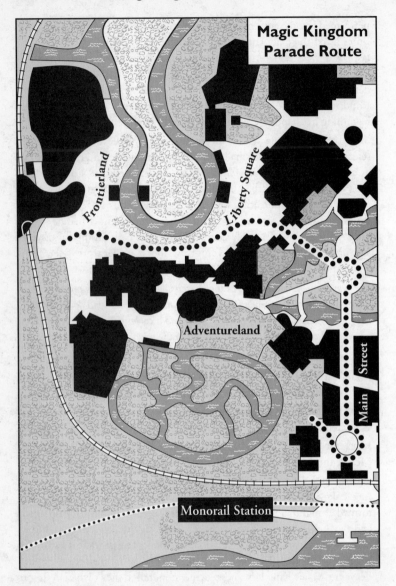

Wishes Fireworks Cruise   For a different view, you can watch the fireworks from the Seven Seas Lagoon aboard a chartered pontoon boat. The charter costs $120 and accommodates up to 12 people. Your Disney cast member captain will take you for a little cruise and then position the boat in a perfect place to watch the fireworks. For an additional $80 per each four persons, the captain will provide deli sandwiches, snacks, and beverages. A major indirect benefit of the charter is that you can enjoy the fireworks without fighting the mob afterwards. Because this is a private charter rather than a tour, only your group will be aboard. Life jackets are provided, but wearing them is at your discretion. Because there are few boats, charters sell out fast. To reserve, call (407) WDW-PLAY at exactly 7 a.m. 90 days before the day you want to charter. Because the Disney reservations system counts days in a somewhat atypical manner, we recommend phoning at about 95 days out to have a Disney agent specify the exact morning to call for reservations. Similar charters are available to watch *IllumiNations* at Epcot.

Disney Character Shows and Appearances   Usually, a number of characters are on hand to greet guests when the park opens. Because they snarl pedestrian traffic and stop most children dead in their tracks, this is sort of a mixed blessing. Most days, a character is on duty for photos and autographs from 9 a.m. to 10 p.m. next to City Hall. Mickey and two or three assortments of other characters are available most of the day at Mickey's Toontown Fair. Shows at the Castle Forecourt Stage feature Disney characters several times daily (check the entertainment schedule/ *Times Guide*). In Fantasyland, Ariel can be found in her Grotto daily, while a host of others can be seen at the Character Festival next to Dumbo. Characters also roam the park. For information on character whereabouts on the day you visit, check the *Character Greeting Guide* printed on the inside of the handout park map or the *Times Guide*.

Magic Kingdom Bands   Banjo, Dixieland, steel drum, marching, and fife-and-drum bands roam the park daily.

Tinker Bell's Flight   This nice special effect in the sky above Cinderella Castle heralds the beginning of the Wishes fireworks show (when the park is open late).

Parades

Parades at the Magic Kingdom are full-fledged spectaculars with dozens of Disney characters and amazing special effects. We rate the afternoon parade as outstanding and the evening parade as "not to be missed."

In addition to providing great entertainment, parades lure guests away from the attractions. If getting on rides appeals to you more than watching a parade, you'll find substantially shorter lines just before and during parades. Because the parade route doesn't pass through Adventureland, Tomorrowland, or Fantasyland, attractions in these lands are particularly good bets. Be forewarned: parades disrupt traffic in the Magic Kingdom. It's nearly impossible, for example, to get to Adventureland from Tomorrowland, or vice versa, during one. Also be advised that the Walt Disney World Railroad shuts down during parades, thus making it impossible to access other lands by train.

Afternoon Parade

Usually staged at 3 p.m., the parade features bands, floats, and marching Disney characters. A new afternoon parade is introduced every year or two. While some elements, such as Disney characters, remain constant, the theme, music, and float design change. Seasonal parades during major holidays round out the mix.

Evening Parade(s)

The evening parade is a high-tech affair employing electroluminescent and fiber-optic technologies, light-spreading thermoplastics (do not try this at home!), and clouds of underlit liquid-nitrogen smoke. Don't worry, you won't need a gas mask or lead underwear to watch. For those who flunked chemistry and physics, the parade also offers music, Mickey Mouse, twinkling lights, and snapshots of classic animated features inside giant snow globes. Disney says the snow globes are just part of the show, but we think maybe the characters are worried about anthrax.

The evening parade is staged once or twice each evening, depending on the time of year. During less busy times of year, the evening parade is presented only on weekends, and sometimes not even then. Call (407) 824-4321 before you go to be sure the parade is on.

Parade Route and Vantage Points

Magic Kingdom parades circle Town Square, head down Main Street, go around the central hub, and cross the bridge to Liberty Square. In Liberty Square, they follow the waterfront and end in Frontierland. Sometimes they begin in Frontierland and run the route in the opposite direction.

Most guests watch from the central hub, or from Main Street. One of the best and most popular vantage points is the upper platform of the Walt Disney World Railroad station at the Town Square end of Main Street. This is also a good place for watching the Wishes fireworks, as well as for ducking out of the park ahead of the crowd when the fireworks end. Problem is, you have to stake out your position 30–45 minutes before the events.

Because most spectators pack Main Street and the central hub, we recommend watching the parade from Liberty Square or Frontierland. Great vantage points, frequently overlooked, are:

1. Sleepy Hollow snack and beverage shop, immediately to your right as you cross the bridge into Liberty Square. If you arrive early, buy refreshments and claim a table by the rail. You'll have a perfect view of the parade as it crosses the Liberty Square bridge but only when the parade begins on Main Street.

2. The pathway on the Liberty Square side of the moat from Sleepy Hollow snack-and-beverage shop to Cinderella Castle. Any point along this path offers a clear and unobstructed view as the parade crosses the Liberty Square bridge. Once again, this spot works only for parades coming from Main Street.

3. The covered walkway between Liberty Tree Tavern and *The Diamond Horseshoe Saloon Revue*. This elevated vantage point is perfect (particularly on rainy days) and usually goes unnoticed until just before the parade starts.

4. Elevated wooden platforms in front of the Frontierland Shootin' Arcade, Frontier Trading Post, and the building with the sign reading FRONTIER MERCANTILE. These spots usually get picked off 10–12 minutes before parade time.

5. Benches on the perimeter of the central hub, between the entrances to Liberty Square and Adventureland. Usually unoccupied until after the parade begins, they offer a comfortable resting place and unobstructed (though somewhat distant) view of the parade as it crosses Liberty Square bridge. What you lose in proximity, you gain in comfort.

6. Liberty Square and Frontierland dockside areas. These spots usually go early.

7. The elevated porch of Tony's Town Square Restaurant on Main Street provides an elevated viewing platform and an easy path to the park exit when the fireworks are over.

Assuming it starts on Main Street (evening parades normally do), the parade takes 16–20 minutes to reach Liberty Square or Frontierland.

On evenings when the parade runs twice, the first parade draws a huge crowd, siphoning guests from attractions. Many folks leave the park after the early parade, with many more departing after the fireworks (scheduled on the hour between the two parades). For optimum touring and less congestion, enjoy attractions during the early parade, then break to watch the fireworks. Continue to tour after the fireworks. This is a particularly good time to see *Stitch's Great Escape,* ride Space Mountain, and enjoy attractions in Adventureland. If you're touring Adventureland and the parade begins on Main Street, you won't have to assume your viewing position in Frontierland until 15 minutes after the parade kicks off (the time it takes the parade to reach Frontierland). If you watch from the Splash Mountain side of the street and head for the attraction as the last float passes, you'll be able to ride with only a couple of minutes' wait. You might even have time to work in a last-minute ride on Big Thunder Mountain Railroad.

Vantage Points for Fireworks

Anywhere along Main Street is fine for the fireworks. If you plan to leave the park immediately afterwards, watch from the train-station end to facilitate a quick departure. Our favorite spot if we intend to remain in the park is the roofless patio of the Plaza Pavilion located in Tomorrowland on the border with Main Street, U.S.A.

Leaving the Park after Evening Parades and Fireworks

Armies of guests leave the Magic Kingdom after evening parades and fireworks. The Disney Transportation System (buses, ferries, and monorail) is overwhelmed, causing long waits in boarding areas.

A mother from Kresgeville, Pennsylvania, pleads:

Please stress how terrifying these crowds can be. Our family of five made the mistake of going to the MK the Saturday night before Columbus Day to watch the parade and fireworks. Afterwards, we lingered at The Crystal Palace to wait for the crowds to lessen, but it was no use. We started walking toward the gates and soon became trapped by the throng, not able to go forward or back. There was no way to cross the hordes to get to the dock for our hotel's launch. Our group became separated, and it became a living nightmare. We left the park at 10:30 p.m. and didn't get back to the Polynesian (less than a mile away) until after midnight. How dare they expose children to that nightmare! Even if they were to raise Walt Disney himself from cryogenic sleep and parade him down Main Street, I would never go to the MK on a Saturday night again!

An Oklahoma City dad offers this advice:

Never, never leave the Magic Kingdom just after the 10 p.m. fireworks. I have never seen so many people in one spot before. Go for another ride—no lines because everyone else is trying to get out!

Congestion persists from the end of the early evening parade until closing time. Most folks watch the early parade and then the fireworks a few minutes later. If you're parked at the Transportation and Ticket Center and are intent on beating the crowd, view the early parade from the Town Square end of Main Street, leaving the park as soon as the parade ends.

If you're staying at a Disney hotel not served by the monorail and must depend on Disney transportation, watch the early parade and fireworks at the park and then enjoy the attractions until about 20–25 minutes before the late parade is scheduled to begin. At this time, leave the park and catch the Disney bus or boat back to your hotel. Don't cut it too close: Main Street will be so congested that you won't be able to reach the exit.

Here's what happened to a family from Cape Coral, Florida:

We tried to leave the park before the parade began. However, Main Street was already packed and we didn't see any way to get out of the park, so we were stuck. In addition, it was impossible to move across the street, and even the shops were so crowded that it was virtually impossible to maneuver a stroller through them to get close to the entrance.

If you don't have a stroller (or are willing to forgo the $1 return refund for rental strollers), catch the Walt Disney World Railroad in Frontierland or Mickey's Toontown Fair and ride to the park exit at Main Street. Be aware that the railroad shuts down during parades because the floats must cross the tracks when entering or exiting the parade route in Frontierland. If you plan to escape by train, don't cut it too close.

If you're on the Tomorrowland side of the park, it's actually possible for you to exit during a parade. Leaving Tomorrowland, cut through The Plaza Pavilion Restaurant to Main Street. Before you reach Main Street, bear left into the side door of the corner shop. Once inside, you'll see that Main Street shops have interior doors allowing you to pass from one shop to the next without having to get on Main Street. Work your way from shop to shop until you reach Town Square (easy, because people will be outside, watching the parade). At Town Square, bear left and move to the train station and the park exit.

This strategy won't work if you're on the Adventureland side of the park. You can make your way through Casey's Corner restaurant to Main Street, then work your way through the interior of the Main Street shops, but when you pop out of the Emporium at Town Square, you'll be trapped by the parade. As soon as the last float passes, however, you can bolt for the exit.

Another strategy for beating the masses out of the park (if your car is at the TTC lot) is to watch the early parade and then leave before the fireworks begin. Line up for the ferry. One will depart about every eight to ten minutes. Try to catch the ferry that will be crossing Seven Seas Lagoon while the fireworks are in progress. The best vantage point is on the top deck to the right of the pilot house as you face the Magic Kingdom, and the sight of fireworks silhouetting the castle and reflecting off Seven Seas Lagoon is unforgettable. While there's no guarantee that a ferry will load and depart within three or four minutes of the fireworks, your chances are about 50/50 of catching it just right. If you're in the front of the line for the ferry and don't want to board the boat that's loading, stop at the gate and let people pass you. You'll be the first to board the next boat.

Behind the Scenes in the Magic Kingdom

Keys to the Kingdom takes guests behind the scenes at the Magic Kingdom. This fascinating guided tour provides an informative and detailed look at the park's logistical, technical, and operational sides. Included are the parade assembly area, the waste treatment plant, and tunnels under the theme park. For additional information, call (407) 939-8687. The program ($58 per person) runs about four to five hours. Advance reservations and payment by credit card are required. Park admission is not included. Discounts are usually available; ask when you call to book.

For those interested in the tour, a reader from Ludington, Michigan, offers the following advice:

People thinking of taking the Keys to the Kingdom tour should know that it is not for the faint of heart. This is a four-hour walking tour with only one 15-minute break plus a few minutes to sit while on Pirates of the Caribbean, The Haunted Mansion, and the Tomorrowland Transit Authority. It wore me out, and I am on my feet most of any given working day. If you do this, make it the last day of your visit—it took me three days to recover. Oh, by the way, it is worth every penny!

Backstage Magic, a seven-hour, $199 tour, goes behind the scenes at all of the parks except the Animal Kingdom. **Disney's Magic behind Our Steam Trains,** a two-hour tour for ages ten and up, takes a backstage look at the steam locomotives of the Walt Disney World Railroad. Cost is $40 per person. For reservations and information on all of the tours described, call (407) WDW-TOUR. A less costly tour is the **Family Magic Tour,** an interactive romp through the park following clues in a sort of treasure hunt. The two-hour tour is offered daily for $25 and is open to all ages.

Traffic Patterns in the Magic Kingdom

When we research the Magic Kingdom, we study its traffic patterns, asking:

1. Which sections of the park and what attractions do guests visit first? When visitors are admitted to the lands during summer and holiday periods, traffic to Tomorrowland and Frontierland is heaviest, followed by Fantasyland, Adventureland, Liberty Square, and Mickey's Toontown Fair.

During the school year, when fewer young people are in the park, early-morning traffic is more evenly distributed but remains heaviest in Tomorrowland, Frontierland, and Fantasyland. Our researchers tested the frequent claim that most people turn right into Tomorrowland and tour the Magic Kingdom in a counterclockwise sequence. We found it to be baseless. As the park fills, visitors head for the top attractions before lines get long. This, more than any other factor, determines morning traffic patterns.

2. How long does it take for the park to fill up? How are the visitors dispersed in the park? A surge of "early birds" arrives before or around opening time but is quickly dispersed throughout the empty park. After the initial wave is absorbed, there's a lull lasting about an hour after opening. Then the park is inundated for about two hours, peaking between 10 a.m. and noon. Arrivals continue in a steady but diminishing stream until around 2 p.m. The lines we sampled were longest between 1 and 2 p.m., indicating more arrivals than departures into the early afternoon. For touring purposes, most attractions develop long lines between 10 and 11:30 a.m.

Attractions that Are Crowded Early

Tomorrowland	Space Mountain
	Buzz Lightyear
	Stitch's Great Escape
Frontierland	Splash Mountain
	Big Thunder Mountain Railroad
Fantasyland	Dumbo the Flying Elephant
	The Many Adventures of Winnie the Pooh
	Mickey's PhilharMagic
	Peter Pan's Flight
Adventureland	Jungle Cruise

From late morning until early afternoon, guests are equally distributed through all of the lands. However, guests concentrate in Fantasyland, Liberty Square, and Frontierland in late afternoon, with a decrease of visitors in Adventureland and Tomorrowland. Adventureland's Jungle Cruise and Tomorrowland's Buzz Lightyear and Space Mountain continue to be crowded, but most other attractions in those lands are readily accessible.

3. How do most visitors tour the park? Do first-time visitors tour differently from repeat guests? Many first-time visitors are guided by friends or relatives familiar with the Magic Kingdom. These tours may or may not follow an orderly sequence. First-time visitors without personal guides tend to be more orderly in their touring. Many first-time visitors, however, are drawn to Cinderella Castle upon entering the park and thus begin their rotation from Fantasyland. Repeat visitors usually go directly to their favorite attractions.

4. How does FASTPASS affect crowd distributions? The effect is subtle and depends somewhat on the time interval between when the FASTPASS is obtained and the FASTPASS return period. For example, guests who receive a FASTPASS for Splash Mountain at 10 a.m. with an 11:05 a.m.–12:05 p.m. return window tend to tour near Splash Mountain during the interim to minimize the inconvenience of backtracking when it's time to use the pass. However, when the return period is several hours distant, guests don't feel compelled to stay in the immediate area. In general, you won't notice much difference in crowd concentrations because of FASTPASS, but empirically speaking, it increases crowds within proximity of the two anchor attractions, Space Mountain and Splash Mountain, throughout the day.

5. How do special events, such as parades and live shows, affect traffic patterns? Parades pull huge numbers of guests away from attractions and provide a window of opportunity for experiencing the more popular attractions with less of a wait. Castle Forecourt Stage shows also attract crowds but only slightly affect lines.

6. What are the traffic patterns near to and at closing time? On our sample days, in busy times and off-season at the park, departures outnumbered arrivals beginning in midafternoon. Many visitors left in late afternoon as the dinner hour approached. When the park closed early, guests departed steadily during the two hours before closing, with a huge exodus at closing time. When the park closed late, a huge exodus began immediately after the early-evening parade and fireworks, with a second mass departure after the late parade, continuing until closing. Because Main Street and the transportation services remain open after the other six lands close, crowds leaving at closing mainly affect conditions on Main Street and at the monorail, ferry, and bus boarding areas. In the hour before closing, the other six lands normally are uncrowded.

7. When there are two or more lines, is the shortest wait always in the left line? We don't recommend the "left-line strategy" because, with the occasional exception of food lines, it doesn't hold up. Disney has techniques for both internal and external crowd control that distribute traffic nearly equally. Placing researchers at the same time in each available line, we could discern no consistent pattern of who was served first. Further, researchers entering the same attraction by different lines almost always would exit the attraction within 30 to 90 seconds of each other.

Occasionally guests ignore a second line that has just opened and stay in the established line. As a rule, if you encounter a waiting area with two lines and no barrier to entry for either, and one line is empty or conspicuously shorter than the other, get in the short line.

Magic Kingdom Touring Plans

Our step-by-step touring plans are field-tested for seeing *as much as possible* in one day with a minimum of time wasted in lines. They're designed to help you avoid crowds and bottlenecks on days of moderate-to-heavy attendance. Understand, however, that there's more to see in the Magic Kingdom than can be experienced in one day. Since we began covering the Magic Kingdom, four headliner attractions and a new land have been added. Today, even if you could experience every attraction without any wait, it would still be virtually impossible to see all of the park in a single day.

On days of lighter attendance (see "Selecting the Time of Year for Your Visit," pages 28–31), our plans will save you time but won't be as critical to successful touring as on busier days. Don't worry that other people will be following the plans and render them useless. Fewer than 1 in every 350 people in the park will have been exposed to this information.

Choosing the Appropriate Touring Plan

We present five Magic Kingdom touring plans:

- Magic Kingdom One-Day Touring Plan for Adults
- Author's Selective Magic Kingdom One-Day Touring Plan for Adults
- Magic Kingdom One-Day Touring Plan for Parents with Young Children
- Magic Kingdom Dumbo-or-Die-in-a-Day Touring Plan for Parents with Young Children
- Magic Kingdom Two-Day Touring Plan

If you have two days (or two mornings) at the Magic Kingdom, the Two-Day Touring Plan is *by far* the most relaxed and efficient. The two-day plan takes advantage of early morning, when lines are short and the park hasn't filled with guests. This plan works well year-round and eliminates much of the extra walking required by the one-day plans. No matter when the park closes, our two-day plan guarantees the most efficient touring and the least time in lines. The plan is perfect for guests who wish to sample both the attractions and the atmosphere of the Magic Kingdom.

If you only have one day but wish to see as much as possible, use the One-Day Touring Plan for Adults. It's exhausting, but it packs in the maximum. If you prefer a more relaxed visit, use the Author's Selective One-Day Touring Plan. It includes the best the park has to offer (in the author's opinion), eliminating some less impressive attractions.

If you have children younger than age eight, adopt the One-Day Touring Plan for Parents with Young Children. It's a compromise, blending the preferences of younger children with those of older siblings and adults. The plan includes many children's rides in Fantasyland but omits roller-coaster rides and other attractions that frighten young children or are off-limits because of height requirements. Or, use the One-Day Touring Plan for Adults or the Author's Selective One-Day Touring Plan and take advantage of switching off, a technique where children accompany adults to the loading area of a ride with age and height requirements but don't board (pages 266–268). Switching off allows adults to enjoy the more adventuresome attractions while keeping the group together.

The Dumbo-or-Die-in-a-Day Touring Plan for Parents with Young Children is designed for parents who will withhold no sacrifice for the children. On the Dumbo-or-Die plan, adults generally stand around, sweat, wipe noses, pay for stuff, and watch the children enjoy themselves. It's great.

Two-Day Touring Plan for Families with Young Children

If you have young children and are looking for a two-day itinerary, combine the Magic Kingdom One-Day Touring Plan for Parents with Young

Children with the second day of the Magic Kingdom Two-Day Touring Plan.

Two-Day Touring Plan for Early Morning Touring on Day One and Afternoon-Evening Touring on Day Two

Many of you enjoy an early start at the Magic Kingdom on one day, followed by a second day with a lazy, sleep-in morning, resuming your touring in the afternoon and/or evening. If this appeals to you, use the Magic Kingdom One-Day Touring Plan for Adults or the Magic Kingdom One-Day Touring Plan for Parents with Young Children on your early day. Adhere to the touring plan for as long as feels comfortable (many folks leave after the afternoon parade). On the second day, pick up where you left off. If you intend to use FASTPASS on your second day, try to arrive at the park by 1 p.m. or the FASTPASSes may be gone. Customize the remaining part of the touring plan to incorporate parades, fireworks, and other live performances according to your preferences.

About Touring Plan Clip-Out Pocket Outlines

Pocket versions of all touring plans presented in this guide begin on page 757. The outlines present the same itineraries as the detailed plans but with vastly abbreviated directions. Select the touring plan appropriate for your party and familiarize yourself with its detailed version. When you understand how the plan works, clip its pocket outline from the back of this guide and carry it as a quick reference when you visit the theme park.

Magic Kingdom Touring Plan Companion

We've consolidated a great deal of information about the Magic Kingdom in the Magic Kingdom Touring Plan Companion, located at the back of the guide just after the various Magic Kingdom Touring Plan Clip-Out Pocket Outlines. Designed to clip out and take with you to the park, the Magic Kingdom Touring Plan Companion includes: the best days to go; the best times to visit each attraction; the author's rating; height requirements; small-child fright potential, and info on dining and cool places to take a break.

The Single-Day Touring Conundrum

Touring the Magic Kingdom in a day is complicated by the fact that the premier attractions are at almost opposite ends of the park: Splash Mountain and Big Thunder Mountain Railroad in Frontierland and Space Mountain and Buzz Lightyear in Tomorrowland. It's virtually impossible to ride all four without encountering lines at one or another. If you ride Space Mountain and see Buzz Lightyear immediately after the park opens, you won't have much wait, if any. By the time you leave Tomorrowland and hurry to Frontierland, however, the line for Splash Mountain will be substantial. The same situation prevails if you ride the Frontierland duo first: Splash Mountain and Big Thunder Mountain Railroad, no problem; Space Mountain and Buzz Lightyear, fair-sized lines. From ten minutes after opening until just before closing, lines are long at these headliners.

The best way to ride all four without long waits is to tour the Magic Kingdom over two mornings: Ride Space Mountain first thing one morning, then ride Buzz Lightyear, Splash Mountain and Big Thunder Mountain first thing on the other. If you have only one day, be present at opening time. Speed immediately to Space Mountain, then take in Buzz Lightyear. After Buzz Lightyear, rush to Frontierland and scope out the situation at Splash Mountain. If the posted wait time is 30 minutes or less, go ahead and hop in line. If the wait exceeds 30 minutes, get a FASTPASS for Splash Mountain, then ride Big Thunder Mountain.

E-Ride Night

Since 2002, Disney has offered a program called E-Ride Night. Only Disney resort guests with multiday passports (and annual and seasonal passholders) are eligible. For about $13 per adult, you can purchase a pass that allows you to remain in the Magic Kingdom for three hours after the official closing time and enjoy the following attractions:

Big Thunder Mountain Railroad	Mickey's PhillharMagic
Buzz Lightyear's Space Ranger Spin	Peter Pan's Flight
Country Bear Jamboree	Space Mountain
The Haunted Mansion	Splash Mountain
The Many Adventures of Winnie the Pooh	

Disney may substitute other attractions when one of the above is closed. Also, *Stitch's Great Escape* may be added to this lineup in the future.

Disney limits the number of E-Ride Night passes sold to four-to-five thousand per night, ensuring short-to-nonexistent waits for most attractions. If you have fantasized about riding Space Mountain ten times in a row with practically no waiting, E-Ride Night makes it possible. E-Ride Night, however, is not good for admission to the park by itself. It must be used with a multiday admission used at any of the major theme parks on the day in question. In other words, you can spend the day at the Animal Kingdom (have your hand stamped upon exiting) and then head to the Magic Kingdom for after-hours fun. On arriving at the Magic Kingdom, enter the park before official closing time, using your multiday pass. Once inside, take your E-Ride Night voucher to either City Hall, the Tomorrowland Arcade, or Splashdown Photo and exchange it for a wristband that identifies you as eligible to stay in the park. After scheduled park closing, only guests with wristbands are allowed to remain in the park. May, June, and July all include E-Ride nights starting at 10 p.m. As with all things Disney, the program is subject to change or cancellation at any time; there is also talk of trying E-Ride Night at the other major theme parks.

Preliminary Instructions for All Magic Kingdom Touring Plans

On days of moderate-to-heavy attendance, follow your chosen touring plan exactly, deviating only:

1. When you aren't interested in an attraction it lists. For example, the plan may tell you to go to Tomorrowland and ride Space Mountain, a roller coaster. If you don't enjoy roller coasters, skip this step and proceed to the next.

2. When you encounter a very long line at an attraction the touring plan calls for. Crowds ebb and flow at the park, and an unusually long line may have gathered at an attraction to which you're directed. For example, you arrive at The Haunted Mansion and find extremely long lines. It's possible that this is a temporary situation caused by several hundred people arriving en masse from a recently concluded performance of *The Hall of Presidents* nearby. If this is the case, skip The Haunted Mansion and go to the next step, returning later to retry The Haunted Mansion.

What to Do if You Get Off Track

If an unexpected interruption or problem throws the touring plan off, consult "Magic Kingdom: Recommended Attraction Visitation Times" (page 757) for preferred times of day to visit attractions.

Park-Opening Procedures

Your success during your first hour of touring will be affected somewhat by the opening procedure Disney uses that day:

1. All guests are held at the turnstiles until the entire park opens (which may or may not be at the official opening time). If this happens on the day you visit, blow past Main Street and head for the first attraction on the touring plan you're following.

2. Guests are admitted to Main Street a half hour to an hour before the remaining lands open. Access to other lands will be blocked by a rope barrier at the central hub end of Main Street. Once admitted, stake out a position at the rope barrier as follows:

If you're going to Frontierland first (Splash Mountain and Big Thunder Mountain Railroad), stand in front of The Crystal Palace restaurant, on the left at the central hub end of Main Street. Wait next to the rope barrier blocking the walkway to Adventureland. When the rope is dropped, move quickly to Frontierland by way of Adventureland. This is also the place to line up if your first stop is Adventureland.

If you're going to Buzz Lightyear and Space Mountain first, wait at the entrance of the bridge to Tomorrowland. When the rope drops, walk quickly across into Tomorrowland.

Between Fantasyland and Tomorrowland is Toontown, which opens at 10 a.m. If you're going to Fantasyland or Liberty Square first, go to the end of Main Street and line up left of center at the rope.

Before You Go

1. Call (407) 824-4321 the day before you go to check the official opening time.

2. Purchase admission before you arrive.

3. Familiarize yourself with park-opening procedures (above) and reread the touring plan you've chosen so that you know what you're likely to encounter.

Magic Kingdom Touring Plans

Magic Kingdom One-Day Touring Plan for Adults

For Adults without young children

Assumes Willingness to experience all major rides (including roller coasters) and shows

This plan requires considerable walking and some backtracking; this is necessary to avoid long lines. Extra walking plus some morning hustle will spare you two to three hours of standing in line. You might not complete the tour. How far you get depends on how quickly you move from ride to ride, how many times you rest or eat, how quickly the park fills, and what time the park closes.

1. If you're a Disney hotel guest, use Disney transportation to commute to the park, arriving 30 minutes before official opening time.

   If you're a day guest, arrive at the Magic Kingdom's parking lot 50 minutes before official opening time. Arrive 70 minutes before official opening time if it's a holiday period. Add 15 minutes to the above if you have to buy your admission. These arrivals give you time to park and catch the tram to the Transportation and Ticket Center. At the TTC, transfer to the monorail or ferry to reach the park's entrance. If the line for the monorail is short, take the monorail; otherwise, catch the ferry.

2. At the park, proceed through the turnstiles and have one person go to City Hall for guidemaps and the daily entertainment schedule (*Times Guide*).

3. Regroup and move quickly down Main Street to the central hub. Because the Magic Kingdom has two opening procedures, you probably will encounter one of the following:
   a. The entire park will be open. In this case, proceed quickly to Space Mountain in Tomorrowland.
   b. Only Main Street will be open. In this case, go to the central hub and position yourself at the entrance to Tomorrowland. When the rope barrier is dropped at opening time, walk as fast as possible to Space Mountain. Ride.

4. Backtrack toward the entrance to Tomorrowland, bearing left to Buzz Lightyear's Space Ranger Spin. Ride.

5. After Buzz, proceed to Fantasyland via Tomorrowland passing the Tomorrowland Speedway en route. In Fantasyland, experience The Many Adventures of Winnie the Pooh.

6. Exit left from Winnie the Pooh and ride Snow White's Adventures next door.

7. Cross Fantasyland Plaza in the direction of Liberty Square and ride Peter Pan's Flight.

8. Across from Peter Pan, ride It's a Small World.

9. Exit Small World and bear right to Liberty Square. Experience The Haunted Mansion.

10. Proceed right after departing The Haunted Mansion and follow the Liberty Square waterfront into Frontierland and on to Splash Mountain. At Splash Mountain, obtain a FASTPASS.

11. Next door to Splash Mountain, ride Big Thunder Mountain Railroad.

12. Proceed to Adventureland via the bridge in front of Splash Mountain. In Adventureland, experience Pirates of the Caribbean.

13. By now it should be time to return and ride Splash Mountain using your FASTPASS. If you still have some time to kill, try the Swiss Family Treehouse in Adventureland.

14. At this point you will have most of the Magic Kingdom bottlenecks in the rearview mirror. Feel free to stop for lunch, a break, or scheduled live entertainment.

15. Catch the Walt Disney Railroad at the Frontierland station next to Splash Mountain. Ride the train to Mickey's Toontown Fair.

16. Tour Mickey's Toontown Fair.

17. Reboard the train at Mickey's Toontown Fair and complete your round-trip, disembarking at the Frontierland Station.

18. Return to Adventureland. Obtain a FASTPASS for the Jungle Cruise.

19. In Adventureland, drop in on the *Enchanted Tiki Birds*.

20. Cross the plaza passing the Aladdin ride and cut through the passage into Frontierland. Bear left (yuk, yuk) and see the *Country Bear Jamboree*.

21. Return to Adventureland through the same passage. Ride the Jungle Cruise using your FASTPASS. Skip to Step 22 if you still have some time to kill before your FASTPASS return window starts.

22. Explore the Swiss Family Treehouse if you didn't see it earlier.

23. Return to Liberty Square via the passage opposite Aladdin. Experience the *Liberty Belle* Riverboat and *The Hall of Presidents* in whichever order is most convenient.

24. Return to Fantasyland and see *Mickey's PhilharMagic*.

25. Return to Tomorrowland via the central hub and experience *Stitch's Great Escape*.

26. Also in Tomorrowland, ride the Tomorrowland Transit Authority.

27. Also in Tomorrowland, see *The Timekeeper* and the *Carousel of Progress* if they are operating (both open only occasionally according to attendance levels).

28. Experience any attractions you might have missed. View any parades, fireworks, or live performances that interest you. Grab a bite. Save Main Street for last because it remains open after the rest of the park closes.

29. Browse Main Street.

Author's Selective Magic Kingdom One-Day Touring Plan for Adults

For Adults touring without young children

Assumes Willingness to experience all major rides (including roller coasters) and shows

This plan includes only those attractions the author believes are the best in the Magic Kingdom. It requires a lot of walking and some backtracking to avoid long lines. Extra walking and morning hustle will spare you three or more hours of standing in line. You might not complete the tour. How far you get depends on how quickly you move from ride to ride, how many times you rest or eat, how quickly the park fills, and what time the park closes.

1. If you're a Disney hotel guest, use Disney transportation to commute to the park, arriving 30 minutes before official opening time.

   If you're a day guest, arrive at the parking lot 50 minutes before the Magic Kingdom's official opening time. Arrive 70 minutes earlier than official opening if it's a holiday period. Add 15 minutes to the above if you must buy your admission. These arrivals will give you time to park and catch the tram to the Transportation and Ticket Center. At the TTC, transfer to the monorail or ferry to reach the park's entrance. If the line for the monorail is short, take the monorail; otherwise, catch the ferry.

2. At the park, proceed through the turnstiles and have one person go to City Hall for guidemaps and the daily entertainment schedule.

3. Regroup and move quickly down Main Street to the central hub. Because the Magic Kingdom has two opening procedures, you probably will encounter one of the following:
   a. The entire park will be open. In this case, proceed quickly to Space Mountain in Tomorrowland.
   b. Only Main Street will be open. In this case, proceed to the central hub and position yourself at the entrance to Tomorrowland. When the rope drops, head to Space Mountain.

4. Backtrack toward the entrance to Tomorrowland, bearing left to Buzz Lightyear's Space Ranger Spin. Ride.

5. After Buzz, proceed to Fantasyland via Tomorrowland, passing the Tomorrowland Speedway en route. In Fantasyland, experience The Many Adventures of Winnie the Pooh.

6. Exit left from Winnie the Pooh, cross Fantasyland Plaza in the direction of Liberty Square, and ride Peter Pan's Flight.

7. Across from Peter Pan, ride It's a Small World.

8. Exit Small World and bear right to Liberty Square. Experience The Haunted Mansion.

9. Proceed right after departing The Haunted Mansion and follow the Liberty Square waterfront into Frontierland and on to Splash Mountain. At Splash Mountain, obtain a FASTPASS.

10. Next door to Splash Mountain, ride Big Thunder Mountain Railroad.

11. Proceed to Adventureland via the bridge in front of Splash Mountain. In Adventureland, experience Pirates of the Caribbean.

12. By now it should be time to return and ride Splash Mountain using your FASTPASS. If you still have some time to kill, try the Swiss Family Treehouse in Adventureland.

13. At this point, you will have most of the Magic Kingdom bottlenecks in the rearview mirror. Feel free to stop for lunch, a break, or scheduled live entertainment.

14. Catch the Walt Disney Railroad at the Frontierland station next to Splash Mountain. Ride the train to Mickey's Toontown Fair. Toontown doesn't hold much appeal for adults. If you think you can live without it, stay on the train for a round-trip all the way back to Frontierland and skip to Step 17.

15. Tour Mickey's Toontown Fair.

16. Reboard the train at Mickey's Toontown Fair and complete your round-trip, disembarking at the Frontierland Station.

17. Return to Adventureland. Obtain a FASTPASS for the Jungle Cruise.

18. In Adventureland, drop in on the *Enchanted Tiki Birds*.

19. Cross the plaza passing the Aladdin ride and cut through the passage into Frontierland. Bear left and see the *Country Bear Jamboree*.

20. Return to Adventureland through the same passage. Ride the Jungle Cruise using your FASTPASS. Skip to Step 21 if you still have some time to kill before your FASTPASS return window starts.

21. Explore the Swiss Family Treehouse if you didn't see it earlier.

22. Return to Liberty Square via the passage opposite Aladdin. Experience the *Liberty Belle* Riverboat and *The Hall of Presidents* in whichever order is most convenient.

23. Return to Fantasyland and see *Mickey's PhilharMagic*.

24. Return to Tomorrowland via the central hub and experience *Stitch's Great Escape*.

25. Also in Tomorrowland, see *The Timekeeper* and the *Carousel of Progress* if they are operating (both open only occasionally according to attendance levels).

26. Experience any attractions you might have missed. View any parades, fireworks, or live performances that interest you. Grab a bite. Save Main Street for last because it remains open after the rest of the park closes.

27. Browse Main Street.

Magic Kingdom One-Day Touring Plan
for Parents with Young Children

For Parents with children younger than age eight

Assumes Periodic stops for rest, rest rooms, and refreshments

This plan represents a compromise between the observed tastes of adults and those of younger children. Included are many amusement park rides that children may have the opportunity to experience at fairs and amusement parks back home. Although these rides are included in the plan, omit them if possible. These cycle-loading rides often have long lines, consuming valuable touring time:

Mad Tea Party	Dumbo the Flying Elephant
Cinderella's Golden Carrousel	Magic Carpets of Aladdin

This time could be better spent experiencing the many attractions that better demonstrate the Disney creative genius and are found only in the Magic Kingdom. Instead of this plan, try either of the one-day plans for adults and take advantage of "switching off." This allows parents and young children to enter the ride together. At the boarding area, one parent watches the children while the other rides.

Before entering the park, decide whether you will return to your hotel for a midday rest. We strongly recommend that you break from touring and return to your hotel for a swim and a nap (even if you aren't lodging in Walt Disney World). You won't see as much, but everyone will be more relaxed and happy.

This touring plan requires a lot of walking and some backtracking to avoid long lines. A little extra walking and some morning hustle will spare you two to three hours of standing in line. You probably won't complete the tour. How far you get depends on how quickly you move from ride to ride, how many times you rest or eat, how quickly the park fills, and what time the park closes.

1. If you're a Disney hotel guest, use Disney transportation to commute to the park, arriving 30 minutes before official opening time.

   If you're a day guest, arrive at the parking lot 50 minutes before the Magic Kingdom's official opening time. Arrive 70 minutes earlier than official opening if it's a holiday period. Add 15 minutes to the above if you must purchase your admission. These arrivals will give you time to park and catch the tram to the Transportation and Ticket Center. At the TTC, transfer to the monorail or ferry to reach the park's entrance. If the line for the monorail is short, take the monorail; otherwise, catch the ferry.

2. At the Magic Kingdom, proceed through the turnstiles and have one person go to City Hall for guidemaps and the daily entertainment schedule.

3. Rent strollers (if necessary). This can be accomplished most days before you pass through the turnstiles.

4. Move briskly to the end of Main Street. If the entire park is open, go quickly to Fantasyland. Otherwise, position your group by the rope barrier at the central hub. When the park opens and the barrier drops, go through the main door of the castle and ride Dumbo the Flying Elephant in Fantasyland.

5. Enjoy The Many Adventures of Winnie the Pooh. Use the standby line—not FASTPASS.

6. Ride Peter Pan's Flight. Use the standby line—not FASTPASS.

7. Across the walkway, ride It's a Small World.

8. Head toward the castle. See *Mickey's PhilharMagic* on your right.

9. Exit Mickey's PhilharMagic and bear left, passing Peter Pan, and cross into Liberty Square. In Liberty Square, experience The Haunted Mansion, directly on your right.

10. On exiting The Haunted Mansion, head towards Frontierland, keeping the waterfront on your right. To the right of the Frontierland Shootin' Arcade is a passageway that leads directly to Adventureland. Continue to Adventureland and ride the Jungle Cruise. If the wait exceeds 30 minutes, use FASTPASS.

11. Turn left on exiting the Jungle Cruise and head for Frontierland. In Frontierland, take the rafts to Tom Sawyer Island. Allocate at least 30 minutes for your kids to explore the island.

12. Return via raft to the mainland. If you have a FASTPASS for the Jungle Cruise, go ahead and ride. If you need to kill some time before your FAST-PASS time slot, explore the Swiss Family Treehouse, next door to the Jungle Cruise. If you've already experienced the Jungle Cruise, skip to Step 13.

13. Proceed to the Frontierland railroad station, situated on the far right side of Splash Mountain. Take the Walt Disney World Railroad from Frontierland to Main Street, U.S.A. Depart the Magic Kingdom for lunch and a nap. If you insist on forgoing the nap, skip the train ride and proceed to Step 15.

14. After your afternoon break, return refreshed to the Magic Kingdom and head for Splash Mountain in Frontierland on foot or via the railroad from the Main Street Station. Be advised that the train is suggested solely to save some walking. There's virtually nothing to see between Main Street and the Frontierland station.

15. In Frontierland, obtain FASTPASSes for Splash Mountain.

16. In Frontierland, see the *Country Bear Jamboree*.

17. Exit the *Country Bear* and turn right, toward the passageway that leads to Adventureland. Return to Adventureland and ride Pirates of the Caribbean.

18. In Adventureland, explore the Swiss Family Treehouse if you didn't see it earlier.

19. Return to Splash Mountain and ride, using your FASTPASSes. If your kids aren't up for Splash Mountain, take advantage of switching off. If you still have some time remaining before your FASTPASS window, ride the *Liberty Belle* Riverboat.

20. After Splash Mountain, cross the park to Tomorrowland via the central hub. On entering Tomorrowland, obtain FASTPASSes for Buzz Lightyear if the return time is acceptable to you. Be aware that on exceedingly busy days, all of the FASTPASSes may have been distributed.

21. In Tomorrowland, ride the Tomorrowland Transit Authority.

22. Keeping the Tomorrowland Indy Speedway on your right, proceed to Mickey's Toontown Fair and explore.

23. If you have FASTPASSes for Buzz Lightyear, return to Tomorrowland and ride. If not, this ends the touring plan. If you have any energy left, check the daily entertainment schedule for live shows, fireworks, and parades.

To Convert This One-Day Touring Plan into a Two-Day Touring Plan

Skip Steps 14–23 on the first day. On the second day, arrive 30 minutes prior to opening, take the Walt Disney World Railroad from Main Street to Frontierland, and pick up the plan with Step 15, but do not use FASTPASS unless the wait exceeds 35 minutes.

Magic Kingdom Dumbo-or-Die-in-a-Day
Touring Plan for Parents with Young Children

For Adults compelled to devote every waking moment to the pleasure and entertainment of their young children, or rich people who are paying someone else to take their children to the theme park

Prerequisite This plan is designed for days when the Magic Kingdom doesn't close until 9 p.m. or later.

Assumes Frequent stops for rest, rest rooms, and refreshment

Note: Name aside, this touring plan is not a joke. Regardless of whether you're loving, guilty, masochistic, selfless, insane, or saintly, this itinerary will provide a young child with about as perfect a day as is possible at the Magic Kingdom.

This plan is a concession to adults determined to give their young children the ultimate Magic Kingdom experience. It addresses the preferences, needs, and desires of young children to the virtual exclusion of those of adults or older siblings. If you left the kids with a sitter yesterday or wouldn't let little Marvin eat barbecue for breakfast, this plan will expiate your guilt. It is also a wonderful itinerary if you're paying a sitter, nanny, or chauffeur to take your children to the Magic Kingdom.

1. If you're a Disney hotel guest, use Disney transportation to commute to the park, arriving 30 minutes before official opening time.

   If you're a day guest, arrive at the parking lot 50 minutes before the Magic Kingdom's official opening time. Arrive 70 minutes earlier than official opening if it's a holiday period. Add 15 minutes to the above if you must purchase your admission. These arrivals will give you time to park and catch the tram to the Transportation and Ticket Center. At the TTC, transfer to the monorail or ferry to reach the park's entrance. If the line for the monorail is short, take the monorail; otherwise, catch the ferry.

2. At the Magic Kingdom, proceed through the turnstiles and have one person go to City Hall for guidemaps and the daily entertainment schedule.

3. Rent a stroller (if needed).

4. Move briskly to the end of Main Street. If the entire park is open, go quickly to Fantasyland. Otherwise, position your group by the rope barrier at the central hub. When the park opens and the barrier is dropped, go through the main door of the castle to Cinderella's Royal Table, on your right as you enter Cinderella Castle.

5. Make a dinner priority seating at the Royal Table for 7 p.m. Eating there will let your kids see the inside of the castle and possibly meet Cinderella. To make your priority seating before you leave home, call (407) 939-3463 90 days in advance.

6. Enter Fantasyland. Ride Dumbo the Flying Elephant.

7. Hey, you're on vacation! Ride again, using the Chuck Bubba Relay if there are two adults in your party (page 268).

8. Experience The Many Adventures of Winnie the Pooh, near Dumbo. Use the standby line—not FASTPASS.

9. Ride Peter Pan's Flight. Use the standby line—not FASTPASS.

10. Ride Cinderella's Golden Carrousel. *then to Toontown*

11. In Tomorrowland, ride the Tomorrowland Speedway. Let your child steer (cars run on a guide rail) while you work the foot pedal.

12. Ride the Astro Orbiter. *Safety note:* Seat your children in the vehicle before you get in. Also, the Astro Orbiter goes higher and faster than Dumbo and may frighten some children.

13. Ride Buzz Lightyear's Space Ranger Spin (near Astro Orbiter). Do not use FASTPASS.

14. Return to Main Street via the central hub and leave the park for your hotel. Eat lunch and rest. (Have your hand stamped for re-entry when you leave the park. Keep your parking receipt to show upon return so you won't have to pay again for parking.) If you elect not to take a break out of the park, skip to Step 17.

15. Return to the Magic Kingdom refreshed about 4 or 4:30 p.m. Take the Walt Disney World Railroad to Frontierland.

16. Take the raft to Tom Sawyer Island. Stay as long as the kids want.

17. After you return from the island, see the *Country Bear Jamboree*. If you're hungry, Pecos Bill's Tall Tale Inn & Café in Frontierland is a good choice for both kids and adults.

18. Return to the Frontierland Station. Ride the train to Mickey's Toontown Fair.

19. Walk through Mickey's Country House and Minnie's Country House and play on Donald's Boat. Meet Disney characters at the Toontown Hall of Fame and pose for photos.

20. You should be within an hour of your dinner priority seating at Cinderella's Royal Table. Take the direct path from Mickey's Toontown Fair to Fantasyland. In Fantasyland, if you have 20 minutes or more before your priority seating, ride It's a Small World. Don't forget to sing.

21. After dinner, see *Mickey's PhilharMagic*, also in Fantasyland.

22. Leave Fantasyland and go to Liberty Square. If your children are up to it, see The Haunted Mansion. If not, skip to Step 23.

23. Evening parades are quite worthwhile. If you're interested, adjust the remainder of the touring plan to allow you to take a viewing position about 10 minutes before the early parade starts (usually 8 or 9 p.m.). See our recommendations for good vantage points (pages 470–471). If you aren't interested in the parade, enjoy attractions in Adventureland while the parade is in progress. Lines will be vastly diminished.

24. Go to Adventureland by way of Liberty Square, Frontierland, or the central hub. Take the Jungle Cruise if the lines aren't long. If they're prohibitive, obtain FASTPASSes and experience *Enchanted Tiki Birds*, Magic Carpets of Aladdin, and Swiss Family Treehouse. If your children can stand a few skeletons, also see Pirates of the Caribbean.

25. After the birds, carpets, treehouse, and pirates, return with your FAST-PASSes to ride the Jungle Cruise.

26. If you have time or energy left, repeat any attractions the kids especially liked, or try ones on the plan you might have bypassed because of long lines. Buy Goofy hats if that cranks your tractor.

27. If you're parked at the Transportation and Ticket Center, catch the ferry or express monorail. If the express monorail line is long, catch the resort monorail and disembark at the TTC.

To Convert This One-Day Touring Plan into a Two-Day Touring Plan

Skip Steps 19 and 20 on the first day. On the second day, arrive 30 minutes prior to opening and take the Walt Disney World Railroad from Main Street to Mickey's Toontown Fair. See Mickey's Toontown Fair in its entirety.

Magic Kingdom Two-Day Touring Plan

For Parties wishing to spread their Magic Kingdom visit over two days

Assumes Willingness to experience all major rides (including roller coasters) and shows

Timing: This two-day touring plan takes advantage of early-morning touring. Each day, you should complete the structured part of the plan by about 4 p.m. This leaves plenty of time for live entertainment. If the park is open late (after 8 p.m.), consider returning to your hotel at mid-day for a swim and a nap. Eat an early dinner outside Walt Disney World and return refreshed to enjoy the park's nighttime festivities.

Day One

1. If you're a Disney hotel guest, use Disney transportation to commute to the park, arriving 30 minutes before official opening time.

   If you're a day guest, arrive at the parking lot 50 minutes before the Magic Kingdom's official opening time. Arrive 70 minutes earlier than official opening if it's a holiday period. Add 15 minutes to the above if you must purchase your admission. These arrivals will give you time to park and catch the tram to the Transportation and Ticket Center. At the TTC, transfer to the monorail or ferry to reach the park's entrance. If the line for the monorail is short, take the monorail; otherwise, catch the ferry.

2. At the park, proceed through the turnstiles and have one person go to City Hall for guidemaps and the daily entertainment schedule.

3. Move as fast as you can down Main Street to the central hub. Because the Magic Kingdom uses two procedures for opening, you probably will encounter one of the following:
   a. The entire park will be open. In this case, proceed quickly to Space Mountain in Tomorrowland.
   b. Only Main Street will be open. In this case, position yourself in the central hub at the entrance to Tomorrowland. When the park opens and the rope barrier drops, walk as fast as possible to Space Mountain.

4. After exiting Space Mountain, proceed to Fantasyland via Tomorrowland, passing the Tomorrowland Speedway en route. In Fantasyland, experience The Many Adventures of Winnie the Pooh.

5. Exit Pooh and bear left past the carousel to Peter Pan's Flight. Ride.

6. Exit Peter Pan to the right and see *Mickey's PhilharMagic*.

7. Also in Fantasyland, ride It's a Small World.

8. Exit Small World to the right and proceed to Liberty Square. Immediately on entering, turn right to The Haunted Mansion. Enjoy.

9. Also in Liberty Square, ride the riverboat.

10. Feel free to stop for lunch from this point on. Fast-food eateries that are generally less crowded include the Columbia Harbour House in Liberty Square and Pecos Bill's Tall Tale Inn & Café in Frontierland.

11. Also in Liberty Square, see *The Hall of Presidents*.

12. Continue along the waterfront into Frontierland. See the *Country Bear Jamboree*. At this point, check the daily entertainment schedule for parades and other live performances that might interest you. Because you already have seen all the attractions that cause bottlenecks and have long lines, interrupting the touring plan here won't cause any problems. Simply pick up where you left off before the parade or show.

13. At the Frontierland waterfront, take a raft to Tom Sawyer Island. Explore.

14. After returning from Tom Sawyer Island, head for Tomorrowland via the central hub.

15. In Tomorrowland, see *Stitch's Great Escape.*

16. Also in Tomorrowland, ride the Tomorrowland Transit Authority.

17. This concludes the touring plan for the day. Enjoy the shops, see some of the live entertainment, or revisit favorite attractions until you're ready to leave.

Day Two

1. If you're a Disney hotel guest, use Disney transportation to commute to the park, arriving 30 minutes before official opening time.

   If you're a day guest, arrive at the parking lot 50 minutes before the Magic Kingdom's official opening time. Arrive 70 minutes earlier than official opening if it's a holiday period. Add 15 minutes to the above if you must purchase your admission. These arrivals will give you time to park and catch the tram to the Transportation and Ticket Center. At the TTC, transfer to the monorail or ferry to reach the park's entrance. If the line for the monorail is short, take the monorail; otherwise, catch the ferry.

2. At the park, proceed through the turnstiles. Stop at City Hall for guidemaps containing the day's entertainment schedule.

3. Proceed to the end of Main Street. If the entire park is open, go immediately to Buzz Lightyear in Tomorrowland and ride. Otherwise, position yourself along the rope at the entrance to Tomorrowland and wait to be admitted. When the rope drops, go directly to Buzz Lightyear.

4. After Buzz Lightyear, head for Frontierland via the central hub. In Frontierland, ride Splash Mountain. Do not use FASTPASS.

5. Ride Big Thunder Mountain Railroad, next to Splash Mountain.

6. Proceed to Adventureland. Ride the Jungle Cruise. If the wait seems prohibitive, use FASTPASS.

7. Across the street, see *Enchanted Tiki Birds.*

8. Walk through the Swiss Family Treehouse.

9. Exit the Treehouse to the left. Enjoy Pirates of the Caribbean. *Note:* At this point, check the daily entertainment schedule to see if any parades or live performances interest you. Note the times, and alter the touring plan accordingly. Since you already have seen all the attractions that cause bottlenecks and have big lines, interrupting the touring plan here won't cause any problems. Simply pick up where you left off before the parade or show.

10. If you're hungry, eat.

11. Exit Adventureland and go to the Frontierland train station between Splash and Big Thunder Mountains. Catch the Walt Disney World Railroad. Disembark at Mickey's Toontown Fair (first stop).

12. Tour the Fair and meet the Disney characters.

13. Exit the Fair via the path to Tomorrowland.

14. In Tomorrowland, if you haven't eaten, try Cosmic Ray's Starlight Café or The Plaza Pavilion.

15. See *Walt Disney's Carousel of Progress* (open seasonally).

16. See *The Timekeeper* (open seasonally).

17. This concludes the touring plan. Enjoy the shops, see live entertainment, or revisit your favorite attractions until you are ready to leave.

Part Eleven

Epcot

Overview

Education, inspiration, and corporate imagery are the focus at Epcot, the most adult of the Disney theme parks. What it gains in taking a futuristic, visionary, and technological look at the world, it loses, just a bit, in warmth, happiness, and charm.

Some people find the attempts at education to be superficial; others want more entertainment and less education. Most visitors, however, are in between, finding plenty of entertainment *and* education.

Epcot is more than twice as big as the Magic Kingdom or Disney-MGM Studios and, though smaller than the Animal Kingdom, has more territory to be covered on foot. Epcot rarely sees the congestion so common to the Magic Kingdom, but it has lines every bit as long as those at the Jungle Cruise or Space Mountain. Visitors must come prepared to do considerable walking among attractions and a comparable amount of standing in line.

Epcot's size means you can't see it all in one day without skipping an attraction or two and giving others a cursory glance. A major difference between Epcot and the other parks, however, is that some Epcot attractions can be savored slowly or skimmed, depending on personal interests. For example, the first section of General Motors' Test Track is a thrill ride, the second a collection of walk-through exhibits. Nearly all visitors take the ride, but many people, lacking time or interest, bypass the exhibits.

We have identified several Epcot attractions as "not to be missed." But part of the enjoyment of the park is that there's something for everyone. Ask your group. They're sure to have a variety of opinions as to which attraction is "best."

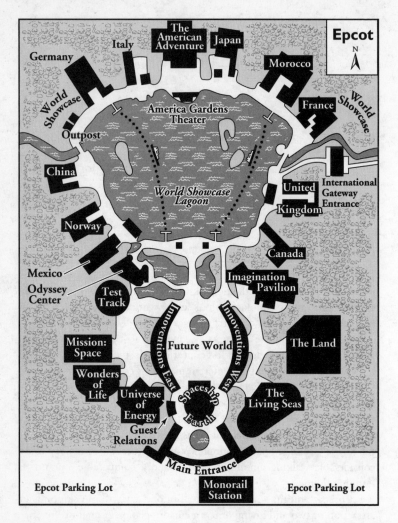

Operating Hours

Epcot has two theme areas: Future World and World Showcase. Each has its own operating hours. Though schedules change throughout the year, Future World always opens before World Showcase in the morning and usually closes before World Showcase in the evening. Most of the year, World Showcase opens two hours later than Future World. Moreover, some attractions open late or close early. For exact park hours during your visit, call (407) 824-4321. For the operating schedule of specific attractions, check the park handout map or the supplemental *Times Guide* available at no charge throughout the park.

Arriving

Plan to arrive at the turnstiles 30–40 minutes prior to official opening time. Give yourself an extra 10 minutes or so to park and make your way to the entrance.

If you are a guest at one of the Epcot resorts, it will take you about 20–30 minutes to walk from your hotel to the International Gateway (back entrance of Epcot) and from there to Future World section of the park. Instead of walking, you can catch a boat from your Epcot resort hotel to the International Gateway and then walk about eight minutes to the Future World section. To reach the front (Future World) entrance of Epcot from the Epcot resorts, either take a boat from your hotel to the MGM-Studios and transfer to an Epcot bus, take a bus to Downtown Disney and transfer to an Epcot bus, or best of all, take a cab.

If you wonder why all the fuss, this reader offers a succinct explanation:

Epcot touring plans don't work well if you stay at an Epcot resort. People from the Epcot resorts enter the park at the International Gateway, far away from Test Track [in Future World]. We were first in the park from the International Gateway, but when we got to Test Track the line was already 95 minutes long.

Arriving at the park by private automobile is easy and direct. Epcot has its own parking lot and, unlike at the Magic Kingdom, there's no need to take a monorail or ferry to reach the entrance. Trams serve the parking lot, or you can walk to the front gate. Monorail service connects Epcot with the Transportation and Ticket Center, the Magic Kingdom (transfer required), and Magic Kingdom resorts (transfer required).

NOT TO BE MISSED AT EPCOT

World Showcase	The American Adventure
	IllumiNations
Future World	Spaceship Earth
	Living with the Land
	Honey, I Shrunk the Audience
	Test Track
	Mission: Space
	Body Wars
	Soarin'
	Cranium Command

Getting Oriented

Epcot's theme areas are distinctly different. Future World examines where mankind has come from and where it's going. World Showcase features landmarks, cuisine, and culture of almost a dozen nations and is meant to be a sort of permanent World's Fair.

Navigating Epcot is unlike getting around at the Magic Kingdom. The Magic Kingdom is designed so that nearly every location is part of a specific environment—Liberty Square or Main Street, U.S.A., for example. All environments are visually separated to preserve the integrity of the theme. It wouldn't do for the Jungle Cruise to pass beneath the futuristic spires of Space Mountain, for instance.

Epcot, by contrast, is visually open. And while it seems strange to see a Japanese pagoda and the Eiffel Tower on the same horizon, getting around is fairly simple. An exception is Future World, where the enormous East and West Innoventions buildings hide everything on their opposite sides.

Cinderella Castle is the central landmark at the Magic Kingdom. At Epcot, the architectural symbol is Spaceship Earth. This shiny, 180-foot geosphere is visible from almost everywhere in the park. Like Cinderella Castle at the Magic Kingdom, Spaceship Earth can help you keep track of where you are in Epcot. But it's in a high-traffic area and isn't centrally located, so it isn't a good meeting place.

Any of the distinctive national pavilions in World Showcase make a good meeting place, but be specific. "Hey, let's meet in Japan!" sounds fun, but each pavilion is a mini-town with buildings, monuments, gardens, and plazas. You could wander quite awhile "in Japan" without finding your group. Pick a specific place in Japan—the sidewalk side of the pagoda, for example.

The EPCOT Acronym

"Epcot" originally was "EPCOT." When envisioned by Walt Disney as a utopian working city of the future, EPCOT was the acronym for Experimental Prototype Community of Tomorrow. Corporate Disney ultimately altered Walt's vision, and the city became a theme park, but the name remained. Because EPCOT, however, was clearly nothing of the sort, the acronym "EPCOT" became the name "Epcot."

Future World

Gleaming, futuristic structures of immense proportions define the first theme area beyond the main entrance. Broad thoroughfares are punctuated with billowing fountains—all reflected in shining, space-age facades. Everything, including landscaping, is sparkling clean and seems bigger than life. Front and center is Spaceship Earth, flanked by Innoventions East and West, while pavilions dedicated to mankind's past, present, and future technological accomplishments ring the perimeter of Future World.

Most Epcot services are concentrated in Future World's Entrance Plaza, near the main gate.

FUTURE WORLD SERVICES

Epcot's service facilities in Future World include:

Wheelchair and Stroller Rental	Inside the main entrance and to the left, toward the rear of the Entrance Plaza
Banking Services	ATMs are outside the main entrance near the kennels, on the Future World bridge, and in World Showcase at the Germany pavilion.
Storage Lockers	Turn right at Spaceship Earth (lockers are emptied nightly).
Lost and Found	At the main entrance at the gift shop
Live Entertainment and Parade Information	At Guest Relations, left of Spaceship Earth
Lost Persons	At Guest Relations and the Baby Center on the World Showcase side of the Odyssey Center
Dining Priority Seating	At Guest Relations
Disney World and Local Attraction Information	At Guest Relations
First Aid	Next to the Baby Center on the World Showcase side of the Odyssey Center
Baby Center/Baby-Care Needs	On the World Showcase side of the Odyssey Center

Guest Relations

Guest Relations, left of the geodesic sphere, is Epcot's equivalent of the Magic Kingdom's City Hall. It serves as park headquarters and as Epcot's primary information center. Attendants staff information booths and take same-day priority seating for Epcot restaurants. If you wish to eat in one of Epcot's sit-down restaurants, you can make your priority seating at Guest Relations.

Spaceship Earth

What It Is Educational dark ride through past, present, and future

Scope and Scale Headliner

When to Go Before 10 a.m. or after 4 p.m.

Special Comments If lines are long when you arrive, try again after 4 p.m.

Author's Rating One of Epcot's best; not to be missed; ★★★★

Appeal by Age Group

Preschool ★★★	Teens ★★★½	Over 30 ★★★★
Grade school ★★★★	Young Adults ★★★½	Seniors ★★★★

Duration of Ride About 16 minutes

Average Wait in Line per 100 People ahead of You 3 minutes

Loading Speed Fast

Description and Comments   This ride spirals through the 18-story interior of Epcot's premier landmark, taking visitors past audio-animatronic scenes depicting mankind's developments in communications, from cave painting to printing to television to space communications and computer networks. The ride is well done and an amazing use of the geosphere's interior.

Touring Tips   Because it's near Epcot's main entrance, Spaceship Earth is inundated with arriving guests throughout the morning. If you're interested in riding Test Track, postpone Spaceship Earth until, say, after 4 p.m. Spaceship Earth loads continuously and quickly. If the line runs only along the right side of the sphere, you'll board in less than 15 minutes.

A PEEK BEHIND THE SCENES WITH JIM HILL

When the Imagineers were building Spaceship Earth, they were told to cut corners wherever they could. So rather than sculpt all new faces for each of this attraction's figures, they just recycled some of the heads from the Magic Kingdom's *Hall of Presidents*. That sleeping monk in the monastery scene? Woodrow Wilson. The large bald slave in the Egyptian set? William Howard Taft.

Innoventions

What It Is   Static and hands-on exhibits relating to products and technologies of the near future

Scope and Scale   Major diversion

When to Go   On your second day at Epcot or after seeing all major attractions

Special Comments   Most exhibits demand time and participation to be rewarding; not much gained here by a quick walk-through

Author's Rating   Vastly improved; ★★★½

Appeal by Age Group

Preschool ★½	Teens ★★★	Over 30 ★★★
Grade school ★★★½	Young Adults ★★★½	Seniors ★★★

Description and Comments   Innoventions consists of two huge, crescent-shaped, glass-walled structures separated by a central plaza. Formerly known as CommuniCore, the complex was designed to be the communications and community hub of Epcot, but something was lost in execution. During Epcot's first 12 years, CommuniCore was, at best, a staid museum of science and industry and, at worst, a huge obstacle to circumnavigate when you wanted to cross from one side of Future World to the other.

In 1994, Disney set out to return it to the original concept, this time with a marketplace rather than communications orientation. The result is a huge, busy collection of industry-sponsored, walk-through, hands-on exhibits. Dynamic, interactive, and forward-looking, Innoventions resembles a high-tech trade show. Products preview consumer and industrial goods of the near future. Electronics, communications, and entertainment technology play a prominent role. Exhibits, many of which are changed each year, demonstrate such products as virtual-reality games, high-definition TV, voice-activated appliances, future cars, medical diagnostic equipment, and Internet applications. Each of the major exhibit areas is sponsored by a different manufacturer or research lab, emphasizing the effect of the products or technology on daily living. The most popular Innovations attraction is an arcade of video and simulator games. One of the coolest exhibits, however, is the demonstration area for the Segway Human Transporter, the much-publicized two-wheeled vehicle where riders look like they're standing on top of a push lawn mower. Guests cannot ride during the demonstrations but can sign up for a Segway driving class. The class costs $80 in addition to your Epcot admission and is offered daily. For reservations call (407) WDW-TOUR.

A welcome development at Innovations is the floorplan introduced recently. For the first time since Innovations debuted almost a decade ago, there's some logic to the layout. Where previously exhibits were jumbled together in truly bewildering juxtapositions with absolutely no regard to traffic flow, there is now a wide aisle, designed to look like a highway, that runs a nice, orderly route through the exhibits. There is even a printed roadmap to help you find and identify exhibits.

Exhibits change periodically, and there is a definite trend toward larger, more elaborate exhibits, almost mini-attractions. The newer exhibits are certainly more compelling, but they require waiting in line to be admitted. Because the theater at each exhibit is quite small, you often wait as long for an Innovations infomercial as for a real attraction elsewhere in the park.

Unofficial Guide reader response to Innovations is mixed. A family from Port Chester, New York, writes:

> The more unstructured "interactive" parts were incredibly noisy and confusing—rather like a crowded video arcade with games that didn't work very well. Crowd control was poor. The setup leads to pushing and shoving to get to control boards. My kids, being small girls, didn't stand a chance of getting near anything. The display portions of the attraction home of the future [House of Innovations], etc., most clearly resembled a trade show at the Javits Center or the fixture displays at Home Depot. This whole pavilion seemed far more commercial than magical.

We receive a lot of complaints about how difficult it is for children (and even adults) to get a turn on Innovations' more high-tech gadgets. This comment from a Michigan dad is typical:

> A warning about Innovations. All those wonderful [electronic] games are there, if you can fight off all the pubescent Sega-geeks. And they're free [the games, that is].

A father of three from Tulsa, Oklahoma, however, liked Innovations:

> The best things at Epcot for my kids were the hands-on exhibits at Innovations. We bumped into the computer games there as we were passing through en route to something else (I don't remember what, because we never got there).

A mom from Bartlesville, Oklahoma, adds:

> My 14-year-old son's favorite attraction was Innovations. He spent hours there and would have spent more if we'd let him. All those free games were a teenage boy's idea of heaven.

Touring Tips Innovations East and West provide visitors an opportunity to preview products of tomorrow in a fun, hands-on manner. Some exhibits are intriguing, while others are less compelling. We observed a wide range of reactions by visitors to the exhibits and can suggest only that you form your own opinion. Regarding touring strategy, spend time at Innovations on your second day at Epcot. If you have only one day, visit later in the day if you have the time and endurance. Many exhibits, however, are technical and may not be compatible with your mood or energy toward the end of a long day. Also, you can't get much out of a walk-through; you have to invest time to understand what's going on.

The Igloo

Attached to (or growing from) the fountain side of Innoventions West is a tacky, besmirched, white igloo called Ice Station Cool. It doesn't look like much, but inside, this Coca Cola–sponsored exhibit provides free unlimited samples of soft drinks from around the world. Some of the selections will taste like medicine to an American, but others will please. Because it's centrally located in Future World, it makes a good meeting or break place, and you can slake your thirst while you wait for the rest of your party to arrive.

A PEEK BEHIND THE SCENES WITH JIM HILL

Beware the Beverly! If you're touring with any practical jokers, they may try to trick you into tasting Beverly, the Italian version of Coca Cola. Our advice is… DON'T DO IT! Beverly is so bitter tasting that many Epcot visitors, rather than swallowing, just spit it out on the ground. If this is really Italy's best-selling soft drink, one wonders what the second bestseller tastes like…

The Living Seas

What It Is A huge saltwater aquarium, plus exhibits on oceanography, ocean ecology, and sea life

Scope and Scale Major attraction

When to Go Before 11:30 a.m. or after 5 p.m.

Author's Rating An excellent marine exhibit; ★★★½

Appeal by Age Group

Preschool ★★★	Teens ★★★	Over 30 ★★★
Grade school ★★★	Young Adults ★★★	Seniors ★★★★

Average Wait in Line per 100 People ahead of You 3½ minutes

Loading Speed Fast

Description and Comments The Living Seas is among Future World's most ambitious offerings. Scientists and divers conduct actual marine experiments in a 200-foot-diameter, 27-foot-deep main tank containing fish, mammals, and crustaceans in a simulation of an ocean ecosystem. Visitors can watch the activity through eight-inch-thick windows below the surface (including some in the Coral Reef restaurant). A two-part adventure consisting of a movie dramatizing the link between the ocean and man's survival and a simulated elevator descent to the bottom of the tank set you up for the underwater viewing.

The Living Seas' fish population is substantial, but the strength of this attraction lies in the dozen or so exhibits offered afterward. Visitors can view fish-breeding experiments, watch short films about sea life, and more. A delightful exhibit showcases clownfish (Nemo), regal blue tang (Dory), and other species featured in *Finding Nemo*. Other highlights include a haunting, hypnotic jellyfish tank, a seahorse aquarium, a stingray petting pool (really!), and a manatee tank.

About two-thirds of the main aquarium is home to reef species, including sharks, rays, and a number of fish that you've seen in quiet repose on your dinner plate. The other third, separated by an inconspicuous divider, houses bottle-nose dolphins and sea turtles. As you face the main aquarium, the most glare-free viewing windows for the dolphins are on the ground floor to the left by the escalators. For the reef species, it's the same floor on the right by the escalators. Stay as long as you wish.

The Living Seas is a high-quality marine/aquarium exhibit, but it's no substitute for SeaWorld, an outstanding marine theme park in Orlando. SeaWorld is on a par with the Disney theme parks in scope, quality, educational value, and entertainment.

Touring Tips   You are given the option when you enter to see the movie first or proceed directly to the marine exhibits. If you've not seen the movie, do so—it's short and very well done. If you're a Living Seas veteran, head straight for the exhibits. The exhibits are the best part of The Living Seas. In the morning, they're often bypassed by guests rushing to stay ahead of the crowd. The Living Seas needs to be lingered over when you aren't in a hurry. Go in late afternoon or evening, or on your second day at Epcot.

A PEEK BEHIND THE SCENES WITH JIM HILL

Thou Shalt Have No Strange God
According to Disney's initial plans for this Future World pavilion, the host for the first half of the attraction would have been Poseidon, the Greek God of the Sea. But then the Living Seas first sponsor, United Technologies, got nervous about offending certain Christian guests and gave Poseidon the flush.

The Land Pavilion

Description and Comments   The Land is a huge pavilion containing three attractions and several restaurants. The original emphasis was on farming, but it now focuses on environmental concerns.

Touring Tips   This is a good place for a fast-food lunch. If you're there to see the attractions, however, don't go during mealtimes.

Living with the Land (FASTPASS)

What It Is   Indoor boat-ride adventure through the past, present, and future of U.S. farming and agriculture

Scope and Scale   Major attraction

When to Go   Before 10:30 a.m., after 5 p.m., or use FASTPASS

Special Comments   Take the ride early in the morning, but save other Land attractions for later in the day. It's located on the pavilion's lower level.

Author's Rating   Interesting and fun; not to be missed; ★★★★

Appeal by Age Group

Preschool ★★½	Teens ★★★½	Over 30 ★★★★
Grade school ★★★	Young Adults ★★★★	Seniors ★★★★

Duration of Ride   About 12 minutes

Average Wait in Line per 100 People ahead of You   3 minutes

Assumes   15 boats operating

Loading Speed   Moderate

Description and Comments   Boat ride takes visitors through swamps, past inhospitable farm environments, and through a futuristic, innovative greenhouse where real crops are grown using the latest agricultural technologies. Inspiring and educational, with excellent effects and good narrative.

Many Epcot guests who read about Living with the Land in guidebooks decide it sounds too dry and educational for their tastes. A woman from Houston, Texas, writes:

> I had a bad attitude about Living with the Land, as I heard it was an agricultural exhibit. I just didn't think I was up for a movie about wheat farming. Wow, was I surprised. I really wished I had not had a preconceived idea about an exhibit. Living with the Land was truly wonderful.

Touring Tips   See this attraction before the lunch crowd hits The Land restaurants, or use FASTPASS. If you really enjoy this ride or have a special interest in the agricultural techniques demonstrated, take the Behind the Seeds Greenhouse Tour. It's a one-hour guided walk behind the scenes for an in-depth examination of advanced and experimental growing methods. It costs $8 for adults and $6 for children ages three to nine. Reservations are made on a space-available basis at the guided tour waiting area (far right of the restaurants on the lower level). *Note:* The tour will be suspended during certain phases of construction for the new attraction, Soarin'.

A PEEK BEHIND THE SCENES WITH JIM HILL

Cut 'Em Out, Put 'Em In, RawHiiiiiiiiddddeeee!!!!
See those mechanical buffalo and prairie dogs in the American desert sequence? They were actually created for Western River Expedition, an elaborate Pirates of the Caribbean–like attraction planned for the Magic Kingdom. The attraction was cancelled at the last minute, and the critters sat in storage for several years before being rounded up and recycled for use in The Land's boat ride.

Soarin' (FASTPASS) Opens 2005

What It Is   Flight simulation ride

Scope and Scale   Super headliner

When to Go   First 30 minutes the park is open or use FASTPASS

Special Comments   Entrance on the lower level of The Land pavilion. May induce motion sickness; 40" minimum-height requirement; switching off available (see pages 266–268).

Author's Rating   Exciting and mellow at the same time; ★★★★½ (rating based on similar attraction at Disney's California Adventure theme park). Not to be missed.

Appeal by Age Group (rating based on similar attraction at Disney's California Adventure theme park).

Preschool —	Teens ★★★★½	Over 30 ★★★★★
Grade school ★★★★★	Young Adults ★★★★★	Seniors ★★★★

Duration of Ride   4½ minutes

Loading Speed   Moderate

Description and Comments   Soarin' is a thrill ride for all ages, exhilarating as a hank on the wing and as mellow as swinging in a hammock. If you are fortunate enough to have experienced "flying dreams" in your sleep, you'll have a sense of how Soarin' feels.

Once you enter the main theater, you are secured in a seat not unlike those on inverted roller coasters (where the coaster is suspended from above). Once everyone is in place, the floor drops away and you are suspended with your legs dangling. Thus hung out to dry, you embark on a hang-glider tour with IMAX quality images projected all around you, and with the flight simulator moving in sync with the movie. The IMAX images are well chosen and drop-dead beautiful. Special effects include wind, sound, and even olfactory stimulation. The ride itself is thrilling but perfectly smooth. We think Soarin' is a must see for guests of any age who meet the height requirement. And yes, seniors we interviewed (in California) were crazy about it.

Touring Tips Soarin' joins Test Track and Mission: Space as an Epcot Super Headliner attraction. Its addition to the Epcot lineup will undoubtedly boost attendance, but also take some of the pressure off the park's other two big attractions. Keep in mind, however, that Test Track and Mission: Space serve up a little too much thrill for some guests. Soarin', conversely, is an almost platonic ride for any age. Expressed differently, guests of all ages will want to ride. For that reason, and because it's new, we predict it will rise quickly to the top of the hit parade. Our advice: see it first thing or use FASTPASS. If you opt for the latter, don't expect there to be any left after 12:30 p.m. or so. Another strategy, if your group doesn't mind splitting up, is to use the singles line.

A PEEK BEHIND THE SCENES WITH JIM HILL

Though this new Future World attraction won't begin entertaining WDW guests until 2005, plans are reportedly already underway to scrap Soarin's IMAX film, originally created for Disney's California Adventure theme park. The replacement version, which is supposedly slated to debut in the fall of 2007 for Epcot's 25th anniversary, will reportedly feature scenery from all over the world.

Circle of Life Theater

What It Is Film exploring man's relationship with his environment

Scope and Scale Minor attraction

When to Go Before 11 a.m. or after 2 p.m.

Author's Rating Highly interesting and enlightening; ★★★½

Appeal by Age Group

Preschool ★★½	Teens ★★½	Over 30 ★★★
Grade school ★★★	Young Adults ★★★	Seniors ★★★

Duration of Presentation About 12½ minutes

Preshow Entertainment None

Probable Waiting Time 10–15 minutes

Description and Comments The featured attraction is The *Circle of Life*, starring Simba, Timon, and Pumbaa from Disney's animated feature *The Lion King*. This playful yet educational film spotlights the environmental interdependency of all creatures on earth, demonstrating how easily the ecological balance can be upset. The message is sobering, but one that enlightens.

Touring Tips Every visitor should see this film. To stay ahead of the crowd, see it in late afternoon. Long lines usually occur at mealtimes.

Imagination Pavilion

Description and Comments Multi-attraction pavilion on the west side of Innoventions West and down the walk from The Land. Outside is an "upside-down waterfall" and one of our favorite Future World landmarks, the "jumping water," a fountain that hops over the heads of unsuspecting passersby.

Touring Tips We recommend early-morning or late-evening touring. See the individual attractions for specifics.

Journey into Imagination with Figment

What It Is Dark fantasy-adventure ride

Scope and Scale Major attraction wannabe

When to Go Before 11:30 a.m. or after 5 p.m.

Author's Rating ★★½

Appeal by Age Group

Preschool ★★	Teens ★★	Over 30 ★★★
Grade school ★★	Young Adults ★★★	Seniors ★★★

Duration of Ride About 6 minutes

Average Wait in Line per 100 People ahead of You 2 minutes

Loading Speed Fast

Description and Comments This attraction replaced its dull and vacuous predecessor in the fall of 1999 and was retooled again in 2002 to add the ever-popular purple dragon, Figment. Drawing on the Imagination Institute theme from *Honey, I Shrunk the Audience* (in the same pavilion), the attraction takes you on a tour of the zany Institute. Sometimes you're a passive observer and sometimes you're a test subject as the ride provides a glimpse of the fictitious lab's inner workings. Stimulating all of your senses and then some, you are hit with optical illusions, an experiment where noise generates colors, a room that defies gravity, and other brain teasers. All along the way, Figment makes surprise appearances. After the ride, you can adjourn to an interactive exhibit area offering the latest in unique, hands-on imagery technology. One of the coolest interactive exhibits is a photo-morphing computer. First the machine takes your picture, then you select an image from several categories into which your photo is integrated. The final result can be e-mailed on the spot to family and friends. Best of all, there's no charge. We sent a number of photos where our faces were morphed into pandas, lions, lizards, and birds. I was a great owl!

   Although Journey into Imagination with Figment is certainly better than the ride it replaced, it pales in comparison to *Honey, I Shrunk the Audience*, the hilarious 3-D film that occupies the other half of the Imagination Pavilion. Pleasant rather than stimulating, the ride falls short of the promise suggested by its name, though each reincarnation has added a little zip. Will you go to sleep? No. Will you find it amusing? Probably. Will you remember it tomorrow? Only Figment.

Touring Tips The standby wait for this attraction rarely exceeds 15 minutes. You can enjoy the interactive exhibit without taking the ride, so save it for later in the day.

Honey, I Shrunk the Audience (FASTPASS)

What It Is 3-D film with special effects

Scope and Scale Headliner

When to Go Before 11:30 a.m., after 6 p.m., or use FASTPASS

Special Comments Adults should not be put off by the sci-fi theme. The loud, intense show with tactile effects frightens some young children.

Author's Rating An absolute hoot! Not to be missed; ★★★★½

Appeal by Age Group

Preschool ★★★½	Teens ★★★★½	Over 30 ★★★★½
Grade school ★★★★½	Young Adults ★★★★½	Seniors ★★★★

Duration of Presentation About 17 minutes

Preshow Entertainment 8 minutes

Probable Waiting Time 12 minutes (at suggested times)

Description and Comments   *Honey, I Shrunk the Audience* is a 3-D offshoot of Disney's feature film, *Honey, I Shrunk the Kids. Honey, I Shrunk the Audience* features an array of special effects, including simulated explosions, smoke, fiber optics, lights, water spray, and moving seats. This attraction is played strictly for laughs, a commodity in short supply in Epcot entertainment.

Touring Tips   The sound level is earsplitting, frightening some young children. Many adults report that the loud soundtrack is distracting, even uncomfortable. While *Honey, I Shrunk the Audience* is a huge hit, it overwhelms some preschoolers. A dad from Lexington, South Carolina, writes:

Honey, I Shrunk the Audience *is too intense for kids. Our four-year-old took off his [3-D] glasses five minutes into the movie. Because of this experience, he would not wear glasses in the Muppet movie at MGM.*

A Tucson, Arizona, mom tells of a similar reaction:

Our three- and four-year-olds loved all the rides. They giggled through Thunder Mountain three times, squealed with delight on Splash Mountain, thought Space Mountain was the coolest, and begged to ride Star Tours over and over. They even "fought ghosts" at the Haunted Mansion. But Honey, I Shrunk the Audience *dissolved them into sobbing, sniveling, shaking, terrified preschoolers.*

Though launched with little fanfare, *Honey, I Shrunk the Audience* has become one of Epcot's most popular attractions. Try to work it into your touring before 10:30 a.m. The show is located to the left of the Journey into Imagination ride; it isn't necessary to ride in order to enter the theater. If the wait is prohibitive (very rare), use FASTPASS. Avoid seats in the first several rows; if you're too close to the screen, the 3-D images don't focus properly.

Test Track

Description and Comments   Test Track, presented by General Motors, contains the Test Track ride and TransCenter, a collection of transportation-themed stationary exhibits and mini-theater productions. The pavilion is the last on the left before crossing into the World Showcase.

Many readers tell us that Test Track "is one big commercial" for General Motors. We agree that promotional hype is more heavy-handed here than in most other business-sponsored attractions. But Test Track is one of the most creatively conceived and executed attractions in Walt Disney World.

Test Track Ride (FASTPASS)

What It Is Automobile test-track simulator ride

Scope and Scale Super headliner

When to Go First 30 minutes the park is open, just before closing, or use FASTPASS

Special Comments 40" height minimum

Author's Rating Not to be missed; ★★★½

Appeal by Age Group

Preschool ★★★★	Teens ★★★★	Over 30 ★★★★
Grade school ★★★★	Young Adults ★★★★	Seniors ★★★★

Duration of Ride About 4 minutes

Average Wait in Line per 100 People ahead of You 4½ minutes

Loading Speed Moderate to fast

Description and Comments Visitors test a future-model car at high speeds through hairpin turns, up and down steep hills, and over rough terrain. The six-guest vehicle is a motion simulator that rocks and pitches. Unlike simulators at Star Tours, Body Wars, and Back to the Future (at Universal Studios), however, the Test Track model is affixed to a track and actually travels.

Though reader comments on Test Track have been mixed, most like it. A Shippensburg, Pennsylvania, couple, for example, gave Test Track two thumbs up:

We did wait about 30 minutes for Test Track and it was worth it! At first we thought it was a bit of a bust, as the beginning of the ride is not very exciting (though it was interesting), but the last minute or so made up for it! It was wonderful!

A Westford, Massachusetts, family agrees:

Test Track was the favorite ride at WDW of all five members of our party. Even my mom (56), who has always refused to go on roller coasters, was coaxed onto Test Track and loved it. Five stars from one preschooler, three over-thirties, and a senior citizen!

But a Monona, Wisconsin, couple were somewhat underwhelmed:

In regard to Test Track, while it was a good ride, it was overrated; or perhaps it just wasn't what I expected. Based on the loud whoosh coming from the ride, the build-up in the preshow area, and your comments, I expected a much more intense experience. As it turned out, it just wasn't all that scary. Compared to the Tower of Terror, Test Track is a Sunday drive in the park.

Touring Tips Some great technology is at work here. Test Track is so complex, in fact, that keeping it running is a constant challenge. When it's working properly, it's one of the park's better attractions. As a Waban, Massachusetts, mother reports, however, it's not always running:

Test Track was the toughest ride to ride. Either it was broken or the lines were one-and-a-half to two hours long.

A Bluemont, Virginia, man put it succinctly:

GM's and Disney's *inability to keep this ride running consistently is no great advertisement for GM products.*

Another reader developed a love-hate relationship with the attraction:

Best ride in WDW. The finale when your open car speeds around the track [is] extremely exhilarating. Unfortunately, getting to the finale can be as frustrating as sitting in snarled rush hour traffic on I-4. Both times we rode Test Track broke down in the middle of our ride.

If you use FASTPASS, be aware that the daily allocation of passes is often distributed by 12:30 or 1 p.m. If all the FASTPASSes are gone, another time-saving technique is to join the singles line. A singles line, thus far only available at Test Track and Mission: Space (and Soarin'—opens 2005), is a separate line for individuals who are alone or who do not object to riding alone. The objective of the singles line is to fill the odd spaces left by groups that don't fill up the ride vehicle. Because there are not many singles, and because most groups are unwilling to split up, singles lines are usually much shorter than the regular line and can save you a bunch of time if you don't mind riding by yourself.

A PEEK BEHIND THE SCENES WITH JIM HILL

Burning Rubber During its first few months of operation, the vehicles in Test Track were taking such a pounding that Disney had to replace all four of each cars' tires every week. Finally weary of spending so much time (and money) replacing tires, Disney turned to GM, who then created a special new tougher type of tire. Disney only has to replace these once every month now.

Wonders of Life Pavilion (Open Seasonally)

Description and Comments   This multifaceted pavilion deals with the human body, health, and medicine. Housed in a 100,000-square-foot, gold-domed structure, Wonders of Life focuses on the capabilities of the human body and the importance of keeping fit.

Body Wars

Motion Sickness

WARNING!

What It Is   Flight-simulator ride through the human body

Scope and Scale   Headliner

When to Go   Before 10:45 a.m. or after 5 p.m.

Special Comments   Not recommended for pregnant women or people prone to motion sickness; 40" height minimum

Author's Rating   Anatomy made fun; not to be missed; ★★★★

Appeal by Age Group

Preschool ★★★	Teens ★★★★	Over 30 ★★★½
Grade school ★★★★	Young Adults ★★★★	Seniors ★★½

Duration of Ride   5 minutes

Average Wait in Line per 100 People ahead of You   4 minutes

Assumes   All simulators operating

Loading Speed Moderate to fast

Description and Comments This thrill ride through the human body was developed along the lines of Disney-MGM Studios' Star Tours space-simulation ride. The story is that you're a passenger in a miniature capsule injected into a human body to pick up a scientist who has been inspecting a splinter in the patient's finger. The scientist, however, is sucked into the circulatory system, and you hurtle through the body to rescue her. The simulator creates a visually graphic experience as it seems to career at fantastic speeds through human organs. The story is more than a little silly, but we nevertheless rate Body Wars as "not to be missed."

Touring Tips Once one of Epcot's premier attractions, Body Wars no longer draws large crowds on a regular basis. Be aware that Body Wars makes a lot of people motion sick; it isn't unusual for a simulator to be taken off-line for attendants to clean up a previous rider's mess. If you're at all susceptible to motion sickness, reconsider riding. If you're on Body Wars and become nauseated, fix your gaze on something other than the screen and as far away as possible (the ceiling or side and back walls). Without the visual effects, the ride isn't rough enough to disturb most guests. If you get queasy, rest rooms are nearby as you get off the ride. Star Tours is just as wild but makes very few people sick. Successfully riding Star Tours doesn't necessarily mean you'll tolerate Body Wars. Conversely, if Body Wars makes you ill, you can't assume that Star Tours will, too.

Reader comments on Body Wars cover the spectrum. These are typical:

The only thing we won't do on this next trip is go on Body Wars in Epcot. The line is so deceptive. We waited almost two hours and then it was only to get motion sickness and feel awful!

and:

Body Wars did not measure up to all the hype and warnings. We expected Space Mountain with visual effects, and it wasn't even close. You weenies!

and:

The ride felt more like the involuntary movements of a hammock.

and finally:

Body Wars at Epcot was great fun. We rode it twice and loved it. A little scary, but exciting. Some of the other things seemed kind of boring after our ride here.

Motion sickness aside, Body Wars is intense—too intense for some, especially preschoolers and seniors. One elderly gentleman confided, "Feeling sick to my stomach took my mind off being terrified."

A PEEK BEHIND THE SCENES WITH JIM HILL

The Way to a Man's Heart Is Through His Stomach; The Way to a Man's Stomach Is Through His Lungs
As you're riding "Body Wars," watch for the abrupt film cut that's made during the trip-through-the-lungs sequence. Why did "Body Wars" director Leonard Nimoy (Yes, THAT Leonard Nimoy) decide to shorten this particular scene? Because the back-and-forth movement of the ride vehicle as it went through the lungs was fomenting a major insurrection in riders' tummies. Once surgery was performed on this sequence, peace (or a semblance thereof) prevailed in the abdominal realm.

Cranium Command

What It Is Audio-animatronic theater show about the brain

Scope and Scale Major attraction

When to Go Before 11 a.m. or after 3 p.m.

Author's Rating Funny, outrageous, and educational; not to be missed; ★★★★½

Appeal by Age Group

Preschool ★★	Teens ★★★★	Over 30 ★★★★½
Grade school ★★★★	Young Adults ★★★★½	Seniors ★★★★½

Duration of Presentation About 20 minutes

Preshow Entertainment Explanatory lead-in to feature presentation

Probable Waiting Time Less than 10 minutes at times suggested

Description and Comments   *Cranium Command* is Epcot's great sleeper attraction. Stuck on the backside of the Wonders of Life pavilion and far less promoted than Body Wars, this humorous Epcot offering is bypassed by many guests. Characters called "Brain Pilots" are trained to operate human brains. The show consists of a day in the life of one of these *Cranium Command*ers as he tries to pilot the brain of an adolescent boy. Epcot and Walt Disney World could use a lot more of this type of humor.

Touring Tips   To understand the program, you need to see the pre-show cartoon. If you arrive in the waiting area while it's in progress, be sure you see enough to get a sense of the story before you enter the theater. While most preschoolers enjoy *Cranium Command,* many don't really understand it.

A PEEK BEHIND THE SCENES WITH JIM HILL

The Making of a Winner
Disney was so impressed with the job that then-fledgling animation directors Kirk Wise and Gary Trousdale did with Cranium Command's pre-show cartoon that they were offered a chance to direct the 1991 hit, *Beauty and the Beast,* the first animated film ever nominated for a "Best Picture" Academy Award.

The Making of Me

What It Iss Humorous movie about human conception and birth

Scope and Scale Minor attraction

When to Go Early in the morning or after 4:30 p.m.

Author's Rating Sanitized sex education; ★★★

Appeal by Age Group

Preschool ★½	Teens ★★½	Over 30 ★★★
Grade school ★★★½	Young Adults ★★★	Seniors ★★★

Duration of Presentation 14 minutes

Preshow Entertainment None

Probable Waiting Time 25 minutes or more, unless you go at suggested times

Description and Comments   This lighthearted and very sensitive movie about human conception, gestation, and birth was considered a controversial addition to

Wonders of Life, but most viewers agree it's tasteful and creative. The plot's main character goes back in time to watch his parents date, fall in love, marry, and, yes, conceive and give birth to him.

Sexual material is well handled, with emphasis on loving relationships, not plumbing. Parents of children younger than age seven tell us the sexual information went over their children's heads for the most part. In older children, however, the film precipitates questions. You be the judge.

A father of two from Connecticut weighed in with this opinion:

> [The Making of Me *is*] *very well done ... but I find it an odd juxtaposition. How many people decide a vacation at Disney World is the time to explain this stuff? Show this in Health Class.*

A gentleman from Cheshire, England, who believes (correctly, in our view) that Americans are sexually repressed, writes:

> *By the standards of sex education programmes shown to English children of ages eight to nine, The Making of Me seemed almost Mary Poppinsish in tone. Certainly other Brits found your warnings over content quite puzzling.*

This reader would have a great time in our hometown (Birmingham, Alabama), where some of the local clergy harangued the city council for months to have Bermuda shorts welded onto the bare buttocks of a large statue depicting Vulcan at his forge.

Touring Tips   *The Making of Me* is excellent and should be moved from its tiny space to a larger theater. Of course, we've been saying that for years.

Mission: Space (FASTPASS)

Motion Sickness

WARNING!

What It Is   Space flight simulation ride

Scope and Scale   Super headliner

When to Go   First 30 minutes the park is open, or use FASTPASS

Special Comments   Not recommended for pregnant women or people prone to motion sickness; 44" minimum-height requirement

Author's Rating   Impressive; ★★★★

Appeal by Age Group

Preschool —	Teens ★★★★½	Over 30 ★★★★
Grade school ★★★★½	Young Adults ★★★★½	Seniors ★★★½

Duration of Ride   About 5 minutes plus pre-show

Average Wait in Line per 100 People ahead of You   4 minutes

Description and Comments   Mission: Space, among other things, is Disney's reply to all the cutting-edge attractions introduced over the past several years by cross-town rival, Universal. The first truly groundbreaking Disney attraction since the Tower of Terror, Mission: Space is one of the hottest tickets at Walt Disney World.

Guests enter the NASA Mission: Space Training Center where they are first introduced to the Mission: Space deep-space exploration program and then divided into groups for introductory space-flight training. After flight orientation, they are strapped into a space capsule for a simulated flight, where, of course, the unexpected happens. Interactive computer controls aboard the capsule allow guests carry out routine flight tasks and to respond to the emergency. The capsules are small and the ride amazingly realistic. Each capsule accommodates a crew consisting of group commander, pilot, navigator, and engineer, with a guest functioning in each role. In contrast to the pre-opening hype, the crew's skill and finesse (or more often, lack thereof) in handling their respective responsibilities have no effect on the outcome of the flight. The queuing area and pre-show are pretty dazzling. En route to the main event guests pass space hardware, astronaut tributes and memorials, a cutaway of a huge spacewheel showing crew working and living compartments, and a manned Mission Control where cast members actually operate the attraction.

The post-show area features an electronic game called Mission: Space Race that almost three-dozen guests, divided into two teams, can play at once. The winning team beats the other team's spaceship back from Mars to the home base. Individuals on each team are responsible for certain tasks essential to the mission and make their ship fly faster by hitting correct keyboard buttons. Making the game even more unique is that folks at home can play in real time by logging onto **www.disneyspacerace.com.**

Touring Tips Having experienced Mission: Space under a variety of circumstances, we always felt icky when riding on an empty stomach, especially first thing in the morning. We came up with a number of potential explanations for this phenomenon, involving everything from low blood sugar and inner-ear disorders to some of us just not being astronaut material. Understandably disturbed by the latter possibility, we looked around for an expert opinion to explain what we were feeling.

The number of organizations with experience studying the effects of high-gravity ("high-g") forces on humans is limited to a select few: NASA, the Air Force, and Mad Tea Party castmembers were the first to come to mind. As NASA is a co-developer of Mission: Space, we called them. Amazingly, the NASA spokesman said NASA no longer does much high-g training these days. And NASA was reluctant to pass along anything resembling medical advice to the general public.

Fortunately, a longtime friend put us in touch with a real NASA astronaut who was willing to share (anonymously) some ideas on what causes the nausea, as well as tips astronauts use to prevent it. Our astronaut guesses, like us, that low blood sugar is the culprit behind the queasiness, and suggests eating a normal meal one to two hours prior to experiencing the ride. Try to avoid milk and tomatoes beforehand; they're difficult to keep down and, as our contact noted with the voice of experience, particularly unpleasant if they resurrect. A banana, we hear, is a good choice for your pre-flight meal. Also, we were told, one trick astronauts use to avoid sickness while in these simulators is to keep a piece of hard candy or a mint in their mouth. It's not clear whether the candy helps keep blood sugar levels high, or is just a placebo.

Be sure to make a rest-room stop before you get in line; you'll feel like your bladder has been to Mars and back for real before you get out of this attraction. In addition to a FASTPASS return line, there is a singles line to expedite traffic flow and loading (yeah!). By our calculations, Mission: Space should be able to handle about 1,600 guests per hour if it is operating at capacity with no breakdowns. This is respectable, but not a huge, number for an attraction of its scope and popularity, so expect long waits unless you ride immediately after the park opens or use FASTPASS. If you intend to use FAST-PASS, assume that all the FASTPASSes for the day will be distributed by about noon.

Universe of Energy: Ellen's Energy Adventure

What It Is Combination ride/theater presentation about energy

Scope and Scale Major attraction

When to Go Before 11:15 a.m. or after 4:30 p.m.

Special Comments Don't be dismayed by long lines; 580 people enter the pavilion each time the theater changes audiences

Author's Rating The most unique theater in Walt Disney World; ★★★★

Appeal by Age Group

Preschool ★★★	Teens ★★★½	Over 30 ★★★★
Grade school ★★★★	Young Adults ★★★★	Seniors ★★★★

Duration of Presentation About 26½ minutes

Preshow Entertainment 8 minutes

Probable Waiting Time 20–40 minutes

Description and Comments   Audio-animatronic dinosaurs and the unique traveling theater make this Exxon pavilion one of Future World's most popular. Because this is a theater with a ride component, the line doesn't move while the show is in progress. When the theater empties, however, a large chunk of the line will disappear as people are admitted for the next show. Visitors are seated in what appears to be an ordinary theater while they watch a film about energy sources. Then the theater seats divide into six 97-passenger traveling cars that glide among the swamps and reptiles of a prehistoric forest. Special effects include the feel of warm, moist air from the swamp, and the smell of sulphur from an erupting volcano.

The accompanying film is a humorous and upbeat flick starring Ellen DeGeneres and Bill Nye that sugarcoats the somewhat ponderous discussion of energy. For kids, Universe of Energy remains a toss-up. The dinosaurs frighten some preschoolers, and kids of all ages lose the thread during the educational segments.

Touring Tips   This attraction draws large crowds beginning early in the morning. Because Universe of Energy can operate more than one show at a time, lines are generally tolerable. If you decide to skip the show, at least check out the great dinosaur topiaries outside the pavilion.

The "Mom, I Can't Believe It's Disney!" Fountain

What It Is Combination fountain and shower

When to Go When it's hot

Scope and Scale Diversion

Special Comments Secretly installed by Martians during *IllumiNations*

Author's Rating Yes!! ★★★★

Appeal by Age Group

Preschool ★★★★★	Teens ★★★★	Over 30 ★★★★
Grade school ★★★★★	Young Adults ★★★★	Seniors ★★★★★

Duration of Experience Indefinite

Probable Waiting Time None

Description and Comments   This simple fountain on the walkway linking Future World to World Showcase isn't much to look at, but it offers a truly spontaneous experience—rare in Walt Disney World, where everything is controlled, from the snow peas in your stir fry to how frequently the crocodile yawns in the Jungle Cruise.

Spouts of water erupt randomly from the sidewalk. You can frolic in the water or let it cascade down on you or blow up your britches. On a broiling Florida day, when you think you might suddenly combust, fling yourself into the fountain and do decidedly un-Disney things. Dance, skip, sing, jump, splash, cavort, roll around, stick your toes down the spouts, or catch the water in your mouth as it descends. You can do all of this with your clothes on or, depending on your age, with your clothes off. It's hard to imagine so much personal freedom at Disney World and almost unthinkable to contemplate soggy people slogging and squishing around the park, but there you have it. Hurrah!

Touring Tips We don't know if the fountain's creator has been drummed out of the corps by the Disney Tribunal of People-Who-Sit-on-Sticks [probably], but we're grateful for his courage in introducing one thing that's not super-controlled. We do know your kids will be right in the middle of this thing before your brain sounds the alert. Our advice: Pack a pair of dry shorts and turn the kids loose. You might even want to bring a spare pair for yourself. Or maybe not—so much advance planning would stifle the spontaneity.

World Showcase

World Showcase, Epcot's second theme area, is an ongoing World's Fair encircling a picturesque 40-acre lagoon. The cuisine, culture, history, and architecture of almost a dozen countries are permanently displayed in individual national pavilions spaced along a 1.2-mile promenade. Pavilions replicate familiar landmarks and present representative street scenes from the host countries.

World Showcase features some of the most lovely gardens in the United States. Located in Germany, France, England, Canada, and to a lesser extent, China, they are sometimes tucked away and out of sight of pedestrian traffic on the World Showcase promenade. They are best appreciated during daylight hours, as a Clio, Michigan, woman explains:

Make sure to visit the World Showcase in the daylight in order to view the beautiful gardens. We were sorry that we did not do this because we were following the guide and riding the rides that we could have done later in the dark.

Most adults enjoy World Showcase, but many children find it boring. To make it more interesting to children, most Epcot retail shops sell Passport Kits for about $10. Each kit contains a blank passport and stamps for every World Showcase country. As kids accompany their folks to each country, they tear out the appropriate stamp and stick it in the passport. The kit also contains basic information on the nations and a Mickey Mouse button. Disney has built a lot of profit into this little product, but I guess that isn't the issue. More importantly, parents, including this dad from Birmingham, Alabama, tell us the Passport Kit helps get the kids through World Showcase with a minimum of impatience, whining, and tantrums.

Adding stamps from the Epcot countries was the only way I was able to see all the displays with cheerful children.

Incidentally, if you do not want to spring for the Passport Kit, the Disney folks will be happy to stamp an autograph book or just about anything else (we saw one four-year-old with a stamp from France right in the middle of his forehead).

Children also enjoy "Kidcot Fun Stops," a program designed to make World Showcase more interesting for the 5–12 crowd. So simple and uncomplicated that you can't believe Disney thought it up, the Fun Stops usually are nothing more than a large table on the sidewalk at each pavilion.

Each table is staffed by a Disney cast member who stamps passports and supervises children in modest craft projects relating to the host country. Reports from parents about the Fun Stops have been uniformly positive.

The World Showcase offers some of the most diverse and interesting shopping at Walt Disney World. Unique shops and merchandise are covered in detail in Part Sixteen, Shopping in and out of Walt Disney World (page 683).

Boats ferry the foot-sore and the weary across the lagoon, although it's almost always less time to walk.

Moving clockwise around the promenade, here are the nations represented and their attractions.

Mexico Pavilion

Description and Comments Pre-Columbian pyramids dominate the architecture of this exhibit. One forms the pavilion's facade, and the other overlooks the restaurant and plaza alongside the boat ride, El Río del Tiempo, inside the pavilion.

Touring Tips Romantic and exciting testimony to Mexico's charms, the pyramids contain a large number of authentic and valuable artifacts. Many people zip past these treasures without stopping to look. The village scene inside the pavilion is beautiful and exquisitely detailed.

El Río del Tiempo

What It Is Indoor scenic boat ride

Scope and Scale Minor attraction

When to Go Before 11 a.m. or after 3 p.m.

Author's Rating Light and relaxing; ★★

Appeal by Age Group

Preschool ★★		Teens ★½		Over 30 ★★
Grade school ★★		Young Adults ★★		Seniors ★★½

Duration of Ride About 7 minutes (plus 1½-minute wait to disembark)

Average Wait in Line per 100 People ahead of You 4½ minutes

Assumes 16 boats in operation

Loading Speed Moderate

Description and Comments El Río del Tiempo (The River of Time) cruises among audio-animatronic and cinematic scenes depicting the history of Mexico from the ancient Maya, Toltec, and Aztec civilizations to modern times. Special effects include fiber-optic projections that simulate fireworks near the ride's end.

The volcano at the entrance suggests great things to come, but the ride disappoints many. A Troy, New York, woman lambasts El Río del Tiempo:

> My worst nightmare would be to get stuck in It's a Small World or El Río del Tiempo. They were both dreadful, boring, and need updating. I thought El Río was an insult to the Mexico Pavilion—it's a cheap tourist's version of Mexico and hardly a reflection on the culture, history, or people.

We agree. Though tranquil and relaxing, El Río del Tiempo is not particularly interesting and definitely is not worth a long wait.

Touring Tips The ride tends to get crowded during early afternoon.

Norway Pavilion

Description and Comments   The Norway pavilion is complex, beautiful, and architecturally diverse. Surrounding a courtyard is an assortment of traditional Scandinavian buildings, including a replica of the fourteenth-century Akershus Castle, a wooden stave church, red-tiled cottages, and replicas of historic buildings representing the traditional designs of Bergen, Alesund, and Oslo. Attractions include an adventure boat ride in the mold of Pirates of the Caribbean, a movie about Norway, and a gallery of art and artifacts in the stave church. For smaller children there is a Viking-ship play area. The pavilion houses Restaurant Akershus, a sit-down eatery (priority seating required) that serves koldtboard (cold buffet) at lunch and dinner. In the morning the restaurant hosts the Princesses character breakfast, one of the most popular in Walt Disney World. An open-air café and a bakery cater to those on the run. Shoppers find abundant native handicrafts.

Maelstrom (FASTPASS)

What It Is   Indoor adventure boat ride

Scope and Scale   Major attraction

When to Go   Before noon, after 4:30 p.m., or use FASTPASS

Author's Rating   Too short, but has its moments; ★★★

Appeal by Age Group

Preschool ★★★½	Teens ★★★	Over 30 ★★★
Grade school ★★★½	Young Adults ★★★	Seniors ★★★

Duration of Ride   4½ minutes, followed by a 5-minute film with a short wait in between; about 14 minutes for the whole show

Average Wait in Line per 100 People ahead of You   4 minutes

Assumes   12 or 13 boats operating

Loading Speed   Fast

Description and Comments   In one of Disney World's shorter water rides, guests board dragon-headed ships for a voyage through the fabled rivers and seas of Viking history and legend. They brave trolls, rocky gorges, waterfalls, and a storm at sea. A second-generation Disney water ride, the Viking voyage assembles an impressive array of special effects, combining visual, tactile, and auditory stimuli in a fast-paced and often humorous odyssey. Afterward, guests see a five-minute film on Norway. We don't have any major problems with Maelstrom, but a vocal minority of our readers consider the ride too brief and resent having to sit through what they characterize as a travelogue.

Touring Tips   Sometimes, several hundred guests from a recently concluded screening of *Reflections of China* arrive at Maelstrom en masse. Should you encounter this horde, postpone Maelstrom. If you don't want to see the Norway film, try to be one of the first to enter the theater. You can follow the preceding audience right through the exit doors on the far side.

China Pavilion

Description and Comments   A half-sized replica of the Temple of Heaven in Beijing identifies this pavilion. Gardens and reflecting ponds simulate those found in Suzhou, and an art gallery features a lotus blossom gate and formal saddle roof line. The China pavilion offers two restaurants: a fast-food eatery and a full-service establishment (priority seating required) that serves lamentably lackluster Chinese food in a lovely setting.

Reflections of China

What It Is Film about the Chinese people and country

Scope and Scale Major attraction

When to Go Anytime

Special Comments Audience stands throughout performance

Author's Rating This beautifully produced film was introduced in 2003; ★★★½

Appeal by Age Group

Preschool ★★	Teens ★★★	Over 30 ★★★★
Grade school ★★½	Young Adults ★★★½	Seniors ★★★★

Duration of Presentation About 14 minutes

Preshow Entertainment None

Probable Waiting Time 10 minutes

Description ans Comments Pass through the Hall of Prayer for Good Harvest to view the Circle-Vision 360 film *Reflections of China*. Warm and appealing, it's a brilliant (albeit politically sanitized) introduction to the people and natural beauty of China.

Touring Tips The pavilion is truly beautiful—serene yet exciting. Reflections of China plays in a theater where guests must stand, but the film can usually be enjoyed anytime without much waiting. If you're touring World Showcase in a counterclockwise rotation and plan next to go to Norway and ride Maelstrom, position yourself on the far left of the theater (as you face the attendant's podium). After the show, be one of the first to exit. Hurry to Maelstrom as fast as you can to arrive ahead of the several hundred other *Reflections of China* patrons who will be right behind you.

Germany Pavilion

Description and Comments A clock tower, adorned with boy and girl figures, rises above the platz (plaza) marking the Germany pavilion. Dominated by a fountain depicting St. George's victory over the dragon, the platz is encircled by buildings done in traditional German architecture. The main attraction is the Biergarten, a buffet restaurant (priority seating required) serving German food and beer. Yodeling, folk dancing, and oompah-band music are included during mealtimes.

Also at Germany, be sure to check out the large and elaborate model railroad located just beyond the rest rooms as you walk from Germany toward Italy.

Touring Tips The pavilion is pleasant and festive. Tour anytime.

A PEEK BEHIND THE SCENES WITH JIM HILL

Et Tour Brewtus One of the more intriguing games guests play is "Drinking 'round the World." This involves walking around World Showcase and downing a beer in every country. The theme park's German pavilion—with its oversized steins of authentic Teutonic ale—has proved to be the undoing of many. Some stop off for a final beer in the Biergarten en route to the Betty Ford Center.

Italy Pavilion

Description and Comments The entrance to Italy is marked by a 105-foot-tall campanile (bell tower) said to mirror the tower in St. Mark's Square in Venice. Left of the campanile is a replica of the fourteenth-century Doge's Palace, also in the famous square. Other buildings are composites of Italian architecture. For example, L'Originale Alfredo di Roma Ristorante is Florentine. Visitors can watch pasta being made in this popular restaurant, which specializes in fettuccini Alfredo. The pavilion has a waterfront on the lagoon where gondolas are tied to striped moorings.

Touring Tips Streets and courtyards in the Italy pavilion are among the most realistic in World Showcase. You really feel as if you're in Italy. Because there's no film or ride, tour at any hour.

A PEEK BEHIND THE SCENES WITH JIM HILL

Gone-Dola with the Wind
Among the many attractions that the Imagineers considered for Epcot's World Showcase was a gondola ride during which guests would be serenaded as they floated by miniature versions of famous Italian landmarks. As Epcot's construction costs began to mount, however, the Imagineers torpedoed the gondolas. A few gondolas intended for this attraction are tied up along Italy's waterfront area.

United States Pavilion

The American Adventure

What It Is Patriotic mixed-media and audio-animatronic theater presentation on U.S. history

Scope and Scale Headliner

When to Go Anytime

Author's Rating Disney's best historic/patriotic attraction; not to be missed; ★★★★

Appeal by Age Group

Preschool ★★	Teens ★★★	Over 30 ★★★★½
Grade school ★★★	Young Adults ★★★★	Seniors ★★★★★

Duration of Presentation About 29 minutes

Preshow Entertainment Voices of Liberty chorale singing

Probable Waiting Time 16 minutes

Description and Comments The United States pavilion, generally referred to as The American Adventure, consists (not surprisingly) of a fast-food restaurant and a patriotic show.

The American Adventure is a composite of everything Disney does best. Located in an imposing brick structure reminiscent of Colonial Philadelphia, the 29-minute production is a stirring, but sanitized, rendition of American history narrated by an audio-animatronic Mark Twain (who carries a smoking cigar) and Ben Franklin (who climbs a set of stairs to visit Thomas Jefferson). Behind a stage (almost half the size of a football field) is a 28 x 55-foot rear-projection screen (the largest ever used) on which motion picture images are interwoven with action on stage.

Though the production stimulates patriotic emotion in some viewers, others find it overstated and boring. A man from Fort Lauderdale, Florida, writes:

I've always disagreed with you about The American Adventure. *I saw it about ten years ago and snoozed through it. We tried it again since you said it was updated. It was still ponderous. Casey used the time for a nap, and I was checking my watch, waiting for it to be over. I'll try it again in ten years.*

An Erie, Pennsylvania, couple resented Disney's squeaky-clean version of American history:

Our biggest gripe was with The American Adventure. *What was that supposed to be? My husband and I were actually embarrassed by that show. They glossed over the dark points of American history and neatly cut out the audio about who bombed Pearl Harbor (after all, Japan is right next door and everyone is happy at WDW). Why do they not focus on the natural beauty of America, the ethnic diversity, immigration, contributions to the world society? No, it's a condensed and Disney-fied history lesson that made us want to pretend to be Canadians after seeing it.*

But an Iowa City father of three thinks a lot of people are missing the point:

Cramming all of American history into a 20-minute flick is no easy task, and face it, a theme park is hardly the place for a wholly objective, serious critique of the United States. I think that it's perfectly appropriate for the film, as an attraction in Epcot, to emphasize what's good about the United States.

Touring Tips   Architecturally, The American Adventure isn't as interesting as most other pavilions. But the presentation, our researchers believe, is the very best patriotic attraction in the Disney repertoire. It usually plays to capacity audiences from around 1:30 to 3:30 p.m., but it isn't hard to get into. Because of the theater's large capacity, the wait during busy times of day seldom approaches an hour, and averages 25–40 minutes. Because of its theme, the presentation is decidedly less compelling to non-Americans.

The adjacent Liberty Inn serves a quick, nonethnic, fast-food meal.

A PEEK BEHIND THE SCENES WITH JIM HILL

A Radically Different America
Had the Imagineers gone with their initial plan, this part of the theme park would have actually served as the gateway to a World Showcase Lagoon extension. Around the extension would have been room for ten more international pavilions. *The American Adventure* would have been located in a futuristic-looking building serving as sort of a bridge between Future World and World Showcase.

Japan Pavilion

Description and Comments   The five-story, blue-roofed pagoda, inspired by a seventeenth-century shrine in Nara, sets this pavilion apart. A hill garden behind it encompasses waterfalls, rocks, flowers, lanterns, paths, and rustic bridges. The building on the right (as one faces the entrance) was inspired by the ceremonial and coronation hall at the Imperial Palace at Kyoto. It contains restaurants and a large retail store. Through the center entrance and to the left is the Bijutsu-kan Gallery, exhibiting some exquisite Japanese artifacts.

Touring Tips   Tasteful and elaborate, the pavilion creatively blends simplicity, architectural grandeur, and natural beauty. Tour anytime.

A PEEK BEHIND THE SCENES WITH JIM HILL

How to Get Bambi out of Your Garden

Drop by the Japanese garden and see the shishi-odoshi or "deer chaser." This simple but elegant device was supposedly developed centuries ago by Japanese farmers eager to keep deer away from their crops. As the primary piece of bamboo fills with water, it suddenly swings forward and strikes a rock while creating a "tonk"-ing sound. This is supposedly enough to frighten even the most sturdy forest creature.

Morocco Pavilion

Description and Comments   The bustling market, winding streets, lofty minarets, and stuccoed archways re-create the romance and intrigue of Marrakesh and Casablanca. Attention to detail makes Morocco one of the most exciting World Show-case pavilions. It also has a museum of Moorish art and the Restaurant Marrakesh, which serves some unusual and difficult-to-find North African specialties.

Touring Tips   Morocco has neither a ride nor theater; tour anytime.

France Pavilion

Description and Comments   Naturally, a replica of the Eiffel Tower (a big one) is this pavilion's centerpiece. In the foreground, streets recall *La Belle Époque*, France's "beautiful time" between 1870 and 1910. The sidewalk café and restaurant are very popular, as is the pastry shop. You won't be the first visitor to buy a croissant to tide you over until your next real meal.

A group from Chicago found the pavilion's realism exceeds what was intended:

There were no public rest rooms in the France part of Epcot—just like Paris. We had to go to Morocco to find facilities.

Impressions de France is an 18-minute movie projected over 200 degrees onto five screens. Unlike at China and Canada, the audience sits to view this well-made film introducing France's people, cities, and natural wonders.

Touring Tips   Detail and the evocation of a bygone era enrich the atmosphere of this pavilion. Streets are small and become quite congested when visitors queue for the film.

Impressions de France

What It Is Film essay on the French people and country

Scope and Scale Major attraction

When to Go Anytime

Author's Rating Exceedingly beautiful film; not to be missed; ★★★½

Appeal by Age Group

Preschool ★½	Teens ★★★	Over 30 ★★★★
Grade school ★★½	Young Adults ★★★★	Seniors ★★★★

Duration of Presentation About 18 minutes

Preshow Entertainment None

Probable Waiting Time 12 minutes (at suggested times)

Ugly Americans

During the war with Iraq, more than a few American visitors became so abusive toward the cast members of the French pavilion that Disney replaced some of the cast members with French-speaking cast members from the Canadian pavilion.

United Kingdom Pavilion

Description and Comments   A variety of period architecture attempts to capture Britain's city, town, and rural atmospheres. One street alone has a thatched-roof cottage, a four-story timber-and-plaster building, a pre-Georgian plaster building, a formal Palladian exterior of dressed stone, and a city square with a Hyde Park bandstand (whew!).

The pavilion is mostly shops. The Rose & Crown Pub and Dining Room is the only World Showcase full-service restaurant with dining on the water side of the promenade.

Touring Tips   There are no attractions, hence minimal congestion; tour anytime. Priority seating isn't required to enjoy the pub section of the Rose & Crown, making it a nice place to stop for a midafternoon beer. Speaking of which, if you can't make up your mind, a beer sampler is available for about $10. Included are six-ounce servings of Bass Ale, Harp Irish Lager, Tennent Scottish Lager, Guinness Stout, and Boddington Crème Ale. In the category of dubious distinctions, the Rose & Crown Pub is the only place at Epcot where smoking is allowed indoors.

Save the Wales

Welsh visitors to World Showcase's U.K. pavilion were outraged when they found not a single item from Wales on sale at the Magic of Wales shop. Instead, the shelves were stocked with Scottish goods. Disney officials apologized for the unintended slight, but explained that—due to the retirement of the store's distributor—the park no longer had a reliable source for authentic Welsh goods.

Canada Pavilion

Canada's cultural, natural, and architectural diversity is reflected in this large and impressive pavilion. Thirty-foot-tall totem poles embellish a Native American village at the foot of a magnificent château-style hotel. Nearby is a rugged stone building said to be modeled after a famous landmark near Niagara Falls and reflecting Britain's influence on Canada. Le Cellier, a steakhouse on the pavilion's lower level, accepts priority seating but also welcomes walk-ins.

O Canada!

What It Is   Film essay on the Canadian people and their country

Scope and Scale   Major attraction

When to Go Anytime

Special Comments Audience stands during performance

Author's Rating Makes you want to catch the first plane to Canada! ★★★½

Appeal by Age Group

Preschool ★★	Teens ★★★	Over 30 ★★★★
Grade school ★★½	Young Adults ★★★½	Seniors ★★★★

Duration of Presentation About 18 minutes

Preshow Entertainment None

Probable Waiting Time 10 minutes

Description and Comments *O Canada!* Showcases Canada's natural beauty and population diversity and demonstrates the immense pride Canadians have in their country. Visitors leave the theater through Victoria Gardens inspired by the famed Butchart Gardens of British Columbia.

Touring Tips *O Canada!*, a large-capacity theater attraction (guests must stand), gets fairly heavy late-morning attendance because Canada is the first pavilion encountered as one travels counterclockwise around World Showcase Lagoon.

A PEEK BEHIND THE SCENES WITH JIM HILL

What to Do with That Grizzly View Epcot visitors have already begun complaining about how Soarin's building looms up over the "mountains" of Canada and ruins the whole scene for this corner of World Showcase. Well, the Imagineers are talking about building a new mountain housing a new raft ride attraction themed around Disney's 2002 animated feature, *Brother Bear.* The proposed mountain will be tall enough to keep the Soarin' building out of sight.

Live Entertainment in Epcot

Live entertainment in Epcot is more diverse than in the Magic Kingdom. In World Showcase, it reflects the nations represented. Future World provides a perfect setting for new and experimental offerings. Information about live entertainment on the day you visit is contained in the Epcot guidemap, often supplemented by a *Time Guide.* Both are available at no charge throughout Epcot.

Here are some performers and performances you're apt to encounter:

In Future World A musical crew of drumming janitors, socializing robots (EpBOTS), and gymnasts in *Alien* attire striking statuesque poses work near the front entrance and at Innoventions Plaza (between the two Innoventions buildings and by the fountain) according to the daily entertainment schedule.

Innoventions Fountain Show Numerous times each day, the fountain situated between the two Innoventions buildings comes alive with pulsating, arching plumes of water synchronized to a musical score. Because there is no posted schedule of performances, the fountain show comes as a surprise to many readers, such as this man from Berwickshire, England:

You don't mention one of the newer joys of Epcot, so the musical fountain came as a real surprise and treat. I sat down and listened to it from start to finish on two different occasions. The music is catchy, and played through the stereo speakers, the soaring effects of both music and water are really beautiful.

A Frankenmuth, Michigan, man was likewise caught off guard:

And, finally, to show that things don't always work out as planned, our children were mesmerized and entertained by something that isn't in any tour plan. At Epcot, there is a fountain between the two Innoventions buildings. During the holidays, the fountain was wonderfully synchronized to Christmas carols. While we [adults] checked our watches to make sure we were on time, our children just wanted to sit and watch the dancing water. Eventually, Mom and Dad sat and watched too. It was better than many of the shows and rides that we encountered during our stay at Disney.

Disney Characters Once believed to be inconsistent with Epcot's educational image, Disney characters have now been imported in significant numbers. In a program called Disney Characters on Holiday, a dozen or so characters roll around the World Showcase in a British double-decker bus, stopping at times and places listed in the park map entertainment schedule. At each stop, the characters sing a song or two and then wander into the crowd for autographs and photos.

Characters also appear in live shows at the American Gardens Theatre and at the Showcase Plaza between Mexico and Canada. Times are listed in the daily entertainment schedule *(Times Guide)* available upon entry and at Guest Relations. Finally, The Garden Grill Restaurant in the Land pavilion and Restaurant Akershus offer character meals.

American Gardens Theatre The site of Epcot's premier live performances is in a large amphitheater near The American Adventure, facing World Showcase Lagoon. International talent plays limited engagements there. Many shows spotlight the music, dance, and costumes of the performer's home country. Other programs feature Disney characters.

IllumiNations An after-dark program of music, fireworks, erupting fountains, special lighting, and laser technology is performed on World Showcase Lagoon (see pages 524–528).

Around World Showcase Impromptu performances take place in and around the World Showcase pavilions. They include a strolling mariachi group in Mexico; street actors in Italy; a fife-and-drum corps or singing group (The Voices of Liberty) at The American Adventure; traditional songs, drums, and dances in Japan; street comedy and a Beatles impersonation band in the United Kingdom; white-faced mimes in France; and bagpipes in Canada, among others. Street entertainment occurs about every half hour (though not necessarily on the hour or half hour).

Live entertainment in World Showcase exceeded the expectations of a mother from Rhode Island and led her son to develop a new talent:

You should stress in the new edition that Epcot's World Showcase is really quite lively now. Street performances are scheduled throughout the day in the different pavilions. The schedules were printed on the daily map we picked up at the ticket booth.

My two-year-old was taken with the Chinese acrobats and the Chinese variety performers. We must have watched their shows four times each! As I write this, he's balancing an empty trash can on his feet.

And an Ayden, North Carolina, woman offers this:

I don't feel that you emphasize the street shows at Epcot enough. My husband and I loved the Japanese drumming, the Chinese and Moroccan acrobats, and the street theatre players in Great Britain. These activities were much more indicative of foreign cultures than the rides.

We think the reader's right on target. The quality of street entertainment throughout Epcot is superb. Our personal favorite is the Living Statues at France—absolutely brilliant.

Kidcot Fun Zones   In the World Showcase there are Kidcot Fun Zones, where younger children can hear a story or make some small craft representative of the host nation. The Fun Zones are quite informal, usually set up right on the walkway. During busy times of year, you'll find Fun Zones at each country. At slower times, only a couple of zones operate. Parents from Nanticoke, Pennsylvania, who thought Epcot would be a drag for their kids, were quite surprised by their experience:

Unfortunately we saved Epcot for the last day, thinking the children (ages five and six) would be bored. This was a mistake. They wanted to sit for every storyteller. And the best part was the Kidcot Fun Zones in each pavilion. Imagine, something free at Disney World. It's only a stick, but it has a little something from each country added by the child at his whim. They had a ball.

Dinner and Lunch Shows   Restaurants in World Showcase serve healthy portions of live entertainment to accompany the victuals. Find folk dancing and an oompah band in Germany, singing waiters in Italy, and belly dancers in Morocco. Shows are performed only at dinner in Italy, but at both lunch and dinner in Germany and Morocco. Priority seating is required.

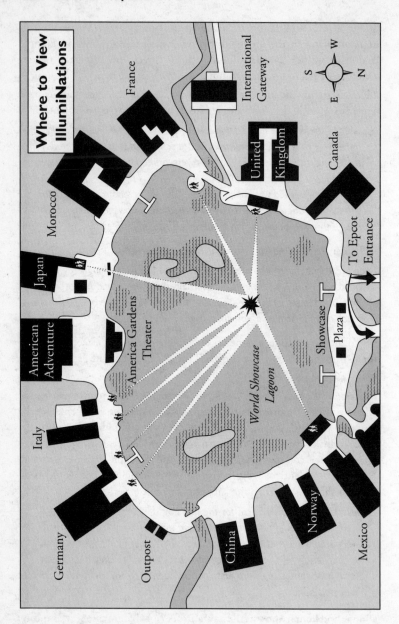

The Best Ways to See IllumiNations

IllumiNations is Epcot's great outdoor spectacle, integrating fireworks, laser lights, neon, and music in a stirring tribute to the nations of the world. It's the climax of every Epcot day when the park is open late. Don't miss it.

Unlike earlier *IllumiNations* renditions, this one has a plot as well as a theme and is loaded with symbolism. We'll provide the Cliffs Notes version here because it all sort of runs together in the show itself. The show kicks off with colliding stars suggesting the big bang, following which "chaos reigns in the universe." This is soon replaced by twittering songbirds and various other manifestations signaling the nativity of the Earth. Next comes a brief history of time from the dinosaurs to ancient Rome, all projected in images on a huge, floating globe. Man's art and inspiration then flash across the globe "in a collage of creativity." All of this stimulates the globe to unfold "like a massive flower," bringing on the fireworks crescendo heralding the dawn of a new age. Although only the artistically sensitive will be able to differentiate all of this from, say, the last five minutes of any Bruce Willis movie, we thought you'd like to know what Disney says is happening.

Getting out of Epcot after IllumiNations (Read This before Selecting a Viewing Spot)

Decide how quickly you want to leave the park after the show, then pick your vantage point. *IllumiNations* ends the day at Epcot. When it's over, only a couple of gift shops remain open. Because there's nothing to do, everyone leaves at once. This creates a great snarl at Package Pick-up, the Epcot monorail station, and the Disney bus stop. It also pushes to the limit the tram system hauling guests to their cars in the parking lot. Stroller return, however, is extraordinarily efficient and doesn't cause any delay.

If you're staying at an Epcot resort (Swan, Dolphin, Yacht and Beach Club Resorts, and BoardWalk Inn and Villas), watch *IllumiNations* from somewhere on the southern half (The American Adventure) of World Showcase Lagoon and then leave through the International Gateway between France and the United Kingdom. You can walk or take a boat back to your hotel from the International Gateway. If you have a car and are visiting Epcot in the evening for dinner and *IllumiNations*, park at the Yacht or Beach Club. After the show, duck out the International Gateway and be on the road to your hotel in 15 minutes. We should warn you that there is a manned security gate at the entrances to most of the Epcot resorts, including the Yacht and Beach Club. You will, of course, be admitted if you have legitimate business, such as dining at one of the hotel restaurants, or, if you park at the BoardWalk Hotel and Villas (requiring a slightly longer walk to Epcot), going to the clubs and restaurants at Disney's BoardWalk. If you're staying at any other Disney hotel and don't have a car, the fastest way home is to join the mass exodus through the main gate after *IllumiNations* and catch a bus or the monorail.

Those who have a car in the Epcot lot have a more problematic situation. If you want to beat the crowd, find a viewing spot at the end of World Showcase Lagoon nearest Future World (and the exits). Leave as soon as *IllumiNations* concludes, trying to exit ahead of the crowd. Be forewarned that thousands of people will be doing exactly the same thing. To get a good vantage point anywhere between Mexico and Canada on the northern end of the lagoon, you'll have to stake out your spot 45–90 minutes before the show. Conceivably, you may squander more time holding your spot before *IllumiNations* than you would if you watched from the less congested southern end of the lagoon and took your chances with the crowd upon departure.

More groups get separated and more children lost after *IllumiNations* than at any other time. In summer, you will be walking in a throng of up to 30,000 people. If you're heading for the parking lot, anticipate this congestion and preselect a point in the Epcot entrance area where you can meet in the event that someone gets separated from the group. We recommend the fountain just inside the main entrance. Everyone in your party should be told not to exit through the turnstiles until all noses have been counted. It can be a nightmare if the group gets split up and you don't know whether the others are inside or outside the park.

For those with a car, the main problem is reaching it. Once there, traffic leaves the parking lot pretty well. If you paid close attention to where you parked, consider skipping the tram and walking. If you walk, watch your children closely and hang on to them for all you're worth. The parking lot is pretty wild at this time of night, with hundreds of moving cars.

Good Locations for Viewing IllumiNations and Other World Showcase Lagoon Performances

The best place to be for any presentation on World Showcase Lagoon is in a seat on the lakeside veranda of the Cantina de San Angel in Mexico. Come early (at least 90 minutes before *IllumiNations*) and relax with a cold drink or snack while you wait for the show.

A woman from Pasadena, California, nailed down the seat but missed the relaxation. She writes:

Stake out a prime site for IllumiNations *at least two hours ahead, and be prepared to defend it. We got a lakeside table at the Cantina de San Angel at 6:30 p.m. and had a great view of* IllumiNations. *Unfortunately, we had to put up with troops of people asking us to share our table and trying to wedge themselves between our table and the fence.*

The Rose & Crown Pub in the United Kingdom also has lagoonside seating. Because of a small wall, however, the view isn't quite as good as from the Cantina. If you want to combine dinner on the Rose &

Crown's veranda with *IllumiNations*, make a dinner priority seating for about 1 hour and 15 minutes before show time. Report a few minutes early for your seating and tell the Rose & Crown host that you want a table outside where you can view *IllumiNations* during or after dinner. Our experience is that the Rose & Crown staff will bend over backward to accommodate you. If you aren't able to obtain a table outside, eat inside, then hang out until show time. When the lights dim, indicating the start of *IllumiNations*, you will be allowed to join the diners on the terrace to watch the show.

Because most guests run for the exits after a presentation, and because islands in the southern half (The American Adventure) of the lagoon block the view from some places, the most popular spectator positions are along the northern waterfront from Norway and Mexico on around to Canada and the United Kingdom. Although the northern half of the lagoon unquestionably offers excellent viewing, it's usually necessary to claim a spot 60–100 minutes before *IllumiNations* begins. For those who are late finishing dinner or don't want to spend an hour or more standing by a rail, here are some good viewing spots along the southern perimeter (moving counterclockwise from the United Kingdom to Germany) that often go unnoticed until 10–30 minutes before show time:

1. **International Gateway Island** The pedestrian bridge across the canal near International Gateway spans an island that offers great viewing. This island normally fills 30 minutes or more before show time.

2. **Second-Floor (Restaurant-Level) Deck of the Mitsukoshi Building in Japan** An Asian arch slightly blocks your sightline, but this covered deck offers a great vantage point, especially if the weather is iffy. Only the Cantina de San Angel in Mexico is more protected. If you take up a position on the Mitsukoshi deck and find the wind blowing directly at you, you can be reasonably sure that the smoke from the fireworks won't be far behind.

3. **Gondola Landing at Italy** An elaborate waterfront promenade offers excellent viewing positions. Claim your spot at least 30 minutes before show time.

4. **The Boat Dock Opposite Germany** Another good vantage point, the dock generally fills 30 minutes before *IllumiNations*.

5. **Waterfront Promenade by Germany** Views are good from the 90-foot-long lagoonside walkway between Germany and China.

Do these suggestions work every time? No. A dad from San Ramon, California, writes:

Your recommendations for IllumiNations didn't work out in the time frame you mentioned. People had the area staked out two hours ahead of time.

None of the above viewing locations are reserved for *Unofficial Guide* readers, and on busier nights, good spots go early. But speaking personally, we refuse to hold down a slab of concrete for two hours before *IllumiNations* as some people do. Most nights, you can find an acceptable vantage point 15–30 minutes before the show. Because most of the action is significantly above ground level, you don't need to be right on the rail or have an unobstructed view of the water. It's important, however, not to position yourself under a tree, awning, or anything else that blocks your overhead view. If *IllumiNations* is a top priority for you and you want to be absolutely certain of getting a good viewing position, claim your place an hour or more before show time.

A New Yorker who staked out his turf well in advance made this suggestion for staying comfortable until show time:

> Your excellent guidebook also served as [a] seat cushion while waiting seated on the ground. Make future editions thicker for greater comfort.

IllumiNations *Cruise*

For a really good view, you can charter a pontoon boat for $120. Captained by a Disney cast member, the boat holds up to ten guests. Your captain will take you for a little cruise and then position the boat in a perfect place to watch *IllumiNations*. Optional food and beverage items are available through Yacht Club Private Dining at (407) 934-3160. Cruises depart from the BoardWalk and Yacht and Beach Club docks. A major indirect benefit of the charter is that you can enjoy *IllumiNations* without fighting the mob afterwards. Because this is a private charter rather than a tour, only your group will be aboard. Life jackets are provided, but you can wear them at your discretion. Because there are few boats, charters sell out fast. To reserve call (407) WDW-PLAY at exactly 7 a.m. 90 days before the day you want to charter. Because the Disney reservations system counts days in a somewhat atypical manner, we recommend phoning about 95 days out to have a Disney agent specify the exact morning to call for reservations. Similar charters are available on the Seven Seas Lagoon to watch the Magic Kingdom fireworks.

Behind the Scenes in Epcot

Epcot's **Gardens of the World** offers adults (ages 16 and over) a glimpse of Disney World's gardens, horticulture, and landscaping. **Hidden Treasures** is a tour exploring the architecture of the international pavilions. A third tour, **Undiscovered Future World,** traces the history of Epcot, including Walt Disney's original concept. Both Hidden Treasures and Undiscovered Future World take guests to behind-the-scene areas. Gardens of the World and Hidden Treasures are a little over three hours long and cost $59. Undiscovered Future World last a bit over 4 hours and costs $49.

Readers rave about guided walking tours at Epcot. A couple from Los Angeles write:

The best-kept secret is the adult tour, Hidden Treasures of World Showcase in Epcot. The description is misleading and sounds like a real bore, but we got a behind-the-scenes tour with lots of information on everything we ever wanted to know or were curious about. Definitely the best part of our trip. (This is a walking tour and is mostly outside in the heat.)

A gentleman in Houston, Texas, tells us:

Keep telling people about the Hidden Treasures of World Showcase tour; we finally got to take it, and it was a real highlight. The cast member who took us on the tour (there were only four of us) told us about a tour of the Magic Kingdom, called Keys to the Kingdom, which we took the very next day. It was similar, with backstage touring and a look at the utilidor system, although it also included going on several rides. Tell people about this one, too.

The **Behind the Seeds Tour** is shorter and takes guests behind the scenes to vegetable gardens in The Land pavilion. It requires same-day reservations; make them on the lower level of The Land (far right of the fast-food windows). The cost of the hour-long tour is $8 for adults and $6 for children ages three to nine.

Dive Quest

The soggiest behind-the-scenes experience available anywhere is Epcot's **Dive Quest,** where open-water scuba-certified divers (ages 15 and over) can swim around with the fish at The Living Seas. Offered twice daily, each tour lasts about two-and-a-half hours, including a 30–40-minute dive. The cost is about $140 per diver and includes all gear, a souvenir T-shirt, a dive log stamp, and refreshments. They will make a video recording of your dive, which you can buy for $30. Reservations are required and can be made with a credit card by calling (407) WDW-TOUR. For recorded information, call (407) 560-5590. The experience is for adults only; no junior certifications are accepted.

Dolphins in Depth

This tour (for guests ages 16 and older) visits the dolphin research facility at the Living Seas. There you'll witness a training session and then wade into the water (but not swim) with the two dolphins. Cost for the three-hour experience is $150. Wet suits are provided. Only eight guests per day can participate, so make reservations 90 days in advance by calling (407) WDW-TOUR.

If you really dig dolphins, keep in mind that for $229, you can visit Discovery Cove, SeaWorld's new park, and actually swim with the dolphins. Though the dolphin swim experience is only about an hour long, the ticket entitles visitors to an entire day at Discovery Cove (where, among other activities, you can snorkel in a manmade coral reef), plus a decent lunch and a seven-day pass to SeaWorld. For more information on Discovery Cove, see pages 651–652.

Epcot Seas Aqua Tour

This recently added tour is sort of a watered down (chuckle) version of Dive Quest. The two-and-a-half-hour tour allows you to swim with goggles/mask (but not scuba) in the main tank for 30 minutes and explore backstage areas at the Living Seas. It costs $100, accepts guests as young as 8 years old, and is the only Epcot tour that does not require separate park admission. Children under 17 must be accompanied by an adult. Seventeen-year-olds are required to bring a waiver from their parent or guardian if not accompanied by an adult.

Additional Information for All Tours

The cost of the tour is in addition to the price of Epcot admission (except as stated). Many of the Epcot tours offer discounts to AAA Diamond Card holders, Disney Visa card holders, Disney Vacation Club members, Annual Passholders, and military. Ask.

For reservations (except for Behind the Seeds) call (407) WDW-TOUR. Reservations must be guaranteed with a credit card, and there is a 48-hour cancellation policy. Taking photographs is generally not allowed in backstage areas. The walking tours involve a lot of walking and standing. For the Living Seas tours, bring a bathing suit; other essential equipment will be provided. The various tours are not offered every day, so call for exact dates and times early in the planning stage of your vacation.

Traffic Patterns in Epcot

In the Magic Kingdom, Main Street, U.S.A., with its shops and eateries, serves as a huge gathering place when the park opens and funnels visitors to the central hub, where entrances branch off to the lands. Thus, crowds are first welcomed and entertained (on Main Street), then distributed almost equally to the Lands.

At Epcot, by contrast, Spaceship Earth, the park's premier landmark and one of its headliner attractions, is just inside the main entrance. When visitors enter the park, they almost irresistibly head for it. Hence, a bottleneck forms less than 75 yards from the turnstiles as soon as the park opens. Visitors aware of the congestion at Spaceship Earth can take advantage of the excellent opportunities it provides for escaping waits at other Future World attractions.

Early-morning crowds form in Future World because most of the park's rides and shows are there. Except at Mission: Space, Test Track, and *Honey, I Shrunk the Audience,* visitors are fairly equally distributed among Future World attractions. In 2005, Soarin' will probably become the primary early-morning magnet.

When Soarin' opens in 2005, it will edge out Test Track at the top of the pop chart, further splitting the crowd. The three biggies, including Mission: Space, will draw so many guests that the other attractions in Future World will not develop long waits until 11 a.m. or later.

Between 9 and 11 a.m., crowds build in Future World. Even when World Showcase opens (usually 11 a.m. but sometimes noon), more people are entering Future World than are leaving for the Showcase. Attendance continues building in Future World between noon and 2 p.m. World Showcase attendance builds rapidly as lunch approaches. Exhibits at the far end of World Showcase Lagoon report capacity audiences from about noon through 6:30 or 7:30 p.m.

The Magic Kingdom's premier attractions are situated on the far perimeters of its lands to distribute crowds evenly. Epcot's cluster of attractions in Future World holds the greater part of the throng in the smaller part of the park. World Showcase has only two major draws (Maelstrom in Norway and The American Adventure), but these are not in the same league as the three Super Headliners in Future World, and consequently there is no compelling reason to rush to see them. The bottom line: crowds build all morning and into early afternoon in Future World. Not until the evening meal approaches do crowds equalize in Future World and World Showcase. Evening crowds in World Showcase, however, don't compare in size to morning and midday crowds in Future World. Attendance throughout Epcot is normally lighter in the evening.

Some guests leave Epcot in the early evening, but the vast majority exit en masse after *IllumiNations.* Upwards of 30,000 people head for the parking lot and monorail station at once. Though quite a mob, closing time congestion at Epcot doesn't compare with the post-fireworks gridlock at the Magic Kingdom. One primary reason for the easier departure from Epcot is that its parking lot is adjacent to the park, not separated from it by a lake as at the Magic Kingdom. At the Magic Kingdom, departing visitors form bottlenecks at the monorail to the Transportation and Ticket Center and main parking lot. At Epcot, they proceed directly to their cars.

Epcot Touring Plans

Our Epcot touring plans are field-tested, step-by-step itineraries for seeing all major attractions at Epcot with a minimum of waiting in line. They're designed to keep you ahead of the crowds while the park is filling in the morning, and to place you at the less-crowded attractions during Epcot's busier hours. They assume you would be happier doing a little extra walking rather than a lot of extra standing in line.

Touring Epcot is much more strenuous and demanding than touring the other theme parks. Epcot requires about twice as much walking. And, unlike the Magic Kingdom, Epcot has no effective in-park transportation; wherever you want to go, it's always quicker to walk. Our plans will help you avoid crowds and bottlenecks on days of moderate to heavy attendance, but they can't shorten the distance you have to walk. (Wear comfortable shoes.) On days of lighter attendance, when crowd conditions aren't a critical factor, the plans will help you organize your tour. We offer four touring plans:

Epcot One-Day Touring Plan   This plan packs as much as possible into one long day and requires a lot of hustle and stamina.

Author's Selective Epcot One-Day Touring Plan   This plan eliminates some lesser attractions (in the author's opinion) and offers a somewhat more relaxed tour if you have only one day.

Epcot Two-Day Sunrise/Starlight Touring Plan   This plan combines the easy touring of early morning on one day with Epcot's festivity and live pageantry at night on the second day. The first day requires some backtracking and hustle but is much more laid-back than either one-day plan.

Epcot Two-Day Early Riser Touring Plan   This is the most efficient Epcot touring plan, eliminating 90% of the backtracking and extra walking required by the other plans while still providing a comprehensive tour.

Preliminary Instructions for All Epcot Touring Plans

1. Call (407) 824-4321 in advance for the hours of operation on the day of your visit.
2. Remember that Wednesday is early-entry day at Epcot. Avoid Epcot on Wednesday unless you are a Disney resort or campground guest taking advantage of your early-entry privileges.
3. Make priority seatings at the Epcot full-service restaurant(s) of your choice in advance of your visit.

Epcot One-Day Touring Plan

For Adults and children eight or older.

Assumes Willingness to experience all major rides and shows.

This plan requires a lot of walking and some backtracking in order to avoid long waits in line. A little extra walking and some early-morning hustle will spare you two to three hours of standing in line. You might not complete the tour. How far you get depends on how quickly you move from attraction to attraction, how many times you rest and eat, how quickly the park fills, and what time it closes.

This plan is not recommended for families with very young children. If you're touring with young children and have only one day, use the

Author's Selective Epcot One-Day Touring Plan. Break after lunch and relax at your hotel, returning to the park in late afternoon. If you can allocate two days to Epcot, use one of the Epcot two-day touring plans.

1. Arrive at the parking lot 40 minutes before official opening time. Soarin', a new Super headliner attraction, is scheduled to open in 2005. We suggest you call Disney information and inquire about the status of Soarin'. Inquire again for an up-to-the-minute report as you pass through the turnstiles.

2. Proceed to the plaza behind Spaceship Earth and then along crescent-shaped Innoventions East building on your left until you see an open passage through the building. Turn left through this passage. After emerging on the far side of Innoventions East, turn right to Test Track. Ride Test Track. Do not use FASTPASS.

3. Mission: Space is next door to Test Track. Enjoy. Do not use FASTPASS.

4. If Soarin' is open, or as they say, "in rehearsal" (not officially open but you can still ride), obtaining FASTPASSes for Soarin' should be your next step. Soarin' is located in the Land pavilion on the far side of Innoventions West (to your right after passing Spaceship Earth). If Soarin' is not operating, skip ahead to Step 5.

5. Ride Living with the Land. Save other attractions in the pavilion for later.

6. Exit the Land pavilion and bear right to the Imagination pavilion. Take the Journey into Your Imagination ride.

7. In the Imagination pavilion, see *Honey, I Shrunk the Audience*.

8. Return to the Land and see the *Circle of Life*.

9. If open, ride Soarin' using the FASTPASSes obtained in Step 4.

10. Exit the Land to the left and experience The Living Seas.

11. Head through Innoventions West toward the front entrance of the park. Ride Spaceship Earth (in the geodesic sphere).

12. Exiting Spaceship Earth, proceed to the Mission: Space side of Future World and visit the Universe of Energy. If you haven't made advance priority seatings for dinner, you can make them now at guest relations (to the left of Spaceship Earth) en route to the Universe of Energy.

13. Exit the Universe of Energy and bear left to the Wonders of Life pavilion. Ride Body Wars (open seasonally).

14. In the Wonders of Life pavilion, see *Cranium Command* (open seasonally).

15. Depart Future World and proceed to the World Showcase section of the park.

16. Initiate a clockwise rotation around the World Showcase Lagoon. Starting at Mexico, ride El Río del Tiempo. If you are primarily interested in the attractions, try to limit your perusal of the dozens of shops. The street scenes at each World Showcase nation, however, are what make the section of Epcot special. Even when there is not a ride or a show, we recommend you spend some time enjoying the architecture, gardens, and street entertainment. The World Showcase is definitely a smell-the-roses kind of place, so try to relax and not hurry through.

17. Exiting Mexico, bear left to Norway. Ride Maelstrom.

18. Continuing clockwise around the lagoon, proceed to China. See *Reflections of China*.

19. Continuing clockwise, tour Germany.

20 Visit Italy next door.

21. Proceed clockwise to *The American Adventure*. See the show.

22. Continue around the lagoon and tour Japan.

23. Next to Japan, visit Morocco.

24. Continue to France and see the movie.

25. Next, cross the bridge to the United Kingdom.

26. Proceed to Canada and see the movie.

27. This concludes the touring plan. Check your watch if you're approaching your priority seating time for dinner. If you plan to stay for *IllumiNations*, give yourself at least 30 minutes to find a good viewing spot. Unless an unusual holiday schedule is in effect, everything at Epcot closes after *IllumiNations* except for a few shops. Thirty- or forty-thousand people bolt for the exits at once. Suggestions for coping with this exodus begin on page 525.

Author's Selective Epcot One-Day Touring Plan

For All parties.

Assumes Willingness to experience major rides and shows.

This touring plan includes only what the author believes is the best Epcot has to offer. However, exclusion of an attraction doesn't mean it isn't worthwhile.

Families with children younger than eight using this touring plan should review Epcot attractions in the Small-Child Fright-Potential Chart (pages 258–261). Rent a stroller for any child small enough to fit in one, and take your young children back to the hotel for a nap after lunch. If you can allocate two days to see Epcot, try one of the Epcot two-day touring plans.

1. Arrive at the parking lot 40 minutes before official opening time. Soarin', a new Super headliner attraction, is scheduled to open in 2005. We suggest you call Disney information and inquire about the status of Soarin'. Inquire again for an up-to-the-minute report as you pass through the turnstiles.

2. Proceed to the plaza behind Spaceship Earth and then along crescent-shaped Innoventions East building on your left until you see an open passage through the building. Turn left through this passage. After emerging on the far side of Innoventions East, turn right to Test Track. Ride Test Track. Do not use FASTPASS.

3. Mission: Space is next door to Test Track. Enjoy. Do not use FASTPASS.

4. If Soarin' is open, or as they say, "in rehearsal" (not officially open but you can still ride), obtaining FASTPASSes for Soarin' should be your next step.

Soarin' is located in the Land pavilion on the far side of Innoventions West (to your right after passing Spaceship Earth). If Soarin' is not operating, skip ahead to Step 5.

5. Ride Living with the Land. Save other attractions in the pavilion for later.

6. Exit the Land pavilion and bear right to the Imagination pavilion. Take the Journey into Your Imagination ride.

7. In the Imagination pavilion, see *Honey, I Shrunk the Audience*.

8. Return to the Land and ride Soarin' using the FASTPASSes obtained in Step 4.

9. Exit the Land to the left and experience the Living Seas.

10. Head through Innoventions West toward the front entrance of the park. Ride Spaceship Earth (in the geodesic sphere).

11. Exiting Spaceship Earth, proceed to the Mission: Space side of Future World and visit the Universe of Energy. If you haven't made advance priority seatings for dinner, you can make them now at guest relations (to the left of Spaceship Earth) en route to the Universe of Energy.

12. Exit the Universe of Energy and bear left to the Wonders of Life pavilion. Ride Body Wars (open seasonally).

13. In the Wonders of Life pavilion see *Cranium Command* (open seasonally).

14. Depart Future World and proceed to the World Showcase section of the park.

15. Initiate a counter-clockwise rotation around the World Showcase Lagoon. If you are primarily interested in the attractions, try to limit your perusal of the dozens of shops. The street scenes at each World Showcase nation, however, are what make the section of Epcot special. Even when there is not a ride or a show, we recommend you spend some time enjoying the architecture, gardens, and street entertainment. The World Showcase is definitely a smell-the-roses kind of place, so try to relax and not hurry through.

16. Continuing counter-clockwise around the World Showcase Lagoon through Great Britain. Stop at France and see the film.

17. Continue on, visiting Morocco and Japan along the way.

18. At The American Adventure, enjoy the show.

19. Stroll through Italy and Germany and then cross the bridge to China. See the *Reflections of China* film.

20. Bear right on exiting China and proceed next door to Norway. At Norway, ride Maelstrom.

21. Bear right and check out Mexico. Try the boat ride inside the pyramid if you're inclined.

22. Check your watch. Is your dinner priority seating soon? Suspend touring and go to the restaurant when it's time. Check the daily entertainment schedule for the times of the Tapestry of Nations parade and *IllumiNations*, both worthwhile. Give yourself at least 30 minutes after dinner to locate a good viewing spot.

23. This concludes the touring plan. Unless an unusual holiday schedule is in effect, everything at Epcot closes after *IllumiNations* except for a few shops. Thirty or forty thousand people bolt for the exits at once. Suggestions for coping with this exodus begin on page 525.

Epcot Two-Day Sunrise/Starlight Touring Plan

For All parties.

This touring plan is for visitors who want to tour Epcot comprehensively over two days. Day One takes advantage of early-morning touring opportunities. Day Two begins in late afternoon and continues until closing.

Many readers spend part of their Disney World arrival day traveling, checking into their hotel, and unpacking: they aren't free to go to the theme parks until the afternoon. The second day of the Epcot Two-Day Sunrise/Starlight Touring Plan is ideal for people who want to commence their Epcot visit later in the day.

Families with children younger than eight using this plan should review Epcot attractions in the Small-Child Fright-Potential Chart (pages 258–261). Rent a stroller for any child small enough to fit into one. Break off Day One no later than 2:30 p.m. and return to your hotel for rest. If you missed attractions called for in Day One, add them to your itinerary on Day Two.

Day One

1. Arrive at the parking lot 40 minutes before official opening time. Soarin', a new Super headliner attraction, is scheduled to open in 2005. We suggest you call Disney information and inquire about the status of Soarin'. Inquire again for an up-to-the-minute report as you pass through the turnstiles. If Soarin' is open, or as they say, "in rehearsal" (not officially open but you can still ride), it should be your first stop. Soarin' is located in the Land pavilion on the far side of Innoventions West (to your right after passing Spaceship Earth). If Soarin' is not operating, skip ahead to Step 2.

2. Proceed to the plaza behind Spaceship Earth and the crescent-shaped Innoventions East building on your left until you see an open passage through the building. Turn left through this passage. After emerging on the far side of Innoventions East, turn right to Test Track. Ride Test Track. If the wait at Test Track when you arrive exceeds 30 minutes, obtain FASTPASSes and return later to ride.

3. Mission: Space is next door to Test Track. Enjoy. If the wait exceeds 35 minutes, use FASTPASS or try the single rider line.

4. If you want to make a priority seating for lunch or dinner do it now at Guests Relations near Spaceship Earth.

5. Cross to the opposite side of Future World passing through Innoventions East and Innoventions West en route. Proceed to the Land pavilion and enjoy the boat ride.

6. Leaving the other Land attractions for later, exit the pavilion, turning right to the Imagination pavilion. Take the Journey into Your Imagination ride first, and then see the 3-D movie, *Honey, I Shrunk the Audience.*

7. Departing the Imagination pavilion, turn right and proceed to the World Showcase section of Epcot.

8. Turn left and proceed clockwise around the World Showcase Lagoon. Experience El Río del Tiempo boat ride in Mexico. The ride is in the far-left corner of the interior courtyard and isn't very well marked. Consign any purchases to Package Pick-up for collection when you leave the park.

9. Continue left to Norway. Ride Maelstrom. Use FASTPASS if the wait exceeds 20 minutes. *Note:* Check your watch. Is your lunch priority seating soon? Suspend touring and go to the restaurant when it's time. After lunch, resume the touring plan where you left off.

10. Continue left to China. See *Reflections of China.*

11. Visit Germany and Italy. Enjoy the settings; there are no rides or films. If you don't have a restaurant priority seating, Sommerfest (fast food) at Germany serves tasty bratwurst, soft pretzels, desserts, and Beck's beer on draft.

12. Continue clockwise to *The American Adventure.* See the show. If you don't have a restaurant priority seating, the Liberty Inn (left side of The American Adventure) serves hamburgers, hot dogs, and chicken sandwiches.

13. Visit Japan and Morocco. Consign any purchases to Package Pick-up for collection when you leave the park.

14. This concludes the touring plan for Day One. Attractions and pavilions not included today will be experienced tomorrow. If you're full of energy and wish to continue touring, follow the Epcot One-Day Touring Plan for steps 11–13. If you've had enough, exit through the International Gateway or leave through the main entrance. To reach the main entrance without walking around the lagoon, catch a boat at the dock near Morocco.

Day Two

1. Enter Epcot about 1 p.m. Get a park guidemap and the daily entertainment schedule/*Times Guide* at Guest Relations.

2. While at Guest Relations, make a dinner priority seating, if you haven't done so already. You can eat your evening meal in any Epcot restaurant without interrupting the sequence and efficiency of the touring plan. We recommend a 7 p.m. priority seating. The timing of the seating is important if you want to see *IllumiNations,* held over the lagoon at 9 p.m.

   If your preferred restaurants and seatings are filled, try for a priority seating at Morocco or Norway. Because these nations' delightful ethnic dishes are little known to most Americans, priority seatings may be available.

3. Ride Spaceship Earth.

4. Cut left through Innoventions East and return to the Wonders of Life pavilion. See *Cranium Command* (open seasonally).

5. In the same pavilion, experience Body Wars (open seasonally).

6. Exiting the Wonders of Life pavilion, turn right to the Universe of Energy and see the show.

7. Pass through Innoventions East and West and proceed to The Living Seas. For maximum efficiency, be one of the last people to enter the theater (where you sit) from the preshow area (where you stand). Sit as close to the end of a middle row as possible. This will position you to be first on the ride that follows the theater presentation. Afterward, enjoy the exhibits of Sea Base Alpha.

8. Exit right from The Living Seas to the Land. See the *Circle of Life*, featuring characters from *The Lion King*. *Note:* Check your watch. Is your dinner priority seating soon? Suspend touring and go to the restaurant when it's time. After dinner, check the daily entertainment schedule for the time of *IllumiNations*. Don't miss it. Give yourself at least a half hour after dinner to find a good viewing spot along the perimeter of World Showcase Lagoon. For details on the best spots, see pages 524–528.

9. Leave Future World and walk counterclockwise around World Showcase Lagoon to Canada. See *O Canada!*

10. Turn right and visit the United Kingdom.

11. Turn right and proceed to France. See the film.

12. This concludes the touring plan. Enjoy your dinner and *IllumiNations*. If you have time, shop or revisit your favorite attractions.

13. Unless a holiday schedule is in effect, everything at Epcot closes after *IllumiNations* except for a few shops. Thirty thousand or more people bolt for the exits at once. Suggestions for coping with this exodus begin on page 525.

Epcot Two-Day Early Riser Touring Plan

For All parties.

The Two-Day Early Riser Touring Plan is the most efficient Epcot touring plan, eliminating much of the backtracking and crisscrossing required by the other plans. It takes advantage of easy touring made possible by morning's light crowds. Most folks will complete each day of the plan by midafternoon. While the plan doesn't include *IllumiNations* or other evening festivities, these activities plus dinner at an Epcot restaurant can be added to the itinerary at your discretion.

Families with children younger than eight using this plan should review Epcot attractions in the Small-Child Fright-Potential Chart (pages 258–261). Rent a stroller for any child small enough to fit.

Day One

1. Arrive at the parking lot 40 minutes before official opening time. Soarin', a new Super headliner attraction, is scheduled to open in 2005. We suggest you call Disney information and inquire about the status of Soarin'. Inquire

again for an up-to-the-minute report as you pass through the turnstiles. If Soarin' is open, or as they say, "in rehearsal" (not officially open but you can still ride), it should be your first stop. Soarin' is located in the Land pavilion on the far side of Innoventions West (to your right after passing Spaceship Earth). If Soarin' is not operating, skip ahead to Step 2.

2. Also in the Land pavilion, ride Living with the Land.

3. Also in the Land pavilion, see the *Circle of Life*.

4. Go to Guest Relations and make priority seatings for the Epcot full-service restaurant of your choice if you did not make them in advance.

5. Tour Innoventions East on the same side of Future World as Guest Relations.

6. Exit Innoventions East on the Mission: Space side of Future World. Bear left and continue to the Universe of Energy. Enjoy the show.

7. Bear left on leaving the Universe of Energy and proceed to the Wonders of Life pavilion. See *Cranium Command* (open seasonally).

8. Ride Body Wars, also in the Wonders of Life pavilion (open seasonally).

9. Depart Future World and enter the World Showcase section of the park. Proceed counter-clockwise around the World Showcase Lagoon to Canada. See the film *O Canada!*

10. Exit Canada to the right and explore the United Kingdom. If you're a beer lover, the Rose & Crown Pub serves a great beer sampler. Priority seatings are not required.

11. Continue counter-clockwise and across the bridge to France. See the film *Impressions de France*.

12. At this juncture, the only thing remaining on the touring plan is to explore the interactive exhibits of Innoventions West, across the central plaza from Innoventions East. If you're inclined, you can continue around the lagoon, explore the various pavilions, and even try a couple of the attractions that are scheduled for Day Two. Be sure to return to Future World and Innoventions West by about 5 p.m., since Future World attractions sometimes close as early as 6 or 7 p.m.

13. Return to Future World and check out the exhibits of Innoventions.

14. This concludes Day One of the touring plan. If you linger over exhibits at The Living Seas and Innoventions East and West, it may be late in the day when you finish, and you might consider staying for dinner and *IllumiNations*. If you toured more briskly, you probably will complete the plan by about 4 p.m., even with a full-service lunch.

Day Two

1. Arrive 40 minutes prior to official opening time. When admitted to the park, proceed to the plaza behind Spaceship Earth and then along crescent-shaped Innoventions East building on your left until you see an open passage through the building. Turn left through this passage. After emerging on

the far side of Innoventions East, turn right to Test Track. If you are held up by a rope barrier anywhere along the route from the park entrance to Test Track, don't worry. Just stay put and proceed to Test Track when permitted. Similarly, if you get to Test Track and it's not operating yet, remain in place and be patient. If you do not want to experience Test Track, skip ahead to Step 2. If the wait at Test Track when you arrive exceeds 35 minutes, obtain FASTPASSes and return later to ride.

2. Mission: Space is next door to Test Track. Enjoy. If the wait exceeds 35 minutes, use FASTPASS.

3. After Test Track, retrace your steps and head for the giant geodesic sphere, Spaceship Earth. Ride.

4. After Spaceship Earth, cross to the opposite side of Future World, passing through Innoventions West en route. Proceed to the Living Seas.

5. Proceed to the Imagination pavilion. Take the Journey into Your Imagination ride first, and then see the 3-D movie, *Honey, I Shrunk the Audience*. After the movie, check out the exhibits at the Image Works, also in the Imagination pavilion.

6. Departing the Imagination pavilion, turn right and proceed to the World Showcase section of Epcot.

7. Turn left and proceed clockwise around World Showcase Lagoon. Experience the El Río del Tiempo boat ride at Mexico. The ride is in the far-left corner of the interior courtyard and isn't very well marked. Consign any purchases to Package Pick-up for collection when you leave the park.

8. Go left to Norway. Ride Maelstrom. Use FASTPASS if wait exceeds 20 minutes.

9. Go left to China. See *Reflections of China*.

10. Visit Germany and Italy. Enjoy the settings; there are no rides or films. If you don't have a restaurant priority seating, Sommerfest (fast food) at Germany serves tasty bratwurst, soft pretzels, desserts, and Beck's beer on draft.

11. Continue clockwise to *The American Adventure*. See the show. If you don't have a restaurant priority seating, the Liberty Inn (left side of *The American Adventure*) serves hamburgers, hot dogs, and chicken sandwiches.

12. Visit Japan and Morocco. Consign any purchases to Package Pick-up for collection when you leave the park.

13. This concludes Day Two of the touring plan. If you futzed around in World Showcase shops and it's late in the day, consider staying for dinner and *IllumiNations*. If you caught *IllumiNations* after Day One, consider exiting Epcot through the International Gateway (between the United Kingdom and France) and exploring the restaurants, shops, and clubs of Disney's Board-Walk. The BoardWalk is a five-minute walk from the International Gateway.

Part Twelve

Disney's Animal Kingdom

With its lush flora, winding streams, meandering paths, and exotic setting, the Animal Kingdom is a stunningly beautiful theme park. The landscaping alone conjures images of rain forest, veldt, and formal gardens. Soothing, mysterious, and exciting, every vista is a feast for the eye. Add to this loveliness a population of more than 1,000 animals, replicas of Africa's and Asia's most intriguing architecture, and a diverse array of singularly original attractions, and you have the most unique of all Disney theme parks. In the Animal Kingdom, Disney has created an environment to savor.

At 500 acres, Disney's Animal Kingdom is five times the size of the Magic Kingdom and more than twice the size of Epcot. But like Disney-MGM Studios, most of the Animal Kingdom's vast geography is only accessible on guided tours or as part of attractions. The Animal Kingdom features six sections or "lands": The Oasis, Discovery Island, DinoLand U.S.A., Camp Minnie-Mickey, Africa, and Asia.

Its size notwithstanding, the Animal Kingdom features a limited number of attractions. To be exact, there are six rides, several walk-through exhibits, an indoor theater, four amphitheaters, a conservation exhibit, and a children's playground. However, two of the attractions—Dinosaur and Kilimanjaro Safaris—are among the best in the Disney repertoire.

The evolution of the Animal Kingdom has been interesting. With regard to the Florida theme-park market, it is seen to be taking dead aim at the recently resurgent Busch Gardens in Tampa, a theme park known for its exceptional zoological exhibits and numerous thrill rides. Disney always preferred the neatly controlled movements of audio-animatronic animals to the unpredictable behaviors of real critters. Disney's only previous foray into zoological exhibits landed the Walt Disney Company in court for exterminating a bunch of indigenous birds that tried to take up residence on Disney property. When it comes to "rides," Disney won't even dignify the term. In Disney parks, there are no rides, you see—only adventures. Attractions such as modern roller coasters, where the thrill of

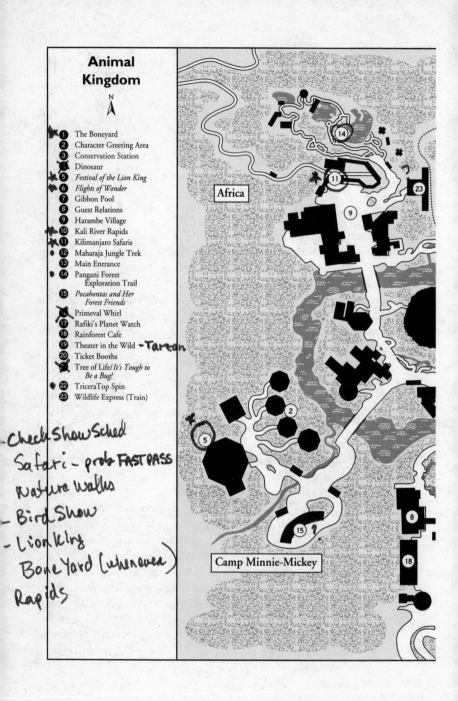

Animal Kingdom

N ↑

1. The Boneyard
2. Character Greeting Area
3. Conservation Station
4. Dinosaur
5. *Festival of the Lion King*
6. *Flights of Wonder*
7. Gibbon Pool
8. Guest Relations
9. Harambe Village
10. Kali River Rapids
11. Kilimanjaro Safaris
12. Maharaja Jungle Trek
13. Main Entrance
14. Pangani Forest
    Exploration Trail
15. *Pocahontas and Her
    Forest Friends*
16. Primeval Whirl
17. Rafiki's Planet Watch
18. Rainforest Cafe
19. Theater in the Wild — Tarzan
20. Ticket Booths
21. Tree of Life/*It's Tough to
    Be a Bug!*
22. TriceraTop Spin
23. Wildlife Express (Train)

Africa

Camp Minnie-Mickey

- Check Show Sched
Safari - prob FASTPASS
Nature Walks
- Bird Show
- Lion King
  Bone Yard (whenever)
Rapids

542

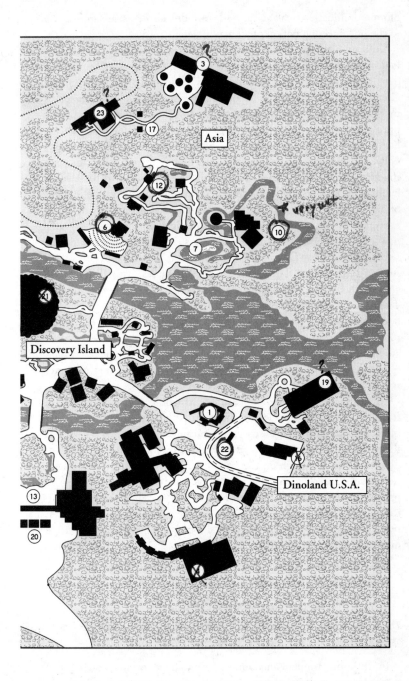

Asia

Discovery Island

Dinoland U.S.A.

motion dominates visual, audio, and story-line elements, are antithetical to the Imagineering notion of attraction design.

Unfortunately for Disney, however, the creative, natural-habitat zoological exhibits and state-of-the-art thrill rides developed by Busch Gardens are immensely popular, and as any student of the Walt Disney Company can attest, there is nothing like a successful competitor to make the Disney folks change their tune. So, all the smoke, mirrors, and press releases aside, here's what you get at the Animal Kingdom: natural-habitat zoological exhibits and state-of-the-art thrill rides. Big surprise!

Even if the recipe is tried and true, the Disney version serves up more than its share of innovations, particularly when it comes to the wildlife habitats. In fact, zoologists worldwide practically salivate at the thought of Disney Imagineers applying their talent to zoo design. Living up to expectations, the wildlife exhibits at the Animal Kingdom do break some new ground. For starters, there's lots of space, thus allowing for the sweeping vistas that Discovery Channel viewers would expect in, say, an African veldt setting. Then there are the enclosures, natural in appearance, with little or no apparent barriers between you and the animals. The operative word, of course, is "apparent." That flimsy stand of bamboo separating you from a gorilla is actually a neatly disguised set of steel rods imbedded in concrete. The Imagineers even take a crack at certain animals' stubborn unwillingness to be on display. A lion that would rather sleep out of sight under a bush, for example, is lured to center stage with nice, cool, climate-controlled artificial rocks.

So far in its short life, the Animal Kingdom has received mixed reviews. Guests complain loudly about the park layout and the necessity of backtracking through Discovery Island in order to access the various theme areas. Congested walkways, lack of shade, and insufficient air conditioning also rank high on the gripe list. However, most of the attractions (with one or two notable exceptions) have been well received. Also praised are the natural habitat animal exhibits as well as the park architecture and landscaping. We marvel at how demographically similar readers come away with such vastly differing opinions. A 36-year-old mother of three, for example, exclaims that:

The Animal Kingdom is a monstrous disappointment! Disney should be ashamed to have their name on it!

While a 34-year-old mom with two children reports:

The Animal Kingdom was our favorite theme park at Disney World. We spent four evenings out of our seven-day vacation there.

In truth, the Animal Kingdom is a park to linger over and savor—two things Disney, with its crowds, lines, and regimentation, has conditioned us not to do. But many people intuit that the Animal Kingdom must be approached in a different way, including this mother of three (ages five, seven, and nine) from Hampton Bays, New York:

Despite the crowds, we really enjoyed Animal Kingdom. In order to enjoy it, you really must have the right attitude. It is an educational experience, not a thrill park. Talk to the employees and you won't regret it. We spoke to an employee who played games with the kids—my daughter found a drawer full of butterflies, and the boys located a hidden ostrich egg and lion skull. If we had not stopped to talk to this guide, we would have joined the hordes running down the trail in search of "something exciting to do."

A Southwestern family agrees, writing:

Animal Kingdom with kids should be approached as you would bird-watching, fossil hunting, or nature walks. To enjoy it, you need to slow down, stop and look, and, especially, engage the cast members. Most have years of experience with animals and are very capable of interacting and sharing their knowledge on any level. Encourage your children to ask questions; the answers are educational, enlightening, and a wonderful alternative to standing in a hot queue.

Arriving

The Animal Kingdom is situated off Osceola Parkway in the southwest corner of Walt Disney World, and is not too far from Blizzard Beach, the Coronado Springs Resort, and the All-Star Resorts. The Animal Kingdom Lodge is about a mile away from the park on its northwest side. From I-4, take Exit 64B, US 192, to the so-called Walt Disney World main entrance (World Drive) and follow the signs to the Animal Kingdom. The Animal Kingdom has its own 6,000-car pay parking lot with close-in parking for the disabled. Once parked, you can walk to the entrance or catch a ride on one of Disney's trademark trams. Be sure to mark the location of your car on your parking receipt and tuck it in a safe place (preferably on your person as opposed to in your car).

The park is connected to other Walt Disney World destinations by the Disney bus system.

Operating Hours

The Animal Kingdom, not unexpectedly, hosted tremendous crowds during its early years. Consequently, Disney management has done a fair amount of fiddling and experimenting with operating hours and opening procedures. Animal Kingdom opening time now roughly corresponds to that of the other parks. Thus, you can expect a 9 a.m. opening during less busy times of the year and an 8 a.m. opening during holidays and high season. The Animal Kingdom usually closes well before the other parks—as early as 5 p.m., in fact, during off-season. More common is a 6 or 7 p.m. closing.

Park opening procedures at the Animal Kingdom vary. Sometimes guests arriving prior to the official opening time are admitted to The Oasis and Discovery Island. The remainder of the park is roped off until official opening time. The rest of the time, those arriving early are held at the entrance turnstiles.

During the financial turmoil of the last few years, Disney laid off a number of cast members and trotted out several cost-cutting initiatives. One of these is to delay the opening of the Asia section of the park, as well as The Boneyard playground, the Wildlife Express train, and Conservation Station until 30 minutes or more after the rest of the Animal Kingdom opens. It's not clear whether these delayed openings are temporary or permanent, or seasonal or year-round.

On holidays and other days of projected heavy attendance, Disney will open the park 30 or 60 minutes early. Our advice is to arrive, admission in hand, 30 minutes before official opening during the summer and holiday periods, and 20 minutes before official opening the rest of the year.

Many guests wrap up their tour and leave by 3:30 or 4 p.m. Lines for the major rides and the 3-D movie in the Tree of Life will usually thin appreciably between 4 p.m. and closing time. If you arrive at 2 p.m. and take in a couple of stage shows (described later), waits should be tolerable by the time you hit the Tree of Life and the rides. As an added bonus for late-afternoon touring, the animals tend to be more active.

The Animal Kingdom has joined the other three major theme parks in the Extra Magic Hour, early entry program. Though participation in the program will probably be a good idea after super-headliner Expedition Everest opens in 2006, it's very counterproductive now. Our testing has shown that the additional attendance on early entry days totally nullifies any advantage associated with being admitted an hour early, and surpasses the time required to see the same set of attractions on a non-early entry day.

ANIMAL KINGDOM SERVICES

Most of the park's service facilities are located inside the main entrance and on Discovery Island as follows:

Wheelchair and Stroller Rentals	Inside the main entrance to the right
Banking Services	ATMs are located at the main entrance and on Discovery Island.
Storage Lockers	Inside the main entrance to the left
Lost and Found	Inside the main entrance to the left
Guest Relations/Information	Inside the main entrance to the left
Live Entertainment/Parade	Included in the park guidemap
Information available free at Guest Relations	

Lost Persons	Lost persons can be reported at Guest Relations and at Baby Services on Discovery Island.
First Aid	On Discovery Island, next to the Creature Comforts Shop
Baby Center/Baby-Care Needs	On Discovery Island, next to the Creature Comforts Shop
Film and Cameras	Just inside the main entrance at Garden Gate Gifts and in Africa at Duka La Filimu

Getting Oriented

At the entrance plaza are ticket kiosks fronting the main entrance. To your right before the turnstiles are the kennel and an ATM. Passing through the turnstiles, wheelchair and stroller rentals are to your right. Guest Relations, the park headquarters for information, handout park maps, entertainment schedules/ *Times Guides*, missing persons, and lost and found, is to the left. Nearby are rest rooms, public phones, and rental lockers. Beyond the entrance plaza you enter The Oasis, a lushly vegetated network of converging pathways winding through a landscape punctuated with streams, waterfalls, and misty glades, and inhabited by what Disney calls "colorful and unusual animals."

The park is arranged somewhat like the Magic Kingdom, in a hub-and-spoke configuration. The lush, tropical Oasis serves as Main Street, funneling visitors to Discovery Island at the center of the park. Dominated by the park's central icon, the 14-story hand-carved Tree of Life, Discovery Island is the park's retail and dining center. From Discovery Island, guests can access the respective theme areas, known as Africa, Camp Minnie-Mickey, Asia, and DinoLand U.S.A. Discovery Island additionally hosts a theater attraction in the Tree of Life, and a number of short nature trails.

To help you plan your day, we have profiled all of the Animal Kingdom's major attractions. We suggest, however, that you be open-minded and try everything. Disney rides and shows are rarely what you would anticipate. For the time being, even if you dawdle in the shops and linger over the wildlife exhibits, you should easily be able to take in the Animal Kingdom in one day.

The Oasis

Though the functional purpose of The Oasis is the same as that of Main Street in the Magic Kingdom (i.e., to funnel guests to the center of the park), it also serves as what Disney calls a "transitional experience." In plain English, this means that it sets the stage and gets you into the right mood to enjoy the Animal Kingdom. You will know the minute you pass through the turnstiles that this is not just another Main Street. Where

Main Street, Hollywood Boulevard, and the Epcot entrance plaza direct you like an arrow straight into the heart of the respective parks, The Oasis immediately envelops you in an environment that is replete with choices. There is not one broad thoroughfare, but rather multiple paths. Each will deliver you to Discovery Island at the center of the park, but which path you choose and what you see along the way is up to you. There is nothing obvious about where you are going, no Cinderella Castle or giant golf ball to beckon you. There is instead a lush, green, canopied landscape with streams, grottos, and waterfalls, an environment that promises adventure without revealing its nature.

The natural-habitat zoological exhibits in The Oasis are representative of those throughout the park. Although extraordinarily lush and beautiful, the exhibits are primarily designed for the comfort and well-being of the animals. This means in essence that you must be patient and look closely if you want to see these animals. A sign will identify the animal(s) in each exhibit, but there's no guarantee the animals will be immediately visible. Because most habitats are large and provide ample terrain for the occupants to hide, you must linger and concentrate, looking for small movements in the vegetation. When you do spot the animal, you may only make out a shadowy figure, or perhaps only a leg or a tail will be visible. In any event, don't expect the animals to stand out like a lump of coal in the snow. Animal-watching Disney-style requires a sharp eye and a bit of effort.

Touring Tips The Oasis is a place to linger and appreciate, and although this is exactly what the designers intended, it will be largely lost on Disney-conditioned guests who blitz through at warp speed to queue up for the big attractions. If you are a blitzer in the morning, plan to spend some time in The Oasis on your way out of the park. The Oasis usually closes 30–60 minutes after the rest of the park.

A PEEK BEHIND THE SCENES WITH JIM HILL

Mixed Messages The Imagineers originally designed the Oasis to be the area where guests learned that the Animal Kingdom was not your typical Disney theme park. The idea was that there were amazing things to be seen here if you took your time. So it's ironic that almost from the Animal Kingdom's opening, cast members were dispatched to hustle visitors through the Oasis by shouting, "THERE'S NO WAIT RIGHT NOW FOR THE AFRICAN SAFARI RIDE!"

NOT TO BE MISSED AT THE ANIMAL KINGDOM

Discovery Island	*It's Tough to Be a Bug!*
Camp Minnie-Mickey	*Festival of the Lion King*
Africa	Kilimanjaro Safaris
DinoLand U.S.A.	Dinosaur

A Word about Animal Kingdom Live Shows

While we were collecting data for our touring-plan software, we discovered that the live performances are scheduled in such a way that it's exceedingly difficult to see all of them in one visit, especially if you want to see all the other stuff too. You will, at least once, need to dart out at the conclusion of one show and run half way across the park to arrive at another show seconds before it begins (and hope that there's enough room at the last minute for you to get a seat). Show times as well as scheduled character appearances and parades are listed in the *Times Guides* available free along with the park guidemap.

A PEEK BEHIND THE SCENES WITH JIM HILL

Follow That Bird
During Animal Kingdom's first few years, so many guests had trouble finding their way back to the parking lot that Disney affixed two enormous, wooden birds over the bridge from Discovery Island to the Oasis pointing the way back to the parking lot.

Discovery Island

Discovery Island is an island of tropical greenery and whimsical equatorial African architecture, executed in vibrant hues of teal, yellow, red, and blue. Connected to the other lands by bridges, the island is the hub from which guests can access the park's various theme areas. A village is arrayed in a crescent around the base of the Animal Kingdom's signature landmark, the Tree of Life. Towering 14 stories above the village, the Tree of Life is this park's version of Cinderella Castle or Spaceship Earth. Flanked by pools, meadows, and exotic gardens populated by a diversity of birds and animals, the Tree of Life houses a theater attraction inspired by the Disney/Pixar film *A Bug's Life.*

As you enter Discovery Island via the bridge from The Oasis and the park entrance, you will see the Tree of Life directly ahead at the 12 o'clock position. The bridge to Asia is to the right of the tree at the 2 o'clock position, with the bridge to DinoLand U.S.A. at roughly 4 o'clock. The bridge connecting The Oasis to Discovery Island is at the 6 o'clock position; the bridge to Camp Minnie-Mickey is at 8 o'clock; and the bridge to Africa is at 11 o'clock.

Discovery Island is the park's central shopping, dining, and services headquarters. It is here that you will find the First Aid and Baby-Care Centers. For the best selection of Disney trademark merchandise, try the Island Mercantile shop. Counter-service food and snacks are available, but there are no full-service restaurants on Discovery Island (the only full-service restaurant in the park is the Rainforest Cafe located to the left of the main entrance).

The Tree of Life/It's Tough to Be a Bug! (FASTPASS)

What It Is 3-D theater show

Scope and Scale Major attraction

When to Go Before 10:30 a.m., after 4 p.m., or use FASTPASS

Special Comments The theater is inside the tree.

Author's Rating Zany and frenetic; ★★★★

Appeal by Age Group

Preschool ★★★½	Teens ★★½	Over 30 ★★★
Grade school ★★★½	Young Adults ★★★	Seniors ★★★

Duration of Presentation Approximately 7½ minutes

Probable Waiting Time 12–30 minutes

Description and Comments The Tree of Life, apart from its size, is quite a work of art. Although from afar it is certainly magnificent and imposing, it is not until you examine the tree at close range that you truly appreciate its rich detail. What appears to be ancient gnarled bark is, in fact, hundreds of carvings depicting all manner of wildlife, each integrated seamlessly into the trunk, roots, and limbs of the tree. A stunning symbol of the interdependence of all living things, the Tree of Life is the most visually compelling structure to be found in any Disney park.

In sharp contrast to the grandeur of the tree is the subject of the attraction housed within its trunk. Called *It's Tough to Be a Bug!*, this humorous 3-D film is about the difficulties of being a very small creature. *It's Tough to Be a Bug!* also contrasts with the relatively serious tone of the Animal Kingdom in general, standing virtually alone in providing some much needed levity and whimsy. *It's Tough To Be A Bug!* is similar to *Honey, I Shrunk the Audience* at Epcot in that it combines a 3-D film with an arsenal of tactile and visual special effects. We rate the *Bugs* as not to be missed.

Touring Tips Because it's situated in the most eye-popping structure in the park, and also because there aren't that many attractions anyway, you can expect *It's Tough to Be a Bug!* to be mobbed most of the day. We recommend going in the morning after Kilimanjaro Safaris, Kali River Rapids, and Dinosaur. If you miss the *Bugs* in the morning, try again in the late afternoon or use FASTPASS.

Be advised that *It's Tough to Be a Bug!* is very intense and that the special effects will do a number on young children as well as anyone who is squeamish about insects. A mother of two from Mobile, Alabama, shared this experience:

It's Tough to Be a Bug! *was too intense for any kid. Our boys are five and seven, and they were scared to death. They love bugs, and they hated this movie. All of the kids in the the-*

ater were screaming and crying. I felt like a terrible mother for taking them into this movie. It is billed as a bug movie for kids, but nothing about it is for kids.

But a Williamsville, New York, woman had it even worse:

We went [to the Animal Kingdom] our very first day and almost lost the girls to any further Disney magic due to the 3-D movie It's Tough to Be a Bug! It was their first Disney experience, and almost their last. The story line was nebulous and difficult to follow—all they were aware of was the torture of sitting in a darkened theater being overrun with bugs. Total chaos, the likes of which I've never experienced, was breaking out around us. A constant stream of parents headed to the exits with terrorized children. Those that were left behind were screaming and crying as well. The 11-year-old refused to talk for 20 minutes after the fiasco, and the three-and-a-half-year-old wanted to go home—not back to the hotel, but home.

Most readers, however, loved the bugs, including this mom from Brentwood, Tennessee:

Comments from your readers make It's Tough to Be a Bug! sound worse than Alien Encounter [now closed]. It's not. It's intense like Honey, I Shrunk the Audience but mostly funny. The bugs are cartoonlike instead of realistic and icky, so I can't understand what all the fuss is about. Disney has conditioned us to think of rodents as cute, so kids think nothing of walking up to a mouse the size of a porta-john, but go nuts over some cartoon bugs. Get a grip!

A PEEK BEHIND THE SCENES WITH JIM HILL

Just One of the Perks of the Job
Michael Eisner himself presided over the meeting where the Imagineers decided what sort of odor Clair de Rume (the stink bug) would emit when it bends over and struts his stuff (so to speak). Of the eight different scents sampled, the one that Eisner found to be the most offensive ended up in the show.

Camp Minnie-Mickey

This land is designed to be the Disney characters' Animal Kingdom headquarters. A small land, Camp Minnie-Mickey is about the size of Mickey's Toontown Fair but has a rustic and woodsy theme like a summer camp. In addition to a character meeting and greeting area, Camp Minnie-Mickey is home to two live stage productions featuring Disney characters.

Situated in a cul-de-sac, Camp Minnie-Mickey is a pedestrian nightmare. Lines for the two stage shows and from the character greeting areas spill out into the congested walkways, making movement almost impossible. To compound the problem, hundreds of parked strollers clog the paths, squeezing the flow of traffic to a trickle. Meanwhile, hordes of guests trying to enter Camp Minnie-Mickey collide with guests trying to exit on the bridge connecting the camp to Discovery Island. To make matters worse, Disney positions vendor carts on the approaches to the bridge. It's a planning error of the first order, one that seems totally avoidable in a theme park with as much usable acreage as the Animal Kingdom.

A PEEK BEHIND THE SCENES WITH JIM HILL

A Coming Attraction?
As you cross the bridge over Safari River into Camp Minnie-Mickey, look on the riverbank to your right for a fearsome creature made of stone and an odd looking cave. This is where the Imagineers eventually hope to build "Beastly Kingdom," a whole new land for Disney's Animal Kingdom. If developed, this area will celebrate mythical creatures like dragons and unicorns. Just don't hold your breath, the idea has been kicking around since 1997.

Character Trails

Description and Comments   Characters can be found at the end of each of several "character trails" named Jungle, Forest, or some such, and Mickey and Minnie. Each trail has its own private reception area and, of course, its own queue. Jungle Characters features characters from *The Lion King* and *The Jungle Book*, and the other trail generally offers characters from Disney's latest movie. The Minnie trail leads to Minnie and the Mickey trail to Mickey. One or two characters are present in the Forest and Jungle greeting areas, while Minnie and Mickey each work solo. Sometimes other characters such as Goofy or Daisy work solo in place of the Jungle and Forest characters.

Touring Tips   Characters usually appear an hour after the rest of the park opens. Waiting in line to see the characters can be very time-consuming. We recommend visiting early in the morning or late in the afternoon. Because there are fewer attractions at the Animal Kingdom than at the other parks, expect to find a disproportionate number of guests in Camp Minnie-Mickey. If the place is really mobbed, you may want to consider meeting the characters in one of the other parks. Ditto for the stage shows.

✷Festival of the Lion King

What It Is   Theater-in-the-round stage show

Scope and Scale   Major attraction

When to Go   Before 11 a.m. or after 4 p.m.

Special Comments   Performance times are listed in the handout park map or *Times Guide*

Author's Rating   Upbeat and spectacular, not to be missed; ★★★★

Appeal by Age Group

Preschool ★★★★	Teens ★★★★	Over 30 ★★★★
Grade school ★★★★½	Young Adults ★★★★	Seniors ★★★★

Duration of Presentation   25 minutes

Preshow Entertainment   None

Probable Waiting Time   20–35 minutes

Description and Comments   This energetic production, inspired by Disney's *Lion King* feature, is part stage show, part parade, part circus. Guests are seated in four sets of bleachers surrounding the stage and organized into separate cheering sections, which are called on to make elephant, warthog, giraffe, and lion noises (you won't be alone if you don't know how to make a giraffe or warthog noise). There is a great deal of parading around, some acrobatics, and a lot of singing and dancing. By our count, every tune from *The Lion King* is belted out and reprised several times. No joke—if you don't know the words to all the songs by the end of the show, you must have been asleep.

Unofficial Guide readers have been almost unanimous in their praise of *Festival of the Lion King*. This letter from a Naples, Florida, mom is typical:

> *Festival of the Lion King is a spectacular show with singers, dancers, fire twirlers, acrobats, robotics, and great set design. My whole family agreed this was the best thing we experienced at Animal Kingdom.*

Touring Tips   This show is both popular and difficult to see. Your best bet is to go to the first show in the morning or to one of the last two performances in the evening. To see the show during the more crowded middle of the day, you'll need to queue up at least 35–45 minutes before show time. There are two separate lines, two for each set of bleachers. The queues fill from left to right and are seated in the same order. To minimize standing in the hot sun, refrain from hopping in line until the Disney people begin directing guests to the far-right queue. If you have small children or short adults in your party, sit higher up in the bleachers. The first five rows in particular have very little rise, making it difficult for those in rows two through five to see. Though the theater is covered and air is circulated by fans, there is no air-conditioning.

A PEEK BEHIND THE SCENES WITH JIM HILL

Parade Float Burial Ground   Folks who've been to Disneyland in the past decade may find parts of the Festival of the Lion King Show show that look very familiar. The enormous Simba, Pumba, giraffe and elephant puppets that appear in the presentation actually started life as pieces of parade floats featured in Disneyland's daily "Lion King Celebration."

Pocahontas and Her Forest Friends

What It Is   Conservation-theme stage show

Scope and Scale   Major attraction

When to Go   Before 11 a.m. or after 4 p.m.

Special Comments   Performance times are listed in the daily entertainment schedule/*Times Guide*.

Author's Rating   A little sappy; ★★½

Appeal by Age Group

Preschool ★★★½	Teens ★★★	Over 30 ★★★
Grade school ★★★½	Young Adults ★★★½	Seniors ★★★

Duration of Presentation   15 minutes

Preshow Entertainment   None

Probable Waiting Time   20–30 minutes

Description and Comments   This show featuring Pocahontas addresses the role of man in protecting the natural world. Various live creatures of the forest, including a raccoon, a snake, and a turkey, as well as a couple of audio-animatronic trees (Grandmother Willow and Twig), assist Pocahontas in making the point. The presentation is gushy and overacted but has its moments nonetheless.

However, as a Michigan reader reports, *Pocahontas* is not in the same league as *Festival of the Lion King:*

Festival of the Lion King was a wonderful show. Unfortunately, we saw it just before seeing the Pocahontas *show. It put* Pocahontas *to shame. Instead of being moved by the show's message, I wondered how much kindling Grandmother Willow would make.*

Touring Tips Because the theater is relatively small, and because Camp Minnie-Mickey stays so mobbed, the *Pocahontas* show is hard to get into. Among other problems, its queuing area adjoins that of *Festival of the Lion King* next door. If you approach when a lot of guests are waiting, which is almost always, it's hard to figure out which show you're lining up for. To avoid the hassle, try to catch *Pocahontas* before 11 a.m. or after 3 p.m. Regardless of time of day, arrive about 20–30 minutes before show time and ask a Disney cast member to steer you to the correct line.

Africa

Africa is the largest of the Animal Kingdom's lands, and guests enter through Harambe, Disney's idealized and immensely sanitized version of a modern, rural African town. There is a market (with modern cash registers), and counter-service food is available. What distinguishes Harambe is its understatement. Far from the stereotypical great-white-hunter image of an African town, Harambe is definitely (and realistically) not exotic. The buildings, while interesting, are quite plain and architecturally simple. Though certainly better maintained and more aseptic than the real McCoy, Disney's Harambe would be a lot more at home in Kenya than the Magic Kingdom's Main Street would be in Missouri.

Harambe serves as the gateway to the African veldt habitat, the Animal Kingdom's largest and most ambitious zoological exhibit. Access to the veldt is via the Kilimanjaro Safaris attraction, located at the end of Harambe's main drag near the fat-trunked baobab tree. Harambe is also the departure point for the train to Rafiki's Planet Watch and Conservation Station, the park's veterinary headquarters.

Kilimanjaro Safaris (FASTPASS)

What It Is Truck ride through an African wildlife reservation

Scope and Scale Super headliner

When to Go As soon as the park opens, in the 2 hours before closing, or use FASTPASS

Author's Rating Truly exceptional; ★★★★★

Appeal by Age Group

Preschool ★★★★	Teens ★★★★½	Over 30 ★★★★½
Grade school ★★★★★	Young Adults ★★★★½	Seniors ★★★★★

Duration of Ride About 20 minutes

Average Wait in Line per 100 People ahead of You 4 minutes

Assumes Full-capacity operation with 18-second dispatch interval

Loading Speed Fast

Description and Comments   The park's premier zoological attraction, Kilimanjaro Safaris offers an exceptionally realistic, albeit brief, imitation of an actual African photo safari. Thirty-two guests at a time board tall, open safari vehicles and are dispatched into a simulated African veldt habitat. Animals such as zebra, wildebeest, impala, Thomson's gazelle, giraffe, and even rhinos roam apparently free, while predators such as lions, as well as potentially dangerous large animals like hippos, are separated from both prey and guests by all-but-invisible, natural-appearing barriers. Although the animals have more than 100 acres of savanna, woodland, streams, and rocky hills to call home, careful placement of water holes, forage, and salt licks ensure that the critters are hanging out by the road when safari vehicles roll by.

A scripted narration provides a story line about finding Big Red and Little Red, a mother elephant and her baby, while an on-board guide points out and identifies the various animals encountered. Toward the end of the ride, the safari chases poachers who have just wounded Big Red.

Having traveled in Kenya and Tanzania, I will tell you that Disney has done an amazing job of replicating the sub-Saharan east African landscape. The main difference that an east African would notice is that Disney's version is greener and (generally speaking) less barren. Like on a real African safari, what animals you see (and how many) is pretty much a matter of luck. We've tried Disney's safari upwards of 50 times and had a different experience on each trip.

If the attraction has a shortcoming, it is the rather strident story line about the poachers and Big Red, which while thought-provoking, is somewhat distracting when you are trying to spot and enjoy the wildlife. Also, because the story is repeated on every trip, it really gets on your nerves after the first couple of times.

Touring Tips   Kilimanjaro Safaris is the Animal Kingdom's top draw. In fact, we've not seen an attraction in any Disney park that so completely channels guest traffic. While Space Mountain, Test Track, and Tower of Terror attract throngs of early-morning guests, there remain a substantial number of additional guests who head for other attractions. At the Animal Kingdom, however, as many as 90% of those on hand at opening head straight for the safari, and later-arriving guests do exactly the same thing. Over the first couple of years, Disney tried any number of ploys to lure guests elsewhere, but to no avail. So, if you want to see Kilimanjaro Safaris without a long wait, be one of the first through the turnstiles and make a beeline for Africa (or use FASTPASS). If you are held up en route by a rope barrier or by cast members, stay put until you are permitted to continue on to the attraction.

As a couple from Laureldale, Pennsylvania, explains, beating the crowd is not the only reason to race to Kilimanjaro Safaris first thing in the morning:

> When I showed my Animal Kingdom photos to a coworker who had recently been to WDW, she remarked how "lucky" I was to see so many animals (she had been disappointed). I promptly told her that "luck" had nothing to do with it! We were willing to sacrifice sleep and breakfast to get there as soon as the gates opened and sprinted (which is no easy feat for two middle-aged, out-of-shape people) to the Safari where we rode twice without waiting. We were rewarded with so many groups of animals it was hard to take pictures of all of them. Twice our truck stopped to let animals cross the road, and even the lions and cheetahs were up and around. If you want to see animals you must get your ample butts there early—it's worth it!

Waits for the Kilimanjaro Safaris diminish in late afternoon, sometimes as early 3:30 p.m., but more commonly somewhat later. As noted above, Kilimanjaro Safaris is a FASTPASS attraction. If the wait exceeds 30 minutes when you arrive, by all means use FASTPASS. The downside to FASTPASS, and the reason we prefer that you ride as soon as the park opens, is that there aren't many other attractions in Africa to occupy your attention while you wait for your FASTPASS return time. This means you will probably be touring somewhere far removed when it's time to backtrack to Safaris. The best way to avoid this disruption is to see the attraction first thing in the morning.

If you want to take photos on your safari, be advised that the vehicle doesn't stop very often, so be prepared to snap while under way. Also, don't worry about the ride itself: it really isn't very rough. Finally, the only thing that a young child might find intimidating is crossing an "old bridge" that pretends to collapse under your truck.

A PEEK BEHIND THE SCENES WITH JIM HILL

A Bit Too Real   During Kilimanjaro Safari's preview period, the tour vehicles actually rolled guests past a giant plastic version of Big Red, clearly showing visitors that poachers had killed Little Red's mom. But so many tourists were upset by the sight of the big fake dead momma elephant that, prior to Animal Kingdom's official opening, Big Red was pulled out of the attraction, never to be seen again.

Pangani Forest Exploration Trail

What It Is Walk-through zoological exhibit

Scope and Scale Major attraction

When to Go Anytime

Author's Rating ★★★

Appeal by Age Group

Preschool ★★½	Teens ★★½	Over 30 ★★★
Grade school ★★★	Young Adults ★★★	Seniors ★★★

Duration of Tour About 20–25 minutes

Description and Comments Because guests disembark from the safari at the entrance to the Pangani Forest Exploration Trail, many guests try the trail immediately after the safari. Winding between the domain of two troops of lowland gorillas, it's hard to see what, if anything, separates you from the primates. Also on the trail are a hippo pool with an underwater viewing area, and a naked mole rat exhibit (I promise I'm not making this up). A highlight of the trail is an exotic bird aviary so craftily designed that you can barely tell you're in an enclosure.

Touring Tips The Pangani Forest Exploration Trail is lush, beautiful, and jammed to the gills with people much of the time. Guests exiting the safari can choose between returning to Harambe or walking the Pangani Forest Exploration Trail. Not unexpectedly, many opt for the trail. Thus, when the safari is operating at full tilt, it spews hundreds of guests every couple of minutes onto the Exploration Trail. The one-way trail in turn becomes so clogged that nobody can move or see much of anything. After a minute or two, however, you catch the feel of the mob moving forward in small lurches. From then on you shift, elbow, grunt, and wriggle your way along, every so often coming to an animal exhibit. Here you endeavor to work your way close to the rail but are opposed by people trapped against the rail who are trying to rejoin the surging crowd. The animals, as well as their natural-habitat enclosures, are pretty nifty if you can fight close enough to see them.

Clearly this attraction is either badly designed, misplaced, or both. Your only real chance for enjoying it is to walk through before 10 a.m. (i.e., before the safari hits full stride) or after 3:30 p.m.

Another strategy, especially if you're more into the wildlife than the thrill rides, is to head for Kilimanjaro Safaris as soon as the park opens and get a FASTPASS instead of riding. Early in the morning, the return window will be short, just short enough in fact for an uncrowded, leisurely tour of the Pangani Forest Exploration Trail before you go on safari.

A PEEK BEHIND THE SCENES WITH JIM HILL

Finger Food   Given that this is a Disney theme park, it's easy to forget that real animals can sometimes be really dangerous. Take, for example, the poor zoo keeper who was hand-feeding grapes to a gorilla. The gorilla mistook the end of one of his handler's fingers as a grape and nipped it right off. So when the signs read "Keep your hands and arms outside the cage," believe them, okay?

Rafiki's Planet Watch

Rafiki's Planet Watch showed up on park maps in 2001. It's not a "land" and not really an attraction either. Our best guess is that Disney is using the name as an umbrella for Conservation Station, the petting zoo, and the environmental exhibits accessible from Harambe via the Wildlife Express train. Presumably, Disney hopes that invoking Rafiki (a beloved character from *The Lion King*) will stimulate guests to make the effort to check out things. As for your kids seeing Rafiki, don't bet on it. The closest likeness we've seen here is a two-dimensional wooden cutout.

Wildlife Express

What It Is   Scenic railroad ride to Rafiki's Planet Watch and Conservation Station

Scope and Scale   Minor attraction

When to Go   Anytime

Special Comments   Opens 30 minutes after the rest of the park

Author's Rating   Ho hum; ★★

Appeal by Age Group

Preschool ★★★	Teens ★½	Over 30 ★★½
Grade school ★★★	Young Adults ★★½	Seniors ★★½

Duration of Ride   About 5–7 minutes one way

Average Wait in Line per 100 People ahead of You   9 minutes

Loading Speed   Moderate

Description and Comments   A transportation ride that snakes behind the African wildlife reserve as it makes its loop connecting Harambe to Rafiki's Planet Watch and Conservation Station. En route, you see the nighttime enclosures for the animals that populate the Kilimanjaro Safaris. Similarly, returning to Harambe, you see the backstage areas of Asia. Regardless which direction you're heading, the sights are not especially interesting.

Touring Tips Most guests will embark for Rafiki's Planet Watch and Conservation Station after experiencing the Kilimanjaro Safaris and the Pangani Forest Exploration Trail. Thus, the train begins to get crowded between 10 and 11 a.m. Though you may catch a glimpse of several species from the train, it can't compare to Kilimanjaro Safaris for seeing the animals.

A PEEK BEHIND THE SCENES WITH JIM HILL

The Best-Laid Plans According to the Imagineers' original plans for Disney's Animal Kingdom, the park was supposed to feature an authentic-looking steam train that took guests out for a scenic trip through the pseudo-savanna. But planners then realized that real animals could be somewhat erratic and possibly dart out in front of the train and get hit, or get scalded by the steam. Ultimately, for safety's sake, the Animal Kingdom ended up with a battery-powered train that basically goes nowhere near the real animals.

Habitat Habit!

Listed on the park map as an attraction is Habitat Habit!, located on the pedestrian path between the train station and Conservation Station. Habitat Habit consists of a tiny collections of signs (about co-existence with wildlife) and a few cotton-top tamarins. To call it an attraction is absurd.

Conservation Station and Affection Section

What It Is Behind-the-scenes walk-through educational exhibit and petting zoo
Scope and Scale Minor attraction
When to Go Anytime
Special Comments Opens 30 minutes after the rest of the park
Author's Rating Evolving; ★★★
Appeal by Age Group

Preschool ★★½	Teens ★½	Over 30 ★★½
Grade school ★★	Young Adults ★★½	Seniors ★★½

Probable Waiting Time None

Description and Comments Conservation Station is the Animal Kingdom's veterinary and conservation headquarters. Located on the perimeter of the African section of the park, Conservation Station is, strictly speaking, a backstage, working facility. Here guests can meet wildlife experts, observe some of the Station's ongoing projects, and learn about the behind-the-scenes operations of the park. The Station includes, among other things, a rehabilitation area for injured animals and a nursery for recently born (or hatched) critters. Vets and other experts are on hand to answer questions.

While there are several permanent exhibits, including Affection Section (an animal petting area), what you see at Conservation Station will largely depend on what's going on when you arrive. On the days we visited, there wasn't enough happening to warrant waiting in line twice (coming and going) for the train. Most of our readers comment that Conservation Station is not worth the hassle. A Tinley Park, Illinois, mom writes:

Skip Conservation Station at the Animal Kingdom. Between the train ride to get to it and being there, we wasted a precious one and a half hours!

A mother of one from Austin, Texas, had a better experience:

Best thing at Conservation Station was the wildlife experts presenting one animal at a time—live, with info—very interesting.

And a reader from Kent in the United Kingdom was amused by both the goings-on and the other guests:

The most memorable part of the Animal Kingdom for me was watching a veterinary surgeon and his team [at Conservation Station] perform an operation on a rat snake that had inadvertently swallowed a golf ball! Presumably believing it to be an egg. This operation took about an hour and caused at least one onlooker to pass out.

You can access Conservation Station by taking the Wildlife Express train directly from Harambe. To return to the center of the park, continue the loop from Conservation Station back to Harambe.

Touring Tips Conservation Station is interesting, but you have to invest a little effort and it helps to be inquisitive. Because it's on the far-flung border of the park, you'll never bump into Conservation Station unless you take the train.

A PEEK BEHIND THE SCENES WITH JIM HILL

OK, Who Can Make the Most Manure?
Of all the informational exhibits at Conservation Station, perhaps the most entertaining ones are the signs you'll discover hanging inside the bathroom stalls and/or over the urinals. The statistics listed here, though admittedly not appropriate for dinner conversation, are fascinating nonetheless.

Asia

Crossing the Asia Bridge from Discovery Island, you enter Asia through the village of Anandapur, a veritable collage of Asian themes inspired by the architecture and ruins of India, Thailand, Indonesia, and Nepal. Situated near the bank of the Chakranadi River (translation: the river that runs in circles) and surrounded by lush vegetation, Anandapur provides access to a gibbon exhibit and to Asia's two feature attractions, the Kali River Rapids whitewater raft ride and the Maharajah Jungle Trek. Also in Asia is *Flights of Wonder,* an educational production about birds.

Coming to Asia in 2006 is a super-headliner roller coaster called Expedition Everest (yep, another mountain, and at 200 feet, the tallest in Florida). You'll board an old mountain railway destined for the foot of Mount Everest that ends up racing both forwards and backwards through caverns and frigid canyons en route to paying a social call on the abominable snowman. Expedition Everest is being billed as a "family thrill ride," which means simply that it will be more like Big Thunder Mountain Railroad than the Rock 'n' Roller Coaster.

A PEEK BEHIND THE SCENES WITH JIM HILL

Large Single Person Seeks Dinner Date with Willing Tourists An abominable Snowman, who'll stand over 20 feet tall, will be the star of Expedition Everest. He will be an unmannerly, ill-tempered creature with pointy fangs, matted fur, and razor sharp claws, who'll take a swipe at every trainload of guests as they whiz backwards (Yikes!) down the mountainside.

Kali River Rapids (FASTPASS)

[handwritten: bring change of clothes or wear poncho]

What It Is Whitewater raft ride

Scope and Scale Headliner

When to Go Before 10:30 a.m., after 4:30 p.m., or use FASTPASS

Special Comments You are guaranteed to get wet. Opens 30 minutes after the rest of the park. Height requirement: 38" tall. Switching off available.

Author's Rating Short but scenic; ★★★½

Appeal by Age Group

Preschool ★★★★	Teens ★★★★	Over 30 ★★★½
Grade school ★★★★	Young Adults ★★★½	Seniors ★★★

Duration of Ride About 5 minutes

Average Wait in Line per 100 People ahead of You 5 minutes

Loading Speed Moderate

Description and Comments Whitewater raft rides have been a hot-weather favorite of theme-park patrons for over 20 years. The ride itself consists of an unguided trip down a man-made river in a circular rubber raft with a platform seating 12 people mounted on top. The raft essentially floats free in the current and is washed downstream through rapids and waves. Because the river is fairly wide, with numerous currents, eddies, and obstacles, there is no telling exactly where the raft will drift. Thus, each trip is different and exciting. At the end of the ride, a conveyor belt hauls the raft up to be unloaded and prepared for the next group of guests.

What distinguishes Kali River Rapids from other theme-park raft rides is Disney's trademark attention to visual detail. Where many raft rides essentially plunge down a concrete ditch, Kali River Rapids flows through a dense rain forest, past waterfalls, temple ruins, and bamboo thickets, emerging into a cleared area where greedy loggers have ravaged the forest, and finally drifting back under the tropical canopy as the river cycles back to Anandapur. Along the way, your raft runs a gauntlet of raging cataracts, log jams, and other dangers.

Disney has done a great job with the visuals on this attraction. The queuing area, which winds through an ancient southeast Asian temple, is one of the most striking and visually interesting settings of any Disney attraction. And though the sights on the raft trip itself are also first class, the attraction is marginal in two important respects. First, it's only about three and a half minutes on the water, and second, well … it's a weenie ride. Sure, you get wet, but otherwise the drops and rapids are not all that exciting. And how wet do you get? A reader from Plymouth, Michigan, has the answer:

The whitewater rafting ride is great fun but beware!! Rather than just getting a little wet, like Splash Mountain, we were <u>soaked to the skin</u> after this ride. It was beyond "fun getting wet," literally drenching you with buckets of water. Poncho sales were brisk the day we were there.

You can use FASTPASS to ride later in the day when it's a little warmer. A family from Humble, Texas, rode early in the morning on a cool day, shares this:

Our plan hit a definite wall upon experiencing Kali River Rapids as number two on the schedule. We did not read about the precautions for this ride in your book until after riding. The six-year-old and mom were COMPLETELY drenched—so much so that we actually had to leave the park and go back to our room at [Port Orleans] to change clothes. Since the temperature was around 60 degrees that morning, we were pretty miserable by the time we got back to our room. Needless to say, our schedule was shot by that time. We would not recommend Kali River Rapids so early in the morning when the weather is chilly.

A couple from Spring, Texas, rode during warmer weather, reporting:

Kali River Rapids gives new meaning to the term "You May Get Wet." More like drenched to the bone! Splash Mountain is nothing close. Four hours of touring later I was only beginning to feel dry. Obviously, Disney needs to lessen the aquatic experience here. This unwelcome bath has resulted in an interesting and undesirable psychological reaction for both of us. [My companion] refused to go on any ride or even into any theater where there was a chance of getting wet. As for me, every time I've been unexpectedly sprayed by water, even after leaving Disney, I withdraw and shudder with fear.

Two self-described "single babes" admonish our soggy readers to "get over it":

If you're going to ride Kali River Rapids, tough it out and get wet. Don't wrap yourself in plastic. Wet butts dry fast and keep you cool in the meantime!

Touring Tips This attraction is hugely popular, especially on hot summer days. Ride Kali River Rapids before 10 a.m., after 4:30 p.m., or use FASTPASS. You can expect to get wet and probably drenched on this ride. Our recommendation is to wear shorts to the park and bring along a jumbo-size trash bag as well as a smaller plastic bag. Before boarding the raft, take off your socks and punch holes in your jumbo bag for your head. Though you can also cut holes for your arms, you will probably stay dryer with your arms inside the bag. Use the smaller plastic bag to wrap around your shoes. If you are worried about mussing your hairdo, bring a third bag for your head.

A Shaker Heights, Ohio, family who adopted our garbage bag attire discovered that staying dry on the Kali River Rapids is not without social consequences:

I must tell you that the Disney cast members and the other people in our raft looked at us like we had just beamed down from Mars. Plus, we didn't cut arm holes in our trash bags because we thought we'd stay drier. Only problem was once we sat down we couldn't fasten our seat belts. The Disney person was quite put out and asked sarcastically whether we needed wetsuits and snorkels. After a lot of wiggling and adjusting and helping each other we finally got belted in and off we went looking like sacks of fertilizer with little heads perched on top. It was very embarrassing, but I must admit that we stayed nice and dry.

Other tips for staying dry (make that drier) include wearing as little as the law and Disney allow and storing a change of clothes in a park rental locker. Sandals are the perfect footwear for water rides. As a last-ditch effort to keep your shoes moderately dry (if you don't have sandals), try to <u>prop your feet up above the bottom of the raft.</u>

A PEEK BEHIND THE SCENES WITH JIM HILL

Play Nicely with the Other Tourists Need to work out a few frustrations after a long day at the park? Then try grabbing one of the water-squirting elephants flanking the exit of the Kali River Rapids. You can easily soak (or resoak) a raft-load of guests as they come floating by. Don't worry about retribution. Chances are that other WDW guests were spraying you when you sailed past.

Maharaja Jungle Trek

What It Is Walk-through zoological exhibit

Scope and Scale Headliner

When to Go Anytime

Special Comments Opens 30 minutes after the rest of the park

Author's Rating A standard-setter for natural habitat design; ★★★★

Appeal by Age Group

Preschool ★★★	Teens ★★★	Over 30 ★★★★
Grade school ★★★½	Young Adults ★★★½	Seniors ★★★★

Duration of Tour About 20–30 minutes

Description and Comments The Maharaja Jungle Trek is a zoological nature walk similar to the Pangani Forest Exploration Trail, but with an Asian setting and Asian animals. You start with Komodo dragons and then work up to Malayan tapirs. Next is a cave with fruit bats. Ruins of the maharaja's palace provide the setting for Bengal tigers. From the top of a parapet in the palace you can view a herd of blackbuck antelope and Asian deer. The trek concludes with an aviary.

Labyrinthine, overgrown, and elaborately detailed, the temple ruin would be a compelling attraction even without the animals. Throw in a few bats, bucks, and Bengals and you're in for a treat.

Most readers agree. From a Tolland, Connecticut, woman:

We went to AK last year and must say—what a difference a year makes! We saw more animals in the first hour this visit than we did the whole day last year. The Bengal tigers were especially exciting—they look so close to where you are in the "ruins." The staff there was so helpful. You truly get the feeling they love their jobs. The kids especially liked the bat exhibit.

And a Washington, D.C., couple chipped in with this:

We went on the Maharaja Jungle Trek, which was absolutely amazing. We were able to see all the animals, which were awake by that time (9:30 a.m.), including the elusive tigers. The part of the jungle trek with the birds was fabulous. If you looked, you could spot hundreds of birds, some of which were eating on the ground a mere three feet away from me. Recommend to future visitors to take their time walking through the jungle, since most of the animals are not obvious to the breezing eye and you must look for them. It is worth the extra time to see such an unusual exhibit.

Touring Tips   The Jungle Trek does not get as jammed up as the Pangani Forest Exploration Trail and is a good choice for midday touring when most other attractions are crowded. The downside, of course, is that the exhibit showcases tigers, tapirs, and other creatures that might not be as active in the heat of the day as proverbial mad dogs and Englishmen.

Flights of Wonder

What It Is   Stadium show about birds

Scope and Scale   Major attraction

When to Go   Anytime

Special Comments   Performance times are listed in the handout park map or *Times Guide*

Author's Rating   Unique; ★★★★

Appeal by Age Group

Preschool ★★★★	Teens ★★★½	Over 30 ★★★★
Grade school ★★★★	Young Adults ★★★★	Seniors ★★★★

Duration of Presentation   30 minutes

Preshow Entertainment   None

Probable Waiting Time   20 minutes

Description and Comments   Both interesting and fun, *Flights of Wonder* is well paced and showcases a surprising number of different bird species. The show has been rescripted, abandoning an improbable plot for a more straightforward educational presentation. The focus of *Flights of Wonder* is on the natural talents and characteristics of the various species, so don't expect to see any parrots riding bicycles. The natural behaviors, however, far surpass any tricks learned from humans. Overall, the presentation is fascinating and exceeds most guests' expectations. A Brattleboro, Vermont, reader found *Flights of Wonder* especially compelling, writing:

In our opinion the highlight of the Animal Kingdom is *Flights of Wonder*. The ornithologist guide is not only a wealth of information but a talented, comedic entertainer. The birds are thrilling, and we especially appreciated the fact that their antics, although fascinating to behold, were not the results of training against the grain but actual survival techniques the birds use in the wild.

Touring Tips   *Flights of Wonder* plays at the stadium located near the Asia Bridge on the walkway into Asia. Though the stadium is covered, it's not air-conditioned, thus, early-morning and late-afternoon performances are more comfortable. To play it safe, arrive about 10–15 minutes before show time.

A PEEK BEHIND THE SCENES WITH JIM HILL

Those of you who suffer from ornithophobia (fear of birds) would be well advised to steer clear of this show. You might also want to give it a pass if you fear high dry cleaning bills. How come? Because *Flights of Wonder's* performers (birds, some quite large) all enter from the rear of the theater, flying in over the heads of the audience. On occasion the birds have been known to drop "a present" on a guest or two.

DinoLand U.S.A.

This most typically Disney of the Animal Kingdom's lands is a cross between an anthropological dig and a quirky roadside attraction. Accessible via the bridge from Discovery Island, DinoLand U.S.A. is home to a children's play area, a nature trail, a 1,500-seat amphitheater, and Dinosaur, one of the Animal Kingdom's two thrill rides.

Also in Dinoland are a couple of natural history exhibits including Dino-Sue, an exact replica of the largest, most complete Tyrannosaurus Rex discovered to date. Named after fossil hunter, Sue Hendrickson, the replica (like the original) is 40 feet long and 13 feet tall. And no, it doesn't dance, sing, or whistle, but it will get your attention nonetheless.

Dinosaur (FASTPASS)

What It Is Motion-simulator dark ride

Scope and Scale Super headliner

When to Go Before 10:30 a.m., in the hour before closing, or use FASTPASS

Special Comments Must be 40" tall to ride. Switching off option provided (see pages 266–268).

Author's Rating Really improved; ★★★★½

Appeal by Age Group

Preschool †	Teens ★★★★½	Over 30 ★★★★½
Grade school ★★★★½	Young Adults ★★★★½	Seniors ★★★½

† *Sample size too small for an accurate rating.*

Duration of Ride 3⅓ minutes

Average Wait in Line per 100 People ahead of You 3 minutes

Assumes Full-capacity operation with 18-second dispatch interval

Loading Speed Fast

Description and Comments Dinosaur, formerly known as Countdown to Extinction, is a combination track ride and motion simulator. In addition to moving along a cleverly hidden track, the ride vehicle also bucks and pitches (the simulator part) in sync with the visuals and special effects encountered. The plot has you traveling back in time on a mission of rescue and conservation. Your objective, believe it or not, is to haul back a living dinosaur before the species becomes extinct. Whoever is operating the clock, however, cuts it a little close, and you arrive on the prehistoric scene just as a giant asteroid is hurling toward Earth. General mayhem ensues as you evade carnivorous predators, catch Barney, and make your escape before the asteroid hits.

Dinosaur is a technological clone of the Indiana Jones ride at Disneyland. A good effort, though not as visually interesting as Indiana Jones, Dinosaur serves up nonstop action from beginning to end with brilliant visual effects. Elaborate even by Disney standards, the attraction provides a tense, frenetic ride embellished by the entire Imagineering arsenal of high-tech gimmickry. Although the ride is jerky, it's not too rough for seniors. The menacing dinosaurs, however, along with the intensity of the experience, make Dinosaur a no-go for younger children.

Dinosaur, to our surprise and joy, has been refined and cranked up a couple of notches on the intensity scale. The latest version is darker, more interesting, and much zippier. A mother from Kansasville, Wisconsin, liked it a lot, commenting:

Dinosaur is the best ride at WDW. Our group of ten, ranging in age from 65 (grandma) to 8 (grandson), immediately—and unanimously!—got back in line immediately after finishing.

A 20-something guy from Muncie, Indiana, however, wasn't so sure:

The Dinosaur attraction was the scariest ride I have ever been on. I'm 24 and love thrill rides, but I didn't open my eyes for half of the ride. I can't believe younger children are permitted to ride.

And speaking of younger children, we got plenty of feedback about their reactions: First, from a Michigan family:

Beware Dinosaur. My seven-year-old son withstood every ride Disney threw at him, from Body Wars to Space Mountain to Tower of Terror. Dinosaur, however, did him in. By the end of the ride, he was riding with his head down, scared to look around. It is intense, combining scary visual dinosaur effects with some demanding roller coaster–like simulation.

Next from a mother of two from Westford, Massachusetts:

My six-year-old felt the Dinosaur ride was far scarier than [now defunct]Alien Encounter or any other ride at Disney. It is very dark (like Alien), but the dinosaurs pop out at you very quickly—I witnessed several adults who were quite shaken by it as well.

From a Florida mom:

This is definitely not for the faint-hearted, and small children should not go on it unless they have nerves of steel!

And finally, a man from Irving, Texas, didn't mind the dinosaurs but got more than he bargained for in the lurching ride vehicle:

One attraction I think you missed the boat on was Dinosaur. I'm 38 and have ridden many roller coasters. I have never ridden anything that tossed me back and forth so far and so quickly as Dinosaur. The preshow was well done, but the ride itself was far too violent. I don't mind that it tossed and tilted me in one direction; my problem is that half a second later, it tossed and tilted me in other directions and kept tossing me back and forth. Aside from the welcome seat belts it was like a bucking bronco. You mentioned that it wasn't too bad for seniors—HA! Talk to my parents or to another couple I overheard disembarking. The violence (of the ride vehicle) was very gratuitous.

Touring Tips   Disney situated Dinosaur in such a remote corner of the park that guests have to poke around to find it. This, in conjunction with the overwhelming popularity of Kilimanjaro Safaris, makes Dinosaur the easiest super-headliner attraction at Disney World to get on. We recommend, nonetheless, that you ride early after experiencing Kilimanjaro Safaris. If you bump into a long line, use FASTPASS.

TriceraTop Spin

What It Is   Hub-and-spoke midway ride

Scope and Scale   Minor attraction

When to Go   First 90 minutes the park is open and in the hour before park closing

Author's Rating   Dumbo's prehistoric forebear; ★★

Appeal by Age Group

Preschool ★★★★	Teens ★★	Over 30 ★★
Grade school ★★★	Young Adults ★★	Seniors ★★

Duration of Ride 1½ minutes

Average Wait in Line per 100 People ahead of You 10 minutes

Loading Speed Slow

Description and Comments Another Dumbo-like ride. Here you spin around a central hub until a dinosaur pops out of the top of the hub. You'd think with the collective imagination of the Walt Disney Company they'd come up with something a little more creative.

Touring Tips An attraction for the children, except they won't appreciate the long wait for this slow-loading ride.

Primeval Whirl (FASTPASS)

What It Is Small coaster

Scope and Scale Minor attraction

When to Go During the first 2 hours the park is open, in the hour before park closing, or use FASTPASS

Special Comments 48" minimum height. Switching off option provided (see pages 266–268).

Author's Rating Wild Mouse on steroids; ★★★

Appeal by Age Group

Preschool ★★★	Teens ★★★½	Over 30 ★★★
Grade school ★★★★½	Young Adults ★★★	Seniors ★★

Duration of Ride Almost 2½ minutes

Average Wait in Line per 100 People ahead of You 4½ minutes

Loading Speed Slow

Description and Comments Primeval Whirl is a small coaster with short drops and curves, and it runs through the jaws of a dinosaur among other things. What makes this coaster different is that the cars also spin. Because guests cannot control the spinning, the cars spin and stop spinning according to how the ride is programmed. Sometimes the spin is braked to a jarring halt after half a revolution, and sometimes it's allowed to make one or two complete turns. The complete spins are fun, but the screeching-stop half-spins are almost painful. If you subtract the time it takes to rachet up the first hill, the actual ride time is about 90 seconds.

Touring Tips Like Space Mountain, the ride is duplicated side by side, but with only one queue. When running smoothly, about 700 people per side can whirl in an hour; a goodly number for this type of attraction, but not enough to preclude long waits on busy-to-moderate days. If you want to ride, try to get on before 11 a.m. or use FASTPASS.

A PEEK BEHIND THE SCENES WITH JIM HILL

Ugly By Design When the expansion of Dinoland U.S.A. first opened in the spring of 2002, some guests were put off by the deliberate tackiness of its "wild mouse" coasters. They complained that a ride that looked this cheap didn't belong in a Disney theme park. The Imagineers' response? "Do you realize how much money it took to make the ride look this bad?"

Theater in the Wild—*Tarzan Rocks!*

What It Is Open-air venue for live stage shows

Scope and Scale Major attraction

When to Go Anytime

Special Comments Performance times are listed in the handout park map or *Times Guide*

Author's Rating Tarzan lays an egg; ★★½

Appeal by Age Group

Preschool ★★★	Teens ★★★	Over 30 ★★★
Grade school ★★★★	Young Adults ★★★	Seniors ★★★

Duration of Presentation 25–35 minutes

Preshow Entertainment None

Probable Waiting Time 20–30 minutes

Description and Comments The Theater in the Wild is a 1,500-seat covered amphitheater. The largest stage production facility in the Animal Kingdom, the theater can host just about any type of stage show. The current production is a rock musical production based on Disney's animated *Tarzan* movie. Called *Tarzan Rocks!*, the show features aerial acts as well as acrobatic stunts, including extreme skating. The musical score is by Phil Collins and drawn from the soundtrack of the film. If this sounds like a hodgepodge, you're right. Although the performers are both talented and enthusiastic, attempting to attach such disparate elements to the *Tarzan* plot (in a musical context yet!) produces a lumbering, uneven, and hugely redundant affair. Simply put, the whole equals significantly less than the sum of its parts. By way of analogy, *Tarzan Rocks!* reminds us of preparations in pretentious restaurants where the chef tries to combine every imaginable delicacy in one fancy dish (seared filet of beef topped with crabmeat au gratin and stuffed with goose pâté and venison medallions—you get the idea). We like parts of the presentation taken individually, but every time the show comes close to taking off, it fumbles into an awkward transition and loses its momentum. And unlike *Festival of the Lion King* in Camp Minnie-Mickey, there's not one single tune that sticks with you when the show's over.

A couple from Dix Hills, New York, concurs:

> Tarzan Rocks! has got to go. Aside from the roller stunts, all in our party were bored to
> tears. A big problem is that the songs from the movie are unmemorable, even when Phil
> Collins sings them, even more so when the cast members sing them.

Touring Tips To get a seat, show up 20–25 minutes in advance for morning and late-afternoon shows, and 30–35 minutes in advance for shows scheduled between noon and 4:30 p.m. Access to the theater is via a relatively narrow pedestrian path. If you arrive as the previous show is letting out, you will feel like a salmon swimming upstream.

A PEEK BEHIND THE SCENES WITH JIM HILL

Lust In the Jungle Owing in some measure to how little the "King of the Jungle" wears in this Animal Kingdom stage show, the performers who play Tarzan have developed quite a following among female Disneyana fans. There are ladies from the Orlando area who have been to *Tarzan Rocks!* literally hundreds of times. There's nothing, it seems, like a guy in a loincloth to stimulate repeat business.

✿ The Boneyard

What It Is Elaborate playground

Scope and Scale Diversion

When to Go Anytime

Special Comments Opens 30 minutes after the rest of the park

Author's Rating Stimulating fun for children; ★★★½

Appeal by Age Group

Preschool ★★★★½	Teens —	Over 30 —
Grade school ★★★★½	Young Adults —	Seniors —

Duration of Visit Varies

Waiting Time None

Description and Comments This attraction is an elaborate playground, particularly appealing to kids age ten and younger, but visually appealing to all ages. Arranged in the form of a rambling open-air dig site, The Boneyard offers plenty of opportunity for exploration and letting off steam. Playground equipment consists of the skeletons of Triceratops, Tyrannosaurus rex, Brachiosaurus, and the like, on which children can swing, slide, and climb. In addition, there are sand pits where little ones can scrounge around for bones and fossils.

Touring Tips Not the cleanest Disney attraction, but certainly one where younger children will want to spend some time. Aside from getting dirty, or at least sandy, be aware that The Boneyard gets mighty hot in the Florida sun. Keep your kids well hydrated and drag them into the shade from time to time. If your children will let you, save the playground until after you have experienced the main attractions. Because The Boneyard is situated so close to the center of the park, it's easy to stop in whenever your kids get itchy. While the little ones clamber around on giant femurs and ribs, you can sip a tall cool one in the shade (still keeping an eye on them, of course).

As a Michigan family attests, kids love The Boneyard:

The highlight for our kids was The Boneyard, especially the dig site. They just kept digging and digging to uncover the bones of the wooly mammoth. It was also in the shade, and there were places for parents to sit, making it a wonderful resting place.

A Woodridge, Illinois, dad thinks maybe children love it too much, warning:

Beware parents, my kid is eight years old, and in Dinoland all he wanted to do was dig up the dino bones in the huge sand box. I saw time and time again parents trying unsuccessfully to drag their kids away from here so they could visit another attraction. This sand box is best left toward the end of the day when you just want to sit and relax while the kids let off energy.

Be aware that The Boneyard rambles over about a half-acre and is multi-storied. It's pretty easy to lose sight of a small child in the playground. Fortunately, there's only one entrance and exit. A mother of two from Stillwater, Minnesota, found the playground too large for her liking:

If you are a parent who likes to have your eyes on your kids at all times, The Boneyard is very scary for adults. Kids climb to the top [of the slides], and you can't see them at the top and you don't know what chute they will be exiting. It made me VERY nervous because I could not see them at all times. We left immediately!

Live Entertainment in the Animal Kingdom

Stage Shows   Stage shows are performed daily at the Theater in the Wild in DinoLand U.S.A., at Grandmother Willow's Grove, at The Lion King Theater in Camp Minnie-Mickey, and at the stadium in Asia. Presentations at Camp Minnie-Mickey and DinoLand U.S.A. feature the Disney characters.

Street Performers   Street performers can be found most of the time at Discovery Island, at Harambe in Africa, at Anandapur in Asia, and in DinoLand U.S.A.

Afternoon Parade   Mickey's Jammin' Jungle Parade is comparable to the parades at the other parks, complete with floats, Disney characters (especially those from *The Lion King, Jungle Book, Tarzan,* and *Pocahontas*), skaters, acrobats, and stilt walkers.

Though subject to change, the parade starts in Africa, crosses the bridge to Discovery Island, proceeds counterclockwise around the island, and then crosses the bridge to Asia. In Asia, the parade turns left and follows the walkway paralleling the river back to Africa. The walking path between Africa and Asia has several small cutouts that offer good views of the parade and excellent sun protection. As it's used primarily as a walkway, the path is also relatively uncrowded. Avoid anything in Harambe around the bridge. The paths on Discovery Island also get very crowded, and it's easier to lose members of your party there.

Kids' Discovery Club   Informal, creative activity stations offer kids ages 4–8 a structured learning experience as they tour the Animal Kingdom. Set up along walkways in six theme areas, Discovery Club stations are manned by cast members who supervise a different activity at each station. A souvenir logbook, available free, is stamped at each station when the child completes the craft or exercise. Children enjoy collecting the stamps and noodling the puzzles in the logbook while in attraction lines.

Animal Encounters   Throughout the day, knowledgeable Disney staff conduct impromptu short lectures on specific animals at the park. Look for a cast member in safari garb holding a bird, reptile, or small mammal.

Goodwill Ambassadors   A number of Asian and African natives are on-hand throughout the park. Both gracious and knowledgeable, they are delighted to discuss their country and its wildlife. Look for them in Harambe and along the Pangani Forest Exploration Trail in Africa, and in Anandapur and along the Maharaja Jungle Trek in Asia. They can also be found near the main entrance and at The Oasis.

Behind the Scenes at the Animal Kingdom

The Animal Kingdom offers two behind-the-scenes tours. **Backstage Safari** is a three-hour guided tour that offer a glimpse of how the animals are housed and cared for. Animal keepers and vets discuss conservation, animal nutrition, behavioral studies, and medicine among other topics. Limited to guests ages 16 and older, the Backstage Safari costs $65 in addition to your paid park admission.

The other tour, **Wild By Design,** offers an inside look at the creation of the Animal Kingdom, telling how architecture, functionality, habitats, themes, and storytelling are combined to provide a complete theme park experience. The tour also runs three hours and costs $58 per person plus park admission. The tour is open to guests ages 14 and older.

For reservations, call (407) WDW-TOUR. Reservations must be guaranteed with a credit card, and there is a 48-hour cancellation policy. Taking photographs is generally not allowed in backstage areas. The tours involve a lot of walking and standing. The tours are not offered every day, so call for exact dates and times early in the planning stage of your vacation.

Traffic Patterns in the Animal Kingdom

The four crowd magnets are *It's Tough to Be a Bug!* in the Tree of Life, Kilimanjaro Safaris in Africa, Dinosaur in DinoLand U.S.A., and Kali River Rapids in Asia.

Because the park hosts large crowds with only a relative handful of attractions, expect for all the attractions to be extremely busy, and for Kilimanjaro Safaris to be mobbed. Most guests arrive in the morning, with a sizable number on hand prior to opening and a larger wave arriving before 10 a.m. Guests continue to stream in through the late morning and into the early afternoon, with the crowds peaking at around 2 p.m. From about 2:30 p.m. on, departing guests outnumber arriving guests by a wide margin, as guests who arrived early complete their tour and leave. Crowds thin appreciably by late afternoon and continue to decline into the early evening.

Because the number of attractions, including theater presentations, is limited, most guests complete a fairly comprehensive tour in two-thirds of a day if they arrive early. Thus, generally speaking, your best bet for easy touring is either to be on-hand when the park opens or to arrive at about 3 p.m. (if the part stays open until 7 or 8 p.m.), when the early birds are heading for the exits. If you decide to visit during the late afternoon, you'll almost certainly have to return on another afternoon to finish seeing everything.

How guests tour the Animal Kingdom depends on their prior knowledge of the park and its attractions. Guests arriving without much prior knowledge make their way to Discovery Island and depend on their handout park map to decide what to do next. Most are drawn to Africa and Kilimanjaro Safaris. A smaller number visit DinoLand U.S.A. first. Those guests who have boned up on the Animal Kingdom make straight for Kilimanjaro Safaris in Africa and Dinosaur in DinoLand U.S.A. Kali River Rapids in Asia and *It's Tough to Be a Bug!* in the Tree of Life are also early-morning favorites.

At the Magic Kingdom, you can tour clockwise or counterclockwise without returning to the central hub. To go from land to land at the Animal Kingdom, however, you usually have to pass through Discovery Island. Discovery Island and its attractions thus draw crowds earlier than the other lands and remain inundated throughout the day. Africa, likewise, draws heavy attendance but is set up to move crowds through in a controlled sequence. Attractions in DinoLand U.S.A., with the exception of Dinosaur, Primeval Whirl, and TriceraTop Spin, will be easily accessible most of the day. Camp Minnie-Mickey is congested from 9:30 a.m. until about 4 p.m., more because of poor traffic design than popularity.

Animal Kingdom Touring Plans

Touring the Animal Kingdom is not as complicated as touring the other parks because it offers a smaller number of attractions. Also, most Animal Kingdom rides, shows, and zoological exhibits are oriented to the entire family, thus eliminating differences of opinion regarding how to spend the day. At the Animal Kingdom, the whole family can pretty much see and enjoy everything together.

Since there are fewer attractions than at the other parks, expect the crowds at the Animal Kingdom to be more concentrated. If a line seems unusually long, ask an Animal Kingdom cast member what the estimated wait is. If the wait exceeds your tolerance, try the same attraction again after 3 p.m., while a show is in progress at the Theater in the Wild in DinoLand U.S.A., or while some special event is going on.

For the time being, the limited number of attractions in the Animal Kingdom can work to your advantage. Many *Unofficial Guide* readers, especially those visiting Disney World for only a few days, have asked for a one-day touring plan that covers the highlights of the Animal Kingdom and another park. The Disney-MGM Studios' size and relative popularity, coupled with FASTPASS at all of its most popular attractions, make it the best choice to combine with the Animal Kingdom into a one-day tour.

The combined touring plan for the Animal Kingdom and Disney-MGM Studios presented here is the result of more than eighteen months of field testing. We believe the plan works best, especially for non-Disney resort guests, on Sunday, Wednesday and Thursday, when Extra Magic Hour is in effect at neither the Animal Kingdom nor the Disney-MGM Studios. While we do not generally recommend visiting the Animal Kingdom when its early entry is in effect (see the beginning of this chapter for our reasoning), Disney resort guests should experience no adverse impact when using this plan on Extra Magic Hour days.

Before You Go

1. Call (407) 824-4321 before you go to learn the park's hours of operation.

2. Purchase your admission prior to arrival.

Animal Kingdom One-Day Touring Plan

The Animal Kingdom One-Day Touring Plan assumes a willingness to experience all major rides and shows. Be forewarned that Dinosaur, Primeval Whirl, and Kali River Rapids are sometimes frightening to children under age eight. Similarly, the theater attraction at the Tree of Life might be too intense for some preschoolers. When following the touring plan, simply skip any attraction you do not wish to experience.

1. Arrive at the park one hour before the official opening time during summer and holiday periods, and 40 minutes before the official opening time the rest of the year. At the entrance plaza, pick up a park map and daily entertainment schedule. Wait at the entrance turnstiles to be admitted.

2. When admitted through the turnstiles, move quickly through The Oasis without stopping and cross the bridge into Discovery Island. Turn left after the bridge and walk clockwise around the Tree of Life until you reach the bridge to Africa. Cross the bridge and continue straight ahead to the entrance of Kilimanjaro Safaris. Experience Kilimanjaro Safaris. Unless the wait exceeds 30 minutes, do not use FASTPASS.

3. After the safari, head back toward the Africa bridge to Discovery Island, but turn left before crossing. Follow the walkway along the river to Asia. In Asia, ride Kali River Rapids.

   As a cost-cutting measure, Disney delayed the opening of Asia until 30 minutes after the rest of the park. If Asia is not yet open when you arrive or if the weather is cool (or you just don't feel like getting wet), proceed to Steps 4–6. Return to Kali River Rapids after seeing *It's Tough to Be a Bug!* (Step 6). If the wait is more than 30 minutes for the raft ride when you return, use FASTPASS.

4. Following the raft trip, return to the entrance of Asia and turn left over the Asia bridge into Discovery Island. Pass the Beastly Bazaar and Flame Tree Barbecue, and then turn left and cross the bridge into DinoLand U.S.A. After passing beneath the brontosaurus skeleton, angle left to Primeval Whirl. Ride. *Note:* If you have children ages eight and younger in your party, they will want to ride TriceraTop Spin (a children's ride straight and to the left) after entering Dinoland. Ride TriceraTop Spin first, then Primeval Whirl.

5. Follow the signs to Dinosaur. Ride.

6. Next, retrace your steps to Discovery Island, bearing left after you cross the DinoLand bridge. See *It's Tough to Be a Bug!* in the Tree of Life. If the wait exceeds 30 minutes, use FASTPASS.

7. By now you will have most of the Animal Kingdom's potential bottlenecks behind you. Check your daily entertainment schedule for shows at the Theater in the Wild in DinoLand U.S.A., for Flights of Wonder in Asia, and for Festival of the Lion King and Pocahontas in Camp Minnie-Mickey. Plan the next part of your day around eating lunch and seeing these four shows. Before 11 a.m., arrive about 15–20 minutes prior to show time. During the middle of the day (11 a.m.–4 p.m.), you will need to queue up as follows:

For the Theater in the Wild:	30 minutes before show time
For the Caravan Stage:	15 minutes before show time
For Pocahontas:	25–30 minutes before show time
For the Lion King Theater:	25–35 minutes before show time

   There is almost always 90 minutes between the first showing of *Flights of Wonder* and the second showing of *Festival of the Lion King*. For example, the first showing of *Flights* is usually at 10:30 a.m., and the second *Festival* is usually at noon. A good sequence for Step 7 is *Flights of Wonder,* lunch (at Flame Tree Barbecue), then *Festival of the Lion King.* If interested in seeing *Tarzan Rocks!* or *Pocahontas,* you will still have several afternoon shows to choose from. We've successfully tested this version of Step 7 at least six times. It does require a bit of clock management during lunch (no more than 45 minutes), but it's a solid sequence for hopping from show to show with little downtime or backtracking between.

8. Between shows, check out The Boneyard in DinoLand U.S.A. and the zoological exhibits around the Tree of Life and in The Oasis. The best time to meet the characters at Camp Minnie-Mickey is while performances are underway at the two Camp Minnie-Mickey amphitheaters.

9. Return to Asia and take the Maharajah Jungle Trek.

10. Return to Africa and take the Wildlife Express train to Rafiki's Planet Watch and Conservation Station. Tour the exhibits. If you want to experience Kilimanjaro Safaris again, obtain a FASTPASS before boarding the train.

11. Depart Rafiki's Planet Watch and Conservation Station and catch the train back to Harambe.

12. In Harambe, walk the Pangani Forest Exploration Trail.

13. Shop, snack, or repeat any attractions you especially enjoyed.

14. This concludes the touring plan. Be sure to allocate some time to visit the zoological exhibits in The Oasis on your way out of the park.

Animal Kingdom / Disney-MGM Studios Combined One-Day Touring Plan

This plan offers a greatest hits tour of both the Animal Kingdom and the Disney-MGM Studios on the same day. It requires that you have a Park Hopper pass and a fair amount of energy. The plan assumes a willingness to experience the "must-see" rides and shows at both parks. This is not an appropriate touring plan for families with children nine years and younger.

1. Arrive at the Animal Kingdom one hour before the official opening time during summer and holiday periods, and 40 minutes before the official opening time the rest of the year. At the entrance plaza, pick up a park map and daily entertainment schedule/*Times Guide*. Wait at the entrance turnstiles to be admitted.

2. When admitted, move quickly through The Oasis without stopping and cross the bridge into Discovery Island. Turn left after the bridge and walk clockwise around the Tree of Life until you reach the bridge to Africa. Cross the bridge and continue straight ahead to Harambe and the entrance of Kilimanjaro Safaris. Experience Kilimanjaro Safaris. Unless the wait exceeds 35 minutes, do not use FASTPASS.

3. Walk the Pangani Forest Exploration Trail.

4. After walking the Pangani Trail, return to the entrance of Harambe and backtrack to Discovery Island. Pass Pizzafari on Discovery Island, and continue around the Tree of Life. Take the third bridge you'll come into DinoLand U.S.A. After passing beneath the brontosaurus skeleton, bear right and follow the signs to Dinosaur. Ride.

5. Return to Discovery Island and check your daily entertainment schedule for the next show time for *Festival of the Lion King*. If the next show is within the next 30 minutes, turn left and continue to the second bridge and Camp Minnie Mickey. If the next show time is more than 60 minutes away, see *It's Tough to Be a Bug!* now, then see *Festival of the Lion King* afterwards.

6. Walk the Maharaja Jungle Trek in Asia.

7. If you have not already done so, see *It's Tough to Be a Bug!* in Discovery Island. This is the last attraction in the touring plan.

8. Return to the entrance of Asia and turn left over the Asia bridge into Discovery Island. If you would like to stop for lunch, Flame Tree Barbecue will be on your left as you enter Discovery Island. A covered gazebo behind the Flame Tree building offers an exceptional view of Asia and the surrounding lake.

9. To exit the Animal Kingdom, continue around Discovery Island. Take the second bridge to your left and pass through The Oasis to the park's main entrance. Depart the Animal Kingdom for Disney-MGM Studios.

10. As you enter Disney-MGM Studios, obtain a park map and daily entertainment schedule.

11. Walk straight down Hollywood Boulevard past the giant hat. On the far side of the hat is the Great Movie Ride.

12. Exit the Great Movie Ride. Check the daily entertainment schedule to see whether the next showing of *Lights! Motors! Action!* or *Beauty and the Beast* will start first. See the show that starts first. *Lights! Motors! Action!* is near New York Street and MuppetVision 3-D, while *Beauty and the Beast* is located just off of Sunset Boulevard by the Tower of Terror.

13. Obtain a FASTPASS for the Rock 'n' Roller Coaster.

14. See the next showing of *Beauty and the Beast* or *Lights! Motors! Action!*, depending on which show you saw in Step 12.

15. See the *Indiana Jones Epic Stunt Spectacular* (FASTPASS).

16. Take the Backlot Tour. The entrance is down Mickey Avenue from *Who Wants to Be a Millionaire*.

17. Exit the Backlot Tour and pass through the Studio Catering Company counter service restaurant, exiting on New York Street. Go left on New York Street and then right at the fake tall buildings. See MuppetVision 3-D.

18. Head in the direction of Echo Lake. Ride Star Tours.

19. Walk past Echo Lake and the big hat towards the Animation Courtyard. See the *Voyage of the Little Mermaid*.

20. Exit the *Little Mermaid* and head down Hollywood Boulevard. Make a left on to Sunset Boulevard, and bear left to the Rock 'n' Roller Coaster. Enter the line marked "FASTPASS Return."

21. After exiting the Rock 'n' Roller Coaster, bear left to the Tower of Terror. Enjoy.

22. If time permits, grab a snack at the refreshment stands at the end of Sunset Boulevard before heading in to see *Fantasmic!*

23. This concludes the touring plan. Do any last-minute shopping and then exit Disney-MGM Studios.

Part Thirteen

Disney-MGM Studios, Universal Orlando, and SeaWorld

Disney-MGM Studios versus Universal Studios Florida

Disney-MGM Studios and Universal Studios Florida are direct competitors. Because both are large and expensive and require at least one day to see, some guests must choose one park over the other. To help you decide, we present a head-to-head comparison of the two parks, followed by a description of each in detail. In the summer of 1999, Universal launched its second major theme park, Universal's Islands of Adventure, which competes directly with Disney's Magic Kingdom. (Universal Studios Florida theme park, Islands of Adventure theme park, the three Universal hotels, and the CityWalk complex are collectively known as Universal Orlando.) Lastly, a summary profile of SeaWorld concludes Part Thirteen.

Both Disney-MGM Studios and Universal Studios Florida draw their theme and inspiration from film and television. Both offer movie- and TV-themed rides and shows, some of which are just for fun, while others provide an educational, behind-the-scenes introduction to the cinematic arts.

Half of Disney-MGM Studios is off-limits to guests except by guided tour, while most all of Universal Studios Florida is open to exploration. Unlike Disney-MGM, Universal Studios Florida's open area includes the entire backlot, where guests can walk at leisure among movie sets. Universal Studios Florida is about twice as large as Disney-MGM, and because almost all of it is open to the public, most of the crowding and congestion so familiar in the streets and plazas of Disney-MGM is eliminated. Universal Studios has plenty of elbowroom.

Both parks include working film and television production studios. Guests are more likely, however, to see a movie or television production in progress at Universal Studios than at Disney-MGM. On any day, production crews will be shooting on the Universal backlot in full view of guests who care to watch.

Attractions are excellent at both parks, though Disney-MGM attractions are on average engineered to move people more efficiently. Each park offers stellar attractions that break new ground, transcending in power, originality, and technology any prior standard for theme-park entertainment. Universal offers Revenge of the Mummy—The Ride, an indoor roller coaster that combines space age robotics with live effects and pyrotechnics; *Terminator 2: 3-D,* which we consider the most extraordinary theater attraction in any American theme park; and Men in Black Alien Attack, an interactive high-tech ride where guests' actions determine the ending of the story. Disney-MGM Studios features The Twilight Zone Tower of Terror, Disney's best attraction to date in our book; Rock 'n' Roller Coaster, an indoor coaster that's launched like a jet off an aircraft deck; and *Muppet Vision 3-D,* a zany theater attraction. Though Universal Studios must be credited with pioneering a number of innovative and technologically advanced rides, we must also point out that Universal's attractions break down more often than Disney-MGM's.

Amazingly, and to the visitor's advantage, each park offers a completely different product mix, so there is little or no redundancy for a person who visits both. Disney-MGM and Universal Studios Florida each provide good exposure to the cinematic arts, though Universal's presentations are generally more informative and comprehensive. Disney-MGM over the years has turned several of its better tours into infomercials for Disney films. At Universal, you can still learn about post-production, soundstages, set creation, special effects, directing, and cinematography without being bludgeoned by promotional hype.

We recommend you try one of the studios. If you enjoy one, you probably will enjoy the other. If you have to choose between them, consider:

1. Touring Time   If you tour efficiently, it takes about eight to ten hours to see Disney-MGM Studios (including a lunch break). Because Universal Studios Florida is larger and contains more rides and shows, touring, including one meal, takes about 9–11 hours. One reader laments:

There is a lot more "standing" at Universal Studios, and it isn't as organized as [Disney-MGM]. Many of the attractions don't open until 10 a.m., and many shows seem to be going at the same time. We were not able to see nearly as many attractions at Universal as we were at [Disney-MGM] during the same amount of time. The one plus here is that there seems to be more property, and things are spaced out better so you have more elbowroom.

As the reader observes, many Universal Studios attractions do not open until 10 a.m. or later. During one research visit, only a third of the major attractions were up and running when the park opened, and most theater attractions didn't schedule performances until 11 a.m. or after. This means that early in the day all park guests are concentrated among the relatively few attractions in operation. The Disney-MGM Studios

also has attractions that open late and shows that schedule no performances until late morning. The number of attractions operating at opening
varies according to season, at both parks. As a postscript, you will not
have to worry about any of this if you tour either park using our touring
plans. We'll keep you one jump ahead of the crowd and make sure that
any given attraction is running by the time you get there.

2. Convenience If you're lodging along International Drive, I-4's
northeast corridor, the Orange Blossom Trail (US 441), or in Orlando,
Universal Studios Florida is closer. If you're lodging along US 27 or
FL 192 or in Kissimmee or Walt Disney World, Disney-MGM Studios is
more convenient.

3. Endurance Universal Studios Florida is larger and requires more
walking than Disney-MGM, but it is also much less congested, so the
walking is easier. Both parks offer wheelchairs and disabled access.

4. Cost Both parks cost about the same for one-day admission, food,
and incidentals, though Universal admission can be purchased in combo
packages that include discounted passes to SeaWorld, Busch Gardens,
and/or Wet 'n' Wild.

5. Best Days to Go In order, Tuesdays, Mondays, Thursdays, and
Wednesdays are best to visit Universal Studios Florida. At Disney-MGM
Studios, visit on Monday or Friday during the summer and on Thursday
or Friday during the off-season.

6. When to Arrive For Disney-MGM, arrive with your ticket in hand
30–40 minutes before official opening time. For Universal Studios, arrive
with your admission already purchased about 40–50 minutes before official opening time.

7. Young Children Both Disney-MGM Studios and Universal Studios Florida are relatively adult entertainment offerings. By our reckon-
ing, half the rides and shows at Disney-MGM and about two-thirds at
Universal Studios have a significant potential for frightening young
children.

8. Food Universal Studios has a decided edge.

9. FASTPASS versus Universal Express Both Disney's FASTPASS
and Universal's Universal Express allow guests to "schedule" a time window to ride crowded attractions; such guests are shunted into shorter lines
that substantially reduce wait times. Notoriously prone to fluctuation,
both programs currently allow you to obtain a second pass at the beginning of the return window of the first pass or two hours after the first pass
was issued, whichever comes first. This means you're not "locked in" to
only one pass if your first-choice attraction has an especially long wait.
However, one important distinction of Universal Express is that guests at
Universal hotels can access the Universal Express lines all day long simply

by flashing their hotel keys. That last perk can be especially valuable during peak season. But if you're staying at a Universal property, you can keep using the Express line even when all the passes are gone.

Also available at Universal is an admission add-on called Universal Express Plus, where for an extra $15 or $25 (depending on season), you can buy a pass that provides line-cutting privileges on each Universal Express attraction at a given park. The Plus feature is good for only one day at one park (in other words, no park hopping), and for one ride only on each participating attraction. Speaking of participating attractions, more than 90% of rides and shows are included in the Universal Express program, a much higher percentage than are included in the FASTPASS program at the Disney parks.

Disney-MGM Studios

Disney-MGM Studios was hatched from a corporate rivalry and a wild, twisted plot. At a time when the Disney Company was weak and fighting off greenmail—hostile takeover bids—Universal's parent company at the time, MCA, announced they were going to build an Orlando clone of their wildly successful Universal Studios Hollywood theme park. Behind the scenes, MCA was courting the real-estate rich Bass brothers of Texas, hoping to secure the brothers' investment in the project. The Bass brothers, however, defected to the Disney camp, helped Disney squelch the hostile takeovers, and were front and center when Michael Eisner suddenly announced that Disney would also build a movie theme park in Florida. A construction race ensued, with Universal and Disney each intent on opening first. Universal, however, was midprocess in the development of a host of new attraction technologies and was no match for Disney, who could import proven concepts and attractions from their other parks. In the end, Disney-MGM Studios opened almost two years before Universal Studios Florida.

The MGM Connection

To broaden the appeal and to lend additional historical impact, Disney obtained the rights to use the MGM (Metro-Goldwyn-Mayer) name, film library, motion-picture and television titles, excerpts, costumes, music, sets, and even Leo, the MGM lion. Probably the two most recognized names in motion pictures, Disney and MGM represent almost a century of movie history.

Comparing Disney-MGM Studios to the Magic Kingdom and Epcot

The Magic Kingdom entertains, modeling its attractions on Disney movies and TV. Epcot educates, pioneering exhibits and rides that teach.

Disney-MGM does both. All three parks rely heavily on Disney special effects and audio-animatronics (robotics) in their entertainment mix.

Disney-MGM Studios is about the size of the Magic Kingdom and about half as large as the sprawling Epcot. Unlike the other parks, Disney-MGM is a working motion-picture and television production facility. This means, among other things, that guests are permitted access to about half of it only on guided tours or observation walkways.

When Epcot opened in 1982, Disney patrons expected a futuristic version of the Magic Kingdom. What they got was humanistic inspiration and a creative educational experience. Since then, Disney has tried to inject more magic, excitement, and surprise into Epcot. Remembering the occasional disappointment of those early Epcot guests, Disney fortified the Studios with megadoses of action, suspense, surprise, and, of course, special effects. The formula has proved so successful that it was trotted out again at the Animal Kingdom theme park. If you want to learn about the history and technology of movies and television, Disney-MGM Studios will teach you plenty. If you just want to be entertained, you won't leave disappointed.

Self-Promotion Run Amok

While it's true that Disney-MGM Studios educates and entertains, what it does best is promote. Self-promotion of Disney films and products was once subtle and in context. It is now blatant, inescapable, and detracting. Although most visitors are willing to forgive Disney its excesses, Studios veterans will lament the changes and remember how good it was when education was the goal instead of the medium.

NOT TO BE MISSED AT DISNEY-MGM STUDIOS

Star Tours	*Fantasmic!*
Disney-MGM Studios Backlot Tour	*Voyage of the Little Mermaid*
Indiana Jones Epic Stunt Spectacular	*The Twilight Zone Tower of Terror*
Jim Henson's MuppetVision 3-D	Rock 'n' Roller Coaster
Lights! Motors! Action! Extreme Stunt Show (opens 2005; recommendation based on a similar attraction at Paris Disneyland)	

How Much Time to Allocate

It's impossible to see all of Epcot or the Magic Kingdom in one day. However, Disney-MGM Studios, is more manageable. There's much less ground to cover by foot. Trams carry guests through much of the backlot and working areas, and attractions in the open-access parts are concentrated in an area about the size of Main Street, Tomorrowland, and Frontierland combined. Someday, no doubt, as Disney-MGM develops and grows, you'll need more than a day to see everything. For now, the Studios is a nice one-day outing.

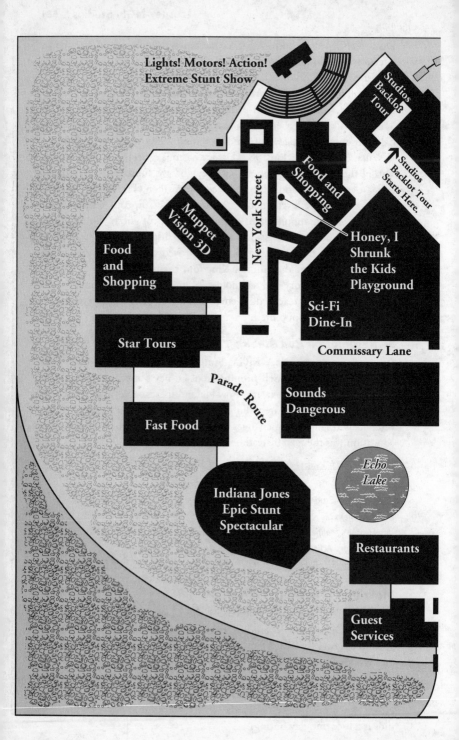

Lights! Motors! Action!
Extreme Stunt Show

Studios Backlot Tour

Food and Shopping

Studios Backlot Tour Starts Here.

Muppet Vision 3D

New York Street

Honey, I Shrunk the Kids Playground

Food and Shopping

Sci-Fi Dine-In

Star Tours

Commissary Lane

Parade Route

Sounds Dangerous

Fast Food

Echo Lake

Indiana Jones Epic Stunt Spectacular

Restaurants

Guest Services

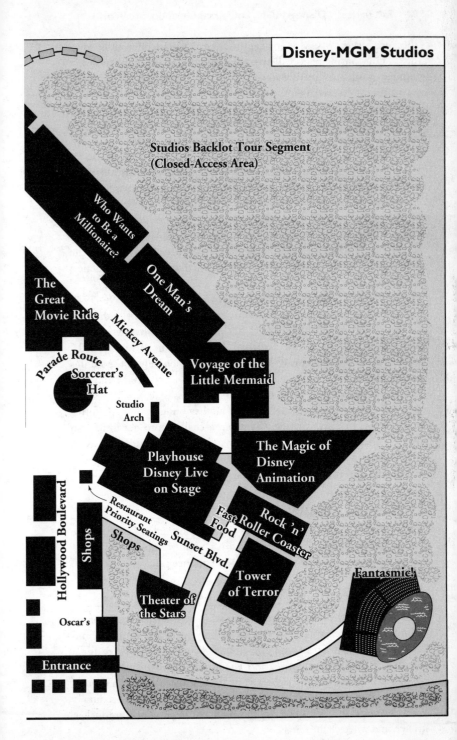

Disney-MGM Studios

Studios Backlot Tour Segment
(Closed-Access Area)

Who Wants to Be a Millionaire?

One Man's Dream

The Great Movie Ride

Mickey Avenue

Parade Route

Sorcerer's Hat

Studio Arch

Voyage of the Little Mermaid

The Magic of Disney Animation

Playhouse Disney Live on Stage

Rock 'n' Roller Coaster

Hollywood Boulevard

Shops

Restaurant Priority Seatings

Fast Food

Sunset Blvd.

Shops

Theater of the Stars

Tower of Terror

Fantasmic!

Oscar's

Entrance

Because Disney-MGM is smaller, however, it's more affected by large crowds. Our touring plans will help you stay a step ahead of the mob and minimize waiting in line. Even when the park is crowded, however, you can see almost everything in a day.

Disney-MGM Studios in the Evening

Because Disney-MGM Studios can be seen in three-fourths of a day, many guests who arrive early in the morning run out of things to do by 4 p.m. or so and leave the park. Their departure greatly thins the crowd and makes the Studios ideal for evening touring. Lines for most attractions are manageable, and the park is cooler and more comfortable. The *Indiana Jones Epic Stunt Spectacular* and productions at other outdoor theaters are infinitely more enjoyable during the evening than in the sweltering heat of the day. A drawback to touring the Studios at night is that there won't be much activity on the production soundstages.

In 1998, the Studios launched *Fantasmic!* (see pages 594–597), arguably the most spectacular nighttime entertainment event in the Disney repertoire. Staged nightly (weather permitting) in its own theater behind the Tower of Terror, *Fantasmic!* is rated as "not to be missed." Unfortunately, evening crowds have increased substantially at the studios because of *Fantasmic!* Some guests stay longer at Disney-MGM and others arrive after dinner from other parks expressly to see the show. Although crowds thin in the late afternoon, they build again as performance time approaches, making *Fantasmic!* a challenge to get into. Also adversely affected are the Tower of Terror and the Rock 'n' Roller Coaster, both situated near the entrance to *Fantasmic!* Crowd levels throughout the remainder of the park, however, are generally light.

Arriving at Disney-MGM Studios

Disney-MGM Studios has its own pay parking lot and is served by the Disney transportation system. If you drive, Disney's ubiquitous trams will transport you to the ticketing area and entrance gate.

Getting Oriented at Disney-MGM Studios

Guest Services, on your left as you enter, serves as the park headquarters and information center, similar to City Hall in the Magic Kingdom and Guest Relations at Epcot and the Animal Kingdom. Go there for a schedule of live performances/ *Times Guide*, lost persons, Package Pickup, lost and found (on the right side of the entrance), general information, or in an emergency. If you haven't received a map of the Studios or a *Times Guide*, get one here. To the right of the entrance are locker, stroller, and wheelchair rentals.

About one-half of the complex is set up as a theme park. As at the Magic Kingdom, you entr the park and pass down a main street. Only, this time it's Hollywood Boulevard of the 1930s and 1940s. At the end of Hollywood Boulevard is a replica of Hollywood's famous Chinese Theater. Lording over the plaza in front of the theater is a 122-foot-tall replica of the sorcerer hat Mickey Mouse wore in the animated classic Fantasia. Besides providing photo ops, the hat is the park's most central landmark, making it a good meeting place if your group becomes separated. In case you're wondering, Mickey would have to be 350 feet tall to wear the hat.

Though modest in size, the open-access areas of the Studios are confusingly arranged (a product of the park's hurried expansion in the early 1990s). As you face the hat, two guest areas—Sunset Boulevard and the Animation Courtyard—branch off Hollywood Boulevard to the right. Branching left off Hollywood Boulevard is the Echo Lake area. The open-access backlot wraps around the back of Echo Lake, the Chinese Theater, and the Animation Courtyard. You can experience all attractions here and in the other open-access sections of the park according to your tastes and time. Still farther to the rear is the limited-access backlot, consisting of the working soundstages, technical facilities, wardrobe shops, administrative offices, and backlot sets. These are accessible to visitors on a guided tour by tram and foot.

HOLLYWOOD BOULEVARD SERVICES

Most of the park's service facilities are on Hollywood Boulevard, including:

Wheelchair and Stroller	Right of the entrance at Oscar's Rental
Banking Services	An ATM is outside the park to the right of the turnstiles.
Storage Lockers	Rental lockers are right of the main entrance, on the left of Oscar's.
Lost and Found	At Package Pick-up, right of the entrance
Live Entertainment/ Parade Information/ Character Information	Available free at Guest Relations and elsewhere in the park
Lost Persons	Report lost persons at Guest Relations
Walt Disney World and Local Attraction Information	At Guest Relations
First Aid	At Guest Relations
Baby Center/Baby-care Needs	At Guest Relations. Oscar's sells baby food and other necessities.
Film	At The Darkroom on the right side of Hollywood Boulevard, just past Oscar's

What to See

Try everything. As we have with the Magic Kingdom, Animal Kingdom, and Epcot, we identify attractions as "not to be missed." But Disney rides and shows usually exceed your expectations and always surprise.

Waiting Times Display

At the corner of Hollywood and Sunset Boulevards is a large display listing current waiting times for all Disney-MGM Studios attractions. It's updated continuously throughout the day. We've found the waiting times listed to be slightly overstated. If the display says the wait for Star Tours is 45 minutes, for example, you probably will have to wait about 35–40 minutes.

Disney-MGM Studios Attractions

Hollywood Boulevard

Hollywood Boulevard is a palm-lined re-creation of Hollywood's main drag during the city's golden age. Architecture is streamlined moderne with art deco embellishments. Most service facilities are here, interspersed with eateries and shops. Merchandise includes Disney trademark items, Hollywood and movie-related souvenirs, and one-of-a-kind collectibles obtained from studio auctions and estate sales.

Hollywood characters and roving performers entertain on the boulevard, and daily parades and other happenings pass this way.

Sunset Boulevard

Sunset Boulevard, evoking the 1940s, is a major addition to Disney-MGM Studios. The first right off Hollywood Boulevard, Sunset Boulevard provides another venue for dining, shopping, and street entertainment.

The Twilight Zone Tower of Terror (FASTPASS)

What It Is Sci-fi-theme indoor thrill ride

Scope and Scale Super headliner

When to Go Before 9:30 a.m., after 6 p.m., or use FASTPASS

Special Comments Must be 40" tall to ride; switching-off option offered.

Author's Rating Walt Disney World's best attraction; not to be missed; ★★★★★

Appeal by Age Group

Preschool ★★★	Teens ★★★★★	Over 30 ★★★★★
Grade school ★★★★★	Young Adults ★★★★★	Seniors ★★★★½

Duration of Ride About 4 minutes plus preshow

Average Wait in Line per 100 People ahead of You 4 minutes

Assumes All elevators operating

Loading Speed Moderate

Description and Comments The Tower of Terror is a new species of Disney thrill ride, though it borrows elements of The Haunted Mansion at the Magic Kingdom. The story is that you're touring a once-famous Hollywood hotel gone to ruin. As at Star Tours, the queuing area integrates guests into the adventure as they pass through the hotel's once-opulent public rooms. From the lobby, guests are escorted into the hotel's library, where Rod Serling, speaking on an old black-and-white television, greets the guests and introduces the plot.

The Tower of Terror is a whopper at 13-plus-stories tall. Breaking tradition in terms of visually isolating themed areas, you can see the entire Studios from atop the tower, but you have to look quick.

The ride vehicle, one of the hotel's service elevators, takes guests to see the haunted hostelry. The tour begins innocuously, but about the fifth floor things get pretty weird. Guests are subjected to a full range of erie effects as they cross into the Twilight Zone. The climax of the adventure occurs when the elevator reaches the top floor (the 13th, of course) and the cable snaps.

The Tower of Terror is an experience to savor. Though the final plunges (yep, make that plural) are calculated to thrill, the meat of the attraction is its extraordinary visual and audio effects. There's richness and subtlety here, enough to keep the ride fresh and stimulating after many repetitions. Disney tinkers with the Tower of Terror incessantly. Recently, random ride and drop sequences were introduced that make the attraction faster and keep you guessing about when, how far, and how many times the elevator drops. We interviewed a family from Toronto who claimed that as they were preparing to disembark at the unloading area the doors suddenly closed and the elevator shot back up for yet another drop! In addition to random sequencing, new visual, auditory, and olfactory effects were added.

A senior from the United Kingdom tried the Tower of Terror and liked it very much, writing:

I was thankful I had read your review of the Tower of Terror, or I would certainly have avoided it. As you say, it is so full of magnificent detail that it is worth riding, even if you don't fancy the drops involved.

The Tower has great potential for terrifying young children and rattling more mature visitors. If you have teenagers in your party, use them as experimental probes. If they report back that they really, really liked the Tower of Terror, run as fast as you can in the opposite direction.

Touring Tips   This one ride is worth your admission to Disney-MGM Studios. Because of its height, the Tower is a veritable beacon, visible from outside the park and luring curious guests as soon as they enter. Because of its popularity with school kids, teens, and young adults, you can count on a foot race to the attraction, as well as to the nearby Rock 'n' Roller Coaster, when the park opens. Expect the Tower to be mobbed most of the day. Experience it first thing in the morning, in the evening before the park closes, or use FASTPASS.

If you're on hand when the park opens and want to ride Tower of Terror first, position yourself on the far right side of Sunset Boulevard as close to the rope barrier as possible. Once in position, wait for the rope drop. When the park opens, cast members will walk the rope up the street toward Rock 'n' Roller Coaster and Tower of Terror. Just stay on the far right sidewalk and you'll be among the first to make the right turn to the entrance of the tower. Usually the Disney people get out of the way and allow you to run the last 100 feet or so. Also, be aware that about 65% of the folks waiting for the rope walk will head for Rock 'n' Roller Coaster. If you are not positioned on the far right, it will be almost impossible to move through the throng of coaster enthusiasts to make a right turn into Tower of Terror.

To save time, when you enter the library waiting area, stand in the far back corner across from the door where you entered and at the opposite end of the room from the TV. When the doors to the loading area open, you'll be one of the first admitted.

If you have young children (or anyone) who are apprehensive about this attraction, ask the attendant about switching off (pages 266–268).

A good strategy for riding both Tower of Terror and Rock 'n' Roller Coaster with minimum waits is to rush first thing after opening to Rock 'n' Roller Coaster and obtain FASTPASSes, then line up for the Tower of Terror. Most days, by the time you finish experiencing the Tower of Terror, it will be time to use your FASTPASS for Rock 'n' Roller Coaster.

A PEEK BEHIND THE SCENES WITH JIM HILL

"If the guests are dead, how will they buy our T-shirts?" One of the first storylines that the Imagineers proposed for the Tower of Terror had theme-park guests being pursued through an abandoned Hollywood hotel by a demented film director. At the very climax of the attraction this director would be seen actually cutting the cable to the elevator car, sending tourists hurtling to their doom.

Disney management eventually nixed this version of the show's storyline. Why? It was thought that if Disney implied the guests had died at the end of the ride, they might be reluctant to buy souvenirs as they exited through the gift shop.

Rock 'n' Roller Coaster (FASTPASS)

What It Is Rock music–themed roller coaster

Scope and Scale Headliner

When to Go Before 10 a.m. or in the hour before closing

Special Comments Must be 48" tall to ride; children younger than age 7 must ride with an adult. Switching off option provided (pages 266–268).

Author's Rating Disney's wildest American coaster; not to be missed; ★★★★

Appeal by Age Group

Preschool ★★★	Teens ★★★★	Over 30 ★★★★
Grade school ★★★★	Young Adults ★★★★	Seniors ★★★

Duration of Ride Almost 1½ minutes

Average Wait in Line per 100 People ahead of You 2½ minutes

Assumes All trains operating

Loading Speed Moderate to fast

Description and Comments This is Disney's answer to the roller-coaster proliferation at Universal's Islands of Adventure and Busch Gardens theme parks. Exponentially wilder than Space Mountain or Big Thunder Mountain in the Magic Kingdom, the Rock 'n' Roller Coaster is an attraction for fans of cutting-edge thrill rides. Although the rock icons and synchronized music add measurably to the experience, the ride itself, as opposed to sights and sounds along the way, is the focus. The Rock 'n' Roller Coaster offers loops, corkscrews, and drops that make Space Mountain seem like the Jungle Cruise. What really makes this metal coaster unusual, however, is that first, it's in the dark (like Space Mountain, only with Southern California nighttime scenes instead of space), and second, you're launched up the first hill like a jet off a carrier deck. By the time you crest the hill, you'll have gone from 0 to 57 miles per hour in less than three seconds. When you enter the first loop, you'll be pulling five g's. By comparison, that's two more g's than astronauts experience at lift-off on a space shuttle.

Reader opinions of Rock 'n' Roller Coaster have been predictably mixed, colored invariably by how the reader feels about roller coasters. These comments are typical. First from a mother of two from High Mills, New York:

You can't warn people enough about Rock 'n' Roller Coaster. My daughter and I refused to go on it at all. My nine-year-old son who had no problems with any ride, including Tower of Terror, went on with my husband first thing in the morning. My son came off so shaken he was "done for" the rest of the day and never fully recuperated. My husband just closed his eyes and hoped for the best.

And from a Longmont, Colorado, dad:

Rock 'n' Roller Coaster: The first 15 seconds of this ride are spectacular. I've never experienced anything like the initial take-off.

From an Australian couple who traveled a long way to ride a coaster:

My wife and I are definitely not roller-coaster people. However, we found Rock 'n' Roller Coaster quite exhilarating—and because it's dark, we didn't always realize that we were being thrown upside down. We rode it twice!

Is Rock 'n' Roller the baddest coaster in Florida? Hard to say. Rock 'n' Roller has the fastest launch acceleration by far, and, as we've discussed, it's a themed ride in the dark, but the Incredible Hulk and the Fire & Ice coasters at Universal's Islands of Adventure, as well as Kraken at SeaWorld, are all higher and offer more inversions (i.e., vertical loops, corkscrews, barrel rolls, etc.). Also, all are much longer coasters. The Disney entry offers great visuals, but the view from Hulk, Fire & Ice, and Kraken (for those with their eyes open) is pretty spectacular. For indoor coasters, Universal Studios' Revenge of the Mummy coaster serves up much more compelling visuals and special effects than Rock 'n' Roller.

Touring Tips   This ride is not for everyone. If Space Mountain or Big Thunder push your limits, stay away from the Rock 'n' Roller Coaster.

It's eye-catching, and it's definitely a zippy albeit deafening ride. Expect long lines except in the first 30 minutes after opening and during the late-evening performance of *Fantasmic!*. Ride first thing in the morning or use FASTPASS.

If you're on hand when the park opens, position yourself on the far left side of Sunset Boulevard as close to the rope barrier as possible. If there's already a crowd at the rope, you can usually work yourself forward by snaking along the wall of the Beverly Sunset Shop. Once in position, wait for the rope drop. When the park opens, cast members will

---

A PEEK BEHIND THE SCENES WITH JIM HILL

Well, how cheap would Cheap Trick be?   When Imagineers first proposed adding the Rock 'n' Roller Coaster to MGM, the band that the Imagineers REALLY wanted to serve as hosts of this attraction was the Rolling Stones. But when Mick, Ron, and Keith proved too pricey for Mickey's tastes, Imagineers were told to find a cheaper alternative.

Those present in Disney's Glendale, California, headquarters that day remember Imagineers running out to their cars, gathering up their CD collections and returning to the building, where conversations then went along the lines of "How much would it cost us to get U2?" "U don't wanna know." Eventually, Aerosmith emerged as the affordable alternative.

walk the rope up the street toward Rock 'n' Roller Coaster and Tower of Terror. Stay on the far left sidewalk and you'll be among the first to make the left turn to the entrance of the coaster. Usually the Disney people get out of the way and allow you to run the last 100 feet or so.

A good strategy for riding both Tower of Terror and Rock 'n' Roller Coaster with minimum waits is to rush first thing after opening to Rock 'n' Roller Coaster and obtain FAST-PASSes, then line up for the Tower of Terror. Most days, by the time you finish experiencing the Tower of Terror it'll be time to use your FASTPASS for Rock 'n' Roller Coaster.

The Great Movie Ride

What It Is Movie-history indoor adventure ride

Scope and Scale Headliner

When to Go Before 11 a.m. or after 4:30 p.m.

Special Comments Elaborate, with several surprises

Author's Rating Unique; ★★★½

Appeal by Age Group

Preschool ★★½	Teens ★★★½	Over 30 ★★★★
Grade school ★★★½	Young Adults ★★★★	Seniors ★★★

Duration of Ride About 19 minutes

Average Wait in Line per 100 People ahead of You 2 minutes

Assumes All trains operating

Loading Speed Fast

Description and Comments Entering through a re-creation of Hollywood's Chinese Theater, guests board vehicles for a fast-paced tour through soundstage sets from classic films including *Casablanca, Tarzan, The Wizard of Oz, Aliens*, and *Raiders of the Lost Ark*. Each set is populated with new-generation Disney audio-animatronic (robot) characters, as well as an occasional human, all augmented by sound and lighting effects. One of Disney's larger and more ambitious dark rides, The Great Movie Ride encompasses 95,000 square feet and showcases some of the most famous scenes in filmmaking. Life-sized audio-animatronic sculptures of stars, including Gene Kelly, John Wayne, James Cagney, and Julie Andrews inhabit some of the largest sets ever constructed for a Disney ride.

Touring Tips The Great Movie Ride draws large crowds (and lines) from midmorning on. As an interval-loading, high-capacity ride, lines disappear quickly. Even so, waits can exceed an hour after midmorning. (Actual waits usually run about one-third shorter than the time posted. If the chalkboard indicates an hour's wait, your actual time will be around 40 minutes.)

A PEEK BEHIND THE SCENES WITH JIM HILL

How Some Guests Get Ahead

Guests experiencing The Great Movie Ride in its first year were sometimes subjected to a gruesome surprise as the ride passed through the *Tarzan* set. Apparently, the constant up-and-down movement of the animatronic chimpanzee in this scene would eventually cause the figure's head to come loose. So periodically Cheetah would literally lose his head. It would tumble off his neck and disappear into the faux foliage, or worse, fall into the lap of a passing guests. How'd you like THAT for a souvenir?

Star Tours (FASTPASS) *Lauren?*

Motion Sickness

WARNING!

What It Is Indoor space flight–simulation ride

Scope and Scale Headliner

When to Go First 90 minutes after opening

Special Comments Expectant mothers and anyone prone to motion sickness are advised against riding. Too intense for many children younger than age 8. Must be 40" tall to ride.

Author's Rating Not to be missed; ★★★★

Appeal by Age Group

Preschool ★★★★	Teens ★★★★	Over 30 ★★★★
Grade school ★★★★	Young Adults ★★★★	Seniors ★★★★

Duration of Ride About 7 minutes

Average Wait in Line per 100 People ahead of You 5 minutes

Assumes All simulators operating

Loading Speed Moderate to fast

Description and Comments Based on the *Star Wars* movie series, this attraction is so much fun that it just makes you grin and giggle. Guests ride in a <u>flight simulator</u> modeled after those used for training pilots and astronauts. You're supposedly on a vacation outing in space, piloted by a droid (android, aka humanoid, aka robot) on his first flight with real passengers. Mayhem ensues almost immediately. Scenery flashes by, and the simulator bucks and pitches. You could swear you were moving at the speed of light. After several minutes of this, the droid somehow lands the spacecraft, and you discover you're about three times happier than you were when you boarded.

Touring Tips Star Tours hasn't been as popular at Disney-MGM Studios as it has been at Disneyland in California. Except on unusually busy days, waits rarely exceed 35–45 minutes. For the first couple of hours the park is open, expect a wait of 25 minutes or less. Even so, see Star Tours before 11 a.m. or use FASTPASS. If you have young children (or anyone) who are apprehensive about this attraction, ask the attendant about switching off (pages 266–268).

Star Tours is near the exit of the 2,000-seat stadium that houses *Indiana Jones*. When an *Indiana Jones* performance lets out, Star Tours is temporarily inundated. Ditto for *MuppetVision 3-D* nearby. If you arrive in the midst of this mayhem, come back later.

Sounds Dangerous

What It Is Show demonstrating sound effects

Scope and Scale Minor attraction

When to Go Before 11 a.m. or after 4 p.m.

Author's Rating Funny and informative; ★★★

Appeal by Age Group

Preschool ★★½	Teens ★★★	Over 30 ★★★
Grade school ★★★½	Young Adults ★★★	Seniors ★★★★

Duration of Presentation 12 minutes

Preshow Entertainment Video introduction to sound effects

Probable Waiting Time 15–30 minutes

Description and Comments *Sounds Dangerous*, a film presentation starring Drew Carey as a blundering detective, is the vehicle for a crash course on movie and TV sound effects. Funny, educational, well paced, and (for once) not hawking some Disney flick or product, *Sounds Dangerous* is both entertaining and worthwhile. Earphones worn throughout the show make the various sounds seem very real, indeed ... perhaps too real for some younger children during a part of the show when the theater is plunged into darkness. A Pasadena, Texas, reader suggests we issue a more emphatic warning about *Sounds Dangerous*, writing:

I would recommend a stronger child warning for Sounds Dangerous. *Of all the attractions [at the Disney-MGM Studios] this had the most screaming children. Since we were plunged in complete darkness, mothers couldn't leave with their screaming children.*

Touring Tips   Because the theater is relatively small, long waits (partially in the hot sun) are common here. Another thing: *Sounds Dangerous* is periodically inundated by guests coming from a just-concluded performance of the *Indiana Jones Epic Stunt Spectacular*. This is not the time to get in line. Wait at least 30 minutes and try again.

A reader from Israel suggests that a good time to catch *Sounds Dangerous* is just before the afternoon parade. If the parade starts on Hollywood Boulevard, it takes about 15–18 minutes to wind over to the theater—just long enough to catch the show and pop out right in time for the parade.

Indiana Jones Epic Stunt Spectacular (FASTPASS)

What It Is   Movie-stunt demonstration and action show

Scope and Scale   Headliner

When to Go   First 3 morning shows or last evening show

Special Comments   Performance times posted on a sign at the entrance to the theater

Author's Rating   Done on a grand scale; ★★★★

Appeal by Age Group

Preschool ★★★	Teens ★★★★	Over 30 ★★★★
Grade school ★★★★	Young Adults ★★★★	Seniors ★★★★

Duration of Presentation   30 minutes

Preshow Entertainment   Selection of "extras" from audience

Probable Waiting Time   None

Description and Comments   Coherent and educational, though somewhat unevenly paced, the popular production showcases professional stunt men and women who demonstrate dangerous stunts with a behind-the-scenes look at how it's done. Sets, props, and special effects are very elaborate.

While most live shows at Walt Disney World are revised from time to time, the *Stunt Spectacular*, as a Hamden, Connecticut, man laments, has not changed for years:

Another bust was the Indy Jones show. The show is the same as it has been since it opened, but the acting grows tired.

Indiana Jones was closed for renovation for several months in 2000. Though the sets and props have been refurbished and the special effects modernized, the content of the show remains essentially the same.

Touring Tips   The Stunt Theater holds 2,000 people; capacity audiences are common. The first performance is always the easiest to see. If the first show is at 9:30 a.m. or earlier, you can usually walk in, even if you arrive five minutes late. If the first show is scheduled for 9:45 a.m. or later, arrive 20 or so minutes early. For the second performance, show up about 20–35 minutes ahead of time. For the third and subsequent shows, arrive 30–45 minutes early. If you plan to tour during late afternoon and evening, attend the last scheduled performance. If you want to beat the crowd out of the stadium, sit on the far right (as you face the staging area) and near the top.

To be chosen from the audience to be an "extra" in the stunt show, arrive early, sit down front, and display unmitigated enthusiasm. A woman from Richmond, Virginia, explains:

Indiana Jones *was far and away the best show—we saw it twice on two different days. After the first performance, I realized the best way to get picked was to stand up, wave my arms, and shout when the "casting director" called for volunteers—sheer enthusiasm wins every time, and sitting towards the front helps, too. We stayed afterwards for autographs of the performers in the obligatory Mickey Mouse autograph book.*

A PEEK BEHIND THE SCENES WITH JIM HILL

What Are We Going to Do With All These People? Back in May of 1989, right after Disney-MGM Studio theme park first opened to the public, the *Indiana Jones Epic Stunt Spectacular* really wasn't ready to be shown to the public. But because the park was really low on shows and rides back then, Disney had to do SOMETHING to occupy the record crowds. So in the spring and summer of 1989, for the first (and only) time, Disney guests were allowed to sit in the arena and watch as the various stunt teams rehearsed for the show's opening on August 25.

Theater of the Stars—*Beauty and the Beast—Live on Stage*

What It Is Live Hollywood-style musical, usually featuring Disney characters; performed in an open-air theater

Scope and Scale Major attraction

When to Go Anytime; evenings are cooler

Special Comments Performances are listed in the daily *Times Guide.*

Author's Rating Excellent; ★★★★

Appeal by Age Group

Preschool ★★★★	Teens ★★★	Over 30 ★★★★
Grade school ★★★★	Young Adults ★★★	Seniors ★★★★

Duration of Presentation 25 minutes

Preshow Entertainment None

Probable Waiting Time 20–30 minutes

Description and Comments The *Theater of the Stars* combines Disney characters with singers and dancers in upbeat and humorous Hollywood musicals. The *Beauty and the Beast* show, in particular, is outstanding. The theater offers a clear field of vision from almost every seat. Best, a canopy protects the audience from the Florida sun (or rain). The theater still gets mighty hot in the summer, but you should make it through a performance without suffering a heatstroke.

Touring Tips Unless you visit during the cooler months, see this show in the late afternoon or the evening. The production is so popular that you should show up 25–45 minutes early to get a seat.

A PEEK BEHIND THE SCENES WITH JIM HILL

Is Dove on the Menu Tonight?

The end of the *Beauty and the Beast* show *used to* feature the dramatic release of an entire flock of white doves. The trained birds would fly out over the audience, circle the theater for a moment, then head back to their coop behind the Magic Kingdom. After a while, indigenous hawks got wise to this ritual and began hanging around the theater waiting to snag a snack as each performance show came to a close. Eventually, the stage staff took pity on the poor doves and removed the birds from the menu..., er, the finale of the show.

Fantasmic!

What It Is Mixed-media nighttime spectacular

Scope and Scale Super headliner

When to Go Only staged in the evening

Special Comments Disney's best nighttime event

Author's Rating Not to be missed; ★★★★★

Appeal by Age Group

Preschool ★★★★	Teens ★★★★½	Over 30 ★★★★½
Grade school ★★★★★	Young Adults ★★★★½	Seniors ★★★★½

Duration of Presentation 25 minutes

Probable Waiting Time 50–90 minutes for a seat; 30–40 minutes for standing room

Description and Comments *Fantasmic!* is a mixed-media show presented one or more times each evening when the park is open late. Located off Sunset Boulevard behind the Tower of Terror, *Fantasmic!* is staged on an island opposite a 6,900-seat amphitheater. By far the largest theater facility ever created by Disney, the amphitheater can accommodate an additional 3,000 standing guests for an audience of nearly 10,000.

Fantasmic! is far and away the most extraordinary and ambitious outdoor spectacle ever attempted in any theme park. Starring Mickey Mouse in his role as the Sorcerer's Apprentice from *Fantasia*, the production uses lasers, images projected on a shroud of mist, fireworks, lighting effects, and music in combinations so stunning you can scarcely believe what you are seeing. The plot is simple: good versus evil. The story gets lost in all the special effects at times, but no matter, it is the spectacle, not the story line, that is so overpowering. While beautiful, stunning, and powerful are words that immediately come to mind, they fail to convey the uniqueness of this presentation. It could be argued, with some validity, that *Fantasmic!* alone is worth the price of the Disney-MGM Studios admission.

Readers, like this Amheart, Massachusetts, woman agree:

Fantasmic! was absolutely the best show any of us had ever seen. It is worth the 90-minute wait to see it. Disney Magic at its best!

From a 30-year-old mother of one from Wake Forest, North Carolina:

Fantasmic! was the high point of the entire trip. We've never seen such an incredible show. It took us three nights to finally get in to it, and it was well worth it.

A Queensbury, New York, dad offers this advice:

Don't see Fantasmic! at MGM before you see the laser/fireworks show at Epcot. Fantasmic! is the most entertaining show we've ever seen, and the technology is beyond belief. It really takes the shine off the other shows, which were truly wonderful.

A Texas reader enjoyed *Fantasmic!* but had some problems with arriving over an hour before the show:

I liked Fantasmic!; the kids around me loved it. They shouted out every character's name as they appeared. But, it wasn't worth the wait. I had to arrive at 8:10 for a 9:30 showing. Nothing is worth an 80-minute wait. The only entertainment in the interim was a couple of cheerleaders urging the crowd to do the wave.

A reader from Down Under found *Fantasmic!* a bit too sentimental:

We were disappointed by this show. While it features boats, characters, water, and light, it was a bit too nostalgic of Disney films. If this is what Mickey thinks about when he dreams, Minnie would be a little disappointed!

Although the reader is dead on about the rogue's gallery of Disney villains, most kids really do take *Fantasmic!* in stride. It is, however, a bit overwhelming for preschoolers. If you have kids ages seven or younger, you should prepare them for what they will see. Also, you can mitigate the fright factor somewhat by sitting back a bit.

Touring Tips *Fantasmic!* provides a whole new dimension to nighttime at Disney-MGM Studios. As a day-capping event, it is to the Studios what *IllumiNations* is to Epcot. While it's hard to imagine running out of space in a 10,000-person stadium, it happens almost every day. On evenings when there are two performances, the second show will always be less crowded. If you attend the first (or only) scheduled performance, show up at least an hour in advance. If you opt for the second show, arrive 50 minutes early. Readers underscore the importance of queuing up early:

From a Yorktown, Virginia, mom:

I think you seriously underestimated the time when people should arrive to see Fantasmic! if they want to get a seat. The stadium was already full when we arrived 45 minutes before the show was scheduled to start, and the remaining seats filled up quickly. Keep in mind this was during the off-season on one of the slower days of the week at Disney-MGM Studios.

A Richmond, Vermont, reader seconds the recommendation, writing:

Cast members at Disney-MGM Studios warned us to get to Fantasmic! at least one hour early. This will only get you the last, far-flung seats. If you want good seats, you'll need to arrive 90 minutes early.

Another reader complains about the treatment of standing guests but also discovered an "upside":

Our only criticism [of Fantasmic!] was that we were in the standing-room-only section where participants were treated like the great unwashed. Employees kept sniping at people to stay in the area, stay away from the fence, stay out of the bushes, etc., etc. The other spectators were great, but the employees really were tough on us. Since the show was [only] 25 minutes, the standing part wasn't so bad. The upside was that it made for a really easy exit from the show.

A father of three from Clarksburg, West Virginia, found that staying for the late performance worked best (note that late shows are offered only during busier times of the year):

Fantasmic! was fantastic. The 9:15 p.m. show was jammed all the time. We chose the 11 p.m. show (three times). The 11 p.m. show was never full. The second and third times we saw the show, we waited until 10:45 and walked right in and sat down. It's a must see!!

A West Wyoming, Pennsylvania (no kidding), dad, thinks the *Fantasmic!* seating situation could use a little Imagineering:

Fantasmic! is wonderful but nuts. The competition for seating rivals a rock show. A Disney worker told us there were hundreds of people in line over 2 hours before the show. We got there one hour prior, no seats. We sat on concrete slabs in the far left corner with other hot, sweaty folks, and then when the show started, everyone stood up in the standing section (no surprise), obliterating my youngest son's view. I tried to hold him up, but 75 lbs. in 90 degree heat; I almost had a hernia and heatstroke. There has GOT to be a better way to do this.

A Cross Junction, Virginia, woman offers this tip:

If planning to go to MGM's Fantasmic!, it's a good idea to buy deli sandwiches outside the park, pack them with snacks and water in your backpack, and get a seat early. Then you can sit and eat your dinner as you wait for a great show. This worked so well.

A mom from Virginia offers a warning about sitting too close to the action:

Avoid sitting near the front. We were stuck in the fourth row and despite no detectable wind, we were constantly sprayed by the fountains during the show. That might feel good after a hot summer day, but it was very unpleasant on a cool fall evening.

Rain and wind conditions sometimes cause *Fantasmic!* to be cancelled. Unfortunately, Disney officials usually do not make a final decision about whether to proceed or cancel until just before show time. We have seen guests wait stoically for over an hour with no assurance that their patience and sacrifice would be rewarded. We do not recommend arriving more than a few minutes before show time on rainy or especially windy nights. On nights like these, pursue your own agenda until ten minutes or so before show time and then head to the stadium to see what happens.

A mom from Pearland, Texas, found *Fantasmic!* too intense for her young child, writing:

Fantasmic! should come with a warning label. The show features a multitude of characters in various vignettes interspersed with water and laser light interludes as Mickey Mouse begins his lighthearted and fanciful dream. Unfortunately for the impressionable and tender-of-mind, the dream becomes a nightmare as the evil villains take over Mickey's imagination. The combination of actual characters, their larger-than-life laser visages, ominous, unbearably loud music, and thundering explosions with blinding flashes of light, fire, and sparks (which went on for a seemingly interminable length of time) sent hordes of parents with screaming children fleeing for the exits. Naturally, good does eventually prevail over evil, and the finale returns to the beautiful, magical Disney style, but not soon enough. Please, please warn parents not to take young children to this show. (For adults and teenagers, it is truly spectacular.)

Though we do not receive many reports of young children being terrified by *Fantasmic!*, the reader's point is well taken. We suggest you spend a little time preparing your younger children for what they will see. Also, make sure to hang on to your children after *Fantasmic!* and to give them explicit instructions for regrouping in the event you are separated.

Fantasmic! **Dinner Package**   If you dine at the Hollywood & Vine buffet or at the Mama Melrose or Brown Derby full-service restaurants, you can obtain a ticket/voucher for the members of your dining party to enter *Fantasmic!* via a special entrance and sit in a reserved section of seats. In return for your patronage of the restaurant, you can avoid 30—90 minutes waiting in the regular line to be admitted.

Here are the rules. You must call (407) WDW-DINE 90 days in advance and request the *Fantasmic!* Dinner Package for the night you want to see the show. This is a reservation rather than a priority seating and must be guaranteed with a credit card at the time of booking. There's a 48-hour cancellation policy.

To keep guests from coming in and ordering the cheapest thing on the menu just to get *Fantasmic!* vouchers, Disney includes a fixed price dinner in the package. At press time the prices were as follows:

	Hollywood Brown Derby	Mama Melrose's Ristorante Italiano	Hollywood & Vine Buffet
Adult	$37	$29	$22
Child (3–11)	$10	$10	$10

The price covers all you care to eat at the Hollywood & Vine Buffet; choice of appetizer, soup or salad, main course, bread, and dessert at the Brown Derby; and flatbread, family-style salad, choice of main course, and dessert at Mama Melrose. Nonalcoholic drinks are included. Park admission, tax, and gratuity are not. With so many courses at the two full-service restaurants, allow yourself a minimum of two hours to eat and make your way to the special theater entrance designated for *Fantasmic!* Dinner Package guests. If you have made ordinary priority seatings for any of the participating restaurants, they will not include reserved seats for *Fantasmic!*. You have to buy the package to get the seats.

You will receive your tickets/vouchers at the restaurant. After dinner, report to the *Fantasmic!* sign on Hollywood Boulevard next to Oscar's Super Service filling station (just inside the front entrance to the park) no later that 35 minutes prior to show time. A cast member will collect your vouchers and direct or escort you to the reserved seating section of the amphitheater. Though you're required to arrive early, you can be seated immediately and won't have to stand in any lines. Be advised that the reserved seats are off to the far right though they afford a good line of sight. You will not have specific assigned seats in the reserved section. It's first-come/first-served, so arrive early for the best choice. Finally, understand that you're out of luck if *Fantasmic!* is cancelled due to weather or other circumstances; you will not receive a refund or even a voucher for another performance.

Voyage of the Little Mermaid (FASTPASS)

What It Is   Musical stage show featuring characters from the Disney movie *The Little Mermaid*

Scope and Scale   Major attraction

When to Go   Before 9:45 a.m., just before closing, or use FASTPASS

Author's Rating   Romantic, lovable, and humorous in the best Disney tradition; not to be missed; ★★★★

Appeal by Age Group

Preschool ★★★★	Teens ★★★½	Over 30 ★★★★
Grade school ★★★★	Young Adults ★★★★	Seniors ★★★★

Duration of Presentation   15 minutes

Preshow Entertainment Taped ramblings about the decor in the preshow holding area

Probable Waiting Time Before 9:30 a.m., 10–30 minutes; after 9:30 a.m., 35–70 minutes

Description and Comments *Voyage of the Little Mermaid* is a winner, appealing to every age. Cute without being silly or saccharine, and infinitely lovable, the *Little Mermaid* show is the most tender and romantic entertainment offered anywhere in Walt Disney World. The story is simple and engaging, the special effects impressive, and the Disney characters memorable.

We receive a lot of mail from Europeans who complain about the "soppy sentimentality" of Americans in general and of Disney attractions in particular. These comments of a man from Bristol, England, are typical:

> *Americans have an ability to think as a child and so enjoy the soppiness of the* Little Mermaid. *English cynicism made it hard for us at times to see Disney stories as anything other than gushing, namby-pamby, and full of stereotypes. Other Brits might also find the sentimentality cloying. Maybe you should prepare them for the need to rethink their wry outlook on life temporarily.*

Touring Tips Because it's well done and located at a busy pedestrian intersection, *Voyage of the Little Mermaid* plays to capacity crowds all day. FASTPASS has helped redistribute crowds at *Voyage of the Little Mermaid*. At least 40–50% of each audience is drawn from the standby line. As a rough approximation, guests in the front third of the queuing area will usually make it into the next performance, and quite often folks in the front half of the queuing area will be admitted. Those in the back half of the queuing area will probably have to wait through two showings before being admitted.

When you enter the preshow lobby, stand near the doors to the theater. When they open, go inside, pick a row of seats, and let six to ten people enter the row ahead of you. The strategy is twofold: to obtain a good seat and be near the exit.

Finally, a Charlotte, North Carolina, mom took exception to our Fright Potential Rating for *Voyage of the Little Mermaid*:

> *The guide let me down on the* Little Mermaid *show at MGM—the huge sea witch portrayed in laser lights, cartoon, and live action TERRIFIED my three-year-old. The description of the show led me to believe it was all sweetness and romance with no scariness.*

A PEEK BEHIND THE SCENES WITH JIM HILL

Who Knew a Mermaid Would Have Such Great Legs? When *Voyage of the Little Mermaid* debuted in January of 1992, the general consensus was that this cute little stage show would run for 18 months. Two years, tops. Over a decade later, Ariel and her finny friends are still going strong. Which is why Disney's Theatrical division is now reportedly readying a radically expanded version of this Disney-MGM show. The new version, we hear, will also see if *The Little Mermaid* has enough drawing power for a run on Broadway.

Jim Henson's MuppetVision 3-D

What It Is 3-D movie starring the Muppets

Scope and Scale Major attraction

When to Go Before 11 a.m. or after 3 p.m.

Author's Rating Uproarious; not to be missed; ★★★★½

Appeal by Age Group

Preschool ★★★★½	Teens ★★★★½	Over 30 ★★★★½
Grade school ★★★★★	Young Adults ★★★★½	Seniors ★★★★½

Duration of Presentation 17 minutes

Preshow Entertainment Muppets on television

Probable Waiting Time 12 minutes

Description and Comments *MuppetVision 3-D* provides a total sensory experience, with wild 3-D action augmented by auditory, visual, and tactile special effects. If you're tired and hot, this zany presentation will make you feel brand new. Arrive early and enjoy the hilarious video preshow.

Touring Tips This production is very popular. Before noon, waits are about 20 minutes. Also, watch for throngs arriving from just-concluded performances of the *Indiana Jones Epic Stunt Spectacular*. If you encounter a long line, try again later.

A PEEK BEHIND THE SCENES WITH JIM HILL

More Muppets On The Way To The Studios?

After more than a decade of trying, the Walt Disney Company was finally able to acquire the Muppets characters from the Jim Henson Company in 2004. Look for Kermit & Co. to become a much bigger presence in the Studios over the next few years. Among the ideas that the Imagineers are supposedly considering is The Great Muppet Movie Ride, an elaborate parody of Disney-MGM's own Great Movie Ride with an animatronic Gonzo serving as your host in a Muppet-ized version of the history of Hollywood.

Honey, I Shrunk the Kids *Movie Set Adventure*

What It Is Small but elaborate playground

Scope and Scale Diversion

When to Go Before 11 a.m. or after dark

Author's Rating Great for young children, more of a curiosity for adults; ★★½

Appeal by Age Group

Preschool ★★★★½	Teens ★★	Over 30 ★★★
Grade school ★★★½	Young Adults ★★½	Seniors ★★½

Duration of Presentation Varies

Average Wait in Line per 100 People ahead of You 20 minutes

Description and Comments This elaborate playground appeals particularly to kids age 11 and younger. The story is that you have been "miniaturized" and have to make your way through a yard full of 20-foot-tall blades of grass, giant ants, lawn sprinklers, and other oversized features.

Touring Tips This imaginative playground has tunnels, slides, rope ladders, and a variety of oversized props. All surface areas are padded, and Disney personnel are on-hand to help keep children in some semblance of control.

While this Movie Set Adventure undoubtedly looked good on paper, the actual attraction has problems that are hard to "miniaturize." First, it isn't nearly large enough to accommodate the children who would like to play. Only 240 people are allowed "on the set" at a time, and many of these are supervising parents or curious adults who hopped in line without knowing what they were waiting for. Frequently by 10:30 or 11 a.m., the playground is full, with dozens waiting outside (some impatiently).

Also, there's no provision for getting people to leave. Kids play as long as parents allow. This creates uneven traffic flow and unpredictable waits. If it weren't for the third flaw, that the attraction is poorly ventilated (as hot and sticky as an Everglades swamp), there's no telling when anyone would leave.

A mom from Shawnee Mission, Kansas, however, disagrees:

Some of the things your book said to skip were our favorites (at least for the kids). We thought the playground from Honey, I Shrunk the Kids was great—definitely worth seeing.

A mom from Tolland, Connecticut, however, found the playground exasperating:

We let the kids hang out at [Honey, I Shrunk the Kids] because we thought it would be relaxing: NOT! You have three choices here: (1) Let your kids go anywhere and hope if they try to get out without your permission someone will stop them. Also hope that some-one else will help your kids if they get caught up in the exhibit. (2) Go everywhere with your kids—this takes a lot of stamina and some athleticism. If you care about appear-ances this could be a problem because you look pretty stupid coming down those slides. But then again, there are women with bright red sailor hats that say "Minnie" and have a yellow flower in the middle of them, so how stupid could you look in comparison? (3) Try to visually keep track of your kids. This is impossible, so you will be either on the edge of or in the middle of an anxiety attack the whole time you are there.

If you visit during warmer months and want your children to experience the play-ground, get them in and out before 11 a.m. By late morning, this attraction is way too hot and crowded for anyone to enjoy. Access the playground via the New York Backlot, or via Mickey Avenue.

Lights! Motors! Action! Extreme Stunt Show (Opens 2005)

What It Is Auto stunt show

Scope and Scale Headliner

When to Go First show of the day or after 4 p.m.

Author's Rating *Not open at press time*

Appeal by Age Group *Not open at press time*

Duration of Presentation 25 minutes

Preshow Entertainment Selection of audience "volunteers"

Description and Comments This show, which originated at Disneyland Paris, fea-tures cars and motorcycles in a blur of chases, crashes, jumps, and explosions. One especially juicy scene culminates with the villain's car being split in half by a guided mis-sile! After each action sequence, the secrets behind the special effects are explained. All of the action takes place in a small town complete with shops, street stalls, and cafes ringing a market square. As in the *Indiana Jones* stunt show, members of the audience will be recruited as "extras." An enormous movie screen in the middle of the set shows auto stunts from classic action films and allows the audience to see how the footage shot during the show is integrated into a finished scene.

Touring Tips The auto stunt show, located at the end of New York Street, is sched-uled to present 4–6 shows daily. As a new attraction, it will be popular, but its remote location (the most distant attraction from the park entrance) will help distribute and moderate the crowds. Seating will be in a 5,000-person stadium, so we don't think it will be difficult to get a seat except on the busiest days. Still, because we haven't actually seen the show in operation, we recommend arriving 30 minutes early.

New York Street Backlot

What It Is Walk-through backlot movie set

Scope and Scale Diversion

When to Go Anytime

Author's Rating Interesting, with great detail; ★★★

Appeal by Age Group

Preschool 1.5	Teens ★★★	Over 30 ★★★
Grade school ★★★	Young Adults ★★★	Seniors ★★★

Duration of Presentation Varies

Average Wait in Line per 100 People ahead of You No waiting

Description and Comments Guests can stroll an elaborate New York Street set and appreciate its rich detail.

Touring Tips There's never a wait to enjoy the New York Street Backlot; save it until you've seen those attractions that develop long lines.

Who Wants to Be a Millionaire (FASTPASS)

What It Is Look-alike version of the TV game show

Scope and Scale Major attraction

When to Go Before noon, or after 4 p.m., or use FASTPASS

Special Comments Contestants play for points, not dollars

Author's Rating No Regis, but good fun; ★★★★

Appeal by Age Group

Preschool ★★	Teens ★★★★	Over 30 ★★★★
Grade school ★★★★	Young Adults ★★★★	Seniors ★★★★

Duration of Presentation 25 minutes

Preshow Entertainment Video of Regis

Probable Waiting Time 20 minutes

Description and Comments It's the familiar ABC television game show sans Regis played on a replica of the real set, including all the snazzy lighting and creepy sound effects. Contestants are selected from among the audience and play for points and prizes. The 600-seat studio is located in Soundstages 2 and 3 on Mickey Avenue. To get there, go to the end of Hollywood Boulevard and turn right through the Studios Arch, then immediately left alongside *Voyage of the Little Mermaid*. The soundstages are about 80 yards down on the right.

Touring Tips Each member of the audience has a small electronic display and keypad to use for recording answers. The keypad has a key for each letter (A, B, C, and D) representing one of the four multiple-choice answers to a given question. When the keypad lights up, typically just as the last choice (D) is revealed, that's your cue to enter your answer. The faster you enter the answer, the better your score. Most people hold their fingers ready and push the letter key designating their answer as fast as humanly possible. You can't change your answer, so once you push the key, you're committed. Getting an answer right but taking longer is better than registering a wrong answer. Your score is tabulated electronically, with points awarded for being both fast and right.

If there is no one from a previous round continuing, the game will start with a "fastest-finger" round, where the audience member who posts the fastest correct answer goes to the hot seat as a contestant. If the contestant wins the ultimate goal of 1 million points, decides to leave, or loses, the audience member with the highest score at that time will be the next contestant. Audience scores are displayed from time to time as the contestant reaches plateaus of 1,000 and 32,000 points. Unlike the real version where Regis gives contestants almost unlimited time to answer, you must answer in less than 30 seconds in the theme-park version. As a contestant you get three "life lines." You can consult the audience or have two wrong choices deleted as in the real game, or phone someone. In the Disney version the person on the other end of the line will be a stranger, someone else in the park. Prizes range from pins, hats, polo shirts, and the like to the grand prize of a 3-night cruise on the Disney Cruise Line.

The first ten questions are fairly easy, with a number of the questions being Disney related. If the show ends while you are a contestant, you may or may not be invited to continue during the next show. Disney has experimented with both options.

Unofficial Guide friend Susan Turner was on hand for a number of shows. Here's her advice for putting yourself in the hot seat:

1. **Answer correctly.** *If you blow a question you can pretty much forget it.*

2. **Answer quickly.** *This is a very close second to answering correctly. If you don't have quick reflexes, it doesn't matter if you answer everything correctly. For the first questions (at least up until the 1,000-point question), this is most critical, as most of the audience will also be answering correctly.*

3. **How to answer quickly.** *The keypad consists of four buttons in a row marked "A, B, C, and D," with lights above each one. This panel will remain unlit until the D answer is put on the screen. This means you really must have the answer figured out before knowing the D answer. I quickly learned to avert my eyes from the screen to the answer panel when they were reading the C answer. By this time I had chosen my answer and had my finger on the correct button. In this way, I could watch for the panel to light and hit the button immediately. If you wait until they finish reading the D answer, or even watch for the D answer to show up on the screen, it's too late. This also means that if the answer is D, you need to figure this out by eliminating A–C. I found (and had this corroborated by others' experiences) that I scored higher when there was a question with D as the answer, perhaps because most guests aren't ready to answer until the correct answer is read. In some ways the game is a bit more difficult as an audience member than as the one in the hot seat. Obviously, you don't have the three lifelines, but also you really don't have time to think through the answers. At the two point plateaus (i.e. 1,000 and 32,000) they pause and show the top ten guest scores, using the seat number for identification. The top ten scores are also shown when they need to refill the hot seat and at the end of a game. I found if I employed this strategy (i.e., immediate and correct answer), I was in the top ten about half of the time when they showed the 1,000-point level, and maybe three-fourths of the time at the 32,000-point level. If you are not in the top ten, you will not know your score. I wish they had little LEDs by each of the answer panels so you could keep up with your scores.*

4. **Go to an early (or maybe late) show.** *The earliest show was reported to be less than half full. I imagine [Millionaire] will be a very popular show and will be full at most if not all shows, but if there is a show that isn't at capacity, it will probably be the [first show of the day]. Fewer people improves your probability of getting in. Unfortunately this didn't occur to me until after I left WDW! If it had, I would most definitely have been at the first show.*

5. A note about the fastest-fingers question. *This will only occur at the start of a game if no one returns from the last game. At the end of the game, if a contestant is in the hot seat and answers the last question correctly, they have the opportunity to return for the next show. For the fastest-finger questions, they read the question and put it on the screen, then all four answers will appear at once. The problem I had with this the first time I played was having to recheck to see if B was to the right of or below A. I saw a couple of kids win this, and I'm not sure if they were just quick and smart, or if they just pushed buttons rapidly and randomly. There is a 1 in 24 chance of answering correctly, so with enough people employing this strategy someone is bound to get it right. Here again, speed is very important. Some of these questions were Disney related (i.e., "Put these Epcot pavilions in the order that they appear starting with the entrance: Spaceship Earth, Innoventions, Imagination, American Pavilion"), while others were not (i.e., "Put these members of the whale family in order of size starting with the smallest: bottlenose dolphin, killer whale, gray whale, blue whale.")*

6. One final note about seating. *It does not matter where you sit—all seats are equipped with an answer pad. Because the studio is a near-replica of the TV studio, they include the ten "fastest-fingers" seats on the floor (the ones with the screens). Guests sitting at these seats have no real advantage over guests in the stands. Also, there is a section of seats on the floor that is largely used as disabled seating. I wondered at first if they had answer keypads as well, and I found that indeed they do, though in the front row you have to hold the keypad (in the stands the keypads are on the back of the chair in front of you).*

We recommend catching a *Millionaire* show after you've experienced all of the park's rides. If waits are intolerable, use FASTPASS. For the record, more than 50% of the audience for each show, come from the standby line.

One Man's Dream

What It Is Tribute to Walt Disney

Scope and Scale Minor attraction

When to Go Anytime

Author's Rating Excellent! ... and about time; ★★★★

Appeal by Age Group

Preschool ★	Teens ★★★	Over 30 ★★★★
Grade school ★★½	Young Adults ★★★½	Seniors ★★★★

Duration of Presentation 25 minutes

Preshow Entertainment Disney memorabilia

Probable Waiting Time For film, 10 minutes

Description and Comments *One Man's Dream* is a long-overdue tribute to Walt Disney. Launched in 2001 to celebrate the 100th anniversary of Walt Disney's birthday, the attraction consists of an exhibit area showcasing Disney memorabilia and recordings, followed by a film documenting Disney's life. The exhibits chronicle Walt Disney's life and business. On display are a replica of Walt's California office, various innovations in animation developed by Disney, and early models and working plans for Walt Disney World, as well as for various Disney theme parks around the world. The film provides a personal glimpse of Disney and offers insights regarding both Disney's successes and failures.

Touring Tips Give yourself some time here. Every minute spent among these extraordinary artifacts will enhance your visit to Walt Disney World, taking you back to a time when the creativity and vision that created Walt Disney World were personified by one struggling entrepreneur. Located to the right of *Millionaire* on Mickey Avenue, *One Man's Dream* will not be difficult to see. Try it during the hot, crowded middle part of the day.

A PEEK BEHIND THE SCENES WITH JIM HILL

Five feet equals 15 years of creative compromise
One of the more poignant moments in the exhibit comes when guests see how Walt's elaborate plans of a futuristic community, EPCOT, were turned into the theme park, Epcot. On one wall you have Disney's last and (some would say) best dream. Five feet away, you have a model of Spaceship Earth, hardly a remnant of the original concept, but still a pointed reminder of how Walt's successors destroyed one of his most cherished visions. You'll often catch people here looking first at the city plans, then at the Spaceship Earth model, then back at the city plans, with this wistful expression on their faces as they reflect on what might have been.

Playhouse Disney Live on Stage

What It Is Live show for children

Scope and Scale Minor attraction

When to Go Per the daily entertainment schedule

Author's Rating A must for families with preschoolers; ★★★★

Appeal by Age Group

Preschool ★★★★★	Teens ★★	Over 30 ★★
Grade school ★★★½	Young Adults ★★★	Seniors ★★★

Duration of Presentation 20 minutes

Special Comments Audience sits on the floor

Probable Waiting Time 10 minutes

Description and Comments The show features characters from the Disney Channel's *Rolie Polie Olie*, *The Book of Pooh*, *Bear in the Big Blue House*, and *Stanley*. A simple plot serves as the platform for singing, dancing, some great puppetry, and a great deal of audience participation. The characters, who ooze love and goodness, rally throngs of tots and preschoolers to sing and dance along with them. All the jumping, squirming, and high-stepping is facilitated by having the audience sit on the floor so that kids can spontaneously erupt into motion when the mood strikes. Even for adults without children, it's a treat to watch the tykes rev up. If you have a younger child in your party, all the better: just stand back and let the video roll.

For preschoolers, *Playhouse Disney* will be the highlight of their day, as a Thomasville, North Carolina, mom attests:

> Playhouse Disney *at MGM was fantastic! My three-year-old loved it. The children danced, sang, and had a great time.*

Touring Tips The show is headquartered in what was formerly the Soundstage Restaurant located to the immediate right of the Animation Tour. Because the tykes just can't get enough, it has become the toughest ticket at the Studios. Show up at least 30 minutes before showtime. Once inside, pick a spot on the floor and take a breather until the performance begins.

A PEEK BEHIND THE SCENES WITH JIM HILL

A Cocktail Would Sure Make This Show Easier To Take. Many guests recall fondly how years back the *Playhouse Disney* building was home to the Catwalk Bar. This was one of the few places in the park that served alcohol. However, the pink elephants gave way to dancing bears when the "Bear in the Big Blue House" took over the facility in October of 2001.

✗ The Magic of Disney Animation

What It Is Overview of Disney Animation process with limited hands-on demonstrations

Scope and Scale Minor attraction

When to Go Before 11 a.m. or after 5 p.m.

Author's Rating Not as good as previous renditions; ★★½

Appeal by Age Group

Preschool ★★★	Teens ★★★	Over 30 ★★★★
Grade school ★★★	Young Adults ★★★★	Seniors ★★★★

Duration of Presentation 30 minutes

Preshow Entertainment Gallery of animation art in waiting area

Average Wait in Line per 100 People ahead of You 7 minutes

Description and Comments The consolidation of Disney Animation at the Burbank, California, studio has left this attraction without a story to tell. Park guests can still get a general overview of the Disney animation process but will not see the detailed work of actual artists, as was possible in previous versions.

The revamped attraction starts in a small theater, where the audience is introduced to a cast-member host and Mushu, the dragon from Mulan. Between the host's speech, Mushu's constant interruptions and a very brief taped segment with real Disney animators, guests are hard pressed to learn anything about actual animation. The audience is shown a plug for current Disney animated releases ("Home on the Range" while we were there), which falls flat.

Next, the audience moves to another room with floor seating, where another cast member gives guests a verbal description of what used to be the walking tour of the actual animation studio. The cast member supplies bits of Disney character trivia (e.g., Buzz Lightyear's original name was Lunar Larry) and fields questions from the audience, but nothing truly enlightening is presented.

Afterwards, guests have the option of exiting the attraction or attending the Animation Academy (space is limited, and is on a first-come, first-served basis). This is by far the most interesting segment of the attraction, but not designed for all guests. The animator works quickly, which seems to frustrate younger guests who need more time or assistance to get their drawing right. For those who do keep up with the animator, this part is interesting and gives a good idea of how difficult hand-drawn animation really is.

Judging by the low wait times, the Animation tour may be in need of yet another overhaul. A mother of two from Oak Ridge, North Carolina, writes:

> The new [Animation] tour is missing the essence of Disney animation, with little to no mention of the modern classics that helped revitalize Disney. The new version is a shell of its former self. It's hard to avoid the word "lame."

Touring Tips Some days, the animation tour doesn't open until 11 a.m., by which time the park is pretty full. The tour is a relatively small-volume attraction, and lines can build on busy days by mid- to late morning.

A PEEK BEHIND THE SCENES WITH JIM HILL

This Is Where They USED to Make the Movies There's been a whole lot less magic to Disney-MGM's Magic of Disney Animation attraction since January of 2004, when Disney management decided to lay off the animators who worked at the Studios and produced great movies like *Mulan, Lilo & Stitch,* and *Brother Bear.*

Lots of people find the ending to this attraction, the Learn to Draw a Disney Character area, to be rather ironic. Now the only drawing going on inside this building is being done by tourists.

Disney-MGM Studios Backlot Tour

What It Is Combination tram and walking tour of modern film and video production

Scope and Scale Headliner

When to Go Anytime

Author's Rating Educational and fun; not to be missed; ★★★★

Appeal by Age Group

Preschool ★★★	Teens ★★★★	Over 30 ★★★★
Grade school ★★★★	Young Adults ★★★★	Seniors ★★★★

Duration of Presentation About 30 minutes

Special Comments Use the rest room before getting in line.

Preshow Entertainment A video before the special effects segment and another video in the tram boarding area

Description and Comments About two-thirds of Disney-MGM Studios is a working film and television facility, where actors, artists, and technicians work on productions year-round. Everything from TV commercials, specials, and game shows to feature motion pictures are produced. Visitors to Disney-MGM can take the backstage studio tour to learn production methods and technologies.

Disney periodically changes the name of this tour. At press time, it was called the Disney-MGM Studios Backlot Tour.

The tour begins on the edge of the backlot with the special effects walking segment, then continues with the tram segment. To reach the Disney-MGM Studios Backlot Tour, turn right off Hollywood Boulevard through the Studio Arch into the Animation Courtyard. Bear left at the corner where *Voyage of the Little Mermaid* is situated. Follow the street until you see a red brick warehouse on your right. Go through the door and up the ramp.

The first stop is a special effects water tank where technicians explain the mechanical and optical tricks that "turn the seemingly impossible into on-screen reality." Included are rain effects and a naval battle. The waiting area for this part of the tour displays miniature naval vessels used in filming famous war movies.

A prop room separates the special effects tank and the tram tour. Trams depart about once every four minutes on busy days, winding among production and shop buildings before stopping at the wardrobe and crafts shops. Here, costumes, sets, and props are designed, created, and stored. Still seated on the tram, you look through large windows to see craftsmen at work.

The tour continues through the backlot, where western desert canyons and New York City brownstones exist side by side with suburban residential streets. The tour's highlight is Catastrophe Canyon, an elaborate special-effects movie set where a thunderstorm, earthquake, oil-field fire, and flash flood are simulated.

Touring Tips   Because the Backlot Tour is one of Disney's most efficient attractions, you will rarely wait more than 15 minutes (usually less than 10). Take the tour at your convenience, but preferably before 5 p.m., when the workday ends for the various workshops.

Live Entertainment at Disney-MGM Studios

When the Studios opened, live entertainment, parades, and special events weren't as fully developed or elaborate as those at the Magic Kingdom or Epcot. With the introduction of an afternoon parade and elaborate shows at *Theater of the Stars,* the Studios joined the big leagues. In 1998, Disney-MGM launched a new edition of *Fantasmic!,* a water, fireworks, and laser show that draws rave reviews. *Fantasmic!,* staged in its own specially designed 10,000-person amphitheater, makes the Studios the park of choice for spectacular nighttime entertainment. *Fantasmic!* is profiled on pages 594–597.

Afternoon Parade   Staged once a day, the parade begins near the park's entrance, continues down Hollywood Boulevard, and circles in front of the giant hat. From there, it passes in front of *Sounds Dangerous* and ends by Star Tours. An alternate route begins at the far end of Sunset Boulevard and turns right onto Hollywood Boulevard.

The parade features floats and characters from Disney's animated features. Excellent parades based on *Mulan, Aladdin, Toy Story,* vintage automobiles, and *Hercules,* among others, have been produced. The current parade showcases Disney characters in vintage autos. Colorful, creative, and totally upbeat, the afternoon parade is great. It does, however, bring pedestrian traffic to a standstill along its route and hampers crossing the park. If you're anywhere on the parade route when the parade begins, your best bet is to stay put and enjoy it. Our favorite vantage point is the steps of the theater next to *Sounds Dangerous.*

Theater of the Stars   This covered amphitheater on Sunset Boulevard is the stage for production reviews, usually featuring music from Disney movies and starring Disney characters. Performances are posted in front of the theater and are listed in the daily entertainment schedule in the handout *Times Guide.*

Disney Characters   Find characters at the Theater of the Stars and Backlot Theater, in parades, Al's Toy Barn near Mama Melrose's on New York Street, in the Animation Courtyard, in Backstage Plaza, and along

Mickey Avenue. Mickey sometimes appears for autographs and photos on Sunset Boulevard. Times and locations for character appearances are listed in the complementary *Times Guide*.

Street Entertainment Film star look-alikes, jugglers, and other roving performers appear on Hollywood and Sunset Boulevards. The Studios' modest marching band and a brass quartet play Hollywood Boulevard, Sunset Boulevard, Studio Courtyard, and the Echo Lake area. Not exactly street entertainment, a piano player performs daily at The Hollywood Brown Derby.

Disney-MGM Studios Touring Plan

Because Disney-MGM offers fewer attractions, touring isn't as complicated as at the Magic Kingdom or Epcot. Most Disney-MGM rides and shows are oriented to the entire family, eliminating disagreements on how to spend the day. Whereas in the Magic Kingdom Mom and Dad want to see *The Hall of Presidents,* Big Sis is revved to ride Space Mountain, and the preschool twins are clamoring for Dumbo the Flying Elephant, at Disney-MGM Studios the whole family can pretty much tour together. Since there are fewer attractions, crowds are more concentrated at Disney-MGM. If a line seems unusually long, ask an attendant what the estimated wait is. If it exceeds your tolerance, retry the attraction while *Indiana Jones* is in progress or during a parade or special event. These draw people away from the lines.

Before You Go

1. Call (407) 824-4321 to verify the park's hours.
2. Buy your admission before arriving.
3. Make lunch and dinner priority seatings or reserve the *Fantasmic!* dinner package (if desired) before you arrive by calling (407) WDW-DINE.
4. The schedule of live entertainment changes from month to month and even from day to day. Review the handout daily *Times Guide* to get a fairly clear picture of your options.

Disney-MGM Studios One-Day Touring Plan

By way of introduction, we didn't believe it when our new touring plan software (see pages 66–71) spit out this plan. It requires a fair amount of backtracking and postpones several big attractions until later in the day. Field testing, however, confirmed that it saves about 40 minutes over all other plans.

Our touring plan assumes a willingness to experience all major rides and shows. Be aware that the Rock 'n' Roller Coaster, Star Tours, The

Great Movie Ride, The Twilight Zone Tower of Terror, and the Catastrophe Canyon segment of the tram tour sometimes frighten children younger than eight. Further, Star Tours and the Rock 'n' Roller Coaster can upset anyone prone to motion sickness. When following the plan, skip any attraction you don't wish to experience.

1. Arrive at the park, admission in hand, 30–40 minutes before official opening time.

2. When you're admitted, grab a park map and a daily entertainment schedule, known as a *Times Guide*, from the little round shop straight ahead and just inside the turnstiles. Then blow down Hollywood Boulevard and turn right onto Sunset Boulevard. Stay to the right side of the street and proceed to the Tower of Terror. Ride. If your route is blocked by a rope barrier, position yourself as near the rope as possible and on the right side of the street. When you are allowed to proceed, go directly to the Tower of Terror.

3. After exiting the Tower of Terror, bear right to Rock 'n' Roller Coaster. Obtain FASTPASSes for the Rock 'n' Roller Coaster if the wait is more than 30 minutes, otherwise ride now.

4. Backtrack down Sunset Boulevard and turn right on Hollywood Boulevard. On the far side of the giant hat is The Great Movie Ride. Enjoy.

5. Exit The Great Movie Ride and bear left. Turn left again just past The Great Movie Ride building and walk the stairs to Mickey Avenue. If the next showing of *Who Wants to Be a Millionaire* is less than 20 minutes from now, see *Who Wants to Be a Millionaire*. If the next showing is between 20 and 40 minutes from now, see *One Man's Dream* first, then *Millionaire*. If the next showing of *Millionaire* is more than an hour away, take the Backlot Tour and see *One Man's Dream* first.

6. Exit *Who Wants to Be a Millionaire* and bear left. Take the Backlot Tour.

7. Exit the Backlot tour and turn right. Walk back down Mickey Avenue and see *One Man's Dream* if you have not already done so.

8. Check the daily entertainment schedule for performance times of *Beauty and the Beast, Playhouse Disney Live,* and *Lights! Motors! Action!* Work these shows in around lunch.

9. See *Muppet-Vision 3-D* near the New York Street Set.

10. Explore the New York Street Set if you didn't see enough en route to the *Muppets*.

11. Head in the direction of the Echo Lake. Ride Star Tours.

12. See *Sounds Dangerous*, which faces Echo Lake near *Indiana Jones*.

13. Checking the daily entertainment schedule for performance times, see the *Indiana Jones Epic Stunt Spectacular* (FASTPASS), as well as the *Voyage of the Little Mermaid* (FASTPASS). Also take the Magic of Disney Animation tour.

14. Tour Hollywood and Sunset Boulevards. Enjoy *Fantasmic!*.

15. This concludes the touring plan. Eat, shop, enjoy live entertainment, or revisit your favorite attractions.

Animal Kingdom / Disney-MGM Studios Combined One-Day Touring Plan

This plan offers a greatest hits tour of both the Animal Kingdom and the Disney-MGM Studios in one day. It requires that you have a Park Hopper pass and a fair amount of energy. The plan assumes a willingness to experience the "must-see" rides and shows at both parks. This is *not* an appropriate touring plan for families with children nine years and younger. The complete plan can be found starting on page 573.

Universal Orlando

Universal Orlando has transformed into a complete destination resort, with two theme parks, three hotels, and a shopping, dining, and entertainment complex. The second theme park, Islands of Adventure, opened in 1999 with five theme areas.

A system of roads and two multistory parking facilities are connected by moving sidewalks to CityWalk, a shopping, dining, and nighttime entertainment complex that also serves as a gateway to both the Universal Studios Florida and Islands of Adventure theme parks. CityWalk includes the world's largest Hard Rock Café, complete with its own concert facility; an Emeril's restaurant; a NASCAR Café, with an auto-racing theme; a Pat O'Brien's New Orleans nightclub, with dueling pianos; a Motown Café; a Bob Marley restaurant and museum; a multifaceted Jazz Center; an E! Entertainment production studio; Jimmy Buffett's Margaritaville; and a 16-screen cinema complex.

The Portofino Bay Hotel opened in 1999 with 750 rooms, followed by the 650-room Hard Rock Hotel in late 2000. The third hotel, the Royal Pacific Resort, opened in 2002 with 1,000 rooms.

Arriving at Universal Orlando

The Universal Orlando complex can be accessed directly from I-4. Once on site, you will be directed to park in one of two multitiered parking garages. Parking runs $8 for cars and $10 for RVs. Be sure to write down the location of your car before heading for the parks. From the garages, moving sidewalks deliver you to the Universal CityWalk dining, shopping, and entertainment venue described above. From CityWalk, you can access the main entrances of both Universal Studios Florida and Islands of Adventure theme parks. Even with the moving walkways, it takes about 10–12 minutes to commute from the garages to the entrances of the theme parks.

Universal offers One-Day, Two-Day, Three-Day, and Annual Passes. Multiday passes allow you to visit both Universal theme parks on the same day, and unused days are good forever. Multiday passes also allow for early entry on select days. Passes can be obtained in advance on the phone with your credit card at (800) 711-0080. All prices are the same whether you buy your admission at the gate or in advance. Prices shown below include tax.

	Adults	Children (3–9)
One-Day, One-Park Pass	$59	$48
Two-Day, Two-Park Pass (w/ third day free)	$106	$95
Three-Day Two-Park Pass	$123	$110
Two-Park Annual Pass Preferred	$181	All guests
Two Park Annual Power Pass	$117	All guests

Be sure to check Universal's Web site (**www.universalorlando.com**) for seasonal deals and specials. As we went to press, Universal was offering a five-day pass good at Universal Studios Florida, Islands of Adventure, and CityWalk for $101 (all guests).

If you want to visit more than one park on a given day, have your park pass and hand stamped when exiting your first park. At the second park use the readmission turnstile, showing your stamped pass and hand.

Combination passes are available: A four-park, 14-day pass allows unlimited entry to Universal Studios, Universal's Islands of Adventure, SeaWorld, and Wet 'n' Wild and costs about $192 for adults and $156 for children (ages three to nine). A five-park, 14-day pass provides unlimited entry to Universal Studios, Universal's Islands of Adventure, SeaWorld, Wet 'n' Wild, and Busch Gardens and costs about $229 for adults and $192 for children.

The main Universal Orlando information number is (407) 363-8000. Reach Guest Services at (407) 224-4233, schedule a character lunch at **www.universalorlando.com,** and order tickets by mail at (800) 224-3838. The number for Lost and Found is (407) 224-4244

Early Entry and Universal Express

Universal no longer operates an early entry program. The Universal Express program is actually two programs, one for Universal hotel guests and one available to everyone. Concerning the latter, there is a basic program, available to all guests at no additional charge (that operates much like Disney's FASTPASS), and an enhanced program that costs extra.

Universal Express Programs Available to All Guests

The basic program works like this: theme-park guests are issued Universal Express return tickets at kiosks set near the entrances of popular attractions. These return tickets have a 1-hour time window printed on them, good for admission during that prescribed time period to the Express queue at a particular attraction. This special queue bypasses much of the main line, and those waiting in it have priority over the proles stuck in the regular queue.

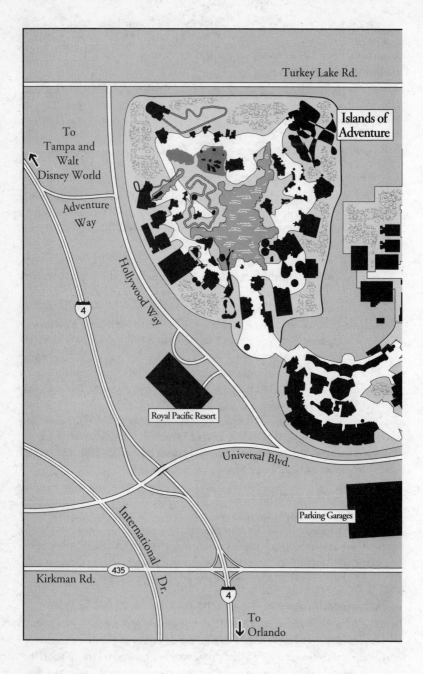

Turkey Lake Rd.

Islands of
Adventure

To
Tampa and
Walt
Disney World

Adventure
Way

Hollywood Way

Royal Pacific Resort

Universal Blvd.

International Dr.

Parking Garages

Kirkman Rd.

435

4

To
Orlando

4

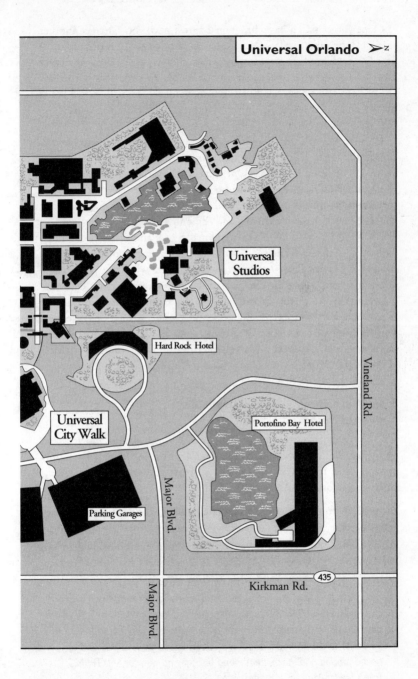

Universal Orlando

Universal Studios

Hard Rock Hotel

Universal City Walk

Portofino Bay Hotel

Parking Garages

Vineland Rd.

Major Blvd.

Major Blvd.

Kirkman Rd.

435

Once you obtain a basic program Express pass, you can't get another until: (1) the time window for you to use your first pass has begun; or (2) two hours after the time you were issued the first pass. The transaction time—the time when you actually obtained the first pass—is printed on the bottom of the pass. So, if your return window is more than two hours away, you can get a second Universal Express pass before you've used the first pass.

If you're willing to drop a little extra cash, you can upgrade to Universal Express Plus. Universal Express Plus allows you to use the Express entrance one time only at each designated Universal Express attraction. With the Plus feature there are no return windows, so you can visit attractions at your convenience. Universal Express Plus is good only for the date of purchase *at one park,* and can only be used by one person.

Universal Express Plus is available for $15 over and above your admission most of the year, and for $25 during peak seasons. You can purchase Universal Express Plus at the theme-park's ticket windows, just outside the front gates. Once in the Universal Studios theme park, Universal Express Plus is available at the Back to the Future Store, the Cartoon Store, Shaiken's Souvenirs, and Nickstuff. Inside Islands of Adventure you can buy Universal Express Plus at Jurassic Outfitters, Toon Extra, Treasures of Poseidon, the Marvel Alterniverse Store, and at Port Merchants Cart. As of the time of his writing, Universal Express Plus was not available on the Internet.

Universal Express Program Available to Universal Resort Guests

The Universal Express program for Universal resort guests allows guests to bypass the regular line anytime, and as often as desired, by simply showing their room key. This perk far surpasses any perk accorded guests of Disney resorts.

How Universal Express Impacts Crowd Conditions at the Attractions

This system dramatically affects crowd movement (and touring plans) in the Universal parks, since all guests can access the Express line to some degree. A woman from Yorktown, Virginia, writes:

People in the [Express] line were let in at a rate of about ten to one over the regular line folks. This created bottlenecks and long waits for people who didn't have the express privilege at the very times when it is supposed to be easier to get around! The fallout from this was that we just kind of poked around until noon, then found basically no wait for ANYTHING (even Spider-Man) in the afternoon.

Unfortunately, especially for attractions that were created before Universal Express was conceived, the Universal Express kiosks are sometimes stuffed in an awkward corner or hidden off to the side. Park guests often crowd around the kiosks, trying to figure out what attraction their pass is for, what time slot to choose, and where the actual express line is. As a woman from Nashua, New Hampshire, complains:

We had to figure out that we needed to go to the terminals at a location other than the ride itself…We were in a "mosh pit" in the heat trying to get to the terminals!

Singles Lines

And there's yet another option: the singles line. Several attractions have this special line for guests riding alone. As Universal employees will tell you, this line is often even faster than the Express line. We strongly recommend you use the singles line or the Express line whenever possible, as it will decrease your overall wait and leave more time for repeat rides or just bumming around the parks.

Universal, Kids, and Scary Stuff

Although there's plenty for younger children to enjoy at the Universal parks, the majority of the major attractions have the potential for wigging out kids under eight years of age. At Universal Studios Florida, forget Revenge of the Mummy, *Twister, Earthquake,* Jaws, Men in Black, Back to the Future, and *Terminator 2: 3-D*. Most young children take the stunt show in stride, though there are gunfire and explosions involved. *E.T.* is a toss-up. The first part of the ride is a little intense for a few preschoolers, but the end is all happiness and harmony. Interestingly, very few families report problems with *Beetlejuice's Rock 'n' Roll Graveyard Revue* or *The Universal Horror Make-up Show.* Anything not listed is pretty benign.

At Universal's Islands of Adventure, watch out for The Incredible Hulk Coaster, Dr. Doom's Fearfall, The Adventures of Spider-Man, the Jurassic Park River Adventure, Dueling Dragons, and *Poseidon's Fury.* Popeye & Bluto's Bilge-Rat Barges is wet and wild, but most younger children handle it well. Dudley Do-Right's Ripsaw Falls is a toss-up, to be considered only if your kids liked water-flume rides. The *Sinbad* stunt show includes some explosions and startling special effects, but once again, children tolerate it well. Nothing else should pose a problem.

Lodging at Universal Orlando

Universal currently has three operating resort hotels. The 750-room Portofino Bay Hotel is a gorgeous property set on an artificial bay and themed like an Italian coastal town. The 650-room Hard Rock Hotel is an ultra-cool "Hotel California" replica, with slick contemporary design and a hip, friendly attitude. The 1,000-room, Polynesian-themed Royal Pacific Resort is sumptuously decorated and richly appointed. All three are excellent hotels; the Portofino and the Hard Rock are on the pricey side and the Royal Pacific ain't exactly cheap.

Like Disney, Universal offers a number of incentives to stay at their hotels. Perks available that mirror those offered by the Mouse include free parking, delivery to your room of purchases made in the parks, tickets and reservation information from hotel concierges, priority dining reservations at Universal restaurants, and the ability to charge purchases to your room account.

Otherwise, Universal offers complementary transportation by bus or water taxi to Universal Studios, Islands of Adventure, CityWalk, SeaWorld, and Wet 'n' Wild. Hotel guests may use the Universal Express program with impunity all day long (see "Universal Express" on pages 611–615). Universal lodging guests are also eligible for "next available" table privileges at CityWalk restaurants and similar priority admission to Universal Orlando theme park shows.

Universal Studios Florida

Universal City Studios Inc. has run a studios tour and movie-theme tourist attraction for more than 30 years, predating all Disney parks except Disneyland. In the early 1980s, Universal announced plans to build a new theme-park complex in Florida. But while Universal labored over its new project, Disney jumped into high gear and rushed its own studios/theme park onto the market, beating Universal by about two years.

Universal Studios Florida opened in June 1990. At that time, it was almost four times the size of Disney-MGM Studios (Disney-MGM has since expanded somewhat), with much more of the facility accessible to visitors. Like its sister facility in Hollywood, Universal Studios Florida is spacious, beautifully landscaped, meticulously clean, and delightfully varied in its entertainment. Rides are exciting and innovative and, as with many Disney rides, focus on familiar and/or beloved movie characters or situations.

On Universal Studios Florida's *E.T.* ride, you escape the authorities on a flying bike and leave Earth to visit *E.T.*'s home planet. In Jaws, the persistent great white shark makes heart-stopping assaults on your small boat, and in *Earthquake—The Big One,* special effects create one of the most realistic earthquake simulation ever produced. Guests also ride in a Delorean-cum-time machine in yet another chase, this one based on the film *Back to the Future,* and fight alien bugs with zapper guns in Men in Black. New attractions based on the *Jimmy Neutron* and *Shrek* movies raised the entertainment stakes even higher. Universal opened in spring 2004 their most ambitious attraction to date: Revenge of the Mummy. Replacing longtime Universal Studios fixture Kong-frontation and based on *The Mummy* film franchise, it's a combination roller coaster/dark ride with maglev coaster tracks, robotics technology adapted from the Mars lander, and a pyrotechnic "ceiling of flame."

While these rides incorporate state-of-the-art technology and live up to their billing in terms of excitement, creativity, uniqueness, and special effects, some lack the capacity to handle the number of guests who frequent major Florida tourist destinations. If a ride has great appeal but can accommodate only a small number of guests per ride or per hour, long lines form. It isn't unusual for the wait to exceed an hour and a quarter for the *E. T.* ride.

Happily, most shows and theater performances at Universal Studios Florida are in theaters that accommodate large numbers of people. Since many shows run continuously, waits usually don't exceed twice the show's performance time (40–50 minutes).

Universal Studios Florida is laid out in an upside-down L configuration. Beyond the main entrance, a wide boulevard stretches past several shows and rides to a New York City backlot set. Branching off this pedestrian thoroughfare to the right are five streets that access other areas of the studios and intersect a promenade circling a large lake.

The park is divided into six sections: Production Central, New York, Hollywood, San Francisco/Amity, Woody Woodpecker's Kid Zone, and World Expo. Where one section begins and another ends is blurry, but no matter. Guests orient themselves by the major rides, sets, and landmarks and refer, for instance, to "New York," "the waterfront," "over by *E. T.*," or "by Mel's Diner." The area of Universal Studios Florida open to visitors is about the size of Epcot.

The park offers all standard services and amenities, including stroller and wheelchair rental, lockers, diaper-changing and infant-nursing facilities, car assistance, and foreign-language assistance. Most of the park is accessible to disabled guests, and TDDs are available for the hearing impaired. Almost all services are in the Front Lot, just inside the main entrance.

NOT TO BE MISSED AT UNIVERSAL STUDIOS FLORIDA

Back to the Future	*Terminator 2: 3-D*
Earthquake—The Big One	Jaws
Men in Black Alien Attack	*Shrek 4-D*
Revenge of the Mummy	

Universal Studios Florida Attractions (Universal Express)

Animal Planet Live! *(Universal Express)*

What It Is Animal tricks and comedy show based on the popular cable network's programs
Scope and Scale Major attraction
When to Go After you have experienced all rides

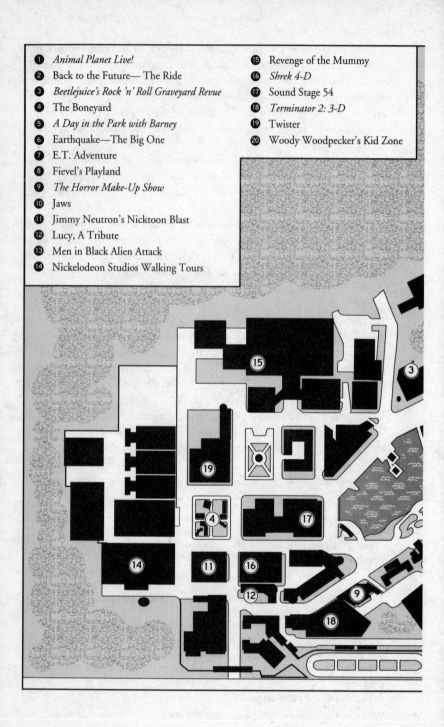

1. *Animal Planet Live!*
2. Back to the Future— The Ride
3. *Beetlejuice's Rock 'n' Roll Graveyard Revue*
4. The Boneyard
5. *A Day in the Park with Barney*
6. Earthquake—The Big One
7. E.T. Adventure
8. Fievel's Playland
9. *The Horror Make-Up Show*
10. Jaws
11. Jimmy Neutron's Nicktoon Blast
12. Lucy, A Tribute
13. Men in Black Alien Attack
14. Nickelodeon Studios Walking Tours
15. Revenge of the Mummy
16. *Shrek 4-D*
17. Sound Stage 54
18. *Terminator 2: 3-D*
19. Twister
20. Woody Woodpecker's Kid Zone

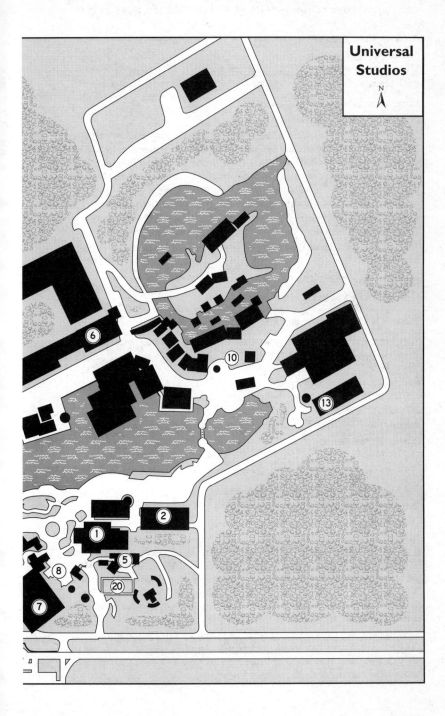

Universal Studios

N

Author's Rating Cute lil' critters; ★★★
Appeal by Age Group

Preschool ★★★★	Teens ★★★	Over 30 ★★★
Grade school ★★★★	Young Adults ★★★	Seniors ★★★½

Duration of Presentation 20 minutes
Probable Waiting Time 25 minutes

Description and Comments This show aims to build on the popularity of Animal Planet's various TV programs and characters, integrating video segments from the TV shows with live sketches, jokes, and animal tricks performed onstage. The idea is to create eco-friendly family entertainment that mirrors the themes of Animal Planet programming. Several of the animal thespians are veterans of television and movies, and many were rescued from shelters. Audience members can participate as well; where else will you get the chance to hold an eight-foot albino reticulated python in your lap?

Touring Tips Check the daily entertainment schedule for show times.

Turing Tips You shouldn't have any trouble getting in to this show. Save it for mid or late afternoon.

Back to the Future—The Ride (Universal Express)

Motion Sickness

WARNING!

What It Is Flight-simulator thrill ride

Scope and Scale Headliner

When to Go First thing in the morning after Mummy and Men in Black

Special Comments Rough ride; may induce motion sickness. Must be 40" tall to ride. Switching off available (pages 266–268).

Author's Rating Not to be missed, if you have a strong stomach; ★★★★
Appeal by Age Group

Preschool †	Teens ★★★★	Over 30 ★★★★
Grade school ★★★★	Young Adults ★★★★	Seniors ★★½

† Sample size too small for an accurate rating.

Duration of Ride 4½ minutes

Loading Speed Moderate

Description and Comments Guests in Doc Brown's lab get caught up in a high-speed chase through time that spans a million years. An extremely intense simulator ride, Back to the Future is similar to Star Tours and Body Wars at Walt Disney World but is much rougher and more jerky. Though the story doesn't make much sense, the visual effects are wild and powerful. The vehicles (Delorean time machines) in Back to the Future are much smaller than those of Star Tours and Body Wars, so the ride feels more personal and less like a group experience.

Touring Tips As soon the park opens, guests stampede to Mummy, Men in Black, and Back to the Future. Our recommendation: Be there when the park opens, and join the rush. If you don't ride before 10:20 a.m., your wait may be exceptionally long. *Note:* Sitting in the rear seat of the car makes the ride more realistic.

Beetlejuice's Rock 'n' Roll Graveyard Revue (*Universal Express*)

What It Is Rock-and-roll stage show

Scope and Scale Almost major attraction

When to Go At your convenience

Author's Rating Outrageous; ★★★½

Appeal by Age Group

Preschool ★★★★	Teens ★★★★	Over 30 ★★★½
Grade school ★★★★	Young Adults ★★★½	Seniors ★★★½

Duration of Presentation 18 minutes

Probable Waiting Time None

Description and Comments High-powered rock-and-roll stage show stars Beetlejuice, Frankenstein, the Bride of Frankenstein, Wolfman, Dracula, and a pair of fly girls called Hip and Hop. The show features contemporary dance and pop songs rather than classic rock. High-energy, silly, bawdy, and generally funnier than it has any right to be, the long running *Revue* just keeps plugging along.

Touring Tips Mercifully, this attraction has been moved under cover.

A Day in the Park with Barney (*Universal Express*)

What It Is Live character stage show

Scope and Scale Major children's attraction

When to Go Anytime

Author's Rating A great hit with preschoolers; ★★★★

Appeal by Age Group

Preschool ★★★★½	Teens ★★	Over 30 ★★★
Grade school ★★★	Young Adults ★★½	Seniors ★★★

Duration of Presentation 12 minutes plus character greeting

Probable Waiting Time 15 minutes

Description and Comments Barney, the purple dinosaur of Public Television fame, leads a sing-along with the help of the audience and sidekicks Baby Bop and BJ. A short preshow gets the kids lathered up before they enter Barney's Park (the theater). Interesting theatrical effects include wind, falling leaves, clouds and stars in the simulated sky, and snow. After the show, Barney exits momentarily to allow parents and children to gather along the stage. He then returns and moves from child to child, hugging each and posing for photos.

Touring Tips If your child likes Barney, this show is a must. It's happy and upbeat, and the character greeting that follows is the best organized we've seen in any theme park. There's no line and no fighting for Barney's attention. Just relax by the rail and await your hug. There's also a great indoor play area nearby, designed especially for wee tykes.

Earthquake—The Big One (*Universal Express*)

What It Is Combination theater presentation and adventure ride

Scope and Scale Major attraction

When to Go In the morning or late afternoon

Special Comments May frighten young children

Author's Rating Not to be missed; ★★★★

Appeal by Age Group

Preschool ★★★	Teens ★★★★	Over 30 ★★★★
Grade school ★★★★	Young Adults ★★★★	Seniors ★★★★

Duration of Presentation 20 minutes

Loading Speed Moderate

Description and Comments Film shows how miniatures are used to create special effects in earthquake movies, followed by a demonstration of how miniatures, blue screen, and matte painting are integrated with live-action stunt sequences (starring audience volunteers) to create a realistic final product. Afterward, guests board a subway from Oakland to San Francisco and experience an earthquake—the big one. Special effects range from fires and runaway trains to exploding tanker trucks and tidal waves. This is Universal's answer to Disney-MGM's Catastrophe Canyon. The special effects are comparable, but the field of vision is better at Catastrophe Canyon. Nonetheless, *Earthquake* is one of Universal's more compelling efforts.

Touring Tips Experience *Earthquake* after tackling the park's other rides.

E.T. Adventure (Universal Express)

What It Is Indoor adventure ride based on the *E.T.* movie

Scope and Scale Major attraction

When to Go Before noon; before 10 a.m. if you have small children

Author's Rating A happy reunion: ★★★½

Appeal by Age Group

Preschool ★★★★	Teens ★★★	Over 30 ★★★½
Grade school ★★★★	Young Adults ★★★	Seniors ★★★½

Duration of Ride 4½ minutes

Loading Speed Moderate

Description and Comments Guests aboard a bicycle-like conveyance escape with E.T. from earthly law enforcement officials and then journey to E.T.'s home planet. The attraction is similar to Peter Pan's Flight at the Magic Kingdom but is longer and has more elaborate special effects and a wilder ride.

Touring Tips Most preschoolers and grade-school children love E.T. We think it worth a 20- to 30-minute wait, but nothing longer. Lines build quickly after 10 a.m., and waits can be more than two hours on busy days. Ride in the morning or late afternoon. Guests who balk at sitting on the bicycle can ride in a comfortable gondola.

A mother from Columbus, Ohio, writes about horrendous lines at E.T.:

> The line for E.T. took two hours! The rest of the family waiting outside thought that we had gone to E.T.'s planet for real.

A woman from Richmond, Virginia, objects to how Universal represents the waiting time:

> We got into E.T. without much wait, but the line is very deceptive. When you see a lot of people waiting outside and the sign says "ten-minute wait from this point," it means ten minutes until you are inside the building. But there's a very long wait inside [before] you get to the moving vehicles.

Fievel's Playland

What It Is Children's play area with water slide

Scope and Scale Minor attraction

When to Go Anytime

Author's Rating A much-needed attraction for preschoolers; ★★★★

Appeal by Age Group

Preschool ★★★★	Teens —	Over 30 —
Grade school ★★★★	Young Adults —	Seniors —

Probable Waiting Time 20–30 minutes for the water slide; otherwise, no waiting

Description and Comments   Imaginative playground features ordinary household items reproduced on a giant scale, as a mouse would experience them. Preschoolers and grade-schoolers can climb nets, walk through a huge boot, splash in a sardine-can fountain, seesaw on huge spoons, and climb onto a cow skull. Most of the playground is reserved for Preschoolers, but a water slide/raft ride is open to all ages.

Touring Tips   Walk into Fievel's Playland without waiting, and stay as long as you want. Younger children love the oversized items, and there's enough to keep teens and adults busy while little ones let off steam. The water slide/raft ride is open to everyone but is extremely slow-loading and carries only 300 riders per hour. With an average wait of 20–30 minutes, we don't think the 16-second ride is worth the trouble. Also, you're highly likely to get soaked.

Lack of shade is a major shortcoming of the entire attraction. Don't go during the heat of the day.

Jaws (Universal Express)

What It Is Adventure boat ride

Scope and Scale Headliner

When to Go Before 11 a.m. or after 5 p.m.

Special Comments Will frighten young children

Author's Rating Not to be missed; ★★★★

Appeal by Age Group

Preschool ★★½	Teens ★★★★	Over 30 ★★★★
Grade school ★★★★	Young Adults ★★★★	Seniors ★★★★

Duration of Ride 5 minutes

Loading Speed Fast

Probable Waiting Time Per 100 People Ahead of You 3 minutes

Assumes All 8 boats are running

Description and Comments   Jaws delivers five minutes of nonstop action, with the huge shark repeatedly attacking. A West Virginia woman, fresh from the Magic Kingdom, told us the shark is "about as pesky as that witch in Snow White." While the story is entirely predictable, the shark fairly realistic and as big as a boxcar. What makes the ride unique is its sense of journey. Jaws builds an amazing degree of suspense. It isn't just a cruise into the middle of a pond where a rubber fish assaults the boat interminably. Add inventive sets and powerful special effects, and you have a first-rate attraction.

A variable at Jaws is the enthusiasm and acting ability of your boat guide. Throughout the ride, the guide must set the tone, elaborate the plot, drive the boat, and fight the shark. Most guides are quite good. They may overact, but you can't fault them for lack of enthusiasm. Consider also that each guide repeats this wrenching ordeal every eight minutes.

Touring Tips Jaws is well designed to handle crowds. People on the boat's left side tend to get splashed more. If you have young children, consider switching off (see pages 266–268).

A mother of two from Williamsville, New York, who believes our warning about getting wet should be more strongly emphasized, has this to say:

> Your warning about the Jaws attraction … is woefully understated. Please warn your readers—we were seated on the first row of the boat. My nine-year-old sat at the end of the boat (first person on the far left), and I was seated next to him. We were wary of these seats as I had read your warning, but I felt prepared. NOT!!!! At "that" moment the water came flooding over the left front side of the boat, thoroughly drenching the two of us and filling our sneakers with water. Unfortunately for us, this was only our third attraction of the day (9:30 a.m.) and we still had a long day ahead of us. It was a rather chilly and windy 62-degree day. We went to the rest rooms, removed our shorts, and squeezed out as much water as we could, but we were very cold and uncomfortable all day. This will be our most vivid and lasting memory of our day at Universal Studios!!!

A dad from Seattle suggests that getting wet takes a backseat to being terrified:

> Our eight-year-old was so frightened by Jaws that we scrapped the rest of the Universal tour and went back to E.T. An employee said she wouldn't recommend it to anyone under ten. Maybe you should change "may frighten small children" to "definitely will scare the pants off most children."

Jimmy Neutron's Nicktoon Blast (Universal Express)

What It Is Cartoon science demonstration and simulation ride

Scope and Scale Major attraction

When to Go The first hour after park opening or after 5 p.m.

Author's Rating Incomprehensible but fun ★★★

Appeal by Age Group

Preschool ★★★	Teens ★★★	Over 30 ★★½
Grade school ★★★★	Young Adults ★★★	Seniors ★★

Duration of Ride A little over 4 minutes

Loading Speed Moderate to slow

Probable Waiting Time Per 100 People Ahead of You 5 minutes

Assumes All 8 simulators in use

Description and Comments This ride features motion simulators that move and react in synch with a cartoon projected onto a huge screen. Based on the Nickelodeon movie *Jimmy Neutron: Boy Genius*, this attraction replaced The Funtastic World of Hanna-Barbera. In addition to Jimmy, the attraction features a mob of other characters from Nickelodeon, including SpongeBob SquarePants, the Rugrats, the Fairly Odd Parents, and the Wild Thornberrys. The story, inasmuch as Universal explains it, takes place in two parts. First, guests are invited to participate in a demonstration of Jimmy's newest invention, which is stolen before the demonstration can proceed. After that, an alien plot is revealed, and guests are strapped into motion-simulator vehicles in order to help Jimmy rescue his invention and defend the Earth. In practice, the plot is absolutely incomprehensible (at least to an adult). All we can report after riding about a dozen times is that there is a frenetic high-speed chase punctuated by an abundance of screaming (also incomprehensible)in piercing, very high pitched, cartoony voices.

Touring Tips This attraction is drawing sizeable crowds primarily because its new, and because its next door to the new *Shrek 4-D* attraction. We think Jimmy Neutron is at best a so-so effort, and not much of an improvement over its predecessor. Except for avid *Jimmy Neutron* cartoon fans, in other words, it's expendable. If you can't live without it, ride during the first hour the park is open, after 5 p.m., or use Universal Express. Be aware that a very small percentage of riders suffer motion sickness. Stationary seating is available.

Lucy, a Tribute

What It Is Walk-through tribute to Lucille Ball

Scope and Scale Diversion

When to Go Anytime

Author's Rating A touching remembrance; ★★★

Appeal by Age Group

Preschool ★	Teens ★★	Over 30 ★★★
Grade school ★★	Young Adults ★★★	Seniors ★★★

Probable Waiting Time None

Description and Comments The life and career of comedienne Lucille Ball are spotlighted, with emphasis on her role as Lucy Ricardo in the long-running television series *I Love Lucy*. Well designed and informative, the exhibit succeeds admirably in recalling the talent and temperament of the beloved redhead.

Touring Tips See Lucy during the hot, crowded midafternoon, or on your way out of the park. Adults could easily stay 15–30 minutes. Children, however, get restless after a couple of minutes.

Men in Black Alien Attack (Universal Express)

What It Is Interactive dark thrill ride

Scope and Scale Super headliner

When to Go In the morning after Revenge of the Mummy

Special Comments May induce motion sickness. Must be 42" tall to ride. Switching off available (pages 266–268).

Author's Rating Buzz Lightyear on steroids; not to be missed; ★★★★½

Appeal by Age Group

Preschool †	Teens ★★★★★	Over 30 ★★★★★
Grade school ★★★★½	Young Adults ★★★★★	Seniors ★★★★

† *Sample size too small for an accurate rating.*

Duration of Ride 2½ minutes

Loading Speed Moderate to Fast

Description and Comments Based on the movie of the same name, Men in Black brings together actors Will Smith and Rip Torn (as Agent J and MIB Director Zed) for an interactive sequel to the hit film. The story line has you volunteering as a Men in Black (MIB) trainee. After an introduction warning that aliens "live among us" and articulating MIB's mission to round them up, Zed expands on the finer points of alien spotting and familiarizes you with your training vehicle and your weapon, an alien "zapper." Following this, you load up and are dispatched on an innocuous training mission that immediately deteriorates into a situation where only you are in a position to prevent aliens from taking over the universe. Now, if you saw the movie, you understand that the aliens are mostly giant, exotic bugs and cockroaches and that zapping the aliens involves exploding them into myriad, gooey body parts. Thus, the meat of the ride (no pun intended) consists of careening around Manhattan in your MIB vehicle and shooting aliens. The technology at work is similar to that used in the Spider-Man attraction at Universal's Islands of Adventure, which is to say that it's both a wild ride and one where movies, sets, robotics, and your vehicle are all integrated into a fairly seamless package.

Men in Black is interactive in that your marksmanship and ability to blast yourself out of some tricky situations will determine how the story ends. Also, you are awarded a personal score (like Disney's Buzz Lightyear's Space Ranger Spin) and a score for your car. There are about three dozen possible outcomes and literally thousands of different ride experiences determined by your pluck, performance, and in the final challenge your intestinal fortitude.

Touring Tips   Each of the 120 or so alien figures has sensors that activate special effects and respond to your zapper. Aim for the eyes and keep shooting until the aliens' eyes turn red. Also, many of the aliens shoot back, causing your vehicle to veer or spin. In the mayhem, you might fail to notice that another vehicle of guests runs along beside you on a dual track. This was included to instill a spirit of competition for anyone who finds blowing up bugs and saving the universe less than stimulating. Note that at a certain point, you can shoot the flashing "vent" on top of this other car and make them spin around. Of course, they can do the same to you . . .

Although there are many possible endings, the long lines at this headliner attraction will probably dissuade you from experiencing all but one or two. To avoid a long wait, hotfoot it to MIB immediately after riding Mummy the first 30 minutes the park is open.

Nickelodeon Studios

What It Is   Nickelodeon Studios Tour

Scope and Scale   Minor attraction

When to Go   When Nickelodeon shows are in production (usually weekdays)

Author's Rating   ★★★

Appeal by Age Group

Preschool ★★½	Teens ★★★	Over 30 ★★★
Grade school ★★★★	Young Adults ★★★	Seniors ★★★

Duration of Tour   36 minutes

Probable Waiting Time   30–45 minutes

Description and Comments   The tour examines set construction, soundstages, wardrobe, props, lighting, video production, and special effects. Much of this information is presented more creatively in the *Horror Make-Up Show* production, but the Nickelodeon tour is tailored for kids. They're made to feel supremely important; their opinions are used to shape future Nickelodeon programming.

The Game Lab, where guests preview strange games being tested for possible inclusion on Nickelodeon, adds some much-needed zip. It ends with a lucky child getting "slimed." If you don't understand, consult your children.

Touring Tips   While grade-schoolers, especially, enjoy this tour, it's expendable for everyone else. Go on a second day or second visit at Universal. If Nickelodeon isn't in production, forget it.

Revenge of the Mummy (Universal Express)

What It Is   Combination dark ride and roller coaster

Scope and Scale   Super headliner

When to Go   The first hour the park is open or after 6 p.m.

Special Comments 54" minimum-height requirement

Author's Rating Killer! ★★★★½

Appeal by Age Group

Preschool ★★	Teens ★★★★	Over 30 ★★★★
Grade school ★★★★	Young Adults ★★★★	Seniors ★★★★

Duration of Ride 4 minutes

Probable Waiting Time Per 100 People Ahead of You 7 minutes

Loading Speed Moderate

Description and Comments   Revenge of the Mummy replaced Kongfrontation in the New York section of the park in spring 2004. It's kinda hard to wrap your mind around the attraction, but trust us when we say you're in for a very strange experience. Here, quoting Universal, are some of the things you can look forward to:

- Authentic Egyptian catacombs

- High-velocity show immersion system (we thing this has something to do with very fast baptism)

- Magnet-propulsion launch wave system

- A "Brain Fire" (!!!!) that hovers [over guests] with temperatures soaring to 2,000 degrees Farenheit

- Canoptic jars containing grisly remains

Reading between the lines, Revenge of the Mummy is an indoor dark ride based on the Mummy flicks, where guests fight off "deadly curses and vengeful creatures" while flying through Egyptian tombs and other spooky places on a high-tech roller coaster. The special effects are cutting edge, integrating the best technology from such attractions as *Terminator 2: 3-D*, Spider-Man (the ride), and Back to the Future, with groundbreaking visuals. It's way cool.

The queuing area serves to establish the story line: You're in a group touring a set from the Mummy films when you enter a tomb where the fantasy world of film gives way to the real thing. Along the way you are warned about a possible curse. The visuals are rich and compelling as the queue makes its way to the loading area where you board a sort of clunky, jeep-looking vehicle. The ride begins as a slow, very elaborate dark ride, passing through various chambers including one where flesh-eating scarab beetles descend on you. Suddenly your vehicle stops, then drops backwards and rotates. Here's where the aforementioned "magnet-propulsion launch wave system" comes in. In more ordinary language, this means you're shot at high speed up the first hill of the roller coaster part of the ride. We don't want to ruin your experience by divulging too much, but the coaster part of the ride offers its own panoply of surprises. We will tell you this, however: there are no barrell rolls or any upside-down stuff. And though it's a wild ride by anyone's definition, the emphasis remains as much on the visuals, robotics, and special effects as on the ride itself.

Touring Tips   Revenge of the Mummy has a very low riders-per-hour capacity for a super-headliner attraction, and especially for the park's top draw. Waits, even using Universal Express, will run longer than an Academy Awards show. Your only prayer for a tolerable wait is to be on hand when the park opens and sprint immediately to the Mummy. Your fallback is to use Universal Express, but even with Univeral Express expect a sizeable wait after 11 a.m. Concerning motion sickness, if you can ride Space Mountain without ill effect, you should be fine on Revenge of the Mummy. Switching off is available.

Shrek 4-D (Universal Express)

What It Is 3-D movie

Scope and Scale Headliner

When to Go The first hour the park is open or after 4 p.m.

Author's Rating Warm, fuzzy mayhem; ★★★★½

Appeal by Age Group

Preschool ★★★★	Teens ★★★★½	Over 30 ★★★★½
Grade school ★★★★½	Young Adults ★★★★½	Seniors ★★★★½

Duration of Presentation 20 minutes

Description and Comments Based on characters from the hit movie *Shrek*, the preshow presents the villain from the movie, Lord Farquaad, as he appears on various screens to describe his posthumous plan to reclaim his lost bride, Princess Fiona, who married *Shrek*. The plan is posthumous since Lord Farquaad ostensibly died in the movie, and it's his ghost making the plans, but never mind. Guests then move into the main theater, don their 3-D glasses, and recline in seats equipped with "tactile transducers" and "pneumatic air propulsion and water spray nodules capable of both vertical and horizontal motion." As the 3-D film plays, guests are also subjected to smells relevant to the on-screen action (oh boy).

Technicalities aside, *Shrek* is a real winner. It's irreverent, frantic, laugh-out-loud funny, and iconoclastic. Concerning the latter, the film takes a good poke at Disney with Pinnocchio, the Three Little Pigs, and Tinkerbelle (among others) all sucked into the mayhem. The film quality and 3-D effects are great, and like the feature film, it's sweet without being sappy. Plus, in contrast to Disney's *Honey, I Shrunk the Audience* or *It's Tough To Be A Bug!*, *Shrek 4-D* doesn't generally frighten children under 7 years of age.

Touring Tips Universal claims they can move 2,400 guests an hour through *Shrek 4-D*. However, its popularity mean that Express passes for the day may be gone as early as 10 a.m., and waits in the regular line may exceed an hour. Bear that in mind when scheduling your day.

Street Scenes

What It Is Elaborate outdoor sets for making films

Scope and Scale Diversion

When to Go Anytime

Special Comments You'll see most sets without special effort as you tour the park

Author's Rating One of the park's great assets; ★★★★★

Appeal by Age Group

Preschool ★★★	Teens ★★★★½	Over 30 ★★★★★
Grade school ★★★★½	Young Adults ★★★★½	Seniors ★★★★★

Probable Waiting Time No waiting

Description and Comments Unlike at Disney-MGM Studios, all Universal Studios Florida's backlot sets are accessible for guest inspection. They include New York City streets, San Francisco's waterfront, a New England coastal town, Rodeo Drive, and Hollywood Boulevard.

Touring Tips You'll see most as you walk through the park.

Terminator 2: 3-D

What It Is 3-D thriller mixed-media presentation

Scope and Scale Super headliner

When to Go After 3:30 p.m.

Special Comments The nation's best theme-park theater attraction; very intense for some preschoolers and grade-schoolers

Author's Rating Furiously paced high-tech experience; not to be missed; ★★★★★

Appeal by Age Group

Preschool ★★★	Teens ★★★★★	Over 30 ★★★★★
Grade school ★★★★	Young Adults ★★★★★	Seniors ★★★★

Duration of Presentation 20 minutes, including an 8-minute preshow

Probable Waiting Time 20–40 minutes

Description and Comments The *Terminator* "cop" from *Terminator 2* morphs to life and battles Arnold Schwarzenegger's T-100 cyborg character. If you missed the *Terminator* flicks, here's the plot: A bad robot arrives from the future to kill a nice boy. Another bad robot (who has been reprogrammed to be good) pops up at the same time to save the boy. The bad robot chases the boy and the rehabilitated robot, menacing the audience in the process.

The attraction, like the films, is all action, and you really don't need to understand much. What's interesting is that it uses 3-D film and a theater full of sophisticated technology to integrate the real with the imaginary. Images seem to move in and out of the film, not only in the manner of traditional 3-D, but also in actuality. Remove your 3-D glasses momentarily and you'll see that the guy on the motorcycle is actually onstage.

We've watched this type of presentation evolve, pioneered by Disney's *Captain EO, Honey, I Shrunk the Audience*, and *MuppetVision 3-D*. *Terminator 2: 3-D*, however, goes way beyond lasers, with moving theater seats, blasts of hot air, and spraying mist. It creates a multidimensional space that blurs the boundary between entertainment and reality. Is it seamless? Not quite, but it's close. We rank *Terminator 2: 3-D* as not to be missed and consider it the absolute best theme-park theater attraction in the United States. If *Terminator 2: 3-D* is the only attraction you see at Universal Studios Florida, you'll have received your money's worth.

Touring Tips The 700-seat theater changes audiences about every 19 minutes. Even so, because the show is hot, expect to wait about 30–45 minutes. The attraction, on Hollywood Boulevard near the park's entrance, receives huge traffic during morning and early afternoon. By about 3 p.m., however, lines diminish somewhat. Though you'll still wait, we recommend holding off on *Terminator 2: 3-D* until then. If you can't stay until late afternoon, see the show first thing in the morning. Families with young children should know that the violence characteristic of the *Terminator* movies is largely absent from the attraction. There's suspense and action but not much blood and guts.

Twister (Universal Express)

What It Is Theater presentation featuring special effects from the movie *Twister*

Scope and Scale Major attraction

When to Go Should be your first show after experiencing all rides

Special Comments High potential for frightening young children

Author's Rating Gusty; ★★★½

Appeal by Age Group

Preschool ★★	Teens ★★★★	Over 30 ★★★★
Grade school ★★★★	Young Adults ★★★★	Seniors ★★★★

Duration of Presentation 15 minutes

Probable Waiting Time 26 minutes

Description and Comments *Twister* combines an elaborate set and special effects, climaxing with a five-story-tall simulated tornado created by circulating more than 2 million cubic feet of air per minute.

Touring Tips The wind, pounding rain, and freight-train sound of the tornado are deafening, and the entire presentation is exceptionally intense. School children are mightily impressed, while younger children are terrified and overwhelmed. Unless you want the kids hopping in your bed whenever they hear thunder, try this attraction yourself before taking your kids.

Universal Horror Make-Up Show *(Universal Express)*

What It Is Theater presentation on the art of make-up

Scope and Scale Major attraction

When to Go After you have experienced all rides

Special Comments May frighten young children

Author's Rating A gory knee-slapper; ★★★½

Appeal by Age Group

Preschool ★★★	Teens ★★★½	Over 30 ★★★½
Grade school ★★★½	Young Adults ★★★½	Seniors ★★★½

Duration of Presentation 25 minutes

Probable Waiting Time 20 minutes

Description and Comments Lively, well-paced look at how make-up artists create film monsters, realistic wounds, severed limbs, and other unmentionables. Funnier and more upbeat than many Universal Studios presentations, the show also presents a wealth of fascinating information. It's excellent and enlightening, if somewhat gory.

Touring Tips Exceeding most guests' expectations, the *Horror Make-Up Show* is the sleeper attraction at Universal. Its humor and tongue-in-cheek style transcend the gruesome effects, and most folks (including preschoolers) take the blood and guts in stride. It usually isn't too hard to get into.

Woody Woodpecker's Nuthouse Coaster and Curious George Goes to Town Playground

What It Is Interactive playground and kid's roller coaster

Scope and Scale Minor attraction

When to Go Anytime

Author's Rating A good place to let off steam; ★★★

Appeal by Age Group

Preschool ★★★★	Teens —	Over 30 —
Grade school —	Young Adults —	Seniors —

Description and Comments Rounding out the selection of other nearby kid-friendly attractions, this KidZone offering consists of Woody Woodpecker's Nuthouse

Coaster and an interactive playground called Curious George Goes to Town. The child-sized roller coaster is small enough for kids to enjoy but sturdy enough for adults, though its moderate speed might unnerve some smaller children (the minimum age to ride is three years old). The Curious George playground exemplifies the Universal obsession with wet stuff; in addition to innumerable spigots, pipes, and spray guns, two giant roof-mounted buckets periodically dump a thousand gallons of water on unsuspecting visitors below. Kids who want to stay dry can mess around in the foam-ball playground, also equipped with chutes, tubes, and ball-blasters.

Touring Tips   After its unveiling, Universal employees dubbed this area "Peckerland." Visit the playground after you've experienced all the major attractions.

Universal Studios Florida Touring Plan

Universal Studios Florida One-Day Touring Plan

This plan is for all visitors. If a ride or show is listed that you don't want to experience, skip that step and proceed to the next. Move quickly from attraction to attraction and, if possible, don't stop for lunch until after Step 9. Minor street shows occur at various times and places throughout the day; check the daily schedule for details.

Buying Admission to Universal Studios Florida

One of our big gripes about Universal Studios is that there are never enough ticket windows open in the morning to accommodate the crowd. You can arrive 45 minutes before official opening time and still be in line to buy your admission when the park opens. Therefore, we strongly recommend you buy your admission in advance. Passes are available by mail from Universal Studios at (800) 224-3838. They are also sold at the concierge desk or attractions box office of many Orlando-area hotels. If your hotel doesn't offer tickets, try Guest Services at the Radisson Twin Towers (407) 351-1000, at the intersection of Major Boulevard and Kirkman Avenue.

Many hotels that sell Universal admissions don't issue actual passes. Instead, the purchaser gets a voucher that can be redeemed for a pass at the theme park. Fortunately, the voucher-redemption window is separate from the park's ticket sales operation. You can quickly exchange your voucher for a pass and be on your way with little or no wait.

Touring Plan

1. Call (407) 363-8000 the day before your visit for the official opening time.

2. On the day of your visit, eat breakfast and arrive at Universal Studios Florida 50 minutes before opening time with your admission pass or an admission voucher in hand. If you have a voucher, exchange it for a pass at the voucher-redemption window. Pick up a map and the daily entertainment schedule.

3. Line up at the turnstile. Ask any attendant whether any rides or shows are closed that day. Adjust the touring plan accordingly.

4. When the park opens, go straight down the Plaza of the Stars. Pass Rodeo Drive on your right. When you reach Nickelodeon Way on your left, you should be standing between Jimmy Neutron's Nicktoon Blast on your left and *Shrek 4-D* on your right. If both are up and running, try to get a Universal Express pass for *Shrek 4-D* usable later in the day (around lunchtime if possible). If you can't get a *Shrek 4-D* pass for that time period, don't sweat it; *Shrek 4-D* has a large enough capacity to keep lines moving even on crowded days. Plan to return to the altogether-expendable Jimmy Neutron later in the day, using Universal Express.

5. Proceed toward the back of the park (past SoundStage 54) to the New York section and ride Revenge of the Mummy.

6. Now head to Men in Black: Alien Attack. From Revenge of the Mummy, proceed with the lagoon on your right along the Embarcadero, along Amity Avenue, and over the bridge to get there. If you're leaving from Jimmy Neutron's Nicktoon Blast or *Shrek 4-D,* take a left on Rodeo Drive to Hollywood Boulevard, pass Mel's Diner (on your left), and (keeping the lagoon on your left) go directly to Men in Black. Ride.

7. After Men in Black, backtrack to Back to the Future and ride.

8. Exit left and pass the International Food Bazaar. If crowds are heavy, this might be about time for lunch, for your *Shrek 4-D* Universal Express pass, or both. If you want to keep going, continue bearing left past *Animal Planet Live!* and go to the E.T. Adventure. Ride.

9. Retrace your steps toward Back to the Future. Keeping the lagoon on your left, cross the bridge to Amity. Ride Jaws.

10. Exit and turn left down The Embarcadero. Ride *Earthquake—The Big One,* which is right next door to Jaws.

11. Work your way back toward the main entrance. Is it time for your Universal Express window for *Shrek 4-D* yet? If so, see *Shrek 4-D.* If not, take a breather and have lunch. Unless your *Shrek 4-D* time window is a long way off, see that show before moving on to Step 12.

12. If you're still intact after various alien assaults, a bike ride to another galaxy, a shark attack, an earthquake, and an encounter with a smelly ogre, take on a tornado. Return to the New York set and see *Twister.* The line will appear long but should move quickly as guests are admitted inside.

13. If you haven't already eaten, do so now. Work in your *Shrek 4-D* visit if that hasn't come along yet.

14. At this point you have four major attractions yet to see:
    Animal Planet Live!
    Beetlejuice's Rock 'n' Roll Graveyard Revue
    The Gory Gruesome and Grotesque Horror Make-Up Show
    Terminator 2: 3-D
        Animal Planet Live!, the *Beetlejuice* show, and the stunt shows are performed several times daily, as listed in the entertainment schedule. Plan the remainder of your itinerary according to the next listed shows for these presentations. The *Horror Make-Up Show* (across from Mel's Diner) runs pretty much

continuously and can be worked in as time permits. Try to see *Terminator 2: 3-D* after 3:30 p.m., but whatever you do, don't miss it.

---

15. Our touring plan doesn't include the Nickelodeon Studios Tour, Woody Woodpecker's KidZone, or *A Day in the Park with Barney*. If you have school-age children in your party, consider taking the Nickelodeon tour in late afternoon or on a second day at the park. If you're touring with preschoolers, see *Barney* after you ride E.T., and then head for KidZone.

---

16. This concludes the touring plan. Spend the remainder of your day revisiting your favorite attractions or inspecting sets and street scenes you may have missed. Also, check your daily entertainment schedule for live performances that interest you.

Universal's Islands of Adventure

When Universal's Islands of Adventure theme park opened in 1999, it provided Universal with enough critical mass to actually compete with Disney. Universal finally has on-site hotels, a shopping and entertainment complex, and two major theme parks. Doubly interesting is that the new Universal park is pretty much just for fun—in other words, a direct competitor to Disney's Magic Kingdom, the most visited theme park in the world. How direct a competitor is it? Check out the box on page 634 for a direct comparison.

And though it may take central Florida tourists awhile to make the connection, here's what will dawn on them when they finally do: Universal's Islands of Adventure is a state-of-the-art park competing with a Disney park that is more than 25 years old and has not added a new super-headliner attraction for many years.

Of course, that's only how it looks on paper. The reality, as they say, is still blowing in the wind. The Magic Kingdom, after all, is graceful in its maturity and much beloved. And then there was the question on everyone's mind: could Universal really pull it off? Recalling the disastrous first year that the Universal Studios Florida park experienced, we held our breath to see if Islands of Adventure's innovative, high-tech attractions would work. Well, not only did they work, they were up and running almost two months ahead of schedule. Thus, the clash of the titans is once again hot. Universal is coming on strong with the potential of sucking up three days of a tourist's week (more, if you include Universal's strategic relationship with SeaWorld and Busch Gardens). And that's more time than anyone has spent off the Disney campus for a long, long time.

Through it all, Disney and Universal spokesmen downplay their fierce competition, pointing out that any new theme park or attraction makes central Florida a more marketable destination. Behind closed doors, however, it's a Pepsi/Coke–type rivalry that will keep both companies working hard to gain a competitive edge. The good news, of course, is that this competition translates into better and better attractions for you to enjoy.

Beware of the Wet and Wild

Although we have described Universal's Islands of Adventure as a direct competitor to the Magic Kingdom, there is one major qualification you should be aware of. Whereas most Magic Kingdom attractions are designed to be enjoyed by guests of any age, attractions at Islands of Adventure are largely created for an under-40 population. The roller coasters at Universal are serious with a capital "S," making Space Mountain and Big Thunder Mountain look about as tough as Dumbo. In fact, seven out of the nine top attractions at Islands are thrill rides, and of these, there are three that not only scare the bejeezus out of you but also drench you with water.

For families, there are three interactive playgrounds as well as six rides that young children will enjoy. Of the thrill rides, only the two in Toon Lagoon (described later) are marginally appropriate for young children, and even on these rides your child needs to be fairly stalwart.

ISLANDS OF ADVENTURE VERSUS THE MAGIC KINGDOM

Islands of Adventure	Magic Kingdom
Six Islands (includes Port of Entry)	Seven Lands (includes Main Street)
Two adult roller-coaster attractions	Two adult roller-coaster attractions
A Dumbo-type ride	Dumbo
One flume ride	One flume ride
Toon Lagoon character area	Mickey's Toontown Fair character area

Getting Oriented at Islands of Adventure

Both Universal theme parks are accessed via the Universal CityWalk entertainment complex. Crossing CityWalk from the parking garages, you can bear right to Universal Studios Florida or left to Universal's Islands of Adventure.

Universal's Islands of Adventure is arranged much like the World Showcase section of Epcot, in a large circle surrounding a lake. Unlike Epcot, however, the Islands of Adventure theme areas evidence the sort of thematic continuity pioneered by Disneyland and the Magic Kingdom. Each land, or island in this case, is self-contained and visually consistent in its theme, though you can see parts of the other islands across the lake.

Passing through the turnstiles, you first encounter the Moroccan-style Port of Entry, where you will find Guest Services, lockers, stroller and wheelchair rentals, ATM banking, lost and found, and, of course, shopping. From the Port of Entry, moving clockwise around the lake, you can access Marvel Super Hero Island, Toon Lagoon, Jurassic Park, the Lost Continent, and Seuss Landing. You can crisscross the lake on small boats, but otherwise there is no in-park transportation.

Islands of Adventure Attractions

Marvel Super Hero Island

This island, with its futuristic and retro-future design and comic book signage, offers shopping and attractions based on Marvel Comics characters.

The Adventures of Spider-Man (Universal Express)

What It Is Indoor adventure simulator ride based on Spider-Man

Scope and Scale Super headliner

When to Go Before 10 a.m.

Special Comments Must be 40" tall to ride

Author's Rating Our choice for the best attraction in the park; ★★★★★

Appeal by Age Group

Preschool ★★★	Teens ★★★★★	Over 30 ★★★★★
Grade school ★★★★½	Young Adults ★★★★★	Seniors ★★★★

Duration of Ride 4½ minutes

Loading Speed Fast

Description and Comments Covering 1½ acres and combining moving ride vehicles, 3-D film, and live action, Spider-Man is frenetic, fluid, and astounding. The visuals are rich, and the ride is wild, but not jerky. Although the attractions are not directly comparable, Spider-Man is technologically on a par with Disney-MGM's Tower of Terror, which is to say that it will leave you in awe. As a personal aside, we love both and would be hard-pressed to choose one over the other.

The storyline is that you are a reporter for the *Daily Bugle* newspaper (where Peter Parker, aka Spider-Man, works as a mild-mannered photographer), when it's discovered that evil villains have stolen (I promise I'm not making this up) the Statue of Liberty. You are drafted on the spot by your cantankerous editor to go get the story. After speeding around and being thrust into "a battle between good and evil," you experience a 400-foot "sensory drop" from a skyscraper roof all the way to the pavement. Because the ride is so wild and the action so continuous, it's hard to understand the plot, but you're so thoroughly entertained that you don't really care. Plus, you'll want to ride again and again. Eventually, with repetition, the story line will begin to make sense.

Touring Tips Ride first thing in the morning after The Incredible Hulk Coaster or in the hour before closing.

Dr. Doom's Fearfall (Universal Express)

What It Is Lunch liberator

Scope and Scale Headliner

When to Go Before 9:15 a.m.

Special Comments Must be 52" tall to ride

Author's Rating More bark than bite; ★★★

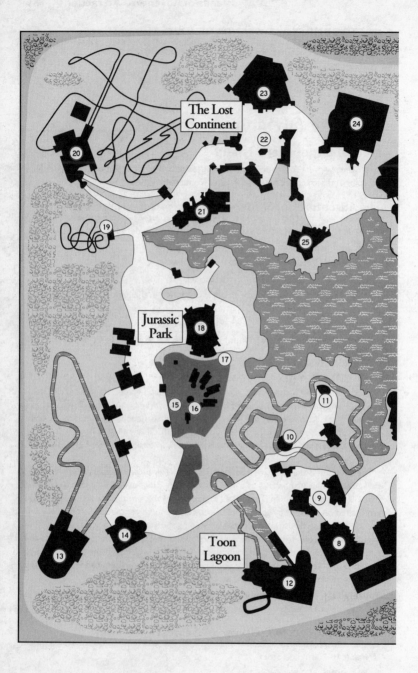

The Lost Continent

Jurassic Park

Toon Lagoon

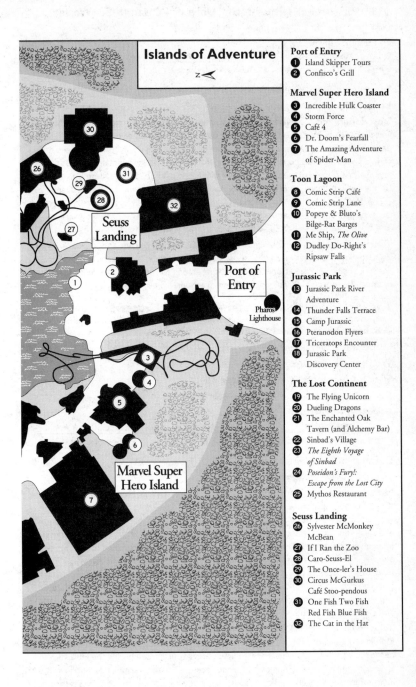

Islands of Adventure

z ◄

Port of Entry
1. Island Skipper Tours
2. Confisco's Grill

Marvel Super Hero Island
3. Incredible Hulk Coaster
4. Storm Force
5. Café 4
6. Dr. Doom's Fearfall
7. The Amazing Adventure of Spider-Man

Toon Lagoon
8. Comic Strip Café
9. Comic Strip Lane
10. Popeye & Bluto's Bilge-Rat Barges
11. Me Ship, *The Olive*
12. Dudley Do-Right's Ripsaw Falls

Jurassic Park
13. Jurassic Park River Adventure
14. Thunder Falls Terrace
15. Camp Jurassic
16. Pteranodon Flyers
17. Triceratops Encounter
18. Jurassic Park Discovery Center

The Lost Continent
19. The Flying Unicorn
20. Dueling Dragons
21. The Enchanted Oak Tavern (and Alchemy Bar)
22. Sinbad's Village
23. *The Eighth Voyage of Sinbad*
24. *Poseidon's Fury!: Escape from the Lost City*
25. Mythos Restaurant

Seuss Landing
26. Sylvester McMonkey McBean
27. If I Ran the Zoo
28. Caro-Seuss-El
29. The Once-ler's House
30. Circus McGurkus Café Stoo-pendous
31. One Fish Two Fish Red Fish Blue Fish
32. The Cat in the Hat

Seuss Landing

Port of Entry

Pharos Lighthouse

Marvel Super Hero Island

Appeal by Age Group

Preschool —	Teens ★★★★	Over 30 ★★★
Grade school ★★★	Young Adults ★★★½	Seniors —

Duration of Ride 40 seconds

Loading Speed Slow

Description and Comments Here you are (again) strapped into a seat with your feet dangling and blasted 200 feet up in the air and then allowed to partially free-fall back down. If you are having trouble forming a mental image of this attraction, picture the midway game where a macho guy swings a sledgehammer, propelling a metal sphere up a vertical shaft. At the top of the shaft is a bell. If the macho man drives the sphere high enough to ring the bell, he wins a prize. Got the idea? OK, on this ride you are the metal sphere.

   The good news is this ride looks much worse than it actually is. The scariest part by far is the apprehension that builds as you sit, strapped in, waiting for the thing to launch. The blasting up and free-falling down parts are really very pleasant.

Touring Tips We've seen glaciers that move faster than the line to Dr. Doom. If you want to ride without investing half a day, be one of the first in the park to ride. Fortunately, if you're on hand at opening time, being among the first isn't too difficult (mainly because the nearby Hulk and Spider-Man attractions are bigger draws).

The Incredible Hulk Coaster (Universal Express)

What It Is Roller coaster

Scope and Scale Super headliner

When to Go Before 9:30 a.m.

Special Comments Must be 54" tall to ride

Author's Rating A coaster-lover's coaster; ★★★★½

Appeal by Age Group

Preschool ★	Teens ★★★★★	Over 30 ★★★★
Grade school ★★★★★	Young Adults ★★★★	Seniors ★★½

Duration of Ride 1½ minutes

Loading Speed Moderate

Description and Comments There is, as always, a story line, but for this attraction it's of no importance whatsoever. What you need to know about this attraction is simple. You will be shot like a cannonball from 0 to 40 miles per hour in two seconds, and then you will be flung upside down 100 feet off the ground, which will, of course, induce weightlessness. From there it's a mere seven rollovers punctuated by two plunges into holes in the ground before you're allowed to get out and throw up.

   Seriously, the Hulk is a great roller coaster, perhaps the best in Florida, providing a ride comparable to Montu (Busch Gardens) with the added thrill of an accelerated launch (instead of the more typical uphill crank). Plus, like Montu, the ride is smooth. You won't be jarred and whiplashed on the Incredible Hulk.

Touring Tips The Hulk gives Spider-Man a run as the park's most popular attraction. Ride first thing in the morning. Universal provides electronic lockers near the entrance of the Hulk to deposit any items that might depart your person during the Hulk's seven inversions. Program the number of your locker into the terminal and follow the instructions. You'll receive a slip of paper with a code you can enter when you return to retrieve your stuff. The locker is free if you only use it for a short time. If you leave things in the locker for a couple of hours, however, you'll have to pay a modest rental charge. When you reach the boarding area, note that there is a separate line for those who want to ride in the first row.

Storm Force Accelatron (Universal Express)

What It Is Indoor spinning ride

Scope and Scale Minor attraction

Special Comments May induce motion sickness

When to Go Before 10:30 a.m.

Author's Rating Teacups in the dark; ★★★

Appeal by Age Group

Preschool ★★★½	Teens ★★★	Over 30 ★★★
Grade school ★★★	Young Adults ★★★	Seniors ★★★

Duration of Ride 1½ minutes

Loading Speed Slow

Description and Comments   Storm Force is a spiffed-up indoor version of Disney's nausea-inducing Mad Tea Party. Here you spin to the accompaniment of a simulated thunderstorm and swirling sound and light. There's a story line that loosely ties this midway-type ride to the Marvel Super Hero theme area, but it's largely irrelevant and offers no advice on keeping your lunch down.

Touring Tips   Ride early or late to avoid long lines. If you're prone to motion sickness, keep your distance.

Toon Lagoon

Toon Lagoon is cartoon art translated into real buildings and settings. Whimsical and gaily colored, with rounded and exaggerated lines, Toon Lagoon is Universal's answer to Mickey's Toontown Fair in the Magic Kingdom. The main difference between the two toon lands is that (as you will see) you have about a 60% chance of going into hypothermia at Universal's version.

Comic Strip Lane

What It Is Walk-through exhibit and shopping/dining venue

Scope and Scale Diversion

When to Go Anytime

Description and Comments   This is the main street of Toon Lagoon. Here you can visit the domains of Beetle Bailey, Hagar the Horrible, Krazy Kat, the Family Circus, and Blondie and Dagwood, among others. Shops and eateries tie into the cartoon strip theme.

Touring Tips   This is a great place for photo ops with cartoon characters in their own environment. It's also a great place to drop a few bucks in the diners and shops, but you probably already figured that out.

Dudley Do-Right's Ripsaw Falls (Universal Express)

What It Is Flume ride

Scope and Scale Major attraction

When to Go Before 11 a.m.

Special Comments Must be 48" tall to ride

Author's Rating A minimalist Splash Mountain; ★★★½

Appeal by Age Group

Preschool ★★½	Teens ★★★½	Over 30 ★★★½
Grade school ★★★★	Young Adults ★★★	Seniors ★★½

Duration of Ride 5 minutes

Loading Speed Moderate

Description and Comments Inspired by the *Rocky and Bullwinkle* cartoon series, this ride features Canadian Mountie Dudley Do-Right as he attempts to save Nell from evil Snidely Whiplash. Story line aside, it's a flume ride, with the inevitable big drop at the end. Universal claims this is the first flume ride to "send riders plummeting 15 feet below the surface of the water." No need to bring diving gear—in reality you're just plummeting into a tunnel.

The only problem with this attraction is that everyone inevitably compares it to Splash Mountain at the Magic Kingdom. The flume is as good as Splash Mountain's, and the final drop is a whopper, but the theming and the visuals aren't even in the same league. The art, sets, audio, and jokes at Dudley Do-Right are minimalist at best; it's Dudley Do-Right's two-dimensional approach versus Splash Mountain's three-dimensional presentation. Taken on its own terms, however, Dudley Do-Right is a darn good flume ride.

Touring Tips This ride will get you wet, but on average not as wet as you might expect (it looks worse than it is). If you want to stay dry, however, arrive prepared with a poncho or at least a big garbage bag with holes cut out for your head and arms. After riding, take a moment to gauge the timing of the water cannons that go off along the exit walk. This is where you can really get drenched. While younger children are often intimidated by the big drop, those who ride generally enjoy themselves. Ride first thing in the morning after experiencing the Marvel Super Hero rides.

Me *Ship,* The Olive

What It Is Interactive playground

Scope and Scale Minor attraction

When to Go Anytime

Author's Rating Colorful and appealing for kids; ★★★

Appeal by Age Group

Preschool ★★★★	Teens ½	Over 30 ½
Grade school ★★★½	Young Adults ½	Seniors —

Description and Comments *The Olive* is Popeye's three-story boat come to life as an interactive playground. Younger children can scramble around in Sweet Pea's Playpen, while older sibs shoot water cannons at riders trying to survive the adjacent Bilge-Rat raft ride.

Touring Tips If you're into the big rides, save this for later in the day.

Popeye & Bluto's Bilge-Rat Barges (Universal Express)

What It Is Whitewater raft ride

Scope and Scale Major attraction

When to Go Before 10:30 a.m.

Special Comments Must be 48" tall to ride

Author's Rating Bring your own soap; ★★★★

Appeal by Age Group

Preschool ★★★	Teens ★★★★	Over 30 ★★★½
Grade school ★★★★½	Young Adults ★★★★	Seniors ★★½

Duration of Ride 4½ minutes

Loading Speed Moderate

Description and Comments This sweetly named attraction is a whitewater raft ride that includes an encounter with an 18-foot-tall octopus. Engineered to ensure that everyone gets drenched, the ride even provides water cannons for highly intelligent nonparticipants ashore to fire at those aboard. The rapids are rougher and more interesting, and the ride longer, than the Animal Kingdom's Kali River Rapids. But nobody surpasses Disney for visuals and theming, though the settings of these two attractions (cartoon set and Asian jungle river, respectively) are hardly comparable.

Touring Tips If you didn't drown on Dudley Do-Right, here's a second chance. You'll get a lot wetter from the knees down on this ride, so use your poncho or garbage bag and ride barefoot with your britches rolled up. In terms of beating the crowds, ride the barges in the morning after experiencing the Marvel Super Hero attractions and Dudley Do-Right. If you are lacking foul weather gear or forgot your trash bag, you might want to put off riding until last thing before leaving the park. Most preschoolers enjoy the raft ride. Those who are frightened react more to the way the rapids look as opposed to the roughness of the ride.

Jurassic Park

Jurassic Park (for anyone who's been asleep for 20 years) is a Steven Spielberg film franchise about a fictitious theme park with real dinosaurs. Jurassic Park at Universal's Islands of Adventure is a real theme park (or at least a section of one) with fictitious dinosaurs.

Camp Jurassic

What It Is Interactive play area

Scope and Scale Minor attraction

When to Go Anytime

Author's Rating Creative playground, confusing layout; ★★★

Appeal by Age Group

Preschool ★★★	Teens —	Over 30 —
Grade school ★★★	Young Adults —	Seniors —

Description and Comments Camp Jurassic is a great place for children to cut loose. Sort of a Jurassic version of Tom Sawyer Island, kids can explore lava pits, caves, mines, and a rain forest.

Touring Tips Camp Jurassic will fire the imaginations of the under-13 set. If you don't impose a time limit on the exploration, you could be here awhile. The layout of the play area is confusing and intersects the queuing area for the Pteranodon Flyers. If your child accidentally lines up for the Pteranodons, he'll be college age before you see him again.

Discovery Center

What It Is Interactive natural history exhibit

Scope and Scale Minor attraction

When to Go Anytime

Author's Rating ★★★

Appeal by Age Group

Preschool ★★½	Teens ★★★	Over 30 ★★★
Grade school ★★★½	Young Adults ★★★	Seniors ★★★

Description and Comments   The Discovery Center is an interactive, educational exhibit that mixes fiction from the movie *Jurassic Park*, such as using fossil DNA to bring dinosaurs to life, with various skeletal remains and other paleontological displays. One exhibit allows guests to watch an animatronic raptor being hatched. Another allows you to digitally "fuse" your DNA with a dinosaur to see what the resultant creature would look like. Other exhibits include dinosaur egg scanning and identification and a quiz called "You Bet Jurassic."

Touring Tips   Cycle back after experiencing all the rides or on a second day. Most folks can digest this exhibit in 10–15 minutes.

Jurassic Park River Adventure (Universal Express)

What It Is   Indoor/outdoor adventure ride based on the *Jurassic Park* movies

Scope and Scale   Super headliner

When to Go   Before 11 a.m.

Special Comments   Must be 42" tall to ride

Author's Rating   Better than its Hollywood cousin; ★★★★

Appeal by Age Group

Preschool ★★★	Teens ★★★★½	Over 30 ★★★★
Grade school ★★★★½	Young Adults ★★★★	Seniors ★★★½

Duration of Ride   6½ minutes

Loading Speed   Fast

Description and Comments   Guests board boats for a water tour of Jurassic Park. Everything is tranquil as the tour begins, and the boat floats among large herbivorous dinosaurs such as brontosaurus and stegosaurus. Then, as word is received that some of the carnivores have escaped their enclosure, the tour boat is accidentally diverted into Jurassic Park's maintenance facilities. Here, the boat and its riders are menaced by an assortment of hungry meat eaters led by the ubiquitous T-Rex. At the climactic moment, the boat and its passengers escape by plummeting over an 85-foot drop billed as the "longest, fastest, steepest water descent ever built" (did anyone other than me notice the omission of the word wettest?).

Touring Tips   Though the boats make a huge splash at the bottom of the 85-foot drop, you don't get all that wet. Unfortunately, before the boat leaves the dock, you must sit in the puddles left by previous riders. Once underway there's a little splashing, but nothing major until the big drop at the end of the ride. When you hit the bottom, however, enough water will cascade into the air to extinguish a three-alarm fire. Fortunately, not all that much lands in the boat.

Young children must endure a double whammy on this ride. First, they are stalked by giant, salivating (sometimes spitting) reptiles, and then they're sent catapulting over the falls. Unless your children are fairly stalwart, wait a year or two before you spring the River Adventure on them.

Pteranodon Flyers

What It Is   Dinosaur version of Dumbo the Flying Elephant

Scope and Scale   Minor attraction

When to Go   When there's no line

Author's Rating   All sizzle, no steak; ½

Appeal by Age Group

Preschool ★★★	Teens ★	Over 30 ★
Grade school ★★★	Young Adults ★½	Seniors ★½

Duration of Ride 1¼ minutes

Loading Speed Slower than a hog in quicksand

Description and Comments This attraction is Islands of Adventure's biggest blunder. Engineered to accommodate only 170 persons per hour (about half the hourly capacity of Dumbo!), the ride swings you along a track that passes over a small part of Jurassic Park. We recommend that you skip this one. Why? Because the Jurassic period will probably end before you reach the front of the line! And your reward for all that waiting? A one minute and fifteen second ride. Plus, the attraction has a name that nobody over 12 years old can pronounce.

Touring Tips Photograph the pteranodon as it flies overhead. You're probably looking at something that will someday be extinct.

Triceratops Encounter

What It Is Prehistoric petting zoo

Scope and Scale Minor attraction

When to Go Before 11:30 a.m.

Author's Rating Well executed; ★★★

Appeal by Age Group

Preschool ★★★★	Teens ★★★½	Over 30 ★★★½
Grade school ★★★★	Young Adults ★★★½	Seniors ★★★½

Duration of Show 5 minutes

Probable Waiting Time 15–25 minutes

Description and Comments Guests are ushered in groups into a "feed and control station," where they can view and pet a 24-foot-long, animatronic triceratops dinosaur. While the trainer lectures about the creature's behaviors, habits, and lifestyle, the triceratops breathes, blinks, chews, and flinches at the touch of the guests.

Touring Tips Nothing is certain, but this may be the only attraction in the park where you won't get wet. Just to be sure, however, stand near the middle of the dinosaur. Though not a major attraction, Triceratops Encounter is popular and develops long lines. Make it your first show/exhibit after experiencing the rides.

The Lost Continent

This area is an exotic mix of Silk Road bazaar and ancient ruins, with Greco-Moroccan accents. And you thought your decorator was nuts. Anyway, this is the land of mythical gods, fabled beasts, and expensive souvenirs.

Dueling Dragons (Universal Express)

What It Is Roller coaster

Scope and Scale Headliner

When to Go Before 10:30 a.m.

Special Comments Must be 54" tall to ride

Author's Rating Almost as good as the Hulk coaster; ★★★★

Appeal by Age Group

Preschool —	Teens ★★★★	Over 30 ★★★★
Grade school ★★★★	Young Adults ★★★★	Seniors ★★

Duration of Ride A minute and 45 seconds

Loading Speed Moderate

Description and Comments This high-tech coaster launches two trains (Fire and Ice) at the same time on tracks that are closely intertwined. Each track is differently configured so that you get a different experience on each. Several times, a collision with the other train seems imminent, a catastrophe that seems all the more real because the coasters are inverted (i.e., suspended from above so that you sit with your feet dangling). At times, the two trains and their passengers are separated by a mere 12 inches.

Because this is an inverted coaster, your view of the action is limited unless you are sitting in the front row. This means that most passengers miss seeing all these near collisions. But don't worry; regardless of where you sit, there's plenty to keep you busy. Dueling Dragons is the highest coaster in the park and also claims the longest drop at 115 feet, not to mention five inversions. And like the Hulk, it's a nice smooth ride all the way.

Coaster cadets argue about which seat on which train provides the wildest ride. We prefer the front row on either train, but coaster loonies hype the front row of Fire and the last row of Ice.

Touring Tips The good news about this ride is that you won't get wet unless you wet yourself. The bad news is that wetting yourself comes pretty naturally. The other bad news is that the queuing area for Dueling Dragons is the longest, most convoluted affair we've ever seen, winding endlessly through a maze of subterranean passages. After what feels like a comprehensive tour of Mammoth Cave, you finally emerge at the loading area where you must choose between riding Fire or Ice. Of course, at this critical juncture, you're as blind as a mole rat from being in the dark for so long. Our advice is to follow the person in front of you until your eyes adjust to the light. Try to ride during the first 90 minutes the park is open. Warn anyone waiting for you that you might be a while. Even if there is no line to speak of, it takes 10–12 minutes just to navigate the caverns and not much less time to exit the attraction after riding. However, if lines are low, park employees will open special doors marked "Re-entry to Fire" or "Re-entry to Ice" (depending on what coaster you just rode) that allow you to get right back to the head of the queue and ride again. Finally, if you don't have time to ride both Fire and Ice, be advised that the *Unofficial* crew unanimously prefers Fire to Ice.

The Eighth Voyage of Sinbad *(Universal Express)*

What It Is Theater stunt show

Scope and Scale Major attraction

When to Go Anytime as per the daily entertainment schedule

Author's Rating Not inspiring; ★★

Appeal by Age Group

Preschool ★★★	Teens ★★½	Over 30 ★★★
Grade school ★★★½	Young Adults ★★★	Seniors ★★½

Duration of Presentation 17 minutes

Probable Waiting Time 15 minutes

Description and Comments A story about Sinbad the Sailor is the glue that (loosely) binds this stunt show featuring water explosions, ten-foot-tall circles of flame, and various other daunting eruptions and perturbations. The show reminds us of those action movies that substitute a mind-numbing succession of explosions, crashes, and special effects for plot and character development. Concerning *Sinbad,* even if you bear in mind that it's billed as a stunt show, the production is so vacuous and redundant that it's hard to get into the action. Fans of the *Hercules* and *Xena* TV shows might appreciate the humor more than the average showgoer.

Touring Tips   See *Sinbad* after you've experienced the rides and the better-rated shows. The theater seats 1,700; performance times are listed in the daily entertainment schedule.

The Flying Unicorn (Universal Express)

What It Is   Children's roller coaster

Scope and Scale   Minor attraction

When to Go   Before 11 a.m.

Author's Rating   A good beginner's coaster; ★★★

Appeal by Age Group

Preschool ★★★★	Teens ★★	Over 30 ★
Grade school ★★★½	Young Adults ★★	Seniors ★

Duration of Ride   1 minute

Loading Speed   Slow

Description and Comments   A child-sized roller coaster through a forest setting, the Unicorn provides a nonthreatening way to introduce young children to the genre.

Touring Tips   This one loads very slowly. Ride before 11 a.m.

Poseidon's Fury! Escape from the Lost City (Universal Express)

What It Is   High-tech theater attraction

Scope and Scale   Headliner

When to Go   After experiencing all the rides

Special Comments   Audience stands throughout

Author's Rating   Much improved; ★★★★

Appeal by Age Group

Preschool ★★	Teens ★★★★	Over 30 ★★★★
Grade school ★★★★	Young Adults ★★★★	Seniors ★★★★

Duration of Presentation   17 minutes including preshow

Probable Waiting Time   25 minutes

Description and Comments   In the first incarnation of this story, the Greek gods Poseidon and Zeus duked it out, with Poseidon as the heavy. Poseidon fought with water, and Zeus fought with fire, though both sometimes resorted to laser beams and smoke machines. In the new version, the rehabilitated Poseidon now tussles with an evil wizardish guy, and everybody uses fire, water, lasers, smoke machines, and angry lemurs (*Note:* lemurs are not actually used—just seeing if you're paying attention). As you might have inferred, the new story is, somewhat incoherent, but the special effects are still amazing, and the theming of the preshow areas is quite imposing. The plot unravels in installments as you pass through a couple of these areas and finally into the main theater. Though the production is a little slow and plodding at first, it wraps up with quite an impressive flourish. There's some great technology at work here. *Poseidon* is by far and away the best of the Islands of Adventure theater attractions.

Touring Tips   If you are still wet from Dudley Do-Right, the Bilge-Rat Barges, and the Jurassic Park River Adventure, you might be tempted to cheer the evil wizard's flame jets in hopes of finally drying out. Our money, however, is on Poseidon. It's legal in Florida for theme parks to get you wet, but setting you on fire is frowned upon.

Frequent explosions and noise may frighten younger children, so exercise caution with preschoolers. Shows run continuously if the technology isn't on the blink. We recommend catching *Poseidon* after experiencing your fill of the rides.

Seuss Landing

A ten-acre theme area based on Dr. Seuss's famous children's books. Like at Mickey's Toontown in the Magic Kingdom, all of the buildings and attractions replicate a whimsical, brightly colored cartoon style with exaggerated features and rounded lines.

Caro-Seuss-El (Universal Express)

What It Is Merry-go-round

Scope and Scale Minor attraction

When to Go Before 10:30 a.m.

Author's Rating Wonderfully unique; ★★★½

Appeal by Age Group

Preschool ★★★★	Teens —	Over 30 —
Grade school ★★★★	Young Adults —	Seniors —

Duration of Ride 2 minutes

Loading Speed Slow

Description and Comments Totally outrageous, the Caro-Seuss-El is a full-scale, 56-mount merry-go-round made up exclusively of Dr. Seuss characters.

Touring Tips Even if you are too old or don't want to ride, this attraction is worth an inspection. Whatever your age, chances are good you'll see some old friends. If you are touring with young children, try to get them on early in the morning.

The Cat in the Hat (Universal Express)

What It Is Indoor adventure ride

Scope and Scale Major attraction

When to Go Before 11:30 a.m.

Author's Rating Seuss would be proud; ★★★½

Appeal by Age Group

Preschool ★★★★	Teens ★★★	Over 30 ★★★½
Grade school ★★★★	Young Adults ★★★½	Seniors ★★★½

Duration of Ride 3½ minutes

Loading Speed Moderate

Description and Comments Guests ride on "couches" through 18 different sets inhabited by animatronic Seuss characters, including The Cat in the Hat, Thing 1, Thing 2, and the beleaguered goldfish who tries to maintain order in the midst of bedlam. Well done overall, with nothing that should frighten younger children.

Touring Tips This is fun for all ages. Try to ride early.

One Fish, Two Fish, Red Fish, Blue Fish (Universal Express)

What It Is Wet version of Dumbo the Flying Elephant

Scope and Scale Minor attraction

When to Go Before 10 a.m.

Author's Rating Who says you can't teach an old ride new tricks?; ★★★½

Appeal by Age Group

Preschool ★★★★	Teens ★★★	Over 30 ★★★
Grade school ★★★★	Young Adults ★★★	Seniors ★★★

Duration of Ride 2 minutes

Loading Speed Slow

Description and Comments   Imagine Dumbo with Seuss-style fish instead of elephants and you've got half the story. The other half of the story involves yet another opportunity to drown. Guests steer their fish up or down 15 feet in the air while traveling in circles. At the same time, they try to avoid streams of water projected from "squirt posts." A catchy song provides clues for avoiding the squirting.

Though ostensibly a children's ride, the song and the challenge of steering your fish away from the water jets make this attraction fun for all ages.

Touring Tips   We don't know what it is about this theme park and water, but you'll get wetter than at a full-immersion baptism.

Islands of Adventure Touring Plan

Islands of Adventure One-Day Touring Plan

Be aware that in this park there are an inordinate number of attractions that will get you wet. If you want to experience them, come armed with ponchos, large plastic garbage bags, or some other protective covering. Failure to follow this prescription will make for a squishy, sodden day.

This plan is for groups of all sizes and ages and includes thrill rides that may induce motion sickness or get you wet. If the plan calls for you to experience an attraction that does not interest you, simply skip that attraction and proceed to the next step. Be aware that the plan calls for some backtracking. If you have young children in your party, customize the plan to fit their needs and take advantage of switching off at thrill rides.

1. Call (407) 363-8000, the main information number, the day before your visit for the official opening time. Try to purchase your admission sometime prior to the day you intend to tour.

2. On the day of your visit, eat breakfast and arrive at Universal Orlando 50 minutes before opening time. Park, buy your admission (if you did not purchase it in advance), and wait at the turnstiles to be admitted.

3. While at the turnstile, ask an attendant whether any rides or shows are closed that day. Adjust the touring plan accordingly.

4. When the park opens, go straight through the Port of Entry and take a left, crossing the bridge into Marvel Super Hero Island. At Super Hero Island, bear left to The Incredible Hulk Coaster.

5. Ride Incredible Hulk.

6. Exiting Hulk, hustle immediately to The Adventures of Spider-Man, also in Marvel Super Hero Island.

7. Dr. Doom's Fearfall, to the left of Spider-Man, is sort of a poor man's Tower of Terror. What's more, it loads about as fast as molasses on a shingle. We suggest you skip it. However, if you're bound and determined to ride, now's the time. *Note:* Steps 8–10 involve attractions where you will get wet. If you're not up for a soaking this early in the morning, skip ahead to Step 11, but be advised that you may have a bit of a wait at the Toon Lagoon attractions later in the day.

8. Continuing clockwise around the lake, depart Super Hero Island and cross into Toon Lagoon.

9. In Toon Lagoon, ride Dudley Do-Right's Ripsaw Falls.

10. Also in Toon Lagoon, subject yourself to Popeye & Bluto's Bilge-Rat Barges.

11. After the barge ride, continue your clockwise circuit around the lake, passing through Jurassic Park without stopping. Continue to the Lost Continent.

12. At the Lost Continent, ride both tracks of Dueling Dragons.

13. While at the Lost Continent, experience *Poseidon's Fury! Escape from the Lost City.*

14. Depart the Lost Continent, moving counterclockwise around the lake, and enter Jurassic Park.

15. In Jurassic Park, try the Jurassic Park River Adventure.

16. Also in Jurassic Park, check out Triceratops Encounter.

17. Return to the Lost Continent. Check the daily entertainment schedule for the next performance of *The Eighth Voyage of Sinbad* stunt show. If a show is scheduled to begin within 30 minutes or so, go ahead and check it out. Otherwise, skip ahead to Step 18 and work *Sinbad* in later.

18. From the Lost Continent, move clockwise around the lake to Seuss Landing. Ride The Cat in the Hat.

19. While in Seuss Landing, ride Sylvester McMonkey McBean if it's operating.

20. At this point, you will have done all the big stuff. Spend the rest of your day experiencing attractions you bypassed earlier or repeating ones you especially enjoyed.

SeaWorld

Many dozens of readers have written to extol the virtues of SeaWorld. The following are representative. An English family writes:

The best organized park [is] SeaWorld. The computer printout we got on arrival had a very useful show schedule, told us which areas were temporarily closed due to construction, and had a readily understandable map. Best of all, there was almost no queuing. Overall, we rated this day so highly that it is the park we would most like to visit again.

A woman in Alberta, Canada, gives her opinion:

We chose SeaWorld as our fifth day at "The World." What a pleasant surprise! It was every bit as good (and in some ways better) than WDW itself. Well worth the admission, an excellent entertainment value, educational, well run, and better value for the dollar in food services. Perhaps expand your coverage to give them their due!

A reader from Sylvania, Georgia, believes Disney could learn a thing or two from SeaWorld:

Disney ought to take a look at how well this place is run. I know they don't have the same crowds or the exciting rides, but there is still a lot of entertainment here and never a wait. This allows you to set your pace without worrying about what you'll have to miss. You'll see it all no matter how you do it, you'll come away feeling you got better value for your dollars, you won't feel as tired as a Disney day, and you will probably learn more, too. Only downside is you'll probably be hungry. Food is not one of the park's assets.

Okay, here's what you need to know (for additional information, call (407) 363-2613 or visit **www.seaworld.com**). SeaWorld is a world-class marine-life theme park near the intersection of I-4 and the Bee Line Expressway. Open daily from 9 a.m. to 10 p.m., SeaWorld charges about $54 admission (plus tax) for adults and $45 (plus tax) for children (ages three to nine). Combination passes, which include admission to Sea-World, Universal Studios, Islands of Adventure, Wet 'n' Wild, and Busch Gardens, are also available. Parking is $6 per car, $7 per RV or camper. Discount coupons for SeaWorld admission are available in the free visitor magazine found in most (but not Disney) hotel lobbies. Figure six to nine hours to see everything, but only five or so if you stick to the big deals.

SeaWorld is about the size of the Magic Kingdom and requires about the same amount of walking. Most attractions are accessible to nonambulatory disabled persons. In terms of size, quality, and creativity, SeaWorld is unequivocally on a par with Disney's major theme parks. Unlike Walt Disney World, however, SeaWorld primarily features stadium shows or walk-through exhibits. This means that you will spend about 80% less time waiting in line during eight hours at SeaWorld than you would for the same-length visit at a Disney park.

Because lines, with one or two exceptions, aren't much of a problem at SeaWorld, you can tour at almost any time of day. We recommend you start about 3:30 or 4 p.m. (when the park is open until 9 p.m. or later). Many of the day's early guests will have left by this hour, and you'll be able to enjoy the outdoor attractions in the relative cool of late afternoon and evening. If you visit in the morning, arrive early or late. Morning arrivals tend to create long waits at the ticket windows, so consider buying your admission in advance.

A daily entertainment schedule is printed conveniently on a placemat-sized map of the park. The three featured shows are:

- *Shamu Killer Whale Show*
- *Sea Lion and Otter Show*
- *Whale and Dolphin Discovery Show*

When you arrive, build your itinerary around these shows. You'll notice immediately as you check the performance times that they're scheduled in a way that makes it almost impossible to see them back to back. The Shamu show, for example, might run from 5 to 5:25 p.m. Ideally, you'd like to bop over to the Sea Lion and Otter Show, which begins at 5:30 p.m. Unfortunately, five minutes isn't enough time to exit Shamu Stadium and cross the park to the Sea Lion & Otter Stadium. SeaWorld, of course, planned it this way so you would stay longer. A Cherry Hill, New Jersey, visitor confirms this rather major problem, complaining:

The shows were timed so we could not catch all the major ones in a seven-hour visit.

It is possible to catch the Shamu show and the Sea Lion and Otter Show in succession by sitting near an exit at Shamu Stadium and leaving a minute or two early (while the performers are taking their bows). Getting a couple of minutes' head start on the crowd and hurrying directly to the Sea Lion & Otter Stadium will get you seated just as the show is beginning. While this strategy allows you to see more in a short time, it makes for a somewhat frenetic and less relaxing tour.

If you're going to a show in Shamu Stadium or at the Atlantis Stadium, don't worry about arriving late. Both stadiums are huge, so you almost certainly will get a seat. Plus, there isn't much in the first few minutes that you can't afford to miss. The same goes for the Whale and Dolphin Discovery Show. The beginning of the Sea Lion and Otter Show, however, is really good; try to be on time.

Kraken and Journey to Atlantis are SeaWorld's entries into the theme-park super-attraction competition. Occupying the equivalent of six football fields, Journey to Atlantis is the world's first attraction to combine elements of a high-speed water ride and a roller coaster. By the way, you'll get soaked. Kraken is the longest, tallest, and fastest roller coaster in Orlando. There's some debate about the smoothness of its ride, though. Catch both rides just after the park opens or be prepared to wait.

Stand-alone exhibits feature dolphins, stingrays, pelicans, spoonbills, flamingos, and the Anheuser-Busch Clydesdale horses, plus a tidal pool and tropical rain forest.

STAR RATINGS FOR SEAWORLD ATTRACTIONS

★★★★½	Kraken (roller coaster)
★★★★½	Terrors of the Deep (shark and eel exhibit)
★★★★	Manatees: The Last Generation (manatee exhibit)
★★★★	Pacific Point Preserve (sea lion exhibit)
★★★★	Penguin Encounter (penguin and puffin exhibit)
★★★★	*Sea Lion and Otter Show*
★★★★	*Shamu Killer Whale Show*
★★★★	Shamu's Happy Harbor (children's play area)
★★★★	*Whale and Dolphin Discovery Show*
★★★★	Wild Arctic (simulation ride and Arctic wildlife polar bears)
★★★½	Tropical Reef (reef-fish aquarium exhibit)
★★★	*Hawaiian Rhythms* (Polynesian dance and music)
★★★	Journey to Atlantis
★★★	*Nautilus Theatre* (musical revue)
★★½	SeaWorld Theater (SeaWorld propaganda and dancing fountains)

Discovery Cove

SeaWorld's intimate new park, Discovery Cove, is a welcome departure from the hustle and bustle of other Orlando parks; the slower pace of this park could be the over-stimulated family's ticket back to mental health. With a focus on personal guest service and one-on-one animal encounters, Discovery Cove admits only 1,000 guests per day.

The main draw at Discovery Cove is the chance to swim with their troupe of 25 Atlantic bottlenose dolphins. The 90-minute dolphin swim experience is open to visitors ages six and up who are comfortable in the water. The experience begins with an orientation led by trainers and an opportunity for participants to ask questions. Next, small groups wade into shallow water for an introduction to the dolphins in their habitat. The experience culminates with two to three guests and a trainer swimming into deeper water for closer interaction with the dolphins. Afterward, swimmers are invited to discuss their experiences with the trainers and, of course, purchase photographs of themselves with the dolphins.

Other exhibits at Discovery Cove include the Coral Reef and the Aviary. You can snorkel or swim in the Coral Reef, which houses thousands of exotic fish as well as an underwater shipwreck and hidden grottos. In the Aviary, you can touch and feed gorgeous tropical birds. The park is threaded by a "tropical river," in which you can float or swim, and dotted with beaches, which serve as pathways to the attractions.

All guests are required to wear flotation vests when swimming, and lifeguards are omnipresent. You'll need your swimsuit, pool shoes, and a cover-up. On rare days when it's too cold to swim in Orlando, guests are provided with free wet suits. Discovery Cove also provides fish-friendly sunscreen samples; guests may not use their own sunscreen.

Discovery Cove is open 9 a.m.–5:30 p.m. daily. Since admission is limited, you should purchase tickets well in advance; call (877) 4-DISCOVERY or visit **www.discoverycove.com.** Admission is $229 per person (there is no children's discount) during the cooler months and $249 per person from March 22 to August 31. Admission includes the dolphin swim, self parking, one meal, and use of beach umbrellas, lounge chairs, towels, lockers, and swim and snorkel gear. Discovery Cove admission also includes a seven-day pass to SeaWorld. If you're not interested in the dolphin swim, you can visit Discovery Cove for the day for $129 per person September through late March, and $149 from March 22 until the end of August.

Part Fourteen

The Water Parks

You're Soaking in It!

Disney has two water parks, and there are two more independent water parks in the area. At Disney World, Typhoon Lagoon is the most diverse Disney splash pad, while Blizzard Beach takes the prize for the most slides and most bizarre theme. Outside the World are Wet 'n' Wild and Water Mania.

At all Disney water parks, the following rules and prices apply: One cooler per family or group is allowed, but no glass and no alcoholic beverages; towels are $1; lockers are $5 small, $7 large (includes $2 refundable deposit); life jacket free with a $25 refundable deposit.

Guests can now use automated ticket-vending machines to purchase admission tickets at Blizzard Beach and Typhoon Lagoon. These automated machines use touch-screen technology and should help reduce the amount of time spent standing in line at the ticket windows.

River Country

The oldest of the Disney swimming parks, River Country was closed during 2002 as a consequence of the soft travel market. It now appears that the closure is permanent.

Blizzard Beach

Blizzard Beach is Disney's most exotic water adventure park and, like Typhoon Lagoon, it arrived with its own legend. This time, the story goes, an entrepreneur tried to open a ski resort in Florida during a particularly savage winter. Alas, the snow melted; the palm trees grew back; and all that remained of the ski resort was its Alpine lodge, the ski lifts, and, of course, the mountain. Plunging off the mountain are ski slopes and bobsled runs transformed into water slides. Visitors to Blizzard Beach catch the thaw—icicles drip and patches of snow remain. The melting snow has formed a lagoon (the wave pool), fed by gushing mountain streams.

Like Typhoon Lagoon, Blizzard Beach is distinguished by its landscaping and the attention paid to executing its theme. As you enter Blizzard Beach, you face the mountain. Coming off the highest peak and bisecting the area at the mountain's base are two long slides. To the left of the slides is the wave pool. To the right are the children's swimming area and the ski lift. Surrounding the layout like a moat is a tranquil stream for floating in tubes. Picnic areas are scattered around the park, as are pleasant places for sunbathing.

On either side of the highest peak are tube, raft, and body slides. Including the two slides coming off the peak, Blizzard Beach has 17 slides. Among them is Summit Plummet, Disney World's longest speed slide, which begins with a 120-foot free-fall, and the Teamboat Springs water bobsled run, 1,200 feet long.

For our money, the most exciting and interesting slides are the Slush Gusher and Teamboat Springs on the front right of the mountain, and Run-Off Rapids on the back side of the mountain. Slush Gusher is an undulating speed slide that we consider as exciting as the more vertical Summit Plummet without being as bone-jarring. On Teamboat Springs, you ride in a raft that looks like a round, children's blow-up wading pool. The more people you load into the raft, the faster it goes. If you have only a couple in it, the slide is kind of a snore.

Run-Off Rapids is accessible from a path that winds around the far left bottom of the mountain. The Rapids consists of three corkscrew tube slides, one of which is enclosed and dark. As at Teamboat Springs, you'll go much faster on a two- or three-person tube than on a one-person tube. If you lean so that you enter curves high and come out low, you'll really fly. Because we like to steer the tube and go fast, we much prefer the open slides (where we can see) to the dark, enclosed tube. We thought crashing through the pitch-dark tube felt disturbingly like being flushed down a toilet.

The Snow Stormer's mat slides on the front of the mountain are fun but not as fast or interesting as Run-Off Rapids or Downhill Double Dipper on the far left front. The Toboggan Racers at front and center on the mountain consists of eight parallel slides where riders are dispatched in heats to race to the bottom. The ride itself is no big deal, and the time needed to get everybody lined up ensures that you'll wait extra long to ride. On one visit, as an added annoyance, we had to line up once to get a mat and again to actually ride. A faster, more exciting race venue can be found on the side-by-side slides of the undulating Downhill Double Dipper. Competitors here can reach speeds of up to 25 miles an hour.

A ski lift carries guests to the mountaintop (you can also walk up), where they can choose from Summit Plummet, Slush Gusher, or Team-boat Springs. For all other slides at Blizzard Beach, the only way to reach the top is on foot. If you're among the first in the park and don't have to wait to ride, the ski lift is fun and provides a bird's-eye view of the park. After riding once to satisfy your curiosity, however, you're better off taking the stairs to the top. There is a minimum-height restriction of 48 inches on Slush Gusher, Summit Plummet, and Downhill Double Dipper.

The wave pool, called Melt-Away Bay, has gentle, bobbing waves. The float creek, Cross Country Creek, circles the park, passing through the mountain. The children's areas, Tike's Peak and Ski Patrol Training Camp, are creatively designed, nicely isolated, and, like the rest of the park, visually interesting.

Like Typhoon Lagoon, Blizzard Beach is a bit convoluted in its layout. With slides on both the front and back of the mountain, it isn't always easy to find a path leading to where you want to go.

At the ski resort's now-converted base area are shops; counter-service food; rest rooms; and tube, towel, and locker rentals. Blizzard Beach has its own parking lot but offers no lodging, though Disney's All-Star and Coro-nado Springs Resorts are almost within walking distance. Disney resort and campground guests can commute to the park aboard Disney buses.

Because it's novel and has popular slides, Blizzard Beach fills early dur-ing hotter months. To stake out a nice sunning spot and to enjoy the slides without long waits, arrive at least 35 minutes before the official opening time. Admission is about $33 per day for adults and $27 per day for children ages three to nine. Children younger than three are admitted free. If you're going primarily for the slides, you'll have about two hours in the early morning to enjoy them before the wait becomes intolerable.

Typhoon Lagoon

Typhoon Lagoon is comparable in size to Blizzard Beach. Ten water slides and streams, some as long as 400 feet, drop from the top of a 100-foot-tall, man-made mountain. Landscaping and an "aftermath-of-a-typhoon" theme add adventure to the wet rides.

Entry to Typhoon Lagoon is through a misty rain forest that emerges in a ramshackle tropical town, where concessions and services are situ-ated. Special sets make every ride an odyssey as swimmers encounter bat caves, lagoons and pools, spinning rocks, formations of dinosaur bones, and many other imponderables.

Typhoon Lagoon has its own parking lot but no lodging. Disney resort and campground guests can commute to the park on Disney buses.

Like Blizzard Beach, Typhoon Lagoon is expensive: about $33 a day for adults and $27 a day for children ages three to nine. Children younger than three are admitted free. If you indulge in all features of Typhoon Lagoon, admission is a fair value. If you go primarily for the slides, you will have only two early-morning hours to enjoy them before the wait becomes prohibitive.

Typhoon Lagoon provides water adventure for all ages. Activity pools for young children and families feature geysers, tame slides, bubble jets, and fountains. For the older and more adventurous are the enclosed Humunga Kowabunga speed slides, corkscrew storm slides, and three whitewater raft rides (plus one children's rapids ride) plopping off Mount Mayday. Of all the Typhoon Lagoon slides, only the Humunga Kowabunga speed slides, where you can hit 30 miles an hour, have a minimum height requirement of 48 inches. Slower metabolisms will enjoy the scenic, meandering, 2,100-foot-long stream that floats tubers through a hidden grotto and rain forest. And, of course, the sedentary will usually find plenty of sun to sleep in. Typhoon Lagoon's surf pool and Shark Reef are unique, and the wave pool is the world's largest inland surf facility, with waves up to six feet high (enough, so Disney says, to "encompass an oceanliner"). Shark Reef is a saltwater snorkeling pool where guests can swim among real fish.

Shark Reef

Fins, mask, snorkel, and wet-suit vest are provided free in the wooden building beside the diving pool. After you obtain the proper equipment (no forms or money involved), you shower and then report to a snorkeling instructor. After a brief lesson, you swim about 60 feet to the other side of the pool. You aren't allowed to paddle aimlessly, but must traverse the pool more or less directly.

The reef is fun in early morning. Equipment collection, shower, instruction, and the quick swim can be accomplished without much hassle. Also, because few guests are present, attendants are more flexible about your lingering in the pool or making minor departures from the charted course.

Later, as crowds build, it becomes increasingly difficult and time-consuming to provide the necessary instruction. The result is platoons of would-be frogmen restlessly awaiting their snorkeling lesson. Guests are grouped in impromptu classes with the entire class briefed and then launched together. What takes four or five minutes shortly after opening can take more than an hour by 11 a.m.

By far the most prevalent species in the pool are the dual-finned *Homo sapiens*. Other denizens include small, colorful tropical fish, some diminutive rays, and a few very small leopard and hammerhead sharks. In terms of numbers, it would be unusual to cross the pool and not see some fish. On the other hand, you aren't exactly bumping into them.

It's very important to fit your diving mask on your face so that it seals around the edges. Brush your hair from your forehead and sniff a couple of times once the mask is in place, to create a vacuum. Mustaches often prevent the mask from sealing properly. The first indication that your mask isn't correctly fitted will be saltwater in your nose.

If you don't want to swim with fish early in the morning or fight crowds later in the day, visit the underwater viewing chamber, accessible anytime without waiting, special equipment, showers, instruction, or water in your nose.

Surf Pool

While Blizzard Beach, Wet 'n' Wild, and Water Mania have wave pools, Typhoon Lagoon has a *surf pool.* Most people will encounter larger waves here than they have in the ocean. The surf machine puts out a wave about every 90 seconds (just about how long it takes to get back in position if you caught the previous wave). Perfectly formed and ideal for riding, each wave is about five to six feet from trough to crest. Before you join the fray, watch two or three waves from shore. Since each wave breaks in almost the same spot, you can get a feel for position and timing. Observing other surfers is also helpful.

The best way to ride the waves is to swim about three-fourths of the way to the wall at the wave-machine end of the surf pool. When the wave comes (you will both feel and hear it), swim vigorously toward the beach, attempting to position yourself one-half to three-fourths of a body length below the breaking crest. The waves are so perfectly engineered that they will either carry you forward or bypass you. Unlike an ocean wave, they won't slam you down.

A teenage girl from Urbana, Illinois, notes that the primary hazard in the surf pool is colliding with other surfers and swimmers:

The surf pool was nice except that I kept landing on really hairy fat guys
   whenever the big waves came.

The best way to avoid collisions while surfing is to paddle out far enough that you will be at the top of the wave as it breaks. This tactic eliminates the possibility of anyone landing on you from above and assures maximum forward visibility. A corollary to this: The worst place to swim is where the wave actually breaks. You will look up to see a six-foot wall of water carrying eight dozen screaming surfers bearing down on you. This is the time to remember every submarine movie you've ever seen. … Dive! Dive! Dive!

Three mornings each week from 6:30 to 9 a.m. (before the park opens), you can take surfing lessons (with a surfboard) from Craig Carroll's Cocoa Beach Surf School. Practice waves range from three to six feet tall. Most of the school's students are first-timers. Cost is $135 per person, and equipment is provided. For reservations and information, call (407) WDW-PLAY.

A final warning: The surf pool has a knack for loosening watchbands, stripping jewelry, and sucking stuff out of your pockets. Don't take anything out there except your swimsuit (and hold on to that).

Disney versus Wet 'n' Wild and Water Mania Swimming Theme Parks

Wet 'n' Wild, on International Drive in Orlando, is on a par with Blizzard Beach and beats Typhoon Lagoon and Water Mania for slides. The headliners at Wet 'n' Wild are the Black Hole, the Surge, the Fuji Flyer, and the Storm. At the Black Hole, guests descend on a two-person tube down a totally enclosed corkscrew slide—sort of a wet version of Space Mountain, only much darker. Our researchers think this is the most exciting slide at any Florida water park (Water Mania, Typhoon Lagoon, and Blizzard Beach have similar slides). The Surge launches groups of five down a 580-foot twisting, turning course. The Fuji Flyer is a 450-foot water-toboggan course. We can only describe the Storm "slide" as a giant toilet bowl that cheerfully flushes its victims through a chute to a splashdown pool. Another Wet 'n' Wild thrill slide is Bomb Bay, which drops guests down a chute angled at 79 degrees.

Water Mania, on US 192 south of I-4, edges out Typhoon Lagoon for slides and is less crowded than its competitors. In addition, it's the only water park to offer a stationary surfing wave.

What sets Disney water parks apart is not so much their slides and individual attractions but the Disney attention to detail in creating an integrated adventure environment. Both eye and body are deluged with the strange, the exotic, the humorous, and the beautiful. Wilder slides and rapids rides can be found elsewhere, but other water parks can't compete with Disney in diversity, variety, adventure, and total impact. Water Mania is nicely landscaped, but it doesn't have a theme. Wet 'n' Wild, though attractive and clean, is cluttered and not especially appealing to the eye.

In the surf and wave pool department, Typhoon Lagoon wins hands down, with Wet 'n' Wild taking second place. All of the parks have an outstanding water activity area for young children, and all feature unique attractions. Wet 'n' Wild has a ride in which guests kneel on water skis, and Blizzard Beach has a 1,200-foot water bobsled. At Typhoon Lagoon, guests can snorkel among live fish, and Water Mania has a surfing wave.

Prices for one-day admission are about the same at Wet 'n' Wild, Blizzard Beach, and Typhoon Lagoon, and slightly less at Water Mania. Discount coupons are often available in local visitor magazines for Water Mania and Wet 'n' Wild.

Wet 'n' Wild is open until 11 p.m. during summer; the Disney swimming parks and Water Mania generally close at 5 p.m. The late closing is a huge plus for Wet 'n' Wild. Warm Florida nights are great for enjoying a water theme park. There's less waiting for slides, and the pavement is cooler under your feet. To top it off, Wet 'n' Wild features live music in the evening at its Wave Pool Stage and sells half-price tickets after 4 p.m. on days when the park is open late. Admission is $33 adults, $27 children ages 3–9, and free for children under age 3.

If you're into slides, Blizzard Beach is tops among the Disney water parks, with Wet 'n' Wild leading the independents. Typhoon Lagoon offers enough slides to keep most folks happy, has its signature surf pool, and provides the most variety. If you like slides but not crowds and are willing to sacrifice exotic surroundings for more elbow room, Water Mania is a good and cheaper choice. For evening and nighttime swimming fun, Wet 'n' Wild is the only game in town.

Typhoon Lagoon versus Blizzard Beach

Many Walt Disney World guests aren't interested in leaving the World. For them, the question is which is better, Typhoon Lagoon or Blizzard Beach? Our readers answer.

A mother of four from Winchester, Virginia, gives her opinion:

At Blizzard Beach, the family raft ride is great, [but] the kids' area is poorly designed. As a parent, when you walk your child to the top of a slide or the tube ride, they are lost to your vision as they go down because of the fake snow drifts. There are no direct ways down to the end of the slides, so little ones are left standing unsupervised [while] parents scramble down from the top. The Typhoon Lagoon kids' area is far superior in design.

A couple from Woodridge, Illinois, writes:

We liked Blizzard Beach much more. It seems like they took everything from Typhoon Lagoon and made it better and faster. Summit Plummet was awesome—a total rush. Worth the half-hour wait. Toboggan and bobsled rides were really exciting—bobsled really throws you around. Family tube ride was really good—much better and much longer than at Typhoon Lagoon. Tube rides were great, especially in enclosed tube. If you have time to go to only one water park, go to Blizzard Beach.

A New England couple agrees:

The slides at Blizzard Beach were longer and [there were] more of them, decreasing wait time. We had planned on spending a day at Typhoon Lagoon but were very bored and disappointed—having to wait in long lines for measly, short rides. We definitely recommend Blizzard Beach over Typhoon Lagoon!

A Waynesboro, Pennsylvania, family recommends both parks:

We got to two of the water parks, Blizzard Beach and Typhoon Lagoon. Both are spectacular, although BB definitely has much better slides, and its family raft ride is easily twice as long. Still, Shark Reef [at Typhoon Lagoon] is an experience not to be missed, as are the waves. Both creeks with tubes were my personal faves. What utter slothdom!

But a hungry reader from Aberdeen, New Jersey, complains:

At Blizzard Beach, there is only one main place to get food (most of the other spots are more for snacks). At lunchtime, it took almost 45 minutes to get some sandwiches and drinks.

A couple from Bowie, Maryland, didn't enjoy Summit Plummet:

The tallest and fastest slide at Blizzard Beach gave me a bunch of bruises. Even my husband hurt for a few days. It wasn't a fun ride, and we both agree that it wasn't worth waiting in line for. Basically, you drop until you hit the slide and that is why everyone comes off rubbing their butts. They say you go 60 mph on a 120-foot drop. I'll never do it again.

A man from Lexington, Massachusetts, who felt like a "hen egg in a skillet" reports:

Blizzard Beach is not well thought out. No shade from the Florida sun and way too much hot concrete.

Typhoon Lagoon won over a Texas family:

The water parks were great! Our favorite for the whole family was Typhoon Lagoon. There was a lot of shade if you wanted, the river around was better [than at Blizzard Beach], and the surf pool was great.

When to Go

The best way to avoid standing in lines is to visit the water parks when they're less crowded. Because the parks are popular among locals, weekends can be tough. We recommend going on a Monday or Tuesday, when most other tourists will be visiting the Magic Kingdom, Epcot, the Animal Kingdom, or Disney-MGM Studios and locals will be at work or school. Fridays are good because people traveling by car commonly use this day to start home. Sunday morning also has lighter crowds. During summer and holiday periods, Typhoon Lagoon and Blizzard Beach fill to capacity and close their gates before 11 a.m.

A Newbury Park, California, reader gives an idea of what "crowded" means:

The only disappointment we had at WDW was Typhoon Lagoon. While WDW was quite uncrowded, Typhoon Lagoon seemed choked with people. I'd hate to see it on a really crowded day. Even the small slides had lines greater than 30 minutes. They weren't worth half the wait. Castaway

*Creek might have been relaxing, but I found it to be a continuous traffic
jam. I [also] would have enjoyed the snorkeling area except we were
forced to go through at warp speed. After half a day we returned to the
Yacht Club, where Stormalong Bay provided much more pleasant water
recreation.*

A mom from Manlius, New York, writes:

*Because we had the 5-Day Park Hopper Plus pass, we also visited Typhoon
Lagoon, arriving before opening so we could stake out a shady spot. The
kids loved it until the lines got long (11 a.m. to noon), but I hated it. It
made Coney Island seem like a deserted island in the Bahamas. Floating
on Castaway Creek was really unpleasant. Whirling around in a chlori-
nated, concrete ditch with some stranger's feet in my face, periodically getting squirted by waterguns, passing under cascades of cold water, and
getting hung up by the crowd is not at all relaxing for me. My husband and
I then decided to "bob" in the surf pool. After about ten minutes of being
tossed around like corks in boiling water, he turned a little green around
the gills and we sought the peace of our shady little territory which, in our
absence, had become much, much smaller. We sat and read our books,
elbow to elbow with other pleasure-seekers, until the kids had their fill.
They, however, loved the body slides and the surf waves, commenting on
how useful your "coach's tip" was.*

A visitor from Middletown, New York, had a somewhat better experience at Typhoon Lagoon:

*On our second trip [to Typhoon Lagoon], we dispensed with the locker rental
(having planned to stay for only the morning when it was least crowded),
and at park's opening just took right off for the Storm Slides before the
masses arrived—it was perfect! We must have ridden the slides at least
five times before any kind of line built up, and then we were also able to
ride the tube and raft rides (Keelhaul and Mayday Falls) in a similar
uncrowded, quick fashion because everyone else was busy getting their
lockers! We also experienced the Shark Reef snorkeling three times with
minimal crowds that day, because, I think, most people overlook this attraction. Shark Reef is lots of fun and a great way to cool off since their water
temp is well below the wave pool's.*

If your schedule is flexible, a good time to visit the swimming parks is
midafternoon to late in the day when the weather has cleared after a
storm. The parks usually close during bad weather. If the storm is prolonged, most guests leave for their hotels. When Typhoon Lagoon or
Blizzard Beach reopen after inclement weather has passed, you almost
have a whole park to yourself.

Planning Your Day at Disney Water Parks

Disney water parks are almost as large and elaborate as the major theme parks. You must be prepared for a lot of walking, exercise, sun, and jostling crowds. If your group really loves the water, schedule your visit early in your vacation. For many families, a visit to a water park is the highlight of their trip. If you go at the beginning of your stay, you'll have more flexibility if you want to return.

To have a great day and beat the crowd at any Disney water park, consider:

1. Getting Information.   Call (407) 828-3058 the night before you go to ask when your chosen park opens.

2. To Picnic or Not to Picnic.   Decide whether you want to carry a picnic lunch. Guests are permitted to take lunches and beverage coolers into the parks. No alcoholic beverages are allowed. Glass containers of any kind (including mayonnaise, mustard, peanut butter, and pickle jars) are likewise forbidden.

3. Getting Started.   If you are going to Blizzard Beach or Typhoon Lagoon, get up early, have breakfast, and arrive at the park 40 minutes before opening. If you have a car, drive instead of taking a Disney bus.

4. Attire.   Wear your bathing suit under shorts and a T-shirt so you don't need to use lockers or dressing rooms. Regarding women's bathing suits, be advised that it is extremely common for women of all ages to part company with the top of their two-piece suit on the slides. Wear shoes. Paths are relatively easy on bare feet, but there's a lot of ground to cover. If you have tender feet, wear your shoes as you move around the park, removing them when you raft, slide, or go into the water. Shops in the parks sell sandals, "Reef Runners," and other protective footwear that can be worn in and out of the water.

5. What to Bring.   You will need a towel, suntan lotion, and money. Since wallets and purses get in the way, lock them in your car's trunk or leave them at your hotel. Carry enough money for the day and your Disney resort ID (if you have one) in a plastic bag or Tupperware container. Though nowhere is completely safe, we felt very comfortable hiding our plastic money bags in our cooler. Nobody disturbed our stuff, and our cash was much easier to reach than if we'd stashed it in a locker across the park. If you're carrying a wad or you worry about money anyway, rent the locker.

A Canadian reader offers another option if you don't feel comfortable stashing your valuables:

> As our admission was from a Park Hopper Plus ticket, I was concerned about our multiday passes being stolen or lost, yet I didn't want the hassle of a locker. Once inside, I noticed several guests wearing small

*plastic boxes on strings around their necks, and was pleased to find
these for sale in the gift shop. They are waterproof and available in
two sizes for around $5, with the smallest being just big enough for
passes/credit cards and a bit of money. I would have spent nearly as
much on locker rental, so I was able to enjoy the rest of the day with
peace of mind and also have it for future days at water parks or the
community pool at home.*

6. What Not to Bring.   Personal swim gear (fins, masks, rafts, etc.)
aren't allowed. Everything you need is either provided or available to rent.
If you forget your towel, you can rent one (cheap!). If you forget your
swimsuit or lotion, they're for sale. Personal flotation devices (life jackets)
are available free of charge, but you must leave a credit card number or a
driver's license as a deposit (held until the equipment is returned).

7. Admissions.   Purchase your admission in advance or about 45 minutes before official opening time. If you're staying at a Disney property,
you may be entitled to an admission discount; bring your hotel or campground ID. Guests staying five or more days should consider the Park
Hopper Plus or Ultimate Park Hopper Passes, which include admission
to all Disney swimming parks.

8. Lockers.   Rental lockers are $5 per day for a small one and $7 per
day for large, of which $2 is refunded when you return your key. Small
lockers are roomy enough for one person or a couple, but a family will
generally need a large locker. Though you can access your locker freely all
day, not all lockers are conveniently located.

Getting a locker at Blizzard Beach or Typhoon Lagoon is truly competitive. When the gates open, guests race to the locker rental desk. Once
there, the rental procedure is somewhat slow. If you aren't among the first
in line, you can waste a lot of time waiting to be served. We recommend
you skip the locker. Carry only as much cash as you will need for the day
in a watertight container you can stash in your cooler. Ditto for personal
items including watches and eyeglasses. With planning, you can manage
nicely without the locker and save time and hassle in the bargain.

9. Tubes.   Tubes for bobbing on the waves, floating in the creeks, and
riding the tube slides are available for free.

10. Getting Settled.   Establish your base for the day. There are many
beautiful sunning and lounging spots scattered throughout all Disney
swimming parks. Arrive early, and you can almost have your pick. The
breeze is best along the beaches of the surf pools at Blizzard Beach and
Typhoon Lagoon. At Typhoon Lagoon, if there are children younger
than six in your party, choose an area to the left of Mount Mayday (ship
on top) near the children's swimming area.

Also available are flat lounges (nonadjustable) and chairs (better for reading), shelters for guests who prefer shade, picnic tables, and a few hammocks.

The best spectator sport at Typhoon Lagoon is the bodysurfing in the surf pool. It's second only to being out there yourself. With this in mind, position yourself to have an unobstructed view of the waves.

11. A Word about the Slides. Water slides come in many shapes and sizes. Some are steep and vertical, some long and undulating. Some resemble corkscrews; others imitate the pool-and-drop nature of whitewater streams. Depending on the slide, swimmers ride mats, inner tubes, or rafts. On body slides, swimmers slosh to the bottom on the seat of their pants.

Modern traffic engineering bows to old-fashioned queuing. At water slides, it's one person, one raft (or tube) at a time, and the swimmer on deck can't go until the person preceding him is safely out of the way. Thus, the slide's hourly capacity is limited compared to the continuously loading rides in the major theme parks. Because a certain interval between swimmers is required for safety, the only way to increase capacity is to increase the number of slides and rapids rides.

Though Typhoon Lagoon and Blizzard Beach are huge parks with many slides, they're overwhelmed almost daily by armies of guests. If your main reason for going to Typhoon Lagoon or Blizzard Beach is the slides, and you hate long lines, be among the first guests to enter the park. Go directly to the slides and ride as many times as you can before the park fills. When lines for the slides become intolerable, head for the surf or wave pool, or the tube-floating streams.

For maximum speed on a body slide, cross your legs at the ankles and cross your arms over your chest. When you take off, arch your back so almost all of your weight is on your shoulder blades and heels (the less contact with the surface, the less resistance). Steer by shifting most of your upper-body weight onto one shoulder blade. For top speed on turns, weight the shoulder blade on the outside of each curve. If you want to go slow (what's the point?), distribute your weight equally as if you were lying on your back in bed. For curving slides, maximize speed by hitting the entrance to each curve high and exiting the curve low.

Some slides and rapids have a minimum height requirement. Riders for Humunga Kowabunga at Typhoon Lagoon and for Slush Gusher and Summit Plummet at Blizzard Beach, for example, must be four feet tall. Pregnant women and persons with back problems or other health difficulties shouldn't ride.

12. Floating Streams. Disney's Blizzard Beach and Typhoon Lagoon and the independent Water Mania and Wet 'n' Wild offer mellow floating streams. A great idea, the floating streams are long, tranquil, inner-tube rides that give you the illusion that you're doing something while you're being sedentary. For wimps, wussies, and exhausted people of all ages, floating streams are an answered prayer.

Disney's streams flow ever so slowly around the entire park, through caves, beneath waterfalls, past gardens, and under bridges. They offer a relaxing alternative to touring a park on foot.

Floating streams can be reached from several put-in and take-out points. There are never lines; just wade into the creek and plop into one of the inner tubes floating by. Ride the gentle current all the way around or get out at any exit. If you lie back and go with the flow, it will take 30–35 minutes to float the full circuit.

Predictably, there will be guests on whom the subtlety of floating streams is lost. They will be racing, screaming, and splashing. Let them pass, stopping a few moments, if necessary, to distance yourself from them.

13. Lunch.   If you didn't bring a picnic, you can buy food. Portions are adequate to generous; quality is comparable to fast-food chains; and prices (as you would expect) are a bit high.

14. More Options.   If you really are a water puppy, consider returning to your hotel for a heat-of-the-day nap and coming back to the water park for some early-evening swimming. Special lighting after dusk makes Typhoon Lagoon and Blizzard Beach enchanting. Crowds tend to be lighter in the evening. If you leave the park and want to return, be sure to keep your admission ticket and have your hand stamped. If you're staying in a hotel served by Disney buses, older children can return on their own to the water parks, giving Mom and Dad a little private quiet time.

15. Bad Weather.   Thunderstorms are common in Florida. During summer afternoons, such storms can be a daily occurrence. Water parks close during a storm. Most storms, however, are short lived, allowing the water park to resume normal operations. If a storm is severe and prolonged, it can cause a great deal of inconvenience. In addition to the park's closing, guests compete aggressively for shelter, and Disney resort guests may have to compete for seats on a bus back to the hotel.

We recommend you monitor the local weather forecast the day before you go, checking again in the morning before leaving for the water park. Scattered thundershowers are to be expected, but moving storm fronts are to be avoided. Because Florida is so flat, approaching weather can be seen from atop the slide platforms at the swimming parks. Particularly if you're dependent on Disney buses, leave the park earlier, rather than later, when you see a storm moving in.

16. Endurance.   The water parks are large and require almost as much walking as one of the theme parks. Add to this wave surfing, swimming, and all the climbing required to reach the slides, and you'll be pooped by day's end. Unless you spend your hours like a lizard on a rock, don't expect to return to the hotel with a lot of energy. Consider something low-key for the evening. You probably will want to hit the hay early.

17. Lost Children and Lost Adults. It's as easy to lose a child or become separated from your party at one of the water parks as it is at a major theme park. Upon arrival, pick a very specific place to meet in the event you are separated. If you split up on purpose, set times for checking in. Lost-children stations at the water parks are so out of the way that neither you nor your lost child will find them without help from a Disney employee. Explain to your children how to recognize a Disney employee (by their distinctive name tags) and how to ask for help.

Part Fifteen

Beyond the Parks

Downtown Disney

Downtown Disney is a shopping, dining, and entertainment development strung out along the banks of the Buena Vista Lagoon. On the far right is the Downtown Disney Marketplace (formerly known as the Disney Village Marketplace). In the middle is the gated (admission required) Pleasure Island nighttime entertainment, and on the far left is Disney's West Side.

Downtown Disney Marketplace

Although the Marketplace offers interactive fountains, a couple of playgrounds, a Lagoon-side amphitheater, and watercraft rentals, it is primarily a shopping and dining venue. The centerpiece of shopping is the **World of Disney,** the largest Disney trademark merchandise store in the world. If you can't find what you are looking for in this 38,000-square-foot Noah's Ark of Disney stuff, it probably doesn't exist. **Pooh Corner** is an entire store devoted to Pooh merchandise. Another noteworthy retailer is the **LEGO Imagination Center,** showcasing a number of huge and unbelievable sculptures made entirely of LEGO "bricks." Spaceships, sea serpents, sleeping tourists, and dinosaurs are just a few of the sculptures on display. **Once Upon a Toy** is a toys, games, and collectibles superstore. Rounding out the selection are stores specializing in resort wear, athletic attire and gear, Christmas decorations, Disney art and collectibles, and handmade craft items. Most retail establishments are open from 9:30 a.m. until 11:30 p.m. Detailed coverage of shopping opportunities can be found in Part Sixteen, Shopping in and out of Walt Disney World (page 683).

Rainforest Café is the headliner restaurant at the Marketplace. There is also **Cap'n Jack's Restaurant, Wolfgang Puck Express,** a soda fountain, a gourmet sandwich shop, and a **McDonald's.** Full-service restaurants are profiled in Part Nine, Dining in and around Walt Disney World (page 337).

Pleasure Island

Pleasure Island is a nighttime entertainment complex. Shops and restaurants, formerly open throughout the day with no admission charge, are now open exclusively in the evening. Detailed coverage of the nightspots is provided in Part Seventeen, Nightlife in and out of Walt Disney World (page 705). Pleasure Island's shops offer more Disney art, casual fashions, Disney character merchandise, movie collectibles, and music memorabilia. **Superstar Studios** is a recording studio where you can make your own music video. There are several full-service restaurants at Pleasure Island. **Fulton's Crab House** and the **Portobello Yacht Club** can be accessed at any time without paying admission to Pleasure Island.

Disney's West Side

The West Side is the newest addition to Downtown Disney and offers a broad range of entertainment, dining, and shopping. Restaurants include the **House of Blues,** which serves Cajun specialties; **Planet Hollywood,** offering movie memorabilia and basic American fare; **Bongo's Cuban Café,** serving Cuban favorites; and **Wolfgang Puck Express,** featuring California cuisine. All four West Side restaurants are profiled in Part Nine, Dining in and around Walt Disney World (page 337).

West Side shopping is some of the most interesting in Walt Disney World. For starters, there's a **Virgin** (records and books) **Megastore.** Across the street is the **Guitar Gallery by George's Music,** specializing in custom, collector, rare, and unique guitars. Other shops include a cigar shop, a rock-and-roll and movie memorabilia store, and a designer eyewear studio.

In the entertainment department, there is **DisneyQuest,** an interactive theme park contained in a building; the **House of Blues,** a concert and dining venue; and a 24-screen **AMC** movie theater. The West Side is also home to Cirque du Soleil's *La Nouba,* an amazing production show with a cast of almost 100 performers and musicians. The House of Blues concert hall and *La Nouba* are described in Part Seventeen, Nightlife in and out of Walt Disney World (page 705). DisneyQuest is described in detail below.

DisneyQuest

For more than a decade, major theme parks have experimented with attractions based on motion-simulation and virtual-reality technologies. Among other things, these technologies have allowed thrill rides with the punch of a roller coaster to be engineered and operated in spaces as small as a one-car garage. Analogous to the computer industry, where the power of a bulky mainframe is now available in a laptop, Disney is pioneering the concept of a theme park in a box, or in the case of DisneyQuest, a modest five-story building.

Opened in the summer of 1998 in the West Side area of Downtown Disney, DisneyQuest contains all the elements of the larger Disney theme parks. There is an entrance area that facilitates your transition into the park environment and leads to the gateways of four distinct themed lands, here referred to as zones. As at other Disney parks, almost everything is included in the price of your admission.

It takes about two to five hours to experience DisneyQuest, once you get in, depending on the crowd. Disney claims that it limits the number of guests admitted to ensure that each person has a positive experience. Right, so does the Super Bowl, and that's about how big the crowd feels much of the time at DisneyQuest. Once DisneyQuest hits capacity, newly arriving guests are lined up outside to wait until departing guests make some room. Weekday mornings are the least crowded times to visit.

DisneyQuest, in concept and attraction mix, is aimed at a youthful audience, say 8–35 years of age, though younger and older patrons will enjoy much of what it offers. The feel is dynamic, bustling, and noisy. Those who haunt the video arcades at shopping malls will feel most at home at DisneyQuest. And like at most malls, when late afternoon turns to evening, the median age at DisneyQuest also rises toward adolescents and teens who have been released from parental supervision for awhile.

You begin your experience in the Departure Lobby, adjacent to admission sales. From the Departure Lobby you enter a "Cyberlator," a "transitional attraction" (read: elevator) hosted by the genie from *Aladdin,* that delivers you to an entrance plaza called Ventureport. From here you can enter the four zones. Like in the larger parks, each zone is distinctively themed. Some zones cover more than one floor, so, looking around, you can see things going on both above and below you. The four zones, in no particular order, are **Explore Zone, Score Zone, Create Zone,** and **Replay Zone.** In addition to the zones, DisneyQuest offers two restaurants and the inevitable gift shop.

Though most kids and adolescents aren't going to care, the zone layout at DisneyQuest may confuse adults trying to orient themselves. Don't count on trapping certain kids in certain zones either, or planning a rendezvous inside one without designating a specific location. Each zone spreads out over multiple levels, with stairways, elevators, slides, and walkways linking them in a variety of ways. Still, as we said, the labyrinthine design of the place won't bother most youngsters, who are usually happy just to wander (or dash madly) between games and rides.

Admission to DisneyQuest is $32 for adults, $26 for children. For more information, call (407) 828-4600.

Explore Zone

The gateway to Explore Zone is the tiger's-head cave from *Aladdin.* You can descend to the attractions area on a 150-foot corkscrew slide or use more traditional means like elevators or ramps. The headline attraction in Explore Zone is the **Virtual Jungle Cruise,** where you paddle a six-person raft. The raft is a motion simulator perched on top of blue air bags that replicate the motion of water. Responding to the film of the river projected before you, you can choose among several routes through the rapids. The motion simulator responds to sensors on your paddle, so the ride you experience simulates the course you choose. As if navigating the river isn't enough, man-eating dinosaurs and a cataclysmic comet are tossed in for good measure. In **Treasure of the Incas,** you pilot a miniature vehicle through a maze in search of hidden treasure. Another Explore Zone attraction, **Aladdin's Magic Carpet Ride,** is a virtual-reality trip through the streets of Agrabah. On **Pirates of the Caribbean,** you fight pirates attacking your ship. The entire battle takes place in 3-D on a motion-base platform, which shudders with every hit by the pirates' cannonballs.

Score Zone

Here you pass through a slash in a giant comic book to enter a theme area based on comic-book characters and competition. The big deal here are enlarged, high-tech versions of electronic and video games where you pit your skill and reflexes against other players. The headliner is **Mighty Ducks Pinball Slam,** where you stand atop a mammoth hockey puck. By manipulating a joystick, you control the motion of your puck as it bounces around a virtual-reality pinball machine. In **Ride the Comix,** you once again don virtual-reality headgear to ride off into comic book scenes and do battle with archvillains.

Create Zone

A digital artist's palette serves as the entrance to Create Zone. Featured here is **CyberSpace Mountain,** an attraction where you can design your own roller coaster—including 360-degree loops—and then go for a virtual-reality motion-simulator ride on your creation. Also in the Create Zone are **Animation Academy,** a sort of crash tutorial on Disney animation, and **Magic Mirror,** where you can perform virtual plastic surgery on yourself. Other creative attractions include painting on an electronic canvas and designing your own toy.

Replay Zone

Replay Zone draws its theme from a 1950s view of the future. Basically, it's three levels of classic midway games with a few futuristic twists. The balls on the **Skeeball** games, for example, glow in the dark. Winners of the various games earn redemption tickets, which can be redeemed for midway-type prizes. The pièce de résistance of Replay Zone is **Buzz Lightyear's Astro Blasters,** a fancy version of bumper cars. Here guests pilot two-person bumper bubbles that suck up grapefruit-sized balls from the floor and fire them from an air cannon at other vehicles. Direct hits cause the other vehicles to spin momentarily out of control.

Reader response to DisneyQuest is very mixed, as evidenced by the following comments.

From a Kendall Park, New Jersey, mother of two:

DisneyQuest was a huge letdown. There were tremendous waits inside and outside.

And from a Pennsylvania family with kids ages 11 and 13:

Our only really big disappointment was DisneyQuest. What a rip-off! My husband and daughters paid $32 to get in because the guy at the window told us that fee covered nearly all the experiences. Once inside, they found that at least half the stuff they wanted to do cost mega-extrabucks. Also, my youngest child, at 50", was one inch too short for the two rides she most wanted to try. Nowhere outside is any of this explained. It's truly an offensive deal for people who have already spent scads in their darned parks. I plan to write and let them know what I think of such tactics.

For a family of five from Cleveland, Ohio, DisneyQuest was a slam dunk:

Your description and reader feedback had us a little skeptical. But with another cold day on hand, we gave it a shot. If you have right brain (creative) kids, you can't miss. Your book said two to three hours for DQ. We had dinner reservations that forced a cutoff at seven hours, otherwise we could have pulled an all-nighter with them! Forget the arcade stuff; our kids focused on the Create Zone. The interactive stuff was fascinating. I think DQ provides parents the best chance to see their kids' brains and personalities in action, since it's so interactive.

A Lebanon, Tennessee, mom shares her experience:

A word of caution about the virtual reality games (especially the Aladdin game). They will make you NAUSEOUS! I was so sick after that dumb game that I literally had to put my head between my knees for upwards of 10 minutes. Yuck!

On an upnote, the Pirates of the Caribbean game was a BLAST and didn't make us sick at all, and the Create Zone 'face morphing' game was the most hilarious part of our trip! There is also a great 'toy making' game in that zone that allows you to create your own toy and then buy it if you like. Of course, most of the creations end up looking like Sid's toys from Toy Story, but that might be what makes it so fun.

This warning from a Centerville, Ohio, mom is good advice:

We went on a Saturday night. Don't do this!!! It is the hangout for local teens and young adults. It was packed. While having lots of neat stuff, [it] was too crowded with teens for our kids to do the best [things].

Finally, a family from Columbia, Maryland, offers this advice to parents with babies and toddlers:

Alert your readers to bring a baby carrier/backpack to DisneyQuest. You're there for several hours, and absolutely no strollers are allowed in the entire building.

Disney's Wide World of Sports

Disney's Wide World of Sports complex is a 200-acre, state-of-the-art competition and training complex consisting of a 7,500-seat ballpark, a fieldhouse, and dedicated venues for baseball, softball, tennis, track and field, beach volleyball, and 27 other sports. From Little League Baseball to rugby to beach volleyball, the complex hosts a mind-boggling calendar of professional and amateur competitions, with one or more events scheduled nearly every day.

During late winter and early spring, the complex is the spring training home of the Atlanta Braves. Although Disney guests are welcome at the sports complex as paid spectators (prices vary according to event), none of the facilities are available for guests unless they are participants in a scheduled, organized competition. To learn what events are scheduled during your visit, call (407) 939-1289.

In addition to scheduled competitive events, a program called the **NFL Experience** is operated daily from 11 a.m. until about 5 p.m. Appealing primarily to school-age boys, the NFL Experience is a supervised activity that allows kids to kick field goals, catch and throw passes, catch punts, and run through a small obstacle course, among other things. Though the NFL Experience is sometimes the only thing going on at the Wide World of Sports complex, Disney nevertheless charges full admission ($11 adults, $8 children ages 3–9). Our advice is to pass on the Wide World of Sports unless there is a specific event you want to see. Call the sports complex directly to confirm event times and venues (as opposed to trusting Disney Guest Relations personnel at the theme parks or hotels).

Counter-service and full-service dining are available at the sports complex, but there's no on-site lodging. Disney's Wide World of Sports is off Osceola Parkway, at the intersection of Victoria Way. The complex has its own parking lot and is accessible via the Disney Transportation System.

The Disney Wilderness Preserve

Located about 40–60 minutes south of Walt Disney World is the Disney Wilderness Preserve, a real wetlands restoration area operated by the Nature Conservancy in partnership with Disney. At 12,000 acres, this is as real as Disney gets. There are hiking trails, an interpretive center, and guided outings on weekends. Trails wind through grassy savannas, beneath ancient cypress trees, and along the banks of pristine Lake Russell. The preserve is open daily from 9 a.m. to 5 p.m., and general admission is $3 for adults and $2 for children ages 6–17. Guided trail walks are offered on Saturday at no extra cost, and "buggy" rides are available on Sunday afternoon. The buggy in question is a mammoth amphibious contraption, and the rides last a few hours. The buggy ride is $10 for adults and $5 for children ages 6–17; reservations are highly recommended. *Note:* Disney Information doesn't know anything about the wilderness preserve, including the fact that it exists. For information and directions, call the preserve directly at (407) 935-0002. Finally, we, *Unofficials,* love the place; it's a delightful change of pace from the artificiality of the theme parks. And as for the buggy ride, it could possibly be the high point of your Disney vacation.

Walt Disney World Speedway

Adjacent to the Transportation and Ticket Center parking lot, the one-mile tri-oval course is host to several races each year. Between competitions, it's home to the **Richard Petty Driving Experience,** where you can ride in a two-seater stock car for $99 or learn to drive one. Courses are by reservation only and cost between $379 (8 laps), $749 (18 laps), and $1,249 (30 laps). You must be age 18 or older, have a valid driver's license, and know how to drive a stick shift to take a course. For information, call (800) 237-3889 or check out **www.1800bepetty.com.**

Walt Disney World Recreation

Most Walt Disney World guests never make it beyond the theme parks, the water parks, and Downtown Disney. Those who do, however, discover an extraordinary selection of recreational opportunities ranging from guided fishing expeditions and water-skiing outings to hayrides, horseback riding, fitness-center workouts, and miniature golf. If it's something you can do at a resort, it's probably available at Walt Disney World.

Boat, bike, and fishing equipment rentals are handled on an hourly basis. Just show up at the rental office during operating hours and they'll fix you up. The same goes for various fitness centers in the resort hotels. Golf, tennis, fishing expeditions, water-ski excursions, hayrides, trail rides, and most spa services must be scheduled in advance. Though every resort features an extensive selection of recreational options, those resorts located on a navigable body of water offer the greatest variety. Also, the more upscale a resort, the more likely it is to have such amenities as a fitness center and spa. In addition, you can rent boats and other recreational equipment at the Marketplace in Downtown Disney.

Walt Disney World Golf

Walt Disney World has six golf courses, all expertly designed and meticulously maintained. The **Magnolia,** the **Palm,** and the **Oak Trail** are across Floridian Way from the Polynesian Resort. They envelop the Shades of Green recreational complex, and the pro shops and support facilities adjoin the Shades of Green hotel (for military personnel and retirees only). **Lake Buena Vista Golf Course** is at Saratoga Springs, near the Downtown Disney Marketplace and across the lake from Pleasure Island. The **Osprey Ridge** and **Eagle Pines** courses are part of the Bonnet Creek Golf Club near the Fort Wilderness Campground. In addition to the golf courses, there are driving ranges and putting greens at each location.

Oak Trail is a nine-hole course for beginners. The other five courses are designed for the mid-handicap player and, while interesting, are quite forgiving. All courses are popular, with morning tee times at a premium, especially January–April. To avoid the crowds, play on a Monday, Tuesday, or Wednesday, and sign up for a late-afternoon tee time.

Peak season for all courses is September–April; off-season is May–August. Off-season and afternoon twilight rates are available. Carts are required (except at Oak Trail) and are included in the greens fee. Tee times may be reserved 60 days in advance by Disney resort guests, 30 days in advance for day guests with a credit card, and 7 days in advance without guarantee. Proper golf attire is required: collared shirt and Bermuda-length shorts or slacks.

Besides the ability to book tee times further in advance, guests of Walt Disney World–owned resorts get other benefits that may sway a golfer's lodging decision. These include discounted greens fees, charge privileges, and the shipping of your clubs between facilities, if, say, you are playing the Lake Buena Vista course one day and a course at one of the other two golf facilities the next. The single most important, and least known, benefit is the provision of free round-trip taxi transportation between the golf courses and your hotel, which lets you avoid moving your car or dragging your clubs on Disney buses. The cabs, which make access to the courses much simpler, are paid by vouchers happily supplied to hotel guests.

Palm Golf Course ★★★★

1950 West Magnolia/Palm Drive, Lake Buena Vista, FL 32830; (407) WDW-GOLF

Established 1970 **Designer** Joe Lee **Status** Resort

Fees Resort guest $94–$99, day visitor $99–$1,119, twilight special $55–$60

Facilities Pro shop, driving range, practice green, locker rooms, snack bar, beverage cart, and club and shoe rentals

Tees   *Blue* 6,957 yards, par 72, USGA 73.0, slope 133

       White 6,461 yards, par 72, USGA 70.7, slope 129

Gold 6,029 yards, par 72, USGA 68.7, slope 124

Red 5,311 yards, par 72, USGA 70.4, slope 124

Comments   The Palm is Disney's best course, with lesser-known architect Joe Lee showing up the marquee designers that headline the Bonnet Creek Golf Club. Home to the Disney/Oldsmobile Classic PGA Tour event, it has numerous lakes coming into play on nine holes, and sand everywhere, with 94 hazards. The highlight, however, is a set of excellent greens, a real surprise, given the heavy volume of play. The defining characteristic is a set of holes where water separates tees from landing areas and landing areas from greens, a wet take on desert-style target golf. The signature 18th, with its island green, caps a fine set of finishing holes and has been ranked as high as fourth in difficulty among all holes on the PGA Tour's many venues. But four sets of well-spaced tees make the course playable for all abilities, and along with its sister course Magnolia, the facility boasts a multilevel natural-grass practice range that is among the largest in the nation.

Magnolia Golf Course   ★★★½

1950 West Magnolia/Palm Drive, Lake Buena Vista, FL 32830; (407) WDW-GOLF

Established 1970 **Designer** Joe Lee **Status** Resort
Fees Resort guest $94–$139, day visitor $99–$144, twilight special $55–$65
Facilities: Pro shop, driving range, practice green, locker rooms, sports bar, beverage cart, and club and shoe rentals
Tees   *Blue* 7,190 yards, par 72, USGA 73.9, slope 133

White 6,642 yards, par 72, USGA 71.6, slope 128

Gold 6,091 yards, par 72, USGA 69.1, slope 123

Red 5,253 yards, par 72, USGA 70.5, slope 123

Comments   Another fine Joe Lee creation, Magnolia shares its best traits with the Palm, including excellent greens, practice facilities, a dramatic finishing sequence, and plenty of water. From the back tees it is Disney's longest course and features a whopping 97 bunkers, including the famous one in the shape of Mickey Mouse's head. But the layout is slightly less challenging than the Palm, with no water on most of the par-3s. Like the Palm, this course hosts the Disney/Oldsmobile Classic.

Osprey Ridge Golf Course   ★★★½

3451 Golf View Drive, Lake Buena Vista, FL 32830; (407) WDW-GOLF

Established 1992 **Designer** Tom Fazio **Status** Resort
Fees Resort guest $114–$174, day visitor $119–$179, twilight special $70–$80
Facilities Pro shop, driving range, practice green, locker rooms, Sand Trap Bar and Grill, beverage cart, and club and shoe rentals
Tees   *Black* 7,101 yards, par 72, USGA 73.9, slope 135

Silver 6,680 yards, par 72, USGA 71.8, slope 128

Gold 6,103 yards, par 72, USGA 68.9, slope 121

Red 5,402 yards, par 72, USGA 70.5, slope 122

Comments   This Tom Fazio layout is a thoroughly modern course that included a large amount of earth-moving in its construction. Its main characteristics are large rolling mounds and elevated tees and greens. The greens are huge, almost to the point of bizarre, making them easy to hit but leaving approaches at four-putt distances where you almost cannot hit the ball hard enough to get it to the hole.

Eagle Pines Golf Course ★★★½

3451 Golf View Drive, Lake Buena Vista, FL 32830; (407) WDW-GOLF

Established 1992 **Designer** Pete Dye **Status** Resort
Fees Resort guest $99–$144, day visitor $109–$154, twilight special $55–$65
Facilities Pro shop, driving range, practice green, locker rooms, Sand Trap Bar and Grill, beverage cart, banquet facilities, and club and shoe rentals
Tees *Black* 6,722 yards, par 72, USGA 72.3, slope 131
Silver 6,309 yards, par 72, USGA 69.9, slope 125
Gold 5,520 yards, par 72, USGA 66.3, slope 115
Red 4,838 yards, par 72, USGA 68, slope 111

Comments In contrast to neighboring Osprey Ridge, Pete Dye crafted a course reminiscent of the Carolina Sandhills, with fairways lined with native grasses and flanked by waste areas of straw and sand. Dish-shaped greens are at or below the levels of the fairway, emphasizing well-struck approach shots to hold the putting surfaces. Water is in play on nearly every hole, and aesthetically, this is the most impressive of the Disney courses with the mix of sand, straw, lush-green fairways, and blue lakes. It is also forgiving for a Dye course, since the waste areas act as buffers to stop errant shots before they reach the water.

Lake Buena Vista Golf Course ★★★

2200 Club Lake Drive, Lake Buena Vista, FL 32830; (407) WDW-GOLF

Established 1971 **Designer** Joe Lee **Status** Resort
Fees Resort guest $94–$99, day visitor $99–$119, twilight special $55–$60
Facilities Pro shop, driving range, practice green, locker rooms, snack bar, beverage cart, and club and shoe rentals
Tees *Blue* 6,819 yards, par 72, USGA 72.7, slope 128
White 6,268 yards, par 72, USGA 70.1, slope 123
Gold 5,919 yards, par 72, USGA 68.2, slope 120
Red 5,194 yards, par 73, USGA 69.4, slope 120

Comments As with the other Joe Lee courses, there are several memorable holes here, and the greens are in fine shape. But this layout is the only one at Disney with housing on it—a lot of housing—which detracts from the golf experience. The course is geographically unique among the other layouts, tucked behind Saratoga Springs, and has a swampy feel reminiscent of the area's pre-Disney everglades with trees dripping Spanish moss. Narrow fairways and small greens emphasize accuracy over length.

Oak Trail Golf Course ★★½

1950 West Magnolia/Palm Drive, Lake Buena Vista, FL 32830; (407) WDW-GOLF

Established 1980 **Designer** Ron Garl **Status** Resort
Fees Resort guest $38; child $20. Includes use of a pull-cart (course is walking only).

To replay the course costs an additional $19 for adults and $10 for children.

Facilities Pro shop, driving range, practice green, locker rooms, sports bar, beverage cart, and club and shoe rentals

Tees   White 2,913 yards, par 36

Red 2,532 yards, par 36

Comments   This Ron Garl nine-holer is a "real" course, not an executive par-3 like many nine-hole designs. Geared towards introducing children to the game, it also makes a good quick-fix or warm-up before a round, and the walking-only layout is the only walkable routing at Walt Disney World.

Golf beyond Walt Disney World

The greater Orlando area has enough high-quality courses to rival better-known golfing Meccas such as Scottsdale and Palm Springs. But unlike these destinations with their endless private country clubs, Orlando is unique because almost all its courses are open for some sort of public play. Because of its easy airport access, wonderful climate, and good golf facilities (along with Florida's lack of a personal income tax), Orlando is the single most popular residence for PGA Tour players, including Tiger Woods, Mark O'Meara, Lee Janzen, Nick Faldo, and Ernie Els.

Of the many golf courses and resorts in the area, one stands head and shoulders above the rest, especially because it actually abuts Walt Disney World. Not only the location of this course is excellent—the sprawling 1,500-acre Hyatt Regency Grand Cypress is superb in every way, with top-notch golf, lodging, dining, grounds, and an enormous fantasy pool complex. One of the world's largest free-form pools, it includes waterfalls, caves, waterslides, and a swim-up grotto bar. The resort also hides a world-class equestrian center with riding and instruction for all abilities. But the standout feature is the golf, which would be worth a trip regardless of where the resort was located. The facilities are first rate, from the luxurious clubhouse with its free shoe shines to the computerized GPS systems on the carts. The golf club is also home to an excellent instructional facility, the Grand Cypress Academy of Golf. Because of the many amenities and the wonderful location, the Hyatt is one of the priciest resorts in Orlando, but since only guests can play the courses, consider making the investment.

Grand Cypress Golf Club, North/East/South Courses ★★★★½

One North Jacaranda, Orlando, FL 32836; (800) 835-7377 or (407) 239-1904

Established 1984 **Designer** Jack Nicklaus **Status** Resort (guests only)

Fees $175 ($115 in summer)

Facilities Pro shop, driving range, practice greens, locker rooms, restaurant, beverage cart, carts equipped with GPS, and club and shoe rentals.

Tees   North/South Tees

      Gold 6,993 yards, par 72, USGA 73.9, slope 130

      Blue 6,335 yards, par 72, USGA 70.7, slope 123

      White 5,823 yards, par 72, USGA 68.5, slope 121

      Red 5,332 yards, par 72, USGA 71.1, slope 119

      North/East Tees

      Gold 6,955 yards, par 72, USGA 73.9, slope 130

      Blue 6,294 yards, par 72, USGA 70.9, slope 124

      White 5,790 yards, par 72, USGA 68.6, slope 121

      Red 5,056 yards, par 72, USGA 69.1, slope 114

      South/East Tees

      Gold 6,906 yards, par 72, USGA 74.4, slope 132

      Blue 6,363 yards, par 72, USGA 71.6, slope 126

      White 5,789 yards, par 72, USGA 69.3, slope 123

      Red 5,130 yards, par 72, USGA 70.2, slope 123

Comments   While the unique Scottish aspect of the New Course and its position as the resort's marquee course make it more popular, the three Nicklaus Nines are actually better. This course can be played in three different 18-hole combinations, but the South is the very best nine at the resort, so try to book either North/South or South/East. The North/South combination hosted the LPGA Tournament of Champions from 1994 to 1996, as well as the PGA Tour Skills Challenge and the Shark Shootout. This course is one of the most beautiful in Orlando, and water is found on 13 of the holes, creating additional peril. There are many unique and interesting holes, several with true risk/reward choices such as shortcuts over lakes. The undulating greens are guarded by pot bunkers and grass depressions and are kept in superb shape. Unlike the New Course, you will have very few opportunities to bump and run the ball onto the green and will have to land the ball on the green with your approach.

Grand Cypress Golf Club, New Course ★★★★

One North Jacaranda, Orlando, FL 32836; (800) 835-7377 or (407) 239-1904

Established 1988 **Designer** Jack Nicklaus **Status** Resort (guests only)
Fees $175 ($115 in summer)
Facilities Pro shop, driving range, practice greens, locker rooms, restaurant, beverage cart, carts equipped with GPS, and club and shoe rentals.

Tees   *Black* 6,773 yards, par 72, USGA 72.1, slope 126

      White 6,181 yards, par 72, USGA 69.4, slope 117

      Red 5,314 yards, par 72, USGA 69.8, slope 117

Comments   The New Course is Jack Nicklaus's homage to the famous Old Course at St. Andrews, Scotland, the birthplace of golf. The first and last two holes are replicas of those at the Old Course, and other features such as the famous Swilcan Bridge and some of the huge bunkers are re-created here. In between are Nicklaus's original holes, done in a links style, with double greens, pot bunkers, tall rough, and wide, hard fairways. As on most Scottish links courses, there are no trees, and the wind will play havoc with your shots when it is blowing. If you've never had a chance to play Scottish courses, the New is a reasonable facsimile that captures the spirit and history of the sport's earliest form.

Other Standout Courses in Orlando

Among the many public courses throughout the area, a handful stand out and are worth leaving Walt Disney World to play. Although there are good-quality golf resorts such as Grenelefe and Mission Hills well outside Orlando, these are all quite convenient to the theme parks:

Championsgate

Three miles from Walt Disney World, and close to Celebration, lies one of the city's newest golf resorts. The complex includes an Omni hotel, but the centerpiece of the $800 million, 1,400-acre facility are the two Greg Norman–designed courses, which are open and worth a visit.

Championsgate International Course ★★★★

1400 Masters Boulevard, Championsgate, FL 33837; (888) 558-9301 or (407) 787-4653

Established 2001 **Designer** Greg Norman **Status** Public
Fees $85 resident ($52 summer), $99 nonresident ($75 summer)
Facilities Pro shop, driving range, practice greens, locker rooms, restaurant, beverage cart, and club and shoe rentals.
Tees   *Trophy* 7,363 yards, par 72, USGA 76.3, slope 143
      Legends 6,792 yards, par 72, USGA 73.7, slope 137
      Champions 6,239 yards, par 72, USGA 71.2, slope 132
      Heritage 5,518 yards, par 72, USGA 72.3, slope 117

Comments   The tougher and more highly ranked of the two layouts, the International lives up to its name by recreating the feel of the championship courses of the British Isles. Laid out in a links style, the course has carpet-like fairways framed by the stark unfinished look of brown dunes, mounds, and severe pot bunkers. From the tips, it is one of the state's most challenging courses, with Florida's highest USGA rating at 76.3.

Championsgate National Course ★★★½

1400 Masters Boulevard, Championsgate, FL 33837; (888) 558-9301 or (407) 787-4653

Established 2001 **Designer** Greg Norman **Status** Public
Fees $85 resident ($45 summer), $89 nonresident ($65 summer)
Facilities Pro shop, driving range, practice greens, locker rooms, restaurant, beverage cart, and club and shoe rentals.
Tees   *Trophy* 7,128 yards, par 70, USGA 75.1, slope 133
      Legends 6,427 yards, par 70, USGA 72.0, slope 126
      Champions 5,937 yards, par 70, USGA 70.9, slope 124
      Heritage 5,150 yards, par 70, USGA 69.8, slope 111

Comments: The kinder, gentler course at Championsgate, the National is a resort-style layout, which ambles through 200-acres of citrus groves in a traditional parkland routing with far less water than the International. Deep greens welcome bump-and-run shots, and the length is manageable from every set of tees.

Orange County National

Five miles south of Disney in Winter Garden lies Orlando's premier daily-fee public facility, winner of numerous industry awards and consistently named among the nation's top public golf clubs by most golf publications. The 45 holes and one of the country's best practice facilities occupy nearly 1,000 verdant acres, with no homes or other distractions, just pure golf. It is also easily the region's best value, and on-site lodging packages run just $92–$101 per night in peak season, including lodging, a round of golf, and free play on the nine-hole course. The par-29 executive Tooth Course is well maintained and has a surprising variety of holes and water hazards for a short course, offering a very satisfying golf fix for those in a hurry. For more information, visit **www.ocngolf.com.**

Panther Lake ★★★★½

16301 Phil Ritson Way, Winter Garden, FL 34787; (888) 727-3672 or (407) 656-2626

Established 1997 **Designer** Phil Ritson and David Harmon **Status** Public
Fees $70–$110 (including lunch and $10 merchandise credit)
Facilities Lodging, pro shop, driving range, practice greens, locker rooms, restaurant, beverage cart, and club and shoe rentals.
Tees Tour 7,295 yards, par 72, USGA 75.7, slope 137
Championship 6,816 yards, par 72, USGA 73.2, slope 132
Member/Guest 6,298 yards, par 72, USGA 70.7, slope 128
Forward 5,073 yards, par 72, USGA 71.5, slope 125

Comments Panther Lake was the nation's first course designed to showcase 18 signature holes, and no expense was spared to make the course beautiful, just as none is spared to keep it in excellent condition. The front nine is carved from Florida wetlands with water at every turn, while the much different back has a Carolinas-like style with surprising elevation changes, stands of pines and oaks, and hard to hold greens emphasizing accuracy. While both courses here are excellent, the sheer beauty makes Panther Lake the first choice for those without time to play both.

Crooked Cat ★★★★

16301 Phil Ritson Way, Winter Garden, FL 34787; (888) 727-3672 or (407) 656-2626

Established 1997 **Designer** Phil Ritson and David Harmon **Status** Public
Fees $70–$95 (including lunch and $10 merchandise credit)
Facilities Lodging, pro shop, driving range, practice greens, locker rooms, restaurant, beverage cart, and club and shoe rentals.
Tees Tour 7,277 yards, par 72, USGA 75.4, slope 140
Championship 6,748 yards, par 72, USGA 72.9, slope 134
Member/Guest 6,035 yards, par 72, USGA 69.3, slope 121
Forward 5,5236 yards, par 72, USGA 70.3, slope 120

Comments Variety is the spice of life, and this partner to the very modern Panther Lake is a throwback to Scottish-style links courses, with few trees, wide fairways, and heather mixed in the rough. Large sloped greens welcome bump-and-run shots, but are protected by deep bunkers of both grass and sand. It is as well maintained as its sibling.

The Best of the Rest

Arnold Palmer's Bay Hill Club & Lodge   ★★★★

9000 Bay Hill Boulevard, Orlando, FL 32819; (888) 422-9445 or (407) 876-2429

Established 1961   **Designer** Dick Wilson   **Status** Resort
Fees $228 (resort guests only); with membership: resident, free; nonresident, $45
Facilities Lodging, pro shop, driving range, practice greens, locker rooms, restaurant, beverage cart, and club and shoe rentals.
Tees   *Palmer* 7,114 yards, par 72, USGA 74.6, slope 141
       Championship 6,586 yards, par 72, USGA 71.8, slope 127
       Men's 6,198 yards, par 72, USGA 70.2, slope 124
       Ladies 5,192 yards, par 72, USGA 72.3, slope 133

Comments   Bay Hill is famous in the golf world as the home club of the King, Arnold Palmer, and is the site of his Bay Hill Invitational each year. The irony is that Palmer's club was built 40 years ago, before Palmer himself became a brand-name golf-course designer, yet the Dick Wilson layout remains equal to or better than anything Palmer has managed on his own. When he is in town, which is most of the time, Palmer makes a point of stopping by the clubhouse daily, and half the attraction of staying and playing here is to see him. The other half is the course. It is comprised of three nines, but it is the Challenger and Champion combination that is the most popular and the one on which the PGA Tour event is played. This combo starts off with a roar, featuring the toughest opening hole on the PGA Tour, a 414-yard par-4 uphill, dogleg left that is heavily bunkered, both in the fairway and around the green. The course ends in similar fashion with one of the toughest closers around, but in between are lots of gentler birdie opportunities. Variety, class, and tradition are the mainstays of Bay Hill.

Metrowest Country Club   ★★★½

2100 S. Hiawassee Road, Orlando, FL 32835; (407) 299-1099

Established 1987   **Designer** Robert Trent Jones, Jr.   **Status** Public
Fees $74–$94
Facilities Pro shop, driving range, practice greens, locker rooms, restaurant, beverage cart, and club and shoe rentals.
Tee   *Blue* 7,051 yards, par 72, USGA 71.7, slope 127
      White 6,467 yards, par 72, USGA 70.3, slope 122
      Red 5,978 yards, par 72, USGA 68.2, slope 117
      Ladies 5,325 yards, par 72, USGA 71.1, slope 110

Comments   Fans of Robert Trent Jones, Jr. will recognize the use of water hazards to make holes more dramatic, such as on approaches to peninsula greens. But there is less water than he usually uses, and far less than on most Florida courses. The result is a less-penal test, with a lower slope and rating than most upscale area layouts. The strength of the course, which is a local favorite, is its variety, mixing doglegs, elevation changes, and interesting green complexes with the wide fairways that make it fun to play.

Miniature Golf

Years ago, the Disney Intelligence Patrol (DIP) noticed that as many as 113 guests a day were sneaking out of Walt Disney World to play Goofy Golf. Applying the logic of the boy who jammed his finger in the dike, Disney feared a hemorrhage of patrons from the theme parks. The thought of those truant guests making instant millionaires of miniature-golf entrepreneurs on International Drive was enough to give a fat mouse ulcers.

The response to this assault on Disney's market share was **Fantasia Gardens Miniature Golf,** an 11-acre complex with two 18-hole dink-and-putt golf courses. One course is an "adventure" course, themed after Disney's animated film *Fantasia.* The other course, geared more toward older children and adults, is an innovative approach-and-putt course with sand traps and water hazards.

Fantasia Gardens is beautifully landscaped and creatively executed. There are fountains, animated statues, topiaries, flower beds, and a multitude of other imponderables that you're unlikely to find at most putt-putt courses.

Fantasia Gardens is on Epcot Resort Boulevard, across the street from the Walt Disney World Swan. To reach Fantasia Gardens via Disney transportation, take a bus or boat to the Swan resort.

The cost to putt at this course is $10.65 for adults and $8.50 for children. If you arrive hungry or naked, Fantasia Gardens has a snack bar and a gift shop. For more information, call (407) WDW-GOLF.

In 1999, Disney opened **Winter Summerland,** a second miniature-golf facility located next to the Blizzard Beach water park. Winter Summerland offers two 18-hole courses—one has a blizzard in Florida theme, while the other sports a tropical holiday theme. The Winter Summerland courses are much easier than the Fantasia courses, which makes them a better choice for families with pre-teen children. It's open daily, 10 a.m.–11 p.m., and the cost is the same as for Fantasia Gardens.

Part Sixteen

Shopping in and out of Walt Disney World

Hey, Big Spender

The *Unofficial Guide* aims to help you see as much as possible, not buy as much as possible. But we acknowledge that for many, a vacation is an extended shopping spree. If you're among these shoppers, you'll love exploring the stores at and around Walt Disney World. You'll notice that our touring plans keep you on-track to see attractions, dissuading you somewhat from shopping. However, to give you a notion of what shopping means to an enthusiast, we share this letter from a Los Angeles couple:

> We would like to point out that, although your book discourages it, the shopping is a divine experience at WDW for those who like to shop. One does not shop in WDW for bargains (that's what flea markets, garage sales, and Target are for), but Disney buyers obtain a large selection of above-average to excellent quality merchandise, much of it not available anywhere else (not even a Disney Store or catalog) and arranged attractively and imaginatively at the exit of almost every attraction. They are marketing geniuses! Not even the largest shops have all the merchandise they have to offer, hence, a shopper can make little discoveries in almost every shop—even the smallest hotel gift shops. That, coupled with congenial, helpful Disney staff, and services like complementary hotel delivery, make shopping an attraction of its own at WDW.

And a woman from, Suffolk, Virginia, offers this:

> Let readers know if they are into shopping to allot at least six hours for Disney Marketplace and West Side.

Central Florida is a shopper's mecca. With more than 52 million square feet of retail space, Orlando is the fastest-growing retail market in the United States, according to the Orlando–Orange County Convention and Visitors Bureau, and millions of visitors from around the globe have retailers scrambling to keep up with demand.

Beyond the ubiquitous mouse ears and T-shirts, avid shoppers can find a wide array of items, from hard-to-find imports from Epcot's World Showcase to designer bargains from hundreds of off-price outlets. Since we figure you are not in Orlando *just* for the shopping, we'll whittle down our lists to the best of the best. We will take a look at all four Disney theme parks, the Disney resorts, and Downtown Disney, then head for the other shopping hot spots around central Florida.

There are too many shops to mention every single one, but we'll tell you what's special and point out the smart buys—and the overpriced merchandise. We'll tell you where to locate hard-to-find goods. If a shop has a special, not-to-be-missed quality, we have marked it with a ★.

Pin Mania

Call it a hobby or an obsession, serious pin traders show up at the theme parks decked out in vests, hats, or sashes decorated with collectible Disney pins, always on the lookout for the one that got away. The mania started in October 1999 with the launch of Disney's Millennium Celebration, and today Disney churns out thousands of pins annually at its resorts around the world. The pins sell for around $6–$8, with one for every occasion, from new attractions to special events.

The spot for the largest collection of pins is **Disney's Pin Traders** at Downtown Disney Marketplace. The store has tables for trading and two Internet stations for visiting the official Disney pin-trading Web site (**officialdisneypintrading.com**) to catch up on the latest pin releases and special events in the theme parks.

There's a real camaraderie in the chase, with traders from around the globe sharing a moment as pins are swapped. Most agree there's no great monetary gain in the trade, just lots of fun. But there is "pin etiquette." (see "Disney Pinformation" below). For instance, pins must be cloisonné, semi-cloisonné, or hard-enamel metal. And they must be traded one at a time, hand to hand.

Some Disney cast members wear lanyards festooned with the ubiquitous pins and happily trade with park visitors. Cast members wearing pin-trading lanyards can be found in all four theme parks, Downtown Disney, and in some of the resorts. If you or your kids want to join the fun, you can save a few bucks on pins for sale at **Character Premiere** at the Belz Factory Outlet World. Pick up a handful, pin them on a hat or vest, and you're in business.

DISNEY PINFORMATION

Since pin trading is such a serious business, here's a primer on Disney's pin-trading etiquette, courtesy of Amelia Kelsall and **www.disneyclubs.com**:

1. Pins should be in good, undamaged condition.

2. You can only trade pins one at a time. The back of the pin must be attached.

DISNEY PINFORMATION *(continued)*

3. Guests may trade a maximum of two pins per cast member.

4. Do not touch a cast member or another individual's pins or lanyard. If you want to view a pin up close, just ask the person you're trading with for a closer look.

5. Certain pins must be traded as sets. If a pin was bought as a set, the entire set must be traded as one pin.

6. Only pins that have a Walt Disney World affiliation will be accepted for trading.

7. "Name pins" cannot be traded with cast members.

8. If the cast member already has the same pin that you want to trade, don't even bother trying.

9. Guests may trade only one pin of the same style with a particular cast member.

10. A pin which is ruled tradable is metal and represents a certain Disney event, place, location, or icon. Don't forget: it must be Disney.

11. Don't try to buy a pin from a cast member—that is unacceptable.

12. Some cast members have what's called a "showcase" pin on their lanyard. These pins are just for show, and cast members are not allowed to trade them. Sorry!

Shopping in Walt Disney World

Tips for Disney Shopping

After exhaustive research in all four Disney theme parks, water parks, and resorts, we can assure you that the Disney-brand merchandise is pretty much the same wherever you go. The only big differences are items with logos for specific resorts or theme parks. So if you are short on time, save your shopping spree for one favorite theme park or for the World of Disney shop in the Downtown Disney Marketplace, the largest Disney shop in the world.

Merchandise costs do not differ across Disney property. A beach towel, for instance, was the same price at every location we checked. Ditto for sale merchandise: if it's on sale at one store, it's on sale in all stores (though you may not be able to find it at all locations).

You pay top dollar for merchandise in Disney stores. However, there are often sales (though almost never at World of Disney, the premier Disney store), generally half-price markdowns. For bathing suits, clothing, and jewelry, you'll pay full retail in every shop—not unlike shopping at any resort anywhere in the world.

If you are staying in a Disney hotel, you can have all of your packages delivered to your resort from any of the four Disney parks—Magic Kingdom, Epcot, Disney-MGM Studios, or the Animal Kingdom. Packages will be delivered to your room by noon of the following day, so this service is not available if you are checking out of your room the same day.

Same-day pickup inside the theme parks is also available. For a nominal charge, you can ship them by FedEx to your home.

If you remember on your flight home that you forgot to buy mouse ears for your nephew, call the Walt Disney Attractions Mail Order Department on weekdays at (407) 363-6200 or the catalog department at (800) 237-5751. Most trademark merchandise sold at Walt Disney World is available.

I Need ...

Where at Disney World is the best selection of a particular item? Here are a few recommendations:

Bathing Suits

Atlantic Wear and Wardrobe Emporium, Disney's Beach Club Resort
Calypso Trading Post, Disney's Caribbean Beach Resort
Polynesian Princess, Disney's Polynesian Resort
Summer Sands, Downtown Disney Marketplace

Men's Clothing

Bally at Disney's Grand Floridian Resort and Spa
Commander Porter's at Disney's Grand Floridian Resort and Spa

Women's Clothing

Commander Porter's, Disney's Grand Floridian
Summer Lace, Disney's Grand Floridian

Sportswear

Bonnet Creek Pro Shop, Bonnet Creek Golf Club
ESPN Club, Disney's BoardWalk
Team Mickey's Athletic Club, Downtown Disney Marketplace

Jewelry

Mitsukoshi Department Store (pearls and watches), the Japan pavilion in Epcot
   World Showcase
Uptown Jewelers, Magic Kingdom
World of Disney (Disney-themed jewelry), Downtown Disney Marketplace

CHEAP (BUT COOL) SOUVENIRS AT WDW FOR UNDER $10	
Character beanie bags	$8
Character-shaped pasta	$3.95
Character back scratcher	$6
Mickey-shaped antenna topper	$3

Downtown Disney

If shopping is an essential part of your Disney vacation, we recommend your first stop be Downtown Disney, with three shopping areas, each with its own special feel: the Marketplace, Pleasure Island, and West Side. If you have time constraints and need to limit your shopping spree to a single stop, this is it. Except for specialty items, like silk rugs from the Japan pavilion at Epcot, you can find a little bit of everything at Downtown Disney.

Downtown Disney stretches along the shore of Buena Vista Lagoon at the intersection of Buena Vista Drive and Hotel Plaza Boulevard. It's a pleasant walk from the Marketplace on the east end to the West Side, with Pleasure Island situated between the two areas. The West Side has smaller shops with trendy merchandise; the Marketplace is loaded with Disney merchandise and a smattering of non-Disney products; Pleasure Island is really a nighttime entertainment district, but there are a few shops worth considering. So, what you're shopping for determines the best place to park—free parking on a surface lot spreads from one end to the other.

The Marketplace

The Marketplace is open Sunday–Thursday, 9:30 a.m.–11 p.m.; Friday and Saturday, 9:30 a.m.–11:30 p.m. There are more than 20 shops and 7 places to eat, including Rainforest Café. Wheelchair and stroller rental are available near Once Upon a Toy. It's a comfortable place to stroll and people-watch. Near the central area is a carousel that runs daily from 9:30 a.m. to 11 p.m.; it's decorated with hand-painted renderings of the Marketplace shops, and cost is a steep $2 per ride. If you don't mind the kids getting wet, check out the free "Fun Fountains" throughout the Marketplace. These streams of water intermittently squirt out of the spongy sidewalk, soaking energetic youngsters on hot summer days. The Marketplace is accessible by Disney bus or boat. Lockers are available for $0.50 on the dock by the steps. Coins must be inserted each time the locker is opened.

In recent years, longtime Marketplace shoppers have complained that the merchandise is "too Disney" and that the unusual shops (a great linen shop, for instance) have all disappeared and been replaced with Disney shops. You'll still find non-Disney merchandise (bathing suits, clothes, etc.), just not in the abundance of the old Marketplace.

Top Shops at the Marketplace

Disney's Wonderful World of Memories   You can start a vacation scrapbook before you even get home. This shop offers Disney scrapbook supplies, stationery, and postcards; tables are available for postcard writing.

Art of Disney   Next door to 2R's, Art of Disney sells limited-edition animation cels and pricey Disney creations, from pottery to crystal. You'll pay dearly for any of the merchandise.

★ **World of Disney**   It's a Disney superstore with 12 rooms—50,000 square feet—stacked with Disney merchandise, from underwear to clocks to Cinderella dresses. Pick up a basket as you walk in, shop

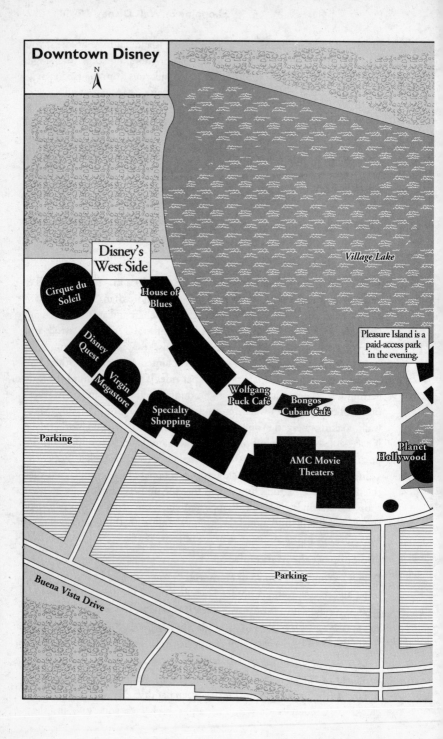

Downtown Disney

N

Village Lake

Disney's West Side

Cirque du Soleil

House of Blues

Disney Quest

Virgin Megastore

Specialty Shopping

Wolfgang Puck Café

Bongos Cuban Café

Pleasure Island is a paid-access park in the evening.

Parking

AMC Movie Theaters

Planet Hollywood

Buena Vista Drive

Parking

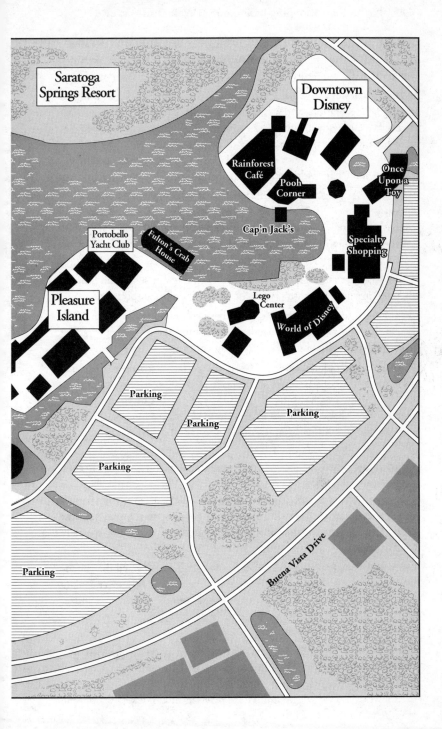

throughout, and check out at any cash register in the store. It's decidedly less crowded and frenetic than theme-park shops, except on evenings when the parks close early.

★ **Disney's Day of Christmas** This shop is just plain fun, with hundreds of holiday decorations and a two-story tree decorated with Disney characters. We especially like the back room of non-Disney baubles, from elegant ornaments to a Lladro nativity. Plenty of ornaments under $5 here make great souvenirs. A hot seller in all of the Christmas shops is the Disney monorail train with tracks to put around the Christmas tree like an old-fashioned train (also carried in some toy stores).

Disney at Home If you want to sleep on expensive Pooh sheets, light expensive Disney candles, or eat on expensive Mickey Mouse plates, you'll find something for every room in the house. It may be a little too cute for anyone but a true Disneyphile.

Basin Browse among metal tubs filled with fragrant soaps and lotions, then scoop your own bath crystals or have a bar of soap specially cut.

Disney Pin Traders The spot for the largest collection of pins, with tables for trading and two Internet stations for visiting the official pin-trading Web site (**www.officialdisneypintrading.com**).

★ **LEGO Imagination Center** This is the perfect rest stop for parents, and you don't even have to go in the store. A 3,000-square-foot outdoor, hands-on play area has bins of LEGOS where kids can go crazy while parents take a break. Inside is all the latest LEGO paraphernalia. Check out the life-size human family made entirely of LEGOs, including a snoring grandpa asleep on a bench.

EUROSPAIN Not the place to take rambunctious kids—there's beautiful glassware and full-lead crystal at every turn. This expensive shop has been a part of the Marketplace for more than 20 years, and you can still watch artisans at work blowing glass, carving monograms on crystal, and practicing the art of Damascene (inlaying gold and silver into specially forged steel).

Ghirardelli Soda Fountain and Chocolate Shop You can smell the chocolate when you walk in for a free sample. There are plenty of chocolate souvenirs, but treat yourself to their "world-famous" hot-fudge sundae, with the decadent hot fudge made daily at the shop. The line for ice cream usually winds out the door.

Once Upon a Toy Five rooms of toys, from choose-your-own Mr. Potato Head parts and Lincoln Logs to popular board games. Several favorites, including G. I. Joe, Lite-Brite, Tonka, and Tinkertoys, are on the shelves. Also for sale are miniature play sets of Cinderella Castle, the Haunted Mansion, and other Disney icons.

Pooh Corner   Winnie the Pooh merchandise, with everything from housewares to clothing, stationery, mugs, and more—all Pooh.

Summer Sands   Cool, hip clothes by Quiksilver, Roxy, Christina, and Op. Also one of the best selections anywhere at Disney of women's bathing suits.

Team Mickey's Athletic Club   From soccer to basketball to golf, this shop features sports apparel. Much of it sports Mickey Mouse and Goofy logos, but there's a decent selection of Nike sportswear and tennis shoes as well.

Pleasure Island

It's best known for its nightclubs, but the shops are open daily from 7 p.m. to 2 a.m. The half-dozen or so small stores carry mostly Disney and Pleasure Island logo merchandise or ordinary goods.

Disney's West Side

The West Side is open every day, 11 a.m.–11 p.m. This is the hip extension of the Marketplace and Pleasure Island, with shops that are full of fun tchotchkes for compulsive buyers. Virgin Megastore towers above the smaller shops on the walkway between Pleasure Island and the West Side.

Top Shops on Disney's West Side

★ **Virgin Megastore**   This giant record/CD/video/book store, with more than 150,000 music titles on CD and cassette and 300 listening stations for previewing CDs, is the biggest hit. A separate classical room features more than 20,000 titles. Music and movie titles on video, laserdisc, and DVD number 20,000, including new releases, classics, international films, and documentaries.

Candy Cauldron   Watch them make gooey treats in the open kitchen. You can buy everything from jellybeans to caramel apples and cotton candy—more than 200 sweets are on the shelves.

★ **Guitar Gallery**   More than 150 custom, collector, and rare guitars and accessories line the walls in this tiny shop tucked between the giant Virgin Megastore and the AMC 24 Theatres. Prices range from $199 for a beginner electric guitar to $25,000 for a Jimmie Rodger Limited Edition. The guitar-shaped checkout counter is inlaid with mother of pearl.

★ **Hoypoloi**   Not a set of mouse ears in sight, but one of our favorite shops, with one-of-a-kind pieces of art from various regions of the United States—Zen water fountains, contemporary art glass, and wooden boxes. To give you a better sense of the merchandise, one of their signature items is a red incense coil from an eighteenth-century Japanese incense maker.

Magnetron   You've got to see this place to believe the funky collection of 20,000 magnets lining the steel walls—magnets that talk, sing, ring, beep, light up, and glow in the dark. Kids love it, and souvenirs are pretty cheap.

Sosa Family Cigars   They hand-roll 'em here and feature great imports, including Arturo Fuente, Cuesta Rey, Diamond Crown, La Gloria Cubana, Macanudo, Puros Indios, Padron, Partagas, and Sosa. A walk-in humidor stores the top brands.

Magic Masters   Elegant little magic shop with decor inspired by Harry Houdini's personal library. Magic tricks, from simple to elaborate, are for sale, with a resident magician to demonstrate and entertain.

Mickey's Groove   An eclectic collection of merchandise, including posters, lamps, handmade greeting cards, and other trendy items.

Starabilias   Great for browsing, as the store is packed with music, movie, political, and historical memorabilia.

Sunglass Icon   Designer sunglasses and eyewear.

THEME-PARK SHOPS WITH THE BEST DISNEY STUFF

Magic Kingdom

Main Street	Emporium (largest selection at Magic Kingdom)
Tomorrowland	Mickey's Star Traders

Epcot

Future World	Mouse Gear (largest selection at Epcot)
World Showcase	Disney Traders (left side of Showcase Plaza)

Disney-MGM Studios

Hollywood Boulevard	Mickey's of Hollywood
Sunset Boulevard	Once Upon a Time
Studio Courtyard	Animation Gallery

Animal Kingdom

Safari Village	Island Mercantile
	Wonders of the Wild

Epcot

We enjoy wandering in and out of the shops in the 11 World Showcase pavilions, looking for unusual finds and bargains. Often you will see sale items, especially in the shops in France and Italy, but most of the imported merchandise is relatively expensive. However, the Epcot shops may be among the few places in the United States that carry some merchandise.

Aside from the World Showcase, two stores in Future World are worth a mention: **Mouse Gear** (the old Centorium) on the east side of Future World is the biggest Disney shop in any of the four theme parks. You can find almost any Disney merchandise here, and there is a substantial selection of adult and children's clothing. Prices are the same as at other Disney merchandise shops. On the other side of Future World is **The Art of Disney Epcot Gallery,** featuring animation production cels, hand-painted cels, character models, and more.

Walking clockwise around the World Showcase, here's what you'll find:

★ **Mexico**   Let your eyes adjust to the dim light in the **Plaza De Los Amigos,** a lovely re-creation of a charming Mexican city at dusk, where a live mariachi band often entertains passersby. Carts are piled with blankets, sombreros, paper flowers, tambourines, and straw bags. Sure, the merchandise may be cheaper south of the border, but these prices aren't bad: piñatas are wildly popular at $5–$11; kids' straw hats are $5.50; and straw bags cost $12, while blankets are $19–$32. Around the perimeter, smaller shops offer higher-priced merchandise, including clay pots, margarita glasses, and elegant silver frames, all imported.

★ **Norway**   **The Puffin's Roost** is a series of small shopping galleries with popular imports such as an entire room of trolls (from $14) and wooden Christmas ornaments (the tiny straw ones are just $3). Other hard-to-find imports include Laila perfume and body lotion and Helly Hansen outerwear. And the Norway pavilion offers Dale of Norway clothing, including thick woolen sweaters (around $260) and pricey but everlasting toboggans. You'll also find pewter, glass, and porcelain.

★ **China**   China features one of our favorite shops, piled with imports from real silk kimonos to cloisonné and thick silk rugs. **Yong Feng Shangdian** is more like a rambling department store than a shop. You'll find everything here from silk fans to $3,000 jade sculptures to antique furniture. The silk dresses and robes are competitively priced in the $100 range. Darling handbags are $18, and silk ties are $19. We always admire the handwoven pure silk carpets, starting at a reasonable $380 for a two-by-four-foot rug and topping out around $2,500 for an eight-by-ten-foot rug. Carpet prices are comparable to what you would pay in a retail shop—if you could find one that imports them. Kids love rummaging through the toy bins in the covered outdoor area, where you also can get your name written in Chinese on a fan for about $4.

Village Traders, a shop between China and Germany, sells Kenyan woodcarvings for about the same price you would pay at the carving center in Mombasa where they're made.

★ **Germany**   Eight small shops interconnect on both sides of the cobblestone central plaza and provide an impressive collection of imports. The tiny **Das Kaufhaus** stocks hundreds of limited-edition steins and glassware. Next door is **Volkskunst,** where the walls are covered with Schneider cuckoo clocks—one of the largest collections in the United States. Prices start at $39, and go up to $1,300. Next is **Der Teddybär,** with lifelike dolls, including Engel Puppe dolls (create your own and watch it made for $137), imported porcelain dolls, and Steiff plush toys. Across the plaza, **Kunstarbeit in Kristall** carries a fabulous collection of Swarovski crystal, including pins, earrings, necklaces, and bracelets. Next is **Süssigkeiten,** full of imported sweets, from Gummy Bears to spicy

Lebkuchen (crisp German Christmas cookies). The **Weinkeller** adjoins Süssigkeiten, with nearly 300 varieties of German wine from the vineyards of H. Schmitt Söhne. You can purchase a bottle of the hard-to-find *Eiswein.* Step through the door to **Die Weihnachts Ecke,** where Christmas ornaments and handmade nutcrackers are on display year-round. The beautiful nutcrackers go all the way to $275. Last stop is **Glas Und Porzellan,** showcasing Goebel glass and porcelain objects. You'll often find a German artist painting the delicate M.I. Hummel figurines, which start at $60 for a tiny version and range up to $26,000.

★ **Italy** **Il Bel Cristallo** showcases Venetian glass, porcelain figurines, Versace toiletries, and Giuseppe Armani figurines from Florence. In the front of the shop is a beautiful collection of handbags in the $150 range, ties, and scarves. Across the walkway, two smaller shops offer Perugina chocolates, Limoncello aperitifs, wines, and elaborate Venetian masks.

American Adventure The **Heritage Manor Gifts** shop carries a few hand-crafted souvenirs and lots of American flag–inspired clothing.

★ **Japan** A U.S. branch of Japan's 300-year-old **Mitsukoshi Department Store** stretches along one entire side of the pavilion. Completely renovated in 2003, kid-friendly merchandise fills the front—Hello Kitty, Gundam, and Yu-Gi-Oh—with kimonos, slippers, handbags, and more at the back of the store. The store has expanded its culinary display and includes a sake-tasting bar along with chopsticks, pretty rice bowls, and sushi-making kits. Pricey Mikimoto pearls (rings, necklaces, earrings, and bracelets) are showcased in a separate room. No bargains here, but cool stuff. And tourists line up for an oyster guaranteed to have a pearl in its shell (pearls are polished for you by the salesperson).

★ **Morocco** Three shops wend through the pavilion: **Tangier Traders** offers woven belts, leather sandals, purses, and fezzes; **Marketplace in the Median** has straw hats, sheepskin wallets, and bags; and **The Brass Bazaar** features brass, of course, and inexpensive ceramic kitchenware (not dishwasher-safe). We like the bottles of refreshing rosewater for $7.

★ **France** We always find a few moments to browse in **Plume et Palette,** a perfume shop with more than 100 imports. You'll find Chanel, Christian Dior, Jean Patou, and Lacoste. Take a minute to admire the sweet collection of fabulous Limoges boxes, all in the $200 range. Across the shaded walkway is **La Signature,** the Guerlain cosmetics and fragrance shop, with a wide selection of lipsticks, makeup, and perfumes. Cross over to **Les Vins de France** and **L'Esprit de la Provence,** two stores in one, with a wine room and a small selection of Provençal goods.

★ **United Kingdom** A handful of interesting imports are scattered throughout a half dozen small shops. Stop in **The Crown & Crest** to look up your family name in the coat of arms book—they will create your family's insignia on paper. You'll also find dart boards and limited-edition chess sets.

Across the street, **The Queen's Table** once carried a large collection of china but is now limited to perfumes, soaps, and powders. Next door is **The Magic of Wales,** a quaint shop with exquisite tea sets, including Scottish thistle ($30 per cup and saucer), and the English dog rose. **The Tea Caddy** stocks English tea, including Fortnum & Mason and Twinings, and biscuits and candies.

★ **Canada**   There's not much shopping here, but the popular **Roots** boutique in **Northwest Mercantile** has a wide selection of merchandise, including caps, jackets, T-shirts, boots, clogs, and backpacks. And we like the pure maple syrup, just $3.50 for a small bottle (enough for one serving of pancakes). Bigger bottles, up to $25, are stocked, too.

Beyond Epcot, shopping is hit-or-miss in the other three theme parks. You'll find the same basic Disney merchandise everywhere, with specialty items for each park tossed in. However, there are still some unusual shops amid all the Disney goods.

Disney-MGM Studios

On Hollywood Boulevard just to the left of the park entrance is a California mission–style house called ★ **Sid Cahuenga's One-of-a-Kind,** which is loosely inspired by junk shops in southern California, the land of movie stars. You'll find plenty of autographed photos of film and TV stars, and old movie posters.

Other fun shops on the right side of the street include: **Celebrity 5 & 10,** with Disney-MGM Studios merchandise (lots of inexpensive souvenirs); **The Darkroom,** for Kodak cameras, including disposable ones, film, and accessories; and **L.A. Prop Cinema Storage,** full of kid's clothing, PJs, and items inspired by recent Disney film releases. Across the boulevard, **Keystone Clothiers** carries an array of Disney clothes for grown-ups, while the adjacent **Mickey's of Hollywood** carries plush toys, watches, more T-shirts, hats, sunglasses, and more—virtually none without a Disney logo. There's plenty to look at but not much to recommend.

On Sunset Boulevard, you'll find more Disney logos in **Legends of Hollywood,** a Winnie the Pooh–themed store and the best stop at Disney-MGM for Pooh collectors. The **Beverly Sunset** features merchandise themed to the villains of Disney films, like Cruella de Vil and Malificent (who buys this stuff?). In **Sunset Boulevard Shops** there's a sizable stock of Disney jewelry and scads of watches, as well as housewares and Disney collectibles.

Elsewhere in the park: ★ **Animation Gallery** in the Animation Building has an impressive collection of cels and other collectibles. You'll pay the same price here as in all the other Disney art galleries. **It's a Wonderful Shop,** near *Jim Henson's MuppetVision 3-D,* features Christmas decoration year round; it's the same merchandise on a smaller scale that's found in the Christmas shops throughout Disney World. You can pick up a decent leather hat just like Harrison Ford's at the **Indiana Jones Adventure Outpost** outside the amphitheater. **Animation Courtyard Shops,** next to *Voyage of the Little Mermaid,* is the best spot in this park for Disney dress-up clothes for little ones.

Animal Kingdom

Though Disney merchandise again dominates, Disney's Animal Kingdom has a fair array of animal-themed items. Most shops are in the centrally located Discovery Island: **Beastly Bazaar** features cute straw safari hats with Mickey, Pluto, or Winnie the Pooh ears, stuffed Disney toys in safari garb, and Animal Kingdom watches; **Disney Outfitters** has men's and women's clothes and jewelry and popular Tree of Life souvenirs; and **Island Mercantile** offers more (yawn) Disney character merchandise. **Creature Comforts** is the stop for children's clothing and toys

In Africa, ★ **Mombasa Marketplace** showcases reasonably priced African-themed pottery, musical instruments, and masks. Often you'll find an artisan from Kenya carving walking sticks on the front porch. From there, if you catch the train to Conservation Station, stop just outside the exit at **Out of the Wild,** featuring an array of conservation-themed souvenirs—books, toys, hats, and more.

Asia has only open-air kiosks, where we found beautiful Bridge to Bali sarongs in one-of-a-kind batik patterns. Also for sale were incense burners, bamboo wind chimes, and paper lamp covers, nicely themed but all easy to pass by.

Our hands-down favorite at the Animal Kingdom is ★ **Chester & Hester's Dinosaur Treasures** in DinoLand U.S.A., inspired by kitschy roadside attractions from the 1950s and 1960s. It's worth a look just to check out the amusing architecture. Chances are you'll find an appropriate Animal Kingdom souvenir—hand-puppet dinosaurs, T-shirts, you name it.

The Magic Kingdom

Bypass the Magic Kingdom shops if you're on a one-day visit. If you have two or more days, browse the shops in early afternoon when many of the attractions are crowded. Store your purchases in lockers at the Main Street rail station while you tour or have them forwarded from shops to Parcel Pick-up and retrieve them when you leave the park.

Much of the non-Disney merchandise that was once available in the Magic Kingdom has disappeared from the shelves. For instance, longtime visitors may remember Liberty Square's Olde World Antiques with unique brass, silver, and pewter, but today it's a shop full of Disney Christmas ornaments. Or remember when the Yankee Trader stocked soufflé dishes and escargot holders? Now it's all Mickey Mouse kitchenware.

Main Street, U.S.A.   Since Main Street, U.S.A., stays open one hour after official park closing, you could save your shopping time until the end of the day. More than a dozen shops line the street, but only two are of note: If you want a monogrammed mouse-ears hat, ★ **The Chapeau** on Main Street is the only place at Walt Disney World to purchase it (there is a hat shop at the Studios, but there you pay extra for the monogramming); at the **Emporium,** the Disney superstore, you can basically count on one-stop shopping if time is of the essence.

Fun for browsing are the **Main Street Market House,** featuring kitchenware; **Crystal Arts,** where the glassblower entertains and the glass and crystal merchandise is similar to that at EUROSPAIN at Downtown Disney Marketplace; and the **Main Street Confectionary,** which occupies prime real estate on the corner of Town Square and is the biggest candy shop in all four theme parks, with every sweet imaginable and employees making fudge and candy apples. For clothes, try **Disney & Co., Main Street Athletic Club,** and **Disney Clothiers,** offering Disney apparel for all ages. For expensive baubles and watches, check out **Uptown Jewelers.** Fans of *101 Dalmatians* might want to check out **The Firehouse Gift Station** next to Town Hall for souvenirs inspired by the film. For animation cels and Disney collectibles, try the **Main Street Gallery.**

For interactive spending, let the artist at **The Shadow Box** snip your silhouette out of black paper or stop in the **Harmony Barber Shop** for a trim—it's open daily 9 a.m.–5 p.m., no reservations necessary. Lots of parents bring babies here for their first haircut.

Adventureland   **Elephant Tales,** across from Aladdin's Magic Carpet, features clothes with a safari theme, *Aladdin*-themed merchandise, and inexpensive imports from Kenya. Near Pirates of the Caribbean, **House of Treasure** carries replicas of famous ships, ships to build in a bottle, and pirate costumes. The adjoining **Plaza Del Sol Caribe Bazaar** has an ample selection of women's sundresses, straw hats, and bags (to us, it's a somewhat odd place to sell women's clothing).

Frontierland   Children gravitate to the cowboy hats, feathered headdresses, moccasins, sheriff's badges, and other play stuff in the **Frontier Trading Post.**

Liberty Square   **Heritage House** has American souvenirs and T-shirts. **Ye Old Christmas Shoppe** is a repeat of the holiday shops in all the other Disney parks. **Yankee Trader,** near the Haunted Mansion, stocks Disney villain–themed merchandise, featuring everyone from Maleficent to Cruella de Vil.

Fantasyland   Shops are themed to the attractions, like **Pooh's Thotful Shop** at The Many Adventures of Winnie the Pooh and **Seven Dwarfs**

Mine near Snow White's Adventures. A favorite for little girls is ★ **Tinker Bell's Treasures,** with a large selection of frilly costumes—Belle, Snow White, Cinderella, and others. **The King's Gallery** in Cinderella Castle offers an odd assortment of knight-wear, swords, and shields; it's one of the old-time shops that has not changed much over the years.

Mickey's Toontown Fair   **County Bounty** is a good place to load up on kid souvenirs.

Tomorrowland   The sci-fi stock in **Merchant of Venus** has been significantly reduced, but they still carry some campy items like glitter lava lamps. However, it's mostly a Tomorrowland souvenir shop, along with adjacent **Mickey's Star Traders,** and both are usually packed with teenagers. Neither is worth a stop unless you're killing time.

Walt Disney World Resorts

Every Disney hotel has gift shops and themed shopping, with specially created Disney merchandise. The Grand Floridian, for instance, sells the thick terrycloth robes you find in the rooms, and Wilderness Lodge and Villas has a line of Wilderness Lodge clothing. The general Disney merchandise is the same at all hotels, and prices do not vary.

Following are some shops worth a stop. We have not mentioned every shop in every resort, only those with something unusual to offer beyond the standard Disney merchandise.

Disney's Grand Floridian Resort and Spa   The best shoe store at Disney is the high-priced ★ **Bally of Switzerland** on the second floor. **Commander Porter's** shop for men and women carries Polo Ralph Lauren, Tommy Hilfiger, golf wear, and even cigars and lighters.

Disney's Polynesian Resort   If you're looking for swimwear or casual clothes, there are two high-quality shops here: **Robinson Crusoe Esq.** for men, with Nautica and Reyn Spooner lines, and the **Polynesian Princess** for women, featuring Liz Claiborne designs among others. **Wyland Galleries,** showcasing art of marine mammals, is just off the lobby.

Disney's BoardWalk Resort   Shopping could be better here; there's nothing out of the ordinary—Disney souvenirs, a handful of bathing suits. One shop worth a stop is **Wyland Galleries,** featuring environmental art that depicts marine animals in their natural setting. The graceful sculptures of dolphins are breathtaking.

Disney's Contemporary Resort   The fourth floor is a good one-stop shopping destination. For souvenirs, **Fantasia** carries a solid selection, including children's clothing and toys. Across the concourse, BVG (short for Bay View Gifts) is stocked with upscale souvenirs like expensive pen sets, men's shirts, and kitchenware.

Disney's Wilderness Lodge and Villas Resort Wilderness Lodge Mercantile is a general catch-all shop, with sundries, souvenirs, and even a substantial line of Wilderness Lodge outdoor clothing. But we always find something fun in the little corner devoted to non-Disney items—scented pine cones for the fireplace, hand-rolled candles, and such. Merchandise changes frequently.

Disney's Yacht and Beach Club Resort The Yacht Club has **Fittings & Fairings Clothes and Notions,** offering souvenirs and a limited selection of casual men's and women's clothing. At the Beach Club, **Atlantic Wear and Wardrobe Emporium** carries more casual clothing and racks of bathing suits. Both are expensive.

Disney's Caribbean Beach Resort We're not sure we'd make the trip to shop here, but the spacious **Calypso Straw Market** has fun casual wear for women and plenty of bathing suits.

Walt Disney World Dolphin Cartier watches and other expensive gems are showcased in **Brittany Jewels.** A small clothing store, **Statements of Fashion,** carries high-end clothing for men and women.

Disney Water Parks

Both water parks—Typhoon Lagoon and Blizzard Beach—have shops for sunning essentials like bathing suits, hats, towels, sunscreen, sandals, beach chairs, sunglasses, and film. Nothing is cheap.

Disney Outlet Stores

There are three notable Disney outlet stores—two in Belz Factory Outlet Mall and one at Orlando Premium Outlets. Belz is on the north end of International Drive, with the **Character Warehouse** in Mall 1, and **Character Premiere** in Mall 2. Liquidation merchandise comes directly from Disney World stores—T-shirts, toys, coffee mugs, holiday ornaments, plush toys, and more—so you never know what you'll find. Both stores get shipments every day of the week except Sunday. Selection is limited, usually featuring less popular Disney characters.

The **Disney Store** in Orlando Premium Outlets off SR 535 has even more sale-price souvenirs of similar selection and vintage. All three stores also carry some full-price merchandise, so shop with care. If you're not picky, you can round up a fair number of inexpensive souvenirs.

A Kentucky family had a hard time getting to the Belz Outlet, warning:

Avoid International Drive between the BeeLine Expressway and Oak Ridge Road. After crawling for what seemed like an hour, we reached the Belz Outlet Stores. We were grinding our teeth at the congestion. Take Interstate 4 directly to the Oak Ridge Road exit. It's much faster. PS: Belz Outlet Stores had some great buys on Disney stuff. Worth the trip.

Shopping beyond Walt Disney World

Celebration

The "town that Disney built" near Walt Disney World on US 192 gets its fair share of tourists who like to stroll the sidewalks. No one shop is worth going out of the way for, but there are good restaurants (including Italian, Spanish, and American), a two-screen theater, and a handful of shops. Because Celebration is an upscale community, the shops are all high-end.

You can purchase fresh coffee beans at **Barnie's Coffee & Tea,** where Celebration residents often gather on the patio for a freshly brewed cup. Specialty stores include: **G. S. Winston Fine Jewelers; Downeast Orvis; Market Street Gallery,** with greeting cards, candles, and gifts for the home; **Soft as a Grape,** with casual clothing for the whole family; **Village Mercantile,** with men's and women's clothing; **Jerard International** with gifts and home accessories; **Day Dreams** collectible dolls and bears; **Hopskotch** women's apparel; **Notingham's** antiques; and **Sherlock's of Celebration,** a wine shop and tearoom.

Most shops are open Monday–Saturday, 10 a.m.–9 p.m. Also on Main Street is a **Gooding's** grocery store that is much smaller than most of their other central Florida stores. Even Celebration residents don't do their regular shopping here but rather use it for impulse buying or lunch items from the deli.

Universal CityWalk

While Downtown Disney is 120 acres (with a strolling area equivalent to about ten city blocks), CityWalk is 30 acres in a relatively compact area between the two Universal theme parks. Downtown Disney has about 32 shops, and CityWalk features 13.

At both destinations, the shopping complements the restaurants and clubs. Without question, Disneyphiles will prefer Downtown Disney where at least a third of the shops are Disney themed. CityWalk is most comparable to the West Side at Downtown Disney, and though the 66-acre West Side is more than twice the size, there are actually a few more shops at CityWalk, covering a broader spectrum of merchandise than the West Side. Nearly all of the CityWalk shops are clustered in front of the Universal Cineplex.

Shop hours at CityWalk are 11 a.m.–11 p.m. Parking is plentiful in the Universal garage; it's a steep $7 before 6 p.m., but free in the evening.

CityWalk shops are fun for browsing and impulse buys. Our favorites include: **Dapy** and **Glow!** for trendy gifts; **Endangered Species,** with merchandise from T-shirts to jewelry to housewares designed to "raise awareness of the plight of endangered species, ecosystems, and cultures worldwide"; **Fresh Produce Sportswear** for colorfully designed clothes for men, women, and children; **Cigarz at CityWalk,** with hand-rolled cigars, cordials, malt scotches, and coffees; **Quiet Flight** for cool customized surfboards and beachwear; and **All Star Collectibles,** where sports fans can find team collectibles, videos, and other sports-related merchandise.

For jewelry, **Fossil** has a notable collection of Fossil-brand watches (also sunglasses and leather goods), **Silver** showcases silver jewelry for men and women, and **Elegant Illusions** sells reasonably priced imitations of expensive designer jewelry.

The **Universal Studios Store** offers one-stop shopping for all theme-park merchandise, from Woody Woodpecker to *Jurassic Park.*

International Drive

"I-Drive" is the heart of central Florida's tourist district, jammed with hotels, motels, discount stores, and cheap restaurants. Locals generally avoid the area except for the outlet malls (which we will discuss separately). Two shopping malls on the more refined south end of the street are worth a look if you're staying on International Drive or nearby.

The Mercado at 8445 International Drive has 60 specialty shops, including apparel shops, jewelry and collectibles stores, and 2 specialty shops, selling candles, kites, toys, electronics, cigars, and coffee. It's a pleasant walk from many I-Drive hotels. The newest addition is the **Hard Rock Vault,** a museum with hundreds of musical instruments, costumes, and other artifacts from Hard Rock's $32-million collection. There are six restaurants and the *Titanic* Ship of Dreams attraction as well. Open seven days a week, 10 a.m.–10 p.m.

Also on the south end of the street at 9101 International Drive is **Pointe Orlando,** with more than 40 stores. This 17-acre complex gets a lot of its business from the convention center, located less than a mile away, rather than from the locals. Hours are Sunday–Thursday, 10 a.m.–10 p.m.; Friday and Saturday, 10 a.m.–11 p.m.

Clothing stores at Pointe Orlando include: **Tommy Hilfiger; Boardwalk Surf & Sport,** carrying Billabong, No Fear, O'Neill, Rip Curl, and Quicksilver; **Abercrombie & Fitch; Everything But Water,** with an excellent selection of bathing suits; **A/X Armani Exchange; Disney Worldport; Gap; Players Golf,** with Tommy Hilfiger, Greg Norman, Bobby Jones, and Tommy Bahama fashions; and **Victoria's Secret.**

Among specialty shops are **Florida Eyeworks,** featuring Cartier, Hilfiger, and Calvin Klein frames; **Touch by Perfumania; Dapy;** and **Bath and Body Works.** Pointe Orlando prices are full retail, but there are always sales.

Outlets

Like every major tourist destination in the United States, central Florida has hundreds of factory outlets, and most are near major attractions. We spent many hours checking prices and merchandise and can generally conclude that in most of the stores you will save about 20% on desirable merchandise and up to 75% on last-season (or older) stock. Some stores in the outlet malls are full retail or sell a few brands at a 20% discount and the rest at full price. If you're picky, you often can do just as well or better at a major department store's end-of-season sales.

The granddaddy of outlet shopping in Orlando is still one of the best: **Belz Factory Outlet World** and **Belz Designer Outlet Centre,** both just off the north end of International Drive. The two comprise the largest of the outlet centers—160 name-brand stores. This is where the locals head for bargains.

★ **Belz Factory Outlet World,** the largest center of its kind in the United States, is at 5401 West Oakridge Road and includes 185 stores in two separate malls and four annexes. Hours are Monday–Saturday, 10 a.m.–9 p.m.; Sunday, 10 a.m.–6 p.m. Major stores include **Anne Klein, Bugle Boy, Danskin, Etienne Aigner, Gap, Guess, Jockey, Levi's, Mikasa, Nike, Oneida, Olga Warner,** and **Reebok.** Again, shop carefully. We found some great buys on current merchandise in the Gap, but meager reductions on the top-of-the-line Nike shoes.

Just around the corner is ★ **Belz Designer Outlet Center** at 5401 West Oakridge Road. Hours are Monday–Saturday, 10 a.m.–9 p.m.; Sunday, 11 a.m.–6 p.m. If you have time to shop only one outlet center, this is the one we prefer, mainly for the great buys at **Off 5th**—the Saks Fifth Avenue outlet. If you're lucky enough to be in town during a sale, the overstuffed racks in the big store offer some great bargains, with designer togs and shoes for up to 75% off. Also in this center are **Coach, Donna Karan, Jones New York, Ann Taylor Loft, Cole Haan, Kenneth Cole,** and **Waterford/Wedgwood.**

The Belz folks have a third center, **Festival Bay,** nearby on International Drive. The mall is designed for 1.1 million square feet of shops, and includes **Hilo Hattie, Sheplers Western Wear, Steve and Barry's University Sportswear, Bass Pro Shops Outdoor World, Ron Jon** surf shop, and a handful of small shops. Other big draws are a 20-screen movie theater and a **Vans Skatepark.**

Another popular outlet is **Lake Buena Vista Factory Stores** on State Route 535 near Disney World (take Exit 68 off I-4, then go two miles south on SR 535). Hours are Monday–Saturday, 10 a.m.–9 p.m.; Sunday, 10 a.m.–6 p.m. We were a little disappointed in the inventory, and the discounts were in the 10–20% range. (We can find scads of markdowns in retail stores that are comparable.) Key tenants include **Gap, Old Navy, Liz Claiborne, Nine West, Oshkosh B'Gosh Superstore,** and **Reebok.**

★ **Orlando Premium Outlets** is setting new standards for outlet shopping, with more than 100 shops at Vineland Avenue off I-4 at Exit 68 near Lake Buena Vista (open Monday–Saturday, 10 a.m.–11 p.m.;

Sunday, 10 a.m.–9 p.m.). An impressive array of shops includes **Banana Republic, Barneys New York, Brooks Brothers, DKNY, Escada, Salvatore Ferragamo, Giorgio Armani, Nautica, Nike, Polo Ralph Lauren, TSE,** and **Versace.** You'll also find **Disney's Character Premiere,** with plenty of Disney merchandise, and a fast-food court.

Traditional Shopping

The premiere shopping experience in Central Florida is the **Mall at Millennia,** anchored by **Bloomingdale's, Macy's,** and **Neiman Marcus.** Of about 150 stores, nearly half are new to the Orlando market, including **Cartier, Burberry, Crate & Barrel, Tiffany & Co., Gucci,** and **Louis Vuitton.** The mall has seven restaurants, a full-service concierge, and a U.S. post office.

We're told that next to Disney World, more tourists visit ★ **Florida Mall** than any other central Florida destination—one of the reasons it offers currency exchange and foreign-language assistance. It's the biggest mall in the area, with about 200 shops, including **Saks Fifth Avenue, Nordstrom's, Lord & Taylor, Brooks Brothers, Pottery Barn,** and **Restoration Hardware.** It's best to go early in the morning and park near one of the major department stores you want to explore. The mall is located at 8001 South Orange Blossom Trail, at the corner of Sand Lake Road (SR 482) and South Orange Blossom Trail (US 441); hours are Monday–Saturday, 10 a.m.–9:30 p.m.; Sunday, 11 a.m.–6 p.m.

Another not-to-be-missed shopping destination in central Florida is ★ **Park Avenue** in Winter Park, a small town just north of Orlando. The street, anchored by Rollins College on the south end, is lovely for strolling, window-shopping, and dining, and has a mix of high-end shops. Favorites include **Restoration Hardware, Pottery Barn, Tuni's** (women's chic apparel), **Bebe's** (trendy children's wear), **Williams-Sonoma, Gap, Talbot's, Caswell-Massey, Timothy's Gallery** (exquisite one-of-a-kind jewelry), and **Birkenstock.** Prices are high, but there are terrific sidewalk sales a few times a year.

If time permits, the **Charles Hosmer Morse Museum of American Art** on the north end of the shopping district has the world's largest collection of Tiffany glass and a wonderful little gift shop.

Most stores open at 10 a.m. but close early, generally by 6 p.m., including weekends. Traffic on the two-lane brick street can be a bear, so avoid driving down Park Avenue; instead, take a side street and search for on-street parking a block or two off the main drag. We also recommend using the new parking garage on the south end of the street.

To get to Park Avenue from the International Drive–WDW–Universal area, take Interstate 4 north, exit at Fairbanks Avenue, and head east. Park Avenue is approximately five miles.

Part Seventeen

Nightlife in and out of Walt Disney World

Walt Disney World at Night

Disney so cleverly contrives to exhaust you during the day that the thought of night activity sends most visitors into shock. Walt Disney World, however, offers much for the hearty and the nocturnal to do in the evenings.

In the Theme Parks

Epcot's major evening event is *IllumiNations,* a laser and fireworks show at World Showcase Lagoon. Show time is listed in the daily entertainment schedule *(Times Guide).*

In the Magic Kingdom are the popular evening parade(s) and *Wishes* fireworks. Consult the daily entertainment schedule *(Times Guide)* for performances.

On nights when the park is open late, Disney-MGM Studios features *Fantasmic!,* a laser, special-effects, and water spectacular. The daily entertainment schedule *(Times Guide)* lists times.

At present there is no nighttime entertainment at the Animal Kingdom.

At the Hotels

The Floating Electrical Pageant is a sort of Main Street Electrical Parade on barges. Starring creatures of the sea, the nightly pageant (backed by Handel played on a doozie of a synthesizer) is one of our favorite Disney productions. The first performance of the short but captivating show is at 9 p.m. off the Polynesian Resort docks. From there, it circles around and repeats at the Grand Floridian at 9:15 p.m., heading afterward to Fort Wilderness Campground, Wilderness Lodge and Villas, and the Contemporary Resort.

For something more elaborate, consider a dinner theater. If you want to go honky-tonkin', many lodgings at the Downtown Disney Resort Area have lively bars.

At Fort Wilderness Campground

The nightly campfire program at Fort Wilderness Campground begins with a sing-along led by Disney characters Chip 'n' Dale and progresses to cartoons and a Disney movie. Only Disney lodging guests may attend. There's no charge.

At Disney's BoardWalk

Jellyrolls at the BoardWalk features dueling pianos and sing-alongs. The BoardWalk also has Disney's first and only brew pub. A sports bar, **Atlantic Dance Hall,** an upscale and largely deserted dance club, and several restaurants complete the BoardWalk's entertainment mix. Access is by foot from Epcot, by launch from Disney-MGM Studios, and by bus from other Disney World locations.

Taste varies, of course, but the *Unofficial Guide* research team rates Jellyrolls as their personal favorite of all the Disney nightspots, including the clubs at Pleasure Island. It's raucous, upbeat, frequently hilarious, and positively rejuvenating. The piano players are outstanding, and they play nonstop with never a break. Best of all, it's strictly adult.

A dad from Troy, Michigan, underscores the last line, stating:

One thing your book doesn't make very clear is that, unlike Pleasure Island, the clubs at the BoardWalk are off-limits to those under 21, even if accompanied by parents, so there really is nothing for teens there.

At Downtown Disney

Pleasure Island   Pleasure Island, Walt Disney World's nighttime entertainment complex, offers eight nightclubs for one admission price. Dance to rock, soul, or country; take in a comedy show; or listen to some jazz. Pleasure Island is in Downtown Disney next to Downtown Disney Marketplace and is accessible from the theme parks and the Transportation and Ticket Center by shuttle bus. For details on Pleasure Island and a touring plan, see pages 713–718.

Downtown Disney Marketplace   It's flog your wallet each night at the Marketplace with shops open until 11:30 p.m.

Disney's West Side   Disney's West Side is a 70-acre shopping, restaurant, and nightlife complex situated to the left of Pleasure Island. Not to be confused with the West End Stage at nearby Pleasure Island, this area features a 24-screen **AMC** movie complex, **Disney Quest** pay-for-play indoor theme park (see pages 668–672), a permanent showplace for the extraordinary **Cirque du Soleil's** *La Nouba,* and a 2,000-capacity **House of Blues** concert hall. Dining options include **Planet Hollywood,** a 450-seat Cajun restaurant at **House of Blues, Wolfgang Puck**

(serving California fare), and **Bongo's** (Cuban cuisine), owned by Gloria and Emilio Estefan. The complex can be accessed via Disney buses from most Disney World locations.

Cirque du Soleil's La Nouba

Type of Show Circus as theater

Tickets and Information (407) 939-7600

Admission Cost with Taxes Category 1: $91 adults, $63 children (ages 3–9); Category 2: $76 adults, $52 children; Category 3: $63 adults, $42 children

Cast Size 72

Night of Lowest Attendance Thursday

Usual Show Times Thursday–Saturday, 6 p.m. and 9 p.m.

Smoking Allowed No

Author's Rating ★★★★★

Appeal by Age Group

  Under 21 ★★★★ | 21–37 ★★★★★ | 38–50 ★★★★★ | 51 and up ★★★★½

Duration of Presentation An hour and a half (no intermission)

Description and Comments   Cirque du Soleil's *La Nouba* is a far cry from a traditional circus but retains all the fun and excitement. It is whimsical, mystical, and sophisticated, yet pleasing to all ages. The action takes place on an elaborate stage that incorporates almost every part of the theater. The original musical score is exotic, like the show.

  Note: In the following paragraph, we get into how the show *feels* and why it's special. If you don't care how it feels, or if you are not up to slogging through a boxcar of adjectives, the bottom line is simple: *La Nouba* is great. See it.

  La Nouba is a most difficult show to describe. To categorize it as a circus does not begin to cover its depth, though its performers could perform with distinction in any circus on earth. *La Nouba* is more, much more than a circus. It combines elements of classical Greek theater, mime, the English morality play, Dali surrealism, Fellini characterization, and Chaplin comedy. *La Nouba* is at once an odyssey, a symphony, and an exploration of human emotions. The show pivots on its humor, which is sometimes black, and engages the audience with its unforgettable characters. Though light and uplifting, it is also poignant and dark. Simple in its presentation, it is at the same time extraordinarily intricate, always operating on multiple levels of meaning. As you laugh and watch the amazingly talented cast, you become aware that your mind has entered a dimension seldom encountered in a waking state. The presentation begins to register in your consciousness more as a seamless dream than as a stage production. You are moved, lulled, and soothed as well as excited and entertained. The sensitive, the imaginative, the literate, and those who love good theater and art will find nothing in all of Walt Disney World that compares with *La Nouba*.

  Thus far, as the following comments suggest, we have not received one negative comment about *La Nouba*.

From a 40-year-old mother of two from Waynesboro, Pennsylvania:

Outside the parks, the only thing we did was explore Downtown Disney and go to Cirque du Soleil one night. We'd made reservations months in advance. It was absolutely incredible, and I'd recommend it to anyone who doesn't mind the extra $$ outlay.

From an Iowa City, Iowa, couple:

In terms of shows and attractions, Cirque du Soleil was absolutely wonderful and any-one with the time should make an attempt to go. I could go on and on about it, but I think just "GO!" is enough.

The comments of a mom from Kansasville, Wisconsin, whose teens reluctantly consented to attend the show:

Even my hard-to-impress MTV-generation teens were awestruck.

From a 40-something mom from Chester, New Hampshire:

Cirque du Soleil was spectacular—plan to arrive a half hour early for the preshow.

From a mother of three from Stafford, Washington:

Cirque du Soleil is fantastic. If you go to Disney World and your kids are older than ten, you should definitely do this. If it means giving up a day at the park due to the expense, Cirque du Soleil is worth it.

From an Andover, Massachusetts, mother:

One of the true highlights of the trip was seeing Cirque du Soleil. The ticket prices were a bit steep and I debated doing it. But I thought it might be enjoyable for my non-Disney-loving husband and decided it was no more expensive than the rest of the trip. In fact, we all loved it, and it was the best money we spent.

Finally, from a Vermont family:

Thank you for singing the praises of Cirque du Soleil. I almost didn't buy tickets, thinking we'd have plenty to do and that there was no need to spend the extra money, but you were right in placing it on a plane of its own. It must be seen to be believed, and our family will never forget it.

Touring Tips   Be forewarned that the audience is an integral part of *La Nouba* and that at almost any time you might be plucked from your seat to participate. Our advice is to loosen up and roll with it. If you are too rigid, repressed, hungover, or whatever to get involved, politely but firmly decline to be conscripted. Then fix a death grip on the arms of your chair. Tickets for reserved seats can be purchased in advance at the Cirque box office or over the phone, using your credit card. Oh yeah, don't wait until the last minute; book well in advance from home.

House of Blues

Type of Show   Live concerts with an emphasis on rock and blues
Tickets and Information   (407) 934-2222
Admission Cost with Taxes $10–$60, depending on who is performing
Nights of Lowest Attendance   Monday and Tuesday

Usual Show Times Monday–Thursday, 8:30; Friday and Saturday, 9:30 **Dark** Sunday

Description and Comments The House of Blues, developed by original Blues Brother Dan Aykroyd, features a restaurant and Blues Bar, as well as the concert hall. The restaurant serves from 11 a.m. until 2 a.m., which makes it one of the few late-night dining options in Walt Disney World. Live music cranks up every night at 11 p.m. in the restaurant/Blues Bar, but even before then, the joint is way beyond ten decibels. The Music Hall next door features concerts by an eclectic array of musicians and groups. During one visit, the showbill listed gospel, blues, funk, ska, dance, salsa, rap, zydeco, hard rock, groove rock, and reggae groups over a two-week period.

Touring Tips Prices vary from night to night according to the fame and drawing power of the featured band. Tickets ranged $7–$35 during our visits but go higher when a really big name is scheduled.

The Music Hall is set up like a nightclub, with tables and bar stools for only about 150 people and standing room for a whopping 1,850 people. Folks dance when there's room and sometimes when there isn't. The tables and stools are first-come, first-served, with doors opening an hour before show time on weekdays and 90 minutes before show time on weekends. Acoustics are good, and the showroom is small enough to provide a relatively intimate concert experience. All shows are all ages unless otherwise indicated.

Walt Disney World Dinner Theaters

Several dinner-theater shows play each night at Walt Disney World, and unlike other Disney dining venues, they make hard reservations instead of priority seatings. You must guarantee advance dinner-show reservations with a credit card. You will receive a confirmation number and be told to pick up your tickets at a Disney hotel Guest Services desk. Unless you cancel your tickets at least 48 hours before your reservation time, your credit card will still be charged the full amount. Dinner-show reservations can be made up to two years in advance; call (407) 939-3463. While getting reservations for *Spirit of Aloha* isn't too tough, booking the *Hoop-Dee-Doo Revue* is a trick of the first order. Call as soon as you're certain of the dates of your visit. The earlier you call, the better your seats will be.

A couple from Bismarck, North Dakota, explains:

I'm glad we made our reservations so early (a year in advance). I was able to reserve space for us at the Luau at the Polynesian and the Hoop-Dee-Doo Revue. At both of these, they seat you according to when you made your reservation. At the Hoop-Dee-Doo Revue, we had a front center table. We were so close to the stage, we could see how many cavities the performers had!

If you can't get reservations and want to see one of the shows:

1. Call (407) 939-3463 at 9 a.m. each morning while you're at Disney World to make a same-day reservation. There are three performances each night,

and for all three combined, only 3 to 24 people total will be admitted with same-day reservations.

2. Arrive at the show of your choice 45 minutes before show time (early and late shows are your best bets) and put your name on the standby list. If someone with reservations fails to show, you may be admitted.

Hoop-Dee-Doo Revue

Pioneer Hall, Fort Wilderness Campground; (407) 939-3463

Show Times 5, 7:15, and 9:30 p.m. nightly **Cost** $49; $25 ages 3–11

Discounts Seasonal; American Express discount at 9:30 show only

Type of Seating Tables of various sizes to fit the number in each party, set in an Old West–style dance hall

Menu All-you-can-eat barbecue ribs, fried chicken, corn-on-the-cob, and strawberry shortcake

Vegetarian Alternative On request (at least 24 hours in advance)

Beverages Unlimited beer, wine, sangria, and soft drinks

Description and Comments Six Wild West performers arrive by stagecoach (sound effects only) to entertain the crowd inside Pioneer Hall. There isn't much plot, just corny jokes interspersed with song or dance. The humor is of the *Hee-Haw* ilk but is presented enthusiastically.

Audience participation includes singalongs, hand-clapping, and a finale that uses volunteers to play parts onstage. Performers are accompanied by a banjo player and pianist who also play quietly while the food is being served. The fried chicken and corn-on-the-cob are good, but the ribs are a bit tough, though tasty. With the all-you-can-eat policy, at least you can get your money's worth by stuffing yourself silly.

Traveling to Fort Wilderness and absorbing the rustic atmosphere of Pioneer Hall augments the adventure. For repeat Disney World visitors, an annual visit to the revue is a tradition of sorts. Plus, warts and all, the revue is all Disney, and for some folks that's enough. The fact that performances sell out far in advance give the experience a special aura.

Most of our readers enjoy the *Hoop-Dee-Doo Revue*, but not all, as this letter from a Texas family attests:

What is all the hoop-dee-doo with the Hoop-Dee-Doo Revue? *The food was okay, if "gut-busting" fare is your idea of a fine night out, and the entertainment was pleasant. As a dinner theater, however, our family of three found it unexceptional in every respect but its cost. Had your review of the Revue tempered its enthusiasm (much as you present its Polynesian counterpart), we probably would have canceled our reservation, pocketed the $100, and spent the evening joyously stunned by another glorious light-and-fireworks spectacle.*

More typical are the remarks of a Carlsile, Pennsylvania, parent:

The Hoop-Dee-Doo-Review *[was] very entertaining, especially for my nine-year-old daughter. The food was not bad, just average, [but] what can you expect? They are making it for such a large crowd.*

A mom from Cambridge, Massachusetts, agreed, adding:

The kids in our group (ages 3 to 8) thought the Hoop-De-Doo Review was just terrific. They watched intently the whole time, laughing hysterically. With them having such a good time, how could the adults not enjoy themselves? But I would not recommend the show for adults on their own. One thing we adults appreciated was the lack of commercialism: no movie tie-in, no merchandise sales. The entire experience, including its setting in the rustic Fort Wilderness campground, brought us back to simpler days and gave the kids exposure to entertainment before there were special effects.

If you go to the *Hoop-Dee-Doo Revue*, allow plenty of time to get there. The experience of a reader from Houston, Texas, makes the point:

We had 7:30 p.m. reservations for the Hoop-Dee-Doo Revue, so we left [Disney-] MGM just before 7 and drove directly to Fort Wilderness. Two important things to note: First, the road direction signs at WDW are terrible. I would recommend a daylight orientation drive upon arrival, except that there are so many ways to get confused that one might be lulled into a false sense of security. Second, when we got to Fort Wilderness, we had great difficulty determining where Pioneer Hall was and how to get there. I accosted several people and found a man who could tell us where we were on the map, and that a bus was the only way to get to Pioneer Hall. I would recommend leaving for Pioneer Hall one hour before your show reservations. Boredom is not nearly so painful as anxiety (reservations are held until 15 minutes after the stated time).

A California dad suggests:

To go to the Hoop-Dee-Doo Revue at Fort Wilderness, take the boat from the Magic Kingdom rather than any bus. This [is] contrary to the "official" directions. The boat dock is a short walk from Pioneer Hall [in Fort Wilderness], while the bus goes to the [main] Fort Wilderness parking lot where one has to transfer to another bus to Pioneer Hall.

Mickey's Backyard Barbecue

Fort Wilderness Campground; (407) 939-3463

Show Times Tuesday and Thursday: 6:30 p.m. **Cost** $39; $25 ages 3–11
Special Comment Operates Tuesday–Thursday
Type of Seating Picnic tables
Menu Baked chicken, barbecued pork ribs, burgers, hot dogs, corn, beans, vegetables, salads and slaw, bread, and watermelon and marble cake for dessert
Vegetarian Alternatives On request
Beverages Unlimited beer, wine, lemonade, and iced tea

Description and Comments   Situated along Bay Lake and held in a covered pavilion next to the now-closed River Country swimming park, *Mickey's Backyard Barbecue* features Mickey, Minnie, Chip 'n' Dale, and Goofy, along with a live country band and line dancing. Though the pavilion gets some breeze off Bay Lake, we recommend going during the spring or fall if possible. The food is pretty good, as is, fortunately, the insect control.

Because the barbecue is seasonal, dates are usually not entered into the WDW-DINE reservations system until late February or early March. Once the dates are in the system, you can make priority seatings for anytime during the dinner show's nine-month season.

The easiest way to get to the barbecue is to take a boat from the Magic Kingdom or from one of the resorts on the Magic Kingdom monorail. Though getting to the barbecue is not nearly as difficult as commuting to the *Hoop-Dee-Doo Revue,* give yourself at least 45 minutes if you plan to arrive by boat.

Spirit of Aloha

Disney's Polynesian Resort; (407) 939-3463

Show Times Tuesday–Saturday, 5:15 and 8 p.m. **Cost** $49; $25 ages 3–11
Discounts Seasonal
Type of Seating Long rows of tables, with some separation between individual parties. The show is performed on an outdoor stage, but all seating is covered. Ceiling fans provide some air movement, but it can get warm, especially at the early show.
Menu Tropical fruit, roasted chicken, island pork ribs, shrimp, mixed vegetables, rice, and pineapple cake; chicken tenders, mini–corn dogs, and mac and cheese are also available for children
Vegetarian Alternative On request
Beverages Beer, wine, and soft drinks

Description and Comments   Formerly the *Polynesian Luau,* this show features South Sea–island native dancing followed by a "Polynesian-style," all-you-can-eat meal. The dancing is interesting and largely authentic, and dancers are attractive though definitely PG in the Disney tradition. We think the show has its moments and the meal is adequate, but neither is particularly special.

Despite the name change, not much else differentiates this show from the old *Polynesian Luau.* The revised show follows (tenuously) the common "girl leaves home for the big city, forgets her roots, and must rediscover them" theme. The performers are uniformly attractive ("Studmuffins!" said an *Unofficial* femme when asked about the men), and the dancing is very good. The story, however, never really makes sense as anything other than a slender thread between musical numbers. Our show lasted for more than two hours and fifteen minutes.

The food does little more than illustrate how difficult it must be to prepare the same meal for hundreds of people simultaneously. The roasted chicken is better than the ribs, but neither is anything special. We conditionally recommend *Spirit of Aloha* for special occasions, when the people celebrating get to go on stage. But go to the early show and get dessert somewhere else in the World.

A well-traveled, married couple from Fond du Lac, Wisconsin, comments:

The Polynesian [Luau] *was a beautiful presentation, better than some shows we have seen in Hawaii! The food, however, lacked in all areas. Better food has come out of Disney kitchens. During our visit, the fruit platter was chintzy, the honey-roasted chicken was a bit fatty, and the pineapple cake was dry.*

Other Area Dinner Theaters

Central Florida probably has more dinner attractions than anywhere else on earth. The name "dinner attraction" is something of a misnomer, because dinner is rarely the attraction. These are audience-participation shows or events with food served along the way. They range from extravagant productions where guests sit in arenas at long tables, to intimate settings at individual tables. Don't expect terrific food, but if you're looking for something entertaining outside Walt Disney World, consider one of these.

If you decide to try a non-Disney dinner show, scavenge local tourist magazines from brochure racks and hotel desks outside the World. These free publications usually have discount coupons for area shows.

Pleasure Island

Pleasure Island is a six-acre nighttime entertainment complex on a man-made island in Downtown Disney. It consists of eight nightclubs, restaurants, and shops. Although it opens at 7 p.m., some of the clubs may not open until 8 p.m. or later, and Pleasure Island doesn't fully come alive until after 9 or even 10 p.m.

Admission Options   One admission (about $22) entitles a guest to enjoy all eight nightclubs. Guests younger than 18 must be accompanied by a parent after 7 p.m. Unlimited eight-day admission to Pleasure Island is included in All-in-One passes.

Alcoholic Beverages   Guests not recognizably older than 21 must provide proof of their age if they wish to buy alcoholic beverages. To avoid repeated checking as the patron club-hops, a color-coded wristband indicates eligibility. All nightclubs serve alcohol. Those under 21, while allowed in all clubs except Mannequins and the BET Soundstage Club, aren't allowed to buy alcoholic beverages. Finally, and gratefully, you don't have to order drinks at all. You can enjoy the entertainment at any club and never buy that first beer. No server will hassle you.

Dress Code   Casual is in, but shirts and shoes are required.

New Variations on an Old Theme   The single-admission nightclub complex was originated in Florida at Orlando's now-defunct Church Street Station in historic downtown Orlando. Starting fresh, Disney eliminated some problems that haunted Church Street Station and other nightspots over the years.

Good News for the Early-to-Bed Crowd   If you aren't nocturnal or you're tired from a long day in the theme parks, you don't have to wait until midnight for Pleasure Island to hit its stride. All bands, dancers, comedians, and showmen come on like gangbusters early in the

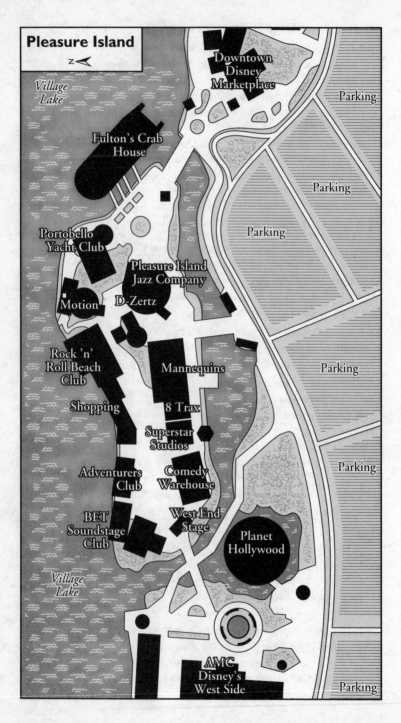

Pleasure Island

Z ◄

Village Lake

Downtown Disney Marketplace

Fulton's Crab House

Parking

Portobello Yacht Club

Parking

Pleasure Island Jazz Company

Parking

Motion   D-Zertz

Rock 'n' Roll Beach Club

Mannequins

Shopping

8 Trax

Parking

Superstar Studios

Adventurers Club

Comedy Warehouse

BET Soundstage Club

West End Stage

Parking

Planet Hollywood

Village Lake

AMC Disney's West Side

Parking

evening. Later in the evening as the crowd builds and becomes more lubricated, Pleasure Island assumes the character of a real adult nightspot. During the transition (that is, after dinner), however, it is not unusual to see a lot of kids in the clubs.

It's Possible to Visit All the Clubs in One Night Whereas performances in nightclubs elsewhere might be an hour or more in duration, at Pleasure Island shows are shorter but more frequent. This allows guests to move among clubs without missing much. Since you can catch the essence of a club pretty quickly, there's no need to hang around for two or three drinks to see what's going on. This format enables guests to have a complete and satisfying experience in a brief time, then move to another club if they want.

The music clubs (Rock 'n' Roll Beach Club, 8TRAX, Motion, BET Soundstage Club, Mannequins Dance Palace, and the Pleasure Island Jazz Company) go nonstop. Sometimes, there are special performances within the ongoing club entertainment. The Adventurers Club and the Comedy Warehouse offer scheduled shows.

We are very high on Pleasure Island. The cover is a little pricey and the drinks aren't cheap, but the entertainment is absolutely top-notch. And if you arrive before 9 p.m., you'll have time to sample all of the clubs, albeit briefly.

A reader reminds us that "sampling" the clubs, as we suggest, isn't the same as spending some time and really appreciating them:

Pleasure Island clubs take much more time to appreciate than you allow. We spent two evenings and only got to four places.

We get considerable mail from couples in their 30s and 40s arguing Pleasure Island's merits (or lack thereof). These quotes are representative.

A reader from Bettendorf, Iowa, writes:

I would not spend the money to go to Pleasure Island again. It is quite obvious that Disney is interested in the 21- to 30-year-old crowd here. There were many people our age (38) and older looking for something to do and not finding it. The Adventurers Club is the only real Disney creation on the island. Walt Disney World crosses all age brackets, and I expected the same from Pleasure Island. What a disappointment! I think you need to go back to the drawing board on your evaluation of Pleasure Island (and so does Disney).

A central Texas couple disagrees:

Your description, even with the statement that you are high on Pleasure Island, didn't prepare my wife and me for what a great place it is. Perhaps our expectations were moderate, but we thought it was an absolute blast, and we are neither under 40 nor club hounds.

For a Duluth, Georgia, man, Pleasure Island was a real eye-opener (at least according to his wife):

My husband couldn't believe the girls in the middle of the road selling Jell-O shooters! (I don't think we're in Disney anymore, Toto!)

Sorry, Invited Guests Only Occasionally, particularly before 9 p.m., certain Pleasure Island clubs are reserved for private parties and are declared temporarily off-limits to paying guests.

Parking Is a Hassle Pleasure Island's parking lot often fills up. On the bright side, the lot is now well marked. If you jot down the location of your space, you'll be able to find your car when it's time to leave. A good strategy is to park in the lot adjacent to the movie theaters and Disney's West Side and enter via the bridge connecting the West Side to Pleasure Island. Because there's an admission booth at the bridge, there's no need to enter through Pleasure Island's main gate.

Pleasure Island Touring Plan

Pleasure Island First-Timers' Touring Plan

This itinerary is for first-timers at Pleasure Island who want to visit all of the clubs in one night. It provides a taste of each venue. If you settle someplace that you really enjoy, you probably won't complete the circuit.

1. Arrive by 6 p.m. if you intend to eat at a Pleasure Island restaurant. If you eat before you go, arrive at about 7:30 or 8 p.m.

2. Buy your admission.

3. **Comedy Warehouse** Go left from the admission windows at the main entrance to the Comedy Warehouse. This is Pleasure Island's toughest ticket. There are normally five shows nightly, with the two earlier shows (usually 7:30 and 8:25 p.m.) easiest to get into. If a show begins within 30 minutes, hop in line. If show time is more than 30 minutes away, check out the Rock n Roll Beach Club down the street. Use your judgment about whether you have time to buy a drink. Return to the Comedy Warehouse 30 minutes before show time. If you don't arrive at Pleasure Island in time to catch either of the first two shows, plan to queue at least 35 minutes before show time for subsequent performances.

4. **Motion** Motion is the newest of the Pleasure Island clubs, replacing the country-western Wildhorse Saloon in 2001 (and leaving the complex without a country-music venue for the first time in its history). Disney says the club features everything from "Top 40 to alternative," but the scene is much more akin to MTV's *Total Request Live.*

5. **Pleasure Island Jazz Company** Turn left from Motion and hit the Pleasure Island Jazz Company next door. The club features live jazz and blues

and hosts jam sessions with local musicians. The crowd, more diverse in age and appearance than at other clubs, sits at tables flanking the stage on three sides.

6. **Adventurers Club**   When you're done at the Jazz Company, walk left and back to the Comedy Warehouse side of the island, and enter the Adventurers Club. Patterned after a stuffy English gentlemen's club, the Adventurers Club is a two-story, turn-of-the-nineteenth-century affair with big armchairs, walls covered with animal heads (some of which talk), and other artifacts.

    Many guests will stroll through the club, inspect the ridiculous decor, and leave, not realizing they missed the main attraction: a show in the club's library downstairs. About once every 30 or 40 minutes, all guests will be ushered into the library for a performance. Nobody tells guests a show is upcoming; they must either hang around long enough to be invited in or intuit that, with Disney, what you see isn't what you get.

    When you arrive at the Adventurers Club, ask an attendant when the next show in the library will begin. If it's in 20 minutes or less, go in and have a drink. If it's a long while, the BET Soundstage Club is next door.

7. **BET Soundstage Club**   Opened in partnership with Black Entertainment Television, this club features hip-hop, soul, and R&B. The dance floor is cool and showy, and the club gets packed as bands finish up at the West End Stage directly outside. The club is restricted to ages 21 and up, so there's a definite adult vibe.

8. **8TRAX**   When Pleasure Island opened, this was an under-21 club called Videopolis East. For various reasons (fights and teenage gang conflicts), it was closed and reopened as Cage, which targeted older (over-21) rockers but never achieved much of an identity. Now it's 8TRAX, a 1970s disco featuring the music of K. C. and the Sunshine Band, the Bee Gees, and Donna Summer. Though the decor during our last visit was the same steel beams, catwalks, and metal mesh that imbued the club's previous incarnations with such charm, it was clear that the 1970s concept had taken root. The place was rocking.

9. **Mannequins Dance Palace**   Backtrack toward Pleasure Island's front entrance to Mannequins, a ritzy, techno-pop, rock dance club with a revolving dance floor, incredible lighting, and wild special effects. The music is all DJ, but the sound system is superb (and very, very loud). There is often a line waiting to enter. This has less to do with the club's popularity than with the fact that Disney prefers guests to enter via an elevator to the second floor. The elevator helps distribute guests throughout the club, but there's a perfectly good entrance on the first floor. For some reason, cast members at the entrance will often invite 40-something (and older) guests to enter directly, without being subjected to the elevator. Patrons younger than 21 aren't allowed in Mannequins through either entrance.

10. **Rock n Roll Beach Club**   Proceed to the Beach Club, featuring oldies and current rock. Bands here are always first-rate, and they raise the roof beginning early in the evening. Electronic games and pool are available for those who don't wish to dance.

11. **West End Stage**   Continue to the West End Stage. It isn't a club, but it's the most happening place on Pleasure Island. Live rock bands perform under the stars in the plaza. The BET Soundstage Club and Adventurers Club are on one side, and Comedy Warehouse stands on the other. Bands are super, as are lighting and sound systems. The high stage provides excellent visibility. Performances usually occur four times each night, with a grand finale at 11:45 p.m., accompanied by fireworks, showers of confetti, and blazing searchlights. Street vendors sell drinks.

12. **Pleasure Island Restaurants**   Though noisy, crowded, and expensive, restaurants here offer a variety of creative and well-prepared dishes. For detailed profiles of Pleasure Island restaurants, see Part Nine, Dining in and around Walt Disney World (page 337).

    Restaurants include Fulton's Crab House, on the *Empress Lilly* riverboat, specializing in shellfish and fresh Florida seafood, and Planet Hollywood, at the entrance to Disney's West Side. While the food is pretty good and the servings large, the main draw is the Hollywood memorabilia decorating the restaurant. Unless you eat at strange times, expect long waits for a table. Our researchers half-jokingly refer to Planet Hollywood as the restaurant with an attitude. A reader from Bartlesville, Oklahoma, agrees:

Planet Hollywood was NOT a pleasant experience. We arrived at 5 p.m. and still had to wait an hour [to be seated]. I had the feeling of being herded like cattle. I also felt the staff manipulated things so there was always a line (i.e., there were several tables that stayed empty during the time we were waiting). The hosts on duty were rude. Our waiter was friendly and the food was good, but by that time I was too stressed out to care. This was the only time at Disney World that we were treated rudely. I understand Planet Hollywood is not owned or operated by Disney, and the contrast in attitude was quite apparent.

    Priority seating is strongly recommended for all full-service restaurants. If you don't have one, arrive by 6 p.m. or eat after 10 p.m. An alternative is to eat sandwiches and snacks in the clubs. It isn't necessary to buy club admission to eat at the restaurants. Most are also open during the day.

    If no Pleasure Island restaurant lights your candle, a number of themed and nonthemed restaurants are within easy walking distance at the Downtown Disney Marketplace and at Disney's West Side. Again, priority seating is advised for the full-service restaurants.

13. **Pleasure Island Shopping**   Some shops on the Island are attractions in themselves. Superstar Studio lets you star in your own music video. Props include keyboard, drums, and guitar. Video technicians record your lipsyncing (or you can actually sing). Post-production adds realism to your tape. Work alone or with a group of your friends. If you don't want your own magazine cover or rock video, watch others make them. It's a hoot!

Universal's CityWalk

CityWalk is Universal's version of Pleasure Island. In addition to a number of restaurants, you'll find a jazz club, a reggae club, a **Pat O'Briens** dueling-pianos club, a **Hard Rock Café** and concert venue, a **Motown Café** with live R&B, **Jimmy Buffett's Margaritaville,** the **Latin Quarter** for Nuevo Latino music, food, and dancing, and a dance club called **The Groove** with high-tech lighting and visual effects. If you do decide to dine at CityWalk, your options include **Jimmy Buffett's Margaritaville, Emeril's Restaurant, Bob Marley—A Tribute to Freedom, Pat O'Brien's, Hard Rock Café, NBA City, NASCAR Café, Motown Café,** and **Pastamoré** (for more information on CityWalk restaurants, see pages 338–339). For dancing, try Motown Café, The Groove, Latin Quarter, or Bob Marley—A Tribute to Freedom. And if you're in the mood for live music, check out Motown Café, Pat O'Brien's, Bob Marley—A Tribute to Freedom, CityJazz, or Jimmy Buffett's Margaritaville.

There's no admission charge to enjoy the shops, restaurants, and street entertainment. As concerns the clubs, you can buy a pass for about $10 that admits you to all the clubs (like at Pleasure Island), or if you prefer, you can pay a cover charge (usually about $5) at each club you visit. In addition to the clubs, shops, and restaurants, there's a 20-screen **Cineplex** movie theater. You can add a movie to your CityWalk pass for $12, or spring for a meal-and-movie deal for $20 more.

CityWalk versus Pleasure Island

Just as Universal's Islands of Adventure theme park allows for more direct competition with Disney's Magic Kingdom, CityWalk squares off with Pleasure Island in the field of nightlife entertainment.

As the underdog, CityWalk tries to catch the wave of the hottest fads in nightclubs and dining. Pleasure Island tends more toward themes and trends with long-established general appeal. Since Pleasure Island has the vast pool of Disney guests to draw from, CityWalk aggressively tries to attract locals in addition to tourists. Overall, Pleasure Island caters to guests who might like to indulge in a little clubbing on their vacation but normally don't make a habit of pub-crawling. CityWalk presents a flashy buffet of premiere nightclubs and restaurants that you might normally find scattered around a large metropolis.

One key difference is that the larger CityWalk is not as physically enclosed as Pleasure Island since it serves as a sort of open portal to the Universal parks. In addition, the CityWalk clubs don't have cover charges until about 9 p.m. So, if you're not interested in jumping around, arrive early, pick the club you like best, and settle in for the rest of the night. More than at Pleasure Island, several CityWalk establishments are both restaurants and clubs, allowing you to have dinner and dance the night away under the same roof. Both complexes have outdoor areas featuring frequent live music, festivals, and other events; both also have large multiscreen movie theaters.

All that said, which entertainment complex you might prefer depends on individual tastes. Consult the chart below.

HOW CITYWALK AND PLEASURE ISLAND COMPARE

CityWalk	Pleasure Island
Adjacent to Universal's theme parks	Adjacent to Downtown Disney
Parking decks free after 6 p.m.	Parking is hectic; use Disney transport
About $9 for pass to all clubs	About $22 for admission to complex
Half local/half tourist; mostly adults ages 20–30	Mostly older teens or curious adults
Ten restaurants	Four restaurants
Three dance clubs	Five dance clubs
Five live music venues	Three live music venues
Upscale mall-fare shopping	Disney memorabilia; hipster clothing

Appendix

Readers' Questions to the Author

Following are questions and comments from *Unofficial Guide* readers. Some frequently asked questions are addressed in every edition of the *Unofficial Guide.*

Question:

When you do your research, are you admitted to the parks free? Do the Disney people know you are there?

Answer:

We pay the regular admission and usually the Disney people do not know we are on-site. Similarly, both in and out of Walt Disney World, we pay for our own meals and lodging.

Question:

How often is the Unofficial Guide *revised?*

Answer:

We publish a new edition once a year, but we make corrections every time we go to press, usually about three times a year.

Question:

Where can I find information about what has changed at Walt Disney World in between published editions of the Unofficial Guide?

Answer:

We post important changes, especially those changes that affect our touring plans, on **www.touringplans.com.**

Question:

Do you write each new edition from scratch?

Answer:

We do not. With a destination the size of Walt Disney World it's hard enough keeping up with what's new. Moreover, we put great effort into communicating the most salient, useful information in the clearest possible language. If an attraction or hotel has not changed, we are very reluctant to tinker with its coverage for the sake of freshening up the writing.

Question:

I have never read any other Unofficial Guides. *Are they all as critical as* The Unofficial Guide to Walt Disney World?

Answer:

What some readers perceive as critical, we see as objective and constructive. Our job is to prepare you for both the best and worst of Walt Disney World. As it happens, some folks are very passionate about what one reader called "the inherent goodness of Disney." These folks might be more comfortable with press releases or the Official Guide than with the strong consumer orientation found in the *Unofficial Guide.* That having been said, we would like to point out that while some readers take us to task for being overly negative about Walt Disney World, others complain that we are too positive.

Question:

How are your age group ratings determined? I am 42 years old. During Star Tours, I was quite worried about hurting my back. If the senior citizens rating is determined only by those brave enough to ride, it will skew the results.

Answer:

The reader makes a good point. Unfortunately, it's impossible to develop a rating unless the guest (of whatever age group) has actually experienced the attraction. So yes, all age group ratings are derived exclusively from members of that age group who have experienced the attraction. Health problems, such as a bad back, however, can affect guests of any age, and Disney provides more than ample warnings on attractions that warrant such admonitions. But if you're in good health, our ratings will give you a sense of how much others in your age group enjoyed the attraction. Our hope, of course, is twofold: first, that you will be stimulated to be adventurous, and second, that a positive experience will help you be more open-minded.

Question:

I have an old edition of the Unofficial Guide. *How much of the information [in it] is still correct?*

Answer:

Veteran travel writers will acknowledge that 5–8% of the information in a guidebook is out of date by the time it comes off the press! Walt Disney World is always changing. If you are using an old edition of the *Unofficial Guide,* descriptions of attractions still existing should be generally accurate. However, many other things change with every edition, particularly the touring plans and the hotel and restaurant reviews. Finally, and obviously, older editions of the *Unofficial Guide* do not include new attractions or developments. Corrections and updates can also be found on the **www.touringplans.com** website.

Question:

How many people have you surveyed for your "age group ratings" on the attractions?

Answer:

Since the publication of the first edition of the *Unofficial Guide* in 1985, we have interviewed or surveyed just over 26,600 Walt Disney World patrons. Even with such a large survey population, however, we continue to have difficulty with certain age groups. Specifically, we love to hear from seniors about their experiences with Splash Mountain, Big Thunder Mountain Railroad, Space Mountain, *Alien Encounter,* Star Tours, Tower of Terror, Rock 'n' Roller Coaster, Body Wars, Test Track, Mission: Space, Kali River Rapids, and Dinosaur.

Question:

Do you stay in Walt Disney World? If not, where do you stay?

Answer:

We do stay at Walt Disney World lodging properties from time to time, usually when a new hotel opens. Since we began writing about Walt Disney World in 1982, we have stayed in over 65 different properties in various locations around Orlando, Lake Buena Vista, and Kissimmee.

Question:

What is your favorite Florida attraction?

Answer:

What attracts me (as opposed to my favorite attraction) is Juniper Springs, a stunningly beautiful stream about one and a half hours north of Orlando in the Ocala National Forest. Originating as a limestone aquifer, crystal clear water erupts from the ground and begins a ten-mile journey to the creek's mouth at Lake George. Winding through palm, cypress, and live oak, the stream is more exotic than the Jungle Cruise, and alive with birds, animals, turtles, and alligators. Put in at the Juniper Springs Recreation Area on FL 40, 36 miles east of Ocala. The seven-mile trip to the FL 19 bridge takes about four and a half hours. Canoe rentals and shuttle service are available at the recreation area. Phone (352) 625-2808 for information.

Readers' Comments

Readers love to share tips. Here's one from a St. Louis mom:

If dining at Downtown Disney, we found it best to arrive before 7 p.m. We ate there twice and had no problem getting seated immediately, but after 7 everywhere was packed. They do not do priority seating at Downtown Disney.

A lot of readers share tips about saving money. Here's a good one from a Canadian reader:

*I highly recommend the website of the Florida Travel and Tourist Bureau (**www.2000orlando-florida.com**). As well as info on area attractions, it has great deals on hotels and car rentals that you can't get elsewhere. I paid $600 less for our hotel than the best price I could get through a travel agent or directly from the hotel!*

For auto club members, I highly recommend getting the free pass for AMA's Diamond Lots at WDW (at your local AMA office before you leave home). The Diamond Lots are usually right next to the park entrance (only the handicapped parking is closer). You are close enough to walk to the park entrance rather than having to wait for the shuttle. A time and hassle saver!

And from an Ann Arbor, Michigan, mother of three:

Even though we stayed on Disney property, we stopped off on [US] 192 and loaded up on the local freebie visitor magazines and coupon books. We estimate they saved us over $200, mostly on food.

From an Annapolis, Maryland, reader:

Have your hotel fax you a confirmation of your reservation. If we had not done this we would have found ourselves without a room over the Easter holiday. Even with confirmation we spent an hour arguing with a totally bone-headed hotel manager.

From a Franklin, Tennessee, dad:

We always use the Florida Turnpike to get to WDW. Usually we exit at Clermont on US 27 and then turn onto US 192 for the rest of the way to Disney. This year we stayed on the Turnpike all the way to I-4 and then took I-4 over. It was faster and much easier on the nerves.

And from an Owensboro, Kentucky, reader:

I cannot express enough the need to bring plenty of film for your camera. I thought I had enough but ran out and had to buy some at the resort. Each 36-exposure roll averaged $9! Take extra rolls from home; you can always use them at Christmas if you don't at Disney.

Taking the long view helped a Texarkana, Texas, family:

I cannot emphasize the importance of realizing that you cannot see all [of WDW] in one trip. I realize that your guide is set up to help people try to accomplish just this for those who feel they can only afford one trip to WDW. But if people can in any way—even if it means staying at a cheaper hotel—get into the mindset that they will not be able to see it all in one trip and just focus on a few most important events/attractions on this trip and plan to come back again, it will save them stress and help make their trip more enjoyable.

An Iowa City, Iowa, couple offers this observation about being in touch with your feelings:

We didn't build rest breaks into our plans but were willing to say, "okay, I'm just not having fun right now; we should leave the park," and go on to something else (like a water park, hotel pool, or shopping trip to Downtown Disney). This is a skill I would like to see more people develop. I can't count the number of people or families who were obviously not having fun. People should remember that yelling at their kids in public ruins the fun for everyone else nearby.

When touring the theme parks, a Baltimore couple discovered that timing is everything:

Waiting time for attractions, food, or anything else, greatly depends on when you do things. For physical reasons my partner doesn't ride thrill rides, so we skipped some of the super headliners (the mountains, Tower of Terror, etc.). At Magic Kingdom opening time, when people are racing (and that's no exaggeration—I saw old ladies body checking teenagers) to Space Mountain, we went to Adventure, Liberty, and Frontier Lands and literally walked on rides we had planned to see (and some we didn't) until lunchtime. (Including Pirates, Jungle Cruise, Haunted Mansion, Country Bears, Tiki Birds, and Tom Sawyer). This type of strategy worked with all of the parks, except for Animal Kingdom, where everyone wants to see the same four things. However, we got there super early and efficiently walked to Safari when the park opened and got right on (saw lots of animals, too). Overall, if hordes of people are sprinting to an attraction, it doesn't take a genius to figure out that you should do something else.

A woman from Suwanee, Georgia, offers a suggestion for the perfect Disney vacation:

Your book made our trip a much more successful one. It also frustrated our male adults, who erroneously believed this was a trip for their enjoyment. We followed your advice to get up early and see as much as possible before an early lunch. But the men refused to go back to the hotel for a nap and a meal outside the park, so we fought the crowds until 3 or 4 p.m., by which time everyone was exhausted and cranky. My mother and I decided our next trip will include your guidebook and the children, but no men!

And if we ever publish an *Unofficial Guide* to weird Disney policies, I'm pretty sure this one, sent by a reader from Ottawa, Canada, will make the cut:

On Splash Mountain there was no one else in our [boat] and so we decided to take our shirts off for the big drop. That way, we wouldn't have to go back to our hotel in wet shirts. When we went to buy our picture, it never showed up. Instead, a cartoon came on the screen saying "Sorry, your picture has been washed away." When we inquired about this, we were told our picture was edited out due to Disney World's "nipple policy." We have no idea about the logic behind such a policy but it didn't seem to be in effect the next day at Typhoon Lagoon!

And so it goes.

Hotel Index

Restaurant Index

Subject Index

Magic Kingdom
Recommended Attraction Visitation Times

It is best to see attractions with visitation times listed as
"anytime" during the more crowded middle part of the day (noon to 4 p.m.).

1. Ariel's Grotto: Before 10 a.m./after 9 p.m.
2. Astro Orbiter: Before 11 a.m./after 5 p.m.
3. Barnstormer: Before 10:30 a.m., during events, or just before closing
4. Big Thunder Mountain Railroad: Before 10 a.m., hour before closing,
   or use FASTPASS
5. Buzz Lightyear's Space Ranger Spin: Before 10:30 a.m./after 6 p.m.
6. Cinderella's Golden Carrousel: Before 11 a.m./after 8 p.m.
7. *Country Bear Jamboree:* Before 11:30 a.m., during parades, or 2 hours before closing
8. *Diamond Horseshoe Saloon Revue:* Per entertainment schedule
9. Donald's Boat: Anytime
10. Dumbo: Before 10 a.m./after 9 p.m.
11. *Enchanted Tiki Birds:* Before 11 a.m./after 3:30 p.m.
12. *The Hall of Presidents:* Anytime
13. The Haunted Mansion: Before 11:30 a.m./after 8 p.m.
14. It's a Small World: Anytime
15. Jungle Cruise: Before 10 a.m., 2 hours before closing, or use FASTPASS
16. *Liberty Belle* Riverboat: Anytime
17. Mad Tea Party: Before 11 a.m./after 5 p.m.
18. Magic Carpets of Aladdin: Before 10 a.m./the hour before closing

—continued on other side—

Magic Kingdom
Recommended Attraction Visitation Times

It is best to see attractions with visitation times listed as
"anytime" during the more crowded middle part of the day (noon to 4 p.m.).

—continued from other side—

19. The Many Adventures of Winnie the Pooh: Before 10 a.m./2 hours before closing

20. Mickey's and Minnie's Country Houses: Before 11:30 a.m./after 4:30 p.m.

21. *Mickey's PhilharMagic:* Before 11 a.m./during parades

22. Peter Pan's Flight: Before 10 a.m./after 6 p.m.

23. Pirates of the Caribbean: Before noon/after 5 p.m.

24. Snow White's Adventures: Before 11 a.m./after 6 p.m.

25. Space Mountain: Opening, 6–7 p.m., hour before closing, or use FASTPASS

26. Splash Mountain: Opening, during parades, just before closing, or use FASTPASS

27. *Stich's Great Escape:* Before 10 a.m., during parades, or after 6 p.m.

28. Swiss Family Treehouse: Before 11:30 a.m./after 5 p.m.

29. Tom Sawyer Island: Midmorning thru late afternoon (closes at dusk)

30. Tomorrowland Speedway: Before 11 a.m./after 5 p.m.

31. Tomorrowland Transit Authority: Between 11:30 a.m. and 4:30 p.m.

32. Toontown Hall of Fame: Before 10:30 a.m./after 5:30 p.m.

33. *Walt Disney's Carousel of Progress:* Anytime

34. Walt Disney World Railroad: Anytime

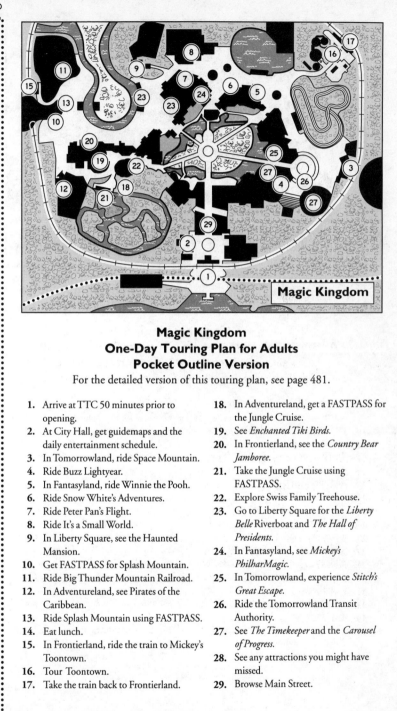

Magic Kingdom
One-Day Touring Plan for Adults
Pocket Outline Version

For the detailed version of this touring plan, see page 481.

1. Arrive at TTC 50 minutes prior to opening.
2. At City Hall, get guidemaps and the daily entertainment schedule.
3. In Tomorrowland, ride Space Mountain.
4. Ride Buzz Lightyear.
5. In Fantasyland, ride Winnie the Pooh.
6. Ride Snow White's Adventures.
7. Ride Peter Pan's Flight.
8. Ride It's a Small World.
9. In Liberty Square, see the Haunted Mansion.
10. Get FASTPASS for Splash Mountain.
11. Ride Big Thunder Mountain Railroad.
12. In Adventureland, see Pirates of the Caribbean.
13. Ride Splash Mountain using FASTPASS.
14. Eat lunch.
15. In Frontierland, ride the train to Mickey's Toontown.
16. Tour Toontown.
17. Take the train back to Frontierland.
18. In Adventureland, get a FASTPASS for the Jungle Cruise.
19. See *Enchanted Tiki Birds*.
20. In Frontierland, see the *Country Bear Jamboree*.
21. Take the Jungle Cruise using FASTPASS.
22. Explore Swiss Family Treehouse.
23. Go to Liberty Square for the *Liberty Belle* Riverboat and *The Hall of Presidents*.
24. In Fantasyland, see *Mickey's PhilharMagic*.
25. In Tomorrowland, experience *Stitch's Great Escape*.
26. Ride the Tomorrowland Transit Authority.
27. See *The Timekeeper* and the *Carousel of Progress*.
28. See any attractions you might have missed.
29. Browse Main Street.

Magic Kingdom
Author's Selective One-Day Touring Plan for Adults
Pocket Outline Version

For the detailed version of this touring plan, see page 483.

1. Arrive at TTC 50 minutes prior to opening.
2. At City Hall, get guidemaps and the daily entertainment schedule.
3. In Tomorrowland, ride Space Mountain.
4. Ride Buzz Lightyear.
5. In Fantasyland, ride Winnie the Pooh.
6. Ride Peter Pan's Flight.
7. Ride It's a Small World.
8. In Liberty Square; see the Haunted Mansion.
9. Get FASTPASS for Splash Mountain.
10. Ride Big Thunder Mountain Railroad.
11. In Adventureland, see Pirates of the Caribbean.
12. Ride Splash Mountain using FASTPASS.
13. Eat lunch.
14. Take the train from Frontierland to Mickey's Toontown.
15. Tour Toontown.
16. Take the train back to Frontierland.
17. In Adventureland, get a FASTPASS for the Jungle Cruise.
18. See *Enchanted Tiki Birds*.
19. In Frontierland, see the *Country Bear Jamboree*.
20. Take the Jungle Cruise using FASTPASS.
21. Explore Swiss Family Treehouse.
22. In Liberty Square, see the *Liberty Belle* Riverboat and *The Hall of Presidents*.
23. In Fantasyland, see *Mickey's PhilharMagic*.
24. In Tomorrowland, see *Stich's Great Escape*.
25. See *The Timekeeper* and the *Carousel of Progress*.
26. See any attractions you might have missed.
27. Browse Main Street.

Magic Kingdom
One-Day Touring Plan for Parents with Young Children
Pocket Outline Version

For the detailed version of this touring plan, see page 485.
Review the Small Child Fright Potential Chart on pages 258–261.

1. Arrive at TTC 50 minutes prior to opening.
2. At City Hall, get guidemaps and the daily entertainment schedule.
3. Rent strollers (if necessary).
4. In Fantasyland, ride Dumbo.
5. Ride Winnie the Pooh (use standby line).
6. Ride Peter Pan's Flight (use standby line).
7. Ride It's a Small World.
8. See *Mickey's PhilharMagic*.
9. In Liberty Square, see the Haunted Mansion.
10. Ride Jungle Cruise (use FASTPASS if wait over 30 minutes).
11. In Frontierland, raft to Tom Sawyer Island.
12. Ride Jungle Cruise if you have a FASTPASS. If not, skip to Step 13.

13. Ride train to Main Street. Leave the park for lunch and nap at hotel.
14. Return to the park. Go to Frontierland on the train.
15. Get FASTPASS for Splash Mountain.
16. See the *Country Bear Jamboree*.
17. Ride Pirates of the Caribbean.
18. Explore the Swiss Family Treehouse.
19. Ride Splash Mountain using FASTPASS.
20. Get FASTPASS for Buzz Lightyear.
21. Ride the Tomorrowland Transit Authority.
22. Explore Mickey's Toontown Fair.
23. Ride Buzz Lightyear using FASTPASS. Check the daily entertainment schedule for events.

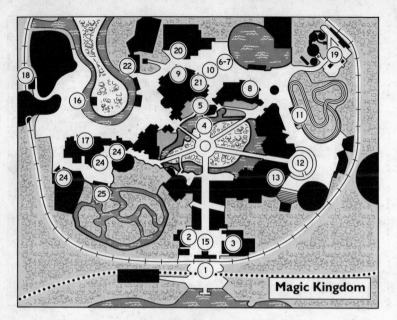

Magic Kingdom
Dumbo-or-Die-in-a-Day Touring Plan
for Parents with Young Children
Pocket Outline Version

For the detailed version of this touring plan, see page 487.
Review the Small Child Fright Potential Chart on pages 258–261.
(Interrupt the touring plan for lunch, rest, and dinner.)

1. Arrive at TTC 50 minutes prior to opening.
2. At City Hall, get guidemaps and the daily entertainment schedule.
3. Rent a stroller (if needed).
4. Go to Fantasyland via Cinderella Castle.
5. Make a dinner priority seating at the castle.
6. Ride Dumbo.
7. Ride Dumbo again.
8. Ride Winnie the Pooh (use standby line).
9. Ride Peter Pan's Flight (use standby line).
10. Ride Cinderella's Golden Carrousel.
11. In Tomorrowland, ride the Speedway.
12. Ride the Astro Orbiter.
13. Ride Buzz Lightyear.
14. Return to hotel for lunch and nap.
15. Return to the park and take the train to Frontierland.
16. Raft to Tom Sawyer Island.
17. See the *Country Bear Jamboree.*
18. Ride the train from Frontierland to Mickey's Toontown.
19. See Mickey's Country House, Minnie's Country House, Donald's Boat. Meet Disney characters and take pictures at the Toontown Hall of Fame.
20. Ride It's a Small World.
21. See *Mickey's PhilharMagic.*
22. In Liberty Square, see the Haunted Mansion.
23. Watch the evening parade.
24. Get FASTPASS for the Jungle Cruise. See the *Enchanted Tiki Birds,* Magic Carpets of Aladdin, Swiss Family Treehouse, and Pirates of the Caribbean.
25. Ride Jungle Cruise using FASTPASS.
26. Repeat favorite attractions.
27. Depart Magic Kingdom.

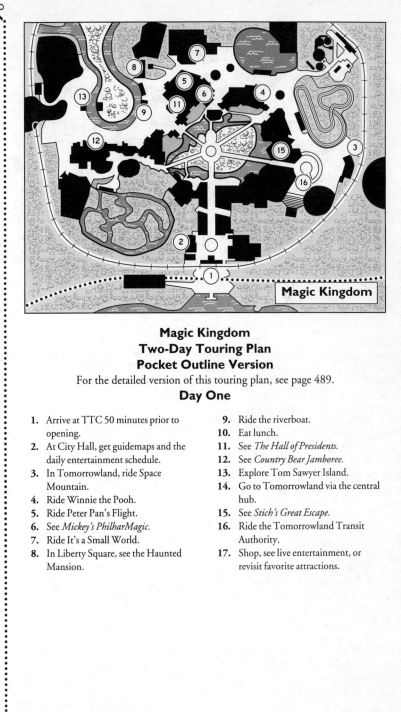

Magic Kingdom
Two-Day Touring Plan
Pocket Outline Version

For the detailed version of this touring plan, see page 489.

Day One

1. Arrive at TTC 50 minutes prior to opening.
2. At City Hall, get guidemaps and the daily entertainment schedule.
3. In Tomorrowland, ride Space Mountain.
4. Ride Winnie the Pooh.
5. Ride Peter Pan's Flight.
6. See *Mickey's PhilharMagic.*
7. Ride It's a Small World.
8. In Liberty Square, see the Haunted Mansion.
9. Ride the riverboat.
10. Eat lunch.
11. See *The Hall of Presidents.*
12. See *Country Bear Jamboree.*
13. Explore Tom Sawyer Island.
14. Go to Tomorrowland via the central hub.
15. See *Stich's Great Escape.*
16. Ride the Tomorrowland Transit Authority.
17. Shop, see live entertainment, or revisit favorite attractions.

Magic Kingdom

Magic Kingdom
Two-Day Touring Plan
Pocket Outline Version

For the detailed version of this touring plan, see page 489.

Day Two

1. Arrive at TTC 50 minutes prior to opening.
2. At City Hall, get guidemaps and the daily entertainment schedule.
3. In Tomorrowland, ride Buzz Lightyear.
4. Ride Splash Mountain. Do not use FASTPASS.
5. Ride Big Thunder Mountain Railroad.
6. Ride the Jungle Cruise. Use FASTPASS, if needed.
7. See *Enchanted Tiki Birds*.
8. See the Swiss Family Treehouse.
9. Ride Pirates of the Caribbean.
10. Eat lunch.
11. Ride the train from Frontierland to Mickey's Toontown Fair.
12. Meet the characters and tour the Fair.
13. Go to Tomorrowland.
14. If you haven't eaten, try Cosmic Ray's or The Plaza Pavilion.
15. See the *Carousel of Progress*.
16. See *The Timekeeper*.
17. Enjoy the shops, live entertainment, or revisit favorite attractions.

Epcot
Recommended Attraction Visitation Times

It is best to see attractions with visitation times listed as "anytime" during the more crowded middle part of the day (noon to 4 p.m.).

1. *The American Adventure:* Anytime
2. Body Wars (Wonders of Life): Before 10:45 a.m./after 5 p.m.
3. *Circle of Life Theater* (The Land): Before 11 a.m./after 2 p.m.
4. *Cranium Command* (Wonders of Life): Before 11 a.m./after 2 p.m.
5. El Rio del Tiempo (Mexico): Before 11 a.m./after 3 p.m.
6. *Honey, I Shrunk the Audience:* Before 11:30 a.m., after 6 p.m., or use FASTPASS
7. *Impressions de France* (France): Before noon/after 4 p.m.
8. Innoventions: Second day or after major attractions
9. Journey into Your Imagination: Before 11:30 a.m./after 6 p.m.
10. Living with the Land (The Land): Before 10:30 a.m., after 7:30 p.m., or use FASTPASS
11. The Living Seas: Before 11:30 a.m./after 3 p.m.
12. Maelstrom (Norway): Before noon, after 4:30 p.m., or use FASTPASS
13. *The Making of Me* (Wonders of Life): Early morning/after 4:30 p.m.
14. Mission: Space: First 30 minutes the park is open or use FASTPASS
15. *O Canada!* (Canada): Anytime
16. *Reflections of China* (China): Anytime
17. Soarin': First 30 minutes the park is open, just before closing, or use FASTPASS
18. Spaceship Earth: Before 11 a.m./after 3 p.m.
19. Test Track: First 30 minutes the park is open, just before closing, or use FASTPASS
20. Universe of Energy: Before 11:15 a.m./after 4:30 p.m.

Epcot

Epcot
One-Day Touring Plan
Pocket Outline Version

For the detailed version of this touring plan, see page 532.
(Interrupt the touring plan for lunch, dinner, and *IllumiNations*.)

1. Arrive 40 minutes before official opening time.
2. Ride Test Track. Do not use FASTPASS.
3. Ride Mission: Space. Do not use FASTPASS.
4. In the Land Pavilion, obtain FASTPASS for Soarin' (if open).
5. Ride Living with the Land.
6. Ride Journey into Your Imagination.
7. See *Honey, I Shrunk the Audience.*
8. Return to the Land Pavilion and see *The Circle of Life.*
9. If open, ride Soarin' using FASTPASS obtained in Step 4.
10. Experience The Living Seas.
11. Ride Spaceship Earth.
12. Make priority seating reservations for dinner at Guest Relations.
13. Visit the Universe of Energy.
14. Ride Body Wars in the Wonders of Life Pavilion (open seasonally).
15. See *Cranium Command* (open seasonally).
16. Go to the World Showcase.
17. Ride El Rio del Tiempo at Mexico.
18. Ride Maelstrom.
19. In China, see *Reflections of China.*
20. Tour Germany.
21. Visit Italy.
22. See *The American Adventure.*
23. Tour Japan.
24. Visit Morocco.
25. Go to France and see the film.
26. Go to the United Kingdom.
27. In Canada, see the film.
28. Check timing for dinner priority seating or allow 30 minutes to find a good viewing spot for *Illuminations.*
29. Depart Epcot.

Epcot

Epcot
Author's Selective One-Day Touring Plan
Pocket Outline Version

For the detailed version of this touring plan, see page 534.
(Interrupt the touring plan for lunch, dinner, and *IllumiNations*.)

1. Arrive 40 minutes before official opening time.
2. Ride Test Track. Do not use FASTPASS.
3. Ride Mission: Space. Do not use FASTPASS.
4. In the Land Pavilion, obtain FASTPASS for Soarin' (if open).
5. Ride Living with the Land.
6. Ride Journey into Your Imagination.
7. See *Honey, I Shrunk the Audience.*
8. If open, ride Soarin' using FASTPASS obtained in Step 4.
9. Experience The Living Seas.
10. Ride Spaceship Earth.
11. Make priority seating reservations for dinner at Guest Relations.
12. Visit the Universe of Energy.
13. Ride Body Wars in the Wonders of Life Pavilion (open seasonally).
14. See *Cranium Command* (open seasonally).
15. Go to the World Showcase.
16. Initiate a counter-clockwise circuit of the World Showcase Lagoon, starting at Canada.
17. Go to France and see the film.
18. Go to Morocco and Japan.
19. Enjoy *The American Adventure.*
20. Go through Italy, Germany, and China. Enjoy *Reflections of China.*
21. In Norway, ride Maelstrom.
22. In Mexico, ride the boat inside the pyramid.
23. Go to dinner. Check the time for *Illuminations.*
24. Depart Epcot.

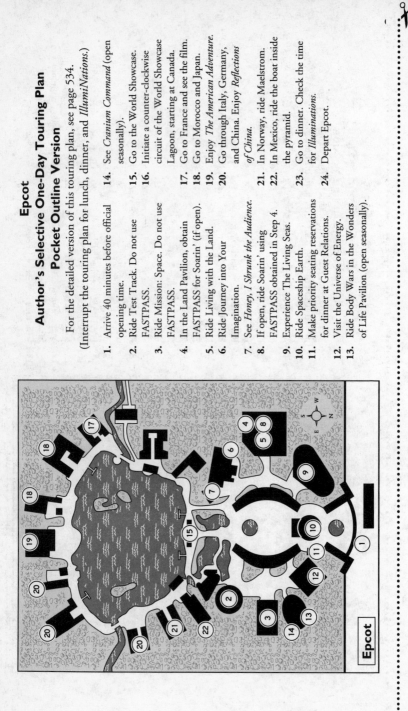

Epcot

768

Epcot
Two-Day Sunrise/Starlight Touring Plan
Pocket Outline Version

For the detailed version of this touring plan, see page 536.
(Interrupt the touring plan for lunch.)

Day One

1. Arrive 40 minutes before official opening time.
2. Ride Soarin'.
3. Go to Test Track. If wait exceeds 30 minutes, use FASTPASS.
4. Ride Mission: Space. If wait exceeds 35 minutes, use FASTPASS or try the single rider line.
5. Make priority seating at Guest Relations for Epcot restaurants.
6. In the Land Pavilion, ride the boat.
7. Ride Journey into Your Imagination. See *Honey, I Shrunk the Audience*.
8. Go to World Showcase.
9. Start a clockwise tour around the World Showcase Lagoon. Experience El Rio del Tiempo.
10. Ride Maelstrom. Use FASTPASS if the wait exceeds 20 minutes.
11. In China, see *Reflections of China*.
12. Visit Germany and Italy.
13. See *The American Adventure*.
14. Visit Japan and Morocco.
15. Depart Epcot.

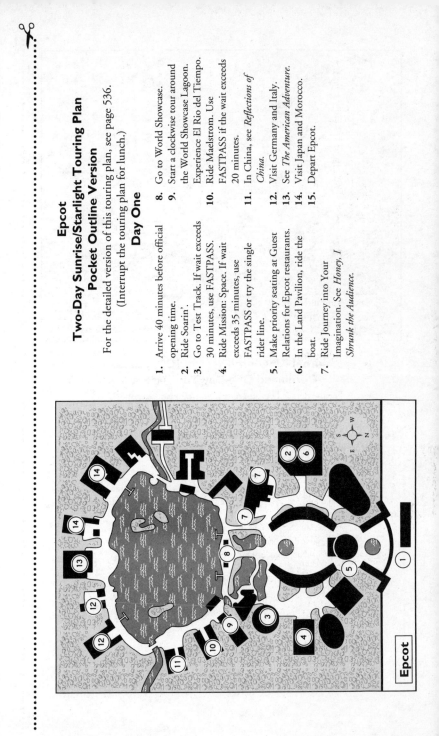

Epcot

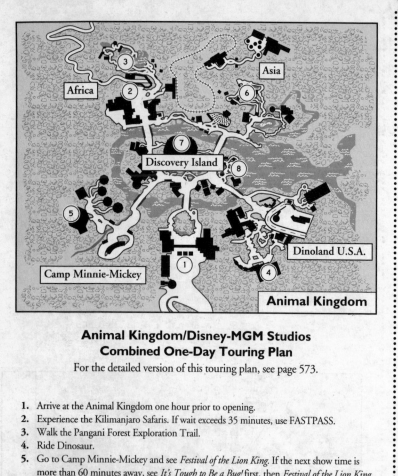

Animal Kingdom/Disney-MGM Studios
Combined One-Day Touring Plan

For the detailed version of this touring plan, see page 573.

1. Arrive at the Animal Kingdom one hour prior to opening.
2. Experience the Kilimanjaro Safaris. If wait exceeds 35 minutes, use FASTPASS.
3. Walk the Pangani Forest Exploration Trail.
4. Ride Dinosaur.
5. Go to Camp Minnie-Mickey and see *Festival of the Lion King*. If the next show time is more than 60 minutes away, see *It's Tough to Be a Bug!* first, then *Festival of the Lion King*.
6. Walk the Maharaja Jungle Trek.
7. See *It's Tough to Be a Bug!* if you haven't already done so.
8. Have lunch at Flame Tree Barbeque.
9. Depart the Animal Kingdom for Disney-MGM Studios.

Epcot
Two-Day Early Riser Touring Plan
Pocket Outline Version

For the detailed version of this touring plan, see page 538.
Parents with young children should review the Small Child Fright
Potential Chart on pages 258–261.

Day One

1. Arrive 40 minutes prior to opening.
2. Ride Soarin'.
3. Ride Living with the Land.
4. See *The Circle of Life*.
5. At Guest Relations, make dinner priority seating arrangements.
6. Tour Innoventions East.
7. See the Universe of Energy.
8. See *Cranium Command* (open seasonally).
9. Ride Body Wars (open seasonally).
10. Start a counter-clockwise tour of World Showcase with the film *O Canada!* at Canada.
11. Explore the United Kingdom.
12. Go to France and see the film.
13. Continue around the lagoon or skip to step 14.
14. Check out the exhibits of Innoventions West.
15. Depart Epcot.

Epcot

Epcot
Two-Day Early Riser Touring Plan
Pocket Outline Version

For the detailed version of this touring plan, see page 538.
Parents with young children should review the Small Child Fright Potential Chart on pages 258–261.

Day Two

1. Arrive 40 minutes prior to opening.
2. Ride Test Track. If wait exceeds 35 minutes, use FASTPASS.
3. Ride Mission: Space. If wait exceeds 35 minutes, use FASTPASS.
4. Ride Spaceship Earth.
5. Proceed to the Living Seas.
6. Ride the Journey into Your Imagination ride and see *Honey, I Shrunk the Audience*.
7. Go to the World Showcase.
8. Take the El Rio del Tiempo boat ride at Mexico.
9. In Norway, ride Maelstrom. If wait exceeds 20 minutes, use FASTPASS.
10. See *Reflections of China*.
11. Visit Germany and Italy.
12. See *The American Adventure*.
13. Visit Japan and Morocco.
14. Enjoy dinner and *Illuminations*. Depart Epcot.

Epcot

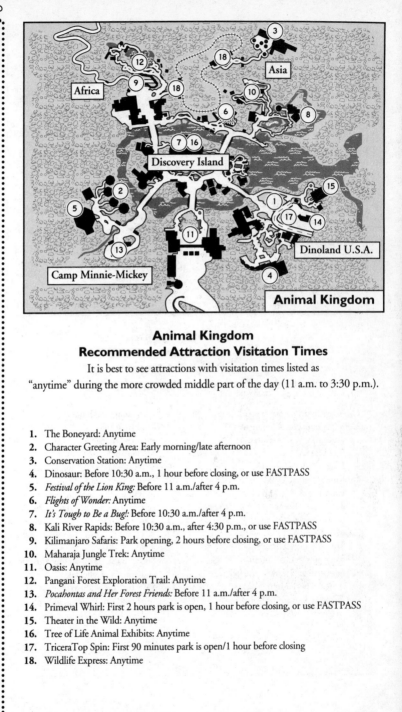

Animal Kingdom
Recommended Attraction Visitation Times

It is best to see attractions with visitation times listed as "anytime" during the more crowded middle part of the day (11 a.m. to 3:30 p.m.).

1. The Boneyard: Anytime
2. Character Greeting Area: Early morning/late afternoon
3. Conservation Station: Anytime
4. Dinosaur: Before 10:30 a.m., 1 hour before closing, or use FASTPASS
5. *Festival of the Lion King:* Before 11 a.m./after 4 p.m.
6. *Flights of Wonder:* Anytime
7. *It's Tough to Be a Bug!:* Before 10:30 a.m./after 4 p.m.
8. Kali River Rapids: Before 10:30 a.m., after 4:30 p.m., or use FASTPASS
9. Kilimanjaro Safaris: Park opening, 2 hours before closing, or use FASTPASS
10. Maharaja Jungle Trek: Anytime
11. Oasis: Anytime
12. Pangani Forest Exploration Trail: Anytime
13. *Pocahontas and Her Forest Friends:* Before 11 a.m./after 4 p.m.
14. Primeval Whirl: First 2 hours park is open, 1 hour before closing, or use FASTPASS
15. Theater in the Wild: Anytime
16. Tree of Life Animal Exhibits: Anytime
17. TriceraTop Spin: First 90 minutes park is open/1 hour before closing
18. Wildlife Express: Anytime

Animal Kingdom
One-Day Touring Plan
Pocket Outline Version

For the detailed version of this touring plan, see page 572.

1. Arrive one hour prior to opening.
2. Experience the Kilimanjaro Safaris. If wait exceeds 30 minutes, use FASTPASS.
3. Ride Kali River Rapids.
4. Ride Primeval Whirl (4a) in Dino-Land U.S.A. If you have small children, ride TriceraTop Spin (4b) before Primeval Whirl.
5. Ride Dinosaur.
6. See *It's Tough to Be a Bug!* If wait exceeds 30 minutes, use FASTPASS.
7. Eat lunch and work in the following shows: Theater in the Wild (7a), *Flights of Wonder* (7b), *Pocahontas* (7c), and *Festival of the Lion King* (7d).

8. Check out The Boneyard (8a) and exhibits at the Tree of Life (8b). Also, meet the characters at Camp Minnie-Mickey (8c).
9. Walk the Maharaja Jungle Trek.
10. Return to Africa and take the train to Rafiki's Planet Watch and Conservation Station. Tour the exhibits.
11. Catch the train back to Harambe.
12. Walk the Pangani Forest Exploration Trail.
13. Shop, snack, or repeat any attractions you especially enjoyed.
14. Visit the zoological exhibits in The Oasis and exit the Animal Kingdom.

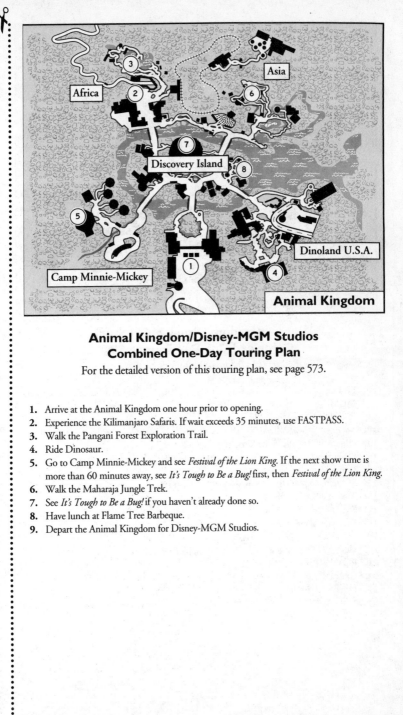

Animal Kingdom/Disney-MGM Studios
Combined One-Day Touring Plan

For the detailed version of this touring plan, see page 573.

1. Arrive at the Animal Kingdom one hour prior to opening.
2. Experience the Kilimanjaro Safaris. If wait exceeds 35 minutes, use FASTPASS.
3. Walk the Pangani Forest Exploration Trail.
4. Ride Dinosaur.
5. Go to Camp Minnie-Mickey and see *Festival of the Lion King*. If the next show time is more than 60 minutes away, see *It's Tough to Be a Bug!* first, then *Festival of the Lion King*.
6. Walk the Maharaja Jungle Trek.
7. See *It's Tough to Be a Bug!* if you haven't already done so.
8. Have lunch at Flame Tree Barbeque.
9. Depart the Animal Kingdom for Disney-MGM Studios.

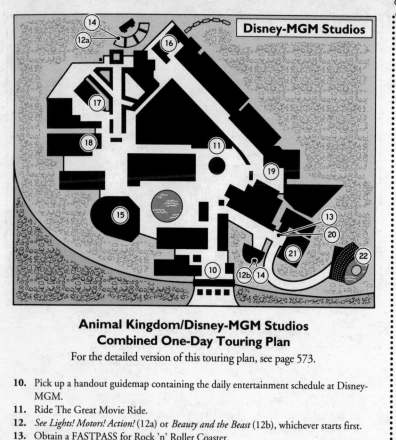

Animal Kingdom/Disney-MGM Studios
Combined One-Day Touring Plan

For the detailed version of this touring plan, see page 573.

10. Pick up a handout guidemap containing the daily entertainment schedule at Disney-MGM.
11. Ride The Great Movie Ride.
12. See *Lights! Motors! Action!* (12a) or *Beauty and the Beast* (12b), whichever starts first.
13. Obtain a FASTPASS for Rock 'n' Roller Coaster.
14. See either *Lights! Motors! Action!* or *Beauty and the Beast,* depending on which you saw in Step 12.
15. See *Indiana Jones Epic Stunt Spectacular* (FASTPASS).
16. Take the Backlot Tour.
17. See *Muppet-Vision 3D.*
18. Ride Star Tours.
19. See *Voyage of the Little Mermaid.*
20. Use FASTPASS and ride the Rock 'n' Roller Coaster.
21. Ride the Tower of Terror.
22. Grab a snack and see *Fantasmic!*
23. Depart the Studios.

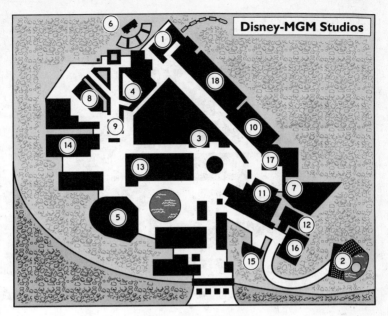

Disney-MGM Studios
Recommended Attraction Visitation Times
It is best to see attractions with visitation times listed as "anytime" during the more crowded middle part of the day (noon to 4 p.m.).

1. Backlot Tour: Anytime
2. *Fantasmic!:* Late show is less crowded
3. The Great Movie Ride: Before 11 a.m./after 4:30 p.m.
4. *Honey, I Shrunk the Kids* playground: Before 11 a.m./after dark
5. *Indiana Jones Epic Stunt Spectacular:* First three morning shows or last evening show
6. *Lights! Motors! Action! Extreme Stunt Show:* Anytime
7. The Magic of Disney Animation: Before 11 a.m./after 5 p.m.
8. *MuppetVision 3-D:* Before 11 a.m./after 3 p.m.
9. New York Street Backlot: Anytime
10. *One Man's Dream:* Anytime
11. *Playhouse Disney Live:* Per entertainment schedule
12. Rock 'n' Roller Coaster: Before 10 a.m., 1 hour before closing, or use FASTPASS
13. *Sounds Dangerous:* Before 11 a.m./after 4 p.m.
14. Star Tours: First hour and a half after opening or use FASTPASS
15. *Theater of the Stars:* Anytime, but arrive 25 minutes early
16. Tower of Terror: Before 9:30 a.m., after 6 p.m., or use FASTPASS
17. *Voyage of the Little Mermaid:* Before 9:45 a.m., just before closing, or use FASTPASS
18. *Who Wants to Be a Millionaire:* Before noon, after 4 p.m., or use FASTPASS

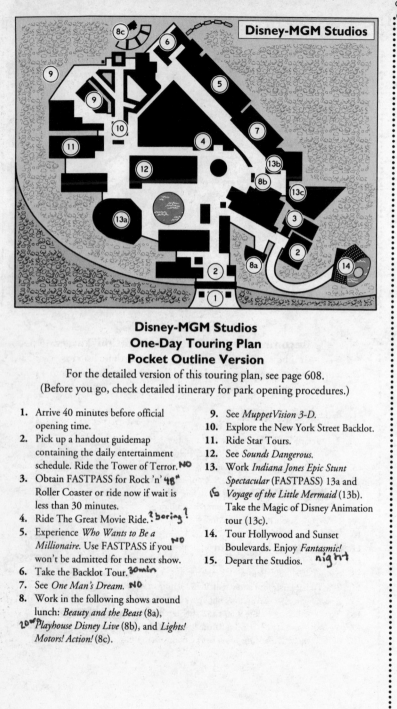

Disney-MGM Studios

Disney-MGM Studios
One-Day Touring Plan
Pocket Outline Version

For the detailed version of this touring plan, see page 608.
(Before you go, check detailed itinerary for park opening procedures.)

1. Arrive 40 minutes before official opening time.
2. Pick up a handout guidemap containing the daily entertainment schedule. Ride the Tower of Terror. **NO**
3. Obtain FASTPASS for Rock 'n' Roller Coaster or ride now if wait is less than 30 minutes. **48"**
4. Ride The Great Movie Ride. **? boring ?**
5. Experience *Who Wants to Be a Millionaire*. Use FASTPASS if you won't be admitted for the next show. **NO**
6. Take the Backlot Tour. **30 min**
7. See *One Man's Dream*. **NO**
8. Work in the following shows around lunch: *Beauty and the Beast* (8a), *Playhouse Disney Live* (8b), and *Lights! Motors! Action!* (8c). **20"**

9. See *MuppetVision 3-D*.
10. Explore the New York Street Backlot.
11. Ride Star Tours.
12. See *Sounds Dangerous*.
13. Work *Indiana Jones Epic Stunt Spectacular* (FASTPASS) 13a and *Voyage of the Little Mermaid* (13b). Take the Magic of Disney Animation tour (13c). **←**
14. Tour Hollywood and Sunset Boulevards. Enjoy *Fantasmic!*
15. Depart the Studios. **night**

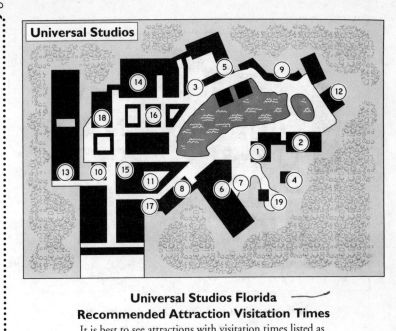

Universal Studios Florida
Recommended Attraction Visitation Times

It is best to see attractions with visitation times listed as "anytime" during the more crowded middle part of the day (noon to 4 p.m.).

1. *Animal Planet Live!:* After experiencing all rides
2. Back to the Future—The Ride: First thing in the morning after Mummy and Men in Black
3. *Beetlejuice's Rock 'n' Roll Graveyard Revue:* At your convenience
4. *A Day in the Park with Barney:* Anytime
5. Earthquake—The Big One: In morning or late afternoon
6. E.T. Adventure: Before noon; before 10 a.m. if you have small children
7. Fievel's Playland: Anytime
8. *The Gory Gruesome & Grotesque Horror Make-Up Show:* After experiencing all rides
9. Jaws: Before 11 a.m. or after 5 p.m.
10. Jimmy Neutron's Nicktoon Blast: First thing in the morning or after 5 p.m.
11. Lucy, a Tribute: Anytime
12. Men in Black Alien Attack: In the morning after Revenge of the Mummy
13. Nickelodeon Studios Walking Tour: When shows are in production
14. Revenge of the Mummy: First thing in the morning or after 6 p.m.
15. *Shrek 4-D:* First thing in the morning or after 4 p.m.
16. Street Scenes: Anytime
17. *Terminator 2: 3-D:* After 3:30 p.m.
18. *Twister:* First show after experiencing all rides
19. Woody Woodpecker's Kid Zone: Anytime

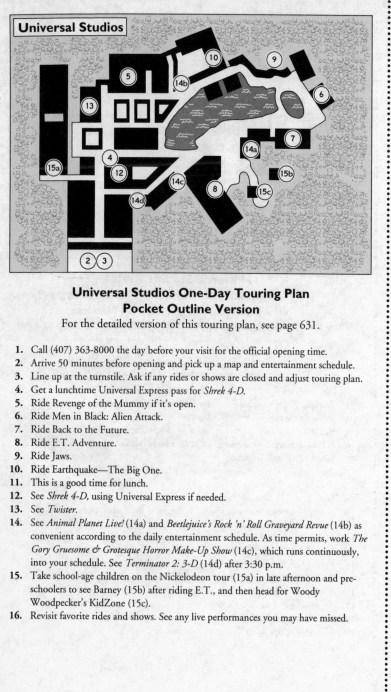

Universal Studios

Universal Studios One-Day Touring Plan
Pocket Outline Version
For the detailed version of this touring plan, see page 631.

1. Call (407) 363-8000 the day before your visit for the official opening time.
2. Arrive 50 minutes before opening and pick up a map and entertainment schedule.
3. Line up at the turnstile. Ask if any rides or shows are closed and adjust touring plan.
4. Get a lunchtime Universal Express pass for *Shrek 4-D.*
5. Ride Revenge of the Mummy if it's open.
6. Ride Men in Black: Alien Attack.
7. Ride Back to the Future.
8. Ride E.T. Adventure.
9. Ride Jaws.
10. Ride Earthquake—The Big One.
11. This is a good time for lunch.
12. See *Shrek 4-D,* using Universal Express if needed.
13. See *Twister.*
14. See *Animal Planet Live!* (14a) and *Beetlejuice's Rock 'n' Roll Graveyard Revue* (14b) as convenient according to the daily entertainment schedule. As time permits, work *The Gory Gruesome & Grotesque Horror Make-Up Show* (14c), which runs continuously, into your schedule. See *Terminator 2: 3-D* (14d) after 3:30 p.m.
15. Take school-age children on the Nickelodeon tour (15a) in late afternoon and pre-schoolers to see Barney (15b) after riding E.T., and then head for Woody Woodpecker's KidZone (15c).
16. Revisit favorite rides and shows. See any live performances you may have missed.

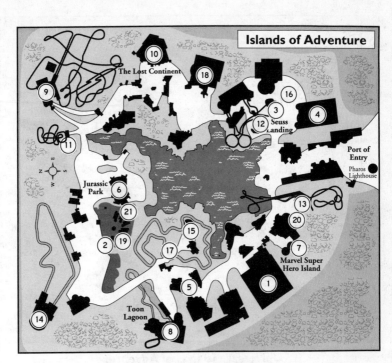

Universal's Islands of Adventure
Recommended Attraction Visitation Times

It is best to see attractions with visitation times listed as "anytime" during the more crowded middle part of the day (noon to 4 p.m.).

1. The Adventures of Spider-Man: Before 10 a.m.
2. Camp Jurassic: Anytime
3. Caro-Seuss-El: Before 10:30 a.m.
4. The Cat in the Hat: Before 11:30 a.m.
5. Comic Strip Lane: Anytime
6. Discovery Center: Anytime
7. Dr. Doom's FearFall: Before 9:15 a.m.
8. Dudley Do-Right's Ripsaw Falls: Before 11 a.m.
9. Dueling Dragons: Before 10:30 a.m.
10. *The Eighth Voyage of Sinbad:* Anytime per the entertainment schedule
11. The Flying Unicorn: Before 11 a.m.
12. If I Ran the Zoo: Anytime
13. The Incredible Hulk Coaster: Before 9:30 a.m.

—continued on other side—

Universal's Islands of Adventure
Recommended Attraction Visitation Times

It is best to see attractions with visitation times listed as "anytime" during the more crowded middle part of the day (noon to 4 p.m.).

—continued from other side—

14. Jurassic Park River Adventure: Before 11 a.m.

15. Me Ship, *The Olive:* Anytime

16. One Fish, Two Fish, Red Fish, Blue Fish: Before 10 a.m.

17. Popeye & Bluto's Blige-Rat Barges: Before 10:30 a.m.

18. *Poseidon's Fury! Escape from the Lost City:* After experiencing all the rides

19. Pteranodon Flyers: When there's no line

20. Storm Force Accelatron: Before 10:30 a.m.

21. Triceratops Encounter: Before 11:30 a.m.

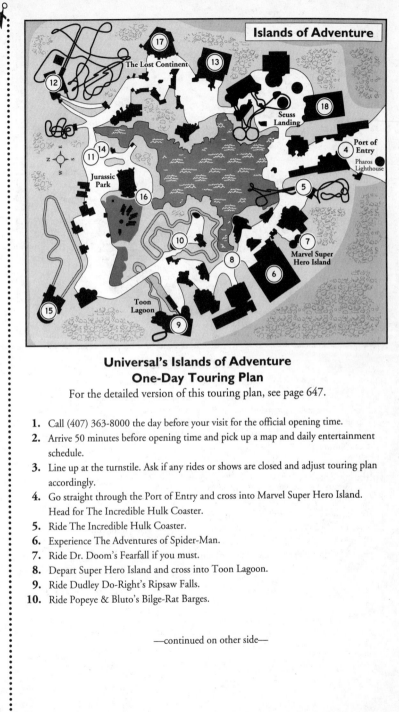

Universal's Islands of Adventure
One-Day Touring Plan

For the detailed version of this touring plan, see page 647.

1. Call (407) 363-8000 the day before your visit for the official opening time.
2. Arrive 50 minutes before opening time and pick up a map and daily entertainment schedule.
3. Line up at the turnstile. Ask if any rides or shows are closed and adjust touring plan accordingly.
4. Go straight through the Port of Entry and cross into Marvel Super Hero Island. Head for The Incredible Hulk Coaster.
5. Ride The Incredible Hulk Coaster.
6. Experience The Adventures of Spider-Man.
7. Ride Dr. Doom's Fearfall if you must.
8. Depart Super Hero Island and cross into Toon Lagoon.
9. Ride Dudley Do-Right's Ripsaw Falls.
10. Ride Popeye & Bluto's Bilge-Rat Barges.

—continued on other side—

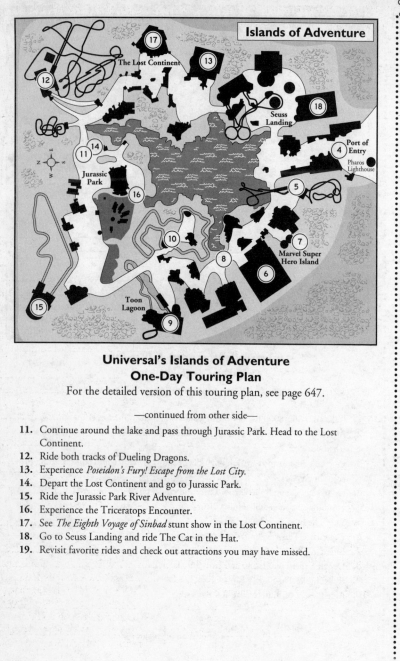

Universal's Islands of Adventure
One-Day Touring Plan

For the detailed version of this touring plan, see page 647.

—continued from other side—

11. Continue around the lake and pass through Jurassic Park. Head to the Lost Continent.
12. Ride both tracks of Dueling Dragons.
13. Experience *Poseidon's Fury! Escape from the Lost City.*
14. Depart the Lost Continent and go to Jurassic Park.
15. Ride the Jurassic Park River Adventure.
16. Experience the Triceratops Encounter.
17. See *The Eighth Voyage of Sinbad* stunt show in the Lost Continent.
18. Go to Seuss Landing and ride The Cat in the Hat.
19. Revisit favorite rides and check out attractions you may have missed.

Attraction	Recommended Visitation Times	Author's Rating	Special Comments
Ariel's Grotto	Before 10 a.m., after 9 p.m.	★★★	
Astro Orbiter	Before 11 a.m., after 5 p.m.	★★	
Barnstormer	Before 10:30 a.m., during events, just before closing	★★	
Big Thunder Mountain Railroad (FASTPASS)	Before 10 a.m., hour before closing	★★★★	40" min.; expectant mothers should not ride.
Buzz Lightyear's Space Ranger Spin (FASTPASS)	Before 10:30 a.m., after 6 p.m.	★★★★	
Cinderella's Golden Carrousel	Before 11 a.m., after 8 p.m.	★★★	
Country Bear Jamboree	Before 11:30 a.m., before parades, 2 hours before closing	★★★	
The Diamond Horseshoe Saloon	Per entertainment schedule	★★★	
Donald's Boat	Anytime	★★½	
Dumbo	Before 10 a.m., after 9 p.m.	★★★	
Enchanted Tiki Birds	Before 11 a.m., after 3:30 p.m.	★★★½	
Frontierland Shootin' Arcade	Anytime	★½	
The Hall of Presidents	Anytime	★★★	
The Haunted Mansion (FASTPASS)	Before 11:30 a.m., after 8 p.m.	★★★★	Fright potential
It's a Small World	Anytime	★★★	
Jungle Cruise	Before 10 a.m., 2 hours before closing	★★★	
Liberty Belle Riverboat	Anytime	★★½	
Mad Tea Party	Before 11 a.m., after 5 p.m.	★★	Expectant mothers should not ride.
Magic Carpets of Aladdin	Before 10 a.m., hour before closing	★★★	
The Many Adventures of Winnie the Pooh (FASTPASS)	Before 10 a.m., 2 hours before closing	★★★½	
Mickey's and Minnie's Country Houses	Before 11:30 a.m., after 4:30 p.m.	★★★/★★	
Mickey's PhilharMagic (FASTPASS)	Before 11 a.m., during parades	★★★★	
Peter Pan's Flight (FASTPASS)	Before 10 a.m., after 6 p.m.	★★★★	
Pirates of the Caribbean	Before noon, after 5 p.m.	★★★★★	
Snow White's Adventures	Before 11 a.m., after 6 p.m.	★★½	Fright potential
Space Mountain (FASTPASS)	At opening, 6–7 p.m., hour before closing	★★★★	44" min.; expectant mothers should not ride.
Splash Mountain (FASTPASS)	At opening, during parades, just before closing	★★★★★	40" min.; expectant mothers should not ride.
Stitch's Great Escape	Before 10 a.m. during parades, after 4 p.m.	t.b.d.	Fright potential; 44" min.
Swiss Family Treehouse	Before 11:30 a.m., after 5 p.m.	★★★	Lots of stairs
The Timekeeper	Anytime	★★★★	Open seasonally
Tom Sawyer Island	Midmorning–late afternoon	★★★	Closes at dusk
Tomorrowland Speedway	Before 11 a.m., after 5 p.m.	★	52" to drive.; expectant mothers should not ride.

Attraction	Recommended Visitation Times	Author's Rating	Special Comments
Tomorrowland Transit Authority	Anytime	★★★	
Toontown Hall of Fame	Before 10:30 a.m., after 5:30 p.m.	★★	
Walt Disney's Carousel of Progress	Anytime	★★★	Open seasonally
WDW Railroad	Anytime	★★½	

Dining Information—*Counter Service*

Restaurant	Location	Quality	Value	Selection
Casey's Corner	Main Street	Good	B	Hot dogs, fries
Columbia Harbor House	Liberty Square	Fair	C+	Fried fish, chicken strips, sandwiches, soups, vegetable chili, garden salad w/ chicken
Cosmic Ray's Starlight Café	Tomorrowland	Good	B	Burgers (veggie avail.) rotisserie chicken, sandwiches, child's plate, some kosher
El Pirata y el Perico	Adventureland	Fair	B	Nachos, taco salad, tacos, beef empanada, chili, churros
The Lunching Pad	Tomorrowland	Good	C	Smoked turkey legs, cookies
Pecos Bill Tall Tale Inn and Cafe	Frontierland	Good	B	Burgers, hot dogs, chicken wraps, chicken salad, chili, child's plate
The Pinocchio Village Haus	Fantasyland	Fair to Good	B	Burgers, hot dogs, garden salads w/ chicken, fresh fruit, child's plate
The Plaza Pavilion	Tomorrowland	Good	B	Mini-pizzas, sandwiches, salads chicken strips, child's plate

Dining Information—*Full Service*

Restaurant	Meals Served	Location	Price	Quality	Value	Selection
Cinderella's Royal Table	B, L, D	Fantasyland	Moderate	★★	★★	Prime rib, steak, seafood
The Crystal Palace	B, L, D	Main Street	Moderate	★★★½	★★★	Buffet, varies
Liberty Tree Tavern	L, D	Frontierland	Moderate	★★★	★★★	Prime rib, ham, roast turkey
The Plaza	L, D	Main Street, U.S.A.	Moderate	★★	★★	Sandwiches, burgers

Priority Seating reservations recommended for Magic Kingdom full-service restaurants; call (407) 939-3463.

Good Rest Areas in the Magic Kingdom

Place	Location	Notes
Covered gazebo	Adventureland	Across from Swiss Family Treehouse; has ceiling fans, nearby refreshments
Movie theater	Main Street	In back of Exposition Hall on Main Street; air-conditioned; refreshments available on Main Street
Shaded benches	Liberty Square	Between central hub and entrance to Liberty Square, on left

EPCOT TOURING PLAN COMPANION

Attraction	Recommended Visitation Times	Author's Rating	Special Comments
The American Adventure	Anytime	★★★	
Body Wars (Wonders of Life)	Before 10:45 a.m., after 5 p.m.	★★★★	40" min., expectant mothers or people prone to motion sickness should not ride; open seasonally
Circle of Life Theater (The Land)	Before 11 a.m., after 2 p.m.	★★★½	
Cranium Command (Wonders of Life)	Before 11 a.m., after 3 p.m.	★★★★½	Open seasonally
El Río del Tiempo (Mexico)	Before 11 a.m., after 3 p.m.	★★	
Global Neighborhood	After riding Spaceship Earth	★★	
Honey, I Shrunk the Audience (FASTPASS)	Before 11:30 a.m., after 6 p.m.	★★★★½	Fright potential
Impressions de France	Anytime	★★★½	
Innoventions	Second day or after major attractions	★★★½	
Journey into Your Imagination	Before 11:30 a.m., after 5 p.m.	★★½	
Living with the Land (The Land) (FASTPASS)	Before 10:30 a.m., after 5 p.m.	★★★★	
The Living Seas	Before 11:30 a.m., after 3 p.m.	★★★½	
Maelstrom (Norway) (FASTPASS)	Before noon, after 4:30 p.m.	★★★	
The Making of Me (Wonders of Life)	Early morning, after 4:30 p.m	★★★	Open seasonally
Mission: Space (FASTPASS)	First 30 minutes the park is open	★★★★	44" min., expectant mothers or people prone to motion sickness should not ride
O Canada! (Canada)	Anytime	★★★	
Reflections of China (China)	Anytime	★★★	Audience stands throughout performance
Soarin' (The Land) (FASTPASS)	First 30 minutes the park is open	t.b.d.	Expectant mothers and people prone to motion sickness should not ride
Spaceship Earth	Before 10 a.m., after 4 p.m.	★★★★	
Test Track (FASTPASS)	First 30 minutes the park is open, just before closing	★★★½	40" min.
Universe of Energy	Before 11:15 a.m., after 4:30 p.m.	★★★★	

Dining Information—*Counter Service*

Restaurant	Location	Quality	Value	Selection
Boulangerie Patisserie	World Showcase France	Good	B	Croissants, pastries, cheese plate, quiche Lorraine, wine, beer
Cantina de San Angel	World Showcase Mexico	Fair	C	Chicken tacos, burritos, child's plate w/ burrito and chips, nachos, beer, margaritas
Electric Umbrella Restaurant	Future World Innoventions Plaza East	Good	B	Breakfast pizza, breakfast burrito, burgers, veggie burgers, chicken tenders w/ fries, child's plate w/ hot dog or cheese & pepperoni pizza, chicken Caesar salad, fruit cup, beer

Dining Information—Counter Service (continued)

Restaurant	Location	Quality	Value	Selection
Kringla Bakeri og Kafe	World Showcase Norway	Good to Excellent	B	Pastries, open-faced sandwiches (smoked ham, smoked turkey, and smoked salmon), green salad, fruit cup, beer
Liberty Inn	World Showcase United States	Fair	C	Burgers, fries, hot dogs, chicken strips, turkey club, chicken Caesar & garden vegetable salad, child's hot dog & child's chicken nugget plate, beer
Lotus Blossom Café	World Showcase China	Fair	D	Stir-fried beef, chicken & vegetable dishes, sweet-and-sour chicken, veggie and sesame noodle plate, child's plate with sweet-and-sour-chicken, beer
Refreshment Port	Between World Showcase and Future World	Good	B	Chicken nuggets, fries, McFlurry desserts; thinly disguised McDonalds; convenient snacks
Rose and Crown Pub	World Showcase United Kingdom	Good	C	Cornish pasties, fish & chips, sausage rolls, shortbread, fruit, cheese, beer, ale, other spirits
Sommerfest	World Showcase Germany	Good	B	Bratwurst & frankfurter sandwiches w/ kraut, chicken schnitzel, apple strudel, Black Forest cake, beer
Sunshine Season Food Fair	Future World The Land	Fair to Good	C	Potatoes w/ fixin's, soups, salads; BBQ chicken & ribs, deli sandwiches, veggie wraps, fruit & yogurt cups, baked goods, beer
Tangierine Café	World Showcase Morocco	Good	B	Chicken & lamb shawarma; hummus; seafood, chicken or tabouleh wraps; child's meal of Mediterranean pizza or hamburger w/ fries; baklava; beer
Yakitori House	World Showcase Japan	Excellent	B	Beef & chicken teriyaki; shrimp; shrimp, chicken, & beef skewers w/ rice; sushi; seafood salad; child's fried chicken w/ vegetables & rice; beer

Dining Information—Full Service

Restaurant	Meals Served	Location	Price	Quality	Value	Selection
Biergarten	L, D	Germany	Moderate	★★★½	★★★	Buffet w/ schnitzel, wurst, spaetzle, roast chicken

Dining Information—Full Service (continued)

Restaurant	Meals Served	Location	Price	Quality	Value	Selection

Restaurant	Meals Served	Location	Price	Quality	Value	Selection
Bistro de Paris	D	France	Expensive	★★★½	★★	Lobster fricassée, roasted duck, veal chop, rack of lamb
Le Cellier Steakhouse	L, D	Canada	Moderate	★★★	★★★	Filet mignon, veal, roast turkey breast, beef brisket, chicken
Chefs de France	L, D	France	Moderate	★★★	★★★	Brochette of prawns, filet of orange roughy, braised beef
Coral Reef	L, D	The Living Seas	Expensive	★★★½	★★	Salmon, whole roasted snapper, bacon-wrapped bass, shrimp
The Garden Grill Restaurant	B, L, D	The Land	Moderate	★★★	★★★	Family style; rotisserie chicken, fish, vegetables, salad
Mitsukoshi Teppanyaki Dining Room	L, D	Japan	Expensive	★★★★	★★★	Chicken, shrimp, beef, scallops, & Oriental vegetables stir-fried on teppan grill
Nine Dragons Restaurant	L, D	China	Expensive	★★★	★	Sweet & sour pork, beef w/ broccoli, moo goo gai pan
L'Originale Alfredo di Roma Restaurante	L, D	Italy	Expensive	★★★	★★	Fettucine Alfredo, pasta e fagiloi, linguine al pesto, pollo alla Milanese, roasted lamb chop
Restaurant Akershus	L, D	Norway	Moderate	★★★★	★★★★	Buffet; salmon, herring, Norwegian salads and cheeses, hot fish & meats
Restaurant Marrakesh	L, D	Morocco	Moderate	★★★½	★★★	Bastila, cornish hen, tangine chicken, roast lamb, kebabs
Rose and Crown Dining Room	L, D	United Kingdom	Moderate	★★★½	★★	Fish and chips, Welsh chicken & leek pie, prime rib, steak & kidney pie, bangers & mash

Dining Information—*Full Service* (continued)

Restaurant	Meals Served	Location	Price	Quality	Value	Selection

San Angel Inn Restaurante	L, D	Mexico	Expensive	★★★★	★★	Enchiladas, tacos, mole poblano, blackened mahimahi, poached red snapper
Tempura Kiku	L, D	Japan	Moderate	★★★★	★★★	Tempura w/ chicken, shrimp, & vegetables; kabuki beef; sushi; sashimi

Priority Seating reservations recommended for Epcot full-service restaurants; call (407) 939-3463.

Good Rest Areas in Epcot

Place	Location	Notes
Seats & benches	Wonders of Life pavilion	Ample room; air-conditioned; usually not crowded; refreshments nearby; pavilion open seasonally
Benches	The Living Seas	Ample room throughout pavilion; air-conditioned
Benches	Innoventions	Air-conditioned; usually not crowded
Covered gazebo	In garden behind shops on left side of United Kingdom	Often empty; refreshments nearby
Rotunda & lobby	The United States pavilion	Ample room; air-conditioned; refreshments nearby; usually quiet unless singers are performing

Attraction	Recommended Visitation Times	Author's Rating	Special Comments
The Boneyard	Anytime	★★★½	
Character Greeting Area	Early morning, late afternoon	n/a	
Conservation Station, Rafiki's Planet Watch	Anytime	★★★	
Dinosaur (FASTPASS)	Before 10:30 a.m., 1 hour before closing	★★★★½	Fright potential, expectant mothers should not ride
Festival of the Lion King	Before 11 a.m., after 4 p.m.	★★★★	
Flights of Wonder	Anytime	★★★★	
It's Tough to Be a Bug!	Before 10:30 a.m., after 4 p.m.	★★★★	Fright potential
Kali River Rapids (FASTPASS)	Before 10:30 a.m., after 4:30 p.m.	★★★½	You will get wet; expectant mothers note that ride is bouncy
Kilimanjaro Safaris (FASTPASS)	Park opening, 2 hours before closing	★★★★★	
Maharaja Jungle Trek	Anytime	★★★★	
Oasis	Anytime		
Pangani Forest Exploration Trail	Anytime	★★★	
Pocahontas and Her Forest Friends	Before 11 a.m., after 4 p.m.	★★½	
Primeval Whirl (FASTPASS)	First 2 hours park is open, 1 hour before closing	★★★	Expectant mothers should not ride
Theater in the Wild	Anytime	★★½	
Tree of Life Animal Exhibits	Anytime	n/a	
TriceraTop Spin	First 90 minutes park is open, 1 hour before closing	★★	
Wildlife Express	Anytime	★★	

Dining Information—*Counter Service*

Restaurant	Location	Quality	Value	Selection
Chakranadi Chicken Shop	Asia	Good	C	Stir-fry chicken, Oriental noodle bowl, pot stickers
Flame Tree Barbecue	Safari Village	Good	B–	Pork shoulder & chicken sandwiches, barbecue ribs, crisp green salad w/ chicken, child's plate of PB&J or franks & beans w/ cookie
Pizzafari	Safari Village	Good	B	Personal pizzas w/ variety of toppings, Mesquite chicken Caesar salad, Italian deli sandwiches
Restaurantosaurus	Dinoland U.S.A.	Good	B+	Cheeseburgers, hot dogs, McDonald's Chicken McNuggets & Happy Meals, turkey wraps, vegetarian platter
Tamu Tamu	Africa	Good	C	Various flavors of yogurt or ice cream, available in cones or as sundaes

Dining Information—*Counter Service* (continued)

Restaurant	Location	Quality	Value	Selection
Tusker House Restaurant	Africa	V. Good	B–	Half rotisserie chicken, fried chicken dinner, turkey & veggie wraps, grilled chicken sandwich, roasted vegetable sandwich, child's plate w/ mac & cheese

Dining Information—*Full Service*

Restaurant	Meals Served	Location	Price	Quality	Value	Selection
Rainforest Café	B, L, D	Park Entrance	Moderate	★★★	★★	Eggroll w/ chicken, red peppers, corn & black beans; seafood pasta; pita quesadilla.

Priority Seating reservations recommended for Animal Kingdom full-service restaurants; call (407) 939-3463.

Good Rest Areas in the Animal Kingdom

Place	Location	Notes
Walkway between Africa & Asia	Between Africa & Asia	Plenty of shaded rest spots; some overlook running streams; refreshments nearby; a favorite of *Unofficial Guide* researchers
Gazebo behind Flame Tree Barbecue	Safari Village	Follow the path towards the water along the left side of Flame Tree Barbecue; gazebo has ceiling fans
Outdoor covered benches near exit from Dinosaur	Dinoland U.S.A.	Gazebo-like structure with nearby water fountain
Tusker House Restaurant	Africa	Note how the panoramic photos are made

Attraction	Recommended Visitation Times	Author's Rating	Special Comments
Backlot Tour	Anytime	★★★★	
Fantasmic!	Evening	★★★★★	
The Great Movie Ride	Before 11 a.m., after 4:30 p.m.	★★★½	
Honey, I Shrunk the Kids playground	Before 11 a.m., after dark	★★½	
Indiana Jones Epic Stunt Spectacular	First 3 morning shows or last evening show	★★★★	
Lights! Motors! Action!	First show, after 4 p.m.	t.b.d.	
The Magic of Disney Animation	Before 11 a.m., after 5 p.m.	★★★½	
MuppetVision 3D	Before 11 a.m., after 3 p.m.	★★★★½	
New York Street Backlot	Anytime	★★★	
One Man's Dream	Anytime	★★★★	
Playhouse Disney Live	Per entertainment schedule	★★★	
Rock 'n' Roller Coaster (FASTPASS)	Before 10 a.m., 1 hour before closing	★★★★	48" min., expectant mothers should not ride
Sounds Dangerous	Before 11 a.m., after 4 p.m.	★★★	
Star Tours (FASTPASS)	First 90 minutes after opening	★★★★	40" min., expectant mothers should not ride, motion-sickness potential
Theater of the Stars	Anytime	★★★★	
Tower of Terror (FASTPASS)	Before 9:30 a.m., after 6 p.m.	★★★★★	40" min., expectant mothers should not ride
Voyage of the Little Mermaid (FASTPASS)	Before 9:45 a.m., just before closing	★★★★	
Who Wants to Be a Millionaire? (FASTPASS)	Before noon, after 4 p.m.	★★★★	

Dining Information—*Counter Service*

Restaurant	Location	Quality	Value	Selection
ABC Commissary	Backlot	Good	B+	Tabouleh wraps, chicken yakitori, vegetable noodle stir-fry, child's chicken-nugget or fish 'n' chips plate
Backlot Express	Backlot	Good	B	Burgers, fries, fruit, chicken strips, hot dogs, chicken Caesar salad, tuna subs
Catalina Eddie's	Sunset Boulevard	Fair	B	Personal pizzas, side salads
Dipsite	Backlot	V. Good	A	Steak sub sandwich, funnel cake with fruit toppings, snow cones; chips; beer and soda.
Min and Bill's Dockside Diner	Echo Lake	Fair	C−	Shakes, beverages, chips, cookies, brownies
Rosie's All American Café	Sunset Boulevard	Good	B	Burgers, chicken strips, veggie burgers, side salads
Starring Rolls Café	Sunset Boulevard	Fair to Good	C	Sandwiches, salads, pastries, baked goods, coffee

Dining Information—*Counter Service* *(continued)*

Restaurant	Location	Quality	Value	Selection
Studio Catering Co.	Backlot	Good	B	Ice cream, soda, popcorn, fruit cup
Toluca Legs Turkey Co.	Sunset Boulevard	Good	B	Smoked turkey legs, hot dogs, Polish sausage, baked potatoes, beer
Toy Story Pizza Planet	Backlot	Excellent	B+	Personal pizzas, salads, chips

Dining Information—*Full Service*

Restaurant	Meals Served	Location	Price	Quality	Value	Selection
50's Prime Time Café	L, D	Echo Lake	Moderate	★★★	★★	Meatloaf, pot roast, chicken, other homey fare
Hollywood & Vine	D	Echo Lake	Inexpensive	★★★	★★★	Buffet; roasted pork loin, smoked seafood, fired rice, salads, fresh fruit
The Hollywood Brown Derby	L, D	Hollywood Boulevard	Expensive	★★★★	★★★	Cobb salad, baked grouper, Udon noodles, grilled steak
Mama Melrose's Ristorante Italiano	L, D	New York Street	Moderate	★★★	★★	Pasta & seafood combos, salads, designer pizzas, veal Parmesan
Sci-Fi Dine-In Theater Restaurant	L, D	Commissary Lane	Moderate	★★½	★★	Sandwiches, burgers, salads, shakes; stick to the simpler fare

Priority Seating reservations recommended for Disney-MGM Studios full-service restaurants; call (407) 939-3463.

Good Rest Areas in Disney-MGM Studios

Place	Location	Notes
Covered seating behind Toluca Legs Turkey Co.	Sunset Boulevard	Refreshments nearby; ample seating
Studios Catering Co.	Backlot	Ample covered seating; refreshments nearby
Benches along Echo Lake	Echo Lake	Some are shaded; refreshments nearby.
Inside *Sounds Dangerous*	Echo Lake	Quiet if you don't wear the headphones; air-conditioned. (Thanks to Matt Hochberg of **mgmstudios.org**)

2005 *Unofficial Guide* Reader Survey

If you would like to express your opinion about Walt Disney World or this guidebook, complete the following survey and mail it to:

Unofficial Guide Reader Survey
P.O. Box 43673
Birmingham, AL 35243

Inclusive dates of your visit _____ Your Hometown _____
Your e-mail address _____

Members of your party: Person 1   Person 2   Person 3   Person 4   Person 5

Gender (M or F) _____
Age _____

How many times have you been to Walt Disney World? _____
On your most recent trip, where did you stay? _____

Concerning accommodations, on a scale with 100 best and 0 worst, how would you rate:

The quality of your room? _____   The value for the money? _____
The quietness of your room? _____   Check-in/checkout efficiency? _____
Shuttle service to the parks? _____   Swimming pool facilities? _____

Did you rent a car? _____   From whom? _____

Concerning your rental car, on a scale with 100 best and 0 worst, how would you rate:

Pickup processing efficiency? _____   Return processing efficiency? _____
Condition of the car? _____   Cleanliness of the car? _____
Airport shuttle efficiency? _____

Concerning your touring:

Who in your party was most responsible for planning the itinerary? _____
What time did you normally get started in the morning? _____
Did you usually arrive at the theme parks prior to opening? _____
Did you return to your hotel for rest during the day? _____
What time did you normally go to bed at night? _____

On a scale with 100 best and 0 worst, rate how the touring plans worked:

Park	Name of Plan	Rating
Magic Kingdom		
Epcot		
Animal Kingdom		
Disney-MGM		
Universal Studios		
Islds. of Adventure		

Concerning your dining experiences (also see WDW Restaurant Survey on following pages):

How many restaurant meals (including fast food) did you average per day? _____

How much (approximately) did your party spend on meals per day? _____

Favorite restaurant outside of Walt Disney World? _____

Did you buy this guide: Before leaving? _____ While on your trip? _____

How did you hear about this guide?

Loaned or recommended by a friend _____ Radio or TV _____

Newspaper or magazine _____ Bookstore salesperson _____

Just picked it out on my own _____ Library _____

Internet _____

What other guidebooks did you use on this trip? _____
_____

On the 100 best and 0 worst scale, how would you rate them? _____
_____

Using the same scale, how would you rate the *Unofficial Guide?* _____

Are *Unofficial Guides* readily available in bookstores in your area? _____

Have you used other *Unofficial Guides?* _____ Which one(s)? _____

Comments about your Walt Disney World vacation or about the *Unofficial Guide:* _____
_____
_____
_____
_____
_____
_____
_____
_____
_____
_____

Walt Disney World Restaurant Survey

Tell us about your Walt Disney World dining experiences. Listed below are the full-service restaurants. Beside each restaurant is a thumbs-up and thumbs-down symbol. If you enjoyed the restaurant enough that you would like to eat there again, circle the thumbs-up symbol. If not, circle the thumbs-down symbol.

Walt Disney World Full-Service Restaurants (in alphabetical order):

Restaurant	Location		
All Star Café	Wide World of Sports	👍	👎
Arthur's 27	Wyndham Palace	👍	👎
Artist Point	Wilderness Lodge Resort	👍	👎
Baskervilles	Grosvenor Resort	👍	👎
Benihana	Hilton	👍	👎
Biergarten	Germany: Epcot	👍	👎
Big River Grille & Brewing Works	Disney's BoardWalk	👍	👎
Bistro de Paris	France: Epcot	👍	👎
bluezoo	WDW Dolphin	👍	👎
Boatwright's Dining Hall	Dixie Landings Resort	👍	👎
Boma	Animal Kingdom Lodge	👍	👎
Bongos Cuban Café	Disney's West Side	👍	👎
California Grill	Contemporary Resort	👍	👎
Cape May Café	Beach Club Resort	👍	👎
Cap'n Jack's Restaurant	Downtown Disney	👍	👎
Le Cellier Steakhouse	Canada: Epcot	👍	👎
Chef Mickey's	Contemporary Resort	👍	👎
Les Chefs de France	France: Epcot	👍	👎
Cinderella's Royal Table	Magic Kingdom	👍	👎
Cítricos	Grand Floridian Resort	👍	👎
Concourse Steakhouse	Contemporary Resort	👍	👎
Coral Reef	Living Seas: Epcot	👍	👎
The Crystal Palace	Magic Kingdom	👍	👎
ESPN Club	Disney's BoardWalk	👍	👎
50's Prime Time Café	Disney-MGM Studios	👍	👎
Finn's Grill	Hilton	👍	👎
Flying Fish Café	Disney's BoardWalk	👍	👎
Fresh	WDW Dolphin	👍	👎
Fulton's Crab House	Pleasure Island	👍	👎
The Garden Grill	Land Pavilion: Epcot	👍	👎
Grand Floridian Café	Grand Floridian Resort	👍	👎
Gulliver's Grill	WDW Swan	👍	👎
Hollywood & Vine	Disney-MGM Studios	👍	👎
Hollywood Brown Derby	Disney-MGM Studios	👍	👎

Check extra day
refrigerator
Still resort guide of Cleveland out?

Walt Disney World Full-Service Restaurants

House of Blues	Disney's West Side	👍	👎
Jiko	Animal Kingdom Lodge	👍	👎
Kimonos	WDW Swan	👍	👎
Kona Café	Polynesian Resort	👍	👎
Liberty Tree Tavern	Magic Kingdom	👍	👎
Mama Melrose's Ristorante	Disney-MGM Studios	👍	👎
Maya Grill	Coronado Springs Resort	👍	👎
Mitsukoshi Teppanyaki Dining Rm.	Japan: Epcot	👍	👎
Narcoossee's	Grand Floridian Resort	👍	👎
Nine Dragons Restaurant	China: Epcot	👍	👎
1900 Park Fare	Grand Floridian Resort	👍	👎
'Ohana	Polynesian Resort	👍	👎
Olivia's Café	Old Key West Resort	👍	👎
L'Originale Alfredo di Roma Ristorante	Italy: Epcot	👍	👎
The Outback	Wyndham Palace	👍	👎
Palio	WDW Swan	👍	👎
Planet Hollywood	Pleasure Island	👍	👎
The Plaza	Magic Kingdom	👍	👎
Portobello Yacht Club	Pleasure Island	👍	👎
Rainforest Café	Downtown Disney and Animal Kingdom	👍	👎
Restaurant Akershus	Norway: Epcot	👍	👎
Restaurant Marrakesh	Morocco: Epcot	👍	👎
Rose & Crown Dining Room	United Kingdom: Epcot	👍	👎
San Angel Inn	Mexico: Epcot	👍	👎
Sci-Fi Dine-In Theater Restaurant	Disney-MGM Studios	👍	👎
Shula's Steak House	WDW Dolphin	👍	👎
Shutters at Old Port Royale	Caribbean Beach Resort	👍	👎
Spoodles	Disney's BoardWalk	👍	👎
Tempura Kiku	Japan: Epcot	👍	👎
Tony's Town Square Restaurant	Magic Kingdom	👍	👎
Victoria & Albert's	Grand Floridian Resort	👍	👎
Whispering Canyon Café	Wilderness Lodge Resort	👍	👎
Wolfgang Puck Café	Disney's West Side	👍	👎
Yacht Club Galley	Yacht Club Resort	👍	👎
Yachtsman Steakhouse	Yacht Club Resort	👍	👎